PLEASE DO NOT
WRITE IN THIS BOOK

AMERICAN GOVERNMENT

THE REPUBLIC IN ACTION

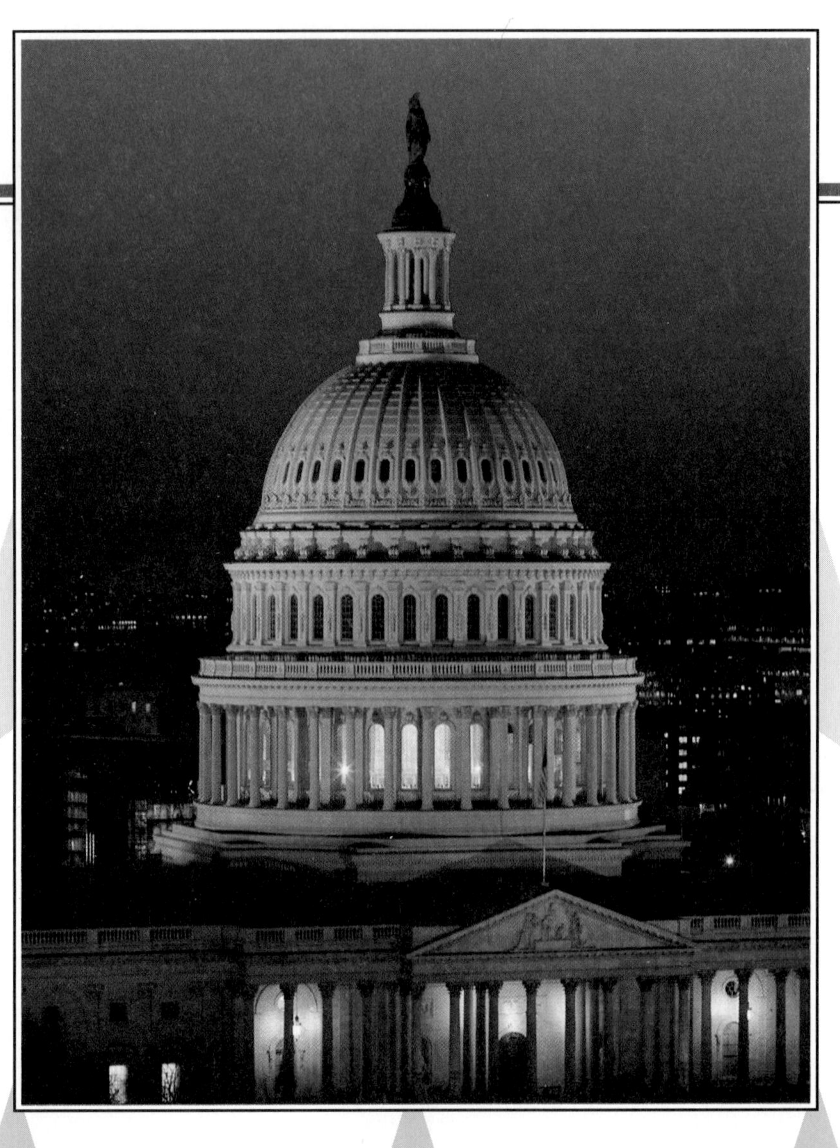

AMERICAN GOVERNMENT

THE REPUBLIC IN ACTION

Robert L. Hardgrave, Jr.

HBJ HARCOURT BRACE JOVANOVICH, PUBLISHERS
Orlando New York Chicago San Diego Atlanta Dallas

THE AUTHOR

Robert L. Hardgrave, Jr., is Professor of Government at the University of Texas at Austin. Dr. Hardgrave earned his B.A. in political science from the University of Texas at Austin and did his graduate study at the University of Chicago, where he received his M.A. and Ph.D. Among the numerous books and articles that Dr. Hardgrave has authored are *Comparative Politics* and *India: Government and Politics in a Developing Nation*. Dr. Hardgrave has recently served as a consultant to the United States Department of State and has also received several awards for his outstanding contributions to teaching in the field of American Government.

Grateful acknowledgment is made to the scholars and teachers who reviewed *American Government: The Republic in Action* in manuscript or in classroom testing.

CONTENT SPECIALISTS

Steven J. Baker
Monterrey Institute of International Studies
Monterrey, California

Lawrence C. Dodd
Indiana University
Bloomington, Indiana

William S. Livingston
University of Texas
Austin, Texas

Janice May
University of Texas
Austin, Texas

Ronald Rapoport
William and Mary College
Williamsburg, Virginia

Walt W. Rostow
University of Texas
Austin, Texas

CURRICULUM SPECIALISTS

John Bowen
Hillsborough High School
Tampa, Florida

Constance Cason
Edward H. White High School
Jacksonville, Florida

Thomas Dunthorn
Dade County Public Schools
Miami, Florida

Ronald Eckstein
Hudson Senior High School
New Port Richey, Florida

Danny Ellis
Edgewater High School
Orlando, Florida

Michael Gallagher
Eisenhower Junior High School
Hoffman Estates, Illinois

Barbara L. Lebda
Lindbloom Technical High School
Chicago, Illinois

William McCracken
Pine View School for the Gifted
Sarasota, Florida

Gloria Sesso
Half Hollow Hills Central Schools
Melville, New York

FIELD TEST TEACHERS

Suzanne Davis
Colonial High School
Orlando, Florida

Robert Leudtke
Lowell High School
San Francisco, California

Robert Mierenfeld
Sycamore High School
Cincinnati, Ohio

Walter Powers
Northwest High School
Cincinnati, Ohio

Sam Romeo
Winter Park High School
Winter Park, Florida

Copyright © 1986 by Harcourt Brace Jovanovich, Inc.

All rights reserved. No part of this publication may be reproduced or transmitted in any form or by any means, electronic or mechanical, including photocopy, recording, or any information storage and retrieval system, without permission in writing from the publisher.

Requests for permission to make copies of any part of the work should be mailed to:
Permissions, Harcourt Brace Jovanovich, Publishers, Orlando, Florida 32887

ACKNOWLEDGMENTS:
For permission to reprint copyrighted material, grateful acknowledgment is made to the following sources:

Allyn and Bacon, Inc.: From *Political Behavior of the American Electorate* by William Flanigan and Nancy Zingale.
Joan Daves: From *I Have a Dream* by Martin Luther King, Jr. Copyright © 1963 by Martin Luther King, Jr.
Harper & Row Publishers, Inc.: From *A Nation of Immigrants* by John F. Kennedy. Copyright © 1964 by Anti-Defamation League of B'nai B'rith.
Holt, Rinehart and Winston, Publishers: From *The Vantage Point* by Lyndon Baines Johnson. Copyright © 1971 by HEC Public Affairs Foundation.
Mrs. Lyndon B. Johnson: White House Memory by Mrs. Lyndon B. Johnson.
Little, Brown and Company: From *The State of the Presidency* by Thomas E. Cronin.
Merriam-Webster Inc.: From the definition of "obscene" in *Webster's Ninth New Collegiate Dictionary.* ©1984 by Merriam-Webster Inc., publisher of the Merriam-Webster® Dictionaries.
Mrs. Maurine Neuberger: From "I Go to the Legislature" by Richard Neuberger.
Prentice-Hall, Inc.: From *Politics in States and Communities,* Fourth Edition, by Thomas R. Dye. Copyright 1980 by Prentice-Hall, Inc.

Printed in the United States of America

ISBN 0-15-371850-1

CONTENTS

CITIZEN'S HANDBOOK OF SKILLS

UNIT 1 THE CONSTITUTIONAL FRAMEWORK

Chapter 2 Founding the Republic 35

Chapter 3 The Constitution: The Framework of Government 60

UNIT 2 GUARANTEES OF CIVIL LIBERTY

UNIT 4 PUBLIC OPINION AND INTEREST GROUPS

BOARD OF ELECTIONS MEETS HERE
JUNTA DE ELECCIONES SE REUNE ACA
94
ELECTION DISTRICT

UNIT 6 THE FEDERAL LEGISLATIVE BRANCH

UNIT 7 THE FEDERAL EXECUTIVE BRANCH

UNIT 8 THE FEDERAL BUREAUCRACY

UNIT 9 THE COURT SYSTEMS AND JUSTICE

Chapter 28 Criminal Justice and the Rights of the Accused 672

UNIT 10 STATE AND LOCAL GOVERNMENT

Chapter 29 State Government 696

Chapter 30 Local Government 733

THE REFERENCE SHELF 765

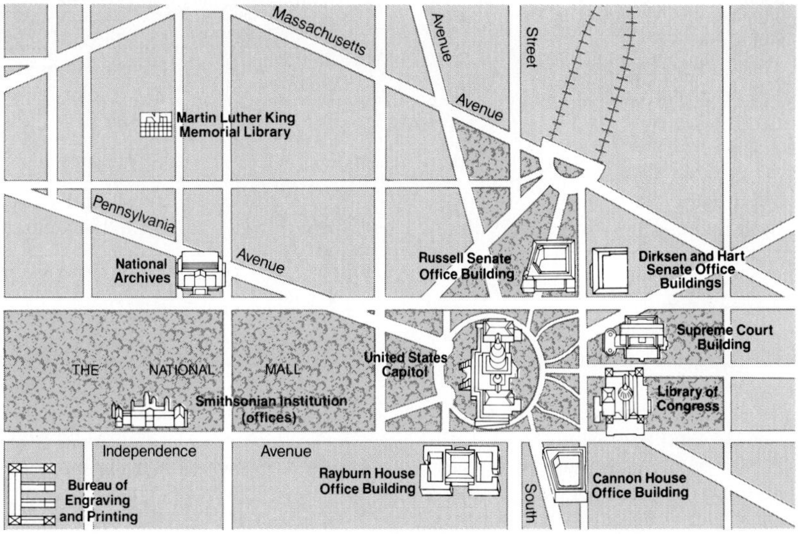

FEATURES

Insight

Issues

Legacy

Lexicon

Profile

CHARTS, TABLES, AND GRAPHS

MAPS

A Letter from the Author

THE CITIZEN IN GOVERNMENT: A WORKING RELATIONSHIP

My interest in politics was awakened when I was in junior high school and watched the Democratic and Republican national conventions on television. I wore the button of my favorite candidate, volunteered to stuff envelopes, and ran errands at the local campaign headquarters. Although I was too young to vote, I felt that I had at least a small part in electing the President. I thought that perhaps I might one day study law or political science, or run for public office. When I was a senior in high school, I wrote to Sam Rayburn—then Speaker of the United States House of Representatives—seeking his advice. In a letter that I now cherish, he wrote: "My advice would be that you study Government, United States History and also read the biographies of our [leaders] from the beginning of the government down to the present time. Everyone in the United States, to be an understanding citizen, must know the background and the history of this country and its people. In order to serve it, we must know . . . what this great nation is and stands for. . . . It is still the best form of government ever devised by the wisdom of statesmen."

Why study American government? The Founders of the Republic believed that the preservation of liberty depends upon citizen participation. Active participation requires an understanding of government and its forms, functions, and processes. James Madison, the father of the Constitution, wrote that "a people who mean to be their own governors must arm themselves with the power which knowledge gives." The study of American government involves the development of knowledge, skills, and positive attitudes that enable a person to participate effectively and responsibly in public life. To be an effective participant, each citizen must know how governmental policy is made. The responsible citizen must also be aware of the role that each individual may play in making that policy. Finally, each citizen must understand the opportunities for participation that are open to all Americans.

There are no more precious rights than those of American citizenship. Americans must be willing to undertake the responsibilities of citizenship, however, if they expect to enjoy the benefits that accompany the rights of citizenship. As American citizens, we participate in shaping the institutions and laws under which we live. We are expected to recognize basic constitutional rights; to be informed about issues; to express well-founded opinions. We are expected to vote; to uphold the law; to pay taxes; to serve on juries; and, when called upon, to defend the nation. Some of these responsibilities, such as voting, come only when citizens reach the age of 18. Young people, however, are not simply persons preparing for citizenship. You are citizens now.

"The qualifications for self-government are not innate," Thomas Jefferson once wrote. "They are the result of habit and long training." The study of American government will enable you to be better informed about the issues that affect your life. It will enable you to develop the skills of critical thinking to judge the arguments on both sides of an issue and to formulate your own opinions. By understanding the structure and the processes of government, you can be a more effective citizen—expressing your views, joining a community action project, volunteering for work in a social-service organization, or working in a political campaign. The rights, privileges, and prosperity that Americans enjoy depend on active citizen participation. That participation is up to you.

Robert L. Hardgrave, Jr.

Citizen's Handbook of Skills

OVERVIEW

Citizen's Handbook of Skills

UNDERSTANDING POLITICAL LABELS: THE MEANING OF REPUBLIC

To know how a government works, it is necessary to understand the political labels that are often applied to different forms of government. In the United States, for example, the term *republic* is very important.

Here are four guidelines that will help you understand political labels and how they are used:

(1) Skim through the material where the labels are used to develop an overview of the material's content.
(2) Read the material carefully. Take notes as you read the material to clarify the major points, the key concepts, and the use of labels in the reading. Organize your notes.
(3) Consult the glossary or a dictionary to check or to learn the meaning of any term used as a label.
(4) Then reread the material. You may discover information that you missed the first time. Review is an essential part of the learning process.

Read the following excerpt from *The Federalist,* No. 39, which discusses the meaning of *republic.* Then answer the questions that follow.

> *What, then, are the distinctive characters of the republican form? ... Holland, in which [there is no authority] derived from the people, has passed almost universally under the [name] of a republic. The same title has been bestowed on Venice, where absolute power over the great body of the people is exercised in the most absolute manner by a small body of hereditary nobles. Poland, which is a mixture of aristocracy and of monarchy in their worst forms, has been dignified with the same [name]. The government of England, which has one republican branch only, combined with an hereditary aristocracy and monarchy, has with equal [inappropriateness,] been frequently placed on the list of republics. These examples ... show the extreme inaccuracy with which the term has been used ...*
>
> *... [W]e may define a republic to be, or at least may bestow that name on, a government which derives all its powers directly or indirectly from the great body of the people, and is administered by persons holding their offices for a limited period, or during good behavior. It is* essential *to such a government that it be derived from the great body of the society, not from [a small portion] or a favored class ... ; otherwise a handful of tyrannical nobles ... [might call themselves republicans]. It is* sufficient *for such a government that the persons administering it be appointed, directly or indirectly, by the people; and that they hold their appointments [for a limited time period,] ... [during] good behavior.*
>
> *On comparing the Constitution planned by the convention ... we perceived at once that it [conforms to the definition of a republic]. The House of Representatives, like that of one branch at least of all State legislatures, is elected immediately by the great body of the people. The Senate,*

like . . . the Senate of Maryland, derives its appointment indirectly from the people. The President is indirectly derived from the choice of the people, according to the example in most of the States. Even the judges. . . will, as in the several States, be the choice, though a remote choice, of the people themselves. The duration of the appointments is equally conformable to the republican standard and to the model of State constitutions. . . .

Could any further proof be required of the republican complexion of this system, the most decisive one might be found in its absolute prohibition of titles of nobility . . . and in its express guaranty of the republican form to each [State].

Checking Your Skill

1. How does *The Federalist* define a republic?
2. According to *The Federalist,* what characteristics of the Constitution make the United States a republic?
3. According to *The Federalist,* what is the most decisive example indicating that the Constitution set up a republic?
4. According to *The Federalist,* what characteristics determine if a nation's government is truly republican in form?
5. Are the characteristics stated in *The Federalist* still valid today? Why or why not?
6. What characteristics of a government would you look for in order to determine if the label *republican* identified a truly republican form of government? Explain your choices.

ANALYZING POLITICAL POSITIONS: DETERMINING BIAS

As an informed citizen, it is important that you are able to determine if candidates, legislators, and other governmental leaders are expressing information fairly. Determining bias is essential because it prevents you from being misled and from making poor decisions. Biased information can be slanted to favor or to oppose a particular position or person.

Biased information can be presented in several forms. It may be inaccurate, distorted, or incomplete. It may present only one side of an issue or slant the facts to favor only one position. Bias may occur in the selective presentation of numbers or statistics; bias may also occur in the speeches of governmental leaders.

To determine bias, the following steps are useful.

(1) Distinguish facts from opinions.
(2) Examine the supporting data for its accuracy and relevance to the issue.
(3) Determine the slant of the position by identifying loaded or emotional words.

The following excerpts are taken from statements that were issued by two members of Congress concerning bills that would limit the Supreme Court's appellate jurisdiction—the Court's authority to decide issues of law. Read each of the excerpts and then answer the questions that follow.

The current attack is . . . serious because it strikes at the independence and integrity of the Supreme Court's most basic function—to review the constitutionality of state laws and actions. This current assault is embodied in 13 bills . . . which are designed to eliminate the jurisdiction of the federal courts to consider any cases relating to state laws on prayer in public schools, abortion or school desegregation plans.

[The Court's] role . . . has been to be the final arbiter of fundamental questions . . . the last best hope for the maintenance of our freedoms. . . .

Congress must not offend or jeopardize the legitimate prerogatives of the other two equal branches of government. [Limiting] the ability of the federal courts to deal with constitutional questions suggests that the judicial branch is not competent to consider such questions.

Representative Robert W. Kastenmeier

... the Constitution must remain supreme. That inspired document specifically obligates Congress to check the judiciary when it steps beyond constitutional limitations. The majesty of the Constitutional framework is that no branch is permitted to become supreme.

The drafters of the Constitution carefully composed Article III to place with Congress the responsibility for ensuring that personal liberties not be endangered by an errant or arrogant judiciary. Section 2 lists the kinds of cases the Supreme Court has the right to decide and then proceeds: 'In all the other cases before mentioned, the Supreme Court shall have the appellate jurisdiction, with such exceptions, and under such regulations, as Congress shall make.'... the Constitution charged Congress to regulate which cases the federal courts could hear on appeal from state courts.

The federal judiciary has been courting constitutional disaster by [reading] its own views into the nation's... document. When the policeman violates the law, a higher authority ... must protect the freedoms of the citizenry. The Constitution is the higher authority.

Senator Orrin G. Hatch

Checking Your Skill

1. What words are "loaded" or "emotional" in Representative Kastenmeier's statement? In Senator Hatch's statement?
2. List two facts from each member of Congress's statement.
3. Do the last paragraphs of each statement contain relevant information? Explain your answer.
4. Which member of Congress supports limiting the Court's appellate jurisdiction? Cite evidence from the excerpt to support your answer.
5. Which position do you support? Write a brief paragraph explaining your answer.

ANALYZING POLITICAL STATISTICS: PARTY AFFILIATION

Statistics are important tools because they provide data that aid students of government in the study of American politics. For example, political statistics help scholars and politicans formulate conclusions about voting patterns and explain various political trends.

A useful way to organize statistics is to group them by such categories as sex, race, or occupation. Grouping statistics this way involves identifying characteristics that the data have in common and putting together similar data. Grouping similar data makes the statistics easier to analyze. Analyzing statistics involves three basic steps.

(1) Identify the facts that are presented.
(2) Explain the interrelationships of the facts.
(3) Draw conclusions about the meaning of the data.

In the following table, statistics concerning political-party affiliation have been grouped together by various categories. Study the data in the table on page 5. Then answer the questions on page 6.

SKILLS

POLITICAL PARTY AFFILIATION

Question: "In politics, as of today, do you consider yourself a Republican, a Democrat, or an Independent?"

	Republicans	Democrats	Independents
National	29%	41%	30%
Sex			
Men	30	38	32
Women	28	43	29
Age			
18-24 years	26	36	38
25-29 years	29	36	35
30-49 years	28	38	34
50-64 years	32	45	23
65 and older	32	48	20
Region			
East	28	43	29
Midwest	31	34	35
South	26	46	28
West	33	40	27
Race			
Whites	32	36	32
Blacks	5	81	14
Hispanics	24	49	27
Education			
College graduates	38	32	30
High school graduates	28	41	31
Less than high school graduates	22	53	25
Occupation			
Professional and business	37	33	30
Clerical and sales	28	35	37
Manual workers/farmers	23	43	34
Non-labor force	30	50	20
Income			
More than $40,000	39	30	31
$30,000 - $39,999	33	36	31
$20,000 - $29,999	32	35	33
$10,000 - $19,999	25	45	30
Less than $10,000	21	53	26
Religion			
Protestants	33	40	27
Catholics	24	44	32
Jews	15	57	28
Urbanization			
Central cities	25	47	28
Suburbs	31	37	32
Rural areas	31	38	31

Checking Your Skill

1. What information do the statistics reveal?
   (a) The voting pattern of the 1984 election;
   (b) A social and economic profile of Democrats, Republicans, and Independents;
   (c) Number of members in the Democratic and in the Republican parties.
2. Use the data to determine which of the following statements are true. Cite the data you used for each determination.
   (a) More college graduates than high-school graduates consider themselves Independents.
   (b) More people under 30 consider themselves to be Democrats rather than Republicans.
   (c) More people who earn less than $10,000 a year consider themselves Democrats than those who earn more than $20,000 a year.
   (d) Republicans and Independents combined outnumber Democrats in the eastern section of the country.
   (e) A Republican is more likely to be a professional than a manual worker.
3. Using the categories of the statistical table, write a paragraph profiling a Republican, a Democrat, or an Independent.
4. If you were a Republican candidate for President, in which regions of the country would you do a large amount of campaigning? Why? To which income and age groups would you appeal? Why? If you were a Democratic candidate for President, in which regions of the country would you do a large amount of campaigning? Why? To which income and age groups would you appeal? Why? In what other ways might your political party affiliation influence your campaign strategy?

ANALYZING A POLL: THE LEVEL OF CITIZEN INVOLVEMENT

A poll is a systematic questioning of randomly selected people, designed to determine the public's opinion concerning a particular topic at a given time. The ability to analyze a poll is a useful tool for all citizens. Understanding how a poll is conducted and the results of a poll prevent citizens from being misled.

Any person or organization may conduct a poll, but an established and well-respected polling organization is more likely to develop accurate and valid poll questions. Thus, the poll results are likely to be more reliable. Three well-known polls are the Gallup Poll, the Harris Poll, and the Roper Poll. Each of these polls specializes in determining public opinion on current issues and political concerns. Professional pollsters often refine their poll statistics on the bases of such variables as age, race, sex, geographic region, income, political party or source of information.

Polls may measure any number of things. Some polls may measure public opinion on an issue; others survey the level of citizen involvement in the community. Pollsters determine the results to their polls by asking questions that are worded in a way that does not influence the respondent's answer. The pollster usually supplies sample answers—*quite a lot, some*, or *very little,* for example—to the questions as well. In this way, all respondents must choose from the same answers; thus, the poll results are easy to tabulate, compare, and analyze.

After the poll is complete, the pollster usually calculates the percentage of people who chose each answer. These percentages, or statistics, are the facts of the poll. Identifying and analyzing the facts should lead you to a conclusion concerning the topic of the poll.

Analyzing a poll often involves two basic steps. The first step is to ask questions of the information presented:

(a) What issue was surveyed?
(b) Who was surveyed?
(c) Were the terms used in the survey defined?

The second step involves interpreting the poll's results. This includes:

(a) Identifying the facts.
(b) Comparing the results.
(c) Formulating a conclusion based on the statistics collected in the poll.

Study the poll results on page 7 from the National Gallup Poll on education. Then answer the questions on page 8.

CHART A

What are the sources of information you use to judge the quality of schools in your local community; that is, where do you get your information about the schools?

	National Totals *	No Children In School *	Public School Parents *	Nonpublic School Parents *
Newspapers	42%	44%	37%	51%
Students	36	28	59	30
Parents of students	29	24	41	33
Other adults	27	25	28	34
School board/faculty	24	19	38	23
Radio and television	19	22	12	13
Personal experience	8	7	8	9
Other	4	3	5	2

CHART B

How much do you know about the local schools — quite a lot, some, or very little?

	National Totals	No Children In School	Public School Parents	Nonpublic School Parents
Quite a lot	22%	19%	31%	21%
Some	42	38	55	47
Very little	29	34	13	24
Nothing	7	9	1	8

CHART C

Since September, which of the following, if any, have you yourself done?

	National Totals *	No Children In School *	Public School Parents *	Nonpublic School Parents *
Received any newsletter, pamphlet, or any other material telling what the local public schools are doing	32%	22%	58%	38%
Attended a local public school athletic event	25	18	42	28
Attended a school play or concert in any local public school	24	16	42	36
Met with any teachers or administrators in the local public school about your own child	21	4	62	44
Attended a PTA meeting	14	4	36	46
Attended a school board meeting	8	4	16	24
None of the above	43	56	14	22

Source: The Gallup Poll

*Percentages add to more than 100 because of multiple answers from some respondents.

SKILLS

SKILLS

Checking Your Skill

1. What is the major source of information about local schools for most people in the nation? For people who have no children in school? For public-school parents?
2. What percentage of public-school parents claim to know "quite a lot" about local schools? To know "some" information about local schools?
3. In what activity did the most public-school parents take part? The most nonpublic-school parents?
4. Based upon your analysis of the poll results, determine which of the following statements are facts and which are opinions. Cite data from the polls to support your conclusions.
   (a) Newspapers are the major source of information about local schools for nonpublic-school parents.
   (b) Most people in the nation claim to know "quite a lot" or "some" information about local schools.
   (c) Greater contact between parents and local school authorities would improve the quality of education
   (d) People with children in school are more likely to attend school-related activities than are people with no children in school.
   (e) A large segment of the American population is not involved in any way in the local schools.

★ ★

ASKING EFFECTIVE QUESTIONS: ARE THE CANDIDATES QUALIFIED?

Asking effective questions enables students of goverment to understand and to gather information about a topic, a person, or an event. Journalistic guidelines should be followed in order to ask effective questions about a topic.

(1) Questions should relate directly to the particular topic.
(2) Questions should be arranged in sequence; each question should ask for information that will lead to the next question.
(3) Two kinds of questions should be asked:
   (a) questions that focus on facts;
   (b) questions that relate the facts to each other.

If you wanted to find out why the Middle East is important to United States foreign policy, you might ask the following questions:

1. What nations make up the Middle East?
2. Which powers are interested in the area?
3. Why is the geographic location of the Middle East important?
4. What natural resources do the nations of the Middle East have?
5. Why are these resources important to the United States?
6. How might a war in the Middle East affect United States foreign policy in the region?

Fact questions often begin with the words *who, which, what, where,* and *when.* Relationship questions often begin with the words *why* or *how.*

You might want to find out information about the candidates in an upcoming election. Below are some sample questions you might ask. Study these questions carefully. Then answer the questions that follow.

1. *What is each candidate's experience in government?*
2. *What kind of education does each candidate have?*
3. *What community awards did each candidate receive?*
4. *What are each of the candidates' qualifications for office?*
5. *Where do the candidates stand on the issue of the economy? The budget deficit? Foreign policy? United States–Soviet relations? The environment?*
6. *Why is each candidate running for office?*
7. *How do the candidates' positions differ?*

Checking Your Skill

1. Which of the questions listed above are fact questions? Which are relationship questions?
2. In what order would you ask these questions? Explain your choice.
3. What other questions might you ask the candidates? Are they fact questions or relationship questions? Why are they relevant to the topic?
4. Choose a topic or issue that you want to find out about. Write five effective questions that you might ask to research the topic or issue.

WRITING TO A MEMBER OF CONGRESS: EXPRESSING YOURSELF EFFECTIVELY

The individual is important to the democratic process of lawmaking. Elected representatives and senators want and need to know your ideas about various issues and the bills that address those issues. Your ideas aid them as they make decisions. For example, writing to your representatives in Congress can have important benefits for you as a citizen and for others in American society. The following guidelines will help you communicate your ideas and opinions to your representatives effectively.

(1) Proper Form
- Address members of Congress properly:

PROPER FORMS OF ADDRESS

	Form of Address	Salutation
representative	The Honorable John Doe United States House of Representatives	Dear Sir: Dear Madam: Dear Representative Doe: Dear Mr. Doe: Dear Ms. (or Mrs.) Doe:
senator	The Honorable Jane Smith United States Senate	Sir: Madam: Dear Senator Smith:

- Type or legibly write your letter.
- Be sure to include your address and sign your name legibly.
- Identify yourself; include the city, state, legislative district or county in which you are a voter.
- Discuss one subject per letter.
- Identify the issue and the bill number, if possible.
- Do not use a form letter.

(2) Organization of Ideas
- In the first paragraph, identify yourself and include your purpose for writing.

- In the second paragraph, state your position.
- In succeeding paragraphs, explain your position.
- Be specific.
- Be constructive—if a bill deals with a problem, offer a solution that you would support.

(3) Timing
- Write while the issue is current, not after a bill concerning the issue has passed.

(4) Courtesy
- Be polite. Never be threatening or abusive. Avoid sarcasm.
- Send a thank-you letter for a reply or for a vote that coincides with your position.

Sample letter

Dear Senator Roberts,

If you do not vote for the immigration bill, I will not vote for you again. Your voting record has been horrible.

I am comparing your votes to the votes of other senators. Make sure that you vote wisely on the immigration bill.

Betty L. Smith

Checking Your Skill

1. Read the sample letter above. Then identify three things that are wrong with it.
2. Choose an issue or a bill that is of concern to you or to your community. After examining the issue, write a letter expressing your view to one of your representatives in Congress.

INTERPRETING POLITICAL CARTOONS: UNDERSTANDING SYMBOLS

Political cartoons have commented on American politics since the beginning of the nation. While often funny, political cartoons can be serious statements of concern about a political issue. Often, political cartoons are satirical—they are drawn to criticize their subject and to do so with humor. The impact of political cartoons is immediate and their message is simple. Many readers who would not bother to read a long editorial will "read" a political cartoon.

Political cartoons can be a powerful force in shaping public opinion because ideas are presented directly and critically. It is important to be able to interpret political cartoons in order to understand how they achieve their effects. Three keys—caricature, symbolism, and labels and captions—help to interpret political cartoons.

(1) Caricature is an exaggeration or extreme distortion of something's or someone's physical features.
(2) Symbolism is the use of one device to stand for another. For example, Uncle Sam represents the United States, an elephant stands for the Republican party, and a donkey stands for the Democratic party.
(3) Labels and captions help readers identify the symbols used in the cartoon. Labels and captions often hint at the main idea of the cartoon, or they may be words spoken by the characters in the cartoon.

Study political cartoons A and B. Then answer the questions that follow.

Cartoon A

Cartoon B

Checking Your Skill

1. What is the major symbol used in cartoon A? What does it symbolize?
2. List the Presidential responsibilities that are illustrated in cartoon A.
3. What do the frayed wires symbolize?
4. What is the caption of cartoon A? Do you think it is an appropriate caption? Why or why not?
5. Write a brief paragraph describing the cartoonist's point of view about Presidential responsibilities shown in cartoon A.
6. What is the subject of cartoon B?
7. What is the cartoonist's point of view shown in cartoon B? What elements in the cartoon helped you reach your conclusion?
8. Write a brief paragraph comparing the two cartoonists' points of view.

INTERPRETING ORGANIZATION CHARTS: WHO CONTROLS THE GOVERNMENT?

Organization charts or flowcharts enable citizens to understand information visually. Such charts are often used to illustrate how a government operates or to explain a political process. These charts provide a framework or outline of the organization. They also show the relationships between the parts or the people of the organization.

The following steps are helpful when interpreting charts.

(a) Identify the title of the chart and the type of chart.
(b) Identify the parts of the chart and their relationships.
(c) Form conclusions based on the information in the chart.

Study the following organization chart and then answer the questions that follow.

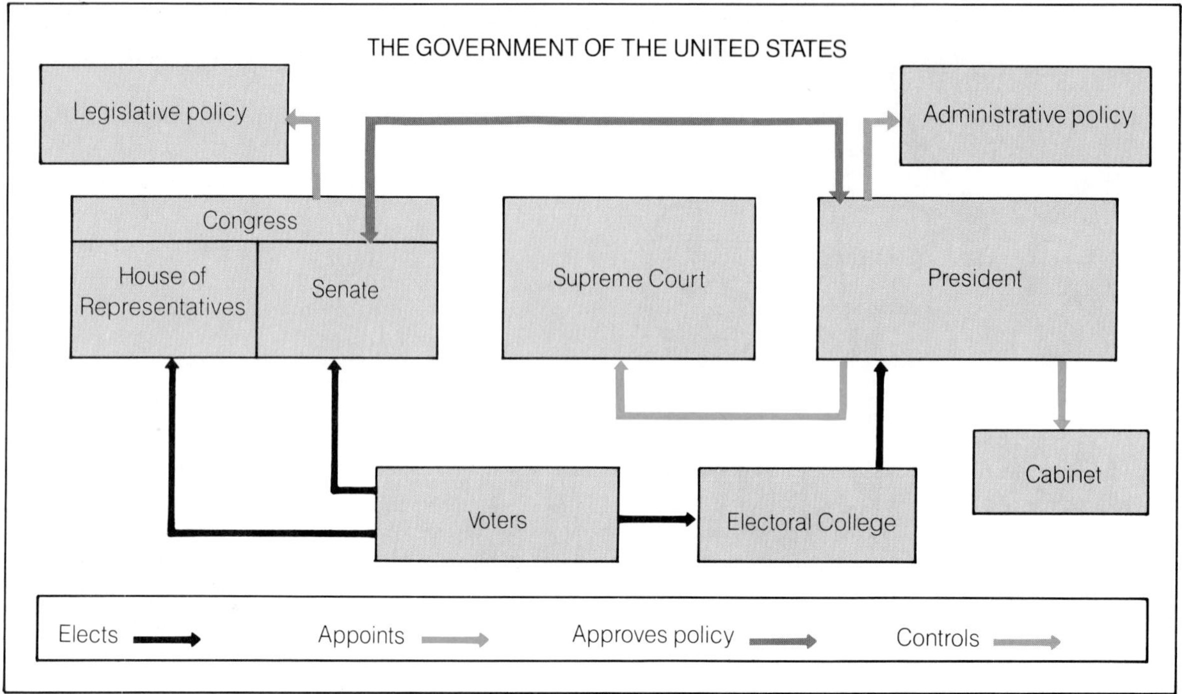

Checking Your Skill

1. What is the title of the chart?
2. What does the title tell you about the information in the chart?
3. What do each of the colors in the key indicate about the structure of the government?
4. How do the colors help you understand the relationships shown on the chart?
5. Based on your interpretation of the chart, write a brief paragraph explaining who controls the government of the United States.
6. How did the information shown on the chart help you reach your conclusion?

ANALYZING A POLITICAL DOCUMENT: PRIMARY SOURCES

Political documents often contain information about the laws and the values of a society. Analyzing a political document enables students of government to gain insight into the reasoning that influences political goals and actions. The following guidelines are helpful when analyzing a political document.

(1) Background
- Who wrote the document?
- When was it written?
- For what purpose was it written?

(2) Terms
- What are the important vocabulary words?
- What do they mean?

(3) Content
- What did the author believe to be most important?
- Can you detect bias in the choice of words?

(4) Significance
- How does the document affect the political situation today?

The following excerpt is from *The Federalist*, No. 10, written by James Madison. The *Federalist Papers* were a defense of the principles and the institutions incorporated into the United States Constitution. Read the excerpt carefully and then answer the questions that follow.

Among the numerous advantages promised by a well-constructed Union, none deserves to be more accurately developed than its tendency to break and control the violence of faction. . . .

There are two methods of curing the mischiefs of faction: the one, by removing its causes; the other, by controlling its effects.

There are again two methods of removing the causes of faction: the one, by destroying the liberty which is essential to its existence; the other, by giving to every citizen the same opinions, the same passions, and the same interests. . . .

[T]he first remedy . . . is worse than the disease. Liberty is to faction what air is to fire. . . . But it could not be a less folly to abolish liberty, which is essential to political life. . . .

The . . . causes of faction are thus sown in the nature of man. . . . A zeal for different opinions concerning religion, concerning government, and many other points . . . have, in turn, divided mankind into parties. . . . But the most common and durable source of factions has been the . . . unequal distribution of property. Those who hold [property] and those who are without property [form] distinct interests in society. Those who are creditors, and those who are debtors, fall under a like discrimination. . . . The regulation of these various and interfering interests forms the principal task of modern legislation and . . . government. . . . The [conclusion] is that the causes *of faction cannot be removed and that relief is only to be sought in the means of controlling its* effects. . . .

A republic, by which I mean a government in which the scheme of representation takes place . . . promises the cure for which we are seeking. . . .

[H]owever small the republic may be the representatives must be raised to a certain number in order to guard against the [intrigues] of a few; and that however large it may be they must be limited to a certain number in order to guard against the confusion of the multitude. . . .

[E]ach representative will be chosen by a greater number of citizens in the large than in the small republic, it will be more difficult for unworthy candidates to practise with success the vicious arts by which elections are too often carried; and the suffrages of the people being more free, will be more likely to center on men who possess the most attractive merit . . . and established characters. . . .

[T]he . . . advantage which a republic has . . . in controlling the effects of faction is enjoyed . . . by the Union over the States composing it. . . .

The influence of factious leaders may kindle a flame within their particular States but will be unable to spread a general [movement] through the other States. . . .

In the extent and proper structure of the Union, therefore, we behold a republican remedy for the diseases most [prevalent in] republican government.

Checking Your Skill

1. Who wrote *The Federalist,* No. 10?
2. What was the author's purpose in writing *The Federalist,* No. 10?
3. Define the following terms:

faction	representatives
republic	suffrage

4. What two causes of faction does the author cite?
5. According to the author, what are the two methods of removing the causes of faction?
6. How does the author define the term *republic*?
7. According to the author, how does a republic provide a cure for the effects of faction?
8. Is the author's viewpoint valid today? Why or why not? Cite examples to justify your answer.

WRITING A PERSUASIVE STATEMENT: STATING YOUR VIEW CLEARLY

Responsibilities of citizens include being informed about issues and taking stands on those issues. If you feel strongly about a governmental policy or a public program, you may want to persuade others to support your view. To do this, you might write a position statement. One way to create a position statement is to follow these guidelines.

(1) List the arguments for and against the issue.
(2) Study the list. Write an opening paragraph that identifies the issue and your position.
(3) Write additional paragraphs that start with your weakest argument and conclude with your strongest. Facts and examples should support the reasoning in each paragraph.
(4) Write one paragraph that summarizes and refutes the opposing arguments.
(5) Develop a concluding paragraph that summarizes the significance of your position and the major reasons for holding that position.

Study the following excerpts from the 1858 Lincoln-Douglas debate. Abraham Lincoln and Stephen A. Douglas were campaigning from Illinois for a seat in the United States Senate. Analyze their persuasiveness by answering the questions below.

. . . [W]hat I understand to be the real issue in this controversy between Judge Douglas and myself. On the point of my wanting to make war between the Free and the Slave states, there has been no issue between us. So, too, when he assumes that I am in favor of introducing a perfect social and political equality between the white and black races. These are false issues. . . . The real issue in this controversy. . . is the sentiment on the part of one class that looks upon the institution of slavery as a wrong, and of another class which does not look upon it as a wrong. The sentiment that contemplates the institution of slavery. . . as a wrong is the sentiment of the Republican Party. They look upon it as being a moral, social, and political wrong;. . . [O]ne of the methods of treating it as a wrong is to make provision that it shall grow no further.

Abraham Lincoln

We ought to extend to the Negro race . . . all the rights, all the privileges and all the immunities which they can exercise consistently with the safety of society. Humanity requires that we should give them all these privileges. . . . What are those privileges, and what is the nature and extent of them? My answer is, that that is a question which each State must answer for itself. . . . If the people of all the States will act on that great principle, and each State mind its own business, attend to its own affairs, take care of its own negroes, and not meddle with its neighbors, then there will be peace between the North and the South, the East and the West, throughout the whole Union.

Stephen A. Douglas

Checking Your Skill

1. What is the issue that Lincoln and Douglas are debating?
2. What is Lincoln's position? Douglas's position?
3. State Lincoln's conclusion. State Douglas's conclusion.
4. Who do you think is more persuasive? Why?
5. Choose a current issue. After researching both viewpoints on the issue, use the guidelines (above) to write a statement that attempts to persuade your classmates to support your view. Read your statement to the class. Then discuss whether your persuasive statement achieved its goal.

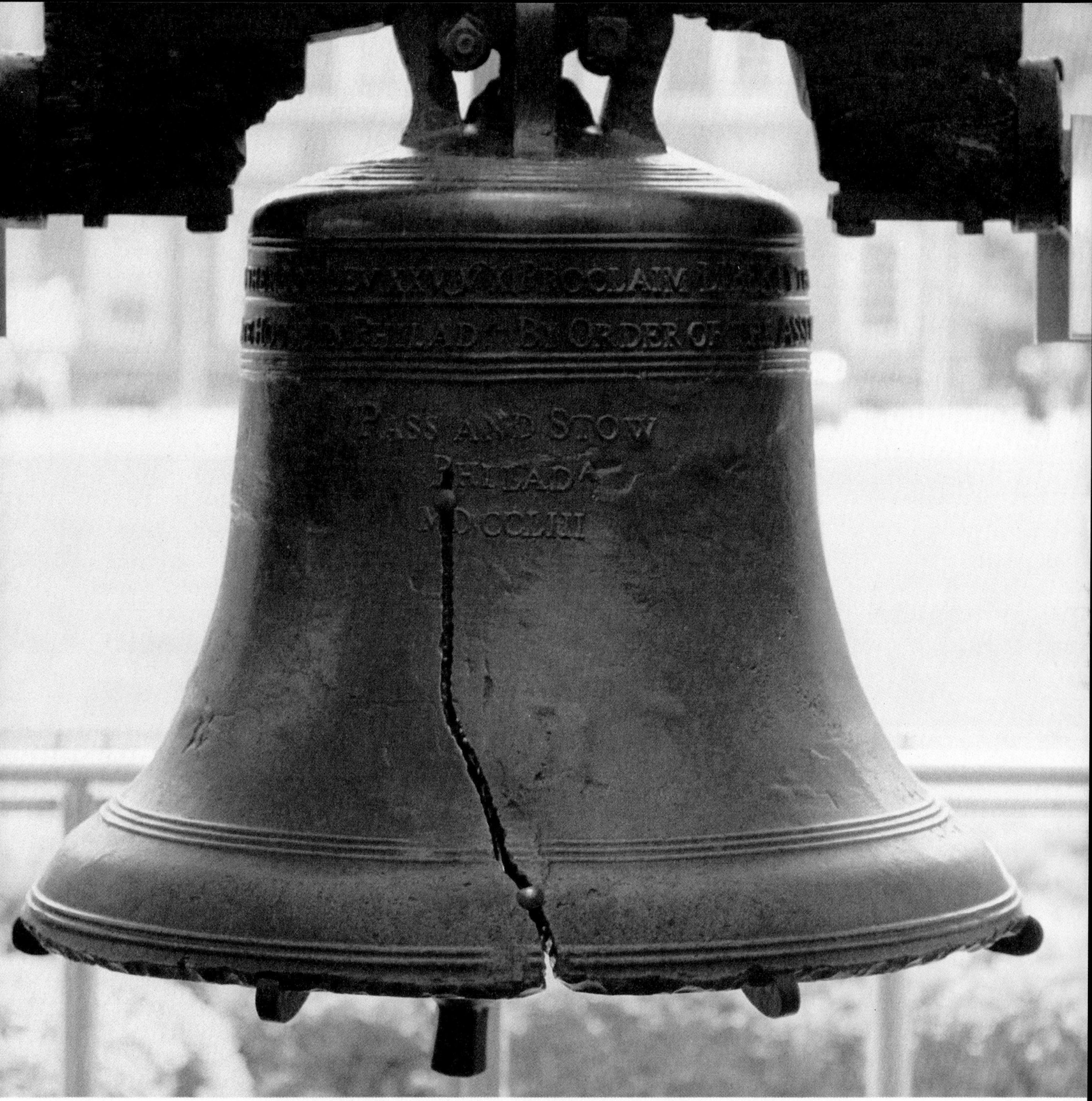

UNIT 1

THE CONSTITUTIONAL FRAMEWORK

Chapter 1

People and Government

If men were angels, no government would be necessary. If angels were to govern men, neither external nor internal controls on government would be necessary. In framing a government which is to be administered by men over men, the great difficulty lies in this: You must first enable the government to control the governed; and in the next place, oblige it to control itself.

JAMES MADISON

CHAPTER OVERVIEW

The customs of many groups of people are based on moral principles. The Ten Commandments, for example, have influenced the customs of Jews and Christians.

1 LAW, GOVERNMENT, AND POLITICS

From birth to death, ***government***—the institutions through which laws are made and enforced—touches every American. When you were born, the doctor filled out a birth certificate, the first recognition from the government of your existence as an individual. At graduation you will receive a diploma in recognition of your educational achievement by a unit of local government. When you begin work for the first time, the government will give you a Social Security number. Each year you will file an income tax return. When you retire, the government will send your monthly Social Security check. When you finally leave this world, you will depart with a death certificate.

There is no ***society,*** or organized group, anywhere in the world—nor has there been at any time—where people simply do as they please. Society depends upon rules, just as does football or any game. Without rules ***anarchy,*** the absence of rules or government, exists. In a society without order "might makes right." No one has security or real freedom. The seventeenth-century English philosopher Thomas Hobbes described life under anarchy as "nasty, brutish, and short."

Rules of Society

The rules by which people live vary from society to society. They also change over time. There are three basic kinds of rules: moral principles, customs, and law.

Moral Principles The rules that are most universally shared among peoples are based on religious or ethical beliefs and are called ***moral principles.*** The Ten Commandments, which are moral principles, proclaim: "Thou shalt not kill," "Thou shalt not steal," and "Honor thy father and thy mother." The Golden Rule says, "Do unto others as you would have them do unto you." Moral principles are found in each of the world's great religions.

Customs People also live according to established ***customs,*** the various cultural patterns that distinguish a society or group from other societies or groups. Customs regulate every aspect of behavior—although people may not realize it. Customs determine the way people dress, what they eat, and the way they behave toward one another. When people do not conform to custom, they are subject to social pressure from other group members. This pressure may be very powerful, and failure to conform may lead to exclusion from the group altogether.

Law Every social organization—family, church, school, company, club, or other group—has rules that apply only to its members. The rules do not extend beyond the group. ***Law*** is a set of rules made and enforced by government that is binding on society as a whole. Government alone has the authority to make laws for society. Law violations may carry severe penalties. Only the government has the legitimate power to fine, imprison, or even put to death lawbreakers.

Legitimacy

Most people obey the law willingly because they believe that their government has ***legitimacy,*** or rightful authority over them. Whether or not a government's legitimacy is accepted by people depends on a number of factors.

This painting, substantially restored after its discovery in Thebes, illustrates the legitimacy of Amenhotep III, who ruled Egypt about 1400 B.C.

In the past legitimacy often depended on tradition or custom. One tradition was the inherited status of the ruler. Birth became an element of legitimacy because people believed that a king or queen was born to rule.

In modern times, especially in most democratic nations, legitimacy rests fundamentally upon four conditions. First, the government officials must be selected in free and competitive elections. Second, the laws must be made according to procedures described in a constitution. Third, the laws enacted must be necessary and just. Fourth, the laws must be enforced fairly, without discrimination or favor.

Essential Functions of Government

Every society, even the most primitive, has some form of government. In the past the Eskimo had one of the simplest forms of government. They lived in small communities scattered across the Arctic from Alaska to Greenland. Survival in the harsh Arctic environment demanded common action by the community which was led by a headman and a priest. There were no separate structures for government, no special officials. It might appear that there was no government at all. But the Eskimo, like all peoples, lived according to rules. Violation of these rules was met by punishment. Disputes within the community were settled by procedures that were understood and accepted. Decisions were also made that affected the lives of each member of the society—decisions about hunting and where to settle. The headman of the community played the most important role in these decisions.

Modern governments are a great deal more complex than the government of the Eskimo. But all societies have the same basic need for government and its three essential functions—maintaining social order, providing necessary services that individuals cannot provide for themselves, and resolving conflicts.

Maintaining Social Order Rules bind the people within a society together. Laws that are made and enforced by government establish the order necessary for social and economic life. Government provides basic security for the lives and property of the people. Without government society would be torn apart by conflict and chaos. People would live in fear. They would be unable to plan for the future. The activities of normal daily life—raising a family, going to school, working, and enjoying leisure time—would be threatened.

INSIGHT

How Government Affects Your Life

Each year national, state, and local governments pass thousands of new laws that cover almost every conceivable subject and that affect almost every aspect of our lives. In a class discussion about the impact of government on daily life, Henry was not convinced that government affected *his* life. "Well, let's see," said Karen. "Let's begin when you got up this morning." In following Henry through his day, this is what the two found.

At 7:00 A.M. the clock radio came on with the weather report. Before Henry rolled over, government had already touched his life. Time zones are set by law. Radio is regulated by the Federal Communications Commission, and the weather report originates with the National Weather Service.

Henry got out of bed and got ready for breakfast and the new day—but not before government had again appeared. The electricity he used came from a public utility. So did the water. The toothpaste he used was inspected and approved by the federal Food and Drug Administration. Its formula is protected by a patent, and its brand name is registered with the Patent and Trademark Office of the U.S. Department of Commerce.

Before Henry even sat down at the table, the Food and Drug Administration and the Department of Agriculture's Consumer and Marketing Service had set standards of quality that had to be met ("U.S. Government Inspected") for each food item he was to eat. Each item had to be constructed, manufactured, or prepared under conditions regulated by law.

After breakfast Henry collected his books and rode the bus to school. Government was with him all the way. His books were under copyright protection by an office of the Library of Congress. His savings account was protected by the Federal Deposit Insurance Corporation. The bus was public transportation, operated by the city and subject to local traffic regulations. The bus, of course, was manufactured to meet federal safety standards.

Henry's public high school was supported by local taxes, state funds, and a number of grants through programs of the federal government. The school was governed by an elected school board and subject to regulation by the state education agency and by standards required by the United States Department of Education.

The review of his activities before class began at 8:30 convinced Henry that government is never very far away from his or anyone's life.

In addition to keeping peace at home by maintaining the social order, the government provides for defense against foreign invasion. National security is a primary goal of every government because each nation seeks to maintain its independence and the security of its territory. Thus a government usually maintains a defense force to ward off invasion and a police force to keep domestic order.

Providing Necessary Services Government provides services that individuals cannot easily provide for themselves. Some governments provide more services than others. In most societies today government services have increased—and so have the taxes to support them. Debates over what services should be provided are frequent. People may want different things. Some may question

In 1849 the United States government purchased Fort Laramie, a former trading post. Situated along the Oregon Trail, the fort housed the troops who helped keep order on the Great Plains. Why might Native Americans and travelers to Oregon have held different views of the fort?

whether a particular service is necessary at all. Abraham Lincoln put it well.

The legitimate object of government is to do for a community of people whatever they need to have done but cannot do at all, or cannot do so well for themselves in their separate and individual capacities. In all that the people can individually do as well for themselves, government ought not to interfere.

Modern government provides a vast number of services. It builds roads, public schools, and parks. It fosters public health through the control of disease. It inspects foods and drugs to ensure their quality and safety. It seeks to prevent the pollution of air and water.

Everyone benefits from these services. Yet few of these services would be provided without government action because only government can make ***binding decisions.*** Only government can make everyone share the costs of government services.

Binding decisions are necessary to assure financial support for government services. People may

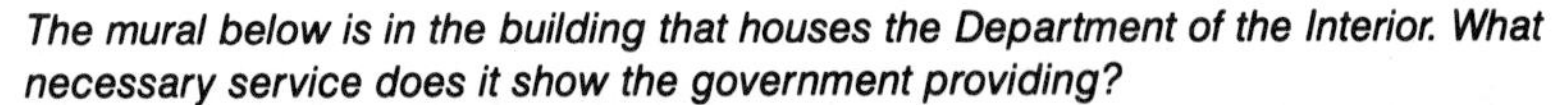

The mural below is in the building that houses the Department of the Interior. What necessary service does it show the government providing?

President Washington reviews the troops before he puts down the Whiskey Rebellion in 1794. What essential function of government does an army provide?

disagree about what services should be provided or what group within society should benefit. Certain groups may strongly oppose some services or activities of government. They may regard them as unwise or even wrong. If it were left to each individual or group to decide which services to support, government would soon collapse. Government cannot depend on voluntary payments. It must have the power to tax.

Binding decisions are also necessary because each service provided by government involves some degree of regulation and control. When government requires all meat to be inspected, it does so to assure the public of its quality. But the producer and the seller may feel inconvenienced by government regulation. Only a binding decision can assure compliance.

Resolving Conflict Fundamental to maintaining social order and providing necessary services is the resolution of ***conflict.*** Conflict is a part of everyday life. It is likely to occur whenever something valued is scarce or limited. It may involve property or a privilege or right. Some kind of procedure is required to settle disputes. Government is necessary to resolve conflict with final authority.

What happens when people have a conflict over the same object? Let us assume that there is a dispute between two families over property ownership. Each family claims full and rightful ownership. Neither is willing to share the disputed property, nor to leave the outcome to chance. But neither wants to act lawlessly. Instead the two families take the issue to the court. The judge and jury hear the arguments on each side, apply the law, and reach a decision. The judgment of the court is binding. It is enforced by the power of the government.

What happens when people conflict over different things? Community conflict usually involves disagreement over what is to be done. Some people want a new freeway; others want a mass transit system. Some people want industrial growth; others want environmental protection. When resources are limited, all of the people are not going to be satisfied. When what is favored by one group is opposed by another, some people necessarily will be unhappy. Government has to make the hard decision, and it does so with final authority. Whatever the outcome, the decision is binding on society.

People obey decisions of government for many reasons. They may feel that it is in their individual interests to do so—that, at least in the long run, they personally benefit. They know too that if they do not obey the government, they may be punished. But most people obey the law willingly. They accept the legitimacy of government authority and understand that order is maintained and conflict peacefully resolved only through binding rules.

LEXICON

The Origins of the State

The term ***state*** refers to a political unit, structured by government and composed of citizens, that has sovereignty within a clearly defined territory. Examples include the United States, Germany, Brazil, and the Soviet Union. ***Sovereignty*** is having absolute power or authority to make final decisions affecting citizens. A state's sovereignty is usually manifested through its government and laws.

Sovereign states such as France, Austria, and Prussia emerged as political bodies during the sixteenth and seventeenth centuries. At that time Western European thinkers sought to explain the origin and nature of a sovereign state. Some thought that a state's ultimate origin was the family, the state being a collection of many families functioning as a whole with a monarch as its head. Other thinkers believed that the state had a divine origin and that monarchs ruled with ***divine right,*** or with authority from God. Thus divine right gave monarchs sovereignty over the citizens of a state.

Scholars such as Thomas Hobbes (1588–1679) believed that people created the state by entering into a ***social contract,*** an agreement whereby they permanently surrendered their individual sovereignty to the state. Hobbes believed that the purpose of the state was to establish peace and order and prevent people from endlessly fighting among themselves. John Locke (1632–1704) also believed that the basis for the state lay in a social contract. But, unlike Hobbes, Locke maintained that the people retained their sovereignty and certain inalienable rights to life, liberty, and property. According to Locke, if the state failed to protect these rights, then the people could change the government—by force or revolution, if necessary. As it shall be shown in Chapter 2, Locke's ideas strongly influenced the Declaration of Independence and the Constitution.

Politics

Many people have a misleading impression of "politics." We have all heard someone say, "Let's keep politics out of this." A leader may be praised for "rising above politics." Yet politics is among the most important activities of public life. Former Senator Howard Baker told an interviewer his idea about politics.

Politics is an honorable undertaking. And I'm proud of it. Politics is an essential part of the self-governing process of the United States. I think it's time we got off this business of saying that politicians in some way or other are unfit to serve or are unworthy of their trust. Politics is the technique by which the people translate their judgments, their political desires, into useful public policy.

Politics is the process of making government decisions. Together government and politics form the ***political system.*** Politics involves conflict between individuals and groups over "who gets what, when, and how." Everyone does not agree on what government should do or on what policies it should pursue. It is through politics that government resolves conflicts.

Politics is "the art of the possible." Politics is a competitive struggle to influence and shape government policy. There is ***compromise*** and conflict. Compromise is settlement or resolution of conflict with each side making concessions. It brings people together in pursuit of common goals. Government would be impossible without compromise.

But conflict is also important. Conflict serves to identify problems within the society. It raises and

President-elect Jackson stops to talk to supporters as he makes his way to his inauguration in 1829. How are politics and the Presidency related?

clarifies issues and makes choice possible. A society without some conflict is very likely to be a society without freedom.

Most political conflict occurs over issues. A political ***issue*** is a matter over which there is public disagreement and debate. Issues vary in intensity. Some are likely to stimulate little interest. Others may arouse great excitement. Conflict also may occur over the nature of the political system itself. Conflict within society involves a delicate balance. For compromise to be possible, conflict must be limited. It must take place within a framework of ***consensus,*** or agreement. Without that agreement intense conflict may lead to civil war—or even revolution.

Section Check

1. Define: government, society, law, state, sovereignty, legitimacy, binding decisions, conflict, consensus
2. What are three kinds of rules by which people live?
3. What three essential functions does government provide for society?
4. What is politics? Why is it important?

2 FORMS OF GOVERNMENT

There are many different ways of classifying governments. A classification is based on a particular characteristic. It tells us about one aspect of government, but it may reveal nothing about other important qualities. A classification also may hide great variation from nation to nation. For this reason governments are usually classified in different ways.

Monarchies and Republics

Governments may be classified as ***monarchies*** or ***republics.*** This distinction turns on the existence of a monarch (a king or queen). Up to the time of World War I (1914–1918), most nations were ruled by monarchs. Many were later defeated in war or overturned by revolution. Today no more than 20 nations can be classified as monarchies. In a very few, like Saudi Arabia, the monarch has real power. Most monarchies that have survived into the twentieth century are limited. These ***constitutional monarchs*** are mainly ceremonial heads of state. They reign but do not rule. Real power lies with an elected parliament. Constitutional monarchies include democratic nations such as Great Britain, Sweden, Norway, the Netherlands, and Japan.

Members of the British Parliament listen to a speech in this eighteenth-century painting. In Great Britain's government, who is head of state? Who is the chief executive?

Republics are those governments that do not have monarchs. They may be parliamentary or presidential, authoritarian or democratic. Among the world's republics are the United States, France, the Union of Soviet Socialist Republics, and the People's Republic of China. To know only that a nation is a republic or a monarchy does not tell us very much about how the government really works or who actually rules.

Unitary, Federal, and Confederal Systems

Another way of classifying governments is according to the distribution of power among governmental units. The focus of attention here is the relation between central government and regional centers of power. There are three basic forms: the unitary system, the federation, and the confederation.

A ***unitary system*** places all legal power in the central government. Lower units of government are created by the center. They derive their power from the center and exist for its administrative convenience. Unitary governments may be either democratic or authoritarian in the exercise of power. Nations with unitary systems include Great Britain, France, Italy, Israel, and Japan.

A ***federal system,*** in contrast, is one in which powers are divided between a central government and certain units of local government. Each level of government exercises some powers independently of the other. Federations take many forms, and the division of powers between the center and local units may be very unequal. Many nations have federal systems. Examples include the United States, Mexico, Canada, West Germany, and India. Some nations are federal only on paper, but in reality are highly centralized.

A ***confederation*** is a league of states. It is a union for limited purposes, and each member keeps its independence. From 1781 until 1789 the 13 American states were associated under the Articles of Confederation. But the task of governing the new nation soon revealed the weakness of confederal government. Today no nation is organized as a confederation. Although it is in no way a true government, the United Nations may be likened to a confederation.

Presidential and Parliamentary Systems

Governments may also be classified according to the relation between the legislative and executive branches—between those who make the law and those who carry it out. There are two basic forms: presidential and parliamentary.

In the ***presidential system*** of government the legislative and executive branches are separate and independent of each other. The chief executive, usually the president, is chosen, either directly or indirectly, in a national election. The president is the national leader and serves a fixed term of office. Neither the president nor any member of the president's cabinet may be members of the legislature. The relation between the executive and the legislature is one in which each checks and balances the actions of the other.

The United States is the leading nation with a presidential form. A few nations have followed the American model, at least on paper. In many countries, for example, the president is in reality a military dictator. In politics form and reality are not always the same.

In the ***parliamentary system*** of government the chief executive, who may be called the prime minister or premier, must be a member of the legislature. The chief executive is formally appointed by the monarch, or in some cases the president, but is responsible to the parliament. Normally the chief executive will be the leader of the majority party. But sometimes a majority must be formed from a ***coalition*** of minority parties that comprise the legislature. If there is not a clear majority in parliament, the monarch may play an important role in choosing the prime minister. Together the chief executive and the cabinet are known as "the government." The chief executive must maintain the confidence of a majority in the legislature. If the government loses that support, the chief executive and the cabinet must resign. If a new government cannot be formed with majority support, elections must be held for a new legislature.

In a presidential system the chief executive, who is normally a president, is also the ceremonial head of state. In parliamentary systems the chief executive and the ceremonial head of state are separate. In constitutional monarchies, Great Britain, for example, the ceremonial head of state is the king or queen. In other parliamentary systems the ceremonial head of state is an elected president. But in a parliamentary system such as France, the president has considerable power. While remaining parliamentary in form, France has adopted features of the presidential system.

Great Britain is the "oldest of parliaments." It has served as the model for governments throughout the world since the thirteenth century. Most of

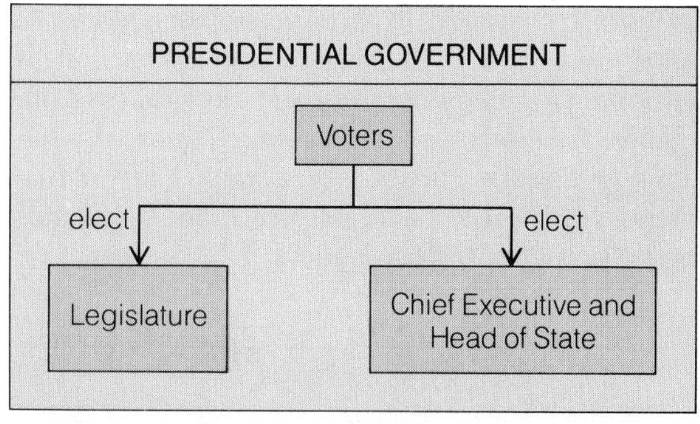

In a presidential form of government, the roles of chief executive and head of state are carried out by the same official. The chief executive, however, must not be a member of the legislature. In a parliamentary form of government, the roles of chief executive and head of state are separate and are carried out by two officials. The chief executive is usually a member of the legislature.

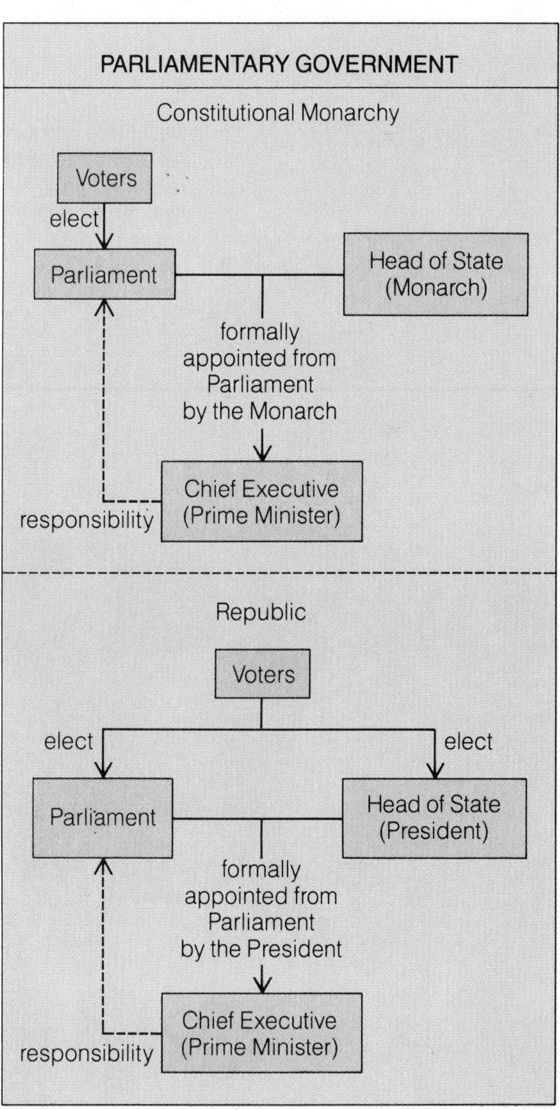

the world's nations have parliamentary forms of government. As with presidential systems, it is important to remember that form often differs from reality. The Soviet Union and the Communist systems of Eastern Europe, for example, are parliamentary in form. But in reality power is in the hands of the Communist party leaders.

Section Check

1. Define: monarchy, republic, constitutional monarchy, parliamentary system, confederation
2. Why are several classifications necessary to describe a government?
3. How does a federal system differ from a unitary system of government?
4. How does a parliamentary form of government differ from a presidential form of government?

3 DICTATORSHIP AND DEMOCRACY

In the study of government one of the most important questions that must be asked is, *"Who governs?"* The ancient Greeks classified governments according to the number of people who held political power—one, a few, or the many. Today, we classify governments in terms of the control and exercise of power. Two basic forms may be distinguished: dictatorship and democracy.

Government by Force

Throughout history most governments have been ***dictatorships*** in which power is concentrated in the hands of one person or an elite—a select few. The rulers are accountable only to themselves, hold power by force, and suppress all opposition. Their exercise of power is unlimited.

Juan Perón, the dictator of Argentina from 1946 to 1955, rides down a street in Buenos Aires after his inauguration for a second six-year term as President. His popular first wife, Eva Perón, stands at his side. How do you think Perón maintained his political control over Argentinians?

Many dictatorships attempt to disguise their true character with a democratic front; for example, they have a constitution and either a presidential or parliamentary structure. There are courts and the appearance of law. There may even be political parties and elections. Behind the democratic front, however, lies power without limits, government without restraint.

Dictatorships vary in the degree of control and in the manner in which power is exercised. Some dictatorships may be relatively mild in their exercise of power. They may be called benevolent because they are disposed to do good. Others may be harsh and oppressive. But even a benevolent dictatorship is no less a dictatorship. Unlimited power is always dangerous. As the Greeks recognized long ago, a wise king can be corrupted and turned into the kind of cruel ruler called a tyrant.

Dictatorships may be described in a wide variety of ways. Some are ***radical*** in that they seek to promote change. Others are ***reactionary*** in that they seek to prevent change. Some dictatorships are run by the military, and others are run by civilians. One way to distinguish among different kinds of dictatorships is according to the scope of their power. ***Authoritarian*** dictatorships usually have limited power. They seek political control but otherwise leave people to themselves. ***Totalitarian*** dictatorships, however, have unlimited power, and they seek to exercise control over almost every aspect of life—political, economic, social, religious, cultural, and personal.

Authoritarianism In dictatorships that are authoritarian, power is concentrated in the hands of one person or an elite and is exercised from the top down. Authoritarian government seeks to control the political behavior of its citizens. Opposition is not permitted. If there are elections, the people have one political party from which to make a choice. If there is a legislative assembly, it is a rubber stamp for those in power. The press, radio, and television are under government control. The people do not enjoy freedom of speech or the right of assembly on political matters. Those who oppose the government can be arrested and jailed without trial.

Some authoritarian governments rule with a fairly light touch, others with a heavy hand. Most authoritarian governments are concerned primarily with political control. Outside of politics, individuals may have considerable freedom. People may even be left to grumble and complain privately—so long as they pose no active threat to the government.

Totalitarianism Totalitarian dictatorships seek a wide range of controls over the individual and society. The ends of the state are taken to justify whatever means are necessary to achieve them. No aspect of life is beyond the control of government. Nothing is private. Even in the fields of music, art, and literature, freedom of expression is not permitted. Rock music and jeans, for example, may be banned as subversive.

Totalitarian government forces people to conform in both action and thought. For those who do not conform, there are prisons, labor camps, and mental hospitals. Secret police create a climate of fear. The mass media—the press, radio, and television—are agents of ***propaganda.*** The people read and hear only what the government wants. They are denied access to foreign newspapers and magazines in which they may read opposition viewpoints. Radio and television broadcasts from abroad are jammed. Only politically approved people are allowed to travel outside the country, and people are rarely allowed to move to another country.

In an authoritarian dictatorship people are free to remain silent. In a totalitarian dictatorship, they must give evidence of their total support. There are elections, but there is only one candidate from a single political party. Opposition and dissent are not permitted. There is an ***ideology***—really a political religion—in which everyone must believe. There is usually a leader who demands total obedience and devotion.

Four dictatorships are most frequently described as totalitarian: Fascist Italy (1922–1943), Nazi Germany (1933–1945), the Soviet Union, and the People's Republic of China.

Fascism arose in Italy under the leadership of Benito Mussolini, who opposed both communism and democracy. Fascism stressed devotion to the glory of the nation and the power of the state. The individual was nothing, the state everything. As *Duce,* or Leader, Mussolini claimed special inspiration and a mystical bond with the people. He glorified war and sought Italian control over the Mediterranean. Fascist rulers were to be an elite—strong in mind, body, and will.

In Germany Adolf Hitler carried fascism to its extreme. Taking power in 1933, Adolf Hitler proclaimed himself *Führer,* or Leader. With the National Socialist, or "Nazi," party he rapidly transformed Germany into a police state. Hitler advanced the idea that the Germans were a "Master Race" and it was Germany's destiny to rule the world. Much of the Nazi racism was directed primarily against the

Jewish people, who were persecuted and forced into concentration camps. Hitler's "final solution" was to destroy 6 million Jews in Nazi gas chambers and ovens, one of the darkest acts in the history of the world.

The rise of three totalitarian governments in the 1930's—Italy, Germany, and Japan—led to World War II. All three powers were defeated by 1945, but only after a staggering toll of lives and property had been taken.

The Communists came to power in Russia in the revolution of 1917. Although the ideals of the new government sounded similar to those of democracy—equality, liberty, and the welfare of the people—the reality of Soviet Communism was quite different. From 1929 to 1953 the dictator Joseph Stalin ruled with brutality and terror. Millions of people were executed or died in prisons and labor camps.

The Soviet Union is still a totalitarian dictatorship, but it is no longer ruled by a single person. Today power is held by a small group of Communist party leaders who have denounced Stalin's dictatorship as tyranny. The secret police, the terror, and the executions of Stalin's time have been replaced by more subtle methods of control and terror.

Soviet society is dominated by the Communist party. Communism is supposed to bring about a "classless society." But equality in the Soviet Union

Benito Mussolini, the fascist dictator of Italy, stands to the right of Adolf Hitler, the dictator of Germany, as they review a military parade. Why were their dictatorships described as totalitarian?

Troops parade in Red Square on the 61st anniversary of the Communist Revolution. Why does the Soviet Union rely so heavily on huge displays of military power?

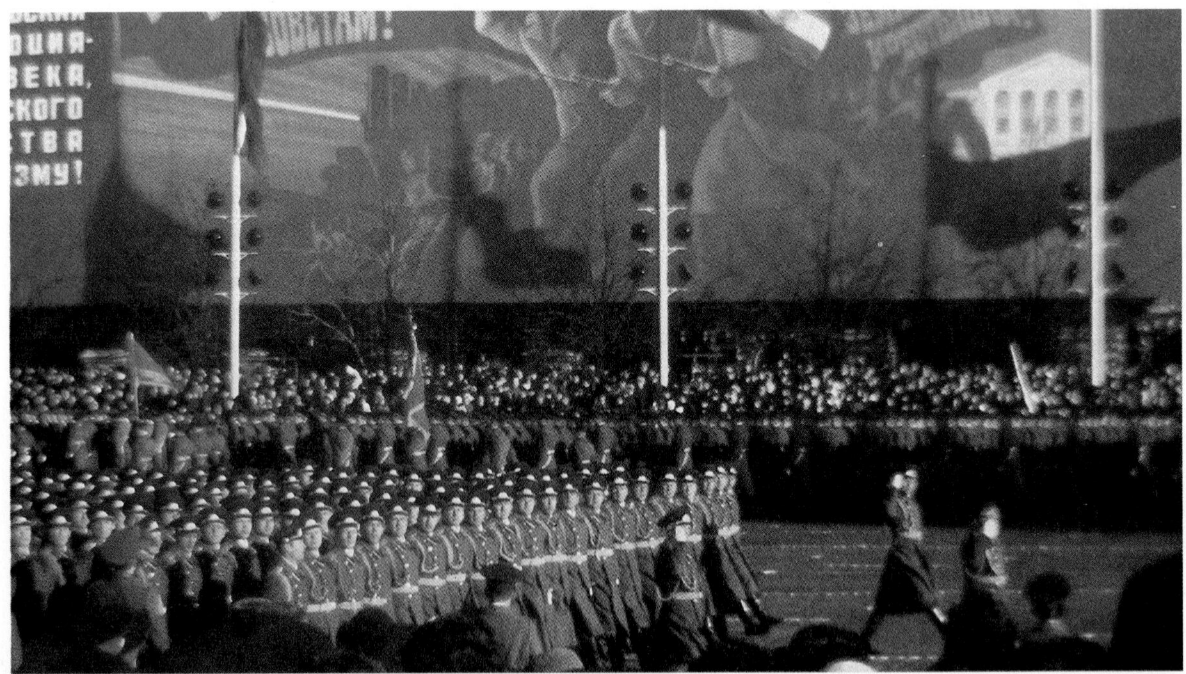

is a myth. Further, personal freedom is sacrificed to the interest of the state, and there are no individual rights in the Soviet Union.

The People's Republic of China was established in 1949 after the Chinese people had engaged in a long civil war. China is the world's largest nation, with more than one billion people. Under the leadership of Mao Zedong the Communists sought to modernize and industrialize China. They organized and accompanied every activity with a political message. Everyone was expected to participate in various mass campaigns. China's success has been remarkable. It is today a great power. The people are adequately housed, clothed, and fed. But China's achievements have come at the cost of freedom.

No political system has fully achieved totalitarian power, although Nazi Germany and the Soviet Union under Stalin came frighteningly close. That the human spirit resists domination can be seen in the courage of Soviet dissidents who today speak out against injustice.

A Chinese wall poster commemorates the takeover of China by Communist forces in 1949. The portrait of a young Mao Zedong may be seen at the lower left.

Government by Consent

Almost every nation in the world claims to be democratic. Communists describe their governments as "people's democracies." An authoritarian government sometimes claims to be a "guided democracy." There are many definitions of ***democracy.***

LEGACY

Democracy in Athens

Democracy began in the small city-state of Athens in ancient Greece. Athens was governed as a ***direct democracy*** in the fifth century B.C. Athenian citizens participated directly in making decisions of government. The statesman Pericles declared, "Our constitution is named a democracy because it is in the hands, not of the few, but of the many." Athenian democracy had four basic features: participation, freedom, equality, and majority rule. Citizens participated directly in making political decisions. Political freedom ensured that all points of view were expressed. All citizens had political equality in public debate, voting, and in eligibility for public office. Decisions were made by majority rule.

Citizenship was limited to free adult males. At its height the total population of Athens was only a little more than 300,000 people. Of these between 40,000 and 50,000 were citizens. Participation in public life was the mark of good citizenship. Its value was personal as well as political. It encouraged the development of moral character, of self-confidence, initiative, and responsibility. Participation also encouraged the development of mutual respect and a sense of community.

Care must be taken because the term *democracy* is used both to describe an ideal system and a political system in the real world. The word *democracy* is a combination of two Greek words: *demos*, meaning "the people," and *kratos*, meaning "rule." Together they mean "rule by the people."

Democratic nations today have millions of people. Direct participation in a great "town meeting" would be impossible. Instead decision making takes place indirectly through elected representatives. This system is known as a representative democracy. Sometimes it is also called a republic. But the essential quality of democracy remains the same. In the words of Abraham Lincoln, it is government "of the people, by the people, and for the people."

Democracy is both a means and an end. As a means democracy is a process. It is concerned with how political decisions are made. As an end democracy is a goal to be achieved. No nation fully achieves the democratic ideal. Governments may be more or less democratic, but each must be judged according to the exercise of its democratic principles. Among the most important principles are these: popular sovereignty, majority rule and minority rights, the dignity of the individual, personal freedom and liberty, mutual respect, public spirit, and equality.

The People Speak Democracy is a process by which decisions are made. In democracy the authority of government is derived from the people. Power is exercised only with the consent of the governed. Government must be by the people—either directly (as in Athenian democracy) or indirectly through elected representatives. This is what is meant by ***popular sovereignty.*** Good laws are most likely to be attained when the people share in the exercise of power. Democracy rests on the assumption that the people are the best judges of their own interests.

In order to ensure that government is responsive to what the people want, there must be free and periodic elections that provide a real choice between alternatives. Once in office, elected representatives are accountable to the people for what they do. If elected representatives abuse their authority, they can be removed from office. If they

An engraving of the 1800's shows Wendell Phillips, an ardent abolitionist, speaking in Boston against the Fugitive Slave Act of 1850. Why is the exercise of popular sovereignty important in a republic?

LEXICON

Majority and Plurality

In majority rule, decisions that count are those made by more than 50 percent of the total voting. But *majority* is often used to mean simply the larger number. When the greater number is less than half of the total, the correct term is *plurality,* not *majority.* For example, in an election that may be decided by a plurality, there may be three candidates. One receives 40 percent of the vote, one 35 percent, and the other 25 percent. The candidate with 40 percent of the votes has a plurality and wins the election.

fail to fulfill their promises, they can be unseated in the next election. Thus, elected representatives work to be responsive to the people.

As self-government, democracy implies the right to know. What goes on in government must be open to public examination. For this reason a free and vigorous press is vital to democracy. Citizens and the press alike must be free to criticize the government when necessary. Everyone must obey the law. But, at the same time, in a democracy people are free to speak out when they believe the law should be changed.

One Out of Many In democracy conflict is resolved by ***majority rule,*** a principle which rests on the belief that more than half of the people will be right most of the time. Majority rule is legitimate only when it is the product of open discussion and free elections. Freedom for all persons to speak their minds and to cast their votes without restraint is essential to the democratic process. Democratic participation rests upon the opportunity to choose among meaningful alternatives. Free choice, in turn, depends on ***minority rights.*** Majority rule and minority rights cannot be separated. In democracy the opinion of the smaller group today may be the opinion of the greater group tomorrow.

Dignity of the Individual In a democracy each person must be recognized as having worth and importance. Each person has reason and can make choices. Each is capable of participating in public affairs and can be educated to the responsibilities of citizenship. One of the goals of democracy is to enable all people to achieve their full potential as individuals. This goal is most likely to be reached when people share in making the decisions that affect their lives.

Fundamental Human Rights Democracy emphasizes that each person has certain fundamental human rights. These rights were not given by government, and they cannot be taken away. Liberty includes both freedom of expression and the right to privacy—the right to be left alone. Individuals should be able to choose for themselves the kind of life they will live. It is not the business of government to choose for them.

Wyoming, the Equality State, granted women the right to vote in 1869. Until Wyoming became a state in 1890, women voted only in territorial elections. Why are voting rights fundamental to a republic?

Liberty is a necessary condition for democracy to exist. People must be free to voice their political opinions—however unpopular they may be. They must be free to organize for political purposes—to be able to join with others in political parties or interest groups. Only under these conditions can there be real and meaningful choice.

Mutual Respect Individual rights are meaningful only in society. Freedom would be meaningless to someone alone on a desert island. People are social, and they exercise their human rights in relation to one another. In order for everyone to have personal freedom, each must respect the rights of others.

Mutual respect involves tolerance for the customs and beliefs of other people. No person has a monopoly on "goodness" or "truth." This recognition provides a basis for compromise when opinions differ. It is also the basis for an openness to change. One must be willing to listen to the other side and to adopt new ideas.

Public Spirit Democracy requires public spirit of its citizens. This is reflected in the sense of community and truth that binds individuals together within a society. People must care about each other. They must have a concern for the welfare of society as a whole. Public spirit involves a willingness to cooperate, to work with others for the common good. It involves a willingness to participate in political life and to accept responsibility for making democracy work.

Equality In democracy there must be political equality. All citizens must have exactly the same opportunity to participate in political life and to hold public office. They must have the right to make their views known and to have their interests considered equally with all others. The vote of each citizen must have equal weight. It may count no more and no less than that of any other citizen.

Democracy also stands for equality before the law. Government must operate according to fixed rules and known procedures. Laws must be applied consistently, fairly, and impartially. No one is above the law. The President and the police officer are subject to the same laws as the average citizen. Whether rich or poor, black or white, male or female, all citizens must have the same rights and be treated equally by the law.

In a democracy there must also be equality of opportunity. All persons must have the chance to develop fully their interests and abilities. People, of course, are not all the same. They differ in interest, ability, and motivation. But no one should be held back because of race, religion, national origin, sex, or social status.

Section Check

1. Define: dictatorship, democracy, radical, reactionary, authoritarian, totalitarian, ideology, fascism
2. Why does "government of the people, by the people, and for the people" best define democracy?
3. What is the difference between a majority and a plurality?
4. Why must minority rights always be respected in a democracy?

---

4 DEMOCRATIC CITIZENSHIP

In a democracy citizens are both rulers and subjects. Citizens are rulers when they elect their representatives or participate in making laws. But as subjects, citizens must obey the laws they have shared in making. The obligation to obey arises from the nature of democratic citizenship. Participation in making law implies a pledge to respect and obey the law.

Participation is the hallmark of democratic citizenship. It is both a right and a responsibility. The strength of democratic government depends on the willingness of the people to be actively involved in public life. Liberty and the rights secured by democratic government can be protected only if they are used. Like muscles of the body, rights must be exercised if they are to remain strong.

In a democracy the people share in making the decisions that affect their lives. They have the capacity to influence, shape, and determine what government does or does not do. Democracy assumes that the people are the best judges of their own interests. The more people are actively involved, the more likely it is that political power will be exercised responsibly and in the public interest.

Participation takes a variety of forms. Democratic participation is voluntary, yet some people are more active than others. At a minimum, participant citizens are informed. They read newspapers and watch the television news. They have the knowledge

Citizens interested in their schools listen attentively to a school-board discussion.

and judgment to evaluate issues and candidates for public office. Participant citizens discuss government and politics. They talk about the issues with their family and friends. Discussion is a forum for learning and understanding. It is a forum for influencing ideas and actions. Participant citizens vote. The right to vote is the power to determine who governs. It is the means by which those in public office are held accountable to the people.

The most active citizens are opinion leaders. They attend public meetings on the issues that concern them most. It may be a hearing on a proposed city zoning change, a school board meeting, or a conference on a major national problem. Opinion leaders speak out on the issues. They write to newspapers, to members of Congress, and to the President.

Citizens may increase their influence when they join with others who share their concerns. Participant citizens are active in interest groups. They seek to shape public opinion and influence government. Participant citizens are active in political parties. They are involved in their local governments. They may attend the county, state, or national party conventions. During campaigns they give time, effort, and money in support of their candidates. They work to get out the vote on election day.

It is in the self-interest of each person to be involved in government and politics. Government touches almost every aspect of our lives—our income, education, and leisure. It determines our freedom and security, and whether we may be called upon to risk our lives in war. Most people want a voice in what affects their lives. Democratic politics provides that opportunity.

If freedom is to be secure, citizens must be active in its defense. Democratic values are learned through participation. If the values of democracy are to be fully achieved, citizens must be willing to participate in government and politics. The most important public office in the United States is that of the private citizen.

Section Check

1. Why can it be said that in a democracy citizens are both rulers and subjects?
2. What are some of the ways that people can participate in a democratic government?
3. What might happen if citizens in a democracy were not informed?
4. How can people in a democracy take part in government and politics?

SUMMARY

Government is the institution through which society makes and enforces its laws, or rules. Society depends upon rules, the most universal of which are moral principles. People also live according to custom and law. People obey the laws of a government that has legitimacy—that is, has rightful authority over them.

Even the most primitive societies have some form of government. Government maintains social order, provides necessary services, and resolves conflicts.

Governments may be classified as monarchies or republics. Their governmental systems may be unitary, federal, or confederal systems. They may also be classified as having presidential or parliamentary systems. Further, the two basic forms of government are dictatorship and democracy.

Democracy is based on the principles of popular sovereignty, majority rule and minority rights, the dignity of individuals, personal freedom and liberty, mutual respect, public spirit, and equality.

In a democracy citizens are both rulers and subjects. Participation is the hallmark of democratic citizenship. Good citizens are informed, discuss the issues, and offer opinions. They may be active in interest groups or in political parties.

Chapter 1 Review

Using Vocabulary

Answer the questions by using the meaning of each underlined term.

1. Why is a compromise often needed to reach a consensus?
2. How does a plurality differ from a majority?
3. Why is choice important in a democracy?
4. Why would you expect popular sovereignty to be a necessary part of self-government?
5. What does legitimacy have to do with a government's binding decisions?
6. Would you expect a radical to have a best friend who is a reactionary? Why or why not?
7. What is the relationship of a government to a political system?
8. Should all conflict be eliminated from politics? Why or why not?
9. What part does a coalition sometimes play in forming a parliamentary system of government?

Understanding American Government

1. Moral principles, customs, and law are three kinds of rules by which people live. Give an example of each.
2. How does life under anarchy differ from life under a system of government?
3. What are the four basic conditions upon which the legitimacy of a government rests?
4. What is meant by the statement, "Only government can make decisions that are binding on society"?
5. Why might politics be considered "the art of the possible"?
6. What is a constitutional monarchy? What are some examples?
7. What is the difference between a unitary system and a federal system? What are some examples of each?
8. In examining systems of government why is it sometimes necessary to look beyond the form a government has on paper to the actual practice of its politics?
9. Explain how democracy is both a means and an end.
10. Explain the importance of majority rule and minority rights in a democracy. How are majority rule and minority rights related?

Extending Your Skills: Comparing Charts

Study the charts on page 25. Then answer the questions that follow.

1. Whom do voters choose in a presidential government? In a parliamentary government?
2. Who selects the prime minister in a constitutional monarchy? In a republic?
3. In a constitutional monarchy, to whom is the chief executive responsible?
4. In a presidential government, to whom is the legislature responsible?
5. Contrast the chief executive's responsibility to the voters in a presidential government with that of a parliamentary government.

Government and You

1. Throughout history people have claimed that there need not be conflict in society. Do you think conflict is part of life? Is government necessary to regulate who gets what, when, and how?
2. Politics has been defined as the process of making government decisions. Yet many people have a misleading impression of politics. Why?
3. Explain how both conflict and cooperation may lead to a better democratic society.

Activities

1. Make a list of ten countries not mentioned in this chapter. Look up each in an encyclopedia to determine what kind of government it has. Prepare a chart to compare and contrast the various governments.
2. Prepare an account of your own day from the time you woke up until school began, indicating all the ways that government has touched your life—from regulating the air waves to ensuring the quality of the foods you eat and the safety of many products you use. Present your account to the class.
3. Do you know someone who has lived under a system of government different from the United States? Interview this person to learn about life under this form of government. Report your findings to the class.

Chapter 2

Founding the Republic

We hold these truths to be self-evident, that all men are created equal, that they are endowed by their Creator with certain unalienable Rights, that among these are Life, Liberty, and the pursuit of Happiness.

THE DECLARATION OF INDEPENDENCE

CHAPTER OVERVIEW

English nobles force King John to sign the Magna Carta. The signing of the Magna Carta was an important first step in the development of the English parliamentary system. Later, settlers from England brought their ideas of government to the New World.

1 THE AMERICAN POLITICAL HERITAGE

The Declaration of Independence proclaims the principles upon which the United States was founded: equality, liberty, and democracy. These principles are rooted deep in America's political heritage, as they were drawn from the political traditions of England and from the colonists' experiences in America. During the years 1776 to 1789 the framework of American government began to take shape. Each state drew up its own constitution which described the way its government would function. A union of states was established under the Articles of Confederation. Finally, to secure a more perfect union, a federal Constitution was drafted and ratified.

Government in England

People from many nations explored and settled the territory that became the United States. The English came in the greatest numbers. Their 13 colonies lined some 1,300 miles (2,100 km) of North America's Atlantic coast. These settlers brought with them a political system that had been developing in England for centuries.

Limited Government The Magna Carta or "Great Charter" of 1215 established the principle of limited government in England by placing restraints on the power of the English king or queen. In 1689 the Bill of Rights, another historic document, set limits on what the crown could do and protected the rights of English people.

Representative Government Fifty years after the Magna Carta was signed, a representative Parliament was established in England. Titled gentlemen and ordinary citizens sat in this body and deliberated about giving their consent to new or higher taxes. Gradually, lawmaking powers passed from the crown to Parliament. By the time the first colonies were established in the Americas, representative government in England was firmly rooted. The Glorious Revolution of 1688—a bloodless revolution in which Parliament replaced the unpopular James II with James's daughter Mary and her husband, William of Orange—secured the supremacy of Parliament over the crown.

Political Institutions By the seventeenth century there were three political institutions in England. Parliament was the source of law; it had

Parliament replaced the unpopular King James II with William III (left) and Mary II (right) in 1689. This action established the supremacy of Parliament.

legislative authority. ***Executive*** authority rested with the monarch. An independent system of courts had ***judicial*** authority.

Parliament was ***bicameral***—that is, divided into two chambers. The House of Lords, the "upper house," represented the nobility. The House of Commons, the "lower house," represented the people with voting rights. In the seventeenth and eighteenth centuries the right to vote, ***suffrage,*** was largely limited to male landowners. Although the House of Lords had the power to ***veto,*** or prevent, an act by the lower house from becoming law, the House of Commons was the more important chamber because it controlled finances.

The role of the crown was limited. The monarch possessed the power to veto acts of Parliament, but this was last used in 1706. It was the responsibility of the crown to see that the laws were enforced and that domestic peace was maintained. Judges were appointed by the monarch. Once in office, however, they could not be removed. Thus, the independence of the courts was secured.

Common Law A body of law developed from decisions made by judges on the basis of local customs. The body of law developed into the ***common law*** as judges, encountering situations similar to those found in earlier cases, applied the rulings from these cases. These decisions from earlier cases are called ***precedents.*** The law of these cases eventually became common throughout England and the English-speaking world.

Colonial Government

The American colonies were part of the British Empire. The first permanent colony established in America was Jamestown, Virginia, in 1607. The Jamestown colony was based on a ***charter,*** an agreement between a commercial company and King James I. Over the next 125 years 12 more colonies were established by written agreements between the colonists and those who granted them the right to colonize. Georgia, settled in 1733, was the last colony.

Although charters issued by the crown differed, in each case the English monarch was the ruler and supervised colonial affairs. The agreement set forth the form of government in the colony and guaranteed settlers the rights and privileges of English people.

Most colonial charters included a statement of rights as an additional safeguard of individual liberty. The Massachusetts "Body of Liberties," adopted

LEGACY

The Mayflower Compact

Winter was beginning. The Pilgrims, a small group of English colonists who had separated from the Church of England, found themselves nearing a distant shore far off course from the land grant of their original charter. No charter existed for Cape Cod Bay, where they would land. The Pilgrims therefore drew up the Mayflower Compact.

"We whose names are underwritten," the Pilgrims wrote, "do covenant and combine ourselves together into a civil body politic." With these words the 41 adults who signed the compact set up a government of their own—one that rested on the consent of the governed. They agreed to obey the officers they would elect and the laws they might pass "for the general good of the colony."

In contrast to the charters of other colonial governments, the government at Plymouth established by the Mayflower Compact was based on a ***social contract,*** an agreement among people to unite for the common good. In fact, the Mayflower Compact represents the first written agreement for self-government made in America.

The Pilgrims write and sign the Mayflower Compact before landing at Cape Cod in November 1620. This document served as the basis of the colonists' government. Why was the Mayflower Compact a social contract?

in 1641, guaranteed free elections, no taxation without representation, trial by jury, and the requirement that no person be deprived of life, liberty, or property without due process of law.

There were variations among the colonies in the specific form of government, but all colonial governments had an executive branch, a legislative branch, and a judicial branch. The colonial governors had executive authority and usually commanded great formal power. In practice, however, the governors' powers were limited by their dependence on the legislatures—especially the lower house, which had control over all appropriations of money. This was "the power of the purse." Most colonial legislatures were bicameral; they were composed of a council (upper house) and an assembly (lower house). Colonial judges were usually appointed by the governors.

The Three Types of Colonies According to the form of government in each, there were three types of colonies: royal, proprietary, and charter.

By the beginning of the Revolutionary War the ***royal colonies*** were Virginia, Massachusetts, New Hampshire, New York, New Jersey, North Carolina, South Carolina, and Georgia. In each royal colony a governor and a council were appointed by the English monarch and an assembly was elected by voters. The governor ruled the colony according to orders from the crown and was usually quite powerful. The lower house provided a place for the colonists to air their grievances. Much of the dissent that led to the Revolutionary War arose in the popular assemblies of the royal colonies.

The ***proprietary colonies*** were Maryland, Pennsylvania, and Delaware. In each of these colonies a ***proprietor***—an individual to whom the monarch had made a grant of land—appointed a governor and authorized a legislature. The proprietor also established courts and created local governments.

The ***charter colonies*** were Connecticut and Rhode Island. Each of these colonies was given the right of self-government through a charter, which was granted by the crown and which established limited and representative government. The colony elected its own governor, council, and assembly each year. The governor had no veto power over the assembly's acts.

The Right to Vote Suffrage was limited in the American colonies. Most white adult male citizens who owned property could vote, but women, indentured servants, slaves, and the very poor could not. Land was considered basic property, but other possessions could be substituted for it. Most colonies also limited voting rights to members of certain church groups. In the royal colonies, for example, all voters had to be members of the Church of England, sometimes called the Anglican Church. Despite these restrictions a large number of colonists could vote. In England and other parts of Great Britain less than ten percent of all adult males had the right to vote. In the colonies between 50 and 75 percent of all adult males were entitled to vote.

Local Government Local government in the colonies was modeled after that in England and played an important role in colonial political life because many matters were wholly within local control. In the South justices of the peace who were appointed by the governors conducted most public business in ***county courts.*** The justices of the peace levied taxes, supervised road construction and ferry service, and organized groups of citizen soldiers called the ***militia.*** They also tried certain civil and criminal cases. In New England, only the courts tried cases. Citizens held ***town meetings*** at which they voted on local laws and elected town officials. In the other colonies, local government operated at the county and town levels. The colonists' participation in local government provided valuable experience for self-government after the Revolutionary War.

The Road to Independence

For more than 150 years the American colonists handled their own affairs with little interference from Britain. Following the British victory over the French in 1763, Britain sought more direct control over the colonies. It had provided military protection to the colonists. Now it demanded that the colonists pay part of the cost. At the same time, the colonists were expected to develop no industry of their own and serve as a market for British manufactures. Parliament levied new taxes to raise revenue and imposed various regulations on trade to help Britain's economy. The new trade limits hurt traders and merchants in the northern colonies and planters in the southern colonies for whom free trade meant greater profits.

The American colonists had no representatives in Parliament. Although they were loyal to the king, the colonists maintained that they had as much right to manage their local affairs as did people in Britain. They argued that the powers of government must

rest on the consent of the governed. The argument gave rise to the famous rallying cry, "No Taxation Without Representation."

Opposition to Britain's tax and trade policies united the colonists, especially after Parliament passed the Stamp Act in 1765. This law required the use of stamps on printed matter such as legal documents and newspapers. Opposition among the colonists was heated and sometimes violent. A Stamp Act Congress, attended by delegates from nine colonies, met in New York in October 1765. The delegates drafted a "Declaration of Rights and Grievances," protesting the stamp taxes and other British policies. Parliament finally repealed the law because it was not bringing in any money.

Still the British government continued to pass laws taxing the colonies. In 1772 Samuel Adams of Massachusetts formed Committees of Correspondence in the colonies to coordinate resistance to Britain's demands. By 1773 these committees provided a network of cooperation and information.

When radicals in Boston resisted Britain's monopoly on tea imports by dumping tea into the harbor, Parliament responded by passing the Coercive Acts. These acts—called the Intolerable Acts in

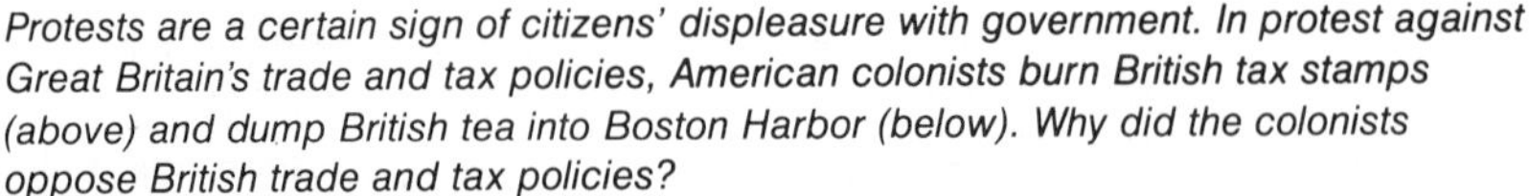

Protests are a certain sign of citizens' displeasure with government. In protest against Great Britain's trade and tax policies, American colonists burn British tax stamps (above) and dump British tea into Boston Harbor (below). Why did the colonists oppose British trade and tax policies?

the colonies—were designed to punish the colonists for the Boston Tea Party and similar acts of resistance. Instead the passing of the Coercive Acts provoked the calling of the First Continental Congress.

The First Continental Congress, attended by 56 delegates from every colony except Georgia, met in Philadelphia in September 1774. The delegates sent a Declaration of Rights to George III, the British king. They recommended a boycott of British goods and called for a Second Congress to meet the following May.

The British, instead of pacifying the colonists, applied even stricter measures. Then, at Lexington and Concord on April 19, 1775, British soldiers and colonial militia fired on each other. The Second Continental Congress met on May 10, 1775, in Independence Hall in Philadelphia to deal with this crisis. Representatives from all 13 colonies attended. Even after the fighting had started and independence had been declared, most colonists felt some compromise with Great Britain was possible. What most of the colonists wanted was a guarantee of their basic rights as subjects of the British crown.

Section Check

---

1. Define: legislative, executive, judicial, suffrage, veto, common law, charter, social contract
2. Identify: the Magna Carta, Parliament, Mayflower Compact, Stamp Act, the Second Continental Congress
3. What patterns of self-government did the colonists develop before independence?
4. Describe three types of colonies founded in North America by the British.

---

2 A NEW NATION: 1776–1787

By June 1776 nearly all members of the Second Continental Congress were in favor of independence. Richard Henry Lee of Virginia introduced a resolution for independence on June 7. A committee was appointed to draft a statement to proclaim independence and explain to the world why the American colonies were rebelling. The committee members were John Adams, Benjamin Franklin, Thomas Jefferson, Robert Livingston, and Roger Sherman. But the Declaration of Independence was mainly the work of the 33-year-old Jefferson. The Second Continental Congress adopted the Declaration of Independence on July 4, 1776. The complete text of the Declaration of Independence begins on page 46.

The Declaration of Independence

In preparing the Declaration of Independence, Jefferson was deeply influenced by the English philosopher John Locke, justifying the Revolutionary War on the basis of Locke's doctrine of the right of revolution.

Most of the Declaration of Independence is a list of grievances the colonists felt toward Britain and George III. But the Declaration also set forth equality, liberty, and democracy as three fundamental principles of the new American nation.

The first principle is ***equality***—"all men are created equal." The term *men* was used at that time, as it is sometimes today, to refer to all people. To Jefferson equality meant human dignity, worth, and self-respect.

Thomas Paine wrote the pamphlet Common Sense *in 1776. It influenced many colonists to favor independence from Great Britain.*

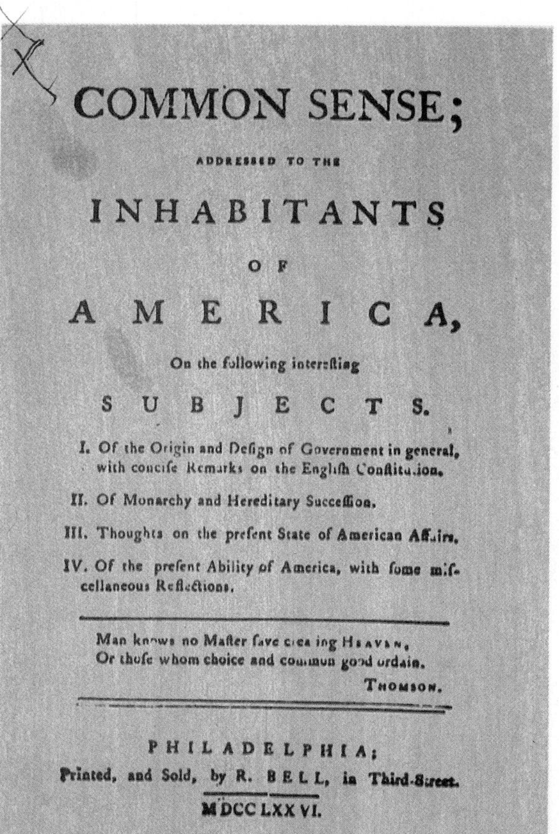

COMMON SENSE;

ADDRESSED TO THE

INHABITANTS

OF

AMERICA,

On the following interesting

SUBJECTS.

I. Of the Origin and Design of Government in general, with concise Remarks on the English Constitution.

II. Of Monarchy and Hereditary Succession.

III. Thoughts on the present State of American Affairs.

IV. Of the present Ability of America, with some miscellaneous Reflections.

Man knows no Master save creating Heaven,
Or those whom choice and common good ordain.

THOMSON.

PHILADELPHIA;
Printed, and Sold, by R. BELL, in Third-Street.
MDCCLXXVI.

PROFILE

John Locke and the Social Contract

Almost 100 years before Thomas Jefferson wrote the Declaration of Independence, the English philosopher John Locke wrote his *Second Treatise on Government.* Locke composed the essay to explain and justify the Glorious Revolution—the English revolution of 1688.

In his essay Locke wrote that government was the product of a social contract, which is an agreement among people to submit themselves to a government of laws. The authority of government, Locke believed, rested on the consent of the governed. The chief purpose of government was to protect the natural rights of human beings—including rights to life, liberty, and property. The power of government, Locke wrote, "is to be directed to no other end but the peace, safety, and public good of the people." Locke believed that the social contract was broken if a government abused its power and the trust of the people who had formed it. The people then had a right to revolt and form a new government.

Locke's ideas made a profound impression on Jefferson, who considered Locke one of the greatest men the world had ever produced. Locke's concept of natural rights inspired Jefferson to write in the Declaration of Independence of the rights of "Life, Liberty, and the Pursuit of Happiness." Jefferson also echoed Locke's words when he wrote that "Governments are instituted among Men, deriving their just powers from the consent of the governed." For a people struggling against the tyranny of British rule, Locke's most powerful idea was the right of revolution. As Jefferson wrote, "whenever any Form of Government becomes destructive . . . it is the Right of the People to alter or to abolish it, and to institute new Government . . . to effect their Safety and Happiness."

The second principle is ***liberty.*** People "are endowed by their Creator with certain unalienable Rights, that among these are Life, Liberty, and the pursuit of Happiness." These are ***natural rights.*** They are "unalienable" because they are not given by government, and they cannot be taken away. Today natural rights are called ***human rights.*** The purpose of government is "to secure these rights."

The third principle is ***democracy.*** The just powers of a democratic government come "from the consent of the governed." In a democracy, ***popular sovereignty,*** or supreme power, rests with the people, who exercise control through elections and the democratic principle of majority rule.

Jefferson asserted that "the will of the majority is in all cases to prevail," but that the rights of the minority must never be lost. To be legitimate, or rightful, majority rule must come out of free and open discussion.

The Declaration of Independence was a superb statement of democratic principles. But it was the task of the Framers of the Constitution in 1787 to shape these principles into a working government.

State Constitutions

After independence, Americans preserved much of their English political heritage. The transition from colony to state was accomplished smoothly, and there were none of the major social, economic, or political upheavals characteristic of a revolution.

With minor changes Connecticut and Rhode Island turned their colonial charters into state constitutions. Most of the other states replaced their colonial charters with written constitutions in 1776 and 1777. The constitutions were written descriptions of the kind of government each state would have and of the powers given by the people to each part of government. Assemblies or conventions were commonly used to draft and approve the new documents. Massachusetts set a precedent by submitting its constitution to the voters for approval.

There were variations in detail among the different constitutions. The constitutions, however, reflected a fundamental agreement on the principles of democratic government. They divided the government into three separate branches: an elected legislature, which was the source of laws; an executive, which administered the laws; and the courts, which enforced the laws. The state constitutions introduced a variety of checks and balances into the relationship of the legislative, executive, and judicial branches. Their purpose was to prevent abuse of power and to guarantee liberty.

State legislatures replaced the colonial assemblies. The state constitutions gave the legislatures a great deal of power because they were regarded as the branch of government that represented the people. Most states adopted bicameral legislatures. Representatives had less power in the state legislatures than in the colonial assemblies because the legislatures were larger than the assemblies and the terms of office were usually only one year.

The governors were given very little power by the state constitutions because experience with royal governors had led most colonists to fear the executive use of authority. The duties of the governors were mainly administrative. Pennsylvania went so far as to abolish the office of governor, replacing it with a council of 12 persons elected by the people. In Virginia the governor was elected by the legislature, not by the people.

Most constitutions contained ***bills of rights*** that limited what state governments could do and that listed those rights guaranteed to the people. The state constitutions also contained statements on equality. The Virginia Constitution stated that by nature all men are "equally free and independent." Nevertheless, all people were not equal in their situation. Slavery still existed, and antislavery feeling was growing. But only in Massachusetts was the constitutional provision that "all men are born free and equal" interpreted to abolish slavery.

Equality was limited in another important sense. Except for New Jersey, where women were permitted to vote, suffrage was restricted to adult white males. The qualifications for voting varied among the states. In some states virtually all white men could vote. In others ownership of property was required. Some states also required substantial property as a qualification to hold elected office. Property ownership was widespread, however. Thus, despite limitations on suffrage, the first state constitutions were the most democratic in the world.

The Articles of Confederation

Soon after the Declaration of Independence was adopted in 1776, the Second Continental Congress began debate on a plan to unite the colonies. Benjamin Franklin had long called for some form of federation among the colonies. "Join, or die," he

A 1774 newspaper includes the slogan "Join or Die," which became a rallying cry for the colonies.

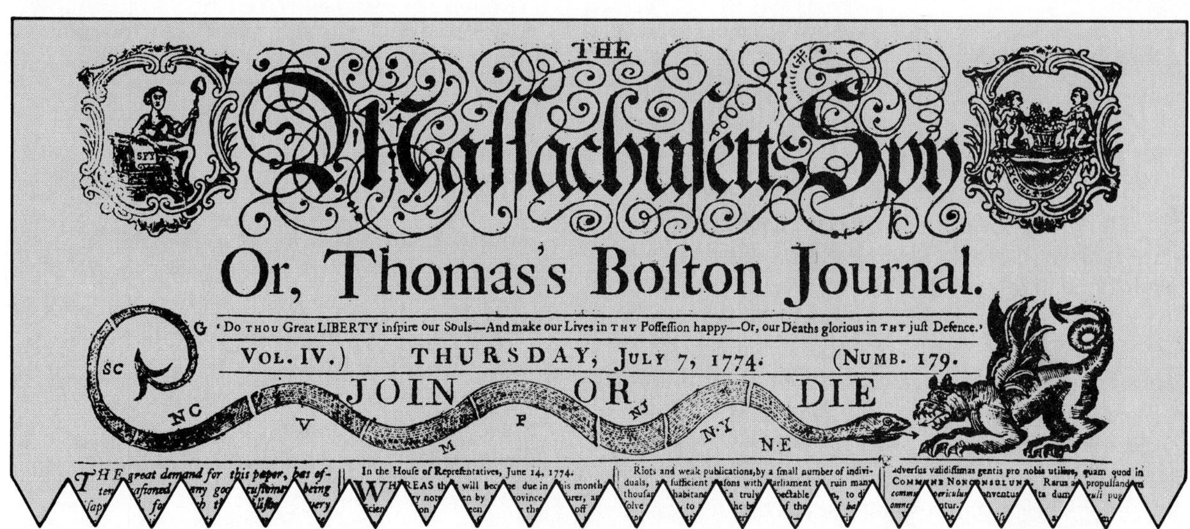

THE Massachusetts Spy

Or, Thomas's Boston Journal.

'Do THOU Great LIBERTY inspire our Souls—And make our Lives in THY Possession happy—Or, our Deaths glorious in THY just Defence.'

VOL. IV.) THURSDAY, JULY 7, 1774. (NUMB. 179.

JOIN OR DIE

had warned. The new nation could not survive unless it was united. The states, however, jealously guarded their independence. People feared concentrating power as it had been under British rule. Most Americans believed that state governments, which were closer to the people, were the best way to preserve equality, liberty, and democracy.

To combine the independent states into a league for defense, the Second Continental Congress drafted the Articles of Confederation and approved them on November 15, 1777. The Articles, however, required unanimous ***ratification,*** or formal approval, by the states, so the Articles did not go into effect until March 1, 1781. At that time the Articles of Confederation established the United States as a union of otherwise independent states.

The Articles of Confederation gave the new nation the name United States of America. The nation was established as a "perpetual Union," with each state retaining its "sovereignty, freedom, and independence, and every Power, Jurisdiction, and right . . . not . . . expressly delegated to the United States." The states entered into a "firm league of friendship with each other, for their common defense, the security of their Liberties, and their mutual and general welfare." As a Confederation it was a limited union.

The structure of government under the Articles followed the existing arrangements of the Second Continental Congress. The Articles established only one body of government, the Congress. There was no executive or judicial branch. These functions were handled by committees of the Congress. Delegates were chosen annually by the state legislatures and could be removed at any time. Each state, regardless of size or population, could be represented by two to seven delegates. The states, however, had only one vote each. Action on important matters required support of at least nine states, and the Articles could be amended only by the consent of all 13 states.

The Articles of Confederation, which established a limited union rather than a central government, had two basic weaknesses. First, Congress was totally dependent on the states for revenue and had no means to make them pay because it was not given the power to raise money. Failure of the states to meet their financial obligations to the Congress left the Confederation in continuous difficulty, unable to meet its debts. Second, Congress had no power to regulate commerce among the states and with foreign countries. As a result the states had separate trade policies. They placed duties on incoming goods from other states and approved tariffs as a barrier to trade. This stunted the growth of a national economy.

Political and Economic Crises: 1781–1787

In October 1781 the last battle of the War for Independence was fought at Yorktown. America was victorious. But under the weak government of the Articles of Confederation, the United States nearly lost the peace it had won. The states quarreled among themselves and often refused to obey laws and treaties made by Congress. Most even raised their own armies and navies and negotiated directly with foreign governments.

In the economic depression that followed the War for Independence, the weakness of the new government became increasingly evident. Each state printed its own currency in large quantities and with little backing in gold or silver. Inflation cheapened the value of the dollar. In the unstable economy, people lost confidence in the Confederation, and conflict grew between various groups.

Some people, among them Alexander Hamilton, had never trusted government by the people. Their worst fears now seemed confirmed. George Washington and James Madison pleaded for a more effective government, arguing that only a strong central government could save the values for which the nation had fought. The states showed little interest in strengthening the union until word came of Shays's Rebellion—an armed uprising by several thousand poor farmers in western Massachusetts. The uprising gave added urgency to the national crisis. Congress now called on the states to appoint delegates to a convention for the "sole and express purpose of revising the Articles of Confederation."

Section Check

1. Define: equality, liberty, natural rights, democracy, state constitution, ratification
2. Identify: John Locke, Thomas Jefferson, Alexander Hamilton, Shays's Rebellion, the Articles of Confederation
3. For which two purposes was the Declaration of Independence written?
4. What are the three basic principles of the Declaration of Independence?

IN CONGRESS, JULY 4, 1776.

The unanimous Declaration of the thirteen united States of America,

When in the Course of human events it becomes necessary for one people to dissolve the political bands which have connected them with another, and to assume among the powers of the earth, the separate and equal station to which the Laws of Nature and of Nature's God entitle them, a decent respect to the opinions of mankind requires that they should declare the causes which impel them to the separation. —— We hold these truths to be self-evident, that all men are created equal, that they are endowed by their Creator with certain unalienable Rights, that among these are Life, Liberty and the pursuit of Happiness. — That to secure these rights, Governments are instituted among Men, deriving their just powers from the consent of the governed, — That whenever any Form of Government becomes destructive of these ends, it is the Right of the People to alter or to abolish it, and to institute new Government, laying its foundation on such principles and organizing its powers in such form, as to them shall seem most likely to effect their Safety and Happiness. Prudence, indeed, will dictate that Governments long established should not be changed for light and transient causes; and accordingly all experience hath shewn, that mankind are more disposed to suffer, while evils are sufferable, than to right themselves by abolishing the forms to which they are accustomed. But when a long train of abuses and usurpations, pursuing invariably the same Object evinces a design to reduce them under absolute Despotism, it is their right, it is their duty, to throw off such Government, and to provide new Guards for their future security. — Such has been the patient sufferance of these Colonies; and such is now the necessity which constrains them to alter their former Systems of Government. The history of the present King of Great Britain is a history of repeated injuries and usurpations, all having in direct object the establishment of an absolute Tyranny over these States. To prove this, let Facts be submitted to a candid world. —— He has refused his Assent to Laws, the most wholesome and necessary for the public good. —— He has forbidden his Governors to pass Laws of immediate and pressing importance, unless suspended in their operation till his Assent should be obtained; and when so suspended, he has utterly neglected to attend to them. —— He has refused to pass other Laws for the accommodation of large districts of people, unless those people would relinquish the right of Representation in the Legislature, a right inestimable to them and formidable to tyrants only. —— He has called together legislative bodies at places unusual, uncomfortable, and distant from the depository of their public Records, for the sole purpose of fatiguing them into compliance with his measures. —— He has dissolved Representative Houses repeatedly, for opposing with manly firmness his invasions on the rights of the people. —— He has refused for a long time, after such dissolutions, to cause others to be elected; whereby the Legislative powers, incapable of Annihilation, have returned to the People at large for their exercise; the State remaining in the mean time exposed to all the dangers of invasion from without, and convulsions within. —— He has endeavoured to prevent the population of these States; for that purpose obstructing the Laws for Naturalization of Foreigners; refusing to pass others to encourage their migrations hither, and raising the conditions of new Appropriations of Lands. —— He has obstructed the Administration of Justice, by refusing his Assent to Laws for establishing Judiciary powers. —— He has made Judges dependent on his Will alone, for the tenure of their offices, and the amount and payment of their salaries. —— He has erected a multitude of New Offices, and sent hither swarms of Officers to harrass our people, and eat out their substance. —— He has kept among us, in times of peace, Standing Armies without the Consent of our legislatures. —— He has affected to render the Military independent of and superior to the Civil power. —— He has combined with others to subject us to a jurisdiction foreign to our constitution, and unacknowledged by our laws; giving his Assent to their Acts of pretended Legislation: — For Quartering large bodies of armed troops among us: — For protecting them, by a mock Trial, from punishment for any Murders which they should commit on the Inhabitants of these States: — For cutting off our Trade with all parts of the world: — For imposing Taxes on us without our Consent: — For depriving us in many cases, of the benefits of Trial by Jury: — For transporting us beyond Seas to be tried for pretended offences — For abolishing the free System of English Laws in a neighbouring Province, establishing therein an Arbitrary government, and enlarging its Boundaries so as to render it at once an example and fit instrument for introducing the same absolute rule into these Colonies: — For taking away our Charters, abolishing our most valuable Laws, and altering fundamentally the Forms of our Governments: — For suspending our own Legislatures, and declaring themselves invested with power to legislate for us in all cases whatsoever. — He has abdicated Government here, by declaring us out of his Protection and waging War against us. —— He has plundered our seas, ravaged our Coasts, burnt our towns, and destroyed the lives of our people. — He is at this time transporting large Armies of foreign Mercenaries to compleat the works of death, desolation and tyranny, already begun with circumstances of Cruelty & perfidy scarcely paralleled in the most barbarous ages, and totally unworthy the Head of a civilized nation. —— He has constrained our fellow Citizens taken Captive on the high Seas to bear Arms against their Country, to become the executioners of their friends and Brethren, or to fall themselves by their Hands. —— He has excited domestic insurrections amongst us, and has endeavoured to bring on the inhabitants of our frontiers, the merciless Indian Savages, whose known rule of warfare, is an undistinguished destruction of all ages, sexes and conditions. In every stage of these Oppressions We have Petitioned for Redress in the most humble terms: Our repeated Petitions have been answered only by repeated injury. A Prince, whose character is thus marked by every act which may define a Tyrant, is unfit to be the ruler of a free people. Nor have We been wanting in attentions to our Brittish brethren. We have warned them from time to time of attempts by their legislature to extend an unwarrantable jurisdiction over us. We have reminded them of the circumstances of our emigration and settlement here. We have appealed to their native justice and magnanimity, and we have conjured them by the ties of our common kindred to disavow these usurpations, which, would inevitably interrupt our connections and correspondence. They too have been deaf to the voice of justice and of consanguinity. We must, therefore, acquiesce in the necessity, which denounces our Separation, and hold them, as we hold the rest of mankind, Enemies in War, in Peace Friends.

We, therefore, the Representatives of the united States of America, in General Congress, Assembled, appealing to the Supreme Judge of the world for the rectitude of our intentions, do, in the Name, and by Authority of the good People of these Colonies, solemnly publish and declare, That these United Colonies are, and of Right ought to be Free and Independent States; that they are Absolved from all Allegiance to the British Crown, and that all political connection between them and the State of Great Britain, is and ought to be totally dissolved; and that as Free and Independent States, they have full Power to levy War, conclude Peace, contract Alliances, establish Commerce, and to do all other Acts and Things which Independent States may of right do. —— And for the support of this Declaration, with a firm reliance on the protection of divine Providence, we mutually pledge to each other our Lives, our Fortunes and our sacred Honor.

John Hancock

Button Gwinnett
Lyman Hall
Geo Walton

Wm Hooper
Joseph Hewes
John Penn
Edward Rutledge
Thos Heyward Junr.
Thomas Lynch Junr.
Arthur Middleton

Samuel Chase
Wm Paca
Thos Stone
Charles Carroll of Carrollton
George Wythe
Richard Henry Lee
Th Jefferson
Benja Harrison
Thos Nelson jr.
Francis Lightfoot Lee
Carter Braxton

Robt Morris
Benjamin Rush
Benja Franklin
John Morton
Geo Clymer
Jas Smith
Geo Taylor
James Wilson
Geo Ross
Caesar Rodney
Geo Read
Thos M:Kean

Wm Floyd
Phil Livingston
Frans Lewis
Lewis Morris
Richd Stockton
Jno Witherspoon
Fras Hopkinson
John Hart
Abra Clark

Josiah Bartlett
Wm Whipple
Saml Adams
John Adams
Robt Treat Paine
Elbridge Gerry
Step Hopkins
William Ellery
Roger Sherman
Saml Huntington
Wm Williams
Oliver Wolcott
Matthew Thornton

The Declaration of Independence

This document explains to the world why Americans had the right to use force to change their government.

In Congress, July 4, 1776
The unanimous Declaration of the thirteen united States of America,

[PREAMBLE]

When in the Course of human events, it becomes necessary for one people to dissolve the political bands which have connected them with another, and to assume among the powers of the earth, the separate and equal station to which the Laws of Nature and of Nature's God entitle them, a decent respect to the opinions of mankind requires that they should declare the causes which impel them to the separation.

impel: force

[A NEW THEORY OF GOVERNMENT]

We hold these truths to be self-evident, that all men are created equal, that they are endowed by their Creator with certain unalienable Rights, that among these are Life, Liberty, and the pursuit of Happiness.

endowed: provided

That to secure these rights, Governments are instituted among Men, deriving their just powers from the consent of the governed,

People create governments to insure that their natural rights are protected. Governments are the servants of the people who establish them.

That whenever any Form of Government becomes destructive of these ends, it is the Right of the People to alter or to abolish it, and to institute new Government, laying its foundation on such principles and organizing its powers in such form, as to them shall seem most likely to effect their Safety and Happiness. Prudence, indeed, will dictate that Governments long established should not be changed for light and transient causes; and accordingly all experience hath shown, that mankind are more disposed to suffer, while evils are sufferable, than to right themselves by abolishing the forms to which they are accustomed. But when a long train of abuses and usurpations, pursuing invariably the same Object evinces a design to reduce them under absolute Despotism, it is their right, it is their duty, to throw off such Government, and to provide new Guards for their future security.

If a government does not serve its purpose, the people have a right to abolish it. Then the people have the right and duty to create a new government that will safeguard their security.

Despotism: unlimited power

[REASONS FOR SEPARATION]

Such has been the patient sufferance of these Colonies; and such is now the necessity which constrains them to alter their former Systems of Government. The history of the present King of Great Britain is a history of repeated injuries and usurpations, all having in direct object the establishment of an absolute Tyranny over these States. To prove this, let Facts be submitted to a candid world.

usurpations: unjust uses of power
Tyranny: absolute power
candid: impartial; fair

He has refused his Assent to Laws, the most wholesome and necessary for the public good.

Twenty-six paragraphs list the supposed crimes of George III.

He has forbidden his Governors to pass Laws of immediate and pressing importance, unless suspended in their operation till his Assent should be obtained; and when so suspended, he has utterly neglected to attend to them.

He has refused to pass other Laws for the accommodation of large districts of people, unless those people would relinquish the right of Representation in the Legislature, a right inestimable to them and formidable to tyrants only.

relinquish: give up
inestimable: priceless
formidable: causing dread

He has called together legislative bodies at places unusual, uncomfortable, and distant from the depository of their public Records, for the sole purpose of fatiguing them into compliance with his measures.

He has dissolved Representative Houses repeatedly, for opposing with manly firmness his invasions on the rights of the people.

He has refused for a long time, after such dissolutions, to cause others to be elected; whereby the Legislative powers, incapable of Annihilation, have returned to the People at large for their exercise; the State remaining in the mean time exposed to all the dangers of invasion from without, and convulsions within.

Annihilation: destruction

convulsions: violent disturbances

He has endeavored to prevent the population of these States; for that purpose obstructing the Laws for Naturalization of Foreigners; refusing to pass others to encourage their migrations hither, and raising the conditions of new Appropriations of Lands.

Naturalization of Foreigners: the process by which foreign-born persons become citizens

He has obstructed the Administration of Justice, by refusing his Assent to Laws for establishing Judiciary powers.

He has made Judges dependent on his Will alone, for the tenure of their offices, and the amount and payment of their salaries.

tenure: term

He has erected a multitude of New Offices, and sent hither swarms of Officers to harrass our people, and eat out their substance.

a multitude of: many

He has kept among us, in times of peace, Standing Armies without the Consent of our legislatures.

He has affected to render the Military independent of and superior to the Civil power.

He has combined with others to subject us to a jurisdiction foreign to our constitution, and unacknowledged by our laws; giving his Assent to their Acts of pretended Legislation:

For quartering large bodies of armed troops among us:

quartering: lodging

For protecting them, by a mock Trial, from punishment for any Murders which they should commit on the Inhabitants of these States:

For cutting off our Trade with all parts of the world:

For imposing Taxes on us without our Consent:

For depriving us in many cases, of the benefits of Trial by Jury:

For transporting us beyond Seas to be tried for pretended offences:

For abolishing the free System of English Laws in a neighboring Province, establishing therein an Arbitrary government, and enlarging its Boundaries so as to render it at once an example and fit instrument for introducing the same absolute rule into these Colonies:

Arbitrary: not based on law
render: make

For taking away our Charters, abolishing our most valuable Laws, and altering fundamentally the Forms of our Governments:

For suspending our own Legislatures, and declaring themselves invested with power to legislate for us in all cases whatsoever.

abdicated: given up

He has abdicated Government here, by declaring us out of his Protection and waging War against us.

He has plundered our seas, ravaged our Coasts, burnt our towns, and destroyed the Lives of our people.

perfidy: violation of trust

He is at this time transporting large Armies of foreign Mercenaries to complete the works of death, desolation and tyranny, already begun with circumstances of Cruelty & perfidy scarcely paralleled in the most barbarous ages, and totally unworthy the Head of a civilized nation.

He has constrained our fellow Citizens taken Captive on the high Seas to bear Arms against their Country, to become the executioners of their friends and Brethren, or to fall themselves by their Hands.

insurrections: rebellions

He has excited domestic insurrections amongst us, and has endeavored to bring on the inhabitants of our frontiers, the merciless Indian Savages, whose known rule of warfare, is an undistinguished destruction of all ages, sexes and conditions.

Petitioned for Redress: asked in a formal manner for a correction of wrongs

In every stage of these Oppressions We have Petitioned for Redress in the most humble terms: Our repeated Petitions have been answered only by repeated injury. A Prince, whose character is thus marked by every act which may define a Tyrant, is unfit to be the ruler of a free people.

unwarrantable jurisdiction: unjustified authority

magnanimity: generous spirit

consanguinity: ancestry

acquiesce in: consent to

Nor have We been wanting in attentions to our British brethren. We have warned them from time to time of attempts by their legislature to extend an unwarrantable jurisdiction over us. We have reminded them of the circumstances of our emigration and settlement here. We have appealed to their native justice and magnanimity, and we have conjured them by the ties of our common kindred to disavow these usurpations, which, would inevitably interrupt our connections and correspondence. They too have been deaf to the voice of justice and of consanguinity. We must, therefore, acquiesce in the necessity, which denounces our Separation, and hold them, as we hold the rest of mankind, Enemies in War, in Peace Friends.

[A PROCLAMATION OF FREE, INDEPENDENT, AND UNITED STATES]

rectitude: rightness

Here is where the signers, as representatives of the people, declared independence from Great Britain.

We, therefore, the Representatives of the united States of America, in General Congress, Assembled, appealing to the Supreme Judge of the world for the rectitude of our intentions, do, in the Name, and by Authority of the good People of these Colonies, solemnly publish and declare, That these United Colonies are, and of Right ought to be Free and Independent States; that they are Absolved from all Allegiance to the British Crown, and that all political connection between them and the State of Great Britain, is and ought to be totally dissolved; and that as Free and Independent States, they have full Power to levy War, conclude Peace, contract Alliances, establish Commerce, and to do all other Acts and Things which Independent States may of right do.

And for the support of this Declaration, with a firm reliance on the protection of divine Providence, we mutually pledge to each other our Lives, our Fortunes and our sacred Honor.

[SIGNERS OF THE DECLARATION]

JOHN HANCOCK
BUTTON GWINNETT
LYMAN HALL
GEORGE WALTON
WILLIAM HOOPER
JOSEPH HEWES
JOHN PENN
EDWARD RUTLEDGE
THOMAS HEYWARD, JR.
THOMAS LYNCH, JR.
ARTHUR MIDDLETON
SAMUEL CHASE
WILLIAM PACA
THOMAS STONE
CHARLES CARROLL OF CARROLLTON
GEORGE WYTHE
RICHARD HENRY LEE
THOMAS JEFFERSON
BENJAMIN HARRISON
THOMAS NELSON, JR.
FRANCIS LIGHTFOOT LEE
CARTER BRAXTON
ROBERT MORRIS
BENJAMIN RUSH
BENJAMIN FRANKLIN
JOHN MORTON
GEORGE CLYMER
JAMES SMITH
GEORGE TAYLOR
JAMES WILSON
GEORGE ROSS
CAESAR RODNEY
GEORGE READ
THOMAS McKEAN
WILLIAM FLOYD
PHILIP LIVINGSTON
FRANCIS LEWIS
LEWIS MORRIS
RICHARD STOCKTON
JOHN WITHERSPOON
FRANCIS HOPKINSON
JOHN HART
ABRAHAM CLARK
JOSIAH BARTLETT
WILLIAM WHIPPLE
SAMUEL ADAMS
JOHN ADAMS
ROBERT TREAT PAINE
ELBRIDGE GERRY
STEPHEN HOPKINS
WILLIAM ELLERY
ROGER SHERMAN
SAMUEL HUNTINGTON
WILLIAM WILLIAMS
OLIVER WOLCOTT
MATTHEW THORNTON

The drafting committee of the Declaration of Independence presents the document to the Second Continental Congress. From left to right are John Adams, Roger Sherman, Robert Livingston, Thomas Jefferson, and Benjamin Franklin. What did the Declaration of Independence tell the world?

3 THE CONSTITUTIONAL CONVENTION

Delegates from each state except Rhode Island convened in Philadelphia on May 25, 1787, in Independence Hall to strengthen the Articles of Confederation. Yet it was immediately apparent to most of the assembled delegates that if the United States was to be preserved, revision would not be sufficient. As a result, the delegates quickly set for themselves another responsibility—framing a constitution.

The Delegates

The meeting in Independence Hall became the Constitutional Convention. Of the 74 delegates appointed, only about 40 actively participated in the proceedings, but they were among the most able and distinguished leaders in America. When Thomas Jefferson—who was in Paris at the time—saw the list of delegates, he wrote to John Adams, then in London, that it was "an assembly of demi-gods."

The delegates were highly educated and were well read in political theory, law, economics, and government affairs. Alexander Hamilton was 30; Gouverneur Morris, 35; and James Madison, 36. George Washington at 55 was one of the few older delegates who played an important role in the convention. Benjamin Franklin, the oldest delegate, was 81.

Important roles in the convention were played by Gouverneur Morris of New York, James Wilson of Pennsylvania, and James Madison and George Washington of Virginia. Alexander Hamilton was instrumental in calling the convention and later in securing ratification of the Constitution. But Hamilton, long an advocate of strong national government, played virtually no role in the framing of the Constitution. His aristocratic views found little support among his fellow delegates.

Gouverneur Morris, like Hamilton a conservative, became the main advocate of strong executive authority. On the other side, James Wilson placed his democratic faith in a legislature elected by the people. Both Morris and Wilson played central roles in framing the Constitution. Wilson, a member of the Committee on Detail, drafted much of its content. Morris, a member of the Committee on Style and Arrangement, was largely responsible for the Constitution's final form and language.

The leading spirit of the convention was James Madison, who is often called the "Father of the Constitution." He had helped draft Virginia's state constitution in 1776. He was a scholar of history and

LEGACY

The Second Continental Congress

The Second Continental Congress, which met in Philadelphia in May 1775, served as the first national government of the United States. It guided the nation through the Revolutionary War, the signing of the Declaration of Independence, and the drafting of the Articles of Confederation. Yet the Second Continental Congress had no constitutional basis. Popular conventions, not the official colonial assemblies, selected the delegates. This meant the delegates lacked any legal power.

The Second Continental Congress was made up of one chamber, which exercised both legislative and executive functions. Each state had one vote. The states remained independent, however, because the Congress could not enforce its decisions on an individual state. Indeed, the Second Continental Congress had little political authority beyond that given by each state to its delegates. The nation's first government depended entirely on the cooperation of the states.

Still, the Second Continental Congress performed many functions of government. It issued paper money, borrowed funds to finance the war, purchased supplies, raised an army and a navy, and negotiated treaties with foreign countries. In its last act the Congress ratified the Articles of Confederation in March 1781.

The painting of James Madison (above) is by Charles Wilson Peale. The painting of George Washington (right) is by Gilbert Stuart. Madison and Washington favored a strong central government for the United States. What roles did these Virginians play at the Constitutional Convention?

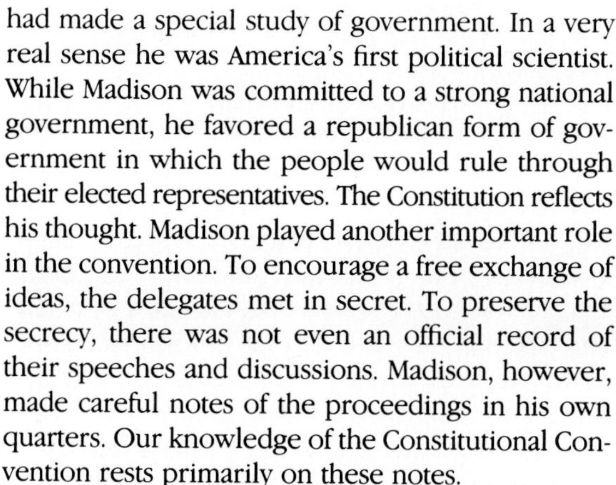

had made a special study of government. In a very real sense he was America's first political scientist. While Madison was committed to a strong national government, he favored a republican form of government in which the people would rule through their elected representatives. The Constitution reflects his thought. Madison played another important role in the convention. To encourage a free exchange of ideas, the delegates met in secret. To preserve the secrecy, there was not even an official record of their speeches and discussions. Madison, however, made careful notes of the proceedings in his own quarters. Our knowledge of the Constitutional Convention rests primarily on these notes.

The most distinguished delegate was George Washington. His presence gave special significance to the gathering. He was unanimously elected to preside over the convention, and he did so with dignity and fairness. As presiding officer, Washington was prevented from taking part in the formal discussions. Yet delegates knew that he favored a strong national government. He used his influence to support Madison and to ensure the convention's success.

The Resolution

The delegates agreed that "a national government ought to be established consisting of a supreme legislative, executive, and judiciary." The delegates knew they must write a constitution creating a central government with greater powers than the Congress of the Confederation. This national government would have power over the state governments. It was to be a representative, republican government, responsible to the people.

The delegates generally agreed on basic principles, but there were two major sources of conflict. First, there was the conflict between the large and small states. Second, there were sectional differences between North and South that reflected their different economic interests.

"A Bundle of Compromises"

The delegates from Virginia had come to the convention prepared. Edmund Randolph presented 15 resolutions, largely written by James Madison, that called for a strong national government. The Virginia Plan called for a new government composed

A NEW PLAN OF GOVERNMENT

The Virginia Plan	The New Jersey Plan
The Legislative Branch	
1. Two-house legislature, one house larger than the other	1. A one-house legislature
2. Members of lower house elected by qualified voters in the states; members of upper house nominated by state legislatures and elected by the lower house	2. All members elected by state legislatures
3. Number of state representatives in each house determined by population of state; each representative has one vote	3. Each state has one vote
4. Each branch able to originate laws and to legislate when states are incompetent or in violation of national laws	4. All acts of the legislature should be considered the supreme law of the land
The Executive Branch	
1. One executive officer	1. Two or more executives
2. Executive officer elected by national legislature for one term, except in the case of impeachment	2. Executive officers elected by national legislature for one term, removable at the will of a majority of states
The Judicial Branch	
1. A Supreme Court and lower courts	1. A Supreme Court only
2. Judges appointed by national legislature to serve for life	2. Judges appointed by the executive branch to serve for life

Study the details of the two competing plans of government that were proposed for the new nation. The two plans reflect the differences of opinion between the large and the small states. How did the Great Compromise resolve these differences?

of three branches—legislative, executive, and judicial. Congress was to be divided into two houses. In each, representation was to be based on population. The greater a state's population, the more representatives it would have in Congress. This would have given the large states—Virginia, Pennsylvania, and New York—a dominant position. The Virginia Plan also called for a "national executive" and a "national judiciary" to be chosen by Congress.

William Paterson of New Jersey presented another plan. The New Jersey Plan favored strengthened government but proposed a single house of Congress. As under the Articles of Confederation, each state would have the same vote, regardless of size. The plan also called for a "federal executive" and a "federal judiciary" to be elected by Congress. The chart on this page outlines the Virginia Plan and the New Jersey Plan.

The Great Compromise The major difference between the two plans concerned representation in Congress. The small states feared they would have little influence in a national government based on the Virginia Plan. After one month's debate the convention adopted the Great Compromise. (Reflecting Roger Sherman of Connecticut's important role, it is sometimes called the Connecticut Compromise.) The Framers resolved the conflict between the large and small states by combining aspects of both plans. Congress would have two houses, a House of Representatives and a Senate. In the House representation would be based on population. Each state would have at least one representative. In the Senate each state, regardless of size, would be represented by two senators and have two votes. Legislation would be approved by a majority vote in both houses of Congress.

Electoral College Compromise The selection of the President represented another compromise. James Wilson favored election of the President directly by the people. Most delegates, however, favored indirect election. The Virginia and New Jersey plans proposed that the President be elected by Congress. Opponents argued that this would lead to legislative domination of the executive branch and destroy the principle of separation of powers. Some delegates from the small states wanted each state to have an equal vote in selecting the President. The compromise that was reached provided for an electoral college in which each state would have as many electors as it had representatives in Congress.

The Three-Fifths Compromise Some of the most serious problems to confront the convention arose from sectional differences on the issue of slavery. Most delegates at the convention regarded slavery as an evil, and they believed that slavery would gradually disappear. Although most delegates saw a compromise on slavery as unpleasant, they thought it was necessary to win southern support for the Constitution. In the Three-Fifths Compromise delegates agreed to determine both taxation and representation in the House of Representatives by counting a slave as three fifths of a free person. In another compromise on slavery delegates agreed that Congress could not ban the slave trade until 1808.

Economic Compromises Economic interests divided the North and the South. The North was increasingly a manufacturing center. The South was predominantly agricultural and heavily dependent on the export of its goods to foreign countries. Yielding to southern demands, the convention delegates agreed that the new Constitution would prohibit ***export duties,*** which were taxes on goods for sale overseas. The South also wanted to ensure that treaties with other nations were favorable to its interests. The delegates agreed that all treaties would require the consent of two thirds of the Senate. On the other hand, the power to regulate

Delegates to the Constitutional Convention debate an important point. Who were some of the delegates at the convention?

commerce within the United States would be subject to an ordinary majority vote of Congress.

Thus the Constitution has been described as "a bundle of compromises." Many different interests had to be considered to win wide support. Compromise—the willingness to negotiate and bargain—is an essential part of democratic politics. Delegates to the Constitutional Convention reached agreement through compromise because they shared the vision of what America was to be.

The Signing of the Constitution

By the end of July the delegates had turned the many resolutions and compromises into a written document. The next several weeks were spent analyzing, debating, and perfecting it. On September 8 the Committee on Style and Arrangement was named to polish the final draft of the Constitution. This group of five, headed by Gouverneur Morris, also included Alexander Hamilton and James Madison. It was this group that put the Constitution into its clear and concise form. The complete text of the Constitution begins on page 69.

The convention ended on September 17, 1787, less than four months after it had opened. Of the 42 delegates present, 39 signed the new Constitution. As Benjamin Franklin stepped from the hall, he was asked by a waiting citizen, "What have we got, Dr. Franklin, a republic or a monarchy?" He replied, "A republic, if you can keep it."

Compare the governmental structure of the Articles of Confederation with the structure of the Constitution. How did the Constitution correct the weaknesses of the Articles of Confederation?

STRUCTURE OF THE NATIONAL GOVERNMENT

Under the Articles of Confederation	Under the Constitution
1. One house of Congress	1. Two houses of Congress: the Senate and the House of Representatives
2. Congress has the power to enact "resolutions," no power to enact laws	2. Congress has power to enact laws
3. Each state has one vote in Congress	3. Each state has two votes in the Senate; number of votes in House of Representatives based on population
4. Delegates elected for one-year term; reelected for no more than three years in every six	4. Senate term of six years; House of Representatives term of two years
5. No power to regulate interstate or foreign commerce	5. Congress can regulate interstate and foreign commerce
6. No power to levy taxes	6. Congress has power to levy taxes
7. No power to act directly against individuals or states	7. Executive and judicial branches have power to act against individuals and (in a more limited way) against states
8. Two-thirds majority required to decide important matters	8. Simple majority of both houses of Congress required to pass laws; laws subject to veto by the President
9. No executive branch; a "Committee of the States" made up of one delegate from each state executes powers of Congress during Congressional recesses	9. An executive branch, headed by the President
10. No national court system	10. A Supreme Court and such lower federal courts as Congress may establish
11. All states must agree to amendments	11. Amendments proposed by national convention or two thirds of both houses of Congress; ratification requires vote by three fourths of state legislatures or state conventions

Section Check

1. Identify: Gouverneur Morris, James Wilson, William Paterson, Edmund Randolph, James Madison
2. For what purpose was the Philadelphia convention originally assembled?
3. Two plans for representation were debated at the Constitutional Convention. What were the main points of each?
4. Another conflict involved the North and South. What is an example of a compromise between those two regions?

4 THE RATIFICATION OF THE CONSTITUTION

The Philadelphia convention had been called to revise the Articles of Confederation. Under the Articles any amendment had to be approved by the legislatures of all 13 states. The delegates, however, devised a new ratification procedure that required approval by specially called conventions in each state. Article 7 of the Constitution says:

The Ratification of the Conventions of nine States shall be sufficient for the Establishment of this Constitution between the States so ratifying the Same.

This procedure was adopted for two reasons. First, the Framers avoided ratification by state legislatures because they believed the state legislatures would object to the weakening of their powers that would result from the creation of a strong national government. Second, they thought that popularly elected conventions would give the Constitution a broad base of popular support. As stated by Madison, "The new constitution should be ratified . . . by the supreme authority of the people themselves."

Federalists and Antifederalists

The new Constitution proposed major changes in the government of the United States. Debate over the Constitution divided the participants into two groups—the Federalists, who supported ratification, and the Antifederalists, who opposed it.

The debate crossed all geographic, social, and economic lines. For example, many farmers of the western back country opposed the Constitution because they feared the new government would be dominated by urban, commercial interests. But there were western farmers who supported the Constitution, just as there were eastern merchants who opposed it. In Virginia, supporters and opponents of the Constitution could be found among persons from the same economic class and social background.

Thomas Jefferson, serving as the American minister to France, was unable to attend the Constitutional Convention. He later called the Constitution "the result of the collected wisdom of our country."

The Federalists were led by many of the people who had attended the Constitutional Convention. Two of their most active leaders were James Madison and Alexander Hamilton. Some of the more famous Antifederalists were important figures in the Revolutionary War such as Patrick Henry, Richard Henry Lee, John Hancock, and Samuel Adams. Criticism focused on three aspects of the Constitution.

First, strong criticism came from people who favored ***states' rights.*** The creation of a strong national government was viewed with alarm by those

LEGACY

The Federalist

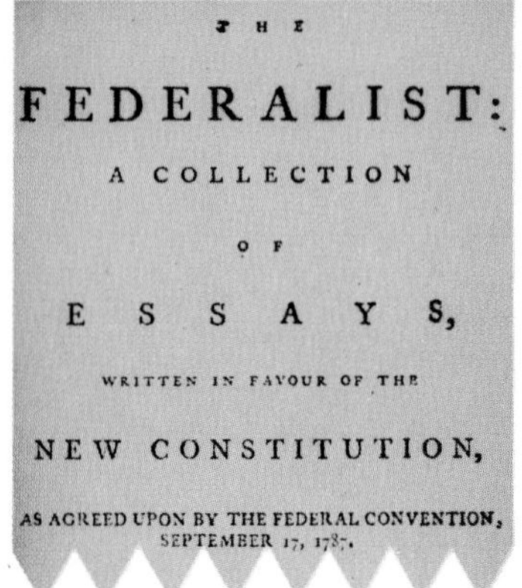
THE

FEDERALIST:

A COLLECTION

OF

ESSAYS,

WRITTEN IN FAVOUR OF THE

NEW CONSTITUTION,

AS AGREED UPON BY THE FEDERAL CONVENTION, SEPTEMBER 17, 1787.

On September 17, 1787, the draft for the Constitution of the United States was at last complete. Now the new Constitution would be put before the people of the states for ratification.

A storm of articles and pamphlets arguing for and against the Constitution swept the country. A powerful opponent, New York Governor George Clinton, began to publish a series of letters against the Constitution under the pen name "Cato" in *The New York Journal*. The articles attracted widespread attention and threatened to turn the American people against the new plan of government.

Alexander Hamilton, a young lawyer who had helped frame the Constitution, took up the challenge of defending it. He enlisted the help of John Jay and James Madison to write a series of articles "To the People of the State of New York" in support of the Constitution. The three men contributed unique abilities to the project. Hamilton, only 30 years old, was already an experienced writer of pamphlets. John Jay, a shrewd and experienced diplomat, knew foreign affairs and the importance of creating a strong union to counteract the danger of foreign powers. Madison, who had attended every session of the Constitutional Convention, intimately understood the complex document and the arguments for and against it.

The articles Hamilton, Jay, and Madison wrote—85 in all—appeared under the pen name "Publius" from October 1787 to March 1788. In the spring of 1788 the articles were gathered together in a two-volume edition called *The Federalist* that proved enormously popular. Today *The Federalist* is widely acknowledged for its brilliant explanation and defense of the Constitution.

who believed that liberty could be protected only by state governments—the governments closest to the people. The Antifederalists argued that the Constitution violated the states' sovereignty and that the states would lose power. The Federalists replied that the choice was between the Constitution and destruction of the Union. The Confederation was defective, and only a strong national government could remedy its problems. The Federalists challenged the notion that only the states could protect liberty. They argued that "an extended republic" composed of different and competing interests was the best guarantee of liberty, for no single group could dominate the whole.

Second, the Antifederalists felt the Constitution was undemocratic. Patrick Henry warned of the danger of a powerful executive—in his eyes, another name for a tyrant. The Federalists met this argument by emphasizing the separation of powers within the constitutional structure. They also pointed out the system of checks and balances that would prevent the concentration of power in the hands of any one branch, executive or legislative.

Third, Antifederalists argued that the Constitution did not contain a bill of rights. They warned that without one, individuals in the states would have no protection against a strong national government. The state constitutions, after all, had such provisions for the guarantee of personal liberty. The Federalists responded by saying that a bill of rights was not necessary. Under the Constitution, the national government had only specifically delegated powers. There was no need to deny to the government what it could not do anyway. But several states approved the Constitution only on the condition that guarantees of such fundamental liberties as freedom of speech and religion be added. The Federalists gave way. The first Congress under the new Constitution enacted a bill of rights. Today the Bill of Rights stands as the first ten amendments to the Constitution.

The Struggle for Ratification

Although ratification by only nine states was required for the Constitution to go into effect, four states—Massachusetts, New York, Pennsylvania, and Virginia—were politically and physically necessary to the Union. By June 1788 nine states had ratified the Constitution, but the critical states of Virginia and New York had not yet acted.

The Virginia debates were the most spirited of all the state conventions. The Federalists were led by George Washington and James Madison. The Antifederalists, led by Patrick Henry, mounted a powerful challenge. Henry's spellbinding oratory was met by the quiet reasoning of Madison. The Federalists prevailed, and Virginia ratified the Constitution. Henry proved a good loser. He pledged to work within the Constitution to remove what he saw

Debate about the Constitution was intense because it proposed major changes. The Federalists had to campaign in several key states to ensure ratification. Which states voted unanimously? In which two states was the vote the closest?

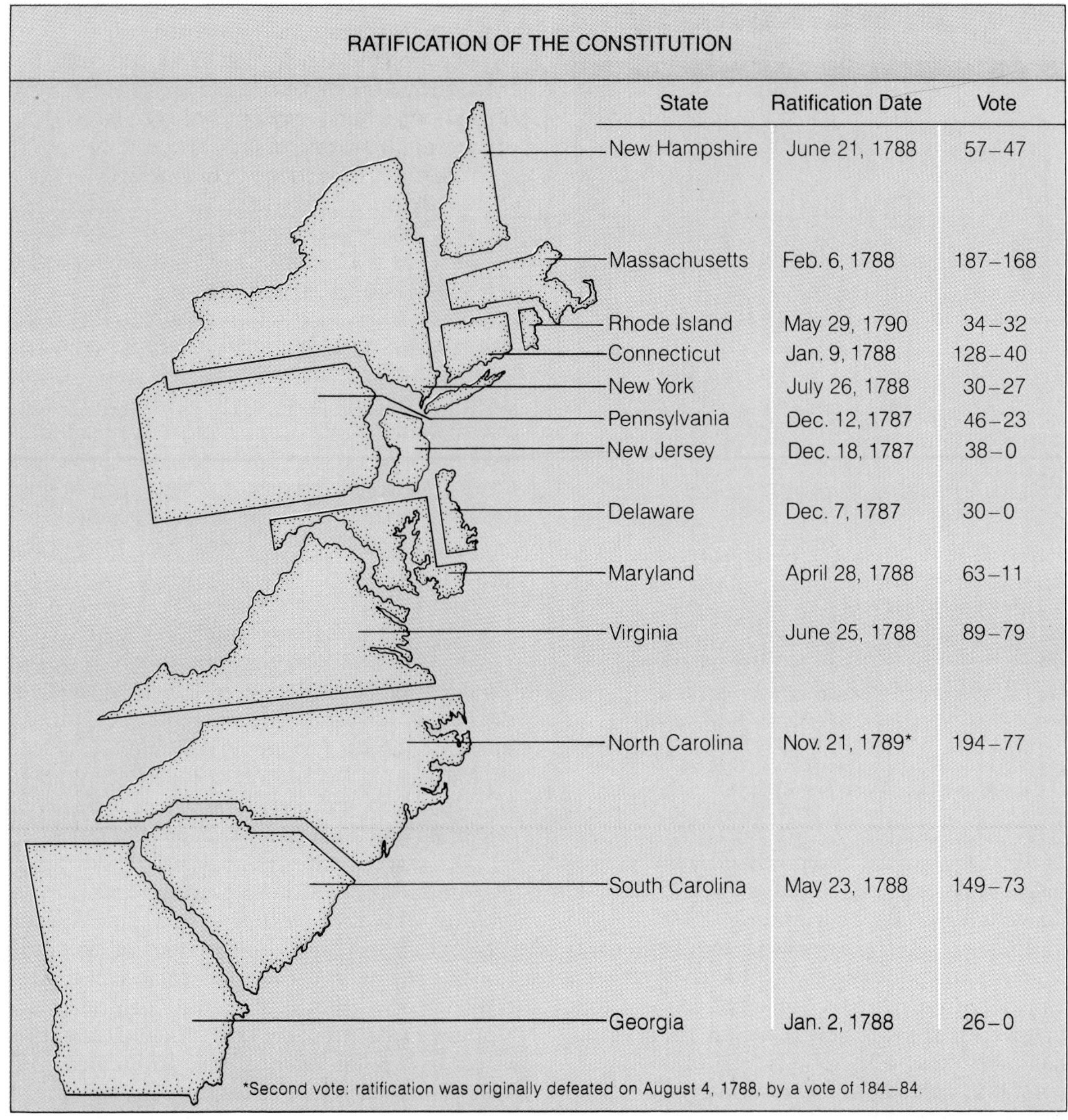

RATIFICATION OF THE CONSTITUTION

State	Ratification Date	Vote
New Hampshire	June 21, 1788	57–47
Massachusetts	Feb. 6, 1788	187–168
Rhode Island	May 29, 1790	34–32
Connecticut	Jan. 9, 1788	128–40
New York	July 26, 1788	30–27
Pennsylvania	Dec. 12, 1787	46–23
New Jersey	Dec. 18, 1787	38–0
Delaware	Dec. 7, 1787	30–0
Maryland	April 28, 1788	63–11
Virginia	June 25, 1788	89–79
North Carolina	Nov. 21, 1789*	194–77
South Carolina	May 23, 1788	149–73
Georgia	Jan. 2, 1788	26–0

*Second vote: ratification was originally defeated on August 4, 1788, by a vote of 184–84.

Patrick Henry (top) opposed the ratification of the Constitution. Alexander Hamilton (bottom) vigorously worked for the Constitution's ratification. Why did Henry and the Antifederalists oppose ratification? How did Hamilton and the Federalists counter this opposition?

as the defects of the system. Other Antifederalists followed his example, and no effort was made to undermine the new government.

In New York, opposition to the Constitution was led by upstate landowners who feared heavy federal taxes. The Federalists, concentrated in New York City, were led by Alexander Hamilton. The battle for ratification was intense, and victory for the Constitution was won only by a narrow margin.

On September 13, 1788, after 11 of the 13 states had ratified the Constitution, the Second Continental Congress met to finish its work. It selected New York City as the nation's temporary capital. On April 30, 1789, George Washington was inaugurated as the first President of the United States under the Constitution. By 1790 all 13 states had ratified the Constitution. The new republic now rested on a firm foundation.

Section Check

1. Define: states' rights
2. Identify: Federalists, Antifederalists, ***Publius***
3. Which two arguments were made for approving the Constitution by specially called conventions rather than state legislatures?
4. What were three arguments of those who opposed the Constitution?
5. What was the purpose of ***The Federalist***?

SUMMARY

During the seventeenth and eighteenth centuries the English established 13 colonies along North America's Atlantic coast. The English settlers contributed much to the shaping of our governmental system: the concepts of limited government and representative government; the separation of government into the three branches of legislative, executive, and judicial; and common law. Three types of colonies existed: royal, proprietary, and charter colonies.

England's tightened control over the colonies in the 1760's provoked colonial objections and the calling of the First Continental Congress. The Revolutionary War had begun when the Second Continental Congress first assembled in May 1776. It proclaimed the Declaration of Independence and by March 1781 had united the independent states under the Articles of Confederation.

The powers of the national government under the Articles of Confederation were too limited to be effective. Delegates meeting to revise the Articles quickly resolved themselves into the Constitutional Convention. After debate and compromise they agreed upon a national government consisting of a "supreme legislative, executive, and judiciary" that would have power over the state governments. By 1790 the 13 states had ratified the Constitution.

Chapter 2 Review

Using Vocabulary

Answer the questions by using the meaning of each underlined term.

1. What makes a representative government a limited government?
2. What role does precedent play in the development of common law?
3. What differences exist between natural rights and states' rights?
4. In what way is the Declaration of Independence a kind of social contract?
5. How is a bill of rights a guarantee of equality?
6. Why is a veto important in a bicameral legislature?
7. What is the relation of county courts and militia to local government?
8. How was the ratification of the Constitution an exercise of popular sovereignty?

Understanding American Government

1. Describe the English Parliament, naming each house, its membership, and its functions.
2. How did the English system of government provide for independent judges?
3. What basic conflict did American colonists have with their government in Britain? What slogan best expressed their concerns?
4. What important economic restriction was placed upon voting in the colonies?
5. After the Revolutionary War, why did states normally limit the power of governors? What role did these state governors usually have?
6. Which branches of government were set up by the new Articles of Confederation?
7. Describe the two major failures of the new government under the Articles of Confederation.
8. At the Constitutional Convention what two proposals were made for representation in Congress? Explain the compromise that resolved the conflict.
9. What were three major criticisms of the Constitution? How did the Federalists respond to these criticisms?
10. Explain why the Constitution was approved by ratifying conventions rather than state legislatures.

Extending Your Skills: Analyzing a Political Document

Study the Declaration of Independence on pages 46–49. Then, to help you analyze the document, answer the questions that follow.

1. Locate each of the main sections of the Declaration of Independence. What is the purpose of each section? How does each relate to the other sections?
2. Find the phrase *a decent respect to the opinions of mankind.* What does it mean? How does it explain the Declaration's purpose?
3. How might the Declaration influence people today?

Government and You

1. Describe how the three great principles of the Constitution—equality, liberty, and democracy—limited the power of government.
2. Was the American Revolution really a revolution? Did the American colonies change fundamental ideas of government or only the location of government? Use examples to explain your answer.
3. If a constitutional convention were to be called today, in what ways do you think it would be different from the meeting in 1787? Who do you think would be chosen as representatives? Would the issues be the same? Explain your answers.
4. Jefferson said "it is the Right of the People to alter or to abolish" a government that is not responsive to the people. Can you name revolutions around the world in which the leaders made a similar claim as their justification?

Activities

1. Prepare a report on one of the Framers of the Constitution. Look particularly at age, education, occupation, and political beliefs. Present your report to the class.
2. Read more about the Constitutional Convention. Then pretend that you were a member of that convention. Write a letter home describing the events that took place as the convention ended.

Chapter 3

The Constitution: The Framework of Government

We the People of the United States, in Order to form a more perfect Union, establish Justice, insure domestic Tranquility, provide for the common defense, promote the general Welfare, and secure the Blessings of Liberty to ourselves and our Posterity, do ordain and establish this Constitution for the United States of America.

PREAMBLE

CHAPTER OVERVIEW

George Washington is inaugurated as first President of the United States. The Presidential oath of office is found in Article 2, Section 2, of the Constitution. It directs the President to "preserve, protect, and defend the Constitution of the United States."

1 BASIC PRINCIPLES OF THE CONSTITUTION

A ***constitution*** is the fundamental laws, ideals, and principles by which a nation is governed. It may be written or unwritten. The term *constitution* usually refers to a single written document. In Great Britain, however, there is no single, written constitutional document as there is in the United States. Instead the British constitution is the product of custom, judicial decisions, and acts of Parliament. It is said to be unwritten because so many documents are a part of it.

The United States Constitution is the oldest written constitution still in effect. It is also one of the shortest, using some 6,700 words to lay down "the supreme Law of the Land" and establish the framework of American government.

The Constitution established a ***republic.*** In *The Federalist,* No. 10, James Madison explained that in a democracy "citizens . . . assemble and administer the government in person." This is the same as they had done in ancient Athens or in New England town meetings. In a republic, however, the people act through their elected representatives. The new government would draw from both traditions.

Limited Government

A constitutional government is usually defined as a government limited by law. As John Adams put it: "Ours is a government of law, not of men." The Constitution both grants and limits the powers of government. It restricts the power of both the national and state governments. The Framers of the Constitution wanted a more effective national government, but they knew that after years of colonial rule the American people would not accept a government that weakened states' rights. Thus they established a system of federalism, which divides the powers of government between the national and state governments.

A large crowd gathers at the White House to greet Andrew Jackson after his inauguration.

The Framers believed that all power to govern must come from the people. Public officials must observe the constitutional limits on their ruling powers, for they are responsible to the people. In a ***representative government*** the people elect their representatives and can vote them out of office if they abuse their power. Yet the Framers thought this popular control of government was not enough. They feared that a majority might use the central government to deprive others of their rights. Therefore they built two basic safeguards into the Constitution: the principles of separation of powers and checks and balances.

The Constitution fully establishes a ***limited government*** by placing restraints on government to protect fundamental human rights. Article 1, Section 9, lists the powers that are denied the national government. Article 1, Section 10, lists the powers denied the state governments. As the Bill of Rights, the first 10 amendments protect human rights by limiting the power of the national government. For example, the First Amendment—which begins with the words "Congress shall make no law"—guarantees freedom of religion, speech, the press, assembly, and petition.

Federalism

The government of the United States divides the powers of government between a central government and regional governments. In the United States the central government is the national government, and the regional governments are the 50 state governments. This form of government is called ***federalism.***

Federalism was an almost natural result of early American history. The colonists had rebelled against the oppressive British government over the right to handle their local affairs. The Americans distrusted central authority. The national government established by the Articles of Confederation was too weak, however, and economic and political chaos troubled the new nation. The Framers of the Constitution resolved the problem by establishing a federal system as a compromise between an all-powerful central government and a system of independent states in loose confederation. As a federal system, the Constitution of the United States distributes powers between the national and state governments.

Popular Sovereignty and Representative Government

"We the People of the United States . . . do ordain and establish this Constitution for the United States of America." These phrases from the Preamble to the Constitution make clear that all government power rests on ***popular sovereignty.*** In the United States, government may act only with the consent of the governed.

Despite their faith in popular sovereignty, most Framers feared that direct democracy would lead to mob rule. They believed that elected representatives, reflecting a wide range of interests and backgrounds, could meet in a calm atmosphere away from crowds and make more reasoned judgments than the people themselves.

Representative government has two essential features. First, the representatives must be selected in free and periodic elections. Second, the representatives must be accountable to the people for their actions. They govern only with "the consent of the governed." If the elected representatives fail to keep the confidence of the people, they will be turned out of office.

Separation of Powers

The Framers of the Constitution distrusted a strong central government in which the same people make the laws, enforce them, and determine their meaning. Their experiences as colonists had taught them that the executive should not dominate the legislature and the courts and that neither the legislature nor the courts should dominate the executive. By keeping the powers of government separate, the Framers sought to ensure that no one branch of government could become too powerful. They were concerned, first, that government be unable to exercise ***tyranny,*** or power, over the people unjustly. Secondly, they wanted to prevent tyranny by the people—tyranny of the majority over the minority. In *The Federalist,* No. 47, Madison wrote:

The accumulation of all powers, legislative, executive, and judiciary, in the same hands, whether of one, a few, or many and whether hereditary, self-appointed, or elective, may justly be pronounced the very definition of tyranny. . . . The preservation of liberty requires that the three great departments of power should be separate.

The principle of ***separation of powers*** is not explicitly stated in the Constitution. Instead it is implied in the framework of government. The first three articles of the Constitution list the specific powers of each branch. Article 1 grants legislative powers to a Congress consisting of a Senate and House of Representatives. Article 2 places executive power in a President. Article 3 gives judicial power to a Supreme Court and a system of lower courts.

Different Constituencies The Framers reinforced the separation of powers by giving each branch of government a different ***constituency***—the body of voters to whom an elected official is politically responsible. The constituency of the President is the entire voting public. Legislators are responsible to the voters of their electoral districts. Senators have a statewide constituency. Representatives are usually responsible to smaller districts within their state. Supreme Court justices are appointed by the President with the consent of the Senate and, as appointees, have no voting constituency to whom they must answer.

Different Terms of Office The Constitution also provides for different terms of office. The President is elected to a four-year term, members of the House of Representatives to two-year terms, and members of the Senate to six-year terms. Supreme Court justices hold office for life. The Framers reasoned that a mixture of different constituencies and terms of office might best prevent a single group from winning control of all institutions of government at one time.

COMPARING THE BRANCHES OF GOVERNMENT

		Mode of Selection	Constituency	Length of Term
Legislative	House of Representatives	Direct election by the people	Local	2 years
	Senate	Election by state legislatures; later, direct election*	Statewide	6 years
Executive	President	Election by a body of electors†	Nationwide	4 years
Judicial	Supreme Court and lower federal courts	Appointment by the President with the consent of the Senate		Life

*The Constitution specified that senators be chosen by the state legislatures. In 1913 the Seventeenth Amendment provided for direct election of senators by the people.

†The states were to determine the manner in which the Presidential electors would be selected. At first they were chosen by the state legislatures. Today electors are chosen by the people in statewide elections.

The Constitution gives each branch of the government its own mode of selection, its own constituency, and its own term of office. Why did the Framers of the Constitution provide for a separation of powers?

The United States Constitution makes each branch of the national government responsible not only to the people but also to each of the other two branches of the government. A system of checks and balances ensures this responsibility within the government. Why must each branch of the government share its powers with the other two branches?

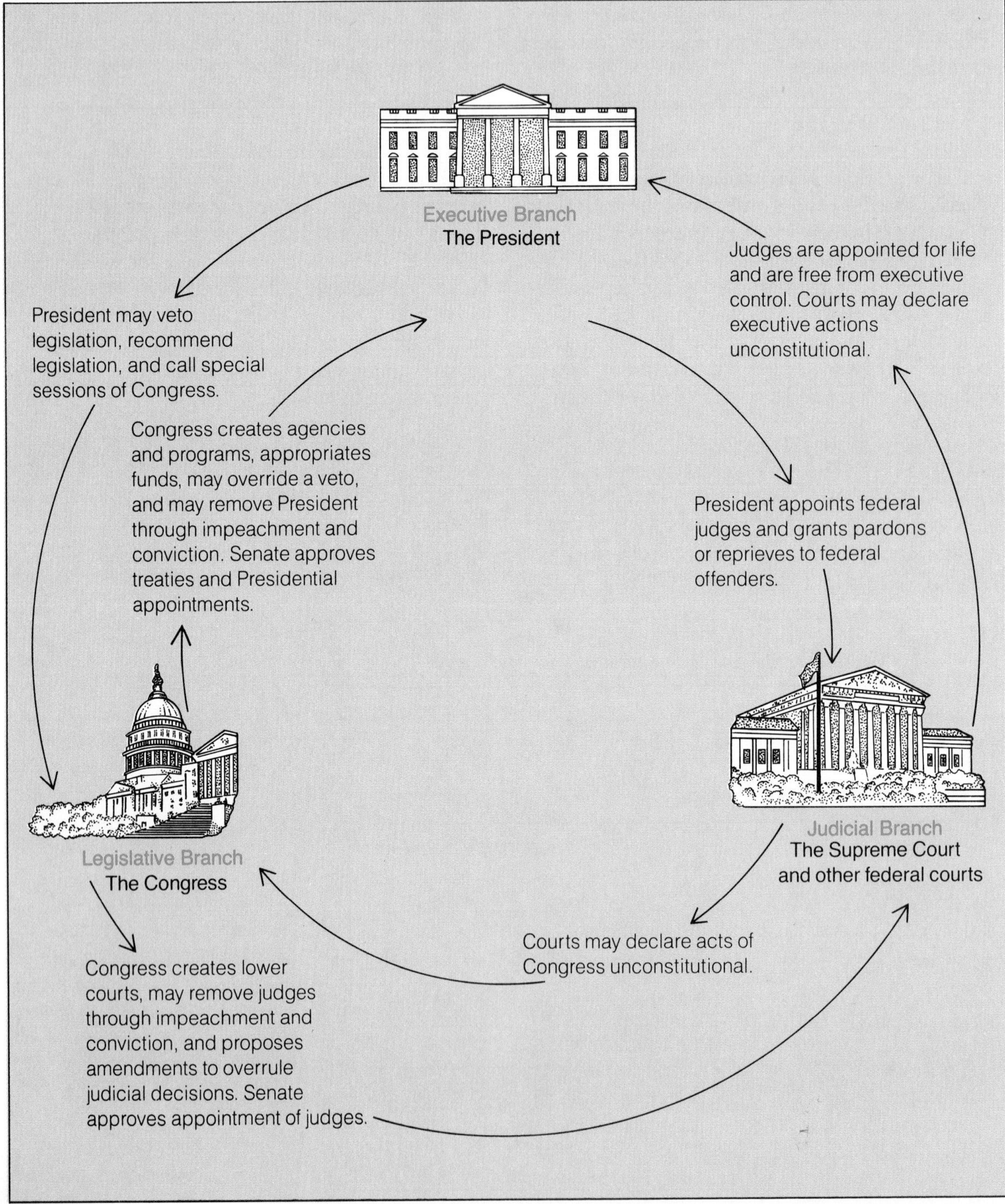

MAJOR FEATURES OF THE SYSTEM OF CHECKS AND BALANCES
Executive Branch
The President
President may veto legislation, recommend legislation, and call special sessions of Congress.
Congress creates agencies and programs, appropriates funds, may override a veto, and may remove President through impeachment and conviction. Senate approves treaties and Presidential appointments.
Judges are appointed for life and are free from executive control. Courts may declare executive actions unconstitutional.
President appoints federal judges and grants pardons or reprieves to federal offenders.
Legislative Branch
The Congress
Judicial Branch
The Supreme Court and other federal courts
Courts may declare acts of Congress unconstitutional.
Congress creates lower courts, may remove judges through impeachment and conviction, and proposes amendments to overrule judicial decisions. Senate approves appointment of judges.

Abuse of Authority Under the Articles of Confederation power had been concentrated in the legislature. Now power was to be divided and shared by the three separate branches of government. The Framers believed that the weaknesses of the Confederation arose in part from its lack of executive authority. There was no leadership to provide unity and direction to national policy. In addition, many Framers feared the abuse of legislative authority.

As a check on legislative power the Framers created a strong and independent executive. In the constitutional system the executive office of the Presidency assumes a central position. It is *the* national institution, responsible to *all* the people. The executive branch, however, also may abuse its power. Executive power was therefore subject to check by the legislative and judicial branches. With the separation of powers each branch was to prevent the others from abusing power or exceeding authority.

Checks and Balances

Each branch of government is ultimately responsible to and controlled by the people. If government officials abuse their authority, periodic elections enable the people to "throw the rascals out." Madison recognized the people as "the primary control on the government." Nonetheless, he pointed out the need for additional precautions—for a system of ***checks and balances.*** In *The Federalist,* No. 51, Madison wrote:

The great security against a gradual concentration of the several powers in the same department consists in giving to those who administer each department the necessary constitutional means and personal motives to resist encroachments of the others.

If the legislative, executive, and judicial powers of government were completely separated—sharply divided among the three branches—then effective government would be impossible. Therefore the Constitution provides for each branch of government to share powers with the other in a system of checks and balances. The following are examples of checks and balances.

1. Only Congress may enact laws, but the President may propose legislation to Congress. As chief legislator the President has in fact become the source of most major legislation.
2. The President may exercise a veto over legislation passed by Congress. However, Congress can override a Presidential veto by repassing the bill with a two-thirds majority in both houses.
3. The President develops programs and policies but depends upon appropriations of money by Congress to carry them out.
4. The President appoints executive officials and federal judges, but the appointments must be confirmed by the Senate.
5. The President is commander in chief of the army and navy, but only Congress can declare war.
6. The President may make treaties with foreign governments, but all treaties require approval by the Senate.
7. Congress has the power to impeach and remove the President or members of the federal judiciary from office.
8. The Supreme Court exercises judicial review, interpreting the law and ruling on the constitutionality of Congressional or executive action.
9. Congress in turn may override Supreme Court rulings by passing an amendment to the Constitution.

Bicameralism In addition to providing checks and balances among the three branches of government, the Constitution divides Congress itself into the House of Representatives and the Senate. ***Bicameralism*** embodies the principle of federalism in that the states are represented equally in the Senate and in proportion to their population in the House of Representatives. Bicameralism also reflects the Framers' concern that the legislative branch might dominate the national government. They established two houses so that each might act as a check on the actions of the other. The two houses were to complement and balance one another. Each was to have an absolute veto over the other. The Senate, originally elected by the state legislatures, mainly represented the interests of wealthy merchants and landowners. The House of Representatives, elected directly by the electorate, was to be the voice of the people.

Two characteristics of the House presented both benefits and problems. First, its relatively large size allowed for representation of a wide variety of interests. On the other hand, its size made debate more difficult. The House could be unwieldy and inefficient. Second, frequency of election—every two years—meant that members of the House would have to answer regularly to their home constituencies. But frequency of elections also had disadvantages. Members might follow short-term interests or passions of the moment, and House membership

INSIGHT

The Constitution Abroad

The Constitution of the United States has served as a model for many nations. In the early nineteenth century it had a strong impact on the newly independent nations of Latin America. It influenced constitutions in Europe in the nineteenth century, particularly in the republican revolutions of 1848. After World War II the United States Constitution influenced the constitution of West Germany. In the former colonial areas of Africa and Asia new nations also looked to the United States Constitution.

A framework of government is not easily exported. Removed from their cultural context, borrowed institutions may work differently. Sometimes they may not work at all. In any case they must be adapted to a new environment.

The Constitution has never been adopted in its entirety. Instead selected features have been borrowed and adapted. Four features that have had the greatest impact are the Presidency, federalism, judicial review, and the emphasis on individual liberty and human rights.

During the nineteenth century the nations of Latin America won their independence from Spain and Portugal. In establishing constitutions, most adopted the presidential form of government. The larger countries—Mexico, Argentina, and Brazil—also adopted federalism. Of all the features of the Constitution, federalism has had the greatest impact abroad. Nations as varied as Canada, Switzerland, Nigeria, and India have adopted it.

India is often described as "the world's largest democracy." Its constitution, adopted in 1950, combines aspects of both the British and American systems. In addition to federalism, it provides for a Supreme Court with the power of judicial review. The Indian constitution also places strong emphasis on human rights. Its preamble echoes that of the United States Constitution:

WE, THE PEOPLE OF INDIA, having solemnly resolved to constitute India into a SOVEREIGN, DEMOCRATIC REPUBLIC and to secure to all its citizens:

JUSTICE, social, economic, and political;

LIBERTY of thought, expression, belief, faith and worship;

EQUALITY of status and opportunity; and to promote among them all

FRATERNITY assuring the dignity of the individual and the unity of the nation;

IN OUR CONSTITUENT ASSEMBLY . . . do HEREBY ADOPT, ENACT AND GIVE TO OURSELVES THIS CONSTITUTION.

President Reagan delivers the State of the Union address before a joint session of Congress. In doing so each January, the President complies with Article 3, Section 3, of the Constitution, which states that the President "shall from time to time give to the Congress information on the state of the Union . . ."

had a potentially high turnover. Therefore the House was viewed as unlikely to provide experienced and stable leadership.

The Senate was to be a chamber of "temperate and respectable" citizens. Its small size would permit reasoned and sober debate. The six-year term of office was meant to encourage a long-range perspective. Overlapping Senate terms served to provide stability and continuity. The large and diverse constituencies that made up each state were believed likely to promote a broad outlook toward the national interest.

Of course, the Senate also had its drawbacks. Critics called it a "rich man's club" that ignored the will of the people. Throughout the nineteenth century some wealthy individuals were able to buy Senate seats by bribing a few state legislators. These abuses led to the passage of the Seventeenth Amendment, which provides for the direct election of senators.

Judicial Review Another major element in the system of checks and balances is ***judicial review.*** This is the power given the courts to declare laws ***unconstitutional***—that is, in violation of the Constitution and therefore void. The courts may act to ensure that neither the legislative branch nor the executive branch exceeds its constitutional authority. The final authority on the meaning of the Constitution is the Supreme Court. Judicial review is discussed in detail in Chapter 4.

Section Check

1. Define: republic, federalism, tyranny, bicameralism, constituency, judicial review, unconstitutional
2. Explain how both the national and state governments are limited governments.
3. What are the two basic safeguards of the Constitution?
4. What is a constituency? How do different constituencies for the three branches of government ensure the separation of powers?
5. What are some examples of the checks and balances of our system of government?

We the People

of the United States, in Order to form a more perfect Union, establish Justice, insure domestic Tranquility, provide for the common defence, promote the general Welfare, and secure the Blessings of Liberty to ourselves and our Posterity, do ordain and establish this Constitution for the United States of America.

Article. I.

Section. 1. All legislative Powers herein granted shall be vested in a Congress of the United States, which shall consist of a Senate and House of Representatives.

Section. 2. The House of Representatives shall be composed of Members chosen every second Year by the People of the several States, and the Electors in each State shall have the Qualifications requisite for Electors of the most numerous Branch of the State Legislature.

No Person shall be a Representative who shall not have attained to the Age of twenty five Years, and been seven Years a Citizen of the United States, and who shall not, when elected, be an Inhabitant of that State in which he shall be chosen.

Representatives and direct Taxes shall be apportioned among the several States which may be included within this Union, according to their respective Numbers, which shall be determined by adding to the whole Number of free Persons, including those bound to Service for a Term of Years, and excluding Indians not taxed, three fifths of all other Persons. The actual Enumeration shall be made within three Years after the first Meeting of the Congress of the United States, and within every subsequent Term of ten Years, in such Manner as they shall by Law direct. The Number of Representatives shall not exceed one for every thirty Thousand, but each State shall have at Least one Representative; and until such enumeration shall be made, the State of New Hampshire shall be entitled to chuse three, Massachusetts eight, Rhode Island and Providence Plantations one, Connecticut five, New York six, New Jersey four, Pennsylvania eight, Delaware one, Maryland six, Virginia ten, North Carolina five, South Carolina five, and Georgia three.

When vacancies happen in the Representation from any State, the Executive Authority thereof shall issue Writs of Election to fill such Vacancies.

The House of Representatives shall chuse their Speaker and other Officers; and shall have the sole Power of Impeachment.

Section. 3. The Senate of the United States shall be composed of two Senators from each State, chosen by the Legislature thereof for six Years; and each Senator shall have one Vote.

Immediately after they shall be assembled in Consequence of the first Election, they shall be divided as equally as may be into three Classes. The Seats of the Senators of the first Class shall be vacated at the Expiration of the second Year, of the second Class at the Expiration of the fourth Year, and of the third Class at the Expiration of the sixth Year, so that one third may be chosen every second Year; and if Vacancies happen by Resignation, or otherwise, during the Recess of the Legislature of any State, the Executive thereof may make temporary Appointments until the next Meeting of the Legislature, which shall then fill such Vacancies.

No Person shall be a Senator who shall not have attained to the Age of thirty Years, and been nine Years a Citizen of the United States, and who shall not, when elected, be an Inhabitant of that State for which he shall be chosen.

The Vice President of the United States shall be President of the Senate, but shall have no Vote, unless they be equally divided.

The Senate shall chuse their other Officers, and also a President pro tempore, in the Absence of the Vice President, or when he shall exercise the Office of President of the United States.

The Senate shall have the sole Power to try all Impeachments. When sitting for that Purpose, they shall be on Oath or Affirmation. When the President of the United States is tried, the Chief Justice shall preside: And no Person shall be convicted without the Concurrence of two thirds of the Members present.

Judgment in Cases of Impeachment shall not extend further than to removal from Office, and disqualification to hold and enjoy any Office of honor, Trust or Profit under the United States: but the Party convicted shall nevertheless be liable and subject to Indictment, Trial, Judgment and Punishment, according to Law.

Section. 4. The Times, Places and Manner of holding Elections for Senators and Representatives, shall be prescribed in each State by the Legislature thereof; but the Congress may at any time by Law make or alter such Regulations, except as to the Places of chusing Senators.

The Congress shall assemble at least once in every Year, and such Meeting shall be on the first Monday in December, unless they shall by Law appoint a different Day.

Section. 5. Each House shall be the Judge of the Elections, Returns and Qualifications of its own Members, and a Majority of each shall constitute a Quorum to do Business; but a smaller Number may adjourn from day to day, and may be authorized to compel the Attendance of absent Members, in such Manner, and under such Penalties as each House may provide.

Each House may determine the Rules of its Proceedings, punish its Members for disorderly Behaviour, and, with the Concurrence of two thirds, expel a Member.

Each House shall keep a Journal of its Proceedings, and from time to time publish the same, excepting such Parts as may in their Judgment require Secrecy; and the Yeas and Nays of the Members of either House on any question shall, at the Desire of one fifth of those Present, be entered on the Journal.

Neither House, during the Session of Congress, shall, without the Consent of the other, adjourn for more than three days, nor to any other Place than that in which the two Houses shall be sitting.

Section. 6. The Senators and Representatives shall receive a Compensation for their Services, to be ascertained by Law, and paid out of the Treasury of the United States. They shall in all Cases, except Treason, Felony and Breach of the Peace, be privileged from Arrest during their Attendance at the Session of their respective Houses, and in going to and returning from the same; and for any Speech or Debate in either House, they shall not be questioned in any other Place.

No Senator or Representative shall, during the Time for which he was elected, be appointed to any civil Office under the Authority of the United States, which shall have been created, or the Emoluments whereof shall have been encreased during such time; and no Person holding any Office under the United States, shall be a Member of either House during his Continuance in Office.

Section. 7. All Bills for raising Revenue shall originate in the House of Representatives; but the Senate may propose or concur with Amendments as on other

Every Bill which shall have passed the House of Representatives and the Senate, shall, before it become a Law, be presented to the President of the

THE CONSTITUTION OF THE UNITED STATES OF AMERICA

[The text of the Constitution is printed on the white background, the commentary on the blue background. Portions of the text printed in brackets and ruled with blue have gone out of date or have been changed by amendment.]

PREAMBLE

We, the people of the United States, in order to form a more perfect Union, establish justice, insure domestic tranquility, provide for the common defense, promote the general welfare, and secure the blessings of liberty to ourselves and our posterity, do ordain and establish this CONSTITUTION for the United States of America.

The Preamble states the purposes of the Constitution, and makes it clear that the government is established by consent of the governed. We, the people, have supreme power in establishing the government of the United States of America.

ARTICLE 1
LEGISLATIVE DEPARTMENT

By separating the functions of government among branches concerned with lawmaking (Article 1), law executing (Article 2), and law interpreting (Article 3), the Framers were applying the principle of separation of powers and developing a system of checks and balances as a defense against tyranny.

Section 1. Congress

All legislative powers herein granted shall be vested in a Congress of the United States, which shall consist of a Senate and House of Representatives.

Practice has modified the provision that all lawmaking powers granted in the Constitution are vested in Congress. For example, such administrative agencies as the Interstate Commerce Commission can issue regulations that in some ways have the force of laws.

Section 2. House of Representatives

1. Election and Term of Members The House of Representatives shall be composed of members chosen every second year by the people of the several States, and the electors in each state shall have the qualifications requisite for electors of the most numerous branch of the state legislature.

Clause 1. The members of the House of Representatives are elected every two years by the "electors" (voters) of the states. Except for the provisions of Amendments 15, 19, 24, and 26, the individual states decide who may or may not vote.

2. Qualifications No person shall be a representative who shall not have attained to the age of twenty-five years, and been seven years a citizen of the United States, and who shall not, when elected, be an inhabitant of that state in which he shall be chosen.

Clause 2. This clause specifies that a member of the House of Representatives must be (1) at least 25 years of age, (2) a United States citizen for at least 7 years, and (3) a resident of the state in which elected. Custom has added the requirement of residency in the Congressional district from which a representative is elected. Each state is divided into Congressional districts for the purpose of electing representatives; each district elects one. TERM OF OFFICE: 2 years.

Clause 3. The portion of this clause begining on line 5 forms what came to be called the Three-Fifths Compromise. Amendment 13 and Section 2 of Amendment 14 overruled this provision in the case of black Americans but not for Native Americans. However, since 1940 Native Americans have been included in the population census. Originally each state was entitled to one Representative for every 30,000 people. Later, membership was limited by law to a total of 435. A census of the United States is taken every ten years to determine the number of Representatives to which each state is entitled. Regardless of its population, however, each state is entitled to at least one representative in the House.

3. Apportionment of Representatives and Direct Taxes Representatives and direct taxes shall be apportioned among the several states which may be included within this Union, according to their respective numbers [which shall be determined by adding to the whole number of free persons, including those bound to service for a term of years, and excluding Indians not taxed, three fifths of all other persons]. The actual enumeration shall be made within three years after the first meeting of the Congress of the United States, and within every subsequent term of ten years, in such manner as they shall by law direct. The number of Representatives shall not exceed one for every 30,000, but each state shall have at least 1 Representative; [and until such enumeration shall be made, the state of New Hampshire shall be entitled to choose 3; Massachusetts, 8; Rhode Island and Providence Plantations, 1; Connecticut, 5; New York, 6; New Jersey, 4; Pennsylvania, 8; Delaware, 1; Maryland, 6; Virginia, 10; North Carolina, 5; South Carolina, 5; and Georgia, 3.]

Clause 4. The *executive authority* refers to the governor of the state; a *writ of election* is an order for a special election to fill the vacant seat.

4. Filling Vacancies When vacancies happen in the representation from any state, the executive authority thereof shall issue writs of election to fill such vacancies.

Clause 5. In actual practice it is the majority party—the political party having the largest number of members in the House—that chooses the Speaker of the House and other House officials (clerk, doorkeeper, sergeant-at-arms, postmaster, and chaplain). The Speaker is the only official chosen from among the members of the House. The House, by a majority vote, can impeach (accuse) an Executive Department officer or a federal judge. The trial of the impeached official takes place in the Senate. (See Section 3, Clause 6.)

5. Officers; Impeachment The House of Representatives shall choose their Speaker and other officers; and shall have the sole power of impeachment.

Section 3. Senate

Clause 1. Under the provisions of Amendment 17, the 100 senators are now elected directly by the voters of the states in the same manner as the representatives. The method of electing senators provided here, by which the state legislatures chose senators, came to be considered undemocratic and was therefore changed.

1. Composition and Term The Senate of the United States shall be composed of two Senators from each state [chosen by the legislature thereof], for six years; and each Senator shall have one vote.

Clause 2. One third of the Senate comes up for election every two years. This procedure was established in the first Senate, whose senators were divided into three groups. One group was to serve for two years, the second for four years, and the third for six years. As a result, the terms of senators today overlap, making the Senate a "continuing" body, in which two thirds of the members are "carried over" through every election. In contrast, every member of the House of Representatives is elected every two years. Under Amendment 17, if a senator resigns or dies, the state governor can call a spe-

2. Classification; Filling Vacancies [Immediately after they shall be assembled in consequence of the first election, they shall be divided as equally as may be into three classes. The seats of the Senators of the first class shall be vacated at the expiration of the second year, of the second class at the expiration of the fourth year, and of the third class at the expiration of the sixth year, so that one third may be chosen every second year; and if vacancies happen by resignation, or otherwise, during the recess of the legislature of any state, the executive thereof may make temporary appointments until the next meeting of the legislature, which shall then fill such vacancies.]

cial election to fill the vacancy. The state legislature, however, may empower the governor to name a temporary senator.

3. Qualifications No person shall be a Senator who shall not have attained to the age of thirty years, and been nine years a citizen of the United States, and who shall not, when elected, be an inhabitant of that state for which he shall be chosen.

Clause 3. This clause specifies that a senator must be (1) at least 30 years of age, (2) a United States citizen for at least 9 years, and (3) a resident of the state in which elected. TERM OF OFFICE: 6 years.

4. President of the Senate The Vice President of the United States shall be President of the Senate, but shall have no vote, unless they be equally divided.

Clause 4. To serve as president of the Senate and vote only in case of a tie is the sole duty the Constitution assigns to the Vice President. In recent years the Vice President has assumed additional duties at the President's request, such as attending cabinet meetings, traveling abroad on good-will tours, and carrying out such ceremonial duties as entertaining leading officials from abroad and representing the government at important events.

5. Other Officers The Senate shall choose their other officers, and also a president *pro tempore,* in the absence of the Vice President, or when he shall exercise the office of President of the United States.

Clause 5. "Other officers" include a secretary, chaplain, and sergeant-at-arms. These officers are not members of the Senate. *Pro tempore* is a Latin expression meaning "for the time being," or "temporarily."

6. Trial of Impeachments The Senate shall have the sole power to try all impeachments. When sitting for that purpose, they shall be on oath or affirmation. When the President of the United States is tried, the Chief Justice shall preside; and no person shall be convicted without the concurrence of two thirds of the members present.

Clause 6. Only the President, Vice President, cabinet officials, and federal judges are subject to impeachment and removal from office. Members of the House and Senate cannot be impeached, but they can be censured and even removed from office by the members of their respective houses. Officials may be impeached only for committing "treason, bribery, or other high crimes and misdemeanors" (see Article 2, Section 4). The Chief Justice of the Supreme Court presides at the impeachment trial of a President. The Vice President presides over all other impeachment trials. The Senate can find an impeached official guilty only if two thirds of the senators present agree on the verdict. The only President ever impeached was Andrew Johnson, in 1867; he was saved from conviction by one vote. In 1974 Richard M. Nixon resigned as President after the Judiciary Committee of the House of Representatives recommended to the House that he be impeached.

7. Penalty for Conviction Judgment in cases of impeachment shall not extend further than to removal from office, and disqualification to hold and enjoy any office of honor, trust, or profit under the United States; but the party convicted shall nevertheless be liable and subject to indictment, trial, judgment and punishment, according to Law.

Clause 7. The punishment for conviction in impeachment cases can consist only of removal from office and disqualification from holding any other federal office. However, the convicted person may also be tried in a regular court of law for this same offense. Although not impeached, President Nixon was granted a Presidential pardon, which spared him a possible criminal court trial.

Section 4. Elections and Meetings

1. Holding Elections The times, places and manner of holding elections for Senators and Representatives shall be prescribed in each state by the legislature thereof; but the Congress may at any time by law make or alter such regulations, except as to the places of choosing senators.

Clause 1. Under this provision Congress has passed a law stating that, unless the constitution of a state provides otherwise, Congressional elections must be held on the Tuesday following the first Monday in November of even-numbered years. (Until 1960 Maine held elections in September.) Congress has also ruled that representatives must be elected by districts, rather than by the state as a whole, and that secret ballots (or voting machines, where required by state law) must be used.

2. Meetings The Congress shall assemble at least once in every year, [and such meeting shall be on the first Monday in December,] unless they shall by law appoint a different day.

Clause 2. Under Amendment 20 Congress now meets on January 3, unless it sets another day by law.

Section 5. Rules of Procedure

1. Organization Each house shall be the judge of the elections, returns and qualifications of its own members, and a majority of each shall constitute a quorum to do business; but a smaller number may adjourn from day to day, and may be authorized to compel the attendance of absent members, in such manner, and under such penalties as each house may provide.

Clause 1. Until 1969 Congress used this clause to disqualify elected candidates who had broken the law or who were charged with gross misconduct and prevent them from taking office. In 1969, the Supreme Court ruled that Congress had to seat all senators and representatives who met the requirements of Article 1, Section 2, Clause 2. A *quorum* is the minimum number of persons required to be present to transact business; a majority of the House or Senate constitutes a quorum. In practice, business is often transacted with less than a quorum present and may go on as long as no member objects to the lack of a quorum.

2. Proceedings Each house may determine the rules of its proceedings, punish its members for disorderly behavior, and, with the concurrence of two thirds, expel a member.

Clause 2. Each house has extensive rules of procedure. Each house can censure, punish, or expel a member. Expulsion requires a two-thirds vote.

3. Journal Each house shall keep a journal of its proceedings, and from time to time publish the same, excepting such parts as may in their judgment require secrecy; and the yeas and nays of the members of either house on any question shall, at the desire of one fifth of those present, be entered on the journal.

Clause 3. Each house is required to keep a journal of its activities. These journals, called the *House Journal* and the *Senate Journal,* are published at the end of each session of Congress. A third journal, called the *Congressional Record,* is published every day that Congress is in session, and furnishes a daily account of what representatives and senators do and say. If one fifth of those present insist on a roll call of the members' votes, each member's vote must be recorded in the proper house journal.

4. Adjournment Neither house, during the session of Congress, shall, without the consent of the other, adjourn for more than three days, nor to any other place than that in which the two houses shall be sitting.

Clause 4. Both houses must remain in session for the same period of time and in the same place.

Section 6. Privileges and Restrictions

1. Pay and Privileges The Senators and Representatives shall receive a compensation for their services, to be ascertained by law, and paid out of the Treasury of the United States. They shall in all cases, except treason, felony and breach of the peace, be privileged from arrest during their attendance at the session of their respective houses, and in going to and returning from the same; and for any speech or debate in either house, they shall not be questioned in any other place.

Clause 1. The provision concerning privilege from arrest establishes the principle of "Congressional immunity." According to this principle, members cannot be arrested or brought into court for what they say in speeches and debates in Congress. The aim of this provision is to enable members of Congress to speak freely. They are subject to arrest, however, if they commit a crime, and, under the laws governing slander and libel, are liable for any false or defamatory statements they may make outside Congress.

2. Restrictions No Senator or Representative shall, during the time for which he was elected, be appointed to any civil office under the authority of the United States, which shall have been created, or the emoluments whereof shall have been increased during such time; and no person holding any office under the United States, shall be a member of either house during his continuance in office.

Clause 2. This clause emphasizes the separation of powers in the federal government. Legislators cannot, while they are members of Congress, hold positions also in the executive or judicial departments. Nor can legislators resign and then accept positions that were created during their term of office. Thus members of Congress cannot set up jobs for themselves in the executive or judicial branches of the government. Furthermore, if a member resigns and is appointed to an existing executive or judicial position, he or she cannot profit from any increase in pay in this position that was voted during the member's term in Congress.

Section 7. Method of Passing Laws

1. Revenue Bills All bills for raising revenue shall originate in the House of Representatives; but the Senate may propose or concur with amendments as on other bills.

Clause 1. All revenue, or money-raising, bills must be introduced in the House of Representatives. This provision grew out of a demand that the popularly elected branch of the legislature should have the "power of the purse." (Until Amendment 17 was ratified, the House was the only popularly elected branch.) It was also felt that the voters had more control over representatives, who are elected for two-year terms, than over senators, who are elected for six-year terms. Thus representatives would be more careful than senators in considering revenue bills. Since the Senate has the power to amend any bill, however, it can amend a revenue bill in such a way as actually to introduce a revenue bill of its own.

2. How a Bill Becomes Law Every bill which shall have passed the House of Representatives and the Senate, shall, before it become a law, be presented to the President of the United States; if he approve he shall sign it, but if not he shall return it, with his objections to that house in which it shall have originated, who shall enter the objections at large on their journal, and proceed to reconsider it. If after such reconsideration two thirds of that house shall agree to pass the bill, it shall be sent, together with the objections, to the other house, by which it shall likewise be reconsidered, and, if approved by two thirds of that house, it shall become a law. But in all

Clause 2. When both houses of Congress pass a law, it is then sent to the President. If the President does not approve of a bill, one of several things may occur. The President may (1) veto, or refuse to sign, the bill; (2) permit the bill to become a law without signing it by holding it for ten days (not counting Sundays) while Congress is in session; (3) hold the bill near the end of a session in the hope that Congress will adjourn within ten days. In that case, the bill fails to become a law, just as though the President had formally vetoed it. This type of veto is called a "pocket veto." A bill vetoed by the President can become a law, however, if two thirds or more of both houses vote for the bill a second time. When this happens, Congress is said to have "overridden the Presidential veto."

such cases the votes of both houses shall be determined by yeas and nays, and the names of the persons voting for and against the bill shall be entered on the journal of each house respectively. If any bill shall not be returned by the President within ten days (Sundays excepted) after it shall have been presented to him, the same shall be a law, in like manner as if he had signed it, unless the Congress by their adjournment prevent its return, in which case it shall not be a law.

Clause 3. A *joint resolution* results from declarations passed by both houses of Congress on the same subject. It becomes a law in the same manner as a bill. A Congressional declaration of war takes the form of a joint resolution. A *concurrent resolution* represents only an expression of opinion on the part of either house of Congress. It does not have the force of law and, therefore, does not require Presidential approval. The process of amending the Constitution may start this way. A vote censuring a representative or senator, or an expression of sympathy, takes the form of a concurrent resolution.

3. Presidential Approval or Veto Every order, resolution, or vote to which the concurrence of the Senate and House of Representatives may be necessary (except on a question of adjournment) shall be presented to the President of the United States; and before the same shall take effect, shall be approved by him, or being disapproved by him, shall be repassed by two thirds of the Senate and House of Representatives, according to the rules and limitations prescribed in the case of a bill.

Section 8 places important powers in the hands of Congress, indicating that the Framers were aware of the weaknesses of the Congress under the Articles of Confederation. This section lists 18 powers granted to Congress—the *delegated* or *enumerated powers.* The first 17 are expressed powers because they clearly designate specific areas in which Congress may exercise its authority. The eighteenth power is contained in the famous elastic clause, from which has come the doctrine of implied powers. The elastic clause permits the stretching of the other 17 powers.

Section 8. Powers Delegated to Congress

The Congress shall have power

Clause 1. This clause gives Congress the power to levy and collect taxes, duties, or tariffs (taxes on imported goods collected at customhouses), and excises (taxes on goods produced, sold, or consumed within the country). The term *imposts* includes duties and excise taxes. Notice that these taxes must be uniform throughout the United States. According to this clause, the power to tax may be used only (1) to pay the government's debts and (2) to provide for the common defense and general welfare. The Social Security tax on payrolls is a present-day use of the power to tax.

1. To lay and collect taxes, duties, imposts and excises, to pay the debts and provide for the common defense and general welfare of the United States; but all duties, imposts and excises shall be uniform throughout the United States;

Clause 2. The power granted in Clause 2 enables the government to borrow money by issuing bonds for sale, on which the government pays interest. This clause, extended by Clause 18, has also given Congress the power to establish national banks and the Federal Reserve System.

2. To borrow money on the credit of the United States;

3. To regulate commerce with foreign nations, and among the several states, [and with the Indian tribes];

Clause 3. Congress is given direct control over interstate and foreign commerce. This provision has been extended, by the use of Clause 18, to give Congress control over transportation, communication, and navigation. In order to exercise this broad power, Congress has set up administrative agencies, such as the Interstate Commerce Commission and the Federal Communications Commission.

4. To establish an uniform rule of naturalization, and uniform laws on the subject of bankruptcies throughout the United States;

Clause 4. This clause provides the power to regulate the methods by which aliens become citizens of the United States and to form rules regarding bankruptcy.

5. To coin money, regulate the value thereof, and of foreign coin, and fix the standard of weights and measures;

Clause 5. Congress is permitted to coin money, to determine the gold and silver content of money, and to order the printing of paper money. It also permits Congress to set up uniform standards for measuring weights and distances.

6. To provide for the punishment of counterfeiting the securities and current coin of the United States;

Clause 6. Under this clause Congress authorizes the Treasury Department to investigate counterfeiting of money or of government bonds.

7. To establish post offices and post roads;

Clause 7. In 1970 Congress transferred authority over the postal system to the executive branch in the Postal Reorganization Act. The Post Office Department was replaced by an independent agency, the United States Postal Service.

8. To promote the progress of science and useful arts by securing for limited times to authors and inventors the exclusive right to their respective writings and discoveries;

Clause 8. This clause shows that the Framers were eager to promote the progress of science and the arts. Under this power Congress has passed laws providing that inventors be granted *patents* (exclusive rights to manufacture and sell their inventions for 17 years) and that authors and composers be granted *copyrights* (exclusive rights to control the publication or performance of their works for their lifetimes plus 50 years).

9. To constitute tribunals inferior to the Supreme Court;

Clause 9. Congress is granted the power to establish the federal district courts, the Courts of Appeals, and special courts.

10. To define and punish piracies and felonies committed on the high seas, and offenses against the law of nations;

Clause 10. Congress protects and controls citizens and ships of the United States when they are out of the country. It may also punish counterfeiting in the United States of bonds and notes of a foreign government.

Clause 11. Congress is given the power to declare war. Although Congress alone has this power, several Presidents have taken military action without prior consent of Congress. In 1846 President Polk sent troops into an area claimed by both the United States and Mexico. In 1950 President Truman ordered American troops into Korea. And in the mid-1960's, through executive order, American troops became involved in the conflict in Vietnam without a formal declaration of war. The 1973 War Powers Resolution requires the President to report to Congress within 48 hours any new commitment of American troops to a foreign war. Unless Congress declares war, the President must end hostilities within 60 days and withdraw the troops within 90 days. Congress can require earlier withdrawal by passing a joint resolution, which the President cannot veto. Letters of marque and reprisal were licenses issued by the government to privateers (armed ships, privately owned), allowing them to attack enemy ships during wartime. In the War of 1812, the government of the United States issued many of the licenses to American privateers, who did extensive damage to British trade. Today, the issuing of such licenses is outlawed by international agreement.

11. To declare war, [grant letters of marque and reprisal,] and make rules concerning captures on land and water;

Clause 12. The two-year limit in Clause 12 on money appropriations for the army was included to keep the major military power under strict civilian control.

12. To raise and support armies, but no appropriation of money to that use shall be for a longer term than two years;

Clause 13. Notice that appropriations for the navy were not limited. An air force, of course, was not dreamed of when the Constitution was written.

13. To provide and maintain a navy;

Clause 14. Under the power granted in this clause, Congress has established rules and regulations governing military discipline and the procedure of courts-martial.

14. To make rules for the government and regulation of the land and naval forces;

Clause 15. The term *militia* now refers to the National Guard units of the states. These units may now be called up by the President to keep law and order. They can become part of the United States Army in emergencies.

15. To provide for calling forth the militia to execute the laws of the Union, suppress insurrections and repel invasions;

Clause 16. Congress is authorized to help states support their militia.

16. To provide for organizing, arming, and disciplining the militia, and for governing such part of them as may be employed in the service of the United States, reserving to the states respectively, the appointment of the officers, and the authority of training the militia according to the discipline prescribed by Congress.

Clause 17. This clause enables Congress to exercise exclusive control over the government of the District of Columbia. In 1973 Congress relinquished some of its control by allowing the District to choose local officials. By this clause Congress also controls all installations owned and operated by the federal government in the various states.

17. To exercise exclusive legislation in all cases whatsoever, over such district (not exceeding ten miles square) as may, by cession of particular states, and the acceptance of Congress, become the seat of the government of the United States, and to exercise like authority over all places purchased by the consent of the legislature of the state in which the same shall be, for the erection of forts, magazines, arsenals, dock-yards, and other needful buildings;—and

18. To make all laws which shall be necessary and proper for carrying into execution the foregoing powers, and all other powers vested by this Constitution in the government of the United States, or in any department or officer thereof.

Clause 18. "Necessary and proper" are the key words in the so-called *elastic clause.* Only by combining the power granted in this clause with one of the other 17 powers can Congress use the implied powers granted to it in the Constitution. Laws based on this clause are, of course, subject to review by the judicial branch.

Section 9. Powers Denied to the Federal Government

Section 9 limits the powers of Congress.

1. [The migration or importation of such persons as any of the states now existing shall think proper to admit, shall not be prohibited by the Congress prior to the year 1808; but a tax or duty may be imposed on such importation, not exceeding $10 for each person.]

Clause 1. Such persons refers to slaves. This provision grew out of the commerce compromise at the Constitutional Convention held in Philadelphia in 1787. It was agreed that Congress would not prohibit the importation of slaves prior to 1808, and that it would not impose an import tax of more than $10 per slave. The importation of slaves into the United States became illegal in 1808.

2. The privilege of the writ of *habeas corpus* shall not be suspended, unless when in cases of rebellion or invasion the public safety may require it.

Clause 2. The guarantee of the *writ of habeas corpus* (meaning "you may have the body, or person") protects a person against being held in jail on insufficient evidence or no evidence at all. The lawyer of a person arrested can obtain a writ, or court order, that requires the arrested person to be brought before a judge who must determine whether there are sufficient grounds to hold the person in jail. If there are no such grounds, the person must be freed.

3. No bill of attainder or *ex post facto* law shall be passed.

Clause 3. A "bill of attainder" is a legislative measure that condemns and punishes a person without a jury trial. Under the Constitution Congress cannot by law single out certain persons and inflict punishment on them. The power to punish belongs to the judiciary. An *ex post facto law* is a law that punishes a person for doing something that was legal before the law was passed, or that increases the penalty for earlier actions. Because of this clause, the Lindbergh kidnaping law of 1932, for example, could not be applied to persons who committed the crime of kidnaping before that year.

4. No capitation or other direct tax shall be laid, unless in proportion to the census herein before directed to be taken.

Clause 4. A capitation tax is a direct tax imposed on each person, such as the poll tax on persons voting. This provision was inserted to prevent Congress from taxing slaves per poll, or per person, for the purpose of abolishing slavery. Amendment 16 makes the income tax an exception to this clause. Amendment 24 outlaws federal poll taxes.

5. No tax or duty shall be laid on articles exported from any state.

Clause 5. The southern states wanted to make sure that Congress could not use its taxing power to impose taxes on southern exports, such as cotton and tobacco.

6. No preference shall be given by any regulation of commerce or revenue to the ports of one state over those of another; nor shall vessels bound to, or from, one state, be obliged to enter, clear, or pay duties in another.

Clause 6. This clause declares that the United States is an open market in which all states have equal trading and commercial opportunities.

Clause 7. This clause concerns the all-important power of the purse. Since Congress controls expenditures, it can limit the powers of the President by limiting the amount of money the Chief Executive may spend to run the government. This clause is perhaps the single most important curb on Presidential power in the Constitution. Furthermore, the requirement to account for money spent and received helps to protect against misuse of funds.

7. No money shall be drawn from the Treasury, but in consequence of appropriations made by law; and a regular statement and account of the receipts and expenditures of all public money shall be published from time to time.

Clause 8. This clause prohibits the establishment of a nobility. It also discourages bribery of American officials by foreign governments.

8. No title of nobility shall be granted by the United States; and no person holding any office of profit or trust under them, shall, without the consent of the Congress, accept of any present, emolument, office, or title, of any kind whatever, from any king, prince or foreign state.

According to Section 10, states cannot (1) make treaties, (2) coin money, (3) pass either bills of attainder or *ex post facto* laws, (4) impair obligations of contract, (5) grant titles of nobility, (6) tax imports or exports without the consent of Congress, (7) keep troops or warships in time of peace. (8) deal with another state or foreign power without the consent of Congress, and (9) engage in war unless invaded.

Section 10. Powers Denied to the States

Clause 1. Because Shays's Rebellion was still fresh in the minds of the delegates to the Constitutional Convention, and since several of the states at that time were being urged to pass legislation relieving debtors from the payment of their debts, the delegates decided to protect creditors once and for all by denying states the right to pass laws that would impair obligations of contract. During the Great Depression, which began in 1929, and the New Deal period (1933–45), the Supreme Court upheld state laws relieving debtors or mortgagees from paying their debts on the due dates, but payments were simply postponed, not canceled.

1. No state shall enter into any treaty, alliance, or confederation; grant letters of marque and reprisal; coin money; emit bills of credit; make any thing but gold and silver coin a tender in payment of debts; pass any bill of attainder, *ex post facto* law, or law impairing the obligation of contracts, or grant any title of nobility.

Clause 2. Forbidden to the states in this clause is the power to vote for taxes on goods sent in or out of a state, unless Congress agrees.

2. No state shall, without the consent of the Congress, lay any imposts or duties on imports or exports, except what may be absolutely necessary for executing its inspection laws; and the net produce of all duties and imposts, laid by any state on imports or exports, shall be for the use of the Treasury of the United States; and all such laws shall be subject to the revision and control of the Congress.

Clause 3. This clause forbids the states to keep troops or warships in peacetime or enter into an agreement with another state or a foreign nation, unless Congress agrees.

3. No state shall, without the consent of Congress, lay any duty of tonnage, keep troops, or ships of war in time of peace, enter into any agreement or compact with another state, or with a foreign power, or engage in war, unless actually invaded, or in such imminent danger as will not admit of delay.

ARTICLE 2
EXECUTIVE DEPARTMENT

Section 1. President and Vice President

1. Term of Office The executive power shall be vested in a President of the United States of America. He shall hold his office during the term of four years, and, together with the Vice President, chosen for the same term, be elected, as follows:

Clause 1. This provision gives the executive power to the President. The President may use all of the means available to carry out the laws or refrain from using some of these means. Of course, the power and prestige of the Presidency depend to some extent on the personality of the person who holds the office.

2. Electoral System Each state shall appoint, in such manner as the legislature thereof may direct, a number of electors, equal to the whole number of Senators and Representatives to which the state may be entitled in the Congress; but no Senator or Representative, or person holding an office of trust or profit under the United States, shall be appointed an elector.

3. Former Electoral Method [The electors shall meet in their respective states, and vote by ballot for two persons, of whom one at least shall not be an inhabitant of the same state with themselves. And they shall make a list of all the persons voted for, and of the number of votes for each; which list they shall sign and certify, and transmit sealed to the seat of the government of the United States, directed to the president of the Senate. The president of the Senate shall, in the presence of the Senate and House of Representatives, open all the certificates, and the votes shall then be counted. The person having the greatest number of votes shall be the President, if such number be a majority of the whole number of electors appointed; and if there be more than one who have such majority, and have an equal number of votes, then the House of Representatives shall immediately choose by ballot one of them for President; and if no person have a majority, then from the five highest on the list the said House shall in like manner choose the President. But in choosing the President, the votes shall be taken by states, the representation from each state having one vote. A quorum for this purpose shall consist of a member or members from two thirds of the states, and a majority of all the states shall be necessary to a choice. In every case, after the choice of the President, the person having the greatest number of votes of the electors shall be the Vice President. But if there should remain two or more who have equal votes, the Senate shall choose from them by ballot the Vice President.]

Clauses 2, 3. These clauses established the electoral system, but very little that the Framers decided about electing a President has survived in the form they intended. The delegates to the Constitutional Convention, still fearful of popular rule, decided that the President and Vice President ought to be elected by a small group of persons called "electors" chosen according to a method determined by each state legislature. Until Andrew Jackson's Presidency, electors were chosen by state legislatures. Since then the people have voted directly for the electors. Some changes in the method of electing a President have been made by formal amendment, as in Amendment 12; other changes have resulted from political practice.

Clause 4. Today Presidential elections are held on the Tuesday after the first Monday in November. Electoral votes are cast on the Monday after the second Wednesday in December.

4. Time of Elections The Congress may determine the time of choosing the electors, and the day on which they shall give their votes; which day shall be the same throughout the United States.

Clause 5. This clause specifies that the President must be (1) a native-born citizen of the United States, (2) at least 35 years of age, and (3) a resident of the United States for at least 14 years. TERM OF OFFICE: 4 years.

5. Qualifications No person except a natural-born citizen, [or a citizen of the United States, at the time of the adoption of this Constitution] shall be eligible to the office of President; neither shall any person be eligible to that office who shall not have attained to the age of thirty-five years, and been fourteen years a resident within the United States.

Clause 6. If a President dies or is removed from office, the Vice President succeeds to the office. John Tyler, in 1841, was the first Vice President to succeed to the Presidency. By assuming the office of President, not simply serving as an acting President, Tyler established a precedent that has since been followed. Under the Presidential Succession Act of 1947, if both the President and the Vice President die or are removed from office, the order of succession is as follows: (1) Speaker of the House, (2) President *pro tempore* of the Senate, and (3) the cabinet members in the order in which their offices were created. Amendment 25, adopted in 1967, clarifies the procedure to be followed in case the President or Vice President is unable to serve or resigns.

6. Filling Vacancies In case of the removal of the President from office, or of his death, resignation, or inability to discharge the powers and duties of the said office, the same shall devolve on the Vice President, and the Congress may by law provide for the case of removal, death, resignation or inability, both of the President and Vice President, declaring what officer shall then act as President, and such officer shall act accordingly, until the disability be removed, or a President shall be elected.

Clause 7. Today the President's salary is $200,000 a year, plus a $50,000 expense account and a nontaxable fund for travel and official entertainment limited to $112,000. The Vice President's salary is $94,200 a year plus a $10,000 expense allowance.

7. Salary The President shall, at stated times, receive for his services, a compensation, which shall neither be increased nor diminished during the period for which he shall have been elected, and he shall not receive within that period any other emolument from the United States, or any of them.

Clause 8. The President assumes office officially only after taking the oath of office, which is administered by the Chief Justice of the United States.

8. Oath of Office Before he enter on the execution of his office, he shall take the following oath or affirmation:—"I do solemnly swear (or affirm) that I will faithfully execute the office of President of the United States, and will to the best of my ability, preserve, protect and defend the Constitution of the United States."

Section 2. Powers of the President

1. Military Powers The President shall be Commander in Chief of the Army and Navy of the United States, and of the militia of the several states, when called into the actual service of the United States; he may require the opinion, in writing, of the principal officer in each of the executive departments, upon any subject relating to the duties of their respective offices, and he shall have power to grant reprieves and pardons for offences against the United States, except in cases of impeachment.

Clause 1. The important point in this provision is that it places the armed forces under civilian control. The President is a civilian but is superior in military power to any military officer. The words *principal officer in each of the executive departments* are the basis for the creation of the President's cabinet. Each cabinet member is the head of one of the executive departments. The President chooses the cabinet members, with the consent of the Senate, and can remove any cabinet official without asking Senate approval.

2. Treaties and Appointments He shall have power, by and with the advice and consent of the Senate, to make treaties, provided two thirds of the Senators present concur; and he shall nominate, and by and with the advice and consent of the Senate, shall appoint ambassadors, other public ministers and consuls, judges of the Supreme Court, and all other officers of the United States, whose appointments are not herein otherwise provided for, and which shall be established by law; but the Congress may by law vest the appointment of such inferior officers, as they think proper, in the President alone, in the courts of law, or in the heads of departments.

Clause 2. The President makes treaties with the advice and consent of two thirds of the Senate. A treaty ratified by the Senate becomes the supreme law of the land. The President can also enter into executive agreements with foreign governments that have the same force as treaties but do not require Senate approval. With the consent of the Senate, the President can appoint ambassadors, public ministers, consuls, and other diplomatic officials, as well as federal judges, military officers, and members of administrative agencies. "Inferior officers" are those subordinate to the cabinet members or to federal judges. At the present time, a majority of federal government positions are filled by men and women who have passed examinations given by the United States Civil Service Commission.

3. Filling Vacancies The President shall have power to fill up all vacancies that may happen during the recess of the Senate, by granting commissions which shall expire at the end of their next session.

Clause 3. If a vacancy in an important position occurs when Congress is not in session, the President has the power to fill such a vacancy with an interim appointment. When Congress meets again, this appointment or a new appointment must be submitted to the Senate so that it may be approved.

Section 3. Duties of the President

He shall from time to time give to the Congress information of the state of the Union, and recommend to their consideration such measures as he shall judge necessary and expedient; he may, on extraordinary occasions, convene both houses, or either of them, and in case of disagreement between them, with respect to the time of adjournment, he may adjourn them to such time as he shall think proper; he shall receive ambassadors and other public ministers; he shall take care that the laws be faithfully executed, and shall commission all the officers of the United States.

The President's duties include the following: (1) *Legislative duties:* delivering annual and special messages to Congress; calling special sessions of Congress; approving or vetoing bills (see Article 1, Section 7). (2) *Diplomatic duties:* receiving (or refusing to receive) ambassadors or ministers of foreign countries to indicate that the United States recognizes (or refuses to recognize) the government of these countries. The President can also send home the ambassador of a foreign country as a sign that the United States is breaking off diplomatic relations with that country. (3) *Executive duties:* executing all the laws. In actual fact the administration and enforcement of the laws are in the hands of the various government departments, commissions, and administrative agencies; but the President is responsible for seeing that they are carried out. (4) *Military duties:* commissioning of United States armed forces officers.

(See annotation of Article 1, Section 3, Clauses 6–7.)

Section 4. Impeachment

The President, Vice President and all civil officers of the United States, shall be removed from office on impeachment for, and conviction of, treason, bribery, or other high crimes and misdemeanors.

By authorizing the establishment of a system of federal courts, Article 3 creates the judicial power—the power to hear and decide cases. Under the judicial powers granted by the Constitution or developed through Supreme Court decisions, the courts have declared unconstitutional certain laws of Congress, acts of the President, laws of the state legislatures, and decisions of the state courts.

ARTICLE 3 JUDICIAL DEPARTMENT

Only the Supreme Court is established by the Constitution itself, but the Constitution gives Congress the authority to establish the lower courts that exist today. Since the Constitution does not state the number of justices to be appointed to the Supreme Court, Congress decides the number by law. Today the Supreme Court has nine justices. Congress has created two types of lower courts. One type includes federal district courts and Courts of Appeals, which review cases sent up by the district courts. District courts and Courts of Appeals are called "constitutional courts" because they are general courts deriving their power directly from the Constitution. The second type of court deals with cases of a specialized nature. The Court of Claims, the Tax Court, and the Court of Customs and Patent Appeals are included in this second group. The Framers of the Constitution wanted to make sure that federal judges would be independent of political influence. Accordingly federal judges are appointed for life, subject to good behavior, and their pay cannot be reduced by law during their term of office.

Section 1. Federal Courts

The judicial power of the United States, shall be vested in one Supreme Court, and in such inferior courts as the Congress may from time to time ordain and establish. The judges, both of the supreme and inferior courts, shall hold their offices during good behaviour, and shall, at stated times, receive for their services, a compensation, which shall not be diminished during their continuance in office.

Clause 1. Here the words *law* and *equity* have special meanings. *Law* means the common law—the laws that originated in England and that have been based on centuries of judicial decisions. *Equity* refers to principles of justice also developed in England to remedy wrongs in situations in which the common law was inadequate. Today, in the United States, law and equity are applied by the same judges in the same courts. The power of the federal courts extends to two types of cases: (1) those involving the interpretation of the Constitution, federal laws, treaties, and laws relating to ships on the high seas and navigable waters; and (2) those involving the United States government itself, foreign diplomatic officials, two or more state governments, citizens of different states when the sum involved is more than $10,000, and a state or its citizens versus foreign countries or citizens of foreign countries.

Section 2. Jurisdiction of Federal Courts

1. General Jurisdiction The judicial power shall extend to all cases, in law and equity, arising under this Constitution, the laws of the United States, and treaties made, or which shall be made, under their authority; to all cases affecting ambassadors, other public ministers and consuls; to all cases of admiralty and maritime jurisdiction; to controversies to which the United States shall be a party; to controversies between two or more states; [between a state and citizens of another state;] between citizens of the same state claiming lands under grants of different states, and between a state or the citizens thereof, and foreign states, citizens or subjects.

2. Supreme Court In all cases affecting ambassadors, other public ministers and consuls, and those in which a state shall be party, the Supreme Court shall have original jurisdiction. In all the other cases before mentioned, the Supreme Court shall have appellate jurisdiction, both as to law and fact, with such exceptions, and under such regulations as the Congress shall make.

Clause 2. Original jurisdiction means the right to try a case before any other court may hear it. *Appellate jurisdiction* means the right of a court to try cases appealed from lower courts. Most of the cases tried by the Supreme Court are cases appealed from lower federal and state courts. Cases involving foreign diplomats and any state of the United States may be started directly in the Supreme Court.

3. Conduct of Trials The trial of all crimes, except in cases of impeachment, shall be by jury; and such trial shall be held in the state where the said crimes shall have been committed; but when not committed within any state, the trial shall be at such place or places as the Congress may by law have directed.

Clause 3. Every person accused of a federal crime is guaranteed a jury trial near the scene of the crime. But accused persons may give up this privilege, if they wish. Amendments 5, 6, and 7 expand the provisions of this clause.

Section 3. Treason

1. Definition Treason against the United States, shall consist only in levying war against them, or in adhering to their enemies, giving them aid and comfort. No person shall be convicted of treason unless on the testimony of two witnesses to the same overt act, or on confession in open court.

Clause 1. Treason is the only crime specifically defined in the Constitution. To be found guilty of treason, a person must be shown to have helped wage war against the United States, or to have given aid and comfort to its enemies. A person cannot be convicted without the testimony of two witnesses to the same act unless the person confesses in open court.

2. Punishment The Congress shall have power to declare the punishment of treason, but no attainder of treason shall work corruption of blood, or forfeiture except during the life of the person attainted.

Clause 2. The punishment for treason, as determined by Congress, is death or a fine of $10,000 and imprisonment for not less than five years. This clause further states that the punishment for treason cannot be extended to the children of a traitor. In 1953, Julius and Ethel Rosenberg became the first American citizens who were convicted and executed for treason in peacetime.

ARTICLE 4
RELATIONS AMONG THE STATES

Section 1. Official Acts

Full faith and credit shall be given in each state to the public acts, records, and judicial proceedings of every other state. And the Congress may by general Laws prescribe the manner in which such acts, records and proceedings shall be proved, and the effect thereof.

The purpose of this provision is to make sure that the official records of one state are respected in all the other states. Official records of this kind include birth certificates, marriage licenses, death certificates, corporation charters, wills, and court decisions. This provision also protects a citizen's right to collect money that has been awarded by a court decision in one state, even if the person who owes the money moves to another state.

Section 2. Privileges of Citizens

1. Privileges The citizens of each state shall be entitled to all privileges and immunities of citizens in the several states.

Clause 1. The terms *privileges* and *immunities* simply mean the rights of citizens. Thus a state cannot discriminate against citizens of other states in favor of its own citizens, except in certain very special areas—such as voting, for example. A state can impose residence requirements for voting, so that citizens of another state must reside in the state for a specified period before they can vote as citizens of their new state.

Clause 2. This provision prevents a prisoner or a person charged with a crime from escaping justice by fleeing across a state line. It provides that a criminal be returned by the state where captured to the state where the crime was committed—a process known as extradition. A governor of a state cannot be forced to extradite, or return, a prisoner, however, if the governor feels that such action will result in injustice to the accused person.

2. Extradition A person charged in any state with treason, felony, or other crime, who shall flee from justice, and be found in another state, shall on demand of the executive authority of the state from which he fled, be delivered up, to be removed to the state having jurisdiction of the crime.

Clause 3. Since the ratification of Amendment 13 in 1865 brought an end to slavery in this country, the clause is now of historical interest only.

3. Fugitive Slaves [No person held in service or labor in one state, under the laws thereof, escaping into another, shall, in consequence of any law or regulation therein, be discharged from such service or labor, but shall be delivered up on claim of the party to whom such service or labor may be due.]

Section 3. New States and Territories

Clause 1. The Northwest Ordinance of 1787 provided that new states be admitted to the Union on completely equal footing with the original thirteen states. Although the Constitution declares here that new states may not be created within the territory of any other state without its consent, an exception did occur in 1863, when West Virginia was formed from the western part of the state of Virginia. This exception occurred during the Civil War, and West Virginia received permission from the loyal, rather than the secessionist, government of Virginia.

1. Admission of New States New states may be admitted by the Congress into this Union; but no new state shall be formed or erected within the jurisdiction of any other state; nor any state be formed by the junction of two or more states, or parts of states, without the consent of the legislatures of the states concerned as well as of the Congress.

Clause 2. Under this provision Congress has the power to control all property belonging to the federal government. It can set up governments for territories and colonies of the United States. It can grant independence to a colony, as it did to the Philippines in 1946. It can set aside land for national parks and build dams for flood control.

2. Powers of Congress The Congress shall have power to dispose of and make all needful rules and regulations respecting the territory or other property belonging to the United States; and nothing in this Constitution shall be so construed as to prejudice any claims of the United States, or of any particular state.

Section 4. Guarantees to the States

If public property is being destroyed and public safety endangered in a state, the President may decide to send troops into that state without having been requested to do so by local authorities. The President may even proclaim martial law in a state. This section also guarantees that states can govern only by consent of the governed.

The United States shall guarantee to every state in this Union a republican form of government, and shall protect each of them against invasion; and on application of the legislature, or of the executive (when the legislature cannot be convened) against domestic violence.

ARTICLE 5
METHODS OF AMENDMENT

The Congress, whenever two thirds of both houses shall deem it necessary, shall propose amendments to this Constitution, or, on the application of legislatures of two thirds of the several states, shall call a convention for proposing amendments, which, in either case, shall be valid to all intents and purposes, as part of this Constitution, when ratified by the legislatures of three fourths of the several states, or by conventions in three fourths thereof, as the one or the other mode of ratification may be proposed by the Congress; provided that [no amendment which may be made prior to the year 1808 shall in any manner affect the first and fourth clauses in the Ninth Section of the First Article; and that] no state, without its consent, shall be deprived of its equal suffrage in the Senate.

One of the most important features of the Constitution is that it can be amended, or changed. An amendment must first be *proposed* and then *ratified.* So far, all amendments have been proposed by Congress and ratified by state legislatures except Amendment 21, which was ratified by the convention method. The fact that only 26 amendments have been adopted since 1789—and only 16 since 1791—indicates that it is not easy to change the Constitution, and that changing it is a serious matter, requiring much thought and discussion in Congress, in the state legislatures, and among the people. Notice that there are two areas in which the Constitution cannot be amended under any circumstances. The first exception is obsolete because it is a reference to the period that preceded 1808. The second exception is still very important because it guarantees that every state shall have equal representation in the Senate.

ARTICLE 6
GENERAL PROVISIONS

1. Public Debts All debts contracted and engagements entered into, before the adoption of this Constitution, shall be as valid against the United States under this Constitution, as under the Confederation.

Clause 1. This provision was important because it announced to all that the new government would assume and pay back all debts of the government under the Articles of Confederation. It was one of several actions favored by Alexander Hamilton and undertaken by Congress in order to establish the credit of the new government.

2. The Supreme Law This Constitution, and the laws of the United States which shall be made in pursuance thereof; and all treaties made, or which shall be made, under the authority of the United States, shall be the supreme law of the land; and the judges in every state shall be bound thereby, anything in the constitution or laws of any state to the contrary notwithstanding.

Clause 2. This is the famous "supremacy clause" of the Constitution. It declares that the "supreme law of the land" is (1) the Constitution, (2) the laws of the United States passed under this Constitution, and (3) the treaties made under the authority of the United States. According to the supremacy clause, the power of the national government is superior to the power of the state governments, provided that the actions of the national government are in accordance with the Constitution. The Supreme Court determines whether the actions of the President and Congress are constitutional.

3. Oaths of Office The Senators and Representatives before mentioned, and the members of the several state legislatures, and all executive and judicial officers, both of the United States and of the several states, shall be bound by oath or affirmation, to support this Constitution; but no religious test shall ever be required as a qualification to any office or public trust under the United States.

Clause 3. No religious qualification shall ever be required as a condition for holding public office. This provision results from the fact that in the United States there is separation of church and state. This means that a person's religion is supposed to remain a private matter, with no bearing on consideration for public office.

The Constitutional Convention was summoned by the Congress of the Confederation to amend the Articles of Confederation. Under the Articles amendments had to be approved by all thirteen states. Instead of amending the Articles, however, the delegates to the Constitutional Convention drafted an entirely new plan of government. Realizing that it would be difficult to get the approval of all the states—Rhode Island, for example, had not even sent delegates to Philadelphia—the Framers provided that the Constitution would go into effect after ratification by only nine states, not thirteen. As a result opponents of the Constitution said it had been adopted by revolutionary means.

ARTICLE 7
RATIFICATION

The ratification of the conventions of nine states, shall be sufficient for the establishment of this Constitution between the states so ratifying the same.

DONE in Convention by the unanimous consent of the States present the seventeenth day of September in the year of our Lord one thousand seven hundred and eighty seven and of the independence of the United States of America the twelfth. IN WITNESS whereof We have hereunto subscribed our names.

GEORGE WASHINGTON—
President and deputy from Virginia

New Hampshire

JOHN LANGDON
NICHOLAS GILMAN

Massachusetts

NATHANIEL GORHAM
RUFUS KING

Connecticut

WILLIAM SAMUEL JOHNSON
ROGER SHERMAN

New York

ALEXANDER HAMILTON

New Jersey

WILLIAM LIVINGSTON
DAVID BREARLEY
WILLIAM PATERSON
JONATHAN DAYTON

Pennsylvania

BENJAMIN FRANKLIN
THOMAS MIFFLIN
ROBERT MORRIS
GEORGE CLYMER
THOMAS FITZSIMONS
JARED INGERSOLL
JAMES WILSON
GOUVERNEUR MORRIS

Delaware

GEORGE READ
GUNNING BEDFORD
JOHN DICKINSON
RICHARD BASSETT
JACOB BROOM

Maryland

JAMES McHENRY
DANIEL OF ST. THOMAS JENIFER
DANIEL CARROLL

Virginia

JOHN BLAIR
JAMES MADISON

North Carolina

WILLIAM BLOUNT
RICHARD DOBBS SPAIGHT
HUGH WILLIAMSON

South Carolina

JOHN RUTLEDGE
CHARLES COTESWORTH PINCKNEY
CHARLES PINCKNEY
PIERCE BUTLER

Georgia

WILLIAM FEW
ABRAHAM BALDWIN

THE AMENDMENTS TO THE CONSTITUTION

[The first ten amendments to the Constitution are called the Bill of Rights. The Bill of Rights limits the powers of the federal government but not the powers of the states. The Supreme Court has ruled, however, that the "due process" clause of Amendment 14 protects individuals against denial by the states of certain rights included in the Bill of Rights. For example, the Supreme Court has decided that neither the federal government nor the states can deprive any individual of freedom of religion, speech, press, petition, assembly, or of several other rights that pertain to the fair treatment of an accused person.]

AMENDMENT 1
FREEDOM OF RELIGION, SPEECH, PRESS, ASSEMBLY, AND PETITION (1791)

Congress shall make no law respecting an establishment of religion, or prohibiting the free exercise thereof; or abridging the freedom of speech, or of the press; or the right of the people peaceably to assemble, and to petition the government for a redress of grievances.

Amendment 1 protects five great civil liberties: (1) Freedom of religion means that Congress cannot interfere with the right to worship as one sees fit. The Supreme Court, however, has ruled that Congress can require "conscientious objectors" to bear arms during wartime. Congress has, however, made special provisions to permit conscientious objectors to participate in war work without bearing arms. In interpreting the phrase *establishment of religion,* the Supreme Court has decided that this phrase erects a wall of separation between church and state. The Supreme Court has prohibited state and local school authorities from requiring prayers or a devotional reading of the Bible in public schools. (2) Freedom of speech means the right to speak out privately and publicly. However, this right does not permit anyone to slander people (make false and malicious remarks about them). Furthermore, the Supreme Court has declared that freedom of speech can be limited by the federal government if there is a "clear and present" danger that what is said may injure the general welfare. (3) Freedom of the press gives newspapers, television, and magazines the right to express ideas and opinions provided they do not libel people (publish false and malicious remarks about them) or incite the violent overthrow of the government. Also, the use of the United States mails may be denied to those publications that spread obscenity and fraudulent ideas. (4) Freedom to assemble is the right to attend meetings and join clubs. (5) The right to petition for redress of grievances means the opportunity to express complaints to any official of the federal government.

AMENDMENT 2
RIGHT TO KEEP ARMS (1791)

A well regulated militia, being necessary to the security of a free state, the right of the people to keep and bear arms, shall not be infringed.

The purpose of this amendment was to prevent Congress from denying states the right to have a militia (or National Guard) of armed citizens. It also protected Americans' right to keep weapons in order to resist a tyrannical government. However, Congress and many states have regulated the ownership and use of weapons by citizens through gun control legislation.

Amendments 3 and 4 guarantee all citizens the right to privacy and security in their own homes. Amendment 3 was designed to prevent the national government from requiring citizens to house and feed military personnel in their homes. The quartering of troops in the colonists' homes by the British government had been a source of friction between the American colonists and the British before the American Revolution.

AMENDMENT 3
QUARTERING OF TROOPS (1791)

No soldier shall, in time of peace, be quartered in any house, without the consent of the owner, nor in time of war, but in a manner to be prescribed by law.

The supporters of this amendment aimed to limit issuance of search warrants to the following conditions: (1) The warrant must be issued by a judge. (2) There must be a good reason for its use. (3) The officer who asks for a search warrant must take an oath affirming reasons for demanding the warrant. (4) The warrant must describe the place to be searched and the persons or things to be seized. The Supreme Court has decided that evidence illegally seized cannot be used in either federal or state courts. Under this amendment the federal government prohibits wiretapping unless a court permit is obtained showing a reasonable certainty that one of a certain list of crimes is being committed. In 1967 the Supreme Court held that eavesdropping and bugging by electronic means are permissible but only within certain limits; for example, police may use eavesdropping devices if they secure a warrant in advance by showing probable cause. In 1968 the Supreme Court forbade the use of criminal evidence obtained by police listening in on a party line, but evidence derived from wiretapping is permitted in federal courts in some crimes.

AMENDMENT 4
SEARCH AND SEIZURE; WARRANTS (1791)

The right of the people to be secure in their persons, houses, papers, and effects, against unreasonable searches and seizures, shall not be violated, and no warrants shall issue, but upon probable cause, supported by oath or affirmation, and particularly describing the place to be searched, and the persons or things to be seized.

This amendment lists the rights of an accused person: (1) A person accused of a capital crime or any other serious crime must first be accused by a grand jury (a jury of 12 to 23 persons) before being brought to trial. An indictment or presentment by a grand jury is merely a formal accusation. (2) A person cannot be tried twice for the same crime. (3) A person cannot be required to give incriminating testimony in a courtroom or before a grand jury or Congressional committee. However, under the Immunity Act of 1954, a witness can be required to testify in certain cases if the evidence he or she may provide cannot be used in any trial of that person. (4) A person cannot be deprived of life, liberty, or property without due process of law—or according to the law of the land. (5) Congress cannot take private property for public use without paying a fair price for it. This provision, an important protection of property rights, establishes the principle of eminent domain. Members of the armed forces are tried by military courts and commissions and are not subject to the provision calling for indictment by a grand jury.

AMENDMENT 5
RIGHTS OF ACCUSED PERSONS (1791)

No person shall be held to answer for a capital, or otherwise infamous crime, unless on a presentment or indictment of a grand jury, except in cases arising in the land or naval forces, or in the militia, when in actual service in time of war or public danger; nor shall any person be subject for the same offense to be twice put in jeopardy of life or limb; nor shall be compelled in any criminal case to be a witness against himself, nor be deprived of life, liberty, or property, without due process of law; nor shall private property be taken for public use, without just compensation.

AMENDMENT 6
RIGHT TO SPEEDY TRIAL (1791)

In all criminal prosecutions, the accused shall enjoy the right to a speedy and public trial, by an impartial jury of the state and district wherein the crime shall have been committed, which district shall have been previously ascertained by law, and to be informed of the nature and cause of the accusation; to be confronted with the witnesses against him; to have compulsory process for obtaining witnesses in his favor, and to have the assistance of counsel for his defense.

This amendment continues the rights of an accused person. Notice that all witnesses against an accused person must appear on the witness stand, and that the government must help the accused to produce favorable witnesses. If an accused person cannot afford to hire a lawyer, the judge will assign one, and the government will pay the lawyer's fee. These provisions under Amendment 6 apply to federal courts. However, under the "due process" clause of Amendment 14, the Supreme Court has decided that state courts must also assign a lawyer to defend an accused person who cannot afford one.

AMENDMENT 7
JURY TRIAL IN CIVIL CASES (1791)

In Suits at common law, where the value in controversy shall exceed $20, the right of trial by jury shall be preserved, and no fact tried by a jury shall be otherwise re-examined in any court of the United States than according to the rules of the common law.

This amendment provides for a jury trial in federal civil cases (trials where one person sues another) in which more than $20 is involved. By custom, however, civil cases are not tried before federal courts unless they involve much larger sums of money.

AMENDMENT 8
BAILS, FINES, PUNISHMENTS (1791)

Excessive bail shall not be required, nor excessive fines imposed, nor cruel and unusual punishments inflicted.

Persons accused of a crime and awaiting trial may be permitted to leave jail if they or someone else posts bail—a sum of money serving as a guarantee that the accused will appear for trial. The courts determine the amount of bail asked for. Cruel and unusual punishments, such as torture and beheading, are prohibited. In a series of rulings, the Supreme Court declared invalid convictions of accused persons based on confessions secured by torture or other "third degree" methods.

AMENDMENT 9
POWERS RESERVED TO THE PEOPLE (1791)

The enumeration in the Constitution, of certain rights, shall not be construed to deny or disparage others retained by the people.

The Constitution does not describe specifically all the rights to be retained by the people. This amendment was added in order to guarantee that those fundamental rights not enumerated must be respected by the national government at all times.

AMENDMENT 10
POWERS RESERVED TO THE STATES (1791)

The powers not delegated to the United States by the Constitution, nor prohibited by it to the states, are reserved to the states respectively, or to the people.

This is known as the reserved power amendment. Powers delegated to the national government are listed in Article 1, Section 8. Powers prohibited to the states are found in Article 1, Section 10. Amendment 10 makes it clear that all other powers—the so-called reserved powers—are left to the states or to the people.

This is the first amendment to the Constitution that was prompted by an unpopular Supreme Court decision. In the case of *Chisholm* v. *Georgia* (1793), the Supreme Court ruled that two citizens of South Carolina could sue Georgia in a federal court for property that Georgia had confiscated. The states objected, arguing that since the states were sovereign, it was undignified to permit a state to be sued by a citizen of another state in a federal court. As a result of this amendment, a citizen of the United States or of a foreign nation who wishes to bring suit against any state is required to introduce the case in the courts of the state that is being sued.

AMENDMENT 11
SUITS AGAINST STATES (1798)

The judicial power of the United States shall not be construed to extend to any suit in law or equity, commenced or prosecuted against one of the United States, by citizens of another state, or by citizens or subjects of any foreign state.

This amendment alters Article 2, Section 1, Clause 3. Before this amendment the electors voted for two persons, without designating which was to be President and which Vice President. As a result in 1796 the people elected a Federalist President (John Adams) and a Republican Vice President (Jefferson). In 1800 the electors of the victorious Republican Party each cast one vote for Jefferson, whom they wanted to be President, and one vote for Burr, whom they wanted to be Vice President. The result, of course, was a tie. Amendment 12, which instructs electors to cast separate ballots for President and Vice President, prevents such situations. (See also Amendment 23, which makes provision for choosing electors of President and Vice President by the District of Columbia.)

AMENDMENT 12
ELECTION OF PRESIDENT AND VICE PRESIDENT (1804)

The electors shall meet in their respective states and vote by ballot for President and Vice President, one of whom, at least, shall not be an inhabitant of the same state with themselves; they shall name in their ballots the person voted for as President, and in distinct ballots the person voted for as Vice President, and they shall make distinct lists of all persons voted for as President, and of all persons voted for as Vice President, and of the number of votes for each, which lists they shall sign and certify, and transmit sealed, to the seat of the government of the United States, directed to the President of the Senate; the President of the Senate shall, in the presence of the Senate and House of Representatives, open all the certificates and the votes shall then be counted; the person having the greatest number of votes for President, shall be the President, if such number be a majority of the whole number of electors appointed; and if no person have such majority, then from the persons having the highest numbers not exceeding three on the list of those voted for as President, the House of Representatives shall choose immediately, by ballot, the President. But in choosing the President, the votes shall be taken by states, the representation from each state having one vote; a quorum for this purpose shall consist of a member or members from two thirds of the states, and a majority of all the states shall be necessary to a choice. [And if the House of Representatives shall not choose a President whenever the right of choice shall devolve upon them, before the fourth day of March next following, then the Vice President shall act as President, as in the case of the death or other constitutional disability of the President.] The person having the greatest number of votes as Vice President, shall be the Vice President, if such number be a majority of the whole number of electors appointed, and if no person have a majority, then from the two highest numbers on the list, the Senate shall choose the Vice President; a quorum for the purpose shall consist of two thirds of the whole number of Senators, and a majority of the whole number shall be necessary to a choice. But no person constitutionally ineligible to the office of President shall be eligible to that of Vice President of the United States.

AMENDMENT 13
SLAVERY ABOLISHED (1865)

Section 1. Neither slavery nor involuntary servitude, except as a punishment for crime whereof the party shall have been duly convicted, shall exist within the United States, or any place subject to their jurisdiction.

Section 2. Congress shall have power to enforce this article by appropriate legislation.

Amendments 13, 14, and 15 resulted from the Civil War. Amendment 13 freed the slaves, Amendment 14 made blacks citizens, and Amendment 15 forbade the states to deny black Americans the right to vote. Amendment 13 forbids slavery, and under Section 2, Congress has the power to enforce this order.

AMENDMENT 14
RIGHTS OF CITIZENS (1868)

Section 1. Citizenship Defined All persons born or naturalized in the United States, and subject to the jurisdiction thereof, are citizens of the United States and of the state wherein they reside. No state shall make or enforce any law which shall abridge the privileges or immunities of citizens of the United States; nor shall any state deprive any person of life, liberty, or property, without due process of law; nor deny to any person within its jurisdiction the equal protection of the laws.

This section contains a number of important provisions. By the definition of citizenship given here, black Americans were granted citizenship. The second sentence, forbidding states to abridge the privileges and immunities—the rights—of citizens, meant that the states could not interfere with the right of black Americans and other citizens to live a peaceful, useful life or to travel. This amendment, like Amendment 5, contains a "due process of law" clause. Amendment 5 denies to Congress and Amendment 14 denies to the states the power to deprive any person of life, liberty, or property without due process of law. This amendment, originally intended to protect black citizenship, has been broadly interpreted by the courts as a protection for corporations. Corporations, under this interpretation, are considered as persons. Their property cannot be taken away except by fair, legal methods. Thus, for example, the Interstate Commerce Commission can fix railroad rates only after giving railroad corporations an opportunity to present their side of the case. The "due process" clause also protects individuals from unfair actions by their state governments. It protects their rights of freedom of religion, speech, press, petition, and peaceful assembly and the rights of persons accused of crimes against state abuses. It prevents a state, in the exercise of its police power (the power to protect its people), from depriving anyone of civil liberties, except during a national emergency. The last provision of Section 1 prevents a state from denying equal protection of the laws. In 1954, in the case of *Brown* v. *Board of Education of Topeka,* the Supreme Court interpreted this provision to mean that segregation in public schools is unconstitutional. Also, in *Baker* v. *Carr* (1962) the Supreme Court ruled that unfair apportionment of representation in state legislatures violates the "equal protection" clause of this amendment.

This section was never implemented, but later civil rights law and Amendment 24 guaranteed the vote to black Americans. Amendment 19 gave women the right to vote. The Dawes Act and the 1924 citizenship law enfranchised Native Americans. And Amendment 26 changed the voting age from 21 to 18. This section dealing with apportionment of Representatives is sometimes called the "dead letter clause" of Amendment 14 since its provisions were never carried out.

Section 2. Apportioning Representatives Representatives shall be apportioned among the several states according to their respective numbers, counting the whole number of persons in each state [excluding Indians not taxed]. But when the right to vote at any election for the choice of electors for President and Vice President of the United States, Representatives in Congress, the executive and judicial officers of a state, or the members of the legislature thereof, is denied to any of the [male] inhabitants of such state, [being twenty-one years of age] and citizens of the United States, or in any way abridged, except for participation in rebellion, or other crime, the basis of representation therein shall be reduced in the proportion which the number of such [male] citizens shall bear to the whole number of male citizens [twenty-one years of age] in such state.

This section aimed to punish the leaders of the Confederacy for having broken their oath to support the Constitution of the United States. All officials who had taken this oath and who later joined the Confederacy in the Civil War were disqualified from holding federal or state offices. Although many southern leaders were excluded under this section from holding office after the war, by 1872 most of them were permitted to return to political life. In 1898 all of the others were pardoned.

Section 3. Disability for Insurrection No person shall be a Senator or Representative in Congress, or elector of President and Vice President, or hold any office, civil or military, under the United States, or under any state, who, having previously taken an oath, as a member of Congress, or as an officer of the United States, or as a member of any state legislature, or as an executive or judicial officer of any state, to support the Constitution of the United States, shall have engaged in insurrection or rebellion against the same, or given aid or comfort to the enemies thereof. But Congress may by vote of two thirds of each house, remove such disability.

This section makes three important points: (1) The public debt of the United States incurred in fighting the Civil War was valid and could never be questioned by southerners. (2) The Confederate debt was void. It was illegal for the federal government or the states to pay any money on Confederate debts. This provision was meant to serve as a harsh lesson to all who had invested money in Confederate bonds. (3) No payment was to be made for the loss of former slaves.

Section 4. Public Debt The validity of the public debt of the United States, authorized by law, including debts incurred for payment of pensions and bounties for services in suppressing insurrection or rebellion, shall not be questioned. But neither the United States nor any state shall assume or pay any debt or obligation incurred in aid of insurrection or rebellion against the United States, [or any claim for the loss or emancipation of any slave]; but all such debts, obligations and claims shall be held illegal and void.

Section 5. Enforcement The Congress shall have power to enforce, by appropriate legislation, the provisions of this article.

AMENDMENT 15
RIGHT OF SUFFRAGE (1870)

Section 1. The right of citizens of the United States to vote shall not be denied or abridged by the United States or by any state on account of race, color, or previous condition of servitude.

Section 2. The Congress shall have power to enforce this article by appropriate legislation.

The purpose of this amendment was to extend the *franchise,* or the right to vote, to blacks. Thus, according to this amendment, any person who can meet all of the qualifications for suffrage in a particular state cannot be deprived of the right to vote simply because of race or color.

AMENDMENT 16
INCOME TAX (1913)

The Congress shall have power to lay and collect taxes on incomes, from whatever source derived, without apportionment among the several states, and without regard to any census or enumeration.

In 1894 Congress passed an income tax law. The following year the Supreme Court declared this tax law unconstitutional. The Court stated that the income tax was a direct tax and, therefore, according to the Constitution (Article 1, Section 2, Clause 3; Article 1, Section 9, Clause 4) should have been apportioned among the states according to their population. This decision was unpopular because it prevented the government from taxing people on the basis of their incomes in order to pay for government expenses, which were already large and growing larger. Amendment 16 is a response to the Supreme Court decision. It gave Congress the power to tax incomes from any source and without apportionment among the states according to population. Today income taxes are the federal government's major source of income.

AMENDMENT 17
ELECTION OF SENATORS (1913)

Section 1. Method of Election The Senate of the United States shall be composed of two Senators from each state, elected by the people thereof, for six years; and each Senator shall have one vote. The electors in each state shall have the qualifications requisite for electors of the most numerous branch of the state legislatures.

Section 2. Filling Vacancies When vacancies happen in the representation of any state in the Senate, the executive authority of such state shall issue writs of election to fill such vacancies: *Provided* that the legislature of any state may empower the executive thereof to make temporary appointments until the people fill the vacancies by election as the legislature may direct.

[**Section 3. Not Retroactive** This amendment shall not be so construed as to affect the election or term of any Senator chosen before it becomes valid as part of the Constitution.]

Before the passage of this amendment, senators were chosen by the state legislatures (see Article 1, Section 3, Clause 1). There was a great deal of dissatisfaction with this method because it gave the voters little control over the Senate. Amendment 17 provides for the direct election of senators by the voters of each state, thus making senators more responsive to the will of the voters who put them in office.

This amendment outlawed the making, sale, or transportation of alcoholic beverages in the United States except for special purposes. This amendment was later repealed by Amendment 21.

AMENDMENT 18
NATIONAL PROHIBITION (1919)

[**Section 1.** After one year from the ratification of this article the manufacture, sale, or transportation of intoxicating liquors within, the importation thereof into, or the exportation thereof from the United States and all territory subject to the jurisdiction thereof for beverage purposes is hereby prohibited.

Section 2. The Congress and the several states shall have concurrent power to enforce this article by appropriate legislation.

Section 3. This article shall be inoperative unless it shall have been ratified as an amendment to the Constitution by the legislatures of the several states, as provided in the Constitution, within seven years from the date of the submission hereof to the states by the Congress.]

This amendment, extending the right to vote to all qualified women, marked the greatest single step in extending the suffrage in the United States. Women's struggle to win this basic right began many years before Amendment 19 was finally ratified.

AMENDMENT 19
WOMEN'S SUFFRAGE (1920)

Section 1. The right of citizens of the United States to vote shall not be denied or abridged by the United States or by any state on account of sex.

Section 2. Congress shall have power to enforce this article by appropriate legislation.

When the Constitution was written, transportation and communication were so slow that a new President and new members of Congress elected in November could not reach the capital to take office until March 4. However, since sessions of Congress began in December, a session including newly elected members could not be held until 13 months after their election. Thus, even if a member running for reelection was defeated in November, he or she would serve in the session of Congress that began the month after this election and continue to serve several more months. Since defeated candidates had been rejected by the voters, they were called "lame ducks," suggesting that their political wings had been clipped. One purpose of Amendment 20 was to limit the term and power of lame duck members.

AMENDMENT 20
"LAME DUCK" AMENDMENT (1933)

Section 1. Beginning of Terms The terms of the President and Vice President shall end at noon on the 20th day of January, and the terms of Senators and Representatives at noon on the 3rd day of January, of the years in which such terms would have ended if this article had not been ratified; and the terms of their successors shall then begin.

Section 2. Congressional Term The Congress shall assemble at least once in every year, and such meeting shall begin at noon on the 3rd day of January, unless they shall by law appoint a different day.

Section 3. Presidential Succession If, at the time fixed for the beginning of the term of the President, the President-elect shall have died, the Vice President-elect shall become President. If a President shall not have been chosen before the time fixed for the beginning of his term, or if the President-elect shall have failed to qualify, then the Vice President-elect shall act as President until a President shall have qualified; and the Congress may by law provide for the case wherein neither a President-elect nor a Vice President-elect shall have qualified, declaring who shall then act as President, or the manner in which one who is to act shall be selected, and such person shall act accordingly until a President or Vice President shall have qualified.

Section 4. Filling Presidential Vacancy The Congress may by law provide for the case of the death of any of the persons from whom the House of Representatives may choose a President whenever the right of choice shall have devolved upon them, and for the case of the death of any of the persons from whom the Senate may choose a Vice President whenever the right of choice shall have devolved upon them.

[**Section 5. Effective Date** Sections 1 and 2 shall take effect on the 15th day of October following the ratification of this article.

Section 6. Time Limit for Ratification This article shall be inoperative unless it shall have been ratified as an amendment to the Constitution by the legislatures of three fourths of the several states within seven years from the date of its submission.]

AMENDMENT 21
REPEAL OF PROHIBITION (1933)

Section 1. The eighteenth article of amendment to the Constitution of the United States is hereby repealed.

Section 2. The transportation or importation into any state, territory, or possession of the United States for delivery or use therein of intoxicating liquors, in violation of the laws thereof, is hereby prohibited.

[**Section 3.** This article shall be inoperative unless it shall have been ratified as an amendment to the Constitution by conventions in the several states, as provided in the Constitution, within seven years from the date of the submission hereof to the States by the Congress.]

This amendment, which repealed Amendment 18, was the only amendment ratified by special state conventions instead of state legislatures. Congress felt that a popular referendum (vote) would give the people a better chance to voice their opinions on prohibition. As in Amendments 18 and 20, Congress included a provision that the amendment, to become law, have a seven-year limit for ratification by the states.

The original Constitution placed no limit on the number of terms a President could be elected to office. Washington and Jefferson, however, set a two-term precedent. In 1940 this tradition was broken when Franklin D. Roosevelt was elected for a third term, and in 1944, when he won a fourth term. The purpose of this amendment was to write the two-term precedent into law. The bracket portion was included so that the amendment would not apply to President Truman, who was in office at the time the amendment was ratified. Note that anyone who succeeds to the Presidency and completes less than two years of another person's term may be elected for two more terms.

AMENDMENT 22 TWO-TERM LIMIT FOR PRESIDENTS (1951)

Section 1. No person shall be elected to the office of the President more than twice, and no person who has held the office of President, or acted as President, for more than two years of a term to which some other person was elected President shall be elected to the office of the President more than once. [But this Article shall not apply to any person holding the office of President when this Article was proposed by the Congress, and shall not prevent any person who may be holding the office of President, or acting as President, during the term within which this Article becomes operative from holding the office of President or acting as President during the remainder of such term.]

[**Section 2.** This Article shall be inoperative unless it shall have been ratified as an amendment to the Constitution by the legislatures of three fourths of the several states within seven years from the date of its submission to the states by the Congress.]

Amendment 23 enabled residents of the District of Columbia to vote for President and Vice President. In effect, it gave the capital city three members in the Electoral College, the same number elected by each of the least populous states.

AMENDMENT 23 PRESIDENTIAL ELECTORS FOR DISTRICT OF COLUMBIA (1961)

Section 1. The District constituting the seat of Government of the United States shall appoint in such manner as the Congress may direct:

A number of electors of President and Vice President equal to the whole number of Senators and Representatives in Congress to which the District would be entitled if it were a State, but in no event more than the least populous state; they shall be in addition to those appointed by the States, but they shall be considered, for the purposes of the election of President and Vice President, to be electors appointed by a State; and they shall meet in the District and perform such duties as provided by the twelfth article of amendment.

Section 2. The Congress shall have power to enforce this article by appropriate legislation.

AMENDMENT 24
POLL TAX BANNED IN NATIONAL ELECTIONS (1964)

Section 1. The right of citizens of the United States to vote in any primary or other election for President or Vice President, for electors for President or Vice President, or for Senator or Representative in Congress, shall not be denied or abridged by the United States or any state by reason of failure to pay any poll tax or other tax.

Section 2. The Congress shall have power to enforce this article by appropriate legislation.

This amendment forbade the collection of poll taxes—taxes persons had to pay before they were able to vote—as a requirement for voting in federal elections (in 1964 five southern states still had poll taxes). In 1966 the Supreme Court ruled that poll taxes were illegal as a requirement for voting in state and local elections as well.

AMENDMENT 25
PRESIDENTIAL DISABILITY AND SUCCESSION (1967)

Section 1. In case of the removal of the President from office or his death or resignation, the Vice President shall become President.

Section 2. Whenever there is a vacancy in the office of the Vice President, the President shall nominate a Vice President who shall take office upon confirmation by a majority vote of both houses of Congress.

Section 3. Whenever the President transmits to the President *pro tempore* of the Senate and the Speaker of the House of Representatives his written declaration that he is unable to discharge the powers and duties of his office, and until he transmits to them a written declaration to the contrary, such powers and duties shall be discharged by the Vice President as Acting President.

Section 4. Whenever the Vice President and a majority of either the principal officers of the executive departments or of such other body as Congress may by law provide, transmit to the President *pro tempore* of the Senate and the Speaker of the House of Representatives their written declaration that the President is unable to discharge the powers and duties of his office, the Vice President shall immediately assume the powers and duties of the office as Acting President.

Thereafter, when the President transmits to the President *pro tempore* of the Senate and the Speaker of the House of Representatives his written declaration that no inability exists, he shall resume the

This amendment was intended to clarify Article 2, Section 1, Clause 6, particularly in the case of the temporary disability of a President. The problem of disability in office existed during the last part of President Wilson's term and occurred again when President Eisenhower was disabled by a heart attack. This amendment provided two ways (see sections 3 and 4) the Vice President could assume the duties of the office of the President, as well as a procedure by which the President could again perform the duties of office when the disability ended.

However, the first use of this amendment did not involve Presidential disability. It involved a Presidential resignation. In 1974 Richard M. Nixon became the first President in American history to resign from office. And Vice President Gerald R. Ford, who succeeded as President, became the first person to become President without being first elected to that office or to the Vice Presidency. This unique situation occurred in the following way. In 1973 Vice President Spiro T. Agnew had resigned, and President Nixon had filled the vacancy according to the provisions of Section 2 of this amendment. Gerald R. Ford, a member of the House of Representatives, had been named Vice President with the approval of Congress. Therefore when Nixon resigned as President during the Watergate scandal, Ford took over the Presidency. A vacancy then existed in the Vice Presidency (see Section 2). President Ford named Nelson A. Rockefeller as Vice President, and this nomination was also approved by a majority vote of both houses of Congress.

powers and duties of his office unless the Vice President and a majority of either the principal officers of the executive department or of such other body as Congress may by law provide, transmit within four days to the President *pro tempore* of the Senate and the Speaker of the House of Representatives their written declaration that the President is unable to discharge the powers and duties of his office. Thereupon Congress shall decide the issue, assembling within 48 hours for that purpose if not in session. If the Congress, within 21 days after receipt of the latter written declaration, or, if Congress is not in session, within 21 days after Congress is required to assemble, determines by two-thirds vote of both houses that the President is unable to discharge the powers and duties of his office, the Vice President shall continue to discharge the same as Acting President; otherwise, the President shall resume the powers and duties of his office.

Congress, in the Voting Rights Act of 1970, had lowered the minimum voting age from 21 to 18, but the Supreme Court ruled that this law applied only to federal elections. Amendment 26 specified that 18 was the legal voting age in state, local, and federal elections.

AMENDMENT 26
VOTING AGE LOWERED TO 18 (1971)

Section 1. The right of citizens of the United States, who are 18 years of age or older, to vote shall not be denied or abridged by the United States or by any State on account of age.

Section 2. The Congress shall have power to enforce this article by appropriate legislation.

This amendment, proposed in 1978, would give the District of Columbia two senators and one or two representatives. The number of Presidential electors—three, at present—would be changed to the total number of senators and representatives. The District would also acquire the power of a state in amending the Constitution. This proposed amendment must be ratified—by three fourths of the states—by August 22, 1985, if it is to become law, unless Congress extends the ratification deadline.

PROPOSED AMENDMENT
REPRESENTATION FOR THE DISTRICT OF COLUMBIA

Section 1. For purposes of representation in the Congress, election of the President and Vice President, and Article 5 of this Constitution, the District constituting the seat of government of the United States shall be treated as though it were a State.

Section 2. The exercise of the rights and powers conferred under this article shall be by the people of the District constituting the seat of government, and as shall be provided by the Congress.

Section 3. The twenty-third article of amendment to the Constitution of the United States is hereby repealed.

2 A LIVING CONSTITUTION

The fundamental principles of American government are firmly rooted in the Constitution of the United States. Yet the Constitution is flexible. It is a *living* constitution, adaptable to conditions never anticipated by the Framers. The United States has experienced dramatic changes since 1787. When the Constitution was drafted, the United States was a rural nation of less than 4 million people. Today it is an urban, industrial society of more than 235 million people. During its almost 200 years of existence, the Constitution has survived the challenges of the Industrial Revolution, the Civil War, economic depression, world wars, and struggles for equal rights. Had the Constitution been rigid, it might well have been broken by any one of these several crises.

Chief Justice John Marshall wrote in 1819 that ours is "a constitution intended to endure for ages to come, and consequently, to be adapted to the various crises of human affairs." The process of adaptation has been both formal and informal and has included sudden change and gradual evolution. Change in the American political system has taken place in five major ways: (1) the development of law, (2) government practice and custom, (3) political development, (4) formal amendment to the Constitution, and (5) judicial interpretation of the Constitution through decisions of the Supreme Court of the United States.

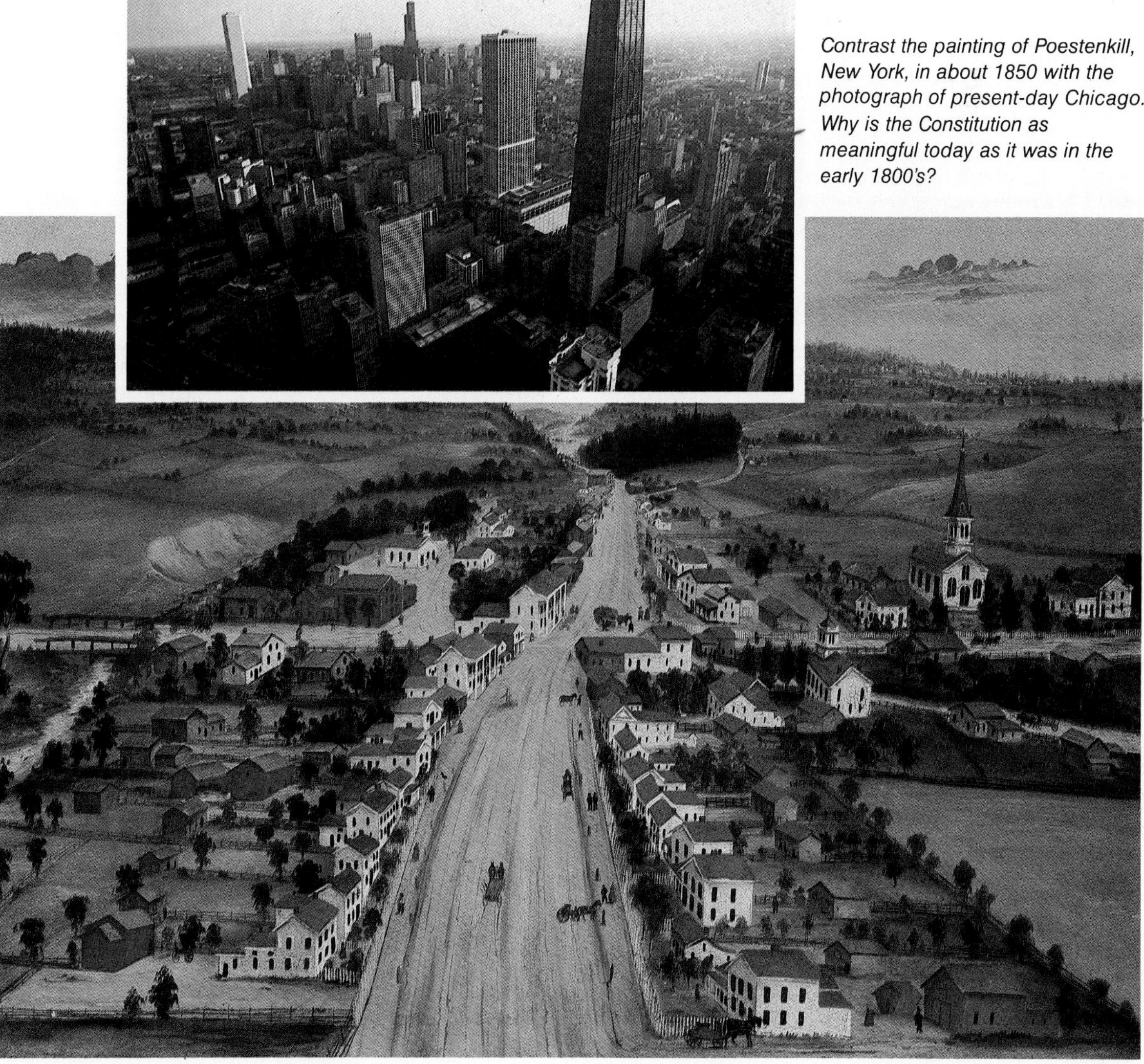

Contrast the painting of Poestenkill, New York, in about 1850 with the photograph of present-day Chicago. Why is the Constitution as meaningful today as it was in the early 1800's?

ISSUES

The Elastic Clause

The Congress shall have Power . . . To make all Laws which shall be necessary and proper for carrying into Execution the foregoing Powers, and all other Powers vested by this Constitution in the Government of the United States, or in any Department or Officer thereof.

Article 1, Section 8, Clause 18, of the Constitution is sometimes called the ***elastic clause*** because it has been used so often to stretch the powers of Congress. Many constitutional scholars consider this single clause one of the most important parts of the Constitution. But even the Framers of the supreme law of the land did not agree on what constituted "necessary and proper" law. When the elastic clause was first invoked to justify the creation of a national bank by Congress—a power not explicitly given Congress in the Constitution—Alexander Hamilton maintained that a national bank had "a natural relation" to the powers explicitly given Congress in the Constitution to collect taxes and regulate trade. Opposing Hamilton, Thomas Jefferson argued that Congress could pass only laws that were *necessary,* "not those which were merely *'convenient.'* " He maintained that government could function without a bank and that the new power assumed by Congress was therefore unauthorized.

In 1819 Chief Justice John Marshall ruled in *McCulloch* v. *Maryland* that a law was "necessary and proper" when both the end, or result, and the means by which it is achieved are consistent "with the letter and spirit of the Constitution."

Marshall's interpretation of the elastic clause has prevailed. During the 1800's the elastic clause was invoked to permit Congress to create a body of maritime legislation—the laws of the sea. Congress has also invoked the elastic clause to create a number of executive departments and agencies—such as the Interstate Commerce Commission and the Federal Communications Commission—with lawmaking powers not explicitly called for in the Constitution. Such agencies have allowed the federal government to manage and control an increasingly complex industrial and technological society.

Development of Law

The Constitution lays down only the basic framework of government. The Framers left to Congress the power to prescribe its details. For example, the Constitution does not specify the various departments and agencies of the executive branch. These have been created, as required, by Congress. Similarly, the Constitution does not fully describe the federal court system. Article 3, Section 1, states only that there shall be a Supreme Court and "such inferior courts as the Congress may from time to time ordain and establish." Since 1789, Congress has passed legislation to set up federal courts.

Practice and Custom

Within the broad framework of the Constitution, practice and custom are part of what is sometimes called "the unwritten Constitution." For example, the Constitution makes no provision for the President's Cabinet. It simply states that the President "may require the Opinion, in writing, of the principal Officer in each of the executive Departments, upon any Subject relating to the Duties of their respective Offices." George Washington called the heads of the executive departments together in a group to advise him on various matters. Out of this practice grew the Cabinet.

George Washington meets with the first Cabinet. From left to right are President Washington, Secretary of War Henry Knox, Secretary of the Treasury Alexander Hamilton, Secretary of State Thomas Jefferson, and Attorney General Edmund Randolph.

Another example is the committee system in Congress. Nowhere does the Constitution mention committees. Yet by the late nineteenth century committees had become important in the legislative process and remain so today, operating largely by custom. The custom that candidates for the House of Representatives live in the district in which they seek election is required neither by the Constitution nor by any law.

Political Development

Among the most important institutions of the American political system are political parties and interest groups. They are not mentioned in the Constitution, nor were they created by any law. Their informal growth represents an adaptation of the political system to change and increasing complexity in American society.

Political parties perform many functions necessary to representative government. They select candidates for elections, stimulate interest in politics, and draw people together behind broad sets of policies. Political parties organize government. They help link the states and national government and the separate branches of the federal government. Political parties serve to make government more responsive and accountable to the people.

Interest groups also play a vital role in American political life. In interest groups individuals join together to protect or promote their common interests. They organize to have a more effective voice in government. Today, almost every interest in American society is represented by an organized group. Interest groups raise issues in the public forum, keep a watchful eye on government and politicians, and help link the people and government.

The Formal Amendment Process

Within the framework of the Constitution the American political system has adapted to change through law, practice, custom, and the development of political institutions. The words of the Constitution have set the boundaries within which these adaptations have taken place. The Framers recognized, however, that the future might require explicit changes in the text of the Constitution itself. Article 5 sets forth the two-step procedure of proposal and ratification for any amendment to the Constitution.

President Nixon signs the Twenty-sixth Amendment. The amendment, which became law on July 5, 1971, made 18 the legal voting age in the United States. The ratification period for this amendment was shorter than that for any previous amendment. How has the Twenty-sixth Amendment made the United States more democratic?

Article 5 provides two methods for proposal. The first—and the only one that has ever been used—is the passage of a proposal by a two-thirds majority of both houses of Congress. The other method of proposal is by a national convention called by Congress at the request of the legislatures of two thirds of the states.

After an amendment has been proposed, it can be ratified by one of two methods. It must be approved either by the legislatures of three fourths of the states or by special ratification conventions in three fourths of the states. In the act proposing an amendment Congress determines which method will be used. Only once—in 1933 for the repeal of prohibition by the Twenty-first Amendment—has Congress specified that an amendment be submitted to ratifying conventions.

Congress may also set a time limit for ratification. Since 1920 Congress has required ratification by the states within seven years of a proposed amendment's passage. In a controversial move in 1978 Congress extended the seven-year deadline for ratification of the Equal Rights Amendment by 39 months. The proposed amendment, however, failed to secure ratification before the extended deadline expired. The Supreme Court has held that after a

In December 1933, newspapers throughout the United States carried the news of the ratification of the Twenty-first Amendment and the end of prohibition. What are two unique characteristics of the Twenty-first Amendment?

"All the News That's Fit to Print."

The New York Times.

LATE CITY EDITION

Copyright, 1933, by The New York Times Company.

VOL. LXXXIII....No. 27,710. NEW YORK, WEDNESDAY, DECEMBER 6, 1933. TWO CENTS

PROHIBITION REPEAL IS RATIFIED AT 5:32 P. M.; ROOSEVELT ASKS NATION TO BAR THE SALOON; NEW YORK CELEBRATES WITH QUIET RESTRAINT

LINDBERGHS AT SEA ON BRAZIL FLIGHT; 'O.K.' SHE REPORTS

630 MILES FROM AFRICA

Breeze Starts Fliers After Twenty Attempts in Dead Calm.

MOON LIGHTS THEIR WAY

10,000 Natives See Take-Off as Motor's Roar Stirs Them From Slumber.

RIDE THROUGH SQUALLS

Wife Radios Every Fifteen Minutes of Progress on 1,800-Mile Flight.

Colonel and Mrs. Charles A. Lindbergh were flying across the South Atlantic from Africa to Brazil this morning, reporting their progress by radio every fifteen minutes and their location every half ho...

Lindbergh Flight to Fame Twice as Long as New Hop

On the morning of May 20, 1927, six years and six months ago, Captain Charles A. Lindbergh, a mail pilot, left Roosevelt Field for Paris.

He flew alone, and veteran pilots shook their heads when they saw him take off. His silver plane, dripping with rain, lumbered slowly—too slowly—down the muddy runway. It gathered speed, bounced from the ground and settled back again. It barely cleared a tractor at the end of the runway and just climbed over low telephone wires at the end of the field.

Thirty-three and a half hours later the young mail pilot brought his gray plane down at Le Bourget. That famous flight covered 3,610 miles. The present flight, also in a single-engined plane, is about 1,875 miles.

PWA READY TO BAR CITY SUBWAY LOAN

Security for $25,000,000 Ad-vance to Fi...h System ... Held ...equate.

TAX PLAN OFFERED TO CURB EVASIONS, RAISE $237,000,000

House Subcommittee Urges a Check on Personal Holding Concerns by 35% Levy.

WOULD INCREASE SURTAX

Normal Income Tax of 4% and Revision of Capital Gains Are Also Proposed.

Special to The New York Times.

WASHINGTON, Dec. 5.—Broad tax reforms designed to increase the Federal revenue $237,000,000 a year and prevent "the avoidance and evasion of the internal revenue laws" were recommended today in a report submitted to the House Ways and Means Committee by a subcommittee.

The full committee immediately began study of the suggestions, and Representative Doughton, the chairman, said a completed bill would probably be ready for presentation soon after Congress meets next month.

Changes sought are aimed principally at persons whose incomes are in the higher brackets, as well as at corporations now legally permitted to take advantage of what committee members said were "unfair but legal" provisions of the revenue laws.

Some discord was apparent within the committee, but no member would publicly express his feelings.

State House Bootlegger Is Barred in Maryland

Special to The New York Times.

ANNAPOLIS, Md., Dec. 5.—Wet legislators here will patriotically support legal liquor. The State House bootlegger received formal notice today to discontinue his trade. The notice was served by a policeman on duty at the Capitol.

Throughout this session, the bootlegger has conducted a thriving business; a business which, he says, has been especially arduous because of the sudden demands made on him by legislators and their desire for prompt service.

While his services were cut off eight hours before post-prohibition stuff could be bought, the bootlegger thought the legislators had obtained a sufficient reserve to carry them through until evening and legal liquor.

RATIFYING BY UTAH ENDS PROHIBITION

With Impressive Ceremony, the 36th State ...llows Ohi... and Penn...ia in ...

CITY TOASTS NEW ERA

Crowds Swamp Licensed Resorts, but the Legal Liquor Is Scarce.

CELEBRATION IN STREETS

Marked by Absence of Undue Hilarity and Only Normal Number of Arrests.

MANY SPEAKEASIES CLOSE

Machine Guns Guard Some Liquor Trucks—Supplies to Be Rushed Out Today.

Slowly gathering momentum from the time when the news began to spread just at nightfall that national prohibition was no more, the public rejoicing at the end of the long dry reign was carried on last night with restraint and absence of ... hilarity.

The Repeal Proclamation

Special to The New York Times.

WASHINGTON, Dec. 5.—The text of the proclamation by William Phillips, Acting Secretary of State, certifying to the adoption of the Twenty-first Amendment repealing prohibition, follows:

WILLIAM PHILLIPS,

Acting Secretary of State of the United States of America.

To all whom these presents shall come, greeting:

KNOW YE, That the Congress of the United States, at the second session, Seventy-second Congress, begun and held at the city of Washington on Monday, the fifth day of December, in the year one thousand nine hundred and thirty-two, passed a joint Resolution in the words and figures as follows:

To wit—

JOINT RESOLUTION.

Proposing an amendment to the Constitution of the United States.

Resolved by the Senate and House of Representatives of the United States of America in Congress assembled (two-thirds of each House concurring therein), That the following article is hereby proposed as an amendment to the Constitution of the United States, which shall be valid to all intents and purposes as part of the Constitution when ratified by conventions in three-fourths of the several States:

ARTICLE.

Section 1. The Eighteenth Article of Amendment to the Constitution of the United States is hereby repealed.

Section 2. The transportation or importation into any State, Territory, or Possession of the United States for delivery or use therein of intoxicating liquors, in violation of the laws thereof, ... hereby prohibited.

FINAL ACTION AT CAPITAL

President Proclaims the Nation's New Policy as Utah Ratifies.

PHILLIPS SIGNS DECREE

Orders 21st Amendment in Effect on Receiving Votes of Three Final States.

RECOVERY TAXES TO END

$227,000,000 a Year Automatically Dropped—Canadian Whisky Quota Is Raised.

Special to The New York Times.

WASHINGTON, Dec. 5.—Legal liquor today was returned to the United States, with President Roosevelt calling on the people to see that "this return of individual freedom shall not ... accompanied by the ...

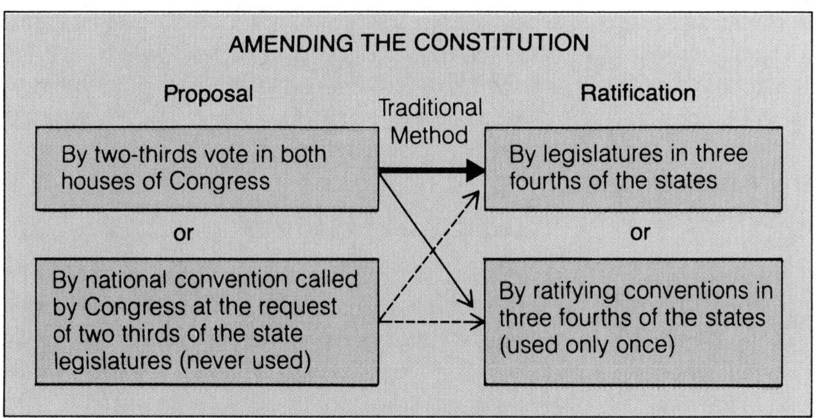

Amending the Constitution is a two-step process that involves both the national and the state governments. The process is usually long and complicated. Which amendments are concerned with the voting rights of Americans? Which are concerned with elections?

AMENDMENTS TO THE CONSTITUTION

Amendment	Year Adopted	Subject
1–10	1791	The Bill of Rights
11	1798	Suits against states
12	1804	Separate election of President and Vice President
13	1865	Abolition of slavery
14	1868	The rights of citizens: privileges and immunities, due process, and equal protection
15	1870	The right to vote without regard to race, color, or previous condition of servitude
16	1913	Income tax
17	1913	Direct election of senators
18	1919	National prohibition on liquor
19	1920	Women's suffrage
20	1933	Change in the dates for Presidential and Congressional terms of office
21	1933	Repeal of prohibition
22	1951	Two-term limit on Presidential tenure
23	1961	Right to vote in Presidential elections for the District of Columbia
24	1964	Poll tax banned in federal elections
25	1967	Presidential disability and succession
26	1971	Voting age lowered to 18
	Proposed	Full representation in Congress for the District of Columbia

state legislature has rejected a proposed amendment it can, if it chooses, reconsider and ratify it. Once a legislature ratifies a proposed amendment, however, the Court has said that it cannot later change its mind and reverse its action.

The formal amendment procedure shows the federal nature of our system of government. Proposal of an amendment is a national function. Ratification of an amendment is a state matter. In order to safeguard the Great Compromise of the Constitutional Convention, the Framers wrote one limitation into the amending clause. No amendment may deprive a state of equal representation in the Senate unless that state gives its consent.

Since 1789 more than 6,000 constitutional amendments have been considered by Congress. Of these only 33 have won the two-thirds majority necessary for proposal. Twenty-six of the 33 amendments proposed by Congress have been ratified by the states. Since the Civil War only two proposed amendments have been defeated—the Child Labor Amendment in 1924 and in 1982 the Equal Rights Amendment. Today one amendment awaits ratification by the states. Proposed by Congress in 1978, it would give the District of Columbia the same representation accorded to a state in the Senate and House of Representatives.

Judicial Interpretation

Oftentimes the Constitution must be interpreted. For example, the Constitution gives Congress the power to regulate interstate commerce, but what precisely does this phrase mean? What about the Fourth Amendment's ban on "unreasonable searches and seizures"? What are the limits to a President's claim of inherent executive powers? What is "necessary and proper" for Congress to carry out its delegated powers?

If interpretation of the Constitution were left to each branch of government, conflict would lead to inevitable crisis. Limited government itself would be threatened. It would be rather like leaving the proverbial fox to guard the hen house. On the other

LEGACY

The Constitution Preserved

The Constitution created a government "to endure for ages to come," but the actual Constitution—four brittle parchment pages penned in ink—is a very fragile document, subject to the deteriorating effects of light, air, and moisture. To preserve the 200-year-old manuscript and still allow visitors to view it, a special exhibit had to be designed.

The Constitution resides in the National Archives, a stately building that stands midway between the White House and the Capitol. Under the Archives' 75-foot-high rotunda, the Constitution, the Declaration of Independence, and the Bill of Rights are displayed. Because bright lights would fade the documents, the light level in the viewing area is kept low. Deep yellow filters block out the more damaging high wavelengths of light. The temperature and humidity of the viewing area are also strictly controlled.

The original parchment pages of the Constitution might well have crumbled to dust by now if each page had not been sealed in its own glass and bronze case. These cases contain inert helium and a carefully measured amount of water vapor to prevent deterioration. Any gas that leaks out is automatically replaced.

Only two pages of the Constitution—the first and the signature pages—are on display throughout the year. Each night these two pages are lowered into a vault 20 feet below the floor of the rotunda, where the remaining pages are stored. Once a year, on Constitution Day, September 17, the complete document is displayed to commemorate the occasion of its signing in 1787.

hand, it is not enough to turn back to see what the Framers intended. To reach compromise, they were often purposely vague. Sometimes they remained silent. In some cases they disagreed among themselves on the meaning of a section of the Constitution. Beyond this, the Framers could not have foreseen all the problems of modern government.

Judicial Review The final authority on the meaning of the Constitution is the Supreme Court. Woodrow Wilson called the Court "a kind of continuous constitutional convention, interpreting, developing, and expanding the basic law." Through its power of judicial review, the Court can declare any law or official act to be in violation of the Constitution and thus void. In the system of checks and balances the Court ensures that neither Congress nor the Presidency exceeds its authority. The Court interprets and applies appropriate sections of the Constitution to the cases it considers. As it does so, the Court adapts the Constitution to changing conditions.

The Constitution does not contain an article expressly stating that the courts have the power of judicial review. But most Framers intended that the federal courts, especially the Supreme Court, should have this power. Article 3, Section 2, and Article 4, Section 2, contain provisions that imply judicial review. In arguing for ratification of the Constitution in *The Federalist,* No. 78, Alexander Hamilton discussed the role of the judiciary, saying it was for the courts to interpret the meaning of the Constitution and legislative acts. When a law is found to be in conflict with the Constitution, Hamilton wrote, it is the duty of the Court to declare that act void.

Marbury* v. *Madison In 1803 the Supreme Court made the power of judicial review explicit in *Marbury* v. *Madison*. This case is one of the most important in constitutional law.

The incident over which the case centered arose after the election of 1800. John Adams, the second President of the United States, was defeated in his bid for reelection by Thomas Jefferson. The Federalist party, of which Adams was leader, also suffered heavy defeat in the elections for Congress. Having lost both Congress and the Presidency, the Federalists were determined to strengthen their hold over the federal courts. Early in 1801 the outgoing Federalist Congress created a number of new judgeships. The Constitution gives the President, with consent of the Senate, the power to appoint federal

William Marbury, one of the Federalist "midnight appointees" who did not receive a commission, turned to the Supreme Court for help. Which of its powers did the Court make explicit in Marbury v. Madison?

judges. In a series of "midnight appointments" made just before leaving office, Adams filled the new judgeships with Federalists.

In another last-minute appointment Adams named John Marshall to the Supreme Court as Chief Justice. Marshall was Adams's Secretary of State. It was his task, before leaving that office, to seal and deliver the commissions for the new judgeships. Marshall worked until the night before Jefferson's inauguration but was unable to deliver all the commissions before the inauguration of the new President. Seventeen remained. He left these to the new Secretary of State, James Madison.

Angered by the Federalists' attempt to maintain a hold on the federal judiciary, Jefferson instructed Madison not to deliver the commissions. Delivery, he claimed, was necessary to complete the appointments.

Among the disappointed office-seekers was William Marbury. He had been appointed as Justice of the Peace for Washington, D.C. In order to get his commission, Marbury turned to the Supreme Court asking it to issue a ***writ of mandamus,*** an order which would compel Madison to deliver the commission. The power to issue the writ of mandamus had been given to the Supreme Court by Congress in a provision of the Judiciary Act of 1789.

The new Chief Justice, John Marshall, spoke for the unanimous Court. He said that Marbury had a right to the commission. This right had been violated by Madison's refusal to make delivery. But the Court refused Marbury's request for a writ of mandamus. Marshall stated that the Supreme Court itself could not compel delivery. The right to issue a writ of mandamus had been given to the Supreme Court by Congress, not by the Constitution. Indeed, the ***original jurisdiction,*** or authority to hear a case first, of the Supreme Court is limited specifically in the Constitution. Therefore, Congress did not have the power to enlarge or decrease that jurisdiction. The provision of the Judiciary Act in question was thus unconstitutional. "The Constitution is superior to any ordinary act of the legislature," Marshall declared, and "a law repugnant to the Constitution is void."

Who then is to determine the constitutionality of a law? Following Hamilton's argument in *The Federalist,* No. 78, Marshall asserted the doctrine of judicial review.

It is emphatically the province and duty of the judicial department to say what the law is. Those who apply the rule to particular cases, must of necessity expound and interpret that rule.

In this landmark decision Marshall established two fundamental principles of constitutional law: (1) that the Constitution of the United States is the supreme law of the land, and (2) that the courts have the power of judicial review. On the basis of this power the Supreme Court is the final authority on the meaning of the Constitution. The Court alone interprets the Constitution.

Opposition to Judicial Review Thomas Jefferson was one of the earliest and most forceful critics of judicial review. He believed that judicial review violated the separation of powers. He argued that it could lead to the supremacy of the Court over the other branches of government. He also regarded judicial review as undemocratic because justices of the Supreme Court were neither elected by nor accountable to the people. To Jefferson, judicial review was a denial of the will of the people as expressed through their elected representatives.

Jefferson's arguments did not prevail. Judicial review was established firmly, but the role of the Court has continued to be a focus of debate.

Section Check

1. Define: the elastic clause, judicial review, original jurisdiction
2. Identify: John Marshall, William Marbury, James Madison, Article 5 of the Constitution
3. What are five ways change takes place in the American political system?
4. What are some examples of practice and custom in "the unwritten Constitution"?
5. What is the two-step process for amendment of the Constitution?
6. What is the significance of *Marbury* v. *Madison?*

SUMMARY

The Constitution is the supreme law of the land. It establishes a limited government by restricting the power of the national and state governments. In the American system of federalism the powers of government are divided between the national government and the 50 state governments. The federal government of the United States is a representative government based on popular sovereignty: all power comes from the people, who govern through their elected representatives.

The legislative, executive, and judicial powers are divided among three independent branches of government; this is the principle of separation of powers. The three branches of government do not exercise their powers independently. They are tied together by a system of checks and balances. An important part of the system of checks and balances is judicial review, which is the courts' power to declare any act of government to be in violation of the Constitution and thus void.

The Constitution provides the framework of American government. It has kept pace with changing times through formal amendment and informal change. Informal change takes place in a number of ways, including government practice and custom, practices of political parties and interest groups, and judicial interpretation.

Chapter 3 Review

Using Vocabulary

Answer the questions by using the meaning of each underlined term.

1. What is the connection between original jurisdiction, writ of mandamus, and *Marbury* v. *Madison*?
2. How does popular sovereignty operate in a constituency?
3. Is every republic a representative government?
4. Why are separation of powers and checks and balances important principles in establishing limited government?
5. What role has the elastic clause and judicial review played in keeping the Constitution a living document?

Understanding American Government

1. Explain why the United States Constitution provides for a limited government.
2. What has been the impact of our Constitution abroad?
3. How does the constituency of the President differ from the constituency of a representative? Of a senator?
4. Who has a longer term of office, a senator or a President? Why were these offices given different terms?
5. How is the frequency of election that House members undergo both an advantage and a disadvantage?
6. How does the Congress embody the principle of federalism?
7. Explain how judicial review is important in the system of checks and balances.
8. What are two ways a formal amendment to the Constitution may be proposed?

Extending Your Skills: Interpeting a Diagram

Study the diagram on page 64. Then name the most likely actor and action in each of the situations. Be prepared to defend your choice.

1. Congress passes a bill the President strongly opposes.
2. The President vetoes a popular bill.
3. A Presidential appointee to the Supreme Court lacks legal experience.
4. The Supreme Court declares a popular law unconstitutional.
5. The President fails to uphold the Constitution of the United States.
6. The Senate finds fault with a treaty that the President negotiated.

Government and You

1. The United States Constitution is one of the shortest constitutions in the world, containing only about 7,000 words. Do you think its length makes the job of governing easier or more difficult? Is a short constitution more or less flexible than a long one?
2. In *The Federalist* James Madison argued that representative government could be superior to direct democracy. He felt that elected officials might better know what was good for the people than the people themselves. What arguments might you make for or against this position?
3. In reading about the case of *Marbury* v. *Madison,* did you notice the unusual role played by John Marshall? As President Adams's Secretary of State, he signed the documents appointing judges like Marbury. But he was also Chief Justice on the court that was to determine whether his successor's actions had been proper. Do you suppose his unusual position influenced the decision he made? Remember that Marshall agreed with Marbury but still denied him a judgeship.

Activities

1. The system of checks and balances in the federal government is quite complicated. Make a chart showing how the different branches of government check and balance each other.
2. Stage a class debate on the following topic: "*Resolved:* The Twenty-sixth Amendment (which gives the right to vote at age 18) should be repealed." Have each side research its position thoroughly.
3. Invite a local judge or attorney to speak to the class about the role of the judicial system in our federal government.

Chapter 4

Federalism: Cooperation and Conflict

The federal and state governments are in fact but different agents and trustees of the people, instituted with different powers, and designated for different purposes.

JAMES MADISON

CHAPTER OVERVIEW

1 **THE DIVISION OF POWERS**
The Powers of the National Government / Limits on National and State Powers / The Powers of the States / Concurrent Powers

2 **THE FOUNDATION OF NATIONAL SUPREMACY**
Strict Construction versus Broad Construction / *McCulloch* v. *Maryland* / National Supremacy

3 **THE NATIONAL GOVERNMENT AND THE STATES**
The National Government's Obligations to the States / Relations Among the States / Admission of New States

4 **NATIONAL-STATE COOPERATION**
The Mix of Governmental Units / Grants-in-Aid / Revenue Sharing / State Aid to the National Government

5 **THE GROWTH OF NATIONAL POWER**
The Constitutional Basis / Politics and Federalism

The Massachusetts state capitol in Boston has been renovated many times since its opening in 1798. A state capitol is symbolic of the federal system of government.

1 THE DIVISION OF POWERS

Just before the Constitutional Convention opened in 1787, James Madison expressed his thoughts on the new government in a letter to George Washington. Madison, like Washington, favored a strong national government. Yet he realized that the states wished to preserve their powers. In loose association under the Articles of Confederation, however, the states had nearly collapsed. If they were to survive and prosper, a stronger union was necessary. "I have sought a middle ground," Madison wrote. That middle ground was federalism.

Madison forecast the structure of American government that emerged through compromise at the Constitutional Convention. That compromise created a ***federal system*** of government in which power is shared by the national government and the 50 states.

Federalism represented a compromise, or "middle ground," between those who favored a centralized government and those who wanted to keep a looser confederation. But federalism was also an important part of the constitutional system of checks and balances. In the separation of powers constitutional authority is divided among the three branches of the national government. In federalism there is a ***division of powers*** between the national government and the states. Separation of powers and federalism are a force for limited government.

The Constitution outlines the federal division of powers. The national government has only those powers delegated, or granted, to it by the Constitution. The Constitution also denies some powers to the national government, some powers to the state governments, and some powers to both the national government and the states. The powers reserved to the states are the powers not delegated to the national government and not denied to the states by the Constitution. Some powers of the national government and the states are concurrent, or shared by both.

The Powers of the National Government

The national government possesses only those powers granted to it by the Constitution. These are called ***delegated powers.*** There are three kinds of delegated powers: expressed powers, implied powers, and inherent powers.

A World War I–era poster (above) illustrates an implied power of the national government. The 1918 poster (below) illustrates an inherent power. What relationship exists between these two kinds of powers?

Expressed Powers Powers that the Constitution actually describes, or enumerates, are called ***expressed powers.*** Most expressed powers are found in Article 1, Section 8. Among these are the power to lay and collect taxes, regulate commerce, coin money, declare war, and raise and support armies and a navy. Certain other expressed powers are granted to the executive and to the judicial branches of government.

Implied Powers The national government also has certain powers that are not described by the Constitution but are suggested by those powers that are described. These are called the ***implied powers.*** The right to establish a national banking system, for example, is implied by the powers to tax and regulate commerce. The constitutional basis of implied powers is the ***elastic clause*** found in Article 1, Section 8, Clause 18.

Congress shall have Power . . . to make all Laws which shall be necessary and proper for carrying into Execution the foregoing [expressed] Powers, and all other Powers vested by this Constitution in the Government of the United States, or in any Department or Officer thereof.

The implied powers of Congress have been a source of unending controversy throughout the nation's history.

Inherent Powers The government of the United States may exercise certain powers in foreign relations simply because it exists as a government in the world community. These are called ***inherent powers.*** Inherent powers include the power to acquire new territory, control immigration and expel undesirable aliens, wage war in defense of the nation, and maintain diplomatic relations with other nations.

Exclusive Powers Most of the delegated powers of the national government are ***exclusive powers;*** that is, they can be exercised only by the national government. Some powers of the national government are exclusive because they are expressly denied to the states by the Constitution—for example, the powers to coin money and make treaties. Other powers of the national government, such as the power to regulate interstate commerce and to control immigration, are not expressly denied to the states but are exclusive because of their inherent nature.

Limits on National and State Powers

The Constitution places certain restrictions on both the national government and the states. The national government, for example, is denied the power to impose export duties. The states are denied the power to levy duties on either exports or imports. The most important limits on government are those designed to safeguard individual liberty: freedom of speech and press, freedom of religion, and the right to a fair trial. Neither the national government nor the states may deny these fundamental rights.

Powers Denied the Nation Some powers are denied to the national government because the Constitution does not mention them. The national government has only those powers granted to it. Amendment 10 makes this clear.

The powers not delegated to the United States by the Constitution, nor prohibited by it to the States, are reserved to the States respectively, or to the people.

Among the ***reserved powers*** are the authority to create a public school system, enact marriage and divorce laws, and establish local units of government.

The national government is not permitted to exercise its powers in a way that would threaten the existence of the federal system. Thus, in the exercise of its power to tax, the national government cannot tax any of the states (or their local units) as they carry out their functions of government. Otherwise the national government could conceivably tax a state out of existence.

Powers Denied the States The Constitution places many restrictions on the states. Most are found in Article 1, Section 10. For example, no state may coin or print money, tax exports or imports without the consent of Congress, keep troops or warships in peacetime, or sign agreements with other states or with foreign nations without the consent of Congress.

Several amendments to the Constitution also limit the powers of the states. The states cannot

The authority to print currency, a power denied to the states, is reserved to the national government. How does a national currency contribute to a country's feeling of unity?

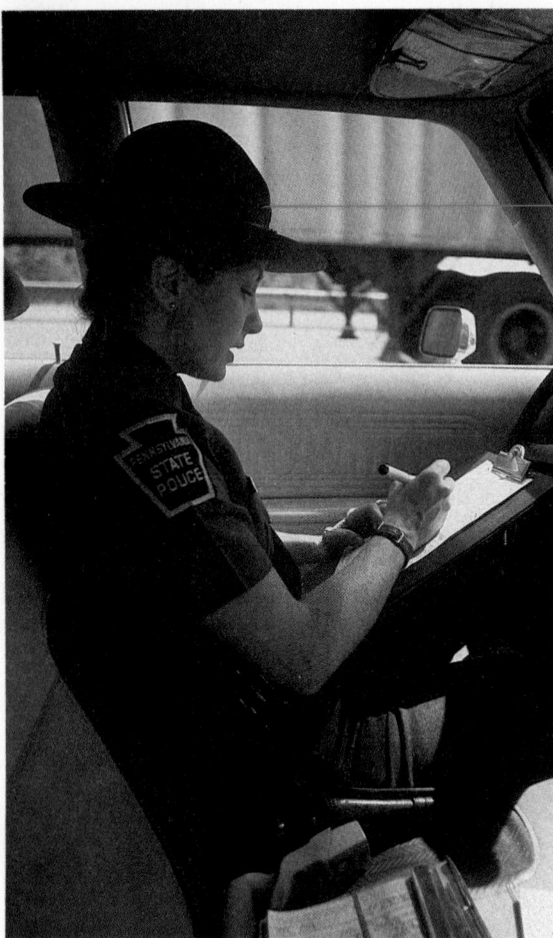

Law enforcement is a concurrent power because the Constitution neither grants law-enforcement activities exclusively nor denies them to any one level of government. What is another concurrent power?

permit slavery (Thirteenth Amendment); deprive a person of life, liberty, or property without due process of law or deny a person equal protection under the law (Fourteenth Amendment); deny a person the right to vote because of race or color (Fifteenth Amendment), sex (Nineteenth Amendment), or age beyond the age of 17 (Twenty-sixth Amendment).

The states—like the national government—cannot exercise their powers in a way that would threaten the existence of the federal system. They cannot, for example, tax the operations of the national government for the same reason that the national government cannot tax their operations.

The powers denied to the states also apply to local governments. All local governments are created by the states and get their powers from the states. They are subject to the same constitutional restrictions as are the states.

The Powers of the States

The Constitution prohibits the states from exercising certain powers, but it does not specifically grant any powers to the states. Amendment 10 makes clear that the powers of the national government are delegated to it by the Constitution and the powers that remain are reserved to the states.

The states' reserved powers—although not listed in the Constitution—cover a vast range of subjects. The states are responsible for public education and welfare, marriage and divorce laws, and the protection of public health and safety. The states may regulate commerce within their borders, regulate local business and labor, and exercise control over the trades and professions. The states also create and change their constitutions, establish local units of government, and conduct elections. To support these activities, the states may collect taxes.

Concurrent Powers

Some powers of the national government and the state governments are ***concurrent,*** or shared. The states may share with the national government any power that is not exclusively granted to the national government by the Constitution and not denied by the Constitution to the states. Both national and state governments have the concurrent power to set up courts, make and enforce laws, collect taxes, borrow money, and spend money for the general welfare. A state may regulate commerce within its boundaries (*intra*state commerce). The national government has the power to regulate commerce among the states (*inter*state commerce).

Section Check

1. Define: federal system, division of power, delegated powers, reserved powers, concurrent powers
2. Identify: The Tenth Amendment; Article 1, Section 8, Clause 18; the Thirteenth Amendment; the Fourteenth Amendment; the Twenty-sixth Amendment
3. What is the difference between delegated and reserved powers?
4. Distinguish between expressed, implied, and inherent powers.
5. Why may governmental units not tax each other?

2 THE FOUNDATION OF NATIONAL SUPREMACY

The division of powers between the national government and the states produces a system in which both governments may have authority over the same area and the same people. This overlapping authority leads to inevitable conflicts between the two levels of government. Anticipating this, the Framers wrote Article 6, Section 2.

This Constitution, and the Laws of the United States which shall be made in Pursuance thereof; and all Treaties made, or which shall be made, under the Authority of the United States, shall be the supreme Law of the Land; and the Judges in every State shall be bound thereby, any Thing in the Constitution or Laws of any State to the Contrary notwithstanding.

Called the ***supremacy clause,*** it makes the Constitution and the acts and treaties of the United States the highest forms of the law.

Strict Construction versus Broad Construction

Less than a year after the ratification of the Constitution, a sharp dispute arose over the powers it granted to Congress. The controversy centered on Article 1, Section 8, Clause 18, which gives Congress the power "to make all Laws which shall be necessary and proper" to carry out its expressly delegated powers. In the debate two classic interpretations emerged: the states' rights position favoring a ***strict construction,*** or reading, of the Constitution, and the nationalist, or Federalist, position favoring a ***broad construction.***

The strict constructionists held that the Constitution was a treaty entered into by sovereign states. They said that the states created the central government and limited its authority to the expressly delegated powers. Because they favored retaining as much power as possible in the states, the strict constructionists wanted to limit Congress to those powers actually stated in the Constitution. They emphasized the word *necessary* in the necessary and proper clause. They argued that Congress has no more authority than is absolutely necessary to carry out its expressed powers.

The broad constructionists held that the Constitution was established by the *people,* not by the states. They said that the powers of the national and the state governments alike were derived from the people. Because the broad constructionists favored a stronger national government, they interpreted the necessary and proper clause broadly to expand the powers of Congress. They held that Congress had the authority to use any proper means to carry out its expressed powers.

McCulloch v. *Maryland*

Strict and broad constructionists met in conflict over the establishment of the Bank of the United States. The issue finally came before the United States Supreme Court in 1819 in the case of *McCulloch* v. *Maryland.* It is one of the most important cases in American constitutional law.

In 1790 Alexander Hamilton, Washington's Secretary of the Treasury, proposed the establishment of a national banking system. The Constitution did not expressly grant the national government the power to do so. Hamilton, a broad constructionist, argued that the power was implied and that the bank was a "necessary and proper" means to carry out the expressed financial and commercial powers of the national government. Thomas Jefferson, a strict constructionist, opposed the national bank as a threat to the states' control of their local economies. He also believed that the bank was unconstitutional, arguing that it "does not stand on the degree of *necessity* that can honestly justify it."

President Washington supported Hamilton, and Congress established the Bank of the United States in 1791. A branch of the bank was set up later in Baltimore—much to the displeasure of the Maryland legislature which tried to cripple the bank by imposing a tax on it. James McCulloch, chief cashier of the Baltimore branch, refused to pay the tax. Maryland then convicted McCulloch for refusing to pay the tax. The case went to the Supreme Court.

McCulloch's lawyers—broad constructionists—agreed that the power to create a bank was not an expressed power of the national government. Nevertheless, they argued, Congress had the power to create a bank as an appropriate way to exercise the enumerated powers of collecting taxes, borrowing money, and caring for United States property. McCulloch's lawyers also argued that although the power to tax was reserved to the states, states cannot exercise their reserved powers in a way that would interfere with the operations of the national government.

Maryland's lawyers, who were strict constructionists, argued that the power to charter a bank was not an expressed power of the national government.

In McCulloch v. Maryland, *Daniel Webster (top) argued the case for the Bank of the United States. Luther Martin (above) the attorney general of Maryland, argued the case for his state. Chief Justice John Marshall (right), speaking for the Court, declared in favor of the bank. Why did this decision strengthen the national government?*

They said that the necessary and proper clause only gave Congress the power to pass laws absolutely necessary to the exercise of its expressed powers. Because a bank was not absolutely necessary to exercise any of its expressed powers, Congress had no authority to establish it. Maryland's lawyers also argued that the state had the right to tax the bank because the power to tax was reserved to the states and could be used as they saw fit.

The Supreme Court unanimously rejected Maryland's arguments. Chief Justice John Marshall spoke for the Court. First, Marshall considered the basic nature of the federal union. Did the national government derive its powers from the states, as the states' rights position held? Or were the powers of the Constitution derived from the people? Marshall gave a classic definition of national sovereignty.

The government of the Union ... is emphatically and truly a government of the people. In form and substance it emanates from them. Its powers are granted by them, and are to be exercised directly on them, and for their benefit.... It can never be in their interest and cannot be presumed to have been their intention, to clog and embarrass its execution, by withholding the most appropriate means.

316 CASES IN THE SUPREME COURT

1819.

M'Culloch v. State of Maryland.

(CONSTITUTIONAL LAW)

M'CULLOCH v. THE STATE OF MARYLAND *et al.*

Congress has power to incorporate a Bank.

The government of the Union is a government of the People; it emanates from them; its powers are granted by them; and are to be exercised directly on them, and for their benefit.

The government of the Union, though limited in its powers, is supremo within its sphere of action; and its laws, when made in pursuance of the constitution, form the supreme law of the land.

There is nothing in the Constitution of the United States, similar to the articles of Confederation, which exclude incidental or implied powers.

If the *end* be legitimate, and within the scope of the constitution, all the *means* which are appropriate, which are plainly adapted to that end, and which are not prohibited, may constitutionally be employed to carry it into effect.

The power of establishing a corporation is not a distinct sovereign power or end of government, but only the means of carrying into effect other powers which are sovereign. Whenever it becomes an appropriate means of exercising any of the powers given by the constitution to the government of the Union, it may be exercised by that government.

If a certain means to carry into effect any of the powers, expressly given by the constitution to the government of the Union, be an appropiate measure, not prohibited by the constitution, the degree of its necessity is a question of legislative discretion, not of judicial cognizanco

The act of the 10th April, 1816, c. 44., to "incorporate the subscribers to the Bank of the United States," is a law made in pursuance of the constitution.

The Bank of the United States has, constitutionally, a right to establish its branches or offices of discount and deposit within any State.

The State, within which such branch may be established, cannot, without violating the constitution, tax that branch.

The State governments have no right to tax any of the constitutional means employed by the goverment of the Union to execute its constitutional powers.

A copy of the first page from the case McCulloch v. Maryland *is shown here. As a result of the Supreme Court's decision in this case, the doctrines of implied powers and national supremacy were firmly established.*

Next, Marshall, addressing the question of the power of the national government to establish a bank, took a broad construction. Marshall admitted that the power to charter a bank was not among the expressed powers of Congress. But he held that such a power could be inferred from the necessary and proper clause. Marshall set forth his views on how the powers of the national government should be broadly interpreted, establishing the doctrine of implied powers.

Let the end be legitimate, let it be within the scope of the Constitution, and all means which are appropriate, which are plainly adapted to that end, which are not prohibited, but consist with the letter and spirit of the Constitution, are constitutional.

The Court then considered whether Maryland had the right to tax the bank. Marshall's opinion set forth the doctrine of national supremacy, which was based on the supremacy clause of Article 6.

If any one proposition could command the universal assent of mankind, we might expect that it would be this—that the government of the Union, though limited in its powers, is supreme within its sphere of action. Hence, no state possesses the power to retard, impede, burden, or in any manner control, the operations of the constitutional laws enacted by Congress.

Thus the Supreme Court held the Maryland law unconstitutional.

National Supremacy

The significance of *McCulloch* v. *Maryland* is enormous. In this case the Supreme Court rejected the states' rights claim that the powers of the national government were derived from the states. The Court established the doctrine of implied powers through a broad construction of the necessary and proper clause. And it held that a state could not interfere with the legal activities of the national government.

Speaking for the Court, Chief Justice John Marshall rested his opinion on the supremacy clause of Article 6 of the Constitution. A state constitution or law cannot conflict with the United States Constitution, national laws, or treaties. The Supreme Court settles conflicts between national and state laws. Since *McCulloch* v. *Maryland,* the Supreme Court has found more than 900 state laws unconstitutional and upheld the constitutionality of thousands of others.

Section Check

1. Define: strict construction, implied power
2. Identify: Article 6, James McCulloch, John Marshall, doctrine of national supremacy
3. How does the supremacy clause of the Constitution resolve conflicts between the national government and the states?
4. What arguments were made by Hamilton and Jefferson for or against a national banking system?
5. Why is *McCulloch* v. *Maryland* considered a case of lasting significance?

---

3 THE NATIONAL GOVERNMENT AND THE STATES

The Constitution sets forth the national government's obligations to the states, provides for relations among the states, and gives Congress the power to admit new states.

The National Government's Obligations to the States

The Constitution sets forth several obligations of the national government to the states. Included among the obligations are territorial integrity, legislative representation, a republican form of government, and protection against violence.

Territorial Integrity Several provisions of the Constitution guarantee the physical boundaries and legal existence of each state. Article 4, Section 3, guarantees the ***territorial integrity*** of the states. In addition, Congress must include in both of its houses members chosen in each of the states, and no state may have its equal representation in the Senate taken away without its consent.

A Republican Government Article 4, Section 4, of the Constitution guarantees every state the right to a republican form of government. Although the phrase *a republican form of government* is not expressly defined by the Constitution, the phrase is generally understood to mean a representative government.

The Supreme Court has held that the question of whether a state has a republican form of government is a political question. In effect Congress decides

President Grover Cleveland sent federal troops to Chicago, Illinois, in 1894 to break the Pullman strike. What authority permits the President to order federal troops into the states?

that a state has a republican form of government when it permits the state's Congressional delegation to take its seats.

Protection Against Violence The national government, under Article 4 of the Constitution, has the responsibility for protecting each state against invasion. This guarantee was necessary to persuade the original 13 states to give up their warmaking powers. The national government pledged that an attack on one state would be seen as an attack on the whole nation.

Keeping law and order is primarily the responsibility of the states. Nevertheless, the Constitution recognizes that a state may find itself unable to control a particular situation and guarantees to protect each state against violence within its own borders. In the late 1960's, for example, President Lyndon Johnson sent troops into three states—Michigan, Maryland, and Illinois—to put down riots. He took action at the request of the state governors. A President usually sends troops into a state only in response to a request from its governor or legislature.

When national laws are being violated, national functions interfered with, or national property endangered, a President need not wait for a request for help. In 1894, over the objections of Illinois Governor John Altgeld, President Grover Cleveland sent federal troops to the Chicago railyards to break the Pullman strike that had paralyzed nearly all railway traffic out of Chicago and resulted in violence. The Supreme Court in the case titled *In re Debs* (1896) ruled that the President's action was justified because of the need to protect federal property, interstate commerce, and the mails. The precedent set by this case was used in 1957 when President Dwight Eisenhower sent troops into Little Rock, Arkansas, to enforce school desegregation orders. It was also used by President John Kennedy in 1962 and 1963 to protect black students entering the University of Mississippi and the University of Alabama.

The national government also regularly aids states stricken by such natural disasters as floods, tornados, and hurricanes.

Relations Among the States

Each state is equal to all other states and has jurisdiction only within its own boundaries. There are, however, three important limitations on the separation of the states from each other's laws. These are found in Article 4 of the Constitution. They are full faith and credit, privileges and immunities, and extradition. In addition, Article 1 allows the states to cooperate through interstate compacts.

Full Faith and Credit Article 4, Section 1, of the Constitution provides:

Full Faith and Credit shall be given in each State to the public Acts, Records, and judicial Proceedings of every other State.

This means that the laws of one state—all legal papers including birth certificates, marriage and drivers' licenses, car registrations, and wills, as well as court rulings—are recognized in all other states. The most common use of the full faith and credit clause has been to force courts in one state to uphold the judgments of courts in other states. If, for example, a person in Montana loses a lawsuit and moves to Texas to avoid paying the judgment, the Texas courts will enforce the Montana decision.

There are two exceptions to full faith and credit. First, it applies only to civil law and not to criminal law. This means that a state is not bound to enforce another state's criminal law. Second, a state does not have to recognize divorces granted by one state to residents of another state.

Privileges and Immunities Article 4, Section 2, Clause 1, of the Constitution provides that "the Citizens of each State shall be entitled to all Privileges and Immunities of Citizens in the several States." This means that the rights a United States citizen has in one state are respected by the other states. A resident of one state cannot be discriminated against by another state. For example, a state may not deny citizens of other states the full protection of the laws, the right to engage in lawful occupations, and access to the courts.

The privileges and immunities clause does not extend to political rights and practicing a profession. As a result, a state may establish residency requirements for voting, serving on juries, running for public office, and practicing law, medicine, or another profession in the state. Also the clause does not give those residing outside the state the same rights as residents of a state to attend publicly supported schools or to be admitted to state-operated hospitals. A state can require nonresident students to pay higher tuitions in state colleges and universities. The Supreme Court has, however, started to set aside some residency requirements that may impose an unconstitutional burden on the right to travel and violate the equal protection clause of Amendment 14. Thus, in *Sosna* v. *Iowa* (1975), it has said a state may not make new residents wait an unreasonable length of time before they are eligible for welfare, voting, seeking a divorce, or attending a state university.

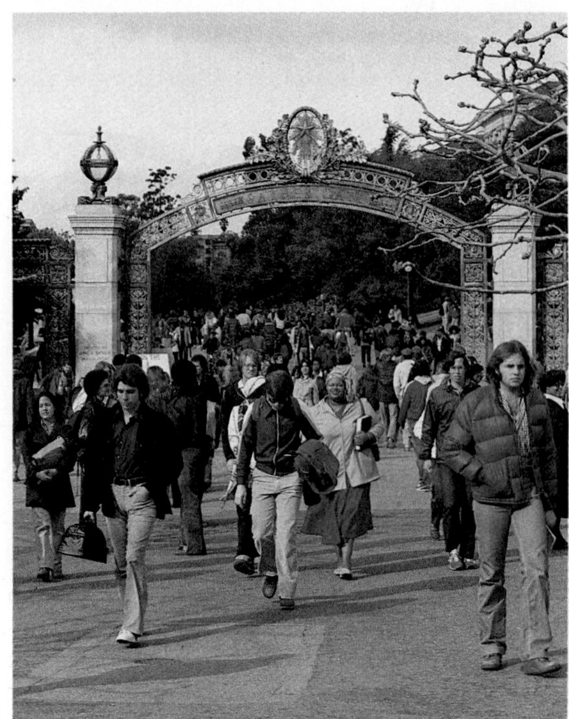

The Constitution guarantees the basic rights of citizens in all the states. How might these constitutional guarantees affect students who choose to attend an out-of-state university?

Extradition Article 4, Section 2, Clause 2, of the Constitution provides the following:

A Person charged in any State with Treason, Felony, or other Crime, who shall flee from Justice, and be found in another State, shall on Demand of the executive Authority of the State from which he fled, be delivered up, to be removed to the State having Jurisdiction of the Crime.

Thus, if a suspect flees to another state, the governor of the state where the crime was committed may request that the suspect be returned. Sending escaped suspects back for trial or punishment is called ***extradition.*** The Supreme Court in *Kentucky* v. *Dennison* (1861) has ruled that a state governor may refuse to give up a fugitive to another state.

Interstate Compacts Article 1, Section 10, of the Constitution provides that "no State shall enter into any Treaty, Alliance, or Confederation" with another state. But this same article gives individual states the right to enter into agreements with each other called ***interstate compacts*** and into agreements with foreign nations. Both can be done only with the consent of Congress.

Interstate compacts were of minor importance until the twentieth century. By 1900 Congress had approved only 19 compacts, all of which involved boundary disputes. In 1921 New York and New Jersey agreed to create the Port of New York Authority. Its purpose was to manage and develop the various types of transportation facilities in the New York City area.

In recent years the number and significance of interstate compacts have increased greatly because of increasing complexity and interdependence in the relations among states. Through interstate compacts the states have sought to tackle a number of regional problems, including flood control and river management, conservation of energy and natural resources, and the protection of air and water from pollution.

The spread of metropolitan areas across state boundaries involves special problems. Greater New York City reaches into the states of Connecticut and New Jersey. Kansas City straddles the borders of Kansas and Missouri. Greater Chicago spills over into Indiana. Urban problems that affect more than one state demand interstate cooperation. Agreements between states may establish agencies for the construction and operation of bridges and tunnels, transportation systems, airports, or similar interstate concerns.

Admission of New States

Article 4, Section 3, of the Constitution gives Congress the power to admit new states to the Union but does not specify the procedure for admission. When admitting new states, the national government must respect the territorial boundaries of the

The 50 states form the basic units of government in the United States federal system. Since 1791, new states have entered the Union on an equal basis with the 13 original states. When were the last 4 states admitted to the Union?

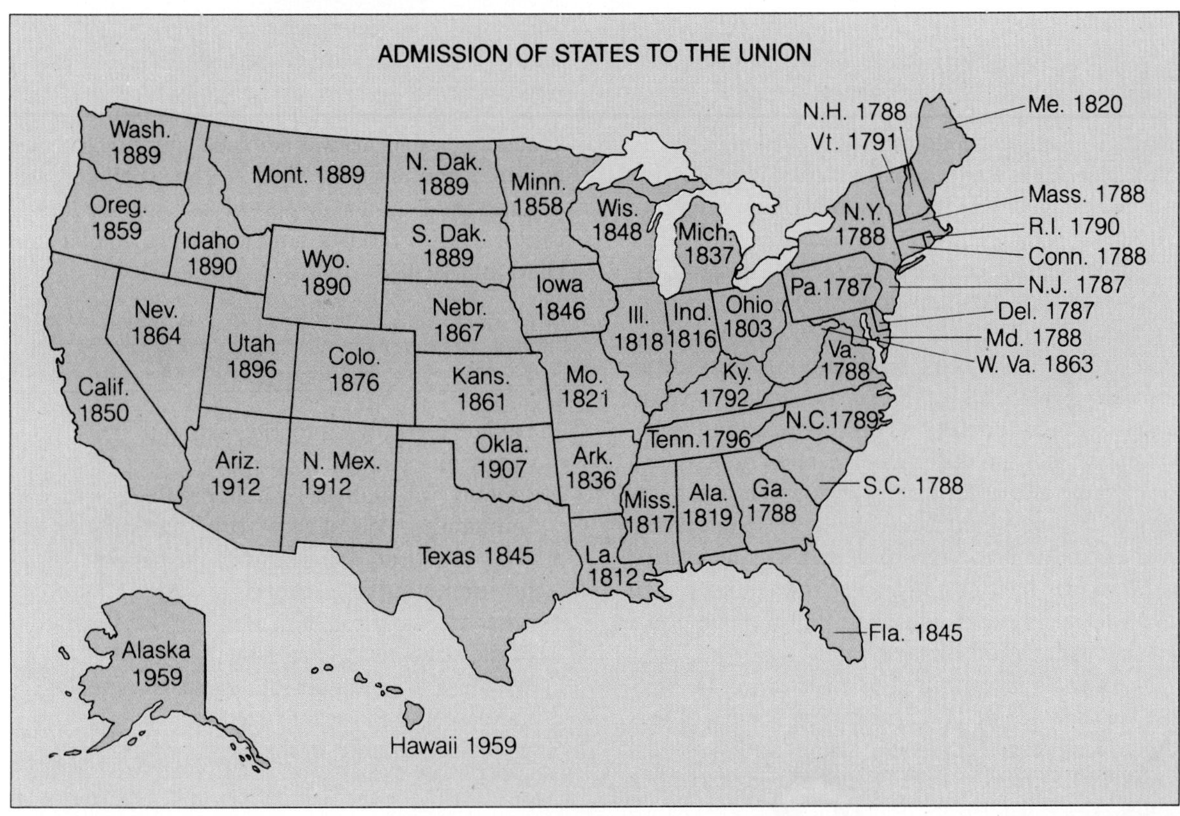

STATEHOOD!

House Sends Bill to Ike

WASHINGTON, D.C., March 12—Congress ended decades of procrastination today and sent to the White House a bill to give Hawaii the Statehood it has so long deserved.

The House overwhelmingly approved the bill this afternoon.

The vote was 323-89.

It was the same bill that passed the Senate 76-15 last night.

The President's approval of the 50th State has been assured and under the bill's machinery Hawaii should join the Union late this year.

WASHINGTON, March 12 (AP)—House Speaker Sam Rayburn, Democrat of Texas, today swung his powerful support to the Hawaii Statehood bill as the House neared a final vote, and almost certain passage.

He said the Territory deserves membership in the union.

"My congratulations to Hawaii," Rayburn said in a statement.

"I opposed this bill in the past when I felt Hawaii was not ready for Statehood. Now, however, the situation has changed and I welcome Statehood because the Territory deserves membership in the Union and will be an asset to the United States."

Representative Walter, Democrat of Pennsylvania, chairman of the House Un-American Activities Committee, told the House that although "Communist labor unions have a very strong hold on the economy of Hawaii," Statehood would give the Islands a chance to "throw off the yoke of those who are so strong and so powerful."

The House, speeding toward passage of the Statehood bill, had shelved its own bill earlier and taken up a Statehood measure passed 76-15 by the Senate last night.

The move made it possible for backers to fulfill their hopes of sending the bill to the White House before nightfall.

If the bill the House passed differed in any respect from the Senate's version, a conference committee appointed by the two chambers would be required to reconcile the varying forms of the bills and make them read exactly the same.

Then re-passage by both chambers of the finally unified form would have been required. This might have taken one day, or even several days more.

All this delay now apparently has been avoided.

The House vote placing the final stamp of approval on legislation turning the Pacific Territory into a 50th state is expected to come around 5:30 p.m. E.S.T. (12:30 p.m. H.S.T.)

Debate began at 11:07 a.m. E.S.T. (6:07 a.m. H.S.T.) today.

SENATE MOVES

Moving with surprising speed, the Senate yesterday approved Statehood on a 76-15 roll call vote, after only four and one-half hours of debate.

10¢

On the Inside

In Statehood Pages

• • •

Statehood in 1849 Whig Paper Urged

• • •

Many Changes Due In Status of Isles

• • •

Statehood Won OK's Four Times Before

• • •

Statehood Reasons Given Over Years

• • •

State Offices Lure Politicians

DIRECTORY

	Page
Bulletin Board	36
Business	19
Classified Ads	32-35

Statehood Extra

Honolulu Star-Bulletin

HONOLULU, TERRITORY OF HAWAII, U. S. A., THURSDAY, MARCH 12, 1959

Honolulu Star-Bulletin, Vol. 48, No. 61 ★★★★★ Phone 57-911

Special Radio, Phone Lines Flash News

Sirens, Bells Herald Statehood Arrival

The wail of civil defense sirens informed Honolulans today that Statehood, long awaited, had finally been approved.

Immediately afterward, church bells pealed, ship's whistles tooted, and motorists leaned on their horns.

Shopping Center, Kalihi Shopping Center and in Palama.

At 7:25 p.m. the international bonfire will be lit at Sand Island.

From 7:30 to 9 p.m. the Armed Forces will set off pyrotechnics off Leeward Oahu.

Armed Forces bands is scheduled for 10 a.m. at the Palace.

At 11 a.m. a Statehood Commemoration Ceremony is to be held there.

At noon a 50-gun salute is to be fired from the Palace grounds.

Mainland entertainers will be flown home by a jet plane in time for tomorrow's events.

And Hawaii will be in the spotlight with several national news outlets sending representatives here to record the occasion.

nor Quinn in Washington that the Statehood bill has passed both Houses of Congress.

The balance of the day will be free for all Territorial employes and public school students.

The next day will also be a holiday.

The process by which Hawaii became a state differed from the usual admission procedure. In 1950 the territory of Hawaii adopted a proposed constitution without waiting for a Congressional enabling act. Congress finally admitted Hawaii as the 50th state in 1959.

states. The only exception to this provision occurred during the Civil War, when the state of West Virginia was formed from the western, pro-Union region of Virginia.

The usual procedure for admission involves the following steps. First, the state applies to Congress for admission. This application is called a ***petition.*** When Congress accepts the petition, it passes an ***enabling act.*** This act directs the territory to draft a state constitution that sets up a representative government. After the document has been drafted by a convention and approved by the people of the territory, it is submitted to Congress. If Congress still wishes to admit the territory, it passes an ***act of admission*** by a majority vote. The territory then becomes a state and enters the Union on an equal footing with the other states.

Congress has admitted 37 states since the original 13 states formed the Union. The 5 states of Vermont, Kentucky, Tennessee, Maine, and West Virginia were formed from territory belonging to other states. Texas was an independent republic before admission. California was admitted after being ceded to the United States by Mexico. The 30 other states entered the Union after periods as organized territories. The last states admitted were Alaska and Hawaii in 1959.

Section Check

1. Define: territorial integrity, extradition, interstate compact
2. Identify: full faith and credit, privileges and immunities, Port of New York Authority
3. What are three obligations of the national government to the states?
4. What are the three limitations on the separation of the states from each other's laws?
5. Why have the number of interstate compacts increased so in recent years?
6. What are the steps in the usual process for admitting a new state?

4 NATIONAL-STATE COOPERATION

There are about 80,000 units of government in the United States. In addition to the national government and 50 state governments, there are approximately 3,000 counties, 19,000 municipalities, 17,000 townships, 15,000 school districts, and 26,000 special districts that regulate water control, fire protection, conservation, rural electrification, sewage treatment, and other needed services. The two basic levels of the federal system are the nation and the 50 states; all of the local units are beneath their respective states.

The Mix of Governmental Units

Many of the 80,000 units of government have overlapping and sometimes conflicting powers and functions. But the American system of federalism is characterized more by cooperation than by conflict. Education provides a good example. In most states the local school district has primary responsibility for the public schools. But these districts depend on county and city governments for services such as special traffic police during school hours. They depend on the state governments for financial aid, teacher certification, and in some states the selection of textbooks. The state determines what must be taught and sets educational standards.

The school districts also depend on the national government. The federal government may assist in the construction of schools. It may supply technical equipment and books. Federal programs fund vocational and agricultural classes in high school. The federal school lunch and milk program provides inexpensive meals for students in all the nation's public schools.

What is true for education is true for almost every function of government. Responsibilities are shared as the different units of government work together in partnership. This mixture of responsibilities has been likened to a "marble cake." No matter how a marble cake is sliced, its different-colored ingredients mix in a swirl of colors so that it is difficult to tell where one ends and the other begins. So it is with federal, state, and local responsibilities in the marble cake of American government.

Grants-in-Aid

State and local governments have grown increasingly dependent on federal assistance. Some 27 percent of state and local government revenue today comes from the federal government. This compares with 10 percent in 1950 and 15 percent in 1960. Federal grants go to state and local governments to support a vast number of programs. By providing funds, the national government may encourage the states to adopt certain projects or to comply with

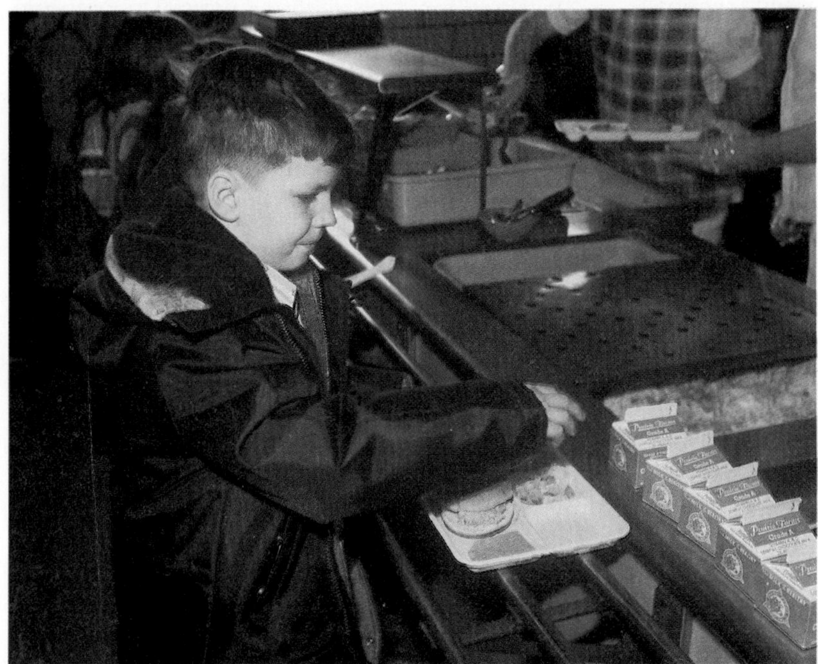

Various aspects of public education depend on the cooperative efforts of national, state, and local levels of government. Federal funds support the school-lunch program. Give examples of state and local support for education.

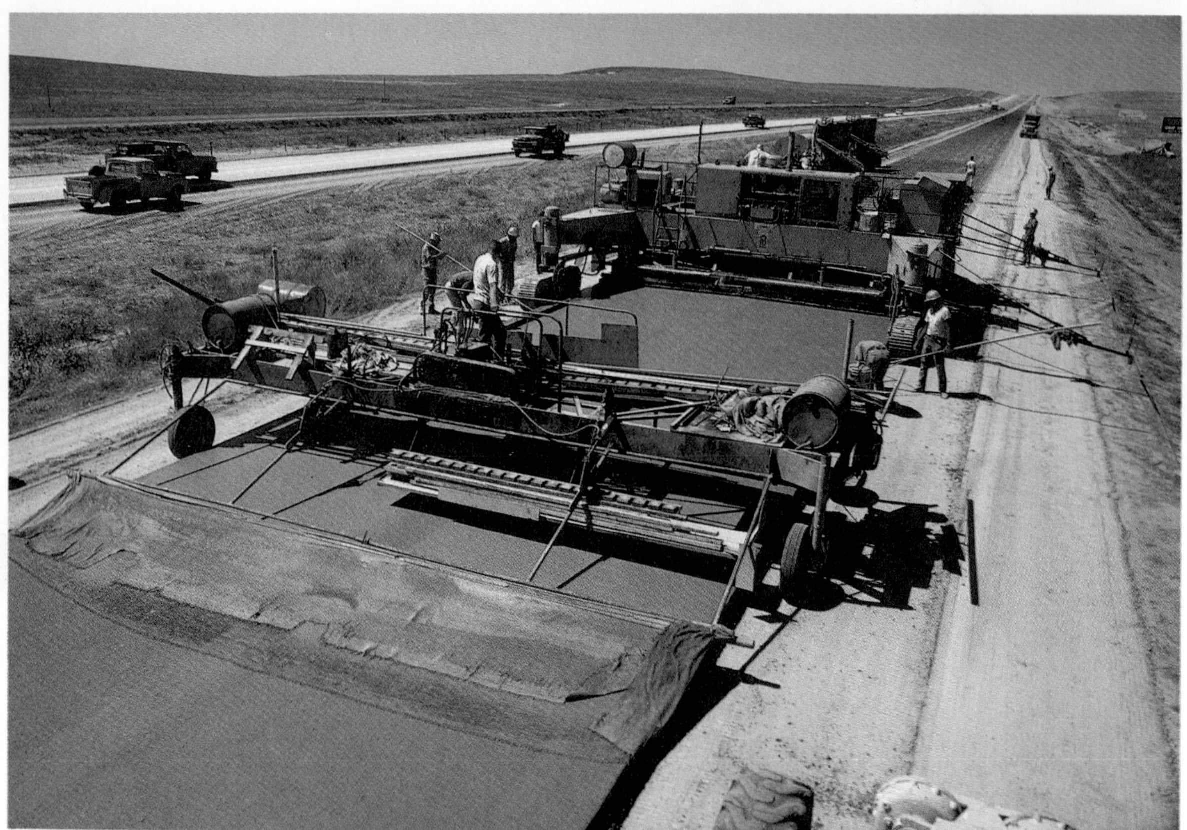

The federal government assists state and local authorities by awarding grants-in-aid for highway construction, public housing, and other projects. What percentage of state and local government revenues comes from federal assistance?

new national standards. Most federal aid has been in the form of grants-in-aid and revenue sharing.

Federal funds given to state and local governments for purposes such as highway construction, education, welfare, and urban renewal are called ***grants-in-aid.*** During the nineteenth and early twentieth century, federal grants amounted to less than 5 million dollars each year. After the income tax was adopted in 1913, federal revenue increased. Grants to the states slowly began to expand, chiefly for agriculture and highway construction. During the Great Depression of the 1930's a number of new programs were begun, including aid for health, welfare, public housing, unemployment insurance, and old-age assistance.

The 1960's brought another expansion under President Lyndon Johnson's War on Poverty and Great Society. Billions of dollars were provided for education, housing, urban renewal, clean air and water, law enforcement, and health care. The expansion of grants brought a shift in focus. Special attention was given to education and aid to the disadvantaged. Urban areas were the main target. Many of the grants bypassed the states and went directly to local communities—particularly to cities facing crisis. As local governments benefited from federal grants, they expanded the area of their responsibility. This has tended to strengthen local government at the expense of the state.

Categorical Grants Most national aid to state as well as local governments is made in the form of ***categorical grants.*** Congress usually sets certain conditions the states must meet to receive the grants. Each grant has its own requirements. There are four common guidelines, or ***strings,*** attached to a categorical grant.

First, the money must be used for the purpose specified by Congress. Second, the state or local government is usually required to put up a certain amount—from 10 to 50 percent—as ***matching funds.*** Third, the state must set up a separate agency and procedures to manage the grant, submit plans for advance approval, meet performance standards, and allow the national government to inspect the results. Aid for school construction, for example, requires the use of certain building materials for maximum safety. There may also be particular requirements for accounting, administration, and reporting. Fourth, the state must obey federal guidelines that establish general standards of conduct. These are not related to the specific purpose of the grant. They include affirmative action in hiring practices to overcome the effects of past discrimination suffered by women and racial minorities, equal access to government benefits and opportunities for the handicapped, and protection of the environment.

Participation in federal grants-in-aid is voluntary. But few state and local governments can resist the opportunity for funds—despite the strings that go along with every grant. Although Congress determines for what purposes states receive federal funds, governors and state legislators have an active role in determining how the programs are carried out.

Block Grants Categorical grants have been criticized for being narrowly defined, having too many strings attached, and giving the national government too much say in policy decisions that should be made at state and local levels. Since the 1960's Congress has combined some categorical grants into larger programs, called ***block grants,*** to meet these objections. These are grants to state and local governments for general use in broad areas. There are few or no strings attached.

In the early 1980's President Ronald Reagan made a series of proposals to reduce the size of the federal government and its influence over the states. Under the name *New Federalism* he pledged to return a number of federal responsibilities to state and local governments. Toward accomplishing that aim, the 1982 budget combined a number of categorical grants into nine new block grants. These are in the areas of public health, social services, community development, energy assistance, and education.

All state and local authorities that accept federal funds must provide equal benefits and opportunities for handicapped persons. What other kinds of guidelines may be imposed upon recipients of federal grants?

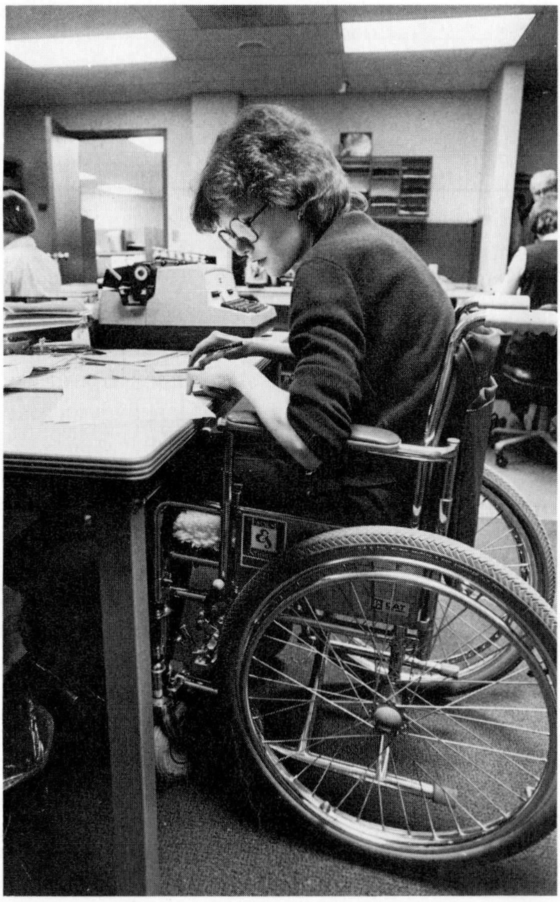

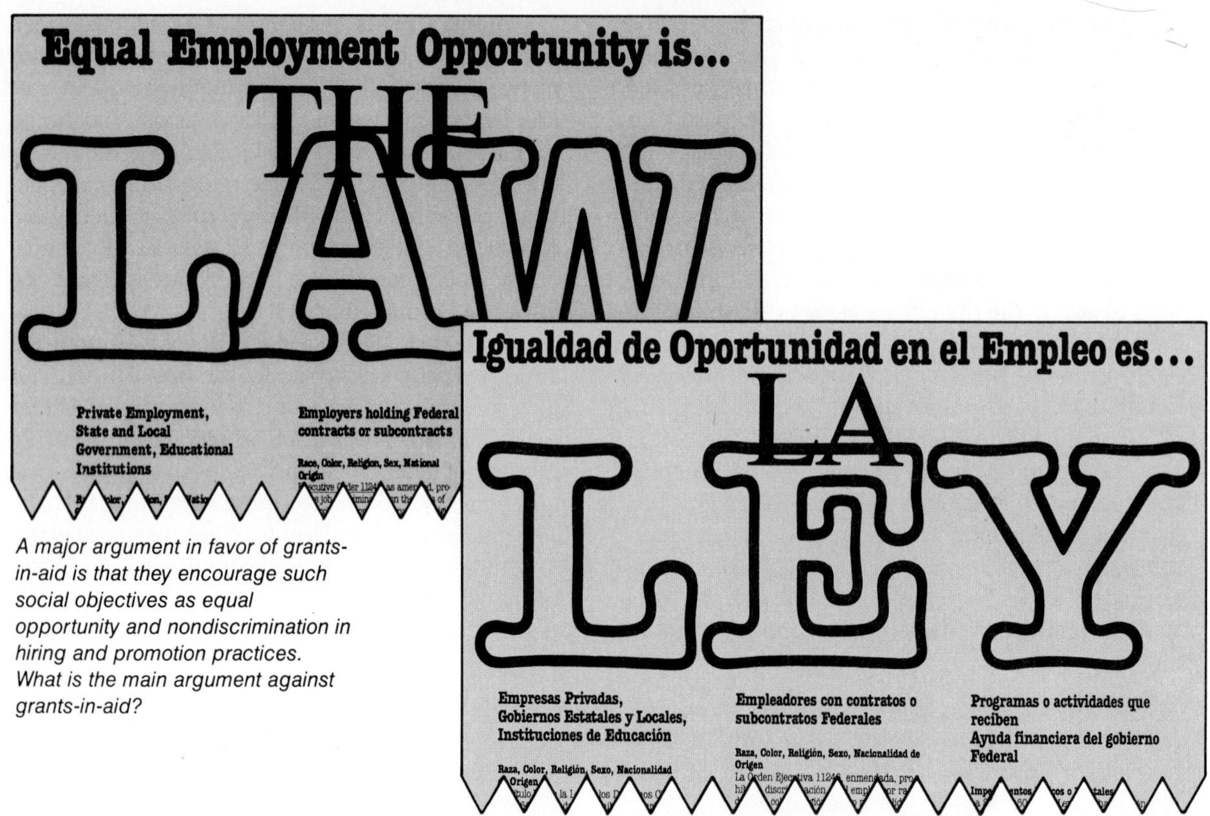

A major argument in favor of grants-in-aid is that they encourage such social objectives as equal opportunity and nondiscrimination in hiring and promotion practices. What is the main argument against grants-in-aid?

Pros and Cons of Grants-in-Aid There are several arguments in favor of grants-in-aid to the states. First, grants-in-aid enable state and local governments to provide services that they otherwise could not afford. Second, they help to maintain minimum standards of services in fields such as health care and welfare. Third, they encourage the achievement of social objectives such as nondiscrimination. Fourth, the grants-in-aid system works to equalize resources among the states. Low-income states receive proportionately more in grants than high-income states.

The main argument against grants-in-aid, particularly categorical grants, is that they allow the national government to exercise authority in areas such as public education that are traditionally reserved to the states. Critics point out that the conditions attached to grants give the national government too much say in state and local affairs. Another argument against grants-in-aid is that they encourage states to undertake programs because of the available federal moneys and not because the programs are needed. Also, critics contend, because states have to put up a specified amount of matching funds, they spend state funds on these unnecessary programs.

Revenue Sharing

In 1969 President Richard Nixon proposed a major change in national-state relations called ***revenue sharing***, an arrangement through which the national government gives an annual share of federal tax money to state and local governments. The revenue-sharing and grants-in-aid programs differ in two important ways. First, states and cities do not put up matching funds in the revenue-sharing program. Second, revenue-sharing funds are provided with almost no strings attached.

Revenue sharing was adopted in 1972 with the passage of the State and Local Fiscal Assistance Act. Congress revised and extended the law in 1976 and again in 1980. Revenue sharing provides for the distribution of almost $7 billion a year in federal funds to state and local governments. One third of the money goes to the states, and two thirds to local governments. The amount of money given to each state is determined by a complex formula based on each state's population and efforts to raise its own tax revenues. There are few restrictions on use.

Revenue sharing is strongly supported by most governors, mayors, and other state and local officials. They argue that revenue-spending decisions should be made at the state and local levels by public officials who are directly accountable to the people.

But revenue sharing does have its critics. Some claim that national goals such as clean air can be achieved only if the national government controls how the money is spent. Critics point out that the money does not always go where it is most needed and cite cases of cities that have used the funds for tennis courts and golf courses.

State Aid to the National Government

Intergovernmental aid does not go in only one direction. State and local governments give aid to the national government in a variety of ways. For example, state and local election officials conduct national elections. The elections are financed by state and local funds and are regulated to a great extent by state laws. Also, the legal process by which aliens become citizens of the United States is done through state courts and is thus paid for by the states.

Section Check

---

1. Define: grant-in-aid, categorical grant, block grant, revenue sharing
2. Identify: War on Poverty, New Federalism
3. How is the mixture of responsibilities in American government described?
4. What are the two types of grants-in-aid?
5. What arguments are made for and against grants-in-aid? Revenue sharing?

---

5 THE GROWTH OF NATIONAL POWER

The formal constitutional powers of the national government have changed very little since 1789. The United States, however, has grown from 13 states with a population of 4 million to a nation of 50 states and a population of more than 235 million. Government has expanded with the nation, and the national government has become increasingly dominant.

The Constitutional Basis

There are a number of reasons for the growth of national power. Oftentimes the national government has stepped in because state and local governments were unable or unwilling to act.

The first factor explaining the expansion of national government is geographic. Problems do not recognize state boundaries. Air and water pollution, for example, do not stop at the state line. A metropolitan area may spread over two or more states. State governments simply may be unable to deal with economic and social problems that are national in scope.

The second factor is economic. A state may not have the financial resources to meet the demands upon it. The states are not equally rich or well-endowed in natural resources. Often the states want the federal government to take over certain burdensome responsibilities. In recent years the states have urged the federal government to assume the full costs of welfare.

The third factor is political. A state may be unwilling to act because of certain powerful interests. Until the 1960's, for example, most state legislatures were dominated by rural interests—even though the great majority of the people lived in cities. While new farm-to-market roads were built, urban problems were largely ignored.

Scientists, with the support of federal funds, test the purity of the Missouri River. Increasingly, the responsibility for pollution control and similar problems has fallen to the national government.

For these reasons people have often looked to the federal government rather than to the states. First business, then agriculture, labor, and other interests turned to the federal government for protection and assistance. They supported federal activity when it was to their advantage. They opposed it—in the name of states' rights—when it was not.

During the debate over ratification of the Constitution, business interests rallied in support of a strong national government. In the early years of the Republic they sought the establishment of a national banking system. Later they called for federal assistance to the nation's developing industry. By the turn of the century farmers were actively pursuing aid from the federal government. They wanted regulation of the railroads, easy credit, and guaranteed support for farm prices. In the twentieth century labor unions made their claim on the national government. They sought improved working conditions, minimum wages, unemployment compensation, and the right to organize.

As America became increasingly an urban society, with urban problems, new groups entered the political arena. They sought federal assistance for education, improved housing, mass transportation, and welfare. Racial minorities and women also turned to the federal government. They sought guarantees of equal opportunity and protection against discrimination.

The history of federalism is a history of the growth of national power. The expansion of the national government rests primarily on three constitutional powers: the war power, the power to tax and spend for the general welfare, and the power to regulate interstate commerce.

The War Power The Constitution gives the national government responsibility for defending the United States against attack by a foreign power. Congress alone has the power to declare war and to raise and support armed forces.

During World War I Justice Charles Evans Hughes wrote, "The power to wage war is the power to wage war successfully." The war power has been used to justify a wide range of activities by the national government. Military strength depends on more than

Throughout American history different groups in society have turned to the national government for protection or assistance. What kinds of assistance have women in the United States sought from the national government?

troops and weapons. When the nation is at war, the power of the national government is limited only by the constitutional protections guaranteed each citizen. In wartime, controls may be extended over almost every aspect of the economy. Price ceilings may be imposed, wages frozen, and strikes forbidden. Materials may be rationed. The national government may do whatever is "necessary and proper" in the war effort.

Even in time of peace the war power may be used to ensure military preparedness. Everything from education to a sound economy affects the nation's military strength. In 1958, Congress passed the National Defense Education Act to promote the study of science, mathematics, and foreign languages. Thus Congress legislated on education, an area traditionally reserved to the states.

The General Welfare Power Congress has the power to tax and spend for the general welfare. This power gives Congress the means to regulate persons and property for the safety, health, and welfare of society.

Congress may use taxes for regulatory purposes. One of the most famous examples was the high tax placed on dangerous white phosphorous matches. The intent of the tax—and its result—was to force the industry out of business. High taxes on such products as cigarettes and liquor may also be imposed to discourage consumption. A classic form of regulatory taxation is the ***protective tariff***, a customs duty that is so high it keeps a particular foreign product out of the country altogether. The purpose of the tax is to protect American industry from foreign competition.

The power of Congress to spend for the general welfare is very important in the growth of national power. Congress appropriates billions of dollars each year to aid education, agriculture, business, and an ever wider range of areas. Conditions attached to grants of money enable Congress to influence state and local operations and regulate individual conduct.

The Commerce Power The Constitution gives Congress the power "to regulate Commerce ... among the several States." This power extends to all commerce that affects more than one state. The term ***interstate commerce*** includes production, buying, selling, and transportation of goods. The power to regulate interstate commerce may be the single most important power of the national government. Interstate commerce is defined so broadly that today it includes virtually all economic activity—and anything that affects economic activity.

Chief Justice John Marshall laid the cornerstone of the commerce power in *Gibbons* v. *Ogden* (1824). Marshall held that interstate commerce was not limited to traffic or the buying and selling of goods across state lines. Interstate commerce involved any trade that affected more than one state. And he held that Congress could use any means "necessary and proper" to regulate interstate commerce.

INSIGHT

Federal Information Centers

People often say that state and local governments are closer to the people than the national government. But the national government is as close as the nearest post office or weather bureau. Ninety percent of all federal employees work outside Washington, D.C. The telephone directory of any city in the nation will have a number of listings under "United States Government." In large cities these may run to several pages. As the telephone listings indicate, the federal government provides many services in every community.

If you need guidance to federal programs and activities, you can call a Federal Information Center. The centers operate in major cities and serve more than half the nation by toll-free telephone numbers. Centers answer more than 8 million questions each year on a wide range of topics, including tax problems, passports, social security benefits, law enforcement, social services, or how to get a job with the federal government.

ISSUES

The Case of Farmer Filburn

The broad scope of the commerce power can be seen in *Wickard* v. *Filburn,* a case that came before the Supreme Court in 1942. Under the Agricultural Adjustment Act, which was passed in 1938, Roscoe C. Filburn, an Ohio farmer, was given a marketing limit, or quota on the amount of wheat he could grow. The purpose of the act was to control the amount of wheat moving into interstate and foreign commerce. Filburn grew more wheat than his quota permitted. In bringing the government to court, he claimed that he was subject to the limit only for the wheat sold—not for the wheat consumed on his own farm. Filburn had used some of the wheat to feed his livestock and make flour for his own use.

Filburn, through his attorneys, held that the Agricultural Adjustment Act of 1938 was unconstitutional. The Supreme Court ruled against Filburn. The Court reasoned that the amount of wheat produced by Filburn for home consumption, by itself, might be trivial. But when similar production by other farmers is considered, the total effect on interstate commerce would be substantial. The Court then held that Congress had the power to regulate any activity that "exerts a substantial effect on interstate commerce." *Wickard* v. *Filburn* is exceptionally noteworthy because it demonstrates the vast power of Congress to oversee commercial activity.

The distinction between commerce that was purely local and commerce that affected more than one state then became critical. Over the years the Supreme Court took various views on the issue. In *National Labor Relations Board* v. *Jones & Laughlin Steel Corp.* (1937), the question before the Court was whether Congress had the power to regulate labor-management relations. This would seem to be an intrastate activity. But, the Court argued, conflict between labor and management had a serious effect on interstate commerce. A strike in the steel industry, for example, might be catastrophic to the nation. The Court held that Congress had the power to control intrastate activities that had a "close and substantial relation" to interstate commerce.

The effect of the decision was to open a wide range of intrastate activities to regulation by the national government. The commerce clause has provided the basis for federal minimum wage laws, the control of child labor, and the regulation of agriculture. In 1964 Congress used its power to regulate interstate commerce as the basis for the Civil Rights Act. The law prohibited restaurants, hotels, and other places of public accommodation from excluding people because of their race, religion, or national origin. In *Heart of Atlanta Motel* v. *United States* (1964), the Supreme Court said, "If it is interstate commerce that feels the pinch, it does not matter how local the operation that applies the squeeze." Thus Congress could legislate against discrimination because it restricted interstate commerce.

Politics and Federalism

Over the years the power of the national government has grown. But the expansion of the national government's activities has not threatened the federal system. The American system of federalism remains as vigorous as American politics.

Political parties in the United States are state-based. The Democratic and Republican parties, in a significant sense, are not national parties. They come together every four years for the Presidential campaign, but even the way the parties nominate Presidential candidates centers on the states.

Federalism accounts, in large part, for the decentralization of American parties. But in turn the party system is one of the most important factors in maintaining the strength of federalism. The parties have a major stake in the federal system. For the party out of power in Washington, the states provide a place to rebuild its strength and prepare for the next election. A party may lose the Presidential election, for example, but win the governorships in a number of states.

The pattern of political representation also reinforces federalism. Senators and representatives in Congress are basically local politicians—and they will likely be defeated if they forget that. They are elected from and accountable to state and local constituencies. Members of Congress are thus strong advocates for their state and local governments.

The federal system established by the Constitution gives the nation and the states the power they need to operate. Because federalism involves both cooperation and conflict, there is a built-in tension between the states and the national government. The Framers intended that tension to be there: It is part of the system of checks and balances, and its purpose is limited government.

Section Check

1. Define: protective tariff, interstate commerce, the war power
2. Identify: *Wickard* v. *Filburn* (1942), *Gibbons* v. *Ogden* (1824), *National Labor Relations Board* v. *Jones & Laughlin Steel Corp.* (1937)
3. What three powers have been especially important in the growth of national government?
4. What are some purposes for which Congress has used regulatory taxes?
5. What are some actions taken by the national government under the commerce power?
6. In *Heart of Atlanta Motel* v. *United States* (1964), how did the Supreme Court justify its ruling against discrimination?

SUMMARY

In the American federal system the Constitution divides power between the national government and the 50 states. The national government has only those powers delegated to it by the Constitution. There are three kinds of delegated powers. (1) The expressed powers are those that the Constitution actually describes. (2) The implied powers are not described by the Constitution but are suggested by those powers that are described. (3) The inherent powers are those that belong to the national government because it is a government in the world community. Most delegated powers are exclusive; that is, they belong only to the national government.

The Constitution also denies certain powers to the national government. Some powers are expressly denied, some are denied because the Constitution does not mention them, and some are denied to preserve the existence of the federal system. The states are also denied certain powers by the Constitution.

The states have reserved powers—those powers that are not delegated to the national government and that are not denied to the states by the Constitution. The concurrent powers are those that may be exercised by both the national government and the states.

Article 6, Section 2—the supremacy clause—makes the Constitution and acts and treaties of the United States the highest forms of law. A state constitution or law cannot conflict with the Constitution, national laws, or treaties. The Supreme Court settles conflicts between national and state laws. *McCulloch* v. *Maryland* established the doctrine of national supremacy.

The national government has certain constitutional obligations to the states. It must respect the territorial integrity of each state, guarantee each state a republican form of government, and protect each state against foreign invasion and domestic violence.

Each of the states is equal to all other states and legally separate from them. There are, however, three important constitutional limitations on the separation of the states from each other's laws: full faith and credit, privileges and immunities, and extradition. The states may also, with the consent of Congress, enter into compacts among themselves.

The national government and the states cooperate in many ways. The national government gives financial assistance to state and local governments through the grants-in-aid program and revenue sharing. The states aid the national government in a variety of ways—for example, conducting national elections.

The national government's powers have grown to meet the needs of a modern industrial nation. The constitutional basis of this growth has been the war power, the power to tax and spend for the general welfare, and the power to regulate interstate commerce. The expansion of the national government's activities has not threatened the federal system because of the nature of American politics.

Chapter 4 Review

Using Vocabulary

Answer the questions by using the meaning of each underlined term.

1. What is the connection between the division of power and federalism?
2. How is it that an expressed power and an implied power are both delegated powers?
3. Why is the supremacy clause a governing principle in national-state relations?
4. Would a broad constructionist or a strict constructionist agree with the doctrine of implied powers? Why?
5. Why can a state expect the federal government to guarantee territorial integrity?
6. What kind of strings might be attached to a categorical grant?
7. How does revenue sharing differ from a program of matching funds?
8. Why does a governor request extradition?
9. Why have interstate compacts increased in recent years?

Understanding American Government

1. Why did James Madison think a compromise might be necessary between a strong central government and control by the states?
2. What is the constitutional basis of implied powers?
3. What are reserved powers?
4. In the controversy between strict and broad constructionists, which side was supported by those favoring states' rights? Why?
5. In *McCulloch* v. *Maryland* did Chief Justice Marshall side with the position of strict or broad construction?
6. What is the meaning of the full faith and credit limitation in the Constitution? What are the exceptions to it?
7. Explain how the American federal system is characterized more by cooperation than by conflict.
8. What did Charles Evan Hughes mean when he wrote, "The power to wage war is the power to wage war successfully"?
9. How may Congress use the power to tax to regulate persons and property? What is an example?

Extending Your Skills: Understanding a Supreme Court Case

Review the discussion of *McCulloch* v. *Maryland* on pages 113–116. Complete each statement. Then explain how each principle added to the strength of the national government.

1. The nature of the federal Union is derived from the (a) people; (b) states.
2. States may use the power to tax (a) in any way they choose; (b) as long as it does not interfere with the operation of the federal government.
3. The necessary and proper clause gives Congress the power to pass (a) whatever laws help it exercise the expressed powers of the Constitution; (b) only those laws that are absolutely necessary to exercise the expressed powers of the Constitution.

Government and You

1. The concept of limited government is central to our political system. Does federalism act as a force for or against limited government? In what ways?
2. How was the case of *Heart of Atlanta Motel* v. *United States* (1964) involved in the fight against racial discrimination?
3. Do you think that Congress was justified in placing a high tax on white phosphorous matches, a product it considered dangerous? Explain the reasons why you believe certain products might merit such a tax. What other products might merit such a tax?

Activities

1. Chief Justice John Marshall was responsible for many crucial decisions in our early political history. Prepare a biographical report on him. Present your report to the class.
2. When was your state admitted to the Union? Make a scrapbook using your state's admission to the Union as a theme. What important events happened that year? Who was your state's first governor? Describe the political process by which your state was admitted to the Union.

UNIT 2

GUARANTEES OF CIVIL LIBERTY

Chapter 5

Personal Freedoms

Since the earliest days philosophers have dreamed of a country where the mind and spirit of man would be free; where there would be no limits of inquiry; where men would be free to explore the unknown and to challenge the most deeply rooted beliefs . . . Our First Amendment was a bold effort to adopt this principle.

JUSTICE HUGO BLACK

CHAPTER OVERVIEW

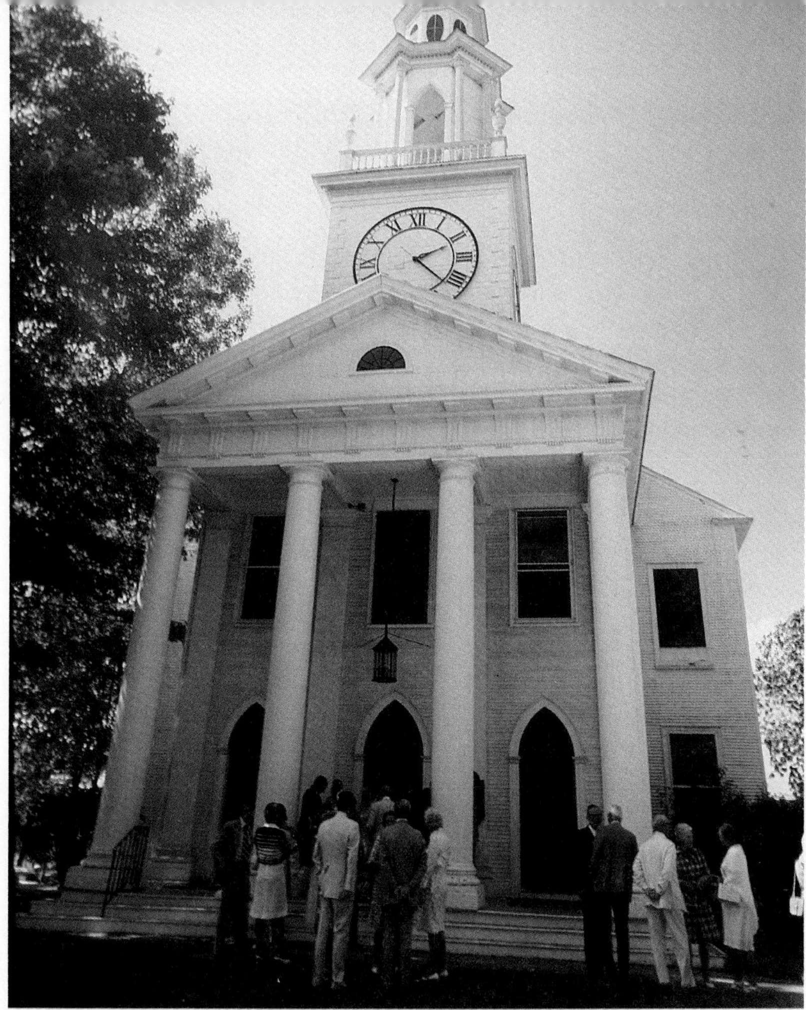

The First Amendment prohibits the government from establishing an official religion. Thus, the First Amendment's guarantee of religious freedom means that the people of the United States may not be compelled to worship. Those who choose to worship may practice the religion of their choice.

1 EXTENDING THE BILL OF RIGHTS

The Framers of the Constitution limited government to protect the liberty of the American people. When the Congress first met in 1789, its members placed further limits on the new government by proposing the Bill of Rights—the first ten amendments to the Constitution. These amendments guarantee our civil liberties. ***Civil liberties,*** or civil rights, are the personal rights of all citizens. Among the most important are those protected by the First Amendment. They include the freedoms of speech, of the press, of assembly, and of religion. The amendment reads:

Congress shall make no law respecting an establishment of religion, or prohibiting the free exercise thereof; or abridging the freedom of speech, or of the press; or the right of the people peaceably to assemble, and to petition the Government for a redress of grievances.

The First Amendment originally protected citizens only against action by the federal government. In *Barron* v. *Baltimore* (1833) the Supreme Court established that the guarantees of the Bill of Rights restricted only the national government and was not applicable to the states. In keeping with the principle of federalism, the states were left free to adopt their own bills of rights. In 1868, however, through the Fourteenth Amendment, the national government placed certain restraints on the states for the protection of individual civil liberties. That amendment said:

No State shall make or enforce any law which shall abridge the privileges or immunities of citizens of the United States; nor shall any State deprive any person of life, liberty, or property, without due process of law; nor deny to any person within its jurisdiction the equal protection of the laws.

The key phrase in the Fourteenth Amendment is "due process of law."

Due Process of Law

Due process of law is guaranteed by the Fifth and Fourteenth amendments. The Fifth Amendment restricts national government and the Fourteenth limits the states. Basically, ***due process*** means that law must be reasonable, regular, and fair.

Due process includes those principles of justice "so rooted in the traditions and conscience of our people as to be ranked as fundamental." These are not fixed in time. They have evolved and expanded. Justice Felix Frankfurter, for example, spoke of due process in terms of "the community's sense of fair play and decency" and "sense of justice."

People argued about the meaning of the due process guarantees. Were the rights now protected against state action by the Fourteenth Amendment the same as those included within the Bill of Rights? The Court dealt with the issue in the *Slaughterhouse Cases* of 1873. It ruled that the requirements of the Bill of Rights applied *only* to the federal government and were not incorporated within the Fourteenth Amendment.

It was not until 1925, in *Gitlow* v. *New York,* that the Supreme Court for the first time applied portions of the Bill of Rights to the states. In its decision, a cornerstone of civil liberties, the Court said:

For present purposes, we may and so assume that freedom of speech and press—which are protected by the First Amendment from abridgment by Congress—are among the fundamental personal rights and liberties protected by the due process clause of the Fourteenth Amendment from impairment by the states.

With *Gitlow* the Court began the gradual process of extending the protections guaranteed in the Bill of Rights to actions by the states. This process is sometimes described as "nationalizing the Bill of Rights." The Court recognized speech and press as fundamental freedoms and thus within the meaning of due process of law. In 1937 the Court included freedom of assembly within due process; in 1940, the free exercise of religion; and in 1947, the prohibition on the establishment of religion. Thus, on a case-by-case basis, various provisions of the Bill of Rights have been gradually included into the due process clause of the Fourteenth Amendment. While most of the Bill of Rights has been extended to the states, only those rights contained within it which the Court regards as fundamental to liberty apply to the states.

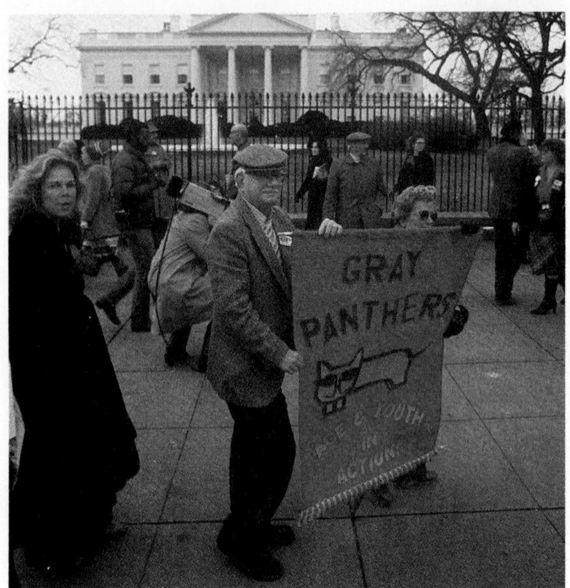

Members of the Gray Panthers, an interest group that represents the elderly, march in front of the White House.

Majority Rule and Minority Rights

Our limited, constitutional government is committed to both majority rule and minority rights. Thomas Jefferson wrote that "the will of the majority is in all cases to prevail," but if it is to be "rightful," majority rule must come from free and open discussion. Jefferson stressed the importance of an open marketplace of ideas, in which all viewpoints—minority as well as majority—might be advanced in free debate.

Jefferson believed that "the will of the people is the only legitimate foundation of any government, and to protect its free expression should be our first object." Jefferson's concern was not so much the individual's right to say something, but rather the public's right to hear what that person has to say. President Harry Truman put this concern very well when he said:

There is no more fundamental axiom of American freedom than the familiar statement: In a free country, we punish men for the crimes they commit, but never for the opinions they have. And the reason this is so fundamental is not, as many suppose, that it protects the few unorthodox from suppression by the majority. To permit freedom of expression is primarily for the benefit of the majority, because it protects criticism, and criticism leads to progress.

The history of limited government is in large measure a history of the judicial interpretation of

Justices Hugo Black (left) and Felix Frankfurter (right) were appointed by President Franklin D. Roosevelt. Contrast Frankfurter's position on First Amendment freedoms with Black's position. How might the two positions conflict?

the scope and limits of individual rights, particularly those liberties found in the First Amendment. These "first freedoms" regarding free expression were described by Justice Benjamin Cardozo as "the indispensable conditions of nearly every other form of freedom." Justice Frankfurter termed them "the well-spring of our civilization." They protect the right of individuals to hold, advocate, and publish their ideas freely.

The Balancing Doctrine

Is democracy best served by balancing First Amendment freedoms against other values, such as national security? Or is it better served by absolute freedom in the areas covered by the First Amendment?

The "absolute freedom" position is expressed by the notion that "to be afraid of ideas, any idea, is to be unfit for self-government." This view is most often associated with Justice Hugo Black. When the First Amendment states that "no law" shall be passed abridging freedom of speech and press, Black argued that that is exactly what the Constitution requires.

The most important view in opposition to Black's hard interpretation of the First Amendment is the ***balancing doctrine*** of Justice Felix Frankfurter. Frankfurter argued that the First Amendment freedoms are not more sacred than other freedoms. Frequently, different rights come into conflict. Competing interests must be balanced.

Undoubtedly even Black would have accepted Justice Oliver Wendell Holmes's view that freedom of speech does not include the right to yell "fire" falsely in a crowded theater and cause panic. The Court has accepted the position that some speech simply is not given the shelter of the First Amendment. How much freedom of speech one may enjoy thus depends on what is said, where, when, how, and even about whom. As Holmes said, it is a question of "proximity and degree." In judging whether speech is protected, he would look to the circumstances of the occasion.

Section Check

1. Define: civil liberty, due process, balancing doctrine
2. Identify: Fourteenth Amendment, Bill of Rights, *Gitlow* v. *New York* (1925), First Amendment Freedoms
3. How has the Fourteenth Amendment been used to extend the Bill of Rights to the states?
4. What did President Truman say was the great benefit of free expression?

A 1799 cartoon criticizes the Federalists' use of the Sedition Act to limit the freedoms of speech and the press. Thomas Jefferson described the act as "an experiment on the American mind to see how far it will bear the avowed violation of the Constitution."

2 FREEDOMS OF SPEECH AND OF THE PRESS

Freedom of speech and freedom of the press are closely related. Each is fundamental to the proper working of our democracy. ***Freedom of speech*** means the right to express even the most unpopular or unusual opinion. ***Freedom of the press*** guarantees that the people will have access to such opinions. Yet these freedoms are neither absolute nor unlimited.

Free Speech and National Security

The first free speech controversy came early in our Republic's history. In 1798 Congress passed the Sedition Act to silence "false, scandalous, and malicious" speech and publications directed against the government.* This bill reflected the view of President John Adams and other Federalists that government must control as well as reflect the opinions of the people. To control potential unrest, they felt it necessary to limit freedom of speech and press.

The Sedition Act was denounced widely as an attack upon liberty. James Madison declared it a violation of the First Amendment. Before any case concerning the Sedition Act reached the Supreme Court, Thomas Jefferson had replaced Adams as President. The act expired, and Jefferson pardoned all who had been convicted under it.

Not until World War I when Congress passed the Espionage Act of 1917 and the Sedition Act of 1918, did the First Amendment again become a subject of controversy. Under these laws some 2,000 persons were prosecuted for subversive activity or criticism of the federal government. The constitutionality of the Espionage Act was considered in *Schenck* v. *United States* (1919).

During the war the general secretary of the Socialist party, Charles Schenck, was arrested and convicted for mailing pamphlets that urged new draftees to refuse military service. Schenck's appeal eventually went to the Supreme Court, which unanimously upheld his conviction. Justice Oliver Wendell Holmes spoke for the Court. "In many places and in ordinary times," he said, "the defendants in saying all that was said in the circular would have been within their constitutional rights." The times, however, were not ordinary. The nation, Holmes emphasized, had been at war.

The question in every case is whether the words used are used in such circumstances and are of such a nature as to create a clear and present danger that they will bring about the substantive evils that Congress has a right to prevent.

The key phrase, *clear and present danger*, was the test Justice Holmes offered. Applying the test, however, soon became a matter of dispute.

**Sedition* refers to language or action undermining legal authority or inciting rebellion against the government. The term *espionage* refers specifically to spying.

Clear-and-Present-Danger Test During the 1920's, shortly after the Russian Revolution, the United States experienced the "Great Red Scare," a national anxiety about the threat of world Communism. In speeches and publications Communists and anarchists advocated the overthrow of the American government. There was widespread fear that foreign radicals were subverting the country.

In several cases involving Communist agitation, the Supreme Court chose to interpret the clear-and-present-danger test broadly. The Court held that "there is no absolute right to speak or publish, without responsibility, whatever one may choose." Justice Holmes dissented. He opposed a weakening of the First Amendment protections. He argued that speech and publication might be limited only if they posed an *immediate* danger to public peace. Words had to be "triggers of action" to violate the law.

Holmes was joined in his dissent by another great justice, Louis D. Brandeis. Like Holmes, Brandeis believed that advocating the overthrow of the government was protected by the First Amendment, unless it involved incitement to immediate action. Brandeis said:

If there be time to expose through discussion the falseness and fallacies, to avert the evil by the processes of education, the remedy to be applied is more speech, not enforced silence. Only an emergency can justify repression. Such must be the rule if authority is to be reconciled with freedom.

The Smith Act During the 1940's and 1950's the Supreme Court again confronted the problem of those who advocated the overthrow of the government. The issue again was Communist subversion. The major case of this period was *Dennis* v. *United States* (1951). Dennis and ten other Communists had been convicted under the Smith Act of 1940—the first peacetime national sedition law since the short-lived act of 1798. The Smith Act made it a crime for any person to advocate or teach the violent overthrow of any government in the United States. It was similarly a crime to publish material advocating the overthrow of the government or to organize any group for that purpose—or even to be a member of such a group.

In *Dennis,* Chief Justice Frederick M. Vinson spoke for the Court. He argued that the clear-and-present-danger test was the proper standard to apply, but that *immediate* danger did not have to be proved when the overthrow of the government was being advocated. The government need not wait to respond

Justice Oliver Wendell Holmes (above), often called the "great dissenter," sat on the Court from 1902 to 1932. Justice Louis Brandeis (below), often called the "people's attorney," sat on the Court from 1916 to 1939.

until such time as its very existence is threatened. "Overthrow of the Government by force and violence," he said, "is certainly a substantial enough interest for the Government to limit speech."

Justice Hugo Black dissented, warning that the Court was diluting the strength of the First Amendment.

The First Amendment is the keystone of our Government [and] the freedoms it guarantees provide the best insurance against the destruction of all freedom. . . . I cannot agree that the First Amendment permits us to sustain laws suppressing freedom of speech and press on the basis of Congress or our own notions of mere 'reasonableness.' The Amendment as so construed is not likely to protect any but those 'safe' or orthodox views which rarely need its protection.

Between 1947 and 1955 the Court shared American society's general hostility toward Communists. Legitimate concern for national security often gave way to an atmosphere of fear, however, which threatened the free expression of all Americans. After 1955 the Supreme Court, under Chief Justice Earl Warren, sought to protect freedom of speech. At the same time, however, the Court recognized that the genuine security interests of the nation must be safeguarded. How was the balance to be struck?

In *Yates* v. *United States* (1957) the Court restricted the use of the Smith Act against alleged Communist sympathizers. The Court held that the Smith Act, under which Dennis had been convicted, did not outlaw advocating the idea of overthrowing the government. To be punishable under the Smith Act, advocacy must go beyond mere belief in violent revolution. "The essential distinction," wrote Justice John Harlan, "is that those to whom the advocacy is addressed must be urged to *do* something, now or in the future, rather than merely to believe in something." Advocacy may be forbidden, the Court ruled in a later decision, only when it is directed toward

Senator Joseph McCarthy of Wisconsin (standing) testifies about the activities of the Communist Party before the House Committee on Un-American Activities in 1954. Later evidence presented at the hearings disproved McCarthy's testimony.

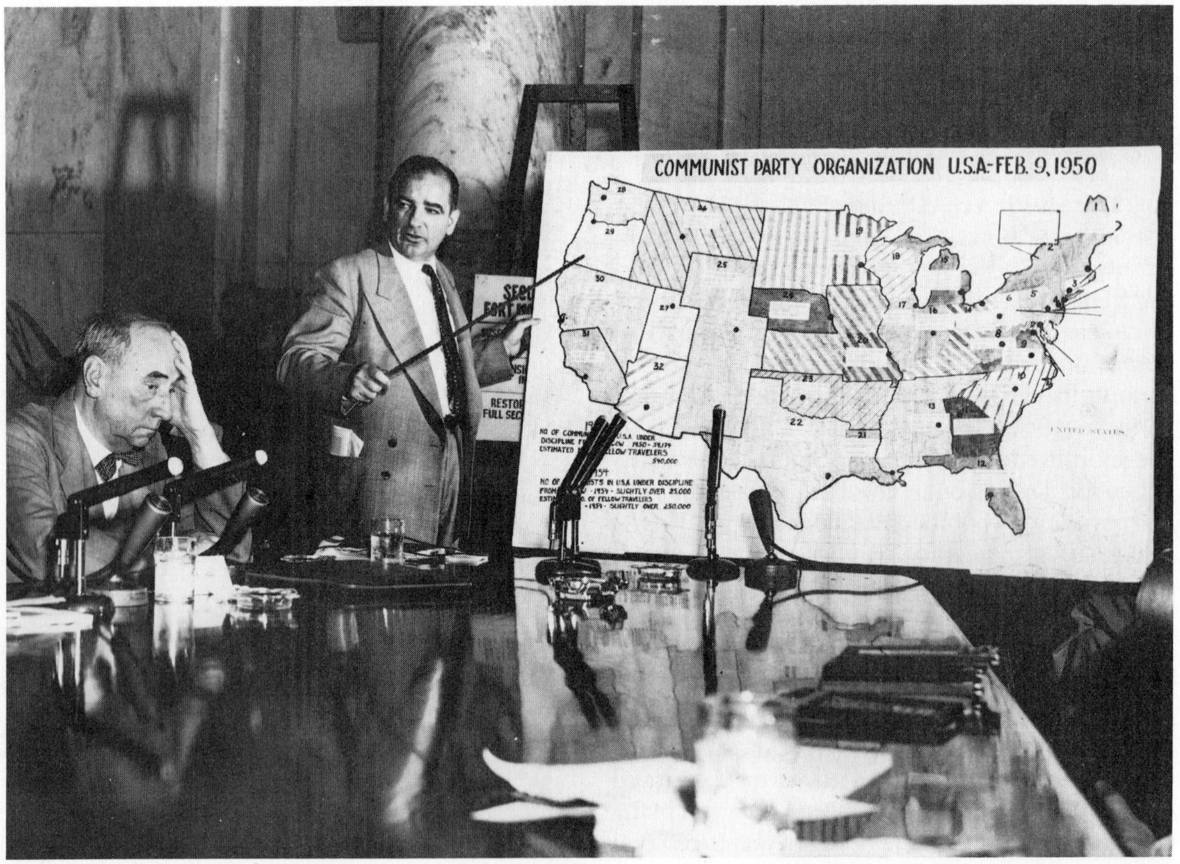

Daniel Ellsberg (left), a former Pentagon researcher, tells a House of Representatives subcommittee that he gave top secret documents concerning the Vietnam War to The New York Times. *How did the Pentagon Papers case illustrate the conflict between national-security interests and First Amendment freedoms?*

inciting *immediate* action in violation of the law and when such action is *likely* to occur. Justice Black, agreeing with the *Yates* decision, took a different line of reasoning. He stated:

The First Amendment provides the only kind of security system that can preserve a free government—one that leaves the way open for people to favor, discuss, advocate or incite to causes and doctrines, however obnoxious and antagonistic such views may be to the rest of us.

In recent years the Court has continued to seek a balance between freedom of expression, as guaranteed by the First Amendment, and the interests of national security. The Court has held that some loyalty and security measures are necessary for the defense of the nation against domestic subversion and espionage. But these measures must be limited to genuine security needs. The legislation stating these measures must be precise and narrow, and the Court has made it clear that special care must be taken to protect the constitutional rights of all citizens.

Free Press and National Security

One of the most difficult balances to secure is that between freedom of the press and the compelling interest in national security. In 1971, in the Pentagon Papers case, the Court dramatically confronted the issue. That year Daniel Ellsberg quit his job at the Department of Defense because of his opposition to United States participation in the Vietnam War. He then released to the press a major portion of a 47-volume Pentagon study of America's involvement in Vietnam. Some 7,000 pages of the material were still classified as "Top Secret—Sensitive." The various documents showed, among other things, that many high officials had deceived the American people about the war. On June 13 *The New York Times* published the first of a series of articles from the so-called Pentagon Papers. Other newspapers soon published parts of the Papers.

The Nixon administration argued that publication of the Papers would endanger national security and do "irreparable injury to the United States." The government secured a temporary restraining order from the federal courts to prevent further publication. In fighting the order, *The New York Times* said that the issue was not one of national security, but the issue was the right of the people to be informed of government's misdeeds.

In a 6–3 decision the Supreme Court held that the government had failed to make its case against publication. After a 15-day waiting period the press was free to publish the Pentagon Papers. Justice Hugo Black spoke for the Court:

In the First Amendment the Founding Fathers gave the free press the protection it must have to fulfill its essential role in our democracy. . . . The press was protected so that it could bare the secrets of government and inform the people. Only a free and unrestrained press can effectively expose deception in government.

Obscenity

The Supreme Court traditionally has distinguished between various forms of speech for purposes of the First Amendment. In the words of Justice Frank Murphy:

There are certain well-defined and narrowly limited classes of speech, the prevention of which have never been thought to raise any Constitutional problem. These include the lewd and obscene, the profane, the libelous, and the insulting or "fighting" *words—those which by their very utterance inflict injury or tend to incite an immediate breach of the peace.*

The Court has taken freedom of speech to mean essentially "discussion," and incitement to riot, libel, and obscenity have not been taken to be discussion. Of all areas of speech, obscenity has been one of the most troublesome and controversial confronted by the Court.

The dictionary defines ***obscenity*** as anything "disgusting to the senses [and]... designed to incite lust." For more than a quarter of a century, the Court has tried to define the line at which material becomes obscene and thus loses its First Amendment protection.

A majority on the Court has always held obscenity to be outside the area protected by the First Amendment. Sensitive to the danger of censorship in a free society, the Court has sought some clear and precise standard by which material might be judged obscene or not. In *Roth* v. *United States* (1957) the Court held that if materials are to be prohibited as obscene, a three-fold test must be met. First, it must be established that "the dominant theme of the material taken as a whole appeals to a prurient interest—that is, that it tends to excite lustful thoughts. Second, the material must be "patently offensive because it affronts contemporary community standards." Finally, it must be "utterly without redeeming social value."

Applying the three-step *Roth* test, the Court upheld Roth's conviction. In subsequent cases, however, the Court split. With no clear majority behind a single rationale, the *Roth* test was ambiguous and ineffective. By a 1966 ruling, the Court held that to be prohibited, material had to be "*utterly* without redeeming social value."

Unhappily for the Court, the social-value test did not settle the issue because it proved extremely difficult to show in court that material was "utterly without redeeming social value." Concern about the obscenity issue rose as pornographic materials became increasingly available in the United States.

With a new, more conservative majority under Chief Justice Warren Burger, the Court again confronted the issue of obscenity in 1973. In *Miller* v. *California* the Court instituted new guidelines emphasizing "community standards" for determining when material was obscene. The Court's decision became a matter of immediate controversy. Dissenters argued that the *Miller* decision presented a serious danger to free speech. Because each community could define obscenity by its own standards, an individual might be prosecuted in one town for selling materials that would have been perfectly legal in a neighboring community. No one would know in advance what was acceptable or where he or she might be prosecuted.

In addition, there was a danger that the majority within a community would be able to impose its moral judgments upon the minority. What one person finds shocking may be taken by another as serious political or artistic expression. This can be seen in a case the Supreme Court heard soon after the *Miller* decision. A Georgia theater manager had been convicted under the state obscenity statute for showing the film *Carnal Knowledge,* which had been nominated for an Academy Award. The jury had been instructed to render its verdict on the basis of "community standards." The Supreme Court justices reviewed the film and ruled that it was not patently offensive. The conviction was overturned.

The problems the Court was encountering had been anticipated by Justices Hugo Black and William O. Douglas in 1957, when they argued that any test for obscenity makes the "legality of a publication turn on the purity of thought which a book instills in the mind of its reader." In a 1977 dissent Justice John Paul Stevens voiced a similar concern.

In the final analysis, the guilt or innocence of a criminal defendant in an obscenity trial is determined primarily by individual jurors' subjective reaction to the materials in question rather than by the predictable application of rules of law. ... The conclusion is especially troubling because the same image—whether created by words, sounds, or pictures—may produce such a wide variety of reactions.

The issue of obscenity today remains no less troublesome and unsettled. Each community tries to find its own standard within the scope permitted by the First Amendment protection of free speech and press.

Newsstands often display publications that carry sensational headlines about public officials and celebrities. Although public personalities can sue the publishers for libel, they must prove that the publishers intended actual malice. Why does the Court make a distinction between public figures and private citizens in libel cases?

Libel and Slander

Freedoms of speech and of the press are restricted in matters of national security and for obscene materials. They are also restricted in matters concerning the injury of a person's reputation through libel or slander. In general libel and slander are false communications that injure "an individual's reputation by lowering the community's regard for that person or by otherwise holding an individual up to hatred, contempt, or ridicule." ***Libel*** is injuring someone's reputation through the printed word. ***Slander*** is injuring through the spoken word.

As complex a problem as obscenity presents, some observers think libel laws may be even more troublesome. The landmark libel case is *The New York Times Company* v. *Sullivan* (1960). A full-page ad had appeared in the *Times* stating that black students in the South were being treated brutally by the police in Montgomery, Alabama. The ad claimed that the police had locked student civil rights demonstrators out of the dining hall to starve them into surrendering. The claim was later proved to be untrue. L. B. Sullivan, police commissioner, sued the *Times* for libel and won $500,000. But the Supreme Court reversed this award.

The Supreme Court decided that libel law may be applied one way to private citizens and another way to public figures and officials. Clearly, a false statement had injured the police chief's reputation, a classic example of libel. Justice William Brennan ruled, however, that a public official, like a chief of police, is prohibited from "recovering damages for a defamatory falsehood relating to his official conduct unless he proves that the statement was made with 'actual malice'—that is, with knowledge that it was false or with reckless disregard of whether it was false or not." In recent years the Court has considered movie stars and other celebrities to be "public figures," making it difficult to sue gossip columnists and other writers for libel.

The reasoning behind the Court's position on libel and public figures is that criticism of public officials is a necessary part of democratic government. The Court also knows that public figures have great access to the media to correct false impressions and misstatements. The Court knows that its position on libel will cause some problems. Still, the current position remains, in the words of Justice Lewis Powell, that "the First Amendment requires that we protect some falsehood in order to protect speech that matters."

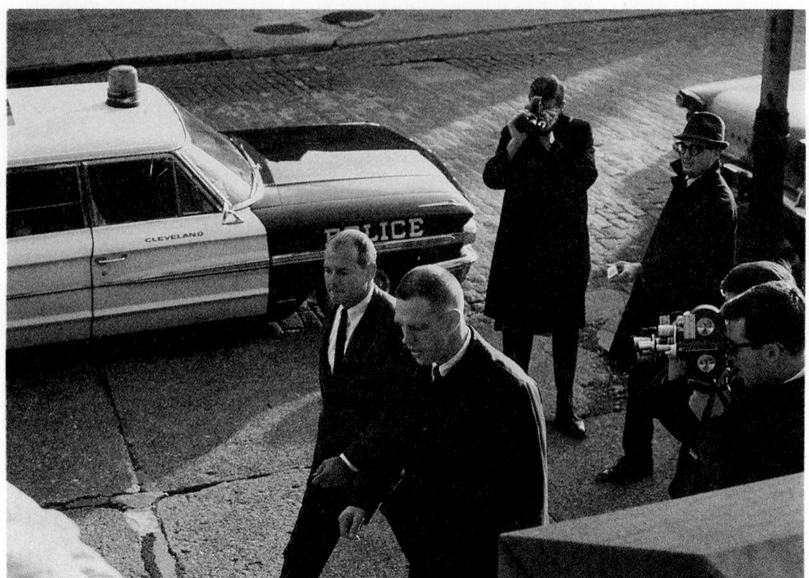

Dr. Sam Sheppard (center left), flanked by reporters, is escorted into court. *What basic freedoms were in conflict in* Sheppard v. Maxwell? *How might a judge resolve this conflict?*

Free Press and the Right to a Fair Trial

Freedom of the press is protected by the First Amendment. The right to a fair trial is guaranteed by the Sixth Amendment. Sometimes the guarantee of a free press conflicts with a person's right to a fair trial. The conflict arises when newspaper, radio, or television coverage before or during a trial might so prejudice potential jurors or a sitting jury as to threaten the impartiality of a verdict.

The most important case—itself the subject of a television dramatization—is *Sheppard* v. *Maxwell* (1966). Dr. Sam Sheppard, a Cleveland osteopath, was convicted of murdering his wife in 1954. Before the trial ever began, a Cleveland newspaper pronounced that the police "have convincing evidence to prove Dr. Sam Sheppard . . . was the killer." The irresponsible manner in which the paper covered the trial turned it into what the Supreme Court later described as "bedlam" and a "Roman holiday." The Court found that "the state trial judge did not fulfill his duty to protect Sheppard from the inherently prejudicial publicity which saturated the community and to control disruptive influences in the courtroom." The Supreme Court demanded that trial courts adopt "strong measures to insure that the balance is never weighed against the accused. . . . If publicity during the proceedings threatens the fairness of the trial, a new trial should be ordered." Sheppard was given a new trial and acquitted.

How is a judge to protect the right to a fair trial, as required by the Court in the *Sheppard* case? Various techniques are available. The judge can order a ***change of venue*** by moving the trial to a place where there has not been so much publicity. The judge can postpone the trial to allow the publicity to lose its immediacy and impact. Once the trial begins, ***sequestering*** of a jury can be ordered. Sequestering means that the members of the jury are kept from being reached by any publicity during the trial itself. It is a drastic measure and is used sparingly. Most jurors, after all, do not appreciate enforced isolation.

In the 1960's courts frequently used the ***gag order.*** This is a court order forbidding the news media from publishing or broadcasting certain information about a case. If a newspaper violates the order, it can be cited for contempt and fined. The media argue that gag orders violate the First Amendment, that they are a fundamental threat to freedom of the press and the public's right to know. What, critics ask, if a gag had been imposed on the press during the Nixon administration when the Watergate break-in had been revealed? *The Washington Post* would never have been able to expose the full ramifications of the break-in. Watergate might have ended as a simple burglary trial instead of bringing on the resignation of a President and the imprisonment of many high officials.

In 1976 the constitutionality of gag orders was challenged before the Supreme Court. In a unanimous decision the Court held a Nebraska gag order unconstitutional. Several justices noted that gags might be permissible in the most compelling circumstances—for example, to prevent a clear threat to national security by the publication of such details as troop movements during wartime. On the whole, however, the Supreme Court took a generally strong stand against all gag orders. "Our liberty depends on the freedom of the press," Chief Justice Warren Burger stated, "and that cannot be limited without being lost."

Section Check

1. Define: freedom of speech, freedom of the press, libel, slander, change of venue, sequestering, and gag order
2. Identify: clear-and-present-danger test, *Schenck* v. *United States,* Great Red Scare, Smith Act of 1940, *Yates* v. *United States* (1957), Pentagon Papers
3. What has been the Supreme Court's position when free speech has conflicted with national security?
4. What has the Court ruled in cases involving the free press and national security?
5. What was the Court's three-fold test in determining which materials are obscene?
6. What are some steps the courts have recommended to guarantee a fair trial?

3 FREEDOM OF ASSEMBLY

The First Amendment guarantees "the right of the people peaceably to assemble, and to petition the government for a redress of grievances." In 1937 the Supreme Court incorporated the right of assembly within the due process clause of the Fourteenth Amendment, recognizing it as fundamental and thus applying to state law.

Freedom of speech would be incomplete without ***freedom of assembly,*** the right of people in a democracy to associate, to form groups, and to unite many different voices as one. In upholding the right of association against state interference in *NAACP* v. *Alabama* (1958), Justice John Harlan spoke for a unanimous Court.

Effective advocacy of both public and private points of view, particularly controversial ones, is undeniably enhanced by group association, as this Court has more than once recognized by remarking upon the close nexus between the freedoms of speech and assembly. . . . It is beyond debate that freedom to engage in association for the advancement of beliefs and ideas is an inseparable aspect of the 'liberty' assured by the Due Process Clause of the Fourteenth Amendment, which embraces freedom of speech.

At an antinuclear-energy rally, peaceful demonstrators exercise two fundamental rights—the freedoms of speech and of assembly. What is the relationship between these two freedoms?

Demonstrations and Protests

During the civil rights movement of the early 1960's a group of young blacks, high school and college students, gathered at the Zion Baptist Church in Columbia, South Carolina. From there they walked in small groups to the grounds of the state capitol to protest racial discrimination. Once on the grounds, they walked around in an orderly manner with signs bearing such messages as "Down with segregation," and "Capitol of Segregated S. C." A crowd of some 200 to 300 onlookers gathered, but there was no evidence of hostility on the part of either the demonstrators or those who watched them. There were no threatening gestures or abusive words. Neither pedestrian nor automobile traffic was obstructed.

PROFILE

Advocates of Civil Disobedience

Throughout history a few remarkable individuals have challenged what they believed to be unjust laws by practicing ***civil disobedience,*** the deliberate and public violation of the law. Civil disobedience focuses public attention on an issue. Three of the most famous advocates of civil disobedience were Henry David Thoreau, Mohandas Gandhi, and Martin Luther King, Jr. Each went to jail for his beliefs, and each shocked the public conscience. All three believed that civil disobedience must be nonviolent. Through ***passive resistance*** they invited arrest to gain sympathy for their causes.

Henry David Thoreau (1817–1862) was a New Englander who worked for the abolition of slavery. He believed that real change would come only when individuals, on the basis of conscience, took direct action. Thoreau did so by refusing to pay his taxes, for which he was arrested. His 1848 essay "Civil Disobedience" had wide influence. Thoreau wrote: "Can there not be a government in which majorities do not virtually decide right and wrong, but conscience? Must the citizen ever for a moment, or in the least degree, resign his conscience to the legislator? . . . I think we should be men first, and subjects afterward."

Mohandas Gandhi (1869–1948) led the struggle for India's independence from Great Britain. Gandhi introduced a form of civil disobedience he called *satyagraha,* or "truth force." This was both a philosophy and a technique for bringing about social and political change. Gandhi believed not only in nonviolent resistance but in "suffering in one's own person" to conquer an adversary. Violence, said Gandhi, is to be met with truth and love.

Martin Luther King, Jr., (1929–1968) drew world attention to his church in Montgomery, Alabama, where he preached against racial discrimination. As a leader of the Civil Rights movement he advocated nonviolent confrontation with injustice. In his struggle for justice and equality for all people, he was jailed, stoned, and beaten. In his "Letters from a Birmingham Jail" King wrote: "I submit that an individual who breaks a law that conscience tells him is unjust, and who willingly accepts the penalty of imprisonment in order to arouse the conscience of the community over its injustice, is in reality expressing the highest respect for law." In 1964, at the age of 35, Martin Luther King received the Nobel Peace Prize for his work. In 1968 King, like Gandhi, was shot to death by an assassin. In October of 1983 the Congress of the United States declared that, beginning in 1986, the third Monday in January shall be a national holiday honoring Dr. King.

Peaceful protests against segregation in Columbia, South Carolina (right), eventually led to the Supreme Court case Edwards v. South Carolina. The wearing of black armbands with peace symbols by Mary Beth and John Tinker (below) led to the case Tinker v. Des Moines School District. The Supreme Court's rulings in these cases reaffirmed First Amendment freedoms.

After about half an hour the police ordered the students to leave within 15 minutes or face arrest. Instead, the students began to sing patriotic songs. When 15 minutes had passed, they were arrested. In state court the demonstrators were convicted of breach of the peace. They appealed to the Supreme Court. In *Edwards* v. *South Carolina* (1963) the Court overturned the convictions. The students had been doing no more than peaceably expressing opinions that "were sufficiently opposed to the views of the majority of the community to attract a crowd and necessitate police protection. . . ." In arresting them, the state had infringed upon the demonstrators' "constitutionally protected rights of speech, free assembly, and freedom to petition for redress of their grievances."

Opposition to the war in Vietnam also took the form of protest demonstrations. The Court considered the limits of such protest in *Tinker* v. *Des Moines School District* (1969). Mary Beth Tinker was a 13-year-old junior high school student in 1965. She wore a black armband to school one day, as did her brother John and her friend Christopher Eckhardt. They had planned with their parents to express opposition to the war in Vietnam by wearing the armbands, despite a ruling by the school authorities forbidding such protests. When they refused to take the armbands off, the students were suspended from school. The school principals thought the issue was closed, but Mary Beth and her friends brought suit against the school in federal court.

The Court found no action or speech that intruded upon the work of the school or the rights of the other students. All that was involved was "a silent, passive expression of opinion, unaccompanied by any disorder or disturbance." Mary Beth's protest was a peaceable assembly. In holding the rule against the armbands to be in violation of the First Amendment, the Court added:

Students in school as well as out of school are 'persons' under our Constitution. They are possessed of fundamental rights which the State must respect, just as they themselves must respect their obligations to the State. . . . They may not be confined to the expression of those sentiments that are officially approved.

Limits on Freedom of Assembly

The First Amendment protects only the right of peaceable assembly. In exercising their rights as citizens, protesters or demonstrators must respect the rights of those who may not agree with them. They are not free to disrupt the classroom or to shout down a speaker. They cannot deny others those rights which they themselves would exercise. As Justice Holmes once said, "My freedom to swing my arm stops where the other man's nose begins."

The Court has never denied government the power to regulate the conduct of demonstrators for the safety of the community and the protection of the rights of other people. Reasonable limits may be imposed on freedom of assembly so long as these laws are "narrowly aimed at that forbidden conduct." People are not free to demonstrate at any time or place or in any manner they choose. Demonstrations may not be conducted in or near a court with the intent of interfering with the administration of justice. Demonstrations on jail premises also may be forbidden. Parades and the use of public parks may be regulated by requiring permits. The Court has upheld carefully worded and reasonably administered local laws against disorderly conduct, even when they regulate speech and assembly.

Section Check

---

1. Define: freedom of assembly, civil disobedience, passive resistance
2. Identify: Henry David Thoreau, Mohandas Gandhi, Martin Luther King, Jr.
3. What protection was extended to students in *Tinker* v. *Des Moines School District?*
4. What are some limits placed on freedom of assembly?

---

4 FREEDOM OF RELIGION

The First Amendment directed Congress to make "no law respecting an establishment of religion, or prohibiting the free exercise thereof." With this simple statement the United States became the first country in the history of the world to build what Thomas Jefferson called "a wall of separation between church and state."

The idea of the ***separation of church and state***—of making no religion an official arm of government—is American in origin. Many settlers of America came in search of religious freedom. All too often, however, like the Puritans of Massachusetts Bay, they then sought to impose their beliefs on others. Roger Williams, the pastor of a Puritan church in Salem, Massachusetts, taught that each individual should have the right to worship according to conscience. Anne Hutchinson, also of Massachusetts, spoke openly against sermons delivered by her minister. Both were banished from the colony. Williams later founded the colony of Rhode Island in 1644. Separating church from state, its charter granted individual religious freedom.

After the War for Independence, Jefferson and Madison struggled to secure the separation of church and state in Virginia. They believed that religion was a private matter. Their success in removing the Anglican Church from its officially established position in Virginia served as a model for other states' and for the federal government's bills of rights.

The Establishment Clause

The First Amendment statement on religion has two aspects: the ***establishment clause*** and the ***free exercise clause.*** In *Everson* v. *Board of Education* (1947) the Court recognized the guarantee against the establishment of religion as so fundamental that it applied to the states through the due process clause of the Fourteenth Amendment. In speaking for the Court, Justice Hugo Black gave a classic definition to the establishment clause.

The "establishment of religion" clause of the First Amendment means at least this: Neither a state nor the Federal Government can set up a church. Neither can pass laws which aid one religion, aid all religions, or prefer one religion over another. Neither can force nor influence a person to go to or remain away from church against his will or force him to profess a belief or disbelief in any religion. No person can be punished for entertaining or professing religious beliefs or disbeliefs, for church attendance or non-attendance. No tax in any amount, large or small, can be levied to support any religious activities or institutions, whatever they may be called, or whatever form they may adopt to teach or practice religion.

The problem with the establishment clause is that people disagree as to what actions can be construed as promoting or establishing religion. Much of the controversy relating to the establishment clause

Roger Williams (left), exiled for his criticism of the government, leaves Massachusetts Bay Colony. Anne Hutchinson (right) defends her religious beliefs before the colony's General Court.

has focused on the nation's schools. Two issues have been involved in the controversy: public aid to church-related private schools and religious exercises in public schools.

Aid to Religious Schools The *Everson* case involved a New Jersey law that provided funds for free bus transportation of students to the school they attended, whether public or parochial. The question before the Court was whether public financing of bus transportation for students in parochial or other church-related schools constituted aid to religion. In a 5–4 decision the Court narrowly upheld the New Jersey law as constitutional. The Court found that the policy was designed to promote the safety and welfare of the school students, not to benefit religion.

In later decisions, the Court upheld the loan of textbooks by a state to students attending parochial schools, but the providing of textbooks directly to parochial schools was found invalid. The Court ruled that state aid to support teachers' salaries in church-related schools was unconstitutional. It also struck down a law providing for reimbursement of tuition costs to parents of parochial school students.

Legislation providing any kind of government aid to church-related private schools has been controversial. In what case was bus transportation for parochial-school students upheld as constitutional by the Supreme Court?

The Constitution requires state neutrality toward religion, but neutrality may be viewed one way as support and another way as opposition. Recognizing the inconsistencies in many of the Court's decisions, Chief Justice Warren Burger remarked that "the line of separation, far from being a 'wall,' is a blurred, indistinct, and variable barrier depending on all the circumstances of a particular relationship."

Through various decisions over the years, the Court has evolved a test to judge the validity of a statute under the establishment clause. Justice Lewis Powell in 1973 stated the test. First, the law must have "a clearly secular legislative purpose"; second, it must have a "primary effect that neither advances nor inhibits religion"; and third, it "must avoid excessive government entanglement with religion."

Religion in Public Schools The Supreme Court held a state educational program invalid on the basis of the establishment clause for the first time in *McCollum* v. *Board of Education* (1948). Illinois permitted religious instruction by religious authorities during school hours within public school buildings. Although attendance at the religious classes was voluntary, students who did not participate had to leave the classroom. Ten-year-old Vashti McCollum protested, and the case reached the highest court. The Court ruled that the religious program was benefited by the state compulsory school attendance law. It thus violated the constitutional separation of church and state. In a later case, however, the Court upheld a New York program that released students from public school in order to attend religious classes off school property. The important distinction was that the program was not held on public property.

The most controversial issue arising from the separation of church and state involves prayer in the public schools. For over 100 years state courts had considered the legality of prayer and Bible readings in public schools. In about 25 percent of the cases, such practices had been found in violation of state constitutions. It was not until *Engle* v. *Vitale* (1962), however, that the Supreme Court confronted the problem.

The students in New Hyde Park, New York, were directed to start each day with a brief, nondenominational prayer: "Almighty God, we acknowledge our dependence upon Thee, and we beg Thy blessings upon us, our parents, our teachers, and our Country." The State Board of Regents had composed the prayer and recommended, though not required, its use in public school classrooms. The parents of 10 pupils challenged it as an official establishment of religion. With only one dissent the Supreme Court upheld their claim and ruled the Regents' prayer "wholly inconsistent with the establishment Clause." Speaking for the Court, Justice Black said:

It is neither sacrilegious nor antireligious to say that each separate government in this country should stay out of the business of writing or sanctioning official prayers and leave that purely religious function to the people themselves and to those the people look to for religious guidance. [The Establishment clause rests] on the belief that a union of government and religion tends to destroy government and to degrade religion.

In two subsequent cases Bible readings and the use of the Lord's Prayer in the public schools were challenged. The Supreme Court ruled that each violated the separation of church and state. Although the Court held that the study of the Bible in a secular context was desirable in the public schools, use of the Bible for religious purposes was ruled unconstitutional. "The place of religion in our society is an exalted one," said Justice Tom Clark, and, for that very reason, "the state is firmly committed to a position of neutrality."

The Free Exercise Clause

The First Amendment guarantees the "free exercise" of religion. Does this mean that *all* religious practices are to be free from government interference or limitation? What happens when people refuse to pay taxes, register for the draft, or send their children to school on the basis of religious beliefs?

Regulating of Actions The first major case on freedom of religion to come before the Supreme Court was *Reynolds* v. *United States* (1879). The Court made a distinction then between "belief" and "action." In this case the action to be regulated was the Mormon practice of polygamy (having several wives), a duty according to Mormon beliefs, but a crime by United States law. The Court held that while belief is always protected, action may be subject to government regulation for the health, safety, and convenience of the community.

In various cases the Court has upheld the protection of life and health against the free exercise of religion. A few religious groups oppose some or all forms of medical treatment as contrary to a belief in faith healing. Though an adult may refuse medical treatment because of religious beliefs, the Court has

Students in a turn-of-the-century classroom pledge allegiance to the flag. In what case was saluting the flag a matter of controversy? What was the constitutional basis of the Supreme Court's decision in the case?

required medical care for children even when opposed by their parents. Compulsory vaccination laws have been upheld, and parents have been prosecuted for refusing to comply.

In the Appalachian Mountains certain religious sects believe that the handling of poisonous snakes is a test of faith. During their worship services rattlesnakes are passed among the devout. On more than one occasion bitten worshippers have died. State laws have been passed against snake handling. These have been upheld by the state supreme courts, despite the claim that they interfere with the free exercise of religion.

While the Supreme Court has imposed certain restraints on the free exercise of religion, it has given special status to many practices based on religious belief. In one case, *West Virginia State Board of Education* v. *Barnette* (1943), the Court considered whether children in the public schools could be expelled for refusal on religious grounds to salute the flag. The children, members of the Jehovah's Witnesses, believed the flag to be a "graven image" and homage to it was forbidden by their religion. The Court reversed an earlier decision, and ruled in favor of the children. Justice Robert H. Jackson spoke for the Court.

If there is any fixed star in our constitutional constellation, it is that no official, high or petty, can prescribe what shall be orthodox in politics, nationalism, religion, or other matters of opinion or force citizens to confess by word or act their faith therein.

Preferential Status Issues In some cases the free exercise clause and the establishment clause conflict, presenting the Supreme Court with a fundamental problem. If certain individuals, because of their religious beliefs, are permitted to engage in behavior forbidden to other citizens, does this then constitute an establishment of religion? If religious practices are accorded special status, does that preference threaten the notion of equal protection under the law?

An additional problem arises when preferential status is given to actions based upon religious rather than ethical or other kinds of beliefs. The Court

An Amish youth in a horse-drawn cart exemplifies the traditional lifestyle of the Amish religious sect. Why has the Supreme Court exempted Amish children from compulsory school-attendance laws?

must decide when a belief is religious and when it is not, and even when and if a group is a religion.

The Court confronted the problem of preferential status in dealing with conscientious objection to war. The Selective Service Act established the draft of young men for military service. It had required that exemption from military service as a conscientious objector be extended only to members of an organized religion who believed in a Supreme Being. In other words, an ethical or philosophical opposition to war was not sufficient to claim status as a conscientious objector. In 1965 the Supreme Court gave religious belief as a basis for exemption a broader interpretation and employed an essentially "religious-blind" test. This meant that religious belief would be treated no differently than other forms of belief. All individuals who held strong beliefs in opposition to war—whether these beliefs were moral, ethical, philosophical, or religious—would be considered for exemption from military service. Then, in *Welsh* v. *United States* (1970), the Court ruled that Elliott Welsh did not have to base his application for status as a conscientious objector on belief in God or religious training. The Court declared that deeply held moral and ethical beliefs were as important as religious beliefs in determining sufficient grounds for exemption from the draft. The Court had recognized a person's moral and ethical beliefs as a form of unorganized personal religion.

The Court encountered a different problem in *Wisconsin* v. *Yoder* (1972). The case involved conflict between Amish people and the state compulsory school attendance policy. The Amish refused to send their children to school for formal education beyond the eighth grade because it was contrary to their beliefs. Compelled attendance, they argued, would destroy their church-community by forcing inappropriate modern values on the Amish children. If the exemption were granted, the state argued, it would give preference to the religious beliefs of the Amish at the expense of a useful social policy, that of education for all children. It would also give preference to the Amish over those who might object to compulsory school laws for nonreligious reasons.

Chief Justice Warren Burger gave the decision for the Court. Employing a balancing test, he argued that "only those interests of the highest order . . . can override legitimate claims to the free exercise of religion." The Chief Justice emphasized the role of tradition among the Amish: "three centuries as an identifiable religious sect and a long history as a successful and self-sufficient segment of American society." In the judgment of the Court the Amish had successfully demonstrated the interrelationship of their religious beliefs with their way of life. Compulsory school attendance threatened the survival of the Amish community. In weighing these values against the state interest in education, the Court sided with the Amish and the free expression of religion.

Over the long history of disputes about freedom of religion, the Supreme Court has established one dominant pattern. When the person involved has demonstrated deep and sincere belief, that person's right to follow his or her belief has by and large been protected.

Section Check

1. Define: separation of church and state, establishment clause, free exercise clause
2. Identify: *Everson* v. *Board of Education* (1947), *Engle* v. *Vitale* (1962), *Reynolds* v. *United States* (1879)
3. What are some foundations of the separation of church and state in America?
4. How has the court dealt with the issue of conscientious objection to military service? Compulsory school attendance *v.* religious beliefs?

---

5 THE RIGHT OF PRIVACY

The right of privacy is not mentioned in the First Amendment, or in fact anywhere in the Constitution. In recent years, however, the Supreme Court has recognized that all Americans have a fundamental right to personal privacy. This right is not absolute and is nowhere specifically defined. Portions of its full meaning have been drawn by judicial interpretation from several sources. These sources include the First Amendment, in its protection of freedom of belief; the Fourth Amendment, which protects the individual from unreasonable searches and seizures; and the Ninth Amendment.

The Ninth Amendment

The First Congress wanted to emphasize that the listing of civil liberties in the Bill of Rights should not be taken as a complete listing of *all* rights belonging to the people. Thus the Ninth Amendment stressed that other, unnamed rights are protected from government interference. The Ninth Amendment reads:

> *The enumeration in the Constitution, of certain rights, shall not be construed to deny or disparage others retained by the people.*

What are these unnamed rights?

Perhaps because it was so broadly written, the Ninth Amendment was virtually ignored until 1965. In that year the Court held the Ninth Amendment to be a foundation of the ***right of privacy***—the right to be left alone, perhaps the most fundamental personal freedom. The Court's decision drew strong dissent from the minority on the bench. Many constitutional scholars also felt uneasy with the notion

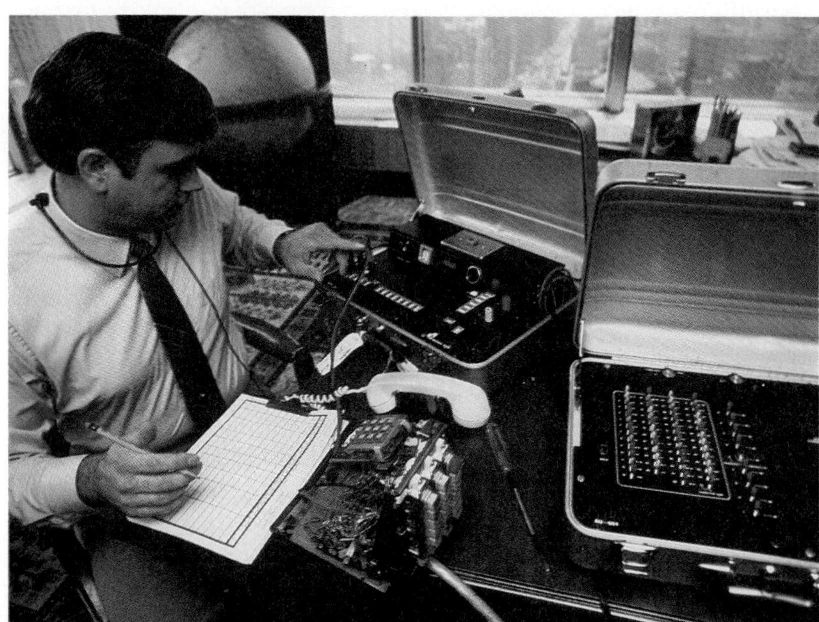

Modern technological equipment makes telephone surveillance, or wiretapping, possible. The Supreme Court has found that some kinds of surveillance violate the right of privacy. What is the constitutional basis of this right?

of a "right of privacy." What did this include? What were its scope and limitations? The possibilities for conflicting rights seemed staggering to some jurists.

Where, for example, is the boundary between a free press and the right to privacy? The right to privacy entered constitutional debate through the efforts of Justice Louis Brandeis to protect individual privacy from invasion by newspapers. He argued that people's private lives should be just that—private. The Court, however, has also been protective of freedom of the press. It has held that if a story is "newsworthy," privacy falls in favor of the press. But in its rulings, the Court has not been consistent. In different cases it has ruled in favor of each side.

Zones of Privacy

Certain "zones of privacy" are now given constitutional protection. Beyond those specifically guaranteed in the Bill of Rights, these include freedom of thought and belief; freedom from government surveillance; privacy of personal information from government disclosure; and privacy of home and family.

Freedom of Thought and Belief This rests on the premise that individuals should be free to develop and express their own personalities, interests, and tastes, free from government control.

ISSUES

Privacy *Versus* Computers

The federal government today maintains more than 3.5 billion separate files on its citizens—or an average of 15 files for each American. Additional files—the total number is not known—are kept by state and local government agencies. Even more data is amassed by private groups. Banks, insurance companies, and other firms keep hundreds of millions of files of information on Americans. This enormous collection of information, stored and transmitted by computers, enables government and business to plan and operate more efficiently. But the great number of computer files on individuals also raises a serious question: Who may use the private information in these files?

A recent study disclosed that 79 percent of all banks, 47 percent of insurance companies, and 58 percent of other large companies voluntarily disclose the information they collect about individual Americans to government agencies. Government agencies also share the data they gather. For example, the Internal Revenue Service and the Social Security Administration are required by law to disclose taxpayers' names and addresses to Selective Service officials to help them locate draft-age men. In 1982 the Social Security Administration gained access to Internal Revenue Service files in order to check the tax records of social security recipients. In many cases information gathered for one purpose was being exchanged and used for other, sometimes very different purposes. And while public and private agencies readily share the information they collect, individuals are often prevented from examining their own files. Though most insurance companies allow individuals to confirm the information contained in their files, only 28 percent of banks and 25 percent of other private firms have similar policies.

As new technology makes the gathering and processing of information even easier, the task of protecting the individual's right of privacy will become more difficult. In the words of the 1977 U.S. Privacy Protection Study Commission, "New avenues and needs for collection of information . . . multiply the dangers of official abuse against which the Constitution seeks to protect."

Government Surveillance In a free society people must be secure in the knowledge that they are not being spied upon by the government. Surveillance by government authorities breeds fear. It undermines the institutions of free expression upon which liberty and democracy rest. This guarantee becomes even more crucial with the development of sophisticated equipment for wiretapping.

Public Disclosure of Personal Data The government amasses a vast amount of information on each citizen. This includes census data, income tax records, and the grades a person receives in school or college. How such information is to be used and by whom are major concerns of all people who value privacy and personal freedom. In 1974 Congress passed the Privacy Act. The law limits the kinds of records that may be kept. It also limits public disclosure of personal information.

In addition, the Privacy Act permits individuals to find out what information the government may have about them. Thus mistaken information may be corrected. Private organizations—banks, insurance companies, and credit bureaus—also maintain files on individuals. The type of information secured, its use, and its availability to others is subject to law. Again, individuals have the right to find out what information is held and whether it is correct.

Privacy of Home and Family This rests on the belief that the privacy of family matters, of the relationship between husband and wife, is fundamental to the family as a social institution.

Justice Abe Fortas expressed his understanding of the right of privacy in these words:

It is, simply stated, the right to be left alone; to live one's life as one chooses, free from assault, intrusion or invasion except as they can be justified by the clear needs of a community living under a government of law.

Section Check

---

1. What does the Ninth Amendment guarantee?
2. What are four zones of privacy?
3. Why is it important for citizens to have freedom of thought and belief?
4. How may the amassing of data in computer files violate zones of privacy?

SUMMARY

The American political system is a form of limited government. The Bill of Rights places some of the most important limitations on government. The first 10 amendments to the Constitution protect the civil liberties of Americans. Among the most important civil liberties are those protected by the First Amendment.

The First Amendment is the foundation of liberty under law. It protects the freedoms of expression, worship, peaceable assembly, and political protest. Although some legal experts disagree, more jurists feel that First Amendment rights are not absolute. Most jurists apply the "balancing doctrine," weighing the basic civil rights against other rights and social considerations with which the basic civil rights may conflict.

The freedoms of speech and of the press are best understood in terms of their limitations. These freedoms have been limited when national security has been threatened, when materials are considered obscene, when the reputation of another has been damaged, and when the right to a fair trial may be affected. Yet, despite some limitations, the Supreme Court has in recent years broadened the protection of these basic freedoms.

Freedom of assembly is fundamental in a democracy to permit individuals to form associations to gain political recognition and power. The key element in assembly rulings is that the First Amendment specifically allows only "peaceable" gatherings. Assemblies may also be forbidden where they may interfere with the process of justice, such as in courtrooms or jails. Parades and other similar assemblies may be regulated by permits.

The First Amendment guarantees religious freedom precisely because the American people so cherish their diverse beliefs. The First Amendment section on religion contains two clauses. One prohibits the state from acting to establish any one religion; the other permits the free exercise of religious practice. The courts have ruled that religion may not be practiced in public schools. The courts have also made a distinction between religious belief and religious action. Belief is always protected, but action may be regulated for the health, safety, and convenience of the community.

The right to privacy is not mentioned anywhere in the Constitution. Nevertheless, recent Supreme Court rulings involving a new interpretation of the Ninth Amendment have recognized privacy as a fundamental right.

Chapter 5 Review

Using Vocabulary

Answer the questions using the meaning of each underlined term.

1. Of what importance is due process as a guarantee of a person's civil liberties?
2. How does change of venue, gag order, and sequestering help assure a person of a fair trial?
3. Where is the boundary between freedom of the press and the right to privacy?
4. How is freedom of speech limited by libel and slander and by community standards of obscenity?
5. What is the relationship between civil disobedience and passive resistance?

Understanding American Government

1. How has the Bill of Rights been extended by the Supreme Court?
2. What is the "balancing doctrine"?
3. What is the meaning of the clear-and-present-danger test?
4. What are some limits on the freedom of assembly?
5. What issues have most often been involved in cases connected with the establishment clause?
6. What are some examples of the Supreme Court upholding protection of life and health over the free exercise of religion?
7. How has the Supreme Court ruled on the conflict between freedom of the press and the right of privacy?
8. What are some zones of privacy? Why have they been given constitutional protection?

Extending Your Skills: Understanding a Quotation

Review the quotation from Justice Hugo Black's dissent in the *Dennis* case on page 138. Then answer the following items.

1. Explain the meaning of the terms *keystone, reasonableness*, and *orthodoxy*.
2. A statement that best expresses the major argument of Justice Black's dissent is (a) The First Amendment particularly protects unpopular ideas. (b) The First Amendment needs to be reinterpreted. (c) The First Amendment guarantees free expression of only popular ideas.
3. A statement that Justice Black might support is (a) "Extremism in defense of liberty is no vice." (b) "I disagree with what you say, but I'll defend your right to say it." (c) "The greater good excuses minor evils."

Government and You

1. How would the United States be different if its citizens were not guaranteed the basic rights protected by the First Amendment? Which one of these fundamental protections do you consider the most important? Why?
2. A few years ago a publication provided a great deal of information on how to construct a hydrogen bomb. Should such information be withheld because of national security? Does freedom of the press guarantee the right to print any story?
3. If the media influence public opinion about persons accused of crimes, would it be better if all criminal cases were closed to the public? What problems might develop from such a practice?

Activities

1. Prepare a report on Supreme Court Justice Oliver Wendell Holmes. Include some of his most famous statements in the report.
2. Interview a local newspaper reporter or editor. Ask his or her opinion on gag rules. Ask what is the most important current issue involving freedom of the press. Then share a report of the interview with the class.
3. Write an essay on the topic "Fundamental rights are limited rights."
4. Make a study chart of the fundamental civil liberties discussed in this chapter. Include the limits of each of these liberties. Include important Supreme Court decisions involving each of these liberties.

Chapter 6

Equality Under Law

Four score and seven years ago, our fathers brought forth on this continent a new nation, conceived in Liberty, and dedicated to the proposition that all men are created equal.

ABRAHAM LINCOLN

CHAPTER OVERVIEW

1 SOCIAL INJUSTICE: A TRAGEDY OF BROKEN PROMISES
The Civil War Amendments / Jim Crow Laws / *Plessy* v. *Ferguson:* "Separate But Equal"

2 SCHOOL DESEGREGATION: STIRRINGS OF EQUALITY
Brown v. *Board of Education* / *De Facto* Segregation and the Busing Controversy

3 THE CIVIL RIGHTS MOVEMENT
The Montgomery Bus Boycott / The Civil Rights Act of 1964 / Urban Violence and Black Militancy

4 VOTING RIGHTS: POWER OF THE BALLOT
Disfranchisement of Southern Blacks / Selma and the Voting Rights Act of 1965

5 THE WOMEN'S MOVEMENT FOR EQUAL RIGHTS
The Equal Rights Struggle / Legislating Women's Rights

6 AFFIRMATIVE ACTION

Slave labor was the basis of the South's economy, but slaves had no economic, social, or political rights. They were in total bondage to their owners. By 1860 almost 4 million slaves were working in the South, mostly in the cotton fields of sprawling plantations.

1 SOCIAL INJUSTICE: A TRAGEDY OF BROKEN PROMISES

First Amendment rights guarantee equality under law. Yet for many Americans equality has been a promise, not a reality. Blacks, Hispanics, Asians, Indians, women—all these groups and more—have been denied "equal protection of the laws" despite the guarantees of the Constitution.

To its credit, American government has grappled earnestly in recent times with problems of inequality. The courts, the Executive Branch, the Congress, and the American people themselves, in this century, have begun the struggle for political and social equality. This chapter is the story of that struggle.

The Declaration of Independence proclaimed that "all men are created equal." Yet in 1776 ours was a society divided between free persons and black slaves. The Framers of the Constitution denied Congress the power to outlaw the slave trade before 1808. Not until 1865 was slavery made illegal by the Thirteenth Amendment. The last two centuries of black American history show not a steady rise to equality, but rather a troubling sequence of bright beginnings and false starts, of victories and setbacks, of honorable vows and broken promises.

The first landmark Supreme Court case involving blacks was the *Dred Scott* decision of 1857. In 1846 a black man named Dred Scott and his wife sued for their freedom from slavery in a Missouri court. Scott claimed that he had become a free man in 1834 when his owner brought him to Illinois, a place where slavery was illegal. The case became quite complicated and finally reached the Supreme Court.

Chief Justice Roger B. Taney led a ruling against Dred Scott. Taney declared that blacks were not American citizens, and thus had no right to bring suit in federal court. Taney went on to add that it was illegal to forbid slavery in the western territories as had been done in Illinois. Such a move would

In 1857 the Supreme Court ruled against Dred Scott. What did Chief Justice Taney and the Court determine about citizenship and slavery in the Dred Scott *case?*

be, Taney said, in violation of the Fifth Amendment, which requires that "no person shall be . . . deprived of life, liberty, or property without due process of law." Slaves, reasoned Taney, were a form of property. The *Dred Scott* decision created a storm of protest from all Americans opposed to slavery.

The Civil War Amendments

In 1863, during the Civil War, President Abraham Lincoln issued the Emancipation Proclamation. It stated that "all persons held as slaves within any States . . . in rebellion against the United States shall be . . . forever free." It did not serve to free the slaves in Maryland, Missouri, Kentucky, or in parts of the South controlled by the Union army.

The total abolition of slavery came with the passage of the Thirteenth Amendment in 1865. The Fourteenth Amendment, ratified in 1868, reversed the *Dred Scott* decision. It gave citizenship to blacks and extended the protection of the Constitution to them. Its words are among the most important in constitutional law.

No state shall make or enforce any law which shall abridge the privileges and immunities of citizens of the United States; nor shall any State deprive any person of life, liberty, or property, without due process of law; nor deny to any person within its jurisdiction the equal protection of the laws.

The Fifteenth Amendment, ratified in 1870, extended the right to vote to freed male slaves. It guaranteed that no citizen could be denied the right to vote "on account of race, color, or previous condition of servitude."

Each of the three Civil War amendments stated that Congress shall have the power to enforce its provisions with appropriate legislation. Between 1866 and 1875 Congress passed a series of civil rights acts that were intended to give blacks immediate equality. The Civil Rights Act of 1875 was the most far-reaching. It sought to prevent discrimination against blacks in such places of public accommodation as hotels, restaurants, and theaters, and in trains and other transport vehicles.

In 1883 the Supreme Court declared the Civil Rights Act of 1875 unconstitutional. The Fourteenth Amendment, it said, applied only to *state* action. It did not permit Congress to forbid discrimination by *private* individuals. In a series of decisions known as the Civil Rights Cases, the Court's narrow interpretation took the heart and force out of the Fourteenth Amendment.

Jim Crow Laws

Federal troops had been withdrawn from the South in 1877 ending the rebuilding period known as Reconstruction. Civil rights protections were then gradually dismantled—first in practice ***(de facto)***, then by law ***(de jure)***. Most blacks were poor and economically dependent upon whites. They had been denied education and lacked organization and leadership. By fraud, force, and economic pressure, blacks were kept from the polls. By law and intimidation, they were excluded from juries. They became second-class citizens.

Injustice in the courts was widespread. Blacks were more likely to be convicted than white defendants and faced far harsher penalties than whites for the same kind of crime. Particularly for crimes against whites, justice had a heavy hand. Mob rule often displaced the law altogether. The hooded knights of the Ku Klux Klan brought terror and death to blacks who dared to assert their constitutional rights. In the 20 years after the Court's 1883 Civil Rights Cases, there were some 2,000 ***lynchings,*** or illegal hangings, of blacks.

Against this backdrop of violence, southern state legislatures began to enact laws to support the practice of racial discrimination and to ensure white supremacy. Known as Jim Crow laws, they required ***segregation*** of the races in public facilities. Many

ABRAHAM LINCOLN

AND HIS

Emancipation Proclamation

Whereas On the Twenty-second day of September, in the year of our Lord one thousand eight hundred and sixty-two, a Proclamation was issued by the President of the United States, containing among other things the following, to-wit:

"That on the first day of January, in the year of our Lord one thousand eight hundred and sixty-three, all persons held as slaves within any State, or designated part of a State, the people whereof shall then be in rebellion against the United States, shall be then, thenceforward and forever free, and the executive government of the United States, including the military and naval authority thereof, will recognize and maintain the freedom of such persons, and will do no act or acts to repress such persons, or any of them, in any efforts they may make for their actual freedom.

"That the executive will, on the first day of January aforesaid, by proclamation, designate the States and parts of States, if any, in which the people thereof respectively shall then be in rebellion against the United States, and the fact that any State, or the people thereof, shall on that day be in good faith represented in the Congress of the United States by members chosen thereto at elections wherein a majority of the qualified voters of such State shall have participated, shall, in the absence of strong countervailing testimony, be deemed conclusive evidence that such State and the people thereof are not then in rebellion against the United States."

Now, therefore, I, ABRAHAM LINCOLN, President of the United States, by virtue of the power in me vested as Commander-in-Chief of the Army and Navy of the United States in time of actual armed rebellion against the authority and government of the United States, and as a fit and necessary war measure for suppressing said rebellion, do, on this first day of January, in the year of our Lord one thousand eight hundred and sixty-three, and in accordance with my purpose so to do, publicly proclaim for the full period of one hundred days from the day the first above mentioned order, and designate as the States and parts of States wherein the people thereof respectively are this day in rebellion against the United States, the following, to-wit:

ARKANSAS, TEXAS, LOUISIANA (except the parishes of St. Bernard, Plaquemines, Jefferson, St. John, St. Charles, St. James, Ascension, Assumption, Terre Bonne, Lafourche, St. Mary, St. Martin, and Orleans, including the city of New Orleans), MISSISSIPPI, ALABAMA, FLORIDA, GEORGIA, SOUTH CAROLINA, NORTH CAROLINA and VIRGINIA (except the forty-eight counties designated as West Virginia, and also the counties of Berkley, Accomac, Northampton, Elizabeth City, York, Princess Ann and Norfolk, including the cities of Norfolk and Portsmouth), and which excepted parts are, for the present, left precisely as if this Proclamation were not issued.

And by virtue of the power and for the purpose aforesaid, I do order and declare that all persons held as slaves within said designated States and parts of States are and henceforward shall be free; and that the executive government of the United States, including the military and naval authorities thereof, will recognize and maintain the freedom of said persons.

And I hereby enjoin upon the people so declared to be free, to abstain from all violence, unless in necessary self-defence, and I recommend to them that in all cases, when allowed, they labor faithfully for reasonable wages.

And I further declare and make known that such persons of suitable condition, will be received into the armed service of the United States to garrison forts, positions, stations and other places, and to man vessels of all sorts in said service.

And upon this act, sincerely believed to be an act of justice, warranted by the Constitution, upon military necessity, I invoke the considerate judgment of mankind, and the gracious favor of Almighty God.

In testimony whereof, I have hereunto set my name, and caused the seal of the United States to be affixed.

L.S.

Done at the City of Washington, this first day of January, in the year of our Lord one thousand eight hundred and sixty-three, and of the Independence of the United States the eighty-Seventh.

By the President: ABRAHAM LINCOLN.

WILLIAM H. SEWARD, Secretary of State.

NOTE.—The rest of the slaves were afterwards freed by Legislation and Constitutional Amendments.

white southerners opposed the bigotry and unfairness of the Jim Crow laws, but their voices were not heeded. Northerners, for the most part, were indifferent to what was going on in the South.

Plessy v. *Ferguson:* "Separate But Equal"

Between 1887 and 1891 eight southern states passed laws requiring railroads to maintain separate cars or sections for white and "colored" races. Then, in 1892, a group of blacks organized a Citizens' Committee to challenge the constitutionality of Louisiana's Jim Crow railroad law. They argued that the segregation laws were a denial of "equal protection," as guaranteed by the Fourteenth Amendment. To bring a test case before the Court, Homer Plessy boarded the train in New Orleans. He took a seat in the "Whites Only" car. When asked to move, Plessy refused and was arrested.

In the landmark case of *Plessy* v. *Ferguson* (1896) the Supreme Court upheld the Louisiana law. The Court declared that the Fourteenth Amendment "could not have been intended to abolish distinctions based upon color, or to enforce social, as distinguished from political equality, or a commingling of the two races upon terms unsatisfactory to either." Segregation could be required by law so long as the separate facilities were equal.

Only one justice, John Marshall Harlan, dissented. He denounced the separation of the races as "a badge of servitude." It was wholly inconsistent, he said, with freedom and equal protection of the laws. In eloquent defense of the rights of all Americans, Harlan stated:

In view of the Constitution, in the eye of the law, there is in this country no superior, dominant, ruling class of citizens. There is no caste here. Our Constitution is color-blind, and neither knows nor tolerates classes among its citizens. In respect of civil rights, all citizens are equal before the law.

The core of the majority opinion in *Plessy* v. *Ferguson* was the ***separate but equal doctrine.*** This became the foundation upon which the institution of segregation in the South was built and extended in the early twentieth century. Racial segregation was required by law in almost every form of public accommodation. There were separate Jim Crow hotels, restaurants, theaters, parks, jails, hospitals, and schools. There were separate restrooms and water fountains. In buses blacks sat at the back in the "colored" section. Where once blacks and whites had freely associated, law now forbade contact. One southern city even passed an ordinance making it "unlawful" for a black and a white person to play checkers or dominoes together.

Justice John Marshall Harlan was a defender of civil rights. His dissent in Plessy v. Ferguson *(1896) foreshadowed the Court's opinion in the landmark decision of* Brown v. Board of Education *(1954).*

In the North, despite laws forbidding discrimination, most hotels, restaurants, and theaters practiced ***de facto segregation*** and refused service to blacks. Contact between the races was limited. Here, too, blacks and whites lived in separate but very unequal worlds.

In housing, de facto segregation retricted blacks to certain neighborhoods. In the South local laws drew distinct boundaries. When blacks moved north, social pressure forced them into urban ghettos. Many areas, particularly in the suburbs, were closed to blacks (and often to Jews and Asian Americans, as well) by ***restrictive covenants.*** These were agreements, enforced by the courts, requiring that certain properties be sold only to whites. Throughout the United States there were communities with no black residents. In some of these, curfew laws made it a crime for a black person even to be in the town after dark.

Racial discrimination restricted employment opportunities for blacks. They were given the jobs no one else wanted. Even for the same work, blacks often received lower wages than whites. They were usually the "last hired and the first fired." Most labor unions excluded blacks from membership. In many cases management limited advancement for black employees, closing white collar and executive positions to them. Blacks fared little better in government employment. Even in the military, blacks were segregated and usually assigned menial tasks.

Section Check

1. Define: de facto segregation, lynching, restrictive covenant
2. Identify: Dred Scott decision, Roger B. Taney, Thirteenth Amendment, Fourteenth Amendment, Fifteenth Amendment, Jim Crow laws
3. Why did Justice Harlan dissent in *Plessy* v. *Ferguson* (1896)?
4. What doctrine provided the central idea for the majority ruling in *Plessy* v. *Ferguson?*

W. E. B. Du Bois was a founder of the National Association for the Advancement of Colored People. He advocated education and political solidarity for blacks.

2 SCHOOL DESEGREGATION: STIRRINGS OF EQUALITY

Despite incredible obstacles, black people sought to overcome the barriers of segregation and prejudice. In 1900, 90 percent of all blacks lived in the South and border states. Most were rural. During World War I they began to move north in search of education and employment. Within the South blacks moved to the cities in hope of advancement. An urban middle class of blacks, determined to secure first-class citizenship, emerged during these years.

Black leaders rightfully saw education as the proper battleground to fight the separate but equal rule. Education was the key to all sorts of opportunities for blacks—to earn a living, to contribute to American culture, and to affect the country's political destiny. "We want our children educated," announced black leader W. E. B. Du Bois as early as 1906. "They have a right to think, to know, to aspire."

Yet educational opportunities for blacks were limited during the first half of the twentieth century. In the South, schools were segregated by law. They were separate, but they were not equal. Black schools were almost always inferior to those of whites. State funding for black schools was meager. The expenditure per pupil for blacks was only one third of that spent for whites. The buildings in black schools typically were old, rundown, and overcrowded. Black teachers were paid less than white teachers. Some counties had no black high school at all. Higher education, when it was available, was often no more than vocational training. Segregated schools tended to keep blacks in ignorance and to perpetuate racial myths and stereotypes that promoted prejudice and segregation.

In the 1930's blacks turned to the courts to challenge discrimination in public schools and universities. The Supreme Court did not overturn the separate but equal doctrine. Instead, on a case-by-case basis, the Court examined the facts of each situation. Where black schools were below standard, the Court ordered that facilities be made equal.

Graduate and professional schools presented a special problem. In 1938 Missouri was required to admit blacks to its white law school because no separate facility for blacks was available. Not until 1950 was there another breakthrough. The case arose from the application of a black for admission to the all-white University of Texas Law School. The Court found that the separate law school provided by Texas for blacks was in no way equal in quality or facilities to that provided for whites. On the basis of the equal protection clause of the Fourteenth Amendment, the Court ordered the admission of qualified blacks to the University of Texas Law School.

Brown v. *Board of Education*

The landmark case in school desegregation was *Brown* v. *Board of Education of Topeka* (1954). A black welder named Oliver Brown was angered when his eight-year-old daughter was forced to attend a distant all-black school, while only seven blocks from Mr. Brown's home was the Sumner Elementary School. Oliver Brown wanted his daughter to go to Sumner, but school officials refused his request. A leading civil rights organization, the National Association for the Advancement of Colored People (NAACP), helped Mr. Brown take his case all the way to the Supreme Court.

In a unanimous decision the Supreme Court declared racial segregation in public schools to be unconstitutional, thus overturning the separate but equal doctrine of *Plessy* v. *Ferguson.* The lone dissent of Justice John Marshall Harlan was finally vindicated. In the *Brown* decision the Court held that segregated schools were not and could never be equal. To separate children "solely because of their race," wrote Chief Justice Earl Warren, "generates a feeling of inferiority as to their status in the community that may affect their hearts and minds in a way unlikely ever to be undone. . . . Separate education facilities are inherently unequal."

The Supreme Court did not order immediate desegregation. It recognized that the historic *Brown* decision involved "problems of considerable complexity." But one year later, school authorities were directed to begin desegregation "with all deliberate speed." Local federal courts were to supervise the transition.

A few school systems voluntarily desegregated. Most resisted in open defiance. Public feeling, especially in the Deep South, was intense. The Court's decision was seen by many whites as a threat to their way of life. By various means southern states sought to avoid desegregation. In some districts the public schools were closed. Segregated private schools were opened in their place. Other schools permitted "token integration," by which no more than, say, half a dozen black students would be admitted to a previously all-white school. The rest of the school system remained fully segregated.

A schoolroom for blacks in the 1940's exemplifies the inherent inequality of segregation. Some states required separate textboks for blacks and for whites. Describe some other forms of discrimination against black students.

In 1957 a Federal judge ordered the admission of nine black students to the white Central High School in Little Rock, Arkansas. Governer Orval Faubus ordered the state National Guard to prevent the black children from entering the school. The federal court ordered the governor to remove the National Guard. When riots broke out, President Eisenhower acted swiftly by sending regular army units to restore law and order and to enforce the court order to desegregate. In 1962 President Kennedy took a similar action to enforce the integration of the University of Mississippi. In a televised address to the nation he said:

Americans are free to disagree with the law, but not to disobey it. For in a government of laws and not of men, no man, however prominent or powerful, and no mob, however unruly or boisterous, is entitled to defy a court of law.

Congress backed the Court decisions with legislation. The Civil Rights Act of 1964 was the most sweeping civil rights bill since Reconstruction. The act authorized the Justice Department to bring legal action to desegregate schools. Private citizens were no longer forced to bring suit on behalf of their children. More important, the act gave the government a powerful weapon for enforcement because it allowed the federal government to withdraw financial support if a school district was found to be practicing discrimination. To receive federal funds, schools had to comply with desegregation orders.

De Facto Segregation and the Busing Controversy

In 1969, 15 years after the *Brown* decision, only 20 percent of all black students in the South attended integrated schools. The Supreme Court, now under Chief Justice Warren Burger, said that continued racial segregation in public schools must end "at once." In rural areas of the South, integration was rapidly achieved without violence simply by assigning pupils of both races to the nearest school. The cities presented a different and more difficult problem. In urban areas both North and South the inner cities were populated more and more by blacks. Middle-class whites were moving to the suburbs. The result was an especially persistent form of de facto segregation.

By escorting black students into Little Rock Central High School, federal troops enforce court-ordered desegregation. President Eisenhower's use of federal troops in this crisis illustrated that national law is the supreme law of the land.

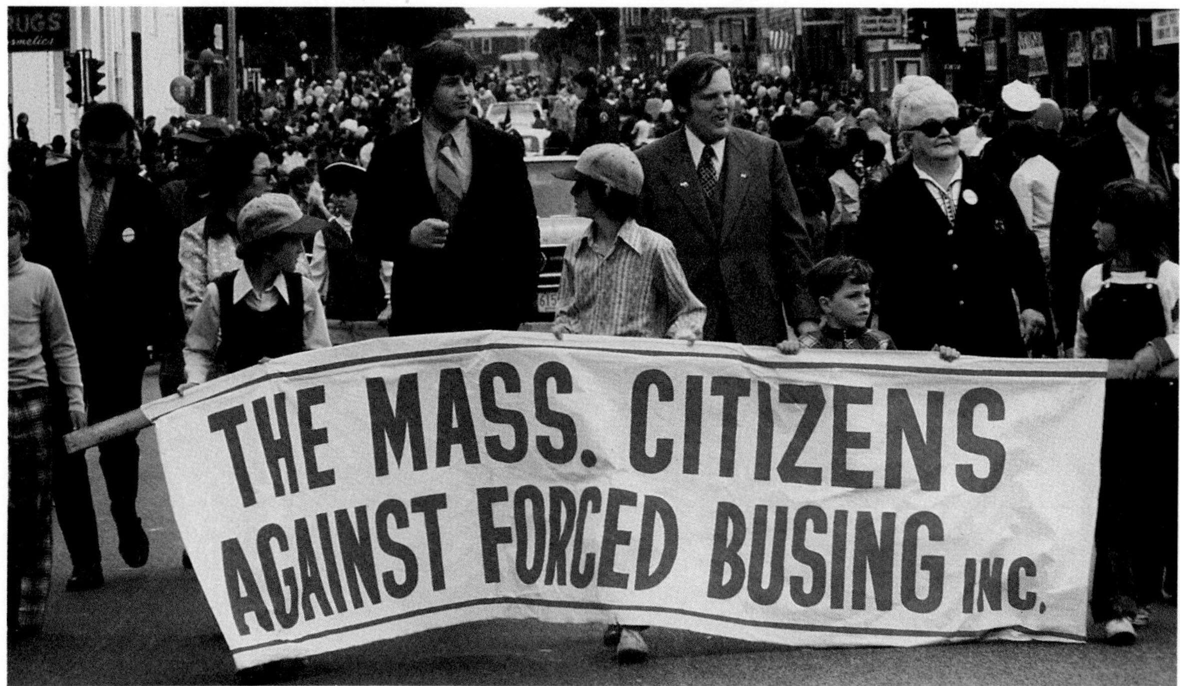

Following the Supreme Court's decision in 1971 to allow busing in order to achieve integration, citizen opposition in urban areas was often intense. Why has the Supreme Court sometimes viewed busing as a tool for achieving racial balance?

In *Swann* v. *Charlotte-Mecklenburg Board of Education* (1971) the Supreme Court decided that busing could be used to integrate urban schools. Busing means that students may be transported far out of their local neighborhoods to achieve racial balance in schools. Chief Justice Burger spoke for the unanimous Court.

All things being equal, with no history of discrimination, it might be desirable to assign pupils to schools nearest their homes. But all things are not equal in a system that has been deliberately constructed and maintained to enforce racial segregation.

The yellow school bus is an American tradition. Each day 20 million students ride it to school. Fewer than 3 percent of these students ride buses due to court orders. Yet when busing was ordered to achieve integration, the school bus became a symbol of bitter controversy. In some cities buses were burned, and angry crowds demonstrated their opposition.

The busing issue is complex. When neighborhoods are themselves segregated, neighborhood schools reinforce racial separation. Busing was seen by the courts as the only reasonable tool for achieving desegregation. But in the mid-1970's polls showed that 75 percent of all whites and 47 percent of all blacks opposed busing for racial integration. Many feared that busing would destroy the integrity and tradition of urban neighborhoods.

Recent decisions indicate that the courts in the United States are not committed to busing at any cost. Other avenues for reducing segregation in urban areas are being explored. Elimination of segregated schools continues to be a high priority. Justice Thurgood Marshall underscored his own commitment to racial integration in these words: "Unless our children begin to learn together, there is little hope that our people will ever learn to live together."

Section Check

1. Identify: *Brown* v. *Board of Education of Topeka*, NAACP, Civil Rights Act of 1964, *Swann* v. *Charlotte-Mecklenburg Board of Education*
2. What reason did Chief Justice Burger give for the Supreme Court's decision that busing could be used to integrate schools?
3. What action did President Eisenhower take to enforce the integration of schools in Little Rock, Arkansas?

3 THE CIVIL RIGHTS MOVEMENT

The desegregation of public schools was but one aspect of a nationwide movement toward racial equality. This struggle is known as the Civil Rights Movement.

In 1947 President Harry S Truman's Committee on Civil Rights issued a report entitled *To Secure These Rights.* It called for strong government action to end racial discrimination. The report challenged the nation to fulfill the promise of equality for black Americans. It demanded first of all that government itself not discriminate. Second, it demanded that government act to protect the civil rights of all citizens against actions by private individuals.

In 1948 President Truman, exercising his duties as commander in chief of the armed forces issued an executive order ending segregation in the armed forces. Another order required that all federal jobs be distributed without regard to "race, color, religion, or national origin." In addition, the government forbade any business holding a government contract to discriminate in hiring practices. The President also recommended civil rights legislation to Congress. In the Senate, however, southern Democrats successfully defeated each measure. Not until 1957 did Congress enact the first civil rights bill since Reconstruction.

The Montgomery Bus Boycott

The 1954 school desegregation decision had been a major legal victory for blacks. Segregation, however, remained a fact of daily life. Progress was slow; blacks were frustrated and impatient. They adopted the slogan "Freedom Now."

One evening in 1955 Rosa Parks, a black woman, boarded an empty city bus in Montgomery, Alabama. Tired, she refused to go to the back of the bus when a white passenger got on. She was arrested. Under the leadership of Ms. Parks's pastor, the Reverend Dr. Martin Luther King, Jr., the blacks of Montgomery united in a boycott of the city's buses. Blacks throughout the nation were inspired by Dr. King and by Parks's show of determination and courage. The boycott continued for more than one year. Dr. King was arrested, and his home was bombed. The bus boycott ended with a decision by the Supreme Court outlawing segregation in public transportation. The message was clear: all forms of state-imposed segregation were unconstitutional.

The civil rights movement began to gather momentum. Dr. King formed the Southern Christian Leadership Conference (SCLC) to continue the struggle. The SCLC was guided by the philosophy of nonviolence, a belief that love was more powerful than hatred or violence. Its commitment was reflected in the spiritual "We Shall Overcome." King

After her arrest for having violated segregation laws in Montgomery, Alabama, Rosa Parks (right) is fingerprinted. How did Rosa Parks's courage lead to progress in the civil rights movement?

The 1963 March on Washington was the largest mass rally ever held on behalf of racial equality. The event drew attention to the concerns of blacks and ultimately prompted Congress to pass the 1964 Civil Rights Act and the 1965 Voting Rights Act.

was soon joined by other groups committed to "direct action"—the Congress of Racial Equality (CORE) and the Student Nonviolent Coordinating Committee (SNCC). This direct approach complemented that of the NAACP, which relied more on court battles and legislative reform to effect change.

The direct action groups used boycotts and demonstrations to focus attention on discrimination and racial injustice. In 1960 the first "sit-in" was staged. A group of black students sat down at a store lunch counter in Greensboro, North Carolina. They were refused service, but they stayed. They were insulted, spat upon, and pelted with food by hostile whites. Each day, joined by other black and white students, they returned to the lunch counter. The sit-in, as a movement, spread throughout the South. Within six months lunch counters and restaurants began serving blacks. "Freedom Riders" employed a similar tactic to expose segregation in interstate bus service and terminals.

In 1963 Dr. Martin Luther King, Jr., began a series of orderly street marches in Birmingham, Alabama. The object was a "minimum program" of racial justice, particularly fair employment opportunities. The marchers were met with fire hoses and police dogs. More than 2,500 demonstrators, including many children, were arrested.

Dr. King then led a "March on Washington for Jobs and Freedom." More than 200,000 Americans, black and white, gathered before the Lincoln Memorial. King's words were to become a classic statement of freedom.

I have a dream that one day this nation will rise up and live out the true meaning of its creed. . . .

I have a dream . . . that my four little children will one day live in a nation where they will not be judged by the color of their skin but by the content of their character. . . .

*So let freedom ring. When we let freedom ring, when we let it ring from every village and every hamlet, from every state and every city, we will be able to speed up that day when all of God's children, black men and white men, Jews and Gentiles, Protestants and Catholics, will be able to join hands and sing in the words of the old Negro spiritual, "Free at last! Free at last! Thank God Almighty, we are free at last!"**

---

*From Martin Luther King, Jr.'s "I Have a Dream" speech. Copyright © 1963 by Martin Luther King, Jr. Reprinted by permission of Joan Daves.

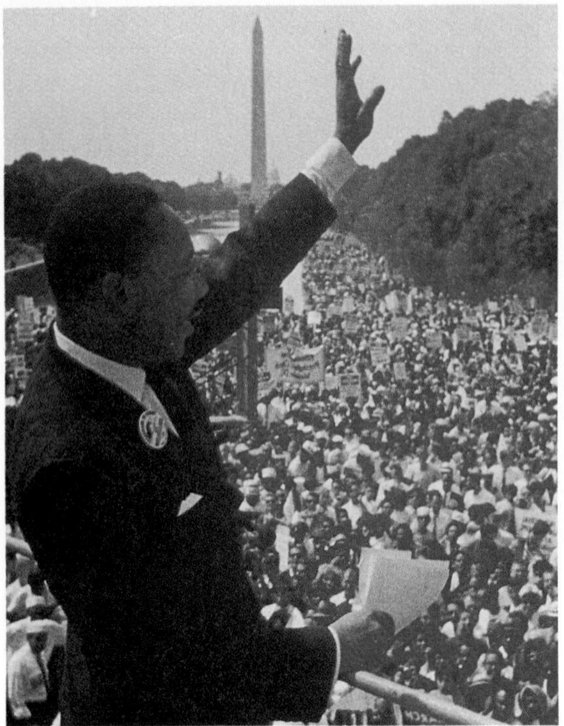

Dr. Martin Luther King, Jr., proclaims, "I have a dream" during the March on Washington. Dr. King won the Nobel Peace Prize in 1964 for his contributions to the civil rights movement. Dr. King led the civil rights movement until his assassination in 1968.

The Civil Rights Act of 1964

During his tragically brief term, President Kennedy had proposed comprehensive civil rights legislation. He was unable to overcome southern opposition in the Senate. Five days after Kennedy's assassination in 1963, President Lyndon Johnson went before Congress. He urged passage of the civil rights bill as the highest priority. After months of intense debate, with support from both Democrats and Republicans, the Civil Rights Act of 1964 was signed into law.

The act was based on the power of Congress to regulate interstate commerce. The act outlawed racial discrimination in all public accommodations affecting interstate commerce. These included hotels, restaurants, and theaters. Discrimination by employers and labor unions was also prohibited. The Attorney General was to enforce these laws by court action. In addition, federal funds could be withheld from any public or private program that practiced discrimination.

Other legislation soon followed. The 1968 Civil Rights Act extended federal criminal laws dealing with the violation of any person's civil rights. The fair housing provision of this act prohibited discrimination in sale or rental on the basis of race, religion, or national origin. Eighty percent of all private housing was covered by the law. Also in 1968 the Supreme Court ruled in *Jones* v. *Mayer* that racial discrimination in the sale or rental of property was unconstitutional. Discrimination was a relic of slavery, expressly forbidden by the Thirteenth Amendment.

Urban Violence and Black Militancy

The 1968 Civil Rights Act became law six days after the assassination of Martin Luther King, Jr. President Johnson proclaimed the act "a memorial to the fallen leader." King had dedicated his life to peace and understanding. Riots broke out, however, in the black neighborhoods of more than 100 cities when news of King's death was announced. In Washington, D.C., rioters set fire to buildings within a few blocks of the White House. For 12 days armed soldiers patroled the streets of the nation's capital.

The 1960's were riddled with urban violence because hope in the black ghettos had been replaced by frustration and anger. Unemployment was high, housing poor. Trapped in poverty, many blacks felt a growing sense of isolation. In the summer of 1965 rioting erupted in the black community of Watts in Los Angeles. Amid gunfire, arson, and looting, 34 people died. Millions of dollars in property was destroyed. In the following summers urban riots grew in intensity. In 1968 the report of the National Advisory Commission on Civil Disorders warned, "Our nation is moving toward two societies, one black, one white—separate and unequal."

Out of this unrest came a number of black militant groups whose leaders urged blacks to develop a sense of Black Power—pride in their racial and cultural heritage, and a desire to control their own destiny. Some black militants called for armed struggle and the creation of a separate black nation. But the great majority of blacks rejected violence and separatism. They continued to share Martin Luther King's dream of one nation, black and white together.

By the 1970's the older civil rights groups—the NAACP, the SCLC, and CORE—regained leadership. Black leaders today are primarily concerned with economic progress—job opportunities and the creation of black-owned business and industry. They seek to develop alliances with other minority groups in the struggle to bring equality to American society.

In a few decades the civil rights movement has made great progress. In Montgomery, Alabama, site of the bus boycott, blacks now attend integrated schools and enjoy equality in public accommodation. Throughout the South and the rest of the nation blacks have advanced rapidly. In education, achievement has been dramatic. Today the average length of schooling is almost the same for blacks and whites—a little more than 12 years. More blacks are attending college.

In economic terms blacks have made great strides. Incomes are rising, and the middle class is expanding as blacks move into better and higher-paying positions. Yet the economic gap between blacks and whites remains. The average black family income is only about two thirds that of white families. Few blacks have top executive positions. Less than 3 percent of the nation's doctors, lawyers, and engineers are black. The number of blacks living in poverty has declined substantially. Nevertheless, about 30 percent of all black families remain below the poverty level. High unemployment rates among black youths is an especially serious problem. Blacks—and whites—without education and skills are falling further behind. The struggle for equality continues.

Section Check

1. Identify: Rosa Parks, SCLC, CORE, sit-ins, Freedom Riders
2. What actions did President Truman take to end racial discrimination?
3. What was the result of the Montgomery Bus boycott?
4. What actions did Dr. Martin Luther King, Jr., take to gain equal rights?
5. What were some provisions of the Civil Rights Act of 1964?
6. Why were the 1960's troubled with urban violence?

4 VOTING RIGHTS: POWER OF THE BALLOT

Among the most important civil rights is the right to vote. In the early years of the Republic, voting was restricted largely to white males who owned property. By the Civil War, property qualifications for voting gradually had been dropped. Women and blacks, however, were still denied the vote. Even in the North, free black men had the right to vote in only a few states. The Fifteenth Amendment to the Constitution, adopted in 1870, ended the racial barrier to voting.

The right of citizens of the United States to vote shall not be denied or abridged by the United States or by any State on account of race, color, or previous condition of servitude.

Despite fraud and threats of violence, blacks did vote in large numbers after the Civil War. During Reconstruction a number of southern state legislatures came under the control of transplanted northern Republicans called carpetbaggers. Along with their southern allies, known as scalawags, they helped blacks assume power. Some Reconstruction leaders were genuinely anxious to promote democracy and to improve the lot of all blacks. Others were completely corrupt.

After the withdrawal of federal troops in 1877 and the end of Reconstruction, conservative white Democratic leadership returned to power in the South. The conservatives offered "protection" to the blacks in exchange for their votes. Blacks were appointed to a few public offices and given a handful of seats in the state legislatures.

An 1874 cartoon in Harper's Weekly *depicts determined white southerners' attempts to prevent blacks from voting. Voting fraud became common in parts of the South.*

In the 1890's southern radicals, the Populists, made a bid for black support. The Populists were mostly poor, rural whites. They recognized their common interest with blacks. "They are in the ditch just like we are," said one Populist leader. Conservatives were alarmed by Populist success, but the Populist racial alliance quickly dissolved.

Disfranchisement of Southern Blacks

Between 1890 and 1910 black voters were denied the right to vote by laws passed in the southern states in a process known as ***disfranchisement.*** The laws called for literacy tests, residency and property requirements, and the poll tax. The laws were upheld by the Supreme Court in 1898 as constitutional. They did not "on their face discriminate between the races," according to the Court. In practice, however, the laws were clearly aimed at blacks.

The ***literacy test*** typically required a prospective voter to read and/or understand a portion of the state constitution. Even the most highly educated black was unlikely to satisfy the local registrar. On the other hand, the laws contained loopholes that allowed almost any white to pass the test. A white illiterate might be asked to explain a simple clause, while a black man could be given a more complicated passage. Whatever the black man said, he would be informed that his explanation was wrong.

Probably the most famous loophole was the ***grandfather clause.*** It permitted a person to vote without taking the literacy test or paying the poll tax if he or one of his ancestors had been entitled to vote in 1866. Since no black could have voted then, only whites could meet the requirement. The grandfather clause was declared unconstitutional in 1915.

These laws, together with economic pressures and the intimidating tactics of the Ku Klux Klan, effectively denied blacks the right to vote. In Louisiana, for example, there were 130,334 registered black voters in 1896. Eight years later, after the adoption of literacy, property, and other requirements, there were only 1,342 registered black voters.

Another means by which blacks were denied a voice in their government was the "white primary." By 1900 nearly all whites in the South were Democrats. The Republicans and Populists offered little competition. The real election took place in the Democratic primary, in which the candidates were selected. Membership in the Democratic party in the South was limited to whites only, as was participation in the primary election. It was argued that this discrimination was legal because the Democratic party was a private association.

Blacks challenged the white primary in the courts. In *Smith* v. *Allwright* (1944) the Supreme Court declared the white primary unconstitutional. The primary was a part of the process by which public officials were chosen, and blacks could not be excluded.

The ***poll tax*** was the next barrier to fall. Eleven southern states had required payment of an annual tax before a citizen could vote. The tax was small, but it was used to discourage voting among blacks. In 1964 the Twenty-fourth Amendment to the Constitution outlawed the poll tax in federal elections. Two years later the Supreme Court held that the poll tax was unconstitutional in all elections. Payment of a tax in order to vote violated the equal protection clause. The Court ruled that "wealth, like race, creed, or color, is not germane to one's ability to participate intelligently in the electoral process."

Discrimination in registration still kept blacks from the polls. Any excuse was used to disqualify blacks. Nevertheless, black registration began to climb. In 1940, 250,000 blacks were registered in eleven southern states—only 5 percent of those eligible to vote. By 1960 the number had climbed to some 1,400,000 (28 percent). Most of the progress had been in the border states. In the Deep South resistance to black registration intensified.

Selma and the Voting Rights Act of 1965

Bolstered by the Civil Rights Act of 1964, blacks began a massive voter registration drive. Selma, Alabama, became a focal point of the voting rights movement. In 1965 only 335 blacks were registered in the county, 2.3 percent of those eligible. To dramatize the issue, Dr. King led a 50-mile (80-km) march from Selma to Montgomery, the state capital. The marchers met with violent resistance from local whites and state police, who used tear gas and clubs on the crowd. The nation, watching on television, was stunned. President Johnson called for federal action to ensure that no citizen would be denied the right to vote because of race. Congress responded with the Voting Rights Act of 1965.

The new legislation provided for direct federal action to guarantee voting rights. (Earlier civil rights acts had required individuals to bring legal action in the courts.) The Voting Rights Act of 1965 suspended literacy tests in those areas where less than 50 percent of the voting-age population had either registered or voted in the 1964 election. The impact

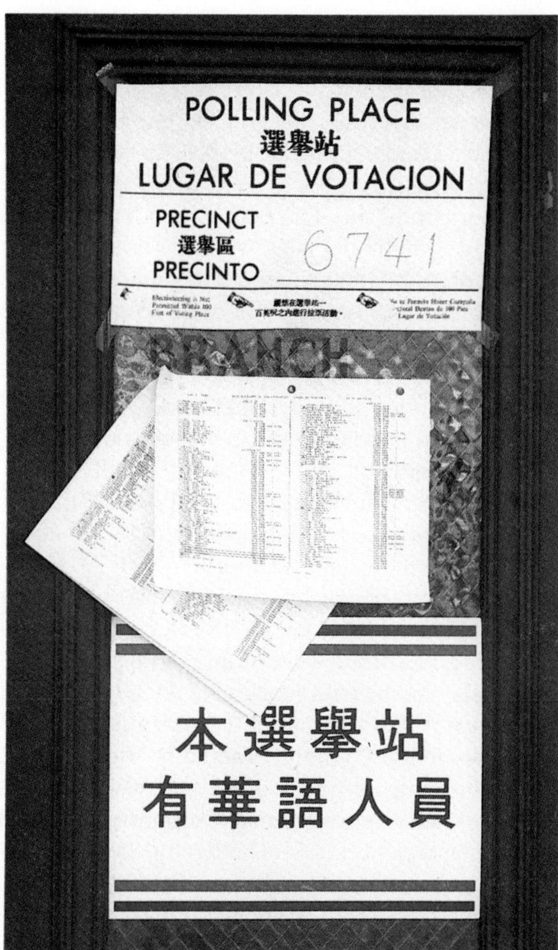

Bilingual polling places have become common since the passage of the Voting Rights Act of 1965. How does the act protect voters who speak little or no English? Name some language-minority groups who are affected by the Voting Rights Act.

was concentrated in about 100 southern counties. Here federal examiners were to enroll qualified voters and supervise elections. Amendments in 1970 and 1975 extended the life of the Voting Rights Act and broadened its provisions. Literacy tests eventually were banned altogether.

The impact of the Voting Rights Act was immediate. In the seven southern states covered by the act, only 29 percent of eligible blacks were registered in 1965. By 1972, 56 percent had registered. In Selma, Alabama, during those seven years, black registration increased from less than 3 percent to 67 percent. In 1972 five of the ten Selma City Council seats were won by blacks. Today, throughout the South and the nation as a whole, the level of voter registration among blacks and whites is roughly the same.

Certain sections of the Voting Rights Act were to have expired in 1982. On June 18 of that year, however, Congress showed a firm and continued commitment to civil rights by extending these provisions for 25 more years. The Senate voted 85 to 8 to extend the act. Only a few southern conservatives opposed it. President Ronald Reagan declared that the Senate vote "sends a strong, bipartisan message: No American's vote shall be defiled, diluted, or denied."

The Voting Rights Act was concerned mainly with discrimination against blacks. But it also extended protections to ***language minorities***—people who spoke little or no English. Included are those who speak Spanish (Mexican-Americans, Puerto Ricans, Cubans, and other Hispanics), Native Americans, Alaskan natives, and Asian Americans. The bill had a provision directed against New York's voting requirement of literacy in English. There were about 750,000 Puerto Ricans in New York City. Many, educated in Puerto Rico, spoke only Spanish. Under New York law they were denied the right to vote. The Voting Rights Act, in effect, guaranteed their right to vote. In areas where these minorities are concentrated, bilingual ballots are required. Today, about 200 counties in 19 states are affected by this provision.

Section Check

1. Define: disfranchisement, literacy test, grandfather clause, poll tax, language minority
2. Identify: Reconstruction, white primary, Selma March, Voting Rights Act of 1965
3. Which groups controlled southern legislatures during Reconstruction?
4. How were literacy tests used to keep blacks from voting?

5 THE WOMEN'S MOVEMENT FOR EQUAL RIGHTS

In 1777 Abigail Adams advised her husband John to "remember the ladies" when he joined in forming the new American government. "If particular care and attention is not paid to the ladies," Adams went on, "we are determined to foment rebellion, and will not hold ourselves bound by any laws in which we have no voice or representation."

American women have been denied, in law and in practice, full social, economic, and political equality with American men. Little more than half a century after Mrs. Adams's dire warning, American women did indeed begin to foment a rebellion. The first movement to grant equal rights to women emerged in the 1830's. For nearly a century this movement focused on a single, simple issue: the right to vote.

The early women's movement gained momentum from three important developments. First, women were starting to receive higher education. They began to seek new careers but were met by surprising resistance from a man's world. Second, women began to move into industrial employment, mostly in textile factories. They worked long shifts, 13 or 14 hours a day. Their wages were low, only a fraction of what men were paid in the same industries. To protest these conditions, women workers formed unions. A third source of inspiration was the abolitionist movement. Women played a major role in the struggle against slavery. In 1840 several women went as delegates from the United States to the World Anti-Slavery Convention in London. There they were denied seats because of their sex and were forced to sit in the visitors' gallery. This experience made them more aware of discrimination against women everywhere.

In 1848 the first Women's Rights Convention was held in Seneca Falls, New York. The delegates resolved: "We hold these truths to be self-evident: that all men and women are created equal." At first the movement concentrated on economic, social, and legal reform. Then, under the leadership of Elizabeth Cady Stanton and Susan B. Anthony, the right to vote became their fundamental concern.

Women who had worked for the abolition of slavery expected equality for blacks *and* women after the Civil War. They were bitterly disappointed when the Fourteenth and Fifteenth Amendments were applied only to black males. Women's liberation was yet to come. In 1869 Stanton and Anthony formed an organization that later became known as the National American Woman Suffrage Association (NAWSA). In 1872 Anthony was arrested and convicted for voting illegally. That same year another woman tried to vote on the grounds that the Fourteenth Amendment granted the vote to all citizens. The Supreme Court disagreed. It held that the states had the power to set voting qualifications and could rightly deny the vote to women.

The efforts of women to gain suffrage were most successful in the West. On the frontier everyone had to work, and women were more readily recognized as equals. The new territories also hoped to attract women as settlers. Wyoming Territory gave women the vote in 1869. When admitted to the Union in 1890, Wyoming became the first state with women's suffrage. The Progressive party, supported by small farmers and city reformers, aided the women's suffrage movement in several states. By 1914, 11 states had given the vote to women. Montana elected the first woman to the United States Congress, Jeannette Rankin, in 1916. Still, women could not vote in most states.

Elizabeth Cady Stanton (left), Susan B. Anthony (center), and Jeannette Rankin (right) were leaders of the women's movement in the United States. Stanton and Anthony led the fight for women's suffrage in the late 1800's. Rankin, who introduced the women's suffrage amendment to Congress in 1918, remained a lifelong champion of women's rights. She was reelected to a second term in the House in 1941.

On the day before Woodrow Wilson's inauguration as President in 1913, 5,000 women paraded in Washington in support of a constitutional amendment for women's suffrage. The more militant among them, led by Alice Paul, formed the National Woman's Party. They marched and staged dramatic protest demonstrations. Jailed, they resorted to hunger strikes. In 1917 they picketed the White House.

The women of NAWSA took a more moderate approach. Led by Carrie Chapman Catt, they continued efforts at political reform on the state level. At the national level they worked closely with President Wilson and won his support for the suffrage amendment. After the nation's entry into World War I, NAWSA emphasized support for the war effort. Its membership grew to about 2 million.

The different tactics of the Woman's Party and NAWSA complemented each other. Together they focused attention on the voting issue. In 1919 the suffrage amendment finally passed both houses of Congress by the necessary two thirds. The amendment now required approval by three fourths of the states to be ratified. By this time 26 states had already given women the right to vote. Approval of the amendment, however, was not assured. Deep opposition remained. NAWSA campaigned for ratification in every state, and in 1920 the Nineteenth Amendment became a part of the Constitution:

The right of citizens of the United States to vote shall not be denied or abridged by the United States or by any State on account of sex.

Carrie Chapman Catt was president of the National American Woman Suffrage Association (NAWSA) for more than 30 years. What tactic did NAWSA use to secure ratification of the Nineteenth Amendment?

The Equal Rights Struggle

After the victory for women's suffrage the women's movement became divided over priorities. The militant Woman's Party saw suffrage as only the first step toward full equality. In its view women remained "subordinate to men before the law, in the professions, in church, in industry, and in the home." The party committed itself to passage of an Equal Rights Amendment (ERA). This proposed amendment read:

Equality of rights under the law shall not be denied or abridged by the United States or by any State on account of sex.

NAWSA became the League of Women Voters. The purpose of the League was "to promote political responsibility through informed and active participation of citizens in government." The League staged nonpartisan get-out-the-vote campaigns. Much of its activity focused on general reform. It campaigned for child labor laws and sought improved conditions for working women through legislation. At the state level it spoke out against laws that discriminated against women. The League, however, opposed the Equal Rights Amendment. So too did the women of the American Federation of Labor. They believed that the ERA would overturn the protective labor laws for which they had worked. These laws—applied only to women—guaranteed minimum wages, imposed restrictions against long hours, and prohibited certain types of dangerous or heavy work.

As protective labor laws were extended to include men, opposition to the ERA declined. The League of Women Voters and numerous other national organizations endorsed the amendment. Both the Republican and Democratic parties extended their support, as did every President from Eisenhower to Carter. Sixteen states have amended their own constitutions to guarantee equality of the sexes under law.

In 1969 the President's Task Force on Women's Rights and Responsibilities called for the immediate passage of the Equal Rights Amendment. Successful passage of the amendment by both the House and the Senate finally occurred in 1972 after the ERA had been introduced into each Congress since 1923. After its introduction in the House in 1971, the amendment was referred to committee. It might have died there. Instead, Representative Martha Griffiths—the amendment's sponsor—succeeded, through skillful parliamentary action, in bringing it to the floor of the House. There, the Equal Rights Amendment passed by an overwhelming vote of 352 to 24. The Senate overcame intense early opposition and passed the ERA in 1972 by a vote of 84 to 8.

An amendment to the Constitution must be approved by three fourths of the states. To become law, the ERA, the prospective Twenty-Seventh Amendment, needed to be ratified by 38 states within seven years. The first states were won easily. By 1974 30 states had ratified the Amendment. With each additional state, however, the supporters of the ERA faced greater opposition.

By 1978, with the deadline one year away, only 35 states had approved. That same year, over strong opposition, Congress voted to extend the deadline by 39 months to June 30, 1982. Various women's groups mounted a major campaign for passage. These included the League of Women Voters, the National Women's Political Caucus, and the National Organization for Women (NOW).

Organized opposition to the ERA came mainly from STOP ERA, an organization headed by Phyllis Schlafly. In the Midwest and South, where most of the nonratifying states were located, STOP ERA waged an effective attack on the amendment. The amendment failed. On June 21, 1982, nine days before the deadline, the Florida Senate voted 22 to 16 against ERA. The vote was bitterly protested by the amendment's supporters. Florida State Senator Gwen Margolis told the Senate: "The women of this country will never forget this vote. They will not give up."

In 1983 the amendment was reintroduced into Congress, but passage by the House failed. The Senate took no action.

Representative Martha W. Griffiths of Michigan served 10 consecutive terms in Congress, during which time she was known for her outspoken defense of human rights and equality. She later became lieutenant governor of her state.

Legislating Women's Rights

The drive for the Equal Rights Amendment in the 1960's and 1970's arose out of an increasing awareness among women that they were subject to various forms of discrimination. This new consciousness was sparked, in part, by the example of the black civil rights movement. The women's movement, which had declined after 1920, again became an important force in American society.

The women's movement voiced demands for equality in all areas of American life. Among its foremost concerns was discrimination against women in employment. World War II had brought a massive increase in the number of women in the nation's work force. By the end of the 1960's a majority of women between the ages of 18 and 65 were employed outside the home. Job opportunities, however, were often restricted. Women were concentrated in the relatively low-paying occupations they traditionally held, so-called "women's jobs" such as nursing, elementary school teaching, and secretarial work. Few women were to be found in professions such as law and medicine, in science or engineering, or in executive business positions. The average salary for women was only about 60 percent of that of men—and it remains very close to that today. Often women were paid less than men for the exact same work.

Women began to demand greater employment opportunities and "equal pay for equal work." The 1963 Equal Pay Act was the first federal law against discrimination in employment on the basis of sex.

During World War II many women took jobs that traditionally had been held by men. After the war, however, women found themselves out of work or underpaid for their efforts. Name some examples of discrimination toward women that still exist in the United States.

Under the act employers were required to pay the same wages to men and women for equal work.

Title VII of the Civil Rights Act of 1964 included women in its employment opportunity provision. The act prohibited "discrimination based on sex as well as race, color, religion and national origin in all terms, conditions, or privileges of employment." The law covered those employers and labor unions whose activities "affect interstate commerce."

Companies or institutions that held government contracts could no longer discriminate on the basis of sex. Administrative guidelines, as well as court decisions, have defined the scope of Title VII. In hiring and promotion, men and women must be considered on their individual merits. No job may be denied to all men or to all women.

Women are now moving into areas of employment that had been closed to them. Jobs that once were regarded for men only, such as engineering, now attract women in increasing numbers. Where once advancement was limited, ability has brought women rapid promotion. More women are assuming top executive positions in business and government. Past discrimination and traditional attitudes about woman's role, however, have left their mark. Women are still not fully represented in all professions. Their average salary is substantially less than that of men, and unemployment is higher among women than men.

Section Check

1. Identify: Elizabeth Cady Stanton, Susan B. Anthony, Nineteenth Amendment, Jeannette Rankin, League of Women Voters, Equal Pay Act
2. What was Abigail Adams's warning in 1777?
3. What did the Women's Rights Convention of 1848 resolve?
4. What did the proposed Equal Rights Amendment guarantee?
5. What guarantees did the 1964 Civil Rights Act provide for women?

6 AFFIRMATIVE ACTION

During the 1970's a series of executive orders were issued by the Labor Department and the Department of Health, Education and Welfare. They required businesses and universities that received federal money to follow a policy of preferential treatment called ***affirmative action*** to ensure nondiscrimination in hiring and promotion. Goals, or targets, were established to increase employment of women and minorities.

Special effort was to be taken to seek out and employ qualified applicants from among underrepresented groups. In addition, an effort was to be made to prepare those who might not yet be qualified. Affirmative action was also required in university admissions in order to increase the number of women and minority students. Special attention was directed to schools of law and medicine, where few women and minority students were accepted.

Affirmative action has stirred bitter controversy. The issue came before the United States Supreme Court in the case of *Bakke* v. *The Regents of the University of California* (1978). Allen Bakke, a white male, had been denied admission to the University of California Medical School at Davis. Among those

ISSUES

Affirmative Action

Supporters of affirmative action believe that preferential treatment must be extended to women and minorities. Only by this means can the effects of past injustice and discrimination be overcome. The aim of affirmative action is to give special help to those who were excluded previously from full and equal participation in American society. When race and sex have been the bases for past discrimination, these factors must be considered in formulating remedies.

Affirmative action sets goals to be attained. It does not impose rigid quotas—specific percentages reserved for women and minorities. No employer is required to hire a less qualified person simply because of sex or race. What is required is that when applicants are of roughly equal qualification, preference be given to women and minority members. In addition, it is emphasized that qualifications be genuinely job-related. Too often qualification requirements may be disguises for discrimination.

Opponents of affirmative action argue that it is a form of reverse discrimination. As such, it is both unjust and unconstitutional. If discrimination *against* women and blacks is wrong, it is equally wrong to discriminate in their favor. Preferential treatment makes some people "more equal" than others. Equal opportunity may be replaced by proportionate representation. Goals may be transformed into quotas.

Each person has a right to be judged on the basis of individual achievement and merit. The equal protection clause of the Fourteenth Amendment protects all citizens. It offers no less protection to whites than to blacks, no less to men than to women. Opponents of affirmative action oppose the use of any racial or sex classifications. They quote Justice Harlan's famous dissent in *Plessy* v. *Ferguson:* "Our Constitution is color-blind. . . . In respect of civil rights, all citizens are equal before the law."

admitted, however, were several minority students with grades lower than Bakke's. This was in keeping with the university's affirmative action policies. Bakke filed suit against the university. He claimed that he was a victim of ***reverse discrimination.*** Bakke argued that the medical school's admission program violated the equal protection clause of the Fourteenth Amendment.

The Supreme Court was deeply divided in the *Bakke* case. The *Bakke* case resulted in a two-part decision with Justice Powell changing sides for each part. In a 5–4 vote, the Court held that the Davis program's use of "quotas"—setting aside a precise number of places for minority students—was unconstitutional. Thus, Allen Bakke was ordered to be admitted to the next entering class at the medical school.

The Court then went on to approve the principle of affirmative action. By another 5–4 vote the Court held that race may be considered as one factor in a university's admissions policy.

Four Justices (Burger, Stewart, Rehnquist, and Stevens) believed that the Davis program violated the Civil Rights Act of 1964: "No person in the United States shall, on the ground of race, color, or national origin, be excluded from participation in, be denied the benefits of, or be subject to discrimination under any program or activity receiving Federal financial assistance."

On the other side, four Justices (Brennan, White, Marshall, and Blackmun) believed that race may be taken into account "when it acts not to demean or insult any racial group, but to remedy disadvantages cast on minorities by past prejudices."

Allen Bakke graduates from the university that initially denied him admission.

Justice Powell, the architect of the Court's split decision, agreed with the first group that the Davis medical school admissions program was unconstitutional. "Equal protection," he said, "cannot mean one thing when applied to one individual and something else when applied to a person of another color. If both are not accorded the same protection, then it is not equal." On the second question, however, Powell sided with the other group. Race and ethnic background could be considered as *one factor* in determining admission. In other words, rigid quotas are not allowed, but more flexible affirmative action programs are permissible.

The significance and meaning of the *Bakke* decision may be debated for many years. In this and other matters of social justice all Americans are faced with difficult decisions. In what manner, at what speed, and at what cost are we to continue our attempts to create a just society?

Section Check

1. What is the meaning of affirmative action?
2. What is meant by "reverse discrimination"?
3. What did the Supreme Court rule in *Bakke* v. *The Regents of the University of California* (1978)?
4. Which justice was the architect of the Court's two-part decision in the *Bakke* case?
5. What did the *Bakke* case determine about race as a factor in college admission?

SUMMARY

Throughout our history, various minority groups have been denied their civil rights, or equality under the law. Mistreatment of black Americans has been one of the most troublesome problems in our history. In 1857 the Supreme Court ruled in the *Dred Scott* decision that blacks were not citizens. Three amendments to the Constitution, passed after the Civil War, freed blacks from slavery, extended them full citizenship, and provided black males the right to vote. Later a Southern backlash removed some of these rights with the passage of Jim Crow laws. The Supreme Court upheld these laws in the case of *Plessy* v. *Ferguson* (1896).

In the twentieth century black America set out to regain its full rights. In *Brown* v. *Board of Education* (1954) the Supreme Court ordered that all school systems be desegregated. Implementing this decision has proved to be difficult in many urban areas because blacks and whites often live in different neighborhoods. The courts have used the controversial tool of busing to overcome this form of de facto segregation.

School desegregation is one aspect of the civil rights movement. Led by Martin Luther King, Jr., blacks effectively used peaceful demonstrations, boycotts, and sit-ins to protest discrimination in public accommodations, housing, transportation, and employment. Many of these civil rights have been achieved, aided by such government legislation as the various Civil Rights Acts. Economically, however, blacks have yet to reach equality.

The Fifteenth Amendment extended the vote to black males in 1870. However, several southern states used literacy tests, poll taxes, and property requirements to deny blacks their voting rights. The Voting Rights Act of 1965 helped restore the guarantees of the Fifteenth Amendment. The voter registration level of blacks is now roughly equal to the level of whites.

Women have also been denied equal treatment. The first organized women's movement began in the 1830's and concentrated for several decades on the issue of suffrage. In 1920 the Nineteenth Amendment gave women the vote. In 1982 a proposed Constitutional amendment to forbid discrimination on the basis of sex—the ERA—failed to gain ratification. A number of other laws, however, have helped women gain equal treatment, equal pay, and equal protection of the laws. But women are still often underpaid and are underrepresented in several important professions.

Chapter 6 Review

Using Vocabulary

Answer the questions by using the meaning of each underlined term.

1. How does *de facto* segregation differ from *de jure* segregation?
2. How did literacy tests, poll taxes, and the grandfather clause bring about the disfranchisement of blacks?
3. How might discrimination against a language minority be avoided?
4. How did a restrictive covenant promote discrimination in housing?
5. What effect does affirmative action sometimes have on reverse discrimination?

Understanding American Government

1. What was the result of each of the following amendments: the Thirteenth, Fourteenth, and Fifteenth?
2. What was the meaning of "separate but equal" in the Supreme Court's ruling in *Plessy* v. *Ferguson?*
3. What did Chief Justice Warren mean when he wrote, in the ruling on *Brown* v. *Board of Education,* that "Separate education facilities are inherently unequal"?
4. How did the Civil Rights Act of 1964 aid those seeking to desegregate schools?
5. What were some of the tactics used by nonviolent, direct action civil rights groups?
6. What were some of the most important provisions of the Civil Rights Act of 1964?
7. What techniques did the southern states use to disfranchise blacks?
8. What developments helped the early women's movement gain momentum?

Extending Your Skills: Comparing Supreme Court Decisions

Reread the information on pages 159–162 about the Supreme Court decisions in *Plessy* v. *Ferguson* and *Brown* v. *Board of Education.* Then complete each statement.

1. A phrase that applies to both cases is (a) The Fourteenth Amendment was its legal basis. (b) The major issue was segregation. (c) The major issue was education.
2. Name the case that each statement describes. (a) Separate facilities are inherently unequal. (b) Separate facilities are allowed if they are equal. (c) The Fourteenth Amendment does not enforce social equality. (d) Separating children because of race generates in them a feeling of inferiority.

Government and You

1. Do violent or nonviolent methods work better to promote social change? How might the civil rights movement have been different if Dr. Martin Luther King, Jr., and other leaders had chosen violence as a tool?
2. Why do you think women were denied the vote for so many years? How may a republic be harmed when many of its citizens are denied the right to vote?
3. Which do you think played a more important role in the civil rights movement, the integration of schools or increasing levels of black voter registration? Which is the more important tool for achieving equality, education or the ballot? Explain your answer.

Activities

1. Make a wall chart showing the history of the struggle by black Americans for equality. Include the birthdates of Abraham Lincoln, Martin Luther King, Jr., and other important historical figures. Include all constitutional amendments that affected this struggle.
2. Interview 10 men and women about the Equal Rights Amendment. Ask whether they believe ERA should have passed. Ask what reasons they may have for supporting or opposing the amendment. Report your results to the class.
3. Prepare a biographical report on the life of Martin Luther King, Jr. Include his childhood and discuss his nonviolent philosophy.
4. Make a scrapbook from newspaper clippings or magazine articles about an issue of social justice in your town or state.

UNIT 3

WE AMERICANS

Chapter 7

Citizenship: A Nation of Nations

The [heart] of America is open to receive not only the opulent and respectable stranger, but the oppressed and persecuted of all nations and religions; whom we shall welcome to a participation of all our rights and privileges, if by decency and propriety of conduct they appear to merit the enjoyment.

GEORGE WASHINGTON

Here is not merely a nation but a teeming nation of nations.

WALT WHITMAN

CHAPTER OVERVIEW

Immigrants wait on Ellis Island to be examined before admission to the United States. Ellis Island was the major immigration station between 1892 and 1943.

1 PATTERNS OF IMMIGRATION

America is a nation of people from every background and from every corner of the earth. In 200 years nearly 50 million immigrants have entered the United States. As President John F. Kennedy wrote:

> *Why they came here and what they did after they arrived make up the story of America. They came for a variety of reasons from every quarter of the world, representing almost every race, almost every religion, and almost every creed. Through their ingenuity, their industry and their imagination, they were able to create out of a wilderness a thriving and prospering nation—and, through their dedication to liberty and freedom, they helped to build a government reflecting man's most cherished ideals.**

Today immigration continues to add richness and variety to life in the United States.

---

*John F. Kennedy, *A Nation of Immigrants.* New York: Harper & Row, 1964, p. 84.

The Colonial Period

At the time of the American Revolution about three fourths of the people in the colonies were of European background. Most colonists were white Anglo-Saxon Protestants—English, Welsh, and Scots. But there were others as well. Dutch and Scandinavian settlers had established colonies along the Hudson and Delaware rivers that were brought under the British Crown in 1664. French Protestants called *Huguenots* had found refuge and religious freedom in the colonies. Germans had settled in large numbers, especially in Pennsylvania. The colonies also included Jews from many European nations.

The Native Americans met the first settlers in friendship. But British expansion soon threatened Native American cultures, and goodwill turned to conflict. The Native Americans, not willing to give up their own way of life, remained apart from the European settlements as a separate people.

By 1776 there were some half million blacks in North America, most concentrated in the southern colonies. Though there were some free blacks, the vast majority were slaves who came from diverse backgrounds and spoke many different languages. They had been brought in chains to America, primarily from the west coast of Africa.

Unlike the Africans, Europeans had willingly come to America. Eager to attract new settlers, the colonies gave most foreigners full civil rights and liberties. Protestants and Jews were admitted to citizenship after seven years' residence. Roman Catholics, though usually tolerated, were denied citizenship in most colonies.

Settlers from different nations were generally welcomed, but there was great pressure to conform to the dominant English culture of the colonies. Those who were not of English stock were often viewed with suspicion and sometimes hostility. Heavy German immigration, for example, aroused alarm among the Anglo-Saxon population of Pennsylvania. The English feared becoming a "colony of aliens" where everyone would soon be learning German.

Old World rivalries between such groups as the English and the Scots were transplanted to American soil, sometimes producing tensions among the various white ethnic groups. Despite their tensions the common experience of being white settlers in colonial America soon bound all white groups together.

The New Americans

In the years from 1776 to 1820 only 250,000 new settlers came to the United States. As the population grew in relative isolation from Europe, old ethnic differences began to blur. A new people, the Americans, came into being. In his famous *Letter from an American Farmer,* written in 1782, Hector St. John Crèvecoeur asked, "What then is the American, this new man?" Crèvecoeur answered his own question.

They are a mixture of English, Scotch, Irish, French, Dutch, Germans, and Swedes. . . .

In this great American asylum the poor of Europe have by some means met together. . . . Everything has tended to regenerate them: new laws, a new mode of living, a new social system. . . . Formerly they were not numbered in any civil list of their country, except in those of the poor; here they rank as citizens.

Here individuals of all nations are melted into a new race of men, whose labors and posterity will one day cause great change in the world.

Early Immigration For more than a century after the American Revolution, immigrants entered the United States without restriction. "In the early nineteenth century," historian Oscar Handlin writes,

An 1880 cartoon favoring unrestricted immigration depicts Uncle Sam warmly welcoming foreigners. What did the United States symbolize to immigrants?

"those already on this side of the ocean regarded immigration as a positive good." America had plenty of land and not enough people to settle it. During the 1860's at least 25 of the 38 states took official action to lure immigrants, offering them land, jobs, and voting rights.

Between 1820 and 1880, nearly 11 million people arrived in America. Most were from northern and western Europe. Seventy-two percent came from three countries: Germany, Ireland, and Great Britain. Three million came from Germany, another 3 million from Ireland, and almost 2 million from Great Britain. By the 1860's Scandinavians, primarily Norwegians and Swedes, began to arrive in large numbers. So too did Chinese, drawn by the promise of work on the West Coast.

A few immigrants came because they sought religious and political freedom. Some fled compulsory military service. Others fled political unrest. But most immigrants came to America in hope of economic improvement. American opportunity—free land and jobs—provided the "pull" for immigration. Population pressure and economic dislocation in Europe provided the "push." The biggest push was the Irish potato famine of the 1840's. During that decade almost half of all immigrants to the United States came from Ireland.

Most immigrants, from whatever nation, arrived without money. But they brought imagination, skills, and a willingness to work hard. Their lot was not easy. In the mid-nineteenth century immigrants often moved into squalid, ghetto-like conditions. In the eastern cities crime was rampant. Confused and often unable to speak English, new immigrants were frequently cheated and exploited. Some immigrants became public charges, depending on charity to escape starvation.

Opposition to Immigration Immigration enriched the United States. The constant supply of cheap labor that immigration provided allowed the economy to expand rapidly. Gangs of immigrant laborers, working under contract at the barest subsistence wages, built America's railroads, canals, harbors, and roads. Immigrant artisans developed the nation's crafts and small industry. With talent and energy immigrants gave a special vitality to the new land.

Yet opposition to immigration was often intense. Many Americans who traced their ancestry to earlier generations of immigrants looked with distaste and fear upon those who came later. One New Yorker, Philip Horn, wrote in his diary.

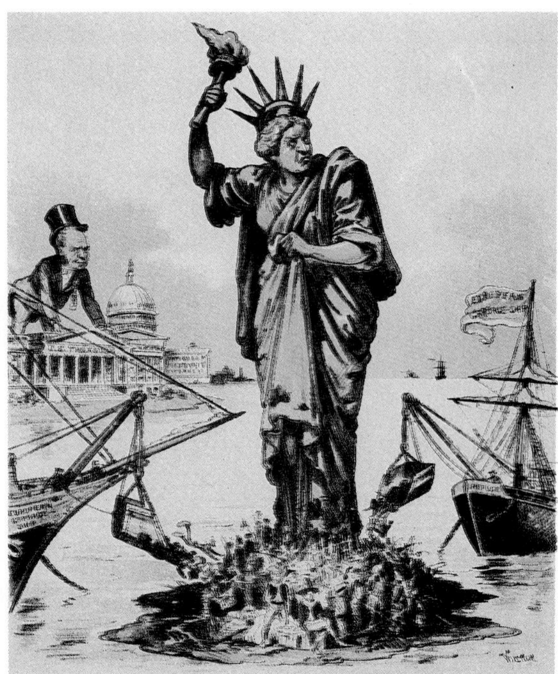

The artist of this 1890 cartoon shows the Statue of Liberty frowning upon immigrants. The cartoon illustrates opposition to unlimited immigration and to immigrants in general. The view of immigrants as undesirables has surfaced often in United States history. Why have some Americans opposed unrestricted immigration?

All Europe is coming across the ocean; all that part at least who cannot make a living at home; and what shall we do with them? They increase our taxes, eat our bread and encumber our streets, and not one in twenty is competent to keep himself.

As the United States headed toward civil war, some "100 percent Americans" tried to blame the nation's ills on foreign influences, especially immigration. This "nativist" movement aimed most of its hostility at Irish and German Catholics. The Irish, called "servants of the Pope," were subject to verbal and physical abuse. Violence and rioting broke out in a number of cities.

During the 1840's and 1850's the American party stirred resentment against the immigrants. Termed the "Know-Nothings," the party wanted to limit political office to native-born Protestants.* It also called for a curb on the rising tide of immigration to American shores. (continued on page 184)

*When members were asked about the party, they replied, "I know nothing." Hence they became known as the "Know-Nothings."

INSIGHT

The Island of Tears

In the early morning hours a shout went up from the small ship's deck. "America!"

The weary, anxious passengers—more than a thousand had crowded aboard the small freighter at the port in Hamburg—rushed to see. Among them a young woman named Katrinka gripped her brother Josef's hand and cried, "Look!" There, like bright beads on a necklace, were the lights of New York strung along the horizon. As the ship neared, they could make out the tall buildings of Manhattan—so big they seemed more like mountains than buildings. And then in the first glow of dawn someone spotted it—the Statue of Liberty! Katrinka's heart flooded with joy. For as long as she could remember, she had dreamed of this sight—the towering woman in long flowing robes, her torch held high. "We have made it!" she whispered breathlessly to her small brother.

The ship entered the harbor. Katrinka could hardly believe her eyes. The harbor was crowded with ships, ships flying the flags of France, Britain, Sweden, Italy, Greece, and Germany—each carrying its own cargo of immigrants to America. It was 1907. Katrinka knew how many people in her native Poland dreamed of coming to America, where some said the streets were paved with gold! But she could not know that she and her brother were part of the greatest mass movement in human history. One million newcomers had made this voyage in 1905, a million more in 1906, and in 1907 more than a million would come to these shores. On this bright spring morning as many as 20,000 immigrants waited on ships and docks to enter the land of liberty.

Katrinka and her brother, carrying everything they owned in a small sack and a suitcase, were loaded onto a ferry for Ellis Island. Like the others, Katrinka knew of Ellis Island—"the island of tears," it was called. Here United States officials would decide who would be allowed to stay in America and who would have to return to their own countries. Since 1892 the great majority of immigrants to America had passed through

Ellis Island. On this day alone nearly 10,000 people would pass through the station.

On Ellis Island the passengers were herded up the stairs to the Great Hall, an immense room teeming with people in long lines. A man in a blue uniform watched them with a stern look as they climbed the stairs. Katrinka grasped Josef's hand. She didn't know, nor did the others, that this man was a doctor, watching the new arrivals for signs of illness. Once past the doctor, they had already passed their first test. Another doctor peered into Katrinka's eyes and examined her for signs of infection. "You're fine," the doctor said, and he pointed Katrinka and her brother toward the Registry Hall. Katrinka's relief at passing the doctor's test was mixed with sadness. Others, because they were too old or too ill, had been taken aside by the doctor to be sent back to their own countries. Katrinka understood, hearing the sound of their crying, why Ellis Island was called the island of tears.

At the end of another long line sat a grim, weary-looking inspector. With the help of an interpreter he asked Katrinka a long list of questions. In a small voice Katrinka answered each question. Her aunt was meeting her, she said. She was going to New York. She showed the inspector the money she had: $25 in German currency. Immigrants without money were often refused entry into the United States. Those who did not have sponsors were also turned back. Nearly two out of every ten people arriving at Ellis Island were refused entry. The inspector nodded. At last he handed her a landing card. "You've made it," the interpreter told her, smiling joyfully.

All around her, as she and Josef made their way to the ferry that would take them to New York City, Katrinka saw the tears of joy and happiness of the others who had made it to the land of liberty. Wiping away her own tears, she understood the other meaning of "the island of tears."

Chinese immigrants endured cold and snow to complete construction of one section of the transcontinental railroad. Why did some Americans regard the Chinese as undesirable aliens? How did legislation passed by Congress reflect this attitude?

Anti-foreign feelings melted in the fires of the Civil War. Over half a million immigrants entered the Union armies. In the North and the South alike, foreign-born soldiers formed their own companies, regiments, and divisions. The Civil War affirmed the importance of immigrant contributions and the patriotism of the newest Americans.

Resentment against immigrants reappeared, however, whenever jobs were scarce. After the depression of 1873 several states passed laws restricting the admission of aliens. The Supreme Court held all such laws to be unconstitutional, saying only Congress had the power to regulate immigration. This power is implied from the Congressional power to regulate foreign commerce. In 1875 Congress passed the first law restricting the admission of undesirable aliens to the United States. Among those excluded were criminals, radicals, the insane, the diseased, and the destitute.

In 1882 Congress further restricted immigration by lengthening the list of undesirables. More drastically, Congress prohibited all Chinese laborers from entering the United States. Chinese had first come to California to work in the gold fields. Later they helped build the transcontinental railroad. As the number of Chinese grew, however, opposition to their presence mounted. Many people feared losing their jobs to lower-paid Chinese workers. Mobs attacked Chinese homes and businesses. Labor groups rallied behind the slogan, "The Chinese Must Go!" The Chinese Exclusion Act passed in 1882 reduced Chinese immigration from 40,000 in 1881 to 10 in 1887. The act remained in force until 1943.

The Great Migration: 1881–1920

From 1881 to 1920 the tide of immigration became a flood. Twenty-three million people were admitted to the United States. In the peak years from 1905 to 1914 more than 10 million immigrants were admitted. In 1914, when World War I began in Europe, 1,218,000 immigrants arrived in the United States. Travel was difficult during the war, and immigration dropped to a low of 110,000 in 1918. After the war immigration again climbed rapidly, reaching nearly half a million by 1920.

LEGACY

Liberty at the Golden Door

For millions of the poor and oppressed who fled Europe to come to the United States, it stands as a symbol of freedom and opportunity. As their ships approached New York Harbor, immigrants crowded the decks for their first glimpse. One refugee from Russia remembered:

The sunshine started, and what do we see? The Statue of Liberty! She was beautiful in the early morning light. Everybody was crying. The whole boat bent toward her because everybody went out, everybody, everybody was in the the same spot. We had been sinking and we survived and now we were looking at the Statue of Liberty. She was beautiful with the sunshine so bright. Beautiful colors, the greenish-like water—and so big, and everybody was crying.

It stands more than 300 feet tall, a crowned figure in classical robes. One hand carries a tablet bearing the date July 4, 1776. The other holds aloft the torch of liberty. At the statue's feet lie the broken chains of slavery. This symbol of liberty was a gift from the people of France to commemorate the achievement of American independence and the friendship of the two nations. Designed by Frederic Auguste Bartholdi, the Statue of Liberty consists of copper sheets pounded and shaped by hand over a framework of four steel supports. The statue's framework, considered an engineering marvel, was the work of Gustave Eiffel, who constructed the Eiffel Tower. Built in Paris, the magnificent structure, weighing over 200 tons, was dismantled and shipped to the United States in 1885. Its size is awesome. The index finger alone measures 8 feet long, the torch-bearing arm a full 42 feet. Set on a huge pedestal on Liberty Island at the mouth of New York Harbor, the Statue of Liberty was dedicated by President Grover Cleveland in 1886.

Today the Statue of Liberty is part of a historical monument that includes the former immigration station on Ellis Island. Visitors climb the 12 flights of stairs to the statue's observation deck, where as many as 30 people can stand at one time. The words of Emma Lazarus, inscribed on a bronze plaque at the base of the statue in 1903, are as true today as when Liberty first raised her torch aloft.

Not like the brazen giant of Greek fame,
With conquering limbs astride from land to land;
Here at our sea-washed, sunset gates shall stand
A mighty woman with a torch, whose flame
Is the imprisoned lightning, and her name
Mother of Exiles. From her beacon-hand
Glows world-wide welcome; her mild eyes command
The air-bridged harbor that twin cities frame.
"Keep, ancient lands, your storied pomp!" cries she
With silent lips. "Give me your tired, your poor,
Your huddled masses yearning to breathe free,
The wretched refuse of your teeming shore.
Send these, the homeless, tempest-tost to me,
I lift my lamp beside the golden door!"

The period from 1881 to 1920 included a major change in the pattern of immigration. Before 1890 most immigrants had come from the countries of northern and western Europe—primarily Germany, Ireland, Great Britain, and Sweden. After 1890 most immigrants came from southern and eastern Europe—Italy, Greece, Austria-Hungary, Poland, and Russia. During the period more than 4 million immigrants arrived from Italy, another 4 million from Austria-Hungary, and 3 million from Russia.

The American frontier had closed. Cheap land was no longer available. Opportunity for new immigrants was now to be found in the industrial cities. The growth of industry increased the demand for labor, but competition was intense. American workers resented the influx of "cheap foreign labor," accusing immigrants of driving down wages, crowding the cities, and increasing crime and disorder.

Immigrants also faced strong social pressure to conform. People calling themselves Americans viewed differences of language, custom, and food with prejudice. They subjected each immigrant group to insults and slurs. They tagged each group with an ethnic stereotype. No group was immune.

In the 1840's and 1850's the Irish had borne the brunt of prejudice and discrimination. Fifty years later the Italians suffered the same treatment. Jews from eastern Europe encountered anti-Semitism in the form of social and economic barriers.

Demands grew for more selective immigration. In 1907 Congress appointed a commission to study the problem. Its report, in 42 volumes, was completed four years later. On the basis of this report Congress in 1917 enacted a restrictive immigation law that added two new provisions to the earlier exclusions. The first provision required that immigrants be able to read and write. The second forbade entry of persons coming from the "Asiatic Barred Zone," an area including most of Asia and the Pacific islands.

Immigration by Quota: 1921–1940

In 1921 Congress for the first time imposed a limit on the number of immigrants who could enter the United States. The Emergency Quota Act was a temporary measure designed to control the flood of immigrants expected to come from the war-ravaged nations of Europe.

The limit on immigration was made permanent in the National Origins Act of 1924. The law was revised in 1929 and governed immigration until 1952. The original law and its revisions had the two basic purposes of limiting immigration and controlling the national origins of immigrants. First, the law restricted the number of immigrants to approximately 150,000 each year. Second, immigration was based on a ***national origins quota system.*** The

Mealtime at Ellis Island involved feeding thousands of people, especially in the years just prior to World War I. As many as 10,000 persons were processed in a day. One immigrant later described the experience as "din, confusion, bewilderment, madness!"

Immigrants in a 1940's citizenship class salute the American flag before beginning lessons. Chief Justice Earl Warren once described citizenship as "the right to have rights." What hardships might these new Americans have faced in their adopted country?

number of immigrants admitted each year from any particular European nation was based on the percentage of people of that national origin already in the United States. The 1920 census was taken as the base for calculation. The formula was like a mirror of the American population. Annual immigration would reflect the peoples who already composed it.

Because most Americans or their ancestors had come from northern and western Europe, the quota system allotted immigrants from Ireland, Great Britain, and Germany 73 percent of the total quota for immigration, a quota that often went unfilled. At the same time, other nations with long waiting lists for immigration to the United States were allotted small quotas—often no more than the minimum 100 persons per year.

The annual quota based on national origins limited southern European immigration. No restrictions were placed on the number of immigrants from countries in the Western Hemisphere—Canada, Mexico, and Central and South America. But the 1924 Act did exclude all people of Asian origin except Filipinos. The racial bar on immigration from Asia and the Pacific islands was not fully lifted until 1952.

According to historian Oscar Handlin, "The new laws put an end to a century of free movement. . . . Probably the whole twenty-five year period after 1925 saw fewer newcomers to the United States than the single year of 1907." America's golden door, which symbolized its long-standing open immigration policy, had slammed shut.

Between 1921 and 1940 only 5 million immigrants came to the United States. Most came during the 1920's. The economic depression of the 1930's brought a drop in immigration to the lowest level in more than 100 years. Between 1932 and 1935 more people left the United States than arrived.

Immigration: 1941–1965

From 1941 to 1945, during World War II, immigration remained low. After the war immigration increased rapidly, though it never again reached the numbers of early years. In the postwar period special legislation relaxed restrictions on the immigration of such groups as "war brides," displaced persons, orphans, and refugees.

The War Brides Act of 1945 aided entry of the foreign brides and grooms of American military personnel. Under the act 120,000 alien brides, grooms, and children of members of the armed forces came to the United States.

The Displaced Persons Act made special provision for the admission of persons dislocated from their homes by war. Some 400,000 displaced persons found a new home in America. They came from many nations and backgrounds, but the largest numbers were from Poland, Germany, the Soviet Union, and Yugoslavia. Since nationality quotas would have limited the number of immigrants from these countries, the Displaced Persons Act provided that persons admitted could be charged to future quotas. Some quotas have been filled to the year 2000.

World War II left thousands of children without parents or family. Special legislation enabled orphaned children to come to America for adoption. Most came from Germany, Italy, Greece, and Japan. (Later, children orphaned by the Korean and Vietnam wars were admitted to the United States for adoption by American families.)

Following World War II the nations of eastern Europe were brought under Soviet domination. Thousands fled Communist dictatorships in search of political and religious freedom. More than 200,000 refugees were admitted to the United States as non-quota immigrants.

War in Europe and the postwar expansion of Communism raised concern for American national security. In 1940 Congress passed the Alien Registration Act. For the first time aliens in the United States were required to register and be fingerprinted. The act also provided for deportation of ***subversives,*** aliens considered potentially dangerous to national security. The Internal Security Act of 1950 expanded the restrictions against subversives.

In 1952 Congress passed the Immigration and Nationality Act, known as the McCarran-Walter Act. The act lifted the racial barrier against Asian immigration but continued the national origins quota system. President Truman, who strongly opposed the use of quotas, vetoed the bill. Truman called the quota system "insulting to large numbers of our finest citizens, irritating to our allies abroad, and foreign to our purposes and ideals." Nevertheless, Congress secured the necessary two-thirds vote and repassed the act over the President's veto.

Under the McCarran-Walter Act immigration from the Western Hemisphere remained without restriction. But for the rest of the world each nationality was allotted a quota, based on the 1920 census. By the new formula more than 90 percent of the total immigration quota went to Europe. The major share—69 percent—went to Great Britain, Germany, and Ireland.

NATIONAL ORIGINS QUOTAS
UNDER THE McCARRAN-WALTER ACT
FOR THE YEAR 1965

	Number	Percent
Total Immigration Quota	158,831	100.0
Total European Quota	149,967	94.4
Great Britain	65,631	41.2
Germany	25,814	16.3
Ireland	17,756	11.2
Poland	6,488	4.0
Italy	5,666	3.6
Sweden	3,295	2.1
Netherlands	3,136	2.0
France	3,069	1.9
Czechoslovakia	2,859	1.8
Soviet Union	2,697	1.7
Norway	2,364	1.5
Other European Nations	11,192	7.1
Other Eastern Hemisphere Nations	8,864	5.6

The 1952 Immigration and Nationality Act, also known as the McCarran-Walter Act, continued the national origins quota system that had been in effect since 1924. This chart shows the 1965 immigration quotas. Which three nations were most favored by the act? Which nations were most discriminated against by the act?

Of the total annual quota of 158,831, Great Britain was allotted 41 percent. Less than half of its 65,361 quota was filled each year. In contrast, Italy was given a quota of only 5,666 persons per year. Yet there were far more Italians who wanted to come to America. There was a backlog of more than 100,000 people waiting for immigration. For those in countries such as India, with a quota of only 100 per year, immigration was an almost impossible dream.

The quota system was harsh and inflexible. Exceptions had to be made by private immigration bills—acts passed by Congress for the admission of a person or family. This was done, for example, to admit Hungarian and Chinese refugees into the United States. Between 1952 and 1965 nearly 5,000 private immigration bills were passed.

Toward a New Immigration Policy

Despite its many restrictions and the discriminatory quota system, American immigration policy remained the most liberal in all the world. No nation permitted more open and free immigration than the United States. Nevertheless, the use of national quotas was clearly at odds with the ideals on which the nation was founded.

President John F. Kennedy, the great-grandson of Irish immigrants, sought a complete revision of immigration law. The issue was not unrestricted immigration. Rather the issue was the national origins quota system. Kennedy believed that the national origins quota system was "without basis in either logic or reason." In 1963 he placed a set of proposals before Congress. The heart of Kennedy's plan was to end the quota system based on national origins, but Congress failed to act.

Section Check

1. Define: national origins quota system, subversives
2. Identify: "Island of Tears," America's Golden Door, McCarran-Walter Act
3. Why did opposition to immigrants grow after the Civil War?
4. How did the pattern of immigration change from the colonial period to after 1890?
5. What were the two basic purposes of immigration laws passed in the 1920's?
6. How did President Kennedy propose to change immigration laws in the 1960's?

President Lyndon B. Johnson stresses the significance of the 1965 Immigration Amendments. Why do you think Johnson chose to sign the amendments at the Statue of Liberty?

2 IMMIGRATION TODAY

In 1964 President Lyndon B. Johnson reintroduced the Kennedy amendments to the Immigration and Nationality Act. After long debate and various changes Congress enacted the amendments in 1965. President Johnson signed the bill into law in a ceremony at the Statue of Liberty.

Immigration Amendments of 1965

The 1965 amendments to the Immigration and Nationality Act abolished the national origins quota system that had been in effect for more than 40 years. They placed an overall limit of 170,000 on immigration from the Eastern Hemisphere. The only restriction that remained was a 20,000-per-country maximum to ensure that no one country or region dominated immigration into the United States.

The new system borrowed the ***preference system,*** a ranking of most-favored immigrants, that had been a part of the old quota system and expanded on it. The new system set up seven categories, giving priority to relatives of United States citizens and resident aliens, to persons with skills needed to fill labor shortages, and to refugees.

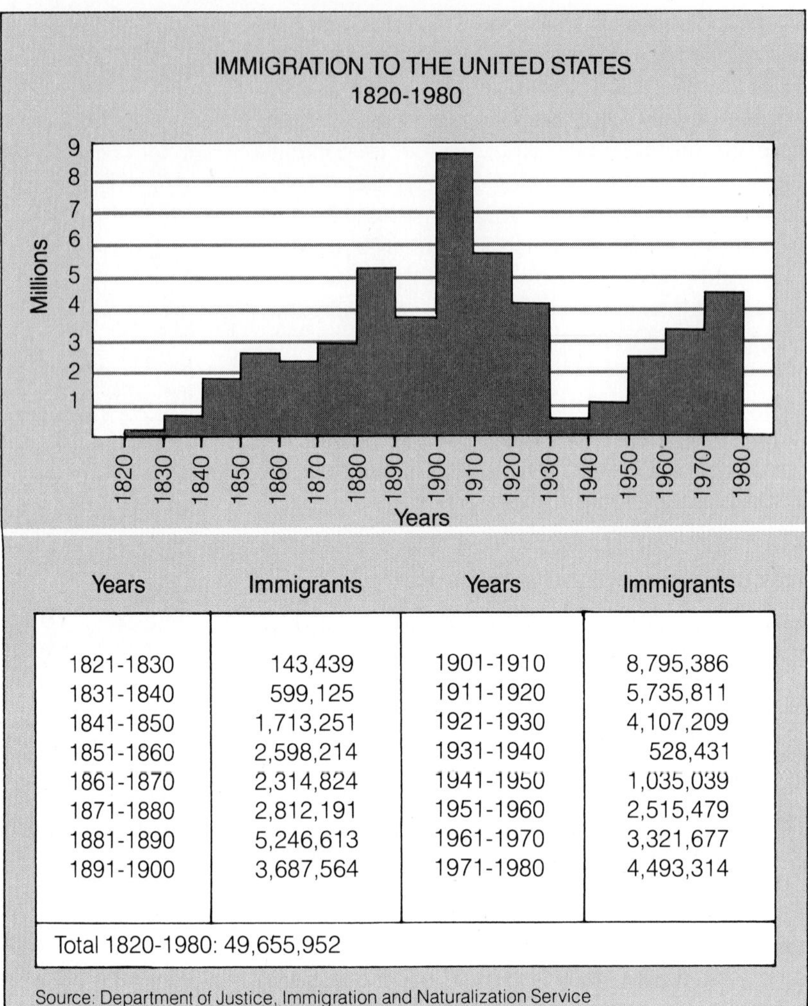

Years	Immigrants	Years	Immigrants
1821-1830	143,439	1901-1910	8,795,386
1831-1840	599,125	1911-1920	5,735,811
1841-1850	1,713,251	1921-1930	4,107,209
1851-1860	2,598,214	1931-1940	528,431
1861-1870	2,314,824	1941-1950	1,035,039
1871-1880	2,812,191	1951-1960	2,515,479
1881-1890	5,246,613	1961-1970	3,321,677
1891-1900	3,687,564	1971-1980	4,493,314
Total 1820-1980: 49,655,952			

Source: Department of Justice, Immigration and Naturalization Service

The number of persons immigrating to the United States has varied widely throughout American history. During what decade since 1820 have the most immigrants come to the United States? During what decade have the fewest immigrants come to this country?

Immigration from the Western Hemisphere, previously unrestricted, was limited to 120,000 per year. Neither the preference system nor the 20,000-per-country maximum, however, was applied to the Western Hemisphere.

Amendments Since 1965

In 1976 the preference system and the 20,000-per-country maximum were applied to the Western Hemisphere. In 1978 the separate hemispheric limits of 170,000 and 120,000 were combined into a single worldwide limitation of 290,000. Now all immigrants compete for immigration visas under a single system.

In 1980 the Refugee Act eliminated the seventh preference category (refugees), replacing it with a separate category of 50,000 refugees per year. A new limit of 270,000 was set on the other six categories.

The Present-Day Preference System

The annual limitation of 270,000 immigrants is divided into six preference classes. Immigrants are admitted to the United States according to such priorities as children of United States citizens, members of the professions, close relatives, and skilled or unskilled workers to fill specified labor requirements.

Whenever any preference class is not filled, the unused portion is available for nonpreference immigrants on a first-come, first-served basis.

In addition to numerical controls on immigration, there continue to be restrictions prohibiting the entry of undesirable aliens. These include criminals, drug addicts, and others who do not measure up to the moral, mental, medical, and economic standards set by law. Members of the Communist party and those who advocate the violent overthrow of the United States government are also excluded.

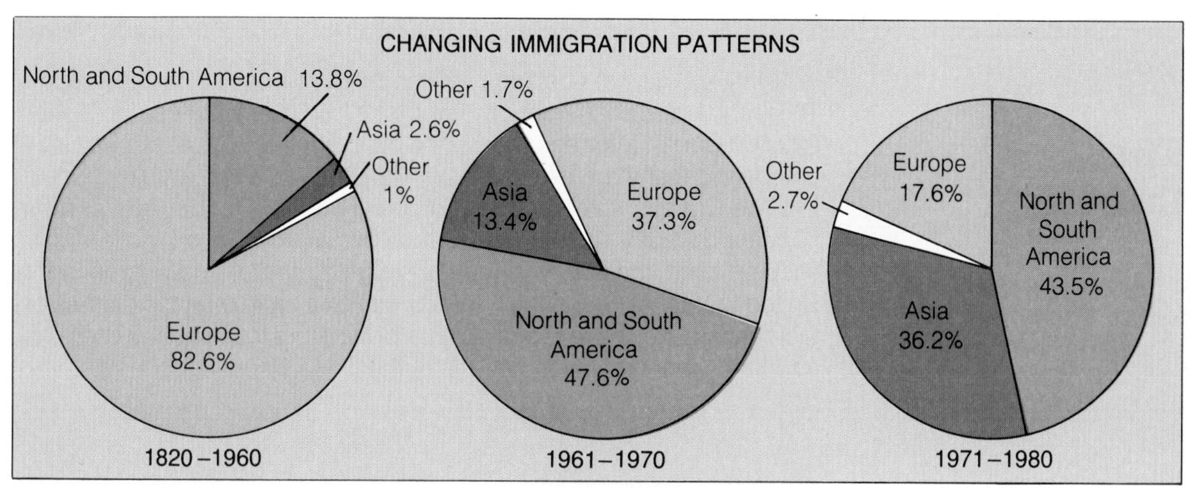

IMMIGRATION TO THE UNITED STATES
1971–1980

Country	Number of Immigrants	Percent of Total Immigration
Mexico	637,163	14.1
Philippines	360,216	8.0
Cuba	276,788	6.1
Korea	271,956	6.0
China*	202,522	4.5
Vietnam	179,681	3.9
India	176,758	3.9
Dominican Republic	148,016	3.2
Jamaica	141,995	3.1
Italy	130,132	2.9
United Kingdom	123,546	2.7
Canada	114,845	2.5
Others	1,729,696	41.6
Total	4,493,314	100.0

*Includes Taiwan
Source: Department of Justice Immigration and Naturalization Service

Study the changes in immigration trends since the early 1800's. What do the circle graphs indicate about immigration from Europe? What do the graphs indicate about immigration from the Americas? Which Latin American country accounted for the highest percentage of total immigration in the period 1971–1980?

The Changing Pattern of Immigration

Following the end of World War II the pattern of immigration began to change. There was a marked increase in the number of immigrants from countries in the Western Hemisphere—particularly from Mexico, Cuba, Jamaica, and the Dominican Republic.

The passage of the Immigration Act of 1965 also brought a dramatic change in immigration from the Eastern Hemisphere. Great Britain, Germany, and Ireland were no longer the countries from which immigrants came in the largest numbers. With the abolition of the national origins quota system, immigration was now led by the Philippines, Korea, and China. Next came Italy, India, Greece, and Portugal.

Refugees

Since its founding, the United States has provided a refuge for those seeking political and religious freedom. According to government policy, refugees are accepted for four reasons. First, the acceptance of

PROFILE

The Cubans

In 1959 Fidel Castro came to power in Cuba in a Communist revolution. Thousands of Cubans sought refuge in the United States. More than 800,000 Cuban refugees have since been admitted. Most are well educated, and many are professionals—doctors, lawyers, architects.

The Cubans settled largely in Dade County, Florida. At first most hoped eventually to return to Cuba. But as the Castro government secured itself, the Cuban refugees sought to make a new home in the United States. Although they arrived with little more than the clothes on their backs, they have rapidly built a prosperous community. Their skill and hard work has given new life to the Dade County economy.

certain refugees often reduces international and domestic frictions that threaten peace. Second, acceptance of refugees may reduce economic and political burdens on other countries. Third, acceptance expresses a deep-seated humanitarian tradition by showing concern for the homeless and persecuted. Fourth, acceptance may help restore to refugees the human rights they have been denied in their homelands, a prime objective of overall United States refugee policy.

Since 1945 the United States has accepted about 2 million refugees. Some 400,000 displaced persons, mostly from Eastern Europe, were admitted after World War II. Another 200,000 persons from Communist Eastern Europe were admitted under the Refugee Relief Act of 1953. In 1956 the people of Hungary rose in revolt against the Communist government and were crushed by the Soviet military, driving 30,000 Hungarian refugees to the United States. Between 1975 and 1980 more than 400,000 refugees from Vietnam and Cambodia entered the United States.

Smaller numbers of refugees have come from all over the world. Among those entering the United States were refugees from Czechoslovakia, after the Soviet invasion in 1968, and Asian residents of Uganda, after their expulsion by Ugandan dictator Idi Amin. Refugees have also come from the Middle East, the People's Republic of China, and the Soviet Union.

Foreign Visitors

Foreign visitors to the United States are not subject to numerical limitation because they are not immigrants. Tourists, business people, government officials, and foreign students come on a ***visa,*** a travel permit for a limited stay. Foreign laborers may also be granted temporary employment permits.

Recent amendments allow foreign visitors with certain types of nonimmigrant visas to apply for immigrant visas while they are in the United States. If they meet all other requirements and if a visa number is available, foreign tourists or temporary workers may now decide to stay.

PROFILE

The Vietnamese

The Vietnamese are the nation's most recent success story. Since the end of the Vietnam War in 1975, more than 400,000 refugees from Indochina have been admitted to the United States. Most of the refugees are educated members of the middle class. More than half could speak English. In a remarkably short time many have been able to find jobs or start their own businesses. The Vietnamese refugees have settled throughout the nation, but about one third are living in California and Texas.

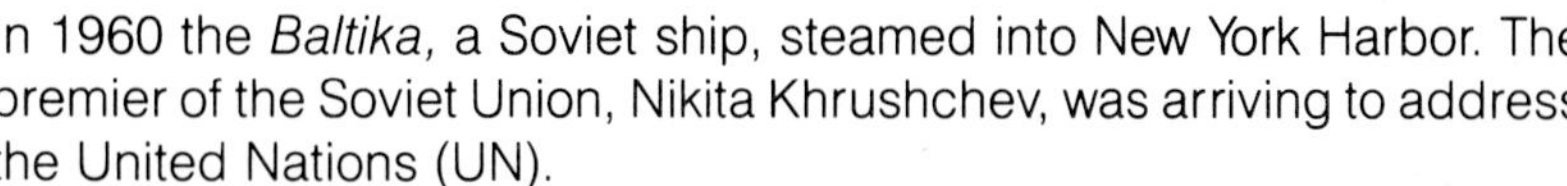

PROFILE

Exiles from Communism

In 1960 the *Baltika,* a Soviet ship, steamed into New York Harbor. The premier of the Soviet Union, Nikita Khrushchev, was arriving to address the United Nations (UN).

Viktor Jaanimets was an ordinary sailor serving on the *Baltika.* Jaanimets, however, soon became the center of an international controversy. For while Khrushchev was speaking at the UN, Jaanimets jumped ship and sought political asylum in the United States. Over the protests of Soviet leaders, Jaanimets was granted asylum and made his home in the United States. He thus became one of thousands of ***defectors,*** citizens of Communist countries who reject the oppression of their homelands.

Unlike the United States and other free countries, the Soviet Union and other Communist countries do not permit their citizens to travel as they choose. Still, more than 135,000 defectors have come to the United States since World War II. Some, like Mstislav Rostropovich, a famous cellist and conductor, and his wife Galina Vishnevskaya, a brilliant ballerina, were able to secure exit visas to leave the Soviet Union. Rostropovich angered Soviet authorities in 1970 when he demanded artistic freedom in a public letter. "Every man must have the right fearlessly to think independently and express his opinions about what he knows," he wrote. In response the Soviet government denied him and his wife the chance to perform. In 1974 the couple fled the Soviet Union for the United States, where Rostropovich later became the highly renowned director of the National Symphony Orchestra in Washington, D.C.

Many other artists have left the Soviet Union for the artistic and personal freedom of the United States. In 1970 the world-famous dancer Natalia Makarova defected from the Kirov Ballet while on tour in the United States. Seven years later, Mikhail Baryshnikov (bottom), another famous dancer, asked for political asylum in the United States. "In Russia a dancer's growth is stunted," Baryshnikov explained after his defection. Highly celebrated, Baryshnikov is now the artistic director of the American Ballet Theater. Also seeking freedom to pursue her career, an 18-year-old Czech tennis star named Martina Navratilova, (center) defected to the United States in 1975. She had come to America, she explained, because here she had the chance to play tennis "whenever I want and wherever I want." Today, she is the world's top-ranked female tennis ace.

Not all Soviet exiles have left their country voluntarily. In 1974 Nobel prize-winning author Alexander Solzhenitsyn (top) was banished from the Soviet Union because he had written about Communist repression. For Solzhenitsyn, like many exiles, the joys of freedom in the United States had to be weighed against the terrible sadness of leaving his homeland. Solzhenitsyn now lives in Vermont. There, he explains, "the simple way of life of the people, the countryside, and the long winters with the snow—remind me of Russia."

Illegal Aliens

According to the Census Bureau there are between 3.5 and 6 million ***illegal aliens*** in the United States. Some estimates go even higher. The number of illegal aliens entering the United States has increased each year over the past decade. In 1979 over 1 million illegal aliens were detained by the Immigration and Naturalization Service and returned to their native countries. This is ten times the number apprehended in 1966. It is believed that only about half of all aliens who enter the country illegally are caught. Thus more than twice as many aliens enter the United States illegally as legally each year. Called "the silent invasion," the flood of illegal immigration is one of the most complex and pressing problems facing the nation.

Illegal aliens enter by a variety of means. Some have counterfeit documents. Some enter on temporary visas—for travel, business, or study—and never leave. Entry without documents is most often made by secretly crossing the borders into the United States. The 2,000-mile (3 200-km) border between the United States and Mexico is too lengthy to be strictly patrolled. More than 80 percent of all undocumented illegal aliens cross the border into the United States from Mexico. They walk, swim, and climb fences. Some are smuggled into the country. The most persistent are caught and returned by the Border Patrol as many as six times a year.

Latin America is the main source of illegal aliens. In addition to the large numbers from Mexico, many undocumented aliens from Central and South America enter the United States across the Mexican border. Another major source of undocumented aliens is the West Indies—especially Haiti, the Dominican Republic, and Jamaica. Most undocumented West Indians enter through Puerto Rico, where they find unrestricted travel to the mainland United States.

Illegal aliens come primarily from countries that are overcrowded, that have high unemployment, and that have very low per capita incomes. They come to the United States—as did immigrants of the past—in search of work and a better life.

The employment of undocumented illegal aliens has stirred fierce controversy. Some people argue that undocumented aliens push American citizens

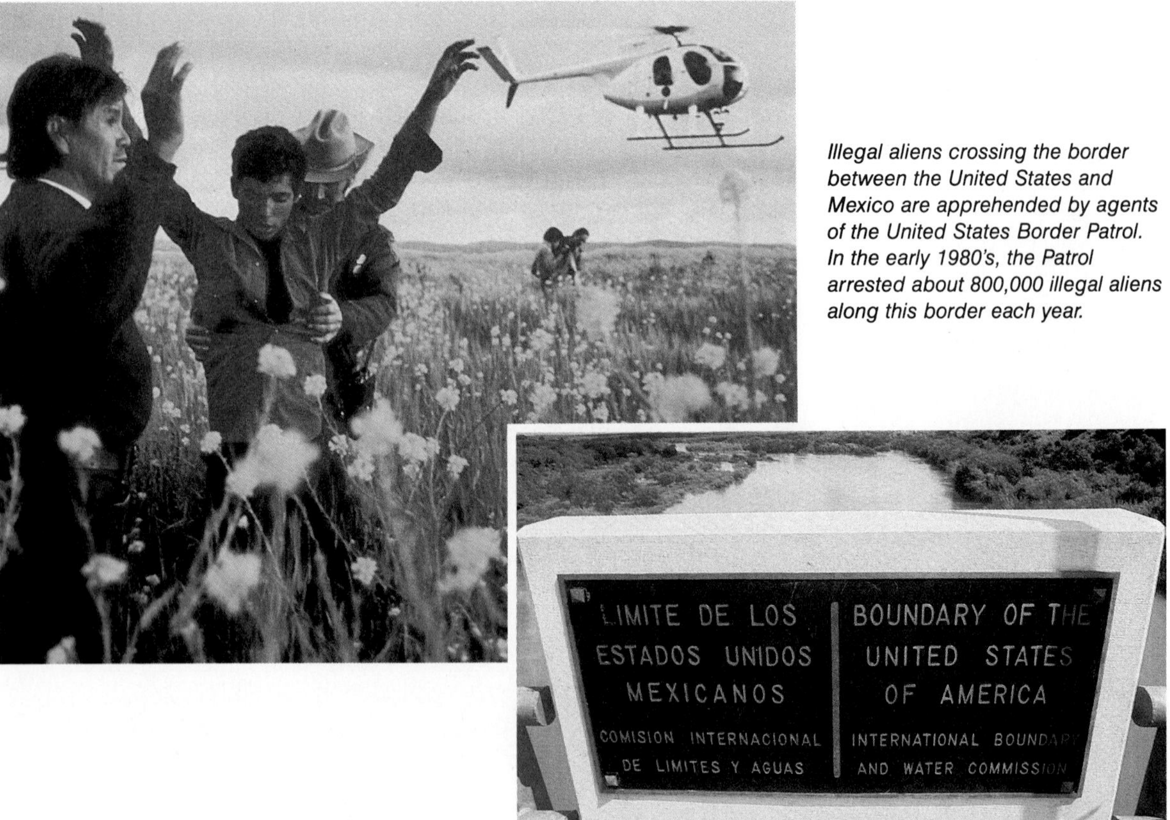

Illegal aliens crossing the border between the United States and Mexico are apprehended by agents of the United States Border Patrol. In the early 1980's, the Patrol arrested about 800,000 illegal aliens along this border each year.

out of jobs, and put them on unemployment relief and welfare. Others respond by saying that most undocumented aliens work at menial jobs that Americans will not take. This is met by the argument that because undocumented aliens often work for low wages, they have lowered the pay rate for certain jobs. Americans, they say, simply cannot afford to take such work.

There are no easy solutions to the problem. One proposal is to cut off the flow of illegal aliens by denying them jobs. This could be done by making it unlawful for an employer to hire them. Any employer who did so would risk punishment. But enforcement for such a law might be difficult. Papers could be forged or counterfeited. Employers, to be on the safe side, might then refuse to hire anyone of Hispanic or Asian ancestry, whether American citizens or legal resident aliens.

The United States Commission on Civil Rights reports that many employers hire undocumented aliens because their illegal status prevents them from organizing or speaking up about unsanitary or unsafe working conditions. According to the Commission, strict enforcement of the Fair Labor Standards Act and other labor laws would remove the employers' temptation to hire illegals.

Another proposal would remove the 20,000-per-country limit imposed on immigration from Western Hemisphere countries since 1976. That limitation was directed at Mexican immigrants, who had numbered about 40,000 per year. With waiting lists for visas backed up for years to come, many Mexicans who want to come north have had to do so illegally. President Reagan has endorsed a bill that would raise immigration from Mexico and Canada to 40,000 per year. But a solution to the undocumented alien problem will not easily be found.

Resident Aliens

Most of the rights guaranteed by the Constitution belong to *persons,* not just to citizens. There are approximately 5 million foreigners legally residing in the United States. There are no restrictions on travel or place of residence, but they must inform the government of any change in address or status. The Bill of Rights protects resident aliens as well as citizens.

Aliens in the United States share most of the obligations of citizens. They must obey the law and pay taxes. Though they may exercise most of the rights enjoyed by citizens, many states place special restrictions on aliens. Most states do not admit aliens into licensed professions such as medicine and law. Some states deny aliens welfare payments and food stamps; others prohibit them from obtaining hunting or fishing licenses. These restrictions are now being challenged in the courts. No state permits aliens to vote—although, oddly enough, aliens voted regularly in the nineteenth century. Aliens may not hold elected public office in any state.

After five years' residence, aliens become eligible for citizenship. But it is not necessary for an alien to become a citizen in order to stay in the United States. Many resident aliens choose to keep the citizenship of their birth—even though they may live in the United States for the rest of their lives.

The most important restriction on aliens is that they do not have a *right* to enter the United States or to stay in the country. These are *privileges,* which the United States government may revoke in certain circumstances. There are three general grounds for ***deportation***—that is, of forcibly requiring aliens to leave the country.

1. Aliens may be sent back to their own country if they have entered the United States illegally.
2. Aliens may be deported if they have violated the terms of their admission. Visas usually specify the length of time an alien may stay. They indicate the purpose of entry—for a visit, study, temporary work, or permanent residence. An alien entering under a tourist or student visa, for example, may not be permitted to take a job while in the United States.
3. Aliens may also be deported if they are proven to be undesirable residents because of immoral, criminal, or subversive acts.

Section Check

1. Define: preference system, defector, visa, illegal alien, deportation
2. Identify: Mstislav Rostropovich, Alexander Solzhenitsyn, resident alien
3. How did the Immigration Amendments of 1965 change immigration to the United States?
4. From which countries have most political refugees come to the United States?
5. What are some problems caused by illegal immigration?

The noted physicist Albert Einstein (center) becomes a naturalized American citizen in 1940. Einstein's daughter Margot (right) and secretary Helen Dukas (left) become citizens at the same time. United States citizenship laws required that Einstein, previously a citizen of both Germany and Switzerland, renounce his allegiance to those countries.

3 CITIZENSHIP

The Constitution refers to ***citizenship*** but does not define it. When the Constitution was ratified in 1789, it awkwardly divided the power to grant citizenship among the states and the federal government. It was not until 1868 and the ratification of the Fourteenth Amendment that citizenship was defined and unified. The amendment states:

All persons born or naturalized in the United States . . . are citizens of the United States and of the State wherein they reside.

The Fourteenth Amendment recognizes citizenship by place of birth. According to the principle of ***jus soli,*** or "right of soil," all persons born in the United States, except the children of high ranking foreign diplomats, are citizens. To be a United States citizen, birth on United States soil suffices. For purposes of citizenship this includes the 50 states, Puerto Rico, the U.S. Virgin Islands, the Marianas, and Guam. It also includes births on vessels within United States territorial waters, or in air carriers in the air space above the United States.

Congress has also provided by statute for citizenship on the basis of ***jus sanguinis,*** or "right of blood." According to *jus sanguinis,* the citizenship of a child is determined by that of the parents. Many American citizens live abroad. Any child born abroad of United States citizen-parents (one of whom has resided in the United States) is a United States citizen.

A child born abroad of one alien parent and one citizen-parent is also a citizen if the citizen-parent has lived in the United States for at least ten years, including five years after the age of 14.

Dual Citizenship

Other countries define citizenship in similar ways—either by *jus soli, jus sanguinis,* or both. This can raise some complicated problems. What happens when someone is born in the United States of foreign parents? What about the situation where one parent is an American citizen, the other foreign? Can a person be a citizen of two nations?

Some countries permit their citizens to claim dual citizenship and to carry the ***passports*** of two nations. The United States rejects the concept of dual citizenship as a matter of policy. It does, however, accept its existence in individual cases. The citizenship laws of other countries cannot be controlled by the United States. Therefore some United States citizens may possess a second citizenship as a result of those laws. They may also possess a passport issued by another country. In most cases, however, United States citizens with two passports are required by law to use their United States passports when entering or departing the United States.

Requirements for Naturalization

The Constitution in Article 1, Section 8, gives Congress the power "to establish a uniform rule of naturalization." ***Naturalization*** is the process by which a person gains citizenship at some time after birth. Naturalized citizens have the same constitutional rights as native-born Americans. The one exception is only native-born citizens may be elected President or Vice President.

In 1790 Congress passed the first naturalization act. Citizenship was limited to "free white persons." Two years' residence in the United States was required before a person could become a naturalized citizen. In 1802 the residency requirement was set at five years, and so it remains today.

Aliens who wish to become citizens of the United States must meet a set of legal requirements. Applicants must be at least 18 years of age. In certain circumstances children under the age of 16 automatically become citizens through the naturalization of their parents. Only aliens who have been lawfully admitted to the United States for permanent residence can be naturalized.

After applicants have been admitted for permanent residence, they must reside continuously in the United States for at least five years. They also must have lived for six months in the state where they have applied for naturalization. For someone who is married to an American citizen, the residency requirement is reduced to three years. Aliens who serve in the United States armed forces for three years may become citizens if they satisfy other legal requirements.

Applicants for citizenship must be able to speak, read, and write simple English. They must show some knowledge of the history and form of the government of the United States. Applicants must also be of good moral character. They must believe in the principles of the Constitution of the United States and be favorable to the "good order and happiness of the United States." Within the ten years before filing for citizenship, applicants must not have advocated the violent overthrow of the government. They must not have been a member of the Communist party or any similar organization.

Before being admitted to citizenship, applicants for naturalization must give up allegiance to any foreign country and any foreign title. They must promise to obey the laws and the Constitution of the United States. They must also promise to bear arms and to defend the United States if called upon to do so. Persons who oppose military service on religious grounds are excused from bearing arms. However, they may be called upon to perform civilian service in the defense of the nation.

Naturalization Procedures

As the first step toward citizenship, aliens must file an application with the Immigration and Naturalization Service of the United States Department of Justice. Applicants are then called before an examiner. Each applicant must bring two United States citizens as witnesses. On the basis of their own personal knowledge, the witnesses must be able to tell the examiner about the applicant's character, loyalty, and residence in the United States.

The applicant then files a petition for naturalization in a state or federal district court. The application triggers an examination process in which examiners send to the court a report of their investigation into the applicant's fitness for citizenship. The last step is an open hearing in the court. If the judge is satisfied that all requirements have been met, the court issues a certificate of naturalization. The judge then administers the oath of allegiance to the United States of America.

Collective Naturalization

From time to time Congress has granted citizenship to a large group of people all at once in a process known as ***collective naturalization.*** It has been used to confer citizenship on the residents of new territories and on racial minorities within the United States.

As the nation expanded, people living in the new territories were naturalized collectively. Thus citizenship was granted to residents of the Louisiana Purchase (1803), Florida (1819), Texas (1845), Alaska (1867), Hawaii (1900), Puerto Rico (1917), the Virgin Islands (1927), and Guam (1950). In 1980 the 16,000 residents of the Northern Mariana Islands were naturalized collectively.

The Fourteenth Amendment conferred citizenship upon blacks in 1868. But it was not until 1924, by an Act of Congress, that Native Americans were made citizens. Originally the government treated groups of Native Americans as separate nations. Treaties were negotiated—and usually broken. In 1871 government policy changed. Native Americans were brought under the direct control of the Federal Bureau of Indian Affairs. They became "wards of the government." Native Americans were naturalized and given voting rights in 1924, but they continued to be treated as "second-class citizens" for many years.

Like Native Americans, the first Mexicans in the United States did not immigrate here. They were a conquered people. What is now the southwestern United States was originally part of Mexico. During the 1830's American settlers in Texas came into conflict and eventual war with Mexico. Joined by some of the Mexican residents of the region, the settlers won independence from Mexico in 1836. In 1845 the Republic of Texas, at its request, was annexed by the United States.

Annexation deepened tensions between the United States and Mexico, and in 1846 the two nations went to war. The terms of peace were set in 1848 by the Treaty of Guadalupe Hidalgo. Mexico, in defeat, was forced to give up two fifths of its territory, including its claim to Texas. The Mexican Cession included the present states of California, Arizona, Nevada, Utah, Texas, and parts of New Mexico, Colorado, and Wyoming. In exchange for the territory

Hunkpapa Sioux Chief Sitting Bull and his family were confined on a United States government reservation in the Dakota Territory at the time of this 1882 photograph. The citizenship principle of jus soli *did not apply to Native Americans until 1924.*

INSIGHT

The Man Without a Country

It is 1805. A young soldier named Philip Nolan has been found guilty of treason against the United States. When the president of the court asks him whether he has anything to say to prove that he has always been faithful to his country, he cries out in a wild frenzy, "I wish I may never hear of the United States again!"

Those words, which shock the court, seal the young soldier's fate. "Prisoner, hear the sentence of the Court!" the judge declares. "The Court decides, subject to the approval of the President, that you never hear the name of the United States again."

And from that moment on, until the day he dies, Philip Nolan is "The Man Without a Country," the title of the story that tells his tale. He is placed on board the *Nautilis,* an American naval ship, with these instructions: "Under no circumstances is he ever to hear of his country or to see any information regarding it. . . . This rule, in which his punishment is involved, shall not be broken."

For more than half a century Nolan's only home is a succession of naval ships—"always at least some hundred miles from the country he had hoped he might never hear of again." He is allowed to engage in conversation—but never once is the United States mentioned. He is allowed to read foreign newspapers—but all advertisements or paragraphs that mention the United States are removed first. Even the map of the United States is removed from the atlas he takes on board. The officers on board begin to call him "Plain-Buttons," because "he was not permitted to wear the army button, for the reason that it bore either the initials or the insignia of the country he had disowned."

Gradually the other sailors come to respect and even feel affection for Philip Nolan. He is courageous in battle, kind to others, and truly repentant. Toward the end of his life he tells a young officer,

No matter what happens to you, no matter who flatters you or who abuses you, never look at another flag, never let a night pass but you pray God to bless that flag. Remember, boy, that behind all these men you have to do with, behind officers, and government, and people even, there is the Country Herself, your Country, and that you belong to Her as you belong to your own mother.

At last, when Nolan is on his deathbed, an officer named Danforth yields to his pleas and tells him what has become of the country he deserted. He tells the dying man that 19 states have been added to the Union. He tries to describe everything that has come into being since Nolan disowned his country. Overcome with emotion, Nolan points to a prayer in a prayerbook at his bedside. "For ourselves and our country, O gracious God," it reads, "we thank Thee."

The story of "The Man Without a Country" is just that—a story written in 1863 by Edward Everett Hale. Philip Nolan never lived; he never betrayed his country; he never suffered the sentence of living without a country. But so moving is Hale's story—and so powerful is the story's patriotic moral—that "The Man Without a Country" has remained for a hundred years a national classic.

the United States paid Mexico $15 million. The Mexican residents had the option to leave, but most chose to stay. By the treaty they were guaranteed "all rights of citizens of the United States." The final territorial adjustment was made in 1853. In the Gadsden Purchase the United States paid Mexico $10 million for a slice of land near El Paso. Under the terms of the agreement Mexican residents of this territory also were granted American citizenship.

Loss of Citizenship

A person who has acquired United States citizenship by naturalization may lose citizenship by proof in a federal court that it was obtained by deceit or willful misrepresentation. Both native-born and naturalized citizens may lose citizenship by performing certain acts specified by Congress if those acts are peformed "with the intention to voluntarily relinquish United States citizenship."

A citizen may also renounce United States citizenship by a formal oath. This declaration, in the form prescribed by the Secretary of State, is made before an American diplomatic or consular officer outside the United States.

Loss of citizenship is not to be taken lightly, for United States citizenship and the rights it confers are among the most valuable possessions a person can have.

One last word should be made on loss of citizenship. It is widely believed that persons convicted of serious crimes can be deprived of their citizenship. This is not so. Many states deny convicted felons the right to vote or hold public office, but their citizenship cannot be taken away.

Travel Abroad

American citizens, native-born and naturalized, have the right to travel freely within the United States and to go abroad. The only restriction on freedom of movement is for people restrained by law—for example, those who are in jail or on bail.

American citizens are free to travel abroad. Visits to Canada and Mexico normally do not require a passport. For most travel elsewhere, Americans must have a valid passport.

All Americans abroad must remember that when traveling in a foreign country they are subject to its laws. These laws may be very different from those of the United States. American ***consulates*** are located in most foreign countries. Consular officers are there to advise and help American citizens who are in serious financial, medical, or legal difficulty. If Americans are arrested overseas, consular officials will advise them of their rights under local law and assist them in getting a lawyer. They will help in contacting family and friends. But what consular officials can do is limited both by the United States laws and by foreign laws.

An exception to the right to travel was made during World War II. On the West Coast people of Japanese ancestry, United States citizens and aliens alike, were forcibly moved from their homes. More than 100,000 men, women, and children—70,000 of whom were United States citizens—were placed in relocation camps. There they remained until their "loyalty" could be established.

The United States was at war with Japan. United States officials justified the relocation in the name of national security and said it was necessary for the

INSIGHT

The Right to Travel

A passport is a formal document issued by a nation to its citizens for travel abroad. A valid passport is usually necessary to exit from and reenter the United States. It is normally required to enter another country. Many countries also require foreigners to have a visa. A visa is an approval placed in the passport by the authorities of a particular country for travel to that country.

Each year some 3 million passports are issued to American citizens. The procedure for getting a passport is simple. For your first passport you must personally present the completed application at a Passport Agency, a federal or state court, or at selected post offices. Proof of identity and citizenship is required, along with two identical photographs and a $35 fee. The passport is valid for ten years.

Members of a Japanese-American family observe mealtime traditions in spite of their internment at a World War II relocation camp. On what grounds did the United States government restrict the movement of Japanese-Americans during the war?

protection and safety of Japanese-Americans. But the United States carried out no relocation in Hawaii, where 32 percent of the population was of Japanese descent. Neither in Hawaii nor on the West Coast was there ever any evidence of disloyalty to the United States by Japanese-Americans. On the contrary, Japanese-American soldiers served heroically in the war. Today the wartime relocation of Japanese on the West Coast is seen as an act of discrimination and prejudice and a tragic mistake.

Section Check

1. Define: citizenship, *jus soli, jus sanguinis,* passport, consulate
2. What is naturalization?
3. What are some requirements for naturalization?
4. What is collective naturalization?
5. What is required for United States citizens to travel abroad?

SUMMARY

The United States is a nation of immigrants. Even the first inhabitants of the continent originally migrated to America from Asia.

For more than a century after the American Revolution, millions of immigrants came to the United States without restriction. After 1882 Congress began to restrict the numbers and types of people who could enter the country.

The national origins quota system, first enacted in 1921, was an attempt to control the racial makeup of the American population. Under the quota system immigration from southern and eastern Europe was cut sharply while immigration from Asia and Africa was nearly eliminated.

The 1965 amendments to the Immigration and Nationality Act shifted the basis of immigration from national origins to reuniting separated relatives and filling the needs of the American labor market.

In addition to legal immigration, thousands of illegal aliens, some undocumented, enter the United States each year, mostly from Latin America.

According to the principle of *jus soli* ("right of soil"), the United States recognizes as citizens all persons born on American soil. Congress has also provided for citizenship on the basis of *jus sanguinis* ("right of blood"). Thus a child born abroad of two citizen-parents is also a citizen.

Naturalization is the process by which a person gains citizenship sometime after birth. Naturalized American citizens have the same constitutional rights as native-born Americans, except that they may not be elected President or Vice President.

Chapter 7 Review

Using Vocabulary

Answer the questions by using the meaning of each underlined term.

1. As an immigrant from Asia, would you prefer to be admitted to the United States under the national origins quota system or the preference system?
2. Is a defector more likely to experience deportation than an illegal alien? Why or why not?
3. For what reason might the government deny a subversive a visa or a passport?
4. How does *jus soli* citizenship differ from *jus sanguinis* citizenship?
5. What are the requirements for naturalization?
6. When might an illegal alien turn to a consulate for help?

Understanding American Government

1. Briefly describe immigration in the colonial period for both whites and blacks.
2. What pushed many European immigrants from their homelands? What attracted them to the United States?
3. Explain how opposition to immigration grew before the Civil War. What forms did the opposition take?
4. What steps did Congress take to restrict immigration in the second half of the nineteenth century?
5. Explain how the tide of immigration rose and fell after 1880. How did the pattern of immigration change?
6. Describe the immigration policy of the United States today.
7. What are some reasons the United States accepts refugees?
8. Discuss the problems caused by the immigration of illegal aliens and some of the proposals to solve it.

Extending Your Skills: Interpreting Graphs

Study the circle graphs on page 191. Then answer the questions that follow.

1. What region was the major source of immigration between 1820 and 1860?
2. What region has contributed most heavily to United States immigration since 1820?
3. What region has contributed most heavily to United States immigration since 1961?
4. What region had the sharpest rate of increase in immigration between 1820 and 1980?
5. Based on the data shown in the graphs, what trend in immigration patterns is likely in the next 20 years? What evidence can you cite from the graphs to support your answer?

Government and You

1. President Truman called the quota system "insulting to large numbers of our finest citizens, irritating to our allies abroad, and foreign to our purposes and ideals." Do you agree? What do you think was wrong with the quota system?
2. Many people have called the influx of illegal aliens one of the most serious problems facing the United States. Do you agree? What do you think can be done to solve this problem?
3. What are some reasons why United States citizenship is so valuable? Why do citizens of countries such as the Soviet Union defect to the United States, while United States citizens seldom defect to the Soviet Union?
4. The process of naturalization requires several years and many steps to complete. Does this process strike you as being fair? What changes, if any, would you suggest?

Activities

1. Make a wall chart showing places in your state that were named by immigrants.
2. Using historical data from the past 200 years, prepare a line graph showing the number of immigrants from a selected country. What events in that country correspond with periods of heavy immigration?
3. Make a list of famous Americans who were naturalized citizens. Use the list to prove or disprove the statement: We gained more from immigration than from limiting entry to the United States.

Chapter 8

The American People: A Statistical Profile

If we could first know where we are, and whither we are tending, we could better judge what to do, and how to do it.

ABRAHAM LINCOLN

We can't know where we're going if we don't know where we are.

BUREAU OF THE CENSUS SLOGAN

CHAPTER OVERVIEW

On a typical workday in New York City, crowds of people of different ages, races, and ethnic backgrounds can be seen on the streets. In 1980 the Census Bureau determined that more than 9 million people lived in the New York metropolitan area.

1 THE CENSUS

Who are the American people? What are the basic characteristics of the population? Its size? Its rate of growth? How is the population distributed by region, by age and sex, by religion, race, and ethnic background, by occupation, income, and education?

To present a profile of the American people we turn to statistics. ***Statistics*** are numerical facts. These figures may seem dry, but behind every population statistic there are real people. These statistics tell not only where we are, but also where we have been and where we are going.

Demography is the statistical study of population. In the United States the primary source of ***demographic data***, or statistical information, is the ***census***—a count of the population taken at a particular time. The Constitution in Article 1, Section 2, directs the government to conduct a census. The first census was taken in 1790, and since then a full census has been conducted every ten years.

The census of 1790 was taken under the supervision of Thomas Jefferson when he was Secretary of State. The first census was little more than a head count to see how many people there were in the United States. It was published in a single slim volume of 56 pages. The census questionnaire now includes a variety of questions. Its purpose is to provide a profile of the population. The 1980 census data was collected and published in a series of volumes that had expanded to more than 15,000 separate books and pamphlets.

The 1980 Census

The census is conducted by the Bureau of the Census, a division of the Department of Commerce. In addition to its 5,000 regular employees, the bureau hired more than 460,000 people to help with the 1980 census. The Census Bureau calls itself the "Fact Finder for the Nation." It counts just about everything that can be counted and provides most of the statistics used by the federal government. Besides the full census taken every ten years, the bureau prepares annual estimates of the population. It also conducts special censuses for various federal agencies. These include surveys of business, industry, agriculture, housing, and transportation.

PROFILE

To Count a Nation

Once every 10 years they set out across America, a small army of census-takers with pens and printed forms. They travel by foot, car, boat, dunebuggy, and snowmobile. They visit homes, hotels, orphanages, prisons, hospitals, and ships at sea—any place in the United States where people live or could live. Their mission: to find and count every person—young and old, citizen and alien, rich and poor—residing in the nation.

The 1980 census was the largest in U.S. history, and perhaps the greatest and most sophisticated gathering of facts ever undertaken. To begin the massive task, the Census Bureau put together the largest mailing list ever compiled for the United States. Mapmakers divided the nation into enumeration districts—areas small enough to be counted by a single census-taker. Within each district every road, every alley, every house was listed and programmed into the bureau's computer. Then, on March 28, 86 million questionnaires were mailed to 35,000 post offices across the country. (In all, the 1980 census used 120 million forms, 5,000 tons of paper, and 85 tons of ink.) Most of these initial questionnaires were returned by mail. On April 1, census-takers set out to reach the people who did not return their questionnaires or who could not be reached by mail. Their job was not an easy one. One census-taker trudged on snowshoes through the north woods of Minnesota, carrying a shotgun to protect himself from hungry wolves. Another sat through a tornado that blew the roof off a house in Oklahoma—but she stayed to get the answers to her questions. Census-takers in the Southwest used aerial photography not simply to locate dwellings on Indian reservations but also to decide whether to go by river, road, or hike over the mountains to reach them.

To encourage people to take part in the census, the Census Bureau mounted the largest advertising campaign in its history. "Answer the census! We're counting on you!" the slogan encouraged—not only in English but in Greek, Vietnamese, Spanish, Cantonese, Russian, and 26 other languages. In states such as Texas and California, Spanish-language radio stations assured millions of migrant workers—many of whom are illegal aliens—that they could take part in the census without fear of being deported. (So strict are the Census Bureau's rules of confidentiality, in fact, that an escaped convict may be interviewed but cannot be turned in, and even federal judges are not allowed to subpoena census records.)

In all, the 1980 census collected more than 3 billion answers. Over the course of the next decade those answers will be examined and interpreted to give a portrait in numbers of the nation and its people.

Census costs have risen dramatically. The 1970 census cost about $222 million. By 1980, the census cost had risen to more than $1 billion. Most likely, the cost of taking the census every 10 years will continue to increase. But most members of Congress believe that the wealth of data collected by the census is well worth the expense. Census data are used by Congress, by agencies of the executive branch, and by the private sector to develop and to evaluate the numerous social and economic programs that affect the nation.

Census Data

The 1980 census was the most extensive ever undertaken. More than 90 percent of all households received a census questionnaire in the mail. Others were visited by census-takers. Certain basic information was gathered about each person in the United States. Each household was to answer 21 questions relating to population characteristics and to housing. These were contained in the short form that most households received. A more detailed form, containing 65 questions, was sent to a 20-percent sample of all households. A ***sample*** is a representative part selected from a larger whole. By studying the characteristics of the sample, it is possible to gain information about the whole from which it was taken.

The facts obtained for all persons in the 1980 census population questionnaire were (1) name, (2) household relationship, (3) sex, (4) race, (5) age, (6) marital status, and (7) Spanish/Hispanic origin or descent. For the more detailed sample further information included birthplace, educational attainment, language, ancestry, citizenship, employment and income, marriage and number of children, veteran status, and physical disability.

The census once asked about religious affiliation, but this question was dropped because it was thought to pry into matters of personal belief. For the same reason the census does not ask political questions. All census data are strictly confidential. The Census Bureau may not give out information about any individual to a private person or to any other government agency—not even the FBI.

How Census Data Are Used

Accurate information about the population is essential for the planning, administration, and evaluation of programs in both the public and the private sector. Decisions must be based upon facts, and the census is a gold mine of data about American society.

INSIGHT

Processing the Census

The Census Bureau has been a leader in developing new and improved methods of statistical tabulation and analysis. The 1890 Census introduced punch card tabulation. For each person information was entered on the card as a hole punched in a particular box. The punched cards were placed over trays containing small cups filled with mercury. Metal pins were then dropped over each card: wherever the pins fell through to a cup, an electronic circuit was completed and the information was recorded. This technique marked the beginning of electronic data processing.

After World War II the automated computer UNIVAC, a machine that could tabulate 4,000 items per minute, was developed for the bureau. By the 1970's new computers had increased speed of tabulation to nearly 1 million items per minute. Today visitors to the Smithsonian Institution in Washington can see the central unit, or brain, of the original UNIVAC.

In the public sector many government policies depend on projected ***trends*** within the population. Needs must be anticipated before they arise. How many young people, for example, can be expected to enter the nation's schools in the next decade? Will additional schools have to be built? Will more teachers be necessary? Census data are also used to gauge the direction of population movements. Such information is necessary to determine the location of new schools, hospitals, libraries, and recreation facilities. The data are used by government to plan roads, sewerage, water, electricity, and fire and police protection.

Businesses use census data to analyze market trends. Changes in the character of the population may require shifts in the kinds of products manufactured. For example, shifts in the population from rural to urban areas bring new consumer needs. Higher average incomes result in a demand for luxury goods and quality merchandise. Successful businesses anticipate these changes before they occur. Census information also helps business leaders decide where to locate new shopping centers, banks, restaurants, and factories.

As prescribed by the Constitution, the primary purpose of the census is for the ***apportionment,*** or division, of seats in the House of Representatives. The total number of seats in the House is fixed by law at 435. Representation for each state is based on its population. The Constitution requires that the seats be reapportioned every 10 years to reflect changes in the population. After each census, the Census Bureau determines the number of seats to which each state is entitled. Congressional districts are then redrawn within the states to reflect these changes. As a result of the 1980 census 11 states gained additional seats, while 10 states lost seats. Census data are also used to apportion seats in state legislatures to reflect shifts in population.

One of the most important uses of census data is for the distribution of federal funds to state and local governments. The distribution of federal funds to the states is based on a number of statistical measures, including population and per capita income. For example, the number of children in poor families determines the amount of federal money going to each county under the Elementary and Secondary School Act. Because as much as $90 billion each year is involved in federal assistance to states and local governments, the accuracy of the census count is of the greatest concern to all involved.

Another important use of census data is in the study of government and politics. Political scientists compare shifts in voting and public opinion with changes in the character of the population. Demographers might ask, for example, whether shifts in voting behavior are related to urbanization, to higher levels of education, or to changing patterns of employment and income, or to combinations of these and other factors. Census data frequently help to identify issues which may become the focus of public policy debate—for example, unemployment, energy requirements, or school finance.

The amusement park on Coney Island, New York, attracts hundreds of thousands of tourists each year. Census data help the tourist industry to predict attendance rates.

The census records a vast amount of information about the United States population. But all of these facts and figures are not of equal importance for political analysis. In this chapter we will look at some of the characteristics of the population which are politically most significant.

Section Check

1. Define: statistics, demography, census, sample, trend, apportionment
2. Identify: Bureau of the Census
3. How was the 1980 census taken? What was the cost?
4. What seven facts were obtained for all persons in the 1980 census?
5. What is the primary purpose of the census as described in the Constitution?

2 POPULATION STATISTICS

In 1980, with a population of 226.5 million, the United States ranked as the fourth most populous nation in the world. In the entrance hall of the Department of Commerce in Washington, a clock records each addition to the nation's population. According to recent Census Bureau calculations, one person is added to the population every 9 seconds, a growth that represents a total increase of about 1 percent each year. The growth of the population of the United States is illustrated on this page.

Although the population of the United States has increased steadily since 1790, the rate of that increase—the growth rate—is slowing down. During the 1960's the nation's 10-year growth rate reached a peak of approximately 16 percent. The growth rate dropped to 9.7 percent in the 1970's, and the Census Bureau expects it to remain at about 9 percent throughout the 1980's. By the year 2000 the 10-year growth rate is projected to drop to about 7 percent. What is the projected population of the United States for the year 2000?

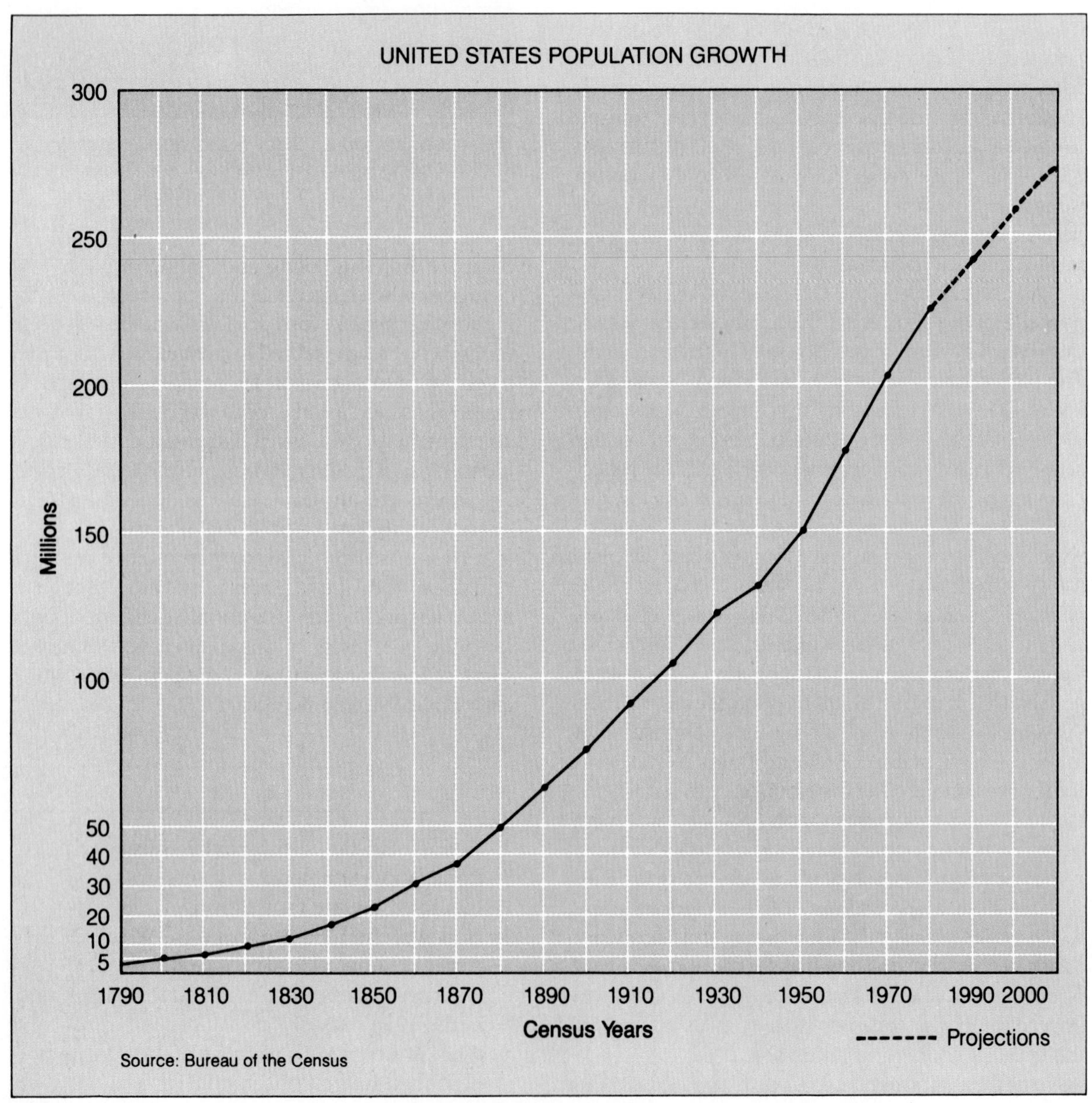

Age and Sex Distribution

The average age of the American population is 30 years. The distribution of the population by age and sex can be seen on the charts on this page.

Since the 1960's the birth rate and death rate in the United States have both fallen. As the large number of young people now between 13 and 19 years of age grows older, the average age of the population as a whole will increase. Improved health care means also that people are living longer. These changes in the age distribution will have an important impact on government and politics. A smaller percentage of people will be in school. Larger numbers will be seeking employment. There will be more people over the age of 65 drawing social security.

A majority of Americans, 51.4 percent of the population, are female. Roughly the same number of male and female babies are born, but females have a longer life expectancy. Today the average American female lives 77.8 years, as compared to 69.9 years for the average male.

SEX DISTRIBUTION

Year	Percent Male	Percent Female
1930	50.6	49.4
1940	50.2	49.8
1950	49.7	50.3
1960	49.3	50.7
1970	48.7	51.3
1980	48.6	51.4

CHANGING AGE DISTRIBUTION (BY PERCENT)

	1980 Average Age 30 Years	2000 Projected Average Age 37 Years
Age 65 and over	11.3%	13.1%
Age 35 – 64	30.9%	39.0%
Age 18 – 34	29.7%	22.8%
Age 5 – 17	20.9%	18.5%
Under Age 5	7.2%	6.6%

Source: Bureau of the Census

Since 1930 the sex-distribution pattern of the United States (above) has shifted steadily. The female population—as a percentage of the total population—has changed from a minority to a majority. The age distribution of the population (left) continues to change. In 1980 persons aged 35 and over made up 42.2 percent of the total population. By 2000 they are projected to make up 52.1 percent of the total.

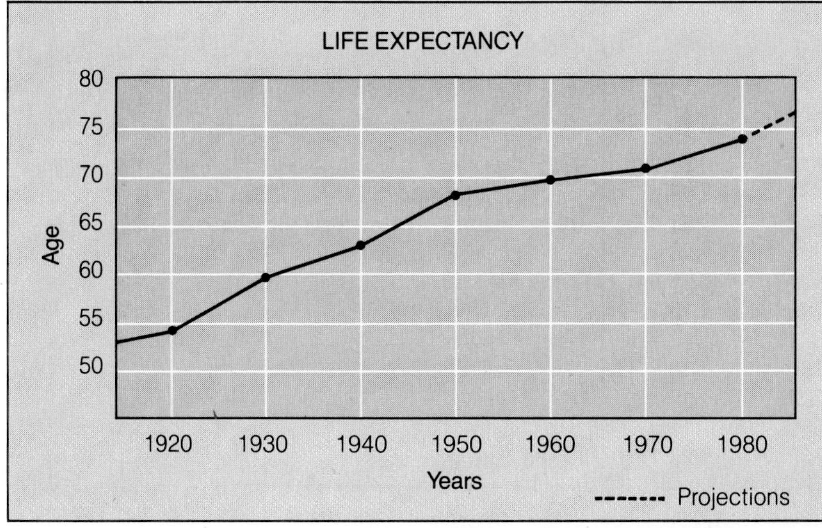

Statistics for life expectancy measure the average length of life from birth. Improvements in nutrition and health care in the United States have enabled people to live longer, leading to a dramatic rise in the average life expectancy. The average life expectancy for 1980—73.8 years—can be calculated by averaging the life expectancies of the average male with the average female.

Population Distribution by Region

One of the most significant population changes has been the shift from rural to urban residence. In 1790, when the census was first taken, 95 percent of the American people lived in rural areas. Philadelphia, then the nation's largest city, had a population of 42,000. Only 33,000 people lived in New York City. Today about 26 percent of all Americans are rural residents. Almost 74 percent of all Americans live in urban areas. About 15 percent of the American people live in cities with a population of 100,000 or more.

Since 1950 urban growth has been primarily in suburbs and in cities of moderate size. Most of the largest central cities, located in the North and East, have lost population. In the Sun Belt of the South

More than half of the total population lives in 9 of the 50 states. In order of population they are (1) California, (2) New York, (3) Texas, (4) Pennsylvania, (5) Illinois, (6) Ohio, (7) Florida, (8) Michigan, and (9) New Jersey. The most rapid population growth is primarily in the Sun Belt states of the South and West. Between 1970 and 1980 three Sun Belt states—California, Florida, and Texas—accounted for two fifths of the total United States population increase of 23 million.

POPULATION BY STATE

	Population in Thousands 1980	Percent Change 1970-1980		Population in Thousands 1980	Percent Change 1970-1980
Northeast			Midwest		
Maine	1,125	13.2	Ohio	10,797	1.3
New Hampshire	921	24.8	Indiana	5,490	5.7
Vermont	511	15.0	Illinois	11,418	2.8
Massachusetts	5,737	0.8	Michigan	9,258	4.2
Rhode Island	947	*0.3	Wisconsin	4,705	6.5
Connecticut	3,108	2.5	Minnesota	4,077	7.1
New York	17,557	*3.8	Iowa	2,913	3.1
New Jersey	7,364	2.7	Missouri	4,917	5.1
Pennsylvania	11,867	0.6	North Dakota	653	5.6
			South Dakota	690	3.6
South			Nebraska	1,570	5.7
Delaware	595	8.6	Kansas	2,363	5.1
Maryland	4,216	7.5			
District of Columbia	638	*15.7	West		
Virginia	5,346	14.9	Montana	787	13.3
West Virginia	1,950	11.8	Idaho	944	32.4
North Carolina	5,874	15.5	Wyoming	471	41.6
South Carolina	3,119	20.4	Colorado	2,889	30.7
Georgia	5,464	19.1	New Mexico	1,300	27.8
Florida	9,740	43.4	Arizona	2,718	53.1
Kentucky	3,661	13.7	Utah	1,461	37.9
Tennessee	4,591	16.9	Nevada	799	63.5
Alabama	3,890	12.9	Washington	4,130	21.0
Mississippi	2,521	13.7	Oregon	2,633	25.9
Arkansas	2,286	18.8	California	23,669	18.5
Louisiana	4,204	15.3	Alaska	400	32.4
Oklahoma	3,025	18.2	Hawaii	965	25.3
Texas	14,228	27.1	United States Total	226,505	11.4

* = Decrease
Source: Bureau of the Census

and West, however, large cities have grown rapidly over the past decade. Of the nation's largest cities, Houston has the highest rate of growth. With more than 1,000 people arriving each week, Houston's 1.6 million population is expected to double by the year 2000.

The dramatic shifts in population from rural to urban areas and the more recent growth of the states and cities in the Sun Belt underscore the fact that Americans are a people on the move. Each year one out of every five Americans changes residence. Most Americans, of course, move from one house or apartment to another within the same area or state. But about 32 percent of all native-born Americans live in a state other than the one in which they were born.

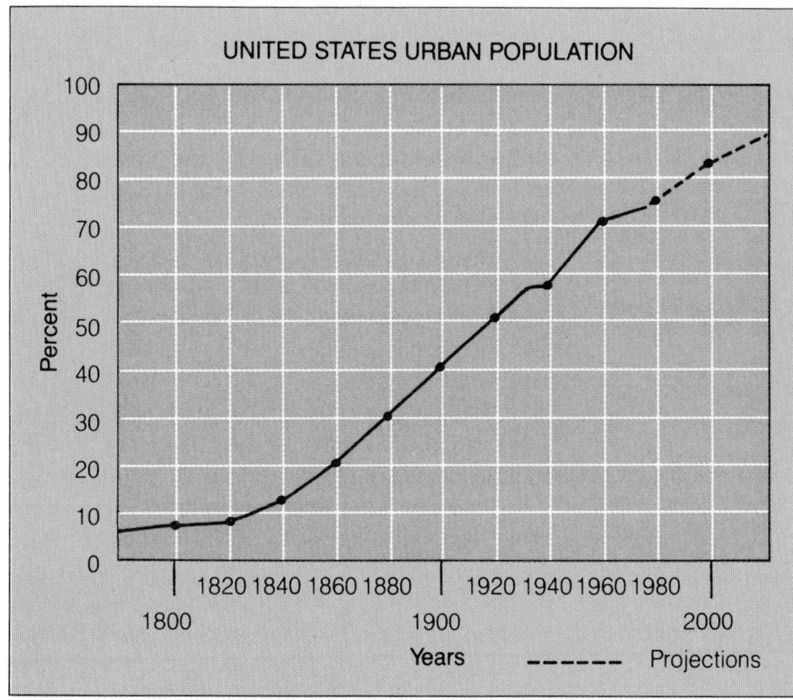

Contrast the Census Bureau projection of urban population for the year 2000 with the urban population of 1900. How much greater will the urban population of the United States be in 2000 than it was in 1900?

TEN LARGEST CITIES IN THE UNITED STATES

City	1980 Population	Percent Change 1970-1980
1. New York City	7,071,000	*10.4
2. Chicago	3,005,000	*10.8
3. Los Angeles	2,967,000	5.5
4. Philadelphia	1,688,000	*13.4
5. Houston	1,594,000	29.2
6. Detroit	1,203,000	*20.5
7. Dallas	904,000	7.1
8. San Diego	876,000	25.5
9. Phoenix	790,000	35.2
10. Baltimore	787,000	*13.1

* = Decrease

Source: Bureau of the Census

Some northern cities are decreasing in population as more Americans move to cities in the Sun Belt. Which Sun Belt city experienced the largest increase in population in the 1970's?

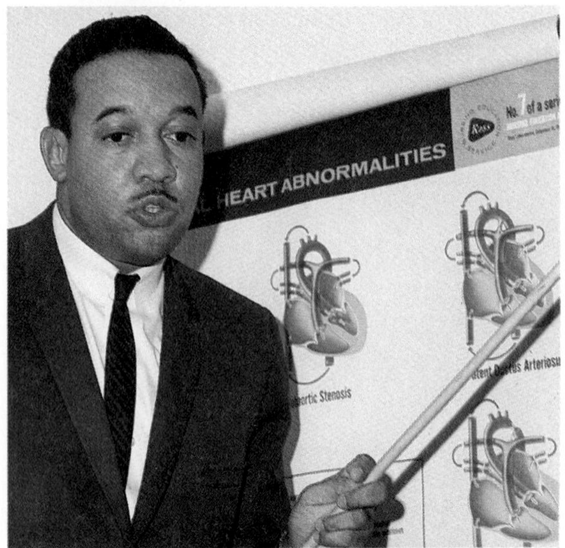

Black Americans have moved into professional positions and higher income levels as the barriers of discrimination have fallen. What percentage of the American population is black?

Population Distribution by Race

The United States has also undergone a significant change in its racial composition. The variety of America's ethnic and racial heritage is seen in the number of different ethnic groups in the United States. It is also reflected in the mixed heritage of most Americans. It is not unusual for an individual American to have ancestors from several different nationality groups. When the census describes the population by its ethnic background, it relies on what each person regards as the most important source of his or her ethnic heritage.

Blacks There are 26 million black Americans—approximately 12 percent of the total population. Before World War I, 90 percent of all blacks lived in the South. During the war blacks began to move north in search of job opportunities. Today 53 percent of blacks live in the South, 38 percent in the North, and 9 percent in the West. Recently, though, the movement of blacks out of the South has slowed. New opportunities have begun to attract blacks, like other Americans, to move to the South.

The rural-urban shift among blacks is even more dramatic. Before World War I blacks were overwhelmingly rural. Today they are predominantly urban. Currently, about 85 percent of all blacks live in cities, compared to 74 percent of all whites. In many cities, such as Atlanta, Detroit, Newark, New Orleans, and Washington, blacks are in the majority.

Hispanics Changes in population distribution have also occurred among the 15 million Americans of Spanish-speaking ancestry. Hispanics—who may be of any race—make up 6.4 percent of the total population. They are the fastest-growing minority in the United States. Hispanics come from many nationality backgrounds. The largest groups are of Mexican, Puerto Rican, and Cuban origin. The 800,000 Cubans, predominantly refugees, are concentrated in southern Florida. Of the 2 million Puerto Ricans in the mainland United States, the vast majority live in the New York metropolitan area, making up 12 percent of the population. The total Hispanic population of the New York metropolitan area is 1.5 million. In addition to Puerto Ricans, other Hispanic groups include Dominicans, Cubans, South Americans, and Mexican-Americans.

Mexican-Americans are the largest Hispanic group in the United States. They number 8.7 million, or about 4 percent of the total population. More than 80 percent of all Mexican-Americans live in the southwestern states of Texas, New Mexico, Colorado, Arizona, and California. In each of these states they form a large portion of the population. In many counties they are in the majority.

Hispanics are predominantly—83 percent—urban. Among Mexican-Americans in the Southwest there has been a major shift from rural areas into the cities. Los Angeles has 816,000 Hispanics (mostly Mexican-Americans)—28 percent of the city's total population. In San Antonio, traditionally a Hispanic city, Mexican-Americans are in the majority. Another major population shift among Mexican-Americans has been their movement to the Midwest and the

Most Hispanic-Americans live in the Southwest. What is the Hispanic population of California? What percentage of California's total population is composed of Hispanics?

HISPANIC POPULATION
(PRIMARILY MEXICAN-AMERICAN)
IN THE SOUTHWEST

State	Hispanic Population	Percent of Total Population
Texas	2,986,000	21.0
New Mexico	477,000	36.6
Colorado	340,000	11.7
Arizona	441,000	16.2
California	4,544,000	19.2

Pacific Northwest. Fifteen states now have Hispanic populations of over 100,000. Over the past two decades many Mexican-Americans have found employment opportunities in northern cities.

Asian-Americans Among the fastest growing groups within the United States population are the Asian-Americans. Today Americans of Japanese, Chinese, Korean, Filipino, and other Asian ancestry total 3.5 million. Though many Chinese-Americans live in New York, most Asian-Americans—71 percent—live in the western United States. About 38 percent of all Asian-Americans live in California; 27 percent live in Hawaii, where they constitute 47.3 percent of the state's population. Nearly 90 percent of all Asian-Americans live in cities.

Native Americans Native Americans (Indian, Eskimo, and Aleut) number 1.4 million—less than 1 percent of the total population. They live all over the United States, but more than half are concentrated in five states: Arizona, California, Oklahoma, New Mexico, and North Carolina. About one third of all Native Americans live on reservations. These are lands reserved for Native American use and held in trust by the government. Each year more and more Native Americans leave the reservations. Like most Americans, they are moving to cities in larger numbers. Today almost half of all Native Americans reside in urban areas.

Other Distribution Factors

There are many other factors by which population within the United States may be studied. Language, religion, employment, occupational status, income, and level of education are among the most important characteristics distinguishing population.

Language English is the dominant language in the United States. Although a knowledge of English is vital to full participation in American life, many Americans speak other languages. Spanish is the second most important language in the United States. In some areas of the country where Hispanics are concentrated, Spanish is the dominant language. In New Mexico, Spanish and English share the status of official languages of the state. All state laws are printed in both languages, and court proceedings may be in either language.

Federal and state laws provide for bilingual education in the primary grades for children without a knowledge of English. As the name implies, ***bilingual education*** involves the use of two languages: the child's native tongue and English. In areas where languages other than English are spoken by more than 5 percent of the population, federal law requires that election ballots be printed in those languages. In addition, many publications of federal, state, and local governments are now printed in both English and Spanish.

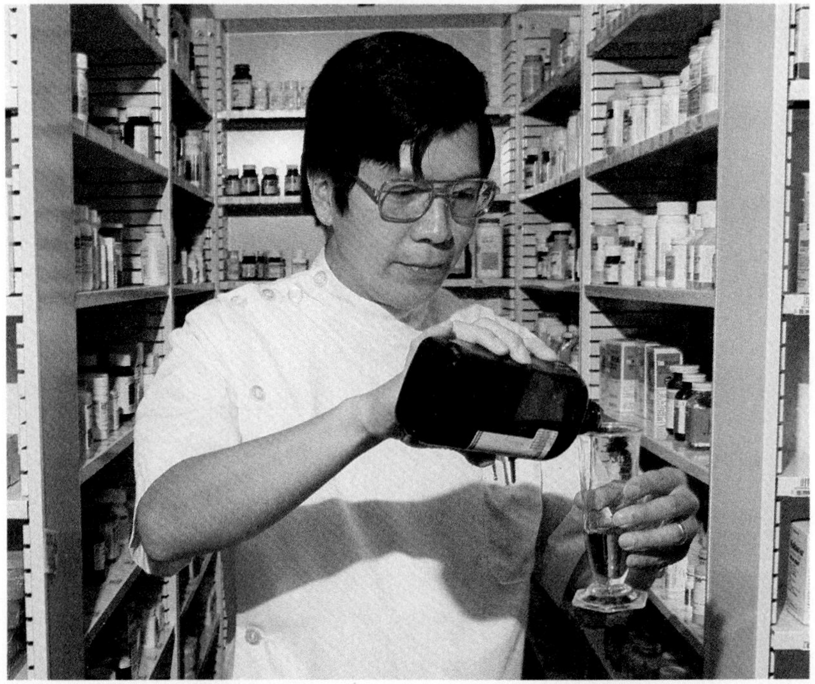

Asian-Americans make up less than 2 percent of the United States population. In what 2 states do the highest percentage of Asian-Americans live?

Religion Most Americans regard themselves as religious. Active church membership in the United States is among the highest in the world. Freedom of religion was one of the founding principles of American democracy. First the Puritans, then Catholics, Jews, and many Protestant groups sought religious freedom in America. The separation of church and state permitted a multitude of religious groups to flourish without government interference.

There are 86 religious sects in the United States with memberships of 50,000 or more. Another 1,400 groups have memberships of less than 50,000. The religious sects range in size from the Roman Catholic Church (50 million members) and the Southern Baptist Convention (13 million) to churches with no more than a handful of members.

RELIGIOUS PREFERENCE

A 1981 Gallup Poll revealed the following distribution of religious preference in America:

Preference	Percent
Protestant	59
Roman Catholic	28
Jewish	2
Eastern Orthodox	1
Other	3
None	7

Source: The Gallup Poll

The vast number and widespread diversity of religious denominations in the United States can be partially explained by the Constitution's guarantee of freedom of religion. What percentage of those Americans surveyed in the Gallup Poll expressed a preference for a religious denomination?

Employment Sixty-four percent of all Americans 16 years of age and over are members of the ***labor force***—they are either employed or actively looking for work. Women make up 42.6 percent of the labor force—a major increase over the past decade. Members of the labor force are employed in a

Many young people join the labor force during the summer months but return to the classroom when the new school year begins. What relationship exists between unemployment and education?

wide range of occupations. The 1980 census reported more than 25,000 different occupations. No single category dominates the labor force. By contrast, in 1820, 83 percent of the labor force was engaged in farming.

Not everyone who wants work finds a job. In recent years, unemployment rates have ranged from a low of 4.9 percent in 1970 to a high of 10.4 percent in 1982. Levels of unemployment are highest among young people entering the labor force—especially those who have not finished high school.

Occupational Status One of the most significant changes in occupation has been the drop in the number of farmers. In 1900, 38 percent of the labor force was in farm occupations. Today only 3 percent is engaged in farming and ranching. At the same time, modern agricultural technology has enabled America's farmers to produce more food than ever before.

Another important change has occurred among blue-collar workers. There are fewer jobs for unskilled workers such as janitors or gas station attendants. Only 7 percent of the labor force is in jobs that require no special skills. On the other hand, skilled and semi-skilled laborers—machinists, carpenters, plumbers, miners, truck drivers—are the core of America's work force. Over the past 30 years working conditions have improved and wages have risen. Today blue-collar workers are solidly part of

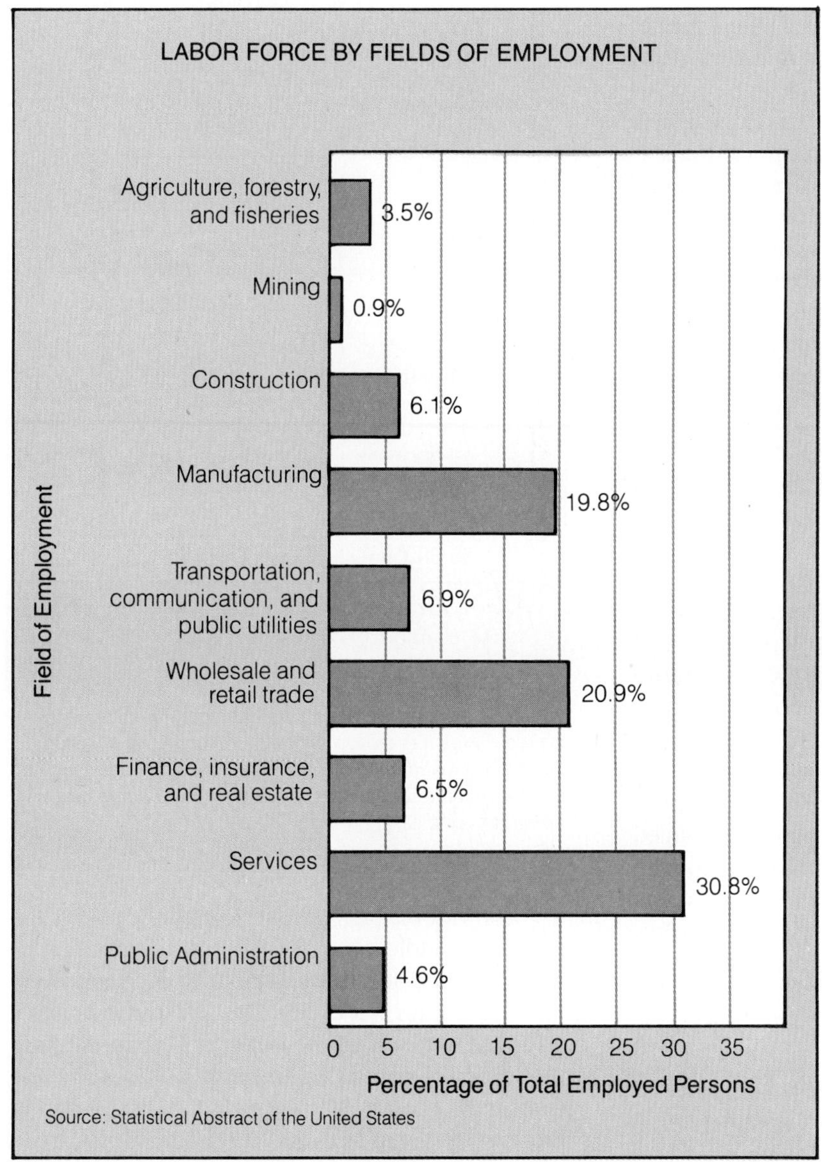

Americans currently work in a wide range of occupations. What percentage of the work force is in the manufacturing industries? In the construction industries? What was the major occupation of American workers in 1820?

WOMEN IN THE LABOR FORCE

Year	Number (millions)	Percent
1950	18.4	29.6
1960	23.2	33.4
1970	31.5	38.1
1980	44.7	42.6

Source: Bureau of Labor Statistics

The number of women in the American work force has increased rapidly since 1950, and this trend is likely to continue. How many more women were in the work force in 1980 than were in the work force in 1950?

FAMILY INCOME: DISTRIBUTION BY INCOME LEVELS

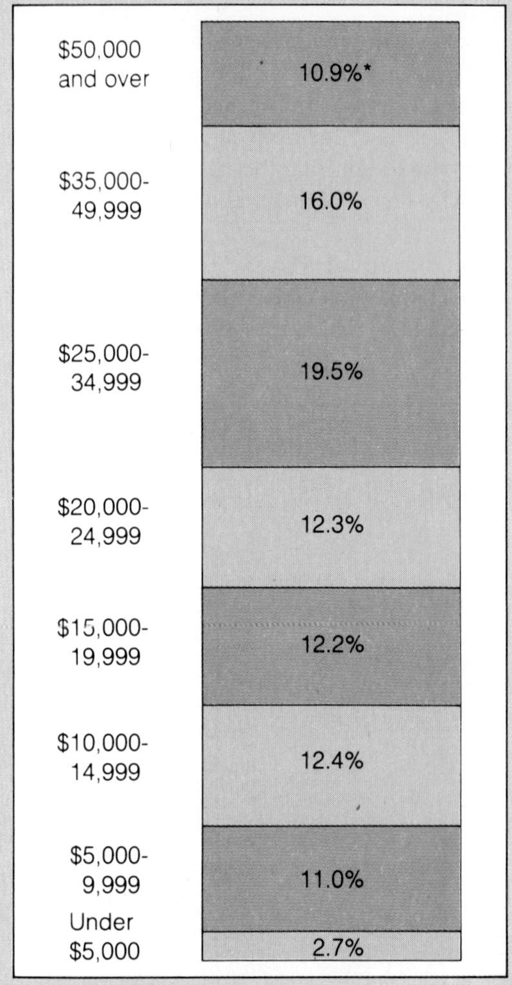

$50,000 and over	10.9%*
$35,000-49,999	16.0%
$25,000-34,999	19.5%
$20,000-24,999	12.3%
$15,000-19,999	12.2%
$10,000-14,999	12.4%
$5,000-9,999	11.0%
Under $5,000	2.7%

*Percentages may not total 100 because of roundings.
Source: Bureau of the Census

In recent years an increasing percentage of families in the United States has moved into higher income levels. Study the current distribution of income among American families. In what income range does the largest percentage of American families lie?

the middle class. Their incomes are often greater than those of white-collar workers, including many professionals.

The professions continue to expand as an area of employment. Professional and technical workers make up 16 percent of the labor force, compared to 4 percent in 1900. Included in this category are doctors, nurses, lawyers, scientists, and teachers.

The most dramatic occupational change in recent years has been the increasing number of women in the labor force. Women have moved primarily into three occupational areas: professional, clerical, and services.

Income Levels In 1980 the average American's per capita income was $9,511. The average family income was $23,204, a sum nearly twice the amount the average family earned in 1950, as calculated in constant 1981 dollars.* Averages, of course, conceal differences in family income. About 3 percent of all American families earn less than $5,000 per year; some 27 percent earn $35,000 or more. Most families fall in the middle-income level.

At one time there were significant differences in average income among the states. Some states were notably poorer than others. Over the past 20 years these differences have been greatly reduced. Wherever Americans live today, they enjoy roughly the same standard of living and per capita income. When differences in cost of living are taken into account, the states are brought even closer together in average personal income.

The vast majority of Americans are a part of the growing middle class. But for the uneducated or unskilled and for those unable to work, poverty remains a grim fact of life. The government uses a statistical scale called the ***poverty line*** to measure the extent of poverty in America. This poverty line takes into account differences in family size and in the cost of living between rural and urban areas.

*Because inflation reduces the value of a dollar, it is necessary to make comparisons in terms of what the dollar buys at a given time.

POVERTY IN THE UNITED STATES

	Number	Percent of all poor people
Age		
Under 24	18,193,000	52.8
24-64	12,454,000	36.2
65 and over	3,751,000	11.0
Residence		
Urban	12,696,000	36.9
Suburban	8,551,000	24.9
Rural	13,152,000	38.2
Region		
Northeast	6,364,000	18.5
North Central	7,772,000	22.6
South	13,967,000	40.6
West	6,296,000	18.3
Race		
White	24,109,000	70.1
Black	10,289,000	29.9

*Based on the official definition of poverty; total number of persons below the poverty level, 1982: 34,398,000.

Source: United States Department of Commerce

Based on the official government definition of poverty, about 15 percent of the United States population is poor (left). Poverty is not restricted to one age group, to one racial group, or to one region of the country. The home of a Kentucky coal miner in the Appalachian Mountains (below) illustrates the extreme poverty that characterized that region until recently.

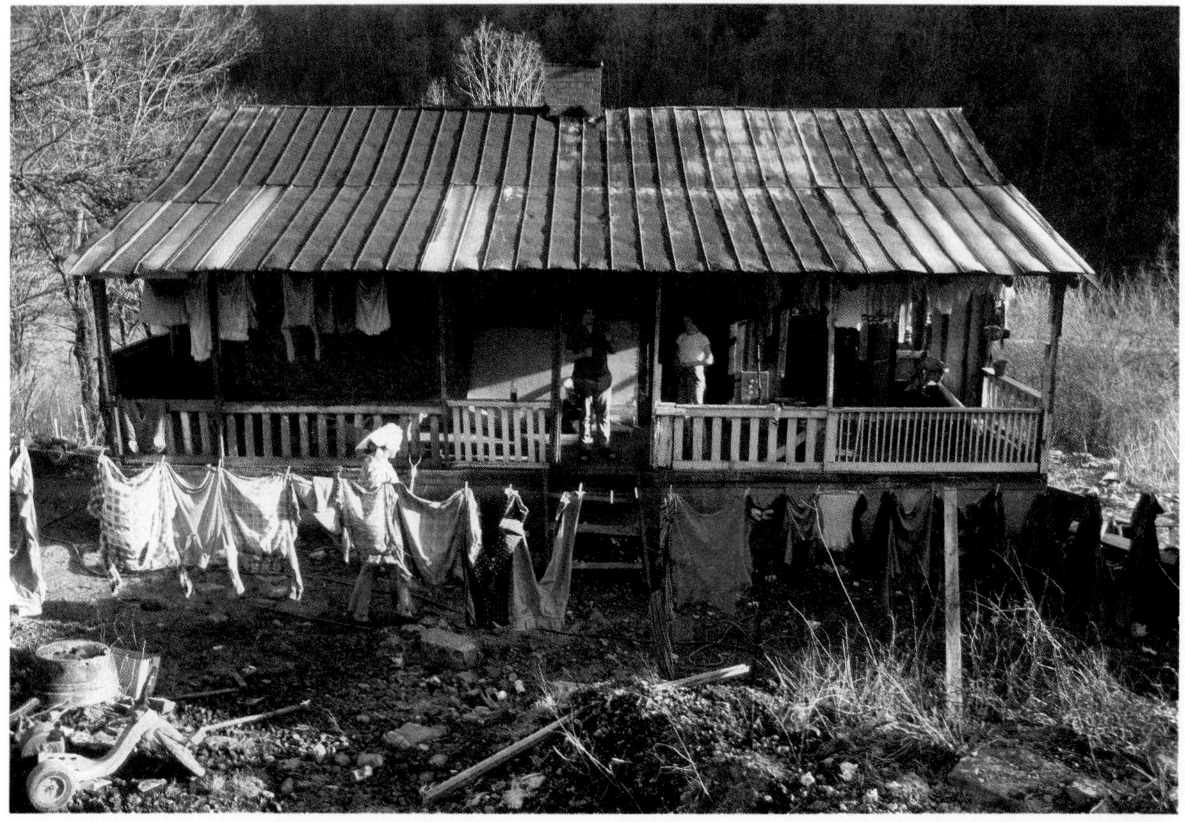

According to this standard, 22 percent of all Americans fell below the poverty line in 1959. By 1973 this figure had been cut in half. But there remain today more than 34 million people—most of them unable to work—who are poor.

A much larger percentage of nonwhites than whites are poor. In absolute numbers, though, twice as many whites as nonwhites are poor. Much of the poverty among whites has been concentrated in rural areas, especially in the Appalachian Mountain region. Long an economically depressed area, Appalachia has again begun to prosper with the renewed importance of the coal industry.

Poverty is also concentrated among those with little education. Among heads of households of poor families, about half did not complete high school.

SCHOOL ENROLLMENT

Grade level	Millions
Elementary (K-8)	31.0
Secondary (9-12)	14.6
Postsecondary	12.1
Total	57.7

Study the distribution of school enrollment in the United States. How many students are enrolled at the secondary level?

Education Levels In 1980, more than 57 million Americans were in school. Most of these students attended public schools.

Over the years a high school education has come to be recognized as the minimum level of schooling required for entry into the middle class. Young people without a diploma usually find that better jobs are closed to them. The importance of education is reflected in the rise in the number of high school and college graduates. More than twice as many students graduate from high school today than did in 1940. In 1980, 86 percent of all persons between 25 and 29 years of age had completed four years of high school; 23 percent had attended four years or more of college. The average number of school years completed was 12.9.

The increase in educational attainment has been especially dramatic among racial and ethnic minorities. The "education gap" that for so long separated blacks and whites has today almost closed.

A Native American woman uses her technical skills in an electronics plant. Minorities are moving into highly paid fields as a result of increased educational opportunities.

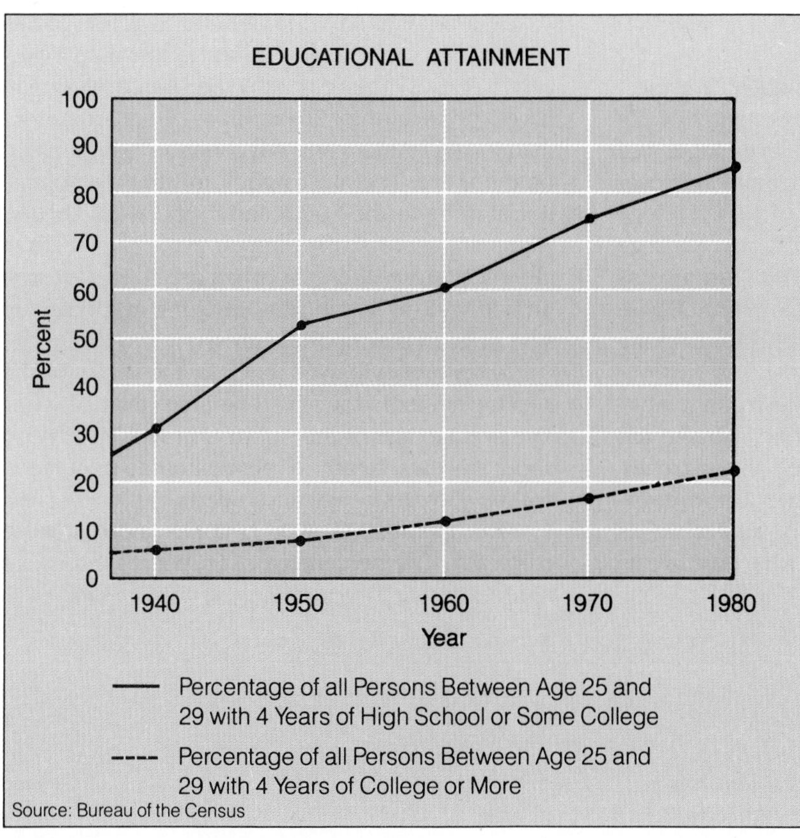

The percentages of Americans completing high school and college (left) have increased steadily since 1940. Significant increases in college enrollment (below) have occurred in recent decades, especially among women and blacks.

COLLEGE ENROLLMENT 1960-1980

	1960	1970	1980	Percent Increase 1960 – 1980
Total	3,570,000	7,413,000	10,180,000	285.2
Women	1,281,000	3,013,000	5,155,000	402.4
Blacks	227,000*	522,000	1,007,000	443.6

*Figure for 1960 includes other nonwhites.

Source: Bureau of the Census

Today more and more high school graduates are going on to college. The increase has been dramatic—from 3.6 million in 1960 to 10 million in 1980. The most significant increases in college enrollment have been among women and blacks. Today 51 percent of all college students are women. Roughly 10 percent of all college students are black—almost the same as the percentage of blacks in the total population.

Education is an investment in future earnings. More than any other factor, education is the key to a good job and a higher income.

Section Check

1. Define: bilingual education, labor force, poverty line
2. What accounts for the fact that a majority of Americans are female?
3. How has the United States population shifted?
4. What is the second most important language in the United States?
5. Why has the percentage of Americans with higher education increased?

3 TOWARD THE YEAR 2000

Census figures reveal a nation in change. They portray continued improvement in the quality of life for nearly all Americans. Americans live longer, are better educated, and enjoy higher incomes than ever before.

On the basis of these statistics, patterns of change can be projected into the future. They can give us an idea of what life will be like in the year 2000—and what problems we are likely to encounter along the way.

A ***forecast,*** or outlook for the future, must always be read with caution. Estimates may be too high—or too low. Since they are based on past trends, they are always subject to error and to the unexpected. With this warning in mind, what changes can the American people expect over the next twenty years?

The population will continue to grow, but its annual increase will slow down to less than 1 percent a year. By the year 2000 the United States will have a population of 264 million—40 million more than in 1980. Americans will continue to be a nation on the move. The most significant shifts in population will be to the South and to the West. Urbanization will increase. By the year 2000, 82 percent of all Americans will live in urban areas. The greatest growth will be in suburbs, resulting in the expansion of great metropolitan areas.

Americans will live longer. By the year 2000 the average life expectancy will be more than 74 years. The average age of the population will increase to about 37 years. Nearly 20 percent of the population will be 65 years of age and older.

The population will become more diverse ethnically. The percentage of Hispanics and Asian-Americans will increase. As their numbers increase,

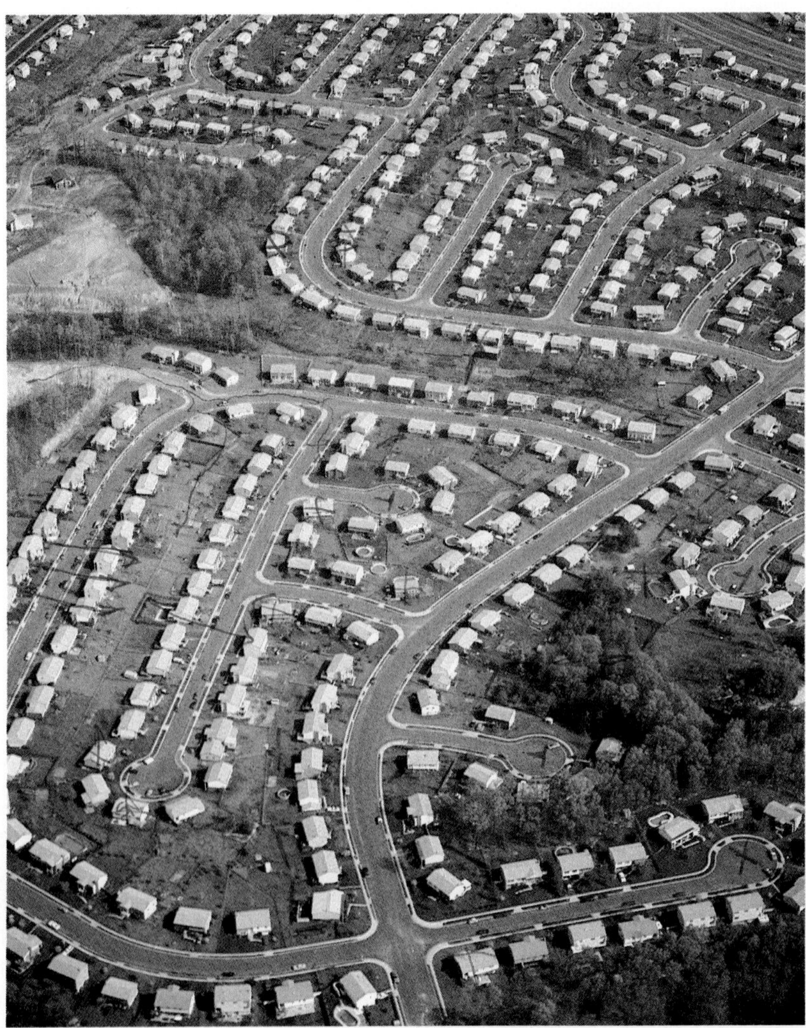

The expansion of a California suburb typifies the trend toward urbanization in the United States. According to recent studies the suburbs in the latter part of this century are expected to continue their expansion into areas where farms and forests now stand.

however, racial and ethnic groups will become more alike in many ways. Differences in education, income, and fields of employment will be reduced. The percentage of blacks and Hispanics in the middle class will continue to grow.

Real incomes for Americans will continue to increase. In today's dollars, taking inflation into account, the average family income in the year 2000 will be $21,000. Income will be distributed more equally, but poverty will not be eliminated.

The patterns of shifts in employment will continue, with shifts from unskilled to skilled occupations and from blue-collar to white-collar jobs. Those with little or no education or skills will find it increasingly difficult to find employment.

Women will work in larger numbers, approaching the percentage of men in the labor force. Differences in fields of employment will decline as more women enter occupations traditionally dominated by men. Differences in income between working men and women will narrow substantially.

Education in the year 2000 will be even more important than it is today. The average level of education for all Americans will continue to rise. More and more young people will graduate from high school and go on to college or a university.

Change produces stress and conflict. Some people may benefit more than others, and some may be adversely affected. What will be the consequences of these changes for the quality of life of the American people? As we look toward the future, choices must be made—political choices. In a democratic society these choices depend in part on what the people want. How do these wants take political form? How are they voiced? We turn to these questions in the following chapters on political behavior.

Section Check

1. Define: forecast
2. What will be the approximate population of the United States in the year 2000?
3. How will racial and ethnic groups within the population change by the year 2000?
4. How will the distribution of income change by the year 2000?
5. What is likely to be the average family income by the year 2000?
6. What patterns of shifts in employment will continue into the year 2000?

SUMMARY

Statistics, or numerical facts, are vital for an understanding of America and the world today. Demography is the statistical study of populations. In the United States the primary source for demographic information, or data, is the census. A census is a count of the population taken at a particular time. The census is taken at regular intervals.

The United States census has expanded greatly over the years. The first census, taken in 1790, was little more than a head count. Today the census includes a variety of questions: its purpose is to provide a profile of the American people.

The primary purpose of the census is for the apportionment of seats in the House of Representatives. Census data are also used to plan, run, and evaluate programs in both government and the private sector. They are used to determine and forecast the need for government services and facilities. They help businesses decide what products to manufacture and where to locate stores and factories. Political scientists study census data to analyze trends in public opinion and voting behavior.

As revealed by census information, the American population is 51.4 percent female, 74 percent urban, averages 30 years of age, and comes from a variety of ethnic and linguistic backgrounds. Most Americans belong to religious groups: two thirds of them are Protestants.

Sixty-four percent of all Americans over the age of 16 belong to the work force. Skilled and semiskilled laborers are the core of America's work force. But the professions continue to expand as an area of employment. Though the vast majority of Americans are part of the growing middle class, poverty remains a fact of life for many.

Nearly 60 million Americans are in school today. More than twice as many students now graduate from high school than did in 1940. The increase in education has been especially dramatic among racial and ethnic minorities.

Census Bureau figures may be used to forecast trends in the American population. The forecasts, like all estimates, must be read cautiously. But some generalizations can be made. For example, if present trends continue, the growth rate of the American population will decrease. It is likely, however, that the average life expectancy of Americans will increase. Overall, the population will become more diverse ethnically. Other trends include shifts in employment patterns and an increase in the education level of all Americans.

Chapter 8 Review

Using Vocabulary

Answer the questions by using the meaning of each underlined term.

1. Why does a demographer need to study statistics?
2. What is demography?
3. What might a sample reveal about the need for a change in a state's apportionment?
4. What kinds of demographic data are obtained in a census?
5. What is needed to make a forecast about the labor force in the year 2000?
6. What relationship might a demographer discover about a trend in bilingual education and the poverty line?

Understanding American Government

1. What are the different functions performed by the Bureau of the Census?
2. How do businesses use census data?
3. What factors account for the increasing life expectancy of Americans?
4. Why can it be said that Americans are a people on the move?
5. How have American job patterns changed over the last few decades?
6. How may the ethnic makeup of the United States have changed by the year 2000?

Extending Your Skills: Using Statistics

Study the Family Income chart on page 216. Then complete each statement.

1. The percentage of Americans who earn $50,000 or more per year is (a) 2.7; (b) 10.9; (c) 19.5.
2. The percentage of Americans who earn less than $10,000 per year is (a) 2.7; (b) 10.9; (c) 13.7.
3. The largest percentage of Americans earn between (a) $20,000 and $24,999 per year; (b) $15,000 and $19,999 per year; (c) $25,000 and $34,999 per year.
4. The percentage of Americans who earn between $15,000 and $24,999 per year is (a) 19.5; (b) 24.5; (c) 23.4.

Government and You

1. The census once asked about a person's religious affiliation, but this question was dropped as an invasion of privacy. Do you agree with this decision? What are your reasons?
2. The census does not ask questions about political beliefs. Do you think such data could serve any important governmental purposes? Do you think it is important that questions about political beliefs are not asked? Why?
3. One of the most significant changes in population distribution has been the shift from rural to urban residences. How has increased urbanization benefited the nation? How has it been a disadvantage to the nation?
4. Federal and state laws provide for bilingual education in the primary grades for children without a knowledge of English. Do you support such a policy? Why or why not?
5. A dramatic increase has occurred during the last few decades in the number of students going to college. Why do you think the increase has taken place? Do you think the trend is likely to continue? Why?

Activities

1. Take a census of your class, using a questionnaire to ask each student's sex, age, and place of birth. Collate the data to find the percentage of males and females, the average age, and the percentage of students whose birthplace is different from their present place of residence.
2. Prepare a series of charts and graphs similar to those in this chapter to give a profile of your town and city, using the latest available census figures.
3. Research the history of your town's population between the year 1900 and the last census or research the history of your state's population in the same span of time. Then make a chart that illustrates the change in population of your town or your state.
4. Make a scrapbook of drawings, charts, and graphs to show the changes the United States will experience by the year 2000. Include your own predictions.

If you think they're dumb then you're just not thinking.
ASPCA
I ♥ NY
GREENPEACE
You Spare The Time?
Say yes to Michigan!
VOTE
COMMUNITY PARTY OF WESTMONT
THE
NOTRE DAME
"WASHINGTON IS A CAPITAL CITY."
AMERICAN LEGION
US
MADD

UNIT 4

PUBLIC OPINION AND INTEREST GROUPS

Chapter 9

Public Opinion: The Voice of the People

What I want is to get done what the people desire to have done, and the question for me is how to find that out exactly.

ABRAHAM LINCOLN

CHAPTER OVERVIEW

Demonstrations, such as this one in New York City for world peace and nuclear disarmament, are used by some groups to bring their opinions to the attention of lawmakers, the media, and the public.

1 THE NATURE OF PUBLIC OPINION

Government in a republic rests upon ***public opinion,*** the preferences expressed by a significant number of people about a particular issue. The strength of any government ultimately depends upon its capacity to respond to public opinion. Even dictatorships must take the opinions of its citizens into account—if only to control or suppress discontent. Napoleon Bonaparte called public opinion "the ruler of the world." No government can ignore public opinion—except at its own peril.

In medieval times the king might disguise himself as a peasant and go into the marketplace to ask, "What think ye of the king?" Early American politicians relied on letters, newspapers, and personal contact to measure the current of opinion. Today there are more accurate ways to find out "what the people desire to have done." But the modern public opinion poll reveals what politicians have always known: there is no one voice speaking for all. The people do not all want the same thing. They do not speak with one voice, and some may not speak at all.

Components of Public Opinion

Public opinion is usually broken down into four specific elements.

Political Issues Public opinion focuses on particular matters of political controversy and public debate. People hold opinions about all kinds of things—movies, cars, or hair styles, for example—but only opinions about matters of government and politics make up public opinion. Political scientist V. O. Key described public opinion as consisting of "those opinions held by private persons which governments find it prudent to heed."

Means of Expression Most opinions are expressed in words, spoken or written. Books, pamphlets, political ads, newspaper editorials, letters to editors and public officials, and lobbying efforts are all methods of expressing opinions on public policy. Voting can be a means of expressing or measuring public opinion—although what opinions a particular vote expresses is often unclear. Sometimes opinions are expressed through gesture—a show of hands, a clenched fist, or "thumbs down."

INSIGHT

Significant Political Knowledge

Almost half of all Americans are unable to name their representative in Congress. Less than half know how their representatives stand on issues. In a Bicentennial survey of 17-year-olds, serious gaps were found in their understanding of the fundamentals of government.

- 53 percent did not understand the meaning of the Fifth Amendment protection against self-incrimination.
- 47 percent did not know that each state had two senators.
- 47 percent believed that the President could appoint people to Congress.
- 28 percent thought it was illegal to start a new political party.
- 14 percent thought that the President did not always have to obey the laws of the United States.

When a person's attitudes are not expressed, they remain private. Only when attitudes are expressed do they enter the public realm as opinion.

The Significance of Numbers Public opinion represents the sum of individual opinions. A meaningful expression of public opinion must involve a significant number of people. It may be the population of the whole country or perhaps just one group within it.

There is no one public but many publics—groups of people who express their views about an issue. These special publics include business, labor, agriculture, and other occupational groups. They also include regional groups, age groups, and racial, ethnic, and religious groups. When an issue fundamentally affects one group, the opinion of that group may be given special consideration. On the question of agricultural price supports, for example, the opinion of farmers is of major importance. Similarly, urban residents would be most concerned with issues relating to public transportation and other city services.

We often hear that the farmers want this, business or labor wants that. But no group is likely to be wholly united in what it wants. There will be differences of opinion. In every public there will be a distribution of individual preferences.

A Matter of Preferences An opinion is an expression of preference, attitude, or judgment. It should reflect a person's knowledge and reasoned evaluation of an issue. No one has the time or resources to be well informed about everything. For each person some issues are more important than others. But even on matters that interest them, many people may not do their homework. Most people are primarily concerned with personal matters—their health, family, job, or income—without realizing how a public issue can affect their lives. They may not have an opinion on the issue—or if they do, it may not be an informed opinion.

Because people want different things, there is a diversity of opinion among individuals on almost every question. They may differ not only in direction—whether they are pro or con—but also in intensity. Some people may feel strongly about an issue, one way or another, while others may hold only weak preferences. Some people may simply have no opinion on the matter. In looking at public opinion, it is important to measure these differences. Public opinion on a particular issue will reveal a distribution of preferences.

Distribution of Opinions

Public opinion is distributed in different ways. To see the variety of ways people answer survey questions, imagine that a public opinion poll is taken in your community. Members of the community are asked whether they favor or oppose various questions, and how strongly they hold their opinions. Each question shows a different distribution of opinions—so many for, so many against—and a different degree of intensity. In order to simplify the results of this hypothetical public opinion poll, the responses of those who have no opinion on a particular issue are not shown.

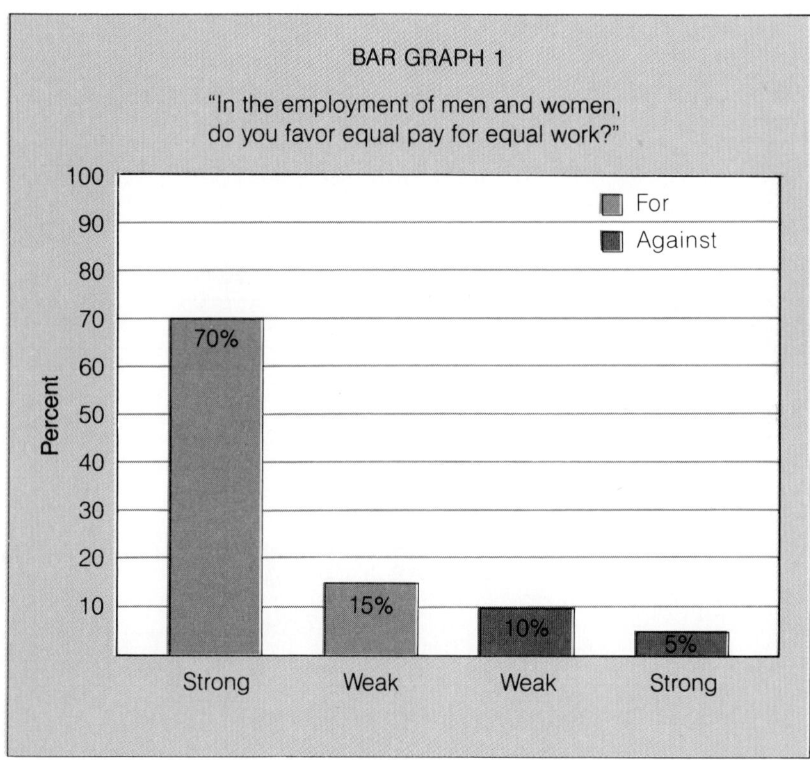

The large percentage of people favoring equal pay for equal work shows a consensus, or general agreement, and a high intensity of feeling about this issue.

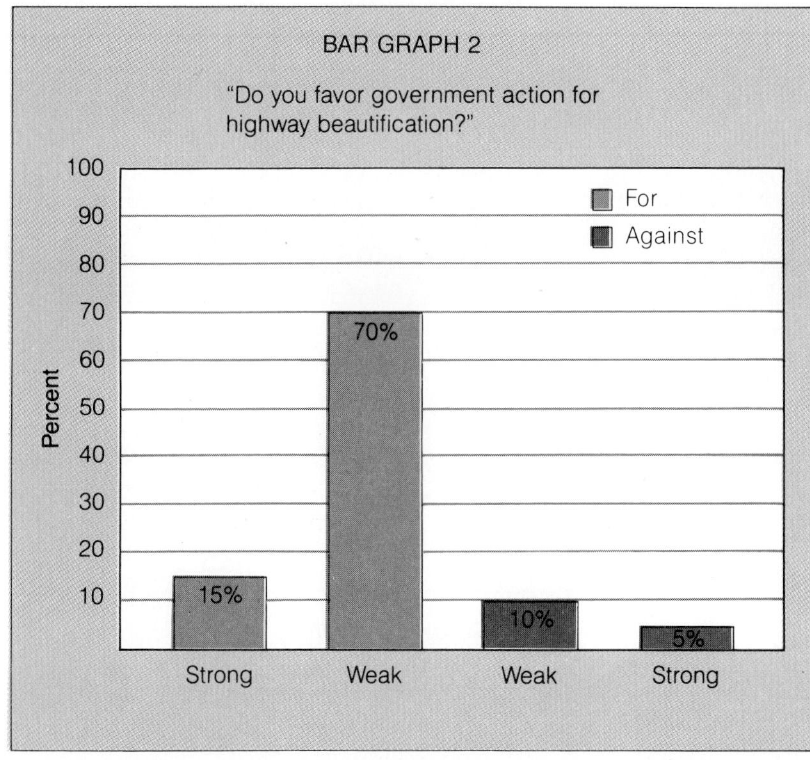

Bar Graph 2 also shows a consensus of public opinion. The public's intensity of feeling is low, however, because most people do not feel strongly about government efforts at highway beautification.

Bar Graph 3 shows a situation in which there is no consensus and a low intensity of feeling. What percentage of those polled have a low intensity of feeling about this issue? What percentage have a high intensity of feeling about the issue?

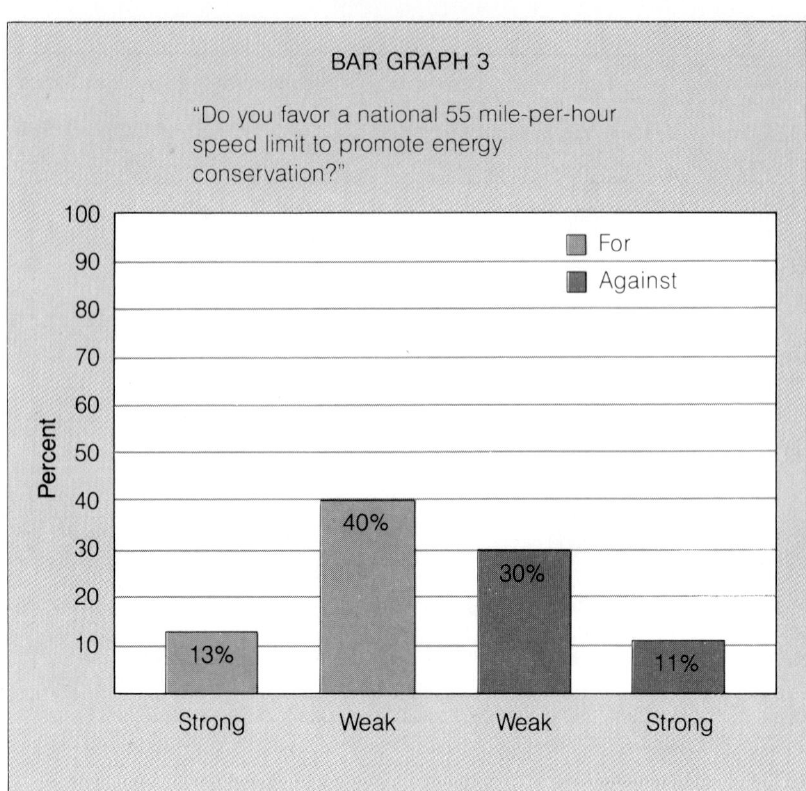

Bar Graph 4 shows a lack of consensus. A near majority on each side, however, expresses a strong preference. Such a distribution of opinion and feeling often indicates an issue of intense controversy.

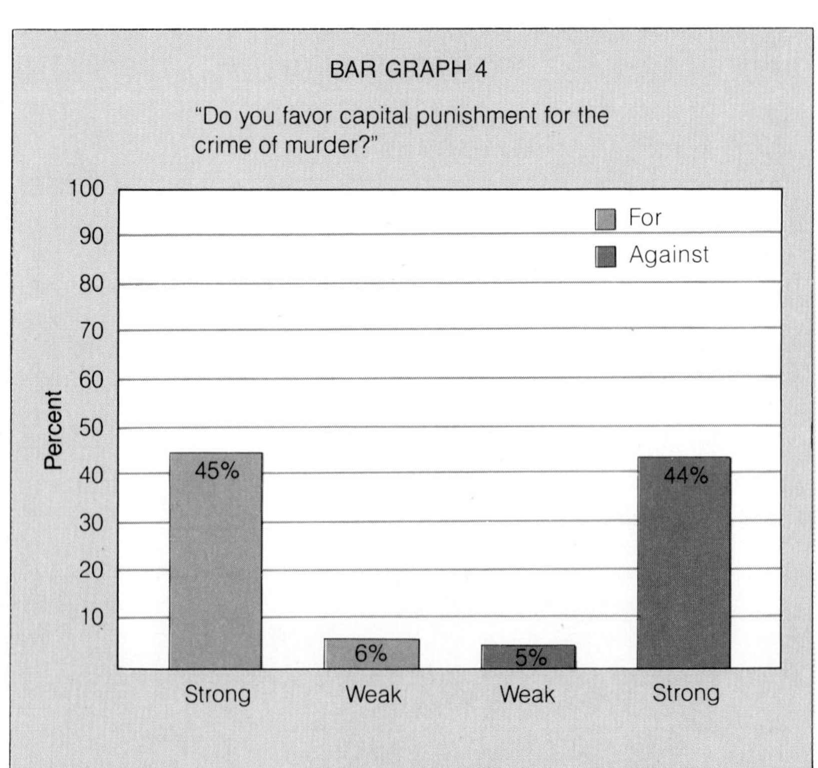

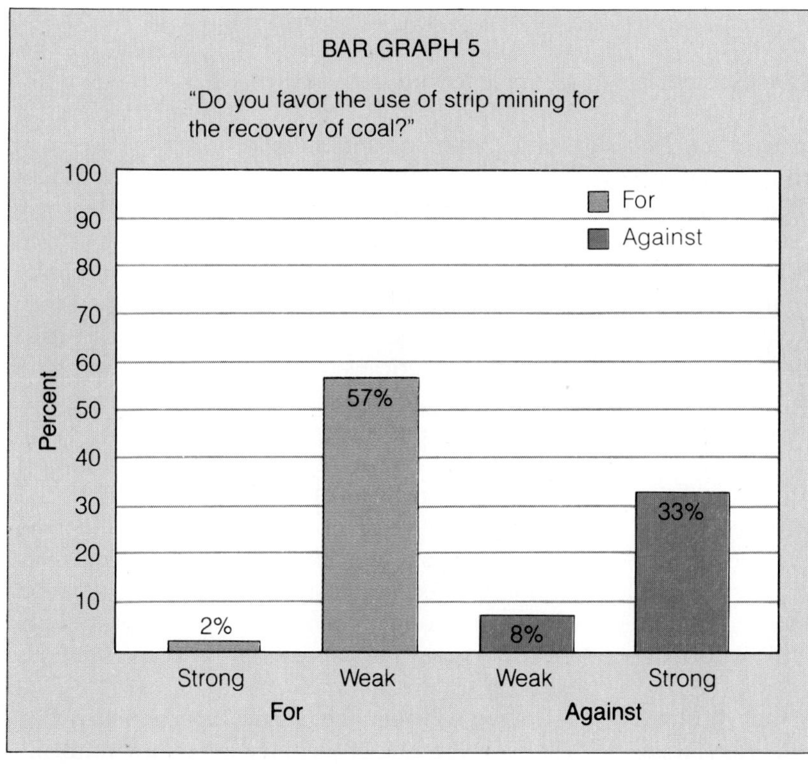

Bar Graph 5 shows a situation in which a minority with strong feelings about an issue may prevail over a majority whose feelings about the issue are weak.

Section Check

1. Define: public opinion
2. What are the four essential components in any public opinion?
3. What four concerns affect most people's preferences on an issue?
4. Why is there a diversity of opinion among individuals on most issues?
5. Give the direction and intensity of public opinion on the question of equal pay for equal work.
6. Give the direction and intensity of public opinion on the question of government action for highway beautification.
7. Give the direction and intensity of public opinion on the question of a national 55 mile-per-hour speed limit to promote energy conservation.
8. Give the direction and intensity of public opinion on the question of capital punishment for the crime of murder.
9. Give the direction and intensity of public opinion on the question of strip mining for the recovery of coal.

2 IDEOLOGY IN AMERICA

The five graphs on pages 227–229 represent distribution of public opinion on particular issues. But each person holds opinions about a number of different issues—energy, welfare, business, taxes, defense spending, and foreign policy, to name just a few. How are these opinions related to each other? Do they form an ***ideology,*** a set of closely related beliefs that fit into a political philosophy? Or is each opinion completely separate from any other and in no way related to a dominant belief?

As we use the term, ideology is a system of ideas that seeks to explain how the social world works. It may also include a program of action for changing the world, as in a revolutionary ideology.

In the United States, Americans tend to base opinions on personal knowledge and experience. Rather than be guided by a rigid ideology, most Americans judge each issue separately and as it comes up. Yet one opinion tends to be related to another. For example, it is contradictory to call for increased welfare or military spending and, at the same time, to favor lower taxes or a balanced budget. Yet many people hold such contradictory opinions. They fail to see the connection among issues or the relationship of one opinion to another.

Ideological Labels

In the United States, issues are posed most often in terms of such ideological labels as right and left, conservative and liberal. The terms *right* and *left* refer to political positions originated in the French National Assembly. The presiding officers seated the ***liberals***—those looking to revolutionary change—on the left, and the ***conservatives***—those seeking to preserve a way of life—on the right. Members with moderate positions in regard to change were seated in the center. Thus today conservatives are often described as "right wing" or "on the right." Liberals are often described as "left wing" or "on the left."

About 35 percent of the people place themselves toward the political center. Another 34 percent are either moderately right or moderately left. These percentages represent a shift over the previous decade toward a more conservative position. But this shift has taken place primarily within the wide center of American politics.

Conservative and liberal labels must be used with caution, for they are misleading in several ways. First, many people have only a vague idea of the meanings of "liberal" and "conservative," and many people disagree about their definitions. All people who describe themselves as conservatives, for example, do not necessarily have a common political philosophy. Nor do they necessarily share the same opinion on a given issue.

Second, many people are conservative in ideology but liberal in practice. For example, they may express the conservative view of opposition to "Big Government." Yet they practice a liberal philosophy by turning to the national government when they want something. Senator Gary Hart of Colorado reminded Americans of this contradiction when he said, "To get the government off your back, get your hands out of the government's pockets."

Third and most important, the beliefs of most Americans usually involve a mixture of both liberal and conservative opinions, depending on the issue at hand. Thus a person may be a liberal on issues of domestic economic policy but a conservative on issues of foreign policy. In short, most people do not fit neatly into ideological packages as liberals and conservatives.

Pragmatism, the practical approach to public affairs or the lack of ideology in political thinking, reflects the overall nature of the American political scene. The choices presented to the American

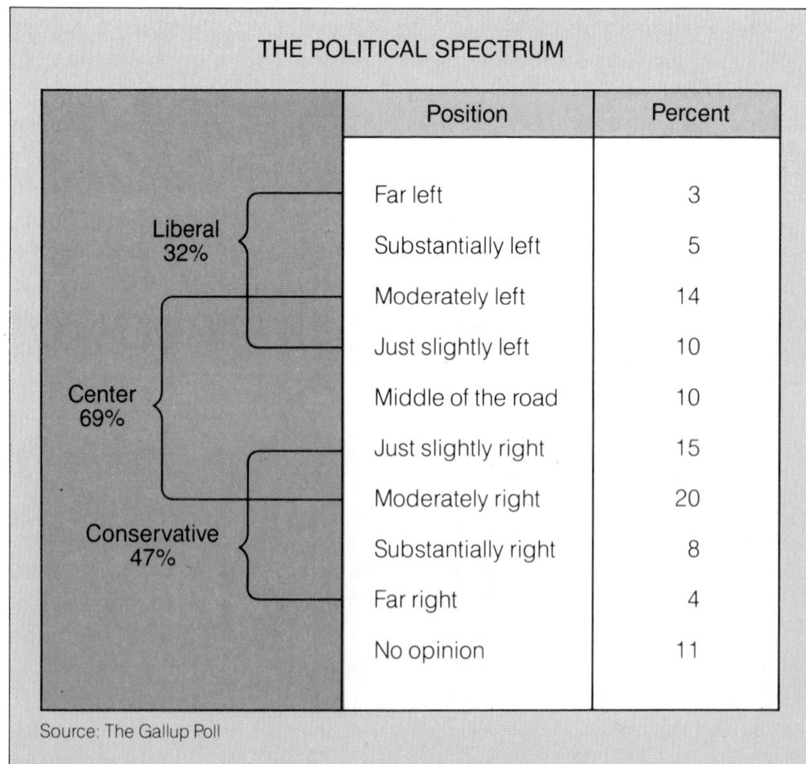
THE POLITICAL SPECTRUM

Position	Percent
Far left	3
Substantially left	5
Moderately left	14
Just slightly left	10
Middle of the road	10
Just slightly right	15
Moderately right	20
Substantially right	8
Far right	4
No opinion	11

Source: The Gallup Poll

The political spectrum refers to the range of political beliefs and positions held by people. This chart illustrates how Americans classify themselves politically. The chart on page 231 classifies the political beliefs of Americans by various social and economic characteristics.

people by candidates and political parties are usually not ideological in character. Most political leaders are practical politicians. Most politicians may wear a conservative or liberal label, but it is rarely a perfect fit. When applied to political parties, however, the use of the labels *liberal* or *conservative* is even more difficult.

Liberalism and Conservatism

Liberalism and conservatism do not represent clear-cut ideologies or programs. The terms themselves mean different things to different people. Adding to this confusion, the words have undergone a change in meaning over the years.

HOW AMERICANS DESCRIBE THEMSELVES

		Left	Percent Moderate	Right
Total Sample		18.0	45.1	30.1*
Sex	Men	16.1	42.9	34.1
	Women	19.8	47.0	26.3
Age	18–24 years	31.8	40.1	19.6
	25–29 years	21.6	41.9	28.6
	30–49 years	14.9	50.6	30.2
	50 years & over	13.5	43.1	35.3
Region	East	15.8	50.8	26.2
	Midwest	18.4	45.8	30.4
	South	16.4	43.2	31.2
	West	23.1	38.2	33.7
Race	White	17.5	45.6	31.0
	Non-White	21.5	41.0	24.0
Education	College	23.7	38.9	35.2
	High school	15.8	48.8	28.9
	Grade school	15.1	43.5	24.2
Income	Over $25,000	17.9	42.0	37.4
	$20,000–24,999	22.2	43.9	30.4
	$15,000–19,999	15.4	52.5	26.9
	$10,000–14,999	15.4	48.3	28.3
	$5,000–9,999	19.1	42.2	24.7
	Under $5,000	19.8	45.4	21.8
Religion	Protestant	16.6	43.7	32.4
	Catholic	16.4	48.2	29.5
	Jewish	31.0	51.7	8.6
Union Membership	Union	16.1	54.6	26.4
	Non-Union	18.6	41.9	31.3
Political Party	Republican	11.4	36.4	48.2
	Democrat	20.8	49.3	20.8
	Independent	20.7	47.2	28.0

*Percentages may not total 100 because of rounding. Source: The Gallup Poll

Both modern liberalism and modern conservatism are rooted in the ***classical liberalism*** of the eighteenth century. In Europe liberalism emerged as the political philosophy of the rising middle classes, who challenged the power and privileges of aristocrats. The cornerstone of classical liberalism was a belief in ***individualism,*** and it included among its important themes the idea of equality, the right to property, and limited government.

Classical liberalism stressed the natural equality of all persons. Each person, given an opportunity to succeed, was to be judged by individual merit and achievement. Classical liberalism held also that all persons possessed certain fundamental rights. Among these was the right to property and, with it, the right to pursue economic interests free from government interference. (This was what the Founders called "the pursuit of happiness"; it was based on the ideal of the free market.) Finally, classical liberalism was committed to the idea of limited government. Government was seen as the major threat to personal liberty, and its powers were to be held in check. In Jefferson's words, "Government is best which governs least."

Modern liberalism and conservatism each draw from the philosophy of classical liberalism, but each emphasizes different themes. Over the years each has given new interpretations to these themes as conditions in American society have changed.

Modern liberalism has roots in the Progressive movement and the Presidencies of Theodore Roosevelt and Woodrow Wilson. The character of liberalism today is essentially the product of Franklin D. Roosevelt's "New Deal." Liberals are advocates of change. They call for government intervention in the economy and the use of governmental powers to promote the public welfare. Liberals have argued that inequality deepened during the course of the Industrial Revolution in the late nineteenth century. They have pointed to the great concentrations of wealth and power that have threatened to control government, to destroy economic competition, and to endanger individual freedom. Liberals have called upon the government to intervene and to restore a balance within society. Strengthened powers of the national government, in their opinion, are to be used to protect the disadvantaged, to promote equality, and to pursue social and economic justice.

Conservatives generally oppose the expanded role of government in promoting welfare. They emphasize self-reliance and a limited role for government. Conservatives urge free enterprise and an economy free from government regulation. They argue that more government means less individual freedom. They are committed to the preservation of private property. Conservatives emphasize the traditional values associated with the family and close communities. They believe in order, loyalty, patriotism, and in a strong military prepared to defend the national interest wherever it may be threatened.

All conservatives, of course, do not share exactly the same beliefs. There is no single conservative or liberal point of view, but instead a general perspective by which each is characterized.

Section Check

1. Define: ideology, pragmatism, classical liberalism, individualism
2. How did the ideological labels of conservative and liberal, right and left originate?
3. What are three reasons for using caution in applying the liberal and conservative labels?
4. How has classical liberalism and its basic themes influenced American political thinking?

---

3 MEASURING PUBLIC OPINION

Public opinion is expressed in many ways. People who feel strongly about a particular issue may send a letter to the editor of a newspaper. They may express their opinion by circulating petitions or participating in rallies and demonstrations. Or they may write to public officials—their city council representative, members of Congress, or even the President.

Elected officials care about what the people are thinking. They know, however, that personal visits or letters from constituents do not reflect the broad distribution of views on an issue. Only those who feel strongly on the issue and know how to express themselves are likely to speak out publicly. Beyond that, more politically active persons usually have a higher income and level of education than the average person. They are not representative of the population as a whole. Their views are not necessarily shared by others in the community.

Elections provide one opportunity for the voice of the people to be heard. What that voice is saying, however, is difficult to interpret. Votes are cast for certain candidates, but the voter's choice is influenced by many factors. A number of issues are likely to arise during an election campaign. The voter may agree with the candidate on some issues but not on others. The vote itself is rarely a clear expression of opinion about a particular issue.

Public Opinion Polls

How then can public opinion be measured? How can political leaders follow Lincoln's advice and find out "what the people desire to have done"? Over the past 40 years candidates and public officials have turned increasingly to public opinion polls.

Polls are not new. For more than 150 years newspapers in the United States have sounded out opinions on the candidates and the issues. These informal ***straw polls***, as they are called, are conducted in several ways. Reporters often stop people on the street or at a shopping center and ask them how they feel about a particular question. Sometimes the interviews are conducted by telephone or by mail. Newspapers and magazines occasionally print questionnaires to be clipped and mailed in by the readers. None of these straw polls is very accurate. There is no way to know how closely the opinions expressed reflect the opinion of the larger population. Scientific polling seeks to overcome these difficulties and measure public opinion more accurately.

Scientific public opinion polls were developed in market research. Manufacturers wanted information about consumer interest in their products. They wanted to find out "who wanted what packaged how." In 1935 George Gallup conducted the first scientifically constructed political opinion poll on a national scale. Since that time polling techniques have been improved and greater accuracy has been obtained. Today there are more than 200 polling organizations in the United States.

How Scientific Polls Are Conducted

Scientific polls measure public opinion by interviewing a small but carefully selected sample of the population. Properly drawn, this sample is representative of the public. The actual number of persons required for a sample in scientific polling is quite small. In a national survey most polling organizations question only 1,500 to 3,500 persons. How can the opinions of so few people accurately represent the opinions of the American people?

The accuracy of a poll depends not on the size of the sample, but on how the sample is chosen. The most accurate samples are drawn in such a way that everyone in the total population being surveyed has an equal chance of being selected. This is known as a ***random sample.*** The population to be surveyed, which is called a universe, may be the whole country, a state, a community, or a particular group. Within the universe a larger sample will give the poll greater accuracy. Beyond a certain number, however, an increase in the size of the sample makes no significant difference in the results of the poll. The necessary size of the sample is determined mathematically, depending on such factors as subgroups to be polled and the number of ways opinion may be divided.

George Gallup, founder of the Gallup Poll, works with an assistant at a machine used to sort responses to a 1941 survey of public opinions and attitudes.

At least two steps are usually involved in drawing a sample for a national survey. First, several hundred sampling units are randomly selected. These are small geographic areas—often electoral precincts or census tracts. Next, within each sampling unit a specific number of persons is chosen at random for interview. The most accurate means of doing this is to put the name of each person in the sampling unit on a slip of paper, mix the slips thoroughly, and draw them out at random. Another method is to choose, say, every tenth (or ten thousandth) member of the sampling unit to be interviewed.

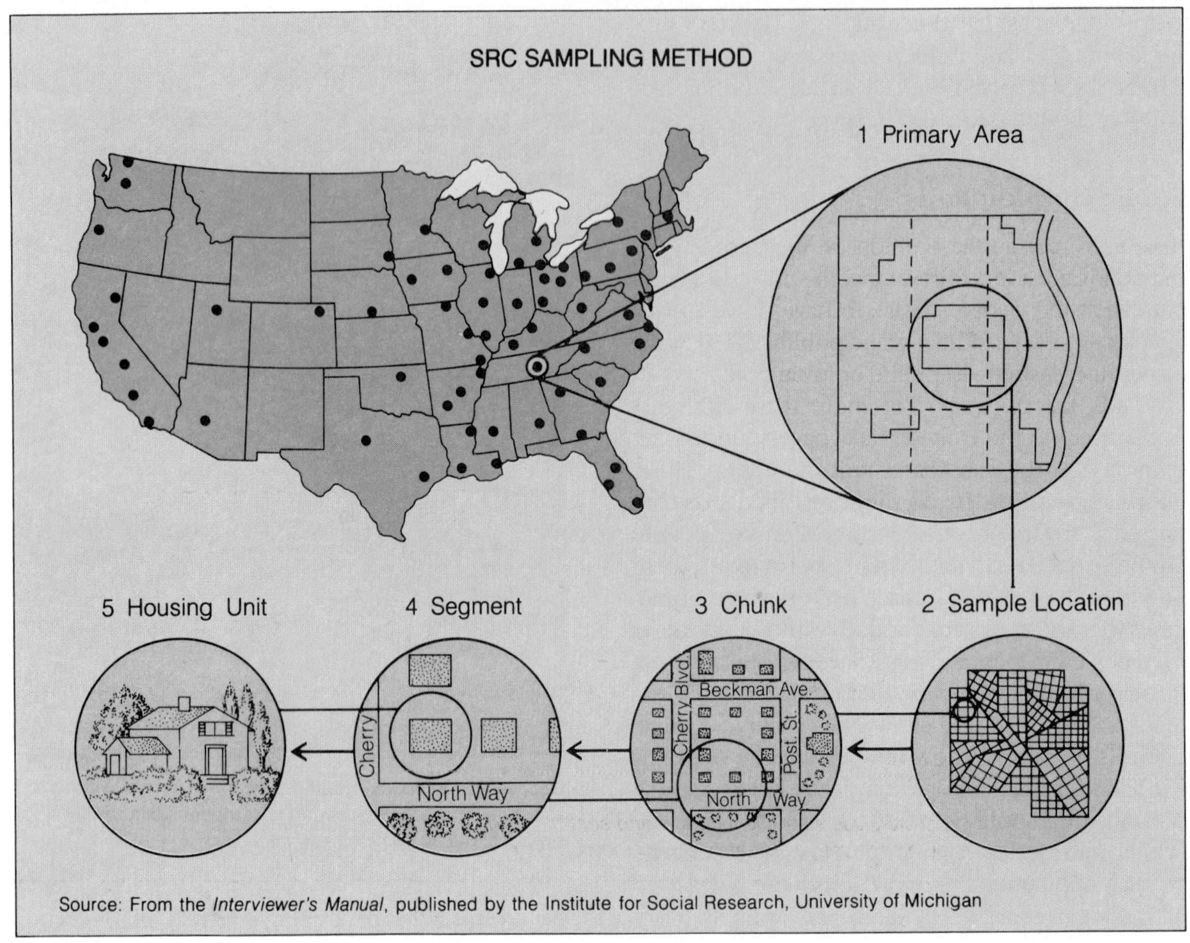

Source: From the *Interviewer's Manual*, published by the Institute for Social Research, University of Michigan

The sampling process has become increasingly refined and the results more accurate. Techniques such as random selection are now used to choose individuals to be interviewed for public opinion polls.

In the sampling process the American population is reduced to a miniature. The mathematical law of probability says that the opinions expressed by this sample are representative of the population as a whole.* The results are a fairly accurate measurement of public opinion. But poll results can never be exact. There is a mathematically determined range of possible ***sampling error***—usually a plus or minus 4 percent in a sample of 1,500 people. Thus a 1984 Gallup Poll stated that 55 percent of the people favored Ronald Reagan for President. With a plus or minus of 4 percent, this meant that Reagan's support was probably somewhere between 51 and 59 percent.

*Probability refers to the likelihood of a possible outcome occurring. If you flip a coin 1,000 times, for example, the law of probability says that it will come up heads about 500 times.

The accuracy of the polls can be seen in predicting recent Presidential elections, as shown in the chart on page 235.

Analyzing the Results

In addition to opinions about candidates and issues, surveys include certain personal questions similar to those asked by the census. These are useful in finding out whether there are patterns in the distribution of opinion. Analysis of results, for example, may show significant differences in the opinions of men and women on a particular question. Or it may show differences of opinion between younger and older people.

Modern computers have made statistical analysis both faster and easier. Poll results can be broken down to see how opinions differ among groups within the population. Opinions can be sorted and

PRESIDENTIAL ELECTIONS: PREDICTIONS AND RESULTS

Election Year	Major Candidates		Percentage Error
1976	Carter	Ford	
Gallup Poll	48.0%	44.0%	2.1
Harris Poll	45.0%	44.0%	5.1
Election Results	50.1%	48.0%	—
1980	Reagan	Carter	
Gallup Poll	47.0%	44.0%	3.8
ABC News/Harris Poll	45.0%	40.0%	5.8
CBS News/New York Times	43.0%	43.0%	7.8
Election Results	50.8%	41.0%	—
1984	Reagan	Mondale	
Gallup Poll	59.0%	41.0%	0.0
Harris Poll	56.0%	40.0%	3.0
CBS News/New York Times	58.0%	37.0%	1.0
Election Results	59.0%	41.0%	—

Most predictions made by pollsters in recent Presidential elections have been reasonably accurate. What is the usual range of sampling error for poll results?

A cartoonist points to the differences between political pollsters' predictions and election results. Although pollsters use scientific methods and sophisticated computers to predict outcomes, the voters ultimately determine election results.

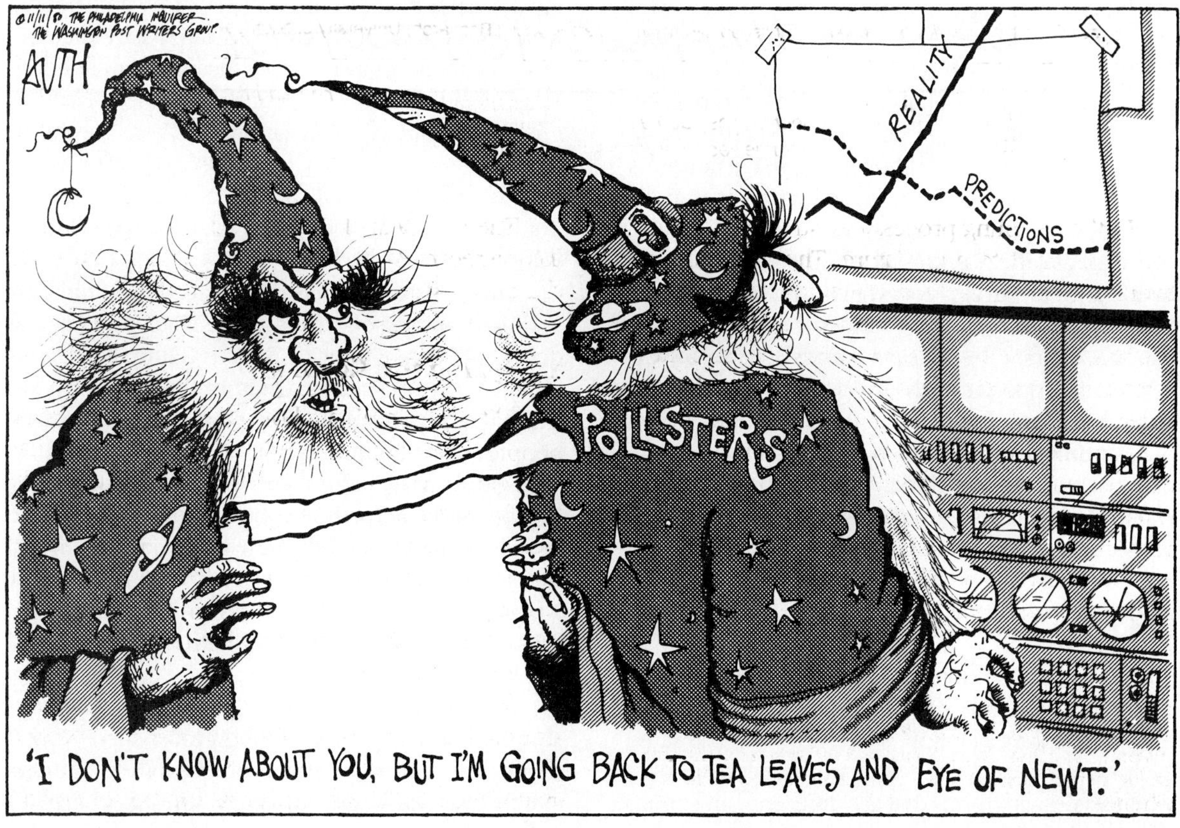
AUTH
REALITY
PREDICTIONS
POLLSTERS
'I DON'T KNOW ABOUT YOU, BUT I'M GOING BACK TO TEA LEAVES AND EYE OF NEWT.'

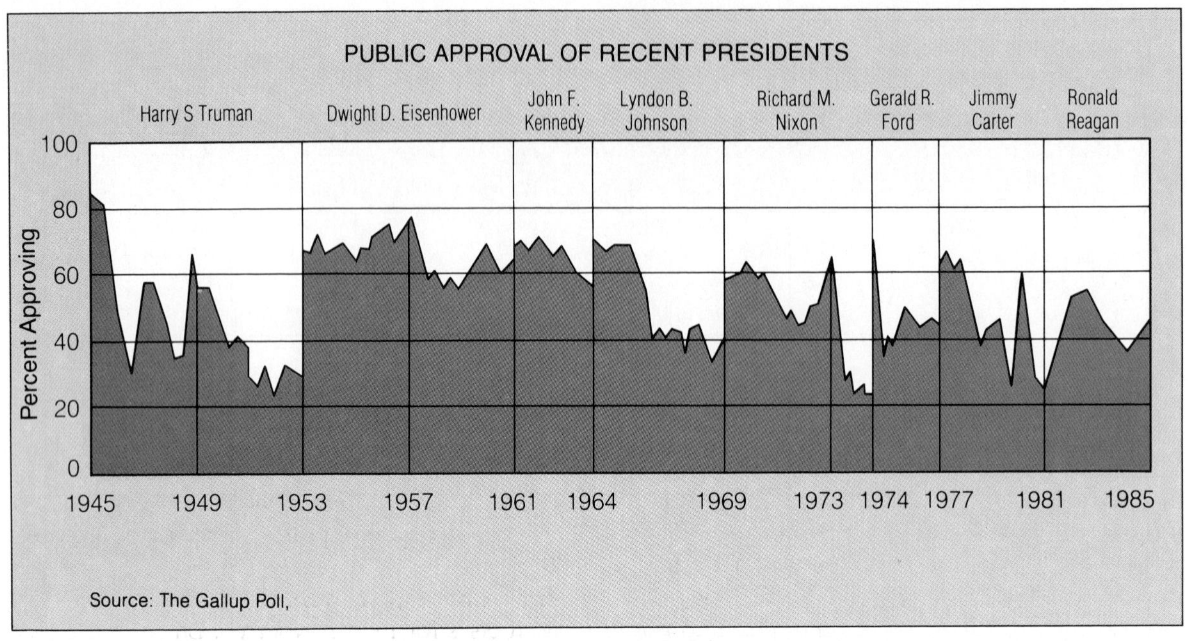

Public approval of the President usually varies during the Presidential term of office. How often does the Gallup Poll survey public attitudes toward the President? Why might a President's approval rating change abruptly?

examined according to geographic regions or urban-rural differences and according to such social and economic factors as race, ethnic origins, religion, education, occupation, income, sex, and age. The analysis of these patterns is vital to an understanding of what public opinion on a given issue really means.

Another kind of analysis involves comparison over time. Have opinions on a particular issue changed? Which way are they moving? The answers can be found by asking the same questions in polls from time to time and then comparing the results. For example, the Gallup Poll asks the same question in a national survey every two weeks: "Do you approve of the way the President is handling the nation's affairs?" Responses vary from survey to survey, but the pattern usually reveals a downward trend. Most Presidents begin their term in office with a high approval rating, which slips gradually until a national or international crisis comes along. Depending on how a crisis is handled, the President's rating then rebounds or drops sharply.

Problems in Polling

Some words of caution about public polling are necessary. First, the way a question is worded can influence the answer a person is likely to give. The same basic question can produce very different responses when asked with terms that are different, but similar in meaning. For example, the question "Do you favor national health insurance?" might reveal wide public support because most people have positive feelings about the term *insurance*. But if the same people were asked, "Do you favor socialized medicine?" more of them would say no because many people have negative feelings about the phrase *socialized medicine*. Polling organizations are very careful to word questions as fairly as possible. Questions are usually tested in a trial run to be sure that they are not biased and that they really ask what the pollsters want to know.

Still pollsters sometimes mislead the public by asking the wrong question. As the Watergate scandal developed throughout 1973, both Gallup and Harris polls asked Americans whether President Nixon should be impeached and removed from office. Many people who wanted Nixon impeached (that is, brought to trial) had to answer "no" because they did not want to presume him guilty without due process of law. The polls were widely and, it turned out, incorrectly interpreted as showing support for Nixon. In the spring of 1974 Gallup caught the error. When people were asked whether they favored impeachment, most said "yes."

Another major problem is that polls may oversimplify the issues. Even though most survey questions deal with complex problems, they demand simple "yes/no," "agree/disagree," or "favor/oppose" answers. Very few questions are open-ended, allowing people to give their opinions. Those who consider different sides of an issue are likely to be recorded as "undecided" or "don't know."

Perhaps the most serious problem in public opinion polls is that some people offer uninformed opinions. Without knowledge or serious thought about the issue, they give a snap judgment. If asked the same question later, they might express a completely different opinion. Because the snap judgments are given the same weight as truly informed opinions, these uninformed answers can distort the results of the poll.

When reading the results of a poll, it is important to note when it was taken because major events may have since changed public opinion. Check out the accuracy of the organization that conducted the poll. Determine how it was conducted—on the street, door-to-door, by phone or mail. Finally note how the sample was chosen. Any poll that fails to give this basic information is not worth reading.

Purposes of Polling

There are three basic purposes for which polls are conducted. The first use is journalistic—to provide the general public with information about what the American people are thinking. Polling organizations conduct regular surveys on a wide range of topics, and the results are carried in newspapers and magazines. The leading journalistic organizations are the Gallup Poll and the Harris Poll.

The second use is scientific. These surveys are conducted by scholars to better understand the nature of attitudes and political behavior. Individual scholars often conduct surveys on particular topics, but these surveys rarely involve national samples. Only a large organization can afford to conduct a national survey. Two important organizations that conduct national scientific polls are the Survey Research Center at the University of Michigan and the National Opinion Research Center at the University of Chicago.

The third use of polls is for private purposes. These polls are conducted for a specific client. Originally, private polls were used almost entirely by businesses for market research. But over the past 20 years political candidates have made increasing use of private polls. The results are usually secret—though when favorable to the candidate they are often leaked to the press. The candidates use private polls to help make election campaign decisions. The most basic decision is whether to run for office at

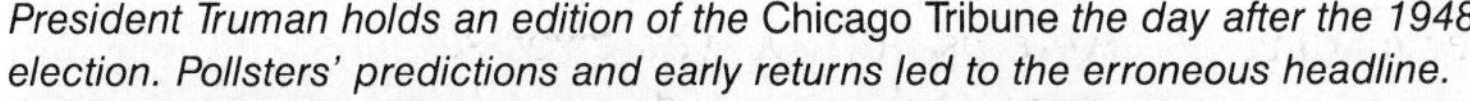
President Truman holds an edition of the Chicago Tribune *the day after the 1948 election. Pollsters' predictions and early returns led to the erroneous headline.*

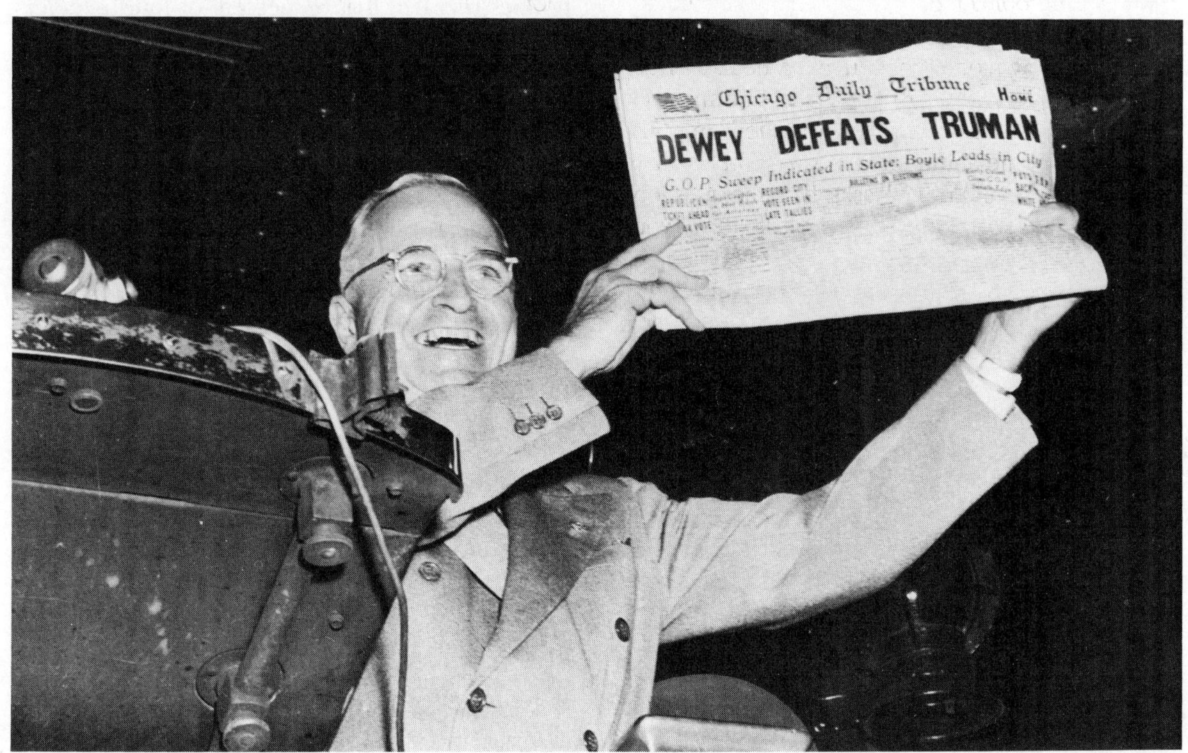

all, and poll results on the level of recognition and support are critical factors in that decision. Polls identify issues of public concern as well as controversial issues that candidates may wish to avoid. They also have a major impact on the candidate's ability to attract campaign contributions. Financial support tends to decrease with a poor showing in the polls.

Some critics charge that public opinion polls have distorted the democratic process. A poor showing in early polls may prevent candidates who lack wide name recognition from running. Polls often force front-runners to compete with poll results, with anything less than a landslide called a "defeat." Polls create bandwagon effects in elections, helping the leading candidate to gain more support. Conversely, a poor poll rating may dishearten a candidate's supporters and even keep them from voting. Thus polls tend to make their own predictions come true. They may influence public opinion rather than simply measure it.

Public opinion polls, however, can give reasonably accurate impressions of public opinion. They can be useful tools for political leaders and for the general public. But they are no substitute for democracy. America's most important polls are still the ones that open on election day.

Section Check

1. Define: straw poll, random sample, sampling error
2. Who conducted the first national, scientifically constructed public opinion poll?
3. Why is it important to be cautious in the interpretation of public opinion polls?
4. What are the three major purposes for which polls are conducted?
5. What are four facts to notice when reading a poll?

---

4 HOW OPINIONS ARE FORMED

Through learning experiences, we gain knowledge, feelings, and judgments about the world and our place within it. Over time we come to share common values, beliefs, and attitudes with others in our society. This learning experience, which is called ***socialization,*** begins in early childhood and continues throughout life.

We acquire our political attitudes in this same learning process. Socialization is both formal and informal, planned and unplanned, and it begins before we are even aware that it is happening. Four sources of influence are especially important in shaping a person's political attitudes: the family, the school, the groups with which one associates and identifies, and the mass media.

Family Influences

Political learning begins in the family. Early experiences have deep influence on later political orientations because they are rooted in family loyalties. Though parents may stress respect for the law, most families do not deliberately teach their children about government and politics. Learning in the family usually takes place less formally. Children may overhear their parents talking about the elections, a political leader, or an important national issue. Parents' opinions are picked up by their children—at first without understanding, but later with greater knowledge and judgment.

In the excitement of a Presidential election year many very young children wear buttons for their favorite candidates or political party. They begin calling themselves Republicans or Democrats long before they know anything about the differences between the two parties. One study of children and politics revealed that 63 percent of fourth-graders identified with a political party. If the parents are politically active and talk about politics in the home, their children are likely to be more politically oriented than children whose parents are less politically involved. The closer the mother and father agree in their political opinions, the more likely it is that their children will grow up to hold similar views.

Attitudes that are learned earliest are the most resistant to change. Most often an outlook acquired in childhood is reinforced and strengthened as the individual enters adult life. Many people continue to share their parents' party loyalty and basic point of view. Of course, children do not always follow the lead of their parents. As adults they may end up on the other side of the political fence. Early family experience remains an important influence, but other conflicting experiences may bring about basic changes in a person's political orientation.

The Influence of Schooling

A child's early school experiences are important elements in the formation of political orientations. A

Marching in a patriotic parade is often a child's first active experience with politics and the political process. What is a child's most basic political orientation? Upon whom does a child's political awareness first focus? Upon entering the teen years, how does a young person's political thinking change?

number of studies show that by the time a child has completed elementary school, many basic political attitudes and values have become firmly established.

Of these orientations the most basic is national loyalty. From kindergarten, children begin to think of themselves as Americans. School children learn to respect the flag, to say the Pledge of Allegiance, and to sing patriotic songs. Like most political learning, patriotism is first based on feeling. The facts come later, but feelings provide the foundation upon which knowledge and judgments are based.

A child's first awareness of the nation's political institutions focuses on persons—the police officer, the mayor, and most of all the President. Many children in the lower elementary grades can name the President and are likely to have fairly strong feelings about anyone holding the office. Children's images of the President vary, depending on their own family background and the views of their parents. Images also vary with the personalities of different Presidents. Generally, though, children have a very positive and idealized view of the President. This highly favorable orientation declines somewhat as they grow older, but the President remains for most people the central focus of government and politics.

As young people enter their teens, they begin to develop greater knowledge about the institutions and processes of government. They become more critical in their thinking and more capable of making informed judgments about politics, politicians, and the issues. They learn to separate the offices of government from the people who occupy them. Thus someone may not approve of a particular President but still respect the office of the Presidency. A person may not agree with decisions of the Supreme Court yet still uphold the Court and defend its constitutional power. Similarly, young people begin to distinguish issues from personalities. Some may disagree with the President or the mayor on a particular issue yet continue to support them on other issues. They learn, too, that it is possible to oppose people politically, to disagree with them on the issues, and still like and respect them as persons.

In high school, students begin to develop a better understanding of basic concepts such as liberty, equality, and democracy. They learn the meaning of majority rule and minority rights. They come to know their constitutional rights and the obligations that go with them. In their teens, young people also become aware of the social and economic problems that face the nation. They come to grapple with the issues that divide America, and express their opinions as citizens.

Citizenship education is an important responsibility of the schools. Classes in American government and politics seek to provide knowledge and skill for effective and responsible citizenship. Schools may sponsor field trips to watch the city council or state legislature in action. Classes may visit a courtroom during a trial. Students may go out for debate or take part in a model legislature. Political learning in school is not limited to the civics curriculum. In the classroom and on the playground the school provides opportunities for participation in the election of class officers or team captains, in student government, and in self-governing extracurricular clubs and organizations. Through such activities students learn citizenship skills that are important in later life.

Not all persons, of course, follow the same patterns of socialization and political development. The pace of political learning varies among individuals, as does the content of political attitudes. Young people, like adults, differ in their interest in politics. The source of these differences is often to be found in the influence of groups to which they belong.

Group Influences

Throughout life from childhood until old age, groups play a vital role in shaping our political opinions. People are social beings, and each person is a member of many different groups. Among the groups with whom we have direct contact are close friends, fellow workers, and the members of a church, club, or other group. Most of these groups are not political, but when members get together they sometimes talk about politics. They may discuss the latest developments in the Middle East, the President's policy to control inflation, or a coming school board election. They may talk about how to get the city to fix the potholes in the street or put up a traffic light at a neighborhood intersection. Perhaps only a few people in the group will express their opinions. If they are well informed on the issues and their judgments are respected, their views are likely to have considerable influence on other members of the group. These people are the ***opinion leaders*** of the community.

How much influence a group has on a person's political opinions depends on a number of factors. A group for which politics is of special importance is likely to have the greatest influence on its members. A politically active labor union or business group, for example, is more likely to be influential than a sports club. The extent of group influence depends on three other factors: how closely a person identifies with the group; the length of time a person has been a member; and how often the members meet.

Group Differences In addition to those groups that demand personal involvement, people identify with larger groups or categories of persons. These groups reflect social and economic differences within the population. Some of the most important differences include geographic differences (regional and urban-rural differences), race, ethnicity, religion, education, occupation, income, age, and sex. The importance of these factors and their influence vary from issue to issue. On some questions these factors may not be important at all.

Party Identification For many Americans one of the most important influences on opinion is their political party. Although party loyalty has declined in recent years, more than half of all Americans identify with either the Republican or Democratic party. The party's position on the issues provides guidance for many people in forming their own opinions. Thus, political parties not only respond to public opinion as they seek support from the voters, but also shape public opinion.

Section Check

1. Define: socialization, opinion leader
2. What four sources strongly influence people's political attitudes?
3. Explain how citizenship education in the schools helps a young person to mature politically.
4. What are some factors that determine the extent of a group's influence on its members?

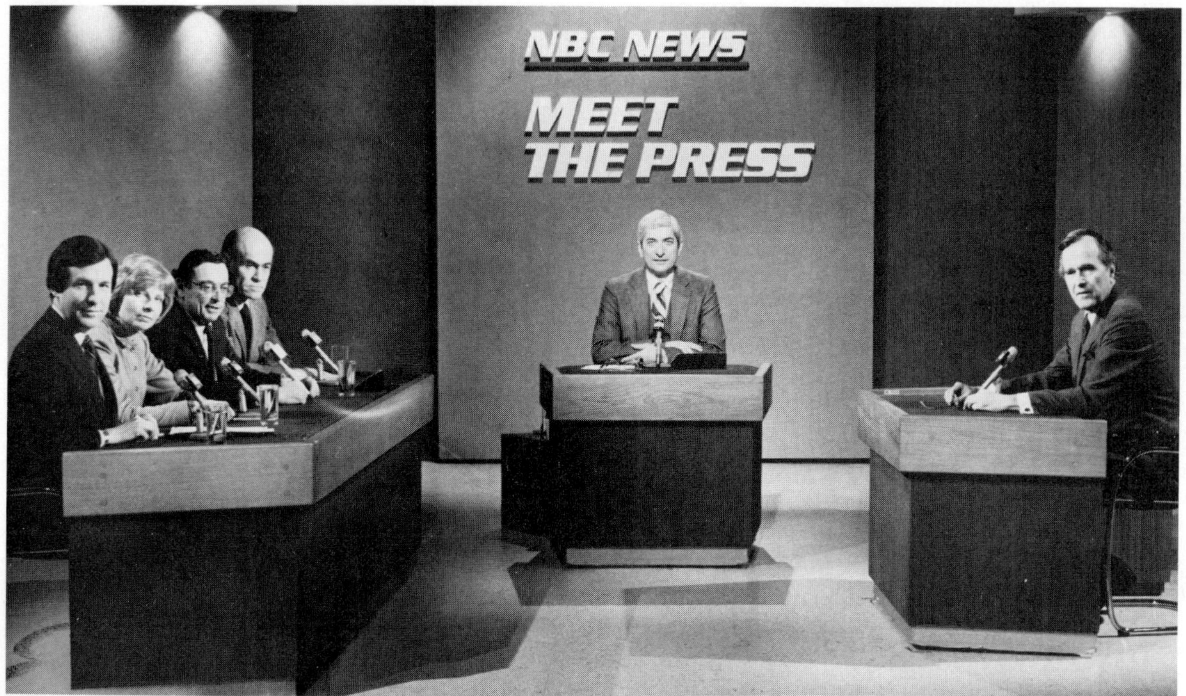

Vice President George Bush (right) appears on a "Meet the Press" telecast. Media presentations provide an opportunity for the public to hear from newsmakers and government officials. How might the mass media help shape public opinion?

5 THE MASS MEDIA AND POLITICAL PROPAGANDA

The ***mass media***—television, radio, newspapers, and magazines—play an important role in shaping political opinion. The media provide information, stimulate interest in politics and public affairs, and influence attitudes.

Television

Of all the mass media, television has the widest impact. Ninety-seven percent of all homes in the United States have at least one television set. Most television programs serve only to entertain, not to inform. But each of the networks has an evening news program. These news programs have a combined audience averaging more than 60 million people each evening.

The network news is presented with an effort to be objective and fair. It does not seek to influence opinion in one direction or another. The networks try to avoid controversy and not offend anyone. Inevitably, though, television news has a crucial impact on people's attitudes about political personalities and the issues.

Because many newscasts last an hour or less, they must be highly selective in their presentations. A single newscast can deal only with a few subjects and cannot provide the depth of coverage and analysis that is possible in a long newspaper article. The text of an entire network newscast, for example, would not fill one page of *The New York Times.*

Selectivity has its influence in a number of ways. The amount of news time given to a particular candidate for election may be critical to success. If candidates receive little or no coverage, they are not likely to be taken seriously by the voters. Television news treatment of the issues is also important. Newscasts generally emphasize certain national and international events and problems that are dramatic and easy to illustrate with film clips. Sometimes one event seems to dominate the news, pushing everything else out of the picture. By focusing on one issue or personality rather than another, the media influence national priorities—what Americans believe to be the most pressing issues of the day or the candidates to be taken most seriously.

In addition to the news, the networks all have regularly scheduled public affairs programs. Some such as *Meet the Press* present panel interviews with political leaders. Others offer investigative reports

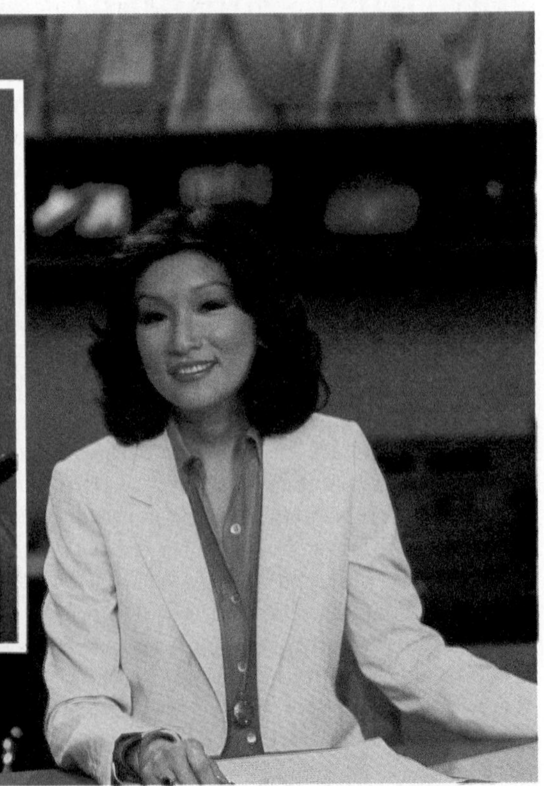

Ted Koppel (top left), Dan Rather (top right), William F. Buckley, Jr., (above), and Connie Chung (right) are newscasters on major television networks. Newscasters frequently host documentaries and special news programs as well.

or in-depth analyses of the issues. Most of these programs draw a relatively small audience, but one program, *Sixty Minutes,* has ranked among the top shows on television.

Periodically television provides prime-time special news reports and documentary features. The networks may carry the President's press conference or a major speech such as the State of the Union Address to Congress. The leader of the opposition party is usually given equal time to respond. Major events are given extensive coverage, as in the televised hearings on the Watergate scandal in 1973 and 1974. The national political party conventions every four years are televised, as are special debates between the major Presidential candidates.

Newspapers and Magazines

There are some 20,000 newspapers and magazines published in the United States. Of these, about 1,800 are daily newspapers with a total circulation of more than 60 million. A few, such as *The New York Times* and the *Washington Post,* provide extensive national and international coverage on a daily basis. They have their own reporters all over the world and a readership throughout the United States. In contrast, many small-town newspapers are weeklies that cover mainly local news, with only a small amount of space, if any, devoted to world affairs. Most daily newspapers have short reports on major news events around the world. For these they rely on ***wire services*** such as United Press International (UPI), the Associated Press (AP), or those connected with major newspapers.

Daily newspapers are no longer the main source of information for most Americans. There are fewer daily papers today than in 1900. As the number of newspapers has declined, most large cities have been left with only one paper. Even in New York City, the nation's largest city, the number of major newspapers has declined over the past 30 years from 8 to 3.

This decline means less competition—not just among newspapers as businesses—but also less competition in ideas and points of view. When a city has only one paper, its citizens are seriously limited in their sources of information. Television partially makes up for this limitation, but only a small number of all television programs is devoted to news and public affairs. Moreover, except for the evening news, most television public affairs programs are aired during "off hours" and do not have large viewing audiences.

The major weekly news magazines—*Time, Newsweek,* and *U.S. News and World Report*—provide additional information for many Americans, but their combined circulation is only about 10 million. Other magazines devoted to public affairs have a much smaller circulation.

The Power of the Media

Many people express concern that the media are controlled by only a small number of persons and that they have undue influence in shaping public opinion. In television, for example, the three major networks dominate the industry. Newspapers, as we have noted, are usually noncompetitive. Few communities have more than one daily paper, and many papers belong to large national chains.

Some people argue that this concentration of power leads to dangerous bias. Because sources of information are limited, they say, public opinion can be manipulated. Former Vice President Spiro Agnew, who served with President Nixon, attacked the media's power over public opinion: "Nowhere in our system are there fewer checks on vast power." During the Watergate investigations President Nixon charged the television networks with distorting the news, and he felt that the press—especially *The New York Times* and the *Washington Post*—treated him unfairly.

To some degree every President has been sensitive to press criticism. One of the most important roles of a free press is that of a watchdog over government. Few political leaders are spared close scrutiny by the press, and the President is watched most closely. President Nixon saw a liberal bias in the press, but many liberals regard the press as conservative. If reporters tend to be liberal, they point out, newspaper owners are generally conservative. In 1980, 443 newspapers supported the Republican candidate Ronald Reagan for President and 126 backed Jimmy Carter, the Democratic nominee.

The news content of telecasts and most newspapers is not readily identifiable as liberal or conservative. There is generally an attempt to present the news fairly and without bias. On their editorial and opinion pages, many newspapers present a variety of viewpoints. In addition to its own views on the candidates and the issues, each paper usually features several nationally known columnists—some conservative and some liberal. These writers, whose columns are carried by newspapers all over the country, analyze major news events and express their individual judgments about the issues.

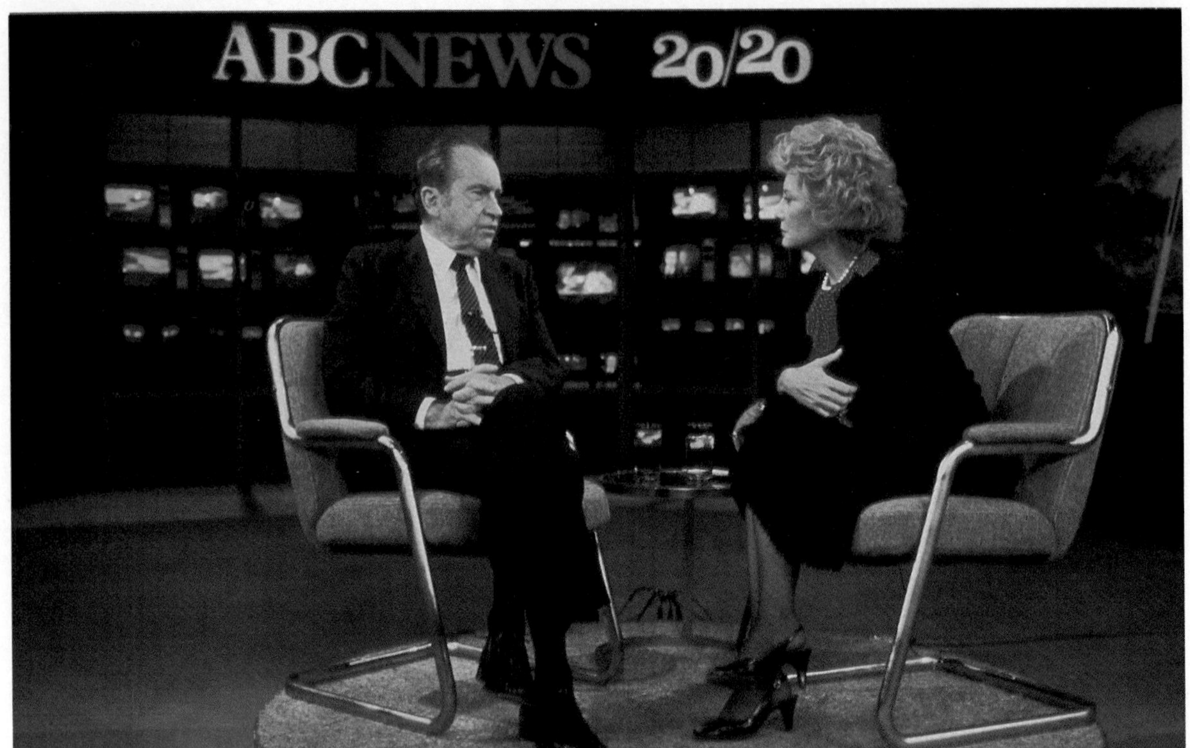

Former President Richard Nixon expresses his views about public issues in an interview with news correspondent Barbara Walters. Public officials are keenly aware of the media's impact on public opinion.

The Influence of the Media

Public opinion is certainly influenced by the mass media, but probably not as much as is generally supposed. The most important factor in weakening the impact of the media is the strong influence of family, school, and group experiences in shaping political opinions. These opinions are deeply rooted and not easily changed.

Another factor in weakening media impact is that people are selective in what they watch and read. It is important to remember that most of the content of television is nonpolitical, and more people watch situation comedies than the evening news or *Meet the Press.* Even when the news is on, people may screen out whatever bores or offends them.

Selectivity is even more clearly evident among newspaper and magazine readers. In the daily newspaper, more people look at the comics and the sports than at the editorial page. Even when reading political news, most people glance at the headlines and then read only those articles which interest them most. A few people, of course, seek out political information, but they generally read publications that support their own political opinions. Instead of changing people's views, the media most often act to reinforce opinions people already have.

Propaganda

Propaganda is a form of communication that manipulates information in order to influence attitudes. As a word *propaganda* carries a negative association, but the actual message of a piece of propaganda itself may be either true or false. It may be used for either good or evil purposes. What distinguishes propaganda from other methods of presenting information is its techniques. Each technique is a one-sided method that attempts to persuade people to support certain ideas, attitudes, or beliefs. There are seven techniques in all.

Propaganda appeals to emotion, fears, and prejudice—not to reason. One technique is ***name-calling.*** Instead of presenting a policy on its logic or merits, the propagandist describes it as "fascist," "extremist," "radical," or "un-American." Political leaders are attacked in the same fashion.

Propagandists use ***glittering generalities***—phrases that sound wonderful but usually have little substance. Political speeches, for example, often contain what is called "Fourth of July rhetoric." Candidates proclaim that they are for Peace and Prosperity, Freedom and Justice. But who isn't? No candidates oppose these values any more than they oppose baseball and apple pie.

Propagandists may distort facts in a technique called ***stacking the deck*** that favors only one side of an argument. Stacking the deck usually oversimplifies an issue and reduces a complex problem to a simple slogan that is mindlessly repeated and easily remembered. It may exaggerate, bend the truth, or contain half-truths. Sometimes it may simply lie.

Another technique is ***false association.*** The propagandist may seek to identify with some favored image or group. Opposing candidates may be smeared by identifying them falsely with unpopular causes. Often this misinformation is circulated by insinuation and rumor.

The use of ***testimonials*** is still another form of propaganda. A movie star or sports personality may endorse a particular candidate or policy. They are not qualified as experts, but their popularity lends appeal to the cause.

Propagandists try to identify with their audience by using a ***plain-folk approach.*** People are more easily persuaded by someone close and familiar. Politicians, for example, usually try to present themselves as "just plain folks." They address the audience as "friends" and try to establish a close relationship with them.

Propaganda often employs an appeal to ***follow the crowd.*** Many people fear that if they do not hop on the bandwagon, they will be left behind. The propagandist's message is: "Everybody's doing it—so you should too!"

The great American humorist Will Rogers used to say that he never believed anything he read and only half of what he saw. Few people are as skeptical as that. And many Americans have learned to recognize propaganda techniques, thus rejecting the propagandists' messages.

Section Check

1. Define: mass media, wire service, propaganda
2. Which of the mass media has the widest impact in our society?
3. What is one result of the decline in the number of daily papers in the United States since 1900?
4. Name the major forms of propaganda commonly used.

SUMMARY

Public opinion is the preference of a significant number of persons about an issue or a number of issues. No government —not even a dictatorship—can ignore public opinion. People usually differ in the direction and the intensity of their opinions on most issues.

Ideology is a set of closely related beliefs that fit together in a political philosophy. In the United States ideologies are most often conservative or liberal. The beliefs of most Americans involve a mixture of both liberal and conservative opinions. In general, conservatism is based on the fundamental right to property and emphasizes gradual development rather than rapid change. Conservatives argue that more government means less freedom. Liberalism seeks to create an equal society with government intervention in the economy and to promote the public welfare.

Public opinion can be measured by surveys known as public opinion polls. These polls have become increasingly important in our political system. Polls are conducted by interviewing people selected from a random sample in which the American population is reduced to a miniature.

There are three major problems to be faced in polling. First, the way a question is worded may influence the answer a person will give. Second, polls tend to oversimplify issues. Third, people will often give uninformed opinions in a poll. Polls are conducted for journalistic, scientific, and private purposes.

Opinions are formed by the process of socialization. This process is the learning of common values, beliefs, and attitudes in the family, in school, and in social or political groups. The values learned in childhood are often deep-rooted and difficult to change. But a person's opinions can change at any time in his or her life.

The mass media play an important role in shaping public opinion. Television has the widest influence, but newspapers, magazines, and radio are also influential. Propaganda is any type of communication that manipulates information to influence public opinion. Propaganda appeals to emotion, fear, and prejudice—not to reason. Among the techniques of propaganda are name-calling, glittering generalities, stacking the deck, false association, testimonials, and audience identification. The information presented to the public by the mass media can help counter the misleading effects of propaganda in a society.

Chapter 9 Review

Using Vocabulary

Answer the questions by using the meaning of each underlined term.

1. Why is individualism the cornerstone of classical liberalism?
2. How might propaganda be a means of promoting an ideology?
3. How would a liberal differ from a conservative on the issue of regulating the environment?
4. What should a person remember about sampling error when reading the results of a straw poll?
5. How does the mass media both shape and reflect public opinion?

Understanding American Government

1. What is the meaning of the statement, "There is no one public but many publics"?
2. What was the basic philosophy of classical liberalism?
3. What two basic steps are involved in drawing a sample for a national survey?
4. According to some critics, how may public opinion polls distort the democratic process?
5. How does the political thinking of young people develop and change as they go through their teenage years?
6. Describe some of the techniques used by propagandists.

Extending Your Skills: Using a Diagram

Indicate whether the text on pages 233–234 or the graphic on page 234 verifies each of the following true statements.

1. Selection of individual housing units takes place on a random basis.
2. The accuracy of a poll depends on how the sampling is done, not on the size of the sample.
3. The necessary size of a sample is determined mathematically.
4. In the SRC sampling method, a primary area is divided into four other areas, each of which comprises a smaller unit.
5. Pollsters rely on the law of probability in analyzing results.

Government and You

1. Of the two political ideologies, liberalism and conservatism, which do you think is better suited to solving today's problems? Do you think a mix of conservative and liberal philosophy is best? What are the reasons for your answers?
2. Socialization is the learning of common values, beliefs, and attitudes. Four influences play a major role in socialization: family, school, group associations, and the mass media. When does each of these have the most influence in a person's life? Which of these influences has most affected you recently? Why do you think influences change at different times in a person's life?
3. The three major purposes of public opinion polls are journalistic, scientific, and private. Which type often gets the greatest publicity? Which often has the greatest impact on society? Why?
4. Can you think of examples in history where propaganda was used to influence public opinion in very important ways? How does propaganda work? How can a person learn to resist its influence?

Activities

1. Select an issue you think is important to you and your classmates. Draw a sample of the members of your class. Poll the ones you chose in your sample on the issue selected. Report the results of your poll to the class.
2. Prepare a biographical report on George Gallup, the conductor of the first national, scientifically constructed public opinion poll. Include details of his life and of the history of public opinion polling.
3. Invite an editor of your local newspaper to speak to the class on the role of newspapers in influencing public opinion and the political process in your state.
4. Make a scrapbook of newspaper clippings and magazine articles showing the results of public opinion polls. Try to include several polls on the same issue. Include such information as who conducted each poll and how the sample for each poll was drawn.

Chapter 10

Interest Groups

As soon as several of the inhabitants of the United States have taken up an opinion or a feeling which they wish to promote in the world, they look around for mutual assistance; and as soon as they have found each other out, they combine. From that moment they are no longer isolated men, but a power seen from afar, whose actions serve for an example, and whose language is listened to.

ALEXIS DE TOCQUEVILLE

CHAPTER OVERVIEW

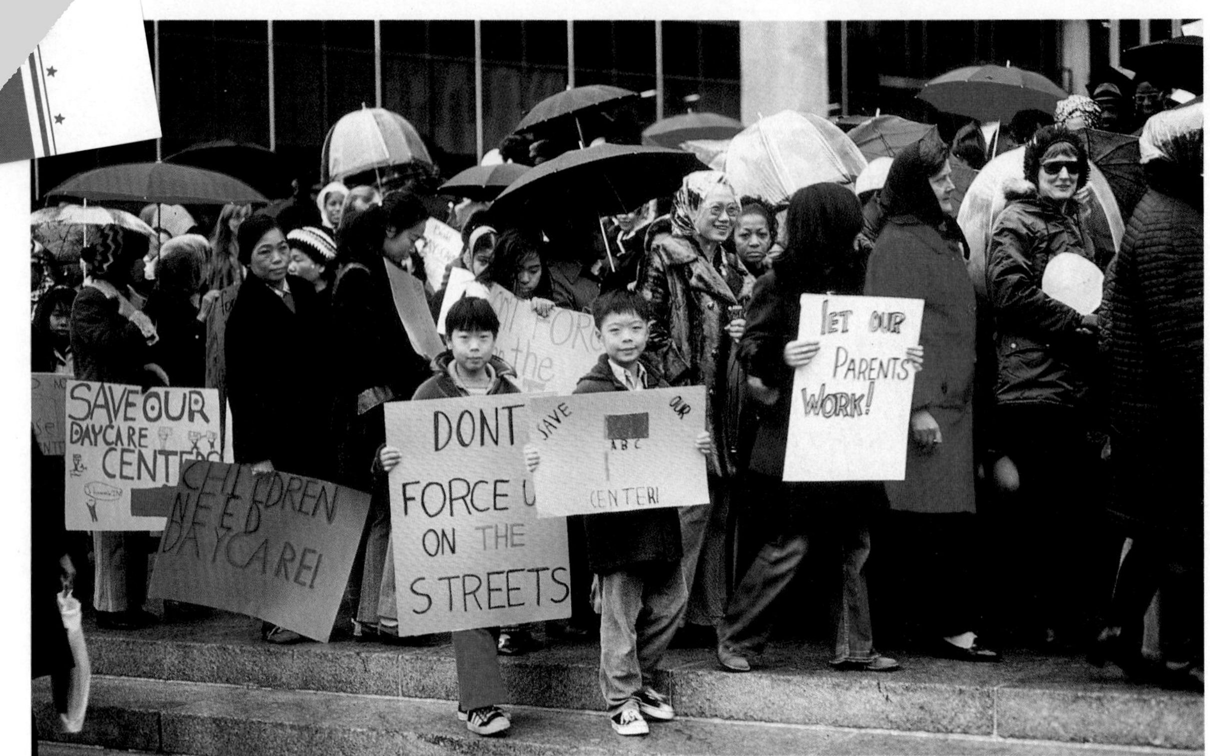

By demonstrating in favor of publicly funded day-care centers, these parents and children seek to influence governmental policy. Their common views and goals bind them together as an interest group, attracting the attention of the public, the media, and the lawmakers.

1 THE GROUP AS A BASIC UNIT OF POLITICS

In his travels through the United States 150 years ago, Alexis de Tocqueville noted the importance of associations in American society. "Americans of all ages, all conditions, and all dispositions, constantly form associations," he wrote. Today, as in the past, Americans join together for every sort of activity—economic, religious, social, and political.

From the founding of the Republic, group activity has played a central role in American government and politics. Through groups people seek to express their opinions, promote their interests, and influence government. This chapter will examine what some writers have called "the group basis of politics."

Hundreds of thousands of groups exist in the United States. They cover a range of almost every conceivable activity and interest—from a neighborhood stamp club to the American Medical Association and the National Association of Manufacturers. Some groups are national, even international, in scope; others are purely local. Some have millions of members, others no more than half a dozen. Some are formal organizations with a charter or written constitution; others are informal, little more than a group of friends who share a common interest.

Politics is the competitive struggle to influence and shape government policy. Conflict arises over "who gets what, when, and how." Groups are the central actors in politics, but not all groups play a politically significant role. For a group to be politically effective, its members must share a common interest which they seek to protect or promote through government policy. At any given time some interests command greater attention than others. Yet each year new groups emerge. With them, new issues are brought before the American people.

What Is an Interest Group?

Any group that seeks to influence what government does becomes a political ***interest group.*** In the broadest sense, an interest group is a collection of people that, on the basis of common views and goals, seeks to influence public policy. The group attempts both to protect and promote its interests. It serves as a "watchdog," keeping an eye on government activities and sounding the alarm whenever its members' interests are threatened. When an interest group is satisfied with the ***status quo,*** with the way things are, it may do no more than try to protect and maintain its interests against the claims of other groups. Frequently, however, a group seeks to advance its interests by making demands on government for positive benefits.

Most organizations are not primarily political, yet each may have political interests. A sports club, for example, wants the city to provide more recreational facilities. It promotes its cause by trying to arouse interest in physical fitness in the community as a whole. Club members contact local officials, urging them to support public tennis courts and swimming pools, a new ball park, or a "hike and bike" trail. Members also contact state and national officials to encourage greater government support for athletic programs. The club also works to prevent cuts in government budgets for recreation and athletics.

Categorical Groups

When we talk about athletes, women, blacks, farmers, or people with red hair, we are classifying people according to specific characteristics. We are placing them in social categories. Each person is a member of a number of different ***categorical groups.*** Some categories—such as those based on income, occupation, or race—are politically important. Others—such as groups based on hair color—are not.

Whether or not a categorical group takes on political significance depends on three important factors:

First, the people within the category must have a sense of attachment and common identity. They must feel that they belong to the group and that they share common interests.

Second, they must see a connection between their group membership and political life. They must feel that their group is affected by what government does.

Third, on the basis of the groups' common interests, groups must be willing to act politically to influence government policy in some way—if only by voting.

Politicians and political scientists tend to view the electorate in terms of categorical groups, not as individual voters. Candidates for office make their appeals in terms of group interests—or what they believe those interests to be. Public officials make decisions taking into account how major groups will respond.

People in the United States belong to many different categorical groups. What three factors determine the political significance of a categorical group? How might the existence of categorical groups affect candidates' appeals to voters?

MAJOR CATEGORICAL GROUPS

Sex	Age	Race	Religion
Men Women	Older Middle Age Youth	White Black Hispanic Asian Native American Other	Protestant Catholic Jew Other
Occupation	**Income**	**Region**	**Residence**
Professional White-collar Labor Farmers	Wealthy Middle-class Poor	Northeast South Midwest Southwest West	Urban Suburban Rural

Categorical groups are politically important, but they must be considered with caution. All members of a categorical group are rarely in agreement about what is in the group's best interest. All women, for example, do not support an Equal Rights Amendment nor do all farmers want price supports. Differences among members of a categorical group arise, in part, because no one group represents all of a person's interests.

Each person is at the same time a member of many different groups. A woman, for example, may be young, black, and rich. She may have been raised in the city in the Southwest as a Catholic. She may have a career and a family. She shares some interests with each of the categorical groups of which she is a member. She may identify with one group on a particular issue, but with another group on another issue. Sometimes, on a given issue, she may be pulled in different directions by divided loyalties.

Because no one group represents all of a person's interests, most people are willing to bargain and compromise. Certain interests may be overriding. For some people one interest may be so important that all others have little meaning. When people feel deeply about one particular issue, they are less likely to compromise. Group conflict becomes more intense.

Any category of persons is likely to embrace a number of different, and sometimes conflicting, interest groups. These groups form to protect and promote special interests. They vary in size, character, and in the goals they pursue. They include informal interest groups and formal organizations.

Informal Interest Groups

Small groups of friends or associates who share the same interests and seek to influence government policy often form informal interest groups. Some groups have a long life, but most form around a particular issue and disappear as quickly as they came into existence. For example, a group of neighbors who get together to urge the city to put in a traffic light at a busy intersection usually disperse after achieving their objective. Another example is a group of friends who find that they share opinions about government energy policy. Rather than just discuss the issue, they write to members of Congress and urge others to do so.

Informal interest groups, as the term implies, are not formal organizations. They have no constitutions or ***bylaws,*** rules that govern the group. There are no officers. Informal groups sometimes develop as ***factions***—groups pursuing particular goals within

Another informal interest group is the President's breakfast meeting with members of Congress. How might informal meetings be important sources of governmental policy decisions?

Formal interest groups are organized to achieve specific goals. The Veterans of Foreign Wars (VFW) promotes veterans' civil service and employment opportunities, a strong national defense, and various patriotic youth activities.

a larger organization. In the Republican and Democratic parties, for example, the liberal and conservative wings can be viewed as factions. In large groups factions often compete for the control of an organization, sometimes in good spirit, sometimes in bitter struggle.

Informal groups also develop within government. In the federal government they are to be found in almost every Executive department and agency. Such groups also exist in Congress, often cutting across party lines. Among the many groups in the House of Representatives, there is a Black Caucus, a Rural Caucus, and an Environmental Caucus. There is the Congressional Prayer Breakfast and the Tuesday luncheon at which women members of the House discuss common concerns. House Republicans have the Chowder and Marching Club, which meets weekly to discuss politics and legislation. Working often behind the scenes, informal groups can exercise great influence over the formation and implementation of government policy.

Formal Organizations

Formal organizations are groups with established goals and structures. They exist to perform certain functions or to achieve specific goals. They usually have a charter or written constitution, bylaws to regulate the conduct of the organization's activities, and officers who are appointed or elected for fixed terms.

Formal organizations include business corporations, departments and agencies of government, the military, churches, schools, and associations of all types. Most formal organizations are not primarily political. But because almost every organization is affected by what government does, they seek to protect and promote their interests through action designed to influence government policy.

When a sports club, a corporation, or a government agency seeks to advance its interests by influencing government policy, it acts as a political interest group, even though the organization exists primarily for other purposes. However, there are other specialized associations which exist primarily to protect and promote the interests of their members. These specialized associations are described frequently as ***pressure groups*** or ***lobbies.**** When people talk about interest groups, it is usually these formal specialized associations that they have in mind.

---

*The word *lobby* may be used as either a noun or verb. As a verb it means to attempt to influence government decisions, especially legislative votes; as a noun it refers to a group organized for this purpose.

According to the *Encyclopedia of Associations* there are some 13,500 separate interest groups in the United States. Some are active only at regional, state, or local levels. But an estimated 4,000 associations are national in scope. With headquarters usually in Washington, D.C., many of these groups also have offices in the state capitals, in addition to local branch chapters.

Recent surveys reveal that about 62 percent of adult Americans belong to at least one organization that may be characterized as an interest group. It is estimated, however, that only 8 percent are members of organizations that are primarily political in concern.

People who join interest groups are not representative of the population as a whole. Such joiners tend to be better educated and more affluent than nonjoiners. Individual voices are amplified through group membership. Moreover, the most active joiners are frequently members of a number of different groups.

Interest groups vary widely in the size of their memberships, ranging from several million to less than a hundred people. The formal membership of an association is an important factor in its influence on government policy. But interest groups almost always claim to speak for a wider population, and all such claims should be investigated carefully. The American Rifle Association has about 1 million dues-paying members, but in its opposition to gun control the association is generally regarded as representing the views of many millions of non-dues-paying gun-owners. The National Association for the Advancement of Colored People (NAACP) has a registered membership of less than half a million, many of whom are white, but it is generally viewed as representing the interests of all black Americans. The Sierra Club has only about 200,000 registered members, but it claims to speak for millions of Americans who are concerned with environmental protection.

Section Check

---

1. Define: interest group, status quo, categorical group, bylaws, faction, pressure group
2. Identify: Black Caucus, National Rifle Association, NAACP, Sierra Club
3. What are the differences between informal groups and formal organizations?
4. What are lobbies?

---

2 A SAMPLING OF MAJOR AMERICAN INTEREST GROUPS

As the role of government has expanded in the twentieth century, interest groups in the United States have increased in number and in the scope of their activities. Most major American interest groups are formed for the economic advancement of business, labor, agriculture, professional, and other specialized groups.

Business Groups

Corporations and businesses are well represented through interest groups. Many large corporations maintain offices and staffs in Washington to keep in regular contact with political leaders. In recent years corporations have also set up their own political action committees (PAC's) to channel financial contributions into political campaigns. But ***trade associations*** serve as the main channels for advancing the interests of American business.

There are some 3,000 trade associations. Most are specialized, such as the National Association of Retail Druggists, the American Tobacco Institute, and the Chocolate Manufacturers Association of the United States. On many issues specialized groups find themselves on opposite sides of the fence. The interests of one are not necessarily those of the other. But there are some associations, such as the National Association of Manufacturers and the Chamber of Commerce of the United States, that represent business interests more generally.

The National Association of Manufacturers (NAM) represents 13,000 member companies, mostly large corporations. After 20 years of declining membership and influence, NAM has rebounded and become very aggressive. It has led business attacks on pro-labor legislation and established a Committee on a Union-Free Environment.

The Chamber of Commerce of the United States is the nation's largest and most influential business organization. It is an ***umbrella association,*** an organization that links many groups together. Its membership includes more than 2,600 local, state, and regional chambers of commerce; about 1,000 trade associations; and nearly 200,000 firms and individuals. The Chamber's Washington headquarters has a staff of about 1,500 persons, with experts on the many issues of concern to business. From its $86 million annual budget the Chamber finances the *Nation's Business,* a monthly magazine; a weekly newspaper, *The Washington Report;* and a

Samuel Gompers (top left) was the founder and first president of the American Federation of Labor (AFL). John L. Lewis (above) organized the Congress of Industrial Organizations in 1935. In 1979, Lane Kirkland (left) was elected president of the AFL-CIO, which was formed in 1955.

cable television network named Biznet for the American Business Network. The Chamber of Commerce provides a wide variety of services to the business community. But according to its president, its "main mission in life is to influence the United States Congress."

Because their members often have conflicting interests, the NAM and the Chamber of Commerce pursue general political goals. They seek "a more favorable business climate" through reduction of taxes and less regulation by government.

More-specialized associations focus on the issues that affect their members' special interests. Often one industry is represented by a number of different interest groups. The oil industry, for example, is represented by a major umbrella association, the American Petroleum Institute (API). Its members include 350 oil and gas companies and associations, plus 7,000 individual members. API members account for over 85 percent of America's total business volume in oil and gas. Among its member groups are the Independent Petroleum Association of America, the American Gas Association, and the American Petroleum Refiners Association.

Labor Groups

Labor unions are among the most active of all interest groups in America. The American Federation of Labor (AFL), was established in 1886 to represent the interests of skilled workers organized in associated craft unions. Other unions, including semiskilled and unskilled workers, were organized on the basis of particular industries. These were brought together in 1935 into the Congress of Industrial Organizations (CIO). In 1955 the AFL and CIO merged into a single labor association of 15 million members.

The AFL-CIO is composed of 106 separate affiliated unions, ranging from plumbers and butchers to government employees. Its national headquarters is in a large marble building near the White House, and offices are maintained in most state capitals. The AFL-CIO has a large research staff and a number of lobbyists engaged in promoting labor interests. Its concerns are primarily economic. These include a wide range of government policy areas of labor-management relations, regulation of wages and working conditions, health, welfare, and social security. In addition to issues directly involving labor, the AFL-CIO takes stands on civil rights, education, and even foreign policy.

The political action arm of the AFL-CIO is its Committee on Political Education (COPE). It undertakes voter registration drives and endorses candidates for public office. Labor support, particularly through financial contributions, can be a critical factor in an election. Although officially bipartisan, the AFL-CIO is closely associated with the Democratic party, and it wields great influence within party circles. But union support for Democratic candidates cannot be taken for granted. Some individual unions, notably the Teamsters, which is outside the AFL-CIO, have in fact been more favorable to the Republican party.

Two important unions not affiliated with the AFL-CIO are the International Brotherhood of Teamsters, with 2 million members, and the United Mine Workers (UMW), with about 220,000 members. Altogether, about one quarter of the American work force belongs to unions.

Farm Groups

American agriculture is represented by a number of interest groups, which are sharply divided in their positions on government policy. The largest group is the American Farm Bureau Federation, with more than 2.8 million members. The dominant group within the Farm Bureau is composed of the owners of large farms of the midwestern Corn Belt. Their influence is reflected in the Bureau's opposition to price support programs.

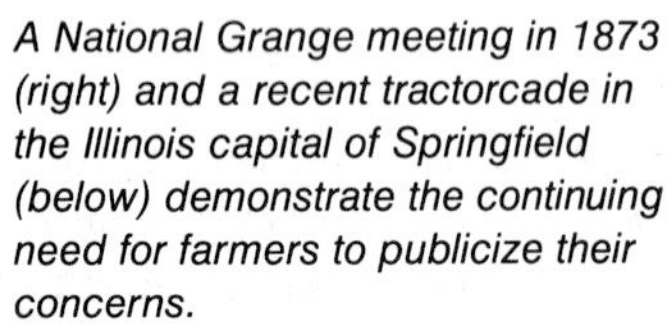

A National Grange meeting in 1873 (right) and a recent tractorcade in the Illinois capital of Springfield (below) demonstrate the continuing need for farmers to publicize their concerns.

The National Education Association (NEA) seeks to further the interests of teachers by making the public aware of educators' concerns and by influencing governmental policy. Among the NEA proposals to improve the quality of education in the United States are rigorous teacher-evaluation programs and well-defined codes of discipline for students.

The National Farmers' Union, with about 250,000 member families, draws its support primarily from small-farm owners, especially wheat growers in the Plains states. The Union sees itself as the champion of the family farm and seeks government protection through price supports for farm products.

The National Grange, founded in 1867, is the oldest American farm organization. Its 600,000 members are concentrated in the Northeast, and the group has strong support among dairy farmers. Although less militant than the Farmers' Union, the Grange shares its commitment to government price support programs.

In addition to broad organizations, interests in particular farm products are represented by various groups. These include the Associated Milk Producers, the National Wool Growers Association, the American Cattlemen's Association, and the National Cotton Council.

Today only about 3 percent of the American labor force is engaged in farming and ranching, and only one farmer in every four is a member of a farm organization. But as a vital part of the American economy, agriculture commands the close attention of those who make government policy.

Professional Groups

The professions are those fields of employment that require specialized knowledge gained through formal education. They include medicine, dentistry, nursing, law, architecture, and teaching. Entry into the professions usually requires an advanced university degree and a license to practice. Each of the professions is represented by a different group or association. These organizations set standards for admission to the profession, provide services to their members, and seek to influence government policy in accord with their interests.

The American Medical Association (AMA) is one of the most prestigious and influential of all interest groups. Although it lost its long battle against national health insurance with the passage of Medicare in 1965, the AMA remains a powerful voice in government health policy.

The most important group representing lawyers is the American Bar Association (ABA). Because of the close links between legal practice and government, the ABA plays a significant role in proposing changes in criminal and civil law and in court procedure. The association also reviews the qualifications of persons nominated for appointment as federal judges and Supreme Court justices. In many states an attorney must be a member of the state bar association in order to practice law.

The largest professional association in the world is the National Education Association (NEA), with a membership of nearly 2 million teachers. Founded in 1857, NEA has only in recent years become politically active. From its headquarters in Washington, NEA lobbyists maintain close ties with Congress and many executive agencies. They seek better schools and higher pay for teachers through increased federal funding for education.

Racial, Ethnic, and Religious Groups

Associations are also formed to represent the interests of particular racial, ethnic, and religious groups. Members of such categorical groups do not all belong to one economic or social class. Their common interests may be as specific as equal rights or as broad as preserving group identity and heritage.

Among black Americans, organizations have been an important force in securing political rights, social justice, and economic advancement. Two prominent groups are the National Association for the Advancement of Colored People (NAACP), founded in 1910, and the National Urban League. The NAACP has 450,000 members and 1,700 chapters. The Urban League has about 50,000 members and 90 local groups. The NAACP has worked through Congress and the courts for the passage and enforcement of civil rights laws. The Urban League, established as a service and counseling agency, later became active in the movement for equal housing and job opportunities.

Hispanics until recently have had little political power or lobbying strength on a national level. This is rapidly changing. Today organizations such as the Mexican American Legal Defense and Education Fund, the League of United Latin American Citizens, and the National Council of La Raza, which represents 58 Hispanic organizations, are addressing a range of issues from national immigration policy and the problems of migrant workers to bilingual education and equal employment opportunity.

Native Americans have also begun to organize. The tribes serve as one base for political action, but new organizations such as the National Tribal Chairmen's Association and the National Indian Youth

PROFILE

The League of Women Voters

In 1920 a young reporter named Anna Steese Richardson traveled to Chicago to report the celebrations that followed passage of the Nineteenth Amendment, which gave women the right to vote. There she attended several meetings called by the feminists who had helped win passage of the amendment—women like Carrie Chapman Catt, Mary Garrett, and Nettie R. Shuler. These women understood that American women, having won the vote, now had to educate themselves in government and politics. They met in a simple classroom for the first session of a class in citizenship. As soon as the first meeting was over, the young reporter telegraphed her editor at *Woman's Home Companion.* Her telegram said *Come to Chicago as soon as possible. These women are making political history.*

In those historic meetings the League of Women Voters was born. Today the organization claims about 140,000 members in 1,300 local chapters in 50 states. More than 3,000 of its members are men. The league's main function continues to be the education of the electorate in political issues. To inform voters, the league publishes *National Voter, Facts and Issues, Current Focus,* and other publications. It initiates and supports research on a variety of controversial issues. In recent years, the League of Women Voters has sponsored television debates between the major presidential candidates.

Although the league remains strictly nonpartisan—it neither endorses nor opposes any candidate or party—it does endorse specific legislation when members reach a consensus. In its lobbying efforts the League of Women Voters has been instrumental in winning passage of a number of landmark bills, including the Social Security Act (1935), the Pure Food, Drug, and Cosmetic Act (1938), ratification of the United Nations Charter (1945), and the Nuclear Nonproliferation Treaty (1969).

BLACK ELECTED OFFICIALS	
Year	Total
1970	1,472
1971	1,860
1972	2,264
1973	2,621
1974	2,991
1975	3,503
1976	3,979
1977	4,311
1978	4,503
1979	4,584
1980	4,890

Source: Statistical Abstract of the United States, 1984

Benjamin Hooks, the executive director of the NAACP, leads the annual Martin Luther King, Jr., Memorial Rally in Washington, D.C., (left). Since its founding, the NAACP has worked for racial equality. One indication of gains by blacks is the steady increase in black elected officials (above) since 1970.

Council have provided more effective voices in speaking for the interests of Native Americans as a whole. But Native Americans, like other categorical groups in American society, do not speak with one voice. Political moderates, for example, have opposed the more militant American Indian Movement (AIM).

Ethnic groups are represented by more than 150 national organizations such as the National Association of Polish-Americans, the American-Italian Congress, and the Japanese American Citizens League. Most ethnic associations are primarily social, but many seek to advance their interests by influencing government policy. Some have been concerned with United States immigration policy. Others have sought to influence American foreign policy toward their ancestral homelands.

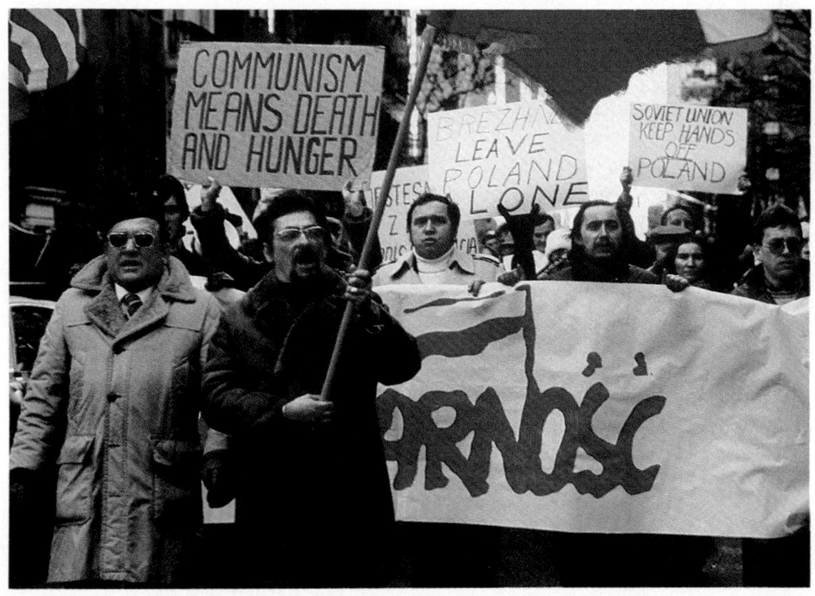

Polish-Americans—here marching to show their support of Solidarity, a labor union in Poland—are but one of hundreds of ethnic groups in the United States. Why might ethnic groups organize?

Religious groups also seek to protect and promote their interests. Broadly based organizations such as the National Council of Churches and the National Conference of Christians and Jews are concerned with such issues as religious freedom and human rights. In addition, the various Protestant denominations each form their own interest groups, as do Catholics and Jews. The National Catholic Education Association and the United States Catholic Conference have been active in lobbying for federal aid to parochial school students. Jewish organizations have taken foreign policy as one of their main political concerns. The American Israel Public Affairs Committee, representing more than 30 separate groups, seeks a favorable American policy toward Israel. Another Jewish concern has been fighting discrimination. Founded to oppose anti-Semitism, the Anti-Defamation League of B'nai B'rith has been a strong advocate for racial equality and social justice.

During the late 1970's a number of Christian fundamentalist political organizations came into prominence. The largest of these evangelical groups is the Moral Majority. With eight full-time lobbyists in Washington, the Moral Majority takes stands on many issues. It supports greater defense spending and prayer in the public schools. It opposes an Equal Rights Amendment. The Moral Majority places great emphasis on local organization and now has chapters in all 50 states. In the 1980 elections, support and campaign contributions from the Moral Majority played an important role in several state and local contests.

Women's Groups

Growing out of the movement for women's suffrage, the League of Women Voters was founded in 1920 to promote informed political participation. Today, with 140,000 members and 1,300 local chapters, the League actively supports passage of an Equal Rights Amendment and works more generally for government reform. Its fundamental purpose remains political education.

More centrally concerned with what are often called "women's issues" are the many organizations that make up the modern feminist movement. The two most prominent are the National Organization of Women (NOW) and the National Women's Political Caucus. NOW, founded in 1966, has about 260,000 members. Its efforts have focused on the issues of

WOMEN IN GOVERNMENT: 1985

	Number	Percent
United States Congress		
Senate	2	2.0
House of Representatives	22	5.1
State Officials		
Governors	2	4.0
Lieutenant Governors	5	12.5
Secretaries of State	17	34.0
State Treasurers	11	22.0
State Legislatures (House and Senate combined)	1,067 (est.)	14.3
County Governing Board Officials	1,427 (est.)	7.8
Mayors of Major Cities	87	12.3
United States Supreme Court Justices	1	11.0
Federal Judges	53	7.7
Members of the Cabinet	2	15.3

Sources: Center for the American Woman and Politics, Rutgers University; U.S.Conference of Mayors.

The number of women at all levels of government has continued to increase in recent years. Several reasons account for this increase. Among them are increased educational opportunities, a significant rise in the number of women in the work force, and a heightened social awareness of women and men as equals.

PROFILE

The Gray Panthers

A group of demonstrators march outside the White House. The signs they carry declare "Save Our Security!" and "Social Security is a right . . . It is not Welfare!" There are angry chants, and fists are raised defiantly. What may seem surprising at first is that most of these demonstrators are in their sixties and seventies, older Americans who have organized as the Gray Panthers to demonstrate and lobby for their rights.

Margaret Kuhn founded the Gray Panthers in 1970 after she had been forced to retire after 25 years of service as a social worker. Angry at what she considered the unfairness of forced retirement, she set out to organize the elderly to fight "ageism"—discrimination based on age. Today there are more than 50,000 Gray Panthers. They have won an impressive series of lobbying victories through techniques of direct action—demonstrations, candlelight vigils, and political rallies. In Pennsylvania, Gray Panthers won a suit to force the Department of Transportation to use barrier-free buses for handicapped commuters. Gray Panthers in California lobbied to pass the "Living Will," which allows people to choose the kinds of medical techniques that will be used to keep them alive in the event of a serious illness. In other states Gray Panthers have protested cuts in the food-stamp program, plans to cut Social Security benefits, and shortcomings in the Medicare program. Gray Panthers lobbying in Washington, D.C., have presented position papers to both the Democratic and Republican national conventions, stressing the needs and demands of the elderly. With more than 47 million Americans over the age of 55—and with elderly Americans, who represent only 29 percent of the voters, casting more than 33 percent of the ballots for President—the voice of the elderly is a powerful one.

political and economic equality for women in all walks of life. The National Women's Political Caucus, with 75,000 members, seeks to increase women's participation in politics. It has worked for the election and appointment of more women to public office.

Senior Citizens' Groups

The social, political, and economic interests of the more than 30 million Americans 65 years of age and older are represented by a number of organizations. The National Council of Senior Citizens, with 4 million members, and the American Association of Retired Persons, with 13 million members, are the largest. Other well-known groups include the conservative National Alliance of Senior Citizens and the activist Gray Panthers.

Citizens' and Public Interest Groups

Many of the citizens' and public interest groups are concerned primarily with various local issues—utility rates, property taxes, new highway construction or zoning, for example. These groups include Fair Share in Massachusetts, San Francisco's Citizens Action League, Community Organized for Public Service (COPS) in San Antonio, and the Arkansas-based Association of Community Organizations for Reform Now (ACORN).

Citizens' lobbies seek goals that they believe will benefit not only their members but everyone in society. But certainly all people are not behind the efforts of these groups. Not everyone agrees on just what "the public interest" is. Everyone wants clean air, for example, but not everyone is prepared to support the strict standards called for by environmental interest groups.

Environmental Groups Some of the most active public interest groups are concerned with conservation and environmental protection. These include the Sierra Club, the National Audubon Society, the National Wildlife Federation, the Wilderness Society, and Friends of the Earth. Some groups focus their efforts on protecting a single species or wilderness area. Others have more general environmental concerns. Environmental groups often work closely together to achieve their common goals, as in the coalition formed in support of the elimination of hazardous-waste sites.

Consumer Protection Everyone is a consumer, and most people at one time or another have purchased a product that proved to be defective or unsafe. In the 1960's, interest groups began to lobby for consumer protection. The Consumer Federation of America is an umbrella association composed of 200 member groups. It has actively sought the establishment of a federal Consumer Protection Agency.

One of the best-known consumer advocates is Ralph Nader. His 1965 book on automobile safety, *Unsafe at Any Speed,* created a sensation and launched his career. Nader's activities rapidly expanded. Today he heads a conglomerate of some 15 different public interest groups, working on a wide range of issues from tax reform to nuclear power. But product safety remains his main concern, and "Nader's Raiders" regularly confront the nation's biggest corporations as well as the federal government.

Common Cause The best known of the citizens' lobbies is Common Cause, founded in 1970 by John Gardner, who served as Secretary of Health, Education, and Welfare in Johnson's administration. Common Cause depends heavily on direct mail fundraising, and its membership fluctuates at about

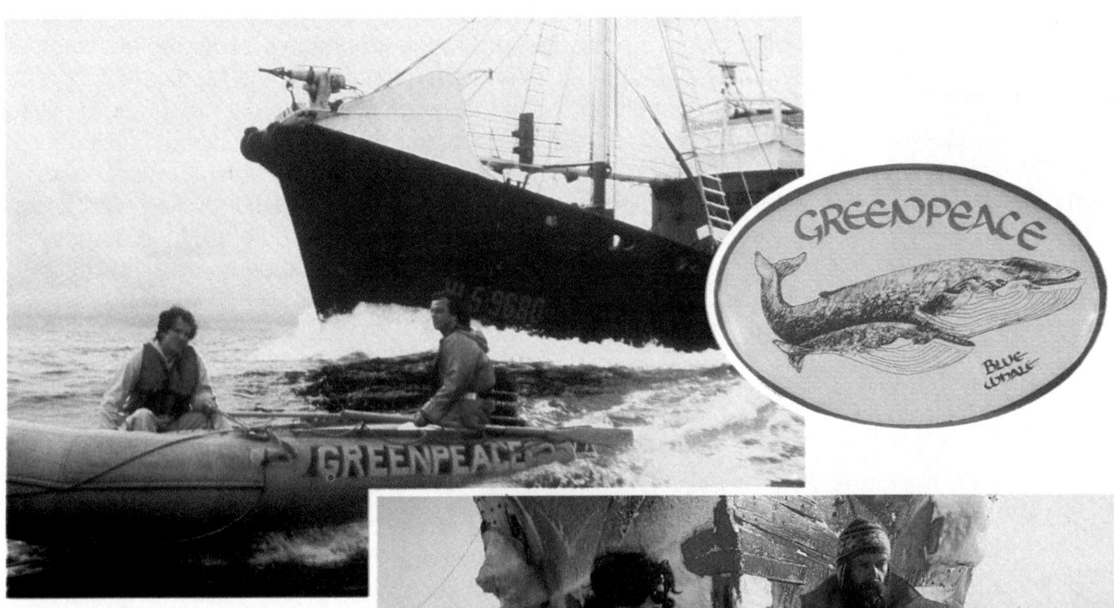

Greenpeace is an environmental group that actively works to save endangered species, such as whales and seals. To inform and educate the public, Greenpeace publishes a quarterly newsletter and maintains libraries in its regional offices.

300,000. Common Cause states as its major goals: "to change political structures so they will be more responsive to social needs and to produce a major reordering of national priorities." Its lobbying efforts have centered on governmental reform—reform of the seniority system in Congress, open meetings and hearings in the legislative and executive branches of government, ease in voter registration, public financing of political campaigns, and disclosure of lobby expenditures.

Ideological Groups

Some interest groups represent particular ideological orientations. The liberal Americans for Democratic Action and the conservative Americans for Constitutional Action each rate members of Congress on how they vote on key issues. Each group uses a scale from 0 to 100 and then scores senators and representatives on how often they voted "liberal" or "conservative."

Public Sector Groups

Groups within the ***public sector***—that is, within government itself—also try to influence what government does. Much of this activity takes place informally, as public officials in competition with each other seek to attain their goals. But bureaucratic agencies and different levels of government also act as interest groups.

The departments of the executive branch do not simply carry out government policy as passed by Congress. They attempt to influence and shape that policy to their own interests. Each department of government sends a ***liaison,*** a kind of "go-between," to represent its interests to Congress. Each department typically seeks a wider scope of authority, a larger staff, and an expanded budget.

Professionals within each government agency—often in cooperation with various private interest groups—also seek to promote particular policies and programs. This is especially true in fields such as health, education, welfare, housing, highways, and defense. Pushing for different programs places the various units of government in competition with each other. Within the Department of Defense, for example, the Army, Navy, and Air Force vie with one another for favored status. The Department of Defense as a whole lobbies for the interests it believes important, such as a new bomber or missile system, competing with other departments for a larger share of the federal budget.

Within the American federal system different levels of government lobby individually for new federal programs. But units of government and public officials also join together to form interest groups. Public officials with specialized functions are organized into such groups as the National Association of State Budget Officers. Other groups represent the basic units of state, county, and city government. Five of the most important associations are the Council of State Governments, the National Governors' Association, the National Association of Counties, the National League of Cities, and the United States Conference of Mayors.

Foreign Interest Groups

Because action by the United States often affects nations throughout the world, foreign governments and private interests abroad seek to influence American policy. Foreign nations have diplomatic representatives at their embassies in Washington, D.C. In addition, some countries set up consulates in major American cities. Foreign nations often send special delegations to this country. They may seek anything from more favorable trade relations to military aid. Recently the British and French governments were active in seeking to open American airports to the Concorde supersonic aircraft.

Sometimes foreign interests hire individuals or firms to represent them in the United States. All foreign agents must register with the government, and normally their activities are legitimate. In 1977, however, the Tongsun Park scandal focused national attention on foreign lobbying. Park, a South Korean business leader, had given cash and favors to some members of Congress in exchange for legislative support for Korean business interests.

Section Check

1. Define: trade association, umbrella association, public sector, liaison
2. Identify: NAM, ABA, Chamber of Commerce, COPE, Grange, NEA, NAACP, Moral Majority, NOW, Gray Panthers
3. Why have interest groups increased in number and in the scope of their activities in the twentieth century?
4. For what reason are most major interest groups formed?
5. What are public sector groups?

3 INTEREST GROUPS AT WORK

Interest groups come in every size and represent almost every conceivable concern. But the wide variety of interest groups that exists does not mean that every person is equally well represented. One group may vary from another in its effectiveness. Whether a group is successful in its efforts to protect and promote its interests depends upon a number of factors.

Goals

The goals an interest group pursues are an important factor in its effectiveness. When a group has a single, specific goal—such as saving the redwoods or promoting a particular industry—its chances for success are usually strengthened. By contrast, the more goals an interest group tries to achieve, the weaker it becomes in the pursuit of any one of its goals.

A group is also more likely to be successful when its goals are widely accepted in the society as a whole. An interest group supporting the status quo or traditional values usually meets with more favorable response than one advocating major changes. An interest group seeking far-reaching change must influence public opinion at the same time it tries to influence public policy.

Tactics: Where and How Interest Groups Operate

The tactics a group uses depend upon its resources and goals. Tactics also depend upon where the group concentrates its activities. Interest groups are active in five main areas: (1) the legislative branch, (2) the executive branch, (3) public opinion, (4) election campaigns, and (5) the courts.

The Legislative Branch Though the term ***lobbying*** can refer to any effort by individuals or groups to influence public policy, it is associated most closely with efforts by interest groups to influence legislative action. Through contact with state legislators or members of Congress and their staffs, lobbyists seek to shape public policy to the advantage of the groups they represent. They work to introduce, modify, pass, or kill legislation.

More than a thousand lobbyists are registered with the House of Representatives and the Senate. Most professional lobbyists are lawyers or public relations specialists. Many with long experience on Capitol Hill have close personal relationships with representatives and senators. Some have served as Congressional staff members. Others are themselves former members of Congress.

The lobbyists' main task is to provide information to those who make government policy. They work closely with the representatives and senators

INSIGHT

How to Be a Lobbyist

Not all lobbyists are full-time professionals. Any concerned citizen who writes to a legislator about some interest is lobbying. Similarly, any citizen who visits a lawmaker to discuss an issue or proposed legislation is lobbying. To be effective, however, all lobbyists should keep certain guidelines in mind. Lester Milbrath, in his book *The Washington Lobbyists,** offers the following guide for successful lobbying:

- Be pleasant and non-offensive.
- Convince officials that it is important for them to listen.
- Be well prepared and well informed.
- Be personally convinced.
- Be succinct, well organized, and direct.
- Use the "soft sell approach."
- Leave a short written summary of the case.

*Lester Milbrath, *The Washington Lobbyists,* Chicago: Rand-McNally, 1963, pp. 220–26.

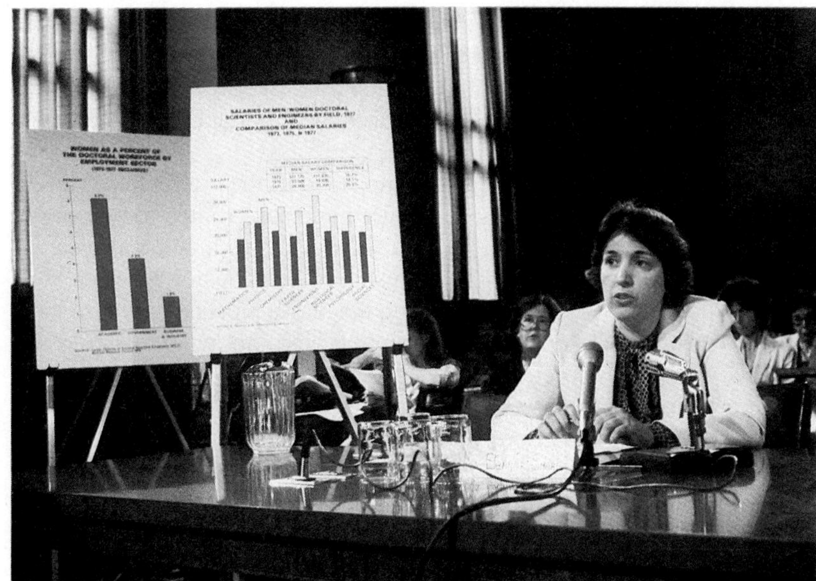

Eleanor Smeal, former president of the National Organization of Women (NOW), lobbies before a Senate hearing on women's rights. Many interest groups employ lobbyists to place their concerns before state and federal lawmakers. How does a lobbyist seek to shape public policy? What is a lobbyist's main task?

who already support their groups' goals. These members of Congress, in turn, seek to persuade their colleagues. Members of Congress often rely heavily on lobbyists with whom they have close ties. Lobbyists supply needed information, and sometimes assist in the drafting of legislation. They compile lists of supporters and opponents of a bill, and help their Congressional allies steer it to victory or defeat by applying pressure to "undecideds."

Much of the lobbyists' attention is focused on specific committees and subcommittees of Congress. It is in committee that some of the most important decisions affecting a group's interests are made. Lobbyists usually try to develop close relationships with members of the key committees—and particularly with the chairpersons. In addition, lobbyists frequently appear as witnesses at committee hearings because the hearings are an opportunity for an interest group to get its views officially "on the record."

The Executive Branch Many interest groups seek direct access to the White House. During the course of a week the President may confer with representatives of business, labor, and agricultural organizations. The President may meet with delegations of women, blacks, and a dozen other groups. Each group seeks to influence Presidential policy.

The impact of government policy is often determined by how it is implemented. Frequently, Congress enacts a law but leaves important details to be worked out by the bureaucracy. Interest groups thus seek to develop close ties with the departments and agencies directly concerned with their activities. Farm interests have links with the Department of Agriculture, business with the Department of Commerce, and unions with the Department of Labor. Powerful interest groups exert influence—often amounting to a veto power—over Presidential appointments to head these departments.

Especially close ties exist between the independent regulatory agencies and the interests which they are supposed to regulate. The Federal Aviation Administration has close ties with the airlines, the Federal Communications Commission with radio and television, and the Interstate Commerce Commission with railroad and trucking interests. So close are the ties that many concerned citizens question who is regulating whom.

Public Opinion Interest groups try to influence government through public opinion, creating a climate of popular support for their goals. In any number of ways, interest groups work to bring issues before the people, arouse their concern, and win their support. Often with the aid of public relations firms, interest groups will conduct publicity campaigns for their causes. Through direct mail, news releases, and advertisements—in the mass media, on billboards, and on bumper stickers—the groups seek to influence public opinion. Sometimes groups will engage in demonstrations to capture attention.

By building up support at the ***grass roots,*** that is, among the people, interest groups hope to bring pressure upon elected officials. They seek to demonstrate public support for their goals, often using the technique of instigating letter-writing campaigns in which group members and the general public are urged to write representatives and senators about an issue or an upcoming vote in Congress. Such campaigns can be effective, but an avalanche of identically worded letters is not likely to be taken very seriously. Elected officials want to know what the people back home are thinking, but they are not easily taken in by manufactured mail.

Election Campaigns Most interest groups actively support candidates for public office who are favorable to their goals. For incumbents, or office-holders, support by an interest group is usually a question of rewarding those candidates who have worked in their interests and opposing those who have not. Single-issue groups have flexed their muscles in nationwide efforts to defeat incumbents who "voted wrong" on their pet issues. For other candidates, support by interest groups depends upon campaign promises. Interest groups seek commitments from candidates, and the candidates themselves make appeals to important groups.

Interest group activities can be crucial to the outcome of an election. The endorsement of a candidate can carry great weight, but campaign contributions are also important. Groups give money to candidates in hopes of electing public officials who are sympathetic to their interests. Political action committees formed by corporations, trade associations, labor unions, and other organizations now raise more money than either the Republican or Democratic party. It is to such groups—not political parties—that candidates turn for financial support. In any election year interest groups contribute millions of dollars to campaigns at every level of government. State and federal law regulates campaign finance, but limits have had little practical effect.

Interest groups also seek to influence political parties. Major groups take part in drafting the campaign platforms of the Democratic and Republican parties. Some groups focus on one party, but many work through both. In turn, each party appeals to a wide variety of groups with promises of something for just about everybody. There are platform planks for business, labor, agriculture, minorities, the aged, and youth. Each party tries to pull together a coalition of groups in order to win the election.

The Courts In the American system of checks and balances, powers are shared by the three branches of government. In the interpretation of laws or of the Constitution, the courts have a great impact on government policy. ***Judicial activism*** in recent years has brought the courts more deeply into a policy-making role. The courts have therefore become an increasingly important focus of interest group activity.

Interest groups turn to the courts for a variety of purposes. Environmental groups, for example, have used court injunctions to block construction of dams and housing projects. Action by a coalition of groups held up the Alaska pipeline until its impact on the environment and on wildlife could be determined.

Groups that are concerned with rights they believe to be protected by the Constitution seek protection through the courts. The Founders of the Republic sought to combine majority rule with minority rights. Often, however, the nature of these rights is in dispute and subject to differing interpretations. Minorities have looked to the courts, as guardians of the Constitution, to defend their rights. An interest group may thus seek to bring a ***test case,*** a legal action to establish some claimed right or to challenge the constitutionality of a law. The American Civil Liberties Union (ACLU), for example, focuses its main activities on the preservation of First Amendment rights.

Resources

Effectiveness depends upon the resources available to group interests—their money, size, and political skill. Groups will have a mix of resources, varying according to their membership and goals.

Money Influencing government policy is expensive. Money is a vital resource for all interest groups. Well-financed groups can bring their interests before the general public through the purchase of advertisements in newspapers and magazines or on radio and television. They can reach each American home through direct mail campaigns. Wealthy interest groups can maintain offices in Washington, D.C., and state capitals. They can hire a professional staff of researchers, public relations specialists, and lobbyists. They can entertain legislators and bureaucrats, and provide them with reports to back up their projects and positions.

For every office at every level of government, groups make campaign contributions to candidates who favor their interests. By supporting candidates who share their views, interest groups seek to assure access to political decision-makers. Money, of course, can also be pumped into a campaign by interest

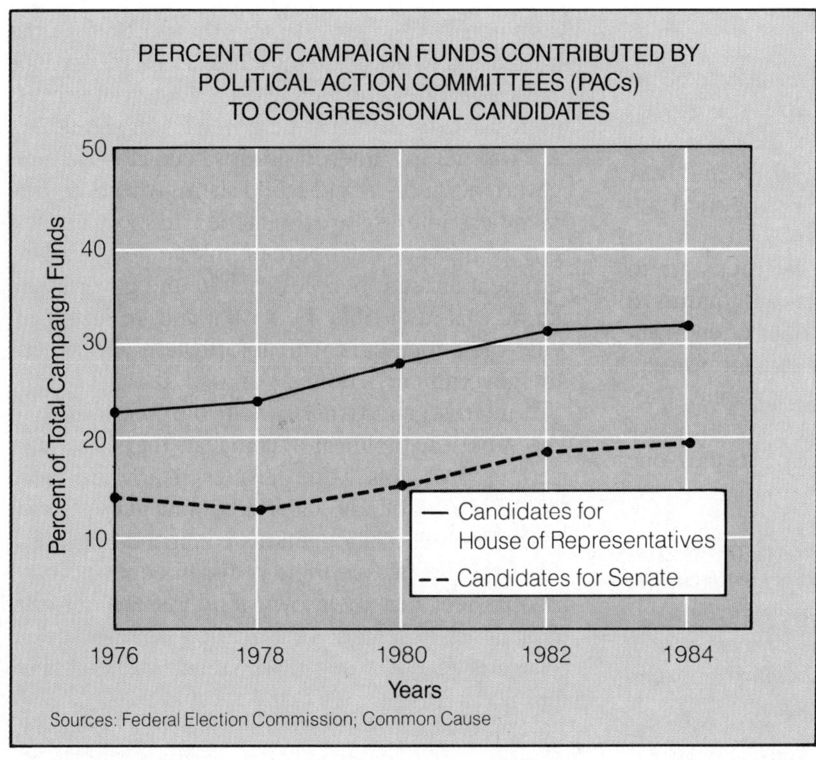

The contributions of interest groups to political campaigns continue to rise. What two restrictions have been placed on campaign contributions?

groups in an effort to defeat unsympathetic candidates. In recent years a number of economic and ideological interest groups have targeted certain elected officials for defeat.

Campaign finance laws now place certain limits on contributions and require disclosure of the amounts spent by individuals and groups. But unaffiliated groups can spend unlimited amounts of money so long as their activities are not authorized by a candidate's official organization.

Groups raise money in many ways. Some are largely financed by membership dues. Many others depend on contributions. Corporations may pay for their own lobbying activities as tax-deductible business expenses. Some groups are obviously richer than others and seem to enjoy almost unlimited funds. Others just scrape by. But the availability of money as a resource is not limited to groups with wealthy members. Many well-financed interest groups are supported by low membership dues and small contributions from many individuals.

Groups can sometimes make up for lack of money through effective use of other resources. Instead of a full-time, paid staff, they can rely on volunteers. Instead of an impressive building, they can have a storefront office. Instead of advertisements and mailings, they can use press releases and telephone calls.

Size An important resource is size. Some associations have only a handful of members. Others have a membership in the millions. Large size can be important in financial terms, but large groups are difficult to organize and maintain. Small groups are often more effective. In larger organizations a core of leaders and activists usually dominates.

Interest groups speak for more than just their members. The larger the number of people for whom they speak, the greater the political weight the interest groups are likely to carry. From the politicians' perspectives, what is important is the capacity of the groups to offer—or withhold—political support in an election. Size means votes. Referring to the AFL-CIO, a Congressional insider said:

*Their sheer size is one of the important reasons for their strength. Labor has a lot of members—a lot of votes—in virtually every Congressional district in the country. Nobody up here can ignore that.**

While size is impressive, the status of a group's members is important. There are relatively few doctors, but the prestige they enjoy expands the political influence of the AMA.

---

*Norman J. Ornstein and Shirley Elder, *Interest Groups, Lobbying and Policymaking,* Washington, D.C.: Congressional Quarterly Press, 1978, p. 73.

Political Skill

Whether money or size will be used effectively as resources depends upon political skill. The groups must be able to determine which of their goals are most important. They must decide where and how best to use their money and effort. Here good leadership is crucial to any organization.

Skill depends on knowledge. If groups are to be effective, they must have the facts and figures to support their positions. Interest groups often maintain research staffs to prepare information for legislators, bureaucrats, and the general public. They depend heavily on their reputations as sources of information. In viewing interest group activities, one member of Congress said:

*It doesn't take very long to figure out which lobbyists are straightforward, and which ones are trying to snow you. The good ones will give you the weak points as well as the strong points of their case. If anyone ever gives me false or misleading information, that's it—I'll never see him again.**

Political "know-how" is also necessary. Group leaders must know the ins and outs of the political process. They must know how to advance their groups' interests.

One crucial skill is mobilization, the ability to call the groups' members and governmental allies into action. Well-timed letter-writing campaigns or subcommittee appearances can spell the difference between success and failure.

Another important lobbying skill is personal knowledge about legislators and their staffs—including their opinions, tastes, and political strengths and weaknesses.

One of the greatest political resources groups can have is their "track records." Their previous successes—in providing useful information, steering their programs through the legislative process, and getting their supporters reelected—add to group prestige and authority. When in doubt, government officials will always favor the groups that can "deliver."

Special Interests and the Public Interest

Interest groups bring issues before the public and expose the strengths and weaknesses of various arguments. They provide information both to the public and to government officials. Interest groups are the channels through which citizens can express their views about what the government should do. As "watchdogs," interest groups keep close tabs on government activity and sound alarms whenever their members' interests are threatened. In short, interest groups provide an important linkage between government and the people. They let the government know what their members want and, in turn, provide their members with information about what the government is doing.

Interest groups make a valuable contribution to the American political system, but they also raise serious problems. Some groups clearly are more powerful than others. Major economic interests such as business and labor unions command enormous resources to pursue their goals. In contrast, many people feel that their own interests are not adequately represented. Competition among special interests does not necessarily result in the general public interest.

Regulating Interest Groups

Special interest groups enjoy a great political advantage over public interest groups and private citizens because of their narrow areas of concern, close relations with government officials, and tremendous resources. Occasionally, lobbyists increase their advantage by influencing officials with bribes or improper "favors." Public concern over lobbying abuses has led to calls for regulation and reform. Today the federal government and most states regulate interest groups through requirements for registration and financial disclosure.

The Federal Regulation of Lobbying Act of 1946 requires paid lobbyists to register with the clerk of the House and the secretary of the Senate. But the act contains several giant loopholes that reduce its effectiveness. Because it applies only to groups whose "principal purpose" is to influence legislation, many of the largest interest groups are not covered. The act does not touch lobbying activities in the executive branch, for example. And a 1954 Supreme Court ruling exempts all "grass-roots" lobbying aimed at bringing indirect pressure on Congress.

Many bills have been proposed to plug these loopholes. Most bills emphasize greater ***public disclosure***—that is, requiring interest groups to reveal where they get and spend their money, who is working for them, and what contacts they have with government officials. Bringing the groups'

*Norman J. Ornstein and Shirley Elder, *Interest Groups, Lobbying and Policymaking,* Washington, D.C.: Congressional Quarterly Press, 1978, p. 77.

A cartoonist expresses the view that the tobacco lobby exerts too much influence in the government. What two steps have been taken to regulate lobbying abuses?

activities out in the open would better enable the public—and Congress—to judge their claims. In contrast, any attempt to control interest groups' activities might have a "chilling effect" on free expression. The Constitution guarantees the right of citizens to petition the government. Lobbying is a legitimate means of influencing public policy and an important way by which people can communicate their views to the government.

One area where interest groups are now regulated is in financial contributions to election campaigns. Certain organizations are prohibited from making contributions to Presidential elections, and others are limited in the amount they can contribute. Congress has been hesitant, however, to regulate contributions to Congressional campaigns.

A number of laws are directed at illegal activity by interest groups. It is a crime for any person to offer members of Congress "anything of value" for the purpose of buying their votes or influencing their actions. It is similarly a crime for members of Congress to accept such offers. The acceptance of a bribe by any public official is not only against the law, it is also a violation of public trust. Corruption and dishonesty among only a few public officials can bring government as a whole into disrespect.

Section Check

1. Define: lobbying, grass roots, test case, judicial activism, public disclosure
2. Identify: Capitol Hill, Federal Registration Lobbying Act of 1946
3. In what five tactical areas are interest groups active?

SUMMARY

An interest group is a collection of people that, on the basis of common views and goals, seeks to influence public policy. The group attempts to protect and promote its interests. It tries to prevent government action that may harm its members, and supports government action that might benefit its members.

Interest groups vary in size, character, and goals. The largest and most influential interest groups—including business, labor, farm, and professional groups—serve their members' economic interests. Other groups are formed according to racial, ethnic, religious, and ideological interests. Some groups seek to advance what they believe to be "public interest" goals for the benefit of society as a whole. Regardless of its primary purpose, any group becomes a political interest group when it seeks to influence the government.

How an interest group functions depends on its goals and resources. Major group resources include money, size, and political skill. A group's tactics depend on where it concentrates its activities. Various groups seek to influence the legislative or executive branches of goverment, directly through lobbying or indirectly through public opinion. Some groups pursue their goals primarily through the courts.

The effectiveness of a group depends on the resources available: money, size, and political skills. One important political skill is mobilization, the ability to call members and allies into action.

Interest groups provide a communications link between government and private citizens. The competition of interest groups in the "political marketplace" helps to form a government policy based on compromise. Many people feel, however, that special interest groups hold unfair political advantages over public interest groups and private citizens. Competition among special interests does not necessarily advance the interests of the general public.

Chapter 10 Review

Using Vocabulary

Answer the questions by using the meaning of each underlined term.

1. Why is an interest group sometimes intent on preserving the status quo?
2. When may a faction within a pressure group lobby for a change within the bylaws of the umbrella association?
3. How does public disclosure regulate the activities of many lobbyists?
4. Why is it important for an organization to build support at the grass roots?
5. Why might a trade association bring a test case before the public sector?

Understanding American Government

1. Which three factors determine whether a categorical group takes on political significance?
2. Explain how each person is at the same time a member of many groups. How may multiple membership require compromise?
3. Are groups such as the Black Caucus, the Rural Caucus, the Congressional Prayer Breakfast, and the Chowder and Marching Club informal groups or formal organizations? Why?
4. Explain the statement, "Those who join interest groups are not representative of the population as a whole."
5. What are Political Action Committees? What are trade associations? Explain how corporations and businesses are represented by these groups.
6. Explain how lobbyists work to influence public policy.
7. Explain how interest groups try to influence government through public opinion.

Extending Your Skills: Comparing Interest Groups

Reread the Profiles on pages 256 and 259. Then identify whether each phrase describes a characteristic of the League of Women Voters or the Gray Panthers or both.

1. Founded by women
2. Organized in 1920
3. Organized to fight ageism
4. Uses lobbying to show support for legislation that it favors
5. Uses direct-action techniques
6. Sponsors Presidential debates
7. Does not endorse a particular political party

Government and You

1. What do you think are the advantages of combining a number of smaller labor unions into a larger organization like the AFL-CIO? What are the disadvantages?
2. The American Farm Bureau Federation opposes price support programs. The National Farmers' Union encourages price supports. Why do these two farm groups take opposing positions? If you were a member of Congress, how would you decide which group to support?
3. Lobbyists have great influence on public policy. What are some pros and cons of lobbies?
4. The effectiveness of an interest group may depend on money, size of membership, and political skill. Which of these resources do you think is the most important? Why?

Activities

1. Write to one of the major American interest groups for literature, using it to write a report on the group's goals.
2. Stage a class debate on the following topic: "*Resolved:* Special interest groups should be more strictly regulated."
3. Invite a representative of a local interest group to class. Ask this person to describe the group's organization, goals, and tactics.
4. Make a wall chart of several citizens' and public interest groups that operate in your area. Include information about the purposes of the groups and how to contact them.
5. Imagine you are a lobbyist trying to influence members of Congress on an issue that you think is important. Your local newspaper may provide a source of such issues. Write down your view on the issue and list the reasons why a legislator should agree with your viewpoint.

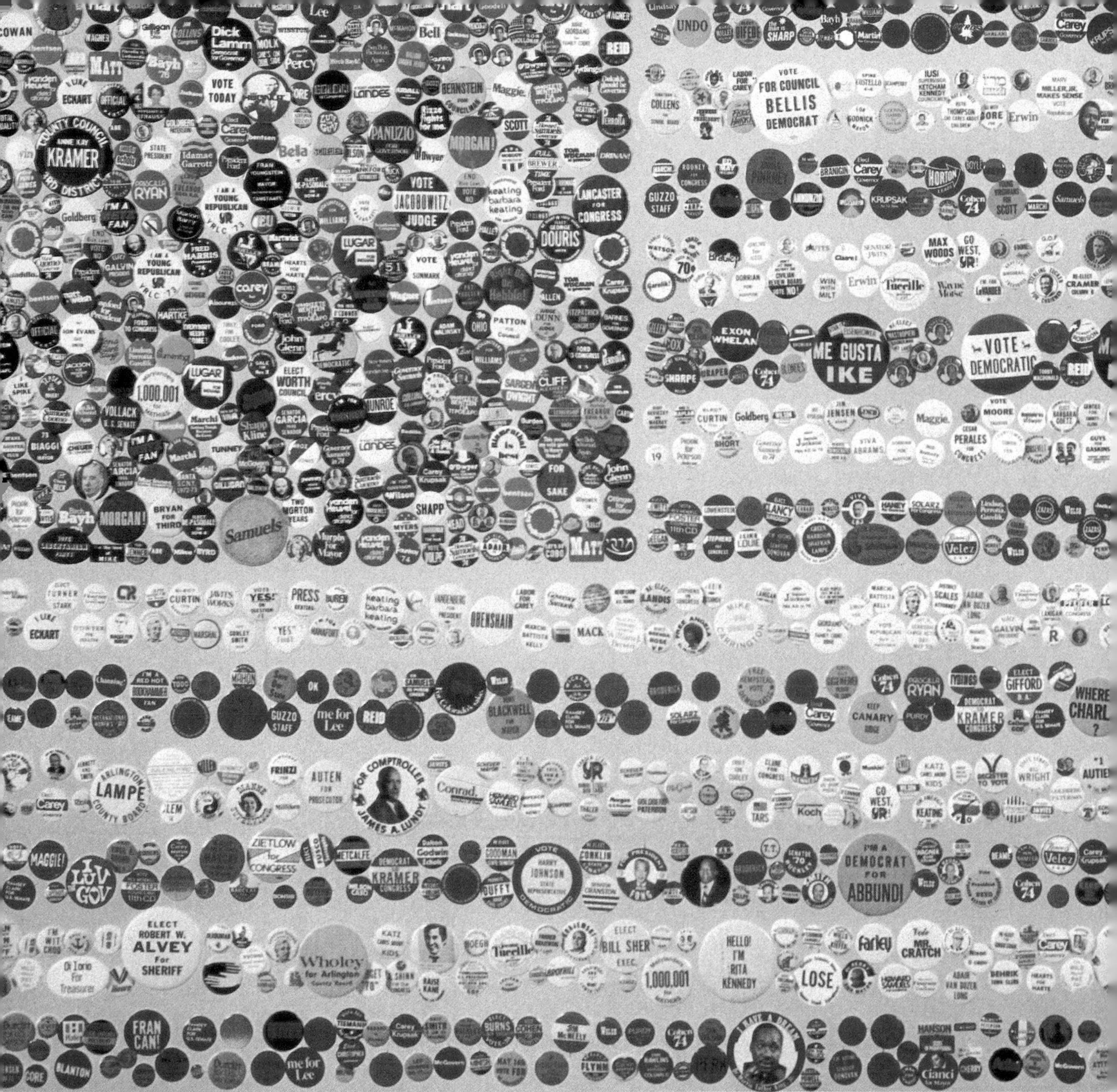

UNIT 5

POLITICAL PARTIES, ELECTORAL PROCESSES, AND VOTING

Chapter 11

Political Parties

The political parties created democracy and modern democracy is unthinkable save in terms of parties. . . . The parties are not therefore merely appendages of modern government; they are in the center of it and play a determinative and creative role in it.

E. E. SCHATTSCHNEIDER

CHAPTER OVERVIEW

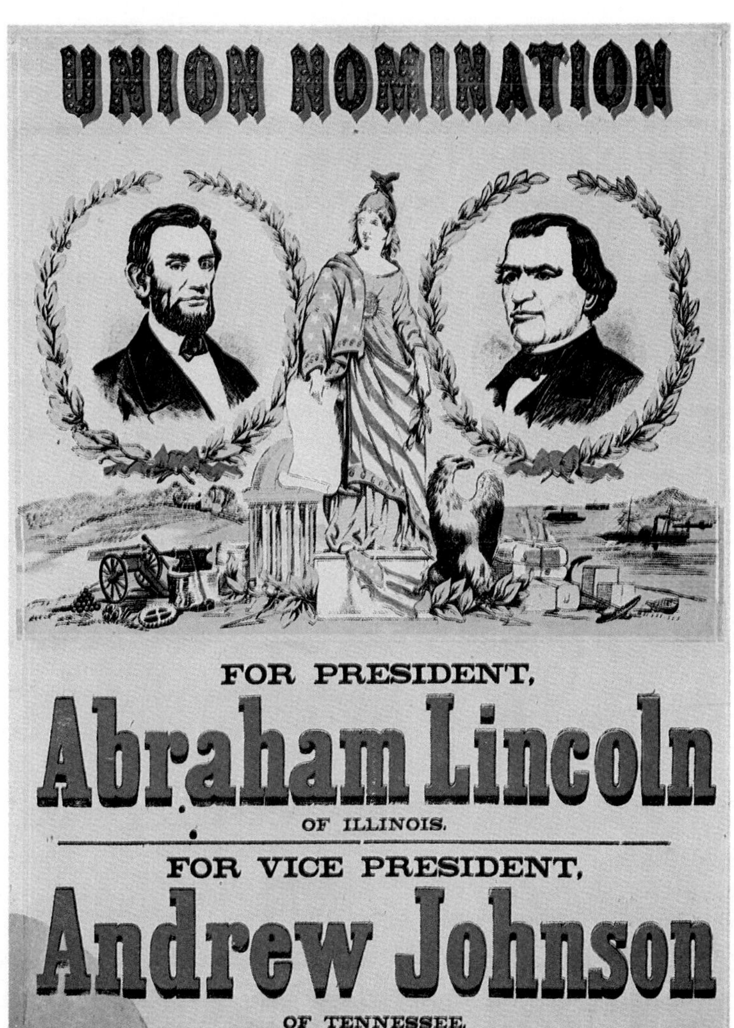

UNION NOMINATION
FOR PRESIDENT,
Abraham Lincoln
OF ILLINOIS.
FOR VICE PRESIDENT,
Andrew Johnson
OF TENNESSEE.

This poster was used in the Presidential election campaign of 1864. At that time issues were more important to the voters than party labels. The issue of preserving the Union became the rallying point for supporters of Abraham Lincoln and his running mate.

1 THE DEVELOPMENT OF AMERICAN POLITICAL PARTIES

Nowhere in the Constitution is there any mention of political parties. No Article sets forth the parties' functions in the framework of government. Yet political parties are central to the American political system. They play a vital role in managing political conflict and in organizing the process of government.

The Nature of Political Parties

Interest groups seek to influence government. Political parties, however, seek to organize and control government. A ***political party*** is an organization of persons who join together in order to win elections, control government, and determine public policy.

Political parties first formed in the United States nearly 200 years ago. Their functions have changed over time, their relative importance has varied, and parties have not always carried them out very well. Nevertheless, it is possible to identify six basic functions of political parties.

Provide a Machinery of Choice Political parties operate "the machinery of choice"—nominations and elections. Choice is essential for democracy. Competitive elections are the means through which the people exercise their sovereign power. Political parties nominate candidates for public office and offer alternative programs. They thus provide the candidates among whom the electorate chooses.

Simplify the Ballot Political parties simplify the voter's choice among rival candidates and programs. Most people today identify with either the

Republican or Democratic party, and the party label on the ballot helps in deciding between candidates for each office. For minor offices the only thing voters may know about the candidates is party affiliation—and this determines which way people vote.

Stimulate Interest Political parties stimulate interest in politics. Election campaigns are exciting. Party competition arouses widespread interest and draws millions of people into active participation. Banners, buttons, and billboards proclaim the names of the candidates. Newspaper advertisements and television and radio spots bring their messages into every home. As in a World Series or a Superbowl game, the fans root for their favorite team. But in politics, by the power of their votes, the fans decide who wins.

Provide a Rallying Point Political parties unite people with different interests and social characteristics. In order to win elections, parties must appeal to a wide variety of groups. Each party seeks a broad base of support among people of different regions, religions, races, occupations, ages, and social classes. Each party tries to form a winning coalition by bringing together different interests. The party's ***platform***, its statement of policy on the issues, represents a compromise reached in a process of bargaining. It offers "something for everybody." Thus, political parties balance the demands of the many interest groups in American society.

Organize the Machinery of Government If each candidate for public office—from the Presidency to justice of the peace—ran without party ties as an Independent, government would be badly divided. Clear and effective policy would be difficult to achieve. Political parties provide a framework within which elected officials can work for common goals. Parties can bridge the separation of powers between the executive and legislative branches of government. They link different levels of government—national, state, and local—within the federal system.

Fix Responsibility Political parties help to make government more accountable to the people. Parties are an important link between the people and their government. The party in power stands on its record in office, and its candidates must answer to the people for what the government does or does not do. Party labels help voters to fix responsibility. If the people approve of what the government is doing, they can express their support by voting to keep the party in office. If they oppose government policy, they can vote the party out of office and give the opposition party a chance to do better.

Federalists and Democratic-Republicans

Political factions developed early in George Washington's administration. Washington tried to stay above factional conflict, but two members of his Cabinet, Alexander Hamilton and Thomas Jefferson, squared off over Hamilton's economic program. Hamilton, then Washington's Secretary of the Treasury, became the leader of a group known as the Federalists, the first American political party. The Federalists favored a strong central government, the interests of banking and commerce, and a pro-British foreign policy. Jefferson, then Washington's Secretary of State, organized the Democratic-Republicans, to which today's Democratic party traces its origin. The Democratic-Republicans favored a weaker central government and the interests of farmers and frontier settlers. In foreign policy they supported Revolutionary France.

In the Presidential election of 1796 John Adams, the Federalist candidate, narrowly defeated Jefferson. But after four years of intense partisan conflict the Democratic-Republicans swept the elections of 1800. Jefferson was elected President, and his party won control of both the Senate and House of Representatives. This election marked the first transfer of power from one party to another.

Federalist support rapidly dwindled, and the party disappeared after 1816. There followed under President James Monroe "the Era of Good Feelings." When Monroe, a Democratic-Republican, ran for reelection in 1820, no one even ran against him. But factions then formed within his party around John Quincy Adams and Andrew Jackson. Adams's election in 1824 had to be settled in the House of Representatives. Thereafter the Democratic-Republican factions emerged as separate parties. Adams led the National Republicans. Jackson, in opposition, led the Democrats.

Whigs and Democrats

Between the elections of 1828 and 1840 political parties took modern form. Two national parties emerged as close competitors, with the Presidency as the focus of political rivalry. In 1832 the parties began to nominate their candidates at national conventions. Property qualifications for voting had almost disappeared by then, and the number of males eligible to vote had greatly increased. To get out the vote among the expanded electorate, political parties staged campaigns that were a lively combination of carnival and organization.

The Jacksonian Democrats represented the common people and called for greater political equality. The United States was then an overwhelmingly agricultural nation. The Democrats appealed to rural interests, winning support both from small western farmers and southern plantation owners. The National Republicans became the Whigs, taking their new name from a British party of the period with whom they shared interests. Representing banking, manufacturing, and commerce, the Whigs were strongest in the urban Northeast. There were class and regional differences between Democrats and Whigs, but these differences must not be exaggerated. Both parties—like Democrats and Republicans today—had a broad basis of support that cut across different regions and social classes.

By the late 1840's the slavery question had begun to divide the nation. On the complicated issue of extending slavery into the new territories, both Whigs and Democrats tried to straddle the fence. In 1848 northern Democrats opposed to the extension of slavery formed a third party, the Free-Soil party. The Free-Soilers were pledged to a "national platform of freedom in opposition to the sectional platform of slavery." Although the Free-Soilers failed to carry a single state, they succeeded in splitting the Democrats and helped elect Zachary Taylor, the Whig candidate to the Presidency. The Democrats returned to power in 1852, but the issue of slavery continued to drive a deepening wedge into both the Democratic and Whig parties.

Republicans and Democrats

In 1854 a group of Free-Soilers, Whigs, and antislavery Democrats met at Ripon, Wisconsin, to urge the creation of a new party to oppose extension of slavery into the new territories. The name Republican party was adopted a few months later at a convention in Jackson, Michigan. The Democrats won again in 1856, but the newly formed Republicans ran a strong second. The Whigs trailed far behind, and their collapse as a party came soon afterward.

Thomas Nast, a political cartoonist who is profiled on page 274, illustrated the power of Tammany Hall—New York City's powerful Democratic machine. The cartoon was published in 1871 on the eve of city and state elections in New York. What point of view did Nast express with this cartoon?

PROFILE

Thomas Nast, Political Cartoonist

Thomas Nast was the first political cartoonist of America, and one of the greatest of all time. In his cartoons he created or popularized many now famous symbols, including the Republican elephant and the Democratic donkey, the top-hatted figure of Uncle Sam, and the jolly figure known as Santa Claus.

Born in 1840, Nast began his career during the Civil War as an artist for *Harper's Weekly*. He sided with the North, and his earliest cartoons served as propaganda for the Union cause. In one example he portrays a kindly Union soldier sharing his military ration with a poor southern family. Another cartoon from the period that is titled *Christmas Eve, 1862,* shows a young wife with her sleeping children praying at the window while her husband, far away on the battlefield, gazes at a picture of his family. So influential was Nast in raising the morale of the North that General Grant claimed Nast had done as much as any man to preserve the Union and end the war. President Lincoln called Nast his "best recruiting sergeant."

Nast's cartoons commented on and influenced every Presidential campaign from 1864 to 1884. Only one of the candidates he supported failed to win the Presidency, and most observers agreed that Nast's support won Grover Cleveland the extremely close Presidential election of 1884. Nast's cartoons touched on issues of the economy, national defense, and corruption in government. But his most rousing subject was the civil rights of minorities. Nast believed the Civil War had been fought both to save the Union and to guarantee equality to blacks. Civil rights, he insisted, were the rights of all minorities, including Native Americans and Asian-Americans. In one cartoon, *Uncle Sam's Thanksgiving Dinner,* Nast portrayed people of many races and nationalities around a table whose centerpiece was "self-government" and "universal suffrage."

Republican Dominance, 1860–1932 The slavery issue so divided the Democrats that in 1860 the northern and southern wings of the party nominated separate candidates for President. The Republicans nominated Abraham Lincoln. The election results followed sectional lines, with the Republicans winning every free state. Soon after Lincoln's victory, the Civil War began.

The defeat of the Confederacy laid the foundation for a long period of Republican dominance. By 1876 the Democrats had recovered sufficient strength to challenge the Republicans and restore two-party competition. But in the seven decades from 1860 to 1932, only two Democrats were elected President—Grover Cleveland in 1884 and again in 1892 and Woodrow Wilson in 1912 and 1916.

As Americans moved West, the Republicans appealed to farmers with the promise of free land for settlers. They also reached out to business, adopting a policy of ***laissez-faire*** that promised no government interference with business and industry. At the same time, the Republicans sought to promote industrial growth through land grants to the railroads, a conservative fiscal policy of "sound money," and a trade policy that called for high protective tariffs.

During the period from 1865 to 1896 the Democrats and Republicans espoused so many of the same policies that cartoons depicted them as "Tweedledee and Tweedledum." Both parties spent much time "sitting on the fence"—that is, avoiding clear stands on the issues for fear of losing votes.

In these two cartoons Thomas Nast used the elephant and the donkey as symbols for the Republican and the Democratic parties, respectively. The elephant cartoon appeared in 1876 during the Hayes-Tilden election campaign. The donkey cartoon appeared in 1880 when Ulysses S. Grant was seeking a third-term nomination for President.

The Democrats, strong in the South, slowly recovered strength in the North and West. The South became solidly Democratic, but leadership within the party shifted to the North, where banking and import interests commanded influence. A major source of Democratic strength was the immigrant vote in the northern cities where urban party organizations—the ***political machines,*** as they were called—welcomed the immigrants with jobs, housing, and financial aid. In exchange, the party counted on the immigrants' votes on election day.

Admittance to the National Convention of the People's party in 1892 was by ticket only. Why was the People's party so short-lived?

Populism and Party Realignment The Democrats sought to avoid the issues that divided the party most deeply, but the issues would not go away. Discontent among farmers, workers, and veterans gave rise to a series of minor parties. The most important of these was the Populist party, or People's party. Founded in 1890 in protest by southern and western farmers, the Populists tried to unite poor farmers and industrial labor behind a common platform of reform. Despite efforts to broaden its base, the party's support remained primarily rural. But in 1896 the Populist faction won control of the Democratic party and nominated William Jennings Bryan for President.

PROFILE

Tammany Hall

The most powerful political machine was New York City's Tammany Hall. Founded in 1789 as a patriotic fraternal order, the Tammany Society grew in political power until, by the early 1800's, it controlled Democratic politics in the city. Tammany's leaders gained power with the arrival of new immigrants, most of whom favored the Democratic party. In return for their political support the local Democratic leaders offered ***patronage***—franchises, contracts, and other forms of assistance. Tammany Hall helped immigrants find work and homes in a new and unfamiliar culture. But the political bosses often demanded bribes in return for their favors. They made deals with contractors, budgeting enormous sums of money for public projects in order to later receive payments known as kickbacks. By 1850 this patronage system had become so widespread and so corrupt that Tammany aldermen were known as the Forty Thieves.

In 1863 William Marcy Tweed was elected Grand Sachem of Tammany Hall. Tweed extended the society's power by electing his own candidate as governor of New York. By then Tammany Hall controlled not only city but also state politics. The construction of the city courthouse in 1871 is the most infamous example of the corruption that was an everyday occurrence. The Tweed Ring pocketed huge sums of public money in kickbacks from contractors. One investigation disclosed a bill for plasterer's wages for nine months that came to nearly $3 million—including wages of $50,000 a day. Forty old chairs and three tables were billed to the city at $179,000. Advertising costs, paid to a Tammany-controlled printing company, totaled well over $7 million. In all, Tweed and his cronies pocketed some $9 million in public funds.

Exposés in *The New York Times* and *Harper's Weekly,* accompanied by political cartoonist Thomas Nast's portraits of Tammany Hall as a tiger devouring New York City, resulted in a public uproar. Tweed was convicted and imprisoned. Yet Tammany Hall continued to exert power within the Democratic organization in New York until the 1950's, when its influence finally faded.

The campaign of 1896 brought a major realignment, or shift, in the patterns of support for the two parties. By the time it was over, large groups of voters had switched sides over the issue of money. American paper money traditionally could be converted into either gold or silver. Both gold and silver coins were minted. In the later part of the nineteenth century, however, the coinage of silver was greatly limited. Bryan favored a ***free silver policy,*** the unlimited minting of silver coins. Republicans favored a return to the ***gold standard,*** however, a policy that opposed the unlimited coinage of silver and favored backing paper money only with gold.

Bryan's money policies divided the Democratic party, scaring away much of its traditional commercial and labor support. However, the Democrats picked up strength among western farmers and miners and held on to people's loyalties in the South, giving rise to the phrase, *the Solid South.*

The Republicans nominated an Ohio Congressman named William McKinley, and they won the 1896 election. Big business contributed heavily to the Republican cause, and campaign manager Marcus Alonzo Hanna used the money brilliantly. Promising "sound money" and prosperity for all, the Republicans built a powerful coalition of various groups including northern business, urban labor, and midwestern farmers. Despite a strong campaign by Bryan, the Republicans swept the election. The Populists, who had also nominated Bryan, ceased to exist as a party after his defeat.

Republican dominance was interrupted in 1912. The party split when former President Theodore Roosevelt, leader of the party's progressive wing, challenged President Taft's conservative leadership. Roosevelt, unable to take the nomination for himself, became the candidate of a new third party called the Progressive, or "Bull Moose" party. The split within the Republican ranks led to a Democratic victory, and Woodrow Wilson was elected President with 42 percent of the vote. But the Democrats held the Presidency for only two terms. During Wilson's administration the nation experienced the shocks of World War I, social unrest, and economic recession. In 1920 the Republican candidate Warren G. Harding offered a "return to normalcy." The Republicans were swept back into office in a landslide. For the decade of "the Golden Twenties" the Republicans were again dominant.

Theodore Roosevelt, only age 42 at the time, succeeded to the Presidency in 1901 when an assassin's bullet killed William McKinley. Roosevelt is shown here in 1903 giving a speech in Newcastle, Wyoming, while campaigning for election in his own right.

LEXICON

A Political Menagerie of Terms

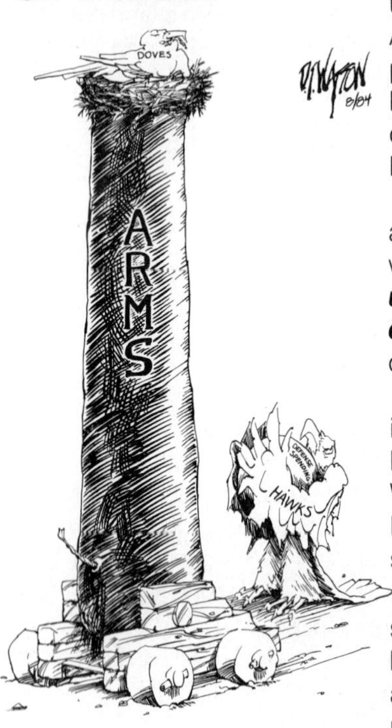

American political slang has created a colorful menagerie of terms. A ***dark horse*** is a little-known candidate who wins a surprise victory. The phrase was borrowed from horse racing, as were other examples of political slang such as ***running mate*** and ***front runner.*** In the same vein, politicians ask voters not to desert their party in times of crisis. Abraham Lincoln told Republicans, "Don't swap horses while crossing the stream." A ***shoo-in*** is a candidate who is a certain and easy winner. A shoo-in is another term borrowed from horse-racing history. In times past jockeys sometimes held back their own mounts. The horse that became the winner was then considered a shoo-in. A ***stalking-horse*** campaigns as a stand-in for a candidate who will come forward at a later time.

The menagerie of political slang includes ***hawks,*** who are pro-war, and ***doves,*** who are antiwar leaders; ***lame ducks,*** who are officials with little power; ***fat cats,*** who are wealthy political contributors; and ***underdogs,*** who are candidates least favored to win. Political ***watch-dog committees*** do just what their name implies—they keep an eye on what other politicians and public officials do.

Sheep have provided other examples of political slang. A ***bellwether*** is a district whose voting pattern sets the trend of voting for the nation because a "*wether*" is a leading male sheep that often wears a bell. Wool dyed in its raw, unfinished state is more likely to hold its color. Hence, a ***dyed-in-the-wool*** Democrat or Republican is someone steadfast in loyalty to the party.

Military terms have also found their place in the lexicon of political slang. ***Campaign,*** which first referred to a series of military operations, has also come to mean a political contest. ***Rally*** means literally to re-ally, or to gather scattered military troops for a new battle. In political rallies the troops are supporters, often called ***party regulars,*** a reference to soldiers of the regular army. ***Rank-and-file,*** originally the enlisted men of an armed force, has come to mean the average members of political parties or labor organizations. The leader of a political party is its ***standard-bearer,*** once the soldier who held the banner at the head of a troop.

Perhaps the most unusual political slang reflects the colorful history of the nation itself. Politicians are said to jump on ***bandwagons,*** the winning side or most popular issue in a campaign. P. T. Barnum used the term to describe the wagon his circus used for traveling. Politicians dip into the ***pork barrel*** when they use state or federal funds for a project that benefits their own constituents. The term comes from the pre-Civil War period, when salt pork was stored in barrels. A survey to discover political opinion is called a ***straw poll*** or ***straw vote***—because, as Ralph Waldo Emerson wrote, "A straw thrown into the air will show how the wind sits." Popular candidates are said to carry less popular candidates into office on their ***coattails,*** another term popularized by Lincoln, who had in mind the long coattails fashionable on men's suits of the period.

Each political campaign brings with it new candidates and issues, and each campaign adds new terms to the political menagerie.

President Franklin D. Roosevelt speaks to the nation in a radio address known as a fireside chat. Through these radio addresses, Roosevelt calmed the fears of the public during the Great Depression and, later, during World War II. How might Roosevelt's fireside chats have added to his popularity?

The Roosevelt Coalition The next major realignment in party support occurred during the Great Depression. Speculators lost vast sums of money in the stock market crash of 1929. The crash dealt the Republicans a political blow from which they did not recover for 20 years. In 1932 the Democratic nominee, Franklin D. Roosevelt, promised the nation a "New Deal" and appealed to the "forgotten Americans" at the bottom of the economic ladder. Roosevelt carried 42 states while Republican President Herbert Hoover carried only 6. The Democrats won overwhelming majorities in both the Senate and House of Representatives.

The Roosevelt coalition was built upon the traditional base of southern Democrats as well as that of urban Roman Catholics. To these two groups Roosevelt added support from labor, small farmers, and minorities. Northern blacks and Jewish voters, ignored by the Republicans, moved into the Democratic ranks.

The sectional divisions of Republican North and Democratic South came to be replaced in the 1930's by economic distinctions. The Democrats gathered strength primarily from the poor and the working class. Republican support came mainly from the rich and middle-income groups. Yet despite this tendency to divide along economic lines, each party had a broad base of support cutting across class, ethnic, and regional differences.

The coalition forged by Franklin D. Roosevelt 50 years ago remains today the foundation of Democratic party support. As time has passed, however, the distinctions between the two parties have become less definite. Since the 1940's the Republicans have made steady inroads into what was once a solidly Democratic South.

The Democratic and Republican parties have had their ups and downs. Each party has been split by internal struggles. Each has suffered crushing defeats. Party loyalty has weakened, and an ever-increasing number of Americans describe themselves as Independents. Yet both Democrats and Republicans have survived—a testimony to the strength of the two-party system in the United States.

Section Check

1. Define: political party, machine, laissez-faire policy, patronage, free silver policy, gold standard, dark horse, bellwether, standard-bearer, pork barrel
2. Identify: Federalists, National Republicans, Whigs, Free-Soilers, Tammany Hall, Thomas Nast, Populists, Progressives, New Deal
3. What are the six basic functions of political parties?
4. How did the first political parties come about?
5. How did the Whigs and Jacksonian Democrats differ?
6. What crucial issue prompted the formation of the Republican party in 1854?

2 THE TWO–PARTY SYSTEM

For over 180 years control of the United States government has shifted back and forth between two major parties. Since 1856 the Republicans and Democrats have dominated the American political scene. Most Americans take two-party competition for granted.

Why Two Parties?

Many democratic nations have ***multi-party systems*** in which three or more parties seriously compete for the control of government. Some of these parties represent specialized interests. Why are there not separate parties to represent each interest in the United States? Among the many factors that help to explain our ***two-party system,*** three are especially important: (1) historical roots, (2) party identification, and (3) the electoral system.

First, historical roots helped shape political parties. The new American nation struggled over the adoption of the Constitution as the country divided into two groups, the Federalists and Anti-Federalists. And from the formation of these two groups the first political parties followed.

Some people, like the worker on the park bench in this cartoon, take a very pragmatic, or practical, view of party identification. Why does he identify with Republicans when he is working?

I'm what you'd call politically flexible: Republican when I'm working, Democrat when I ain't.
Houston Chronicle

Second, most Americans have grown up with a sense of party identification. Party loyalty, like church membership, has tended to be passed on from generation to generation. This has given stability and continuity to the political system. Party identification has weakened, however, as the number of Independents has increased, but the majority of American voters still regard themselves as either Democrats or Republicans.

Third, institutions have shaped political behavior in significant ways. The electoral system has promoted two-party politics because one of the most important institutional features of the American political system is the division of the nation into districts from which one legislator is elected. In the ***single-member districts*** the candidate with the most votes—a ***plurality***—wins the seat. Although a number of parties may enter the race, the system offers little chance except to the strongest competitors. Voters are rarely willing to "waste" their votes on a party that does not have a chance to win. Even though some voters may prefer a third party, they are likely to cast their votes for a candidate of one of the two major parties, thus discouraging minor parties and strengthening the two-party system.

In marked contrast to single-member districts, countries such as West Germany use a system of ***proportional representation.*** Under this system membership in legislative bodies reflects the popular voting strength of each party. If, for example, a minor party wins 5 percent of the vote nationwide, it receives about 5 percent of the legislative seats. The system of proportional representation varies somewhat from country to country, but the result is the same: It tends to encourage a multiparty system.

Two-party politics in the United States is also strengthened by the manner in which the President is elected. Under the Electoral College system the candidate who receives the most popular votes in each state wins all the state's electoral votes. Like the single-member district, it is a case of winner-take-all. Minor parties, with little chance of winning the Presidency, rarely attract more than a handful of votes. Sometimes people vote for a third party as a form of protest, but when people care who wins, they almost always vote Republican or Democratic.

Patterns of Political Conflict

In the United States the two-party system rests upon a fundamental consensus of commitment to democratic values and to the constitutional framework

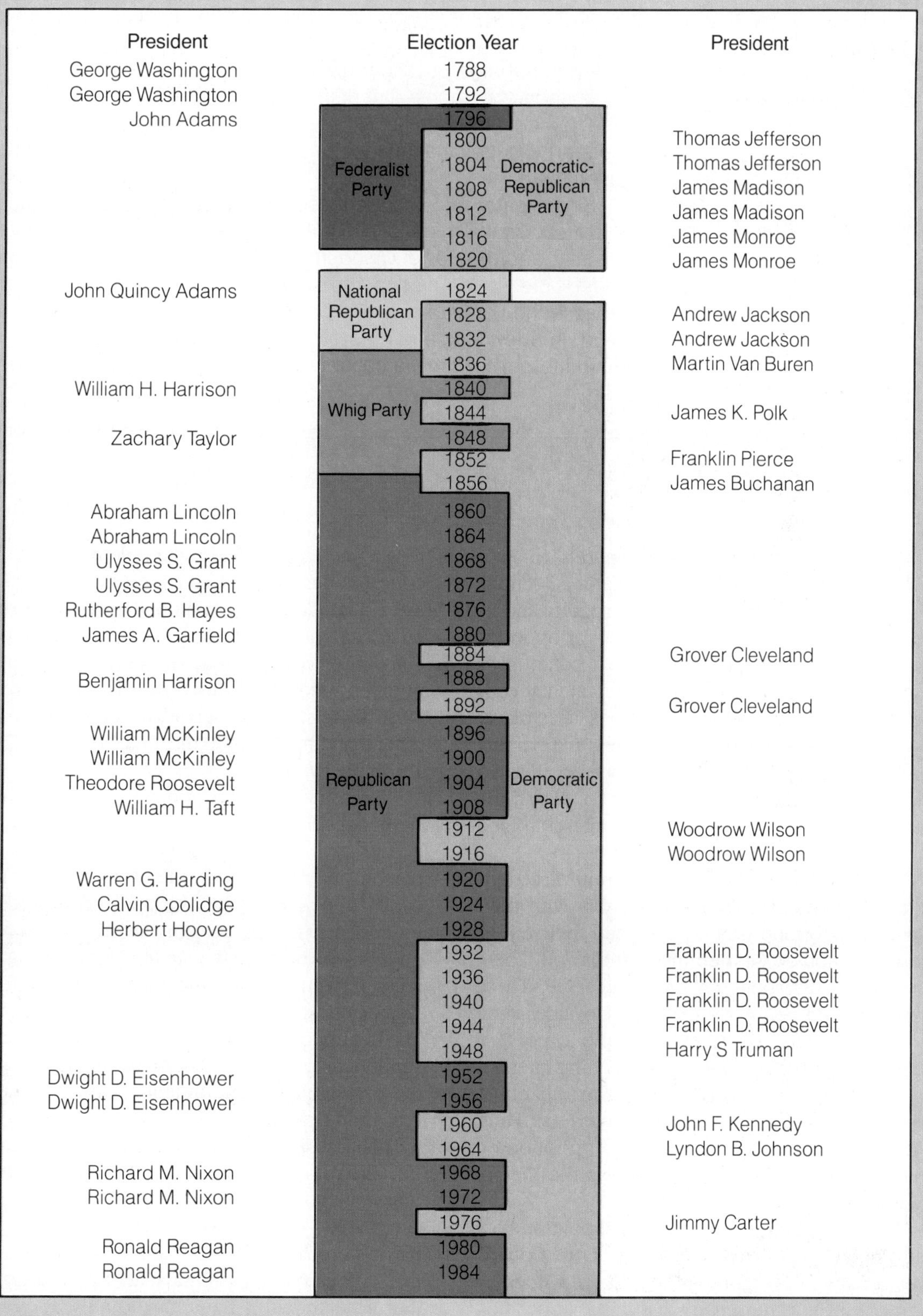
POLITICAL PARTIES AND PRESIDENTIAL ELECTIONS
President
Election Year
President
George Washington
1788
George Washington
1792
John Adams
1796
1800
Thomas Jefferson
1804
Thomas Jefferson
1808
James Madison
1812
James Madison
1816
James Monroe
1820
James Monroe
Federalist Party
Democratic-Republican Party
John Quincy Adams
1824
1828
Andrew Jackson
1832
Andrew Jackson
1836
Martin Van Buren
National Republican Party
William H. Harrison
1840
1844
James K. Polk
Zachary Taylor
1848
1852
Franklin Pierce
1856
James Buchanan
Whig Party
Abraham Lincoln
1860
Abraham Lincoln
1864
Ulysses S. Grant
1868
Ulysses S. Grant
1872
Rutherford B. Hayes
1876
James A. Garfield
1880
1884
Grover Cleveland
Benjamin Harrison
1888
1892
Grover Cleveland
William McKinley
1896
William McKinley
1900
Theodore Roosevelt
1904
William H. Taft
1908
1912
Woodrow Wilson
1916
Woodrow Wilson
Warren G. Harding
1920
Calvin Coolidge
1924
Herbert Hoover
1928
1932
Franklin D. Roosevelt
1936
Franklin D. Roosevelt
1940
Franklin D. Roosevelt
1944
Franklin D. Roosevelt
1948
Harry S Truman
Dwight D. Eisenhower
1952
Dwight D. Eisenhower
1956
1960
John F. Kennedy
1964
Lyndon B. Johnson
Richard M. Nixon
1968
Richard M. Nixon
1972
1976
Jimmy Carter
Ronald Reagan
1980
Ronald Reagan
1984
Republican Party
Democratic Party

LEGACY

Party Systems

In parliamentary democracies, multi-party systems often exist in which the political parties are based on ideological, economic, regional, or religious interests. Since no one party is likely to win a majority of seats in parliament, it is usually necessary to form a coalition government with a cabinet composed of members of different parties.

A few countries, notably Mexico, have minor opposition parties, but one party is dominant, and that party is in continuous control of government.

Single-party systems are those in which no opposition parties are permitted. Typically found in dictatorships such as Nazi Germany, Fascist Italy, and the Soviet Union, the party is controlled by a handful of leaders. Elections are conducted, but the people are offered no choice because the name of only one party and candidate appears for each office. In a few single-party systems opposition is allowed to develop within the party. In these cases a faction may serve as an opposition "party."

of government. This consensus extends to economic and social values as well. Nearly all Americans believe in the right to private property and in free enterprise. They support equality of opportunity for all persons and uphold the separation of church and state. It is within this fundamental consensus that conflict over specific issues takes place.

Americans do differ on the issues, and conflict among opposing interests is often heated. But two important characteristics of political conflict in the United States are cross-cutting interests and moderation.

Most people are pulled in different directions by divided loyalties. They may identify with their occupational group on one issue and their ethnic group on another. Or their interests may pull them in opposite directions on the same issue. These ***cross-cutting interests***, or divided loyalties, tend to reduce conflict and to open people to political bargaining and compromise. Cross-cutting interests also mean that one political party is not likely to best represent all of a person's interests. Thus, someone might prefer the Republican position on domestic economic policy, but favor the Democratic stand on foreign policy.

The second basic characteristic of political conflict in the United States is moderation. Conflict over certain issues has been intense, as witnessed in the civil rights movement and in the opposition to the Vietnam War. Protest and civil disobedience reveal the depth of feeling people may have about critical issues. In most elections, however, conflict takes a moderate form, and the vast majority of American voters will stand on the middle ground. The differences that separate them are not great, and no deep ideological differences divide the nation. Most liberals and conservatives are closer to each other than liberals are to the far left or conservatives are to the far right.

Even though there are about twice as many Democrats as Republicans, neither party commands a majority. In a recent Gallup Poll, 45 percent of all persons interviewed regarded themselves as Democrats, 25 percent as Republicans, and 30 percent as Independents. This pattern has important consequences for each party's strategy for winning Presidential elections. The fundamental problem for the Democrats is to hold on to their base of support. The Republicans, on the other hand, must try to win support away from the Democrats. Finally, both parties must appeal to the Independents. Both Republicans and Democrats must direct their appeal toward the political center or risk a substantial loss of support.

The pattern of conflict within consensus has an important consequence: The victory of one party is acceptable—or at least tolerable—to the other. Each party is prepared to accept defeat because it knows that in four years it will have another chance. Furthermore, though a party may lose the Presidency, it can (as the Democrats have so often done) retain control of Congress. The federal system also helps to nourish the hope of a return to power. When a party is defeated at the national level, it may still be able to maintain its hold in the states and cities.

Two-Party Competition

Elections are won and lost on the middle ground of American politics. Since both the Republicans and Democrats seek a majority of votes, each must appeal to the political center. When the parties move too far to the right or to the left, they run the risk of losing moderate support. This is precisely what happened in 1964 and in 1972. In 1964 the Republicans nominated Senator Barry Goldwater for President. A conservative, Goldwater offered the voters "a choice, not an echo." Many people—Republicans and Independents as well as Democrats—viewed Goldwater as an extremist, and he suffered a massive defeat. In 1972 the Democrats nominated Senator George McGovern, whom some called "a liberal in radical clothing." Many moderate Democrats and most Independents went over to the Republican candidate, Richard Nixon. On Election Day, George McGovern was soundly defeated.

In 1980 Ronald Reagan won the Republican Presidential nomination as a right-wing candidate of his party. After the convention, however, Reagan moderated his conservative image. He chose his running mate and drew many of his advisers from among the Republicans' moderate wing. By making his way to the center of the political stage, Reagan won a landslide victory in November of 1980.

Party Differences

Despite the overlap and similarities between the two parties, there are important differences between Democrats and Republicans. Though often blurred, in the electoral competition for the middle ground, these differences are real and clearly evident in the political beliefs of those most active within each party. Differences between Democrats and Republicans are revealed in their basic philosophies, campaign platforms, in legislative action, and in party support.

The Democrats are the liberal party. Democrats, on the whole, accept an active role for government, with a willingness to use federal funds to solve social problems. They have generally supported the interests of labor, minorities, and the poor. They have favored government regulation of the economy. Franklin D. Roosevelt's New Deal shaped the character of the modern Democratic party. Its program for social justice and welfare was extended through Truman's Fair Deal, Kennedy's New Frontier, and Johnson's Great Society.

Both Barry Goldwater (left) and George McGovern (right) were nominated by their parties for the Presidency. Both lost. Why do you think most "elections are won and lost on the middle ground of American politics"?

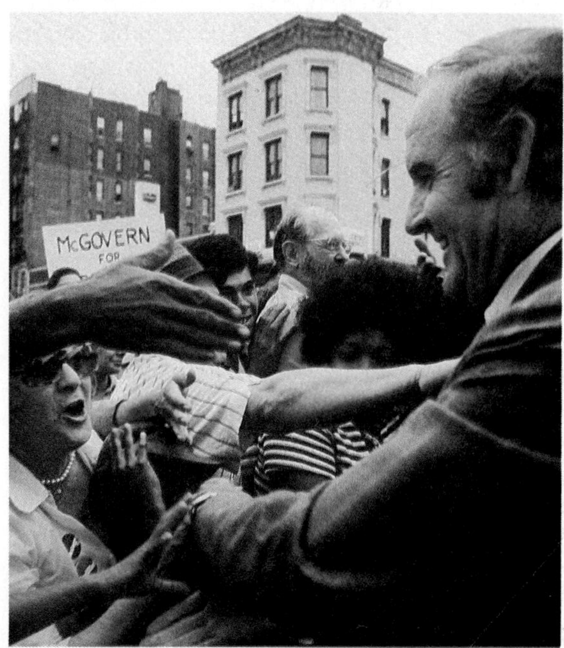

The Republicans are basically the conservative party. They oppose "big government" and favor the reduction of federal spending—except for national defense. They support the interests of business and stress the value of a market economy free from government regulation. Republicans place their faith in the traditional values of middle-class and small-town citizens, emphasizing self-reliance and initiative.

Party differences are revealed in each party's national campaign platform. The platform, hammered out during the Presidential nominating convention, states the party's position on the major issues before the nation. The differences between recent Republican and Democratic platforms have been significant.

Policy differences between the two parties are recorded in votes by senators and representatives in Congress. There are almost always differences within each party, but members of the same party tend to vote the same way on bills before Congress. On issues such as government regulation and social welfare the majority of Republicans will be on one side and the majority of Democrats on the other. Often the differences are dramatic, as in 1964 when 84 percent of the Democrats in the House of Representatives voted for President Lyndon Johnson's anti-poverty program and 87 percent of the Republicans voted against it.

Party Competition at State and Local Levels

The two-party system operates most clearly at the national level in Presidential elections. The pattern of competition is often very different at state and local levels. At the local level one party frequently dominates the political scene for decades. Only about half the states have close two-party competition. The others tend to be dominated by either the Republican or Democratic party. The South, for example, remains overwhelmingly Democratic. The Midwest is primarily Republican. But fewer states today are completely safe for one party. Traditional bases of strength have begun to break down, as can be seen in the dramatic rise of Republican support in the South.

For almost a century after the Civil War, the deep South was solidly Democratic. The Republican party had virtually no support in southern states and did not even contest most state offices. Instead of competition between two parties, competition in these southern states was between factions within the Democratic party. Because nomination as the Democratic candidate assured election, the party primary was the "real" election for state office. The Solid South began to break in the 1950's, when Southerners split their tickets to vote for the Republican Presidential candidate. State offices remained largely in the hands of Democrats until the 1970's, when Republicans began a serious effort to win southern governorships. Most local offices today are still "safe" for the Democrats, but two-party competition has changed the face of southern politics.

Third Parties

Throughout American history new parties have arisen to challenge the two major parties. The Republican party was successful in replacing the Whigs, but most ***third parties*** disappear or decline to insignificance after an unsuccessful bid for power. Such parties include the Anti-Masons in the 1830's, the Greenback party in the 1880's, the Populists in the 1890's, and the Progressives in the 1920's.

DEMOCRATIC AND REPUBLICAN STRENGTH: 1985

Office	Democrats	Republicans
Members of Congress		
House of Representatives	252	183
Senate	47	53
Governors	34	16
Members of State Legislatures	4,318	3,038

A reflection of two-party competition at the national level is the struggle for majority control in Congress. Which party is in the majority in the House? In the Senate? How does majority control strengthen a party's national position?

LEGACY

Third Parties

ELECTORAL VOTES OF THIRD PARTIES IN SELECTED PRESIDENTIAL ELECTIONS	
Party (Year)	Number of Electoral Votes
Populist (1892)	22
Progressive (1912)	88
Socialist (1912)	0
Progressive (1924)	13
States' Rights (1948)	39
American Independent (1968)	46

No third party in the United States has ever won a significant victory in national politics. Yet more than a hundred third-party movements have sprung up to challenge the candidates and platforms of the two major parties. What accounts for the variety and vitality of third parties?

Some third parties have arisen in response to events of the time. The Jobless party, for example, founded in 1932 at the height of the Great Depression, spoke out for political reform to end unemployment. Its influence lasted only as long as the economic crisis it sought to solve. During the period of the Vietnam War the People's party was created by radical and antiwar activists to protest United States involvement in Southeast Asia. In 1972 the People's party nominated Presidential and Vice-Presidential candidates. But four years later, with the war at an end, the party had all but disappeared.

Other third parties have appeared in response to a single issue. "LOOK HERE!—Over Thirty Thousand American People Destroyed Annually by Intoxicating Drinks . . . To the Rescue, Sons and Daughters of Liberty," proclaims an early broadside that led to the establishment of the Prohibition party in 1869. The Prohibition party has run a Presidential candidate in every national election since 1872. It has also expanded its platform to include the issue of equal pay for women, but it remains largely identified with the single issue of temperance. Not many single-issue parties have lasted as long. The American Vegetarian party was founded in 1948 to promote vegetarianism in the United States. It won only four votes in its first Presidential election and was disbanded by 1960.

The most colorful third parties have existed largely to give voice to their founders. The Poor Man's party, for example, was founded in 1952 by Henry Krajewski, a hog farmer who nominated himself the party's Presidential candidate. Krajewski ran on a platform that included a mandatory year of work on a farm for every youth in the nation. The Tax Cut party has been identified almost exclusively with its founder, Lar Daly, who usually appears in public as Uncle Sam.

Though some third parties may seem merely eccentric, others play a significant role in American political life. The Libertarian party has remained a visible force in American politics since 1971 with its platform to "defend the rights of the individual" against the excesses of government. And many third parties—short-lived and largely unsupported—have served the very important role of bringing attention to controversial issues that were later to be addressed by the major parties. The Liberty party was formed on the platform that "slavery is against natural rights." That issue in 1839 won the party little support, but it served to draw attention to a conflict that would later divide the nation and its political parties. The Equal Rights party, established in 1884 by Belva A. Bennett Lockwood, a lawyer, won barely 4,000 votes. Today the highly controversial planks of the Equal Rights party's platform are accepted without question—women's suffrage and equal rights for blacks, Native Americans, and immigrants. By giving voice to new ideas and controversial issues during election campaigns, third parties enrich political thought.

Many third parties emerge as ***splinter groups,*** or breakaway movements, from one of the two major parties. Often they have been organized around particular political personalities. The American Independents, the most recent third party to win any sizeable following, formed around the 1968 Presidential candidacy of Alabama Governor George Wallace. With 13.6 percent of the popular vote Wallace carried five states and won 46 electoral votes. Other "personality" parties have included the various Progressive parties, organized around Theodore Roosevelt (1912), Robert LaFollette (1924), and Henry A. Wallace (1948). Such parties are based on one candidate's bid for the Presidency and tend to disappear once the campaign is over.

Other minor parties are based on ideas—either a single issue or a general ideology. Unlike the major parties, which are loose coalitions formed to win elections, these "idea" parties are generally tightly-knit groups committed to a set of principles or to a particular doctrine. They suffer accordingly at the polls. With no hope of winning major elections, they function very much like interest groups. Election campaigns help to publicize their programs and goals. Single-issue parties such as the Anti-Masons and Greenbacks tend to rise and fall with public interest in their particular issue. Ideological parties may survive through the efforts of a dedicated few. Such parties include the Libertarian, Prohibition, Communist, Socialist Workers, and Citizens parties.

Some minor parties, like the Liberal and Conservative parties of New York, are active only at state levels.

Although minor parties rarely win more than a handful of votes, they perform important functions in the American political system. Minor parties act as political barometers, measuring the climate of public opinion. They frequently take stands on controversial issues and draw attention to problems that the major parties may choose to side-step or ignore. They offer new ideas and programs. If a minor party begins to gain popularity, one of the major parties almost always moves to absorb it, adopt its programs, and "steal its thunder." Just a few of the issues that the major parties "stole" from minor-party platforms are extension of voting rights to women and blacks, abolition of slavery, the eight-hour workday, direct election of senators, prohibition of alcoholic beverages, and progressive income taxes.

Third parties can sometimes play the role of the "spoiler" in a Presidential election. In 1912 Teddy Roosevelt's Progressive party divided the Republican vote and gave the election to the Democrats and

George Wallace was also a third-party Presidential candidate in 1972. He was unable to campaign, however, because an assassination attempt left him paralyzed from the waist down. Most of his supporters voted for Nixon rather than for McGovern. How else might a third-party candidate play a spoiler role in an election?

Woodrow Wilson. Third parties can sometimes create special problems. Under the Electoral College system, if no candidate receives a majority of electoral votes, the election is decided by the House of Representatives. In 1968 many people feared that George Wallace might carry enough states to prevent either the Republican or Democratic candidate from gaining a majority of electoral votes. If this had happened, Wallace might have been able to bargain his votes and, in effect, name the next President.

Section Check

1. Define: multi-party system, single-member district, plurality, proportional representation, cross-cutting interests, splinter group
2. What three important factors explain the development of the two-party system?
3. What are the two most important characteristics of political conflict in the United States?
4. Explain the basic philosophies of the Democratic and Republican parties.
5. What are some issues in third-party platforms "stolen" by the major parties?

3 PARTY ORGANIZATION

American political parties are not what they seem. On paper each party appears to be set up as a unified national political organization. The national convention meets every four years to nominate Presidential and Vice Presidential candidates and to form party policy. The permanent party organization has the form of a pyramid, with the party chairperson and the national committee at the peak. Below are the state, county, and city committees, and near the base are the ward and precinct committees. But appearances are misleading. In reality each party is a loose ***coalition*** of state and local units. Organization is highly decentralized, and party units at each level exercise considerable independence.

The loose and decentralized organization of the Republican and Democratic parties reflects the federal structure of American government. Party units are organized around elective offices—local, state, and national. Their principal reason for existence is to win elections to these offices. The national party organization exists primarily to operate the machinery of Presidential elections. Otherwise it has little authority and not much to do.

National Party Structures

In theory the ***national convention*** is the supreme authority in the Republican and Democratic parties. Its most important task is the nomination of candidates for President and Vice President—a process that shall be examined closely in the next chapter. The convention also ratifies the party platform, adopts rules governing party organization, and elects officers.

Although the convention is the highest authority in each party, its real power is limited. It meets just once every four years—and then only for a few days of confusion and excitement. Such a gathering can hardly be expected to provide clear and stable leadership. Many key decisions already will have been made. At the convention itself, leadership rests primarily with elected public officials—many of whom lead their states' delegations—and with the candidates for the Presidential nomination. Oftentimes, the party nominee is determined in the primary elections and state conventions. In addition, the Vice-Presidential nominee is often known before the national convention even opens.

On-going national party leadership is provided by the ***national committees*** of the Democrats

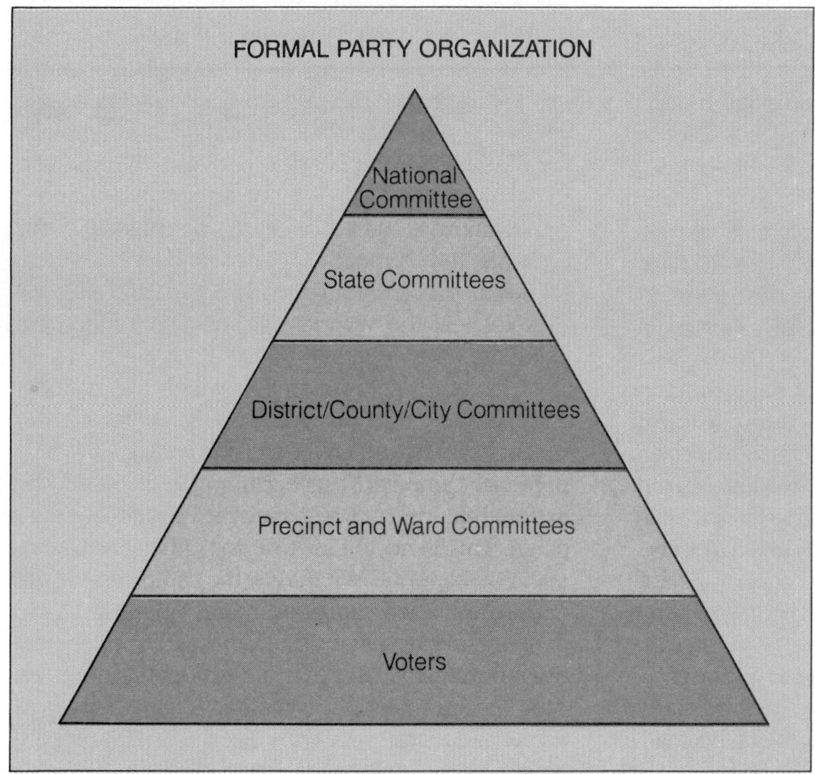

Voters make up the broad base of a political party's formal organization. Ultimately, then, the effectiveness of a party's organization relies on citizens who are willing to participate in one or more of the party's levels of organization.

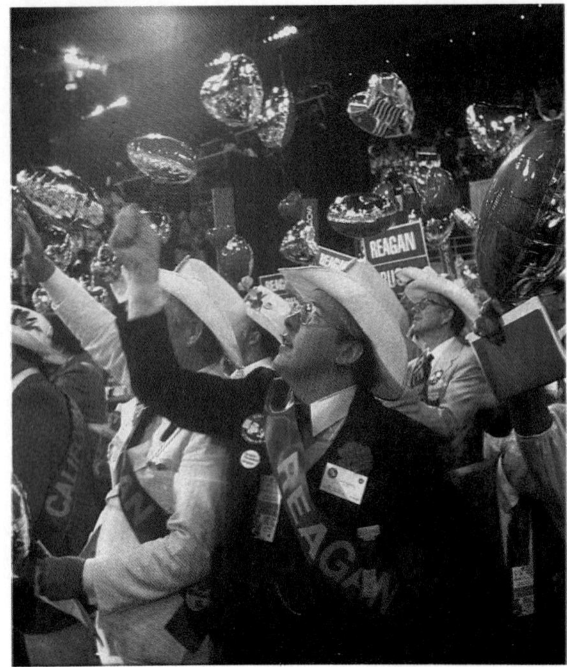

Presidential nominating conventions frequently take on a circus air, especially after a candidate's name has been placed in nomination and seconded by one or more orators. How did these 1980 convention delegates show their enthusiasm and loyalties for their parties' nominees?

and Republicans. The national committee consists of one man and one woman from each state, the District of Columbia, Puerto Rico, and the Virgin Islands. Additional members are also chosen according to population and party strength in each state and to make the committee more representative. Procedures vary among the states in selecting national committee members. They are chosen according to state law by primary election, state party convention, state committee, or by the state delegation to the national convention. The members selected by each state are then formally elected by the national convention.

The full membership of the national committee rarely meets. Responsibility for the day-to-day operations of the party rests with the national chairperson and the staff of the party headquarters in Washington. The chairperson, though officially selected by the national committee, is actually chosen at the end of the convention by a party's Presidential nominee. It is through the chairperson that the successful candidate, as President, dominates the party. On the other hand, a defeated Presidential candidate usually has little influence over the party, and the national committee often replaces the chairperson with someone of its own choosing.

The chairperson works to raise funds for the party, polish its image in public relations, and coordinate its Presidential campaign. As the party's chief administrator, the chairperson manages the national headquarters. For the party in the White House the chairperson is often little more than a mouthpiece for the President. When the party is out of power, the chairperson has an opportunity to play a more significant role. After McGovern's defeat in 1972, for example, the Democratic party was deeply divided. Chairman Robert Strauss worked hard and successfully to heal the wounds of factional conflict and bring the party together.

The unity and leadership which the national chairperson could provide has been weakened in recent years by the Presidential nominee's use of a personal campaign organization. Traditionally the national chairperson managed the Presidential campaign. This is no longer true for either the Democratic or Republican party. In the campaign for the nomination each candidate builds up an independent organization. It is usually through this personal organization that the party's Presidential nominee runs the campaign. The national chairperson and party headquarters are bypassed, and a winning candidate owes little to the party itself. In 1976, for example, Hamilton Jordon, a young aide and political adviser to Jimmy Carter, managed the Carter Presidential campaign. Four years earlier, Richard Nixon's successful bid for reelection was staged by the Committee to Reelect the President (CREEP). This reelection organization, which was later linked to the Watergate break-in, was distinct and completely separate from the Republican National Committee.

The national committees of the Republican and Democratic parties play no role in selecting the nominees for public office. By contrast, in Europe most political party candidates are handpicked and carefully screened by the national organization. The party manages and finances the campaign. In turn, the successful candidate is expected to be loyal to the party and to vote along party lines in parliament. If a member of parliament votes with the opposition on a crucial issue, the party organization may exercise its discipline by denying the member a place on the party ticket in the next election.

Nothing of this sort is possible in the United States. For the Senate and the House of Representatives, for state and local offices, candidates for nomination run their own campaigns. They raise their own funds and build their own organizations. They owe little to the party and nothing to each other. Victory in the primary is enough to take the party label. Once in office it is to the home constituency, not the party organization, that the elected official must answer.

The decentralization of American party organization is seen in the separate campaign committees each party organizes in the Senate and House of Representatives. The Republican and Democratic Congressional committees are composed of members elected by their party colleagues in each house. They help fellow senators and representatives in their reelection campaigns by providing speakers, money, and advice. In ***off-year elections***—when the Presidency is not contested—these committees provide almost the only coordination at the national level for the campaign effort by the two major parties. Otherwise, party activity is focused on the election campaign for each office at the state and the local levels.

State and Local Party Structures

Among the 50 states there is considerable variation in party organization and operation. The state parties are quite similar, however, in their formal structure. At the top is the ***state committee,*** made up of members chosen according to state law at the district or county level. State committees and state chairpersons generally have little power. This is because the committees tend to be dominated by politicians holding elective office. The governor usually controls his or her state party organization. In the party out of power a United States senator, a mayor, or a coalition of local leaders may dominate the state organization.

Below the state committee are the various district and county committees, varying widely in the power they command. Party politics has operated most effectively at the county level through tightly organized groups called ***political machines.*** At the top of the machine is the party boss, who controls the precinct captains responsible for getting out the vote on election day. Local machines still exist, but today most are only a shadow of what they were 50 or 100 years ago. Machines depend on ***patronage***—the reward of jobs, contracts, and favors to the party faithful. Although patronage has been greatly reduced by the growth of civil service, many patronage jobs remain on the public payroll. The Chicago Democratic machine, for example, controls several thousand government jobs, as well as other benefits it can bestow in exchange for political support. But few counties or cities have the powerful party organization of Chicago. Most local organizations are poorly financed and inactive except around election time.

Party Membership: Leaders and Activists

At the base of the Democratic and Republican party organizations are the members who vote in the primary, attend precinct meetings, contribute money, work in campaigns, and run for office. It is upon these participant citizens that each party depends. But what does it mean to be a member of the Democratic or Republican party? Unlike most European parties, the two American parties do not have formal memberships. No one has to apply. There are no cards or dues. In the United States membership is a matter of party identification. You are a Republican or Democrat if you say you are.*

The leadership within each party is composed of elected public officials, full-time party officials (such as national, state, and county chairpersons),

*Depending on the state, this may involve registering as a party member, voting in a party caucus, or merely voting in a primary election and asking for one party's ballot.

Within the individual states, the strength of a party's power can often be found at the most local of levels—the precinct meeting. Through participation in precinct meetings, voters can express opinions on a variety of concerns. Here Mexican Americans in Texas have gathered to plan strategy for an upcoming election.

and the party activists. The most important party leaders are almost always public officials—the President, governors, and senators. At the national level the recognized leader of the party in the White House is the President. Leadership in the opposition party is usually dispersed among senators, governors, and those seeking the Presidential nomination. But whether in power or out, each party has its rivals for leadership. Sometimes the battle lines are drawn in terms of liberal and conservative ideology. More often the question of leadership settles on who can best lead the party to the White House or who can keep the party in the White House.

Party activists are of two types: the regulars and the purists. ***Party regulars*** are committed primarily to the party itself. Their first interest is in winning the election, and their concern is to select candidates with wide popular appeal. Their approach to the issues is practical. In order to forge a winning coalition of various interests, they are prepared to bargain and compromise.

Party purists are oriented to candidates and issues rather than to the party. They rally around their favorite candidate or pursue their commitment to a particular issue. They tend to be more ideological and to view compromise as suspect if not immoral. Purists frequently give only conditional support to the party. Their loyalty is to the candidate. Their commitment is to the cause.

Both parties have long included regulars and purists, just as both have liberal and conservative wings and rivals for party leadership. All of these divisions can be signs of health in a party, showing that it can bring together divergent interests and types of people. Recently, however, the number of purists found within each party has risen sharply. To many observers the increasing importance of candidate- and issue-orientation is a symptom of the decline of political parties.

Decline and Disarray in Political Parties

In most states parties are loose coalitions of local organizations. Few state committees have much power over local levels. Those that do are usually in states with close competition between the two parties. Competition acts to bring the various units and factions of the party together in order to win elections. The greatest disarray occurs in those states where a single party is dominant. Here the main arena of conflict is within the party itself.

The growth of the ***primary system*** is a major factor in the weakness of party organization. The primary election (which shall be discussed in the next chapter) is the most widely used method of selecting party nominees for each office. Formerly nominees were chosen at ***party caucuses,*** or meetings of party leaders. The primary was introduced as a reform to make parties more democratic, allowing party members themselves to choose among the candidates. But, ironically, the primary system has weakened party organization and the capacity of each party to offer the voters a slate of candidates who stand together behind a common program.

Overall there are important differences between the Republican and Democratic parties. But because party nominees do not stand together behind a common program, these differences are blurred. Party label is still important for most voters, but increasingly voters split their ticket, voting Republican for one office, Democratic for another. As parties have weakened, special interests have grown in power. Concerned citizens and party leaders have called for a strengthening of party politics. They do so in the belief that a strong two-party system is the best guarantee the people have for responsive and accountable democratic government.

Weak political parties make clear and effective policy difficult to achieve. Candidates depend on personal campaign organizations. They have different electorates. Public officials have little incentive to work together—even with members of their own party. More importantly, weak parties reduce accountability. When each party is itself divided, the voters cannot fix responsibility. It becomes more difficult to hold government answerable to the people.

Several years ago journalist David Broder entitled his book on American politics, *The Party's Over*. Broder was certainly not the first to warn of the decline of political parties. One observer or another for nearly a century has described American parties as "in crisis." But the major parties have not collapsed. They are under stress, but they are also undergoing reform and change as they respond to new demands and go about their central concern—winning elections.

Section Check

1. Define: coalition, patronage, off-year election, state committee, party activist, primary system, caucus
2. Identify: Democratic National Committee, CREEP, Republican Congressional Campaign Committee
3. What groups provide ongoing party leadership between national conventions?
4. What effect has the primary system had on party organization?

SUMMARY

Although never mentioned in the Constitution, political parties are central to the American system of government. Parties operate the "machinery of choice" (nominations and elections), stimulate interest in politics, simplify the voters' choices, help organize the machinery of government, make government more accountable to the people, and unite different interests and social groups.

For over 180 years control of the government has shifted back and forth between two major competing parties. Since 1856 the Republicans and Democrats have dominated the political scene. The electoral system—particularly the single-member district and the Electoral College—serves to perpetuate the two-party system by making it difficult for minor parties to arise. Only one third party—the Republicans—has ever replaced a major party. However, third parties have contributed to American politics by raising controversial issues that the major parties have tried to ignore or avoid.

Both major parties are broad coalitions of regional and interest groups. This variety of membership and the general moderation of the electorate mean that both parties must seek to control the middle ground of American politics. This tends to blur the differences between the parties.

Though formally a national organization, each party is actually a loose coalition of state and local units organized to control elective offices. This decentralization reflects the federal structure of American government. Political parties have been weakened by the primary elections system, which takes the nominating process away from the party organization. Special interests have grown in power and have taken over many party functions.

Chapter 11 Review

Using Vocabulary

Answer the questions by using the meaning of each underlined term.

1. What role does patronage play in the development of a political machine?
2. What part in a political campaign would a dark horse, a front runner, an underdog, and a shoo-in have?
3. How might the rank-and-file of a political party view the standard bearer's choice of a hawk for a running mate?
4. How might a fat cat influence a party's political platform?
5. What role might a splinter group play in the formation of a multi-party system?
6. Why can the two-party system in the United States be described as a coalition of party regulars and party purists?
7. How does proportional representation influence the outcome of a national convention?

Understanding American Government

1. What are the six basic functions of political parties?
2. How did the campaign of 1896 realign political patterns of support in the United States?
3. What basic values provide a fundamental political consensus in the United States?
4. Explain why elections are won or lost on the middle ground of American politics.
5. In what ways are the Democrats described as the liberal party?
6. In what ways are the Republicans described as the conservative party?
7. What important functions do minor parties perform in American politics?
8. How has the primary system weakened party organization?

Extending Your Skills: Generalizing from Data

Study the chart on page 281. Then complete each generalization.

1. Between 1860 and 1932, the Presidency was dominated by the (a) Democratic party; (b) Republican party; (c) Whig party.
2. Since 1952 the control of the Presidency has (a) been dominated by the Democratic party; (b) been dominated by the Republican party; (c) shifted between the two major parties.
3. Since 1796 two major parties have controlled the Presidency. During certain periods, however, (a) one party has dominated the Presidency; (b) a third party has controlled the Presidency; (c) the party in power has always won the Presidency by a large electoral majority.

Government and You

1. The development of political parties in the United States has been affected by such important historical events as the struggle over the meaning of the Constitution, the Civil War, and the Great Depression. Which historical event do you think has had the greatest effect on political parties? What effect did this event have?
2. What replaced sectional divisions of Republican North and Democratic South in the 1930's? How would you divide the country politically today?
3. Most Americans describe themselves as political moderates. Why do you think this is so? Does this tendency make the United States resist political change?
4. Some observers say that our major political parties are in decline. Do you agree? What are the reasons for your answer? How would such a decline affect American politics?

Activities

1. Prepare a report on one of the third parties that seeks power today or sought power in the past.
2. Make a wall chart showing the history of the major political parties. Include the Whigs and major factions such as the Populists. The chart should serve as a family tree for the parties.
3. Prepare a biographical report on Franklin D. Roosevelt. Include a description of the New Deal. Tell what impact New Deal programs have on our lives today.

The Electoral Process: Nominations, Campaigns, and Elections

The election is a solemn periodical appeal to the nation to review its condition, the way in which its business has been carried on, the conduct of the two great parties. It stirs and rouses the nation as nothing else does, forces everyone not merely to think about public affairs but to decide how he judges the parties. It is a direct expression of the will of millions of voters, a force before which everything must bow. It refreshes the sense of national duty; and at great crises it intensifies national patriotism.

JAMES VISCOUNT BRYCE

CHAPTER OVERVIEW

Presidential candidate Walter Mondale and Vice-Presidential candidate Geraldine Ferraro acknowledge delegates' cheers after accepting their nominations to the 1984 Democratic ticket.

1 NOMINATIONS

Elections are the heartbeat of democratic government, the means by which the people choose public officials and hold government accountable. An election is a celebration of democracy, a confirmation of self-government as well as a vote of confidence in representative government. As important as Election Day is, however, it is just the final solidifying link of a long and complicated chain of events known as the ***electoral process.*** This process consists of three elements: nominations, campaigns, and elections.

Most important elected officials—including the President, members of Congress, governors, and state legislators—are chosen in partisan elections. In the ***nominating process*** each political party chooses its candidates for public office from among many contenders—each of whom belongs to the party. On Election Day the voters are offered a choice from among candidates representing various political parties.

Caucus

Parties originally selected their candidates by caucus—that is, in closed meetings of party leaders. In the early years of the Republic, the members of each party in Congress met separately as a caucus to select their party's Presidential candidate. Candidates for state offices were chosen by caucuses composed of party members in the state legislatures.

In the 1820's the caucus as a nominating device began to fall into disfavor. It was criticized as being secretive, unrepresentative, and easily dominated by small cliques. Furthermore, by permitting members of the legislature to nominate candidates for the executive branch, it violated the constitutional separation of powers. Denied the Democratic nomination in 1824, Andrew Jackson set out to dethrone "King Caucus." Four years later Jackson was nominated for President by a state convention of Tennessee Democrats. His election hastened the end of the caucus system. During the 1830's the legislative caucus was replaced at both national and state levels by nominating conventions.

Conventions

The first national nominating convention was held by the tiny Anti-Mason party in 1831. The following year the two major parties, the Democrats and the National Republicans, held conventions to select their Presidential candidates.

The convention rapidly became the standard method for selecting state and national candidates. The system was popular because it seemed more democratic than the party caucus. Typically, party members met at local levels to choose delegates to the state convention. The state party convention nominated candidates for state offices and also named the delegates to the national convention. This system offered an opportunity for rank-and-file party workers to participate in the selection of delegates. However, the delegates themselves were almost always party leaders and others most active in the party organization.

During the late nineteenth century, with the rise of political machines, the convention system increasingly came to be dominated by party bosses. Local party meetings were called without prior notice and packed with people loyal to the organization. Delegates to the county, state, and national conventions were in the pockets of a few party leaders. The actual selection of candidates was made by these leaders off the floor of the convention in smoke-filled rooms. There, convention leaders bargained and compromised, traded votes and made deals. The end product was a slate of party candidates chosen on the basis of wide voter appeal and its willingness to work with the machine.

After the turn of the century progressive reformers called for greater public participation in the nominating process. They sought to take control away from the bosses and place it in the hands of the people. Rather than change convention rules, the reformers introduced the direct primary.

Direct Primaries

A ***direct primary*** is an election within the party in which voters select the party's candidates for the general election. Today each party uses the national convention for selecting its Presidential and Vice-Presidential candidates. But beginning with Wisconsin in 1903, all states have adopted some form of direct primary for choosing candidates for Congress and state offices. There is considerable variation in law from state to state, and a few states still nominate candidates for some offices at conventions or use a combination of primary and convention.

The direct primary is a party activity, but because it is a vital part of the electoral process, it is regulated by state law. The state normally provides the ballots, and it officially supervises conduct of the primary election. The primary is held some time before the November general election—usually in late spring.

An editorial cartoon of the early 1900's attacks political bosses. What techniques did political bosses use to maintain control of the political machine?

Any person legally qualified for the office can run. To get on the primary ballot, a candidate must file a petition signed by a required number of voters, as set by state law.

There are two basic types of direct primary: closed and open. Thirty-eight states have ***closed primaries,*** permitting only declared members of the party to vote. In other words, only Republicans may vote in the Republican primary and only Democrats may vote in the Democratic primary. In most states voters are required to declare their party affiliation at the time of voter registration. In other states voters may declare themselves at the time of the primary. If challenged, they must pledge to support the party's candidate in the general election. The closed primary seeks to discourage the ***crossover vote*** in which members of one party vote in the other party's primary. Crossover "raids" are made in hopes of nominating a weak opponent or defeating a particularly undesirable candidate before the general election.

Twelve states have ***open primaries.*** Voters in an open primary do not have to make a public declaration of party affiliation. All qualified voters, including Independents, may participate, and the choice of party is made in the privacy of the voting booth. Each voter, however, may choose among the candidates of only one party.

Two states, Alaska and Washington, have what is known as a ***blanket*** or ***wide-open primary.*** Candidates for the same office are grouped together on the ballot without regard to party. Voters may choose one for each office, and they may cross party lines, voting Republican for one office, Democratic for another.

In most states the candidate in the primary with a ***plurality***—the largest number of votes—wins the nomination. The vote may be split among a number of candidates, and frequently the winner has less than a majority. Some states, primarily in the South, provide for a ***runoff election*** if no candidate receives a majority of votes in the primary. This is a second primary between the two candidates with the most votes. For almost one hundred years after Reconstruction, the Democratic party was dominant in the South. Because the party nominee faced no real opposition in the November election, victory in the Democratic primary usually was a guarantee of election. The runoff primary was introduced to ensure that the winner had a majority.

The direct primary was intended as a reform to give the people a greater voice in selecting party candidates. But despite the importance of primaries, voter turnout has generally been low. People who vote in primaries have tended to be older, richer, and better educated. They are more politically aware and usually more ideological in orientation than the general electorate. In short, they are not representative of the people as a whole. Low turnout in primaries gives a special advantage to activists who rally

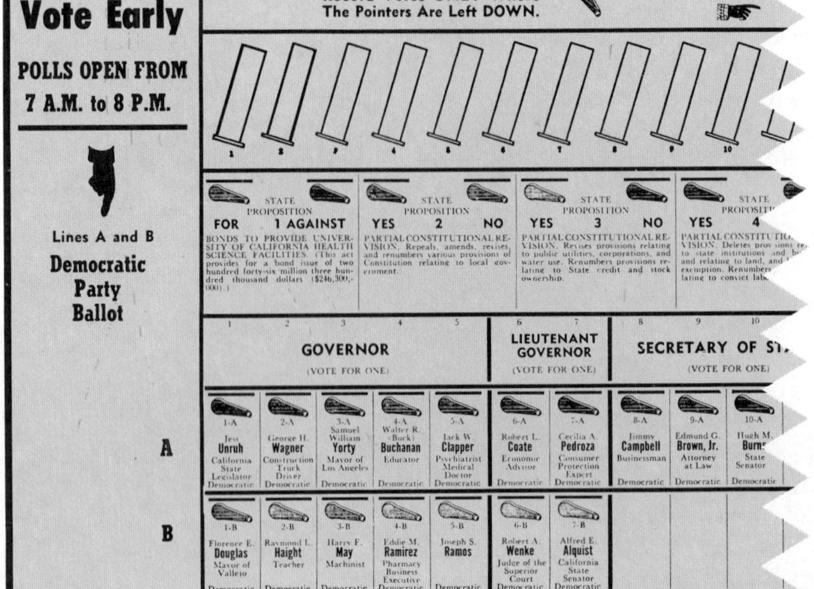

This sample ballot is similar to ballots found in voting machines, which were common until the 1970's. Today, cards that voters punch with a stylus and that computers tabulate are replacing voting machines throughout the United States.

The Reverend Jesse Jackson (left) speaks in Philadelphia and Senator Gary Hart (right) greets supporters in Mobile, Alabama, as each candidate campaigns in the 1984 Democratic Presidential primaries. What are three criticisms of primaries?

behind a particular candidate or who pursue commitment to a single issue.

Most political scientists believe that primaries have contributed to the decline of party organization. In contesting the primary, candidates must build their own campaign organizations and raise their own funds. The party remains neutral until the nominee is selected. Party leaders have little control over nominations, and the nominees owe little to the party or to each other. After the primary it is usually the candidate's personal organization—not the party—that runs the campaign. Primaries thus tend to fragment political parties and to deepen the divisions within them.

Primaries also increase the cost of running for public office. Primary campaigns are enormously expensive and personally exhausting. They require personal appearances, direct mailings, and media (especially television) advertising. Defeated candidates and their supporters may be too tired, bitter, or disappointed to support their party's nominee. And even the winners have won only the right to begin again: they still face the grueling campaign for the election itself.

Petition and Self-Announcement

In addition to conventions and primaries, two other methods are commonly used to nominate candidates for public office. They are petition and self-announcement.

Nomination by petition is generally used in local, nonpartisan elections. In order to get their names on the ballot, candidates must submit petitions signed by a certain number of voters registered in the district. The petition method is also used in many states and voting districts to nominate Independent and minor-party candidates in partisan elections.

Nomination by self-announcement is just what the term implies. A candidate merely states that he or she wishes to run in a general election without participating in a party primary. Self-announced candidates may in some cases win a place on the ballot through petitioning or by law; if not, voters may still write in the candidate's name on the election ballot.

Section Check

1. What process was used by political parties in the early 1800's for nominating political candidates?
2. How is a direct primary different from a nominating convention?
3. Which primary system—open or closed—is preferred by most states?
4. What kind of voter usually votes in primary elections?

2 NOMINATING THE PRESIDENT

Of all candidates for public office, those running for President of the United States face the greatest challenge. The American Presidency is the most powerful office in the world. It is the focal point of American government and politics. For this reason, and because the race for the White House is the most interesting and complex event in American politics, the electoral process emphasizing the nomination, campaign, and election of the President is discussed in this chapter.

Republican and Democratic candidates for President and Vice President are chosen by national party convention. But the most important part of the nominating process occurs in the selection of delegates to the convention.

The Selection of Delegates

The Republican and Democratic national conventions are held every four years in July or August. Delegates from the 50 states, the District of Columbia, Guam, Puerto Rico, and the Virgin Islands gather to nominate their candidates for President and Vice President.

The two parties use similar principles in determining the number of delegates to which each state is entitled. Each uses population as the basis for delegate allocation, with bonus delegates awarded for past party support. In 1984 the Republicans gave extra delegates to states that had voted Republican in the previous Presidential election and to those which had elected Republican governors, senators, and representatives. The Democrats alloted bonus delegates according to the number of Democratic votes cast in each state. The actual number of delegates has varied from year to year.

The process of delegate selection is spread over six months. State law determines when and how delegates are selected. Two basic methods are employed: state conventions and Presidential primaries. A few states use a combination of the two methods in delegate selection.

State Conventions At one time the state convention was the most widely used method of selecting delegates to the national party conventions. Today

John F. Kennedy campaigns for the Democratic nomination in the 1960 West Virginia primary election. His primary-election victory in overwhelmingly Protestant West Virginia proved that Kennedy—a Roman Catholic—could win the votes of non-Catholics.

Candidates for the 1984 Democratic Presidential nomination engage in a televised debate before the New Hampshire primary. Seated, left to right, are Senators John Glenn (Ohio), Alan Cranston (California), and Ernest Hollings (South Carolina); former Senator George McGovern (South Dakota); Senator Gary Hart (Colorado); former Vice President Walter Mondale; the Reverend Jesse Jackson; and former Governor of Florida Reubin Askew.

only about 25 percent of all delegates are chosen by convention. The method begins at the local precinct level, where a caucus open to all party members chooses delegates to the county convention. The county convention in turn picks delegates to the state convention, where finally the national delegates are chosen. The foundation of this multilevel system is the precinct caucus. If only a few people attend, these neighborhood meetings are easily dominated by party organization regulars or those out in support of a particular candidate. To encourage greater participation, recent party reforms now require proper advance notice of precinct meetings. By 1980 participation in the Iowa caucuses had risen so much that they became the functional equivalent of a primary.

Until 1972 the Democratic party permitted state delegations to operate under the ***unit rule.*** This was a winner-take-all system in which all delegates were bound to support the candidate favored by the majority. Beginning what was to become a wave of party reform, the 1968 Democratic National Convention abolished the unit rule. The new rules require that at every level, from the precinct on up, delegates be selected in proportion to the support given to each candidate. Thus, at each stage of the nominating process—precinct caucus, county convention, or state convention—each candidate may win as many delegates as are proportional to the amount of his or her support.

Presidential Primaries In Presidential primaries the voters directly elect delegates to the national party conventions. In 1984, 27 states, the District of Columbia, and Puerto Rico, selected delegates by primary. The percentage of convention delegates chosen by Presidential primary climbed rapidly from about 40 percent in 1968 to more than 70 percent in 1984.

Presidential primaries are conducted according to the law of each state. In some states the primary ballot simply presents the voter with a choice among candidates for nomination. In others only the names of the candidate's convention delegates appear. A few states combine the two procedures, requiring the voter both to indicate a preference among candidates and to vote for the candidate's delegates.

As more and more states adopted the Presidential primary, the Democratic and Republican parties each set out to reform the procedure in delegate selection. The Democrats were the most ambitious, and their reforms were the most extensive in the party's history.

The Democratic National Convention appointed commissions in 1968 and in 1972 to develop guidelines for the state parties on delegate selection. Under the rules adopted for the 1976 convention, each state was to take ***affirmative action*** to encourage greater participation by minorities, women, and traditionally underrepresented groups in delegate selection and in all party affairs.

A further change in the Democratic rules barred the "winner-take-all" primary, which gave the candidate with a plurality of the vote all of the state's delegates to the national convention. The rules now require that if a state uses the Presidential primary, delegates are to be selected in proportion to the primary vote received by each candidate. To qualify for a share of the delegates, a candidate must receive at least 15 percent of the primary vote. The cutoff was designed to eliminate marginal candidates and to narrow the race to the leading contenders for the nomination. Recent Democratic party reforms no longer require the delegates to vote for the Presidential candidate they were elected to support on the first ballot taken at the national convention.

Republican party reforms also sought to expand representation of women and minorities in the national convention. The Republicans have not attempted to regulate delegate selection as extensively as have the Democrats, nor have they eliminated the "winner-take-all" primary still used in a few states. But, like the Democrats, Republican delegates are no longer pledged to particular candidates for whom they must vote on the first ballot.

The Nominating Campaign

In order to gain the party nomination, a Presidential candidate must be able to win a majority of the delegate votes at the national convention. If a candidate wins a majority of delegates through the primaries and state conventions, the party's choice is determined before the gavel ever falls to open the national convention. For this reason much of the struggle that once took place during the convention now occurs in the preconvention period of the nominating campaign.

The formal process of delegate selection lasts about six months. It begins in January of each Presidential election year when Iowa chooses its delegates by the caucus convention method. A few more convention states follow before the first Presidential primary is held in March in New Hampshire. Then, in rapid succession, one state after another holds its convention or primary. The process of delegate selection ends with a crucial round of primaries in early June.

In the months before the New Hampshire primary Presidential hopefuls within each party begin to emerge. ***Trial balloons*** are sent up to test the political wind. Potential candidates watch the public opinion polls to gauge their popularity and chances of winning. Well-known candidates begin with a great advantage, and a major elective political office has

1984 NATIONAL CONVENTION DELEGATES

	Democratic	Republican
Women	50%	44%
Blacks	18%	4%
Hispanics	6%	4%
Protestant	49%	71%
Catholic	29%	22%
Jewish	8%	2%
Liberal	48%	1%
Moderate	42%	35%
Conservative	4%	60%
Average age	43	51
Number of governors	28	13
Number of senators	28	29
Number of representatives	182	72

Source: CBS News Delegate Survey, 1984.

The distribution of the various groups that comprised the delegates at the 1984 Democratic and Republican national conventions reflects recent party reforms. How have new party rules affected the representation of minority groups at the national conventions?

ISSUES

A National Presidential Primary

Critics of the long and complicated process of delegate selection have proposed a national Presidential primary to choose each party's candidates. If no candidate emerges with a clear majority, a runoff primary would then be held. Advocates argue that a national primary would be more "democratic." Moreover, they say, it would shorten the exhausting preconvention campaign and conserve the candidate's energy for the election campaign ahead.

But the proposal of a national primary has its critics too. Some argue that a national Presidential primary would favor candidates who are already well-known. Candidates who start out without much national visibility would have to spend an enormous amount of money for television and direct mailings to gain public attention. Another objection is that in virtually removing the party from the nominating process, a primary would further weaken political parties. After the divisive struggle for delegates, the national convention provides the opportunity for the party to reunite around the party nominee.

Another proposal suggests a series of four or five regional primaries to select convention delegates. By grouping adjoining states for a primary held on the same day, it is argued that candidates might better concentrate their campaign efforts.

been the base from which most contenders seek the nomination. A prominent governor, senator, or the Vice President is likely to be among the leading candidates. For a President who seeks another term in office, nomination traditionally has been assured. But revolts within the party can occur, as witnessed in the challenges to President Ford by Ronald Reagan in 1976 and to President Carter by Edward Kennedy in 1980. Both incumbents won renomination, but not without struggles, and neither won reelection.

The problem for less well-known candidates is gaining public attention. The media plays a critical role in the early stages, and television is especially important. The drawn-out series of primary elections may be grueling, but it also provides an opportunity for little-known candidates to gain visibility and to prove themselves. In a small state such as New Hampshire the candidate does not need a large campaign budget. A good showing will draw ***media coverage,*** supporters, and money. The candidate then can move on to the larger primaries with added strength.

With three quarters of the delegates now selected by Presidential primary, serious contenders must go into the primaries. Here the element of strategy is crucial. The candidates must decide which of the primaries they will enter. Limits of time and money mean that most candidates will concentrate their energy in selected states. A number of factors go into choosing which primaries to enter. Most candidates feel that they must enter the first primary in New Hampshire. Although only a few delegates are at stake, the primary provides the first opportunity to test popular sentiment. The results of the early primaries can shape the course of the campaign for nomination. Candidates who do poorly are likely to withdraw, narrowing the field in the later primaries. A substantial or unexpected victory can produce a ***bandwagon effect,*** as more and more people rally in support of the winner.

Another factor affecting the candidates' choice of which primaries to enter is delegate strength. The large primaries, such as California's, are generally considered a must for serious contenders. Candidates also enter primaries with an eye on demonstrating their strength among various sections of the population. They thus seek to contest primaries in different parts of the country and in states with different characteristics. In 1960, John Kennedy staked his campaign on the West Virginia primary in order to prove that a Catholic could carry an overwhelmingly Protestant state. Candidates generally try to avoid primaries that they think they will lose. But a number of states now have laws that automatically place recognized candidates on the ballot. If this trend continues, candidates for the nomination will have less choice about the primaries they enter.

The National Conventions

The national conventions are held in July or August of Presidential election years. The site is selected by each party's national committee from among those cities bidding for the opportunity to host the convention. The city's physical facilities—a large convention hall, sufficient hotel space, security, and convenient transportation—are of prime consideration. Political factors also weigh in the party's choice. Convention cities are usually in large states where there is close two-party competition. By holding the convention in such a state, the party hopes to gain interest and support among local voters.

Before the convention opens, the rival candidates set up their headquarters in hotels around the city. Television crews and press reporters converge on the city to cover the convention. In the hall itself miles of television cable are laid, and hundreds of telephones are installed.

The convention usually lasts four days. Its atmosphere is a mixture of carnival and serious business, excitement and boredom. Many important decisions already will have been made. The party's Presidential nominee may have been determined in the primaries and state conventions. Even during the convention many major decisions are made "off the floor"—out of the convention hall, at the candidates' headquarters, or in the delegate caucuses. The candidates usually do not attend the convention. Instead, from their hotel suites, the candidates keep in constant contact with their floor managers in the convention hall. Along with the interested American public, the candidates stay glued to their television sets watching the convention through each day's events.

William Jennings Bryan (standing), a fiery speaker and the youngest Presidential candidate, made more than 600 speeches throughout the United States in 1896. One of them was this speech in New York's Madison Square Garden.

LEGACY

Memorable Keynote Speeches

"The humblest citizen in all the land, when clad in the armor of a righteous cause, is stronger than all the hosts of error," William Jennings Bryan proclaimed from the podium of the 1896 Democratic national convention. Before Bryan delivered what would come to be known as the "Cross of Gold" speech, he was a little-known Congressman from Nebraska. After he finished, he was carried through the hall on the shoulders of several delegates while the entire convention thundered its applause. His words still rang in the convention hall: "You shall not press down upon the brow of labor this crown of thorns. You shall not crucify mankind upon a cross of gold." The following day the convention named 36-year-old William Jennings Bryan the Democratic Presidential nominee.

Bryan's "Cross of Gold" speech is one of the most famous speeches delivered to a national political convention. But other orators have held tremendous power over the emotions and opinions of the nominating delegates. In 1944, for example, Connecticut Congresswoman Clare Booth Luce addressed the Republican party in a speech that brought the delegates to their feet. America was fighting World War II. Blaming the Democrats for getting the nation into the war, Luce asked, "Who is G.I. Jim? Ask rather, who was G.I. Jim . . . Jim was the fellow who lived next door. . . . Jim was, you see, immobilized by enemy gunfire, immobilized for all eternity."

In 1976 a black Congresswoman named Barbara Jordan electrified delegates and captured the spotlight with her keynote address to the Democratic national convention. Jordan told the assembly, "Notwithstanding the past, my presence here is one additional bit of evidence that the American dream need not forever be deferred." She went on to a rousing conclusion in which she quoted Abraham Lincoln. "As I would not be a slave," she declared, "so would I not be a master. This expresses my idea of democracy. Whatever differs from this, to the extent of the difference is no democracy."

On the first day, after the opening ceremonies, the ***credentials committee*** presents its report to the convention. This committee decides which delegates may participate in the convention. In most cases the committee simply certifies, or approves, each state delegation. Sometimes, however, a rival group may charge that the official delegation was improperly selected. When these challenges occur, the credentials committee makes its recommendations to the convention. These are usually accepted without debate, but a dispute over seating a delegation can become a test of the candidates' strength among convention delegates, with rival candidates supporting rival delegations. In a close race for the nomination, the result of a credentials fight may be crucial.

In the evening of the first day the ***keynote speaker*** praises the party in grand oratorical tradition. The keynote speaker is often an up-and-coming politician being given a first chance at national attention. In 1896 the Democrats were so carried away by William Jennings Bryan's "Cross of Gold" speech that the convention nominated the young Nebraskan for President.

On the second day the convention debates and votes on the platform—the statement of principles, policies, and promises upon which the party stands in the campaign. The platform is used to appeal to various groups in hopes of winning their support. Although not binding, it is taken seriously both by the convention and by the candidate. In the week before the convention, the platform committee holds

John W. Davis, a New York lawyer, was nominated after a record 103 ballots at the 1924 Democratic convention. He lost the election to incumbent President Calvin Coolidge.

public hearings. Here representatives of differing interests have the opportunity to present their views. The committee prepares the draft of the platform, with each ***plank,*** or position, hammered out among the party's factions. Every effort is made to unite the party. This often means taking a middle-ground stance, watering down a position, or avoiding an issue altogether. Sometimes, however, a controversial stand is unavoidable. In 1948, for example, most Democrats felt that the party must campaign for the rights of black Americans. Their strong civil rights plank led some southern delegates to abandon the Democrats and form the Southern Democrats (States' Rights) party. Failure to reach a compromise in the committee may lead to a fight on the convention floor over adoption of the platform. This becomes an important test of candidate strength among the delegates. It is usually the strongest candidate who shapes the party platform.

Nominations and balloting ordinarily take place on the third day. In the traditional nominating speech the candidate's name is not mentioned until the very end. The speaker reels off a long list of the candidate's accomplishments and qualifications before introducing "the next President of the United States." The candidate's name is the signal for a boisterous and carefully planned demonstration of support—complete with marching bands, noisemakers, and cheers. Meanwhile, behind the scenes, candidates make last-minute efforts to win over uncommitted delegates and to forge alliances. (Nowadays, most delegates are personally committed to a candidate, and before the first ballot, there is little opportunity for maneuvering).

After all nominating and seconding speeches have been made, the balloting begins. The secretary calls the roll of the states. A complete roll call constitutes one ballot. As each state is called, its chairperson announces the vote within the delegation. Excitement builds as a candidate approaches the majority needed to win. When the "magic number" is reached, the convention becomes a wild victory celebration. As order returns and balloting resumes, delegates begin to switch their votes to the winning candidate. By the end of the ballot, the winner frequently emerges as the "unanimous" choice of the convention.

The party nominee is often determined in the primaries and state conventions before the national convention ever opens. The national convention then acts, in effect, to ratify that choice. In fact, since 1956 the nominees of both parties have been designated on the first ballot.

Under Democratic party reforms, delegates are now based on proportional representation of each candidate's strength. Nearly every state convention and primary now awards delegates to two or more candidates. This reduces the chance of a candidate coming to the convention with a first-ballot victory.

If no candidate is nominated on the first ballot, delegates may switch their support to another candidate. However, delegates usually remain loyal until they are released by the candidate. One candidate may step down in favor of another, urging his or her delegates to shift their vote. It is a period of intense negotiation and bargaining. If none of the leading candidates gives way, a ***deadlock*** among the candidates can result. The delegates may then turn to a ***dark horse,*** a marginal candidate or someone totally unexpected.

The choice of the running mate is traditionally left to the Presidential nominee. Among the most

Dwight D. Eisenhower (right), nominated on the second ballot, acknowledges delegates' cheers at the 1952 Republican convention. Eisenhower is joined by (left to right) Mrs. Pat Nixon, Governor John W. Bricker of Ohio, Mrs. Mamie Eisenhower, Vice-Presidential candidate Richard Nixon, and convention leader Joseph Martin.

important considerations in selecting the Vice Presidential candidate is a ***balanced ticket***. A balanced ticket results by choosing a person whose background is different from that of the Presidential candidate. The balanced ticket is designed to broaden the party's appeal and strengthen its chances of winning the election. Factors typically taken into account are geographic region, ideology, ethnic background, and religion. A conservative Presidential candidate might be balanced with a more liberal running mate, a southerner matched with a northerner, a Protestant teamed with a Catholic. Thus in 1960 John F. Kennedy, a liberal Irish Catholic from Massachusetts, selected Lyndon Johnson, a conservative Protestant from Texas, as his running mate.

In 1980 Ronald Reagan chose George Bush as his running mate. Bush himself had sought the Republican nomination. In selecting Bush, Reagan sought to unite the party for the coming campaign and at the same time to strengthen the ticket with a Vice-Presidential candidate experienced in national government.

In 1984 Democratic nominee Walter Mondale made a historic Vice-Presidential choice. Mondale selected three-term Congresswoman Geraldine Ferraro as his running mate. This choice marked the first time that a woman was nominated for the Vice Presidency by a major party. Ferraro brought a hard-driving campaign style to the ticket.

The balloting for Vice President takes place on the last day of the convention. That night, climaxing the long struggle for the nomination, the party nominees make their acceptance speeches. Joined by their families on the stage, they welcome the cheers of the delegates, whose task is now over. The convention closes as a giant pep rally—the end of the nominating process, the beginning of the Presidential campaign.

Section Check

1. Define: unit rule, trial balloon, bandwagon effect, credentials committee, keynote speaker, plank, deadlock, balanced ticket
2. Identify: National Presidential Primary, "Cross of Gold" speech, Barbara Jordan
3. What factors are considered by each political party in assigning the number of delegates for each state?
4. What are the two methods for selecting delegates to national conventions?
5. What are some factors candidates must consider in deciding which primaries to enter?
6. What are the major events of each day of a national convention?

3 THE PRESIDENTIAL CAMPAIGN

Winning the party nomination is only one step on the long road to the Presidency. The rough-and-tumble battle through the primaries to the national convention is expensive and exhausting. It may also divide the party. The party nominee's first task is to try to reunite the party for the campaign ahead. Traditionally, the losing candidates pledge their support to the winner. Disappointed staff members and activists often find making peace more difficult. The nominee's organization makes a major effort to include these people. Failure to bind party wounds can seriously weaken the campaign from its beginning.

Organization

As soon as the national conventions are over, the nominees go into seclusion with their advisers to plan the strategy of the campaign. During the struggle for the nomination, candidates build their own campaign organizations. It is the nominee's ***personal organization,*** not the party national committee, that now takes chief responsibility for the Presidential campaign.

At the top of the organization is the campaign manager and a small group of aides and advisers. They give overall direction to the campaign and make decisions about campaign strategy. Among the candidate's closest advisers is the person in charge of fund-raising—one of the principal tasks in the campaign. Within the organization there are a press secretary, speech writers, and media specialists who handle television and advertising. On the campaign trail ***advance personnel*** keep ahead of the candidate, preparing the details for each personal appearance.

State and local campaign organizations are set up, as are various citizens' groups representing diverse interests. Among such groups have been Texans for Eisenhower, Viva Kennedy (Mexican-Americans for JFK), and Democrats for Reagan. With so many different groups, as well as the national, state, and local party organizations, the candidate's organization must include skilled ***field managers*** to coordinate campaign efforts.

A successful campaign depends upon thousands of volunteer workers who are willing to stuff envelopes, make telephone calls, and canvass neighborhoods in a house-to-house effort on behalf of the candidate. In addition to this volunteer army the candidates increasingly have turned to professionals to run their campaigns—and this, of course, takes money. Since 1952 Republicans and Democrats have hired professional campaign consultants and firms providing a variety of specialized services. They conduct public opinion surveys, research and develop stands on the issues, help write speeches, handle advertising and public relations, and raise campaign funds.

The candidates depend heavily on public opinion polls. Throughout the course of the campaign the candidates use polls to help them identify issues, judge voter sentiment, and plan strategy. The pollster may become one of the candidate's closest advisers.

Public relations firms first applied their advertising skills to politics in California in the 1930's. Since 1952 they have played a major role in Presidential campaigns. Public relations firms are concerned with "selling" the candidate. These firms coordinate the media campaign. With a television set in practically every American home, the influence of media specialists has grown enormously. However, one must be careful not to exaggerate the influence of public relations firms. They are limited in a number of ways—by campaign spending laws, by the issues, and most importantly by the strengths and weaknesses of the candidates themselves.

Campaign Strategy

Each candidate must make decisions about campaign strategy—about how the campaign will be conducted. Among these decisions are the campaign's image and style; when and how to attack the opposition; which themes and issues to emphasize; which appeals to make to which voting groups; where to campaign; and how much time to spend in each state and city.

Candidate Image How candidates appear to the electorate is of vital importance. All candidates try to project a particular image. Dwight Eisenhower was presented as a benevolent father figure. John F. Kennedy brought "vigor." Jimmy Carter was a "new face" on the political scene in 1976. The Reagan campaign underscored the candidate's experience as governor of the nation's most populated state. While candidates seek to project favorable images of themselves, they may also try to cast their opponents in an unfavorable light. Gerald Ford, for example, described Carter as indecisive: "He wavers, he wanders, he wiggles, he waffles."

A TIPPECANOE PROCESSION.

The expression keep the ball rolling *originated in 1840 with these William Henry Harrison supporters who rolled a ball covered with campaign slogans from town to town to publicize their candidate. Why are campaign slogans helpful?*

Events themselves also serve to shape the voters' image of the candidates. How a candidate responds to a crisis situation, deals with sensitive issues, and handles different groups are all critical factors in the public mind. The campaign is a political tightrope. Candidates are often accused of saying one thing to one group and something else to another. In appealing to the various groups within the electorate, each candidate must be careful not to offend anyone. Yet the candidate must also appear decisive and consistent.

Campaign Theme Most campaigns develop a central theme to give the voters an overall impression of where the candidate stands. Often it is embodied in a simple message or slogan—something easily remembered and repeated. In 1960 John F. Kennedy promised "to get this country moving again." Eight years later, with the issues of crime in the streets and urban disorder haunting the middle class, Richard Nixon appealed to these "forgotten Americans." Following Nixon's Watergate scandals Jimmy Carter ran on a theme of trust and openness. In 1980 and in 1984 Reagan promised to get government "off people's backs and out of their pockets."

The theme is sometimes planned in early strategy sessions, but often it emerges during the course of the campaign. The theme is determined, in part, by whether the candidate's party is in or out of power. The candidate of the out party takes the offensive, attacking the party in the White House for its actions or lack of action. The candidate of the "in" party—often the incumbent President—must defend the accomplishments of the administration. In 1956, for example, President Eisenhower ran for a second term on the theme of "peace and prosperity."

Incumbency A President in office who seeks another term traditionally commands the prestige and power of the White House itself. The incumbent receives a tremendous amount of free publicity, and Presidential actions can be timed for political advantage. But incumbency also carries a disadvantage. The President can be blamed for whatever is wrong in the country—inflation, unemployment, or gas shortages—as President Carter discovered in 1980. The incumbent can even be held responsible for unrest and revolution in other countries. Political analyst Louis Harris writes: "The job of President may now be so complex, and the problems the country faces so difficult, that any future occupant of the White House might find that incumbency is no longer an asset in seeking reelection."

An incumbent who enjoys a high level of national popularity may decide to campaign from the White House. The incumbent may cite the pressing needs

Democrat John F. Kennedy (left) and Republican Richard M. Nixon (right) participate in a televised debate during the 1960 Presidential campaign. Why has television become important to Presidential campaigns?

of the country as a reason for making only a few personal appearances outside of Washington. But an incumbent with a low standing in the polls will be forced onto the campaign trail.

Party Identification In planning the campaign, party identification among most voters is an important consideration. The Democratic candidate, representing the majority party, stresses party label. Democratic campaign strategy gives great attention to "getting out the vote" for a heavy turnout on Election Day.

The Republicans face a very different problem. As the minority party, the Republicans must reach out for the support of Independents and Democrats in order to win. The Republican candidate tends to play down party label, urging people to vote for the best candidate.

Surveys show that about 60 to 65 percent of all voters have already decided how to vote by the end of the national conventions. These voters tend to be the party faithful and are unlikely to switch to the opposition candidate. The campaign acts to reinforce and strengthen their preferences.

The Undecided Identifying with a party is no guarantee that a person will vote for that party's candidate. In recent years party loyalty has weakened, and more and more people split their tickets. These party members, along with Independents, are among the most likely to be undecided as to how they will vote. It is the undecided voters—approximately one third of the electorate—for whom both parties compete. They hold the key to victory, and the campaign is directed primarily toward them.

On the Campaign Trail

Since the national conventions were first televised in 1948, television has played an increasingly important role in Presidential campaigns. Its major impact has come through the Presidential debates.

The first televised debates between Presidential candidates were held in 1960 between John F. Kennedy and Richard Nixon. Kennedy's cool and effective presentations in the debates proved to be a key factor in his election victory. In several Presidential campaigns since Kennedy's 1960 success, televised debates between the incumbent and the challenger have been held. The television networks cover the debates as a news event—thus getting around the provision of the Federal Communications Act that requires equal time for all candidates, even those from the smallest parties. When a challenger outshines the incumbent, as Reagan did in 1980, the campaign often swings in the challenger's favor.

Television enables the candidates to reach a far greater number of people than ever before in history. Nonetheless, personal contact with the voters is still a vital ingredient of the campaign. Speeches and personal appearances fill the candidate's schedule. From early morning until late at night the candidate is on the move, in the push of the crowd, shaking hands and kissing babies. By the end of the day, physically exhausted, a candidate may have given a dozen speeches in as many cities.

The candidates' resources are limited. The candidates must decide how and where time and money are to be spent. They must pace themselves carefully through the long months of campaigning, building up to the last two weeks of intense activity before the election. Most candidates concentrate their energies in the heavily populated, closely contested states of California, New York, Texas, Pennsylvania, Illinois, Ohio, Michigan, and Florida.

Campaign Finance

Candidates and their organizations spend tremendous amounts on advertising, travel, direct mailings, and telephoning. Even the old-style door-to-door canvassing, done by volunteers, requires large outlays for pamphlets and bumper stickers. In 1980 candidates at all levels spent a record $800 million, up 60 percent from four years before. Television accounted for much of the cost increase. Another major factor was the rising expense of professional polling and public relations services. As costs have gone up, campaign finance has become a matter of growing concern. When so much money is involved, there is always the danger of abuse.

The role of big contributors—the "fat cats," as they are called—has long been a source of controversy. Perhaps the largest contribution ever made by one person was in 1968, when Chicago insurance executive W. Clement Stone gave $2.8 million for the nomination and election of Richard Nixon. In addition to hefty individual contributions, special interest groups, especially business and labor, pour millions of dollars into campaigns. The adage "He who pays the piper calls the tune" brings a number of questions to mind. Do big contributors receive special consideration from those elected to office? Can wealthy interests dominate the political process?

Still another issue relates to how money is distributed among candidates. Clearly some candidates have more money than others. In 1972, for example, President Nixon spent $61 million dollars in his campaign, compared to $30 million by George McGovern. The high cost of political campaigns may keep some qualified people out of the race altogether.

Controlling Campaign Finance Reform efforts to control abuses in campaign finance go back to the turn of the century. In 1907 Congress enacted a law prohibiting corporations from contributing money to campaigns for national office. The Taft-Hartley Act of 1947 extended the prohibition to labor unions. But these laws were easily evaded. Companies gave bonuses to their executives to be used for contributions in their own names. Labor unions encouraged their members to make voluntary donations to political action committees, with the funds going into campaigns. Federal laws required public disclosure of campaign contributions above a certain amount and imposed limits on

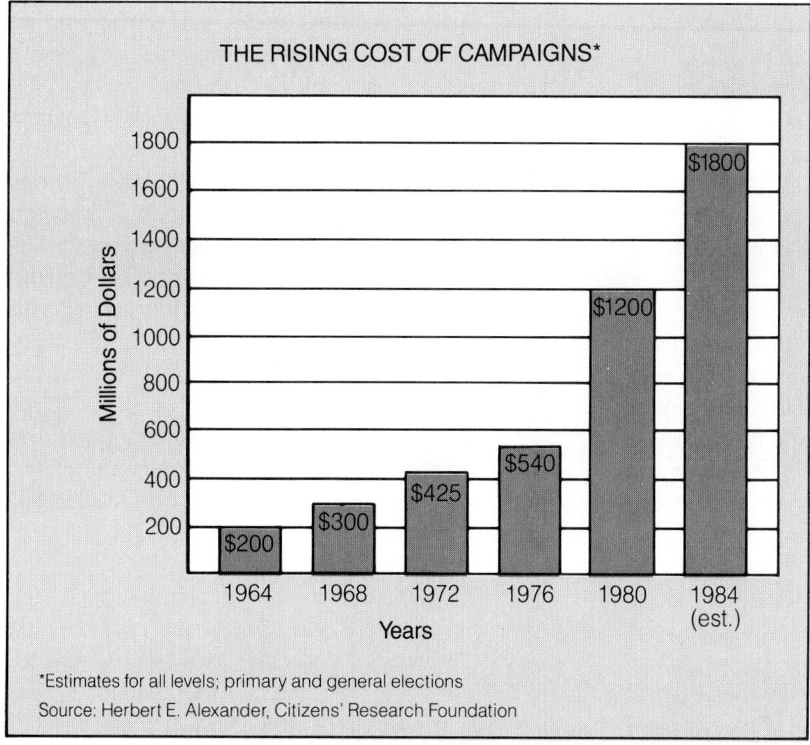

The cost of campaigning for public office continues to rise. Some experts have suggested that all campaign spending be equalized and limited by law before campaigning becomes so costly it allows only the wealthy to run for public office.

Ohio business leader and Republican party chief Mark Hanna (left) directs President William McKinley (right) to disregard the statement attributed to Henry Clay: "I'd rather be right than President." Hanna, nicknamed "Dollar Mark," helped raise more than $2 million for McKinley's reelection in 1900.

individual contributions. Again, these laws were filled with loopholes and easily evaded. In practice, legislation to control campaign finance simply was not very effective.

In the 1970's Congress enacted a series of major reforms for the control of campaign finance. Today, campaign funding is regulated under the Federal Election Campaign Act of 1971 and the amendments of 1974 and 1976.

The passage of the 1971 law had little impact on the following year's campaign. More money was spent in the 1972 Presidential campaign than ever before ($120 million dollars, including the primaries), and financial abuse led to national scandal. At the center of the scandal—exposed only after the election—was the Committee to Reelect the President (CREEP), President Nixon's campaign committee. In the early months of the Nixon campaign CREEP raised an enormous amount of money. Much of this money came in large cash gifts from people who wished to remain unidentified and in illegal contributions from corporations. Some of these unreported funds were used to finance the Watergate break-in and other dirty tricks against the leading Democratic candidates in the primaries and for the cover-up of the national scandal.

In response to the Watergate scandal Congress enacted tough new controls on campaign finance. The Supreme Court, however, held that the portions of the 1974 law which placed limits on campaign spending restricted political speech and were thus unconstitutional. In 1976 Congress revised the Federal Election Campaign Act to bring it in accord with the Court's ruling. The act applies only to Presidential and Congressional elections. It controls the use of money in campaigns in four ways: (1) requires public disclosure of campaign contributions and expenditures; (2) limits campaign contributions; (3) limits campaign expenses; and (4) provides public financing of campaigns.

Public Disclosure Candidates must file periodic reports with the government on campaign finance. The names and addresses of all contributors of more than $100, and all expenditures of more than $100, must be reported. Disclosure is expected to reduce abuse in campaign finance and the influence of big contributors because the public knows who is giving how much to whom.

Limits on Contributions The amount of money any one person or group can donate to a candidate in a Presidential or Congressional election is limited by law. Individuals may give up to $1,000 to each candidate in both the primary and the general election. An individual may contribute up to $5,000 to a political action committee (PAC) set up by an association, corporation, or labor union, and up to $20,000 to a political party. Each person is limited to a total of $25,000 in contributions in any one year. There is no limit, however, on the amount of money a person may spend independently on behalf of a candidate or party. Expenditures of more than $100 must be reported.

Interest groups may contribute up to $5,000 per candidate in both primaries and elections. A similar restriction applies to political action committees. Companies and unions are prohibited from making direct contributions to campaigns, but they are permitted to use their own funds to pay PAC operating expenses. There is no overall limit on the amount of money PAC's can spend. As individual contributions have been sharply restricted, the role of PAC's has increased. PAC contributions to federal election campaigns reached $50 million in 1980. With each successive election PAC contributions have continued to rise rapidly. New proposals have been put forward in Congress to place tighter limits on special interest PAC contributions.

Limits on Spending There are no limits on how much candidates may spend, nor on how much candidates may contribute to their own campaigns. The Supreme Court has held that limits on spending impose an unconstitutional restriction on freedom of speech. There is one important exception: Presidential candidates who accept public financing must abide by spending limits.

Public Financing The Federal Election Campaign Act of 1971 for the first time provided optional public financing for Presidential candidates. The plan is funded by taxpayers who check a box on their income tax form, agreeing to have $1 of their tax payment set aside for this purpose. To qualify for public financing in the primaries, a candidate must first demonstrate broad-based popular support by raising at least $100,000—$5,000 in 20 or more states and in contributions of $250 or less. Under a matching formula, each candidate may receive up to $5 million in public funds for the primary campaign. But in accepting public financing the candidate must agree to a spending limit for the primaries.

For the general election the major party candidates automatically qualify for public financing.* But Presidential candidates who accept public funds cannot accept private contributions. In 1976, when the plan came into operation, both Republican and Democratic candidates opted for public financing. Each received $21.8 million to cover the cost of the campaign. No additional money from private sources could be spent. Because of these limits both parties conducted far more restricted campaigns than they had in 1972, when the Republicans spent $61 million and the Democrats $30 million. In 1984 the Republican and Democratic Presidential candidates could spend (with a few exceptions) only the $40.4 million in public funds each received.

In addition to public funding for the candidates in 1984, each party received $3.2 million to conduct its national convention.

The Federal Election Commission To enforce federal election law and administer the public finance program, the 1974 legislation created the Federal Election Commission. It is an independent, bipartisan commission, composed of both Republicans and Democrats. Its six members are appointed by the President and confirmed by the Senate.

---

*Minor party and independent candidates can also qualify for public financing. To be eligible, the party or candidate must have won at least 5 percent of the popular vote in the last presidential election. Candidates may receive public funds after the election to pay expenses if they received 5 percent of the vote.

Section Check

1. Define: personal organization, advance personnel, field managers
2. Identify: Federal Communications Act, W. Clement Stone, Taft-Hartley Act, PAC, Federal Election Commission
3. What are some ways candidates use public opinion polls?
4. Why does the Democratic party stress party identification more than does the Republican party?

4 ELECTING THE PRESIDENT

The climax of the Presidential campaign is Election Day. Election officials arrive at the polls in the early morning and may spend as long as 24 hours there. Campaign volunteers stage last-minute rallies, run messages, make phone calls and go door-to-door urging party members to vote, drive voters to the polls, babysit for voters, and watch the polls for voting irregularities or for clues about how the vote is going.

When the polls close, local and state officials begin the count. As the results for each precinct come in, the votes are tabulated in a running count for each candidate. The returns come in slowly at first, and it is usually well into the next morning before they are complete.

Election Night Coverage

The election results are collected and reported to the nation through the News Election Service, operated jointly by the three major television networks and the the two major news services, Associated Press and United Press International. In their election night coverage the television networks do more than just report the official returns. Each network has developed a ***vote projection and prediction system*** that names a winner when only a handful of votes are in. The system is based upon a computer analysis of a few selected precincts across the nation. The vote is projected by comparing incoming returns with the results of past elections for each of the sample precincts.

Any projection is subject to error, and the computers have made mistakes in predicting how a particular state will go. The technique, however, is remarkably accurate. On election night 1980, for example, little more than an hour after the polls closed in the East and while millions of people were still voting in the western states, NBC News declared Ronald Reagan the next President of the United States. On the basis of television network projections President Jimmy Carter formally conceded defeat. Because of Carter's concession many Democrats in the western states where the polls had not yet closed did not bother to vote. This in turn led to the defeat of many Democratic candidates for Congress and state offices. Furious politicians demanded that the networks withhold their projections until all the polls across the nation have closed. Whether the networks withhold their predictions in future elections remains to be seen.

The Electoral College

Voters do not directly elect the President. In casting a ballot, the voter is really selecting a slate of electors pledged to a particular candidate. Most voters are probably unaware of this, because in two thirds of the states the names of the electors do not appear on the ballot.

Each state has one electoral vote for each senator and representative. Thus even the smallest state has at least three electoral votes. In addition, the Twenty-third Amendment gives three electoral votes to the District of Columbia. The candidate winning the most popular votes in each state gets all of that state's electoral votes.

About one month after the election the chosen electors meet in the state capitals to cast their ballots. These Presidential electors together constitute the ***electoral college.*** The Presidential electors never meet as a national body. Instead, each state sends its results to Washington, D.C., where the ballots are counted before a joint session of Congress in early January.

There are a total of 538 electoral votes. In order to be elected, a candidate must receive a majority of the electoral votes—270 votes. If no candidate receives the necessary majority of electoral votes, the House of Representatives then chooses the President from among the three candidates with the largest number of electoral votes. Members of the House vote as a delegation, with each state having one vote. If no candidate for Vice President receives a majority of electoral votes, the Senate then chooses between the two leading candidates, with each senator having one vote.

Origin and History The electoral college system was devised as a compromise by the Framers of the Constitution. There was little support among the delegates at the Constitutional Convention for direct popular election of the President. They believed that the people lacked the knowledge and experience to make an informed choice, and that direct election gave an unfair advantage to the more populous states.

At first, most Framers favored the selection of the President by Congress. But this idea was rejected when the large and small states were unable to agree on the manner of voting. The "one state, one vote" proposal put forward by the smaller states was unacceptable to delegates from the larger states. Moreover, selection of the President by Congress violated the principle of the separation of powers to which the delegates were committed.

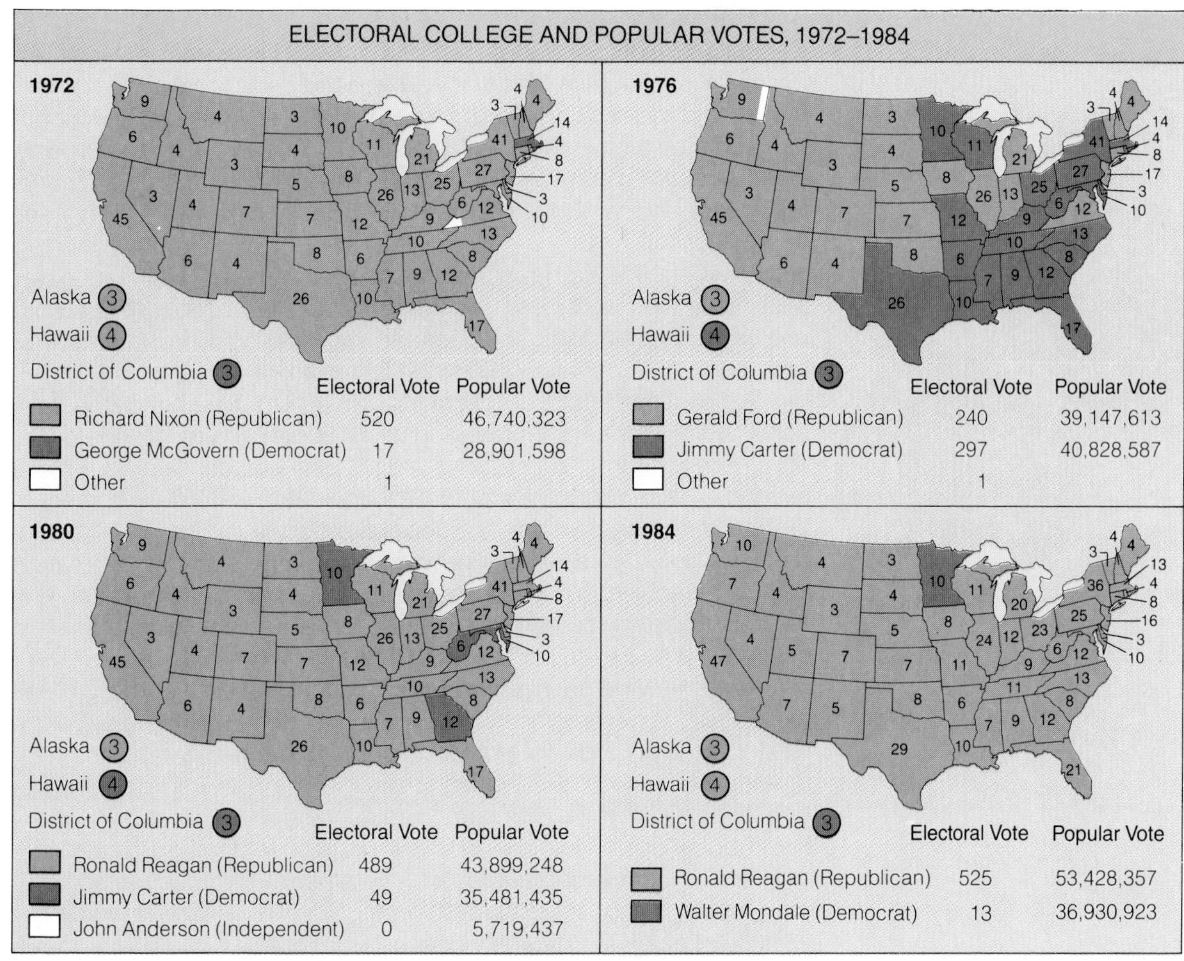

Electoral-vote distribution and popular-vote totals for the major candidates in the four most recent Presidential elections reflect the differences between popular and electoral votes. In 1980, for example, Republican Ronald Reagan received nearly 51 percent of the popular vote and 91 percent of the electoral vote; Democrat Jimmy Carter received 41 percent of the popular vote but only about 9 percent of the electoral vote.

After long debate the Constitutional Convention adopted the electoral college as a compromise. By basing electoral votes on the number of senators and representatives, small states benefited because every state had two senators. On the other hand, large states benefited because representatives were apportioned according to population.

As originally set forth in the Constitution, each elector cast two votes. The candidate receiving a majority of electoral votes would be declared President. The runner-up would be declared Vice President. But the emergence of parties with Presidential and Vice-Presidential candidates created an immediate problem. In the election of 1800 each Democratic-Republican elector cast one ballot for Thomas Jefferson and one for Aaron Burr. It was intended, of course, that Jefferson be elected President and Burr, Vice President. But the result was a tie vote, which threw the election into the House of Representatives. Jefferson ultimately won, but to prevent a similar situation from again occurring, the Twelfth Amendment, adopted in 1804, provides that separate electoral ballots be cast for President and Vice President.

In devising the electoral college, the Framers expected the electors to be the most respected and enlightened citizens in each state. It was assumed that each elector would exercise independent judgment in selecting the most qualified person for the Presidency. The Constitution, however, gives each

(continued on page 316)

PROFILE

Campaign '84

Campaign '84 officially began in February 1983 when former Vice President Walter Mondale announced his candidacy for the Democratic Presidential nomination. By the end of 1983, seven more Democrats had declared their Presidential intentions—Senators John Glenn, Gary Hart, Alan Cranston, and Ernest Hollings; former Senator George McGovern; former Governor of Florida Rubin Askew; and Reverend Jesse Jackson.

President Ronald Reagan announced in January 1984 that he was seeking a second term in the White House. In contrast to the hotly contested Democratic race, Reagan ran unopposed and was thus assured of the Republican Presidential nomination.

The excitement of Campaign '84 came from the eight Democratic contenders. When the primary contests began, Walter Mondale was considered the front runner and John Glenn was considered a close second. The remaining Democratic candidates were dark horses. In the February Iowa caucus—the first contest of the campaign—the candidates worked hard, each hoping to win a large share of Iowa's convention delegates. Mondale predictably captured the largest share of the caucus vote. The surprise of the caucus was Gary Hart's finish in second place. John Glenn finished fifth.

As the New Hampshire primary approached in late February, Hart's candidacy gained momentum and Glenn's began slipping. About a week before the New Hampshire primary, the eight Democratic candidates expressed their political positions in a televised debate. The debate between all the Democratic contenders was a historic first. Gary Hart won an upset victory in the New Hampshire primary, Walter Mondale finished in second place, and the other candidates trailed. Senators Hollings and Cranston and former Governor Askew immediately withdrew because of their low primary-vote totals. By the end of March candidates Glenn and McGovern also ended their campaigns.

Throughout April and May, the three remaining candidates campaigned to win primary elections and caucuses. For the most part, either Mondale or Hart won the contests. Jesse Jackson, however, won victories in the District of Columbia and Louisiana. The strength of Jackson's candidacy and his Rainbow Coalition surprised political analysts. His candidacy greatly increased the turnout of black voters and proved that a black could run as a strong Presidential candidate. As the last primaries approached in early June, the candidacies of Jackson, Hart, and Mondale each gained support.

After the votes of the June primaries were tallied, Mondale claimed the nomination. At a press conference, he declared, "Today, I am pleased to claim victory . . . I am the nominee. I've got the votes." Mondale had won enough delegates to secure the Democratic nomination.

After Walter Mondale won the Democratic party's nomination, he moved boldly to capture the public's attention. For his running mate, Mondale chose Congresswoman Geraldine Ferraro—the first woman nominated for Vice President by a major party. In July, at the Democratic Convention in San Francisco, candidates Mondale and Ferraro formally accepted their party's nominations.

Experts had expected Walter Mondale and Ronald Reagan to win the nominations of their respective political parties. Political analysts, however, have pointed to two events that made Campaign '84 unique in the Republic's election history. First, the candidacy of Jesse Jackson marked the first Presidential campaign by a black to win nationwide support and a significant number of convention delegates. Second, the Vice-Presidential candidacy of Geraldine Ferraro proved to be an election milestone. Her candidacy ended the long-standing tradition that only men are chosen to run for national office by a major party.

Early in the campaign season, Senator John Glenn (far left) appeals to voters during a parade. The Reverend Jesse Jackson (top) meets with voters before the crucial New Hampshire primary. Senator Gary Hart and former Vice-President Walter Mondale (above) debate the issues in Atlanta. President Ronald Reagan (left) speaks to supporters in January 1984 after announcing his decision to seek a second term.

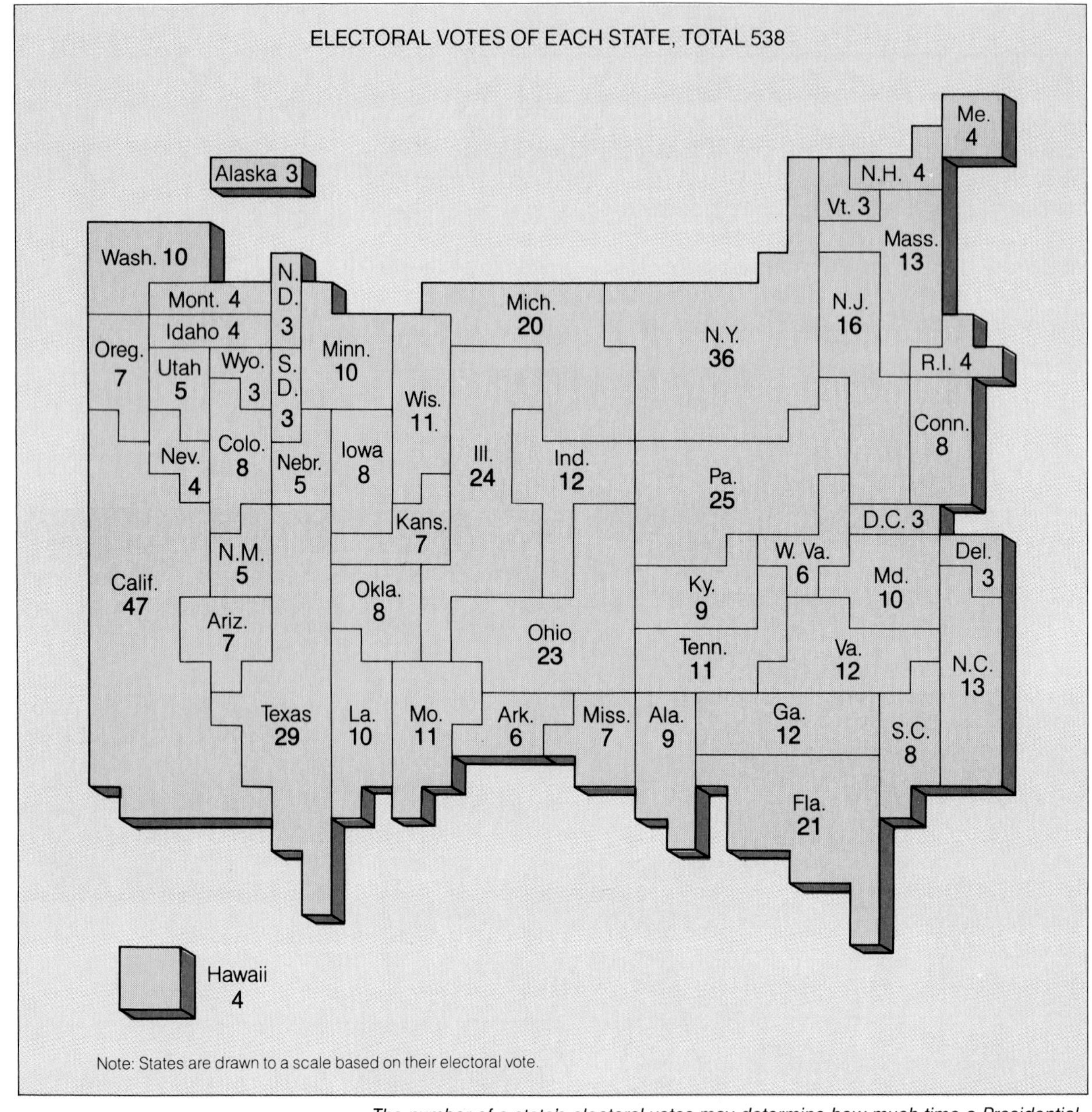

The number of a state's electoral votes may determine how much time a Presidential candidate spends campaigning in that state. How does the electoral college system and the unit rule reinforce the role of federalism in Presidential elections? What is one criticism of the unit rule?

state legislature the power to determine how the electors are to be chosen. By 1804 most states had placed the selection of electors in the hands of the people through popular elections. The electors were pledged to their party's candidates.

The states also adopted the ***unit rule,*** and by 1832 all had done so. Under this system, all of the state's electoral votes go to the candidate receiving the largest number of popular votes. The unit rule enhanced the influence of the states in Presidential elections and served to reinforce federalism.

Criticism of the Electoral College Over the years the electoral college has been harshly criticized. Various proposals for its reform or abolition have been put forward. Four major criticisms are discussed here.

The first focuses on the unit rule—the "winner-take-all" feature of the system. A candidate needs only one vote more than the closest opponent in order to get all of the state's electoral votes. The result has sometimes distorted the will of the people. Three Presidents have been elected with a majority of electoral votes even though they trailed their opponents in popular votes. They are John Quincy Adams in 1824, Rutherford B. Hayes in 1876, and Benjamin Harrison in 1888. It could easily have happened again in 1976. If 9,000 people in Hawaii and Ohio had voted for Ford instead of Carter, the two states would have gone to Ford. Gerald Ford would have won reelection to the Presidency with an electoral vote of 270 to 268, even though Carter would still have led in popular votes.

The second criticism concerns political equality—the principle of "one person, one vote." The unit rule gives the large, populous states a dominant role in Presidential elections. In order to win, candidates tend to concentrate their efforts in the states with the most electoral votes. Moreover, in states where there is close two-party competition, a small group voting as a bloc may command great influence. Its swing one way or the other often determines who gets all of the state's electoral votes.

Campaigns tend to focus on the larger, pivotal states, but the electoral college system is also criticized because voters in the smallest states are overrepresented. Every state, no matter how small, has at least three electoral votes. This gives the individual voters in small states a stronger voice than they would have on the basis of popular votes alone.

The third criticism centers on the role of the electors themselves. The Constitution does not require electors to vote for the candidate to whom they are pledged. In 1976 one elector pledged to Ford voted for Ronald Reagan. Although such "faithlessness" might be cause for alarm, only six electors since 1820, out of a total of more than 16,000, have failed to honor their pledge. None even came close to altering an election.

The fourth criticism arises from the chance of an election being thrown into the House. If no candidate receives a majority of electoral votes, the House of Representatives chooses the President from among the top three candidates, with each state delegation

Two Presidential elections have been determined by the House of Representatives. After 36 ballots, the House chose Thomas Jefferson (left) as President to break the electoral deadlock in 1800. John Quincy Adams (right) was chosen by the House in 1824 when no candidate received the necessary majority of electoral votes.

PRESIDENTIAL ELECTION OF 1800

Candidates	Parties*	Electoral Votes**
T. Jefferson	D–R	73
A. Burr	D–R	73
J. Adams	F	65
C. Pinckney	F	64
J. Jay	F	1

*D–R = Democratic-Republican; F = Federalist
**Electoral votes needed to win election: 70

PRESIDENTIAL ELECTION OF 1824

Candidates	Parties*	Electoral Votes**
J. Q. Adams	D–R	84
A. Jackson	D–R	99
W. Crawford	D–R	41
H. Clay	D–R	37

* D–R = Democratic-Republican
**Electoral votes needed to win election: 131

having a single vote. This has happened only twice—in 1800 and in 1824. But in 1960 a shift of some 9,000 voters in Illinois and Missouri from Kennedy to Nixon would have forced the election into the House of Representatives.

Proposals for Change Various proposals have been made to reform or abolish the electoral college. One plan would allocate electoral votes by Congressional district rather than by state. Another plan would divide a state's electoral votes in proportion to the popular votes received by each candidate. Thus a candidate who received 55 percent of the popular vote would get 55 percent of the electoral vote. But under this plan there is an increased chance that an election might be forced into the House. For this reason recent proposals have focused on the ***direct popular election*** of the President and Vice President.

In 1968 a constitutional amendment was proposed to abolish the electoral college and substitute direct election. According to the proposal, if no candidate received 40 percent of the vote, a runoff election between the two leading candidates would be held. The amendment passed the House of Representatives, 339–70, but failed to win the necessary two-thirds vote for passage in the Senate. Another big push for direct election came in 1979, but Congress again failed to pass the amendment. Why? What reasons are advanced for keeping the electoral college system?

There are three basic arguments for the electoral college. The first is that the electoral college supports the federal system. The blocs of electoral votes give the states an important role in Presidential elections. Second, the electoral college helps to preserve a two-party system and encourage moderation. Because all of the electoral votes go to the winner of each state, third parties have little chance of drawing much support. Most voters feel that they are wasting their vote if they vote for a minor party candidate. Defenders of the electoral college point out that direct election would tend to encourage third parties. They argue that it would allow ideological or single-issue candidates to gather enough votes around the country to force a runoff election, in which their support might be exchanged for political influence. The third argument for keeping the electoral college is simply that the system has served the United States very well. Direct election of the President and Vice President raises unanswered questions and may bring about deep and unforeseen changes in the political system.

Section Check

1. Identify: electoral college, vote projection and prediction system, direct popular election
2. Why were some people upset by television coverage of the 1980 Presidential election?
3. If no candidate for President receives a majority of the electoral votes, how is the President chosen?
4. What are three arguments in favor of retaining the electoral college system?

SUMMARY

The electoral process is composed of three elements: nominations, campaigns, and elections.

In the nominating process each party chooses its candidates for public office from among many contenders. Parties originally selected candidates in caucuses—closed meetings of party leaders. In the 1830's this system was replaced by the convention system. Around 1900 progressive reformers in many states introduced the direct primary, in which the people themselves select the nominees.

Republican and Democratic candidates for President and Vice President are chosen by national party conventions. Delegates to the conventions are selected, according to state laws, by state conventions, by primary election, or by a combination of these two methods. Recent party reforms have increased minority participation and proportional representation in delegate selection. The national convention chooses or ratifies the party's nominees and drafts the party platform.

Political campaigns are very expensive. Recent scandals and undue influence from wealthy contributors have led to strengthening of campaign finance laws. The use of money in campaigns is controlled by public disclosure of campaign contributions and spending, limits on campaign contributions, and public financing of campaigns.

Voters do not directly elect the President; they vote for a slate of electors pledged to a particular candidate. The candidate who receives the most votes in any state wins all that state's electoral votes. To be elected, a candidate must win a majority—270 votes—in the electoral college. Though the electoral college system has been criticized, efforts to replace it with direct election of the President have thus far been unsuccessful.

Chapter 12 Review

Using Vocabulary

Answer the questions by using the meaning of each underlined term.

1. What effect has the closed primary on the crossover vote?
2. When might a candidate send up a trial balloon?
3. What is the role of the credentials committee in a national convention?
4. How does media coverage often contribute to a bandwagon effect in a runoff election?
5. How does the unit rule govern the work of the electoral college?
6. At what stage of the electoral process does a keynote speaker function?
7. Why is it important to have a balanced ticket in a Presidential election?

Understanding American Government

1. What were the main criticisms directed against the caucus method of nominating candidates?
2. Why do most candidates feel that they must enter the New Hampshire primary?
3. In what way is the selection of a Vice Presidential candidate often an attempt to "balance the ticket"?
4. What are the advantages and disadvantages of an incumbent President running for reelection?
5. What factors caused campaign spending to reach record levels?
6. What are the four ways in which the Federal Election Campaign Act controls campaign spending?
7. Why was the electoral college system adopted by the Constitutional Convention?
8. What are the four major criticisms of the electoral college?
9. What three arguments are used to support the electoral college?

Extending Your Skills: Using Election Data

Complete each item as indicated.

1. Examine the electoral-vote map for 1984 on page 313. Find and name the swing states—those with 20 or more electoral votes.
2. Total the votes of the swing states. Compare their total with the 270 votes needed to secure the Presidency.
3. Write a paragraph detailing the strategy you would follow if you were a Presidential candidate in 1988.

Government and You

1. There are two basic types of direct primaries, open and closed. Which type do you prefer? Why? Which type does your state have? What effect does each type have on our two-party system?
2. Some observers have suggested replacing the many state primaries with one national primary. Do you agree? What advantages might such a national primary have? What disadvantages?
3. If you were a candidate for President with limited funds, which primaries would you plan to enter? Are there any primaries you might want to avoid? What are the reasons for your answers?
4. Think of the ways that television has changed our electoral process, listing as many as you can. Which of these is the most important? Has the effect of television been mostly positive or negative?
5. Do you favor keeping the electoral college? Why or why not?

Activities

1. Stage a class debate on the following topic: "*Resolved:* That Americans should nominate Presidential candidates through a national primary rather than a national convention."
2. Prepare a biographical report on Andrew Jackson. Pay special attention to the Presidential campaigns of 1824 and 1828, including Jackson's defeat of "King Caucus."
3. Write a report about the Kennedy-Nixon televised debates of 1960, using information from newspapers and magazines. Include the results of the election and several opinions on the effect of the debates on voters' choices.

Chapter 13

Voting

Nobody will ever deprive the American people of the right to vote except the American people themselves—and the only way they could do that is by not voting.

FRANKLIN D. ROOSEVELT

CHAPTER OVERVIEW

In this 1889 engraving of a Boston polling place, voters receive an Australian, or secret, ballot (right). After marking the ballot in a voting booth (center rear), they deposit it in a ballot box (left), where a poll watcher stands to prevent fraud.

1 SUFFRAGE: THE RIGHT TO VOTE

The right to vote is fundamental to government in a republic. It is through the vote that government is held accountable to the people. But who are "the people" who pass judgment at the polls? In an ideal government every citizen would participate equally in public affairs and decision making. In the United States today almost every adult citizen has the right to vote. The ***electorate,*** those eligible to vote, numbers over 160 million people. Yet in each election many people do not vote. Even in Presidential elections, barely half the electorate actually votes. Clearly the democratic ideal of the participant citizen is not met by reality. What accounts for this relatively low turnout for elections? Who votes and who does not?

The Expansion of Suffrage

Throughout most of our history less than half the nation's adults have been eligible to vote. The Constitution originally left each state free to determine who was entitled to vote. Qualification requirements varied from state to state. ***Suffrage,*** the right to vote, was generally restricted to adult white males who owned a certain amount of property. In some states fewer than 10 percent of the adults could vote. By the middle of the nineteenth century most states had abolished property qualifications. However, three major groups, blacks, women, and Native Americans were still denied the right to vote.

The Fifteenth Amendment, adopted in 1870, extended suffrage to black males. But by the 1890's measures such as the poll tax and the "white primary" were used to disenfranchise black males. Only after passage of the Voting Rights Act of 1965 was the promise of the Fifteenth Amendment secured for blacks of both sexes in the North and the South.

Voting rights for women came only after a century of struggle. Wyoming was the first state to give full voting rights to women, granting suffrage in 1869 when it was still a territory. During the next 50 years a strong women's suffrage movement won the vote in more than half the states. Finally, in 1920, passage of the Nineteenth Amendment extended women's voting rights to all elections.

The electorate was further expanded in 1924, when Native Americans gained the right to vote, and in 1961, when the Twenty-third Amendment gave District of Columbia voters the right to participate in Presidential elections.

The most recent extension of suffrage came in 1971, when the minimum voting age was lowered from 21 to 18. For many years Georgia had been the only state to permit young people between 18 and 21 years of age to vote. In the late 1960's, during the war in Vietnam, some states began to lower their

Like women in other states, these New Yorkers cast their first Presidential ballots in 1920. More than 9 million women—37 percent of the total number of voters and 43 percent of the women eligible to vote—cast ballots in the 1920 Presidential election.

voting age requirements. Most people then agreed that anyone old enough to be drafted into military service was old enough to vote. In 1971 Congress passed the Twenty-sixth Amendment, which was quickly ratified by the states. The voting age was lowered to 18 for all elections, and more than 10 million young voters were added to the electorate in the United States.

Voter Qualifications

In order to vote, each person must meet certain minimum qualifications set by the states. All 50 states require a voter to be a citizen, to be 18 years of age, and to have maintained residence within the state for a certain length of time. Forty-nine states also require registration.

Citizenship, Age, and Residence During the nineteenth century a number of states permitted aliens to vote if they had applied for citizenship. These states, mostly in the West, were eager to attract new settlers. Today only citizens may vote.

Each state sets a minimum voting age. The Twenty-sixth Amendment states that no citizen 18 years of age or older can be denied the right to vote on account of age. A state is free to lower the voting age if it chooses, but today all states follow the 18-years-of-age requirement.

To be qualified to vote, a person must live in the state for a specific period of time. The residence requirement was instituted to prevent voters from outside a state being brought in to influence an election and to ensure that voters were acquainted with local issues and candidates.

At one time the states had lengthy residence requirements. Most required one year's residence in the state, 90 days in the county, and 30 days in the local precinct. As Americans became increasingly mobile, moving from one state or community to another, residence requirements temporarily disenfranchised millions of people. In the Voting Rights Act of 1970 Congress set a 30-day residence requirement to vote in Presidential elections. In 1972 the Supreme Court ruled that lengthy residence requirements for state elections interfered with the right to travel. Today about half the states follow the Court's suggestion of a 30-day residence requirement. Other states vary in the requirement, but the Court has held that it may be no longer than 50 days.

LEGACY

The Polling Place

The highest ideals of democracy become reality in the most commonplace settings: a firehouse, a public school, a private home, even the lobby of a large hotel—any place where Americans gather to vote. According to election codes, the location of a polling place must be convenient to all voters in a precinct. Usually the number of voters assigned to a single polling place is kept small—no more than a thousand—to prevent crowding. Polling places may not be located in a place where alcoholic beverages are sold. To protect individual voters from undue pressure while voting, most state election codes also prohibit the distribution of campaign literature within a prescribed distance of the polling place, usually 100 feet (30 meters).

Election Day is a legal holiday in 18 states. In 30 states election codes guarantee all workers a certain amount of paid time off in which to vote. So important is voting in our democracy that almost all election codes protect a voter from arrest on the way to the polls except for the most serious crimes. Special regulations also provide for the assistance of handicapped voters at the polling place. Some state codes specify that only officials at the polling place can provide help. Other states allow handicapped voters to select people to assist them. To protect the handicapped voter from pressure, some states require the presence of two officials—one from each of the main parties—during voting.

Registration In most nations citizens are automatically entered on to the electoral roles. In every state except North Dakota a person must first register in order to be able to vote. When they register, potential voters are required to give their age, place of residence, and proof of citizenship. Voter registration was introduced in the late nineteenth century in order to prevent fraud. Without registration a person might cast a vote at several different polling places. Registration also sought to prevent voting by noncitizens.

Because of concern about low voter turnout, registration has been simplified in recent years. In many states and cities voter registration booths are set up in shopping centers, banks, and schools. A number of states permit registration by mail.

Several states still have a system of periodic registration. Under this system people must reregister every few years in order to remain qualified voters. Most states, however, now use a system of permanent registration. The details vary from state to state, but the basic procedure is similar. Once registered, voters are kept on the state's electoral rolls unless they move or do not vote within a certain period of time.

A New York City resident hands naturalization papers to voter registration officials in 1884. What does voter registration help prevent?

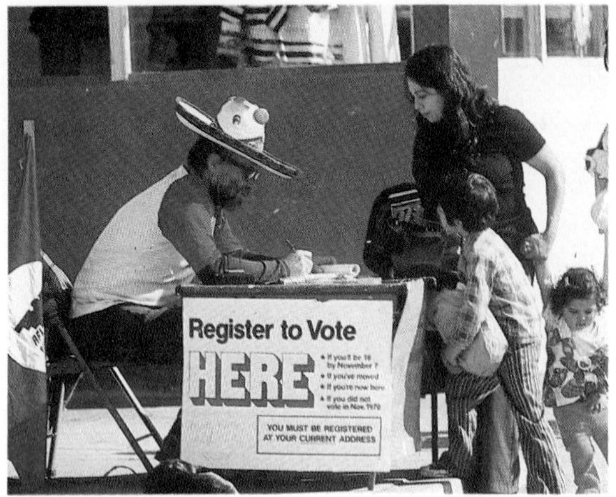

Making registration more convenient has increased the number of registered voters in recent years, particularly among minorities.

Various proposals have been put forward for a system of national registration. Many political leaders favor a national registration system similar to the election-day registration used in Minnesota and Wisconsin. Advocates of such a national registration system claim that it could increase voter turnout by as much as 10 percent. Opponents stress the increased possibility of fraud. Any proposal for national registration is likely to provoke some controversy, if only in terms of federalism, because the Constitution reserves to the states the power to determine voter eligibility.

Ineligibility Each state holds certain classes of people ineligible to vote. Those barred from voting usually include inmates of mental institutions, persons judged to be mentally incompetent, and those convicted of serious crimes.

Section Check

1. Explain how suffrage was extended to blacks, women, and Native Americans.
2. What argument was made for lowering the voting age to 18?
3. Why did the states and later the Supreme Court lower residency requirements for voters?
4. What is the purpose of voter registration? What is periodic registration?
5. What arguments are made for a system of national voter registration?

2 HOW ELECTIONS ARE CONDUCTED

More elections are held in the United States than in any other nation in the world. More than 500,000 public officials—from the President to members of local school boards—are elected. The Constitution gives the state legislatures the power to regulate the time, place, and manner of holding elections. Congress retains the power to alter state regulations that affect Congressional and Presidential elections. This overlapping authority has resulted in a complicated pattern of federal and state election laws.

When Elections Are Held

Congressional elections are held every two years in even-numbered years. The date set by Congress is the Tuesday following the first Monday in November. Presidential elections, held on the same day, take place every four years in even-numbered years. Thus, Election Day for 1984 was November 6. In 1988 it will fall on November 8.

Most states hold elections for state offices at the same time as national elections although a few states elect their officials in odd-numbered years. Local elections are held at various times throughout the year. In addition to regularly scheduled elections of public officials, other elections are held from time to time to place issues before the voters. The people may be asked to vote on an amendment to the state constitution or a proposal for the construction of a city convention center. The large number of different elections contributes to voter confusion and may account for low voter turnout in many elections.

The Polling Place

According to state law, each city or county is divided into voting districts called ***precincts.*** Voters register in their home precinct and must vote where they are registered. The election is conducted at a designated polling place. The polls are open for 12 hours, typically from 7 o'clock in the morning until 7 o'clock in the evening. Voters may come at any time, usually with only a short wait in line.

Local election officers supervise the polling place. They check to ensure that each voter is registered and that there are no irregularities in voting. In addition each political party may assign ***poll watchers*** to make sure that the election is conducted fairly. When the polls close, the votes are counted and the precinct results are officially reported.

Voting Procedures

Fairness and honesty are basic ingredients in democratic elections. One of the most important requirements is that the voters are able to make their choice without pressure or fear. To ensure free elections, the ***secret ballot*** was introduced in the nineteenth century. Under this system printed ballots listing the names of all candidates are prepared at public expense. At the polling place on Election Day each qualified voter receives one ballot and marks his or her choices on the ballot in secret.

The Ballot

How the names of the candidates are listed on the ballot is important. Two different forms are used: the office-group ballot and the party-column ballot. On the ***office-group ballot,*** candidates of all parties are grouped together according to the office for which they are running. Most political scientists believe that this arrangement encourages ***ticket splitting***—voting for candidates of different parties for different offices. In contrast, candidates on the ***party-column ballot*** are listed by party in columns. The voter can vote a ***straight ticket*** for all of one party's candidates by making one mark on the paper ballot or by punching a single box on a computer-tabulated ballot.

Whatever the style of ballot or voting procedure, the voter is free to write in the name of someone not listed on the ballot for any office. Often, a ***write-in campaign*** will be staged in hopes of electing someone not on the ballot. Such efforts rarely succeed because of the amount of organization and publicity required.

Long and Short Ballots Many states have what is called a ***long ballot.*** Introduced in the 1830's during the era of Jacksonian democracy, the long ballot provides for the election of a vast number of officials. The idea was to expand democracy by making virtually every public official—even the local dogcatcher—directly accountable to the people.

LEGACY

Casting the Ballot

The first votes cast in America used ballots of corn and beans, a system passed down from Indian custom in which a piece of corn meant "yes" and a bean meant "nay." In colonial America paper ballots, known as "papers," were the predominant method of voting. Although the first printed ballots were used in 1629 by the congregation of Salem Church to elect a minister, it was not until the eighteenth century that printed ballots were widely used. Printed ballots of the eighteenth and nineteenth centuries, designed by the political parties themselves, were seldom uniform. Only by the late 1920's had all states accepted the idea of an official ballot printed at public expense.

Until the turn of the century, ballots were counted by hand. But in 1892 mechanical voting machines were introduced, and by 1972 all but two states used machines to tally votes. The Presidential election of 1964 marked the first use of punch card ballots tallied by computers. Computers can count the vote more quickly and accurately than any other method. Today some modern ballots use fluorescent ink or special pencil marks that can be read and tallied by computer. With each election the use of computers to tally votes grows.

New technological developments promise to change even more dramatically the way Americans cast their votes. Cable television systems in some communities already allow two-way communication between viewers and broadcasting stations. Some experts predict that soon we may vote in our own homes, viewing electronic ballots on a television screen and transmitting our choice to a computer via a two-way cable.

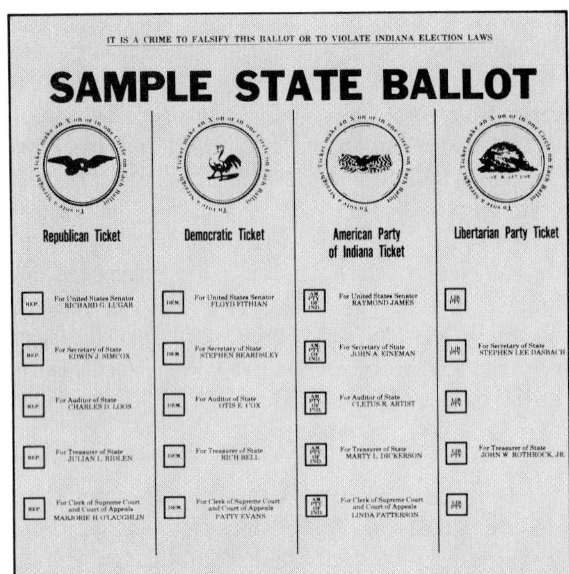

IT IS A CRIME TO FALSIFY THIS BALLOT OR TO VIOLATE INDIANA ELECTION LAWS

SAMPLE STATE BALLOT

Republican Ticket	Democratic Ticket	American Party of Indiana Ticket	Libertarian Party Ticket
REP. For United States Senator RICHARD G. LUGAR	DEM. For United States Senator FLOYD FITHIAN	AM. PTY. OF IND. For United States Senator RAYMOND JAMES	LIB. PTY.
REP. For Secretary of State EDWIN J. SIMCOX	DEM. For Secretary of State STEPHEN BEARDSLEY	AM. PTY. OF IND. For Secretary of State JOHN A. EINEMAN	LIB. PTY. For Secretary of State STEPHEN LEE DASBACH
REP. For Auditor of State CHARLES D. LOOS	DEM. For Auditor of State OTIS E. COX	AM. PTY. OF IND. For Auditor of State CLETUS R. ARTIST	LIB. PTY.
REP. For Treasurer of State JULIAN L. RIDLEN	DEM. For Treasurer of State RICH BELL	AM. PTY. OF IND. For Treasurer of State MARTY L. DICKERSON	LIB. PTY. For Treasurer of State JOHN W. ROTHROCK, JR.
REP. For Clerk of Supreme Court and Court of Appeals MARJORIE H. O'LAUGHLIN	DEM. For Clerk of Supreme Court and Court of Appeals PATTY EVANS	AM. PTY. OF IND. For Clerk of Supreme Court and Court of Appeals LINDA PATTERSON	LIB. PTY.

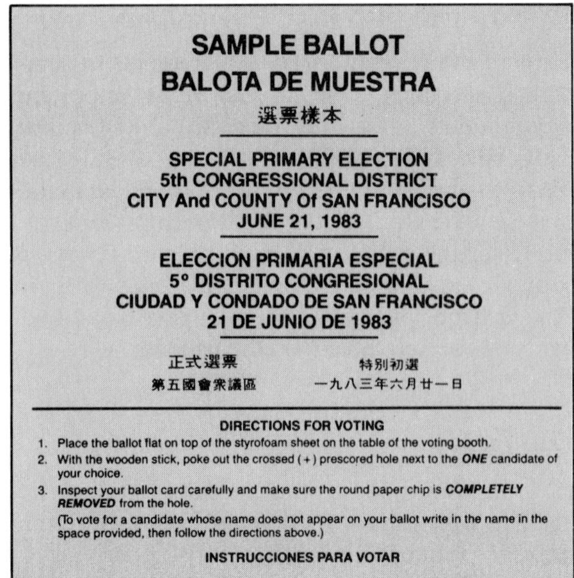

SAMPLE BALLOT
BALOTA DE MUESTRA
選票樣本

SPECIAL PRIMARY ELECTION
5th CONGRESSIONAL DISTRICT
CITY And COUNTY Of SAN FRANCISCO
JUNE 21, 1983

ELECCION PRIMARIA ESPECIAL
5° DISTRITO CONGRESIONAL
CIUDAD Y CONDADO DE SAN FRANCISCO
21 DE JUNIO DE 1983

正式選票　　特別初選
第五國會衆議區　　一九八三年六月廿一日

DIRECTIONS FOR VOTING

1. Place the ballot flat on top of the styrofoam sheet on the table of the voting booth.
2. With the wooden stick, poke out the crossed (+) prescored hole next to the ***ONE*** candidate of your choice.
3. Inspect your ballot card carefully and make sure the round paper chip is ***COMPLETELY REMOVED*** from the hole.

(To vote for a candidate whose name does not appear on your ballot write in the name in the space provided, then follow the directions above.)

INSTRUCCIONES PARA VOTAR

Party-column ballots (top left) help voters identify the party affiliation of the candidates. Federal law provides that ballots must be printed in English and in a minority language in areas where minority groups do not speak or read English well (top right). In some polling places (below) bilingual poll workers assist non-English speaking voters.

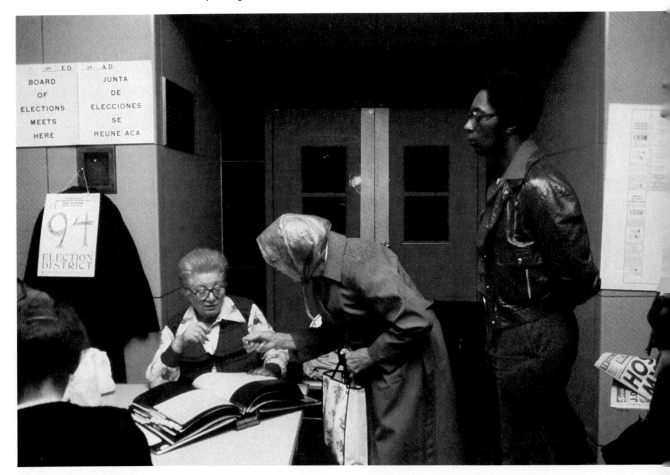

INSIGHT

Bilingual Ballots

The right to vote extends to nearly all Americans, including those who speak languages other than English. To protect the rights of "language minorities"—including Spanish-speaking Americans, Alaskan natives, Native Americans, and Asian-Americans—the Voting Act of 1975 requires that ballots and related election materials be printed in the languages of voting minorities as well as in English. This ruling applies in areas where illiteracy in English is high or where the 1972 voting turnout was exceptionally low.

Spanish-speaking Americans make up the largest language minority. In New York City and in parts of Florida, California, Texas, and other southwestern states, election materials are available in both English and Spanish. In San Francisco, with its large Asian population, ballots and other election materials are printed in three languages—English, Spanish, and Chinese. Because of its unique population mix, Hawaii translated its 1976 ballots and election materials into four different languages—Cantonese, Ilacao, Japanese, and English.

Some paper ballots actually reached a length of twelve feet, with hundreds of candidates listed for dozens of offices.

Rather than expanding democracy, however, the long ballot may actually weaken it. Voters are unlikely to be familiar with the candidates for minor offices on the ballot. They may vote for a name they recognize or, more likely, not vote at all. The result is that for lower offices, well-organized special interest groups often can elect whomever they want.

A few states have adopted a ***short ballot*** by reducing the number of elective offices. Those officials who make public policy are elected. Those who simply carry out policy are appointed.

Sample Ballots In most states sample ballots are mailed or published some time before each election. The sample ballot lists all the candidates and propositions as they will appear on the official ballot. Thus the voters are able to study and consider the choices available to them on election day. The sample ballots may not be used for actual voting. Neither may they be confused with absentee ballots.

Nonpartisan Elections

Reformers in the early part of the century often tried to eliminate political parties from state and local elections. In a ***nonpartisan election*** parties are prohibited from naming candidates, and no party labels appear on the ballot. One state, Nebraska, elects its legislators on a nonpartisan basis: Candidates run without party label. In most states local elections for mayor, city council, judges, and school board are conducted in a similar manner. Typically, an open primary is held. If one candidate receives an absolute majority, he or she is declared elected. Otherwise the top two candidates for each office face each other in a runoff election.

Nonpartisan elections help keep state and national party considerations out of local politics. But by taking away party labels, they deny the voters an important source of information about the candidates and the policies they favor.

Section Check

1. Define: poll watcher, precinct, ticket-splitting, write-in campaign, long ballot, short ballot
2. How often are Congressional elections held? Presidential elections?
3. Why was the secret ballot introduced in the United States?
4. What are the two kinds of ballots according to how candidates are listed?
5. What is the purpose of sample ballots?

3 TURNOUT: WHO VOTES AND WHY

Since 1960 voter turnout in American Presidential elections has averaged about 58 percent. In the 1980 election only 53.2 percent of all eligible voters went to the polls. In off-year elections—those held for Congress when the Presidency is not at stake—turnout is even lower. (The 1982 turnout was only 40 percent.) Turnout for state and local elections is lower still. It is not unusual for less than 20 percent of the electorate to vote in an important school board or city bond election. The pattern in voter participation for Presidential and off-year Congressional elections can be seen in the chart on this page.

The level of voter participation in the United States is considerably lower than in many other democratic nations. One reason, already noted, is that most other countries do not require voter registration. In some countries voting is even required by law. But these reasons are not enough to explain why so few Americans vote. In order to understand "the empty polling booth," it is necessary to examine how the nature of an election influences turnout in the United States. It is necessary to look closely at who votes in the United States, who does not, why some people vote, and why others do not.

VOTER TURNOUT BY NATION

Nation	Vote as a Percentage of Voting-Age Population
Italy	94.0%
Belgium	88.7
Sweden	86.8
Australia	83.1
West Germany	81.1
France	78.0
United Kingdom	76.0
Japan	74.4
United States	52.9
Switzerland	39.4

Source: *Public Opinion*

A comparison of voter turnout in selected democratic nations (above) illustrates the relatively low percentage of eligible voters who actually vote in the United States. Data on voter participation in Presidential and off-year elections (below) shows that more voters turn out in Presidential election years than in off-year elections. Why does a Presidential election influence voter turnout?

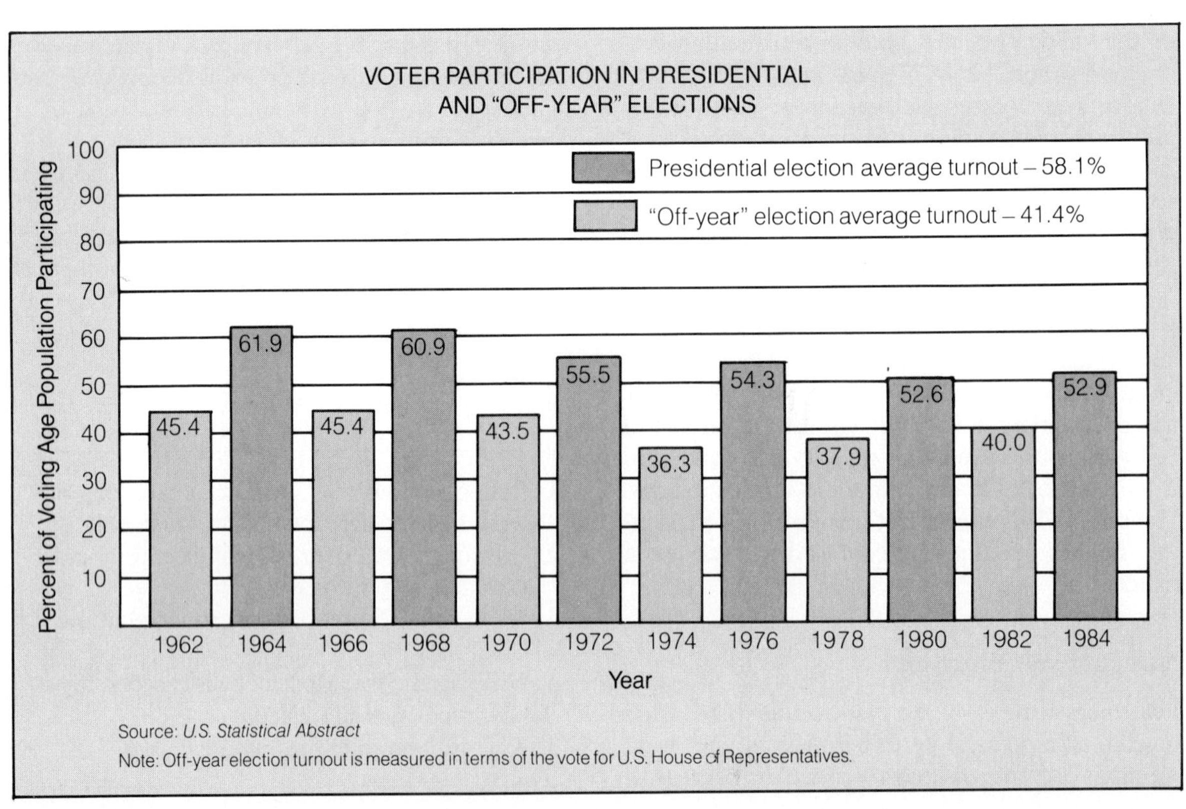

How Elections Influence Turnout

One of the most important factors influencing voter turnout is the nature of the election. Different kinds of elections produce very different levels of participation. Two general patterns can be identified.

First, Presidential elections bring out the largest numbers of voters. A Presidential campaign involves intense political activity. The issues raised touch the lives of everyone in the country. Voters attach great importance to the office of the President. With wide media coverage the campaign captures the public's interest. In contrast, local elections often pass with little notice. A local election may be decided by a handful of people. Only the most interested and informed people are likely to turn out—even though everyone may be affected by the outcome.

Second, the less competitive an election, the lower voter turnout is likely to be. The lowest turnout is in those states and communities that are dominated by one political party. When an election is not seriously contested—that is, when a candidate faces no real opposition—there is little incentive to vote.

Similarly, if the outcome of an election seems certain, many people may not bother to vote. But taking the results of an election for granted can be dangerous. Believing their candidate the sure winner, people who do not vote are sometimes shocked by the victory of the opponent. This happened in Texas in 1978, when most Texans believed that the Democratic candidate for governor would win the election easily. The polls gave him a strong lead. Some Democrats no doubt felt safe in not voting. Only 42 percent of the predominantly Democratic electorate went to the polls. By a margin of less than 1 percent, the Republican candidate won.

As elections become more competitive, voter turnout increases. Strong competition results in higher levels of participation and greater political interest. In the South, for example, the growth of two-party politics has been accompanied by higher turnouts on Election Day.

A Voter Profile

The study of voting behavior indicates that participation is related to a number of social and economic factors. These include age, education, income, occupation, and race. Of these personal characteristics, age and education are the most important in predicting who is most likely to vote.

Age Age is one of the most important characteristics associated with voting. The pattern shows young people are the least likely to vote. Voting increases with age, reaching a peak in middle age after which it declines.

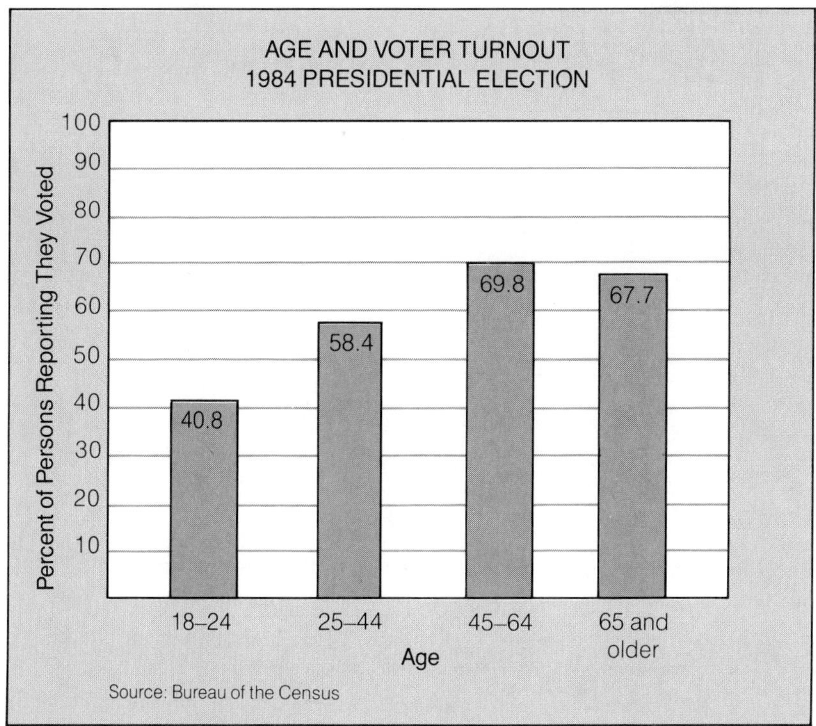

Study the data on age and voter turnout. Which age group had the highest turnout? Which group had the lowest turnout? What other personal factors are indicators of voting behavior? Which factors are considered the most important indicators of voting behavior?

Some young people, of course, are active in politics and are eager to cast their first vote. Those with higher levels of education are more likely to participate. But, as the chart on page 329 indicates, less than half of all people ages 18 to 24 reported that they voted in 1984.

Why do so few young people vote? Probably the most important reason is that they are not yet settled in their lives. They are distracted by the immediate concerns of education or military service, finding jobs, and starting families. Many young people fail to register because they have a low interest in politics. Another reason is that young people have not yet acquired the habit of voting. One reason voting increases with age is that each time a person votes, participation becomes more deeply a part of regular behavior.

Education Education is closely related to voter turnout. Voting increases with higher levels of education. College-educated persons are more likely to vote than those who never attended college. High school graduates are more likely to vote than those with only a grade school education. The lowest level of voter participation is among those who never completed grade school.

Through education, people acquire knowledge of government and politics. They learn basic skills for more effective participation. They also gain confidence to take part in the public affairs of their community, state, and nation. People with higher levels of education are more likely to follow public affairs in the newspapers and on television. They have greater knowledge of the candidates and the issues. They are likely to have a greater sense of civic duty and feel an obligation to vote. Furthermore, they are likely to have a heightened awareness of the impact of government on their lives. Their greater political interest increases the likelihood of voting.

Other Personal Factors Income and occupation are directly associated with high voter participation. Those with high incomes are much more likely to vote than those who make less money. Similarly, professionals and other white-collar workers are much more likely to vote than blue-collar workers. When income and occupation are looked at more closely, though, it becomes strikingly apparent that differences in income and occupation reflect differences in education. And education is the key factor in the development of political interest and the likelihood of voting. Better-educated people in the professions and in many other white-collar jobs are more likely to vote.

Differences in voter participation according to race are also significantly related to education. As barriers to participation by blacks have been lifted,

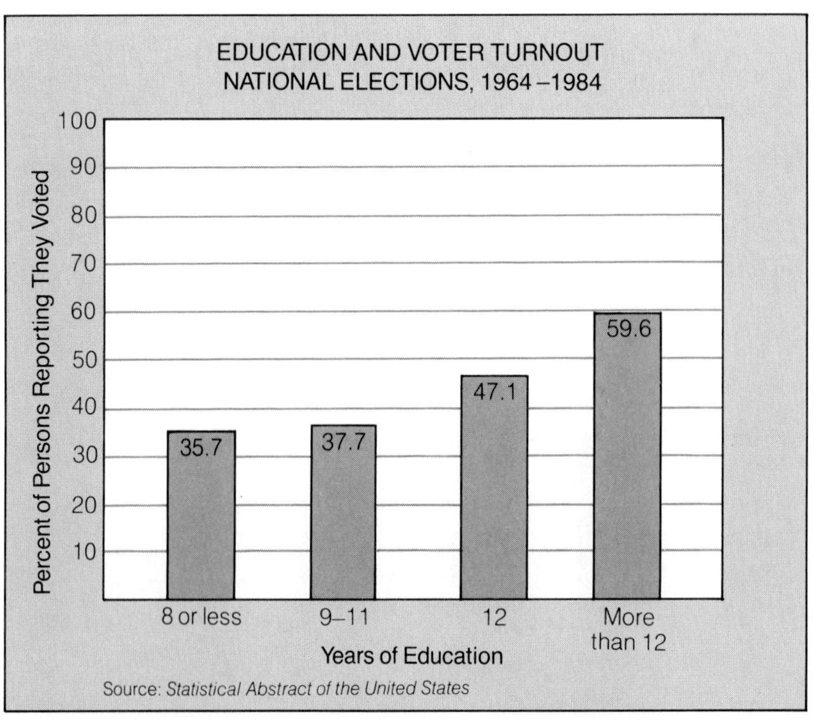

Study the relationship of educational level to voter participation. What reasons may account for the effects of higher levels of education on voter participation?

INSIGHT

The Weather and Voter Turnout

Weather conditions can have a serious effect on voter participation. Rain, snow, or ice almost always reduces turnout. People who do not have a high interest in politics may choose to stay at home. When the weather is good, they will be more inclined to go to the polls.

A heavy turnout has been traditionally regarded as good for the Democrats. Poor people and those with less education are more likely to be Democrats than Republicans. They also have the lowest level of political interest and are the least likely to vote if the weather is bad. If the weather is good and more people vote, the Democrats benefit—or so it is believed. Whether this in fact happens is a matter of debate.

blacks have voted in larger numbers. Passage of the Voting Rights Act of 1965 gave rise to a dramatic increase in the black electorate. Today, for blacks and whites with the same amount of education, there is no significant difference in voter participation.

What about differences between men and women? In the years immediately after women won the right to vote, there was a wide gap between the sexes in voter participation. Women were less likely to vote because they had been taught to believe that politics was "a man's business." Women first turned out in large numbers in 1932 to elect Franklin D. Roosevelt to the Presidency. Since then there has been almost no difference between men and women in the rate of voting. The difference that does remain is closely related to education. Among persons with a college education, women tend to be more politically active than men.

Why People Do Not Vote

Whether people vote or not depends upon a number of factors. Among these factors are voter apathy, alienation, cross-pressure, illness, and the need to travel.

Apathy Probably the most important reason why people do not vote is apathy, a lack of interest. Nonvoters are usually uninformed about public affairs because they have little interest in government and politics. Nonvoters are more likely to be young, less educated, and poor. They feel powerless, and often express the view that their participation would not make any difference. Typically, they say, "What's *one* vote anyway?" But in failing to participate, apathetic nonvoters give up the power to influence the affairs that affect their lives.

Alienation Some people do not vote because they are alienated, or "turned off," by politics. They have little trust in government and often express disgust with politics and politicians. They may point to corruption in government—to the Watergate scandal or to the bribery convictions of members of Congress. Alienated persons usually have a high interest in politics and are often well educated. Many alienated citizens *do* vote, and many are active in interest groups and party politics. Some take part in demonstrations and protest movements. But many other alienated persons withdraw entirely from politics in frustration and cynicism. They may gripe, but they do nothing.

The response given to the poll-taker in this cartoon highlights a major reason why some Americans do not vote. What is voter apathy? Which segments of the voting public are likely to be apathetic? Why?

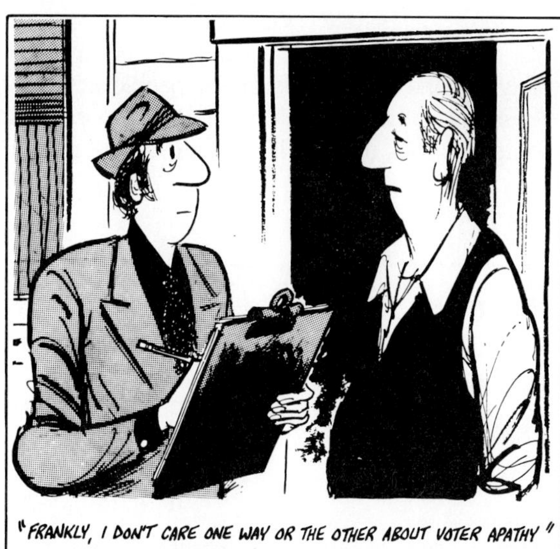

"FRANKLY, I DON'T CARE ONE WAY OR THE OTHER ABOUT VOTER APATHY"

REASONS FOR NOT VOTING

	Percent
Not registered	42
Did not like candidates	17
No particular reason	10
Not interested in politics	5
Illness	8
Not an American citizen	5
New resident	4
Traveling out of town	3
Working	3
No way to get to polls	1
Did not get absentee ballot	*
Other reasons	2

Source: The Gallup Poll *Less than 1%

Citizens who provided reasons for not voting such as "New resident" and "Traveling out of town" may have been able to vote in many elections. How may they have voted?

A few people do not vote because they feel that they do not have a meaningful choice between candidates. They may not like any of the candidates, or they may feel that the major parties do not represent their views. Even when the differences between candidates or parties may seem small, most people prefer one to the other. But some people choose to stay home, perhaps as an act of silent protest against the candidates.

Cross-Pressure Most people hold opinions that are more closely associated with one political party than the other. However, few people are wholly consistent in their political beliefs. Most people hold some opinions that are liberal and others that are conservative. On one issue they may favor the Republican, on another, the Democratic party. When these cross-pressures become intense, a person may be undecided or indifferent to the outcome of the election. In either case nonvoting may result.

Other Factors There are many other reasons why people do not vote. Some may be ill on election day. Others may have to leave town for work or personal reasons. Some people are physically unable to leave home to vote. Physical handicap need not be a barrier to voting. Special assistance in getting to the polls and in voting is available for the blind and other handicapped persons. Any qualified voter unable to go to the polls may vote in advance through the mail by ***absentee ballot.***

Why People Do Vote

The reason most people give for voting is ***civic duty.*** They feel that it is their obligation as citizens to vote. The primary form of political participation for most citizens is voting. It is their opportunity to express judgments on political leadership. It is through elections that government is held accountable to the people.

The vote of each citizen counts equally. The vote of an 18-year-old going to the polls for the first time counts as much as the vote of an older person. How much difference can one vote make? One vote alone rarely decides an election, but together with others, it makes the difference between who wins and who loses.

In many elections the shift of only a few votes can be critical. In 21 Presidential elections the results were so close that a shift of one vote in every hundred would have changed the outcome. In the 1968 Presidential election a change of one vote in each precinct of only three states would have resulted in victory for Hubert Humphrey instead of Richard Nixon.

INSIGHT

Absentee Ballots

If a person expects to be unable to vote on election day, a ballot may be obtained at a specified time before the election. The citizen marks the ballot and returns it to the proper official—most often by mail. Members of the armed forces usually vote by absentee ballot. American citizens who are in foreign countries also can vote in this manner. Casting an absentee ballot is worth the effort. Many close elections have been decided by absentee votes.

Of course, few elections are this close, and few people expect to cast the deciding vote in any election. However, as political scientists William Flanigan and Nancy Zingale point out, each person's vote also counts as an expression of preference for a candidate or party, regardless of who wins the election. They state:

Elections are more than simply a mechanism for selecting public officials; they are also a means for communicating, albeit somewhat dimly, a set of attitudes to government. For most Americans, voting remains the only means of influence regularly employed; many see it as the only avenue open to ordinary citizens to make government listen to their needs. The desire to be counted on one side of the fence or the other and the feeling that one ought *to be so counted are perhaps the greatest spurs to voting, even when interest is low and the candidates not too appealing.**

As fewer and fewer Americans vote, it becomes easier for special interests to dominate politics and influence public policy. This is nowhere more evident than in local elections. In an important bond election—to fund the construction of a new airport, for example—frequently less than 20 percent of the eligible voters go to the polls. Those most intensely concerned about the issue will vote, but their interests are not necessarily those of the community as a whole. Low turnouts can, in effect, give control of the community to a handful of well-organized special interests. When people do not vote on election day, the real losers are the people themselves.

---

*Flanigan and Zingale, *Political Behavior of the American Electorate* (Boston: Allyn and Bacon, 1979), p. 30.

Section Check

---

1. Define: apathy, alienation, cross-pressure, absentee ballot, civic duty
2. Is voter participation higher among young people or middle-aged people?
3. How is education related to the level of voter participation?
4. What are some of the major reasons why people do not vote?
5. What is the reason most people give to explain why they vote?

---

4 THE VOTER DECIDES

Voters reach their decisions on the basis of three factors: party identification, the candidates, and the issues.

Party Identification

Party loyalty is the most powerful long-run influence on how people vote. The majority of voters feel a sense of attachment to either the Republican or Democratic party. Often rooted in early learning experience in the family, party identification usually persists over time. Candidates and issues change from election to election, but for most people party preference remains constant. The longer a person remains attached to one party, the deeper party identification becomes.

Party identification gives order to political life. It helps people make sense out of confusing issues and complicated political events. It provides a guideline for judging the candidates. In short, party identification provides most people with a kind of road map to politics.

Party identification is the best single indicator of how people will vote. But whether voters will support *all* their party's candidates in *all* elections depends on ***partisanship,*** or party loyalty.

The more strongly people identify with a party, the greater their party loyalty in voting. Strong partisans are not only more loyal to the party, but they are also more likely to vote than either weak partisans or independents. Weak identifiers are more likely to cross party lines or not vote at all.

Identifying with a party is not the same as voting for that party's candidates in every election. If it were, then the Democrats—who outnumber Republicans by two to one—would win every Presidential election. In any Presidential campaign the Democrats need only to fan the fires of partisanship. If they can hold on to their weak identifiers, they will win the election. For the Republicans to win, they must win over an element of Democratic support.

Split Tickets Since 1952, the winning Republican candidates—Dwight Eisenhower, Richard Nixon, and Ronald Reagan—have won with support from people who describe themselves as Democrats. In every election some people cross party lines to vote a split ticket for a candidate in the other party. They do so without changing their own party identification. In other words, they remain Democrats but vote Republican for some offices (or vice

The percentage of Americans identifying themselves as either Democrats, Republicans, or Independents varies from year to year. What reason is cited for the growth in the number of voters identifying themselves as Independents?

PARTY IDENTIFICATION
HOW PEOPLE IDENTIFY THEMSELVES

Year	Democrats	Independents	Republicans
1968	53%	22%	25%
1970	46%	27%	27%
1972	43%	29%	28%
1974	44%	33%	23%
1976	48%	29%	23%
1978	46%	31%	23%
1980	45%	29%	26%
1982	45%	29%	26%
1984	42%	30%	28%

Source: The Gallup Poll

versa). Organizations like "Democrats for Reagan," for example, draw support from traditional Democratic voters. The number of people who vote split tickets has increased dramatically in recent years. The personality of the candidate has always been an important factor. The influence of issues has also contributed to the decline in party loyalty.

Some people, of course, vote a straight ticket. That is, they vote for all the candidates running under their party's label. The party-column ballot used in many states makes it easier to vote along straight party lines. People who vote a straight ticket usually do so because they believe that the party best represents their interests. For many less important offices, perhaps the only thing known about the candidates is their party label.

Independents In a recent survey only 70 percent of the people interviewed described themselves as Republicans or Democrats. Although figures vary from year to year, there has been some growth in the number of Independents. This growth has primarily resulted from young voters entering the electorate without a sense of party identification rather than people leaving the Republican and Democratic parties.

Many Independents feel closer to one party or the other. However, about half of those who describe themselves as Independents have no partisan attachment at all. These people are "pure" Independents. In addition, a few people—usually grouped with the Independents—identify with minor parties such as the American Independent party, the Libertarian party, and the Socialist Workers party.

Independents generally show a lower level of political interest than do strong Republican and Democratic partisans. But not all Independents are alike. This category includes those who are most apathetic—the uninformed and the uninvolved. But also found among the Independents are some of the best-informed and most politically active voters.

Candidates

When people cross party lines by voting a split ticket, they often do so because of ***candidate appeal.*** They may dislike the candidate of their own party, or they may be attracted to the candidate of the other party. Appeal often has little to do with the policies the candidate advocates. Instead, the popularity of the candidate may be based on past achievements or on public image.

In 1952 the Republicans nominated Dwight D. Eisenhower for President. "Ike," as he was called, had led the Allies to victory in World War II. He was an enormously popular military hero. Many people of differing political beliefs were attracted by his fatherly image. Without even knowing where Eisenhower stood on the issues, people liked him. "I Like Ike" became the slogan of his victorious campaign.

In the 1952 presidential campaign the Republicans capitalized on the image of Dwight D. Eisenhower as a military hero. They also used a positive campaign slogan. What other techniques are used to project a candidate's image to the voters?

Candidates can also "turn off" the electorate. George McGovern succeeded in winning the 1972 Democratic nomination. But many people viewed McGovern as weak, indecisive, and "too liberal." His Republican opponent, Richard Nixon, won a landslide victory, with the largest share of the popular vote for any Presidential candidate since 1936. Nixon won with the support of almost all Republicans, 66 percent of the Independents, and 42 percent of those who described themselves as Democrats.

Candidate appeal is most important in elections for President. In the course of the campaign, through wide media coverage, the candidates become well known. Their backgrounds, personalities, and lifestyles are bared before the public. Few candidates for other offices ever undergo such intense personal examination by the electorate. The less important the office, the less knowledge the voter is likely to have about the candidate. Most voters fall back on what they do know: party label, and whether or not the candidate is an ***incumbent,*** a person who holds office. Incumbents usually have an advantage in running for reelection, because they already have a following. They also are generally better known among the voters than their opponents.

Over the past few years, there has been a good deal of attention given to ***candidate image.*** Some campaign aides believe that Presidential candidates can be created, packaged, and marketed through the mass media in the same manner as a breakfast cereal. Political campaigns are more sophisticated today than in the past. The candidates use modern public relations and advertising techniques and rely heavily on the mass media, particularly television. But today's voters are not easily manipulated or taken in by a slick, well-financed media campaign. A candidate cannot really be "sold" to the voters because in a free society the image-makers do not control all available information. What the voter thinks about the candidate ultimately will be influenced by various information from many sources.

Democrat Jimmy Carter (above) and Republican Ronald Reagan (left) greet their supporters during the 1980 Presidential election campaign. What were two important campaign issues in 1980? What limits the impact of issues on a particular election? How might single-issue voting affect a voter's choice of a candidate?

Issues

In recent years issues have become increasingly important as a basis for the voters' choice. For many voters the candidates' positions on various questions of public policy mean more than the party labels they wear. However, the importance of issues varies from election to election. In order for issue-voting to have a major impact on an election, several conditions must be present.

First, voters must have knowledge of the issues and where the candidates stand on them. Many people are unaware of the major issues in a campaign, and others have only a dim notion as to the candidates' positions. Sometimes, of course, the candidates do not have clear positions on an issue. They may prefer to "sit on the fence" rather than take a stand on a controversial issue. Candidates may also waver back and forth between issues, or even say one thing to one group of voters and something else to another group of voters.

Secondly, issues are more important in some Presidential campaigns than in others. In 1964, 1968, and 1972 controversial issues such as recognition of civil rights for blacks and the nation's participation in the Vietnam War divided the nation and determined many voters' choices. But in 1976 issues were hard to identify, and the Presidential campaign often seemed to be waged in vague terms of personal "trust." In the 1980's economic issues such as employment, government spending, and taxation have played important roles in determining election returns.

A third limit on issue-voting is that in any major campaign there are likely to be a number of issues. A voter might well support the stand of one candidate on domestic economic issues, for example, but favor another candidate's position on foreign policy. There may be many issues, but there is only one vote. This is one reason why many people fall back on party identification and a judgment that one party better represents their overall interests.

When issues do play a role in the voters' decisions, certain issues assume critical importance. These may be major campaign issues or simply those about which the individual voter feels most strongly. Traditionally, the issue-oriented voter chooses among the candidates according to how they stand on several important issues. More recently, ***single-issue voting*** has been on the rise. Many people become so absorbed with one issue—nuclear energy, for example—that all other questions fade into the background. Candidates are judged by their position on that issue and that issue alone. But single-issue voting can be a booby trap. Each voter has many interests and concerns. When candidates are evaluated in terms of only one issue, other important interests are likely to be sacrificed.

Verdict or Mandate

In voting, people do not endorse everything their candidate advocates. An election rarely provides a clear ***mandate***—an authorization or "go-ahead"—to carry out specific policies. Rather than a mandate for the future, most elections serve as a ***verdict*** on the past performance of the candidate or the party.

The average voter makes an overall evaluation of how well the government has performed. The evaluations are personal, made in terms of the issues about which there is most concern. Deeds, not words, count in the final analysis. Is the voter generally satisfied with the performance of the party in power and with those who hold public office? A voter may not be familiar with policies pursued or even with the stands taken by various leaders. But, to use an old adage, the voter knows where the shoe hurts. An unpopular war, crime in the streets, racial unrest, scandal and corruption, high taxes, unemployment, and inflation are likely to have a far greater impact on the voter's decision than campaign rhetoric or promises for the future.

Section Check

1. Define: partisanship, candidate appeal, candidate image, single-issue voting
2. What is meant by voting a straight ticket?
3. Why has the number of independent voters increased recently?
4. Why is an election more likely to be a verdict than a mandate?

SUMMARY

The right to vote is a fundamental part of a republican form of government. Throughout much of our history less than half of all Americans have had the right to vote. The Fifteenth, Nineteenth, Twenty-third, and Twenty-sixth Amendments, however, have extended the right to vote to almost all Americans over the age of 18. The Twenty-fourth Amendment has eliminated the poll tax as a requirement for voting. In order to vote, a person must meet certain minimum qualifications, including citizenship, age, and residence. Forty-nine of the 50 states require that a voter register on either a periodic or a permanent basis.

Congressional elections are held every two years. Presidential elections take place every four years. To ensure free elections, the secret ballot was introduced in the nineteenth century. Most cities or counties are divided into voting districts called precincts. Precincts may use either paper ballots or voting machines to record votes. Some states have very long ballots, which provide for the election of a vast number of officials. Most political scientists argue, however, that voters often make more informed choices when faced with a short ballot for the election of policy-making officials.

The level of voter participation in the United States is considerably lower than in many other democratic nations. Presidential elections bring out more voters. Highly competitive elections also increase voter turnout. Young people have a low turnout rate. Voter participation increases among more highly educated groups.

People fail to vote for several reasons. One is apathy, or lack of interest. Another is a sense of powerlessness. Many potential voters feel mistrustful of politics. Others may be torn by such cross-pressures as conflicting opinions and beliefs. The majority of Americans do vote, however. They do so out of a sense of civic duty or because they feel their vote may make a difference in elections.

Voters generally base their choices on three primary factors: party identification, the candidates, and the issues. Overall, the number of independent voters is increasing. This is largely because young voters are entering the electorate without a strong sense of party identification. In recent years issues have become an increasingly important component in a voter's decision. More recently single-issue voting has been on the rise. Many people become so absorbed with one issue that other issues fade into the background.

Chapter 13 Review

Using Vocabulary

Answer the questions by using the meaning of each underlined term.

1. Why is there a poll watcher in every precinct at election time?
2. How does voting a straight ticket differ from ticket splitting?
3. Why is a write-in campaign often unsuccessful, even in a nonpartisan election?
4. Is it possible for a long ballot as well as a short ballot to be a secret ballot? Why?
5. How does an incumbent show candidate appeal?
6. What effect does single-issue voting have on partisanship?

Understanding American Government

1. Why were residency requirements for voting first instituted? Why has the Supreme Court limited the length of these requirements?
2. How has voter registration been simplified in recent years?
3. The long ballot was introduced to expand democracy in America. In what ways might the long ballot weaken democracy?
4. What are some reasons for low voter participation among young people?
5. Why is voter participation high among well-educated people?
6. In what ways do many voters use party identification as "a kind of road map to politics"?
7. Why is candidate appeal most important in Presidential elections?
8. What conditions must exist for issue-voting to have an impact on an election?

Extending Your Skills: Reading a Bar Graph

Study the graph on page 329. Then complete each item.

1. The age group that reported the smallest voter turnout was (a) 18–24; (b) 25–44; (c) 45–64; (d) 65 and older.
2. The age group 45–64 reported a turnout of (a) 40.8 percent; (b) 58.4 percent; (c) 69.8 percent.
3. The age groups that reported a voter turnout of more than 60 percent were (a) 18–24 and 65 and older; (b) 18–24 and 45–64; (c) 45–64 and 65 and older.
4. Based on the graph, what relationship exists between age and voter turnout? Explain your answer.

Government and You

1. Do you think that voter registration requirements serve an important function in reducing fraud and confusion? Or do you think these requirements serve to reduce voter participation? What do you think is the ideal system for registering voters?
2. In a nonpartisan election no party labels appear on the ballot. Many people feel these elections help keep state and national party politics out of local elections. Do you agree? Or do you feel that by taking away party labels the voters are denied an important source of information? What are the reasons for your answer?
3. Is party identification a sound method of choosing a candidate? Why or why not? What do you think is the most reliable method of choosing a candidate? May the method of selection change with the type of election?
4. What politicians do you think have great candidate appeal? What is behind this appeal?

Activities

1. Prepare a biographical report on a recent candidate for President. Tell whether or not the candidate was popular and give reasons to support your conclusion.
2. Stage a class debate on the topic "*Resolved:* That Election-Day voter registration should be instituted nationwide."
3. Invite to class a voter registration officer, such as the county registrar of voters. Ask this official to speak about what methods are being used locally to increase voter participation.
4. Make a scrapbook of newspaper and magazine articles on a recent election in your area.
5. Make a wall chart on the results of the last five Presidential elections, showing how the nation voted and how your state voted.

UNIT 6

THE FEDERAL LEGISLATIVE BRANCH

Congress: The Lawmakers

All legislative Powers herein granted shall be vested in a Congress of the United States, which shall consist of a Senate and a House of Representatives.

THE CONSTITUTION

CHAPTER OVERVIEW

1 **REPRESENTATION IN CONGRESS**
A Bicameral System / Apportionment

2 **CONGRESSIONAL ELECTIONS**
Qualifications / Incumbency / Congressional Nominations / Congressional Campaigns and Elections / Campaign Finance

3 **MEMBERSHIP IN CONGRESS**
The Philosophies of Representation / Legislators and Their Constituents / The Public Image of Congress / Congress at Work / Salaries and Benefits / Political Patronage / Congress as a Career

Congress meets in the Capitol—the Senate in the north wing and the House of Representatives in the south wing. The statue on top of the dome—titled "Freedom"—was placed there in 1863. The Capitol is a symbol of the American system of republican government.

1 REPRESENTATION IN CONGRESS

By far the longest passage in the Constitution is Article 1. It is devoted entirely to the establishment of the United States Congress. Why did the Framers place Congress first? The Declaration of Independence states that "Governments are instituted among Men, deriving their just powers from the consent of the governed." Nowhere is this consent of the governed more clearly reflected than in Congress.

A Bicameral System

Congress is a ***bicameral legislature***—that is, it is composed of two houses. In the House of Representatives each state is represented according to its population. In the Senate each state is accorded two members.

This system resulted from the so-called Great Compromise at the Constitutional Convention. The large states favored the Virginia Plan. This provided for two houses, with representation in each house based upon population. The greater a state's population, the more representatives it would have in Congress. The small states feared, however, that they would be overpowered by such an arrangement. They offered an alternative proposal. Under the New Jersey Plan, there would be a single house, and each state—regardless of size—would have the same number of votes.

After one month's debate the conflict between the large and small states was resolved by an agreement to combine aspects of both plans. The result was our present system. The House of Representatives satisfied the larger states. The Senate eased the fears of the smaller states.

Members of the House of Representatives are elected every two years from local constituencies. Senators are elected for terms of six years from statewide constituencies. The terms of senators are staggered so that every two years one third of the seats are filled by election. These longer, overlapping terms were designed to provide stability and continuity in the Senate. The composition of the House, however, may change quite rapidly.

The size of the Senate is determined by the number of states in the Union. With each state having two senators, there are now 100 members. Membership in the House of Representatives is based upon population, and during the nineteenth century the House grew along with the nation. Expanding membership weakened efficiency, though, as the size of the House threatened to become too large. In 1911 membership was fixed at 435.

In addition to the regular members of the House, there are three delegates (representing the District of Columbia, Guam, and the Virgin Islands) and one Resident Commissioner for Puerto Rico. The four territorial delegates may introduce bills, serve on committees, and participate in debate. But they are not entitled to vote.

Apportionment

The 435 seats of the House of Representatives are divided among the states according to population, with each state guaranteed at least one representative. While America's population has grown each year, some state populations have grown more rapidly than others. Today, for example, the Sun Belt states of the South and West have the highest rates of population growth. During the 1970's 53 percent of the nation's population growth occurred in the South. Thirty-six percent took place in the West.

To allow for such changes in population, the Constitution requires that ***reapportionment*** of the seats in the House be undertaken every ten years. The number of seats to which each state is entitled is determined by the Bureau of the Census. Reapportionment thus reflects shifts in population as recorded by the 1980 Census. As a result of population shifts, 11 states gained additional representatives, while 10 states lost seats in the House.

Once the reapportionment of seats has been made, the state legislatures are responsible for drawing district boundaries. From the beginning, "districting" has been a highly political process. Within each state the party in power normally seeks to draw district lines to its own advantage. Two basic problems arise during this process: malapportionment and gerrymandering.

Unequal Districts When districts are unequal in size or population, ***malapportionment*** results. The Constitution requires reapportionment of seats among the states every ten years to reflect changes in population. But no provision was made to deal with population changes within each state. Over the years there has been a dramatic shift in population from rural to urban and suburban areas. But until the 1960's state legislatures failed to redraw district lines to account for these changes. Most state legislatures were themselves dominated by rural interests, and Congressional districts were drawn in

Study the changes in representation in the House of Representatives that occurred as a result of the 1980 census. In which state did representation increase the most? In which state did representation decrease the most?

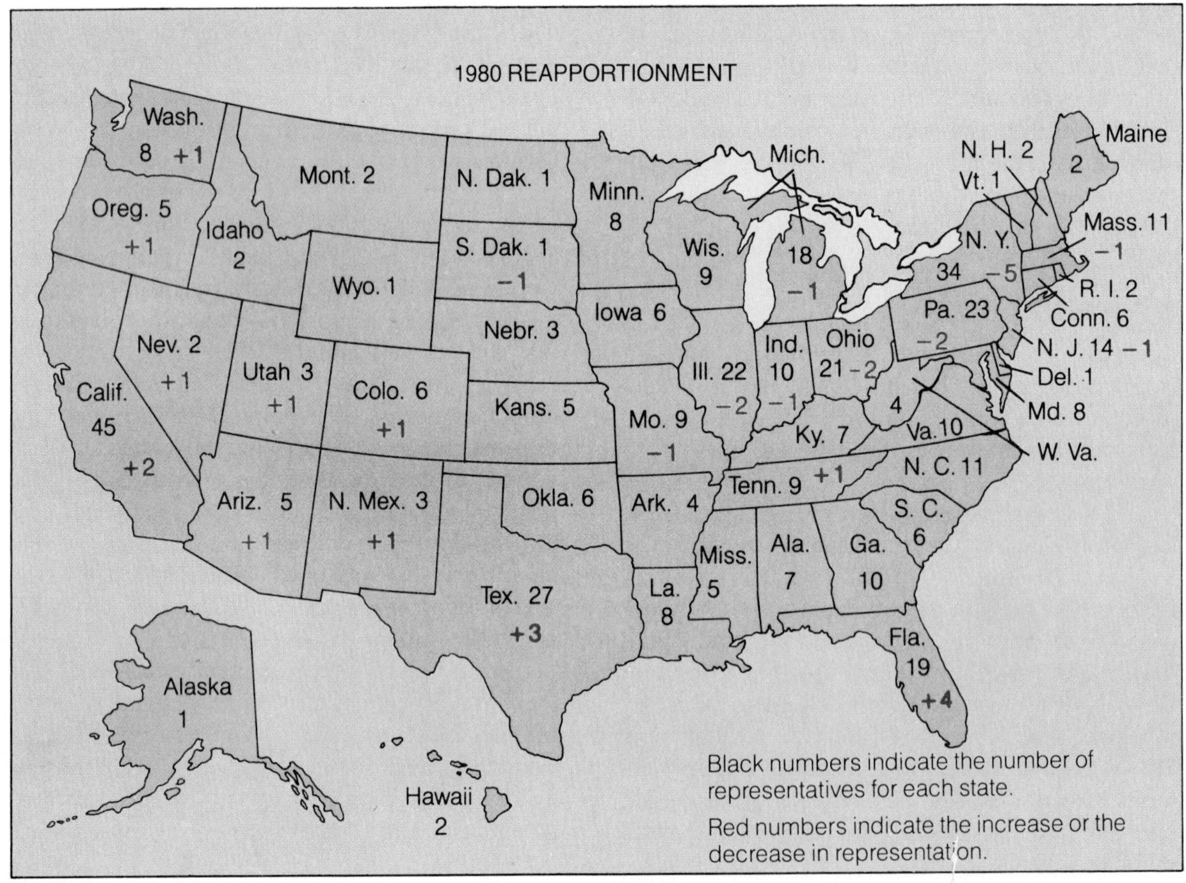

such a way as to overrepresent rural areas. The resulting inequality between rural and urban districts was striking. In 1960 the smallest Congressional districts had fewer than 180,000 residents, while the largest approached 1 million. Consequently the bias in representation increased the power of rural and farming interests at the expense of more populous urban districts.

The Supreme Court in a series of decisions in the 1960's moved to correct the malapportionment bias. In *Wesberry* v. *Sanders* (1964) the Court held that district boundaries must be drawn so that each contains approximately the same number of people. One person's vote in a Congressional election, the Court said, is to be worth as much as any other's. The goal was political equality: "One person, one vote."

Congressional districts today are of roughly equal size, each with about 500,000 people. A state legislature must make "a good faith effort" to achieve strict equality, and any variation must be justified. The Court stated:

While it may not be possible to draw congressional districts with mathematical precision, that is no excuse for ignoring our Constitution's plain objective of making equal representation for equal numbers of people the fundamental goal for the House of Representatives. That is the high standard of justice and common sense which the Founders set for us.

Unusual Boundaries The problem of malapportionment has been corrected, but the problem of how district lines are drawn remains. The party in power in the state legislature usually draws the boundary lines to its own advantage. This practice is known as ***gerrymandering.***

The aim of gerrymandering is to secure as many legislative seats as possible for one's own party. Two

LEGACY

The Gerrymander

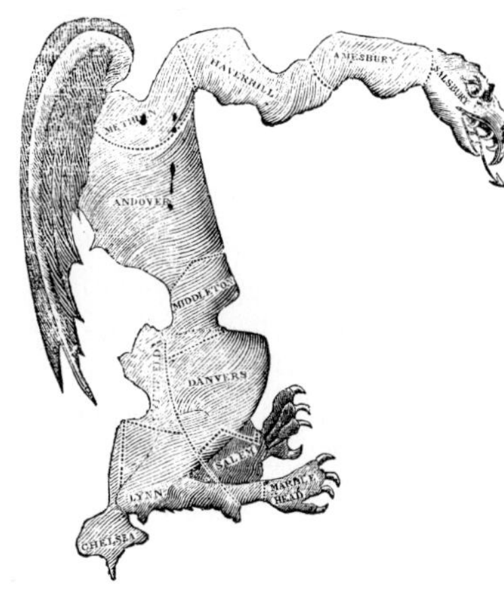

In 1812 Massachusetts Democrats holding office signed into law a plan that reorganized their election districts. The plan strengthened the Democrats by creating as many Democratic districts as possible, and weakened the Federalists by lumping them together in as few districts as possible. Among the oddly-shaped districts that resulted was one that zigged and zagged wildly over the map. When the map was displayed at a party, an artist present added wings, claws, an eye, and a tongue. "It's a salamander," someone declared. Remembering that Governor Elbridge Gerry had signed the redistricting plan into law, another member of the party spoke up: "It's not a salamander, it's a gerrymander!" From then on the unnatural division of election districts has gone by the name of gerrymander.

The first gerrymander was a success. Although the Democrats received 51,000 votes and the Federalists 50,000, the Democrats managed to elect 29 state senators, the Federalists only 11. Since then the gerrymander has had many offspring.

In one redistricting plan a Massachusetts district was carved into the shape of a snake—25 miles long and as narrow as 2 miles wide. Residents of another Congressional district could leave their own district, travel 15 miles due east through another, and then find themselves right back in their home district. Mississippi once had a district called the "shoestring"—300 miles long and only 40 miles wide—created to concentrate the largest number of black voters in one area. Although some voters and lawmakers have tried to control gerrymanders, this particular political beast continues to appear in different forms and in different places with each reapportionment.

techniques are used. The first seeks to concentrate the strength of the opposition party in the fewest districts possible. This then leaves the remaining districts "safe" for the majority party. The other technique seeks to divide the strength of the opposition among as many districts as possible. This is designed to reduce their chance for victory in any district. Thus district lines are drawn to include some groups and exclude others—or to divide groups right down the middle.

Gerrymandering is clearly unfair, but how should district lines be drawn? What standards should be used? Should district lines follow natural boundaries? Should cities be kept together as separate urban districts, or should they be divided and combined with suburban and rural areas? Should districts be socially and economically diverse, or should they be homogeneous (composed of one group) and thus give representation to particular interests? The problem is that however the lines are drawn, some groups gain politically and others lose.

Voters have begun to express their opposition to gerrymandering. In 1982 California voters rejected the gerrymandered apportionment of their state legislature. Reforms have been proposed that would shift the job of redistricting from state legislatures to permanent bipartisan commissions. Several states, including Colorado, Hawaii, and Montana, have already established reapportionment commissions to end partisan bias in drawing district lines and end gerrymandering.

Section Check

1. Define: bicameral legislature, reapportionment, malapportionment
2. Identify: Virginia Plan, New Jersey Plan, *Wesberry* v. *Sanders*
3. How often are Congressional districts reapportioned?
4. Approximately how many people live in each Congressional district?
5. What is gerrymandering?

2 CONGRESSIONAL ELECTIONS

The people of the United States elect the President indirectly through the electoral college. In contrast, the people directly elect members of Congress. Originally the Constitution allowed each state to determine the procedure by which its senators were selected. During the early years of the Republic, states allowed their legislatures to select senators. It was believed that this procedure would best ensure the selection of persons of judgment and distinction. Shielded from the pressures of political campaigns, the Senate would serve as a check on the popularly elected House. The Senate could prevent hasty, ill-considered actions.

By the late nineteenth century pressure began to grow for direct election of senators. The Senate was attacked as a "Millionaires' Club." Individual senators were accused of serving big business instead of the people. A number of states then turned to popular elections to choose their senators, with the legislatures giving formal ratification to the results. Finally, in 1913, the Seventeenth Amendment required that all senators be elected directly by the people.

Qualifications

The Constitution states the qualifications necessary for Congressional office. Representatives must be at least 25 years old, United States citizens for at least 7 years, and residents of the state in which they are elected. Senators must be at least 30 years of age, United States citizens for at least 9 years, and state residents.

The requirement of residency in a district or state is applied loosely. Voters normally prefer someone with close ties to the constituency, but occasionally a well-known national figure establishes residence in a state with the express purpose of running for office. Daniel Patrick Moynihan was a resident voter in Massachusetts until he decided to run for the Senate in New York. Robert F. Kennedy, brother of John F. Kennedy, served from 1964 to 1968 as a senator from New York, though he too had lived in Massachusetts.

Article 1, Section 5, of the Constitution states:

Each house of Congress shall be the judge of the elections, returns, and qualifications of its own members.

Before 1969 Congress had on occasion used its power to judge qualifications as the basis for refusing to seat an elected member. In 1969, however, the Supreme Court ruled that the House and Senate may exclude an elected member only if the constitutional requirements of age, citizenship, and residency are not met.

In the event of the death or resignation of a representative, the home-state governor may call a special election to choose a successor to serve out the remaining portion of the term. The governor may also call a special election for the Senate. Most state legislatures, however, have granted their governors the power to appoint a successor to serve in the Senate until the next regular election.

Incumbency

In most Congressional districts elections are usually won by a hefty majority. No more than 10 to 15 percent of all House seats are closely contested. Most districts thus tend to be "safe" for one party or the other. One reason for this is the relatively small size of House districts. In addition the House districts are often dominated by interests closely associated with one party.

One of the most important factors accounting for the large number of ***safe seats*** is that incumbents are almost always reelected. In nearly every Congressional election more than 90 percent of all representatives seeking reelection are returned to office. Typically these incumbents win by wide margins. They have a powerful advantage over their challengers for a number of reasons.

First and most important, the incumbent is likely to be better known than the opposing candidate. People tend to vote for a familiar name. As a general rule the longer representatives have served in Congress, the more likely they are to be reelected.

Second, as members of Congress, incumbents have many material advantages. They have a staff of aides paid with public funds who see that they get media exposure. A number of free or inexpensive services are also provided, such as postage and stationery. Challengers, however, must build their own organizations. The high costs of direct mailings, advertisements, and television time are a great burden to challengers.

Third, incumbents can raise campaign funds more easily than their challengers. Because members of Congress are already in a position of influence, they draw contributions from a number of interests seeking favor. Incumbents usually outspend their opponents during the campaign by a two-to-one margin.

Fourth, another advantage for incumbents results from party identification. A great many voters do not know the name of either candidate—even their incumbent member of Congress. When people do not know who the candidates are or where they stand on the issues, they fall back on party identification. In general, voters in House elections follow party lines much more closely than they do in elections for the Senate and the Presidency, where the candidates are better known.

After the death of Senator Hubert H. Humphrey in 1978, the governor of Minnesota appointed Muriel Humphrey to fill her husband's unexpired term.

Voting by party identification has two principal results. First, it favors the incumbent because few people change party identification. Second, party voting favors the Democrats because Democrats outnumber Republicans two-to-one nationally. The impact of this pattern is dramatic: Since 1932 the Democrats have been in the majority in the House of Representatives for all but four years. Even when the Republicans have won the Presidency, the Democrats have kept control of the House. The margin of Democratic strength is also substantial. Even with Republican gains in 1980, the Democrats won 243 seats as compared to 192 for the Republicans.

Senate seats are generally more competitive than those in the House because the built-in advantages of the incumbent are lessened. Candidates for the Senate must appeal to statewide constituencies with many varied and competing interests. All Senate candidates tend to be better known by the voters than are those for the House. A Senate challenger's party organization is more likely to supply campaign services. For these reasons Senate elections tend to be closer, and incumbents sometimes go down in defeat. In 1980, for example, Republicans won control of the Senate for the first time in 28 years. Nine Democratic incumbents were defeated, many of them in powerful positions on Senate committees.

Congressional Nominations

Nearly all states today use the direct primary for the nomination of candidates for the House and Senate. Although procedures vary from state to state, generally, any qualified person may enter a party primary. Some are "self-starters" who decide on their own to contest the primary. Others are urged to run by party leaders or by interest groups and thus begin with substantial support.

Most candidates for the Senate are already well known when they enter the race. The prestige of the Senate attracts prominent persons from all walks of life. Most frequently a senatorial candidate has served in high public office as a governor, a member of the House of Representatives, or as a Cabinet member. A few candidates run for the Senate with no background in politics. Senator John Glenn of Ohio was a pioneer astronaut. Senator Bill Bradley of New Jersey played professional basketball for the New York Knicks.

Candidates for the House of Representatives most often come from lower public office—from state legislatures or from local government. Sometimes they enter without political experience from business or the legal profession. Representative Jack Kemp of New York came from a career in professional football.

Congressional primaries—especially for the House—are rarely competitive. Incumbents are almost always renominated and often run unopposed in the primary. In recent years fewer than 2 percent of all House members seeking reelection have lost their party's nomination. The incumbent's advantage also has an impact on the minority party's nomination. Unless there is a reasonable chance of defeating an incumbent representative in the general election, serious candidates are unlikely to enter

Representative Jack Kemp (left), Senator Bill Bradley (center), and Senator John Glenn (right) had no experience in government before their election to Congress. Most often, however, senators and representatives have held other public offices before winning a Congressional election.

the opposition party's primary. Thus, primaries for nomination by both parties tend to be noncompetitive.

Elections for the Senate are generally more competitive than House races, and so too are senatorial primaries. But incumbents still enjoy a powerful advantage. Only 7 percent of those senators seeking reelection lose in the primaries. In the few instances when members of the House or Senate fail to be renominated, it is often because of their age. This was a major factor in the 1980 primary defeat of Jacob Javits, a New York Republican. Javits, 76 years old, had served 24 years in the Senate. Occasionally incumbents are defeated in the primary because of their stand on a controversial issue. Some have lost because of personal scandal. In House races, redistricting sometimes forces two incumbent representatives of the same party into a single Congressional district. The result is that in the primary one incumbent is defeated by another.

The most competitive nomination contests normally are those in which the incumbent is not seeking reelection. The Congressional seat is "open," and the primaries and general election usually involve lively campaigns.

President Reagan (left) campaigns on behalf of a fellow Republican, Representative Jim Collins of Texas (right), who ran unsuccessfully for the Senate in 1982.

Congressional Campaigns and Elections

Candidates for the House and Senate face many of the same problems as Presidential candidates in mounting a campaign. They must put together a campaign organization. They must plan a strategy and raise funds. They rely increasingly on professional consultants—polling firms, media specialists, and fund-raisers. Like Presidential candidates, they are concerned about image and campaign themes, about where to stand on the issues, and about winning support from a variety of groups.

The incumbent in Congressional elections, as we have seen, enjoys a great advantage. But another factor that also weighs heavily in elections for the House and Senate is the popularity of the President or of the parties' Presidential candidates. For better or worse, the electoral fortunes of candidates for the House and Senate are closely tied to their party's Presidential candidate in Presidential election years. If the candidate at the head of the ticket wins, that provides a boost to other party candidates. Sometimes weak Congressional candidates are elected on the strength of the Presidential candidate. This is the ***coattail effect***—so called because it is said that party candidates are carried into office on the President's coattails. This effect is strengthened by the use of party column ballots, which make it easier for people to vote a straight ticket.

The impact of Presidential candidates on House and Senate elections can, of course, work the other way. A losing candidate at the head of the ticket may drag others down to defeat. In 1980 President Carter's massive defeat contributed to Democratic losses of 33 seats in the House and 12 seats in the Senate.

Presidential popularity is also an important factor in off-year Congressional elections. To a degree, off-year elections express the voters' judgment on Presidential performance. Candidates for the House and Senate seek to identify themselves closely with a popular President of their own party. Photographs portray the candidate with the President, with a clear message that he or she is part of the President's team. The President may even make personal appearances on behalf of the candidate—especially in crucial Senate races. Of course, candidates are likely to be hurt by an unpopular President in their own party. House and Senate candidates usually seek to keep an unpopular President at a distance and to separate their own positions from that of Presidential policy.

Campaign Finance

Political campaigns are expensive, and the cost of running for office has grown as television has taken on greater importance. In 1974 the average cost of campaigning for a House seat was $50,000. By 1980 the average was $150,000. In recent years, the average was more than $250,000, and campaign expenses of $500,000 were not unusual for House races. Recent Senate races averaged $1.7 million, but went as high as $7 million. Campaign costs, of course, depend upon a number of factors such as the size of the state, the strength of the incumbent, and just how close the election is likely to be. Unlike Presidential campaigns, Congressional campaigns are not publicly financed. Candidates for the House and Senate must raise most of their own funds. The House Democratic and House Republican campaign committees provide some assistance, but most campaign money comes from private contributions and from the candidate's own pocket or purse.

Congressional candidates must raise money from a wide variety of sources. Campaign finance law now limits the amount an individual or group may give to each candidate in both the primary and general election campaigns. Individuals may contribute no more than $1,000 for each campaign, while political action committees have a $5,000 limit. No limit is placed on the amount candidates may contribute to their own campaign.

These laws have helped cause a dramatic rise in the number of special interest group political action committees (PAC's). Representing business, labor, and other interests, PAC's increased in number from some 600 in 1974 to more than 3,500 in the early 1980's. PAC contributions to Congressional candidates went from $12.5 million in 1974 to more than $80 million in recent years. Furthermore in recent campaigns PAC's spent about $160 million on local races, independent political advertising, and on administrative activities.

PAC's represent several diverse special interests. For example, in one recent Congressional campaign, business PAC's contributed approximately $30 million, labor PAC's gave $20 million, PAC's representing trade and health professional associations gave $22 million, and ideological and other special interest PAC's gave an estimated $8 million.

Eighty percent of these contributions went to incumbent candidates. Representatives received an average of 35 percent of their campaign money from PAC's, averaging $93,000. Senators received a smaller portion of their total campaign funds from PAC's, but the amounts involved were often hefty—reaching upwards of $1 million in several cases.

Many people—including members of the House—believe that there is an unhealthy dependence on special interest money. The increased influence of PAC's, says former Representative John J. Cavanaugh of Nebraska, "greatly usurps the independence, the judgment, and, ultimately, the integrity of senators and representatives."

Two proposals for reform have received wide attention. One would introduce partial public financing of Congressional campaigns, with limits imposed on campaign spending. The other proposal would place tighter limits on the amount of money PAC's may contribute. A limit of $50,000 would also be imposed on the total amount a candidate could receive from all PAC's. The intent is to reduce the dependence of House candidates on powerful special interest groups and to diversify the sources of campaign contributions.

Section Check

1. Define: safe seat, coattail effect
2. Identify: Political Action Committee
3. How has the procedure for electing senators changed over the years?
4. What are the qualifications for election to the Senate? To the House?
5. What method is used by most states to select Congressional candidates?
6. What impact do political action committees (PAC's) have on Congressional elections?

---

3 MEMBERSHIP IN CONGRESS

Each term of Congress lasts two years, with two regular sessions.* The 1st Congress came into being in 1789, and terms have been numbered consecutively ever since. The 99th Congress came into session in January 1985 and will terminate in January 1987.

The membership of the House and the Senate does not resemble the population as a whole. The membership of Congress has hardly been proportionate to the number of women or minorities in

*The Constitution gives the President the power to call Congress into *special session* on "extraordinary occasions." Today, however, Congress meets almost year round.

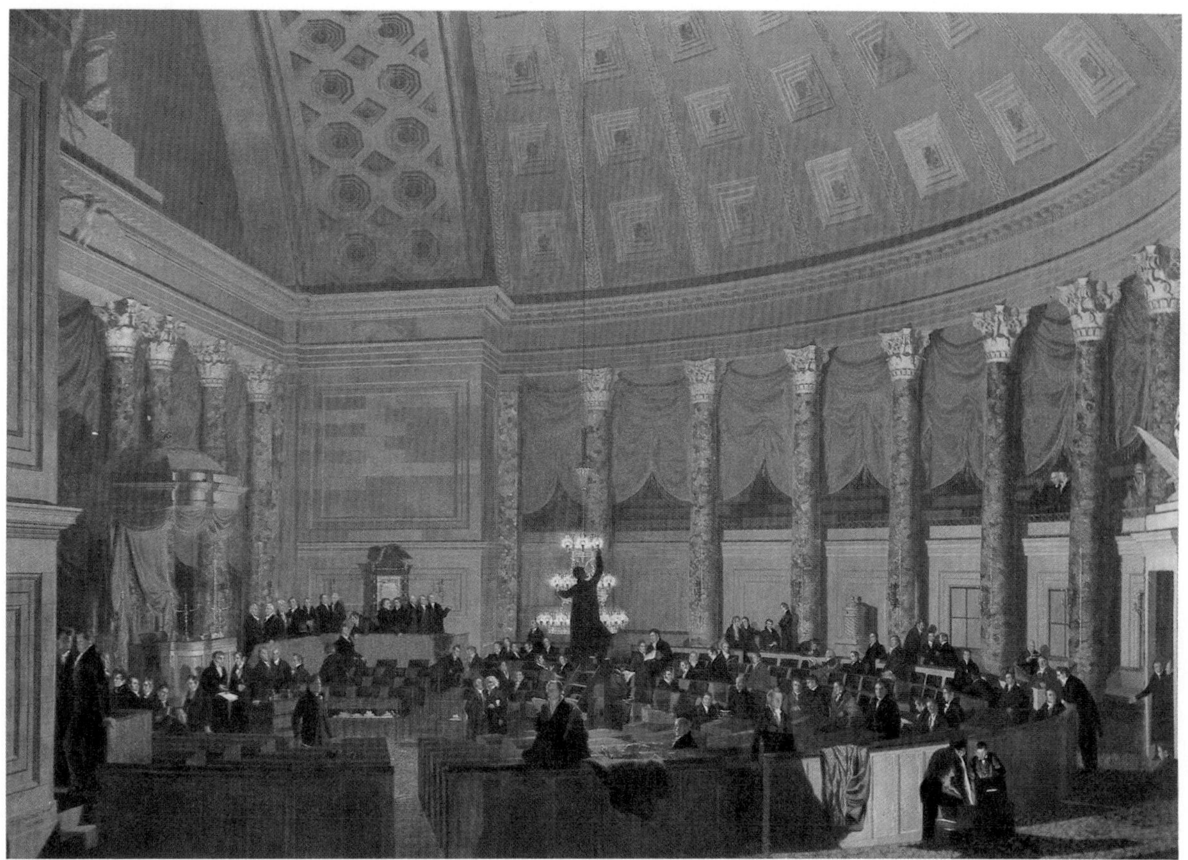

"The Old House of Representatives" by the noted artist and inventor Samuel F. B. Morse shows the 17th Congress, which was in session from 1821 until 1823. At that time the House had 183 members representing 24 states.

the general population, to say nothing of representation by different occupations or ages.

It is unrealistic to expect Congress to be a mirror image of the American people. Most observers agree, however, that increased representation of minorities and of women is a necessity. Congress must hear a range of perspectives based on different experiences.

However, members of Congress do represent specific geographic constituencies. It is not necessary to be a farmer to represent a predominantly rural district. What is necessary is to represent the wide range of interests of "the folks back home." Representatives who fail to answer to the people will be defeated in the next election.

The Philosophies of Representation

Three basic philosophies of representative government have been expressed at one time or another. These three are independence, mandate, and party responsibility. The ***independence of judgment***, or "Burkean," approach, was articulated by the great English statesman Edmund Burke. Burke believed that the actions of representatives should be based primarily on independent judgment. In his view representatives are not agents of local interests. Rather they are elected to exercise their own wisdom and conscience for the public good and the national interest.

In sharp contrast is the second approach, that of the instructed or ***mandated delegate.*** According to this view, representatives are elected to express the will of their constituents. They are bound by an electoral mandate (or command) to follow the wishes of the people who place them in office. Government by an assembly of all citizens is impossible. Thus, in place of direct democracy, the people express their will through elected representatives. According to this approach, representatives are an instrument of the people and should vote only as they are instructed by the people. (continued on page 352)

PROFILE

The 99th Congress

Representatives Cardiss Collins of Illinois (top), Matthew G. Martinez of California (center), and Eligio de la Garza of Texas (bottom); Senator Nancy Landon Kassebaum of Kansas (right)

Control of the 99th Congress, which began in January 1985, was split—the Democrats holding a majority in the House of Representatives and Republicans, a majority in the Senate. In the House, Democrats reelected Thomas P. ("Tip") O'Neill, Jr., of Massachusetts as Speaker of the House. In the Senate, Republicans elected Robert Dole of Kansas as Majority Leader to succeed Tennessee's Howard Baker, who retired from the Senate in 1985.

The 99th Congress convened with 44 new representatives and 7 new senators present. Overall, incumbency proved to be an advantage to those Congressional candidates who sought reelection. In the House, 391 incumbents were reelected. In the Senate, 27 incumbents were reelected.

At the beginning of the 99th Congress the oldest senator, at 83, was John C. Stennis of Mississippi; the youngest senator, at 37, was Daniel Quayle of Indiana. The oldest representative, at 84, was Claude Pepper of Florida; the youngest representative, at 27, was John G. Rowland of Connecticut.

The majority of the members of the 99th Congress were lawyers, but the occupations of the members varied widely. Two former pro athletes served in the 99th Congress, and at least three representatives formerly worked for the Federal Bureau of Investigation (FBI). Other occupations represented in the 99th Congress included probation officer, newscaster, social worker, mortician, ice cream maker, automobile dealer, and exterminator.

The occupations of the members of Congress, however, do not reflect every working group in the United States. Similarly, the composition of Congress does not perfectly reflect all the characteristics of the United States population, as the chart on page 351 shows. Nevertheless, legislators draw upon their own experience and expertise as they consider the interests of their constituents and the nation.

PROFILE OF THE 99TH CONGRESS

Senate			House	
		Party		
Republicans	53		Democrats	252
Democrats	47		Republicans	183
		Sex		
Men	98		Men	413
Women	2		Women	22
		Race		
Whites	98		Whites	403
Orientals	2		Blacks	19
Blacks	0		Hispanics	10
Hispanics	0		Orientals	2
Polynesians	0		Polynesians	1
		Average Age		
98th Congress	53.6		98th Congress	48.6
99th Congress	54.2		99th Congress	49.4
		Religion		
Protestants	69		Protestants	263
Roman Catholics	19		Roman Catholics	122
Jews	8		Jews	30
Others	4		Others	20
		Profession		
Lawyers	53		Lawyers	159
Business people	24		Business people	109
Public officials	8		Public officials	78
Farmers, ranchers	4		Educators	30
Educators	3		Farmers, ranchers	15
Airline pilots	1		Journalists	12
Admirals	1		Congressional aides	10
Astronauts	1		Clergy	2
Economists	1		Judges	2
Journalists	1		Dentists	1
Judges	1		Pro athletes	1
Pro athletes	1		Others	16
Veterinarians	1			

The third approach, ***party responsibility,*** emphasizes the importance of a national party program and leadership. Rather than being bound by the will of a local constituency, representatives are seen as members of a party delegation. In voting the people choose between alternative party policies and political philosophies. Representatives are elected to support the party program.

Representation in the United States is a mixture of all three approaches. On issues most closely touching the interests of their constituents, representatives ordinarily feel bound by an electoral mandate. They vote according to the will of the people. When constituents feel strongly about an issue, it is a rare legislator who will vote the other way. To do so is to risk defeat in the next election. But in matters of conscience, there are always courageous political leaders who are prepared to speak out for what they believe to be right—whether or not their constituents agree.

Constituents, however, do not have clear or strong views on most issues. During a legislative session members of Congress consider hundreds of different bills. Constituents are likely to take a deep interest in only a few. Not surprisingly, people care most about what affects them most directly. On those issues without a clear mandate from the voters, legislators have considerable freedom to vote as they choose. Most make every effort to follow party lines. When they do break party ranks, it is because they feel bound by constituency pressure to do so—or because of their independent judgment on an issue about which they are personally concerned.

With thousands of bills before Congress each year, no legislator is able to study each bill fully before deciding how to vote. On issues beyond their own expertise legislators look for guidance, or cues, on how to vote. Members of Congress say that the most important guidance they receive about how to vote comes from their fellow party members—especially those from their own state. But on issues affecting constituency interests, the views of the people back home are the major influence on legislative action.

Legislators and Their Constituents

Members of Congress want to know what their constituents, the people back home, are thinking. They rely on conversations with friends, local party leaders, and the people who are most influential in the community and the state. They read mail from constituents concerned about a particular issue. They watch the editorial pages of the home papers and keep close tabs on public opinion polls. Many members of Congress also send out their own questionnaires to gauge the views of their constituents on a variety of issues. They often find that their constituency is divided. The larger the constituency, the more varied its interests are likely to be. But whatever the size or character of the constituency, people will always differ on issues. However legislators vote on a bill, some people will be pleased and others will be unhappy.

Politically sensitive and concerned about re-election, legislators must weigh the impact of their votes on their home constituencies. Some observers criticize legislators for always looking over their shoulders, worried about what the people back home will think. Most members of Congress act as if their every vote is watched closely by the voters. However, studies reveal that most people have little knowledge of their legislator's voting record. Only if a member of the House or Senate votes "wrong" on an important or controversial issue are most people likely to hear how their legislators vote.

The Public Image of Congress

Public opinion polls regularly ask people to rate the performance of Congress as an institution. Over the years Congress has not gotten very high marks in public confidence. Approval ratings tend to rise and fall in close relationship to the nation's economy, but more often than not, the judgment has been negative. In contrast to their evaluation of Congress as an institution, people generally give their own representatives and senators the stamp of approval.

The favorable image most people have of individual members of Congress is related to what representatives do for their home constituencies. In addition to their role as lawmakers, representatives and senators provide a number of important constituency services. They get government grants or federal contracts for their district or state—perhaps a military base, a dam, or a large government office—which create jobs and give a boost to the local economy. Members of Congress also help individual constituents with a wide range of problems.

Congress at Work

Members of the House and Senate are among the hardest working people in any occupation. Some are concerned mainly with lawmaking. Their time is taken largely by committee hearings, activity on

Representative James Wright, Jr., of Texas confers with members of his staff. Most Congressional staffs include administrative assistants, legislative assistants, office managers, case workers, and press officers.

the floor of the House or Senate chamber, and in conferences with their staffs and colleagues. Others, usually freshman legislators or those who are unsure of reelection, may spend more time building support in their constituency. They tend to emphasize "errand running" for the people back home.

Whatever their emphasis or personal style, representatives and senators spend a good deal of their time helping constituents with their problems. This is often called ***case work.*** As government bureaucracy becomes more complicated, people often turn to legislators for assistance. People may write to find out how a new law affects them or their business. They may seek advice about Social Security, veterans' benefits, or tax difficulties. Most legislators make every possible effort to assist constituents. They see it as a part of their job, but also as a way of creating good will and winning support for reelection.

Each member of Congress has a personal staff to assist in answering mail, helping constituents, writing speeches and newsletters, in legislative research, and in press relations. As the workload has increased, legislators must rely more and more on their staffs—both in Washington, D.C., and in their district or state offices. Washington Congressional staffs have grown rapidly, and their members now number more than 10,000. The personal staffs of representatives average about 15. Senators' staffs vary in size from 13 to 71, depending on the population of their state.

In order to keep in close touch with their constituents, representatives and senators return frequently to their home districts or states. The average representative makes 30 to 40 such trips each year, and some go back home every weekend. These trips are rarely for relaxation but instead involve busy schedules with constituents. Members of Congress may be cutting the ribbon on a new school, giving a speech, attending a barbecue, or meeting citizen delegations. They listen to the people and try to get a feel for their problems and concerns. But as leaders they speak out on the issues—explaining their

INSIGHT

A Representative's Day

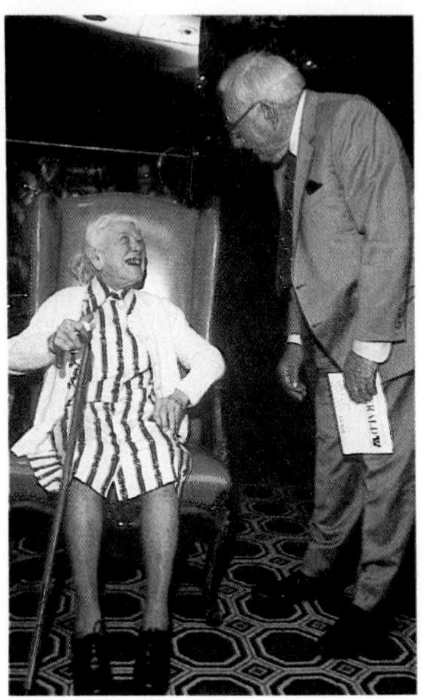

Representative Claude Pepper of Florida

Location	Activity	Average Time hours	minutes
In the House chamber	Voting, speechmaking	2	53
In committees/ subcommittees	Drafting legislation	1	24
In the office	Meeting constituents		17
	Meeting organizations and other groups		29
	Directing staff aides and conferring with other House members		58
	Preparing legislation/ speeches and answering mail		58
	Reading or talking on the telephone		37
	subtotal	3	19
In other Washington locations	Meeting constituents at the Capitol or at political events		42
	Conferring with party leadership and other members of Congress		14
	Meeting in informal groups		13
	Personal time and other activities		53
	subtotal	2	02
Other locations	Miscellaneous activities	1	40
Total average time for a Representative's day		11	18

Representative Delbert Latta of Ohio (left) and Senator Phil Gramm of Texas

Representative Barbara Mikulski of Maryland

Speaker of the House Thomas P. ("Tip") O'Neill, Jr., is the chief parliamentary officer and the leader of the majority party in the House. The salary of the Speaker is higher than that of other House members because of the additional responsibilities of the office.

own positions and those of their party, arguing the merits of different policy proposals, and seeking to inform the people about government in action.

Despite all the time they spend with constituents, three fourths of all representatives report that they devote even more effort to legislative tasks in Washington, D.C. Visitors to the House and Senate galleries are often surprised to see only a handful of legislators on the floor. During the course of a day representatives and senators come into House and Senate chambers to vote, to join in debate, or just to listen. But much of a legislator's work takes place off the floor, in committees and in Congressional offices. Even after a work day of 11 or 12 hours, members of Congress usually have "homework," such as a bill or committee report to read or a speech to prepare.

Salaries and Benefits

Members of the House and Senate each receive a yearly salary of $72,243. Congressional leaders are paid somewhat more. The Speaker of the House, like the Vice President, receives $94,200, and the House and the Senate majority and minority leaders are paid $81,700. In addition, members of Congress receive a number of benefits, including insurance, medical care, and a retirement program. Although these salaries and benefits may seem substantial, members of Congress have heavy expenses that swallow up their incomes, and many feel financially pressed. For example, most representatives and senators maintain a house or apartment in their hometown as well as in Washington, D.C.

Most representatives and senators supplement their salaries with outside income. The House requires its members to file a report on certain outside earnings. Senators must report fees received for speeches, writings, or television appearances. In 1977 the House and Senate each adopted a set of rules called a ***code of ethics*** that governs the activities of their members. The codes of ethics require members to make a full public disclosure of their wealth and personal income. In addition, the codes place limits on the amount of outside income members may earn from certain sources. Members, for example, may receive no more than $2,000 for giving a speech or writing an article. Furthermore, the income earned from these outside sources may not exceed 30 percent of the member's salary.

LEXICON

Censure and Expulsion

The Constitution gives Congress the power to discipline its own members for wrongdoing. Action ranges from **censure,** a formal reprimand or condemnation, all the way to ***expulsion*** or removal from the House or Senate. Although the need is infrequent, each house may vote to censure a member for such misconduct as financial corruption, misuse of public funds, or abuse of privileges. A member may be stripped of privileges, fined, and removed from positions of leadership. Expulsion requires the concurrence of two thirds of the membership of the chamber. In 1980, for the first time since the Civil War, the House of Representatives took the extreme measure of expelling a member. The representative was convicted of bribery after an FBI undercover operation, code-named ABSCAM, in which a bureau agent posed as a wealthy Arab sheik seeking various favors.

The intent of the codes of ethics is to erase any suspicion of ***conflict of interest.*** A conflict of interest may arise when a public official benefits personally from a government action in which he or she takes part. A conflict of interest may occur, for example, if a legislator holds stock in a company that is regulated by the government or with which the government does business. The codes also seek to eliminate possible scandal associated with gifts from lobbyists to members of Congress. Outside income remains a question of controversy and concern. But while a few instances of corruption have been uncovered, the vast majority of legislators maintain a record of honesty and integrity.

Each member of Congress is provided with a suite of offices in one of the House or Senate office buildings next to the Capitol. Representatives are allotted suites of three rooms, while senators have five-room suites. All members of Congress are also given an allowance for an office in their home district or state. Members of Congress receive a payroll allowance for their staffs, a stationery and telephone allowance, and free postage for official mail in what is called the ***franking privilege.*** Members may produce and send a periodic newsletter or questionnaire to their constituents. Political mailings, however, are printed and mailed at the members' own expense.

Paula Hawkins (left) was the first woman elected to the United States Senate from Florida. On a letter, the facsimile of Hawkins's signature, or frank (above), takes the place of a postage stamp. The privilege of franking was first employed by the Continental Congress in 1775. How does the franking privilege help members of Congress maintain contact with their constituents?

Political Patronage

Political patronage refers to government appointments made for political favor or reward. At one time senators and representatives had thousands of federal jobs that they could give to their supporters. These included such jobs back home as the local postmaster and health inspector. Today most of these old patronage jobs come under ***civil service,*** a program of public employment through merit.

On Capitol Hill there are now about 1,000 patronage jobs. Most require no special training. They include doorkeepers, mail carriers, clerks, and the pages who serve the House and Senate. Members of Congress are responsible for filling these positions. By a complicated formula, each member is awarded certain patronage jobs to give out. These jobs provide members little political benefit, and many go to college students needing financial assistance.

Members of Congress are permitted a number of trips to their home constituencies at government expense each year. In addition, ***junkets,*** or trips abroad, may be paid for by the government. Usually the junkets are for the purpose of obtaining information relating to legislative matters. It is important that representatives and senators have first-hand knowledge of conditions in foreign countries and be able to meet with officials of other governments. Frequently, however, the line between business and pleasure is hard to draw, and rather than "fact-finding," junkets often serve political, social, or entertainment purposes.

Congress as a Career

During the nineteenth century members of Congress typically served one or two terms and returned home to pursue their careers in local or state politics. In the twentieth century the greater power and prestige of Congressional positions has made service in Congress more attractive. The incumbency advantage has enabled representatives and senators to be reelected again and again and to build political careers within Congress. As of the beginning of the 99th Congress, the average House member had served 5 years, the average Senator, 9 years.

For a few members Congress is the springboard to higher office. A senator, for example, may aspire to the Presidency. A member of the House of Representatives may run for the Senate. But most members of Congress seek only to be reelected and to build their careers within the House or Senate. They may aspire to assume positions of power and influence—perhaps the chair of an important committee or leadership within the chamber itself. The leadership and organization of Congress will be discussed in the next chapter.

PROFILE

Colorado's Patricia Schroeder

Patricia Schroeder, Democrat of Colorado, has served in the United States House of Representatives since 1973. She came to Congress with impressive credentials—earning an undergraduate degree with highest honors from the University of Minnesota, and a law degree from Harvard. She also had experience as an attorney in Denver. Representative Schroeder has made a name for herself among fellow House members for her intelligence, sense of humor, and outspoken independence.

Representative Schroeder is a member of the Armed Services Committee, the Judiciary Committee, and chairs the Civil Service Subcommittee, which prepares legislation to improve government performance. In 1981 the Speaker of the House appointed her a Majority At-Large Whip, and she serves as a member of the Democratic Steering and Policy Committee. She is also co-chair of the Congresswomen's Caucus. On top of her many responsibilities as a member of Congress, Schroeder spends as much time as possible with her family: her husband James, a lawyer in Washington, D.C., and their two school-age children—Scott and Jamie.

PROFILE
Indiana's Richard Lugar

Richard Lugar, Republican of Indiana, was elected to the Senate in 1976, just 12 years after he first entered public life as a member of the Indianapolis school board. In 1967 he was elected Mayor of Indianapolis, and during his two terms he gained national attention for effective leadership. While serving as mayor, Lugar was elected president of the National League of Cities.

Senator Lugar chairs the important Senate Foreign Relations Committee and thus plays a key role in shaping United States foreign policy. He also serves on the Senate Agriculture Committee. He has established a reputation as one of the Senate's "brightest, sharpest members." His pragmatic approach to politics is seen in his willingness to listen to all sides and in his openness to compromise. Senator Lugar has moved quickly into the ranks of the Senate Republican leadership.

Senator Lugar is a physical fitness advocate and an ardent runner. The focus of his private life is his family—his wife, Charlene, their four sons, and a grandson.

Section Check

1. Define: case work, code of ethics, censure, expulsion, conflict of interest, franking privilege, civil service, junket
2. Identify: Edmund Burke, Congressional staff, ABSCAM
3. What are some characteristics of an average member of Congress?
4. What are some benefits, other than salary, that members of Congress receive?
5. What are some areas in which members of Congress might face conflicts of interest?

SUMMARY

The legislature is the most representative of the three branches of American government. Nowhere is "the consent of the governed" more clearly reflected than in Congress. The Congress is bicameral; that is, it is made up of the Senate and the House of Representatives. In the House representation is based on population. In the Senate each state is accorded two members.

When shifts in population occur, House seats must be reapportioned. The party in power usually seeks to make reapportionment to its own advantage. This can result in malapportionment, the creation of districts with unequal populations, or in gerrymandering, the drawing of odd, unnaturally shaped districts.

Both senators and representatives are now elected directly by the people. Direct election for senators was made law by the Seventeenth Amendment in 1913. Incumbents, those holding office already, are generally reelected in both the House and the Senate.

Modern politics can be a very expensive proposition. New campaign laws that limit individual contributions have tended to promote the growth of political action committees (PAC's). These special-interest organizations have come to play a powerful role in many elections.

There are three dominant philosophies of political representation: independence of judgment, mandated delegates, and party responsibility. In the United States all three philosophies are blended. Most members of Congress act independently on certain issues, consult constituents on others, and follow party lines when possible.

Members of Congress divide their time between lawmaking and helping their constituents. Members of Congress receive a salary of $72,243 per year, plus many fringe benefits. But heavy expenses swallow up their income, and many feel financially pressed.

For a few members Congress is a springboard to higher office. But most seek to build a career within the House or the Senate.

Chapter 14 Review

Using Vocabulary

Answer the questions by using the meaning of each underlined term.

1. In which house of the bicameral legislature may malapportionment occur?
2. Why is gerrymandering considered a problem resulting from reapportionment?
3. Why is a member of Congress occupying a safe seat unlikely to be elected through the coattail effect?
4. What connection is there between the codes of ethics set by Congress and the possibility of conflict of interest?
5. Why is a representative about to take a junket also likely to make use of the franking privilege?
6. What is the difference between a censure and expulsion from Congress?

Understanding American Government

1. Why was there disagreement among the states at the Constitutional Convention over the form the United States legislature would take?
2. What are the two techniques used to gerrymander Congressional districts?
3. Why do incumbents in Congress have such a powerful advantage over their challengers?
4. Why are Senate seats generally more competitive than those in the House?
5. What two proposals have been made to reduce the impact of PAC's on Congressional elections?
6. Briefly describe the three basic philosophies of representation. How is representation in the United States a mixture of all three?
7. In what ways do members of Congress stay in touch with their constituents?

Extending Your Skills: Interpreting a Political Map

Study the map on page 342. Then complete the items that follow.

1. Indicate whether the population of the following states most likely increased, decreased, or remained about the same: Oregon, Pennsylvania, Washington, California, New York, Texas, Wyoming, Ohio.
2. Based on the map, which of the following statements are true? (a) Ten states lost seats in the House of Representatives. (b) Prosperity is increasing in the Southwest. (c) States in the Southwest have increased their share of representation in the House of Representatives.
3. Write a brief paragraph explaining the relationship that exists between population growth and reapportionment.

Government and You

1. What effect does the practice of gerrymandering have on American politics? Do you think something should be done to limit the effects of gerrymandering? Would you favor the establishment of apportionment commissions? Why or why not?
2. Some people believe that Congress should have a higher percentage of women and minorities among its members. What steps might be taken to increase the numbers of women and minorities in Congress?
3. There are three basic philosophies of representative government: independence, mandate, and party responsibility. With which philosophy are you most in agreement? Why?

Activities

1. Prepare a biographical report on one of your state's two senators. You may want to consult the *Congressional Directory.*
2. Make a chart that lists the senators and representatives serving your state in Congress. Show how many years each has served. Figure out the average number of years your state's senators and representatives have served. Also list the committees to which your senators and representatives belong. Other data you may show are schooling, area of residence, and important legislation sponsored.
3. Invite a member of a Congressional staff to speak to the class. Ask this person to speak about how average citizens can best assist their members of Congress in performing the functions of government.

Chapter 15

Congress: Leadership and Organization

Like a vast picture thronged with figures of equal prominence and crowded with elaborate and obtrusive details, Congress is hard to see satisfactorily and appreciatively at a single view or from a single standpoint. Its complicated forms and diversified structures confuse the vision, and conceal the system which underlies its composition. It is too complex to be understood without an effort, without a careful and systematic process of analysis.

WOODROW WILSON

CHAPTER OVERVIEW

When Henry Clay (standing, center) presented the Compromise of 1850 to the Senate, it was composed of 60 senators. The Constitution states that there shall be 2 senators from each state. Thus, there are currently 100 senators.

1 PARTY LEADERSHIP AND ORGANIZATION

The Constitution vests the national legislative powers in Congress. But as part of the system of checks and balances, Congress is bicameral. It has two separate chambers—the Senate and the House of Representatives. A bill must pass both these chambers to become law. In essence each chamber has veto power over the other. These two legislative bodies are quite different in character and tradition. In the early days of the Republic these differences were even more marked than they are today.

Of the House of Representatives, Alexis de Tocqueville wrote in 1831: "Its members are almost all obscure individuals . . . they are mostly village lawyers, men in trade or even persons belonging to the lower classes of society." The Frenchman saw the other chamber differently. "The Senate," he wrote, "is composed of eloquent advocates, distinguished generals, wise magistrates and statesmen of note, whose language would at all times do honor to the most remarkable parliamentary debates of Europe."

Today the distinction separating the House and the Senate is reversed. The Senate, with 100 members, has the atmosphere of a club. Power is widely shared, and rules are flexible. In contrast, the House, with 435 members, has become a more formal institution. It has a tradition of stronger leadership, and its large size requires stricter rules and procedures.

Organization within each house of Congress is based on party affiliation. Almost every member is elected as a Democrat or Republican. In each chamber the Republicans sit on one side of the center aisle, and the Democrats on the other.

The party holding a majority of seats within each house is said to be "in control." The minority party is "in opposition." For most of the past 50 years the Democrats have been in control of both the House and the Senate—even when a Republican President was serving in the White House. The Republicans have controlled Congress only four years since 1933—the 80th Congress (1947–1949) when Democrat Harry S Truman was in the White House, and the 83rd Congress (1953–1955), when Republican Dwight D. Eisenhower was President. The 1980, 1982 and 1984 elections split the control of Congress. The Republicans held a majority in the Senate, while the Democrats kept control of the House.

House Leadership

Members of Congress are responsive to the varied interests of their home constituencies, but they are of independent mind. It is the task of party leadership to bring party members together to support a legislative program.

The leaders of the House manage party organization, schedule the business of the chamber, and provide members with information on current legislation. But their most important function is to persuade the members of their party to support and vote for the party's legislative program. Not all leaders are equally successful. Political circumstances change, and there are significant differences in the skill, personality, and style of the leaders themselves.

The leaders of the House are chosen by the members of each party—the House Democratic Caucus and the Republican Conference. For the majority party the three key leaders are the Speaker of the House, the Majority Leader, and the Majority Whip. The key leaders for the minority party are the Minority Leader and the Minority Whip.

Party leaders are almost always members with long service in the House. They have the respect of their colleagues and a record of party loyalty. They are usually political moderates, and they are masters of the art of compromise.

One responsibility of the House Speaker is to swear in the membership of the House each January after a Congressional election has been held. For what other tasks are House leaders responsible?

Sam Rayburn of Texas (left), who served as Speaker of the House for 17 years, held the position longer than any other representative. Thomas P. ("Tip") O'Neill, Jr., of Massachusetts (right) has served as Speaker since 1977.

The Speaker of the House

The Speaker of the House is the presiding officer of the House of Representatives. Formally elected by the House as a whole, the Speaker is actually chosen by the caucus of the majority party and is the leader of that party in the House. According to legislation the Speaker is second in line for succession to the Presidency when both the offices of President and Vice President become vacant at the same time. The office of the Speaker commands great power, but its formal powers today are only a shadow of what they were at the turn of the century.

From 1889 to 1910 Republican Speakers "Czar" Thomas Reed and "Uncle Joe" Cannon exercised authority with an iron hand. In 1910 Progressive Republicans and Democrats joined together in a revolt against Cannon. The formal powers of the Speaker were sharply limited in a reform effort to share power more broadly among House members. Among other changes, the Speaker lost the right to appoint members to House committees.

In decentralizing power among the chairpersons of the various committees, the House became increasingly fragmented. It lacked coherence and direction. Sam Rayburn of Texas, a Democratic Speaker of the House for 17 years, beginning in 1940, was sometimes able to use persuasion and gentle arm-twisting to bring effective leadership to the House. On the whole, though, the restriction of the formal powers of the Speaker weakened the House and contributed to the decline of Congress as the central institution of American government.

In a series of reforms in the 1970's the House increased the formal powers of the Speaker. The Speaker can now influence certain committee appointments and can select the committee to which a bill should be referred. To these reforms the present Speaker, Thomas P. ("Tip") O'Neill, Jr., added his own political skills to restore forceful leadership to the House.

As the presiding officer the Speaker manages the business of the House, recognizing members on the floor—that is, granting them the right to speak.

LEXICON

Rules of Procedure

We have all been in situations where everyone tried to talk at once and nothing got done. Rules of procedure bring order to the conduct of meetings. Many organizations conduct their business according to *Robert's Rules of Order,* a manual of parliamentary procedure.

The House of Representatives and the Senate each have drawn up their own rules of procedure. They are complicated, and senior members of Congress tell incoming members to master the rules if they want to become effective legislators. Skill in the use of the rules can make the difference between success or failure in legislative activity.

The House and the Senate each have a ***parliamentarian,*** a specialist in the rules of procedure and in technicalities of the legislative process. The parliamentarians are appointed by the leadership in each chamber, but once appointed, it is traditional that they remain in office regardless of which party controls Congress.

The Speaker interprets and applies the rules of procedure in the House and is responsible for maintaining order. The Speaker puts questions to a vote and, on a voice vote, determines whether the "ayes" or the "nays" have it. It is expected that the Speaker will exercise these powers in a fair and impartial manner.

The Speaker may vote on any issue and can step down from the chair to participate in debate. These privileges are used rarely and are taken to emphasize the party's strong interest in particular bills. The House rules do require, however, that the Speaker vote to break a tie.

The Speaker appoints members of the select and conference committees and refers, or assigns, bills to the standing (permanent) committees. The assignment of a bill to committee can have a significant impact on its outcome. Legislation often involves the concerns of several different committees. One committee may view a bill more favorably than another. The Speaker has the power to decide which committee gets each bill. The Speaker may even decide to refer a bill to more than one committee. The Speaker can split up a bill and send portions to different committees. The Speaker can even create special committees to consider bills of an especially broad character.

The Speaker, together with the Majority Leader, provides a link between Congress and the White House on policy matters. The Speaker and the President may work in close cooperation. Often, though, even when they are of the same party, these two leaders become entangled in a tug-of-war between the executive and legislative branches. Ultimately Congress and the President must work together if effective and coherent policy is to be enacted into law. In a process of bargaining and compromise, Congressional leadership plays a critical role.

As leader of the majority party in the House, the Speaker has important powers, both formal and informal. The Speaker is the key figure in shaping strategy and in guiding the majority party's legislative programs through the House.

The Speaker selects the majority-party members of the House Rules Committee, chooses its chairperson and consults with the Minority Leader concerning the appointment of minority party members. This committee plays a major role in directing the flow of bills from standing committees to the floor for debate and voting. The Speaker also chairs his or her respective party's committee on committee assignments—the Democrats' Steering and Policy Committee or the Republican's Committee on Committees and takes a dominant role in selecting its members. These committees nominate members to standing committees and the committee chairpersons. The Speaker's role in committee assignments gives the office considerable influence over the House's members.

The office also has informal powers. The Speaker can offer rewards in exchange for political support—an important committee assignment, assistance in passing legislation favorable to a member's home constituency, or help in a close election campaign. But the effectiveness of a Speaker depends largely on individual personality and political skill.

The Speaker must have a capacity to bargain and a willingness to compromise.

Floor Leaders and Whips

The Speaker's chief assistant is the House Majority Leader, who by tradition succeeds the Speaker whenever the office becomes vacant during the life of a Congressional session. Elected by the party caucus, the Majority Leader works with the Speaker in scheduling legislation and debate and is the party's key spokesperson and strategist on the floor. The Majority Leader is responsible for developing and holding majority support for the party's legislative program.

The Majority Leader is aided by the Majority Whip and a number of deputy whips. When the Democrats control the House, the Majority Whip is appointed by the Speaker and the Majority Leader. Whips provide a vital communications link between the party leadership and the rank-and-file House membership. Through weekly "whip notices" they keep members informed of business pending before the House. They run polls of members ("whip checks") to be sure that the party has the necessary majority on a particular bill. Finally, they try to see that members are on the floor to vote on important bills.

Party leadership on the minority side follows a similar pattern. The Minority Leader is the party's chief spokesperson and strategist, and the Minority Whip and deputy whips assist the Minority Leader. Among Republicans—who have been the minority in the House for all but four years over the past 50 years—the whips as well as the floor leader are elected by the party conference.

Representative Robert Michel of Illinois (left) has served as House Minority Leader since 1980. Representative James Wright, Jr., of Texas (right) has served as House Majority Leader since 1976.

LEXICON

Keeping the Party Together

Both Democrats and Republicans in the House of Representatives have leaders known as party whips. The term *whip* is borrowed from the British Parliament. It originally comes from "whipper-in," the person who keeps the hounds from straying during a fox hunt. In the House the whip tries to keep party members together. Given the weak and fragmented character of political parties in the United States, this is no easy task.

Party members do vote together most of the time, but constituency interests or personal judgment may lead a member to break party ranks on a particular bill. In a close vote on an issue of importance to the party, the Whip, the Majority Leader, and even the Speaker will do what they can to persuade members to vote with the party. They may try to strike a bargain or simply appeal to party loyalty. But leaders are sensitive to the pressures on individual members. House leaders recognize the members' needs to be responsive to the interests of their home districts if they are to be reelected.

Party Caucuses and Committees

The ultimate authority in each party within the House is the caucus, or conference. Before the opening of a new Congress, all members of each party meet to elect leaders and to ratify the assignments of committee members and chairpersons.

The House Democratic Caucus, once powerful, fell into disuse over the years. A move to give new life to the caucus came in the late 1960's from the House Democratic Study Group, an organization of moderate and liberal Democrats who sought reform in House procedure. In 1969 the Speaker approved regular monthly meetings for the caucus. A series of reforms soon followed. The most dramatic reform brought the selection of committee chairpersons under the control of the caucus. The caucus also created the 24-member Steering and Policy Committee to assist the Speaker in the development of the Democratic legislative program. The committee was later given the power to nominate members to the House standing committees. Final approval of committee assignments lies with the caucus.

The Republican Conference holds periodic meetings to plan legislative strategy. One of its main functions is to provide information to members on legislation before the House. Two committees of the conference carry on this task on a regular basis. The Republican Research Committee prepares reports analyzing the issues, while the Policy Committee adopts positions on legislation and plans strategy.

House Groups

There are a number of clubs and informal groups within the House of Representatives. A few are strictly for fun, such as the House baseball team. Some combine social life with business, such as the Republicans' Chowder and Marching Club, S.O.S., and the Acorns. Most informal groups have a political focus, and members often vote together as a bloc.

Within each party, groups are organized along liberal and conservative lines. Among the Democrats the liberals have the Democratic Study Group. To counter its influence, there is the conservative Democratic Forum. The conservative Republican organization is the Republican Study Committee. More moderate and liberal Republicans meet as the Wednesday Group. Then there are the "Gypsy Moths," who emerged during the Reagan administration as an informal group of 20 to 30 moderate Republicans. Conservative Democrats supporting Reagan's economic program were dubbed "Boll Weevils."

Many House groups are organized in terms of particular issues or interests. Some are ***bipartisan groups*** because members of both parties belong to them. Among the bipartisan groups are the Environmental Study Conference, the Rural Caucus, the New England Congressional Caucus, the Southern Caucus, the Women's Rights Group, the Black Caucus, and the Hispanic Caucus. State delegations also meet from time to time to discuss matters of common interest.

Senate Leadership

The smaller size of the United States Senate permits a more informal atmosphere, and traditionally its leaders have not been as strong as those in the House of Representatives. Power in the Senate is more broadly shared.

The Constitution provides that the Vice President shall preside over the Senate as "President of the Senate." But the Vice President may vote only in the case of a tie. In the absence of the Vice President the presiding officer is the President pro tempore,* who is elected by the Senate. The President pro tempore is an honorary position, given by custom to the most senior member of the majority party in the Senate. Unlike the Speaker of the House, the presiding officer in the Senate has little formal power. Other members of the Senate take turns presiding over that body.

Floor Leaders and Whips

As in the House, Senate leadership is organized along party lines. The Majority Leader is the most powerful elected leader in the Senate and is responsible for directing the party's legislative program. The Senate Majority Leader, however, does not command the formal powers of the Speaker of the House. The effectiveness of the Senate Majority Leader depends to a greater extent on political skill, personality, and style.

As in the House, the leadership in the Senate acts as a link to the White House. When the Majority Leader and the President are of the same party, there is normally a close working relationship. The Majority Leader is in charge of the President's program in the Senate. But the Majority Leader also speaks for party interests and may not always see eye to eye with the President.

The Minority Leader is the chief spokesperson and strategist for the opposition party. This senator also works closely with the Majority Leader in setting the schedule for Senate debate.

The Senate Majority and Minority Whips have duties similar to their counterparts in the House. As assistants to the floor leaders, they have three main tasks: (1) to provide information on pending legislation, (2) to count noses to see how party members stand on a particular bill, and (3) to get out the party's full strength on a key vote.

Senator Howard Baker of Tennessee (above) was Senate Minority Leader from 1977 until 1981 and Majority Leader from 1981 until 1985. Senator Robert C. Byrd of West Virginia (below) was Senate Majority Leader from 1977 until 1981 and has been Minority Leader since 1981. What are the functions of the Senate Majority and Minority Leaders?

**Pro tempore* (or *pro tem,* for short) is a Latin term meaning "for the time being."

LEGACY

Symbols of Authority

In its first session in 1789 the House of Representatives adopted the ***mace*** as the symbol of its legislative authority. The original mace was destroyed when the British burned the Capitol in 1814 during the War of 1812. The present mace has been in use by the House of Representatives since 1841. The mace is a bundle of ebony rods bound in silver and topped with a silver globe on which an eagle perches with wings outstretched.

When the House is in regular session, the mace rests on a tall marble pedestal to the right of the Speaker. If a member of the House is unruly, the Sergeant at Arms will bear the mace before the member to restore order.

The Senate cherishes another symbol—a small silver-capped ivory gavel, now without a handle. The government of India presented the Senate with a replica in 1954, and the new gavel is used by the presiding officer. The old gavel remains on the desk, a symbol of Senate tradition.

Party Conferences and Committees

In the Senate, both parties use the term *conference*, rather than *caucus*, to refer to a closed meeting of party members. The conferences elect the floor leaders and whips and ratify the nominations for membership on standing committees. Actual committee assignments, however, are made by the Democratic Steering Committee and the Republican Committee on Committees. Each party also has a Policy Committee. The majority Policy Committee, working closely with the Majority Leader, prepares reports on the issues and recommends policy positions for the party. On the minority side the Policy Committee is chaired by the Minority Leader and formulates and coordinates policy for its senators.

The Senate Club

Up until the 1960's the Senate was dominated by an "inner club," an informal group of senior senators who worked together behind the scenes. This club included both Democrats and Republicans, conservatives and liberals. They operated through bargaining and compromise to put together a legislative program. Today the inner club no longer exists. ***Seniority***—length of service—is not as important as it once was. Junior senators are now assigned to important committees, and committee and subcommittee chairs are widely distributed. No longer must an incoming senator serve out an apprenticeship period before gaining influence.

Although the Senate is relaxed and informal in its rules and procedures, senators address each other with elaborate courtesy on the floor of the chamber. Instead of calling each other by name, they typically speak of "the distinguished senator" or "the able senator" from whatever state. These flowery phrases may seem outdated, but they serve a useful purpose. This decorum helps keep a polite, friendly tone during even the most intense debate.

Section Check

1. Define: rules of procedure, parliamentarian, mace, bipartisan group, seniority
2. Identify: Speaker of the House, Majority Leader, Majority Whip, Minority Leader, House Rules Committee, Steering and Policy Committee, Republican Research Committee
3. On what basis are both houses of Congress organized?
4. How is the Speaker of the House chosen?
5. What official serves as the Speaker's chief assistant?
6. In the absence of the Vice President, who serves as the presiding officer of the Senate?

2 THE COMMITTEE SYSTEM

In 1885, long before he became President, Woodrow Wilson wrote a book entitled *Congressional Government.* He observed that Congressional government is committee government. He saw the committees as "little legislatures" where the real work of Congress took place. "Congress in session is Congress on public exhibition," Wilson wrote, "whilst Congress in its committee rooms is Congress at work." A century later much of Wilson's analysis still holds true. Committees are the center of legislative activity in both the House and the Senate.

The workload of Congress is enormous. In a two-year term upwards of 20,000 bills and resolutions are introduced. As many as 1,000 may be enacted into law. Congress must also appropriate money for the operation of the federal government and act as a watchdog to see how that money is spent. To help with the handling of so many responsibilities, each house of Congress is organized into a system of committees and subcommittees. There are several types of committees, but the most important are the permanent ones called ***standing committees.***

Standing Committees

When a bill is introduced, it is referred to a standing committee for consideration and action. There are 22 standing committees in the House and 16 in the Senate. The subject matter, or jurisdiction, of each is fixed. In most cases a committee's name indicates the area of policy with which it is concerned. Agriculture, Armed Services, Education and Labor, and Foreign Affairs are obvious examples. In some cases, though, the label is not obvious. For example, the jurisdiction of the House Ways and Means Committee is taxation.

STANDING COMMITTEES OF THE HOUSE OF REPRESENTATIVES

Committee	Number of Members	Number of Subcommittees
Agriculture	41	8
Appropriations	57	13
Armed Services	44	7
Banking, Finance, and Urban Affairs	46	8
Budget	31	9
District of Columbia	11	3
Education and Labor	31	8
Energy and Commerce	42	6
Foreign Affairs	37	8
Government Operations	39	7
House Administration	19	5
Interior and Insular Affairs	39	6
Judiciary	31	7
Merchant Marine and Fisheries	39	5
Post Office and Civil Service	24	7
Public Works and Transportation	48	6
Rules	13	2
Science and Technology	41	7
Small Business	41	6
Standards of Official Conduct	12	0
Veterans' Affairs	33	5
Ways and Means	35	6

The work load of the House of Representatives is currently divided among 22 standing committees. Only the House can reorganize its committees or set up new committees. What is the jurisdiction of the House Ways and Means Committee?

The Senate currently has 16 standing committees. Which committee has the most members? Which committee has the most subcommittees? Which Senate committees are considered the most important?

STANDING COMMITTEES OF THE SENATE

Committee	Number of Members	Number of Subcommittees
Agriculture, Nutrition, and Forestry	18	7
Appropriations	29	13
Armed Services	18	6
Banking, Housing, and Urban Affairs	18	9
Budget	22	0
Commerce, Science, and Transportation	17	8
Energy and Natural Resources	20	6
Environment and Public Works	16	6
Finance	20	9
Foreign Relations	17	7
Governmental Affairs	18	7
Judiciary	18	9
Labor and Human Resources	18	7
Rules and Administration	12	0
Small Business	19	9
Veterans' Affairs	12	0

Standing committees are considered permanent, and their memberships are fairly stable. Once appointed, members normally remain on the same committee throughout their careers in Congress. Membership on each committee is divided along party lines roughly proportionate to the number of Democrats and Republicans in each house. If, for example, some two thirds of the members of the House are Democrats, then two thirds of the members of each House committee will be Democrats. The chairperson of each committee in the House and Senate is selected from the majority party.

Some committees are considered more attractive, prestigious, or important than others. In the House the most important committees are Rules, Ways and Means, Appropriations, and Armed Services. In the Senate they are Foreign Relations, Finance, Appropriations, Judiciary, and Armed Services. These committees often bring their members—and especially their chairpersons—into national prominence.

Most standing committees today work through ***subcommittees,*** smaller bodies with specialized areas of concern. Subcommittees have become increasingly numerous. In recent Congresses, there were about 140 subcommittees in the House and more than 100 in the Senate. On the whole, subcommittees are more important in the House than in the Senate. Subcommittees are the centers of legislative activity. Here most of the work of Congress is done. In recent years they have become increasingly independent of their parent committees and are major powers in their own right.

Other Committees

In addition to standing committees, there are three other types of committees: select, joint, and conference.

Select Committees Special committees known as ***select committees*** are set up from time to time to deal with a particular problem or conduct a study or an investigation. Normally they exist for only a limited time. Among the most important select committees in recent years have been the Senate Watergate Committee, the House Ethics Committee, and the Senate Intelligence Committee. In the 98th

Congress there were four select committees in the House and four in the Senate.

Joint Committees A ***joint committee*** is composed of an equal number of members from both houses. Like select committees, they are sometimes created for a special purpose and for a limited time. There are, however, four standing joint committees. Library and Printing handle "housekeeping" concerns. The Joint Committee on Taxation prepares reports and recommendations on taxes for the House of Representatives and the Senate. The Joint Economic Committee, through its reports and hearings, helps shape overall economic policy for the nation.

Joint committees promote close cooperation between the two houses of Congress. Each house, however, jealously guards its own powers, so the use of joint committees has been limited.

Conference Committees A special joint committee created to resolve differences between the House and Senate versions of the same bill is called a ***conference committee.*** Each house often passes its own version of the same bill. Differences among the two versions must be ironed out before final passage. About 15 percent of all bills passed go to conference. The conference committee is typically made up of a few senior members of the House and Senate standing committees that reported the bill. They are appointed by the presiding officer in each house, and both political parties are represented. The compromise version they reach is then returned to the House and Senate for approval or rejection. In most cases the conference report is accepted. If not, the bill returns to the conference committee for further negotiation.

Committee Assignments

Members of Congress—especially in the House—tend to build their careers based on their work in committees. Assignment to the right committee is of major importance to most members of the Congress. Three kinds of committee assignments are most sought after.

First, some committees help members work for their constituents. These include committees that directly concern the major interests of a district or state. A representative from a farming region, for

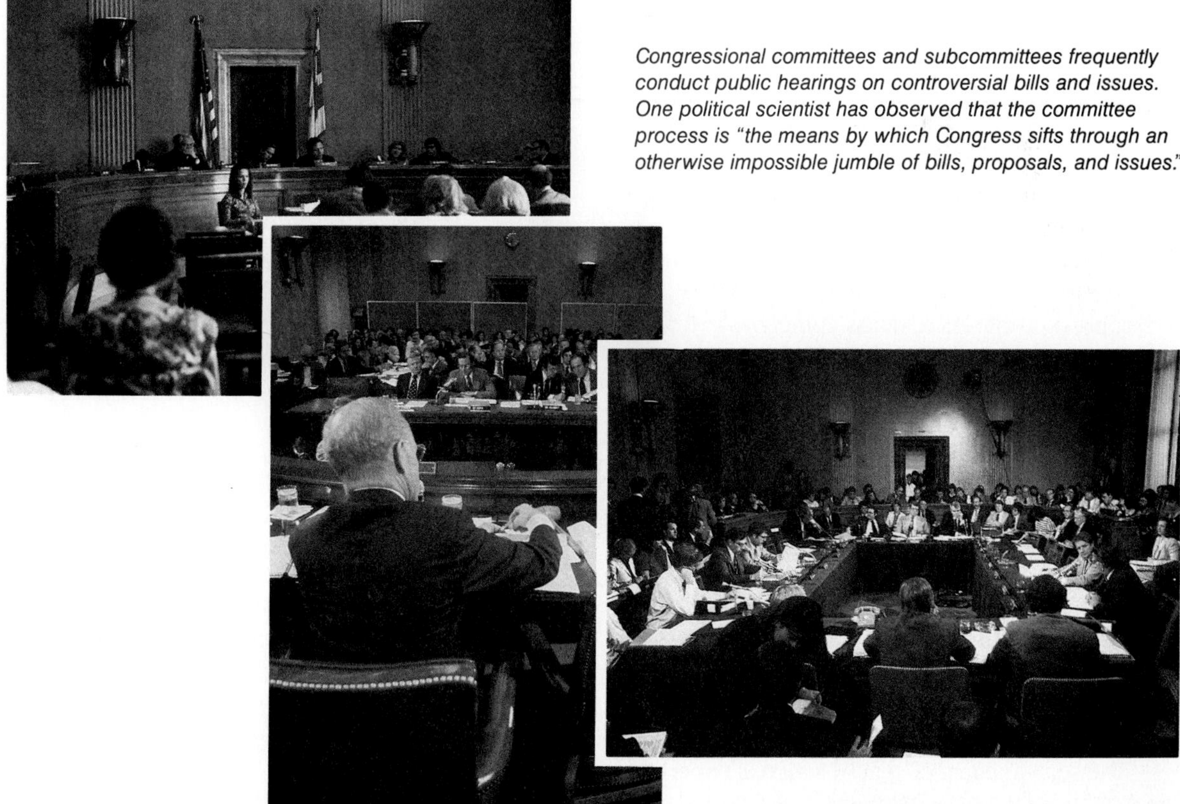

Congressional committees and subcommittees frequently conduct public hearings on controversial bills and issues. One political scientist has observed that the committee process is "the means by which Congress sifts through an otherwise impossible jumble of bills, proposals, and issues."

example, would probably want to be on the House Agriculture Committee. Membership on a committee directly related to constituency interests is often critical for reelection. Some committees, such as Public Works and Transportation, offer the chance for members to get major federal construction projects—such as highways or dams—for their home areas. The projects may be important and necessary, but often they are not. Public money may be wasted on so-called ***pork barrel projects*** to help a member's chances for reelection.

A second type of committee enables representatives and senators to help shape national policy in areas of their special interest. A member of Congress concerned about national defense might seek assignment to the Armed Services Committee. Another might want to serve on the Energy and Natural Resources, Foreign Relations, or the Judiciary Committee.

Third, some committees provide avenues to power within the House and Senate. They are bases from which members may exert influence over their colleagues. Such committees include those on taxing (Senate Finance and House Ways and Means) and spending (Appropriation). Another is the House Rules Committee. Although no longer as powerful as it once was, the Rules Committee continues to play an important role in setting the agenda and time for debate on major bills in the House of Representatives.

Effects of Specialization

Each member of the House serves on either one or two standing committees and an average of four subcommittees. The average senator serves on two or three committees and some ten subcommittees. Members of Congress seek assignment to the committees that interest them most, and most become specialists in a particular legislative subject. This is especially true of the House.

Specialization has two important effects. First, it tends to fragment legislative activity. Each of the committees becomes its own little world. Each works closely with concerned interest groups and government agencies to hammer out policy on a particular legislative matter. Each committee goes its own way, often with little vision of overall national policy goals. It is the task of the party leadership to provide that vision and to coordinate committee action behind a cohesive legislative program.

The second effect of specialization is expertise. As experts, committee members command special influence over their colleagues. Knowledge commands respect. Thus, when a bill comes to the floor for a vote, most legislators take their cues from the committee specialists. The result is that some 90 percent of all bills that are favorably reported out of committee pass the House and the Senate. Furthermore, a majority of committee bills pass without any amendments. Woodrow Wilson's analysis is perhaps truer than ever: Congress does its work in committee.

How Committee Assignments Are Made

The two political parties have similar ways of making assignments to standing committees. Democrats are nominated by the party's steering committee in each house, with final approval by the House Democratic Caucus and the Senate Conference. Republican assignments are made by the Committee on Committees.

Committee assignments are based on seniority, region, and political ideology. Each party tries to meet the members' requests for particular committees insofar as possible. Special consideration is given to assigning members to committees that will help in their reelection.

New members of Congress cannot expect to get on every committee they want. New senators, by custom, are assigned to one of the more powerful committees and one or two with less prestige. First-time representatives must often work entirely on less attractive committees before they can serve on those with more power and prestige.

When a vacancy occurs on one of the more important committees, a representative or senator may request a transfer. Once members find the right committee, they normally remain there throughout their careers in Congress. Through continued service on the same committee, they gain the knowledge and power that comes with seniority.

Section Check

1. Define: pork barrel project, subcommittee
2. Identify: standing committee, select committee, joint committee, conference committee
3. What percentage of bills favorably reported out of committee pass the House and Senate? Why is this percentage so high?
4. What are the most important factors in making committee assignments?

Senator John McClellan of Arkansas (left), Senator James Eastland of Mississippi (center), and Representative L. Mendel Rivers of South Carolina (right) were powerful, conservative Democrats who, because of the seniority system, were able to control several key Congressional committees from the 1950's until the 1970's.

3 COMMITTEE CHAIRPERSONS

Because so much of Congress's work is done in committee, the chairpersons of committees wield great power. For many years committee chairpersons were selected according to the unwritten rule of seniority. By custom the majority party member with the longest continuous service on a committee became its chairperson. But the seniority system came in for sharp criticism, and beginning in 1971, a series of reforms weakened its hold. In practice most committee chairpersons are still selected by seniority, but selection by seniority is no longer automatic.

The Seniority System

From the mid-nineteenth century chairpersons in the Senate were selected on the basis of their committee seniority. (The senior minority party member was known as the *ranking member.*) Committee members were ranked by length of service for purposes of succession. On the death, retirement, or defeat of a chairperson, the next member of the majority party on the ladder of seniority would move up to take the chair.

In the House, by contrast, the seniority system was not established securely until after the reforms of 1910. Before that time the Speaker appointed committee chairpersons. Appointment by the Speaker was tolerated while members served only a term or two and then returned to state and local politics. As members began to make their political careers within Congress, though, discontent with the procedure grew. In 1910 members of the House voted to strip the Speaker of the power to appoint chairpersons. From then until the 1970's, with only a few exceptions, chairpersons were selected according to the principle of seniority.

There are two main arguments for the seniority system. First, automatic selection by seniority may promote harmony by eliminating conflict over who should be chairperson. Second, seniority may ensure that the chairperson will be most experienced in the legislative concerns of the committee.

The argument against the seniority system is that it rewards the survivors—those who serve the longest time—not necessarily the best legislator. Leadership may be placed in the hands of elderly representatives and senators, ignoring the talents of younger members.

The real problem with the seniority system, however, is not a matter of age. It is that the seniority system enables people to chair committees even when they are opposed to the policies favored by the majority in their own party.

The most senior members of Congress—the "survivors"—are most likely to come from safe districts where they face little or no opposition. From the late 1930's until the mid-1960's these safe districts were located primarily in the South, especially in the more conservative rural areas. The South was still solidly Democratic, and incumbents were virtually assured of reelection. The result in both the Senate and the House was that conservative southern Democrats gained the chairs of a large number of committees.

The southern conservative chairpersons were often at odds with the majority of their fellow Democrats, and they frequently voted with the Republicans. Moreover, they used their powerful positions to block legislation they did not like. The attack on the seniority system by reform Democrats was primarily directed against these powerful southern conservatives.

Ironically, by the early 1970's the conservative bias of the seniority system was rapidly disappearing. Many of the southern chairpersons who had ruled their committees with an iron hand had died or retired. In many instances their chairs were taken by liberals from the Northeast or the West. And the South itself was changing, becoming more urban and more Republican.

Reforming the Selection Process

The reforms of the early 1970's sought to break the hold of the seniority system over the selection of committee leaders. In place of the strict rule of seniority, Republicans and Democrats in each chamber adopted some form of election, with final authority in the party caucus.

Among House Democrats nominations for committee chairpersons are made by the Steering and Policy Committee. Each nominee is then voted on in secret ballot by the Democratic Caucus. The Republican Committee on Committees nominates ranking committee members. The nominees are then voted on in secret ballot by the Republican Conference.

The Senate follows a somewhat different procedure in selecting committee leadership. The Democratic nominations are made by the Steering Committee, chaired by the party floor leader. If at least 20 percent of all Democratic Senators want a vote on any nominee, a secret ballot is held. The Republicans on each committee meet to elect their ranking member. The committee choices are subject to final approval by the Republican Conference.

These reforms were adopted to place control over the selection of committee leadership in the hands of the party caucuses. In practice, however, the seniority system was modified but not overturned. Chairpersons and ranking members continue to be selected on the basis of seniority. In 1975, though, the House Democratic Caucus voted in an historic action to replace three long-time committee chairpersons. This action served as a warning to all chairpersons that they must be responsive to the views of the majority in the party.

Powers of the Chairperson

The roles of chairpersons vary from committee to committee. Some are more powerful than others, but all chairpersons have a major role in shaping legislation. Though their powers have been reduced in recent years, they remain key figures in the leadership of Congress.

At one time the power of the chairpersons was almost absolute. Protected by the seniority system, many ruled over their committees like tyrants. They controlled the schedule, called meetings, selected the staff, and appointed subcommittees. As legislative gatekeepers, chairpersons often had total control over the bills referred to their committees. The chairpersons could push through a bill they liked or ***pigeonhole***—hold back—a bill they opposed.

The powers of the chairpersons were brought under control by the reforms of the 1970's. The secret ballot and election procedure made the chairpersons accountable to their colleagues for their conduct. Abuse of authority could result in replacement of a chairperson.

Specific powers of the chairpersons—especially in the House—were also limited in a number of ways. The most important action was taken by the

A 1970 cartoon by Herblock satirizes some abuses of the seniority system. Public legislation is portrayed as a casualty of the system, which was characterized by closed committee meetings and off-the-record voting.

The staff of the House Select Committee on Aging prepares for a day of hearings. A portrait of the committee's former chairperson—Representative Claude Pepper of Florida, who is more than 80 years of age—hangs in the staff's office. How do committee staffs assist in the work of Congressional committees?

House Democrats to give subcommittees greater independence. The Democratic members of each committee, meeting as a caucus, now determine the number of subcommittees to be established and select their chairpersons. The jurisdiction, or subject matter, of each subcommittee is also fixed. These reforms—part of a "bill of rights" for subcommittees—protect House subcommittees from domination by the chairperson of the standing committee.

The House and Senate also placed limits on the number of committees and subcommittees any one person could chair. No senator can be chairperson of more than one full committee and one major subcommittee. House Democrats adopted a rule that no member may chair more than one subcommittee. As a result of these restrictions, leadership and power in Congress are more widely shared. In the House almost half of all Democratic members now chair subcommittees.

Committee Staffs

Congressional committees and subcommittees are assisted by professional staffs. These have grown rapidly over the past 30 years, and each house now has more than 1,500 committee staff members. Reflecting the division within Congress, the majority and minority party members on each committee have separate staffs.

Staff members perform a number of different tasks relating to committee work. They plan hearings and arrange for witnesses to appear. They also conduct investigations and gather information for committee use. They analyze legislation, draft bills, and prepare committee reports. Many staff members are experts in the legislative matters before the committee. Their judgment is respected, and they are often influential in shaping policy. Indeed, critics sometimes express alarm at the extent of staff power. Despite the importance of committee staffs in lawmaking, however, the final decisions are made by elected representatives and senators.

Committee staffs maintain close contact with both the executive branch and interest groups. These ties provide a valuable exchange of information and viewpoints. Staffs also serve to bridge the gap between the two houses of Congress. House and Senate staffs concerned with the same subject matter work closely together. This is especially important in preparing conference committee reports, where the differences between House and Senate versions of a bill must be ironed out.

Section Check

1. What was the sole basis for selecting committee chairpersons before the 1970's?
2. Which group nominates candidates for chairperson among House Democrats? Which group nominates Republicans in the House?
3. How are Senate chairpersons selected by the Democrats? By the Republicans?
4. What are some tasks performed by committee staff members?

4 CONGRESSIONAL SUPPORT

With its heavy workload Congress requires the assistance of "housekeeping" staffs and various supporting organizations.

Capitol Housekeeping

In both the House and Senate certain appointed officials are responsible for making sure that the business of Congress goes smoothly. The Sergeants-at-Arms enforce order on the floor of the House and Senate chambers. They also oversee the Capitol Police. In the Senate the Sergeant-at-Arms also supervises the Senate pages, doorkeepers, the visitors and press galleries, and various Senate employees. In the House most of these supervisory functions are handled by the Office of the Doorkeeper.

Still another member of the housekeeping staff is the Architect of the Capitol. This official is the administrative officer in charge of the care and maintenance of the buildings on Capitol Hill. The buildings include the Capitol and its grounds, the House and Senate office buildings, the Library of Congress, and the Supreme Court.

Capitol Pages

Members of Congress are served by a force of young men and women called ***pages.*** There are 30 pages in the Senate and 71 in the House of Representatives. Senate and House pages are between 16 and 18 years of age and must be at least juniors in high school. They are appointed under patronage by representatives and senators. Because only a small number can be selected, most pages serve for only a six-month period.

The pages have a number of duties. They must, of course, attend school. Classes in the Capitol Page School, located on the third floor of the Library of Congress, begin at 6:15 in the morning. At 9:45 classes are over, and the pages report for duty to the House and Senate cloakrooms. Democrats and Republicans each have separate cloakrooms next to the House and Senate chambers, and these are headquarters for the pages in each house. While the pages are appointed along party lines, their duties are nonpartisan.

Before the House and Senate sessions begin, the pages prepare each member's desk for the business of the day. There they place a copy of the

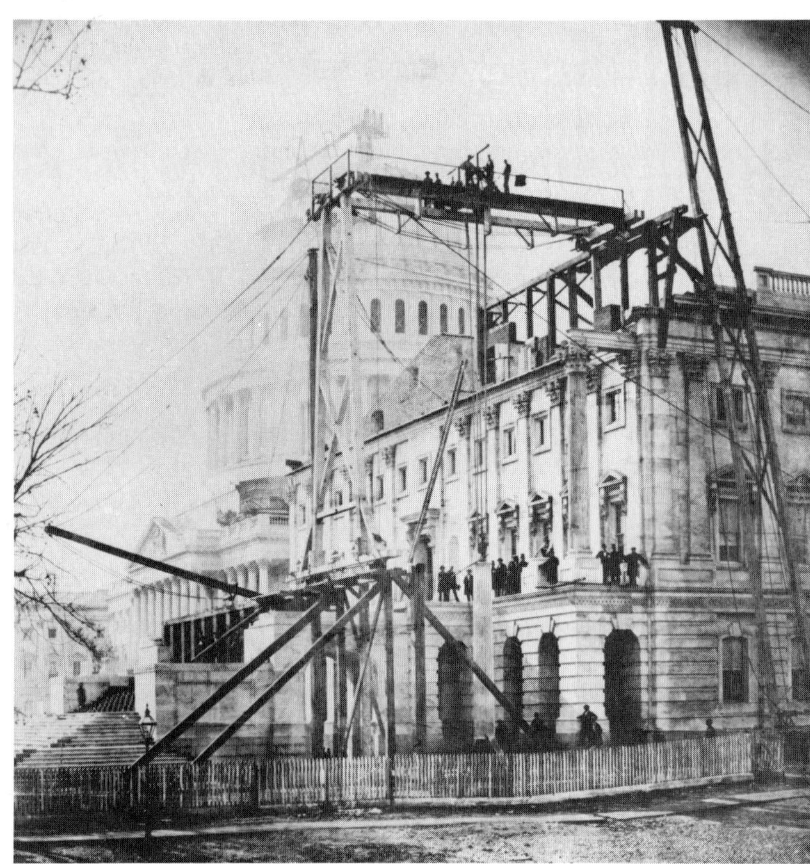

Congress is responsible for the maintenance of the Capitol. This photograph, taken in the 1860's, shows the expansion of the Capitol that was authorized by Congress in 1850.

The Library of Congress is composed of three buildings. The main reading room of the Library of Congress (above) is housed in the Thomas Jefferson Building, which was built in 1897 after the Library outgrew its original location in the Capitol. What services does the Library provide to Congress and to the nation?

Congressional Record, the calendar of business, and the bills, resolutions, documents, and reports that may come before the chamber.

In the House, pages are given special assignments. One is assigned exclusively to the Speaker. Two are in charge of supplying members with bills and reports as they come before the House. These pages are also responsible for the legislative bells that call members for votes on the floor. Several pages are assigned to the cloakroom, where they answer the telephones. They call members to the phone, take messages, and place calls for members. Most House pages are floor pages, or "runners." They are the messengers of Capitol Hill, constantly on the move between the House floor and Congressional offices. Senate pages do not have such a sharp division of labor, but their duties are very similar: running errands, carrying messages, distributing documents, and answering the telephone.

When the House is in session, floor pages take their places at the back of the chamber. There they wait for the representative's call. This is made by the push of a button at the member's desk, which lights a board at the pages' station. In the Senate the pages sit on the steps of the rostrum at the front. A senator calls by a motion of the hand or a snapping of fingers. Pages must be able to identify members on sight and are expected to attend immediately to a member's request.

The Library of Congress

The Library of Congress was founded in 1800 to provide "such books as may be necessary for the use of Congress." Congress appropriated $5,000 for the new Library. The Library was originally housed, together with Congress and the Supreme Court, in the first Capitol.

During the War of 1812, British troops burned the Capitol in 1814, destroying the Library's collection of 3,000 volumes. Congress rebuilt its Library in 1815 by purchasing Thomas Jefferson's private collection of about 6,000 volumes for $23,950. At that time Jefferson noted, "There is no subject to which a Member of Congress may not have occasion to refer."

PROFILE

Congressional Research Service

The Congressional Research Service (CRS) is a department within the Library of Congress. With a staff of more than 700 persons, the CRS handles about 2,000 requests for information from Congress each day. These range from answers to specific questions that may be provided in a few minutes to the preparation of reading lists, analyses of policy issues, and detailed legal research that takes anywhere from a few hours to many days.

Twice more—in 1825 and 1851—fire destroyed parts of the Library's collections. In 1866, the Library of Congress expanded to include the Library of the Smithsonian Institution. In 1870, Congress decided that copies of all copyrighted works in the United States would be kept in the Library of Congress. The nation's library grew rapidly and in 1897 moved into the new Thomas Jefferson Building.

Congress added a major collection to the Library in 1930 when it purchased more than 3,000 rare fifteenth-century books, including a Gutenberg Bible. As the library's collections continued to grow throughout the twentieth century, two new buildings were added—the John Adams Annex in 1938 and the James Madison Building in 1981. Indeed, the vast collections of the Library of Congress bring to mind Thomas Jefferson's observation of 1815.

Today it is the world's largest library. Its collection includes more than 18 million books and pamphlets, 32 million pieces of music and 9 million photographs. Its materials are in 468 different languages. Jefferson's rough draft of the Declaration of Independence and Madison's personal notes on the Constitutional Convention are among its treasures.

The Library is open to the general public, but books may not be removed from the reading rooms. The Library provides a wide range of services to the public. One of the most important is the provision of special materials for the blind and those unable to read regular printed matter. The Library of Congress and 160 cooperating regional libraries throughout the country have books with raised characters (braille), large-print books, and "talking books" on tape and record.

The Library of Congress also provides a number of services to other libraries. In cataloging new books, for example, it prepares printed cards which may be purchased. Its own classification system for identifying and numbering books is used by many libraries instead of, or in addition to, the Dewey Decimal System. Furthermore, most new books have the Library of Congress number printed on the copyright page.

The Government Printing Office

Within the legislative branch of the federal government is the world's largest publishing house, the Government Printing Office. The departments and agencies of the national government publish thousands of pamphlets and books each year. Some of these materials are available free and others are for sale. Almost every conceivable topic is covered among the 25,000 available titles—from accident prevention to zoology. The most popular publications are sold through the Government Printing Office

LEXICON

Copyright

Have you ever wondered what that little © is in the front of books and magazines and on record jackets? It is the symbol for ***copyright.*** A copyright is an exclusive legal right to produce and sell a written, musical, or artistic work. Since 1870 the Library of Congress has been responsible for copyrights in the United States. Works to be copyrighted—and thus protected by law—are registered with the Library's Copyright Office.

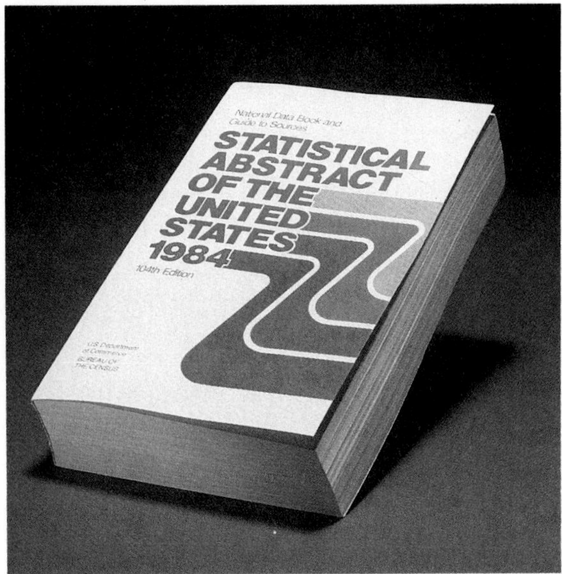

The Statistical Abstract *has been published since 1878 and is sold through the Government Printing Office.*

bookstores in Washington, D.C., and in 19 cities around the country.

One of the major responsibilities of the Government Printing Office is the publication of the *Congressional Record.* This is the official transcript of the daily debate and proceedings in the House and Senate. Each copy averages more than 200 pages in length, and the speed of its publication is astounding. At the close of each day, the *Record* goes to press. In the morning—some 13 hours later—copies are delivered to Capitol Hill.

In addition to the proceedings on the floor of the House and Senate, the *Congressional Record* contains "Extensions of Remarks"—insertions into the official record made by senators and representatives. These often include speeches made outside Congress, editorials from hometown newspapers, or letters from constituents. The *Record* also carries a "Daily Digest" of the activities of Congressional committees. In short, the *Congressional Record* is a daily report of Congress in action.

Section Check

---

1. Which officials preserve order in the House and the Senate?
2. Why was the Library of Congress founded?
3. What publication is a daily report of Congress in action?

SUMMARY

The organization of Congress is bicameral. There are two separate chambers—the House of Representatives and the Senate. Each must approve a bill for it to become law. Within each chamber the organization is based on party affiliation. In each house the Republicans sit on one side, the Democrats on the other.

The House is led by the Speaker of the House. This powerful official is chosen by the caucus (meeting) of the majority party. The office of Speaker had much of its power removed in 1910, but some power was restored in the 1970's. The Speaker is the presiding officer of the House and the leader of the majority party. Power in the House is also shared by the Majority Leader, the Majority Whip, the Minority Leader, and the Minority Whip.

The Vice President presides over the Senate. In the Vice President's absence the President pro tempore of the Senate presides over that body but lacks the power of the Speaker of the House. The Senate also has floor leaders and whips for both parties.

Congress does much of its real work in committees. The most important are the standing committees. There are 22 standing committees in the House and 16 in the Senate. In the House the most prestigious committees are Rules; Ways and Means; Appropriations; and Armed Services. In the Senate the most important are Foreign Relations; Finance; Appropriations; Judiciary; and Armed Services. Both houses also employ select committees for special issues and investigations, as well as joint and conference committees.

Because so much work is done in committees, the chairpersons of these committees are important figures. For many years the chairs have been chosen by the unwritten rule of seniority; the majority party member with the longest continuous service on the committee was chosen. Critics point out that the seniority system enables people to become committee chairpersons even when they are opposed to the policies favored by the majority in their own party. Recent reforms have kept the seniority rule from being used automatically, but it is still the dominant method of chairperson selection.

Congressional support services help the members with the business of legislation. These services include Capitol housekeeping, Capitol pages, the Library of Congress, and the Government Printing Office. The entire organizational structure of Congress is designed to help the members put the wishes of the American people into law.

Chapter 15 Review

Using Vocabulary

Answer the questions by using the meaning of each underlined term.

1. What is the function of the parliamentarian in regard to rules of procedures?
2. Why is a joint committee a bipartisan group?
3. Why does the mace stand next to the Speaker's platform in the House of Representatives?
4. What would you expect to take place in a select committee that you would not expect to take place in a conference committee?
5. When would a ranking member of a standing committee favor a pork barrel project?
6. What does it mean if a chairperson pigeonholes a bill?

Understanding American Government

1. What are the most important powers that the Speaker of the House derives from being the leader of the majority party?
2. What are the three main tasks of Senate whips?
3. What three types of committee assignments are most sought after?
4. What are the two most important effects of specialization in Congress?
5. What are the two leading arguments for the use of the seniority system in appointing committee chairpersons?
6. What powers are held by committee chairpersons in both houses of Congress?
7. What are the most important services provided by the Library of Congress?

Extending Your Skills: Understanding a Political Role

Reread the section "The Speaker of the House" on pages 363–365. Then complete the items that follow.

1. Identify the phrases that indicate a responsibility of the Speaker of the House: (a) Recognizes members to speak; (b) Determines the outcomes of voice votes; (c) Enters into all floor debates; (d) Breaks tie votes; (e) Determines which bills are referred to which committees.
2. Explain why the following generalization is true: The Speaker of the House can determine the outcome of key votes.

Government and You

1. Members of Congress are becoming increasingly specialized. A few become experts on a particular topic, while others may know very little about it. Do you think this specialization is necessary? Do you think it has a positive or a negative effect on Congress? Why?
2. The seniority system is no longer used automatically to make appointments of committee chairpersons. Would you limit its use even more? Do you think its advantages outweigh its disadvantages? What are the reasons for your answers?
3. Name the member of Congress whose name you know the best. What position does this person hold? What factors help a member of Congress become well known?
4. Rivalry exists between the House and the Senate. How is this rivalry part of our political system? How could it have been anticipated from the founding of the Republic? Do you think America would be better off with a one-house Congress? Why or why not?

Activities

1. Prepare a biographical report on a former Speaker of the House such as Sam Rayburn or Thomas Reed.
2. Stage a class debate on the following topic: "*Resolved:* That the automatic seniority rule for the selection of committee chairpersons should be reinstituted."
3. Make a wall chart showing the committees to which your representative and your two senators belong.
4. Interview your representative or a member of your representative's staff. Ask about the effect of increased specialization on legislative programs. Ask this person what is the greatest challenge facing Congress today. Report your findings to the class.

Chapter 16

Congress in Action

Once begin the dance of legislation, and you must struggle through its mazes as best you can to the breathless end—if any end there be.

WOODROW WILSON

The Old Senate Chamber was restored to its mid-nineteenth-century elegance in 1976. The Senate, which had outgrown this chamber by 1840, moved into a new wing in the Capitol in 1859. The Supreme Court occupied the Old Senate Chamber from 1859 until 1935. The Old Senate Chamber is now a museum.

1 THE POWERS OF CONGRESS

Article 1 of the Constitution describes the United States Congress, the lawmaking branch of our government. This first Article is more than twice as long as any other part of the Constitution. Its length reflects the complicated makeup of the legislature. The United States is ruled by a government of laws. For each law passed, a majority of 435 representatives and 100 senators must agree on its exact wording. This is no simple feat. Committees, subcommittees, and conference committees come into play. The interests of lobbyists, constituents, and members of the executive branch further complicate the legislative process. This chapter looks at the inner workings of Congress and the manner in which it deals with the executive branch.

Congressional powers may be classified as legislative and nonlegislative. ***Legislative powers*** derive from Article 1 of the Constitution. They involve the many areas about which Congress may make laws. The ***nonlegislative powers*** may all be found in other parts of the Constitution. These promote the system of checks and balances by giving Congress certain authority with regard to the executive branch.

Legislative Powers

Article 1, Section 1, of the Constitution begins:

All legislative powers granted herein shall be vested in a Congress of the United States.

Then follows a list of specific powers that are known as the ***expressed powers*** of Congress. They include the power to tax, to regulate commerce, to coin money, and to declare war.

This list, however, does not exhaust the powers of Congress. As noted in Chapter 4, Congress has ***implied powers*** given to it by the Constitution. For example, the powers to regulate commerce and maintain a navy are taken to imply the power to improve harbors and other waterways.

The constitutional source of the implied powers is Clause 18 of Article 1, Section 8. This is also known as the "necessary and proper clause," or the ***elastic clause.*** This clause states:

Congress shall have power . . . to make all laws which shall be necessary and proper for carrying into execution the foregoing expressed powers, and all other powers vested by this Constitution in the government of the United States, or in any department or officer thereof.

The elastic clause enables Congress to adapt to the needs of a changing society.

In Chapter 4 it was noted that, early in our history, members of two schools of thought began to debate the meaning of Clause 18. One school was known as the ***strict constructionists.*** The other was the ***broad constructionists.*** Secretary of the Treasury Alexander Hamilton and other broad constructionists convinced Congress to create a National Bank in 1791. Hamilton argued successfully that such authority was implied by Congress's fiscal powers and by Clause 18, the elastic clause.

In 1819 the State of Maryland challenged this power in the Supreme Court. Maryland took a strict constructionist position, asserting that the elastic clause could not have intended such drastic steps

THE POWERS OF CONGRESS

Expressed Powers

1. To lay and collect taxes
2. To borrow money
3. To regulate foreign and interstate commerce
4. To establish naturalization and bankruptcy laws
5. To coin money and to regulate its value; to regulate weights and measures
6. To punish counterfeiters
7. To establish post offices
8. To grant patents and copyrights
9. To set up courts inferior to the Supreme Court
10. To define and to punish piracies and felonies on the high seas, and offenses against the law of nations
11. To declare war, to grant letters of marque and reprisal, and to make rules concerning captures on land and water
12. To raise and support armies
13. To provide and maintain a navy
14. To make laws governing land and naval forces
15. To provide for calling forth the militia to execute federal laws, suppress insurrections, and repel invasions
16. To provide for organizing, arming, and disciplining the militia, and to provide for its governing when in the federal government's service
17. To exercise exclusive jurisdiction of the District of Columbia; to exercise authority over forts, dockyards, and other needful buildings

Implied Powers

To make all laws which shall be necessary and proper for carrying into execution the foregoing powers

Article 1, Section 8, of the Constitution defines the powers of Congress. The "necessary and proper" clause of the implied powers provides the Constitution with a high degree of flexibility. Thus, Congress is able to enact legislation concerning areas not specifically listed in the expressed powers. The basis for any implied power, however, must always be found in the expressed powers.

as the creation of a National Bank. In *McCulloch* v. *Maryland* (1819), the high court sided with Congress and the broad constructionists' position. Chief Justice John Marshall wrote:

We think . . . the sound construction of the Constitution must allow . . . the national legislature . . . to perform the high duties assigned to it, in the manner most beneficial to the people.

This interpretation has held up in succeeding years. The power and scope of Congress has been immeasurably increased by this landmark ruling.

Nonlegislative Powers

The primary function of Congress is to make laws. In the constitutional system of checks and balances, however, the three branches of government—legislative, executive, and judicial—share powers. Thus, the Constitution gives to Congress certain nonlegislative powers. These powers are expressed in different parts of the Constitution. A majority of these powers are detailed in Article 2.

Electoral Power Under the electoral college system, if no candidate for President or Vice President receives a majority of the electoral votes, the election is decided by Congress. The House of Representatives elects the President from among the three candidates with the largest number of electoral votes. The Senate chooses between the two leading candidates for Vice President. These powers are expressed in the Twelfth Amendment.

Congress gained an additional electoral duty with the adoption of the Twenty-fifth Amendment in 1967. The amendment provides that whenever there is a vacancy in the office of the Vice President, the President shall nominate a successor. A majority in both houses of Congress must then confirm the nomination.

Since this amendment was ratified, Congress has acted twice to fill the vacancies. The first occurred in 1973, when Vice President Spiro Agnew resigned after being indicted for accepting bribes. President Richard Nixon nominated House Minority Leader Gerald Ford to take Agnew's place, and Ford was confirmed as Vice President by Congress. Less than a year later, upon Nixon's resignation from office, Ford succeeded to the Presidency. He nominated former New York governor Nelson Rockefeller to the Vice Presidency. After lengthy hearings in both the House and Senate, Rockefeller was confirmed.

Impeachment Power As stated in Article 2, Section 4, Congress has the special judicial power of ***impeachment.*** By this power, Congress may remove the President, Vice President, or other

Gerald R. Ford (right) announces the Congressional confirmation of Nelson A. Rockefeller (left) as Vice President in 1974. Under what circumstances does Congress confirm Vice-Presidential nominees?

An 1868 engraving (left) portrays the Senate as the court of impeachment in the trial of President Andrew Johnson. The House Judiciary Committee (above) recommends the impeachment of President Richard Nixon in April 1974.

federal officials of the United States from office for "treason, bribery, and other high crimes and misdemeanors." The phrase *high crimes and misdemeanors* comes from English tradition. It means simply abuse of authority or official misconduct. An impeachable offense need not be a crime. It is enough that it be a violation of the public trust upon which democratic government depends.

There are two stages in the removal of a public official by impeachment. The House of Representatives prepares the bill of impeachment, a list of charges against the official. Then hearings are held and witnesses examined. The House must decide whether the evidence of misconduct is sufficient to justify trial. If a majority of the House votes to impeach the official, the case then goes to the Senate for trial.

The Senate tries the official on the specific charges brought by the House. Evidence is heard and witnesses may be called just as in a criminal case. If the President is to be tried, the Chief Justice of the Supreme Court presides. The Senate sits as the jury, with a two-thirds vote needed for conviction.

Conviction in an impeachment results in removal from office and bars the person from holding future office. The purpose of the impeachment proceeding is not to punish the offender. Instead, it is to protect the public from official misconduct. Punishment is a matter for the regular courts. An official who has been removed from office by a conviction on impeachment charges remains subject to criminal prosecution.

In the nation's history only four officials, all of whom were federal judges, have been convicted by the Senate and removed from office. Altogether, only 12 impeachment trials have been held. The most famous was that of President Andrew Johnson in 1868. Radical Republicans were angry with Johnson for vetoing several Reconstruction bills. They felt Johnson was unwilling to punish southern plantation owners. Most of the Republican charges against Johnson, though, were without merit. Still, Johnson was saved from conviction by only a single vote.

In 1974 the House began impeachment proceedings against President Richard Nixon. The House Judiciary Committee held hearings to consider the range of charges against the President. The main charges arose from events surrounding the Watergate break-in and an associated attempt to cover up the facts of the case. The committee, composed of both Democrats and Republicans, voted to recommend that Nixon be impeached. There were three counts: obstruction of justice, abuse of power, and contempt of Congress. Facing certain impeachment by the House and likely conviction by the Senate, President Nixon resigned.

Confirmation Power Article 2, Section 2, gives two executive powers to the Senate. The first of these is the power to approve Presidential appointments. The Senate has ***confirmation power*** over the following Presidential appointments: Supreme Court justices, federal judges, Cabinet members, ambassadors, members of independent boards and regulatory commissions, United States attorneys, United States marshals, public health service officials, foreign service officers, and military officers. In recent times, more than 100,000 nominations have been placed before the Senate. Most of these—some 97 percent—have been military officers, whose appointment and promotion are normally confirmed as a bloc. Of the remaining appointments, most have won routine confirmation. Some 500 major appointments, however, have involved detailed inquiry into the qualifications of the nominee.

Traditionally, Cabinet nominations are confirmed with little difficulty, on the theory that Presidents should be able to select their own advisers. Appointments to independent boards and regulatory commissions are examined much more closely. In recent years, nominations of Supreme Court Justices have received the closest scrutiny because, once confirmed, a Justice may serve on the Court for life.

The nomination procedure begins informally. On major appointments, the President normally consults with key members of Congress and with the leaders of political organizations and interest groups that may be affected by the appointment. If a candidate runs into serious opposition at this stage, the President is likely to choose someone else. When a nomination is submitted to the Senate, it goes to committee. Hearings are held at which the nominee and others may testify. Most such hearings are routine, but on important nominations, senators ask tough and probing questions.

After the hearings, the committee votes on the nomination. It may report the nomination favorably or unfavorably, or it may take no action at all. Normally only nominees recommended by the committee go to the Senate floor for a vote. Most are confirmed without objection. The President may withdraw a nomination if approval seems doubtful. Nominations are rarely brought to the floor unless confirmation is assured. Occasionally, a highly controversial nomination is debated on the floor.

Many executive appointees fill federal offices outside Washington, D.C. These include, for example, federal judges and United States attorneys. When Presidents want to appoint someone to serve in a particular state, they follow the unwritten rule of ***senatorial courtesy.*** This rule requires, for example, that a Republican President, making an appointment in Iowa, first secure the approval of any Republican senator from that state. If such a senator objects to the nominee, the Senate will almost always refuse to confirm the appointment. In practice, this means that the senators often choose who will serve in federal offices in their own states.

The Senate Committee on Environment and Public Works holds confirmation hearings for William Ruckleshaus (with glasses, far left), President Reagan's nominee as administrator of the Environmental Protection Agency. List the steps in the Senate's confirmation process.

President Jimmy Carter (seated fourth from left) and Panamanian President Omar Torrijos Herrera (seated fifth from left) sign the Panama Canal Treaties on June 16, 1978. The signing, which followed the Senate's ratification of the treaties, took place at a meeting of the Organization of American States. Describe the Senate's "advice and consent" role in the treaty-making process.

The Treaty Power The Constitution gives the President the power to make treaties with "the advice and consent of the Senate." Approval must be by a two-thirds majority of the senators present.

Treaties with foreign governments are negotiated by the President and the Department of State. During negotiations, the President normally consults with the members of the Senate Foreign Relations Committee and with influential senators of both parties. When a treaty is submitted to the Senate, it goes first to the Foreign Relations Committee. Hearings are held, and the committee votes to recommend adoption, modification, or rejection. The treaty then goes before the full Senate for consideration. Debate can be intense, as in the controversies over control of the Panama Canal and the second round of the Strategic Arms Limitation Treaties (SALT II) in 1978–79. Often the battle focuses on proposed amendments to the treaty. The Senate may require changes in the treaty before accepting it. Amendments often are designed, however, to sabotage the treaty or kill it altogether.

In the exercise of its treaty power, the Senate can accept, amend, or reject the treaty. Outright rejection is rare; only 11 treaties have failed to win the necessary two-thirds vote. On the other hand, Senate amendment of treaties has become increasingly common. This can present the executive branch with serious problems, because an amended treaty must go back to each nation signing the treaty for final agreement. Nevertheless, the power to amend treaties is an important means by which Congress can exercise influence and control over the conduct of American foreign policy.

Amendment Power

Article 5 of the Constitution gives to Congress the power to propose amendments to the Constitution. A two-thirds vote by each house is required for passage. The amendment then goes to the states for approval. The only restriction in Article 5 is that no amendment be proposed to deprive any state of equal representation in the Senate.

Section Check

1. Define: legislative power, nonlegislative power, expressed power, implied power, elastic clause, impeachment, senatorial courtesy
2. Give examples of the electoral powers of Congress.
3. How is the power of impeachment an illustration of the system of checks and balances?
4. What two executive powers are given to the Senate?

2 THE MAKING OF A LAW

Since the 1st Congress in 1789, more than 1 million bills have been introduced in Congress. But of this total, fewer than 100,000 have been enacted into law. In recent years some 15,000 bills and resolutions have been introduced in each two-year session of Congress. Of these, fewer than 5 percent have become public laws. In the 1983 and 1984 sessions of the 98th Congress, for example, 12,201 bills were introduced but only 623 public laws were enacted. For those bills to be passed into law, each must go through several different stages of the complicated ***legislative process.***

Introducing a Bill

A proposal for legislation can begin in many different ways. The idea, of course, may begin with a member of Congress. In preparing the bill, a representative or senator is usually assisted by a staff or by a support agency such as the Congressional Research Service. The House and Senate also provide special legal services to help members in drafting bills. Sometimes individuals or groups from a member's home constituency suggest legislation. Such a proposal may come in a letter from a private citizen. Often such interest groups as business associations, labor unions, and farm groups are the source

A bill is sent to the President for approval or veto only after passage by both Houses. What happens to most bills introduced in Congress?

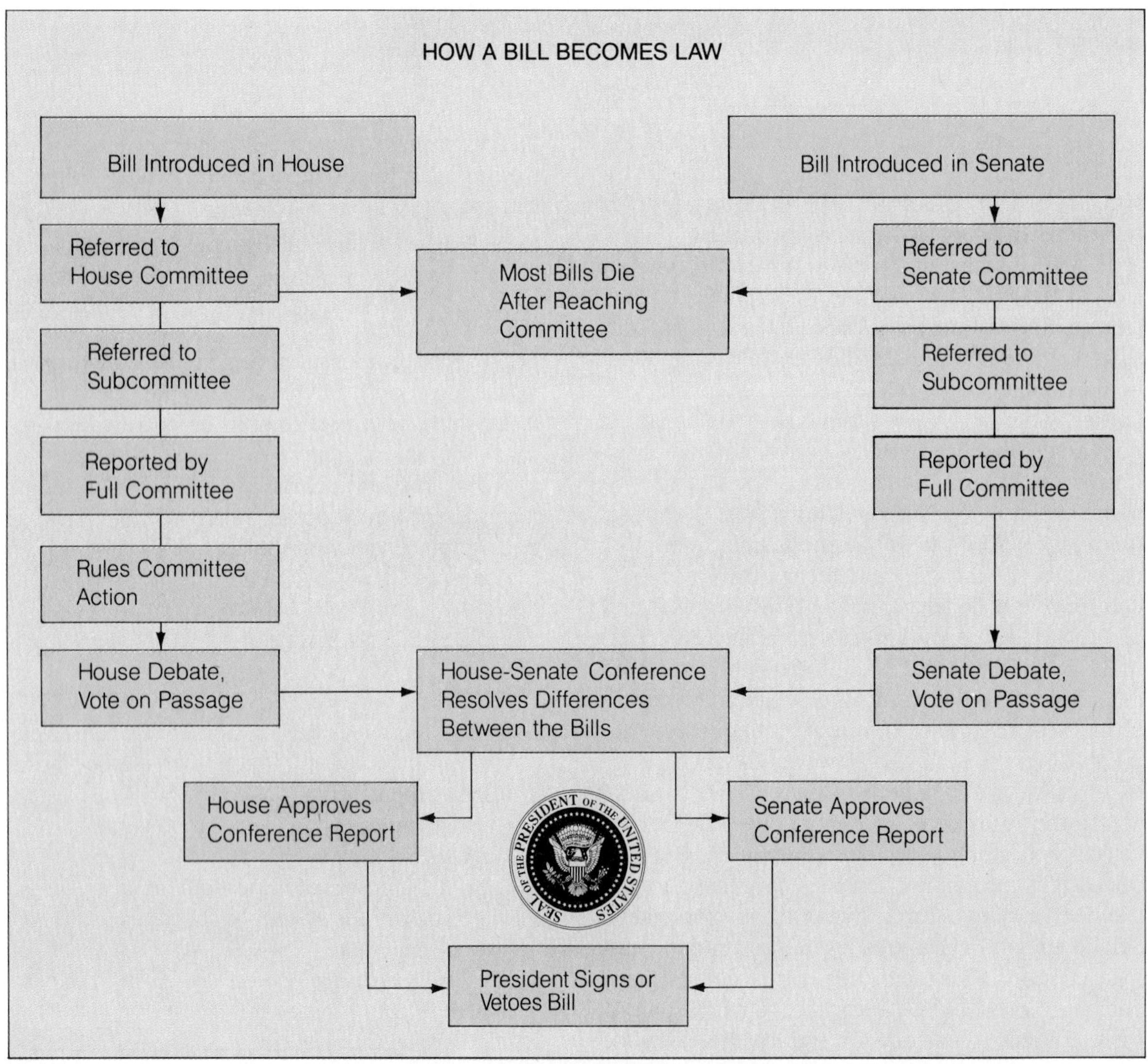

of legislative proposals. Most of the larger lobbies employ experts whose main job is to draft bills on subjects affecting the interests of the group.

The major source of legislation today, however, is the executive branch. In formulating the administration's proposals, the President consults with key members of Congress. Each year, in the State of the Union Address, the President presents the outline of the administration's legislative program. Executive departments and agencies draft the bills to carry out the program. In preparing these bills, they work closely with Congressional committee staffs. Each bill is usually introduced by the chairperson of the committee or subcommittee having jurisdiction over the subject. If the chairperson is not of the President's party, the ranking minority member introduces the bill.

Whatever the original source of a legislative proposal, only a member of Congress can introduce a bill. Members of the House introduce a bill by dropping it in the ***hopper,*** a large box on the Clerk's desk. Senators introduce bills by addressing the chair.

The Constitution in Article 1, Section 7, requires that "all bills raising revenue shall originate in the

LEXICON

Bills and Resolutions

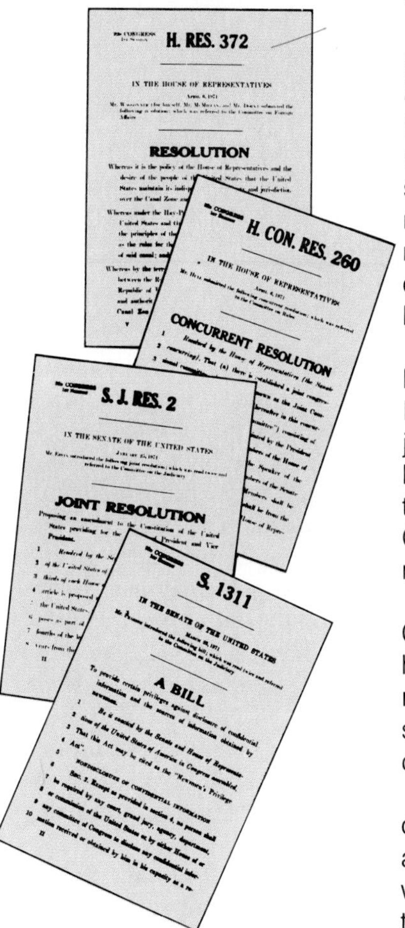

Legislative proposals may take the form of bills or resolutions.

Bills are proposed laws and are the form used for most legislation. House bills have the prefix "H.R." followed by a number. The numbers are assigned in the order of introduction from the beginning of each Congress. Bills introduced in the Senate have the prefix "S." followed by their assigned numbers.

Bills are either public or private. ***Public bills*** deal with matters of general concern and apply to the nation as a whole. In contrast, ***private bills*** are introduced on behalf of a specific person or with regard to a particular place. Typically they seek to correct some wrong inflicted by government or to deal with some matter not covered by a general statute. The largest number of private bills provide for immigration and naturalization of specific persons and for claims against the government. Whether private or public, a bill must be passed by both houses of Congress in identical form and signed by the President before it becomes law.

Joint resolutions start with the prefix H. J. Res. or S. J. Res., must be passed by both houses, and require the signature of the President. If approved, they have the force of law. There is little difference between joint resolutions and bills, except that joint resolutions usually deal with limited or temporary matters. On occasion, joint resolutions are used to approve executive actions in foreign affairs. Amendments to the Constitution are proposed in the form of joint resolutions, but these do not require Presidential approval.

Concurrent resolutions start with the prefix H. Con. Res. or S. Con. Res. and are used on matters affecting the operation of both houses of Congress, for example, the date for adjournment. Concurrent resolutions also are used to express the opinion of the two houses on some question. They do not require the President's signature, and they do not have the force of law.

Resolutions start with the prefix H. Res. or S. Res. and concern only the matters of the chamber in which they pass. They require neither approval by the other house nor by the President. Most resolutions deal with rules for the House or Senate, but they can be used to express the opinion of the chamber on a current issue.

Members of the House Ethics Committee (right) prepare to hear testimony from witnesses. Defense Secretary Caspar Weinberger (below, left) testifies during a 1982 House Appropriations Committee hearing. What role do committee hearings play in the legislative process?

House of Representatives." This requirement has been interpreted to mean that both tax and spending bills, which are called appropriations bills, must be introduced first in the House. All others bills may originate in either the House or the Senate. After passing one chamber, each bill then goes to the other house. Major legislation, however, is introduced in both houses at the same time in what are called "companion bills."

Committee Action

After a bill is introduced, it is referred to a standing committee. The standing committee often acts as a mini-legislature. Its action determines the fate of most legislative proposals. Many bills referred to committee are pigeonholed—simply set aside and not considered. Bills important enough to be considered are usually assigned to a subcommittee for study and hearings.

Hearings To obtain information about a proposed law or resolution, subcommittees hold hearings. Government officials and representatives of private interests are invited to testify as witnesses. These witnesses usually begin with a prepared statement of their views on the issue. They may then be questioned by the subcommittee members. Hearings may be brief—perhaps no more than a few hours—or they may go on for months. Sometimes hearings are held outside Washington, D.C., in order to get the views of people who are most closely affected by the proposal.

Some hearings capture national interest and are closely followed by television and the press. Most hearings are open to the public, but some are held in closed sessions. The closed hearings generally concern bills for which public testimony would endanger national security. The House Armed Services Committee, for example, holds closed hearings when dealing with "Top Secret" military matters.

Hearings serve a variety of purposes. They enable Congress to gather information and different points of view about the issue under consideration. They provide an opportunity to focus national attention on a problem or to build support for a bill. They can also be used to test whether public opinion favors the proposed legislation.

Mark-Up Session After hearings are over, the subcommittee meets in what is called a ***mark-up session***—a working session in which each provision of the bill is debated. The subcommittee may approve the bill just as it is, amend it, or completely rewrite it. The subcommittee may also decide to do nothing and in that way block the bill from any further consideration. The subcommittee reports its recommendation to the full committee.

Committee Vote and Report The full committee may again debate the provisions of the bill, in whole or in part. The committee then votes to determine what recommendation it should make to the House or Senate. In most cases, it follows the subcommittee recommendations. The committee may report the original bill, with or without amendments, or it may report its own "committee bill" as a substitute. The committee sends the bill to the chamber floor with an accompanying ***committee report.*** This report describes the reasons for the committee's action and explains the scope and purpose of the bill. Often committee members who oppose the bill attach a "minority report," in which they present their own dissenting views.

Bypassing Committee If a committee fails to act on a bill, that bill is usually dead, at least for that session of Congress. More than 90 percent of all bills die in committee. The rules of the House and Senate, however, provide ways to bypass the committee and bring a bill to the floor of the chamber for consideration. In the House, this may be done by a ***discharge petition*** signed by a majority of the House membership. In the Senate, a majority vote on a special resolution is required.

Attempts to bring to the floor legislation blocked by a committee are rarely successful. First of all, committees generally reflect the will of the chamber. Committee members rarely oppose a bill they know is supported by a clear majority in the chamber. Second, members of Congress generally accept the expertise and informed judgment of the committee members. Legislators, especially in the House, are specialists in the subject matter of the various committees on which they serve. Each legislator tends to respect the expertise of the others, and a challenge to one may be viewed as a threat to all.

House and Senate Calendars

When a bill is reported from committee to the House or Senate, it is placed on a ***legislative calendar,*** the official list of business for each chamber. There are actually five calendars for the House, each listing bills in different categories. In the Senate, all bills go on a single calendar. Nonlegislative matters, such as treaties and confirmation of appointments, are listed on a separate ***executive calendar.***

Bills need not be called up for debate in the order in which they are listed on the calendar. Nor is placement of a bill on a calendar any guarantee that it will be considered on the floor. The decisions on scheduling debate are made, for the most part, by the leadership within each chamber. In the House, the Rules Committee has primary responsibility for scheduling floor action. In the Senate, the Majority Leader plays the dominant role in setting the schedule.

The House Rules Committee After being reported from committee, most House bills are routed through the Rules Committee before going to the floor for debate. This additional legislative hurdle is an important difference between the House and Senate. The House Rules Committee acts as a "traffic cop" to regulate the flow of business. Most major bills cannot be taken to the floor of the House for action without a special "rule" from the Rules Committee. The rule for each bill sets the conditions for debate, indicating the amount of time allowed for discussion on the floor and whether or not amendments will be permitted.

The Rules Committee exercises great influence because the nature of the rule granted can affect a bill's chances for passage. Also, in the last days of the session, there are always more bills awaiting action than can be considered. The Rules Committee decides which bills will go to the floor and which will die.

Today the Rules Committee is an arm of the Speaker of the House and the majority party leadership. The Speaker appoints the majority-party members of the Committee and consults with the Minority Leader concerning the appointment of minority-party members. The Speaker uses the Rules Committee to control House procedure and to advance the majority party's legislative program.

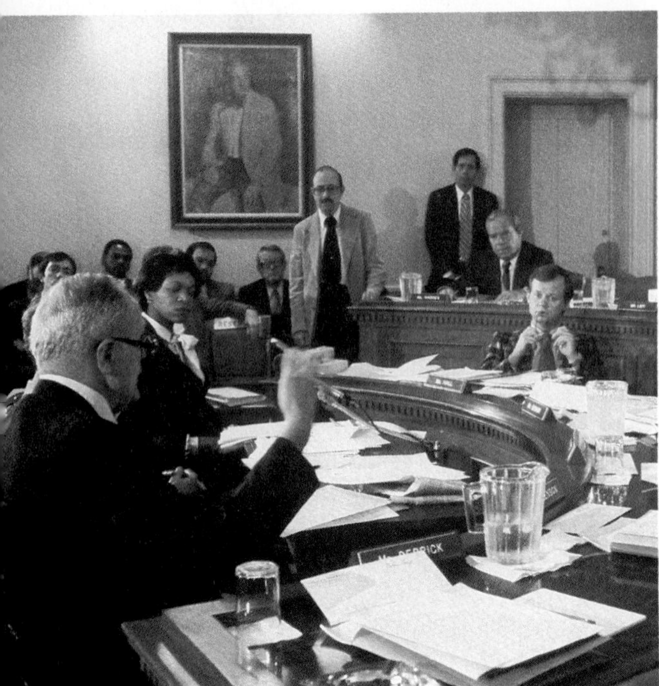

The House Rules Committee was organized as a standing committee in 1880. Since that time, the Rules Committee has developed into a major source of power, often dominating the legislative agenda of the House.

At one time, the Rules Committee was a major roadblock in the legislative process. For some 30 years, up until the mid-1960's, the committee was dominated by a coalition of conservative Democrats and Republicans. The coalition was able to use its position to block liberal legislation its members did not like. By refusing to grant a rule, the coalition could effectively kill a bill. In the 1960's, however, a series of reforms brought the Rules Committee under the control of the Speaker. Additional procedures now enable a majority in the House to bypass the Rules Committee in order to bring a bill to the floor.

Senate Scheduling Unlike the House, with its complicated rules for bringing bills to the floor, the Senate operates in a relaxed and informal manner. This is made possible by its much smaller size. After a Senate bill has been reported from committee, the bill may be called up for debate by unanimous consent—that is, without objection. In practice, floor action is scheduled by the Senate Majority Leader, with the help of the party's policy committee and in consultation with the Minority Leader. No rules limit the time for debate or restrict the amendments that can be made in the Senate.

Floor Action

By the time a bill comes to the floor of the House or Senate for debate, it has already been studied extensively in committee. For most bills, committee approval assures speedy passage. On controversial legislation, though, floor debate is often crucial.

In debate, supporters and opponents of a bill argue its pros and cons. On occasion, debate on a bill can be a time of tension and high drama, as the fate of major legislation hangs in the balance. The reality of routine debate, however, rarely lives up to this colorful image. Instead of great oratory, one is more likely to hear a member reading from a prepared text. Most of the time, only a handful of members are in the chamber and, more likely than not, those present are not paying much attention to what is being said. Some may wander around conferring with colleagues; others work at their desks, reading constituents' letters, checking over a committee report, or preparing a speech.

Tourists who pass through the House and Senate visitors' galleries are often bewildered by what they see. It is important to remember, in most cases, that floor debate is simply a replay of what went on in committee. The main function of debate is to bring up the issues on which key votes are taken.

When an amendment or a bill comes up for a vote, the members of the House and Senate are summoned by bells that ring throughout the Capitol. The number of bells indicates whether a member's presence is needed for a quorum or for a vote. A ***quorum*** is the minimum number of members who must be present in order to conduct business. According to the Constitution, the quorum for each house of Congress is a majority of its membership—218 for the House and 51 for the Senate. In practice, a full quorum need not be on the floor for business to go on. But if a quorum call is made, members assemble in the chamber for a head count. Business may proceed only if a quorum is present. Once the vote has been recorded, most members return to their offices or to the committee sessions from which they were called.

In each chamber, a bill is guided through debate by the ***floor manager,*** usually the chairperson of the committee or subcommittee that previously reported out the bill. The ranking minority member of the committee usually leads opposition to the bill. In the House, the "rule" sets the number of hours for general debate on the bill, dividing the time equally between supporters and opponents. Much of the debate is likely to focus on amendments to the bill. Amendments may be introduced to improve legislation, but often they are designed to weaken or even kill a bill.

Debate in the House Procedures for floor debate differ widely between the House and Senate. In the House, most legislation is considered by what is called the Committee of the Whole. This is an informal session of the House designed to speed debate under relaxed rules. At this time, the Speaker appoints a temporary chairperson. Formal rules are suspended. Only 100 members need to be present to make a quorum. Meeting as a large committee, House members debate the merits of the bill and its amendments. The Committee of the Whole, however, cannot take final action on a bill. The passage of any bill or amendment requires formal action by the House in regular session.

Votes in the House may be taken in one of three ways. The most common form is the ***voice vote.*** Members call out "aye" or "no" in chorus. A member may also call for a ***standing vote,*** also known as a "division of the House." Those in favor stand up and are counted, followed by those opposed. Finally, the ***roll-call vote*** is becoming increasingly common. This used to be a time-consuming process, given the size of the House. Today, however, a computer-operated electronic system speeds up the vote greatly. Members simply push a button, and their votes are recorded automatically. In contrast, the Senate, because of its smaller size, continues to use the traditional roll-call vote.

Debate in the Senate Because of its large size, the House employs tight rules to control debate. In the smaller, more informal Senate, debate is unlimited. Freedom of debate is designed to encourage the full exploration of the merits of a bill before it is brought to a vote. This freedom, however, is sometimes abused by a minority of determined senators. Opponents of a bill favored by the majority can resort to the tactic of ***filibuster.*** In a filibuster, one or more senators continue talking as long as possible. This may win concessions or force withdrawal of the bill. Sometimes just the threat of a filibuster can have its effect. The tactic is especially effective at the end of a legislative session when time is short and business is pressing.

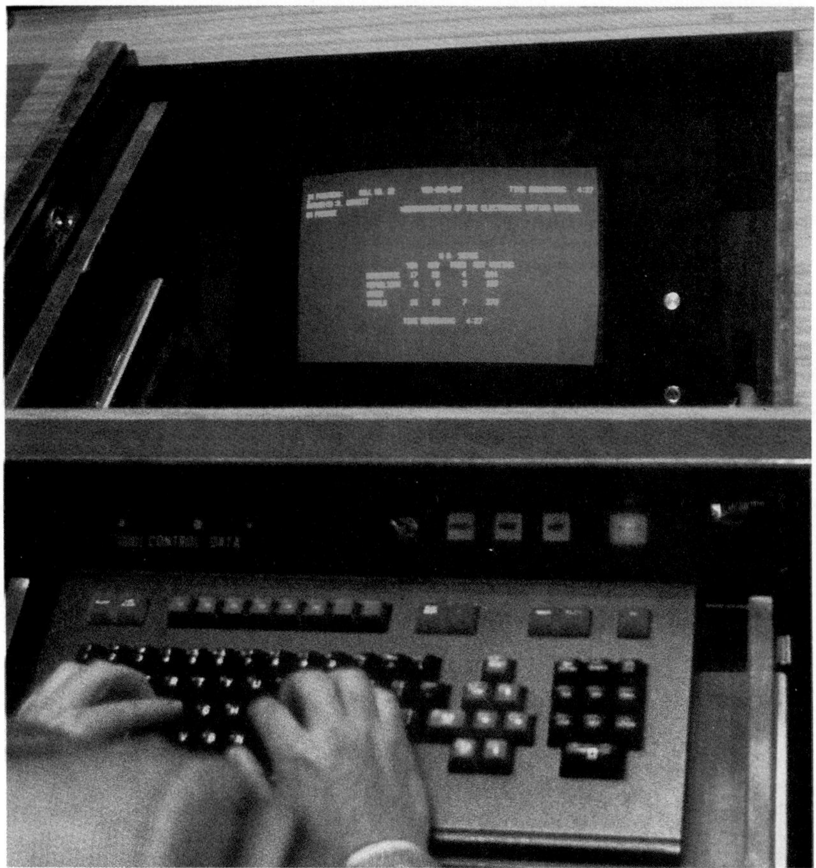

Sessions of the House of Representatives—and the tallies of members' votes—are televised via cable from the House television control room.

To filibuster, a senator must remain standing and keep talking. The speech need not even be on the subject of the bill. Some senators have read poetry; others, the telephone book. The record for the longest individual filibuster is held by Senator Strom Thurmond of South Carolina. He spoke continuously for more than 24 hours in opposition to the 1957 Civil Rights Bill. But his tactic failed to block debate on the bill. Usually several senators join in a filibuster. When one senator grows tired, he or she yields to another. In this manner, the filibuster can go on for days.

A filibuster can sometimes be broken by keeping the Senate in continuous session in hope of wearing down the filibusterers. The best weapon against a filibuster is Senate Rule 22, the ***Cloture Rule,*** a special motion to stop debate. For many years, cloture required a two-thirds vote and was very difficult to obtain. Between 1917, when the Cloture Rule was adopted, and 1975, cloture votes were taken 123 times. Only 34 were successful. To make it easier to end a filibuster, the Senate revised the Cloture Rule in 1975. Today, 16 senators can file a cloture motion. A three-fifths majority of the entire Senate membership—60 votes—is required for adoption. If the motion passes, no senator may speak for more than 1 hour. The bill is then brought to a vote.

South Carolina Senator Strom Thurmond waves to onlookers after his record-setting filibuster on August 19, 1957.

Conference Committee

Each bill must pass both the House and the Senate. House and Senate bills, however, rarely emerge from committee and floor action in the same form. For most bills, these differences do not present a serious problem. One chamber simply agrees to the version adopted by the other. For major legislation, however, differences between House and Senate bills are resolved by a committee composed of senior Democrats and Republicans from the committees responsible for the bill. Usually, between three and nine members are appointed by the Speaker of the House and the presiding officer of the Senate.

The task of the ***conference committee*** is to work out a compromise version of the bill that will be acceptable to both houses. The committee exercises great power. Some of the hardest bargaining in the legislative process takes place in conference committees. When the conferees from each house reach agreement, the compromise bill is sent to the House and Senate in the form of a ***conference report.*** Rarely does either house reject this report. If that happens, the report returns to the conference for further negotiation. If the report is approved, the bill is then ready for Presidential action.

Presidential Action

After a bill has passed each house in identical form, it is signed by the Speaker of the House and the President of the Senate. The bill is then sent to the White House for Presidential action. Upon receiving the bill, the President has four options.

The first option is to sign the bill, whereupon it becomes law. The second option is to ***veto,*** or reject, the bill. The President then returns the bill to the chamber where it was first introduced, accompanied by a message stating the President's objections. If Congress takes no action, the bill dies. Congress may override the President's veto by repassing the bill with a two-thirds vote of those present within each house. The bill then becomes law.

After receiving it, if the President does not sign the bill within 10 days, not including Sundays, the bill becomes law without a Presidential signature. The President may choose this third option when the preference is neither to approve the bill nor to veto it.

Fourth, if, before the 10 days are up, Congress adjourns at the end of its session, then a bill not signed by the President is dead. This is known as a ***pocket veto.***

After Senate ratification, President John F. Kennedy (above) signs into law the 1963 Nuclear Test Ban Treaty with the United Kingdom and the Soviet Union. President Lyndon B. Johnson (right) signs the Civil Rights Act of 1964.

In the next section these options will be looked at more closely. In addition, the relationship between Congress and the President will be studied.

Section Check

---

1. Define: hopper, bill, joint resolution, legislative calendar, quorum, voice vote, standing vote, filibuster, pocket veto
2. Identify: private bill, mark-up session, Rules Committee, floor manager, Committee of the Whole, conference committee
3. List some of the sources of bills that are introduced by members of Congress.
4. List the steps in committee action on a bill. How may a bill bypass committee?
5. Compare floor action in the Senate and House.
6. How may a filibuster be defeated?
7. What four options does the President have after receiving a bill from Congress?

---

3 CONGRESSIONAL CONTROL OVER THE EXECUTIVE BRANCH

The three branches of the federal government are separate from but not independent of each other. Power is shared and dispersed in a system of checks and balances. Other than the executive powers discussed earlier in this chapter, Congress has two "watchdog" powers that give it substantial control over the executive branch. One is ***legislative oversight,*** the power to watch over, or supervise, executive activities. The other is the ***power of the purse,*** Congressional control over the money that pays for the activities of the federal government.

Legislative Oversight

After it makes a law, Congress is not forced simply to trust the executive branch to carry that law out. Congress has the power to see how laws are administered. Congressional oversight is performed in a number of ways, but not always successfully.

Each standing committee of Congress has responsibility for supervising the executive agencies that come within its area of concern. Specifically, the Legislative Reorganization Act of 1970 provides:

Each standing committee shall review and study, on a continuing basis, the application, administration, and execution of those laws, or parts of laws, the subject matter of which is within the jurisdiction of the committee.

Recent legislation has strengthened this power, giving certain committees wide responsibilities.

Many committees have a permanent subcommittee concerned with oversight. Committee staffs often include specialists who monitor the efficiency and effectiveness of administrative agencies and government programs. A few committees play especially important roles in legislative oversight. The 26 appropriations subcommittees of the House and Senate keep close tabs on how the various executive agencies spend their money. The Government Operations Committees of the House and Senate keep watchful eyes on the economy and efficiency of federal government activities at all levels. In addition, the General Accounting Office assists Congress through its audits and investigations of executive spending practices.

In committee hearings held every day on Capitol Hill, members of Congress question executive officials about their conduct and the activities of their agencies. Departments and agencies must file annual reports with Congress, and Congress may request special reports from the executive branch—even from the President—on a variety of topics.

Congressional Investigations Congress has the power to investigate any subject that is properly within the scope of its legislative authority. Standing committees regularly conduct investigations as a part of their fact-finding duties. They do so to aid in lawmaking, to provide effective oversight, and to inform the public. From time to time, special investigating committees are created to inquire into specific instances of probable wrongdoing.

The first Congressional investigation, conducted in 1792, looked into the causes of a defeat of the Army by the Wabash Indians. Since that time, there have been more than 600 investigations. Some have been to the credit of Congress. Others have been shabby affairs, used for partisan advantage or to promote the personal career of the investigator. Often, investigations have brought Congress into major clashes with the executive branch. At times the President has claimed a special executive privilege in refusing to permit government officials to appear before a committee.

Major Congressional investigations over the past 30 years include the following:

- The Kefauver Crime Hearings held in 1951 and 1952 investigated organized crime. The televised hearings focused national attention on the committee chairman, Senator Estes Kefauver, of Tennessee.
- The McCarthy Investigations took place in 1953 and 1954. They inquired into Communist influence and subversive activities in the United States. The subcommittee was chaired by Joseph R. McCarthy, a Republican senator from Wisconsin. An accumulation of unfounded charges, abuse of committee powers, and, ultimately, his attack on

INSIGHT

General Accounting Office

The General Accounting Office (GAO) is the Congressional watchdog over spending by the executive branch. It is headed by the Comptroller general, who is appointed by the President with the advice and consent of the Senate for a term of 15 years. The GAO conducts official examinations called audits to see how government agencies use the taxpayers' money. It conducts investigations for Congress into the effectiveness of government programs, and it makes recommendations for greater economy and efficiency. The GAO has responsibility for settling claims against the federal government and for collecting debts. It also provides legal services, and the Comptroller General has the final say on the legal use of public funds.

The Senate Crime Investigation Committee Hearings held in 1951 and 1952 (left) were chaired by Senator Estes Kefauver (with hand upraised, left). The 1973 Watergate Hearings (below) were chaired by Senator Sam J. Ervin, Jr. (left), of the Senate Select Commission on Presidential Campaign Activities.

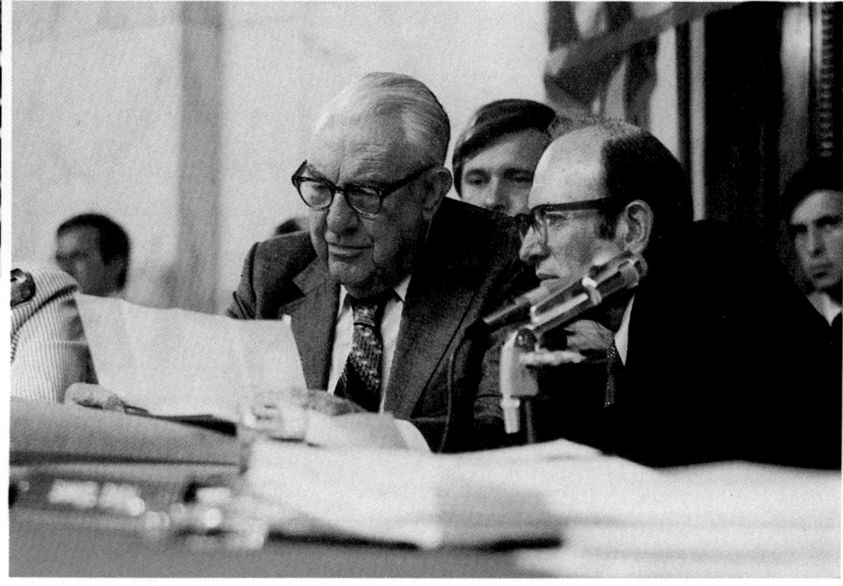

the Army brought about McCarthy's downfall. The Senate eventually passed a motion of censure against McCarthy for his actions during the subcommittee hearings.

- The Watergate Hearings that took place in 1973 investigated illegal campaign practices. Disclosures made before the Senate committee sent shock waves through the nation, brought on a constitutional crisis, and, ultimately, the resignation of President Richard Nixon.
- The CIA Investigations that occurred in 1975 were a penetrating inquiry by both the House and Senate into the activities of the Central Intelligence Agency. Many instances of illegal and improper spying by the CIA were documented.

The Effectiveness of Oversight In recent years, Congress has given increasing attention to its oversight functions. This has come about for two main reasons. First, laws often impart broad authority to the executive branch. Congress cannot anticipate every situation and spell out every detail. This forces Congress to give administrators greater leeway in implementing laws. To ensure that laws are carried out according to its intentions, Congress engages more and more in legislative oversight. Second, Congress realizes that it has lost considerable power to the executive branch during the last century. Legislators see increased oversight as a means of regaining some of that power.

Congressional oversight has been haphazard and sporadic. Few committees really keep a continuously watchful eye on the administrative agencies within their jurisdiction. At best, the committees make spot checks on program effectiveness and agency efficiency. More often than not, years pass before Congress makes any comprehensive study of a program to see how it is working. Most members of

INSIGHT

Sunset Legislation

One way of holding agencies in check and, at the same time, reducing the growth of bureaucracy is through ***sunset legislation,*** laws that provide for the operation of an agency or program only for a limited time. At the end of its term, five years, for example, the agency or program must be reviewed. If it is not renewed, the "sun sets" and the agency or program is ended.

Congress, in fact, regard their job as making laws. Checking to see how those laws are carried out is left to the bureaucrats. But administrative performance is hard to measure objectively. Also, the number and complexity of government programs has put effective oversight beyond the capacity of Congress.

The Power of the Purse

Of all Congress's executive control powers, the most important is the power of the purse. Through its powers to tax and spend, Congress controls the business of government. In Chapter 22, taxes, the national budget, and how government spends the public's money will be examined. This section is concerned with how Congress exercises its power over the budget.

The Power to Tax Tax laws are terribly complicated, as every taxpayer can readily testify. The making of these laws and their enforcement require close cooperation between the legislative and executive branches. Tax bills usually begin as administration proposals and are presented to Congress by the President. The Constitution requires that all tax bills first be introduced in the House of Representatives. Tax legislation in the House is handled by the Ways and Means Committee. It is one of the most powerful and prestigious of all committees, and its members are experts on matters of taxation.

After passage by the House, a tax bill goes to the Senate, where it is referred to the Finance Committee. The Senate may amend the bill, but as with all legislation, a conference committee resolves any differences between the House and Senate versions. When the final version is approved by each house, the bill goes to the President to be signed into law. By the time a tax bill returns to the White House, however, it often looks very different from the original proposal.

The Power to Spend The Constitution gives Congress the power to decide how money collected by the government is to be spent. Article 1, Section 9, reads:

No money shall be drawn from the Treasury, but in consequence of appropriations made by law.

An ***appropriation*** is a legislative grant of money for a specific purpose. It is through the power of appropriations that Congress exercises its strongest control over the executive branch.

The appropriations process is among the most complicated operations of government. Congress appropriates funds only for those programs that are permitted by law. Accordingly, an ***authorization act*** legally establishes a program, specifies its general purpose, and indicates approximately how much money will be needed to finance it. The authorization act does not, however, provide the money to pay for the program. This must be done separately through an appropriation.

Each year, the President's budget request is presented to Congress in the form of a series of appropriation bills. By tradition, the House acts first. Each bill is assigned to one of the 13 House appropriations subcommittees, where it is examined closely. In hearings, the chief officers of various executive agencies defend their budget requests and justify their agencies' programs and operations over the previous year.

The members of the House Appropriations Committee are dedicated to the control of government spending. Some agencies and programs fare better than others, but in any case, the subcommittees cut most budget requests. Because administrators do not expect to get what they ask for, they usually ask for more than they really expect to receive. The task of the Appropriations Committee is to pare down each request to what is necessary to run the agency and carry out its programs.

As director of the Congressional Budget Office, Rudolph G. Penner oversees a staff of more than 200 economists, lawyers, and computer specialists. The Congressional Budget Office was created by Congress in 1974 to assist lawmakers with federal budget decisions.

The House almost always approves the reports of the appropriations subcommittees. The bills then go to the Senate, where the executive agencies have a second chance to make their case for funding. The Senate Appropriations Committee serves as an "appeals court." It may restore some of the money cut by the House. The conference committee smooths out the differences between the House and Senate appropriation bills to produce a compromise version.

Limitations on the Power of the Purse The power of the purse gives Congress control over government spending, but this power is limited in a number of ways. One limitation comes from the long-term, binding commitments to spending that have been made by earlier Congresses. Some 75 percent of the money spent by the federal government is fixed by long-term, binding commitments such as social security payments, veterans' benefits, and interest on the national debt. They also include defense contracts and public works projects, such as the construction of a dam or highway system. New appropriations must always be made in the light of these long-term commitments.

Another limitation on control of spending results from the fragmentation of Congress itself. Tax and appropriations bills, for example, are handled by separate committees. Ideally, governmental spending should not exceed the amount of revenue raised. But a balanced budget is difficult to achieve in our complex society. A balanced budget is almost impossible without coordination between the tax programs and spending bills.

The appropriations process itself is also fragmented. Congress also authorizes programs with little regard for available money. Funding is handled separately. Moreover, the appropriations subcommittees operate independently, so there is little opportunity to weigh the importance of competing claims for funding.

Congressional Budget Reform Historically there has never been much coordination between the Congressional powers of taxation and spending. As a result, the task of balancing spending and income has fallen to the executive branch. In effect, Congress surrendered control over the purse to the President. In the early 1970's the legislative and executive branches came into increasing conflict over the budget. President Nixon accused Congress of financial irresponsibility and refused to spend billions of dollars appropriated by Congress. He impounded the money. But most members of Congress viewed impoundment as an improper, if not unconstitutional, exercise of Presidential power. ***Impoundment*** refers to Presidential refusal to allow executive agencies to spend money appropriated by Congress. Earlier Presidents had impounded funds, but never to the extent held back by President Nixon.

Congress was aware that its failure to coordinate spending and income had caused a forfeiture of power. Congress enacted the Congressional Budget and Impoundment Control Act of 1974. This act was designed to coordinate Congressional action on the federal budget. It aimed at more effective control over spending and at establishing priorities in funding. The act gave Congress power to require the executive branch to spend the money authorized for specific projects.

To achieve these goals, the act established House and Senate budget committees and a Congressional Budget Office to provide the committees with information and technical assistance. The Budget Office provides data on economic aspects of government policies and programs. It also prepares national economic forecasts and analyzes alternative policy choices. After close study of the President's budget and the data submitted by the Congressional Budget Office, the House and Senate committees prepare a concurrent resolution. This sets the targets for total spending and for the needed tax revenue and debt limit. The resolution provides guidance for action by the appropriations committees. A later resolution then sets binding figures for the final budget.

Congressional budget reform has brought greater coherence to what had long been a fragmented and piecemeal process. But the budget remains the subject of intense battle between the legislative and the executive branches. In the early 1980's the Reagan administration tried to pressure Congress into accepting the President's economic

INSIGHT

The Legislative Veto

The legislative veto, which prevents or postpones executive actions, is one of the most controversial tools that Congress has ever used to exert control over the executive branch. The Constitution makes no provision for legislative vetoes. But legislative vetoes have, over the years, been carefully built into certain laws.

An early legislative veto was included in an 1895 bill that authorized the House Committee on Printing to review and disapprove, if it so chose, the publication list of the public printer. Although the legislative veto was first used for such routine "housekeeping" matters, it eventually evolved into a more important tool.

One of the most well known legislative vetoes is included in the War Powers Resolution of 1973. This Resolution was passed in reaction to the Vietnam War policies of Presidents Johnson and Nixon. It permitted Congress, under certain circumstances, to force the President to withdraw United States troops from overseas military conflicts. President Nixon and succeeding executives have held that the resolution conflicts with the President's power as commander in chief.

The constitutionality of the legislative veto was tested in the Supreme Court case *Immigration and Naturalization Service* v. *Chadha* (1983). This case involved a Kenyan student, J. Chadha, whose visa had expired. Ultimately, the United States Attorney General ruled that Chadha could remain in the United States. The House of Representatives, however, used the legislative veto provisions of the immigration laws to order his deportation.

Eventually, Chadha's case reached the Supreme Court. The Court ruled that Chadha could stay in the United States. The Court also ruled that, in this case, Congress's use of the legislative veto was unconstitutional. The Court's ruling, however, left in doubt the constitutionality of other legislative vetoes.

program. In most cases, appropriations turned out to be a compromise between Congress and the President. A balanced budget, however, remained an elusive goal.

Congress in Perspective

The United States embodies many varied and often competing interests. Members of Congress are pulled in different directions as they respond to their constituents' claims and to their own judgments of the public interest. To get things done, members must negotiate, bargain, and compromise. Congress reflects the decentralization and diversity of the United States political system. This diversity is Congress's great strength, but it is also a source of weakness. Fragmentation and disunity of purpose have contributed to what many observers have described as "the decline of Congress" in relation to the Presidency.

During much of the nineteenth century, Congress was the dominant branch of government. In this century, the Presidency has become one of the most powerful offices in the world.

In recent years, Congress has sought to reassert its power and leadership. Reforms over the past decade—greater power for the Speaker of the House, changes in the seniority system, and congressional budget reform—have given Congress more cohesion and renewed strength.

Which of the two branches will be the stronger? Ideally, neither will eclipse the other. In the constitutional system of the United States, the legislative and executive branches, while separate, must share powers. Although Congress and the President may come into conflict over policy goals, cooperation is the keystone of their relationship. Responsive and effective government depends on the capacity of Congress and the President to work together.

Section Check

---

1. Define: legislative oversight, power of the purse, sunset legislation, appropriation, authorization act, impoundment
2. Identify: Legislative Reorganization Act of 1970, General Accounting Office, McCarthy Investigations, Congressional Budget Office
3. Give examples of power of the purse.
4. What is the purpose of the Congressional Budget and Impoundment Control Act of 1974?

SUMMARY

The Constitution gives Congress both legislative and nonlegislative powers. The legislative powers are of two types: those expressly written in the Constitution and those implied by the elastic clause, Clause 18 in Article 1, Section 8, of the Constitution. Congressional nonlegislative powers are primarily designed as checks and balances on the power of the executive branch. For example, Congress has the power to impeach, or remove, high federal officials for violation of public trust. Congress must also confirm executive appointments and treaties. Additional powers are the right to propose amendments to the Constitution and the authority to elect the President in the absence of a majority in the electoral college.

The process by which Congress passes laws is a complicated affair. The first step is introduction of a bill. There are many sources of legislation, but only a member of Congress can introduce a bill. All bills that raise revenue must originate in the House of Representatives. After introduction, a bill is referred to a standing committee and then to a subcommittee for study and hearings. More than 90 percent of all proposed bills die in committee.

The real business of the Congress is done in committee. Floor action is often a formality. There are three types of floor votes in the House: a voice vote, a standing vote, and an electronic roll-call vote. The Senate uses a traditional roll-call vote. Because the Senate is smaller and less formal than the House, it has no limit on floor debate time. This sometimes gives rise to the tactic of a filibuster. In a filibuster, one or more senators continue talking as long as possible. This may win concessions from opponents or force the withdrawal of a bill. To stop a filibuster, a vote of cloture must be passed. Recent reforms have made cloture a more effective tool, and the filibuster has declined in use.

Congress has two watchdog powers that lend it added control over the executive branch. They are legislative oversight and the power of the purse. Oversight gives Congress the authority to conduct investigations and observe how its laws are carried out. Famous oversight investigations have included the Watergate hearings and the McCarthy investigations. The power of the purse gives Congress the right to control government spending. This power is limited, but is still an important lever in Congress's interactions with the executive branch. Ideally, effective government depends on the capacity of Congress and the President to work together.

Chapter 16 Review

Using Vocabulary

Answer the questions by using the meaning of each underlined term.

1. What role does legislative oversight play in the legislative process?
2. Why might a roll-call vote be used to determine a quorum in the Senate?
3. Can a bill be pigeonholed and put in the hopper?
4. What might the reaction of a floor manager be to the start of a filibuster?
5. Is the power of the purse a legislative power or an executive power of Congress?

Understanding American Government

1. What does the length of Article 1 suggest about the nature of Congress? Give examples to support your answer.
2. Why did the Framers give Congress nonlegislative powers?
3. Describe the stages in the impeachment process. How is the power of impeachment an illustration of the system of checks and balances?
4. Why is the Senate's power to amend treaties so important?
5. Why do so few of the bills introduced in Congress become law?
6. Why is the executive branch the major source of legislation?
7. Why do you think the Framers decided that only the House could introduce revenue raising bills?
8. In what ways has the House Rules Committee been a major roadblock in the legislative process?
9. Why is the Senate able to operate in a more relaxed, less formal manner than the House?
10. What different purposes are served by Congressional hearings and investigations?
11. Why has Congress recently given increased attention to legislative oversight? Why has Congressional oversight not been an effective tool?
12. How is the power of the purse limited?
13. What are the goals of Congressional budget reforms?

Extending Your Skills: Understanding a Flow Chart

Study the chart on page 388. Then complete the items that follow.

1. Place in correct order the following steps through which a bill in the House of Representatives must pass: (a) House debate, vote on passage; (b) Report by full committee; (c) Referred to House committee; (d) Rules committee action.
2. When the House and the Senate pass different versions of the same bill, the (a) President vetoes one version; (b) House-Senate Conference resolves differences between the bills.
3. Most often, the President's signature is (a) the final step before a bill becomes law; (b) required only if the House and the Senate pass different versions of a bill.

Government and You

1. Why do you think that all of Congress's nonlegislative powers are expressed powers, not implied?
2. If the executive branch proposes most bills and executes all of them, perhaps the executive branch should just make the laws. What problems do you see in such an arrangement?
3. Which powers of Congress do you think are the most important? Can you see the impact of Congressional powers on your everyday life or on that of your parents?
4. Most Cabinet appointments have been confirmed with little difficulty. Supreme Court appointments, however, have been scrutinized closely, especially in recent times. Why do you think this discrepancy exists?

Activities

1. Prepare a biographical report on Senator Joseph McCarthy. Pay special attention to the investigations he conducted in the 1950's.
2. Make a wall chart showing the expressed powers of Congress and the more powerful committees involved in the exercise of these powers.

UNIT 7

THE FEDERAL EXECUTIVE BRANCH

The Presidency

No one can experience with the President of the United States the glory and agony of his office. No one can share the majestic view from his pinnacle of power. No one can share the burden of his decisions or the scope of his duties. A Cabinet officer, no matter how broad his mandate, has a limited responsibility. A senator, no matter how varied his interests, has a limited constituency. But the President represents all the people and must face up to all the problems. He must be responsible, as he sees it, for the welfare of every citizen and must be sensitive to the will of every group. He cannot pick and choose the issues. They all come with the job. So his experience is unique among his fellow Americans.

LYNDON B. JOHNSON

CHAPTER OVERVIEW

President Ronald Reagan welcomes Canadian Prime Minister Brian Mulroney to the White House. When meeting with the leaders of other nations, the President serves as the chief diplomat of the United States.

1 THE POWER OF THE PRESIDENCY

The Presidency is the central institution of the American political system. It is at once the highest office of government and a symbol of the American nation. It is an office of great power, but that power is limited. What the President can do is bounded by the Constitution, by political considerations, and by the reality that no human being is all-powerful.

From the earliest days of the Republic, the power of the Presidency has expanded. Indeed, some observers believe that the Presidency has gone beyond its constitutional bounds and that the delicate system of checks and balances has been upset. Yet, whenever Congress moves to reassert its authority and to restore the balance, there is a new call for strong Presidential leadership. The President must have the capacity to lead and the power to govern. But that power must be exercised in accordance with the law and with the Constitution of the United States. In the oath of office the President swears to "preserve, protect, and defend the Constitution of the United States."

The Presidency Established

The American Revolution was, in part, a struggle against the British king and the authority of his colonial governors. When independence was won, Americans viewed executive power with suspicion. The new state constitutions placed nearly all power in popularly-elected legislatures, very little in governors. The Articles of Confederation vested power in the Congress. Under the Articles, Congress appointed the executive departments and a presiding officer. But government under the Articles of Confederation soon proved to be weak and ineffective. A principal source of that weakness was lack of executive authority.

The earliest known engraving of the Constitutional Convention shows George Washington presiding with pen and scroll in hand. Why did some Framers of the Constitution favor a "weak" President for the new nation?

In 1787 delegates from 12 states gathered in Philadelphia to consider revising the Articles of Confederation. Instead, they produced a new constitution. At this Constitutional Convention, delegates such as James Wilson and Gouverneur Morris called for a single, independent chief executive. James Madison, cautious at first, added his support. Those against the argument for a strong and energetic executive favored a "weak" president. They wanted a chief executive appointed by, responsible to, and dependent upon Congress.

Through compromise the Framers of the Constitution resolved the question of the executive. Their practical solution embodied the two fundamental principles of American government: the separation of powers and the system of checks and balances. The key to the system was that the separate branches would share power. As Madison wrote in *The Federalist,* No. 48, the arrangement was such that "these departments be so far connected and blended as to give each a constitutional control over the others."

The Framers gave form to the Presidency through a series of decisions.

First, Article 2 of the Constitution provides for a separate executive branch. In contrast, in a parliamentary government the executive is not separate from the legislature. The prime minister is a member of the legislature and the leader of the majority party.

Second, after lengthy debate, the Framers of the Constitution decided on a single chief executive, the President of the United States. Many delegates expressed fears that the Presidency would be turned into a monarchy. To reduce that possibility, there was wide support for a plural executive composed of three persons. But the views of Wilson and Morris prevailed—in large part because it was assumed by all that the highly respected George Washington would be chosen as the first President.

Third, the President is elected independently, not by Congress. The Framers devoted a great deal of discussion to this matter. Most delegates initially shared Roger Sherman's view that the executive "ought to be appointed by and accountable to the legislature only." Both the Virginia and New Jersey plans had provided for election of the executive by Congress. In the debates Gouverneur Morris carried the day and secured the compromise electoral college system by which the President is selected.

Fourth, to provide stability, the President serves a fixed term of office and may be reelected. As a protection against the abuse of executive authority, however, the Constitution gives to Congress the power to remove a President by impeachment for "high crimes and misdemeanors."

Fifth, the powers of the President are granted by the Constitution. They do not come from Congress. In contrast to those powers granted by the Constitution to Congress, the list of Presidential powers is short and sketchy. The President is the commander in chief of the armed forces and may pardon persons convicted of federal crimes. The

President may, with the advice and consent of the Senate, make treaties and appoint executive officials, federal judges, and ambassadors—that is, to recognize foreign governments. Among the Presidential duties defined by the Constitution, the President is required to inform Congress as to "the state of the Union" and to recommend legislative measures for their consideration. The President's executive responsibility is underscored by the requirement that "he shall take care that the laws be faithfully executed."

These provisions reveal little about the nature of the Presidency. They are vague and often ambiguous. Yet the basic framework of the office is clear: (1) a separate executive branch (2) with a single executive (3) elected independently of Congress (4) for a fixed term (5) with limited powers. The constitutional limits on Presidential power are fundamentally those of checks and balances. In sharing power, the three branches of government must work together. But at the same time they remain in constant tension, as each branch moves to check and control the other branch.

The Expansion of Presidential Power

With George Washington clearly in mind, most delegates to the Constitutional Convention envisioned a strong, dignified chief of state—someone above political strife and factional rivalries. Alexander

George Washington is portrayed during the American Revolution in a 1790 painting. The leadership qualities that had made Washington a war hero led to his unanimous election as first President of the United States.

Thomas Jefferson (above) and Andrew Jackson (below) each served two terms as President. Jefferson and Jackson were well-known to most Americans before election to the nation's highest office.

Hamilton, an advocate of strong government, foresaw a more active role for the Presidency. In *The Federalist,* No. 70, he wrote: "Energy in the Executive is a leading characteristic in the definition of good government."

Throughout the history of the Presidency, there has been continuing debate between those who emphasize the limits of Presidential power and those who underscore its strengths. So too, like a pendulum, there has been a swing back and forth between weak and strong Presidents. But with each swing, the power of the Presidency has grown. Indeed, the history of the Presidency is largely a history of the expansion of Presidential power. It is written in terms of the Presidents who have shaped the office by the force of their personal character and their executive actions.

George Washington (1789–1797) As the most respected man in America, Washington gave the Presidency his own personal prestige. And, as the first President of the United States, he established many precedents for the scope of Presidential power. Washington did not simply rest on his dignity. At times he assumed an active role that brought him into conflict with Congress. Washington's actions as President served to establish the principle that the Presidency is vested with broad and independent executive authority. The President is neither a creature of Congress nor a mere figurehead.

Thomas Jefferson (1801–1809) Jefferson, as national party leader, gave the Presidency a popular, democratic base. Like Washington, Jefferson made independent use of the executive power. The most dramatic use and most far-reaching in its impact was the Louisiana Purchase. In one act, Jefferson doubled the size of the United States—and nowhere was the purchase of territory a power expressly granted in the Constitution. The purchase, Jefferson believed, was justified by national emergency. In going beyond the Constitution, Jefferson invoked the laws of "necessity" and "self-preservation." In contrast, Madison and Monroe took a less vigorous Presidential role.

Andrew Jackson (1829–1837) The Presidency gained strength with the election of Andrew Jackson. The hero of the Battle of New Orleans, Jackson had national popular appeal and he used that popularity as an instrument of Presidential power. He was an active President and was the first to make extensive use of the veto in his battles with Congress.

PROFILE

His Accidency the President

When William Henry Harrison died one month after taking office in 1841, his Vice President, John Tyler, became the first to succeed to the Presidency. He was an unpopular leader whom his detractors called "His Accidency" instead of "His Excellency."

Since Tyler's time, seven other Vice Presidents have taken the oath of office upon the death of the President.* Millard Fillmore succeeded Zachary Taylor, who died of cholera. Calvin Coolidge became President upon the death, from undetermined causes, of Warren Harding, and Harry Truman succeeded Franklin Roosevelt, who died of a massive cerebral hemorrhage during his fourth term in office.

The assassinations of four Presidents thrust their Vice Presidents into the high office. Andrew Johnson succeeded Abraham Lincoln, who was shot only five days after the Civil War ended. James Garfield was shot by a disgruntled office seeker and died six months after taking office. He was succeeded by Chester Arthur. Theodore Roosevelt became President when William McKinley was assassinated early in his second term, and Lyndon Johnson succeeded John Kennedy, who was slain by a sniper.

Six Presidents—Andrew Jackson, both Roosevelts, Harry Truman, Gerald Ford, and Ronald Reagan—survived attempts on their lives.

*A ninth Vice President succeeded to office when Gerald R. Ford became President upon the resignation of Richard M. Nixon.

To manage the crisis of a nation divided by war, Abraham Lincoln extended Presidential authority. An 1865 Matthew Brady photograph portrays Lincoln with his son, Tad.

Jackson gave form to the modern Cabinet and successfully argued that its members were responsible to the President and not directly to Congress. He made extensive use of the appointment power, bringing his own people into office at every level of the federal government. Jackson also relied heavily on close, informal advisers who became known as the Kitchen Cabinet. Although they held no major government offices, their influence was great. They had a reputation for unpolished manners, but one favorable Washington newspaper described them as "men fresh from the ranks of the people, acquainted with their wants and understanding the current of their opinions." The Kitchen Cabinet was the forerunner of today's White House staff.

Abraham Lincoln (1861–1865) After a period of Presidential weakness, Lincoln took office at a time of crisis. Confronted by the destruction of the Union and civil war, Lincoln assumed the role of national leader. Invoking the "war power" of the President, he exercised almost unlimited authority. By his own admission, he took measures that in ordinary times would be beyond the constitutional limits of Presidential power. He was attacked by critics as a "dictator" and "despot," yet Abraham Lincoln waged war to defend the Constitution and save the Union. No President had ever before taken such sweeping action—nor has any since. But in his use of the war powers, Lincoln established the precedent that in times of crisis the President commands extraordinary power.

Theodore Roosevelt (1901–1909) After Lincoln the Presidency again declined. For nearly 40 years Congress was the dominant branch of government—so much so that in 1885, Woodrow Wilson, then a young political scientist, entitled his study of the American political system *Congressional Government.* The Presidency seemed to glow with new life under Theodore Roosevelt, a former cowboy and war hero, who captured popular imagination with his energy and enthusiasm. His was an activist Presidency. He wrote:

My belief was that it was not only [the President's] right but his duty to do anything that the needs of the nation demanded unless such action was forbidden by the Constitution or by the laws.

Roosevelt's successor, William Howard Taft, took a very different approach.

The true view of the Executive is, as I conceive it, that the President can exercise no power which cannot be fairly and reasonably traced to some specific grant of power or justly implied and included within such express grant as proper and necessary to its exercise.

The two views reflected very different conceptions of Presidential power. Roosevelt believed that the President had reserves of power that should be used *except* as specifically limited by law and the Constitution. In contrast, Taft believed that Presidential power was limited to that which was specifically granted by law and the Constitution. Roosevelt and Taft differed in politics as well. In 1912 Roosevelt challenged Taft's bid for reelection. The Republican party split, and in a three-way race for the Presidency, the Democratic candidate, Woodrow Wilson, won the election.

Woodrow Wilson (1913–1921) Wilson became President just before the beginning of World War I, and it was the "war power" that gave strength to his Presidency. In mobilizing industry and labor for the war effort, Wilson assumed wide control over the nation's economy. Rationing, wage and price controls, and a ban on strikes were among the many domestic actions taken under his Presidential leadership. International crisis brought the American Presidency to the forefront of domestic politics and foreign relations. The power of the United States came into focus in the office of the Presidency—a power of consequence for the whole world.

Earlier, Wilson had written:

When foreign affairs play a prominent part in the politics and policy of a nation, its Executive must of necessity be its guide: must utter every initial judgment, take every first step of action, supply the information upon which it is to act, suggest and in large measure control its conduct.

It is ironic that it was in foreign relations that Wilson came up against the limits of Presidential power. His proposal for a League of Nations won acceptance from allies of the United States, but at home Wilson could not gain its acceptance by Congress.

The election of 1920 brought a "return to normalcy," and the pendulum swing brought a succession of passive Presidents. The Twenties was a decade of prosperity. But not all Americans shared the nation's plenty; many of those who did lived beyond their means. The economy was dangerously inflated, and with the crash of the stock market in 1929, the United States entered the Great Depression.

Franklin D. Roosevelt (1933–1945) In 12 years in the White House, Franklin D. Roosevelt left his strong imprint on the modern Presidency. FDR was a "doer" and a "pusher," and he made vigorous use of Presidential power. In his first hundred days in office, Roosevelt persuaded Congress to pass a package of major bills that provided the foundation of his New Deal program. In an expanded role for the federal government, he supported such programs as subsidies for the farmers, welfare payments for the unemployed, and social security for the aged. One of Roosevelt's advisers later wrote the New Deal:

The legislative record it set, the impression it created on the public, its impact on the economy of the nation, and the incredible speed with which important legislation was planned, considered, proposed, and enacted has no parallel in the earlier history of the Republic.

The foreign-policy motto of Theodore Roosevelt (above, left) was, "Speak softly and carry a big stick." Woodrow Wilson (above, right) called the United States entrance into World War I a crusade "to make the world safe for democracy."

The popular Franklin D. Roosevelt (left) was elected four times to the Presidency. The crises that confronted Roosevelt—the Great Depression and World War II—required strong Presidential action. What were some of the programs created by Roosevelt's New Deal?

The Presidents of the United States

	President	Years in Office	Party	Age at Inauguration	Vice President(s)
1	George Washington	1789-1797	Federalist	57	John Adams
2	John Adams	1797-1801	Federalist	61	Thomas Jefferson
3	Thomas Jefferson	1801-1809	Democratic-Republican	57	Aaron Burr George Clinton
4	James Madison	1809-1817	Democratic-Republican	57	George Clinton Elbridge Gerry
5	James Monroe	1817-1825	Democratic-Republican	58	Daniel D. Tompkins
6	John Quincy Adams	1825-1829	Democratic-Republican	57	John C. Calhoun
7	Andrew Jackson	1829-1837	Democrat	61	John C. Calhoun Martin Van Buren
8	Martin Van Buren	1837-1841	Democrat	54	Richard M. Johnson
9	William H. Harrison	1841-1841	Whig	68	John Tyler
10	John Tyler	1841-1845	Whig	51	—
11	James K. Polk	1845-1849	Democrat	49	George M. Dallas
12	Zachary Taylor	1849-1850	Whig	64	Millard Fillmore
13	Millard Fillmore	1850-1853	Whig	50	—
14	Franklin Pierce	1853-1857	Democrat	48	William R. King
15	James Buchanan	1858-1861	Democrat	65	John C. Breckinridge
16	Abraham Lincoln	1861-1865	Republican	52	Hannibal Hamlin Andrew Johnson
17	Andrew Johnson	1865-1869	Democrat	56	—
18	Ulysses S. Grant	1869-1877	Republican	46	Schuyler Colfax Henry Wilson
19	Rutherford B. Hayes	1877-1881	Republican	54	William A. Wheeler
20	James A. Garfield	1881-1881	Republican	49	Chester A. Arthur
21	Chester A. Arthur	1881-1885	Republican	50	—
22	Grover Cleveland	1885-1889	Democrat	47	Thomas A. Hendricks
23	Benjamin Harrison	1889-1893	Republican	55	Levi P. Morton
24	Grover Cleveland	1893-1897	Democrat	55	Adlai E. Stevenson
25	William McKinley	1897-1901	Republican	54	Garret A. Hobart Theodore Roosevelt
26	Theodore Roosevelt	1901-1909	Republican	42	Charles W. Fairbanks
27	William H. Taft	1909-1913	Republican	51	James S. Sherman
28	Woodrow Wilson	1913-1921	Democrat	56	Thomas R. Marshall
29	Warren G. Harding	1921-1923	Republican	55	Calvin Coolidge
30	Calvin Coolidge	1923-1929	Republican	51	Charles G. Dawes
31	Herbert Hoover	1929-1933	Republican	54	Charles Curtis
32	Franklin D. Roosevelt	1933-1945	Democrat	51	John N. Garner Henry A. Wallace Harry S Truman
33	Harry S Truman	1945-1953	Democrat	60	Alben Barkley
34	Dwight D. Eisenhower	1953-1961	Republican	62	Richard M. Nixon
35	John F. Kennedy	1961-1963	Democrat	43	Lyndon B. Johnson
36	Lyndon B. Johnson	1963-1969	Democrat	55	Hubert H. Humphrey
37	Richard M. Nixon	1969-1974	Republican	55	Spiro T. Agnew Gerald R. Ford
38	Gerald R. Ford	1974-1977	Republican	61	Nelson A. Rockefeller
39	Jimmy Carter	1977-1981	Democrat	52	Walter F. Mondale
40	Ronald Reagan	1981-	Republican	69	George Bush

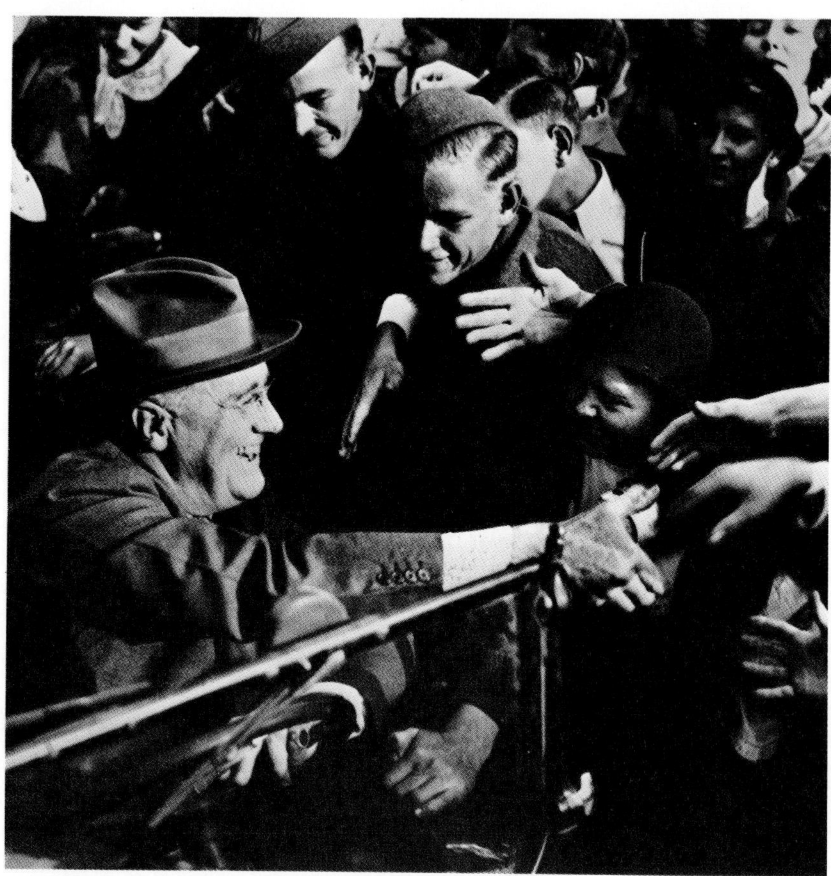

Franklin D. Roosevelt greets admirers at Warm Springs, Georgia, in 1933. Roosevelt often visited Warm Springs to treat the paralysis resulting from the polio he had contracted in 1921. Roosevelt's physical limitations did not prevent him from being one of America's strongest Presidents.

With the entry of the United States into World War II in 1941, Roosevelt relied upon the Presidential "war power" to strengthen his hand. Under direction by the President, as the nation mobilized for war, the government assumed extensive control over the economy. Roosevelt claimed ***emergency powers*** for the President as commander in chief.

The President has the powers, under the Constitution and under Congressional acts, to take measures necessary to avert a disaster which would interfere with the winning of the war.... When the war is won, the powers under which I act automatically revert to the people—to whom they belong.

Roosevelt came in for sharp criticism from his opponents. But in exercising Presidential power, he drew upon his resources as leader of the Democratic party and upon his great political skill. He sought support for his actions among the American people through his public speeches and radio "fireside chats." Roosevelt's leadership made the Presidency the most powerful office in the world.

Section Check

1. Define: emergency power
2. What was the principal problem concerning the chief executive faced by the Framers of the Constitution?
3. Identify four important powers of the President as described in the Constitution.
4. Which President created both a formal and informal group of advisers?
5. What did Franklin Roosevelt say would happen to his "war powers" when World War II was over?

2 THE PRESIDENCY IN MODERN TIMES

By the time Roosevelt had died in 1945, just a few months before the end of the war, the United States was the most powerful nation on earth. The Presidency had grown, and the scope of its power had expanded. Not only had the Presidency become the central institution of the national government, but the national government itself had grown enormously under Presidential leadership. From 1932 to 1945, the federal budget grew from $5 billion to $95 billion. The number of federal government employees increased from 605,000 to 3.8 million.

The Roosevelt model of the strong President has had a profound influence upon all who have followed in the White House. Whatever the personal style or political philosophy, each succeeding President has been shaped by the demand for leadership in a complex economy and a dangerous world.

Healing Wartime Wounds

The power of the Presidency has expanded in times of crisis and especially in times of war. Great Presidents have shaped the office with their energy and vision, but Presidents are shaped by the office as well. The President today is expected to be a national problem-solver. Whether the issue is energy, inflation, unemployment, or racial injustice, most people look to the President for leadership.

"I felt like the moon, the stars, and the planets had fallen on me," said Harry S Truman following his succession to the Presidency upon the death of Franklin Roosevelt. List four major foreign policy decisions made by Truman.

The demands of the office for leadership in international affairs is even more pressing. Under the Constitution, the President has central responsibility for the foreign relations of the United States. As one of the two most powerful nations in the world, the United States has commitments and responsibilities around the globe. In an age of nuclear weapons, when the future of all humanity is in the balance, the White House is the focus of international concern. The President is not only a national leader but a world leader as well.

Whatever a President's personal philosophy about the role of government, each incumbent is burdened today with great responsibilities—domestic and foreign. "Being a President is like riding a tiger," Harry S Truman once wrote. "A man has to keep on riding or be swallowed."

Harry S Truman (1945–1953) Truman succeeded to the Presidency on the death of Franklin Roosevelt in 1945. He immediately was confronted by one of the most awesome questions any President has ever had to resolve—the decision to drop the atomic bomb in order to bring an end to World War II. As President, Truman took the initiative in both foreign and domestic affairs. He was the architect of the Marshall Plan to assist in the economic recovery of Europe after the war. He moved to check Soviet expansion around the world and committed American troops to war in Korea to stop Communist expansion. In the Korean conflict Truman asserted his power as commander in chief by dismissing General Douglas MacArthur—leader of American forces in Korea—when the popular war hero refused to follow Presidential orders.

Truman was active, as well, in domestic policy—though not always successful. His Fair Deal program, which proposed national health insurance and civil rights guarantees, ran into strong opposition in Congress. Truman struggled with what he termed a "do-nothing" Congress and sometimes had to use the full power of the Presidency to obtain his goals. In 1948, when Congress refused to consider civil rights legislation, he issued executive orders to end discrimination in federal government employment and to desegregate the United States armed forces. Although elected to his own term in 1948, his effectiveness as President was weakened by low levels of public support. Perhaps the essential characteristic of the Truman Presidency was decisiveness. This was symbolized in the motto President Truman had on his desk in the Oval Office: "The Buck Stops Here."

Dwight D. Eisenhower (1953–1961) As commander of the Allied forces in Europe during World War II, Dwight ("Ike") Eisenhower was a national hero. He was a father figure for the American people, and his election reflected a desire for stability, peace, and prosperity. His was basically a moderate, conservative Presidency—both in policy and style.

Eisenhower believed that Roosevelt and Truman had reached beyond their constitutional powers. He took a more passive role in Presidential leadership. He viewed the Presidential office in terms of limited powers, as had William Howard Taft a half century before. Eisenhower presented few legislative programs and held back from the arm-twisting and persuasion that had come to mark Presidential relations with Congress. Yet Eisenhower was not a weak President. When necessary, he stood firm, notably in his decision to send the National Guard into Little Rock, Arkansas, to enforce court-ordered school desegregation.

Eisenhower remained popular throughout his two terms in office. He brought United States troops home from Korea and guided the nation in peace in world affairs. At home Eisenhower held down defense costs, kept a lid on inflation, and presided over eight years of prosperity and domestic tranquility.

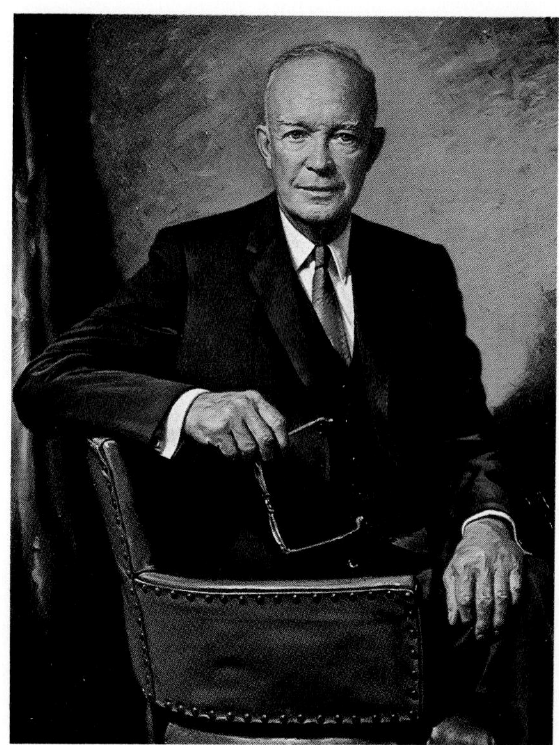

President Dwight D. Eisenhower—a strict constructionist—guided the nation for eight years. His style of governing was characterized by the delegation of authority to subordinates. List two domestic accomplishments of the Eisenhower administration.

LEGACY

Presidential Libraries

The papers and mementos of most recent Presidents are housed in Presidential libraries located across the United States. These are wonderful structures, maintained by the National Archives and Record Service, that reflect the personalities of the leaders whose names they bear. Some contain replicas of the Oval Office that give visitors a sense of the power of the Presidency. Gifts from heads of states are housed in the libraries along with souvenirs from lifetimes in politics and public service.

The Presidential libraries and their locations are:

Herbert Hoover, West Branch, Iowa
Franklin D. Roosevelt, Hyde Park, New York
Harry S Truman, Independence, Missouri
Dwight D. Eisenhower, Abilene, Kansas
John F. Kennedy, Boston, Massachusetts
Lyndon B. Johnson, Austin, Texas
Gerald R. Ford, Ann Arbor and Grand Rapids, Michigan
Jimmy Carter, Atlanta, Georgia (proposed)

John F. Kennedy, in his January 1961 inaugural address, challenged all Americans to "Ask not what your country can do for you—ask what you can do for your country." Give two examples of United States activism abroad during Kennedy's administration.

Soothing Domestic Turmoil

The 1960's and the early 1970's were often times of domestic turmoil. During these years, many Americans demonstrated for civil rights. Other Americans protested United States policies in Vietnam and in other parts of Southeast Asia. Later, the scandals of Watergate raised questions about Presidential leadership. During these eventful years, Americans looked to the Presidency to end domestic strife.

John F. Kennedy (1961–1963) With the vow to "get America moving again," Kennedy brought youth and vigor to the White House. In foreign affairs, he dramatically confronted the Soviet Union in Berlin in 1961 and in the Cuban missile crisis of 1962. A new American activism abroad was seen in the creation of the Peace Corps and in the Alliance for Progress to aid in the economic development of Latin America. But where Eisenhower had kept the United States out of Vietnam, Kennedy took the first steps toward America's involvement in that long and tragic war.

In the domestic sphere, Kennedy proposed a wide range of social and economic programs under the banner of the New Frontier. Few of the Kennedy programs passed Congress, but the Kennedy years later came to be idealized as Camelot—a reference to the romantic legend of King Arthur and the Knights of the Round Table. The Kennedy Presidency ended with an assassin's bullet on November 22, 1963.

Lyndon B. Johnson (1963–1969) Shocked by the Kennedy assassination, the nation rallied in support behind the new President, Lyndon B. Johnson. Drawing upon his great skill as a legislative leader, LBJ pushed a wide range of social and economic programs through Congress. Legislation included the civil rights bills, national health insurance (Medicare and Medicaid), and massive increases in federal support for education. Johnson called for a Great Society—the slogan of his administration. He declared "war on poverty." Federal aid to the poor doubled, with a proliferation of new government programs. But as people came to expect and demand more from government, some became increasingly impatient. Frustration spilled over into violence and social unrest.

The domestic turmoil of the 1960's was deepened by growing opposition to United States involvement in Vietnam. As military activity increased, the antiwar movement gained intensity. The nation was divided, and debate turned to confrontation between the hawks, who favored fighting the war until it was won, and the doves, who wanted the fighting stopped. Opposition to the war focused on President Johnson and on what some had come to call "the imperial Presidency."

In March 1968 Johnson stunned the country by his announcement that he would not seek a second full term as President. His decision was shaped by social unrest, political opposition, personal health, and his desire to unite the nation.

Richard M. Nixon (1969–1974) The war continued, as did the turmoil at home, when Nixon became the President in 1969. Nixon promised stability, conservatism, and an end to the war. But the war dragged on for another four years, while the movement against it grew. In foreign policy two achievements of the Nixon Presidency stand out. The first was the easing of world tension by an improvement in the relations between the United States and the Soviet Union. The second was the President's journey to China in 1972, opening relations between the United States and China.

The Vietnam War posed foreign-policy dilemmas for President Lyndon B. Johnson (left) and Richard M. Nixon (right). Yet despite the war, these two Presidents achieved success in other areas. Describe some of the presidential successes of Johnson and Nixon.

Nixon's success in foreign relations was not matched in the domestic sphere. His efforts to dismantle the Great Society programs ran into strong Democratic opposition in Congress. The issue of ***impoundment,*** involving the President's refusal to spend money appropriated by Congress, brought the two branches of government into collision. But it was the Watergate cover-up that brought the nation to constitutional crisis. The issue involved the two basic principles of American government: the separation of powers and the system of checks and balances. As the Presidency had grown in power, the balance had tipped. The Watergate investigations revealed abuses of Presidential power and a violation of law and the public trust. Facing impeachment by the House of Representatives and likely conviction by the Senate, Richard Nixon resigned as President in August 1974.

Setting New Directions

Through the late 1970's and the 1980's, the nation has continued to look to the Presidency as the source of leadership. Economic uncertainties and new foreign challenges have faced the Republic. To meet the needs of the times, recent Presidents have led the nation in new directions.

Gerald R. Ford (1974–1977) In the whirl of events in 1973 and 1974, within one year Gerald Ford moved from the House of Representatives to the Vice Presidency and then to the Presidency itself. Ford was the Republican Minority Leader in the House when, in October 1973, President Nixon nominated him to replace Spiro Agnew, who resigned as Vice President because of scandal. Eight months later, on August 9, 1974, Gerald Ford was sworn in as President of the United States. He sought to heal the wounds of Watergate and restore confidence in the institutions of government. President Ford's first words to the nation were those of reassurance: "My fellow Americans, our long national nightmare is over."

Ford was respected as a decent and honorable man, but he was viewed by many as an "accidental" President. He had never sought the Presidency and had entered the White House without a national base of support. Ford was thus at a political disadvantage—especially in facing the opposition of a Democratic Congress. His greatest problem over the

(continued on page 420)

INSIGHT

Lady Bird Johnson's White House Memory*

Since the White House was first occupied in 1800 by our second President, John Adams, every Presidential family has called it home. The Johnsons—Lyndon, Lynda, Luci, and I—were the 36th family in the succession of its residents.

My White House introduction came when I journeyed to Washington as a tourist in 1934. I remember the awe and affectionate regard with which I viewed that handsome structure—taking pictures through the iron gates which surround it, as countless visitors have done across a long span of decades. I thought, too, of the many families who had been its occupants—never dreaming that much later mine would number among them. A few months after that trip I met and soon married Lyndon, who was then Secretary to Congressman Richard Kleberg, and his job, of course, meant that we would live partly in Washington.

That respect I first felt is permanently engraved on my heart. It grew as I took Lyndon's constituents on sight-seeing rounds and when I returned as a guest at official functions. It intensified during the years we lived there.

In the White House memories of previous administrations are an almost tangible part of the surroundings. I walked through the halls with a rich sense of the past, knowing that my own family's footsteps would lengthen history's long journey. If the walls could talk, I know they would have enforced our determination to use the days fully—wisely and productively—and to savor them with excitement and anticipation for each new opportunity and experience!

Those days were a rich blend of a multitude of public and private moments. They were consistent only in their diverseness. All kinds of activities were included—from greeting a visiting head of state, entertaining a group of young Presidential Scholars or a delegation of labor leaders—to helping Lynda or Luci choose just the right dress for a special event, quiet dinners at 11:00 at night or later when Lyndon finally brought to a close a grueling day at the office, or stolen time for a fast game of bowling in the basement of the Executive Office Building next door!

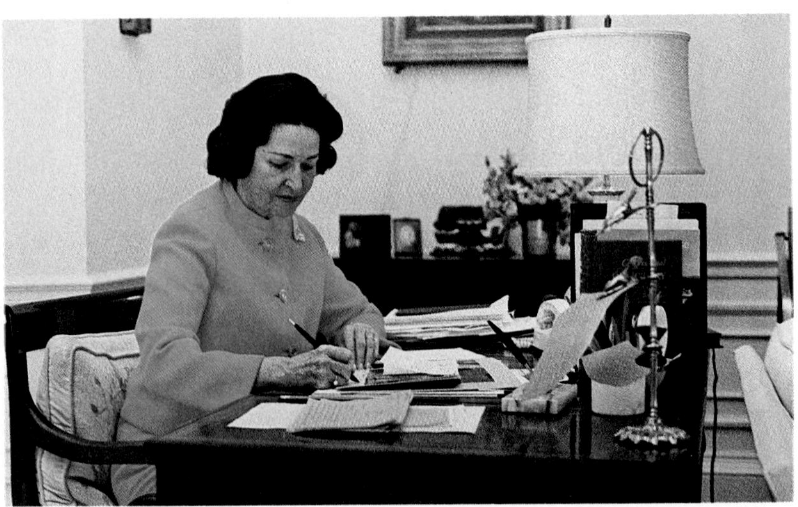

A montage of scenes march across my mind—of the first floor rooms, through which thousands of tourists poured every morning, frantically being readied for the day's scheduled events, of a meeting which would ultimately give birth to Project Head Start or one which would result in the settlement of a railroad industry crisis, homework papers spilling over the massive table in the Treaty Room, the Rose Garden glowing with lights on a balmy evening, framing an inviting setting for a special dinner party.

Life in the President's House is having a front row seat watching the constantly unfolding drama of national and international events, and at the same instant, finding yourselves as principal characters on the stage with the world as your audience—all without the chance to rehearse! This "glass house" is constantly reflected in the eye of the media.

For Lynda and Luci, who arrived at 1600 Pennsylvania Avenue at ages 19 and 16, it was a challenge to achieve normal personal lives with an inordinate amount of attention focused on them—not to mention dating under the watchful eyes of the Secret Service! When Lynda commented about the spotlight once, she said: "I sometimes think of those Roman slaves I read about in my history lessons. They had to stand in the chariot behind a general or emperor when he rode in triumph through the streets, and murmur, 'You are mortal, you are mortal.' "

One of the great rewards of those years for them (and their parents!) was the opportunity to become acquainted with the finest minds and talents within and without government. That glorious parade included such names as Carl Sandburg, Helen Hayes, Charles Lindbergh, Roy Wilkins, and Earl Warren. Cabinet officials and Congressmen were an everyday part of their lives, and outstanding writers, scientists, businessmen, educators, artists, and performers were frequent visitors.

Much of my time in the nation's home was centered around dispensing its hospitality to foreign visitors and our own countrymen. On the reverse side of that coin, it is also the private residence of the family who lives there, and I tried to make it an island of peace for my husband and children, balancing those duties with my own pursuits and trips to help focus public attention on Lyndon's programs or my own work in the beautification/conservation "vineyard."

It was to my husband that the crush of burdens of this house fell. As consuming as they often were, Lyndon believed it was the greatest honor that could befall a man in his lifetime to serve his country in its highest office, to be able to put his ideas into practice, and to devote himself to helping every individual raise himself to a life of dignity and independence.

It is a house of high aspirations, and the centerpiece of the continuing story that unfolds with each administration—a saga of many circumstances and personalities, of pain and triumph, of grand successes and bitter disappointments—lending strength and refreshment to its occupants with its enduring qualities, its serenity and expansiveness, and as a living symbol of the greatness of our nation's past.

*The above account of life in the White House during the Johnson Presidency was written especially for this book by the former First Lady at her ranch in Texas.

Gerald R. Ford (above) was the only person to have served as both Vice President and President without having been elected to either office. Jimmy Carter (below), a Georgia peanut farmer and state politician, entered national politics in 1976. What factors may have accounted for Ford's defeat in 1976? For Carter's defeat in 1980?

next two years was the economy, weakened by both recession and inflation. In 1976, when he sought election to a term of his own, Ford was far behind in the public opinion polls. But with the advantage of incumbency, he waged a strong campaign and was only narrowly defeated by his Democratic challenger, Jimmy Carter.

Jimmy Carter (1977–1981) Jimmy Carter's rise to the Presidency was against all odds. When he began his campaign for the nation's highest office, he was virtually unknown outside his native state of Georgia, where he had served one term as governor. Carter campaigned against the "insiders" of the Washington establishment, but once in the White House his lack of national political experience weakened his capacity to provide effective leadership. Many of Carter's closest aides were similarly inexperienced, contributing to the isolation of the White House.

The President's programs bogged down in Congress. Within the executive branch, both in domestic and foreign policy, administration officials often seemed to be at odds with one another in their public pronouncements. The President had scored real achievements in civil service reform, but these were overshadowed by the continuing problems of energy and inflation. Carter's popularity dropped even faster than the value of the dollar. By August 1979, in the Gallup Poll's approval rating for the President's performance, only 20 percent felt that he had done an excellent or good job. At the same time, however, 80 percent of those surveyed believed Carter to be a "man of high moral principles." The problem was one of leadership. Most people did not see Carter as having "strong leadership qualities"—a commanding presence, forceful speech, and the ability to persuade.

Incumbency is normally a great advantage, and no President who has sought renomination in this century has been denied it by his party. But incumbency also has a built-in disadvantage. Rightly or wrongly, when things go badly, the President gets the blame. As Carter's rating in the polls declined, Senator Edward Kennedy gained increasing support for his challenge to the President's renomination. In late 1979, however, two events—the seizure of American hostages in Iran and the Soviet invasion of Afghanistan—focused attention on the White House. International crisis became the stage for the President to demonstrate strong leadership. As the nation rallied in support of the President, Carter's approval ratings shot up dramatically. From the doldrums Carter's Presidency emerged with new energy and power. But the hostage crisis dragged on, and the nation's economy showed no relief from inflation and unemployment. Carter's standing again fell, and on November 4, 1980, he suffered a massive defeat at the polls. President Carter, with 41 percent of the vote, carried only six states and the District of Columbia.

Ronald Reagan (1981–   ) Ronald Reagan was born in 1911 in Tampico, Illinois. After graduation from Eureka College in his home state and a brief stint as a sports announcer for an Iowa radio station, Reagan began his acting career in California. He appeared in more than 50 films and served six terms as president of the Screen Actors Guild. From movies Reagan went into television and then into politics.

In 1966 Reagan contested public office for the first time and was elected governor of California. He served for eight years as governor of the nation's most populous state. Reagan gained a national reputation as a champion of conservatism. In 1976 he came close to taking the Republican Presidential nomination. Four years later, the nomination his, Reagan was elected the 40th President of the United States.

In the White House, Reagan faced the task of translating his political philosophy into public policy. He had long believed that the size of the government must be reduced, and his first official act as President was to place a freeze on federal hiring. Within a month of taking office, Reagan went before Congress to present his economic program. The plan called for deep budget cuts and reduced taxes. Its goal was to slow the growth of government, to bring inflation under control, and to encourage investment for renewed economic productivity. In foreign policy, President Reagan issued stern warnings to the Soviet Union and underscored America's resolve to resist the expansion of Communist influence. To build the nation's military strength, Reagan called for major increases in the defense budget.

The early momentum of the Reagan Presidency was sustained by wide popular support and by the skill of the President and his White House aides in dealing with Congress.

On March 30, 1981—less than one hundred days after taking office—President Reagan was shot in an attempted assassination. He made a rapid recovery and two months later was again horseback riding on his California ranch and fully in control of the White House. An already friendly Congress rallied to his side, giving the President victory after victory on Capitol Hill. Gradually, the economy recovered. Interest rates fell, the stock market soared, but unemployment hovered at about 7.5 percent.

In the Presidential elections of 1980 and 1984, Ronald Reagan was able to appeal not only to Republican voters but also to conservative southern Democrats. The Reagan Presidency emphasized economic recovery and a strong defense.

Reagan, once an admirer of Franklin Roosevelt, proved, like Roosevelt, to be a flexible leader willing to experiment with a variety of approaches to solve economic woes, including tax reform. Unlike Roosevelt, however, he often seemed content to leave decision making to his White House staff.

Section Check

1. Define: impoundment
2. What was the first major decision President Truman faced after taking office?
3. What names were given to the programs of Truman, Kennedy, and Johnson?
4. Which two achievements in foreign affairs stand out from the Nixon Presidency?
5. What was Ronald Reagan's experience in government before becoming President?

PROFILE

The 1984 Presidential Election

The 1984 Presidential election between Ronald Reagan and Walter Mondale offered voters the clearest choice between political philosophies since the 1972 contest between Richard Nixon and George McGovern. During the election campaign, the candidates made their political preferences clear.

President Reagan expressed the view that the federal bureaucracy is too large and must be cut back. In Reagan's view, government should be kept in check and the federal deficit reduced by cutting taxes in a way that stimulates economic growth. On foreign policy, Reagan called for a strong military and increased defense spending. Thus, he contended, the United States could negotiate arms-control treaties with the Soviet Union from a position of strength.

Walter Mondale, on the other hand, stated his view that the federal government should be an instrument for social improvement. In Mondale's view, a properly managed government could cure the ills of American society and make the country a better place. Mondale also called for a reduction of the federal deficit. He proposed, however, a tax increase and a decrease in military spending to achieve the reduction. On foreign policy, Mondale called for renewed arms-control talks with the Soviet Union.

The positions of the candidates were highlighted in two televised Presidential debates, sponsored by the League of Women Voters.

The first debate, held in early October, focused on domestic issues. As the date of the first debate approached, the political pollsters determined that President Reagan led former Vice President Mondale by as much as 20 percent. Mondale viewed this debate as a key opportunity

Democratic candidates Walter Mondale and Geraldine Ferraro (above) campaign in Mondale's home state of Minnesota.

President Reagan addresses Republican women officeholders at the White House.

to close the gap. Throughout the 90-minute debate, the candidates restated their positions on the issues. During this first debate, however, President Reagan sometimes seemed hesitant and unsure of his answers. The President also seemed to be overburdened with statistics. Conversely, Mondale appeared confident throughout the debate. Most significantly, the debate had raised a serious issue—the President's age. The post-debate polls showed that Mondale had made impressive gains into Reagan's lead.

In the second debate, Reagan—at 73 years of age, the oldest Presidential candidate ever—needed to prove that his age did not impair his ability to lead the nation. Mondale hoped to show that he held a vision of the nation's future which the President lacked. During the debate, both contenders generally restated their positions on the issue of foreign policy. Mondale, clear and articulate throughout the debate, demonstrated his sharp debating skills. Reagan, however, effectively diffused the age issue, appearing confident and in control. In the post-debate assessment, analysts agreed that the President had regained an impressive lead over his challenger.

George Bush (top) and Geraldine Ferraro (bottom) address the issues during their historic televised Vice-Presidential debate.

One 90-minute Vice-Presidential debate was sponsored by the League of Women Voters. The debate between the candidates—Vice President George Bush, Republican, and Congresswoman Geraldine Ferraro, Democrat—was historic because it was the first time that a woman contender for a nationwide office met her opponent on national television. The debate covered issues of domestic and foreign policy. Many political experts believed that the candidates scored a tie, but each side claimed that its candidate won the debate.

About a week before the Presidential election, public opinion polls indicated that Reagan's lead was between 16 and 20 percent. On election night, the pollsters' predictions proved to be reliable. Reagan won 59 percent of the popular vote to Mondale's 41 percent—a margin of 18 percent. In the electoral college, Reagan won 525 electoral votes from 49 states—the greatest sweep by any Presidential candidate. Mondale won a total of 13 electoral votes, gaining the votes of only Minnesota and the District of Columbia.

Analyses of the 1984 Presidential election show that Reagan won the majority of the popular vote in every region of the country. He also won the majority of votes of men, of women, and of every voting-age group. Reagan carried the votes of Roman Catholics and Protestants, but Mondale won the ballots of most Jewish voters. Blacks—a categorical group that is traditionally Democratic—voted overwhelmingly for Mondale.

Many political analysts believed that Reagan's landslide reelection was a mandate for him to continue the policies of his first term. Other analysts saw Reagan's victory as an indication of a trend toward a more conservative electorate. Still others viewed the election results as part of a realignment of the parties' traditional bases of support. Analysts agree, however, that the Reagan win resulted from three main factors—the President's popular appeal, the nation's economic prosperity, and a relatively peaceful world.

President Reagan (far right) faces microphones and cameras on the White House lawn. The media bring the President's image into homes throughout the United States. What does the President symbolize to most Americans?

3 THE PRESIDENTIAL IMAGE

How people view the Presidency—their image of that high office and those who occupy it—is a major factor in the exercise of Presidential power. Without popular support the constitutional powers of the President carry little weight. As the one elected national leader, the President commands public attention in whatever is said or done. This visibility is a valuable resource that, with skill, can be used to win approval and support. But with all eyes on the White House, the President's actions are under constant scrutiny, and Presidential performance is measured by high expectations.

Great Expectations

The Presidency is a uniquely personal institution. The office and the person are not easily separated. The President is the symbol of the nation, of government and authority. For most Americans this image is rooted in childhood. As children our first awareness of government is likely to be in terms of the President. Studies show that most children have an image of the President as a benevolent leader and protector. As they grow older, they exercise more critical judgment, but the image remains deeply personal. As the representative of the people, the President is the embodiment of their hopes and aspirations.

As the Presidency has grown more powerful, especially over the past 50 years, more people have looked to the President as the nation's problem solver. Indeed, the expansion of Presidential power has been encouraged by popular demands and expectations. Whether it is energy, inflation, unemployment at home, or unrest and revolution abroad, people expect the President to *do* something. Too often these expectations are unrealistic. The President is not all-powerful—and few people, surely, would want such a tyrant. The President is the nation's most powerful leader and has an impressive array of powers, both formal and informal. But Presidential powers are limited. They are bounded by the Constitution and by what is politically possible. No President can satisfy all of the people all of the time.

The power of the Presidency is limited in yet another way. Complex problems rarely have quick and simple solutions. The solution to one problem may only create problems in other areas. Efforts to protect the environment, for example, may reduce our access to energy resources. Efforts to control inflation may lead to higher levels of unemployment. Finally, there are some problems over which the President has little control. The United States may seek to influence the course of world events, but it cannot control what other nations do. For all their efforts, a succession of Presidents has been unable to bring peace to the troubled Middle East. Neither have recent Presidents been able to settle the continuing unrest in Central America.

A President is judged according to performance—by what gets done. But public expectations today may be so high that no President can possibly meet them. The President is the lightning rod of public dissatisfaction. When things go wrong—when the economy falters or the government stumbles—the President is likely to get the blame.

Presidential Popularity

Public judgment of the President's performance is measured by the polls—the "fever chart" of Presidential popularity. For more than 40 years, survey research organizations have studied public opinion on Presidential performance. Once every two weeks, the Gallup Poll asks the same question: "Do you approve or disapprove of the way (name) is handling the job as President?" The result is a zigzag line recording the highs and lows of Presidential popularity. The typical pattern is for a President to begin a term with a high approval rating. After the initial "honeymoon" period, the ratings begin a choppy decline. A notable exception was President Eisenhower, who maintained relatively high approval ratings throughout his two terms. President Kennedy's popularity also remained fairly steady, but in the last year of his Presidency, his ratings, too, began to decline.

President Carter's approval rating hit a high of 75 percent in March 1977, soon after he took office. A year later, it had fallen below 50 percent, and in July 1979, it plunged to 28 percent. Yet, like a roller coaster, within six months Carter's approval rating soared to 58 percent as a result of his handling of the Iranian and Afghan crises. It then fell to the lowest rating given any President in more than 40 years—21 percent in January 1980.

Political scientists have determined that there are 5 significant factors that account for the abrupt changes in the public's judgment of Presidential performance.

Reaction to Presidential Decisions During the campaign candidates make promises about what they will do if elected. Almost always, they promise more than any President can deliver. Not only may a President be unable to keep campaign promises, but in office a President's judgment of what is needed may change. Either way, many people are likely to be disappointed. In addition, whatever the President does, some groups inevitably will be dissatisfied. As the President takes action on an increasing variety of issues, the number of groups in opposition is likely to grow. This will be reflected in a decline in the President's approval rating.

"Rally-Round-the-Flag" International events—especially crises—typically give a boost to Presidential popularity. The nation unites behind the President in what is described as a "rally-round-

(continued on page 428)

APPROVAL RATINGS OF PRESIDENTS

President	Favorable Ratings (In Percent) High	Low	Average
Roosevelt (1933-45)	84	54	68
Truman (1945-53)	87	23	46
Eisenhower (1953-61)	79	49	66
Kennedy (1961-63)	83	57	70
Johnson (1963-69)	80	35	54
Nixon (1969-74)	68	24	48
Ford (1974-77)	71	37	46
Carter (1977-81)	75	21	47
Reagan (1981-)	68	41	—

SOURCE: The Gallup Poll

Since the first administration of Franklin Roosevelt, polls have measured Presidential popularity. What is Roosevelt's average rating? Which President has achieved the highest rating? Which President has the highest average rating?

PROFILE

America's First Ladies

The First Lady is not a public official, but as the President's wife she has great influence. Martha Washington, one of the richest women in America, gave her husband financial independence. Dolley Madison was a tactful White House hostess for 16 years, assisting first the widowed Thomas Jefferson and then her husband. Mary Todd Lincoln gave social graces to her husband, in his own words "a poor nobody" when he met her. Grace Coolidge used her wit and vivacity to soften the dour image of her husband, Calvin.

Although Robert Kennedy once quipped of his sister-in-law Jacqueline Kennedy that she would be most unlikely to greet her husband with the question "What's new in Laos?" her lack of interest in government did not deter her from an ambitious restoration of the public rooms of the White House. Lady Bird Johnson worked tirelessly for a cleaner and more beautiful environment. Betty Ford actively sought passage of the Equal Rights Amendment.

Martha Washington

The range of these activities has led to concern by some that the First Lady has too much influence. Such criticism is not new. During the administration of John Adams, Abigail Adams was her husband's chief adviser. She had a strong voice in major decisions, and political opponents questioned the role of this "unelected" woman. But there is no requirement that the President's advisers be elected officials. Each President is free to pick his own advisers, and many have relied heavily upon their wives.

Sarah Polk was a full partner in the Presidency of her husband James. She shared the President's office and assisted him in many of the duties now performed by the White House staff.

One of the most influential First Ladies was Edith Wilson, Woodrow Wilson's second wife. They were married in 1915, during Wilson's first term as President. Wilson brought the First Lady into his war councils and turned to her for advice on foreign policy. When he suffered a disabling stroke in 1919, Mrs. Wilson assumed a critical role. Some

Abigail Adams

Sarah Polk

Dolley Madison

historians argue that for the 17 months until the end of Wilson's term, she was, in fact, Acting President.

Eleanor Roosevelt, the wife of Franklin Roosevelt and niece of Theodore Roosevelt, was a prominent and controversial figure in public life. As First Lady she overcame great shyness to speak strongly for liberal causes. She was a champion of human rights and racial justice. President Truman appointed her to the United Nations Commission on Human Rights in 1946, which she chaired until 1951.

Little was known about the very private Bess Truman during her eight years in the White House. Yet Harry Truman later said that he had consulted with her about every major decision of his administration. President Truman summed up the First Lady's influence by calling her "my chief adviser" and "a full partner in all my transactions—politically and otherwise."

Recent First Ladies have continued to be influential in American life. Rosalynn Carter was an invaluable assistant to her husband. She sometimes attended Cabinet meetings, and served as the President's personal ambassador to numerous occasions of state. Mrs. Carter influenced her husband's views on women's rights, federal hiring practices, and the needs of the elderly.

Nancy Reagan has focused attention on the problems of drug and alcohol abuse among young Americans. She is also a strong advocate of ACTION's Foster Grandparents, a program through which elderly persons volunteer to care for disadvantaged children. Mrs. Reagan has addressed these issues on television and in speeches to school and civic groups.

Each of these women demonstrated strong leadership qualities. Had the times been different, perhaps each might have been elected President. But times change, and as Americans look to the future, it may not be so very long before they speak—instead of the First Lady—of the President's Husband.

Grace Coolidge

Eleanor Roosevelt

Betty Ford

Jacqueline Kennedy

the-flag" effect. These events must involve the United States and the President particularly. They must be dramatic and sharply focused. The Japanese attack on Pearl Harbor in 1941, for example, brought a major rise in Roosevelt's popularity. In the years since, there have been a number of similar rallying points—the Cuban missile crisis in 1962, the Vietnam peace accords in 1973, and the Iranian and Afghan crises in 1979. These rallying points usually have only short-term effects and account for the bumps and wiggles on the President's "fever chart."

Economic Slump A President's popularity is closely tied to the condition of the economy. An economic slump—as measured by the rate of unemployment, for example—is likely to be recorded in a decline in the President's approval rating. Unfortunately the President gets the blame for the nation's economic woes but gets little credit when things improve.

Another feature of the public's reaction to economic changes should be noted. Most people pass judgment on Presidential performance in terms of the economic outlook for the nation as a whole—not, as might be expected, according to their own personal economic situation.

War Presidential popularity is affected by war. When the nation is behind the war effort, as in World War II, the President gains support. An unpopular war, however, lowers the President's approval rating. The Korean War hurt Truman, and President Johnson believed that the Vietnam War cost him 20 points in the polls.

Scandal Scandal within the executive branch can cut deeply into a President's standing in the polls. As a result of the Watergate investigations, for example, Nixon's approval rating fell rapidly from 60 percent to a low of 24 percent.

HOW HISTORIANS RATE THE PRESIDENTS

Great	Near Great
1. Abraham Lincoln	5. Theodore Roosevelt
2. Franklin D. Roosevelt	6. Woodrow Wilson
3. George Washington	7. Andrew Jackson
4. Thomas Jefferson	8. Harry S Truman

Above Average	Average
9. John Adams	18. William McKinley
10. Lyndon B. Johnson	19. William Howard Taft
11. Dwight D. Eisenhower	20. Martin Van Buren
	21. Herbert Hoover
12. James K. Polk	22. Rutherford B. Hayes
13. John F. Kennedy	
14. James Madison	23. Chester A. Arthur
15. James Monroe	24. Gerald Ford
16. John Quincy Adams	25. Jimmy Carter
17. Grover Cleveland	26. Benjamin Harrison

Below Average	Failures
27. Zachary Taylor	32. Andrew Johnson
28. John Tyler	33. James Buchanan
29. Millard Fillmore	34. Richard Nixon
30. Calvin Coolidge	35. Ulysses S. Grant
31. Franklin Pierce	36. Warren G. Harding

Not rated are Ronald Reagan and two Chief Executives who died early in office: William Henry Harrison and James Garfield.
Source: *U.S. News & World Report*, Nov. 21, 1983

Historians' opinions of Presidential greatness are measured in a 1983 poll. Which Presidents are considered failures? Which are considered below average?

Presidential Greatness

The Vietnam War and Watergate weakened public confidence in government and in the Presidency specifically. In the mid-1970's the American people valued honesty and trustworthiness as the most important qualities a President should have. By the end of the decade, however, leadership was the quality most sought in a President.

Emphasis on leadership ability is reflected in the judgment of Presidential greatness. In 1983 a panel of historians ranked the Presidents. Their four "great" Presidents were (1) Abraham Lincoln, (2) Franklin D. Roosevelt, (3) George Washington, and (4) Thomas Jefferson. These were followed by "near greats," (5) Theodore Roosevelt, (6) Woodrow Wilson, (7) Andrew Jackson, and (8) Harry S Truman.

People, of course, disagree on what makes a President great, and any list is likely to provoke controversy. Historians' views of Presidents change over time. A President who gets relatively low marks today may in another 20 years be seen in very different terms. But when asked to rank the Presidents, the public and historians alike tend to give highest place to strong and active Presidents.

The expectations surrounding the modern Presidency demand strong leadership ability. No President, of course, chooses to be weak, but Presidents do differ in their skills and personalities.

Presidential Personality

Personality plays an important role in shaping Presidential performance. One political scientist, James David Barber, identifies style, world view, and character as three elements in the pattern of Presidential personality. Style refers to how the President goes about the job of responding to the demands of the office. Style is the President's way of acting. A President's world view is composed of basic beliefs about human nature, society, and politics. World view is a President's way of seeing. Character is the President's enduring orientation toward life. According to Barber, Presidential character is deeply rooted in childhood experience. At its core is how the President understands and judges self-image and sense of self-esteem or worth.

Barber believes that character is the key to understanding why our Presidents act as they do. In studying Presidential character, Barber divides Presidents according to (1) how active they are, and (2) how they feel about political life. On the first point, active Presidents are full of energy, while passive ones rarely take initiative. On the second point, positive Presidents are optimists, with a love of politics. Negative Presidents are pessimists and take power as a burden. Thus Franklin Roosevelt was an active-positive President. Calvin Coolidge was a passive-negative President.

Barber recognizes that no President fits perfectly into any single type. The four character types represent general tendencies. Nevertheless, there is considerable disagreement about how different Presidents should be classified.

The Presidential Experience

Can an understanding of character help us predict a candidate's likely performance as President? Barber believes that it can, but performance is not shaped by personality alone. How personality influences Presidential performance depends upon a number of factors. Three factors are briefly discussed in the paragraphs that follow. These three factors are the power situation, the climate of expectations, and the pressure of the Presidency itself.

One theory of Presidential character divides Presidents according to their activity and their feelings about politics. Give an example of an active-negative President. Give an example of a passive-negative President.

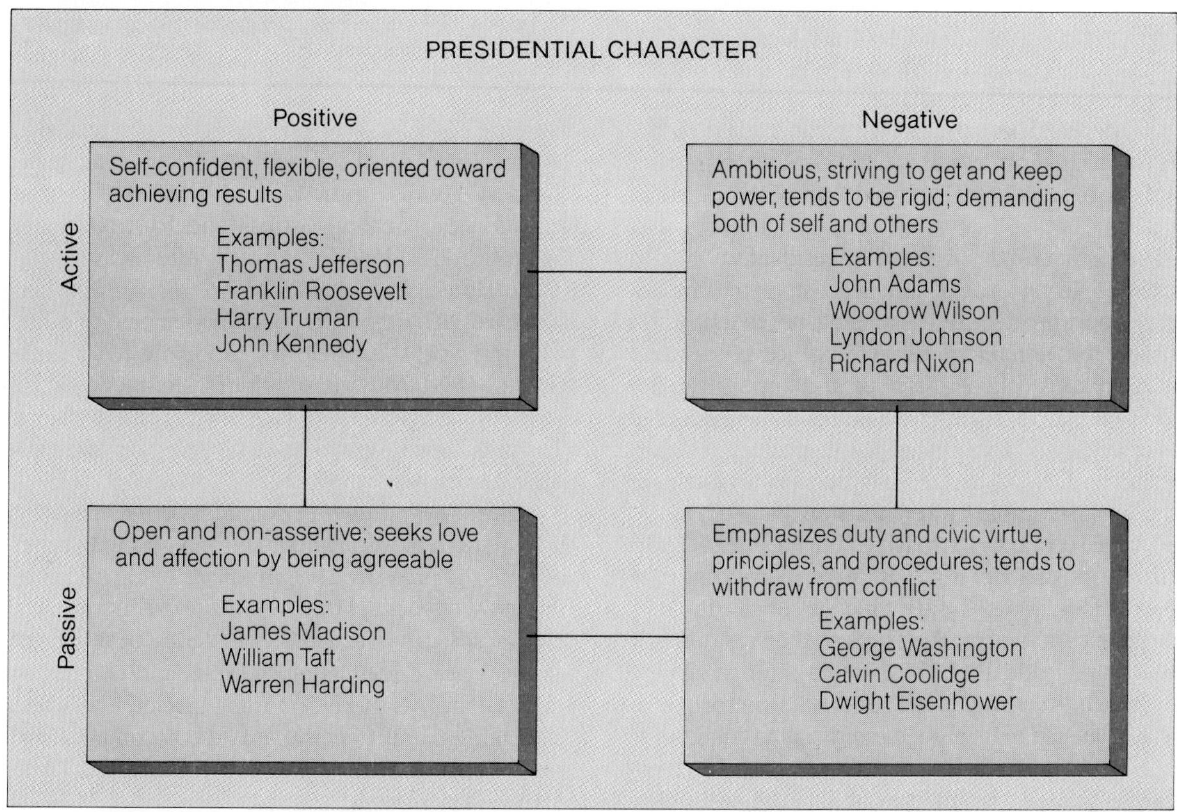

PRESIDENTIAL CHARACTER
Positive
Negative
Active
Self-confident, flexible, oriented toward achieving results
Examples:
Thomas Jefferson
Franklin Roosevelt
Harry Truman
John Kennedy
Ambitious, striving to get and keep power, tends to be rigid; demanding both of self and others
Examples:
John Adams
Woodrow Wilson
Lyndon Johnson
Richard Nixon
Passive
Open and non-assertive; seeks love and affection by being agreeable
Examples:
James Madison
William Taft
Warren Harding
Emphasizes duty and civic virtue, principles, and procedures; tends to withdraw from conflict
Examples:
George Washington
Calvin Coolidge
Dwight Eisenhower

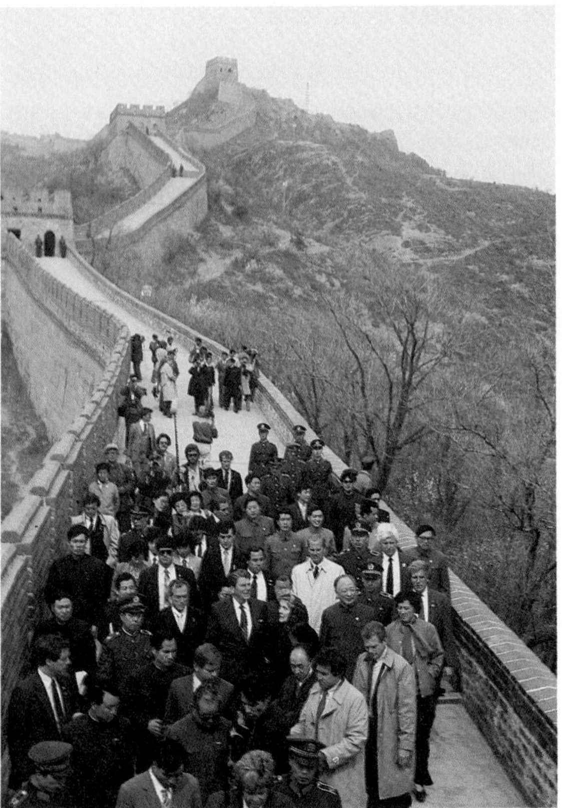

During a 1984 visit to the People's Republic of China, President and Mrs. Ronald Reagan visit an outdoor market (left) and tour the Great Wall of China (right). Presidential trips to foreign countries are an important means through which the United States carries out diplomatic relations.

The President must respond and adapt to the "power situation" that is at hand—the support from the public and Congress. Presidential power, as noted earlier is limited in a variety of ways, but even within the constitutional powers, the President's ability to exercise strong leadership depends upon the amount of support received. A President is not in a position simply to command the system. An active President is likely to run into resistance and opposition. On the other hand, a person who sees the Presidential role largely as a caretaker, above politics and partisan conflict, may not even try to take advantage of the most favorable power situation.

The second factor to which the Presidential personality must adapt is the "climate of expectations." People look to the President for reassurance in times of unrest and worry. They look to the President for action and leadership. The expectations may change from time to time, and Presidential performance will be judged in terms of these changing conditions.

The power situation and the climate of expectations change, but the pressures of the Presidency itself are constant. Truman offered a word of advice to those who sought the office: "If you can't stand the heat, get out of the kitchen." But even for the strongest personalities, stress and frustration can make the Presidency an ordeal. After leaving the White House, Lyndon Johnson recalled that when he heard Richard Nixon conclude his oath of office with the words "so help me God," he felt a great burden lifted from his shoulders. He knew that he would no longer have to face the terrible decisions that might lead the world to nuclear war and possible destruction.

The sheer number of demands on the President impose both physical and emotional strain. In times of crisis the pressure for immediate action becomes intense. Presidential decision making is never easy. The issues that reach the President's desk almost always involve conflicting interests and competing values. Rarely is there one right answer. The stress of making painful decisions is often compounded by the incessant publicity that follows the President's every move.

A measure of stress can be invigorating, as every athlete has experienced in competition. It can provide the push toward excellence. But intense and unrelieved stress may lead to exhaustion and breakdown. Coupled with frustration, it can result in a distortion of reality and rash action. Herein lies one of the great dangers to the American Presidency. How the President copes with the inevitable stress and frustrations of the office is critical. How, for example, will a President react in a crisis—remain calm, decisive, and in control? Or will the President be provoked to anger, overreaction, and serious error?

Character can tell us a great deal, but it is not the whole story of Presidential performance. Presidents have shaped the office through the force of their character and actions, but each, in turn, has been shaped by the Presidency. The Presidency is, in a sense, both a person and an institution. To help you understand the impact of the office on Presidential performance, the next chapter will discuss the President at work.

Section Check

1. What are some limits on the power of the President to be a problem solver?
2. What is meant by the phrase "the President is the lightning rod of public dissatisfaction"?
3. Which President, of the past nine, had the highest average favorable rating, as measured by the Gallup Poll? Which had the lowest?
4. Which two events of the 1970's particularly weakened public confidence in the Presidency?
5. Which four Presidents were rated "great" by a panel of historians? Which four "near great"?

SUMMARY

The Presidency is the central institution of the American political system. Yet the power of the office is limited by the Constitution and by custom. The Framers of the Constitution resolved the role of the Presidency by the two fundamental principles of American government: separation of powers and the system of checks and balances. Thus, a separate executive branch is headed by a single executive, independently elected for a fixed term of office, with limited powers. The powers of the Presidency are granted by the Constitution, not by Congress.

The President is commander in chief of the armed forces; may grant pardons to those convicted of federal crimes; may make treaties, with the advice and consent of the Senate; may appoint executive officials, federal judges, and ambassadors, again with Senate approval; and may recognize foreign governments by receiving their ambassadors. Among the office's constitutional duties are the State of the Union message to Congress and recommending legislation. The President, finally, is responsible for the faithful execution of all laws.

Presidential power has steadily expanded, even as the pendulum has swung between weak and strong Presidents. George Washington established many precedents for the office by his dignity and resolve. Thomas Jefferson gave the Presidency a popular, democratic base. Andrew Jackson used his national popularity as an instrument of Presidential power. Abraham Lincoln exercised almost unlimited authority by invoking the "war power" of the Presidency. Theodore Roosevelt gave the office new vitality. Woodrow Wilson assumed wide control over the nation's economy during World War I. Franklin Roosevelt greatly expanded the role of the federal government in social and economic programs during the Great Depression.

Since 1945 the power and prestige of the office have continued to expand. Under the Constitution the President has central responsibility for foreign relations of the United States. As one of the two most powerful nations in the world, the United States has commitments and responsibilities around the globe. The President has become a world leader.

A major factor in the exercise of Presidential power is the public image of the high office and those who occupy it. Constant public scrutiny and high expectations accompany the office. The President is expected to be the nation's problem solver and is, at the same time, the lightning rod of public dissatisfaction.

Presidential popularity tends to zigzag in reaction to Presidential decisions and actions during times of international crisis, economic slump, war, or scandal.

Presidential personality, which plays an important role in shaping performance in office, is partly based on style, world view, and character. Presidents may be actives, full of energy, or passives, who rarely take initiative. They may be positives, with a love of politics, or negatives, who take power as a burden. Other influences on Presidential performance are the power situation, the climate of expectations, and the pressure of the Presidency itself.

Chapter 17 Review

Using Vocabulary

Answer the questions by using the meaning of each underlined term.

1. What is the difference between an active President and a passive President, according to James David Barber?
2. Why do political scientists consider style, world view, and character as important elements by which to judge Presidential leadership?
3. How did Franklin Roosevelt view his role in regard to emergency powers?
4. What does climate of expectations have to do with the way people perceive executive leadership?
5. What did Richard Nixon do with regard to impoundment?

Understanding American Government

1. Explain why some Framers of the Constitution favored a weak chief executive. How were the objections of these Framers overcome?
2. Briefly describe the expansion of Presidential power under Washington, Jefferson, Jackson, Lincoln, Theodore Roosevelt, Wilson, and Franklin Roosevelt.
3. How did Theodore Roosevelt and William Howard Taft differ in their views of Presidential power?
4. What are five factors that affect the public's judgment of Presidential performance? Explain the role that these factors play in the public's assessment of Presidential performance.

Extending Your Skills: Reading a Chart

Study the chart on page 412. Then answer the questions that follow.

1. To what political party did John Adams belong? To what political party did William Henry Harrison belong? To what political party did Abraham Lincoln belong?
2. Who was the oldest President at the time of inauguration? Who was the youngest President to take office?
3. How many Vice Presidents have become President?
4. Who served the longest term as President? How long did he serve?
5. Since 1829, how many Presidents have belonged to the Democratic party? To the Republican party?

Government and You

1. Presidential power has changed through the years largely because of the personality of the various Presidents. What if the Constitutional Convention met again today? How might it change the office of President? What additional limits might be placed on the office?
2. Some political scientists have argued that war has been responsible for the tremendous growth in the power of the Presidency. Do you agree or disagree? Explain your answer.
3. From newspapers and television news, list the activities of the President in two columns: *Domestic* and *Foreign.* Which occupies the greater amount of news coverage? On the basis of this short-term observation, what can you conclude about the role of the Presidency in modern times?

Activities

1. You might plan a class visit to a Presidential library or museum if one is close. In addition to the Presidential libraries described in this chapter, many of the Presidents' homes or birthplaces have been restored and are open to the public. Write to the General Services Administration in Washington, D.C., for information on the Presidential libraries and museums and report on the nearest one.
2. Moments of national crisis—war, assassination, economic disaster—all produce vivid memories for those who live through them. Interview an adult who recalls the assassination in 1963 of John F. Kennedy. You might tape-record highlights to share with the class. Other subjects for oral history might include memories of Franklin D. Roosevelt, Lyndon Johnson, or Richard Nixon or the assassination attempt on President Reagan.

Chapter 18

The President in Action

He is the vital center of action in the system, whether he accepts it or not, and the office is the measure of the man—of his wisdom as well as of his force.

WOODROW WILSON

CHAPTER OVERVIEW

George Washington's 1789 inaugural ceremony at Federal Hall in New York City is illustrated in an 1876 Currier and Ives print. Robert Livingston, the Chief Judge of New York State (in the red and black robe), administers the oath.

1 THE AMERICAN PRESIDENCY

George Washington took the oath of office on April 30, 1789, to become the first President of the United States. The oath he recited has been repeated by every President, for it is part of the Constitution.

I do solemnly swear that I will faithfully execute the office of the President of the United States, and will, to the best of my ability, preserve, protect, and defend the Constitution of the United States.

By tradition the Chief Justice of the United States administers the oath of office. This is simply custom, however, and in an emergency a judge may give the oath. After the oath, the President delivers the ***inaugural address,*** setting the tone and spirit of the new administration.

The American Presidency has been described as the toughest job in the world. Before looking at the President in action, this chapter will first consider the following: qualifications, compensation, term of office, impeachment, succession, disability, and the Vice President.

Qualifications

Article 2, Section 1, of the Constitution lays down the only three requirements for eligibility. First, the President must be a natural-born citizen—that is, a citizen born in the United States. An immigrant who becomes a citizen through naturalization is not eligible for the office. Although it is debated, most constitutional experts include persons born on foreign soil as natural-born citizens if their parents are American citizens. Second, the President must be at least 35 years old. Theodore Roosevelt, who took office at 42, was the youngest President. There is no bar based on age beyond 35. Ronald Reagan, taking office at 69, was the oldest person to take the Presidential oath. Third, the President must have lived in the United States for at least 14 years. Meeting these formal requirements, any citizen is eligible to run for President.

Neither race, religion, nor sex is a barrier. John Kennedy was the first Roman Catholic to be elected President. His religion was an issue in the campaign, but Kennedy effectively defused the issue by showing that religious affiliation had no bearing on his actions as President. Up to now all Presidents have been men, but it is entirely possible for a woman to be elected President of the United States. Women have held the highest office and provided effective leadership in such nations as Great Britain, India, and Israel.

Compensation

The President receives a salary of $200,000 a year and, like everyone else, must pay an annual income tax. Congress sets the President's salary, but to safeguard the independence of the executive branch, the amount may not be changed during the President's term. Salary alone would never be enough to meet the expenses of official duties, entertainment, and travel. For this the President receives an expense account, plus additional funding. The President's family is given official residence in the White House, where the President maintains offices. The President is also provided with a mountain retreat at Camp David, Maryland, and with a fleet of automobiles, jets, and helicopters.

Term of Office

In the debates at the Constitutional Convention the Framers considered limiting the President to a single term of six or seven years. In the end they agreed on a four-year term of office, with the President eligible for reelection to any number of terms. In *The Federalist,* No. 72, Alexander Hamilton presented the argument for reelection. It would, he believed, provide an incentive for the President to act in the public's interest. Moreover it would enable the people to review the President's conduct and to continue the President in office if they so decided. The Framers also provided that the President be elected by an Electoral College rather than directly by the people.

Since 1800 the White House has served as the President's official residence. In addition to the use of the White House, what other compensation does the President receive?

Franklin Roosevelt (above) is inaugurated for a fourth time on January 21, 1945. Lyndon Johnson (below) takes the Presidential oath after the assassination of John Kennedy on November 22, 1963. What amendment made Johnson eligible for two full terms? Why was it passed?

Many people hoped that George Washington would remain President for the rest of his life. Instead he chose not to seek a third term. His action served to establish an unwritten no-third-term tradition. The tradition remained unbroken until 1940, when Franklin Roosevelt sought and won a third term. In 1944, in the midst of World War II, Roosevelt was elected to a fourth term.

The Twenty-second Amendment was adopted in 1951 in reaction to Roosevelt's four terms. It limits a President to two terms and provides for a person who succeeds to the Presidency in midterm.

No person shall be elected to the office of the President more than twice, and no person who has held the office of President, or acted as President, for more than two years of a term to which some other person was elected President shall be elected to the office of the President more than once.

Thus, Lyndon Johnson, who served less than two years of John Kennedy's uncompleted term, was eligible for two full terms. On the other hand, because Gerald Ford served more than two years of Richard Nixon's uncompleted second term, he was eligible to serve only one full term.

As provided by the Twentieth Amendment to the Constitution, the Presidential term begins at noon on January 20 every four years. Before the adoption of the amendment in 1933, the term began on March 4—more than four months after the election. During this waiting period the outgoing President, who was termed a ***lame duck,*** could do little but mark time. In reducing this period, the Twentieth Amendment came to be called the "Lame-Duck Amendment."

Impeachment

To prevent the abuse of authority, the Framers gave Congress the power to impeach a corrupt or oppressive President. Only one President has ever been impeached—Andrew Johnson in 1868—and he was not convicted. In 1974, facing likely impeachment and probable conviction as a result of the Watergate scandal, Richard Nixon resigned from the Presidency.

Succession, Disability, and the Vice President

Article 2, Section 1, of the Constitution provides that in the event of the President's removal from office, or the President's death, resignation, or disability,

★ ★

ISSUES

A Six-Year Term

In recent years, support has grown for a single six-year term for the President. The hope is that it would give the President time to develop and carry out a program without having to worry about reelection. Lyndon Johnson supported the idea in his memoirs:

*The growing burdens of the office exact an enormous physical toll on the man himself and place incredible demands on his time. Under these circumstances the old belief that a President can carry out the responsibilities of the office and at the same time undergo the rigors of campaigning is, in my opinion, no longer valid.**

But taking politics out of the White House—if that were really possible—might install a President who was unresponsive to the people. Former Presidential aide Thomas Cronin makes this point:

The Presidency must be a highly political office, and the President an expert practitioner of the art of politics. Quite simply, there is no other way for Presidents to negotiate favorable coalitions within the country, Congress, and the executive branch and to gather the authority needed to translate ideas into accomplishments. A President who remains aloof from politics, campaigns, and partisan alliances does so at the risk of becoming a prisoner of events, special interests, or his own wishes.†

*Lyndon B. Johnson, *The Vantage Point* (New York: Holt, Rinehart & Winston, 1971), p. 344.

†Thomas E. Cronin, *The State of the Presidency*, 2nd ed. (Boston: Little, Brown, 1980), pp. 356–357.

★ ★

the powers and duties of the office pass on to the Vice President. Congress is authorized to designate the line of succession in case both the President and Vice President are unable to serve. Under the Presidential Succession Act of 1947, the Speaker of the House is next in line, followed by the president pro tempore of the Senate and members of the Cabinet.

The adoption of the Twenty-fifth Amendment in 1967, however, greatly reduces the importance of this line of succession because it provides for filling a vacancy in the office of the Vice President. On 18 occasions, the Vice Presidency has been vacant because of succession to the Presidency, death, or resignation. The Twenty-fifth Amendment provides that in the event of such vacancy, the President shall appoint a Vice President, with the approval of a majority in each house of Congress. The provision was first used in 1973, when Richard Nixon appointed Gerald Ford to replace Vice President Spiro Agnew. A year later, having succeeded to the Presidency, Gerald Ford appointed Nelson Rockefeller as Vice President.

What would happen if the ***President elect,*** an elected President who has not yet taken office, were to die before taking office? This has never happened, but the Twentieth Amendment (1933) provides that the Vice President shall take the oath of office as President on inauguration day.

Disability One of the most serious problems relating to succession is ***Presidential disability.*** The Constitution makes no clear provision for a situation in which the President is unable to perform the duties of the office. The issue was raised when Woodrow Wilson suffered a stroke in September 1919. Although disabled, he remained in office until March 1921. Dwight Eisenhower's heart attack in 1955 again raised the question of disability.

The Twenty-fifth Amendment, adopted in 1967, replaced informal agreements between the President and Vice President about what to do. If the President is unable to perform the duties of the office, Congress must be informed of this in writing by the President. The Vice President becomes Acting

President. If the President is unable or unwilling to make such a notification, the Vice President and a majority of the Cabinet may inform Congress that the President is disabled. Again, the Vice President becomes Acting President. Congress must again be informed in writing when the President feels able to resume the duties of the office. If the Vice President and a majority of the Cabinet believe that the President is still disabled, Congress must decide the issue within three weeks. A two-thirds majority in both houses is necessary for the Vice President to continue as Acting President. Otherwise, the President resumes the full powers and duties of the office.

The Vice President The Vice President is the nation's second highest executive official and assumes the Presidency in case of the death, resignation, or removal of the President. The Vice President's only constitutional duty is as president of the Senate (Article 1, Section 3). As the Senate's presiding officer, the Vice President can vote only in case of a tie. In practice, however, the Vice President may be engaged in any number of activities on behalf of the President.

For most of the nation's history, the Vice Presidency was regarded as a useless office. The Vice President was ignored by just about everyone, including the President, and was rarely taken into confidence on anything that mattered. The low regard for the Vice Presidency came about largely as a result of the way in which the President's running mate was selected. Typically, the Vice-Presidential candidate was chosen to give geographic and political balance to the party ticket or to eliminate a troublesome rival. Balance was also sought between the liberal and conservative factions of the party.

The assassination of John Kennedy underscored the fact that the Vice President is only a heartbeat away from the Presidency. In recent years, Presidents have increasingly used their Vice Presidents in ceremonial, diplomatic, and political activities. Jimmy Carter gave Vice President Walter Mondale major responsibilities on domestic policy issues. Mondale was really an assistant to the President. Ronald Reagan has also made Vice President George Bush an active participant in the governmental process, appointing him to chair several commissions.

PROFILE

Vice President George Bush

George Bush, Ronald Reagan's Vice President, is a man of almost boundless energy and enthusiasm. He brings to the office a wide range of experience, especially in foreign affairs. Bush is the son of a United States senator. He was born and educated in the Northeast, and moved to Texas in 1948. Having achieved success in the oil business, he ran successfully for the House of Representatives in 1966 and served two years.

Over the next decade, Bush served as United States ambassador to the United Nations, chairman of the Republican National Committee, United States liaison to the People's Republic of China, and the Director of Central Intelligence. In 1978, Bush announced his candidacy for the Republican Presidential nomination. He was Ronald Reagan's strongest rival in the primary campaign, but it was to George Bush, a political moderate, that Reagan turned in choosing his running mate in 1980 and 1984.

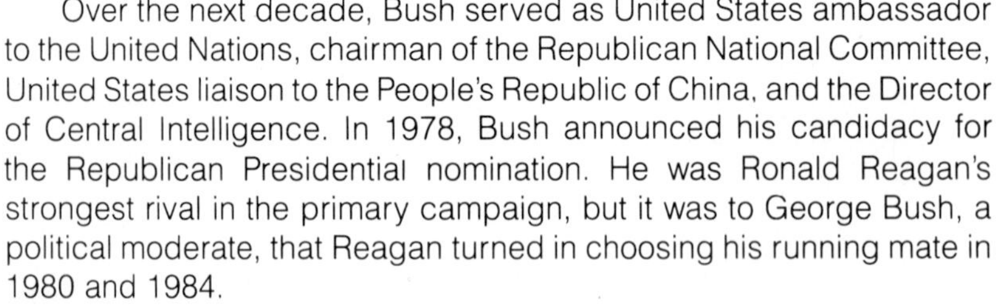

Section Check

1. Define inaugural address, lame-duck President, President-elect, Presidential disability
2. Identify: Article 2, Twentieth Amendment, Twenty-second Amendment, Twenty-fifth Amendment
3. What are the three constitutional qualifications for the Presidency?
4. What is the Vice President's only constitutional duty?
5. Why has the Vice Presidency assumed a greater importance in recent years?

2 PRESIDENTIAL ROLES

The American President bears an awesome burden of responsibility. Among the many functions the President performs it is possible to identify six major roles. They are chief of state, chief executive, chief diplomat, commander in chief, chief legislator, and political party leader. The roles are closely connected. Sometimes they support each other, and sometimes they conflict.

Chief of State

The President of the United States is the ceremonial head of the nation as well as the working head of the government.

In many countries the two roles are separate. In Great Britain, for example, the queen is chief of state, but the prime minister is chief executive. In the United States, the Presidency combines the two roles. The President is, as Theodore Roosevelt wrote, both "a king and a prime minister."

As chief of state, the President is the representative and symbol of the nation, its laws, and its people. In this ceremonial role, the President receives distinguished visitors from all over the world, hosts elaborate state dinners, lays the wreath at the Tomb of the Unknown Soldier, and lights the nation's Christmas tree. The President greets delegations from every walk of life, from school children to athletes and astronauts. The President buys the first Easter Seal, and officially proclaims holidays and observances in honor of interests and causes.

In these various ceremonies, significant and trivial, the President stands above politics. Yet ceremonies and rituals are an important political resource. They give dignity and sometimes grandeur to the office of the Presidency. The respect and

President and Mrs. Gerald Ford receive Great Britain's Queen Elizabeth II (far right) and Prince Philip (far left) on the south portico of the White House. On this occasion President Ford acted as chief of state, chief executive, and chief diplomat.

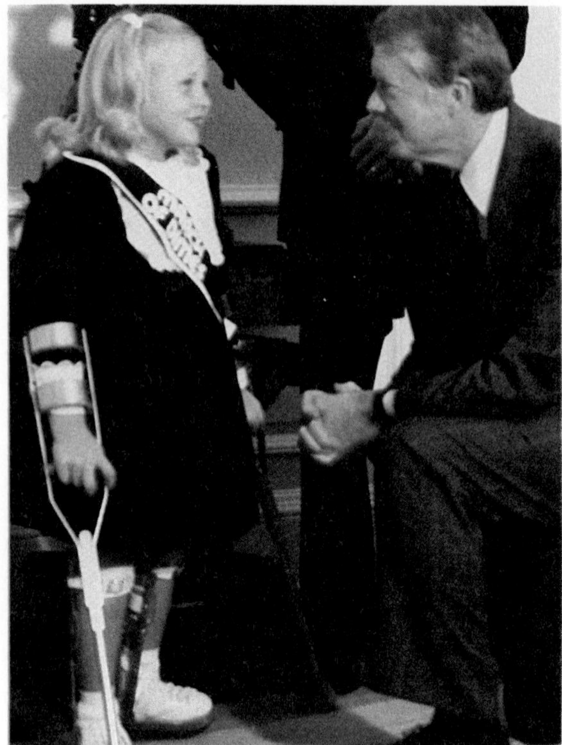

President Jimmy Carter (right) welcomes Melanie Brockington (left), a March of Dimes Poster Child, to the White House. What role is the President exercising?

awe that surround the executive office give the President an important vantage point from which to exert influence. The President may also use the grandeur of the office to develop popular support, as in times of crisis when the exercise of national leadership is called for.

Chief Executive

The role of the President as chief executive rests on Article 2 of the Constitution.

The executive power shall be vested in a President of the United States of America.

The executive powers are not precisely defined. At the heart of the executive function, however, is the President's constitutional duty to carry out the laws of the United States.

As chief executive, the President is head of the executive branch of government. The President has the responsibility of running the vast federal bureaucracy, with 3 million civilian employees and a budget of $700 billion. Like the head of a giant corporation, the President delegates administrative authority to lower officials for the day-to-day operation of the government. These include members of the Cabinet and advisers on the White House staff. But final authority rests with the President. The President lays down the basic principles and policies of the administration, and in matters of major disagreement or conflict within the bureaucracy, the President has the last say.

The President exercises formal control over the bureaucracy through the powers of appointment and removal. These powers, however, are limited in a number of ways. Most significantly, the vast majority of employees—including many high officials—within the executive branch are appointed and promoted under the Civil Service. These employees may be removed only "for cause." Nevertheless, there remain some 6,500 important federal appointments under the direct or indirect control of the President. Of these, a large portion may be appointed only with the ***advice and consent*** of the Senate. Even when Senate approval is not required, it is customary for the President to clear appointments informally through the senators who represent the home states of the appointees or who have jurisdiction over important committees.

Senate approval is not required for the President to remove an appointed official, but the President must consider any political costs the removal may have. The President, of course, may benefit politically by removing a controversial or unpopular official, but there are almost always some political costs. One formal limitation on the President's power to remove appointed officials concerns members of the independent regulatory agencies, such as the Federal Reserve Board and the Interstate Commerce Commission. Although appointed by the President, the members of independent regulatory agencies serve a fixed term and may not be removed from office.

As part of the executive role, the President is empowered by the Constitution to grant reprieves and pardons for offenses committed under federal law. A ***reprieve*** postpones punishment that has been legally imposed. A ***pardon*** is a legal release from imposed punishment. A famous use of the pardon was in 1974, when President Gerald Ford granted a full pardon to former President Richard Nixon for any offenses he may have committed while in office. ***Amnesty*** is a general pardon, before arrest or conviction, to all members of a group who have violated the law. In 1977, President Jimmy Carter gave amnesty to those who had evaded the draft during the Vietnam War.

Chief Diplomat

The role of the President as chief diplomat rests on the Constitution, law, custom, and the practice of other nations. The President is empowered by the Constitution to appoint ambassadors, receive foreign ambassadors, and make treaties. But beyond the provisions of the Constitution, the President has assumed the dominant position in foreign relations because the President alone can speak with one voice for the nation.

Foreign relations involve both the making of policy and the conduct of foreign affairs. The President shares responsibility for making policy with Congress because the Constitution provides that the Senate shall give its advice and consent to all treaties negotiated by the President. But the real power of Congress in foreign relations lies in its control over the purse strings. The ability of the President to control foreign affairs depends on cooperation with Congress. Traditionally, however, Presidential leadership has prevailed.

The House and Senate committees on foreign relations also keep a watchful eye on the President. They receive official reports and background briefings. They also hold hearings on many aspects of American foreign policy. In recent years, largely as a result of United States military involvement in Vietnam, Congress has sought a greater voice in foreign relations. Indeed, members of Congress, especially the Senate, have been some of the strongest critics of American foreign policy. But without full access to the reports from the Department of State, the Pentagon, and the Central Intelligence Agency—important information upon which the President acts—it is often difficult for members of Congress to effectively challenge the President's conduct of foreign affairs.

The actual conduct of foreign affairs is an exclusive power of the President. In *United States* v. *Curtiss-Wright* (1936), the Supreme Court held that the President is "the sole organ of the federal government in the field of international relations—a power which does not require as a basis for its exercise an act of Congress." Within the executive branch, the Department of State is responsible for foreign relations, and it carries on its activities, which are discussed in Chapter 19, in the name of the President. But whether American foreign relations is conducted through the Secretary of State, through the National Security Adviser, or by the President, it is the President who bears final responsibility for it.

As the nation's chief diplomat, President Harry S Truman met at Potsdam, Germany, in 1945 with the British Prime Minister, Clement Attlee (left), and the Soviet leader, Joseph Stalin (right) to discuss the peace terms of Japan's surrender.

Prime Minister Menachem Begin of Israel (left), President Jimmy Carter (center), and President Anwar as-Sadat of Egypt (right) celebrate the 1979 signing of the Camp David Accords, a peace treaty Carter arranged between Israel and Egypt.

The Treaty Power A ***treaty*** is a formal agreement between two or more nations that has the force of law. In the United States, the President alone has the power to negotiate and sign treaties. The Constitution, however, provides that all treaties be made "by and with the advice and consent of the Senate." No treaty has the force of law unless, or until, it is approved by a two-thirds vote of the Senate.

George Washington established the precedent that the President may negotiate treaties without prior advice from the Senate. But to win passage for the treaty, the President must be responsive to the views of the Senate. In practice the President normally consults with Senate leaders of key committees throughout a treaty's negotiations.

Over the years, the Senate has rejected or refused to act on about 10 percent of all treaties submitted for approval. Among the treaties rejected was the Treaty of Versailles, the treaty ending World War I, that President Wilson had a major part in preparing. The Senate modifies treaties through amendments or reservations more frequently than it rejects them. Sometimes the result is unacceptable to the President or to the other nations involved.

Executive Agreements Over the past half century, the President has turned increasingly to executive agreements with foreign heads of state. ***Executive agreements*** are legally similar to treaties, but they do not require the consent of the Senate. They are often negotiated by the President under the authority of Congress, as in the case of most trade agreements. Others, however, are made by the President's power in foreign relations.

Today the United States is party to some 1,000 treaties and more than 4,000 executive agreements. In any one year the President may sign several hundred executive agreements and a dozen treaties. The 1973 Paris Peace Accords, ending the war in Vietnam, is an example of an executive agreement. An executive agreement avoids the delay and possible defeat or crippling by Senate action on a treaty. It can also be made in secrecy, as in time of war. A secret agreement, however, arouses both Congressional and public suspicion. In 1972, Congress adopted a resolution known as the Case Amendment. This resolution requires the President to inform Congress of every foreign commitment that is made.

Most executive agreements are of minor importance. But some are of great consequence—for example, the President's commitment of military aid to Vietnam. In cases where substantial public support is required, however, it is in the best interests of the President's political future to use the treaty procedure.

Recognition The President has the sole power to establish diplomatic relations with foreign nations. This power of ***diplomatic recognition*** is based on the President's constitutional authority to appoint and receive ambassadors. Diplomatic recognition involves the exchange of diplomatic representatives and does not signify approval of the government. At the same time, diplomatic recognition can be used as an instrument of foreign policy.

The power of diplomatic recognition implies the ability to refuse to accept a state within the family of nations. The United States, for example, did not recognize the Soviet Union until 1933, 16 years after the Russian Revolution. American recognition of the People's Republic of China involved a series of delicate and controversial moves. President Nixon's historic visit to China in 1972 was followed by the exchange of "liaison officers" without the formal rank of ambassador. Full recognition came in 1979, with the establishment of embassies in Washington and Beijing (Peking).

Normal diplomatic relations between nations provide the advantage of direct communication and observation. But the President can deliver a strong diplomatic "slap in the face" to a nation by withdrawing recognition. Such action is extreme and may be the first step to war. Diplomacy is backed by military power, and the President's role as chief diplomat is strengthened by the equally important role of commander in chief. The two roles are closely connected and are symbolically depicted in the olive branch and the arrows of the Presidential seal.

Commander in Chief

The third major role of the President is as Article 2, Section 2, of the Constitution states.

The President shall be Commander in Chief of the Army and Navy of the United States and of the militia of the several states. . . .

In peace and war, the President is the supreme commander of the American armed forces. The principle of ***civilian supremacy*** over the military is based on this constitutional foundation.

The Constitution gives Congress the power to declare war, but the President bears responsibility for the nation's defense. Since the early days of the Republic, Presidents have sent troops into action around the world on more than 200 occasions. The reasons have varied, but the justification has normally been to protect American lives and property and to defend the nation's vital interests. Congress has declared war only five times—1812, 1846, 1898, 1917, and 1941. In each case war has been declared at the request of the President. In the Korean War and the Vietnam War Congress made no formal declaration of war. Instead, the two wars were "police actions" undertaken by Presidential order.

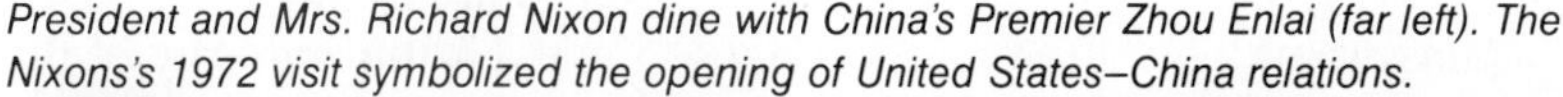
President and Mrs. Richard Nixon dine with China's Premier Zhou Enlai (far left). The Nixons's 1972 visit symbolized the opening of United States–China relations.

LEGACY

Executive Privilege

Presidents have claimed the right to withhold information from Congress and the courts. It is argued that this ***executive privilege*** is an inherent right based on the separation of powers. Executive privilege was used during the Dwight Eisenhower administration in defending the executive branch against the McCarthy investigations. The practice of withholding information from Congress, however, goes back to George Washington.

Over the years, the claim for executive privilege has expanded. Its use is no longer limited to the protection of military secrets or confidential treaty negotiations with foreign nations. Executive privilege is now used to protect decision-making processes within the executive branch from Congressional scrutiny. It is held that disclosure of conversations and documents would inhibit the free flow of information and debate necessary for wise decisions. Congress, on the other hand, argues that its legislative power includes the right to conduct investigations into the executive branch and to obtain all necessary information.

President Nixon invoked executive privilege in an attempt to keep Congress from digging into White House involvement in the Watergate scandal. In *United States* v. *Nixon* (1974), the Supreme Court for the first time recognized executive privilege. But it held that the right of the President to keep certain matters confidential must yield to the rule of law and the need for evidence in a criminal trial.

The President delegates most military decisions to the military command. But the President may take active command at any time. During the Whiskey Rebellion of 1794, President George Washington personally led federal troops into Pennsylvania. President Abraham Lincoln took an active role in military planning during the Civil War and actually instructed generals in the field. President Franklin D. Roosevelt conferred with British Prime Minister Winston Churchill on the overall strategy of World War II. The major decisions of war are made by civilian authority. President Harry Truman made the decision to drop the atomic bomb on Japan in 1945, and it was again his decision that brought the United States into the Korean War. During American involvement in Vietnam, Presidents Lyndon Johnson and Richard Nixon each made critical decisions on the bombing of targets, the escalation of the war, and the withdrawal of forces.

The President's use of the war powers is not unchecked. The Constitution gives to Congress not only the power to declare war, but also the power to tax for the common defense and to raise and support an army and navy. The President as commander in chief is thus ultimately dependent upon Congress. Yet by resolution and military appropriations, Congress historically has given wide scope to the President's power to wage war. During the war in Vietnam, however, Congress sought to assert itself and to impose limits on the authority of the President as commander in chief.

Vietnam was the longest war in the nation's history. Each year of frustration brought mounting opposition within Congress. Many critics felt the United States should make the commitment to win or else get out of Vietnam. Others challenged the undeclared war as unwise, immoral, and illegal. In 1973, overriding President Nixon's veto, Congress passed the War Powers Resolution. Its passage was a declaration of Congressional authority to share with the President decisions about future military involvements. Congress wanted to be sure that it had a say in when, where, and under what circumstances American forces would be used overseas. Under the War Powers Resolution, the President must report to Congress within 48 hours after committing forces to combat abroad, explaining the circumstances of the commitment. If Congress does not approve of the action within 60 to 90 days, the President is required to withdraw the troops.

Critics of the War Powers Resolution argue that it is an unconstitutional limit on the President's inherent warmaking power as commander in chief. They express concern that the resolution weakens the ability of the President to act decisively in a crisis. In practice, however, the resolution may have little effect on the President's power to commit troops abroad. It does give to Congress a role in the commitment of American troops abroad. But rather than weakening the President's hand, it gives Presidential action greater legitimacy. Congress recognized that emergency conditions may require the President to act immediately. For the first time, the President has legal authority to commit troops to combat without prior approval by Congress or a declaration of war. Ultimately, however, the President's power to wage war depends upon popular support.

In times of war Presidents have used their role as commander in chief to assume extraordinary powers at home. Lincoln exercised almost unlimited authority during the Civil War. He governed by executive order and Presidential proclamation. The Emancipation Proclamation, for example, was issued under the President's war powers, not by an act of Congress. During World War I, President Wilson assumed wide control over the economy, with rationing, wage and price controls, and a ban on strikes. During World War II, Franklin D. Roosevelt claimed "emergency powers" for a range of Presidential actions. By order of the President, for example, the government seized and operated more than 60 plants and industries threatened by strike.

Presidential action taken under the war powers has its limits and is bounded by the constitutional system of checks and balances. In 1952, during the Korean War, the steel mills faced a possible shutdown because of a labor dispute. President Truman ordered the seizure of the mills and the steelworkers back to the job. He did so on his authority as President and as commander in chief of the armed forces. "The President", he said, "has very great inherent powers to meet national emergencies." The Supreme Court, however, held the seizure unconstitutional. Truman's action also lacked support by the public and by Congress because the situation simply did not seem to warrant drastic action. Had a genuine emergency existed the Court in all likelihood would have upheld the seizure as within the President's power.

Chief Legislator

Article 2, Section 3, of the Constitution lays the groundwork for the President's role of chief legislator. It states:

He shall from time to time give to the Congress information on the state of the Union and recommend to their consideration such measures as he shall judge necessary and expedient.

This is the ***message power,*** and it places the President fully in the legislative process.

The President gives the annual State of the Union Address in January before a joint session of Congress assembled in the House of Representatives. In the televised address, the President presents the major foreign and domestic policy goals of the administration. The President draws in broad outline the basic legislative program that will be placed before

In 1983 President Reagan used his authority as commander in chief to dispatch American Marines to Lebanon. Many members of Congress criticized the President's action as an improper extension of the war powers. What constitutional powers enable Congress to check Presidential war powers?

Congress in the coming year. The details of proposed legislation follow in a series of specific Presidential messages sent to Congress.

The President's annual Budget Message spells out the President's program in dollars and cents. It underscores the President's priorities—the particular areas to which the President is most committed. The annual Economic Message is a report on the condition of the nation's economy. It is concerned with inflation, unemployment, production, and overall economic trends.

In recent decades, the President has played an increasingly important role as the chief source of major legislation. Each year, the President sends to Congress between 100 and 400 bills as a part of the legislative program. Indeed, some 80 percent of the most important laws passed since World War II have begun within the executive branch.

Congress has come to expect strong Presidential leadership in matters of legislation. But no President can railroad a program through Congress because Congress insists on being treated as an equal partner. As chief legislator, the President must be prepared to consult, bargain, and compromise with the members of the House and Senate. Congress, fragmented as it often is, is simply not very good at developing comprehensive programs on its own. Congress and the President must work together in making law.

Congress usually passes a major portion of the President's program, but rarely does the President get exactly what was requested. Sometimes the only similarity between what goes "in" and what comes "out" of the Congressional lawmaking process is the title of the bill itself. When a bill is sent to Congress, for example, the President usually asks for broad authority to work out the details of the legislative program. Congress, on the other hand, tries to limit the authority of executive officials and provide for a measure of Congressional control.

Presidential legislative leadership requires consultation with the Speaker of the House and the Majority Leaders of Congress about the content and timing of the proposed program. But working closely with Congressional leaders—even when they are of the President's party—is no guarantee of success for the White House. The fate of a bill is almost always determined in committee and subcommittee. The President and other officials of the executive branch must negotiate with the committee leaders who are specialists in the subject matter of the committee and masters of legislative detail. To save the core of any Presidential proposal, the President must be prepared to bargain and compromise. In dealing with Congress while he was President, John F. Kennedy said, "When I was a Congressman, I never realized how important Congress was. But now I do."*

In building support for a legislative program, the President must know the mood of each house. The President must have a detailed knowledge of the legislative process and demonstrate a mastery of strategy and tactics. Effective leadership requires that the White House maintain close contact with important members of the House and Senate. President Lyndon Johnson said that "there is but only one way to deal with Congress, and that is continuously, incessantly, and without interruption."†

Continuous contact between the President and members of Congress is maintained through White House officials who are close advisers to the President and who can both speak for the President and, in turn, bring to the Oval Office accurate information about what members of Congress are thinking. The President is also likely to keep in personal touch with certain key legislators. It is customary for the President to invite members of Congress to the White House for breakfast or buffet briefing sessions. President Eisenhower had the entire Congress to a series of luncheons. Such attention is unlikely to change votes, but it serves to show that the President does not take the Congress for granted.

When the President's program is on the line, it takes more than gentle persuasion to get it through Congress. The President can try a little "armtwisting" by asking individual legislators for support and by reminding them of past Presidential favors. The President, for example, may mention an upcoming federal appointment—perhaps a judgeship—in which the member is interested or a government contract that would benefit the member's home state or district. The President may try to strike a bargain for an exchange of support: If you support my program, I'll support yours. When persuasion, negotiation, and compromise fail, the President may turn from Congress to the public, going before the nation in a television address. The President may leave the capital for speeches across the country in an effort to win popular support for Presidential policies and thereby bring constituency pressure on legislators to vote for the President's program.

---

*Quoted in Tom Wicker, *JFK and LBJ: The Influence of Personality Upon Politics* (Baltimore: Penguin, 1968), p. 23.

†Quoted in Doris Kearns, *Lyndon Johnson and the American Dream* (New York: Harper and Row, 1976), p. 226.

The Veto The President has an important constitutional power in the veto. The ***veto power*** is the right of the President to reject a bill that Congress has approved. After a bill passes both the House and Senate, it goes to the President for action. As noted in Chapter 16, the President has four options.

1. The President may sign the bill, whereupon it becomes law.
2. The President may choose not to sign the bill. If the President does not sign the bill within ten working days, it becomes law without a signature. If the President does not approve of a bill but does not want to go so far as to veto it or run the risk of having a veto overridden by Congress, the President may choose this option.
3. If Congress adjourns during this ten-day period, the bill dies by what is called a ***pocket veto.*** The bill, of course, can be reintroduced in the next session of Congress, but it must go through the full legislative process all over again.
4. The President may veto the bill and send it back to the house where it originated. The President vetoes a bill by writing *veto* (Latin for "I forbid") across the front of it. The President returns the bill to Congress with a list of objections.

Congress may amend the bill to meet the President's demands and then repass it. But it may also

President John Kennedy (above center), surrounded by Congressional leaders, signs a bill into law. In what three ways may a President demonstrate disapproval of legislation passed by Congress?

Presidents have varied widely in their use of the veto power. Which President cast the most regular vetoes? Which President cast the most pocket vetoes? Which Presidents were overridden on 12 vetoes?

PRESIDENTIAL VETOES

Period	President	Regular Vetoes	Pocket Vetoes	Total Vetoes	Vetoes Overridden
1945-1953	Truman	180	70	250	12
1953-1961	Eisenhower	73	108	181	2
1961-1963	Kennedy	12	9	21	0
1963-1969	Johnson	16	14	30	0
1969-1974	Nixon	24	18	42	5
1974-1977	Ford	48	18	66	12
1977-1981	Carter	13	16	29	2
1981-1985	Reagan (first term)	27	12	39	4

Source: Statistical Abstract of the United States

attempt a ***veto override*** by repassing the bill by a two-thirds vote in each house, a majority that is relatively difficult to achieve. Only about 4 percent of all Presidential vetoes have been overridden by Congress.

Because a veto override is so hard to achieve, the President can use the threat of a veto in bargaining with Congress. Unlike most state governors, the President lacks the ***item veto,*** the power to reject a particular portion, or item, within a bill. The President must approve or veto the entire bill. This fact sometimes leads Congress to attach riders to important bills. The ***rider*** is a provision unrelated to the subject of a bill and unlikely to pass on its own merit. It is expected to "ride" through the legislative process because the President cannot veto it without killing the whole bill.

Executive-Legislative Relations Most Presidents fare best in their relations with Congress early in their first terms—during the "honeymoon" period. The President and Congress are also more likely to get along when the President and the majority in the House and Senate are of the same party. The political party is a bridge between the executive and legislative branches. The President can often appeal for Congressional support on the basis of party loyalty. But party bonds are not enough to ensure passage of a President's program, as each President has discovered. Party loyalty does not guarantee Congressional support for the President's program. John Kennedy had difficulty with a Democratic Congress, as did Jimmy Carter.

A President's problems in dealing with Congress are magnified when the President and Congress are of different parties. Republican Presidents Dwight Eisenhower, Richard Nixon, and Gerald Ford faced Democratic Congresses throughout their terms in office. Ronald Reagan came into office with a Republican Senate and a Democratic House. But American parties are neither highly disciplined nor ideological opposites. Although members of the same party vote together most of the time, individual members may cross to the other side on a particular issue.

The fluid character of American parties gives flexibility to the political system, but the really critical element that makes government possible is compromise. The President and Congress must be prepared to work together—to consult, bargain, and compromise. The President's task is surely more difficult when there is political opposition in Congress. But even with party members, the President must rely on persuasion. "Presidential *power*," writes Richard Neustadt, "is the power to persuade."* The effectiveness of persuasion in one area affects the President's strength in others.

*Richard E. Neustadt, *Presidential Power* (New York: John Wiley & Sons, 1960), p. 10.

President Ronald Reagan (left) and Vice President George Bush (center) meet with Speaker of the House Thomas P. ("Tip") O'Neill, Jr. (right). During what period of an administration does the President seem best able to manage relations with Congress?

Party Leader

American political parties are loosely organized. The President has little control over the party, and the party has no real control over the President. At the same time, however, the President is the party leader. The President is closely identified with the party in the voter's minds, and the fortunes of the President and other party candidates tend to go together at the polls. Presidential popularity affects the whole of the party ticket. Members of Congress have a strong incentive to support a popular President. On the other hand, members of Congress may try to put as much distance as possible between themselves and a President who has a low standing in the polls.

The President's standing as a party leader and the President's effectiveness as chief executive and chief legislator depend to a significant extent upon the support in the country as a whole. But a successful President does not simply respond to public opinion. The mark of Presidential leadership is the capacity to shape and direct public opinion—to educate the people. "The Presidency," Franklin D. Roosevelt said, "is not merely an administrative office. That is the least of it. It is preeminently a place of moral leadership."*

Section Check

---

1. Define: advice and consent, treaty, executive agreement, message power, veto power, rider
2. Identify: the principle of civilian supremacy, State of the Union Address, Budget Message, Economic Message, War Powers Resolution
3. Briefly describe the six major Presidential roles.
4. Why was the President designated commander in chief?
5. What are the main distinctions between a reprieve, a pardon, and amnesty?

---

3 DECISON MAKING IN THE WHITE HOUSE

In each of the various roles the President confronts decisions of major importance. The President makes decisions under the pressure of conflicting demands, limited time, and often inadequate information. In making decisions, the President relies heavily on close advisers for information. But whatever the sources of advice, the President bears the responsibility for the final decision.

The President not only makes decisions, but also sees that they are carried out. Here again the President is dependent upon others in the Executive Office of the President, the Cabinet, and the vast complex of the ***federal bureaucracy,*** which is discussed in Chapter 21.

The Executive Office of the President

For 150 years, Presidents managed the White House with little assistance. Thomas Jefferson had a staff of two—a secretary and a messenger, both of whom he paid with his own money. Abraham Lincoln personally answered official mail, and Woodrow Wilson typed most of his speeches. In 1939 the President's Commission on Administrative Management concluded that the President needed help. Following the commission's recommendations, President Franklin Roosevelt established the Executive Office of the President. It was to consist of six administrative assistants to the President and three advisory bodies. In the years since it was created, the Executive Office has expanded. At the time Ronald Reagan took office in 1981, the White House bureaucracy had some 1,900 employees—down from a peak of 4,700 in 1970. The staff has long since outgrown the White House, and most members are located in the elegant Executive Office Building next door and in the annex a block away.

The Executive Office has grown as the power and responsibility of the President have expanded. Its various units serve to advise the President and to coordinate policy among the hundreds of departments and agencies of the federal government. But the size and coordination of the Executive Office has become a problem. President Jimmy Carter reorganized the Executive Office in an attempt to reduce its size and improve decision-making processes in the White House. Ronald Reagan made further reductions. There are now 10 units within the Executive Office (see chart on page 450). The most important units are the White House Office, the Office of Management and Budget, the National Security Council, the Domestic Policy Staff, and the Council of Economic Advisers. Other units include the Office of the United States Trade Representative, the Council on Environmental Quality, and the Office of Science and Technology Policy.

---

*Quoted in Clinton Rossiter, *The American Presidency,* rev. ed. (New York: Harcourt Brace Jovanovich, 1960), p. 148.

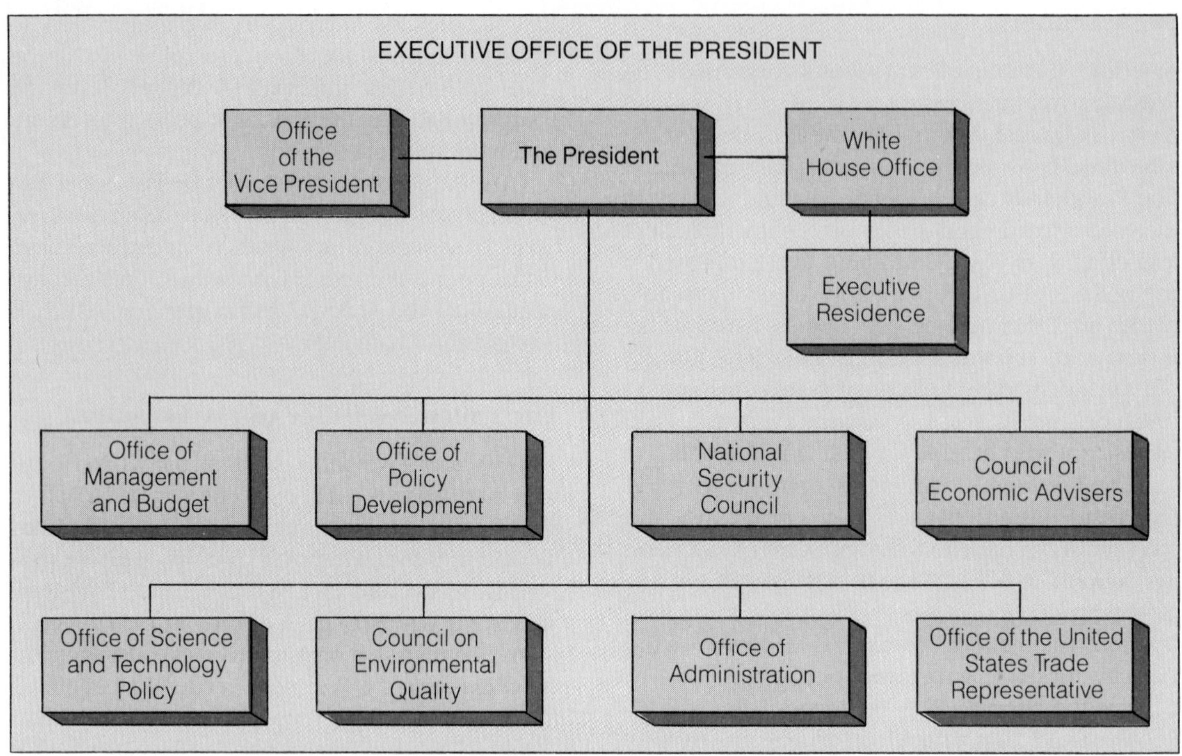

The Executive Office of the President was established by the Reorganization Act of 1939. Since then, Presidents have changed the composition of the Executive Office to suit their own administrative needs and styles.

The White House Office The White House Office is made up of the personal assistants to the President. The number of people in the White House Office has ranged over the past two decades from 300 to 600. Staffers perform a wide variety of functions and include senior advisers, administrative aides, appointment secretaries, speech writers, the President's physician, and the White House chef. Most of the staff closest to the President work in the West Wing of the White House, where the President's Oval Office is located. Fewer than a dozen can be counted as senior advisers. They are among the most powerful people in government because they have direct and immediate access to the President.

Presidents have organized their staffs in different ways. Despite these differences, the President's assistants perform three general functions: gatekeeping, advising, and liaison.

First, some members of the White House staff act as ***gatekeepers*** to the President. The President is besieged by letters, memoranda, reports, and people. The President's personal assistants, to a considerable degree, determine which people get to see the President. They screen written material, passing on only that which is important.

Second, there are White House staff members who are ***advisers.*** Presidents frequently delegate considerable power to senior White House advisers in making and implementing policy. The delegation of Presidential power can be a source of serious problems and deep resentment by department and agency heads. A dramatic example can be seen in the relationship between the President's National Security Adviser and the Secretary of State. During the Nixon administration, before becoming Secretary of State, Henry Kissinger served the President as National Security Adviser. His dominant role in the making and conduct of American foreign policy overshadowed that of the Secretary of State. A similar problem arose under President Carter—this time between National Security Adviser Zbigniew Brzezinski and Secretary of State Cyrus Vance. A major concern is accountability. Unlike members of the Cabinet, White House advisers are not confirmed by the Senate and are not subject to periodic questioning by Congressional committees. They are answerable only to the President.

The President's chief advisers—at least ideally—perform four important roles that help the President govern the nation.

Secretary of the Interior William Clark (left) and White House Chief of Staff James A. Baker III (right) advised President Reagan during his first term. Reagan appointed Baker Secretary of the Treasury in 1985.

1. They are channels of information flowing into the White House from outside.
2. They help the President formulate the range of options possible in the face of a given problem.
3. They act as personal advisers to the President in both policy and political matters, offering their own ideas and suggestions.
4. They act as sounding boards for the President's ideas.

Third, some Presidential assistants maintain White House ***liaison,*** or contact, with the executive departments and agencies, Congress, the mass media, various interest groups, and the general public. These aides speak for the President and, in turn, relay back to the White House the views they hear expressed.

White House and other executive liaison aides keep in close touch with the heads of departments and agencies. They provide a two-way channel of communication between the President and the bureaucracy. The problem in executive supervision is that White House aides often have little understanding of the problems involved in running the executive departments. Moreover, there is a tendency for supervision to turn into direct control, with White House members giving orders to senior department officials or even Cabinet officers.

Faith Ryan Whittlesey serves as Assistant to the President for Public Liaison. What is the purpose of the White House Liaison?

INSIGHT

The President's Schedule

THE WHITE HOUSE

WASHINGTON

THE PRESIDENT'S SCHEDULE*

8:00 a.m. (15 min.)	Staff meeting with personal aides.	Oval Office
8:15 a.m. (60 min.)	Breakfast with a group of labor leaders.	Family Dining Room
9:30 a.m. (15 min.)	National security briefing by National Security Adviser.	Oval Office
9:45 a.m. (15 min.)	Meeting with National Security Council.	Oval Office
10:00 a.m. (60 min.)	Cabinet meeting.	Cabinet Room
11:00 a.m. (40 min.)	Personal staff time.	Oval Office
11:40 a.m. (20 min.)	Meeting with Executive Committee, National Governors Association.	Roosevelt Room
Noon (75 min.)	The President escorts the governors to luncheon in the residence.	Family Dining Room
3:00 p.m. (30 min.)	Meeting with labor leaders.	Oval Office
5:45 p.m. (30 min.)	Videotaped interview with news correspondent.	Library
8:00 p.m.	The President and the First Lady attend a performance at the Kennedy Center.	Kennedy Center Opera House
10:45 p.m.	Return to the White House.	

*reconstructed

8:00 A.M.

8:00 P.M.

11:40 A.M.

Liaison with Congress is handled by members of a special staff under the President's assistant for legislative affairs. Congressional-liaison aides keep in day-to-day contact with the members of Congress and their staffs. Again, it is a two-way flow of communication, but on really important matters, members of Congress want direct access to the President. Similarly, the President can get a message across to Congress most effectively on a personal basis. One of the most important liaison functions is to advise the President of possible Congressional reactions to Presidential decisions.

The White House ***press staff*** is in charge of the President's relations with the news media. It handles the President's press conferences and makes arrangements for the media during trips around the country and abroad. A section of the staff prepares a daily press summary of major news stories and editorials for the President each morning. The press secretary heads the White House press staff, speaks for the President, and holds daily briefings for the White House press corps.

The President may appoint aides to maintain liaison with such specific groups as state governors, mayors, minorities, and women. These special liaison aides keep the President in touch with the many interest groups that make up the Presidential constituency.

Office of Management and Budget The Office of Management and Budget (OMB) was established in 1970 to replace the old Bureau of the Budget. It is the largest unit within the Executive Office of the President. The OMB is the President's right arm in managing the federal bureaucracy and in improving its performance. It is headed by a Director who is responsible to the President. The OMB has four main functions.

1. It assists the President in preparing the budget submitted to Congress each year by reviewing budget requests from the various agencies of government and by making recommendations to the President.
2. It supervises and controls the administration of the budget. In other words, it watches over how the government spends the taxpayer's money.
3. It reviews the structure and operation of the executive branch and recommends reforms for greater efficiency and effectiveness.
4. It clears and coordinates all proposed legislation coming from the various executive departments and agencies.

National Security Council Congress established the National Security Council (NSC) in 1947 to advise the President "with respect to the integration of domestic, foreign and military policies relating to the national security." By law, its membership consists of the President, the Vice President, and the Secretaries of State and Defense. The director of the Central Intelligence Agency (CIA) and the chairman of the Joint Chiefs of Staff are advisers to the Council. The President may appoint other members to the National Security Council and, over the years, it has expanded in size. The President's National Security Adviser has responsibility for directing the activities of the staff. With access to intelligence from the State Department, the Defense Department, and the CIA, the NSC has a central role in shaping American foreign policy.

The CIA is under the direction of the National Security Council. The director of the CIA is appointed by the President with the advice and consent of the Senate and reports directly to the President. The CIA advises the President and the NSC on matters of intelligence—information about activities and events in foreign countries that affect the national security of the United States. (Chapter 19 looks more closely at the National Security Council and at the intelligence-gathering network of the Central Intelligence Agency).

Domestic Policy Staff Established in 1978 as a part of the Executive Office of the President, the Domestic Policy Staff functions under the direction of the President's Domestic Affairs and Policy Adviser. Its purpose is to formulate and coordinate domestic policy recommendations to the President. The Staff maintains a continuous review of ongoing domestic programs. It assesses national needs and priorities and advises the President on various policy choices.

Council of Economic Advisers Congress created the Council of Economic Advisers to assist the President in making economic policy. Its three members are appointed by the President and confirmed by the Senate. Its chairperson typically functions as one of the President's key policy advisers. The Council studies trends and appraises developments in the national economy. It also makes recommendations for federal economic policy and programs. The Council advises the President on economic growth and stability and assists the President in the preparation of the annual Economic Message to Congress.

The Cabinet

The Constitution makes no mention of the Cabinet. The term was first used by news reporters in referring to George Washington's four department heads. By custom, the ***Cabinet*** consists of the secretaries who head the major executive departments. Each secretary is appointed by the President and confirmed by the Senate. Only 9 of the more than 500 Cabinet appointments that have been made over the years have failed to win Senate approval. Cabinet officers serve at "the pleasure of the President," and may be removed at any time. In addition to the 13 department secretaries, the President may expand the Cabinet to include other executive officials. Today, there are 18 members of the Cabinet. The Vice President sits in on the meetings, and other officials may be invited to attend. Each of the 13 Cabinet departments and its various functions is discussed in Unit 8.

The President's Cabinet is an American political tradition that has endured since 1789. What are the two principal functions of Cabinet members?

THE PRESIDENT'S CABINET
Secretary of State
Secretary of the Treasury
Secretary of Defense
Attorney General
Secretary of the Interior
Secretary of Agriculture
Secretary of Commerce
Secretary of Labor
Secretary of Health and Human Services
Secretary of Housing and Urban Development
Secretary of Transportation
Secretary of Energy
Secretary of Education
Counselor to the President
Director of the Office of Management and Budget
Director of Central Intelligence
United Nations Ambassador
United States Trade Representative

Cabinet members have two principal functions. First, the Cabinet officers serve as the administrative heads of the executive departments. Second, they serve as advisers to the President. Presidents have varied in their use of the Cabinet. Meetings of the full membership are infrequent, however. The Cabinet is not a decision-making body, and it has limited usefulness to the President as a source of advice. Its weakness as a body is illustrated by the often-told story of how President Lincoln counted when his whole Cabinet opposed him: "Seven nays, one aye—the ayes have it."

Two major factors account for the limited role played by the Cabinet. First, in making Cabinet appointments, the President is guided by a number of political considerations such as sectional balance, interest groups, and party affiliations. In recent years, the President has sought to include women and minorities and to attain religious and ethnic balance in making Cabinet appointments. Several departments are identified closely with particular segments of society, and the President's appointments are made with sensitivity to the groups affected. The Secretary of the Treasury is usually drawn from the world of banking and finance and the Secretary of Commerce from business. The Secretary of Agriculture must meet the approval of the farm interests, just as the Secretary of Labor must be acceptable to the unions. Traditionally, the President names a westerner as Secretary of the Interior. The President frequently has never before met the people considered for appointment to the Cabinet.

Second, Cabinet members, as department heads, have divided loyalties. They are accountable to both the President and Congress. Congress creates the departments of the executive branch, and it appropriates the funds by which they operate. The secretaries are called from time to time before Congressional committees to answer for their actions and to defend their departments' programs. Inevitably, Cabinet members become advocates for the departments they head. Unlike the President's personal assistants, they do not necessarily share the Presidential perspective. In addition Cabinet officers are frequently rivals for the President's favor, competing with each other for a bigger share of the budget. They are not inclined to bring up major

LEXICON

The Kitchen Cabinet

Before the creation of the White House Office, Presidents frequently turned to an informal group of personal advisers. Thomas Jefferson was accused of forming "an invisible, inscrutable, unconstitutional cabinet" that dealt in "back-stairs influence."* Jackson met regularly with a group of friends in the White House kitchen. Inevitably, they were dubbed "the Kitchen Cabinet." Franklin Roosevelt relied heavily for advice on a group of university professors—"The Brain Trust."

*William Safire, *Safire's Political Dictionary* (New York: Random House, 1978), p. 357.

matters concerning their departments before the entire Cabinet. They prefer to confer with the President alone.

While the Cabinet as a body does not play a significant role in White House decision making, individual Cabinet members may have great influence as Presidential advisers. In recent years, the Secretaries of State, Defense, and the Treasury and the Attorney General have had close contact with the President. They constitute an "inner Cabinet" and may be brought into a wide range of policy decisions.

The role of the Cabinet varies with each administration and is determined by the President. The frequency of Cabinet meetings is also determined by the President. Some Presidents have given the Cabinet an important role, while other Presidents have given it a less important role. Some Presidents meet with certain Cabinet heads on a regular basis.

Section Check

1. Define: liaison, Cabinet, federal bureaucracy
2. Identify: Executive Office of the White House, Office of Management and Budget, the Central Intelligence Agency, the National Security Council, the Council of Economic Advisers
3. Briefly describe the three different functions of the President's assistants in the White House Office.
4. What are the four main functions of the Office of Management and Budget?
5. What factors limit the advisory role of the Cabinet?

SUMMARY

The Constitution provides that the President must be a natural-born citizen, must be at least 35 years old, and must have resided in the United States for at least 14 years. The President receives an annual salary of $200,000 and many other compensations. The President is elected to a four-year term. The Twenty-second Amendment limits the President to serving two full terms or not more than ten years.

A vacancy in the Presidency is filled by the Vice President. Under the Presidential Succession Act, the line of succession passes to the Speaker of the House, president pro tempore of the Senate, and members of the Cabinet. The Twenty-fifth Amendment provides for filling a vacancy in the Vice Presidency. The problems of Presidential disability are also treated by this amendment.

The Vice President's only constitutional duty is to preside over the Senate. In the past, the Vice Presidency was regarded as a useless office. Recent Presidents, however, have made increasing use of their Vice Presidents.

The President performs many functions. It is, however, possible to identify six major roles: chief of state, chief executive, chief diplomat, commander in chief, chief legislator, and party leader.

In making decisions, the President relies on advisers for information. Members of the Executive Office of the President advise the President and coordinate policy among the hundreds of departments and agencies of the federal government. Members of the Cabinet also serve as advisers to the President. The Cabinet membership consists of the secretaries who head the major executive departments. The President may expand the Cabinet to include other executive officials. The importance of the Cabinet varies with each administration.

Chapter 18 Review

Using Vocabulary

Answer the questions by using the meaning of each underlined term.

1. How does treaty power differ from veto power?
2. Why is civilian supremacy an important part of the President's role as commander in chief?
3. What takes place in a Congressional veto override?
4. Why does the President sometimes negotiate an executive agreement rather than a treaty?
5. What effect might a rider have on the President's use of the pocket veto?
6. How might a gatekeeper function as a liaison?
7. Is it possible for a lame-duck President to exercise diplomatic recognition? Why or why not?

Understanding American Government

1. What is the distinction between a treaty and an executive agreement?
2. What four options does the President have when Congress sends a completed bill to the White House?
3. Why would a pardon be more desirable than a reprieve?
4. What are the arguments for and against executive privilege?
5. Briefly describe the most important units of the Executive Office of the President.
6. Describe the development of the President's Cabinet.

Extending Your Skills: Identifying Presidential Roles

Reread pages 439–449. Then identify which of the Presidential roles the President would most likely fulfill in each of the following hypothetical situations.

1. Appointing a special bipartisan commission to study the possible reorganization of the executive branch
2. Appointing a new ambassador
3. Ordering warships from home port to a specific location
4. Recommending sweeping tax-reform legislation to Congress
5. Campaigning on behalf of party members running for reelection to Congress
6. Signing a treaty improving trade relations with United States allies
7. Vetoing a bill
8. Meeting with the Cabinet

Government and You

1. Study the chart of Presidential vetoes on page 447. Can you conclude from the chart that the President with the most vetoes had the greatest problems with Congress and that the President with the fewest vetoes got along best with Congress? Why or why not?
2. Why is Congressional control of appointments important? For example, is it better to have the Secretary of State or the National Security Adviser control foreign affairs?
3. Should a President be limited to two terms? What is wrong with serving for as long as possible?
4. Suppose you were the President of the United States and you decided on a legislative program that centered around one key bill. How would you go about influencing members of Congress to support that bill?

Activities

1. Women such as Margaret Thatcher of England, Indira Gandhi of India, and Golda Meir of Israel have made strong leaders of their countries. Write a report on one of these women. Present your report to the class.
2. The White House has had a long and colorful history. Write a report on the history of the White House or on some specific event, such as the fire in 1814.
3. Many excellent books detail the lives of recent Presidents. Read one of these books and write a brief report on it.
4. Stage a debate entitled "Resolved: Recent Supreme Court Decisions on Executive Privilege Are Destroying the Power of the President." Use the *United States* v. *Nixon* as a basic source of information.

Chapter 19

Making Foreign Policy and Defending the Nation

Let every nation know, whether it wishes us well or ill, that we shall pay any price, bear any burden, meet any hardship, support any friend, oppose any foe to assure the survival and the success of liberty.

JOHN F. KENNEDY

President Ronald Reagan (right) and Chinese Premier Zhao Ziyang (left) hold a conference in Beijing, China, in April 1984, to discuss defense and trade policies. Traditionally, the President has been primarily responsible for United States diplomacy.

1 THE UNITED STATES AND WORLD AFFAIRS

Setting foreign policy consists of formulating goals, making decisions, and carrying out the actions that characterize a nation's relations with the rest of the world. The President, the Secretary of State, and other Presidential advisers shape foreign policy to meet new situations and changing world conditions. The national interests that guide policy also change. But always underlying any President's foreign policy is a concern for national security and the defense of the nation against outside threat. Indeed, it was in part to "provide for the common defense" that the United States was founded.

This chapter examines the role of the President and the United States in world affairs. The two Cabinet departments most directly responsible for the conduct of foreign policy and national defense are the Department of State and the Department of Defense.

The Conduct of Foreign Affairs—1776 to 1945

The foreign relations of the United States go back to the days of the Continental Congress in 1776. The leaders of the American Revolution saw the need for support from other nations if the colonies were to gain their independence from Great Britain. Accordingly, the Congress voted to send Benjamin Franklin, one of the most widely known and respected Americans of the time, to Paris. His mission was to gain official French recognition for the new nation, to secure loans, and to forge an alliance. As a result of Franklin's efforts, French troops and warships helped ensure the British surrender at Yorktown.

Diplomacy, the art and practice of international negotiations, thus contributed significantly to American independence. But for much of the nineteenth and part of the twentieth century, the United States pursued a policy of ***isolationism,*** minimal involvement in foreign affairs. The Atlantic Ocean was a wide enough barrier to protect the United States from Europe's wars. In 1835 the French visitor Alexis de Tocqueville wrote the following while visiting the United States:

The United States is a nation without neighbors. Separated from the rest of the world by the ocean, and too weak as yet to aim at domination of the seas, it has no enemies, and its interests rarely come into contact with those of any other nation of the globe.

America's interests changed, however, as the nation expanded and as the steamship reduced the traveling time across the oceans. By the late 1800's, an industrialized United States had assumed an active role in the Pacific area and had opened relations with China and Japan. As a result of the Spanish-American War, the United States had become a world power. It acquired Guam and Puerto Rico. It established a protectorate over Cuba. It also governed the Philippines for nearly half a century. In the early twentieth century, the United States government intervened militarily in Mexico, in various Caribbean nations including Nicaragua and Haiti, and in South America.

It was not until World War I that the United States became militarily involved in Europe. At the outbreak of the war in 1914 the United States adopted a position of neutrality, but events at home and abroad moved the country slowly toward war. In 1917 President Woodrow Wilson called for America's entry into the conflict to make the world "safe for democracy."

The fighting in World War I ended with the signing of the armistice on November 11, 1918. But President Wilson's efforts to build a lasting peace were unsuccessful. The Senate rejected the Treaty of Versailles and kept the United States out of the League of Nations. Wilson warned that the Senate's refusal to accept a position of world leadership for the country was a retreat into "sullen and selfish isolation."

Thus the United States returned to the policies of "normalcy" and isolationism. In his inaugural address as President in 1921, Warren G. Harding stated, "We seek no part in directing the destinies of the world."

In the early 1930's, aggression by Japan, Italy, and Germany moved the world again toward war. American isolationists were determined to keep the United States out of any conflict. Congress, reflecting public sentiment, passed a series of neutrality acts. But as the armies of Germany's Adolf Hitler pushed across Europe, pressure mounted for United States intervention on behalf of France, Great Britain, and other countries known as the Allies.

In February 1917, President Wilson tells Congress that diplomatic relations with Germany have been broken because of German submarine attacks on American merchant ships. The President's power to conduct diplomatic relations derives from Article 2, Sections 2 and 3, of the Constitution.

The entry of the United States into World War II, a direct result of the Japanese attack on Pearl Harbor, signaled the beginning of a new period of internationalism. Name two ways in which the United States maintained a policy of internationalism after World War II.

While Hitler pursued the domination of Europe, the Japanese extended their control over Asia and the Pacific. On December 7, 1941, Japanese planes bombed Pearl Harbor and shattered the hopes of isolationists. On December 8, 1941, President Franklin D. Roosevelt asked the Congress to declare war on Japan, Germany, and the other Axis powers.

The Conduct of Foreign Affairs Since 1945

The United States emerged from World War II as the most powerful nation on earth. After the war, President Harry S Truman committed the United States to a policy of ***internationalism.*** It entered into cooperative relations with other nations for defense and to solve common political, economic, and social problems. One sign of the United States' renewed interest in international affairs was its participation in the creation of the United Nations (UN) in 1945.

The Marshall Plan—named for its creator, Secretary of State George C. Marshall—helped Western Europe regain economic and political stability. Between 1948 and 1952, the United States poured almost $13 billion in economic aid into some 16 nations, including France, Great Britain, Italy, and West Germany. Through the Marshall Plan and other programs, the United States has provided grants and loans to more than 100 countries, including the developing nations of Asia, the Middle East, Africa, and Latin America.

In the years following World War II the spirit of ***nationalism***—the common spirit that unites people in the desire to be self-governing—brought independence to many of the peoples who had once been under colonial rule. Following independence, most developing nations experienced political instability, and many faced the threat of revolution. They soon became arenas in which the United States and the Soviet Union competed for power and influence.

The Cold War Speaking in 1946 at Fulton, Missouri, Sir Winston Churchill—the Prime Minister of Great Britain during World War II—declared that the Soviet Union had brought down "an iron curtain" across the continent of Europe. The nations of Eastern Europe with their Communist governments had become Soviet satellites. A new phrase was coined to characterize the nonshooting struggle for power and prestige between the United States and the Soviet Union. The struggle became known as the ***cold war.***

As cold war tensions mounted, the United States adopted a policy of ***containment,*** designed to stop Soviet expansion and to "contain" Communism within its existing boundaries. Underlying containment was the hope that if Communism did not spread to other countries, it would then collapse from internal weaknesses. The policy of containment was first applied in 1947 under President Truman, when the United States supplied military aid to Greece and Turkey. In a statement that became known as the Truman Doctrine, President Truman said, "I believe it must be the policy of the United States to support free peoples who are resisting [aggression] by armed minorities or by outside pressures."

As the United States rearmed, it entered into a series of ***collective security agreements*** with non-Communist nations around the world. Each signatory to such an agreement pledged to defend the others against armed attack. The most important collective security agreement was the North Atlantic Treaty. Under it, the signatory nations formed the North Atlantic Treaty Organization (NATO) in 1949 to safeguard Western Europe and North America. Today, the United States is pledged under regional security pacts and by individual military alliances to defend 41 other nations.

A basic component of American defense policy since 1945 has been ***deterrence,*** the discouragement of aggression by the threat of retaliation. The

The United States has formal defense commitments with countries throughout the world. Many of these commitments are collective security agreements which were signed during the 1940's and 1950's as part of the strategy of containment. What was the purpose of containment? Who was the first President to apply containment to United States foreign policy?

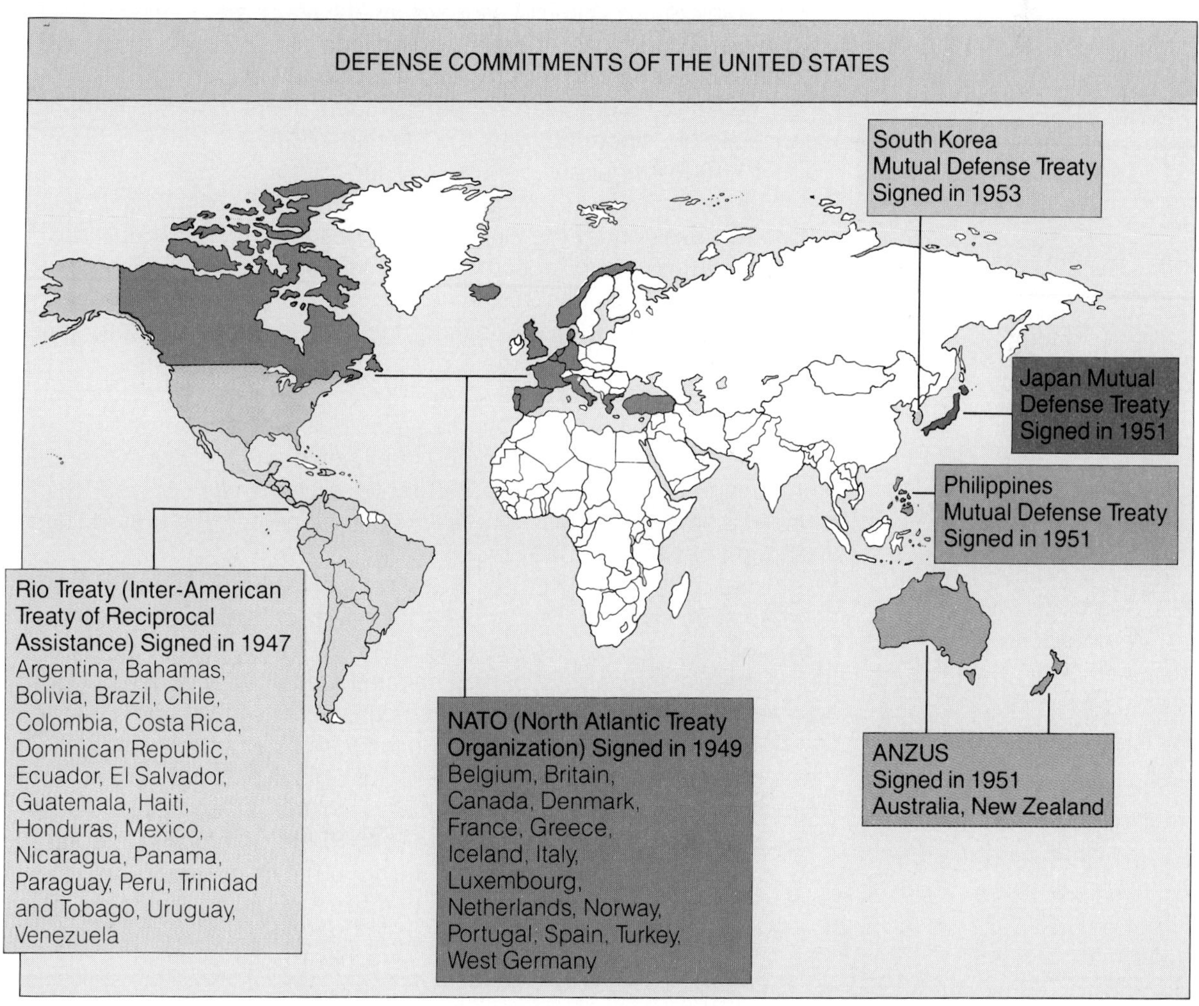

purpose of deterrence is to prevent war. Deterrence also means that the United States must be prepared to take military action when its vital interests are threatened. Based on the twin policies of containment and deterrence, the United States fought in Korea (1950–1953) and in Vietnam (1965–1973).

Relaxation of Cold War Tensions The cold war has been viewed essentially as a two-sided conflict between the United States with its allies and the Soviet Union with its allies. But the language of the cold war sometimes has clouded the complexity of the changing postwar world. Cold war language has

INSIGHT

Vietnam

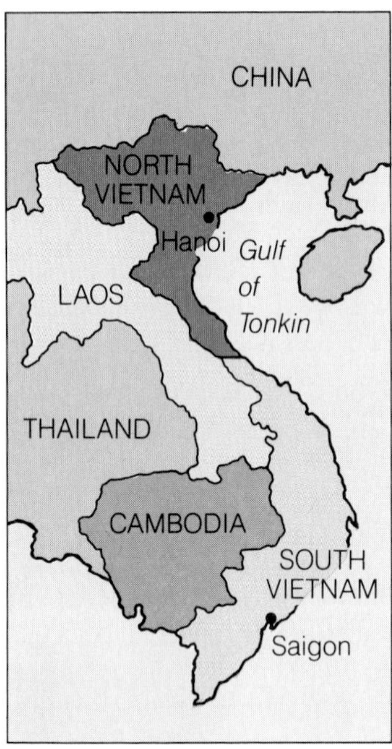

From the late nineteenth century, Vietnam had been a part of French Indochina. At the end of World War II the Vietnamese Communist leader Ho Chi Minh proclaimed the country's independence. From his stronghold in the north he led a war against the French and their Vietnamese supporters, which ended in 1954 with a French defeat. Under the Geneva Accords, Vietnam was temporarily divided, pending elections. A Communist government was established in North Vietnam with Hanoi as its capital. A non-Communist government was established in South Vietnam with Saigon as its capital. When the time came for Vietnam's national elections, the leader of South Vietnam refused to hold them. So opposition forces, known as the Viet Cong, began a guerrilla campaign against the South Vietnamese government. Many members of the Viet Cong were Buddhists, liberals, and nationalists. But the majority were Communists receiving military help from North Vietnam.

The United States had supported South Vietnam with military and economic aid since 1950. In 1961 President John F. Kennedy sent in about 16,000 American troops as advisers. But little ground was gained in the effort to lessen Communist influence. In 1965, with authorization from Congress under the Gulf of Tonkin Resolution, President Johnson escalated the military action against the Communists. Subsequently, the number of American troops increased rapidly to more than one half million. In air strikes over Vietnam, the United States dropped three times the total bomb tonnage dropped in World War II. By the time the United States withdrew in 1973, 47,000 Americans had been killed and another 300,000 wounded. As many as 1 million Vietnamese died, and an additional 2 million were forced from their homes. About 20 percent of the landscape was devastated by toxic chemicals sprayed by the United States. Estimates of the dollar cost of the war to the United States ranged from $120 to $200 billion.

United States involvement in the Vietnam War had seriously divided the American people. During the war, antiwar protestors demonstrated against the United States role in Vietnam. In Congress and in the executive branch, the nation's leaders debated fundamental issues of United States involvement: What were American interests in Vietnam? Was the struggle in Vietnam a civil war to be left to the Vietnamese people? Or was it a war of aggression by the Communist North against the non-Communist South and thus in the interests of the United States to counter Communist aggression in Asia? In 1975 the Communists captured Saigon and unified Vietnam under the government of Hanoi. Even then, the questions and the implications of the use of United States power in world affairs had not been answered.

Demonstrators against the Vietnam War rally to show their opposition to United States military policy. Upon what foreign policy principles did the United States government base its involvement in the Vietnam War?

failed to give due recognition to the forces of nationalism throughout the world, especially in Asia, Africa, and parts of Latin America. It has also tended to obscure tensions within the Communist bloc.

As early as 1948 Yugoslavia's President Tito broke with the Soviet Union. In the years since 1948 other Communist nations of Eastern Europe have tried to chart a more independent course from the Soviet Union. In 1956 Hungary tried to assert its independence from Soviet control, but the Soviet leadership crushed Hungary with a massive outlay of power. In 1968 Czechoslovakia suffered the same fate as Hungary. But other Communist nations were more successful in opening contacts and economic ties with the West. The major break in Communist unity came in the early 1960's. At that time the Soviet Union came into open and bitter conflict with its former ally, the People's Republic of China.

In the changing world environment of the early 1970's, the United States sought to promote its interests through improved relations with China and with the Soviet Union. In 1972 President Richard M. Nixon made a historic trip to China. Later that same year he went to Moscow for a ***summit conference,*** or face-to-face meeting, with Soviet party chief Leonid Brezhnev. The world leaders signed agreements

The 1972 summit conference between President Richard Nixon (left) and Soviet leader Leonid Brezhnev (right) signaled a temporary improvement in American-Soviet relations.

Henry Kissinger was Secretary of State during the Nixon and Ford Presidencies. What was Kissinger's policy of détente? Why did some people criticize it?

based on the first round of the Strategic Arms Limitation Talks (SALT). As a step toward the reduction of arms, the two sides agreed to certain limits on nuclear missiles. The arms-control negotiations continued, and during the next two years the United States and the Soviet Union reached a number of agreements for improved trade and for technical, scientific, and economic cooperation.

The relaxation of tensions between the two superpowers became known as ***détente*** and was hailed by many as the beginning of a new era. But by 1976 many Americans grew suspicious of détente. Soviet involvement in conflicts in the Middle East and in Africa renewed tension and again brought the two great powers into confrontation. The renewal of tension resulted in sharp criticism of the policy of détente and of Secretary of State Henry Kissinger, its architect. Critics charged that the Soviet Union was using détente as a tactic to gain military advantages over the United States.

In the second half of the 1970's caution marked Soviet-American relations. The United States spoke out against violations of human rights in the Soviet Union, as well as in other nations around the world. The United States, however, cooperated with the Soviets where possible and emphasized arms control to reduce the threat of nuclear war. But the Soviet invasion of Afghanistan in December 1979 shook hopes for progress toward world peace. Reacting strongly to the invasion, President Jimmy Carter imposed an embargo on American grain shipments to the Soviet Union. As another symbol of protest, he withdrew United States teams from the 1980 Summer Olympics in Moscow, a boycott followed by more than 50 other nations.

Following his inauguration in January 1981 President Ronald Reagan took an equally tough stance toward the Soviet Union. His stance reflected a determination to contain the expansion of Soviet influence in the Third World.

In 1983 United States troops invaded Grenada and expelled about 650 Cubans who were building an airstrip there. The Reagan administration justified its action primarily on the grounds of protecting American students at the local medical school. But the administration's action also eliminated the potential use of the airstrip by Cuban soldiers who might have intervened in the guerrilla warfare in Central America. At the same time, the Reagan administration continued supplying economic and military aid to the government forces of El Salvador and to the forces trying to overthrow the government of Nicaragua. In both instances, President Reagan argued that the United States was supporting non-Communists against Communists.

Section Check

1. Define: diplomacy, isolationism, internationalism, nationalism, cold war, containment, collective security agreement, deterrence, summit conference, détente
2. Identify: George C. Marshall, Sir Winston Churchill, Truman Doctrine, North Atlantic Treaty Organization, Ho Chi Minh
3. How did diplomacy contribute to American independence?
4. Why did the United States follow a policy of isolationism until the early part of the twentieth century? Why did it change that policy?
5. When did the United States become militarily involved in Europe for the first time?
6. What did Sir Winston Churchill mean when he declared that the Soviet Union had brought down "an iron curtain" across the continent of Europe?
7. What foreign policies led to United States involvement in Korea and in Vietnam?
8. Why did many Americans grow suspicious of détente by 1976?

2 HOW FOREIGN POLICY IS MADE

Foreign policy is a process that undergoes continuous review in response to changing world conditions. The central figure in the making and conduct of American foreign policy is the President, who is both chief diplomat and commander in chief. Helping the President are a variety of agencies, the most important of which are the Department of State and the National Security Council. Congress also plays a major role.

The President's chief foreign policy adviser is usually the Secretary of State. The degree of a Secretary's influence, however, usually depends upon each President. Some Presidents have left matters of foreign policy largely in the hands of the Secretary of State. Other Presidents have taken an active interest in foreign policy and kept decision making in their own hands.

Beyond the Department of State, many government agencies have interests in various aspects of foreign affairs. Much of the concern of international relations today is economic, and this brings in the Departments of the Treasury, Commerce, Labor, and Agriculture. Even more important, because of the close link between foreign policy and national defense, is the Department of Defense. In addition, other agencies include the Central Intelligence Agency (CIA), the Arms Control and Disarmament Agency (ACDA), the United States Information Agency (USIA), and the Agency for International Development (AID). These various agencies have different policy concerns, and each views American interests from its own perspective. The result is that the President, when making policy decisions, often receives conflicting advice from different groups.

The Role of the National Security Council

Established in 1947, the National Security Council (NSC) advises the President on "the integration of domestic, foreign, and military policies relating to national security." The President chairs the NSC, and its members include the Vice President, the Secretary of State, and the Secretary of Defense. The director of the Central Intelligence Agency and the head of the Joint Chiefs of Staff are advisers to the Council. The President appoints and the Senate confirms the National Security Adviser. The National Security Adviser directs the various activities of the NSC staff.

George Schultz was appointed Secretary of State by President Reagan. Schultz has been influential in formulating United States foreign policies toward the Soviet Union, the Middle East, and Central America.

Presidents have made varying use of the National Security Council. Under President Eisenhower, the NSC met on a regular basis. Presidents Kennedy and Johnson preferred to use the NSC more informally. The NSC staff, however, took on increasing importance, so much so that many critics called it "a little State Department." President Nixon directed that the NSC function "as the principal forum for Presidential consideration of foreign policy issues."

As the issues of foreign policy have grown more complex, Presidents have relied on personal advisers to assist them in decision making. Presidents have used their advisers in different ways. Under Nixon, Henry Kissinger, as National Security Adviser, became the chief architect of American foreign policy—a role he continued as Secretary of State in Nixon's second term and in Ford's administration. Zbigniew Brzezinski, President Carter's National Security Adviser, also took a major role in making foreign policy. With an office in the White House, the National Security Adviser has access to the President around the clock, and at times he has come into competition with the Secretary of State. Conflict between the views of Brzezinski and Secretary of State Cyrus Vance, for example, was one of the main factors leading to the latter's resignation in 1980.

The Vance resignation raised a serious question as to the proper role of the National Security Adviser. Originally, the National Security Adviser was to operate in a neutral way as a manager, with the task of shaping and bringing order to the policy options available to the President. But in recent years, the National Security Adviser has become an outspoken advocate for specific foreign-policy issues, sometimes in opposition to the Secretary of State. One result is that Congress and foreign governments are often unsure who is speaking for the administration—the National Security Adviser or the Secretary of State. Ultimately, however, the responsibility for the direction of American foreign policy rests with the President.

The Role of Congress

The Constitution gives Congress a major role in making foreign policy. All treaties must be approved by a two-thirds vote in the Senate. The Senate also gives its "advice and consent" to the appointment of ambassadors and senior officials of the Department of State. Congress has the power to provide for the common defense, to raise and support armies, and to declare war. Congress also has the power to regulate commerce with foreign nations.

The most important source of Congressional influence over foreign policy lies in the legislative control over the purse strings. The President depends upon Congress for the appropriation of money to support the conduct of foreign relations. Through its power of investigation Congress oversees how that money is spent. In the system of checks and balances Congress acts as a watchdog over American foreign policy.

More than half of all Congressional committees have some impact on foreign affairs. The most important are the Senate Foreign Relations and the House Foreign Affairs committees. The Armed Services and Appropriations committees of both houses are equally important. Administration officials, including the Secretary of State, consult frequently with these committees. They brief Congressional members informally on foreign policy developments and give formal testimony in Congressional committee hearings.

Members of Congress make trips abroad to inspect American programs firsthand and to meet with foreign leaders. The President often invites senators and representatives to participate in diplomatic negotiations, such as the SALT talks, and to serve as members of American delegations to international conferences.

In creating the separation of powers system, the Constitution created "an invitation to struggle" between the President and Congress for the control of foreign policy. For most of the nation's history the President has taken the dominant role in foreign policy. From time to time, however, Congress has asserted its independence. During the 1970's, largely as a response to the Vietnam War, Congress became increasingly active in foreign policy.

Large, decentralized, and often exceedingly slow, Congress is not well-suited to the conduct of foreign relations. Yet it plays a vital role in setting the goals of American foreign policy and in charting its direction. Congress, as the voice of the people, gives legitimacy to foreign policy and helps shape the popular support upon which a successful foreign policy must ultimately rest.

The Department of State

The Department of State is responsible for advising the President and carrying out American foreign policy. The State Department is the oldest executive department, having been established in 1781 under the Articles of Confederation as the Department of Foreign Affairs. When the Constitution was adopted in 1789, it was reorganized as the Department of State. President George Washington named Thomas Jefferson as the first Secretary of State.

The Secretary of State is the President's official adviser on foreign policy and is the highest ranking member of the Cabinet. The Secretary is in charge of State Department operations and is responsible for the overall direction, coordination, and supervision of American foreign relations.

The Secretary of State is aided by a Deputy Secretary, four Under Secretaries, and a number of special assistants who furnish advice on such matters as international terrorism, refugees, and long-range policy planning. There are also ambassadors-at-large who undertake special missions at the request of the Secretary or the President.

Most of the day-to-day work of the department is handled through regional bureaus, each headed by an Assistant Secretary of State or an equivalent. The five regional bureaus are responsible for United

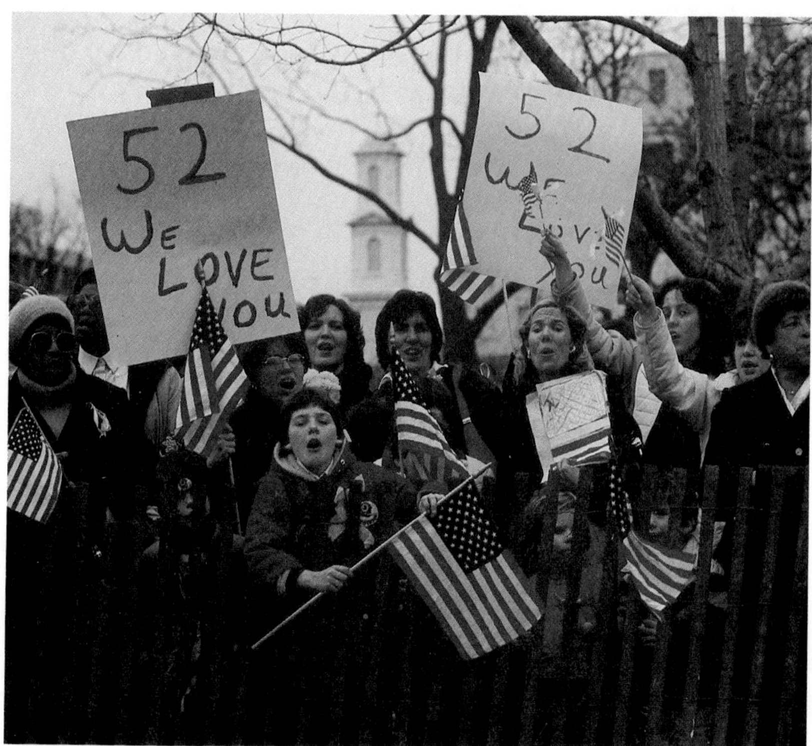

On January 24, 1981, crowds gathered to welcome home 52 Americans who had been held hostage for 444 days in the United States Embassy in Tehran, Iran. The Department of State played a key role in securing the release of the hostages.

States foreign relations activities in the major regions of the world. They are Africa, East Asia and the Pacific, Latin America, Europe, and the Near East and South Asia. For the most part, the assignment of countries to each bureau follows the map. There are some exceptions, however. Canada, with its close ties to the Atlantic nations, comes under the Bureau of European Affairs. Egypt and the Arab countries of North Africa are a part of the Bureau of Near Eastern and South Asian Affairs.

The Assistant Secretaries in charge of the regional bureaus advise the Secretary of State on foreign policy concerning their regions. The bureaus are divided into subregional offices that handle relations with individual countries. The country desks are the main point of contact between Washington and America's embassies abroad and foreign embassies in Washington, D.C. Each office is staffed by specialists in political, economic, and military affairs. Most often these specialists are Foreign Service Officers who have served in the countries for which they are responsible.

A number of bureaus are organized along functional lines. They are concerned with particular kinds of activities. Economic and Business Affairs deals with such areas as trade policy, international finance and development, and international resources, including food and energy. Intelligence and Research analyzes the flow of information coming into the State Department and other agencies from around the world and prepares reports on problems and trends in international affairs.

International Organization Affairs coordinates American participation in the United Nations and the other international organizations to which the United States belongs. It also supports the work of United States delegates to more than 800 international conferences each year.

Still another functional bureau is Consular Affairs. It is the most familiar bureau of the State Department for many Americans. Its Passport Office issues 3.5 million passports to American citizens each year. Through some 170 consular offices in major cities around the world, the bureau provides a number of services to assist and protect Americans and their interests in foreign countries. United States consulates take special concern in the welfare and whereabouts of Americans abroad. They also issue visas to foreign nationals who wish to come to the United States to live, to work, to study, or to visit.

The Work of Embassies

The United States maintains embassies in about 150 nations with which it has diplomatic relations. An ambassador, who is appointed by the President and confirmed by the Senate, heads each embassy and serves as the personal representative of the President to the foreign host government. Ambassadors report to the President through the Secretary of State. Their responsibilities include negotiating agreements between the United States and the host government, explaining official United States policy, reporting to Washington on conditions of the host country, and maintaining cordial relations with that country's government and people.

The size of a diplomatic post depends upon the importance of the host nation to the United States and the number of activities that take place between the two countries. The largest embassies have several hundred American employees and as many host-country employees.

The work of an embassy is divided into four sections: administrative, consular, economic/commercial, and political. Economic and commercial officers analyze and report economic trends in the host country. They also seek to advance United States trade and investment opportunities. Political officers, through a wide range of contacts, keep a close watch on local politics and keep Washington informed of important developments. They convey the views of the United States government to the host government and negotiate agreements between the two governments.

A number of federal agencies assign personnel to foreign countries to represent their interests. In most embassies, the United States Information Agency has cultural and information officers who arrange educational and cultural exchanges and provide information about life in the United States and its foreign policy. Officials of the Agency for International Development provide technical assistance to the host country. The Peace Corps conducts programs in economic and social development based on the host country's needs. The Foreign Agricultural Service and the Foreign Commercial Service represent the Departments of Agriculture and Commerce, respectively. The Department of Defense assigns military attachés to the embassy to maintain liaison with the local military. Marine Corps guards protect America's embassies abroad. With the exception of military commands, all United States agencies abroad report to the ambassador.

The embassies are in continuous contact with Washington. Some 1 million telegrams flow in and out of the Operations Center of the State Department each year. Nearly 100,000 messages are coded high priority and secret. The Center's telephone system is in direct contact with diplomatic and military posts throughout the world. It also maintains direct links to the White House, the Department of Defense, and the Central Intelligence Agency. In a crisis situation, the CIA officials keep the President and the Secretary of State constantly informed.

Before the American Embassy in Beirut, Lebanon, was bombed by terrorists in April 1983, it headquartered various federal agencies working in Lebanon. List the federal agencies that may be represented in American embassies.

The Foreign Service

The Department of State employs people in a wide range of professions, specialties, and skills. Some are regular members of the civil service and remain on permanent duty in Washington. Nearly 3,000 Foreign Service Officers form the elite diplomatic corps. Entry into the Foreign Service is by competitive examination, and between 100 and 200 new officers are appointed each year.

The men and women of the Foreign Service represent the United States abroad and staff key positions within the State Department. Normally officers rotate every four years between an assignment in Washington and a tour of duty overseas. Foreign Service officers generally become specialists in a particular geographic region of the world and gain a command of local languages. It is State Department policy, however, that officers serve a major portion of their time in regions other than their specialty in order to broaden their perspectives.

Ambassadors do not have to be members of the Foreign Service. Until recently, ambassadorial posts were handed out in return for large campaign contributions or as a reward for party service. This has changed dramatically. Today two thirds of United States ambassadors are career diplomats. Ambassadors appointed from outside the Foreign Service are sometimes distinguished university professors, but certain posts typically go to prominent political supporters. For example, the ambassador to the Court of St. James in Great Britain is usually a political appointment. The post is often given to a wealthy individual, because the expense of maintaining the American embassy is so much greater than the public funds available.

Section Check

1. Identify: National Security Council, National Security Adviser, Operations Center, Foreign Service
2. What determines how much influence the Secretary of State has on foreign policy?
3. How has the role of the National Security Adviser changed since the position was first established?
4. What is the most important source of Congressional influence over foreign policy, and how does it operate?
5. What is an argument for and an argument against Congress's participation in the making of foreign policy?
6. What is the most familiar bureau of the State Department for many Americans? Why?
7. On what does the size of the United States diplomatic posts depend?
8. How were ambassadorial posts generally awarded in the past? How are most of these posts awarded today?

3 SPECIALIZED AGENCIES

Several areas of foreign policy—the acquisition and dissemination of information, foreign aid, and arms control and disarmament—are handled by specialized agencies. These agencies include the Central Intelligence Agency, the United States Information Agency, the Agency for International Development, the Peace Corps, and the Arms Control and Disarmament Agency.

The Central Intelligence Agency

Since the days of George Washington, the United States has, both openly and secretly, acquired and evaluated information about the capabilities and intentions of foreign governments. Only since World War II, however, have these ***foreign-intelligence activities*** been coordinated on a government-wide basis. During the war the Office of Strategic Services (OSS) gathered information and conducted political warfare and sabotage operations behind enemy lines. In 1945 the OSS was disbanded. In 1947 the Central Intelligence Agency (CIA) was established. The Director of Central Intelligence heads the CIA and coordinates the larger intelligence community.

William Casey serves as Director of Central Intelligence for the Reagan administration. The Director of Central Intelligence is also a member of the President's Cabinet.

The covert activities of the Central Intelligence Agency (CIA) include spying on foreign nations. The downing of an American U-2 spy plane (right) by the Soviet Union in May 1960 created new tensions in Soviet-American relations. What other activities of the CIA have been attacked by critics?

A primary function of the Central Intelligence Agency is to gather and analyze political, economic, and military information about other countries. Making successful foreign policy decisions depends upon complete and accurate information. At the CIA headquarters in Langley, Virginia, intelligence experts evaluate vast amounts of data from all over the world. Most of it is from published sources. But some of it is top secret information acquired by undercover agents.

The secrecy surrounding the CIA gives it a certain mystique and has contributed to its "cloak-and-dagger" image. This image is reinforced by the agency's ***covert actions,*** which are separate and distinct from its intelligence gathering. The CIA defines covert actions as special activities conducted abroad to influence opinions and events in support of American foreign-policy objectives. Covert actions are conducted in such a manner that the role of the American government is not apparent. In short, covert actions are secret political warfare, somewhere between diplomacy and military action. Covert actions are carried out under the direction of the National Security Council and must have the prior approval of the President. Through its covert actions the CIA helped to overthrow the governments of Iran and Guatemala in 1954 and of Chile in 1971. It organized the unsuccessful invasion of Cuba at the Bay of Pigs in 1961. It also supported a secret army against Communist forces in Laos. The CIA makes no public comment on such activities, and the agency is often associated with assassinations, coups, and revolts, whether or not it is actually involved.

Critics have attacked the CIA as an invisible government that is protected by secrecy from public scrutiny and Congressional control. In the mid-1970s, House and Senate investigating committees and a Presidential commission headed by Vice President Nelson Rockefeller disclosed tales of CIA plots. They also revealed that the CIA had spied on American citizens in this country and had infiltrated antiwar groups and other dissident groups. These domestic intelligence-gathering activities and covert actions were in clear violation of the agency's charter, which prohibits the CIA from operations within the United States.

Congress reacted to the CIA revelations by creating permanent committees in the House and the Senate to oversee the intelligence community. The House and the Senate Appropriations Committees also monitor CIA activities. Within the White House, an independent Intelligence Oversight Board monitors CIA activities and reports to the President those intelligence activities that raise serious questions of legality.

The conduct of intelligence activity in a democratic society poses a major dilemma. On the one hand, democratic government requires public accountability. On the other hand, opening the CIA to public inquiry may result in weakening its capacity to gather the intelligence information upon which successful foreign and defense policy depends. Today the CIA walks a fine line between an openness in government that Americans have come to expect and the secrecy that intelligence, by its very nature, demands.

The United States Information Agency

The United States Information Agency (USIA) is an independent executive agency closely associated with the Department of State. Its mission is to tell the world about American society and policies and to tell Americans about the world.

Through its offices in 127 countries, the USIA sponsors publications, films, cultural programs, exhibits, lectures, and seminars about the United States. It promotes personal contact between foreign leaders and visiting American experts in a number of fields. Libraries at American Centers in nearly 90 countries provide materials about the United States, its culture, history, and government. The USIA operates international exchange programs for students and teachers. It brings foreign leaders in labor, in science, in the mass media, and in other fields to the United States to meet their counterparts and to observe American society and institutions.

The Voice of America (VOA), which is the USIA's global radio network, broadcasts in English and in 38 other languages to an estimated world audience of 75 million listeners. Its programming includes comprehensive news reports, programs on various aspects of American society, and a mix of popular music and jazz.

A Voice of America (VOA) newscaster delivers an address concerning life in the United States to listeners in the Soviet Union. How does the VOA help carry out the mission of the United States Information Agency?

The Agency for International Development

The Agency for International Development (AID) administers most of the foreign economic assistance programs of the United States government. AID is part of the larger United States International Development Cooperation Agency. AID programs are carried out through field missions in about 60 countries of Africa, Asia, Latin America, and the Middle East. The programs—mostly long-range—deal with

American soldiers in El Salvador distribute surplus corn to victims of the Salvadoran civil war. United States emergency food assistance abroad involves the cooperative efforts of the Agency for International Development (AID), private organizations, and international organizations such as the Red Cross.

LEGACY

Disaster Relief

The first United States foreign aid appropriation was for disaster relief to Venezuela in 1812, after an earthquake killed 25,000 people and left thousands injured and homeless. Since 1964 the United States has helped the victims of nearly 600 disasters throughout the world. Most disaster relief is channeled through American volunteer agencies and international organizations, such as the Red Cross and the Cooperative for American Relief Everywhere, Inc. (CARE).

food, nutrition, and rural development; health care; and education and human resources development. AID also provides technical assistance in a wide range of projects, such as energy development and urban planning. AID has achieved notable successes, but the problems of world poverty, malnutrition, and hunger remain staggering.

Many Americans ask why the United States government should help people in developing countries when this country has its own pressing problems. Apart from traditional humanitarian concerns, economic assistance to less developed countries serves United States national interests. The welfare and the security of the United States are closely linked to the stability and the progress of developing nations. Several reasons account for this link.

First, the United States is dependent on developing countries for such essential raw materials as bauxite, cobalt, and tin. Second, economic progress in the developing nations means bigger markets for American farm and industrial products. The Third World countries already receive 30 percent of United States exports. More exports go to Third World nations than to all of Europe, and the amount of these exports is three times greater than our exports to Japan. About 1.2 million Americans work at jobs that depend on exports to developing countries. Third, no nation in the world—including the United States—will be secure unless the problems of the Third World are effectively addressed.

By the year 2000, the world's population will have increased from 4.5 to about 6 billion. Almost 80 percent of the world's population will live in Third World nations. Overpopulation in Third World nations often breeds such grim conditions as poverty, unemployment, illiteracy, disease, malnutrition, and famine. These conditions, in turn, may lead to violence, to terrorism, or to guerrilla warfare. Aiding the progress of developing nations helps to secure world peace.

About a third of all United States aid consists of low-interest loans. The rest takes the form of grants, mostly of food from American farms, equipment from United States factories, and technical assistance from American universities. Thus, a large portion of the money spent on foreign aid stays in the United States in payment for goods and services provided for Third World countries.

The cost of United States foreign aid is small—about 1 percent of the federal budget and one fourth of 1 percent of the Gross National Product. The United States contribution to foreign aid comprises the largest dollar amount. But 14 other industrial nations devote a greater percentage of their wealth than the United States to assist developing countries. In the 1980's, annual American government aid to developing countries added up to about $11 billion. By contrast, that same year the American people spent $46 billion on alcoholic beverages, $23 billion on tobacco products, and more than $5 billion on pet food.

The Peace Corps

The Peace Corps sends volunteers to developing countries that request help in economic and social development. Since the Peace Corps was created in 1961, more than 70,000 volunteers have served two-year terms in various projects in countries around the world.

Today, 6,000 volunteers serve in 63 countries, living among the people with whom they work and becoming a part of the community. They learn the local language and adapt to the customs and living conditions of their host countries. Almost half of all Peace Corps volunteers are engaged in some kind of educational project. About one fourth are involved in agriculture and rural development. The rest work in public health, civil engineering, city planning, and business management.

A team of nuclear experts (left) conducts surveillance of worldwide nuclear activity from a United States military base in Colorado Springs. The US Redstone *(below), a naval missile tracking ship based at Port Canaveral, Florida, monitors the activities of the space shuttle and satellites.*

The Arms Control and Disarmament Agency

The Arms Control and Disarmament Agency (ACDA) provides advice concerning arms control. It also implements arms control and disarmament policies. Its director is a principal adviser to the President and to the Secretary of State on disarmament matters.

The ACDA has played a major role in negotiations with the Soviet Union and other countries on such issues as the nuclear test ban, strategic arms limitations, the spread of nuclear weapons, chemical and germ warfare, and the peaceful exploration of outer space. The ACDA also keeps close watch on the movement of the arms trade throughout the world.

As a step toward reducing the threat of nuclear war, the United States and the Soviet Union conducted Strategic Arms Limitation Talks (SALT), signing two agreements in 1972. One agreement resulted in the freeze of offensive missiles at near-existing levels for a five-year period. The other placed a limit on the size of land-based and submarine-based missile forces and limited each nation to two antiballistic missile sites. A second round of negotiations (SALT II) resulted in a treaty that was not ratified by the Senate. For the most part, however, both nations abide by the terms of the treaty.

Section Check

1. Define: foreign-intelligence activities, covert actions
2. Identify: Central Intelligence Agency, Voice of America, Agency for International Development, Peace Corps
3. Why is it important for the United States to obtain intelligence about other countries?
4. What is the purpose of the covert actions of the CIA? Who must approve such actions before they occur?
5. About what percent of the federal budget does foreign aid represent?
6. What is the purpose of the Arms Control and Disarmament Agency?

4 THE NATION'S DEFENSE

The Department of Defense (DOD) is responsible for providing the military forces needed to deter aggression and protect the security of the United States. Its origin goes back to the War Department (1789) and the Navy Department (1798). World War II underscored the need for closer coordination of the nation's defense agencies, and in 1947 Congress created the National Military Establishment. At its head was a Secretary of Defense, who was responsible for coordinating and developing general policy for the Cabinet departments of the Army, the Navy, and the Air Force. The arrangement proved unwieldy, however, and in 1949 the three armed services lost their separate Cabinet status and became military departments within a single Department of Defense.

Civilian Control Over the Military

Civilian supremacy over the military is a principle of democratic government. In giving the President and Congress ultimate control over the military, the Framers of the Constitution gave elected officials supremacy in military matters because they, not military commanders, are accountable to the people.

As the commander in chief of the armed forces, the President is the superior of all generals and admirals and can remove them from their posts. The

The Department of Defense is headquartered in the Pentagon Building, located in Arlington, Virginia, directly across the Potomac River from Washington, D.C. About 26,700 military and civilian employees work at the Pentagon, which has been called "the largest office building in the world." The Pentagon serves as the command center for all Department of Defense operations throughout the world.

President commissions all officers, with the consent of the Senate. Within the limits of the War Powers Resolution, the President may order the armed forces into action in any part of the world. Only Congress, however, has the power to declare war. Congress makes the rules governing the armed forces, and it decides whether or not there will be a draft. With control over the purse strings, Congress determines the size of the armed forces, their pay, and their weapons. The Constitution restricts appropriations to a period of no more than two years.

The Secretary of Defense and the Secretaries of the Army, the Navy, and the Air Force must, by law, be civilians. Military influence, however, is considerable. Each of the Joint Chiefs of Staff has direct access to the President. Each may make recommendations to Congress, even when those recommendations are contrary to Presidential policy. President Eisenhower, one of the generals of World War II, opposed an independent role for the military in shaping defense policy. In his final speech to the nation as President, Eisenhower warned against the consequences of the close connection between America's military establishment and the huge arms industry that he called the ***military-industrial complex.*** "We must never let the weight of this [military-industrial] combination endanger our liberties or democratic processes."

An American soldier participates in NATO military maneuvers in West Germany. Describe the roles of the President and of Congress in maintaining civilian control over United States military forces.

The Organization of the Department of Defense

The Department of Defense (DOD) is the largest of the 13 Cabinet departments. It employs about 1 million civilian employees. It also has more than 2 million military personnel on active duty. The defense budget amounts to nearly 25 percent of all federal expenditures. The DOD includes the Office of the Secretary of Defense, the Joint Chiefs of Staff, the military departments, and the specialized defense agencies.

Office of the Secretary of Defense The Secretary of Defense exercises direction, authority, and control over the DOD. The Secretary is always a civilian appointed by the President, with the advice and consent of the Senate. The Secretary of Defense is a member of the National Security Council and advises the President on defense policy. A Deputy Secretary is responsible for the supervision and coordination of department activities. A special Assistant, two Under Secretaries, and seven Assistant Secretaries also have major staff responsibilities.

In matters relating to defense legislation the Legislative Affairs division provides liaison with Congress, the Executive Office of the President, and other government agencies. It provides information for members of Congress and Congressional committees, and it handles arrangements for witnesses from the department at Congressional hearings.

The Armed Forces Policy Council advises the Secretary of Defense on matters of broad policy relating to the armed forces. The Council members include the Secretaries of the Army, the Navy, and the Air Force, and the Joint Chiefs of Staff.

The Joint Chiefs of Staff The Joint Chiefs of Staff (JCS) are the principal military advisers to the President, the National Security Council, and the Secretary of Defense. The President, with the consent of the Senate, appoints the chairman of the Joint Chiefs of Staff for a two-year term. The chairman takes precedence over all other officers of the armed forces. The other members of the JCS are the Army Chief of Staff, the Chief of Naval Operations, the Air Force Chief of Staff, and the Commandant of the Marine Corps. The Joint Chiefs are assisted by a staff of 400 officers selected in approximately equal numbers from the Army, the Navy (including the Marines), and the Air Force.

The Joint Chiefs have three main functions. They advise civilian decision makers, they prepare strategic plans for the armed forces in the event of war, and they direct combat operations. The chain of command runs from the President to the Secretary of Defense through the Joint Chiefs of Staff.

The members of the JCS, except for the chairman, also serve as the military head of the service to which each belongs. Serving as the head of a service and advising the President builds in a potential conflict of interest. The members of the Joint Chiefs of Staff are to be unbiased in their advice to the President. Yet, inevitably they become advocates for their own branch of the military.

The Armed Services

A civilian Secretary heads each of the departments of the Army, the Navy, and the Air Force—the military departments within the Department of Defense. Each Secretary has a principal military adviser who is the Chief of Staff for that branch of the armed services. Each of the Chiefs of Staff is responsible

ISSUES

Selective Service

On America's entry into World War I in 1917 Congress passed the Selective Service Act, establishing a system of conscription to draft men into military service. The actual selection was by a national lottery. It was based on the patriotic principle that all young men had an equal obligation to serve their country and that each should have the same chance to be called for active duty. Of the 24 million men who registered, 2.8 million were drafted. In 1940 the United States again used the draft to build its military strength. During World War II more than 10 million men were inducted into the Army as draftees.

In 1948, as cold war tensions increased, Congress enacted a peacetime draft. Its object was to ensure that American troop levels were sufficient to deter aggression and to meet sudden attack. During the period from 1948 to 1973, some 5 million young men were drafted, most during the Vietnam War. Vietnam sharpened opposition to the draft, however, and President Nixon's call for an all-volunteer Army won wide support. The draft ended in 1973, and registration was suspended two years later.

In 1980, following the Soviet invasion of Afghanistan, Congress reinstated registration but not the draft. The purpose of registration is to speed military mobilization in the event of an emergency. The law requires that all young men register on or about their 18th birthday. They may do so at any United States post office by filling out a brief form. Those who fail to register are subject to fine and possible imprisonment.

The United States today relies upon an all-volunteer Army. But the adequacy of a volunteer Army to meet the nation's defense needs has become an issue of public debate. The central issue focuses on how the Army can best maintain the necessary numbers of qualified men and women. For some, the answer to an all-volunteer Army of high quality lies in higher pay and more attractive benefits. Others, however, argue that numbers and quality can be met only by a return to the draft.

A division of United States Marines lands on the coast of Lebanon in 1983. The Marines—part of an international peacekeeping force—were to help reestablish order in Lebanon, which had been divided by a lengthy and violent civil war. What roles do the Marines fulfill in naval campaigns?

for personnel recruitment and weapons procurement, the planning and development of service programs, and combat readiness.

The United States Army The United States Army traces its origin to the American Continental Army of 1775. The Army has primary responsibility for military operations on land. Its basic combat units are infantry, armor, and artillery. The infantry remains the Army's backbone. Transported to the front lines by helicopter or personnel carrier, foot soldiers engage the enemy in direct small-arms combat in order to seize and hold ground. Armor is the cavalry of the modern army, except that the armored soldiers today move into battle in tanks instead of on horseback. Artillery operates the cannons of the battlefield and antiaircraft missile installations. But the Army is more than rifles and tanks. Less than 15 percent of the Army's personnel have ground combat functions. The vast majority are involved in the various support and service roles that include transport, mechanics, electronics, and clerical work.

The United States Navy Responsibility for military operations at sea and, with the Marine Corps, for the defense or seizure of naval bases belongs to the United States Navy. From its founding in 1775, when it had only a few small sailing vessels, the United States Navy has grown to a powerful force that includes hundreds of ships, as many as 6,000 aircraft, and more than 500,000 uniformed personnel. It has ships that are nuclear-powered, submarines that carry surface-to-air missiles, and aircraft carriers that exceed the length of three football fields.

As a division of the Department of the Navy, the United States Marine Corps provides combat troops to secure and fortify land bases in naval campaigns. Marine aviation provides close air support for ground forces as they make their landings on foreign shores.

The United States Air Force The defense of the United States depends heavily upon air power, and the United States Air Force provides the first line of defense against sudden enemy attack. The Air Force began as a part of the Army but became a

The United States maintains three military academies that train officers for service in the Army, the Navy, and the Air Force. In addition, ROTC programs at selected universities throughout the nation provide Army officer training for students. Shown below (counterclockwise, from top) are a cadet at the Air Force Academy in Colorado Springs, Colorado; cadets in formation at the United States Military Academy (Army) at West Point, New York; new recruits at the Naval Academy in Annapolis, Maryland; and ROTC students at Texas Christian University.

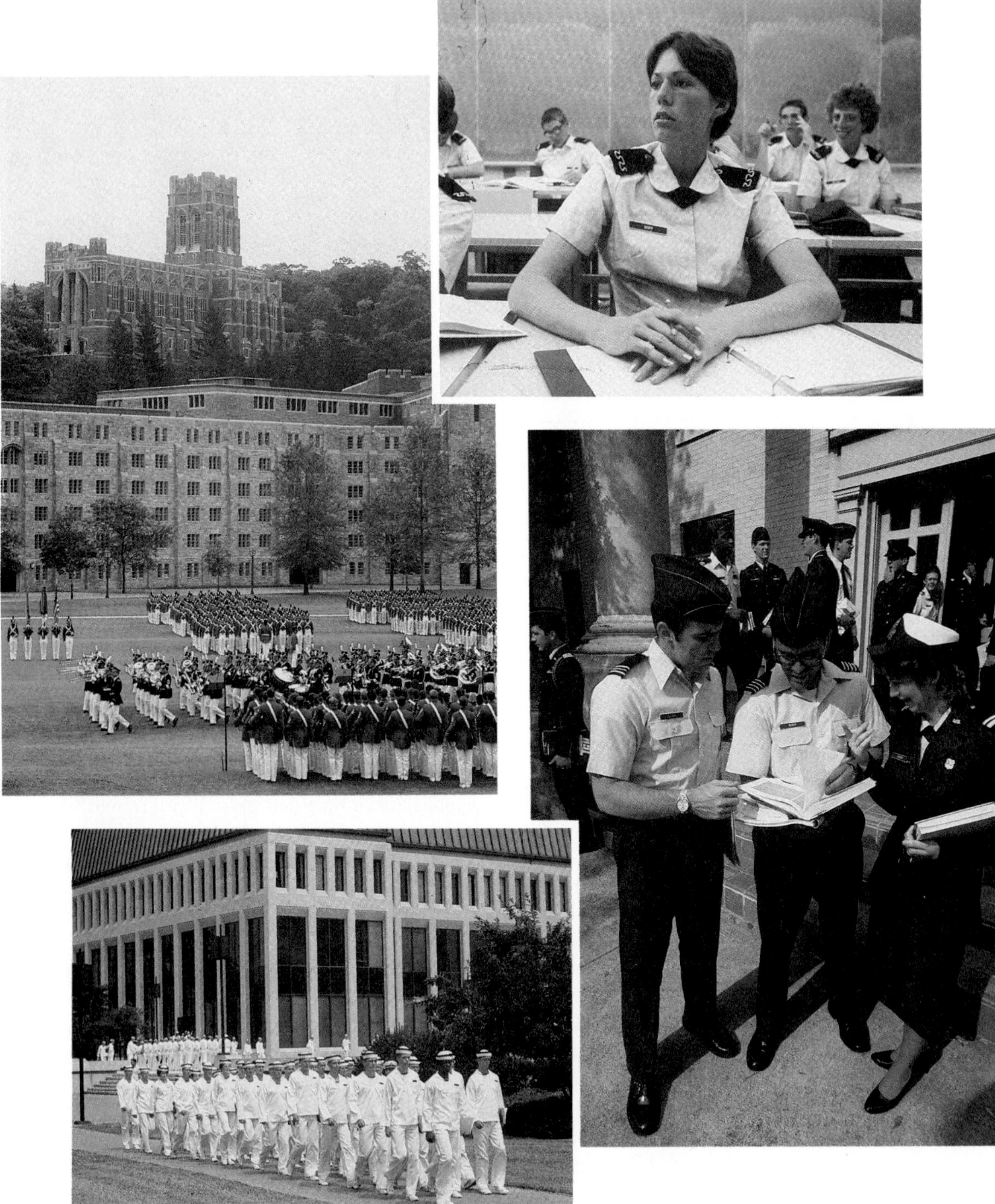

separate service in 1947. It has primary responsibility for military air operations. It conducts air reconnaissance missions, provides military air transportation, and gives air support to land and naval combat forces. The United States Air Force, especially the Strategic Air Command, is on constant alert to defend United States territory and to carry out, on a few minutes' notice, long-range attacks against enemy targets. Air power includes nearly 6,000 planes and nearly 2,000 high-technology missiles.

Nuclear weapons may be used only on the direct coded instruction of the President. Sometimes called the nuclear button, the code is designed to prevent the use of nuclear weapons except in response to a nuclear attack upon the United States. No nuclear weapons have been used since the United States dropped two atomic bombs on Japan in 1945.

The Specialized Defense Agencies

There are 12 specialized agencies in the Department of Defense. The oldest is the Defense Nuclear Agency (DNA). It was created in 1942 to direct the Manhattan Project, which developed the first atomic bomb. The DNA coordinates weapons development and testing with the Department of Energy and manages the nation's stockpile of nuclear weapons.

The Department of Defense operates an extensive intelligence network for gathering information about the military capabilities and intentions of foreign governments. In addition to the Defense Intelligence Agency, the Army, the Navy, and the Air Force each have their own intelligence units. The supersecret National Security Agency (NSA) is responsible for the making and breaking of codes and for electronic surveillance.

Section Check

---

1. Define: military-industrial complex
2. Identify: Joint Chiefs of Staff, United States Marine Corps, Strategic Air Command
3. Why was the Department of Defense created?
4. What controls does the President exercise over the military? What controls does Congress exercise?
5. Why did President Eisenhower warn against the military-industrial complex?
6. What is the first line of defense of the United States against sudden enemy attack, and how does that defense operate?

SUMMARY

Over the years, the foreign policy of the United States has shifted from one of isolationism to one of internationalism. Since the end of World War II, the main task confronting the United States has been how to protect its national interests and security while at the same time promoting international peace and cooperation. The United States was instrumental in the creation of the United Nations (UN). The United States also launched the Marshall Plan, which helped Western Europe regain economic and political stability, and it provided grants and loans to more than 100 countries.

The central figure in the making and the conduct of United States foreign policy is the President. The President is assisted in the making of foreign policy by the Secretary of State and the National Security Adviser. Congress also plays a major role in making foreign policy through Senate approval of treaties and personnel appointments, through its powers to declare war and to regulate international commerce, and especially through its control of government purse strings.

The Secretary of State is the highest-ranking member of the Cabinet. Most of the department's diplomatic work is handled through its five geographic bureaus—Africa, East Asia and the Pacific, Latin America, Europe, and the Near East and South Asia—and through its functional bureaus and embassies.

Several specialized agencies are involved in certain areas of foreign policy. The Central Intelligence Agency acquires and evaluates political, economic, and military information about other countries. In support of United States foreign policy objectives, it also carries out covert actions. Other specialized agencies include the United States Information Agency, the agency for International Development, the Peace Corps, and the Arms Control and Disarmament Agency.

The Department of Defense was formed in 1949 by combining the three Cabinet departments of the Army, the Navy, and the Air Force. According to the Constitution, ultimate control over the military rests in the civilian hands of the President and Congress. The Department of Defense is the largest Cabinet department. The Secretary of Defense, by law, must be a civilian. As head of the Department, the Secretary receives military advice from the Joint Chiefs of Staff. The latter are the highest-ranking officers of the Army, the Navy, the Marine Corps, and the Air Force.

Chapter 19 Review

Using Vocabulary

Answer the questions by using the meaning of each underlined term.

1. How do collective security agreements support the policy of containment?
2. What is the relationship between diplomacy and détente?
3. Why might a strong military-industrial complex favor a policy of deterrence?
4. What role do covert actions play in a cold war?

Understanding American Government

1. What are the two Cabinet departments most directly responsible for assisting the President in the conduct of foreign policy? Compare and contrast their spheres of operation.
2. What conditions brought about the cold war?
3. Why did the United States become involved in Korea and Vietnam?
4. What actions in recent years are outgrowths of the twin policies of containment and deterrence?
5. How has the role of the National Security Adviser changed since 1949? Why has there sometimes been a conflict between the Secretary of State and the National Security Adviser?
6. How did the Constitution create an "invitation to struggle" between the President and Congress for the control of foreign policy?
7. List four ways in which foreign aid benefits the United States conduct of foreign policy.
8. Why are the military departments of the Department of Defense headed by civilian Secretaries? Where do they obtain the military advice they need?

Extending Your Skills: Understanding the Chronology of Events

Reread "The Cold War" on pages 460–462 and the "Vietnam" insight on page 462. Then arrange the following events in the correct chronological order.

1. Vietnam divides into a Communist North and a non-Communist South.
2. President Kennedy sends about 16,000 American advisers to South Vietnam.
3. Winston Churchill declares that an "iron curtain" has divided Europe.
4. Saigon falls to the North Vietnamese forces.
5. The United States joins NATO.
6. President Johnson escalates military action against the Communists.
7. The United States applies a policy of containment for the first time.
8. The United States withdraws its forces from Vietnam.

Government and You

1. What are the advantages and disadvantages of the President receiving conflicting advice from such staff members as the National Security Adviser, the Secretary of State, and the Director of Central Intelligence?
2. What are the arguments for and against an all-volunteer Army? Which set of arguments do you feel carries the most weight?
3. Do you think the United States should continue to maintain its policies of containment and deterrence? Why or why not?
4. Do you agree that there should be civilian control over the military? Defend your position.

Activities

1. Research the amount of economic aid and the amount of military aid the United States has given to foreign countries in five-year periods since the end of World War II. Group the data on a geographic basis, i.e., Africa, East Asia and the Pacific, Latin America, Europe, and the Near East and South Asia. Then construct two series of bar graphs, one for each category of aid.
2. Find out what the requirements are for enlisting in the armed forces and what the pay scales and job opportunities are.
3. Interview someone who is participating in a college Reserve Officers' Training Corps (ROTC) program, and write a brief description of that person's experiences.

Chapter 20

The President, the United States, and the World

Modern science and technology have created so close a network of communication, transport, economic interdependence—and potential nuclear destruction—that planet earth, on its journey through infinity, has acquired the intimacy, the fellowship, and the vulnerability of a spaceship.

BARBARA WARD

CHAPTER OVERVIEW

1 **INFLUENCES SHAPING WORLD EVENTS**
Nationalism / Population Pressure / The Wealth and Poverty of Nations / Freedom in the World

2 **THE CLASH OF IDEOLOGIES**
Capitalism / Socialism / Communism

3 **THE UNITED NATIONS**
Organization / Membership

In President Harry S Truman's address to the United Nations in June 1945, he stated that the creation of the UN symbolized a "faith that war is not inevitable." The first UN meeting was held in San Francisco.

1 INFLUENCES SHAPING WORLD EVENTS

The analogy of the earth as a spaceship and the whole of humanity as its crew emphasizes the interdependence of people and nations. But nations in the world are separated by wide gaps in power, wealth, and ideology. It is the task of the world's leaders to bridge the wide gaps and divisions in order to promote peaceful cooperation.

Foremost among the world's leaders is the President of the United States. President Woodrow Wilson proposed the idea for a League of Nations in his Fourteen Points, but the Senate rejected his dream of United States participation in the international organization. Franklin D. Roosevelt laid the early groundwork for the United Nations (UN) through his conferences with Winston Churchill. Harry S Truman carried on the idea of a world organization dedicated to peace and became the first President of the United States to address the United Nations.

Since then other Presidents have addressed the UN and have carried out United States responsibilities in the world arena. They have appointed ambassadors to the United Nations and representatives to other international organizations. They have also appointed diplomatic officials to the many new countries that have joined the community of nations. In addition, they have participated in summit conferences with other world leaders.

Since 1945, the world community has undergone considerable change. Former imperial powers lost their vast colonial possessions as the forces of nationalism spread around the globe. New nations carved from these possessions have taken their places in the global community. Some have looked to the United States for political friendship. Others have firmly wedded themselves to Communism and the influence of the Soviet Union. Still others have found it to their advantage to court both the United States and the Soviet Union without tying themselves to either side. Today the people of the world are divided into about 170 nations. Great and small, powerful and weak, rich and poor, free and unfree—nations are the principal actors upon the stage of international politics.

Nations are often grouped for comparison into three "worlds." The First World includes the United States, Canada, Japan, and the advanced industrial nations of Europe. The nations of the First World are democratic and have essentially capitalist economies that are based on individual initiative and free enterprise. The Second World includes the Soviet Union and its bloc of Communist nations. Their governments are authoritarian, and their economies are controlled by the state. The Third World refers to the newly independent and developing nations of Africa, Asia, and Latin America. Having gained their independence from colonial rule, they seek to modernize and to develop economically and industrially. Most are ***nonaligned nations;*** that is, they are not allied with either the United States or the Soviet Union. Nonaligned nations seek to be an independent force in international affairs. Most are authoritarian, typically under military rule or the control of a single party. Only a few have constitutional and democratic governments with free elections and protected liberties.

The President, as the chief diplomat of the United States, is ultimately responsible for the nation's relations with the rest of the world. The President may represent the United States at high-level meetings with other nations and may conclude treaties or executive agreements with these nations. Another important responsibility of the President is the appointment of ambassadors, diplomats, and consular officers—subject, of course, to Senate approval. The President's appointment of a diplomat to a particular nation may deeply affect relations with that nation. Because the President is the leader of the most powerful democratic nation on earth, people of many countries look to the President to ease international tensions and maintain world peace.

Nationalism

Approximately half of the nations in the world today have achieved their independence since 1945. These new nations were once colonies of European empires. In 1776, the United States became the first major colony to break away from imperial rule.

Following the American Revolution, in the early decades of the nineteenth century, 20 nations of Central and South America won their independence from Spain and Portugal. After World War I, new nations emerged from the defeated empires in Europe and in the Middle East. In the years since World War II, more than 70 nations, mostly in Africa and Asia, have achieved independence. Some, such as India, Ghana, and Nigeria, won independence through peaceful political struggle. Others had to fight for independence in bitter colonial wars, as in Indochina, Indonesia, Algeria, and Angola.

The driving force behind the aspiration for independence is ***nationalism,*** the spirit that binds people together on the basis of a common identity in culture, language, or territory. Nationalism is expressed in loyalty to the nation-state. For the people within a nation, nationalism is a source of unity, pride, and purpose. For the global community, however, nationalism tends to emphasize the divisions and the differences between people.

INSIGHT

Presidential Appointments

Beginning with the administration of George Washington, the President has been in charge of the nation's relations with the rest of the world. The President's selection of an ambassador to a particular country, to the UN, or to another international organization often characterizes a concern of the administration. For example, the appointment of the first woman ambassador—to Denmark in 1949 by President Truman—and the appointment of the first black ambassador—to Luxembourg in 1965 by President Johnson—are representative of Truman's and Johnson's concerns about equal opportunities. Similarly, the appointment of a black—Andrew Young—as ambassador to the UN in the late 1970's reflected President Carter's concern for human rights in world affairs.

Many of the world's newly independent nations do not have a secure national identity. Their people are often divided by religion, language, or ethnic background and have little sense of loyalty to the nation-state. These divisions may give rise to separatist movements and even civil war. But problems of national unity are by no means limited to the new nations. Quebec separatism, for example, threatens the unity of Canada. Basque nationalists in Spain seek independence. Catholics and Protestants battle over the future of Northern Ireland.

On the other hand one of the great strengths of the United States is its diversity. Americans are of many races, religions, and ethnic backgrounds. But despite these differences, they are united as one nation. The President of the United States serves as a living symbol of the nation. As chief of state, the President functions as ceremonial head of the nation. This function of the Presidency contributes to American national unity.

Population Pressure

Nations vary in area and population. The United States ranks fourth in the size of its territory and its population. The largest nation is the Soviet Union. Its 8,649,500 square miles (22,402,000 square kilometers) make it more than twice the size of the United States. The most populous nation is China, with more than 1 billion people.

Altogether there are some 4.5 billion people in the world today. For thousands of years the world's population grew slowly, reaching 1 billion in the early 1800's. During the 1900's improvements in hygiene, nutrition, and medical care brought a decline in the death rate and a rapid growth in population. By 1930 the world's population had reached 2 billion. By 1975 it had topped 4 billion. In only 45 years the world's population had doubled. By the year 2000, estimates place the world's population at about 6 billion.

Per capita GNP—the total value of goods and services produced yearly by a nation, divided by that nation's population—is a statistical measure of a nation's wealth. Per capita GNP is often used to compare the wealth of various nations.

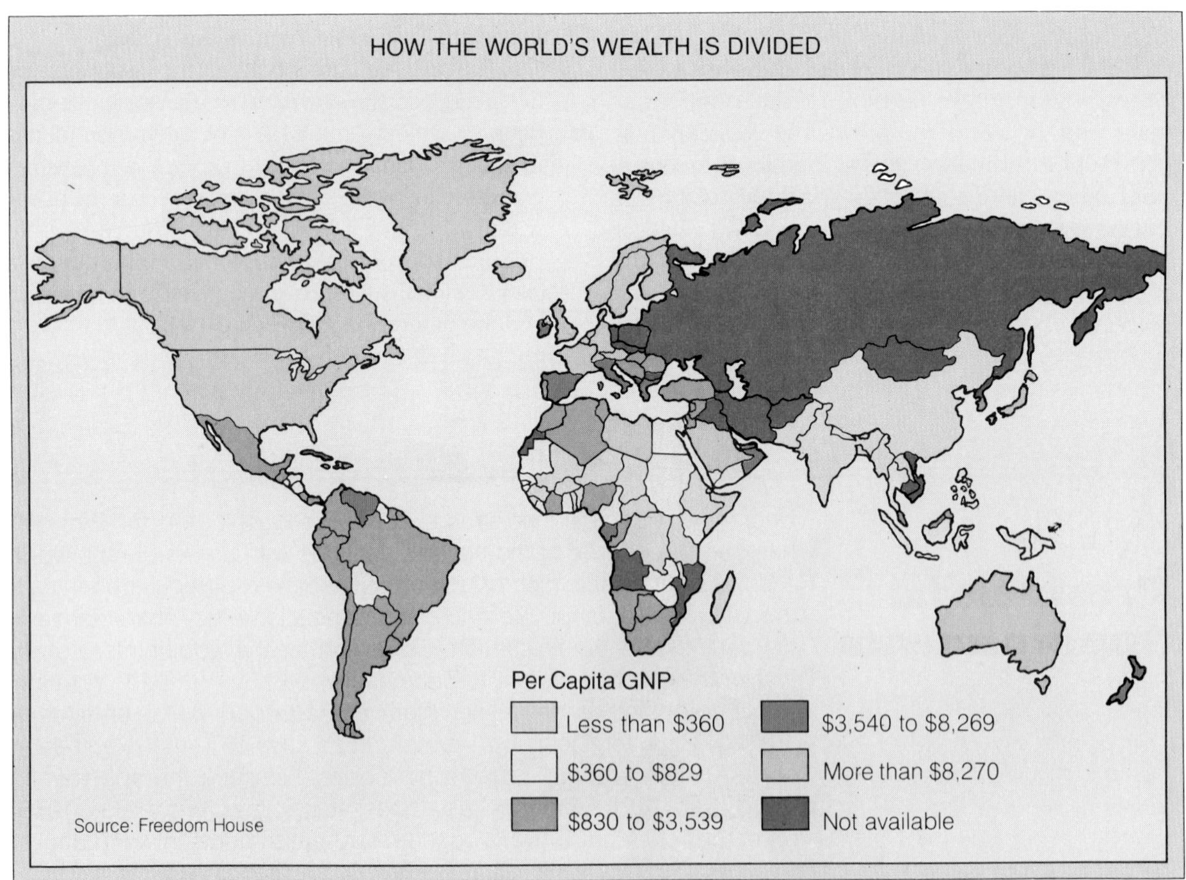

Population growth heightens competition for the world's scarce resources both between and within nations. The problem is especially critical in the developing nations of Africa, Asia, and Latin America, where more than 80 percent of the world's people live. These nations are already beset by poverty, severe unemployment, low productivity, and limited resources. Increases in population only hamper efforts to improve the quality of life. Every additional mouth to feed places a greater burden on food and energy supplies and on the environment. All too often, the hard-won gains of agricultural and industrial development go simply toward supporting more people. Population pressure spreads poverty and widens the gap between rich and poor.

As a world leader, the President is often called upon to aid developing nations combat the problems of hunger and population growth. The President, together with Cabinet heads and other advisers, frequently proposes additional monetary help for nations stricken by other problems as well. For example, in the early 1980's President Reagan promised additional assistance to African nations struck by a severe drought.

The Wealth and Poverty of Nations

The wealth of nations can be measured and compared in terms of per capita Gross National Product (GNP). The gap between rich and poor nations is enormous, and it grows wider each year. The chart on this page contrasts the per capita GNP of the United States with that of other selected nations.

Two thirds of the world's nations, embracing more than 70 percent of all humanity, have a per capita GNP of less than $2,000. Of these, 62 countries are in the lowest income group, having less than $500 per capita GNP. In these nations 700 million people are seriously undernourished, 550 million cannot read or write, and 220 million are without adequate shelter. Life expectancy averages 52 years, compared to about 73 years in the United States. One of every five children will not live to reach the age of five.

Despite these problems, many developing countries have made real progress. Industrial and food production have risen, health and nutrition have improved, and the number of children in schools has doubled. But rates of economic growth and social change tell only part of the whole story. Income and opportunity in most developing countries are unevenly distributed. Just as there is a gap between rich and poor nations, there is also a gap within the developing nations between the "haves" and the "have-nots." Often fabulous wealth can be found side-by-side with unbelievable poverty. Certain social groups or particular regions of a country may enjoy prosperity, while others sink deeper into poverty.

The harsh inequalities that exist in much of the developing world often lead to political unrest, violence, and revolution. In the 1980's the bipartisan Kissinger Commission, appointed by President Reagan, noted that political stability will not become a reality in Central America until the widespread poverty of the region is reduced. Widespread poverty is often a cause of political unrest in other regions of the world as well.

PER CAPITA GNP FOR SELECTED NATIONS

United Arab Emirates	$28,110
Kuwait	24,160
Switzerland	15,980
Sweden	13,730
West Germany	12,320
United States	11,590
France	11,200
Canada	10,180
Australia	10,070
Japan	9,020
United Kingdom	8,590
Italy	6,400
Argentina	2,590
Yugoslavia	2,540
Mexico	1,980
South Korea	1,490
Nigeria	870
El Salvador	670
Egypt	550
China	270
India	230
Zaire	200
Bangladesh	130
Laos	70

Source: World Bank Atlas

Many factors contribute to the vast differences in per capita GNP among nations. These factors include scarcity of resources, inefficient agricultural production, lack of highly trained workers, and little or no industrialization.

Freedom in the World

In its annual survey, Freedom House, a private organization, compares nations in terms of political rights and civil liberties. ***Political rights*** allow people to participate freely and effectively in choosing their own leaders or in voting directly on legislation. At the core of political rights are competitive elections, in which the majority can replace leaders and challenge their policies. ***Civil liberties*** include the freedoms of speech, assembly, religion, and the press; the right of privacy; the right to travel; and the right to a fair trial.

In the mid-1980's, more people than ever were living in countries that granted political rights and civil liberties to their citizens; yet these people constitute only 36 percent of the world's population.

Government troops march in the streets of Warsaw, Poland, to enforce martial law—military rule—during the summer of 1982. Under martial law, civil rights are suspended, military law replaces civil law, and military courts replace civil courts.

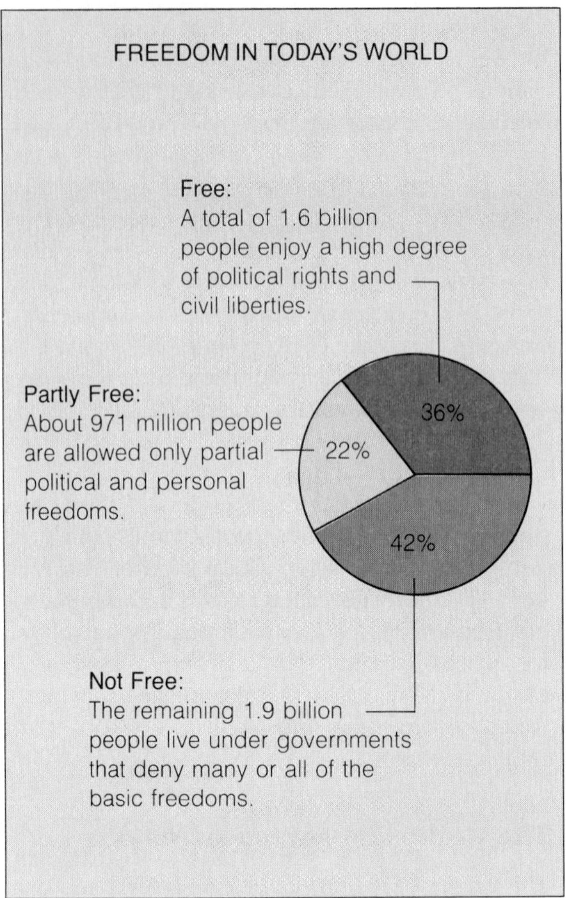

FREEDOM IN TODAY'S WORLD
Free:
A total of 1.6 billion people enjoy a high degree of political rights and civil liberties.
36%
Partly Free:
About 971 million people are allowed only partial political and personal freedoms.
22%
42%
Not Free:
The remaining 1.9 billion people live under governments that deny many or all of the basic freedoms.

Each year Freedom House conducts a survey of freedom. According to Freedom House, what percentage of the world's population is free? What percentage is not free?

The United States was founded on a commitment to individual human freedom. Liberty is its greatest strength. Its liberty is also a source of inspiration and encouragement to other nations and peoples throughout the world. Commitment to human rights is a fundamental element of United States foreign policy. In his 1976 inaugural address, President Jimmy Carter said, "Because we are free we can never be indifferent to the fate of freedom elsewhere."

The commitment of the United States to freedom goes back to its early history. One important example of this commitment is the Monroe Doctrine, in which President James Monroe warned European powers against further colonization in the Western Hemisphere. Later, in the early part of this century, President Woodrow Wilson in his Fourteen Points called for national self-determination for the peoples formerly under the domination of empires in Eastern Europe and the Middle East.

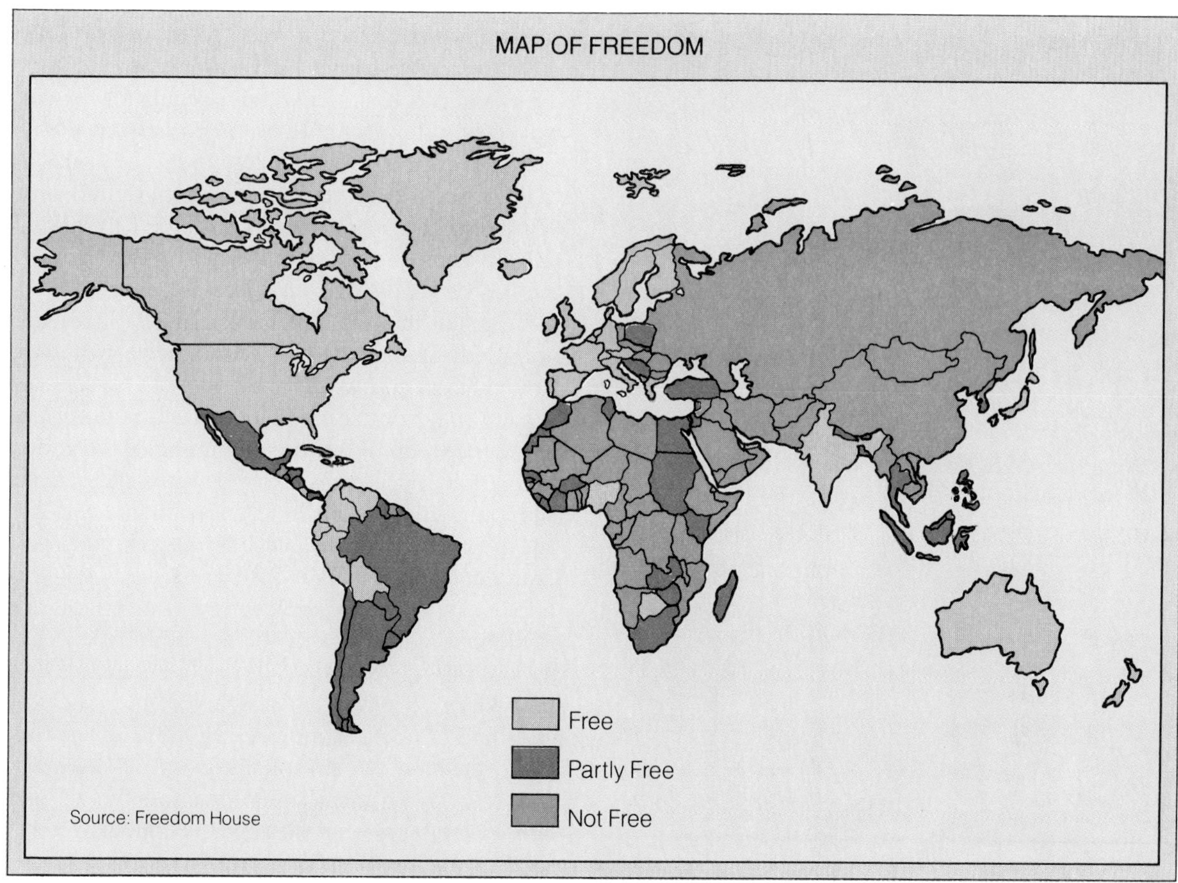

The method Freedom House uses to conduct its freedom survey requires ranking nations on a seven-point scale that measures political rights and civil liberties. A high ranking in political rights means that a nation has competing political parties and enforces political equality. A nation with a high civil-liberties ranking permits the freedoms of speech, press, assembly, and religion.

Section Check

1. Define: political rights, civil liberties
2. Identify: First World, Second World, Third World
3. What percentage of the world's nations have achieved their independence since 1945? In what two ways has independence been achieved?
4. What may happen when a nation does not have a secure national identity?
5. Why is population growth a serious world problem?
6. List five results of poverty in developing nations.
7. What percentage of the world's population enjoys political rights and civil liberties?

2 THE CLASH OF IDEOLOGIES

Ideology is a set of closely related beliefs that fit together into a political philosophy that expresses a way of life, values, and goals. People use ideology to explain the world and to change it. They use ideology, in particular, to explain political and economic systems. In the international marketplace of ideas, proponents of different ideologies compete for the hearts and minds of the world's peoples. The dominant ideologies today are capitalism, socialism, and Communism.

Capitalism

Both a political ideology and an economic system, ***capitalism*** is based on private ownership and competition in a market economy. In the market, based upon supply and demand, buyers and sellers

Adam Smith, the Scottish philosopher, author, teacher, and economist, is regarded as the founder of modern capitalist philosophy. What was Smith's view of the government's role in a nation's economy?

come together in exchanges for profit. The market system developed in Europe and the United States and matured in the late eighteenth and early nineteenth centuries. The philosopher Adam Smith examined the nature of the capitalist system in his influential book *An Inquiry into the Nature and Causes of the Wealth of Nations,* published in 1776. Smith wrote that individuals who were free to choose their own economic activity would be eager to get ahead and would thus strive to produce better goods and provide better services. Smith said that competition would determine what was produced, ensure quality, establish just wages and prices, and stimulate enterprise and invention. In this way, he said, the "invisible hand" of the market would operate in the interest of the whole society.

In Smith's view the role of government should be minimal, providing only the basic conditions for free competition. The government should maintain law and order, defend the nation against foreign attack, enforce contracts, and protect private property. Within these limits, government should allow the market to function without regulation or control. This system came to be called ***laissez-faire,*** a French expression meaning "to let do"—that is, to let people do as they choose. Smith's philosophy of unfettered capitalism was grounded in individualism. Thus, it embodied the notion that "government is best which governs least."

Capitalism fueled the Industrial Revolution and provided the incentives for economic growth in the United States and Western Europe. But laissez-faire capitalism never existed in the pure form described by Adam Smith. From the beginning of the Industrial Revolution, especially in the United States, major economic groups looked to government to protect and promote their special interests. In time, government stepped in to impose tariffs, break up monopolies, provide subsidies, regulate wages and working conditions, and correct the imbalances of the business cycle. Today, all capitalist countries have ***mixed economies,*** in which private ownership and market competition are regulated extensively by government. Most capitalist countries have also adopted various measures to promote human welfare, including programs for public education, social security, national health insurance, and subsidized housing.

Through the years Presidents have worked to preserve capitalism in the United States. At various times in the nation's history the President has called for legislation extending government protection to business or decreasing certain government regulations. These and other measures reflect the Presidents' concern for the United States capitalistic economic system.

Socialism

As an ideology, ***socialism*** opposes the private ownership of property and the capitalist system. Socialism seeks to replace the ownership of private property with a system of public ownership. In this system all or most of the means of production and distribution are owned by society as a whole and are administered by the state for the good of all. In place of competition for profit, socialism calls for cooperation and social responsibility. Its goal is equality, and its promise is to provide for the basic material needs of the people. Approaches to socialism vary from the peaceful and democratic ideas of utopian and Christian socialists to the violence of revolutionary Marxists.

Under ***democratic socialism,*** free elections determine the government's role in the economy. Democratic socialism seeks a gradual, evolutionary extension of public control over such major sectors of the economy as banking, communications, transportation, steel, and coal. Originally, public control was to be achieved by ***nationalization,*** with the government taking over ownership and management of private companies in key industries. Nationalization of industry, however, has generally proven inefficient, and the Social Democratic parties of Western Europe have rejected massive nationalization. Instead, they have combined private ownership of major industries with extensive government planning, regulation, and control of the economy. High taxes support an array of welfare and social services that are used as a means to equalize incomes. Several countries, notably Great Britain, France, West Germany, Norway, Sweden, and Denmark, have moved toward democratic socialism. But their mixed economies are more properly described as capitalist welfare states.

Most Third World nations are socialist, at least in theory and rhetoric if not always in practice. In the developing countries that are predominantly agricultural, farming generally remains in private hands. Most Third World governments, however, have control over modern industry and assume primary responsibility for economic development.

Clement Attlee served as the Prime Minister of Great Britain from 1945 until 1951. As Great Britain's first socialist Prime Minister, he brought key industries under state control and introduced a national welfare system.

Karl Marx, a German social scientist, believed that capitalist societies would be overthrown by the workers. Communism, as envisioned by Marx, does not exist.

Communism

The ideological foundations of ***Communism*** rest upon the writings of Karl Marx. In his *Communist Manifesto,* published in 1848, Marx called upon the workers of the world to unite and to throw off the chains of capitalism. In the book *Das Kapital,* Marx's major work, he developed his political and economic theories.

Marx believed that the ***proletariat,*** or working class, is exploited by the owners of private property in the capitalist system. Marx felt that this exploitation occurs because capitalists do not pay workers full value for the labor by which they produce goods. As a result, workers cannot afford to buy goods. This causes capitalists to reduce production and employment, which eventually results in a depression. Marx predicted that repeated depressions inevitably would bring about the collapse of the capitalist system. The ***class struggle*** between those with economic power and those without it would intensify, and after a time, the workers would rise up in revolution. They would seize the ***means of production***—land and factories—and establish a ***dictatorship of the proletariat*** to achieve the ideals of socialism.

Marx assumed that after the revolution, the national wealth would be shared among all the

The All-Union Communist Party Congress met in December 1982 to commemorate the 60th anniversary of the founding of the Soviet Union. At the rear of the stage is a sculpture of V. I. Lenin, founder of Soviet Communist ideology. How does the Communism practiced in the Soviet Union differ from that envisioned by Marx?

workers. He thought that once a [illegible]ssless society was achieved government would wither away and true Communism would emerge.

The Communism practiced in the Soviet Union is very different from the Communism envisioned by Marx. In the Soviet Union the state, rather than withering away, has grown ever more powerful. Rather than a government by the workers, the Soviet Union is a dictatorship under the control of the top leaders of the Communist party. Instead of a classless society, there is a new class of party officials and government bureaucrats who command both power and prestige. The Soviet government dominates almost every aspect of the lives of the people and denies them the political rights and civil liberties Americans take for granted.

Today nearly a third of the world's population is under Communist rule. But the Communist world is itself divided. From the Russian Revolution in 1917 until 1945, Moscow was the command center of the international Communist movement. In 1948, however, Yugoslavia broke from the grip of the Soviet Union. China also charted a separate course following Mao Zedong's version of Communist doctrine. By the early 1960's China and the Soviet Union were in open conflict.

Section Check

1. Define: capitalism, laissez-faire, mixed economies, socialism, democratic socialism, nationalization, proletariat, class struggle, means of production, dictatorship of the proletariat
2. Identify: Adam Smith, *An Inquiry into the Nature and Causes of the Wealth of Nations,* Karl Marx, *The Communist Manifesto, Das Kapital*
3. What is the "invisible hand" of the market, and how does it operate in a capitalist society?
4. According to Adam Smith, what is the role of government in a capitalist society?
5. What welfare programs do the governments of capitalist countries provide today?
6. Why have the Social Democratic parties of Western Europe rejected massive nationalization? What has taken its place?
7. What type of government did Marx foresee after the workers' revolution? What types of government actually exist in Communist nations today?

3 THE UNITED NATIONS

"We the peoples of the United Nations..." These are the opening words of the United Nations Charter, drawn up in San Francisco in 1945 and ratified by 51 nations. The charter serves as the constitution for the United Nations Organization. It sets forth the basic purposes of the UN:

- To maintain international peace and security through effective, collective measures and through peaceful settlement of disputes;
- To develop friendly relations among nations based on respect for the principles of equal rights and self-determination of peoples;
- To achieve cooperation in solving international economic, social, cultural, and humanitarian problems, and in promoting human rights for all without distinction as to race, sex, language or religion; and
- To be a center for harmonizing the action of nations in achieving these ends.

The UN was founded to "save succeeding generations from the scourge of war." It is an international community dedicated to peace, justice, and progress for all humanity. The UN provides a place where national leaders can talk out their problems instead of fighting over them. Through its various agencies, the UN has contributed to improving the education, health, and welfare of people throughout the world.

Organization

The United Nations is an organization of sovereign nations. The sole exceptions are the Byelorussian and Ukranian Soviet Socialist Republics, which are part of the Soviet Union and which were admitted to the UN through a political compromise when the UN was founded. Since the United Nations is not a world government, it does not legislate in the sense of enacting laws that nations must accept. Instead, it provides the machinery to help solve disputes and to deal with a range of problems of concern to people throughout the world. The UN has six main organs: the General Assembly, the Security Council, the Economic and Social Council, the Trusteeship Council, the International Court of Justice, and the Secretariat (see page 494). Except for the International Court of Justice, which sits at The Hague in the Netherlands, all are based in New York City.

The General Assembly The General Assembly is the UN's central organ. All member-nations of the UN are represented in it, and each of

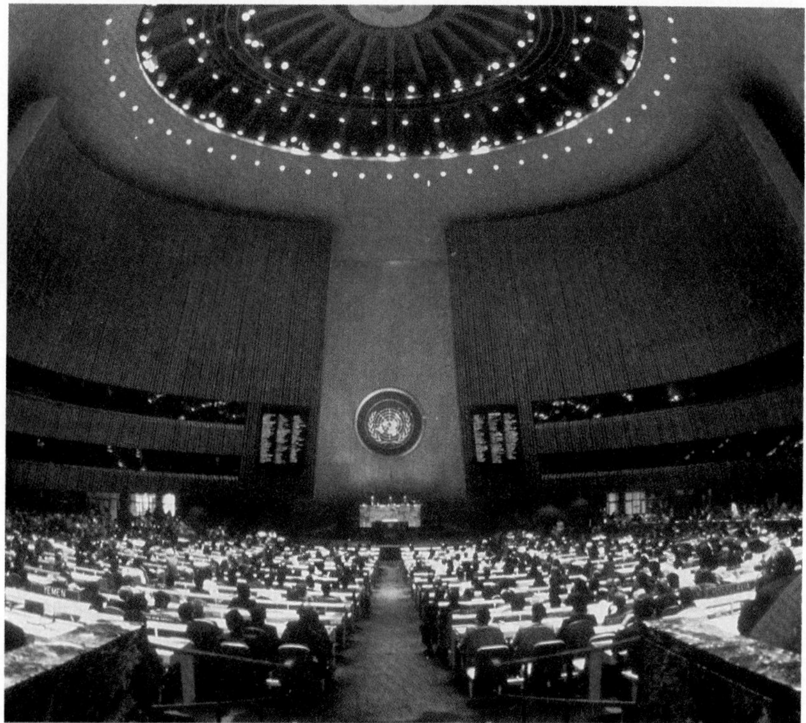

A regular session of the UN General Assembly meets at its headquarters in New York. Each regular session usually lasts about three months. Emergency sessions of the assembly may be called by the Secretary-General when crises occur.

MEMBERSHIP OF THE UNITED NATIONS

Charter Members

Argentina
Australia
Belgium
Bolivia
Brazil
Byelorussian S.S.R.
Canada
Chile
China*
Colombia
Costa Rica
Cuba
Czechoslovakia
Denmark
Dominican Republic
Ecuador
Egypt
El Salvador
Ethiopia
France
Greece
Guatemala
Haiti
Honduras
India
Iran
Iraq
Lebanon
Liberia
Luxembourg
Mexico
Netherlands
New Zealand
Nicaragua
Norway
Panama
Paraguay
Peru
Philippines
Poland
Saudi Arabia
South Africa
Syria
Turkey
Ukrainian S.S.R.
Union of Soviet Socialist Republics
United Kingdom
United States
Uruguay
Venezuela
Yugoslavia

Admitted Since 1945

Afghanistan
Albania
Algeria
Angola
Antigua and Barbuda
Austria
Bahamas
Bahrain
Bangladesh
Barbados
Belize
Benin
Bhutan
Botswana
Bourkina Fasso (Upper Volta)
Brunei
Bulgaria
Burma
Burundi
Cameroon
Cape Verde Islands
Central African Republic
Chad
Comoros
Congo
Cyprus
Democratic Kampuchea (Cambodia)
Democratic Yemen (South)
Djibouti
Dominica
Equatorial Guinea
Fiji
Finland
Gabon
Gambia
German Democratic Republic (East Germany)
Germany, Federal Republic of (West Germany)
Ghana
Grenada
Guinea
Guinea-Bissau
Guyana
Hungary
Iceland
Indonesia
Ireland
Israel
Italy
Ivory Coast
Jamaica
Japan
Jordan
Kenya
Kuwait
Laos
Lesotho
Libya
Madagascar
Malawi
Malaysia
Maldives
Mali
Malta
Mauritania
Mauritius
Mongolia
Morocco
Mozambique
Nepal
Niger
Nigeria
Oman
Pakistan
Papua-New Guinea
Portugal
Qatar
Romania
Rwanda
Saint Christopher and Nevis
Saint Lucia
Saint Vincent and the Grenadines
Samoa
São Tomé and Principe
Senegal
Seychelles
Sierra Leone
Singapore
Solomon Islands
Somalia
Spain
Sri Lanka
Sudan
Suriname
Swaziland
Sweden
Tanzania
Thailand
Togo
Trinidad and Tobago
Tunisia
Uganda
United Arab Emirates
Vanuatu
Vietnam
Yemen (North)
Zaire
Zambia
Zimbabwe

*In 1971, the General Assembly voted to seat the People's Republic of China in place of the Republic of China (Taiwan).

Source: The United Nations

the member-nations (listed on page 492) has one vote. The General Assembly holds its regular session from mid-September to mid-December each year. Special or emergency sessions are held when necessary. When the General Assembly is not in session, committees carry on its work.

The General Assembly has been called a "town meeting of the world." It is an international forum where nations can discuss world problems and make recommendations on all matters within the scope of the UN Charter. For many years after 1945, when the UN was founded, the United States had the most influence in the General Assembly and could count on member-nations to support the American position. As the UN gained new members from nations formed from former colonial empires, voting power shifted to a Third World majority. The General Assembly today is a major forum for the ***North-South dialogue*** between the non-Communist industrialized nations, most of which are in the Northern Hemisphere, and the developing nations of the Third World, most of which lie south of the industrial belt. The principal goal of the Third World majority is a new economic order, designed to reduce the gap between the rich and the poor nations of the world.

Tractors and other equipment supplied by the UN Development Program improve the efficiency of workers in Nigeria. Many African countries rely on UN agencies for technical and economic assistance.

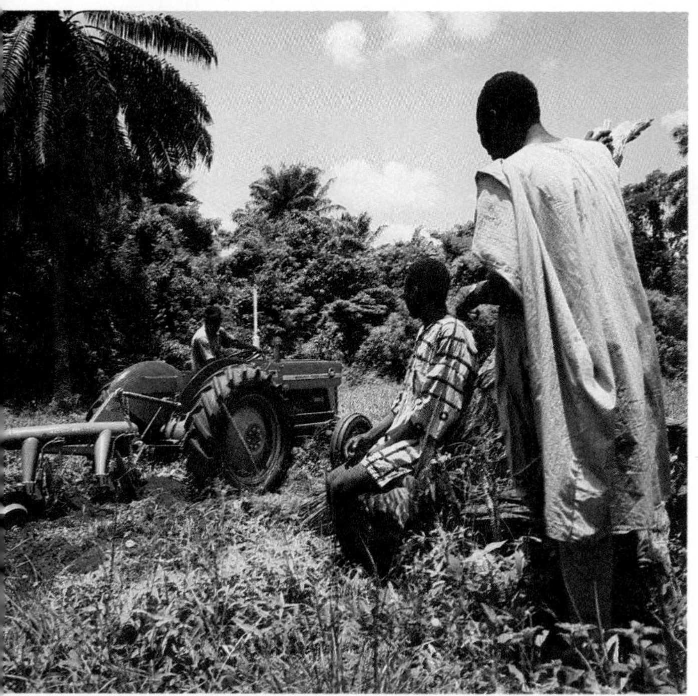

The General Assembly has no power to enforce any of its decisions; however, General Assembly recommendations are often influential in forming world opinion. The General Assembly ordinarily adopts its decisions by a simple majority vote, but on important questions it requires a two-thirds majority.

The General Assembly sets the policies and programs of the United Nations. It has general supervisory control over UN organs and receives annual reports on their activities. Its financial power is exercised through control over the UN budget and the assessments levied on member-nations.

The General Assembly chooses all members of the Economic and Social Council, the elective members of the Security Council, and the members of the Trusteeship Council. Along with the Security Council, the General Assembly participates in the selection of judges for the International Court of Justice. It also has a major say in the appointment of the Secretary-General of the United Nations.

The Security Council The UN Charter gives the Security Council primary responsibility for maintaining world peace and security. The UN's founders did so on the assumption that the Great Powers—the United States, the Soviet Union, the United Kingdom, France, and China, which had been allies in World War II—would cooperate for the preservation of peace. Yet conflict between the Western democracies and the Soviet Union has characterized the years of the cold war.

The Security Council has 15 members. Five nations—the United States, France, the United Kingdom, China, and the Soviet Union—are permanent members of the Security Council. The other 10 members are elected by the General Assembly for two-year terms. They choose 5 each year, taking geographical distribution into account. The presidency of the Council is held by each member in turn for one month.

Under the Charter, members of the United Nations have agreed to carry out the decisions of the Security Council, which require the support of at least nine members. On matters of substance, a unanimous decision of all permanent members is required. Thus a "no" vote by any permanent member can prevent a Security Council action. This veto power has been used more than 100 times, most often by the Soviet Union, and has reduced the effectiveness of the Council in resolving international conflicts. The Uniting for Peace Resolution, adopted in 1950, empowers the General Assembly to deal with a threat to peace when the Security

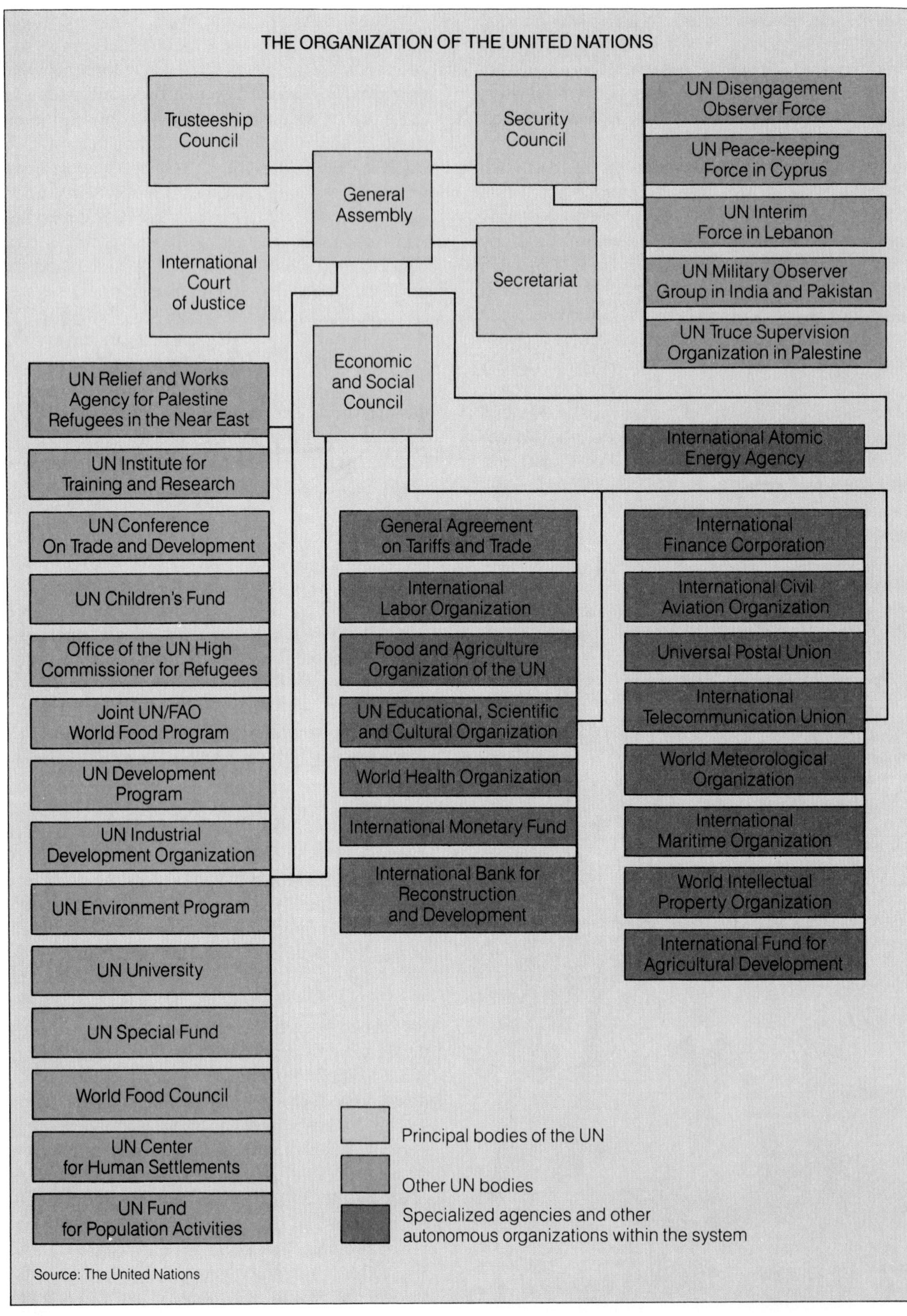
THE ORGANIZATION OF THE UNITED NATIONS
Trusteeship Council
General Assembly
Security Council
International Court of Justice
Secretariat
UN Disengagement Observer Force
UN Peace-keeping Force in Cyprus
UN Interim Force in Lebanon
UN Military Observer Group in India and Pakistan
UN Truce Supervision Organization in Palestine
Economic and Social Council
UN Relief and Works Agency for Palestine Refugees in the Near East
UN Institute for Training and Research
UN Conference On Trade and Development
UN Children's Fund
Office of the UN High Commissioner for Refugees
Joint UN/FAO World Food Program
UN Development Program
UN Industrial Development Organization
UN Environment Program
UN University
UN Special Fund
World Food Council
UN Center for Human Settlements
UN Fund for Population Activities
International Atomic Energy Agency
General Agreement on Tariffs and Trade
International Labor Organization
Food and Agriculture Organization of the UN
UN Educational, Scientific and Cultural Organization
World Health Organization
International Monetary Fund
International Bank for Reconstruction and Development
International Finance Corporation
International Civil Aviation Organization
Universal Postal Union
International Telecommunication Union
World Meteorological Organization
International Maritime Organization
World Intellectual Property Organization
International Fund for Agricultural Development
Principal bodies of the UN
Other UN bodies
Specialized agencies and other autonomous organizations within the system
Source: The United Nations

The UN Security Council held many special sessions between 1979 and 1981 in an attempt to settle the Iranian-American hostage crisis. The Security Council's repeated condemnation of Iran was ineffective in resolving the crisis, as were attempts to enforce economic sanctions against Iran. Through what other means may the Security Council attempt to enforce its decisions?

Council is unable to act because of a veto. No nation has veto power in the General Assembly.

When a threat to peace is brought before the Security Council, first it usually asks the parties involved to reach an agreement by peaceful means. In some cases, the Council requests the Secretary-General to investigate and report on the situation. The Council may undertake its own investigation and seek to mediate a settlement of the dispute. If fighting breaks out, the Council tries to secure a cease-fire and bring the parties to the negotiating table. The Council can send peacekeeping units to troubled areas to reduce tensions and keep opposing forces apart. It can also enforce its decisions by imposing ***economic sanctions,*** or collective boycotts and trade restrictions, or by ordering collective military action, as it did in Korea in 1950.

The commitment of armed forces under UN command to repel aggression by North Korea was possible because the Soviet Union at that time was boycotting the Security Council. When the Soviet Union, armed with its veto power, returned to block further action by the Council, the General Assembly took responsibility for Korea under the Uniting for Peace Resolution brought by the United States. The Resolution has since provided the basis for UN peacekeeping operations in the Middle East.

The Economic and Social Council The 54 members of the Economic and Social Council are elected by the General Assembly. The Council coordinates the work of the specialized agencies and bodies of the United Nations system, such as the World Health Organization (WHO) and the Food and Agricultural Organization (FAO). The Economic and Social Council promotes the worldwide observance of human rights, improvement in the status of women, and an end to discrimination against minorities. Under its umbrella, five regional commissions foster economic and social cooperation in Africa, Asia and the Pacific, Europe, Latin America, and the Middle East.

The Trusteeship Council The international trusteeship system was established to administer the former colonies of Germany, Italy, and Japan. The UN Trusteeship Council ensured that the governments responsible for the territories took adequate steps to prepare them for self-government and, ultimately, independence. The Trusteeship Council has sought to conduct negotiations between South Africa and Angola over the status of Namibia, the last major trust territory theoretically under UN auspices. The UN has worked to end South Africa's administrative control of Namibia.

The International Court of Justice Fifteen judges sit on the International Court of Justice, also known as the World Court. They are elected by the UN General Assembly and the Security Council for terms of nine years. No two judges may be from the same country.

The UN Charter calls for the peaceful settlement of disputes in accordance with principles of international law. But recourse to the Court as an agency for dispensing justice is optional. Since its creation

SPECIALIZED UNITED NATIONS AGENCIES

Food and Agriculture Organization (FAO) Seeks improved production and distribution of food and agricultural products, promotes improved nutrition, and provides food for famine relief	International Civil Aviation Organization (ICAO) Sets international air safety standards and operates navigation services	UN Education, Scientific and Cultural Organization (UNESCO) Promotes mutual understanding among peoples and the free flow of ideas, expansion of education and literacy, advancement of science and the arts.
Inter-Governmental Maritime Consultative Organization (IMCO) Promotes international cooperation on shipping, maritime safety, and navigation	International Labor Organization (ILO) Promotes full employment and improvement in working conditions throughout the world	Universal Postal Union (UPU) Unites countries throughout the world in the reciprocal delivery of mail and promotes improved services between nations
International Bank for Reconstruction and Development (World Bank) Provides member countries with loans and technical assistance to advance economic development	International Monetary Fund (IMF) Promotes monetary cooperation and stable currency exchange rates	World Health Organization (WHO) Works to control disease, train health workers, and advance medical research
International Development Association (IDA) World Bank affiliate; makes loans on liberal terms to promote development in poor countries	International Telecommunication Union (ITU) Coordinates and regulates international radio, telegraph, telephone, and space telecommunications	World Intellectual Property Organization (WIPO) Promotes protection of such intellectual property as inventions and literary and artistic works
International Finance Corporation (IFC) World Bank affiliate; promotes private enterprise in developing countries		World Meteorological Organization (WMO) Promotes international cooperation in the establishment of a worldwide network of weather stations and the rapid exchange of information on weather conditions

Specialized UN agencies are separate intergovernmental organizations that are linked to the UN through special agreements and through the UN Economic and Social Council. Which UN agencies deal with financial and monetary issues?

in 1945, however, the Court has decided fewer than 50 cases. Unless required by special treaty provisions, a country does not have to take part in a case before the Court. But a country that agrees to take a case before the Court must accept the Court's judgment as final. Less than half of the UN members have agreed to accept jurisdiction of the Court in legal disputes. In addition to deciding cases, the Court gives advisory opinions on legal questions at the request of UN agencies.

The Secretariat The Secretariat is the administrative arm of the UN. The 14,000 staff members of the Secretariat, who are selected on the basis of personal competence and geographic distribution, are drawn from more than 130 countries.

The Secretary-General heads the Secretariat and is the chief administrative officer of the United Nations. The Secretary-General is chosen by the General Assembly upon the recommendation of the Security Council and serves a five-year term. Among

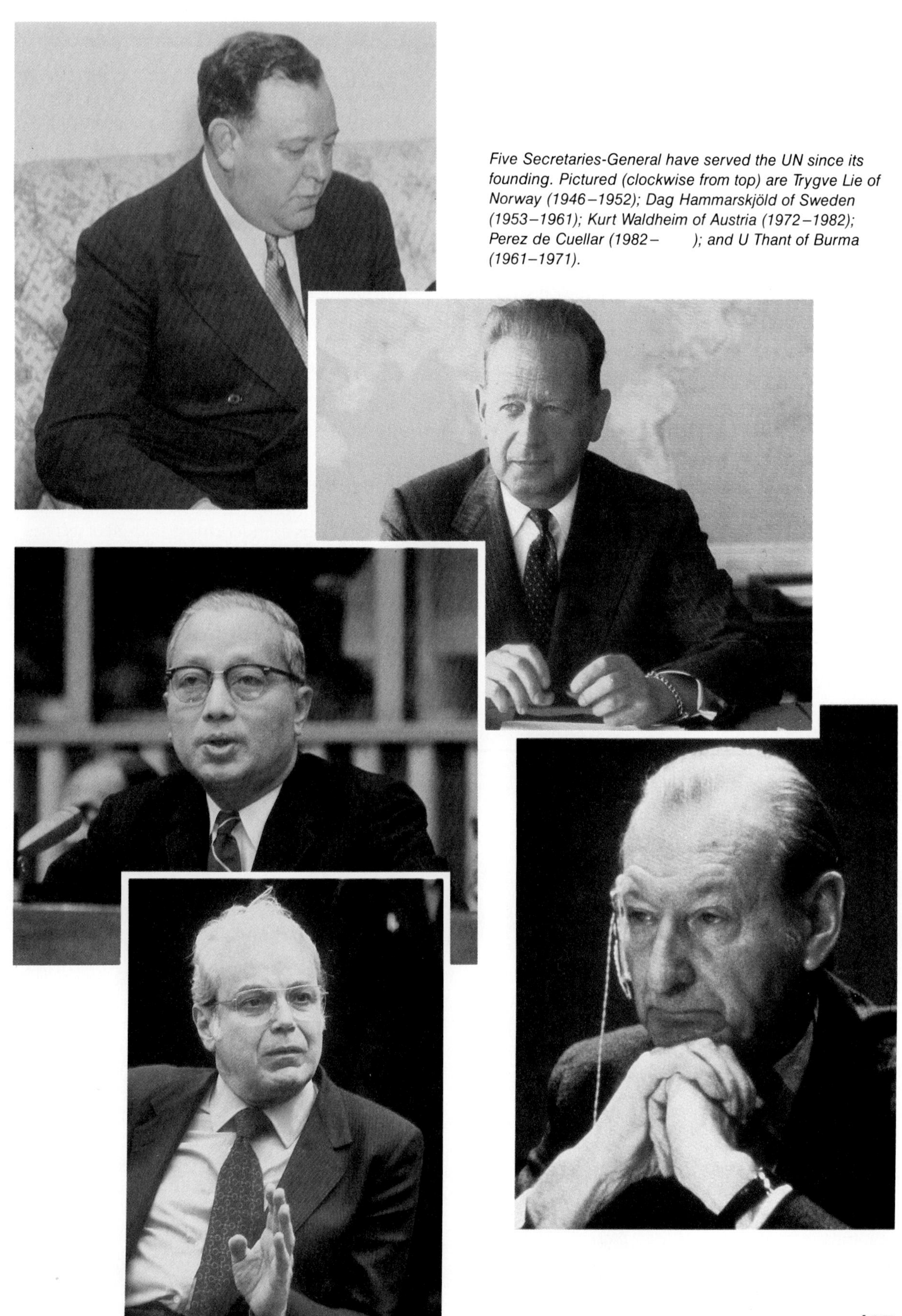

Five Secretaries-General have served the UN since its founding. Pictured (clockwise from top) are Trygve Lie of Norway (1946–1952); Dag Hammarskjöld of Sweden (1953–1961); Kurt Waldheim of Austria (1972–1982); Perez de Cuellar (1982–); and U Thant of Burma (1961–1971).

INSIGHT

Financing the United Nations

All members of the UN share in its expenses. The General Assembly assesses each member-nation, using its national income as a basis for its ability to pay. The General Assembly levies higher assessments on wealthier countries and lower assessments on poorer countries. The United States is the largest contributor, but a few countries pay more in terms of per capita contributions. In addition to paying the mandatory assessments, many countries make voluntary contributions to various UN programs and funds. The specialized agencies of the United Nations, such as the World Health Organization (WHO) and the United Nations Educational, Scientific, and Cultural Organization (UNESCO), have separate budgets and control their own purse strings. All of their funding comes from members' voluntary contributions.

other functions, the Secretary-General may bring to the attention of the Security Council any matter that threatens world peace and security. The role of the Secretary-General has expanded over the years, and the position has become one of real leadership. Since 1945, the Secretaries-General of the UN have played an important part in directing UN peacekeeping operations throughout the world and in mediating international disputes.

Membership

When the UN was founded, more than 70 of its present members were under colonial rule. In many cases, the UN helped these nations to achieve independence. Today, more than 155 independent nations are members of the UN. New members are admitted on the recommendation of the Security Council and by two thirds of the General Assembly. The General

The sculpture "Let Us Beat Swords into Ploughshares" stands outside UN Headquarters in New York City. The sculpture, a gift from the Soviet Union to the UN, was installed in 1959. It symbolizes humankind's determination to put an end to war and to turn the elements of destruction to peaceful purposes.

Assembly may also suspend or expel any nation by a two-thirds vote if the Security Council recommends such action.

UN members range in population from China, with more than 1 billion people, to Seychelles, with only 60,000. Nearly every independent nation in the world today belongs to the UN. The notable exceptions are Switzerland, the Republic of China (Taiwan), North Korea, and South Korea.

The delegates to the United Nations speak many languages. But the UN avoids a babel of tongues by translating speeches and documents into six official languages: Arabic, Chinese, English, French, Russian, and Spanish. The administrative staff of the UN Secretariat uses English and French in most of its daily work.

Section Check

1. Define: North-South dialogue, economic sanctions
2. Identify: United Nations Charter, General Assembly, Security Council, Economic and Social Council, International Court of Justice, Trusteeship Council, Secretary-General
3. What are the four basic purposes of the United Nations?
4. How does the UN avoid a babel of tongues in its daily operations?
5. How has the General Assembly changed since the UN was founded? What effect has this change had?
6. Why was the Security Council given primary responsibility for maintaining world peace and security? Why has it not always succeeded in keeping the peace?
7. Why has the usefulness of the International Court of Justice been limited?

SUMMARY

Nations are the principal actors in international politics. They are often grouped for comparison into three worlds. The First World includes advanced industrial nations, which are democratic and have essentially capitalist economies. The Second World includes the Communist nations, which are authoritarian and have state-controlled economies. The Third World includes developing nations, many of which have authoritarian governments.

Since 1945, about half of the nations in the world, driven by the forces of nationalism, have achieved independence from colonial rule. Some nations fought for independence; others achieved it through peaceful political struggle. Many of the world's nations do not have a secure national identity, which sometimes leads to separatist movements or civil war.

Three economic ideologies dominate the world scene: capitalism, socialism, and Communism. Capitalism is based on private ownership and competition in a market economy. Its principles were described by Adam Smith in *An Inquiry into the Nature and Causes of the Wealth of Nations.* Although Smith favored a minimal role for government, all capitalist countries today have extensive government regulation of their economies. They can be considered to have mixed economies. Many have adopted such welfare measures as public education, social security, national health insurance, and subsidized housing.

Socialism seeks to replace private property and competition for profit with public ownership. Socialism includes democratic socialism, in which free elections determine the government's role in the economy.

The third ideology is Communism. Communism is based on the writings of Karl Marx, especially *The Communist Manifesto* and *Das Kapital.* Marx believed that a class struggle would result in the establishment of a dictatorship of the proletariat and that government would eventually wither away. In practice, the governments of Communist nations are strongly authoritarian.

The United Nations was organized in 1945. It has helped settle various international disputes, provided a forum for discussion of international problems, and helped improve the education, the health, and the welfare of people throughout the world.

Two of the most important organs of the UN are the General Assembly and the Security Council. The General Assembly has more than 155 member-nations. In recent years it has been a major forum for the North-South dialogue between the First World and the Third World. The Security Council has 5 permanent members and 10 rotating members. It is generally concerned with preventing war by mediating disputes, sending peacekeeping units to troubled areas, applying economic sanctions, or ordering collective military action. Other important organs of the UN are the Economic and Social Council, the Trusteeship Council, and the International Court of Justice.

Chapter 20 Review

Using Vocabulary

Answer the questions below by using the meaning of each underlined term.

1. According to Adam Smith, what is the relationship between laissez-faire and capitalism?
2. According to Karl Marx, why does the class struggle lead to the dictatorship of the proletariat?
3. What role does nationalization play in democratic socialism?
4. What kinds of discussions about political rights or sanctions might the North-South dialogue include?

Understanding American Government

1. What are some positive aspects of nationalism? What are some negative aspects?
2. Compare the First World, the Second World, and the Third World with respect to each of the following: (a) typical form of government; (b) typical economic system; (c) degree of industrialization; (d) per capita GNP.
3. Would Adam Smith approve of or disapprove of the role of the federal government in the American economy today? Explain.
4. Why is the United States said to have a mixed economy?
5. Compare and contrast the American attitude toward political rights and civil liberties with that of the Soviet Union.
6. How did the United States help obtain UN military action in Korea in 1950?
7. Why does the United States have a unified identity despite the diverse racial, religious, and ethnic backgrounds of its people?

Extending Your Skills: Comparing Ideologies

Reread pages 487–490. Then identify whether the following phrases characterize capitalism, socialism, or Communism.

1. Is based upon private ownership
2. Dominates almost every aspect of the lives of the people and denies them most political and civil rights
3. Seeks to replace private ownership with public ownership
4. Is based upon the Marxist belief that the working class is exploited by the owners of private property
5. Achieves its goals through the nationalization of key industries
6. Utilizes a market system in which buyers and sellers freely come together in exchange for profit

Government and You

1. Should the United States reduce its contributions to the UN? Give reasons for your opinion.
2. Would you be willing to have the United States accept the jurisdiction of the International Court of Justice? Why or why not?
3. The United States commitment to human rights is a fundamental element of its foreign policy. Does this mean that the United States should form alliances with or otherwise support only democratic governments? Explain.
4. Do you agree that "government is best which governs least"? Why or why not?
5. How can a capitalist society encourage cooperation and social responsibility without adopting socialism?

Activities

1. Skim one of Charles Dickens' novels, such as *Nicholas Nickleby, Hard Times, David Copperfield,* or *Oliver Twist.* Find an excerpt that depicts living conditions among the English proletariat during the Industrial Revolution.
2. Research and write a short biography of one of the following: (a) Adam Smith; (b) Karl Marx; (c) Robert Owen; (d) Thomas Malthus.
3. Write a letter to the editor expressing an opinion either for or against the withdrawal of the United States from the United Nations.
4. Research the history and write a short account of one of the following examples of a modern nationalistic movement, choosing one of the following: (a) Quebec separatism; (b) Basque nationalism; (c) the struggle in Northern Ireland between Catholics and Protestants; (d) the Nigeria-Biafra civil war; (e) the creation of Bangladesh.

UNIT 8

THE FEDERAL BUREAUCRACY

Chapter 21

The Bureaucracy: Government at Work

To be responsive to a wide spectrum of problems, governments consist of large organizations, among which primary responsibility for particular tasks is divided. Each organization attends to a special set of problems and acts in quasi-independence on these problems. . . . Government leaders can substantially disturb, but not substantially control, the behavior of these organizations.

GRAHAM T. ALLISON

CHAPTER OVERVIEW

The Social Security Administration is one of the largest agencies in the federal bureaucracy. Its 10 regional offices, 6 special service centers, and more than 1,300 local offices bring a wide variety of important government services to people across the country.

1 THE BUREAUCRATIC SYSTEM

The federal bureaucracy consists of 2.9 million employees. It provides Americans with thousands of services and with the rules and regulations that inevitably accompany them. It leaves virtually no aspect of our lives untouched.

The Nature of Bureaucracy

To most people *bureaucracy* brings to mind paper shuffling, rigidity, and big government. But the term has a neutral, technical meaning that we shall use in this chapter. A ***bureaucracy*** is any large organization that has specialization of function, hierarchical form, and standardized procedures as its basic characteristics.

Specialization of Function A bureaucracy performs its functions, or tasks, through a number of separate, specialized units that are variously called departments, agencies, bureaus, or offices. This ***specialization of function*** enables the people in the organization—the ***bureaucrats***—to concentrate on a limited range of activities. Bureaucrats tend to develop a highly specialized knowledge of a subject area which becomes for them a main source of power.

Hierarchical Form A bureaucracy is organized as a ***hierarchy,*** a ranking of bureaucrats with authority flowing downward from the top. Work at each level of the bureaucracy is checked and directed by supervisors who, in turn, are checked by bureaucrats at higher levels. Information goes up the hierarchy and orders come down. The organizational chart of a bureaucracy usually resembles a layered pyramid because of these successive levels of command. Hierarchy enables a bureaucracy to maintain a unified system and to speak with one voice.

Standardized Procedures A bureaucracy operates according to various ***standardized procedures***—that is, by fixed rules and regulations. Communications consist mostly of written memos and official forms that are kept in files and that become the permanent record of bureaucratic action. Standardization tells everyone what is required and enables the bureaucracy to function clearly and routinely. It also reduces complexity and makes problems more manageable. Most importantly, it limits the personal judgment of individual bureaucrats in making decisions. Standardized procedures specify what is required in each situation and thus ensure that citizens are treated equally.

Specialization, hierarchy, and standardized procedures can be seen in any bureaucratic organization, whether it be a large corporation or the federal government. The main characteristics of bureaucracy reflect both strengths and weaknesses. When a bureaucratic organization is working well, it functions in an orderly and predictable way, providing efficient and effective administration. Employees are hired and promoted on the basis of merit—the ability to perform tasks well. Clients—the people with whom the bureaucrats deal—are treated fairly and equally.

Problems of Bureaucracy

All too often, however, problems plague bureaucracies and transform an orderly, well structured, administrative organization into a frightening, impersonal machine. Listed below are some of the problems that have given bureaucracy a negative image.

1. Divisions within the bureaucracy have often resisted change and control from above, becoming worlds unto themselves. The result has been fragmentation and ineffective coordination within the bureaucracy.
2. Procedures have become rigid, with everything done "by the book," so that no exceptions have been made for special cases.
3. Regulations have often been written in a language that confuses rather than clarifies. It seems that many bureaucrats never use one word where three can be used, or a short word if a long one can be found.
4. Delay—under the label of ***red tape***—has become accepted operating procedure. The shuffling of paper from desk to desk often has buried bureaucrats under unnecessary paperwork and an endless number of forms.
5. Promotions have been based more on time in service than on merit.
6. Clients have been treated impersonally as "cases" rather than as people with real problems because bureaucrats normally have dealt with only one aspect of their clients' lives.

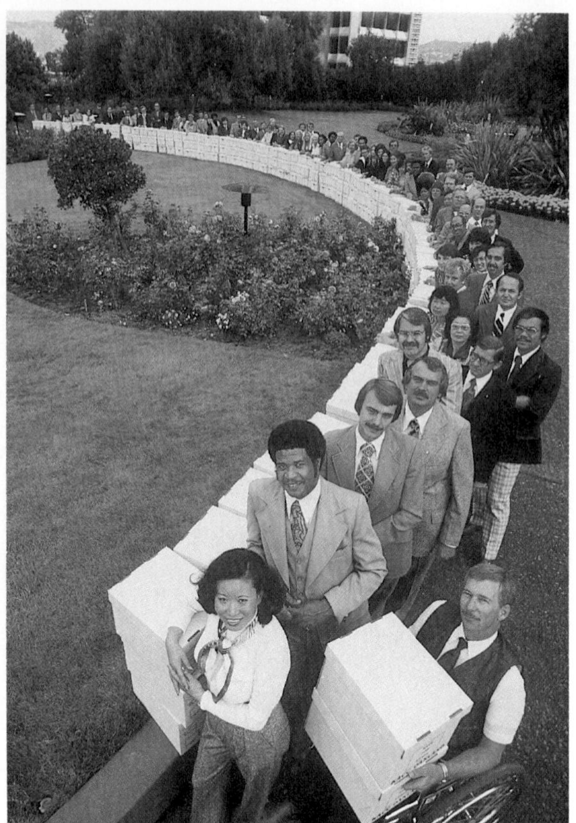

The annual files of one agency demonstrate a characteristic problem of bureaucracies—paperwork that often results in delays. The paperwork also contributes to the idea that bureaucracies treat clients impersonally. Name four other problems of many bureaucracies.

Aware of its problems, government officials keep the federal bureaucracy under constant review. They seek greater efficiency and effectiveness through reorganization and reform. They try to ensure that bureaucratic agencies are accountable for their actions to Congress and to the White House and that bureaucrats are responsive to the public they serve.

The Constitutional Foundation of the Bureaucracy

The federal bureaucracy is an inviting target for opponents of government waste and inefficiency. When Jimmy Carter ran for President in 1976, he promised to "release our civil servants from bureaucratic chaos." President Gerald Ford complained that bureaucrats had prepared a "Mulligan stew of government rules and regulations." Ford warned that "a government big enough to give you everything you want is big enough to take from you everything you have." Most Americans claim to be against big

LEXICON

Red Tape

During the nineteenth century the British developed an elaborate bureaucracy to administer their empire in India. As official forms piled up, the files were tied with a string or tape that was reddish in color. As a result, bureaucratic routine and its standardized procedures came to be called red tape. The term suggests excessive devotion to rules and regulations, where procedures become ends in themselves.

government, yet they expect and demand all kinds of government services. Over the past century, people have turned to government for solutions to an ever-widening range of problems. This is, in fact, the reason the bureaucracy exists.

The President and Congress share responsibility for the creation and operation of the federal bureaucracy. The Constitution gives to the President the duty to "take care that the laws be faithfully executed." It gives to Congress the authority to make all laws that are "necessary and proper" for carrying out its own delegated powers and "all other powers vested by this Constitution in the Government of the United States, or in any Department or Officer thereof."

In 1789 Congress created the Department of State to assist Secretary of State Thomas Jefferson in carrying out his duties. Persons appointed to the department were to be nominated by the President with the advice and consent of the Senate. But they were "to be removable by the President" alone to ensure the President's control over subordinates. Congress, however, retained a powerful hold over the administrative branch. Only Congress could create new departments and determine their structure and duties. The administration could implement only those laws enacted by Congress. And it was Congress that controlled the appropriation of money and had the power to investigate how that money was spent.

The Growth of the Federal Bureaucracy

The federal executive branch began in 1789 with three departments and two offices. Each was created to fulfill a basic function. Diplomacy was conducted by the State Department. National defense was in the care of the War Department. The collection of taxes and payment of debts were handled by the Treasury Department. The Office of the Attorney General, which became the Justice Department in 1870, was in charge of the government's legal matters. The Office of the Postmaster General handled the mail.

During the first half of the nineteenth century the federal bureaucracy grew as the nation expanded in area and population. The increased size of the executive branch was not the result of new tasks assumed by the government. It came with the expansion of basic services—primarily postal service—to meet increased demand.

The Pony Express, established in 1860, carried the mail to the outlying areas between St. Joseph, Missouri, and Sacramento, California. What is one major reason the federal bureaucracy grew during the nineteenth century?

The Civil War marked a turning point in the growth of the federal government. The conduct of the war itself required an increase in the size of the bureaucracy. Furthermore, the emergence of a new united national economy accounted for major changes in the role of government. Government began promoting specific sectors of the economy such as agriculture, commerce, and labor. In 1862 Congress created the Department of Agriculture to help farmers. It founded the Department of Commerce in 1903 to protect and promote the interests of American business. It established the Department of Labor in 1913 to serve the needs of working people. These departments conducted research, gathered statistics, and provided benefits. Their primary goal was to serve their clients rather than to regulate their activities.

Until the end of the nineteenth century, regulation of business and commerce—insofar as it existed at all—remained a matter for the states. There was a general belief that the proper role for the federal government was to promote the economy, not to police it. Moreover, the Supreme Court denied to the federal government any general "police power" by which it could regulate business. The Constitution, however, gave Congress the power to regulate interstate commerce. By using the commerce power the federal government gradually assumed a major role in regulating the economy. The growth of the federal bureaucracy over the past century came in three waves of regulatory activity.

The First Wave: 1880–1920 The first surge of bureaucratic growth came with the government's drive to regulate business and industry. The first federal regulatory agency, the Interstate Commerce Commission (ICC), was established in 1887 to regulate the railroads. The Food and Drug Administration, created in 1906, was also regulatory in intent. The government also took regulatory action against

Beginning in the late 1800's Congress used its commerce power to regulate industries. The need for national railroad regulation is expressed in an 1874 cartoon (below). Federal regulations prevent the false advertising of medicines, as in this movie-set "medicine show" (right).

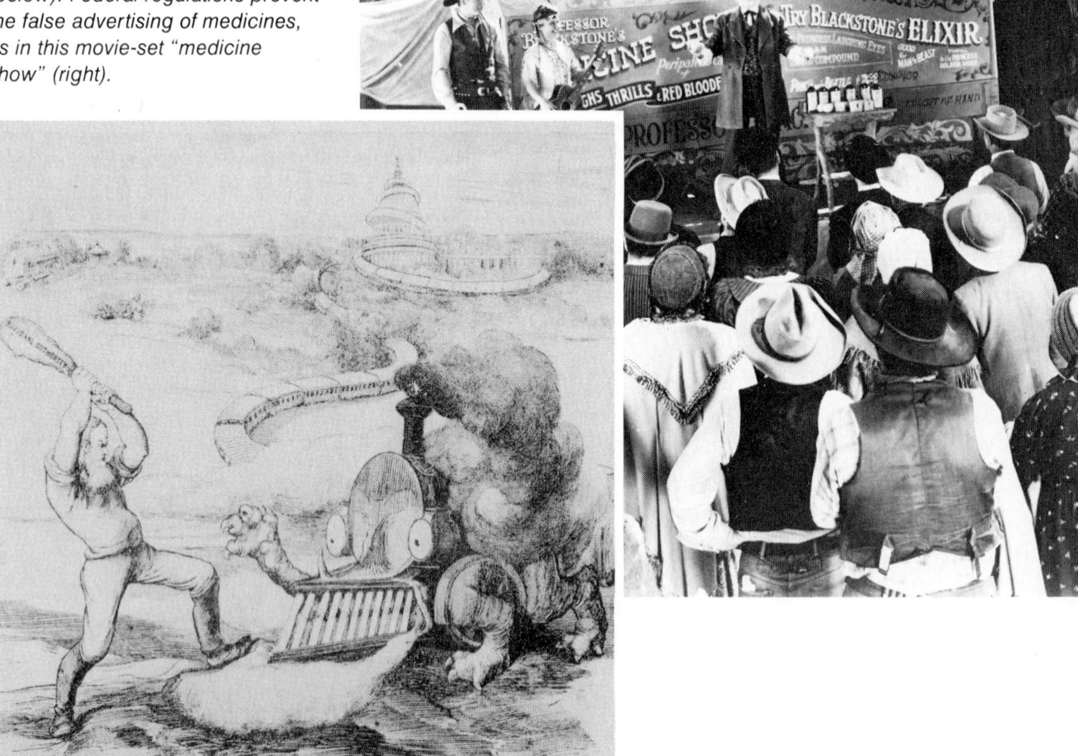

Between 1935 and 1943, employees of the Works Progress Administration (WPA) built or repaired about 600,000 miles (960 000 kilometers) of roads (above). The WPA spent more than $11 billion on the construction projects. A 1933 National Recovery Administration (NRA) parade (right) promoted fair labor and business practices.

the excessive power of big business. Seeking to control monopoly, Congress enacted the Sherman Anti-Trust Act of 1890. Its provisions were enforced by the Department of Justice. Expanded efforts to control restraints of trade came with the creation of the Federal Trade Commission (FTC) in 1914.

The Second Wave: 1933–1953 The biggest expansion of the federal bureaucracy began under Franklin D. Roosevelt's New Deal when the government took an active role in trying to solve the nation's economic and social problems. Many new agencies, known generally by their initials and called "the alphabet agencies," were created to administer the various New Deal programs. Among the best known were the AAA (Agricultural Adjustment Administration), the CCC (Civilian Conservation Corps), the NRA (National Recovery Administration), and the WPA (Works Progress Administration).

United States participation in World War II brought on an enormous expansion in the activity of the federal government. Between 1940 and 1945 federal tax collections rose from $5 billion to $44 billion. New agencies were created to direct the war effort and coordinate the domestic economy. The number of civilian federal employees reached record levels. By the end of the war the modern bureaucracy had taken its basic form.

LEXICON

Guns and Butter

The phrase *guns and butter* refers to the competing priorities of war supplies and domestic consumer products. In times of war, leaders traditionally call on the people to put "guns before butter"—that is, to make economic sacrifices for the war effort. But in his 1966 State of the Union Address, President Lyndon Johnson declared:

Time may require further sacrifices. If so, we will make them. But we will not heed those who will wring it from the hopes of the unfortunate in a land of plenty. I believe we can continue the Great Society while we fight in Vietnam.

The news media therefore described the policy as one of "guns *and* butter."

The Third Wave: 1961 to the Present The most recent period of bureaucratic growth began with the Presidency of John F. Kennedy and expanded under that of Lyndon Johnson. Between 1961 and 1969 the administration pushed new domestic programs and at the same time conducted the war in Vietnam under a policy of ***guns and butter.*** The pace of bureaucratic growth slowed under Presidents Nixon, Ford, and Carter. But throughout the 1970's demands for environmental protection and energy conservation spurred the creation of new programs and agencies. The period also saw a surge in government regulation. Federal standards were established for safety in the workplace, truth in advertising, consumer product safety, and air and water quality.

Since 1961, new federal programs have included assistance to depressed areas, massive support for education, job training for the disadvantaged, housing, community action programs, federal medical insurance for the poor and the elderly, promotion of consumer interests, medical research, the exploration of space, and the development of new energy sources. The number of executive agencies has also grown. Three new Cabinet-level departments were established: Housing and Urban Development, Transportation, and Energy. The Department of Health, Education and Welfare (HEW) was divided into the Department of Education and the Department of Health and Human Services.

Taking office in 1981, President Ronald Reagan sought to reverse the trend of bureaucratic growth by reducing the size of government. One of his first actions was to place a freeze on government hiring.

Scientists working for the Department of Energy set up a laser data converter for use in physics research. What other Cabinet-level departments have been established since 1961 to oversee new federal programs?

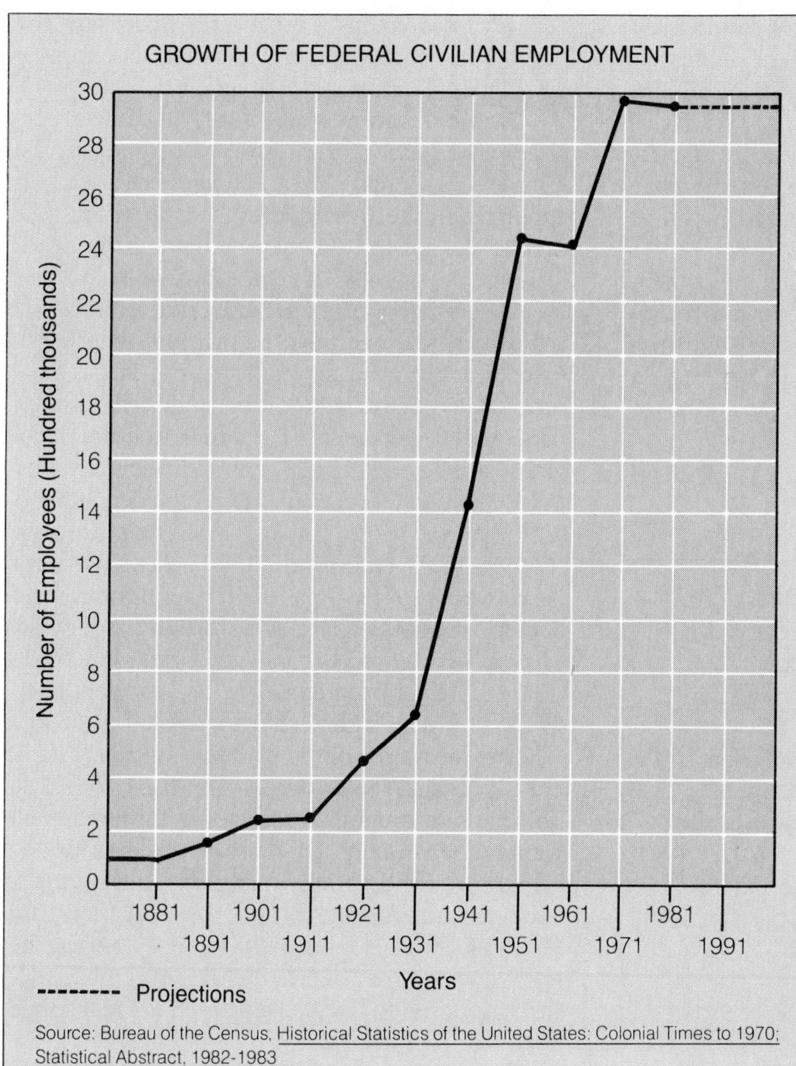

The number of federal civilian employees has increased with the demand for additional government services. During what years was the increase in federal civilian employment the greatest? What is one reason there has been no significant increase in federal civilian employment since 1980?

Reagan also cut back domestic spending and targeted various social programs for elimination. He brought regulatory agencies under close scrutiny and vowed to free the economy from government waste, bureaucratic red tape, and overregulation.

The Size of the Bureaucracy

The growth of the federal bureaucracy can be measured by the increase in the number of civilian employees. In 1792 only 780 people worked for the national government. In 1821 there were fewer than 7,000 employees. But with each decade the number of federal employees steadily expanded as indicated by the graph on this page. Some surprising facts are a part of the federal employment statistics.

- Only 12 percent of the 2.9 million federal employees work in the Washington, D.C., area. The remaining 88 percent work in regional offices.
- Three federal agencies account for 65 percent of all civilian employees. They are the Department of Defense (34 percent), the Postal Service (23 percent), and the Veterans Administration (8 percent).
- Federal employees number less than 20 percent of all government employees in the United States. Many more people work for state and local governments than for the federal government.
- The number of federal civilian employees has remained stable over the past 30 years. But the number of state and local employees has increased by more than 300 percent. Causes of this rapid

growth are the expansion of services provided by state and local governments and the increased role of state and local governments in the administration of federal programs.

- State and local employees are often paid indirectly with federal funds because a large number of federal programs are administered by other levels of government.
- Another form of indirect federal employment involves government contracts. Some 6 to 8 million persons in the private sector are paid from the federal treasury. They include workers in defense industries and research scientists in universities.

Section Check

---

1. Define: bureaucracy, bureaucrat, hierarchy, specialization of function, standardized procedures, red tape, guns and butter
2. Identify: Interstate Commerce Commission, New Deal's alphabet agencies
3. What are some problems that have given bureaucracy a negative image?
4. Explain the constitutional foundation of the federal bureaucracy.
5. About what percentage of all government employees work for the federal government?

---

2 THE STRUCTURE OF THE BUREAUCRACY

Four basic types of agencies make up the federal bureaucracy. They are Cabinet departments, independent executive agencies, independent regulatory commissions, and government corporations—as the chart on page 511 shows. Besides the 13 departments and some 55 agencies and commissions, there are several hundred federal boards, citizen advisory groups, task forces, and Presidential commissions. Altogether the extensive bureaucracy that is a part of the executive branch includes more than 2,000 bureaus, services, and other administrative units.

The Cabinet Departments

The 13 Cabinet departments are the main agencies of the federal bureaucracy. Most of the work of the federal government is conducted through them. Each department oversees a broad area of activity. The number of departments has grown as the scope of government activity has widened.

Twelve department heads carry the title of secretary. The head of the Justice Department is the Attorney General.* Each department head is appointed by the President with the advice and consent of the Senate. Together the department heads form the President's Cabinet. Individually they are the officers through whom the President directs the activities of the executive branch. But the department heads do not simply carry out Presidential orders. They are ***advocates,*** or supporters, for their particular departments. They push for new programs and defend the old ones against budget cuts.

Despite differences in size, all the departments are organized along similar lines. Their structure resembles a layered pyramid, with the department head, who is aided in overall responsibility by a deputy or undersecretary, at the top. The layer below consists of several assistant secretaries who are in charge of major programs. They are also appointed by the President with Senate approval.

The next layer of the pyramid contains a number of bureaus. The ***bureau***—sometimes called an office, administration, or service—is the largest unit within a department. The bureaus are the working agencies of the federal government. They normally have specific functions, and their directors are responsible to the department secretary. Among the best-known bureaus are the Federal Bureau of Investigation (FBI) in the Department of Justice and the Bureau of the Census in the Department of Commerce. A bureau is usually subdivided into various divisions, branches, and sections, each with specialized activities. These subdivisions make up the bottom layer in the pyramid structure.

Most bureaus maintain regional and field offices throughout the country. The listing under "United States Government" in the telephone directories for many cities may include dozens of entries.

The Independent Executive Agencies

The ***independent executive agencies*** are not a part of any Cabinet department. Their heads report directly to the President, who appoints them.

One important independent executive agency is ACTION, which includes the Peace Corps and other volunteer service programs. Other agencies are the

---

*Twelve departments are discussed in chapters 22–26; the Department of Justice is discussed in Chapter 27.

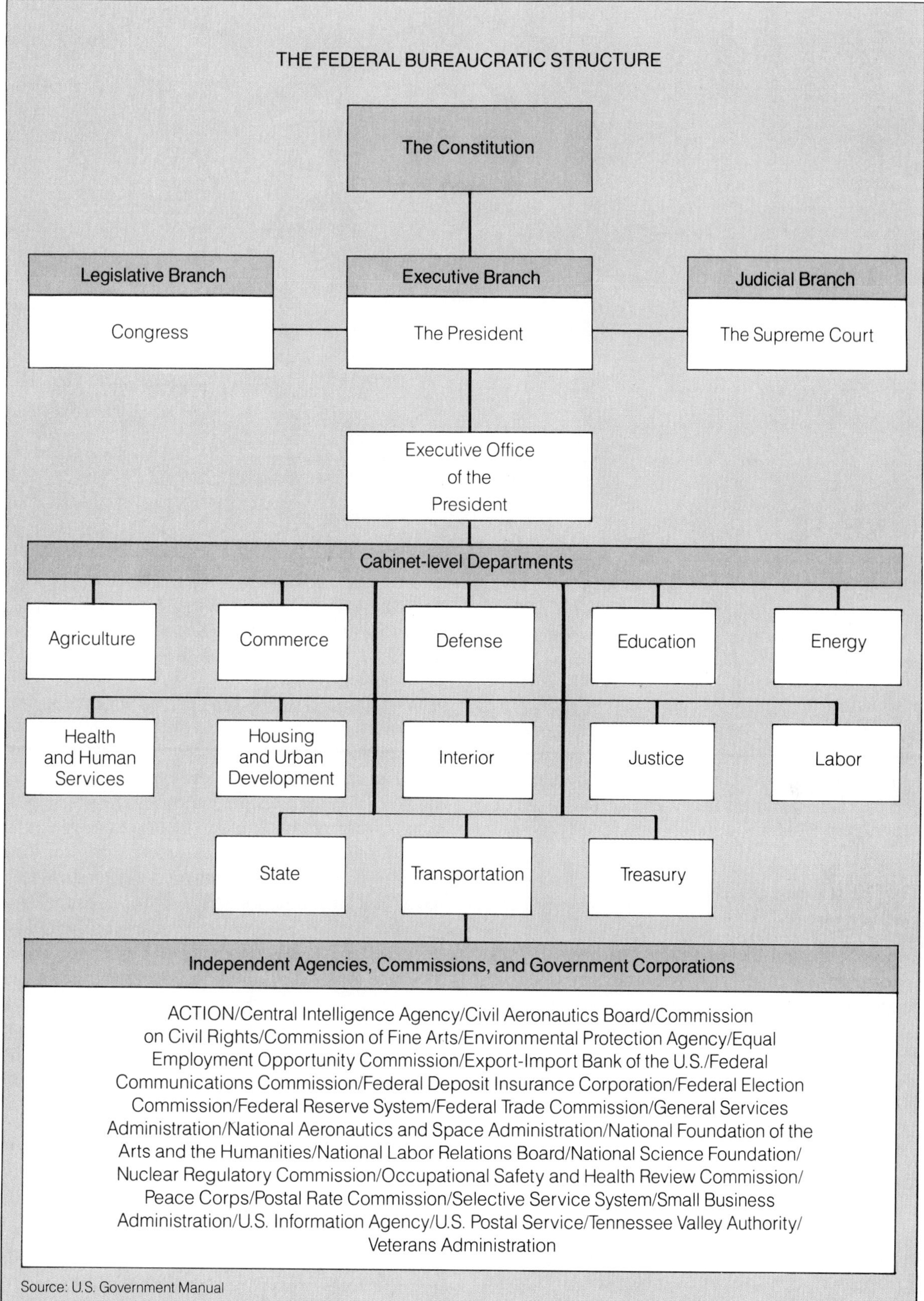
THE FEDERAL BUREAUCRATIC STRUCTURE
The Constitution
Legislative Branch
Congress
Executive Branch
The President
Judicial Branch
The Supreme Court
Executive Office of the President
Cabinet-level Departments
Agriculture
Commerce
Defense
Education
Energy
Health and Human Services
Housing and Urban Development
Interior
Justice
Labor
State
Transportation
Treasury
Independent Agencies, Commissions, and Government Corporations
ACTION/Central Intelligence Agency/Civil Aeronautics Board/Commission on Civil Rights/Commission of Fine Arts/Environmental Protection Agency/Equal Employment Opportunity Commission/Export-Import Bank of the U.S./Federal Communications Commission/Federal Deposit Insurance Corporation/Federal Election Commission/Federal Reserve System/Federal Trade Commission/General Services Administration/National Aeronautics and Space Administration/National Foundation of the Arts and the Humanities/National Labor Relations Board/National Science Foundation/Nuclear Regulatory Commission/Occupational Safety and Health Review Commission/Peace Corps/Postal Rate Commission/Selective Service System/Small Business Administration/U.S. Information Agency/U.S. Postal Service/Tennessee Valley Authority/Veterans Administration
Source: U.S. Government Manual

Each agency of the federal bureaucracy is identified by a specific seal or logo that usually symbolizes the agency's function.

Environmental Protection Agency (EPA), the National Aeronautics and Space Administration (NASA), the Selective Service System, and the Veterans Administration (VA). Still other independent agencies that provide services for government are the General Services Administration (GSA) and the Office of Personnel Management.

The Independent Regulatory Commissions

Congress created the ***independent regulatory commissions*** to oversee important areas of the economy. The 10 regulatory commissions (see chart on page 513) occupy a unique place in the federal government. Although not accountable to the President, they are a part of the executive branch. They also have *quasi*-legislative and *quasi*-judicial functions. They combine aspects of all three branches.

The commissions are run by boards, which vary in size from 5 to 11 members. Board members are appointed by the President with the consent of the Senate and may be removed only "for cause." Terms on the boards range from 5 to 14 years and are usually overlapping so that an entire board does not have to be replaced at the same time. Also, the overlapping terms keep any one President from dominating a board. A further requirement is that boards be ***bipartisan,*** with members drawn from both political parties.

The commissions are administratively independent of both the President and Congress. The purpose of freeing the commissions from Presidential and Congressional control is to ensure that they conduct their regulating activities fairly and without favor. But such independence gives rise to the danger that they may become "captives" of the industries they are supposed to regulate. This danger arises because most board members are drawn from the industries they are intended to regulate. Their closeness to the industries they regulate may make them too sympathetic to industry needs and interests. In some cases, though, regulatory commissions keep such tight control that the affected industries complain of government interference.

Special problems may also arise when the policies of a regulatory commission are in conflict with those of the President and Congress. For example, the Federal Reserve Board is an independent regulatory commission that oversees the nation's banking system and controls the flow of money within the economy. The President's efforts to direct the

INDEPENDENT REGULATORY COMMISSIONS

Name	Date created	Members	Term (Years)	Function
Interstate Commerce Commission (ICC)	1887	11	7	Regulates railroads, buses, trucks, and waterway and coastal shipping.
Board of Governors, Federal Reserve Board	1913	7	14	Supervises the nation's banking system and controls the flow of money and the use of credit.
Federal Trade Commission (FTC)	1914	5	7	Seeks to prevent unfair or deceptive trade practices, such as price-fixing, false advertising, and mislabeling or packaging of products.
Securities and Exchange Commission (SEC)	1934	5	5	Regulates the buying and selling of securities (stocks and bonds) to protect the public against malpractice; regulates the stock exchanges.
Federal Communications Commission (FCC)	1934	7	7	Grants licenses and regulates all radio and television stations; sets rates for telephone and telegraph companies in interstate service.
National Labor Relations Board (NLRB)	1935	5	5	Administers federal laws relating to labor-management relations; prevents unfair labor practices by employers and unions; supervises labor union elections.
Federal Maritime Commission (FMC)	1961	5	4	Regulates the rates and services of shippers engaged in waterborne foreign and off-shore domestic commerce.
Consumer Product Safety Commission (CPSC)	1972	5	5	Sets mandatory standards for product safety and has authority to ban dangerous consumer products.
Commodity Futures Trading Commission (CFTC)	1974	5	5	Regulates the market in agricultural, lumber, and mining products sold for future delivery.
Nuclear Regulatory Commission (NRC)	1974	5	5	Licenses and regulates the civilian uses of atomic energy — the design, construction, and operation of nuclear power plants and the handling of nuclear materials.

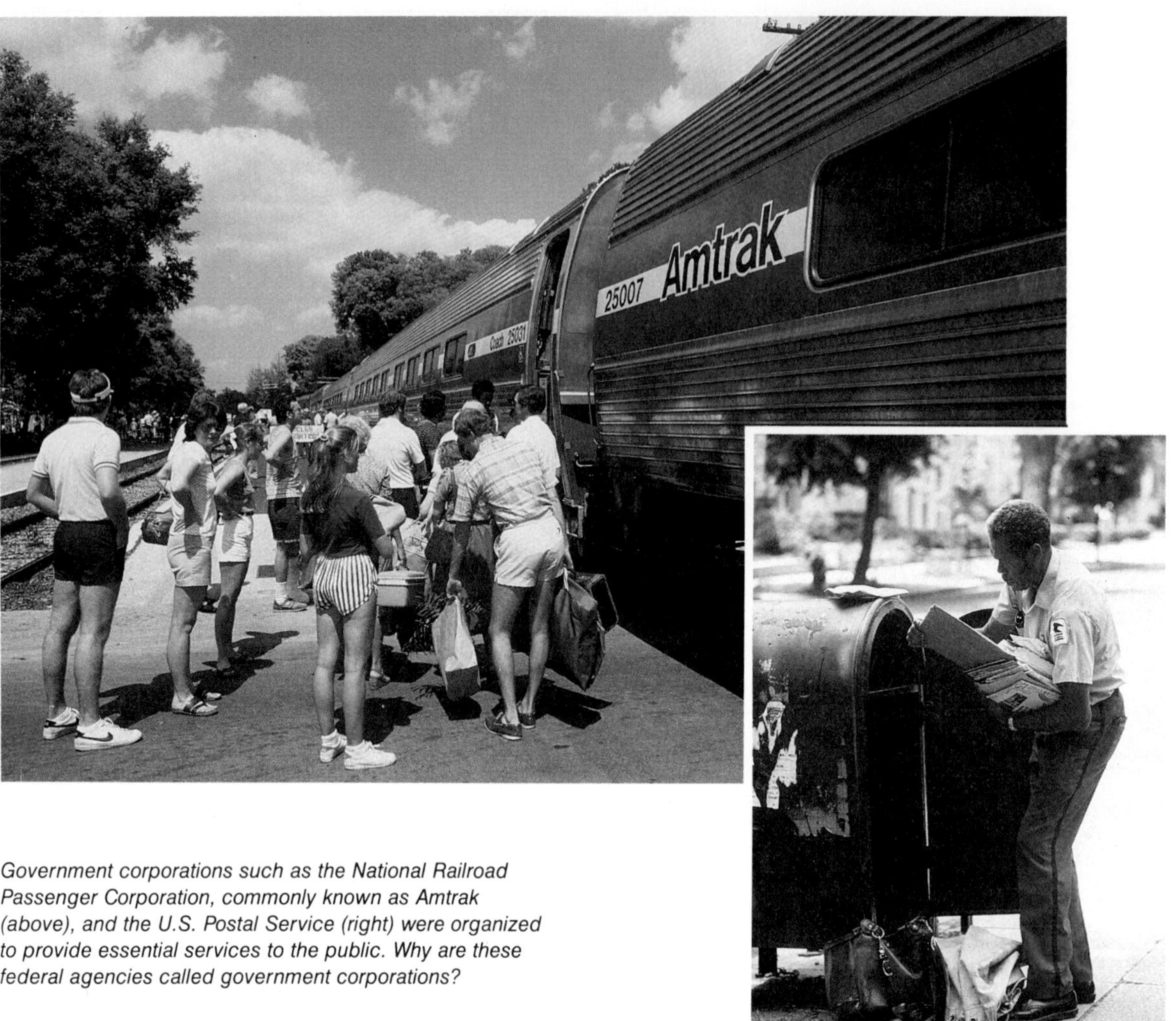

Government corporations such as the National Railroad Passenger Corporation, commonly known as Amtrak (above), and the U.S. Postal Service (right) were organized to provide essential services to the public. Why are these federal agencies called government corporations?

economy, however, may be seriously weakened without the cooperation of the Federal Reserve Board. If the President and the "Fed," as the Board is often called, work at cross-purposes, the economy is likely to be pulled one way and then another.

The Government Corporations

Government corporations operate commercial enterprises and are run just like private businesses. Policy is set by a board of governors whose members serve overlapping terms after appointment by the President with the consent of the Senate. The corporations are subject to Presidential authority and the scrutiny of Congress. But they usually have greater independence and flexibility than other government agencies because they earn a major portion of their operating expenses.

Four well-known government corporations are Amtrak, the Federal Deposit Insurance Corporation (FDIC), the Tennessee Valley Authority (TVA), and the U.S. Postal Service.

The U.S. Postal Service, which delivers the nation's mail, was reorganized as a self-supporting corporation in 1970. It replaced the Post Office Department, which had been directed by the Postmaster General, who was a member of the President's Cabinet. Today the Postal Service is run by a board of governors. With Senate approval, the President appoints nine board members who serve nine-year, overlapping terms. They, in turn, appoint the Postmaster General. The Postal Service has 40,000 post offices and 650,000 employees who handle more than 114 billion pieces of mail each year. To provide swift and reliable mail delivery, the Postal Service operates its own planning and research programs.

Section Check

1. Define: advocate, bureau, bipartisan, independent executive agency, independent regulatory commission, government corporation
2. Identify: Federal Bureau of Investigation, General Services Administration, Federal Reserve Board, U.S. Postal Service
3. How many Cabinet departments are there in the federal bureaucracy?
4. What two main functions does a department head have?
5. Give one example of an independent executive agency, an independent regulatory commission, and a government corporation.
6. Why do independent regulatory commissions occupy a unique place in the federal government?

The Arms Control and Disarmament Agency is an independent executive agency that was established in 1961 to advise the President on arms-control policy. It also assists in the negotiation of international arms-control treaties.

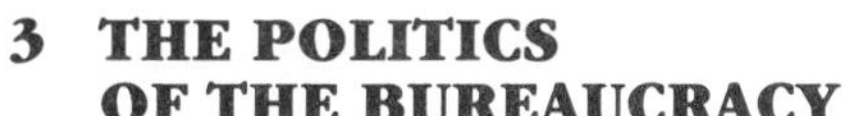

3 THE POLITICS OF THE BUREAUCRACY

The bureaucracy not only implements policy and administers programs, it also plays an important role in shaping policy. The bureaucracy shapes government policy in three ways.

First, agencies often have a wide range of choices in carrying out policy. Because Congress cannot anticipate every situation or problem, it normally frames laws in a broad manner. The details are worked out in federal rules and regulations that are formulated by the various bureaus. These rules and regulations have the force of law. They also have major political consequences in determining who gets what, when, and how.

Second, how a policy or program is administered determines what gets done. An agency may implement a policy with enthusiasm and commitment, or it may drag its feet in carrying out a program it does not like.

Third, the bureaucracy plays a major part in shaping policy because proposals for new government programs often originate within federal agencies. For example, executive agencies in recent years have initiated more than half of the major bills passed by Congress. Each agency has a number of experts who make policy recommendations, draft bills, and exert influence upon those who can put their plans into action.

INSIGHT

The Federal Register

The *Federal Register* is the executive branch's equivalent of the *Congressional Record.* Published daily, the *Federal Register* contains new regulations and other legal documents of the executive branch. In 1980 the *Register* comprised some 87,000 pages and listed more than 5,000 new rules and regulations. Agency regulations are collected and published annually in the *Code of Federal Regulations.* The regulations are divided into 50 groups, each representing a broad subject area. The *Code* runs to more than 175 volumes.

In shaping government policy, each agency seeks to advance its own interests. It does so in its relations with the groups and individual clients with which it deals, with Congress, and with the President.

The Bureaucracy and Its Clients

Agencies and bureaus of the federal government often develop close relationships with their ***clients***—the groups they serve. Their clients may have sought the establishment of the agency in the first place, as when organized labor sought a separate Department of Labor. More recently, the National Education Association lobbied for the establishment of the Department of Education and has fought to prevent its abolition. On the other hand, government agencies have sometimes fostered the development of outside support groups. For example, the Department of Agriculture helped to establish the American Farm Bureau Federation.

The ties between an agency and its clients may be reinforced by sharing personnel at different times. Many employees move back and forth between government and the private sector. Top agency officials are often drawn from client groups, and many key figures outside the government are former government employees. For example, a number of Defense Department officials have taken jobs with defense contractors—private companies with which the department deals.

The Department of Education administers federal education programs, sponsors research, and collects data on educational trends.

The Small Business Administration, an independent federal agency, promotes and protects the interests of small businesses. It also provides special programs and loans for minorities entering business.

An agency and its clients frequently have common interests and agree on policy. Agencies may come to identify with the groups they serve. The Department of Agriculture sees itself as representing the interests of the American farmer within government. Similarly, the Department of Labor takes the part of wage earners, and the Department of Commerce speaks for business. Agencies that engage primarily in regulation rather than in the provision of services are likely to be less sympathetic toward outside groups than the service-oriented departments of Labor, Agriculture, and Commerce. But even with regulatory agencies, relationships with client groups may be close and mutually supportive.

The Bureaucracy and Congress

The many departments, agencies, and bureaus of the executive branch keep in close touch with Congress over a wide range of matters including budget, agency organization, program performance, and new programs. Interaction takes place primarily at the committee, and especially subcommittee, levels of Congress where critical decisions affecting the agency are made. Department secretaries and agency heads regularly testify in formal Congressional committee hearings. They may also seek to influence Congressional decision making more informally through personal contacts with committee chairpersons.

The Office of Management and Budget (OMB) evaluates federal programs and makes recommendations on spending. The director of OMB often testifies before Congress on the budget recommendations of the executive branch.

To build political support in Congress for more programs and higher budgets, federal agencies maintain liaison officers who work on a continuous basis with staff members of House and Senate committees. Of more than 500 department liaison personnel working in Congress over half, for example, are from the Department of Defense. Liaison officers keep their agencies informed of action before Congress. They supply committees with information on department and agency programs. They work with committee staffs in drafting and revising bills. In addition, liaison officers work to maintain very good relations with the appropriations subcommittees.

Members of Congressional committees want the agencies of the executive branch to know that Congress oversees their activities. At the same time they seek cordial relations with the bureaucracy, hoping to gain benefits for their home districts, states, and individual constituents.

Members of Congressional committees and agency officials thus have an interest in reaching decisions agreeable to everyone involved. They are joined in this partnership by the interest groups affected by these decisions. These three sectors—the Congressional subcommittee, the executive bureau, and the interest group—work together through bargaining and compromise for common advantage, a relationship that has been described as a "cozy little triangle," a "policy whirlpool," or a "subgovernment." By whatever name, the relationship of these three groups is at the core of the governmental process.

The Bureaucracy and the President

As chief executive, the President attempts to coordinate and control the federal bureaucracy. The President does so through the department heads that constitute the Cabinet and through the Executive Office of the President—notably the White House Office and the Office of Management and Budget. The President's lines of control reach through each layer in the structure of the bureaucracy. But the sheer size and complexity of the executive branch make supervision by the White House Office very difficult.

Presidential concerns are likely to focus on pressing issues of foreign and economic policy. Presidential control is therefore selective. In routine matters the bureaucracy operates largely on its own. But even on the most important matters, agencies are not easily brought under Presidential control. The execution of the President's orders may be delayed, weakened, or simply ignored. President Kennedy complained that the State Department was "a bowl of jelly." Franklin D. Roosevelt said it was "almost impossible" to get results from the Treasury Department. But, he added, "the Treasury and the State Department put together are nothing compared with the Na–a–vy. . . . To change anything in the Na–a–vy is like punching a feather bed."

There are three basic controls that the President exercises over the bureaucracy. These basic controls are the budget, reorganization, and bureaucratic appointments.

The Budget The President's most important tool for controlling the bureaucracy is the budget. Through the budget process the President sets priorities and holds executive agencies accountable for what they do. Here the President is assisted by the Office of Management and Budget (OMB). The OMB also reviews the organizational structure and management procedures of the executive branch to ensure efficiency and effectiveness.

Any attempt to cut the budget, eliminate a program, or abolish an agency meets strong resistance from interest groups, from members of Congress, and from the agency itself. The first law of bureaucracy is survival. So once an agency or program is in place, it is very difficult to bring about change.

Senator John McClellan of Arkansas (left) meets with former President Herbert Hoover (right) during a session of the Commission on the Reorganization of the Executive Branch in 1949. After two years of study, the commission recommended combining many federal agencies and eliminating overlapping powers.

Executive Reorganization The President also tries to gain more effective control over the bureaucracy through administrative reform. Periodically Congress has given the President authority to reorganize the structure of the executive branch, subject to Congressional veto. Some of the most extensive reforms were made on the recommendation of a commission chaired by former President Herbert Hoover. The Commission on The Reorganization of the Executive Branch was set up in 1949 to find ways to end bureaucratic waste. Between 1949 and 1973, five Presidents submitted 91 reorganization plans to Congress. Of these, 72 went into effect. Most involved relatively minor changes because of limitations imposed by Congress.

One of Jimmy Carter's campaign promises in 1976 was to streamline the bureaucracy and "to make government more responsive, efficient, and open." In 1977 Congress renewed Presidential authority to reorganize the executive branch. Under the current

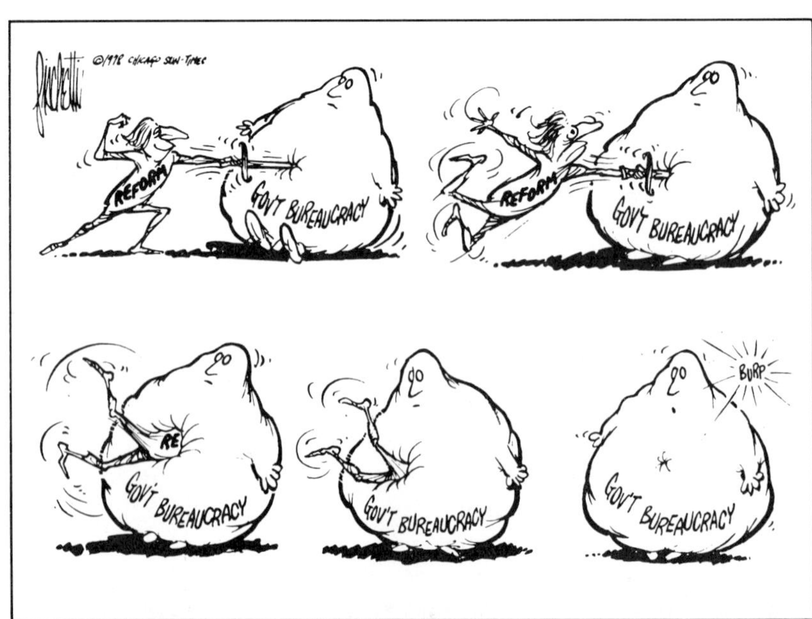

Attempts to reform the government bureaucracy are often difficult and unsuccessful. How does this cartoonist explain the lack of success of bureaucratic reform efforts?

Reorganization Act the President may submit to Congress plans for creating or abolishing agencies or for changing their structure or functions. Either the House or the Senate can veto the Presidential plan within 60 days after it is submitted. If Congress takes no action within that period, the reorganization goes into effect. Among the changes brought about by President Carter were an effort to consolidate overlapping agency functions and a reorganization of the Executive Office of the President.

Presidential Appointment The President seeks to control the bureaucracy through appointments to key positions within each executive department. In addition to department secretaries and undersecretaries, the President appoints agency and major bureau heads. These officials hold the top policy-making jobs within the bureaucracy. Many of these officials are chosen from outside the government. Also, at the upper levels within each department, some changes in career personnel are permitted. This allows the President to appoint high-ranking civil service personnel from within the department to major policy-making positions. Together with appointments brought in from outside, they form the President's team. They are accountable to the President and may be removed only by Presidential order. But these appointments number less than 1,500. The vast majority of the 2.9 million civilians employed by the federal government are not appointed and cannot be removed by the President. They hold their positions under the protection of the civil service.

Section Check

1. Define: client
2. Identify: *Federal Register,* Office of Management and Budget, Herbert Hoover
3. Why does Congress frame laws in a broad rather than a detailed manner?
4. What are three ways in which the bureaucracy shapes government policy?
5. What is the function of department liaison personnel who work in Congress? What are some of their activities?
6. What is the President's most important tool for controlling the bureaucracy?

4 THE CIVIL SERVICE

Most federal employees are career civil servants. Presidential administrations come and go, but the ***civil service*** is a permanent institution.

The Spoils System

Government employees today are hired on the basis of their abilities and remain secure in their jobs. This was not always so. George Washington and John Adams favored members of the Federalist party. When Jefferson came into office, he replaced the Federalists with members of his own party. In 1829 Andrew Jackson replaced about 1,000 government employees with his political supporters.

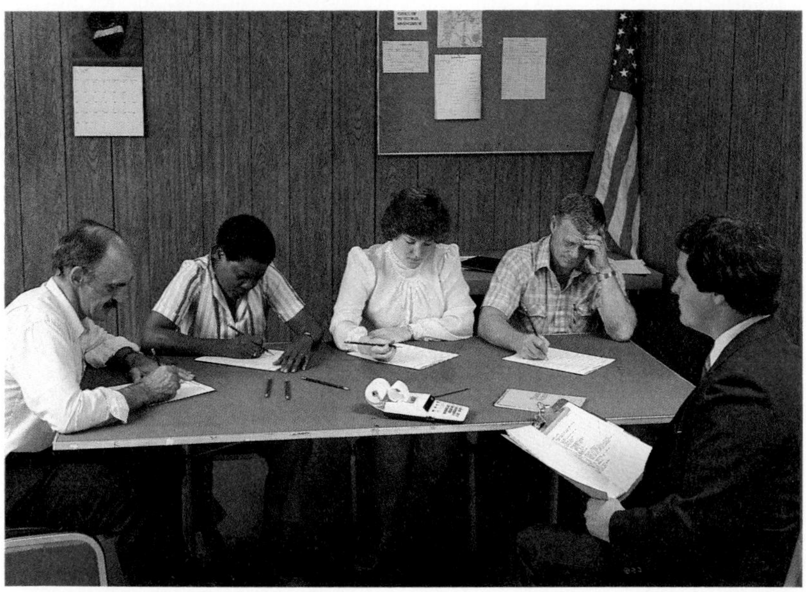

Applicants for positions in the civil service are tested by the Office of Personnel Management (OPM). A primary role of the OPM is to guarantee that civil service applicants are hired only on the basis of their knowledge and skills.

The assassination of President James A. Garfield in 1881 spurred Congress to pass the Civil Service Reform Act. This act brought reform to governmental hiring procedures. What did the Civil Service Reform Act require?

Defending President Jackson, Senator William Marcy of New York declared, "To the victor belong the spoils"—a reference to the plunder taken in conquest. Jackson's enemies adopted the phrase and used it to attack the practice of awarding government jobs on a partisan basis—dubbing this the ***spoils system.***

Over the next 50 years political workers came to expect government jobs as a reward for their loyalty. The spoils system bred inefficiency and corruption, which led to demands for reform. Finally, after President James A. Garfield was assassinated in 1881 by a disappointed office-seeker, Congress took action. In 1883 the Civil Service Reform Act, popularly known as the Pendleton Act, established the original framework for a system of government employment based upon merit.

The Merit System

The Pendleton Act required that the recruitment and promotion of federal employees be based on merit. Entry into the civil service was by competitive examination. Employees were to be politically neutral in office and were protected from political pressure. They could be dismissed only for proven incompetence, inefficiency, or violation of the law. The operation of the system was supervised by an independent, bipartisan Civil Service Commission.

The Pendleton Act originally covered only 10 percent of all federal employees. Over the years more and more government workers have been brought into the civil service. Today more than 95 percent of all federal civilian employees are covered by the ***merit system.*** The largest number—about 2.1 million—are in the regular civil service. In addition, several agencies maintain their own recruitment and merit systems. These agencies include the U.S. Postal Service, the Foreign Service of the Department of State, the Forest Service, the Public Health Service, and the Federal Bureau of Investigation.

Civil Service Reform

The first major reform in the civil service was enacted almost a century after the passage of the Pendleton Act. The new law, known as the Civil Service Reform Act of 1978, was described by President Carter as "the centerpiece of government reorganization."

Under the Reform Act, which took effect in January 1979, the Civil Service Commission was abolished. Its functions were divided between the Office of Personnel Management and the Merit Systems Protection Board.

The Office of Personnel Management (OPM) is in charge of the recruitment, training, and promotion of federal employees. It administers civil service examinations and conducts investigations into each applicant's reputation, character, and loyalty to the United States. The OPM also manages the government's ***affirmative action hiring program.*** To ensure equal opportunity, this program seeks to eliminate from all aspects of federal employment such nonmerit considerations as race, religion, sex, age, and political influence.

★ ★

LEXICON

Whistle-blower

A **whistle-blower** is a government employee who draws public attention to mismanagement, waste, corruption, or other wrongdoing by a government agency. A whistle-blower cannot be fired or otherwise punished because of his or her disclosures.

★ ★

The Merit Systems Protection Board is an independent agency created to protect the federal merit systems and the rights of individual employees. It hears cases of wrongdoing and orders corrective action where appropriate.

A third agency, the Federal Labor Relations Authority, is charged with settling various labor-management disputes within the government. It oversees federal employee unions and investigates complaints of unfair labor practices.

Merit System Principles

The Civil Service Reform Act gives more flexibility and responsibility to individual federal agencies. All government personnel practices, however, must follow the nine ***merit system principles**** that have been established by law.

1. Recruitment must come from all segments of society, and selection and advancement must be on the basis of ability, knowledge, and skills, under fair and open competition. This means that people from all walks of life and all parts of society must have an equal chance for a federal job, and that people chosen to be hired or promoted must be the best qualified.
2. There must be fair and equitable treatment in all personnel management matters, without regard to politics, race, color, religion, national origin, sex, marital status, age, or handicapped condition, and with proper regard for individual privacy and constitutional rights. Thus, this principle forbids discrimination in any form.
3. There must be equal pay for work of equal value, considering both national and local rates paid by private employers, with incentives and recognition for excellent performance. This principle stipulates that the government must keep the salaries it pays comparable to those paid outside. The government fulfills this requirement by using a variety of different pay systems for different groups of workers. Some systems are based on what private employers throughout the nation pay for similar work. Other pay systems have different pay rates in each locality, based on local wage levels among private employers. This principle also requires that government employees who do especially well at their jobs be rewarded for their excellence.
4. Employees must maintain high standards of integrity, conduct, and concern for the public interest. No action can be taken by employees that is not moral, ethical, and for the ultimate benefit of the public.
5. There must be efficient and effective use of the federal work force. All personnel actions must be aimed at getting the best possible performance from federal employees.
6. Employees must be judged by the quality of their performance on the job. This means that employees control their own fate by how well they do their jobs. Those who perform at or above specified minimum standards for the job will continue working. Those not meeting the standards will be given help to meet the acceptable level. Those who still do not meet the standards will lose their jobs.
7. Improved performance must be accomplished through effective education and training. The government must provide opportunities and assistance to federal employees if it seeks to improve their performance.
8. Protection of employees from arbitrary action, personal favoritism, or political coercion, must be maintained. Government workers must not be subject to personnel actions that are unreasonable or based only on personal or political considerations.
9. There must be protection of employees against reprisal for lawful disclosures of information. No personnel action can be taken to punish an employee who is a "whistle-blower."

*Source: Office of Personnel Management, *Fed Facts 20* (1979).

Government—at all levels—employs thousands of workers in a variety of functions (right). As a federal employee the forest ranger, speaking to students about conserving natural resources (below), holds a civil service position. What percentage of federal employees are concerned with natural resources? What percentage of state employees?

GOVERNMENT EMPLOYMENT BY FUNCTION

Function	Percent of Employees		
	Federal (civilian)	State	Local
National defense and international relations	35	—	—
Postal service	23	—	—
Education	*	43	55
Highways	*	7	3
Health and hospitals	9	18	8
Public welfare	—	5	2
Police protection	2	2	6
Fire protection	—	—	3
Sanitation and sewerage	—	*	2
Parks and recreation	—	*	2
Natural resources	10	4	*
Financial administration	4	3	2
All others	16	17	16

* less than 1%
Source: *Statistical Abstract of the United States*, 1984

A Profile of the Civil Service

There are more than 2,000 different kinds of jobs within the civil service. Federal employees work in offices, laboratories, national parks, hospitals, military bases, and many other settings across the country and around the world. The government employs some 150,000 engineers and architects; 120,000 doctors and others in health care; 92,000 scientists; 58,000 social scientists and welfare workers; and 10,000 librarians. More than 500,000 civilians are blue-collar workers ranging from truck drivers to skilled carpenters, mechanics, and electricians.

Women make up about 33 percent of the federal work force. About 4 percent of federal employees are black, and about 3 percent are Hispanic. Although women and minorities are still concentrated in the lower ranks of the civil service, each year brings more and more women and minorities into the top levels of the bureaucracy of the federal government.

Recruitment and Classification

The Office of Personnel Management has a network of Federal Job Information Centers throughout the country. The centers, most of which are listed under "United States Government" in metropolitan area telephone directories, provide information about employment opportunities with the government. For some positions a written examination is required to test the ability of the applicants to do a particular job or measure their ability to learn how to do it.

Applicants for positions that do not require a written test are evaluated on the basis of training and experience.

Those who qualify are placed on the list of eligibles that exists for each type of job. When a position opens in a federal agency, the OPM provides the top three names on the appropriate list. The agency must choose one of the three. In hiring for government jobs, there is a ***veterans' preference.*** Honorably discharged veterans receive a five-point addition to their examination scores. Disabled veterans and certain members of their families receive an additional ten points. This preference is given in recognition of the service veterans have provided to their country.

Civil service grades and salaries are classified according to a general schedule in which grades range from GS–1 to GS–18 and salaries from a little over $7,000 to more than $50,000. Career opportunities and pay scales are generally competitive with those in the private sector. Persons qualify for grades according to experience and training. College graduates, for example, usually qualify for jobs at the GS–5 or GS–7 level. Those with advanced degrees and extensive experience may qualify for higher grades.

Within each grade there are ten steps, or pay levels. Pay rates are adjusted each year to keep government competitive with private industry. Under the old civil service system, salary raises were made mainly by automatic, specified increments. Years of service, rather than quality of work, determined pay for most federal employees. But the 1978 Reform Act determined that the major portion of any pay increase must be based upon performance. Employees are now evaluated according to how well they perform their specific jobs. On-the-job training is provided for federal employees who seek to advance.

Most civil servants pursue a career within a single agency. The Reform Act, however, created a new Senior Executive Service (SES) for managers in the top GS grades. Some 7,000 eligible persons joined the SES, which opened top executive jobs in the federal government to competition among civil servants for the first time. The SES offers greater opportunity for professional advancement.

Civil servants have a high degree of job security. A government employee may be dismissed only "for cause," such as inefficiency or misconduct. Furthermore, firing a civil servant involves a complex and lengthy process of hearings and appeals which protects employees from arbitrary dismissal.

Restriction on Political Activity

In establishing the civil service Congress sought to ensure political neutrality and the protection of government employees from political pressure. Such pressure might include "suggestions" that employees contribute money to the political party in power or work in a political campaign. The Hatch Act, passed in 1939, imposed restrictions on the political activities of federal employees. Under the provisions of the act, civil servants cannot actively participate in party politics or election campaigns, nor can they run for political office.

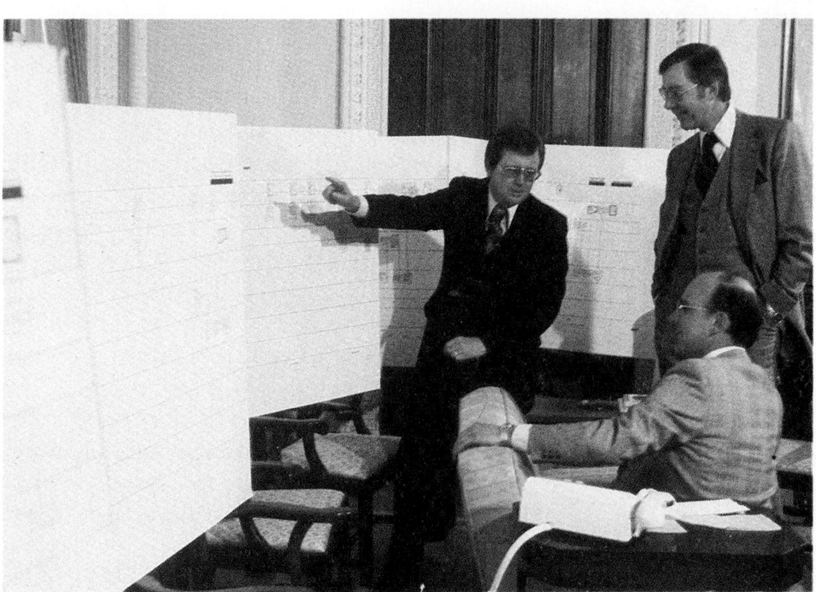

A series of charts illustrate the lengthy procedure that bureaucrats must follow before dismissing a civil service employee. The specific procedure was outlined in the Civil Service Reform Act of 1978.

Many federal employees feel that these restrictions are a denial of their constitutional rights. The Supreme Court, however, has upheld the Hatch Act. Its restrictions on political activity, the Court noted, were designed to make sure that politics could not influence promotion and job security. Government workers are still free to express their opinions on any political issue, to wear campaign buttons, to attend political rallies, and to make voluntary contributions of time or money to the party and candidates they support.

Control of the Bureaucracy

Civil servants are not elected. They are not accountable directly to the voters. Elected politicians come and go, but the bureaucracy remains as a permanent government. The bureaucracy, as we have seen, not only administers programs and carries out the law. It also plays a major role in shaping the policies it is called to implement.

The independence of the federal bureaucracy is drawn in part from the expert knowledge and abilities of its members. But its independence is also the result of the sheer size and complexity of the executive branch. The bureaucracy is accountable both to the President and to Congress, yet neither exercises effective control over it. The question of who controls the bureaucracy—and for what purposes—remains fundamental. Bureaucracy must be efficient and effective, but in a democracy it must also be responsive to the people and the public interest.

Section Check

---

1. Define: civil service, spoils system, affirmative action hiring program, merit system principles, whistle-blower, veterans' preference
2. Identify: Pendleton Act, Civil Service Reform Act of 1978, Federal Job Information Center, Hatch Act
3. What two things helped bring about establishment of the merit system for federal employment?
4. About what percentage of federal civilian employees are covered by the merit system?
5. What two things may a written examination for a government job test?
6. How are applicants for positions that do not require a written test evaluated?

SUMMARY

A bureaucracy is any large organization with three basic characteristics: specialization of function, a hierarchy of form, and standardized procedures. The federal executive branch, headed by the President, is a vast bureaucracy with nearly 3 million employees in hundreds of departments and bureaus.

The Constitution makes no specific provision for a bureaucracy. But under the "necessary and proper" clause, Congress assumed the right to create new departments, determine their structures and duties, and control their budgets. The President has the right to appoint department heads with the consent of the Senate and to remove them at will.

During the first half of the nineteenth century the executive branch expanded as the nation placed greater demands on the Post Office and other basic services. The Civil War marked a turning point in bureaucratic growth. At that time the federal government took an active role in promoting specific sectors of the economy.

The subsequent growth of the federal bureaucracy came in three waves. The first wave began in 1887 when the Interstate Commerce Commission was established to regulate the railroads. The expansion of regulatory activity gave rise to many federal agencies. The second wave of bureaucratic growth, which represented the biggest expansion of the bureaucracy, began during the Great Depression of the 1930's and continued through World War II. The bureaucracy's third and most recent wave of growth began in the 1960's with the domestic programs of the Kennedy and Johnson administrations and the Vietnam War.

The federal bureaucracy consists of the Cabinet departments, the independent executive agencies, the independent regulatory commissions, and the government corporations. Altogether the executive branch includes more than 2,000 bureaus, services, and other administrative units.

Most federal bureaucrats are career employees who hold their position under the civil service. These employees are hired and promoted under the merit system established by the Pendleton Act of 1883. The Civil Service Reform Act of 1978 was the first major reform of the civil service system.

The Hatch Act, passed in 1939, attempted to protect civil service employees from political pressure. It did this by restricting the employees' political activities. Some employees believe that these restrictions are unfair, but the Supreme Court has upheld the Hatch Act.

Chapter 21 Review

Using Vocabulary

Answer the questions by using the meaning of each underlined term.

1. Why are hierarchy, standardized procedures, and specialization of function important characteristics of bureaucracy?
2. Why are most regulatory commissions bipartisan in membership?
3. What relationship often exists between an independent executive agency and the civil service?
4. What effect might red tape and a whistle-blower have on a bureaucrat?
5. How might veterans' preference and affirmative action affect the merit system?
6. When does a bureaucrat sometimes act as a lobbyist?

Understanding American Government

1. What are the three basic characteristics of a bureaucracy?
2. What might government be like in the absence of a bureaucracy?
3. How did the attitude of the federal government toward business and commerce change toward the end of the nineteenth century? How did this change affect the bureaucracy?
4. Describe the relationship that often develops between a federal agency and the group it serves. Do you think such a relationship is desirable? Why or why not?
5. Why might a government agency be tempted to take action against a whistle-blower? What protection does a whistle-blower have?

Extending Your Skills: Reading a Line Graph

Study the graph on page 509. Based on the data in the graph, determine which statements are true and which are false. Then use the graph to make the false statements true.

1. Federal hiring remained stable between 1881 and 1921.
2. The number of federal civilian employees in 1881 was less than 200,000.
3. The greatest increase in federal civilian employment occurred between 1931 and 1951.
4. The number of federal civilian employees tripled between 1941 and 1981.
5. The number of federal civilian employees has decreased since 1961.

Government and You

1. If you were President of the United States and were instituting an executive reorganization, which, if any, of the Cabinet departments would you abolish? Explain your answer.
2. If you wanted a job with the federal government, do you think your chances for getting it would be better under the spoils system or the merit system? Why?
3. Do you think there are advantages to working for the federal government rather than in the private sector? Give reasons for your opinion.
4. Do you approve or disapprove of the creation of the Senior Executive Service in the federal bureaucracy? Justify your opinion.
5. Would you be in favor of modifying the Hatch Act? Why or why not?
6. Do you think that employees should be allowed to move back and forth between government and the private sector? Why or why not?
7. List five ways in which the federal bureaucracy affects your daily life.

Activities

1. Find out what GS-level job and salary you would be eligible for upon graduation from high school; upon graduation from college.
2. Look in your local telephone directory and list ten of the entries under "United States Government." Describe how the agencies listed under those entries might be useful to you.
3. Choose one of the independent regulatory commissions. Look in *Readers' Guide to Periodical Literature* and research a controversial action taken by this commission during the past three years. Indicate which groups favored or opposed the action, and why they did so.
4. Choose a Cabinet department, determine who the head of the department is, and what his or her policies are.

Chapter 22

Government and Finance

Money is, with propriety, considered as the vital principle of the body politic; as that which sustains its life and motion, and enables it to perform its most essential function.

ALEXANDER HAMILTON

CHAPTER OVERVIEW

The Department of the Treasury is a law enforcement agency and the financial agency of the federal government. The seal of the Department of the Treasury includes the scales of justice and a key, representing authority.

1 THE DEPARTMENT OF THE TREASURY

The Treasury Department was one of the three departments created during President George Washington's first term in office. The Treasury Department collected taxes and paid debts, printed currency and minted coins, and established a national banking system. Over the years it took on new responsibilities, and its role within the economy expanded. At the same time, new agencies concerned with government finance were created outside the Treasury Department. These included the Bureau of the Budget—now the Office of Management and Budget within the Executive Office of the President—and the independent Federal Reserve Board.

The Secretary of the Treasury is the head of the Treasury Department and the chief financial officer of the government. As a major adviser to the President, the Treasury Secretary plays an important role in making decisions that affect taxing, spending, borrowing, lending, and other financial operations of the federal government. These decisions also influence the national economy.

As chief financial officer the Secretary of the Treasury serves on numerous committees and boards, both domestic and international. The Secretary officially represents the United States in such organizations as the World Bank and the International Monetary Fund.

Besides making policy, the Secretary oversees the eleven major bureaus and offices within the Treasury Department. The agencies of the Treasury Department have five basic duties. They collect taxes. They enforce the law. They provide the government with various financial services. They manufacture coins, stamps, and paper money. And they supervise the nation's complex banking system. The rest of this section examines each of these five duties in detail.

Tax Collection

The Constitution gives Congress the power to tax. Collecting taxes is done, for the most part, by the United States Customs Service and the Internal Revenue Service. The Bureau of Alcohol, Tobacco, and Firearms also collects taxes, but its major duty is law enforcement.

Notable Secretaries of the Treasury have included (clockwise, from top center) Andrew Mellon, who reduced the nation's World War I debt; Henry Morgenthau, whose financial policies contributed to Allied victory in World War II; Roger B. Taney, who served President Andrew Jackson for a year but was denied Senate confirmation; Salmon P. Chase, who raised the revenues that enabled the Union to win the Civil War; and Albert Gallatin, who served Presidents Thomas Jefferson and James Madison.

United States Customs Service Established in 1789, the Customs Service processes all persons, carriers, cargo, and mail in and out of the country. Its head is the Commissioner of Customs.

The Customs Service assesses and collects ***duties***, or ***tariffs***, which are taxes on goods imported into the United States. These taxes are designed to produce revenue and sometimes also to protect American industry.

The Customs Service maintains offices at some 300 ***ports of entry***—border crossings, seaports, and airports at which international flights are scheduled. All imports must be brought into the United States through one of these ports of entry and must pass through customs.

The Customs Service searches for smuggled goods and seizes them. Often it cooperates with other branches of the federal government. With the Department of Agriculture, for example, it enforces a waiting period of isolation, or a ***quarantine***, on plants and animals being brought into the country. With the Department of Justice, as well as with foreign governments, it works to suppress the traffic in illegal drugs. The Customs Service also works closely with the Immigration and Naturalization Service to process people entering the United States.

Customs Service officials at the Hartsfield Atlanta International Airport check the baggage of passengers entering the United States. What financial function does the Customs Service perform?

Internal Revenue Service Created in 1862, the Internal Revenue Service (IRS) is the largest bureau within the Treasury Department. Most of the government's ***revenue,*** or income, comes from taxes collected by the IRS.

The IRS operates in a decentralized way. Although the national office in Washington, D.C., makes overall policy, most activities of the IRS are conducted through 60 district offices. In these district offices IRS agents answer taxpayers' questions and help them to fill out their tax returns. The agents also examine tax returns and investigate possible cases of tax evasion and other violations of the tax laws. The IRS also maintains 10 Service Centers throughout the nation that process tax returns and various other related documents.

Law Enforcement

Two agencies divide the law enforcement activities of the Treasury Department. They are the Bureau of Alcohol, Tobacco, and Firearms and the United States Secret Service.

The Bureau of Alcohol, Tobacco, and Firearms administers and enforces two sets of laws. One set regulates the production, use, and distribution of alcohol and tobacco. The other set regulates the production, use, and distribution of firearms and explosives. The bureau collects taxes on liquor and tobacco products. It also seeks to suppress illegal traffic in liquor and cigarettes. But above all, it works to keep guns out of the hands of criminals by enforcing the Gun Control Act of 1968. This law forbids

The Internal Revenue Service (IRS) is responsible for administering and enforcing United States tax laws and for encouraging voluntary compliance with these laws.

the sale of handguns to persons under 21 and of shotguns and rifles to persons under 18. It also prohibits the sale of firearms by mail. Finally, it requires the licensing of certain kinds of firearms.

The Secret Service was established in 1865. In its early years, before the creation of the Federal Bureau of Investigation, the Secret Service was the general law enforcement agency of the federal government. Today the Secret Service has two primary duties. First, it protects the President and the First Family. Second, it protects the United States against the counterfeiting of coins, currency, stamps, government bonds, government checks, and other government securities. The Secret Service handles

PROFILE

To Protect the President

The President of the United States is about to deliver a speech in a large metropolitan area. For more than a week Secret Service agents have been at work. With the help of local police officials, the agents have checked the backgrounds of everyone who may meet the President during the visit, comparing the names with a computer list of nearly 27,000 people considered potentially dangerous because of criminal records. Meanwhile other agents have investigated the auditorium where the President will speak. They have a detailed map of all entrances and exits and a plan of action for almost any conceivable emergency. They have also checked the entrances and exits to make certain the building is secure. And just in case the President should be wounded or injured, Secret Service agents have made sure that local hospitals have a supply of blood of the President's type.

As the President's limousine pulls up outside the auditorium, agents search faces in the crowd. The agents have been trained to react immediately to the erratic movements or suspicious gestures of onlookers. Meanwhile other agents surround the limousine as the President steps down. They have been trained to give their own lives in order to save the President from harm.

President Abraham Lincoln established the Secret Service in 1865 a month before he was assassinated. At that time, however, the main task of the Secret Service was fighting counterfeiters. Ironically, it was not until 1901—after two other Presidents, James A. Garfield and William McKinley, had been assassinated—that protection of the President was added to the duties of the Secret Service.

Today more than 1,500 men and women serve as Secret Service agents. One branch of the Secret Service continues to fight counterfeiters of United States coins and currency. Another branch protects not only the President but also the First Family, the Vice President, the Vice President's family, major Presidential and Vice-Presidential candidates, and, on occasion, visiting heads of state. Secret Service agents accompany their assigned political leaders and their families at virtually every waking moment. Secret Service agents accompanied President Woodrow Wilson as he courted his wife. Agents stood near President Calvin Coolidge as he kept vigil at his dying son's bedside. Secret Service agents joined President Franklin D. Roosevelt as he traveled through enemy waters during World War II. To protect the President's and Vice President's children, agents go to school with them, accompany them on their dates, and are always nearby—even on their honeymoons.

The United States government raises billions of dollars in revenue by selling savings bonds in small dollar amounts to investors. People who buy savings bonds are loaning money to the federal government for a specific length of time.

thousands of counterfeiting and forgery cases a year, destroying all the counterfeit money it confiscates. It also tracks down people who steal government checks, make false claims to federal lending agencies, and commit a variety of other federal offenses.

Financial Services

The Department of the Treasury serves as a financial agent for the federal government. Three agencies—the Office of the Treasurer, the Bureau of Government Financial Operations, and the Bureau of Public Debt—share this responsibility.

The Treasurer of the United States was originally responsible for receiving, holding, and spending the government's money and for keeping the government's accounts. Today most of this work is done by other agencies, and the post of Treasurer is largely ceremonial. One of the Treasurer's main jobs is to promote the sale of United States Savings Bonds. The Treasurer's signature also appears on all paper money.

Many of the tasks nominally assigned to the Office of the Treasurer are performed by the Bureau of Government Financial Operations. For example, as the government's bookkeeper, it maintains a central

Katherine Ortega serves as Treasurer of the United States for the Reagan administration. The Treasurer supervises the Bureau of Engraving and Printing, the United States Mint, and the United States Savings Bond Division.

accounting system for the government's money. It also pays out public money under orders drawn by the Secretary of the Treasury and approved by the Comptroller General. Each year its disbursing service mails out more than 600 million checks to pay federal salaries and wages, to pay for goods and services purchased by the federal government, and to pay benefits under Social Security and other federal programs.

The bureau publishes daily, monthly, and annual reports on the government's financial operations. These reports tell the President, Congress, and the public where the government's money comes from and where it goes.

The Bureau of Public Debt manages the national debt, which is discussed later in this chapter. Specifically, the bureau supervises the loans that the government takes out to pay its expenses.

PROFILE

The Bureau of Engraving and Printing

At the Bureau of Engraving and Printing in Washington, D.C., the presses are rolling. Large sheets of specially prepared paper—a blend of cotton and linen fibers mixed with millions of tiny red and blue silk threads—are fed into the presses. Only a few people at the bureau know the formula for the special ink used in the presses. On a typical day the bureau produces 9 million bills in denominations of $1, $5, $10, $20, $50, and $100. Each bill—from the one-dollar bill to the hundred-dollar bill—costs only about two cents to produce. Over the course of one year the bureau prints an average of 1.5 billion one-dollar bills and 1 billion of all other denominations.

New money is distributed by the 12 main Federal Reserve Banks and their 25 branch banks. There is an average of nearly $170 billion worth of currency in circulation at all times. As the currency passes from hand to hand, it deteriorates. A dollar bill, for example, lasts only about 18 months in circulation. By contrast, a coin may circulate as long as 40 years. When currency has become badly worn, it is removed from circulation and returned to the Treasury Department in Washington. There, under the careful scrutiny of Federal Reserve and Treasury officials, the worn-out currency is burned. The Treasury Department keeps track of currency that has been damaged or destroyed in order to know how much currency remains in circulation.

Occasionally a bill is damaged or torn by accident. Banks will replace a torn bill if three fifths or more of the bill remains intact. If only as much as two fifths remains, the bill is worth half its original value and its exchange can be authorized only by the Treasurer of the United States.

Experts in a special division of the Treasury Department are trained to examine severely damaged or mutilated bills. Using advanced scientific techniques, examiners can determine the original denominations of bills that have been burned or even shredded. In one case a Minnesota farmer had buried a strongbox of paper money in a field. Over time, moisture seeped into the box and the bills hardened into a solid mass. The farmer brought the damaged bills to the Treasury Department, claiming that the bills totaled $20,000. Treasury experts set to work. They soaked the money in moist cotton. As the hardened mass of bills grew soft, they removed them one by one. Every bill the experts could identify was replaced with a crisp new bill, much to the delight of the farmer. In the end, investigators identified and returned to the farmer $27,000.

Gold coins similar to this $10 coin—called an eagle—were minted by the United States between 1795 and 1933. Today these coins are worth far more than their face value, partly because of the increased value of gold.

The General Accounting Office (GAO) is an agency of the Congress. It is mentioned here because it acts as a watchdog on the Treasury. The GAO checks to make sure that federal money is being spent legally. It also designs the various federal accounting systems and supervises the recovery of debts owed to the federal government.

The GAO is headed by the Comptroller General, who is appointed by the President. To ensure independence from the President, the Comptroller General is appointed for a 15-year term. The GAO's head cannot be reappointed. But Congress may remove the Comptroller from office by a joint resolution. To further ensure independence, the GAO is not part of the executive branch but is a legislative agency.

The Currency System

The Constitution gives Congress the power "to coin money [and] regulate the value thereof." This power has been interpreted to include the issuing of paper money, or ***currency.*** The Bureau of the Mint and the Bureau of Engraving and Printing produce all of the nation's coins and currency.

The Gold Standard By granting Congress the power to coin money and regulate the value thereof, and by denying this power to the states, the Constitution gives Congress the power to establish a national currency system. In the Mint Act of 1792, Congress set up a ***bimetallic system*** based on gold and silver. Both gold and silver coins were issued, and each contained metal approximately equal in value to the stated value of the coin. Paper money was first issued by the federal government in 1862 to finance the Civil War. The notes could be redeemed for either gold or silver.

During the late nineteenth century the bimetallic system was thrown into chaos by a decline in the value of silver and an increase in the value of gold. As a result of the fluctuating values, debtors preferred to pay their debts in silver dollars, while creditors wanted to receive gold dollars.

Between 1873 and 1878, Congress stopped the minting of silver coins altogether, provoking violent debate over the issue of ***free silver.*** Democrats fought for the free coinage of silver, insisting that Congress authorize the minting of an unlimited amount of silver coins. Republicans supported the use of gold coins and the ban on silver. For the next 25 years the nation was bitterly divided over the free-silver issue.

Following the Republican victory in the 1896 Presidential election, Congress passed the Gold Standard Act of 1900. Under the ***gold standard*** all coins and paper currency were valued in terms of gold. Silver and paper money could be redeemed at face value for gold. Consequently the Treasury Department and the national banks had to keep enough gold on hand to back the money in circulation.

Much of the gold that is owned by the federal government is stored in the United States Bullion Depository in Fort Knox, Kentucky. The gold at Fort Knox is in the form of almost pure gold bars that are slightly smaller than ordinary bricks. Each bar contains approximately 400 troy ounces of gold.

The Gold Reserve System The gold standard remained in effect until the 1930's. Then, as the financial crisis of the Great Depression weakened public confidence in the exchange of currency, people began to hoard gold. Gold disappeared from circulation, and the nation's gold reserves declined.

When President Franklin D. Roosevelt took office in 1933, the government adopted the gold reserve system in place of the gold standard. The Treasury was directed to build up a ***gold reserve,*** or a supply of gold, equal to at least 25 percent of all the paper money in circulation. Thus, coins and currency were partly to be based on gold, but money could no longer be redeemed for gold. Gold coins were no longer minted, and people who owned them had to exchange them for paper money. Private citizens could no longer buy and sell gold. Except for gold jewelry, dental fillings, and collector's coins, the federal government owned all the gold in the United States .

On the international scene, however, gold remained the basis of currency exchange. Gold moved from one nation to another in payment of international debts. The United States dollar was freely exchanged for gold at a fixed price.

The Currency System Today In the 1960's the United States bought more goods than it sold on the international market. As a result, more gold left the country than came in, and federal gold reserves declined. In the 1970's gold reserves declined still further as the United States began spending more and more money to import increasingly expensive foreign oil.

To counter the decline in gold reserves, Congress declared in 1968 that the Treasury need no longer hold gold to back the nation's currency. In 1971 President Richard M. Nixon announced that foreign governments could no longer exchange dollars for gold at a fixed price. These two governmental actions totally abolished the gold reserve system as a basis for national currency. In 1974 Congress restored to United States citizens the right to own gold and to buy and sell gold in the open market.

Today, paper currency in circulation totals about $170 billion. The paper bills may not be redeemed for either gold or silver. United States currency—like that of every other nation in the world—is based on the trust and confidence people have in their government.

The Banking System

The history of banking in the United States may be divided into three periods. In the first period, from 1791 to 1836, Congress set up a national bank with branches located in major cities. The national bank served as a depository for the nation's money. Funds were drawn and loans made from the depository. The national bank issued its own paper money.

Critics of the national bank thought its charter had been issued unconstitutionally by Congress. Even after the bank's constitutionality was upheld in the landmark decision of *McCulloch* v. *Maryland* (1819), opponents continued to call for its elimination. The charter for the Bank of the United States expired in 1836, four years after President Andrew Jackson had vetoed a bill to extend its life.

The second period, from 1836 to 1863, was one in which there was no national banking system. The Constitution forbids the states to issue money. But it does not forbid them to authorize private banks to issue paper money. So the states chartered banks that had the authority to issue paper currency. But the currency was as varied as the banking laws of the different states. Some bank notes were backed by gold. Others were worth little more than the paper on which they were printed. The result was unsound currency and many bank failures that caused severe financial distress for businesses and people.

The National Banking System The third period, from 1863 to the present, began when Congress created a new national banking system. Under this system national and state banks exist side by side. National banks are chartered under federal law and state banks are chartered under state law. There are about 10,000 banks under state charters and almost 5,000 banks under national charter. The nationally chartered banks have 14,000 branches, more than 600 of them in more than 70 countries.

Banks today are closely regulated on both the national and state levels. One federal regulatory

INSIGHT

Coins Today

There are five coins minted by the United States government today—the penny, the nickel, the dime, the quarter, and the half-dollar. The present system of coinage is basically the same as the one authorized by Congress in 1792. In the early years of the Republic, the worth of the metal in each coin was the same as the stated value of the coin. In other words, a half-dollar coin actually contained 50 cents worth of silver.

As the price of metal rose, however, the value of the metal content of each coin became higher than the face value of the coin. Thus, a half-dollar coin contained more than 50 cents worth of silver. To keep coins in circulation, Congress in 1965 changed the metallic content of the coins. Since then, all the "silver" coins—the dime, the quarter, and the half-dollar—have actually been minted from copper and nickel. In 1982, after the price of copper increased, Congress changed the content of the penny. Since then, pennies have been minted from 97.6 percent zinc.

Thus coins, like currency in the United States, are today based on the trust and confidence Americans have in their government.

agency is the Treasury Department's Office of the Comptroller of the Currency. The Comptroller approves bank charters and mergers and the creation of bank branches. The Comptroller's Office examines regularly the financial condition, operation, and management of each national bank. It makes sure that all banks are complying with federal laws.

The Federal Reserve System The second agency charged with bank supervision is the Board of Governors of the Federal Reserve System, which was created in 1913. The Federal Reserve Board, frequently called the Fed, has two jobs. First, it supervises and controls the operations of all banks. Second, it sets and administers the nation's monetary policy.

Under the Federal Reserve System the United States is divided geographically into Federal Reserve Districts. Within each district is a Federal Reserve Bank that is governed by a nine-member board of directors, six of whom are chosen by the bank and three by the Fed. Each Federal Reserve Bank serves as a bank for the member banks in its district. It acts as a central clearinghouse for collecting and cashing

INSIGHT

Dust Bowl Days

It was 1934. It could have been any state in the Great Plains, especially Kansas, Oklahoma, or Texas. Three years of drought and scorching temperatures had left the farmland bare, cracked, and bone-dry. Wheat struggled to grow. Farmers throughout the plains wondered how much wheat they would harvest and how much lower the price of wheat would get. Last year's crop was half what it was the year before. This year's crop would be half that of last year. Farmers with tractor and mortgage payments to make faced a bleak future.

The thought of the dark clouds that rolled in ever more frequently made the future bleaker still. The dark clouds brought no rain—only wind and dust that had been picked up from the topsoil and carried for miles. The dust blotted out the daylight, beat against windows and doors, and seeped through the tiniest cracks. In all, the dust storms swept nearly 350 million tons of topsoil into the air from the Dust Bowl plains of Kansas, Oklahoma, and Texas.

Many farmers lost their homes, their land, and many of their possessions before help came through the New Deal programs of President Franklin D. Roosevelt. One act established the Federal Home Loan Bank System to provide money for home loans. The system consists of 12 regional banks, each of which makes loans to member institutions. These, in turn, make loans directly to home buyers. There are 4,500 member institutions, mostly savings and loan associations, with a total of more than $500 billion in assets. The system is directed by the Federal Home Loan Bank Board, an independent executive agency.

Other New Deal acts established agencies to give farmers help in securing credit and in selling their crops and livestock. Some of these agencies operate under the Department of Agriculture. Others are independent agencies devoted to farm interests. One such agency is the Farm Credit Administration. It supervises the Federal Land Banks, which have a regional organization similar to the Federal Home Loan Banks. The Federal Land Banks loan money to member banks, which, in turn, loan money to individual farmers to buy or improve land, buildings, and farm equipment. Should the Dust Bowl days return or another disaster bring ruin to farmers, help is as close as the nearest Federal Land Bank. Its loans to farmers total about $20 billion a year.

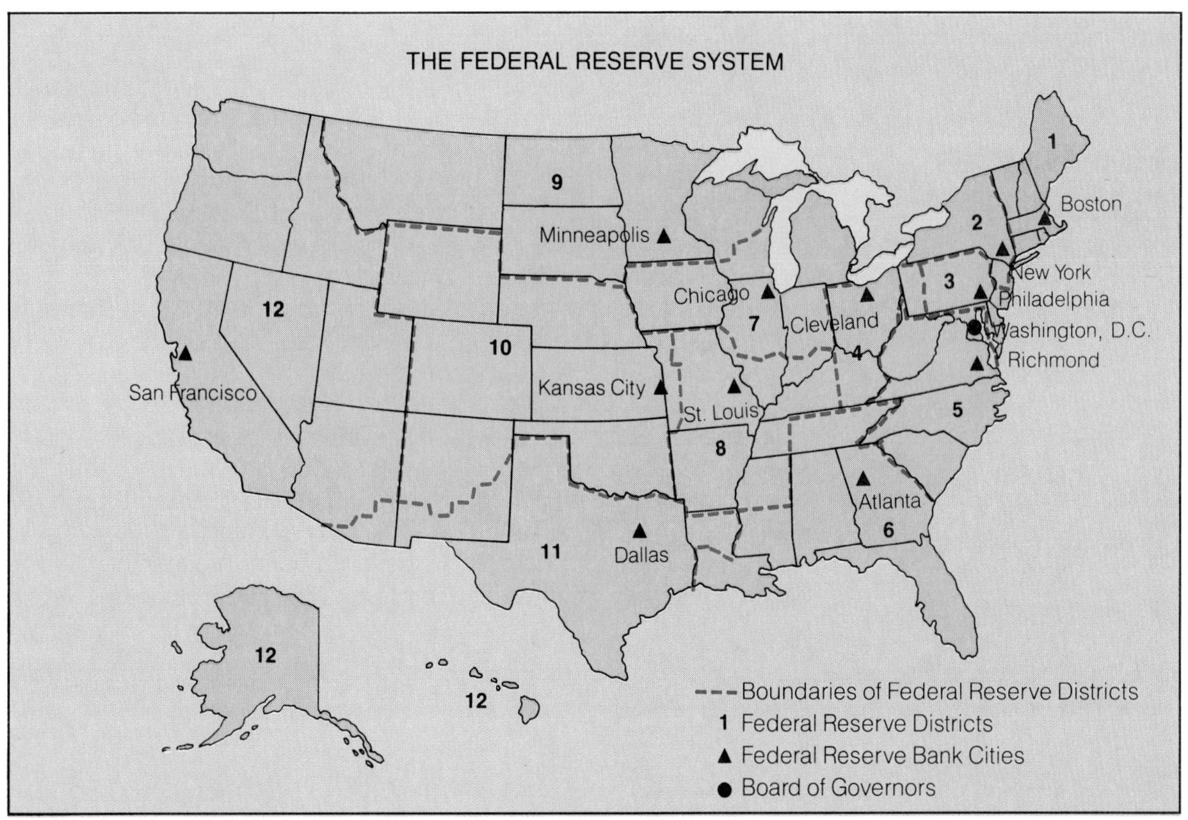

The Federal Reserve System is composed of 12 Federal Reserve Districts, each of which has a Federal Reserve Bank. These banks issue Federal Reserve Notes—paper money. Name three major functions of the Federal Reserve Banks.

checks. It holds on deposit the reserves of its member banks and makes loans to them as needed.

The Federal Reserve Banks issue most of the paper money in circulation. Federal Reserve Banks also provide banking services to the federal government. They hold the Treasury Department's money on deposit, handle the sale and redemption of government securities, and conduct many other transactions for the federal government.

All national banks must belong to the Federal Reserve System. State banks may join if they meet the same standards as the national banks. In practice, most state banks are members of the Federal Reserve System.

The Fed controls the operations of all Federal Reserve Banks. It examines these banks regularly to ensure that they comply with federal laws. It requires member banks to make periodic reports. It admits national and state banks to membership in the Federal Reserve System and suspends them for unsound practices. It also limits the rates of interest that member banks may pay, preventing them from offering higher rates than they can safely afford to pay.

The Fed also makes ***monetary policy*** and administers it by expanding or contracting the money supply. In a period of ***inflation,*** prices rise because there is more money available than there are goods to buy. So if the Fed wishes to fight inflation, it tightens credit. It may do this in three ways.

First, it can raise the ***discount rate,*** the interest that member banks pay when they borrow money from their district's Federal Reserve Bank to make loans to their own borrowers. The higher the discount rate, the less willing member banks are to make loans to their customers.

Second, the Fed can increase the ***reserve requirement,*** the percentage of its funds that each member bank must deposit with its Federal Reserve Bank. By increasing the reserve requirement, the Fed leaves member banks with less money for making loans.

Third, the Fed can authorize the Federal Reserve Banks to sell the ***government securities,*** or interest-bearing bonds and notes, that they hold. This ***open-market operation*** in effect drains money away from other kinds of investment.

LEGACY

The Banks Take a Holiday

In February 1933 the economy of the United States seemed about to collapse. Depositors began a rush to withdraw their savings from banks, which by law had to redeem currency in gold. Unable to meet the staggering demand for gold, banks all over the country shut their doors. Shortly after taking office in March, President Franklin D. Roosevelt declared a four-day bank holiday. He issued the order to gain time for a reorganization of the nation's banking system.

The bank holiday ended officially on March 9, 1933. At that time Congress passed the Emergency Banking Act, giving the Federal Reserve Board greater control over the nation's banking system. A later act set up the Federal Deposit Insurance Corporation (FDIC). As an independent executive agency the FDIC provides depositors insurance on the full value of all accounts up to $100,000. The reorganization of the banking system and the creation of the FDIC restored people's confidence in banks as safe places for their deposits.

Bank failures still occur. But if the failed banks are members of the Federal Reserve System and are insured by the FDIC, depositors never lose a cent.

All of these actions are designed to slow down the rate of inflation by reducing the money supply. Conversely, the Fed may try to bring the country out of a recession or reduce unemployment by loosening credit and thus stimulating economic growth.

Since most of the money in circulation is issued by the Federal Reserve Banks, the Fed can also influence the money supply simply by issuing more or less money. Its ability to control credit and to issue money gives the Fed enormous power over the nation's economy.

Section Check

1. Define: duties, tariffs, ports of entry, revenue, bimetallic system, free silver, gold standard, gold reserve, monetary policy, inflation, discount rate, reserve requirement, government security, open-market operation
2. Identify: United States Customs Service, Internal Revenue Service, Secret Service, Federal Reserve System
3. Why did the bimetallic system run into trouble during the late nineteenth century?
4. Why did the government abandon the gold standard in the 1930's?

2 TAXES AND THE FEDERAL BUDGET

The federal government takes in about $30 billion a year from nontax sources. Much of this nontax money comes from interest on loans made by the Federal Reserve System. The sale or lease of public lands, a wide variety of fees and fines, and the sale of surplus government property account for most of the rest. It is through taxation, however, that the federal government finances the majority of its activities and programs. As Benjamin Franklin said, "In this world nothing is certain but death and taxes." But Oliver Wendell Holmes reminded people that "taxes are the price we pay for civilized society." It is a high price—more than $630 billion in 1985. What all this money is spent on is the other side of the taxation picture. Which programs get the money determines to a large extent the shape of life for the taxpayers themselves.

Taxation

The power to tax is granted to the government in Article 1, Section 8, Clause 1, of the Constitution. But the Constitution also places limits on the power to tax. Taxes may not be imposed if the result is to deny persons their constitutional rights. For example, no tax may be imposed on churches, temples, or synagogues because such taxation would limit the free exercise of religion, a right guaranteed by the First Amendment.

Specifically, the Constitution states four limitations on the federal government's power to tax.

- As Article 1, Section 8, Clause 1, states, taxes may be levied only for public purposes. Thus, taxes may not be used to benefit any private group.
- As Article 1, Section 9, Clause 4, states, direct taxes must be apportioned, or divided, equally among the states according to population.
- As Article 1, Section 9, Clause 5, states, no tax may be levied on exports. But taxes may be levied on imports.
- As Article 1, Section 8, Clause 1, states, indirect taxes must be uniform.

A fifth limitation, which is implied rather than stated specifically, is that federal taxes may not be imposed on state and local governments. Conversely, the states may not tax the federal government. As Chief Justice John Marshall stated in *McCulloch* v. *Maryland* (1819), "The power to tax involves the power to destroy." Congress, however, may tax the business activities of state and local governments.

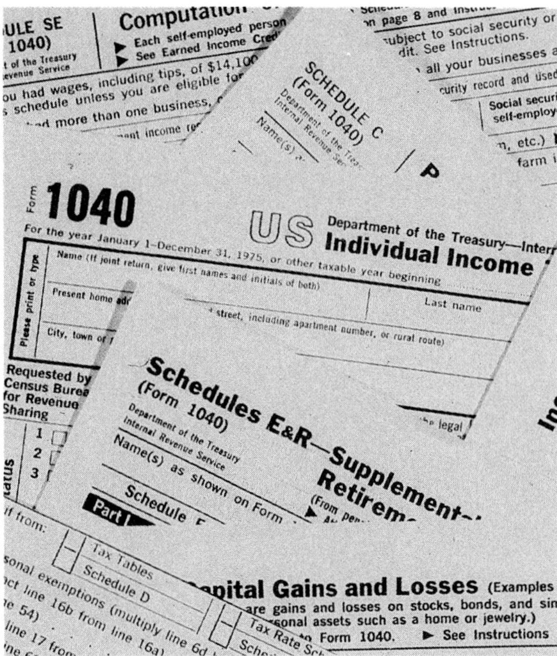

Most American workers fill out one or more tax forms each year as they comply with the nation's income tax laws. Is the income tax a direct or an indirect tax?

Income Taxes Before 1913 most of the government's revenue came from customs duties on imported goods. Nearly 90 percent of the revenue collected within the country came from excise taxes on tobacco and liquor.

By the late nineteenth century, however, the growth of the federal government's expenses forced Congress to look for new sources of revenue. In 1894, Congress enacted an income tax, but the following year the Supreme Court struck it down as unconstitutional. The Court held that the federal income tax was a direct tax. Under Article 1, Section 9, Clause 4, all direct taxes must be apportioned equally among the states. But such a tax would be grossly unfair because of the great differences in wealth among the states.

The Sixteenth Amendment, adopted in 1913, settled the question. It states:

Congress shall have the power to lay and collect taxes on incomes, from whatever source derived, without apportionment among the several States, and without regard to any census or enumeration.

LEXICON

Direct and Indirect Taxes

A ***direct tax*** is levied directly on an individual or business and is paid directly to the government. Income and property taxes are examples of direct taxes. An ***indirect tax*** is levied on manufactured goods and is paid by a purchaser of those goods. It is usually collected by a business and then passed on to the government. Sales and excise taxes are examples of indirect taxes.

The constitutional requirement for uniformity of indirect taxes means, for example, that the federal excise tax on gasoline must be the same in New York, Texas, Florida, and every other state in the Union.

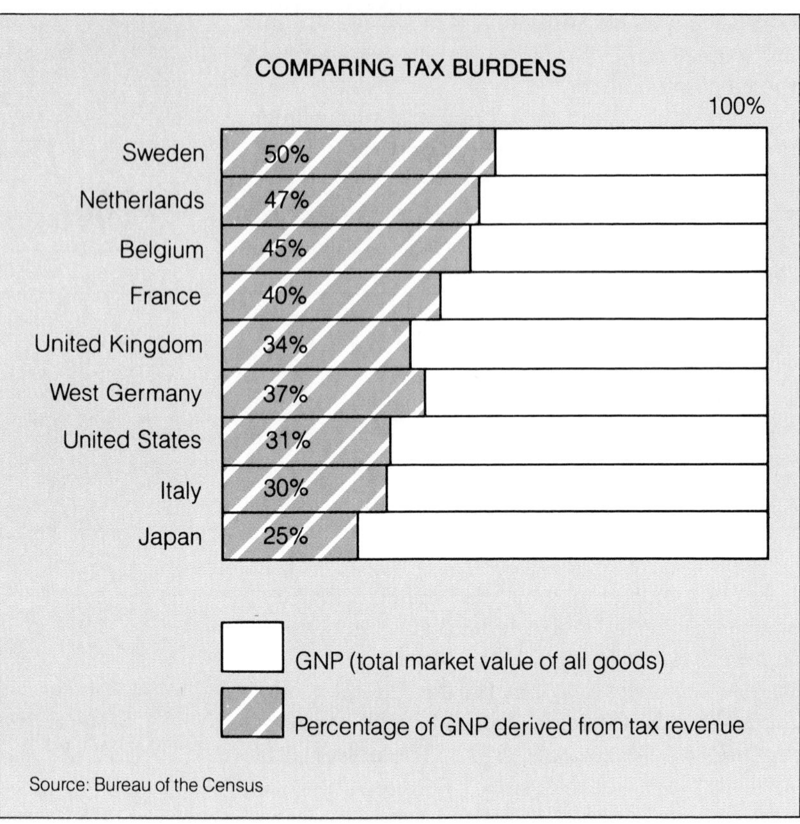

When compared to the tax burdens of other industrialized countries, the tax burden of the United States does not appear to be particularly severe. Some Americans avoid paying their fair share of taxes by taking advantage of loopholes in the tax laws.

Today the personal income tax is the federal government's largest single source of revenue. It accounts for 75 percent of federal revenue, if Social Security taxes are excluded. Revenue from the personal income tax also accounts for about 45 percent of the budget dollar.

The personal income tax is a ***graduated tax*** because the tax rate increases as income rises. For example, in 1982, people earning the lowest taxable income paid a tax rate of 12 percent, while those earning the highest taxable income paid a tax rate of 50 percent.

Tax rates apply only to ***taxable income***—a person's total income minus exemptions and deductions. Each individual is allowed a personal exemption of $1,500, with additional exemptions for the elderly and the blind. The interest paid on a home mortgage is a deduction. So are contributions to certain charities, as well as certain medical and business expenses. While exemptions are straightforward, determining which deductions are allowable may be complicated. The Internal Revenue Service publishes a whole library of pamphlets to help people cope with the thousands of rules governing deductions.

In addition to standard deductions, there are inconsistencies in the tax laws called ***loopholes*** that make it possible for some people to avoid paying taxes. Many loopholes are unintentional, but some are deliberately written into the law to benefit a particular activity or group. By taking advantage of deductions and loopholes, a millionaire may end up paying no income taxes at all.

Tax reform efforts seek to close loopholes and eliminate the deductions that stem from them. One proposed solution is a proportional tax. In this flat-rate system there are no loopholes or deductions because everyone is taxed at the same rate. Supporters of a proportional tax argue that it would be simpler and in some ways fairer than the graduated tax system presently in use. Opponents argue that a flat-rate system would not be based on ability to pay. Still other experts feel that the real answer may be some compromise between the graduated tax and the flat-rate, or proportional, tax. Everyone agrees that the goal is a tax system in which each wage earner pays a fair share.

Most individuals with taxable income must file an annual income tax return before midnight on April 15. Most wage earners pay their taxes through

withholding, an automatic deduction from wages or salary. The employer issues a W–2 form on which the total amount withheld for the calendar year is indicated. The employer sends one copy of this form to the IRS, and the taxpayer sends in another copy along with the tax return. A taxpayer who owes more than the amount withheld sends the IRS a check for the difference. If too much money has been withheld, the IRS sends the taxpayer a refund check.

Most people honestly report all their earnings. The IRS, however, keeps a watchful eye out for taxpayers who fail to report all taxable income, who take nonallowable deductions or misrepresent the amount of legal deductions, or who take exemptions for which they do not qualify. Intentional failure to file an accurate return is a crime punishable by fine and imprisonment.

The ***corporate income tax*** accounts for approximately 16 percent of federal revenue. Like individuals, corporations are subject to a graduated income tax. Similarly, they are entitled to a wide and complicated variety of deductions.

Nonprofit organizations such as schools, religious institutions, charities, unions, and cooperatives are exempt from income taxes.

Payroll Taxes There are two types of federal ***payroll taxes*** levied on employers and on their employees. Social Security taxes are levied to finance Old-Age, Survivors, and Disability Insurance (OASDI) and Medicare. At present the employee pays a tax of 6.7 percent of the first $32,400 of annual salary, and the employer pays an identical amount. The employer deducts the employee's tax from each paycheck and sends it, along with his or her own payment, to the IRS.

A second tax, levied on the payrolls of businesses with one or more employees, supports the Federal-State Unemployment Compensation Program. Although the cost of this program is shared by the state and federal governments, the amount and duration of the benefits vary from state to state. At present the tax rate is 3.4 percent on the first $6,000 earned.

Receipts from Social Security and federal unemployment taxes comprise about 33 percent of all federal revenue.

Excise Taxes A levy on the manufacture, sale, use, or transfer of certain goods and services is called an ***excise tax.*** Such taxes are typically imposed on luxury items, such as liquor and tobacco. They are also imposed on firearms, gasoline, air travel, and telephone service.

Because excise taxes on the manufacture of goods are figured into the price of the item, they are in reality a form of sales tax. Excise taxes comprise about 7 percent of all federal revenue.

Employee earnings and the federal income tax withheld from those earnings are reported on the W–2 form. Many states have a state income tax and withholding as well.

OMB No. 1545-0008

1 Control number 308058

4 Employer's State number C02500

1985

Wage and Tax Statement
Copy 1 for State, City, or Local Tax Department.

2 Employer's name, address, and ZIP code
JONES SUPPLY CO.
1535 WEST 9TH STREET
CHICAGO IL 60601

3 Employer's identification number 36-2659374

5 Stat. employee · Deceased · Legal rep. · 942 emp. · Subtotal · Void

6 Allocated tips

7 Advance EIC payment

8 Employee's social security number 33A-48-C123

9 Federal income tax withheld 113.37

10 Wages, tips, other compensation 1529.67

11 Social security tax withheld 102.49

12 Employee's name
DARRELL J. WILLIAMS
10053 SOUTH STREET
WESTMONT IL 60559
Employees' address and ZIP code

13 Social security wages 1529.67

14 Social security tips

16

17 State income tax 42.77

18 State wages, tips, etc. 1529.67

19 Name of State IL

20 Local income tax

21 Local wages, tips, etc.

22 Name of locality

Form **W-2 Wage and Tax Statement**

LEXICON

Three Types of Taxes

A ***progressive tax*** is the same as a graduated tax. In the United States, which uses a progressive tax system to produce most federal revenue, the tax rate rises as income increases. A person with a high income pays a larger percentage of income in taxes than a person with a lower income.

A government that uses a ***proportional tax*** system taxes each person's income at the same rate regardless of the amount earned. For example, all incomes might be taxed at a uniform rate of 20 percent.

A ***regressive tax*** is one in which each person, regardless of income, pays the same amount. An example is a general sales tax. Traditionally, lower-income families spend a proportionately higher percentage of their income on such necessities as food, milk, and clothing. A sales tax is regressive because it imposes a heavier burden on lower-income families than on those with higher incomes.

Customs Duties Before the income tax was legalized most of the government's revenue came from ***customs duties,*** the taxes levied on imports. Today, however, customs duties account for just slightly more than 1 percent of all the federal government's revenue.

Customs duties vary with the item being taxed. Some items—for example, diamonds—are taxed at a low rate "for revenue only." Other items—for example, shoes—are taxed at a high rate "for protection." The customs duty serves to protect American industry—in this case, the shoe industry—from the low prices of foreign-made goods. Finally, some goods—for example, books—are "duty free," or not taxed at all.

Transfer of Property Taxes The federal government places two kinds of taxes on the transfer of property. An ***estate tax*** is levied on property left by someone who dies. The federal government first levied estate taxes in 1916. The tax is applied to the value of a person's estate after certain exemptions and deductions have been subtracted. A 1983 law has made the first $275,000 of a person's estate exempt from any estate taxes. So only estates with a value greater than $275,000 will have estate taxes levied on them. An estate tax may also be levied by state governments.

The second kind of tax placed on the transfer of property is the ***gift tax.*** It is levied on a cash gift made by a living person if the amount of the gift is greater than $10,000 and the gift is to someone other than the donor's spouse.

Regulatory Taxes The use of taxes to promote desirable activities or to suppress dangerous or undesirable ones is the main goal of ***regulatory taxation.*** For example, higher taxes on gasoline tend to reduce consumption and promote energy conservation. High excise taxes on the sale of liquor and tobacco may discourage their use. A classic example of regulatory taxation occurred in 1912, when Congress imposed a tax on white phosphorous matches. The phosphorous was poisoning workers in the factories where the matches were produced. The tax, which made the production of white phosphorus matches unprofitable, destroyed the industry. The Supreme Court has upheld such regulatory taxes as constitutional, declaring that it is not the business of the courts to inquire into the motives behind a legally imposed tax.

Customs duties and excise taxes have been used for regulatory purposes. In the past, ***protective tariffs*** on certain items were set so high that they kept out foreign goods altogether. Today tariffs have been reduced in favor of freer international trade. Domestic industries are protected against foreign competition by import quotas and by product standards, such as the emission requirements on imported automobiles that the Environmental Protection Agency has set.

Income taxes also serve a regulatory function. The graduated income tax tends to level incomes by imposing a heavier tax on higher incomes. Reducing income taxes overall supposedly increases the demand for goods, while increasing income taxes is believed to reduce consumer spending. These actions, in turn, theoretically affect the rate of inflation and the level of unemployment. The actual effects of such policies have come into increasing dispute.

The Federal Budget

The ***federal budget*** may be looked at in two ways. First, it is an estimate of the amount of money the government expects to collect and spend during the coming ***fiscal year,*** the twelve-month accounting period that begins October 1 and ends September 30. Second, the federal budget is a plan that determines how the government will implement its policies. The budget specifies how much money will be spent on the government's existing programs and includes proposals for new programs.

The ways in which the federal budget dollar is spent—approved by both the President and Congress—are an indication of the nation's priorities. What priorities are indicated by the expenditures shown on the chart?

SPENDING THE BUDGET DOLLAR
Amount of Each Budget Dollar

National Defense: all military expenses, including personnel, weapons, and other equipment (26 cents)

International Affairs: foreign aid and diplomatic operations; information and exchange programs (2 cents)

Science, Space, and Technology: research, development and testing of space and other scientific programs (1 cent)

Energy: research and development of energy supplies with emphasis on the conservation of energy (½ cent)

Natural Resources and the Environment: development, management, and conservation of natural resources and recreational areas; pollution control (1 cent)

Agriculture: aid to farmers; quality control of food products for consumers (1½ cents)

Commerce and Housing Credit: support for mortgage credit and thrift insurance; subsidies to Postal Service; aid to small business (½ cent)

Transportation: aid for highway, mass transit, and airport construction; Coast Guard operations; aid to airways, rail and shipping lines (3 cents)

Community and Regional Development: aid for urban renewal and rural development (1 cent)

Education, Training, Employment, and Social Service: grants for elementary secondary, vocational, and higher education; job and safety training; care for needy, elderly, and disabled (2½ cents)

Health: Medicaid; consumer safety (3½ cents)

Income Security: Social Security and other retirement payments; Medicare; unemployment insurance; food stamps; housing subsidies; school breakfast and lunch programs (40 cents)

Veterans' Benefits and Services: support to families of disabled, aged, or deceased veterans (3 cents)

Administration of Justice: law enforcement; judicial and correctional activities; federal aid to state and local law enforcement groups (½ cent)

General Government: revenue collection; general property and records management; legislative functions (½ cent)

Revenue Sharing: return of tax dollars to state and local governments (½ cent)

Interest on Federal Debt: (13 cents)

Source: *The United States Budget in Brief, Fiscal Year 1985*

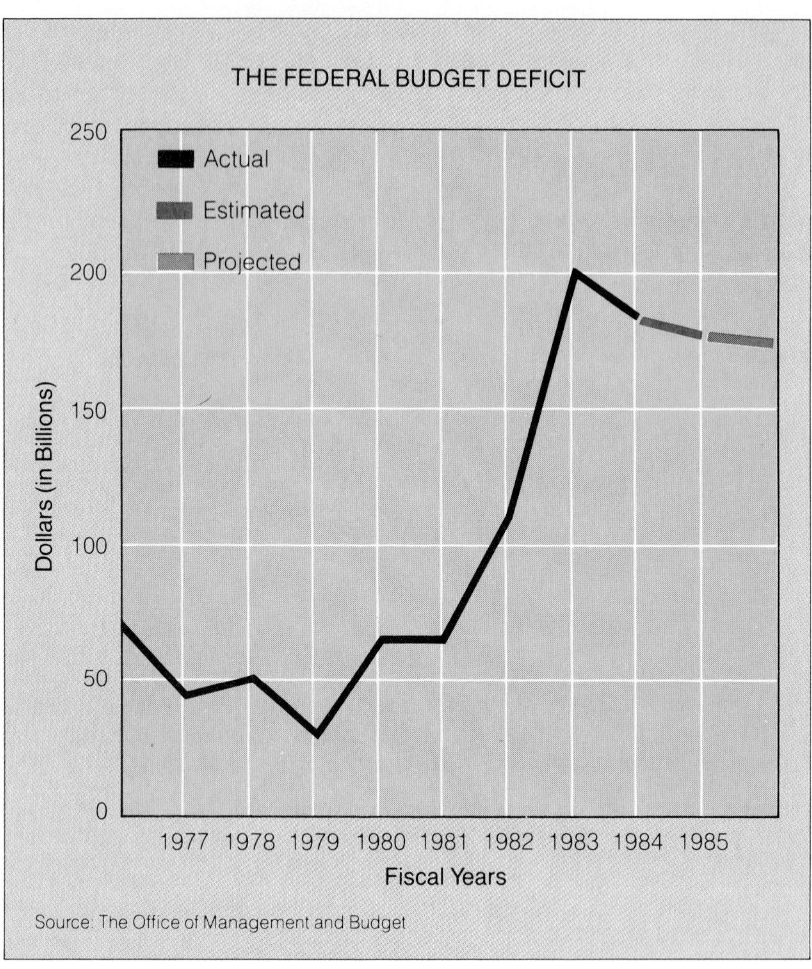

"Uncontrollable" items in the federal budget make accurate estimates and predictions of the deficit almost impossible. What are some of the "uncontrollable" items that contribute to the size of the budget deficit?

Preparation of the Budget The federal budget is prepared by the President's Office of Management and Budget (OMB). Each federal agency submits to the OMB a detailed estimate of its expenses for the coming fiscal year. After reviewing all of these estimates at a series of budget hearings, the OMB combines them into a single budget proposal.

At the beginning of each calendar year, the President sends budget proposals to Congress for the upcoming fiscal year. Congress examines the budget closely and makes cuts and additions. But a major portion of the budget is not easily controlled—either by the President or by Congress—because a great deal of spending is locked in by long-term, binding commitments. Examples of "uncontrollable" items include Social Security payments, civil service pensions, veterans' benefits, payments for Medicare and Medicaid, and interest on the national debt.

The federal budget reflects the nation's values. As they change, so does the budget. Thus, from 1970 to 1980, the portion of the budget devoted to human resource programs—income security, health, education, social services, and veterans programs—rose from 37 percent to 52 percent. During this same period the portion of the budget devoted to defense declined from 40 percent to 23 percent. A shift in priorities occurred with the election of President Ronald Reagan in 1980. In the 1984 budget he submitted to Congress, national defense expenditures rose from 23 percent to 29 percent.

Federal Expenditures To gain a better understanding of how the federal government spends the taxpayers' money, we can look at how the budget dollar for the fiscal year 1984 was to be expended. Government spending for the year was estimated at $849 billion, and revenues at $660 billion. This left a deficit of $189 billion, which would be made up by borrowing. The difference, or deficit, represents that year's contribution to the ***national debt,*** the total amount of money owed by the federal government.

The federal government makes up its budget deficit by borrowing. The Constitution—in Article 1, Section 8, Clause 2—gives Congress the power "to borrow money on the credit of the United States." The government does this by issuing short-term or long-term securities that may be purchased by private individuals, commercial banks and insurance companies, and Federal Reserve Banks. Government securities are a safe, guaranteed investment—as sound as the government itself.

The United States government came into being with a debt of $75 million from the Revolutionary War. As of 1982 the national debt was just over $1 trillion ($1,000,000,000,000), or some $4,300 for every person in the country. The 1982 interest alone on this astronomical sum came to $85 billion. Historically, the greatest increases in the national debt have come in times of such national crises as the Civil War, World War I, and World War II. In recent years tax cuts, combined with increased military spending, have created massive deficits. The 1984 deficit, for example, was almost $200 billion.

Management of the Economy

As noted earlier in this chapter, inflation occurs when there is more money in circulation than there are goods to buy. Because of the unmet demand for goods, inflation generally stimulates business and increases employment. In a recession, on the other hand, prices fall, business productivity slows down, and unemployment increases. A severe and prolonged recession is known as a ***depression.*** Inflation and recession tend to occur in cycles. Economists have termed this sequential rising and falling of the economy the business cycle.

Before the 1930's the government did not attempt to stabilize these economic cycles. But during the Great Depression and especially after World War II, the government began playing a major role in managing the economy. It began the attempt to steer a middle course between inflation and recession. To achieve this goal, the government today relies on three tools: fiscal policy, monetary policy, and wage and price controls.

Many economists note that economic activity in the United States appears to follow a specific business cycle—a pattern of alternating periods of prosperity and recession. What three economic tools are used by the federal government to stabilize the business cycle?

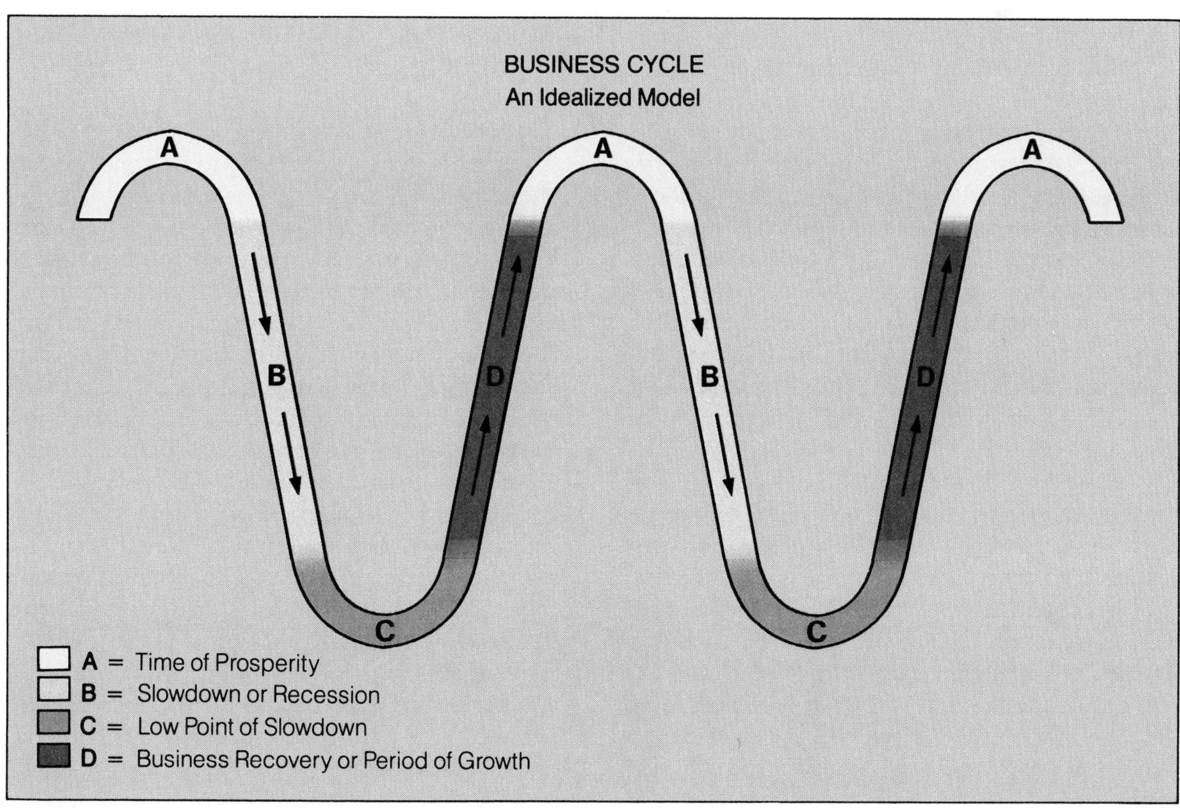

ISSUES

Deficit Spending

The national debt has long been the subject of controversy. Although Congress puts a ceiling on the debt, the ceiling is often raised. Many economists believe that ***deficit spending,*** or spending beyond income, is a good way to stimulate a sluggish economy and thus an important tool of government economic policy. They are not worried by the size of the national debt because, they say, we owe it to ourselves. These economists see deficit spending as an investment in America's future. Moreover, they point out that the economy has grown faster than the national debt.

Critics of deficit spending argue that the policy is responsible for runaway inflation and thus threatens the health of the economy. These experts are unimpressed by the "we owe it to ourselves" argument. Rather than seeing the debt as an investment in America's future, they see it as a burden passed on to future generations.

Fiscal Policy Through its ***fiscal policy*** the government uses its taxing and spending powers to influence the economy. To fight a recession, the government reduces taxes, increases spending, and increases the national debt. To combat inflation, the government reverses its policies. Thus it increases taxes, reduces spending, and attempts to balance the budget.

Monetary Policy Monetary policy, which was discussed earlier in this chapter, seeks to stabilize the economy by making changes in the money supply. The Federal Reserve Board uses tight-money policies to fight inflation and loose-money policies to move the economy out of recession.

Some economists prefer fiscal policy as a tool, while others prefer monetary policy. Both policies may be implemented at the same time. To be effective, of course, the two policies must not conflict with each other but must be used to achieve the same economic goals.

Wage and Price Controls Limits on how much workers can earn and how much businesses can charge are called ***wage and price controls.*** They are regarded as a drastic measure and therefore are seldom used. As a rule, they are only imposed during wartime. For example, they were used during World War II and during the Korean War, but not during the Vietnam War. They have been used in peacetime only once: in 1971, when President Richard M. Nixon imposed a 90-day freeze on wages and prices.

Rather than set actual controls, most Presidents have preferred to establish ***wage and price guidelines,*** or recommendations that the President's economic advisers consider acceptable. The White House uses persuasion, pressure, and publicity—usually called jawboning—to bring unions and corporations to accept these guidelines. But, as Presidents have discovered again and again, the task of securing acceptance by all parties is not easily accomplished.

Economic Stabilization Any policy used to stabilize the economy is likely to be controversial. The most controversial issue is whether to stabilize the economy at all. And even if the decision is made to do so, controversy arises over the best way to achieve the goal. In fighting inflation, for example, should taxes be raised, spending decreased, or both? Should the money supply be tightened by raising interest rates? Should wage and price controls be imposed? Each choice carries with it certain gains and certain losses—or gains for one group and losses for another group. And these gains and losses are not always predictable. Since the 1970's, policy choices have been made even more difficult by ***stagflation,*** a combination of economic stagnation and inflation. The dilemma is that any policy that stimulates the sluggish economy is also likely to increase inflation.

Tuning the machinery of the economy is complicated; there is no getting around it. Economics is not an exact science, and the impact of economic policy is always uncertain.

Section Check

1. Define: direct tax, indirect tax, graduated tax, proportional tax, regressive tax, taxable income, loophole, withholding, payroll tax, excise tax, estate tax, gift tax, regulatory taxation, federal budget, fiscal year, national debt, deficit spending, depression, fiscal policy, wage and price controls, wage and price guidelines, stagflation
2. Identify: Office of Management and Budget, Social Security, federal tax dollar
3. Where did most federal revenue come from before 1913? Where does it come from today?
4. What is one argument in favor of and one argument against a flat-rate income tax system?
5. In what ways do income taxes serve a regulatory function?
6. Why is a major portion of the federal budget considered to be "uncontrollable" by either the President or Congress?
7. What is one argument in favor of deficit spending? What is one argument against it?

SUMMARY

Financing the operations of government is an important domestic function of the executive branch. The Treasury Department manages the government's finances. It is headed by the Secretary of the Treasury, and it has five major functions.

Tax collection is carried out by the Internal Revenue Service and the United States Customs Service. The Customs Service processes all persons and goods in and out of the country and collects taxes on imports. The IRS collects individual and corporate income taxes and enforces the tax laws.

Law enforcement is also carried out by two agencies. The main job of the Bureau of Alcohol, Tobacco, and Firearms is to enforce the gun laws. The main law enforcement activity of the Secret Service is to stop counterfeiting.

Three agencies provide financial services to the federal government. The Treasurer's post is now largely ceremonial. The Bureau of Government Financial Operations acts as the government's bookkeeper and financial reporting agency. The Bureau of Public Debt manages the national debt. The General Accounting Office, which audits all federal expenditures, is not part of the Treasury Department but is a legislative agency.

The Bureau of the Mint manufactures and distributes coins, and the Bureau of Engraving and Printing designs, engraves, and prints paper money. The national currency system was originally based on a bimetallic system of gold and silver. This system was followed by the gold standard in 1900 and the gold reserve system in 1933. Today the nation's currency system is no longer based on gold or silver. Rather it is based on the people's faith in the government.

The banking system, which includes both national banks and state banks, is supervised by the Office of the Comptroller of the Currency. The banking system also includes several independent agencies. The Federal Reserve System coordinates banking activities in the United States. Its Board of Governors, often called the Fed, supervises the operations of the banks and makes and administers monetary policy. The Federal Deposit Insurance Corporation insures deposits in all national and many state banks. The Federal Home Loan Bank System provides money for home loans. The Farm Credit System provides money for farm loans. Its most important program is the Federal Land Banks.

The federal government finances its activities and programs through taxation. The power to tax is granted to the government by the Constitution, which also places certain limitations on that power. The individual income tax is the government's largest single source of revenue. Other federal taxes are the corporate income tax, Social Security and the federal unemployment payroll taxes, the excise tax, the customs duty or tariff, the estate tax, and the gift tax. Regulatory taxes may also be imposed to suppress or promote certain activities.

The federal budget is an estimate of the government's income and expenses. It is prepared by the President's Office of Management and Budget and then submitted to Congress, which revises it and appropriates the necessary funds. The portion of the federal budget devoted to each of the government's many programs reflects the nation's current priorities.

The national debt is the total amount of money owed by the federal government. At present it totals about $1 trillion. The national debt and the policy of deficit spending are the controversial issues among economists.

Since the 1930's the government has attempted to manage the economy through the use of fiscal and monetary policy. Fiscal policy makes use of the government's taxing and spending powers. Monetary policy regulates the money supply.

Chapter 22 Review

Using Vocabulary

Answer the questions below by using the meaning of each underlined term.

1. What does the Fed do with government securities in carrying on its open-market operations?
2. How did the importance of duties in raising revenue for the federal government change between 1790 and 1913?
3. Describe the relationship between the gold standard and the issue of free silver.
4. What is the relationship between deficit spending, the federal budget, and the national debt?
5. What effect do loopholes in the tax laws have on taxable income?
6. How can the federal budget be used to combat a depression?
7. Why should monetary policy and fiscal policy have the same goal?

Understanding American Government

1. What is the main purpose of the General Accounting Office? How is this purpose carried out?
2. Why is the chairman of the Federal Reserve Board often considered the most important person in the federal government besides the President?
3. Tell which federal agency is responsible for each of the following: (a) collecting tariffs; (b) keeping guns out of the hands of criminals; (c) promoting the sale of United States Savings Bonds; (d) manufacturing coins; (e) printing the nation's currency; (f) insuring bank deposits.
4. Indicate whether the following taxes are progressive, proportional, or regressive: (a) Social Security tax; (b) personal income tax; (c) flat-rate income tax; (d) general sales tax.
5. How does the federal budget reflect the nation's values?
6. How does a tight-money policy on the part of the Fed affect consumers?
7. Describe how fiscal policy and monetary policy might be used together to fight a recession.
8. What difficulties are involved in trying to stabilize the economy?

Extending Your Skills: Interpreting a Divided Bar Graph

Study the graph on page 540. Then complete the items that follow.

1. What does the left part of the graph represent? The right part?
2. The graph shows (a) the tax revenues of European nations; (b) the relationship of tax revenues to GNP in selected nations; (c) a comparison of inflation in selected nations.
3. Two nations that each derive more than 45 percent of their GNP from tax revenues are (a) Belgium and Japan; (b) Sweden and the Netherlands.
4. Two nations that each derive less of their GNP from tax revenues than the United States are (a) France and West Germany; (b) Italy and Japan.

Government and You

1. Why does the government exempt nonprofit organizations from income taxes? Why do some people oppose this exemption? Can you think of some other way that the federal government might encourage such organizations? Explain your answer.
2. What are the advantages of having the Fed independent of the President? What are the disadvantages?
3. What do you think Oliver Wendell Holmes meant when he said that "taxes are the price we pay for civilized society"?
4. If you were drawing up the federal budget, what changes, if any, would you make in the ways in which the government spends money? Give reasons for your decision.

Activities

1. Find out what the per capita share of the national debt was last year and compare it with the per capita corporate debt for the same year.
2. Read William Jennings Bryan's "Cross of Gold" speech delivered in 1896, research its background and consequences, and explain why historians consider it one of the most influential speeches ever delivered.

Chapter 23

Agriculture and Labor

Here in the United States individuals of all nations are melted into a new race . . . whose labors and posterity will one day cause great changes in the world.

MICHEL-GUILLAUME JEAN DE CREVECOEUR

The habits of life are those of an exclusively working people. From the moment of awakening, the American is at . . . work, and . . . is engaged in it till the hour of sleep.

MICHAEL CHEVALIER

CHAPTER OVERVIEW

American farmers depend upon the Department of Agriculture for many services, including rural development, business loans, and conservation programs. All Americans benefit from the research activities of the department.

1 THE DEPARTMENT OF AGRICULTURE

Throughout the history of the United States, the federal government has been concerned with economic policy. To carry out economic policy, it uses promotion and regulation. ***Promotion*** is the effort to encourage, strengthen, protect, and advance the interests of particular groups, industries, or sectors of the economy, or of the economy as a whole. Promotion takes the form of grants of financial aid called ***subsidies,*** special favors, and the provision of services. ***Regulation*** is government control over particular activities. Regulation takes a variety of forms. It may be an outright ban on a certain activity, such as price-fixing or false advertising. It may require that an activity be conducted only under license or permit. It may set standards that must be met, as in automobile emissions or the quality of food.

Promotion often requires regulation. When the government provides subsidies or special services to a group, it sets ***eligibility requirements,*** regulations specifying who is entitled to receive the benefits. In many instances regulation itself achieves promotion by bringing order and prosperity to a particular economic area. An example is the government's program to stabilize agricultural prices. Finally, to promote the interests of one group, it may be necessary to regulate another. To promote the interests of agriculture, for example, the government may impose restrictions on business.

A Client-Centered Department

The United States began as a predominantly agricultural society. In 1790, when the first census was taken, 95 percent of the population was rural. As late as 1910, farm families still made up the majority of our population. But as modern agricultural technology reduced the need for farm laborers, the farm population declined. Today only about 25 percent of the population lives in rural areas, and the people who live on farms number only 6 million, or less than 3 percent of the nation's total population. Yet agricultural abundance in the United States has never been greater, because of American farming techniques that improve every year. Today American farmers produce more food more efficiently than ever before.

Over the past 40 years there have been many changes in American farming. First, the farm population has declined from 23.2 percent of the total population in 1940 to 2.7 percent in 1980. Second, the total number of farms has shrunk by more than half from 6.5 million in 1940 to 2.4 million today. Third, during this same 40-year period, the size of the average farm has almost tripled—from 167 acres (67.5 hectares) to 430 acres (174 hectares). Fourth, productivity has skyrocketed. American farmers today get 64 percent more crops per acre than they did just 30 years ago. In 1950 a single farmer's output supplied food and fiber for 16 people. Today the same farmer's output can supply the needs of 59 people—an increase of 370 percent.

From the beginning the federal government looked for ways to help farmers, but it was not until 1862 during the Civil War that Congress created the Department of Agriculture. At that time Congress was controlled by the Republicans, who relied heavily on midwestern farmers for political support. The new department gave farmers a forum in which they might voice their interests and through which they might secure the services of government.

Also in 1862 Congress passed two other major laws for the benefit of farmers. The Homestead Act gave 160 acres of public land in the Midwest and West to anyone who agreed to settle the land and farm it for five years. The Morrill Act gave 11 million acres of public land to the states to establish agricultural colleges. In 1887 a land-grant system of state agricultural experiment stations was established in cooperation with the Department of Agriculture. The land-grant universities and experiment stations provided the foundation for a wide range of research and extension services. These services have helped to make United States agriculture the most productive in the world.

The United States Department of Agriculture (USDA) was the first Cabinet department created to serve the interests of a particular group of clients. Later, as its activities grew, the department took on regulatory functions as well.

From 1862 to 1889 the Department of Agriculture was administered by a commissioner who was not a member of the Cabinet. Under increasing pressure from such farm groups as the Grange and the Farmers Alliance, however, Congress raised the Department of Agriculture to Cabinet rank in 1889. The commissioner then became the Secretary of Agriculture.

Norman Coleman (top, left) became the first Secretary of Agriculture in 1889. Henry A. Wallace (above) headed the department during Roosevelt's four terms. Ezra Taft Benson (left), who served under President Eisenhower, favored less government aid to farmers.

As a member of the Cabinet, the Secretary—usually a farmer—is appointed by the President and confirmed by the Senate. As head of the department the Secretary directs the work of its various agencies and bureaus.

Major Department Functions

Today the Department of Agriculture through some 20 bureaus performs five functions. It regulates and stabilizes farm prices. It provides marketing services to farmers. It promotes research, education, and conservation in agriculture and related fields. It provides food and consumer services to the general public. And it promotes rural development.

Price Stabilization Farm prices have always been unstable—affected by weather, blight, foreign markets, and a host of factors over which the farmer has little or no control. Following World War I, American agriculture fell on hard times. By 1933, when the Great Depression was at its worst, farm prices had fallen dramatically. As a result farmers sank deeper into debt. Many were unable to make their mortgage payments and lost their farms.

In 1933 Congress passed the first Agricultural Adjustment Act (AAA), legislation designed to reduce agricultural production in order to force prices up. The act provided for payments to farmers who took land out of production. The plan worked. In three years farm prices rose by some 60 percent. But in 1936 the Supreme Court declared AAA unconstitutional. Congress thereupon passed the Soil Conservation Act. It paid farmers for planting soil-building crops instead of staple crops.

In 1938 Congress passed the second Agricultural Adjustment Act. This act continued the payments for soil conservation and also established a system of loans to farmers using stored crops as ***collateral,*** or security.

With the outbreak of World War II, the agricultural situation changed. It became necessary for farmers to grow more food rather than less. Congress encouraged farmers to increase production by guaranteeing minimum prices for certain crops. These minimum prices were designed to give farmers ***parity,*** or the same purchasing power as city dwellers. The parity prices were figured on the base period of 1910–1914, a period often described as the golden age of agriculture. Farmers who could

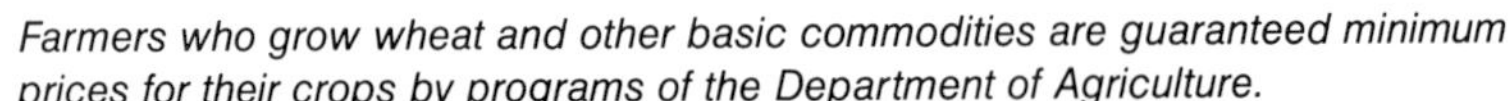
Farmers who grow wheat and other basic commodities are guaranteed minimum prices for their crops by programs of the Department of Agriculture.

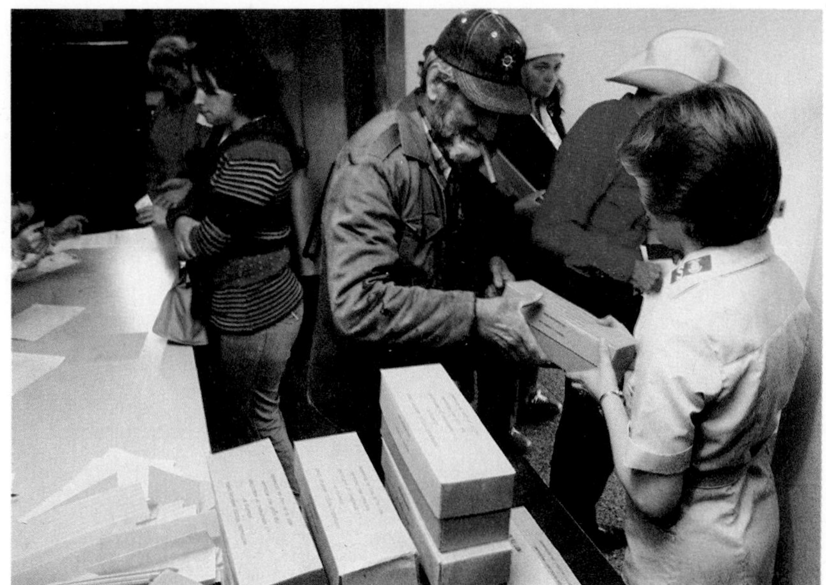

A program of the Food and Nutrition Service (FNS)—an agency of the Department of Agriculture—makes surplus food available to elderly citizens and to needy families. Other FNS programs provide free or reduced cost meals to school children.

not get the minimum price on the open market could sell their crops to the government. After the war Congress changed the system of rigid price supports to a system in which the kind and amount of support depended on the supply of each year's crop.

Today the federal government maintains stable prices for basic commodities* through a combination of payments, purchases, and loans. Farmers who grow one of the basic crops receive a payment of up to $50,000 if the market price for that crop falls below the established or "target" price, a modified parity price. The target price is figured on the 10-year period immediately preceding the year for which it is being set. Thus parity prices set in 1985 were figured on the base period 1974–1984. Because the subsidy depends on a variable—in this case, the market price—it is a flexible rather than a rigid price support.

The price of milk is stabilized through direct government purchases of processed dairy products. Other commodities are stabilized through loans to farmers based on stored crops. If the market price of the crop rises above the loan level, the farmer sells the crop and pays off the loan. If the market price fails to rise above the loan level, the farmer turns the crop over to the Commodity Credit Corporation (CCC), a government agency that buys the crop.

*Basic commodities are wheat, corn, rice, barley, rye, oats, grain sorghum, tobacco, peanuts, tung nuts, cotton, wool, mohair, honey, milk, and butterfat. The Secretary of Agriculture may order price supports for other commodities if it is believed necessary.

The stored crops that the government buys became known as ***surplus crops.*** The buildup of surplus crops was a real problem throughout the 1950's. As the productivity of American farmers increased, farm prices declined. Farmers became heavily dependent on price supports. The result was an enormous surplus of stored crops, over $6 billion worth by 1960.

The government could not sell its surplus crops, either at home or abroad, without disrupting the market. So the government had to find other ways to dispose of them. Some of the surplus was kept as reserves to ensure a stable supply of farm products. Some was sold abroad through the Food for Peace program. Some was used to provide food for the lunch, breakfast, and milk programs in American schools. And some of the surplus farm crops were donated to disaster victims, needy persons, and public institutions.

Another government strategy for stabilizing prices is controlling production through ***acreage allotments.*** When there is an oversupply of a basic commodity such as wheat, the Department of Agriculture estimates the probable market demand for that commodity. Next the department estimates the number of acres needed to produce that amount. This total acreage is then divided among participating farmers. The allotment, or division, is made by state and county committees elected by the farmers themselves. Participation in the acreage allotment program is voluntary, but farmers who ignore the allotments are ineligible to receive government price supports.

INSIGHT

Public Law 480

In 1954 Congress enacted the Food for Peace program under Public Law (P.L.) 480. This program has helped to reduce American farm surpluses, provide food for developing nations, and strengthen United States foreign policy. Under the P.L. 480 program, surplus products—especially wheat—are sold to developing nations for local currencies. The United States spends the sale money in the aided country to support its own embassy, to promote educational and cultural exchanges, and to pay for development programs. Sometimes the government returns part of the sale money to the aided country. P.L. 480 also gives the President the power to provide emergency food aid throughout the world in times of famine or natural disaster.

The Agricultural Marketing Service (AMS) is responsible for the standards that are used to grade and certify basic commodities like peanuts. These standards ensure that buyers and sellers trade according to agreed-upon quality levels. What other services does the AMS provide?

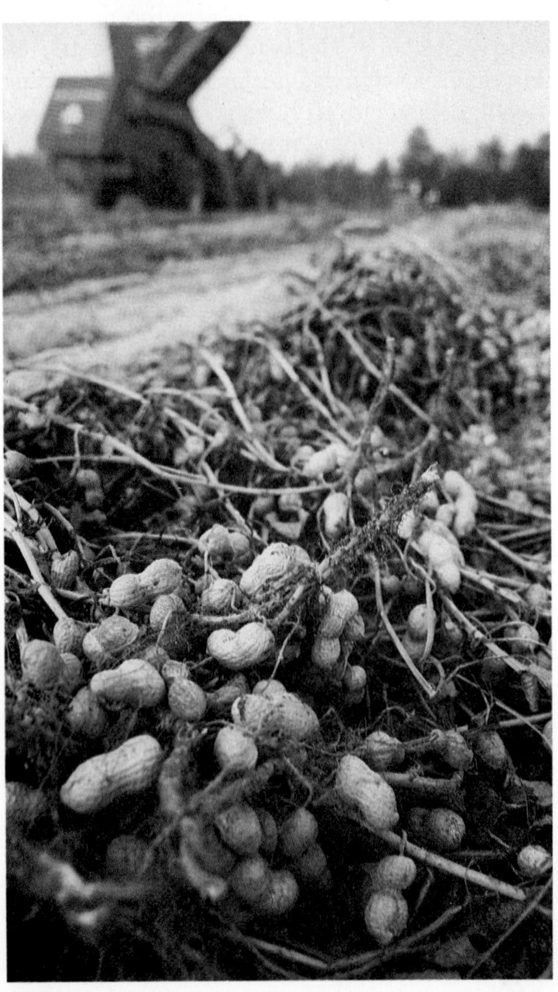

When there is a surplus of a supported crop, the government may set a ***market quota,*** or a limitation on the amount of the crop that each farmer may sell. These quotas must be approved by the farmers themselves, who vote in a national referendum. If two thirds of the farmers approve, the quota is imposed, and anyone violating it may be fined. If the quota is voted down, however, no price supports are paid for the crop that year. Since there have been no surpluses in recent years, neither acreage allotments nor market quotas are currently being imposed.

Grants to farmers for not growing crops or grazing animals on their land are called ***conservation payments.*** Conservation payments serve two purposes. First, like other forms of price stabilization, they help to match supply with demand. Second, they promote soil conservation by letting the land rest, or lie fallow.

Marketing Services The Department of Agriculture provides marketing, grading, pest control, and inspection services. The various services provide valuable assistance to farmers and ensure an orderly market, open competition, and fair business practices. The department assists farmers in marketing their crops worldwide, staffing agricultural offices in 65 embassies and consulates. It also provides insurance against crop loss from such uncontrollable causes as weather, pests, and diseases.

Information Services The Department of Agriculture engages in scientific research in all phases of livestock and plant production. It issues bulletins and other publications that inform farmers

One of the major projects of the Extension Service, the Department of Agriculture's educational agency, is the 4–H program. Through the 4–H program, young people develop leadership skills and explore careers.

and other interested members of the agricultural community about laboratory findings, various new agricultural developments, and other experimental research.

The department employs ***county extension agents*** that communicate new techniques and useful information to farmers by coming directly into farm communities, even into farmers' homes. County extension agents work with students in 4–H Clubs and provide farmers with up-to-date information on nutrition and other areas of interest.

In the area of conservation the department has several responsibilities. It teaches farmers how to apply appropriate soil conservation methods. It also promotes the wise use and conservation of 134 national forests and 19 grasslands.

ISSUES

Price Stabilization

The stabilization of farm prices has always been a controversial issue. One criticism, voiced by some conservative economists, is that government interference with supply and demand causes price instabilities in the first place. These economists would prefer the government to stay out of the economy altogether and let prices find their own level. Another criticism is that subsidies benefit mostly the owners of large farms, while the owners of small farms are left with the crumbs. This criticism arises because subsidies are based on production—the more a farmer produces, or the more land taken out of production, the bigger the subsidy. A third criticism is that city people carry the burden of farm support programs because price stabilizing programs raise the prices that people in the city pay for food.

Supporters of the program argue that farmers will be forced out of business if they do not get a fair price for their products. They also point out that, despite rising food costs, Americans get more food for their money today than ever before. There are two reasons why. First, agriculture is more efficient, which keeps costs down. Second, personal income has risen faster than the food prices. Thus, while food may cost more, the average consumer is spending less of his or her total income on food.

Consumer Services The Department of Agriculture sets standards for more than 300 food products. It then inspects these products at various stages of the production process to assure consumers that they are receiving quality products from the nation's farmers and food processors. The Department of Agriculture also approves labels to make sure the information on them is adequate and accurate.

An important service run by the Department of Agriculture in cooperation with state and local welfare agencies is the food stamp program. The food stamp program enables low-income families to purchase coupons that increase their buying power at grocery stores. For example, how much a person has to pay for $100 worth of food stamps depends on the person's income level. One person may pay as little as $10 while another person may pay $50. The department also provides cash grants to public and private schools, as well as day-care centers, for the purpose of supplying nutritional breakfasts and lunches at moderate prices.

Rural Development The Department of Agriculture works to improve economic opportunities and community facilities and services for people living in rural areas of the United States. One of its programs provides credit for the owners of small farms to enable them to be competitive with larger farm operations.

Another program makes loans to farm cooperatives and local governments to provide electricity and telephone service to rural areas. When ***rural electrification*** began in 1935, only 10 percent of the nation's farms had electricity. Today more than 29 million rural Americans are served by power and telephone systems that have been financed through the program's loans.

The food stamp program, which was started in 1964, is the principal food-assistance activity of the Department of Agriculture. The coupons issued to low-income families are used to buy food at any retail store that has been approved by the Department of Agriculture.

PROFILE

Electrification of Rural America

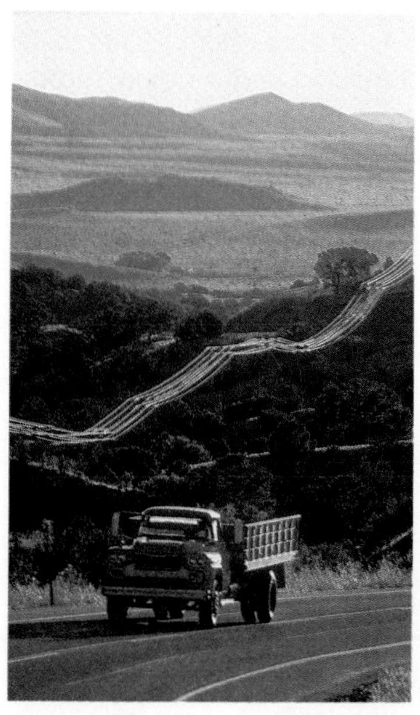

When Thomas Edison perfected the light bulb in 1879, a revolution began that transformed the way Americans worked and played. Within a few years American cities glowed with electric lights and hummed with the sound of electric motors operating everything from trains to small household appliances.

But for rural Americans the revolution of electrification was tragically slow. Utility companies eagerly supplied power to cities and towns where large populations assured the companies a profitable return on their investment. But electric companies were reluctant and often unwilling to supply power to rural areas where a small population was scattered over a wide area. At a cost of $1,255 a mile, extending power lines into the countryside was a poor investment.

As late as 1935 more than 6 million farm families—about 9 out of 10—lived entirely without electricity. In Mississippi only 1 in 100 families had electricity. Without electric power, life on the farms was backbreaking. Obtaining water serves as one example. Without electricity to run a pump, a farm family had to obtain water for washing, bathing, and cooking from outdoor wells. The water had to be pumped by hand and often carried bucket by bucket across the yard to the house. In one year a farm family of five might have lugged 73,000 gallons of water.

In 1935, to end the silent suffering of farm families, President Franklin D. Roosevelt issued an executive order that established the Rural Electrification Administration (REA). He determined that electricity would "become a standard article of use...for every home within reach of an electric light line." Within 18 months the REA had brought electricity to 500,000 American farms across the nation. Today, the REA continues to bring electricity and telephone service to rural areas by guaranteeing loans made to power and telephone companies.

Section Check

1. Define: promotion, subsidy, regulation, eligibility requirement, collateral, parity, surplus crop, acreage allotment, market quota, conservation payment, county extension agent, rural electrification
2. Identify: Homestead Act, Morrill Act, Agricultural Adjustment Acts, Food for Peace, REA
3. In what four ways has American farming changed over the years?
4. What are the five major functions of the Department of Agriculture?
5. Why do some people believe in stabilizing farm prices? Why do some people oppose price stabilization?

2 THE DEPARTMENT OF LABOR

In the last quarter of the nineteenth century, industrialization advanced at a rapid pace. Unions grew stronger. They pushed for a direct voice in the federal government, receiving that voice in 1884 when the Bureau of Labor was established and placed within the Department of the Interior. In 1888 the Bureau of Labor became the Department of Labor, but it did not receive Cabinet status.

Toward the turn of the century, a decline in public support badly hurt the labor movement and resulted in the merger in 1903 of the Department of Labor into the new Department of Commerce and Labor. Labor resented the merger because it feared that its interests would be subordinated to those of business. But the American Federation of Labor (AFL), a rising power within the labor movement, gained the support of the Democratic party for a separate Department of Labor with Cabinet rank, a status it received from Congress in 1913. The act creating the Department of Labor stated its purpose.

To foster, promote and develop the welfare of the wage earners of the United States, to improve their working conditions, and to advance their opportunities for profitable employment.

Secretary of Labor

The Secretary of Labor has three responsibilities. First, as head of the department the Secretary manages its various agencies. Second, the Secretary serves as the President's chief adviser on labor matters. Third, the Secretary acts as a mediator in important labor disputes, especially those that threaten to disrupt the nation's economy. Like other Cabinet officers, the Secretary of Labor is appointed by the President with Senate confirmation.

Major Department Functions

Today the Department of Labor administers more than 130 federal labor laws and a variety of programs. The department has five main functions. It provides unemployment compensation and matches

Notable Secretaries of Labor include (clockwise, from top left) Frances Perkins (1933–1945), the first woman Cabinet member; Arthur Goldberg (1961–1962), later appointed to the Supreme Court; George Schultz (1969–1970), later Secretary of State in the Reagan administration; and Raymond Donovan (1981–1985).

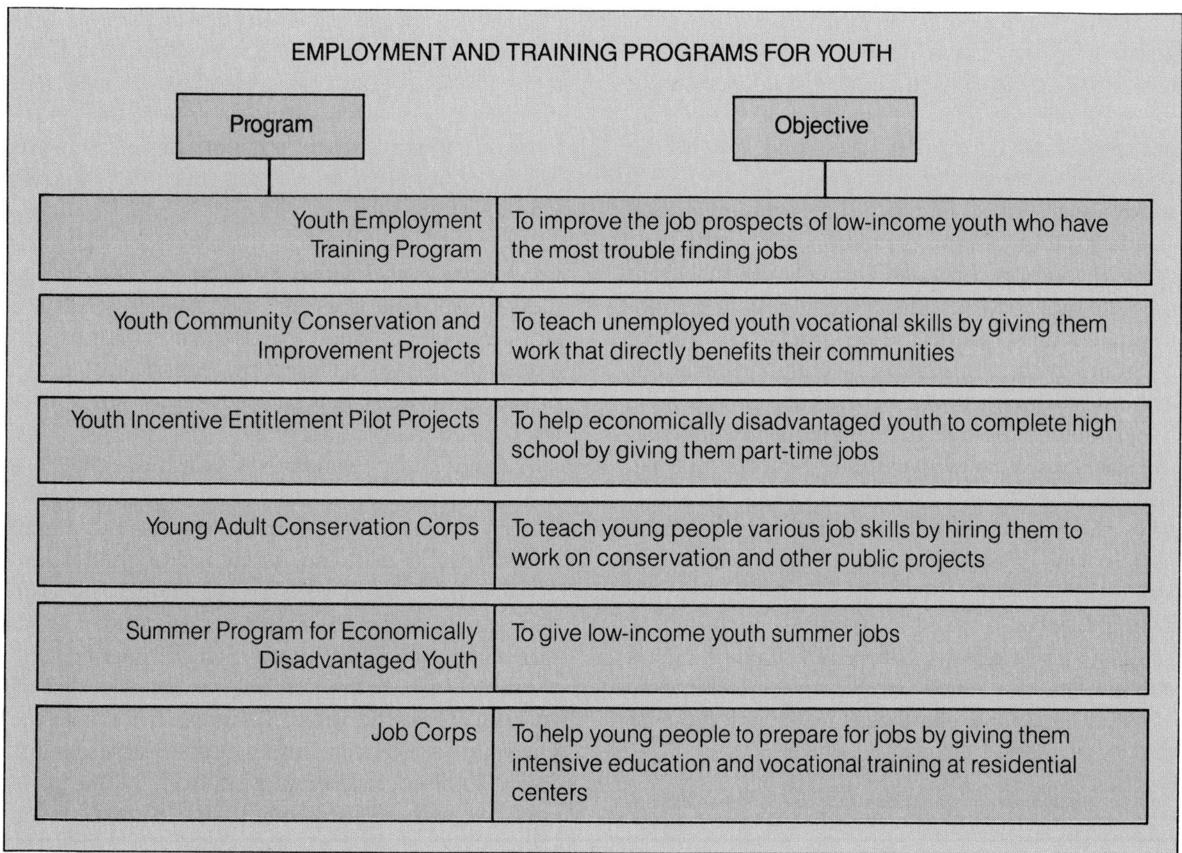

EMPLOYMENT AND TRAINING PROGRAMS FOR YOUTH

Program	Objective
Youth Employment Training Program	To improve the job prospects of low-income youth who have the most trouble finding jobs
Youth Community Conservation and Improvement Projects	To teach unemployed youth vocational skills by giving them work that directly benefits their communities
Youth Incentive Entitlement Pilot Projects	To help economically disadvantaged youth to complete high school by giving them part-time jobs
Young Adult Conservation Corps	To teach young people various job skills by hiring them to work on conservation and other public projects
Summer Program for Economically Disadvantaged Youth	To give low-income youth summer jobs
Job Corps	To help young people to prepare for jobs by giving them intensive education and vocational training at residential centers

Study the list of employment and training programs offered by the Department of Labor. How do these programs propose to help young people increase their opportunities to get jobs?

job seekers to jobs. It sets and administers fair employment standards and occupational safety standards. It collects and publishes labor statistics. It represents the interests of the United States in the field of international labor. And the department helps to promote sound labor-management relations, although it does not itself settle labor disputes.

Job and Unemployment Services The Department of Labor is in charge of various federal programs for people who are out of work or who are seeking new employment. Programs include placement services, job training, and federal-state unemployment insurance.

The department operates a nationwide network of 2,400 local employment offices that make some 6 million job placements annually. It offers job counseling, skill testing, training, and job placement services for such special-interest groups as young people seeking part-time and summer employment, the chronically unemployed, veterans, seasonal farm workers, the handicapped, and older workers. Many of the department's programs are funded through federal grants but are operated in cooperation with state and local governments.

The Labor Department provides a program of ***unemployment insurance*** through which it makes payment for a limited period of time to workers who have lost their jobs because of seasonal changes, plant closings, job elimination, or other reasons beyond an individual's control. Approximately three fourths of the American work force is covered by unemployment insurance.

Employers now pay a 3.4 percent tax on the first $6,000 of each employee's annual wage—a payment that employers deduct on their federal corporate tax returns. The payments from employers are credited to state accounts in a special Unemployment Compensation Trust Fund that is administered by the Treasury. States also contribute to the fund.

Each state sets the standards for its own program, deciding who is eligible, for how long, and under what conditions. If a state's standards do not meet the minimum federal standards, the state cannot draw money from the Trust Fund; instead the state must finance its own program.

If a state's program meets the minimum federal standards, the state can draw money from the trust fund. In addition, the federal government will grant the state money to administer its program. The minimum federal standards are designed to ensure that programs are administered efficiently and fairly. For example, workers whose benefits are denied must be guaranteed the right to an impartial hearing. And the states must pay workers their benefits on time. On the other hand, the fairness rule works both ways. Unemployment compensation is designed for people who are willing and able to work. Thus workers can lose their benefits if they refuse to take a suitable job.

Not all workers are covered by unemployment compensation. Certain farm workers, domestic workers, and public employees are excluded. So are people who are self-employed, as well as employees of firms with fewer than four workers. And there are separate programs for railroad workers and federal employees. Even with these exceptions, however, the unemployment compensation system has helped enormously to ease the suffering of people who lose their jobs.

The unemployment compensation program is administered jointly by the Department of Labor and the states. How do the minimum standards of the Department of Labor ensure that workers in the states are receiving their benefits equitably?

Fairness and Safety Standards The Department of Labor enforces fair labor standards, handles workers' compensation for job-related injuries, diseases, and deaths suffered by federal and certain private employees, and enforces equal opportunity laws on federal contract work.

The Fair Labor Standards Act, established in 1938, protects workers against unfair employment practices by setting a maximum work week and a minimum wage. It also restricts the use of child labor.

The basic standard is an 8-hour day, or a 40-hour week, at a ***minimum wage.*** Anyone who works more than 40 hours a week must be paid overtime. In 1938 the minimum wage was 25 cents an hour. Over the years, Congress has raised the minimum wage from time to time. Currently it is $3.35. To discourage employers from asking workers to work excessively long hours, overtime pay is set at "time-and-a-half." Originally the Fair Labor Standards Act covered only workers engaged in interstate or foreign commerce. Today its provisions have been broadened to cover nearly all working people. Self-employed workers and state and federal employees are the only important exceptions.

The act also restricts child labor. Workers engaged in interstate or foreign commerce must be at least 16. If the work is classed as dangerous, they must be 18. Certain jobs—acting, newspaper delivery, and most kinds of farm work—are exempted as long as the children receive schooling. Also the law does not apply to children who work for their parents.

The Department of Labor also administers various laws aimed at eliminating discrimination based on age or sex. The most important of these is the Equal Pay Act of 1963, which specifies that men and women receive equal pay for equal work.

Currently, women make up about 43 percent of the nation's work force. A special division within the Labor Department, the Women's Bureau, is specifically concerned with the needs of the 49 million women in the work force. It investigates women's employment opportunities and working conditions. It then advises the federal and state governments on them. Specifically, it studies such issues as equal

At the turn of the century, boys as young as 9 years old worked for 12 hours a day in coal mines. The early twentieth-century attempts of the federal government to restrict child labor were declared unconstitutional.

pay, child care for working mothers, job training and career counseling, occupational safety, and family law.

Federal employees are protected against job-related injuries by their own workers' compensation program. This program is administered by the Office of Worker's Compensation. The office determines whether an injured worker is eligible for benefits, and what benefits a worker should receive. It also handles benefits for certain nonfederal employees, notably longshoremen and coal miners.

Any private company that works for the federal government under contract must comply with the requirements of federal civil rights legislation. A company may not discriminate against any person on the basis of race, religion, ethnic background, sex, handicap, or veteran status. Moreover, government contractors must take ***affirmative action***—preferential treatment of women and minorities to ensure nondiscrimination—when hiring and promoting workers. A division within the Department of Labor makes sure that all government contractors obey these laws.

Two offices within the Labor Department enforce federal safety standards. The Occupational Safety and Health Administration (OSHA) is one of these. The second is the Mine Safety and Health Administration. It is charged with enforcing mine safety standards and protecting the health of miners throughout the nation.

Distribution of Labor Statistics The Department of Labor provides policymakers with accurate and up-to-date information through its

PROFILE

Guardian of Safety and Health

The Occupational Safety and Health Administration (OSHA) administers a comprehensive program to protect workers from health and safety hazards in the workplace. The hazards include fire traps, unsafe equipment, poor ventilation, and other unhealthy or dangerous conditions. And they include the workers' failure to observe safety requirements as well as the employer's failure to enforce them.

For many years organized labor sought passage of enforceable safety legislation. In 1969 more than 15,000 people were killed at work, while serious injuries numbered an estimated 2 million. In 1970 the Occupational Safety and Health Act created OSHA.

OSHA protects workers in several ways. It develops and issues safety and health regulations. It conducts inspections to make sure that employers are complying with safety and health standards. Finally, it issues citations and imposes penalties for noncompliance. Today OSHA regulations and standards cover approximately 65 million workers in more than 5 million companies engaged in interstate commerce.

Although no one disputes the need for job safety, OSHA has drawn strong criticism from Congress, business, and industry. Controversy has centered on three issues. The first is the rigidity and detail of OSHA regulations, many of which critics say are unnecessary. The second is the extent to which these regulations intrude on the rights of private business. The third is the high cost of complying with OSHA regulations.

Bureau of Labor Statistics (BLS). As the government's major fact-finding agency in the field of labor economics, it conducts research and publishes data on the labor force, on employment and unemployment, on work hours and wages, and on various other labor-related matters. It publishes surveys of employee benefits that labor and management use in collective bargaining. And it publishes surveys of employment trends that tell what kinds of jobs are currently needed. These surveys are especially useful to young people who are just entering the job market.

The BLS gets most of its data from other government agencies, from business, and from labor organizations. These organizations supply the data voluntarily because they, in turn, need the data that the bureau publishes in its *Monthly Labor Review* and in an assortment of periodic bulletins.

One of the most widely used of the bureau's statistics is the monthly Consumer Price Index (CPI). The CPI is a measure of changes in the cost of living from a base year of 1967. It is determined by taking prices for some 400 common consumer goods and services, such as food, clothing, medical care, transportation, and housing. Union leaders who are negotiating wage agreements with management keep a close eye on the CPI, because it is an accurate measure of inflation. Indeed, the CPI is a valuable tool for anyone who wants to know where the economy is going.

Labor's Goodwill Ambassador The Bureau of International Labor Affairs represents the Labor Department's interests in the international arena.

The bureau acts as a sort of goodwill ambassador, sponsoring exchange programs with union officials of other countries and conducting training programs for foreign labor leaders. In addition it encourages the exchange of technical information and provides consultants for foreign assignments.

The bureau also directs the foreign activities of the Department of Labor. The bureau supervises labor attachés in United States embassies abroad and acts as an advisory and fact-finding agency for the United States government and foreign governments. Finally, it represents the United States in the International Labor Organization (ILO). The ILO is an independent specialized agency of the United Nations that promotes the interests of workers throughout the world.

Labor-Management Relations In the field of labor-management relations, the department exercises a threefold responsibility through its Office of Labor-Management Relations. As a fact-finding agency, the office conducts and publishes research on the collective bargaining process in general and on specific disputes in particular. As an advisory agency, it helps state and local governments to resolve labor-management disputes. It provides assistance to employers and to unions in meeting problems caused by economic and technological change. As a crisis intervention agency, it helps Presidential emergency boards to settle strikes under the provisions of the Taft-Hartley Act.

Through other offices the Labor Department administers laws relating to pension and benefit plans maintained under labor contracts. It also enforces the guarantees of the 1940 Selective Service Act that ensures military veterans the right to return to their civilian jobs.

Section Check

1. Define: unemployment insurance, minimum wage, affirmative action
2. Identify: Unemployment Compensation Trust Fund, Equal Pay Act of 1963, the Women's Bureau, OSHA, Bureau of Labor Statistics, Consumer Price Index
3. What are the three major responsibilities of the Secretary of Labor?
4. What are the five major functions of the Department of Labor?
5. How does the Fair Labor Standards Act protect workers against unfair employment practices?
6. What is the main purpose of OSHA? Why has it been criticized?

3 A HISTORY OF LABOR–MANAGEMENT RELATIONS

Although the first labor unions were formed in the late eighteenth century, it was not until the Industrial Revolution in the mid-nineteenth century that unionization began in earnest. Between the 1830's and the 1870's the factory system was introduced, and the new mass-production techniques relied heavily on cheap labor. As industry grew more powerful, factory workers began to organize to protect their own interests.

The Knights of Labor

The most successful of the early national unions was the Knights of Labor. It was the first to combine many small local unions into one large group. Founded in 1869, the Knights of Labor at its peak of power in 1886 had 700,000 members—men and women of all races, skilled and unskilled workers alike. It even included employers. Only stockholders, bankers, lawyers, and gamblers were excluded. The Knights fought for such improvements as equal pay for men and women, and the abolition of child labor, both of which were considered radical for the time. But internal differences and a series of unsuccessful strikes weakened the organization. It lost still more prestige when the press unfairly blamed it for a bloody riot in Chicago that became known as the Haymarket Affair. Mismanagement and disputes with other unions weakened the Knights still further. By the turn of the century it had ceased to be a major force in the American labor movement. In 1917 the union was officially dissolved.

The leadership of Terrence Powderly (center) led to the growth of the Knights of Labor in the 1880's. Powderly's efforts also led to the establishment of labor bureaus in several states. What were some of the goals that Powderly and the Knights of Labor worked to achieve?

The AFL–CIO

The American Federation of Labor (AFL) was the nation's first federation of ***craft unions,*** or unions of skilled workers, whose members practice the same trade. It began in 1881 as the Federation of Organized Trade and Labor Unions of America and Canada. The name was shortened six years later.

Unlike the Knights of Labor, which believed that labor's success lay in political activity, the AFL believed in "bread-and-butter unionism." Under the leadership of Samuel Gompers, the AFL concentrated on improving wages and working conditions. Although successful, the results were limited because only about 30 percent of the labor force consisted of skilled workers. The great majority were unskilled or semiskilled. Also, except for the United Mine Workers, no AFL union allowed blacks or women to join.

The Congress of Industrial Organizations (CIO) was the nation's first federation of ***industrial unions,*** or unions whose members—both skilled and unskilled—all worked in the same industry. The CIO—originally the Committee for Industrial Organization—had its beginnings in an organizing drive that started in 1935. The drive was aimed at workers in such mass-production industries as automobiles, steel, oil, rubber, and textiles. The CIO encouraged the inclusion of black as well as white workers in its unions. It also developed the ***sit-down strike.*** Instead of walking off their jobs and organizing picket lines, workers remained inside the plant but did not work. This kept employers from using strikebreakers to carry on production.

A. Philip Randolph founded the predominantly black Brotherhood of Sleeping Car Porters in 1925. Randolph remained active in union affairs and later served as vice president of the AFL–CIO from 1955 until 1973.

The CIO's organizing drive was so successful that the older craft unions became jealous, and in 1937 the older unions expelled the industrial unions from the AFL. In 1938 the CIO, led by John L. Lewis, changed its name to the Congress of Industrial Organizations. By 1940 it had as many members as the AFL. The two federations remained rivals until 1955. Then they merged to form the AFL–CIO, the American Federation of Labor and Congress of Industrial Organizations.

Today this gigantic federation includes 105 different unions. Its executive council is made up of leaders from both of the old groups. And its membership in the early 1980's numbered a staggering 17 million, or nearly 16 percent of the American labor force. Another 4.5 million workers, or about 4 percent of the labor force, belonged to the International Brotherhood of Teamsters, the United Mine Workers of America, the United Steel Workers, and the International Brotherhood of Electrical Workers. These four unions, as well as twelve other small ones, are ***independent unions*** not affiliated with the AFL–CIO.

Government Regulation

Few domestic issues have inspired more controversy than government regulation of labor disputes. A serious and prolonged labor dispute, especially in a major industry, can have a devastating effect on the economy. At some point, then, most people would probably agree that the government must step in. But when? And how far may the government go in its attempts to settle such disputes? Or, to put it another way, what are the rights of labor? The rights of management? And what should the government do to protect the rights of each? Over the years the passage of several landmark acts has gone a long way toward answering these questions.

Labor-management relations today are based on a system of ***collective bargaining,*** in which a union representing the employees negotiates with the employer on the terms of a contract. Today the right of collective bargaining is taken for granted. Early unions, however, were often prosecuted if they made any organized effort to promote their own interests. Even though the unions themselves were legal, they had few legal means of enforcing their demands. And while the federal government did not

Women, members of the Amalgamated Clothing Workers, demonstrate in favor of the closed shop in the early 1920's. The closed shop—outlawed in 1947—was favored as a means of strengthening the labor movement.

prohibit unions, neither did it go out of its way to protect the unions' rights. Furthermore, federal and state troops were often used to put down strikes.

This gave employers the upper hand, and they found many ways to oppose unions. Employers formed ***company unions*** under their control in order to undercut legitimate unions. They made workers sign ***yellow-dog contracts***—promising not to join a union. They blacklisted union organizers to prevent them from getting jobs. They used strikebreakers. Often the courts would back employers by issuing an ***injunction,*** or order, requiring employees to refrain from striking on the grounds that doing so injured an employer's property rights. Injunctions were also issued against picketing, paying strike benefits out of union funds, and even holding meetings to discuss a strike.

In spite of all this, unions continued to grow. By the early 1900's they were numerous enough to have some real political influence. In 1914 they were exempted from antitrust laws by the Clayton Act. The act gave the unions a legal right to exist, and also to strike, to picket peacefully, and to pay strike benefits to their members. But court decisions soon took the teeth out of these rights.

In the 1930's the federal government began passing laws that directly protected the interests of labor. These laws established the right of collective bargaining and also placed various restrictions on employers. Additional labor laws were passed after World War II.

In all, there are five landmark acts that deal with the rights of labor. One of these, the Fair Labor Standards Act of 1938, has already been discussed. The other four acts are discussed here.

Norris-LaGuardia Act In 1932 labor won its first major victory with the passage of the Norris-LaGuardia Act. This act outlawed yellow-dog contracts, restricted the power of the courts to issue injunctions against unions, and guaranteed workers the right to join a union and to engage in its normal activities. These guaranteed activities specifically included the right to strike and the right to urge other workers to strike.

Wagner Act In 1935 Congress passed the National Labor Relations Act. Commonly called the Wagner Act, it gave workers in industries engaged in interstate commerce the right to organize and bargain collectively. It also outlawed certain unfair labor practices, including the establishment of company unions and discrimination against union workers.

(continued on page 568)

PROFILE

Champions of Labor

"I am a workingman," Samuel Gompers once declared, "and in every nerve, in every fibre, in every aspiration, I am on the side which will advance the interests of my fellow workingman." Apprenticed as a cigar maker at the age of 13, Samuel Gompers knew the worker's life well. At the age of 25 he became head of the Cigar Makers Union's largest local, and in 1881 he helped to found the American Federation of Labor (AFL). For 38 years the stocky, powerful Gompers dominated the AFL, which became a national force under his leadership. He traveled the country, averaging 30,000 miles a year, and everywhere he went he spoke out for unions. Both his flamboyant rhetoric and his devotion to the laborer are captured in these lines from one of his speeches.

So long as man shall live...so long as there is in the human mind the germ of the belief in human justice and human liberty, so long as there is in the whole makeup of man a desire to be a brother to his fellow man, so long will there be the labor movement.

In 1911, at a union gathering, Samuel Gompers met a young miner whose energy and ambition were so impressive that Gompers made him a field representative for the AFL. The young miner was John Llewellyn Lewis. The son of a Welsh miner, Lewis had entered the mines at the age of 15. When he was 25, he helped carry out the bodies of more than 200 miners killed in a terrible mine disaster. Perhaps it was that experience that made him a champion of oppressed workers and a lifelong advocate of mine safety. Lewis went on to become president of the United Mine Workers (UMW) and then vice president of the AFL. A towering six-footer, Lewis cut a commanding and self-confident figure. "He who tooteth not his own horn," he once said, describing his grandiose style, "the same shall not be tooted." In 1935, Lewis broke with the AFL over the issue of admitting semiskilled and unskilled laborers into the union. Then, with other union leaders, he proceeded to set up the rival Congress of Industrial Organizations (CIO). After 20 years the two rival unions merged in 1955 to form the AFL–CIO.

One of the most powerful advocates of the AFL–CIO merger was George Meany. The son of a plumber, Meany himself became an apprentice plumber at age 15. He went on to serve as secretary-treasurer of the AFL and in 1952 was elected president. Along with Walter P. Reuther, then head of the CIO, he negotiated the AFL–CIO merger. For the next 24 years, Meany served as president of the AFL–CIO controlling 110 separate unions. "My No. 1 job," he once said, "is holding the boys together." Meany became a national figure. He was always outspoken. In a clash over foreign policy with the Ford administration, Meany declared, "Foreign policy is too important to be left to the Secretary of State." He once explained to a young visitor why his office was located across the street from the White House. "Because the people of the country need me to watch over whoever is living there," he said. When George Meany died in 1980, President Jimmy Carter declared, "Like seven of my predecessors, I was privileged to benefit from his straightforward counsel."

American Federation of Labor (AFL) founder Samuel Gompers (above, center) leads a 1919 workers' parade in Washington, D.C. John L. Lewis (right), leader of the newly formed Congress of Industrial Organizations (CIO), speaks to Congress in 1936. CIO President Walter Reuther (below, right) and AFL leader George Meany (below) united the two unions into the AFL–CIO in 1955.

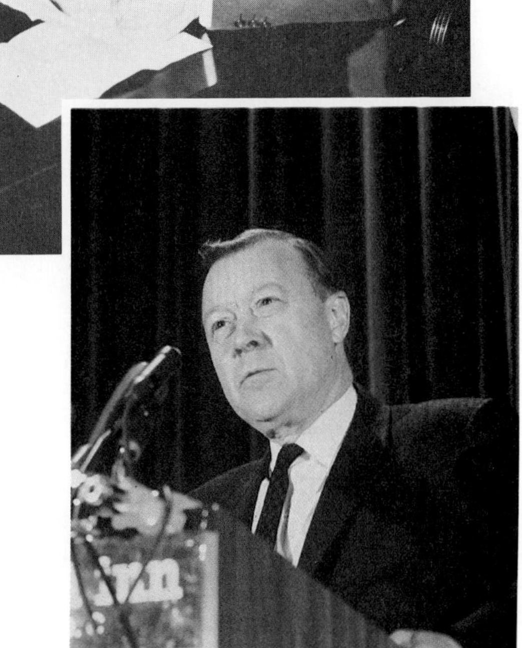

The Wagner Act also established the independent National Labor Relations Board (NLRB). Originally composed of three members, who are appointed by the President and confirmed by the Senate, the NLRB now has five. The Board conducts elections among employees to determine whether or not they wish to be represented by a union. It enforces the ban on unfair labor practices, and it administers the various federal laws relating to labor-management relations. Further, it prevents unfair labor practices by unions as well as employers. And finally, the NLRB supervises labor union elections.

The Wagner Act inspired enormous controversy. Its supporters hailed it as the Magna Carta of labor. Under its protection unions grew in economic and political power. But critics argued that the act was one-sided, imposing restrictions on management but none on unions. These critics claimed that unions sometimes engaged in unfair labor practices.

After World War II, railroad and coal-mining strikes sharpened criticism of labor unions. Many people felt that government should control as well as protect labor. The result was the Labor Management Relations Act of 1947, better known as the Taft-Hartley Act.

Taft-Hartley Act The Taft-Hartley Act provided several amendments to the Wagner Act. It prohibited certain labor union practices, such as featherbedding and secondary boycotts. In featherbedding, for example, the union takes advantage of safety laws to oblige employers to limit production or to hire more workers than are really needed. In a secondary boycott, for example, the union takes action against employer A indirectly. In order to prevent employer B from doing business with employer A, the union strikes against employer B. The act said that employers had the right to seek injunctions to end strikes and to sue union officials for contract violations.

The act also banned strikes against the federal government and prohibited unions from making contributions to political campaigns. Individual members may do so, however, and they may also fund political action committees, which then support candidates who support unions.

The Taft-Hartley Act strengthened the position of the individual worker. It obliged union leaders to file periodic financial reports with the Secretary of Labor and to make these reports available to union members. It also obliged union leaders to file an affidavit with the NLRB swearing that they were not members of the Communist party.

Under the provisions of the Taft-Hartley Act, states may pass right-to-work laws. How might right-to-work laws lessen the power of labor unions?

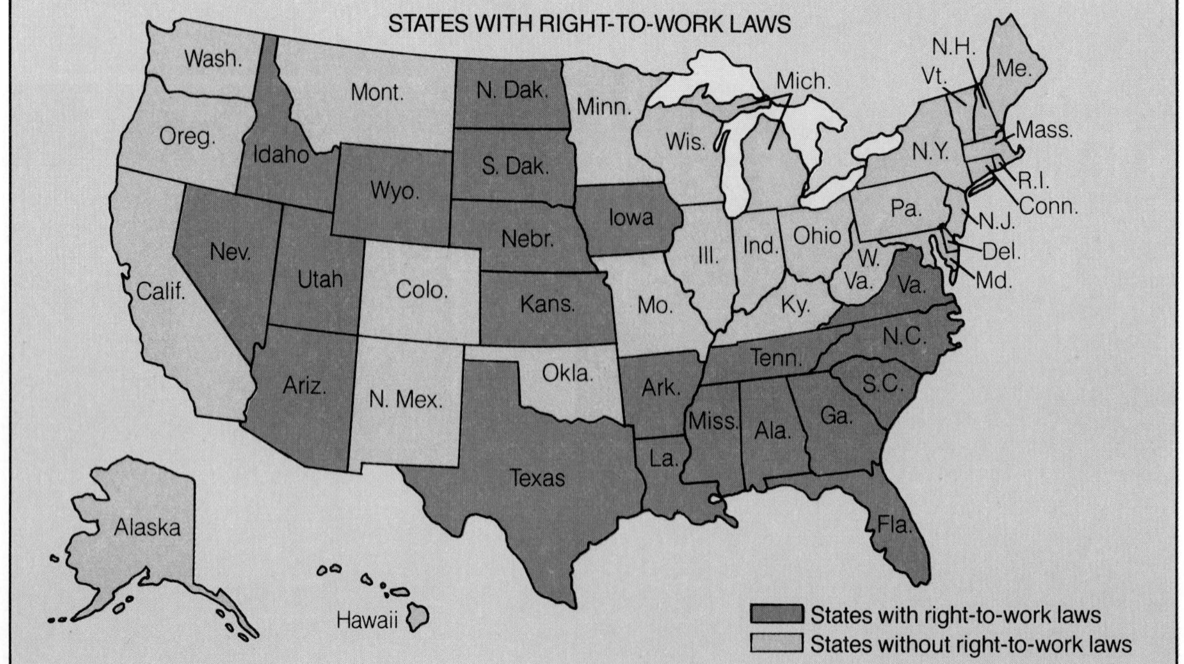

Workers demonstrate in 1947 to urge President Truman to veto the Taft-Hartley Act. Truman, agreeing with the workers, vetoed the act, saying that it "contributes neither to industrial peace nor to economic stability and progress." Congress passed the Taft-Hartley Act over President Truman's veto.

Among the act's most important provisions was the one outlawing the ***closed shop,*** a workplace where only union members are hired. The ***union shop,*** however, was permitted, provided a majority of the workers voted to have it. Under union shop rules, workers need not be union members in order to be hired. But they must join the union within a certain period of time in order to keep their jobs. The purpose of these rules is to eliminate ***free riders,*** or workers who benefit from collective bargaining without paying union dues or supporting the union in other ways.

But some workers object to being forced to join a union in order to keep their jobs. So the Taft-Hartley Act gave the states the power to forbid union shops by passing right-to-work laws. ***Right-to-work laws*** establish the ***open shop,*** in which workers may join a union but are not required to do so. To date, 20 states have passed right-to-work laws.

The Taft-Hartley Act also established rules governing labor disputes. Unions that wish to negotiate a new contract or change an existing one must give at least 60 days notice before calling a strike. During this cooling-off period, management cannot impose a ***lockout,*** an action closing a plant in order to force the union to accept its terms. If a settlement on a new contract is not reached within 30 days, the Federal Mediation and Conciliation Service, an independent executive agency, is called in. The service seeks to prevent or shorten strikes by mediating a settlement. Although the service cannot compel labor and management to compromise, it often convinces both sides to submit a dispute for ***arbitration,*** or binding settlement by an impartial third party.

In a serious labor dispute, especially one that imposes inconvenience or hardships on millions of people, the President may call representatives of labor and management to the White House. But even the President's full powers of persuasion are not always sufficient to mediate a settlement. If a strike poses a threat to the national health or safety, the Taft-Hartley Act permits the President to seek an 80-day cooling-off period. If no agreement is reached after 80 days, a strike or lockout may take place unless Congress intervenes.

Landrum-Griffin Act In the late 1950's Senate investigations into labor racketeering disclosed a variety of corrupt practices on the part of some union leaders. The Senate uncovered links to organized crime, misuse of union funds, extortion, fraud, and the rigging of union elections. To protect the integrity of organized labor and the rights of individual union members, Congress passed the Labor Reform Act of 1959, also known as the Landrum-Griffin Act.

The Landrum-Griffin Act required unions to file financial reports on their pension and welfare funds with the Department of Labor. The act also required unions to file copies of their constitutions and bylaws. The act barred ex-convicts and Communist party members from holding union office and made misuse of union funds a federal crime. It strengthened certain provisions of the Taft-Hartley Act that forbade the unions to engage in unfair labor practices. And it guaranteed members the right to participate freely in union meetings and to vote in union elections by secret ballots.

Policy Shift Between the passage of the Norris-LaGuardia Act in 1932 and the passage of the Landrum-Griffin Act in 1959, a significant shift in the government's labor-management relations occurred. The government's policy shifted from the promotion of the worker's rights to the promotion of the public interest. It also shifted from the regulation of powerful and sometimes unscrupulous employers to regulation of the powerful and sometimes unscrupulous unions.

Section Check

1. Define: craft union, industrial union, sit-down strike, independent union, collective bargaining, company union, yellow-dog contract, injunction, closed shop, union shop, free rider, right to work, open shop, lockout, arbitration
2. Identify: Knights of Labor, Committee for Industrial Organization, Samuel Gompers, John L. Lewis, George Meany, AFL–CIO, Federal Mediation and Conciliation Service
3. About what percentage of the American labor force is unionized?
4. What basic rights did labor obtain under the Wagner Act?
5. Why did Congress pass the Taft-Hartley Act?
6. What is the main argument in favor of right-to-work laws? What is the main argument against right-to-work laws?

SUMMARY

The government uses promotion and regulation to carry out its economic policy, especially in the areas of agriculture and labor.

The Department of Agriculture promotes the interests of farmers and regulates their activities. The department, headed by the Secretary of Agriculture, performs five major functions.

(1) It stabilizes prices paid to farmers for the goods they produce through a system that includes price supports, acreage allotments, market quotas, and conservation payments. (2) It provides marketing services, informing farmers about new crop and livestock developments and establishes standards of quality. It also insures farmers against unavoidable losses. (3) It conducts research in all phases of plant and livestock production. It educates through the publication of books, bulletins, and newsletters. It conducts activities through county extension agents. (4) It protects the interests of consumers by inspecting and grading goods. It also administers federal programs that give food to the needy. (5) It promotes rural development through such activities as making loans available to owners of small farms and providing electricity and phone service to rural areas.

The Department of Labor promotes improved labor conditions and sound labor-management relations. It has five major functions. (1) It provides funds for unemployment compensation programs administered by the states. It matches job seekers to jobs through such services as job counseling, job training, and job placement. (2) It enforces fair labor standards, equal-opportunity laws, and safety and health standards in the workplace. (3) It conducts research and publishes data on labor-related subjects. One such service is the Consumer Price Index, which is a valuable tool for the measurement of inflation. (4) It represents labor interests of the United States in the international field. (5) It helps promote sound labor-management practices.

The history of labor-management relations is a stormy one. Unions began to organize during the Industrial Revolution. The most successful of the early national unions was the Knights of Labor. The Knights was supplanted by the American Federation of Labor (AFL), made up of craft unions, and the Congress of Industrial Organizations (CIO), made up of industrial unions. In 1955 the two unions merged to form the AFL–CIO. In the early 1980's the AFL–CIO represented some 17 million workers. An additional 4.5 million workers belonged to independent unions.

Collective bargaining and government regulation of labor disputes are based on five landmark acts. They are the Norris-LaGuardia Act of 1932, the Wagner Act of 1935, the Fair Labor Standards Act of 1938, the Taft-Hartley Act of 1947, and the Landrum-Griffin Act of 1959. The first three acts protect labor and regulate management. The last two acts protect management and regulate unions.

Chapter 23 Review

Using Vocabulary

Answer the questions by using the meaning of each underlined term.

1. How does the government use parity, acreage allotments, and market quotas to reduce surplus crops and to set price supports?
2. What is the difference between a craft union and an industrial union?
3. How does a union shop differ from a closed shop?
4. How do right-to-work laws promote the open shop?
5. What is the role of arbitration in collective bargaining?
6. How might a lockout, a yellow-dog contract, or an injunction be used against union activities?

Understanding American Government

1. Why did the federal government originally give help to farmers? Why does it continue to do so today?
2. How has the government's attitude toward farm production changed over the years? Why?
3. What effect has the Rural Electrification Administration had on farmers' daily lives?
4. How does the federal government help farmers market their crops?
5. Why did Congress establish a Department of Labor?
6. When and why did the federal government establish an unemployment compensation program? How is the unemployment compensation program funded?
7. What is the relationship between the Consumer Price Index published by the Bureau of Labor Statistics and the wage demands of unions?

Extending Your Skills: Identifying Leaders

Reread the "Champions of Labor" profile on page 566. Then identify the labor leader that each phrase describes.

1. Head of the largest local of the Cigar Makers Union
2. President of the United Mine Workers (UMW)
3. A founder of the American Federation of Labor (AFL)
4. Elected president of the AFL in 1952
5. A founder of the Congress of Industrial Organizations (CIO)
6. President of the AFL–CIO for 24 years

Government and You

1. Discuss the reasons why the federal government should continue to stabilize farm prices. What arguments might be proposed for discontinuing the program?
2. Why does labor compare the Wagner Act to the Magna Carta? What group might view it differently? Why?
3. What can the President do to prevent a strike that threatens the national health or safety? What might be some political results of these actions?
4. Do you think that local government employees, as well as federal employees, should be prohibited from striking? Give reasons for your opinion.

Activities

1. Choose one of the agencies in the Department of Agriculture and find out what kinds of jobs are available in that agency and what the qualifications for those jobs are.
2. Make a collage of newspaper photographs or drawings dealing with the activities of the 4–H Clubs in your state.
3. Research and write a short biography on one of the following: (a) Eugene V. Debs; (b) Walter P. Reuther; (d) Frances Perkins.
4. Research and write an account of the Haymarket Affair. Be sure to discuss the effect it had on the political career of Governor John P. Altgeld of Illinois.
5. Interview a local labor leader about the major concerns of his or her union. Prepare a report of the interview to present to the class.
6. Prepare a report on your state's right-to-work law or a report on whether such a law has ever come up in your state legislature.

Transportation and Commerce

The business of America is business.

CALVIN COOLIDGE

CHAPTER OVERVIEW

The Federal Aviation Administration (FAA), an agency of the Department of Transportation, sets safety standards and supervises the operations of more than 1,000 airports in the United States.

1 THE DEPARTMENT OF TRANSPORTATION

Since the early days of the United States, the government has promoted the development of transportation, because it is the life stream of agriculture, commerce, and industry. As early as 1817 Senator John C. Calhoun of South Carolina said, "Let us bind the Republic together with a perfect system of roads and canals." And when the West was opened to settlement, the federal government helped to build the roads, canals, and railways that took settlers into new territories. Today, although airline, bus line, trucking, and railroad systems in the United States are privately owned, they depend heavily on government assistance and regulation.

The Department of Transportation was created in 1966. The government had been regulating commercial transportation for many years and had subsidized such programs as the Interstate Highway System. But the government had lacked a coordinated transportation policy. Programs had been administered by more than 30 separate agencies and bureaus. The new Department of Transportation brought all these programs under one roof. Its mission was, first, "to assure the coordinated, effective administration" of the federal government's transportation programs, and second, to develop policies and programs that would help provide "fast, safe, efficient, and convenient transportation."

The Department of Transportation performs three functions. It enforces federal law on the high seas. It promotes air, highway, and railroad safety. Finally, it helps construct and maintain federal highways and urban mass-transit systems and maintains and operates part of the Saint Lawrence Seaway.

Law Enforcement

Enforcing federal law on the high seas and in our coastal waters is the province of the United States Coast Guard. Originally called the Revenue Marine, it was established by Alexander Hamilton in 1790 to combat smuggling. In 1915 it was renamed the Coast Guard and made part of the Treasury Department. Then in 1967 the Coast Guard became part of the Department of Transportation.

As a branch of the armed forces, the Coast Guard operates within the Department of Transportation only in peacetime. In wartime it becomes a part of

Elizabeth Dole (below) served as commissioner of the Federal Trade Commission and as White House liaison before being appointed the Secretary of Transportation in 1983. Department of Transportation objectives include the promotion of transportation research in cooperation with private industry and the development of high-quality, low-cost public transportation.

the United States Navy. Its 40,000 officers and enlisted men and women serve under a commandant appointed by the President with Senate confirmation.

The Coast Guard has a wide range of law enforcement duties. It patrols for smuggling and enforces the laws that protect the United States coastal fisheries. It maintains such aids to navigation as lighthouses, buoys, and radio signals. It enforces maritime safety regulations by inspecting pleasure boats and commercial vehicles for seaworthiness and offshore structures for safety.

The Coast Guard helps protect the marine environment and has a special strike force to fight oil spills. It also transmits weather reports from the North Atlantic and the Pacific, helps oceangoing vessels and airplanes, and conducts oceanographic research. Its International Ice Patrol keeps watch on icebergs in the shipping lanes of the North Atlantic. Coast Guard personnel also go out on more than 70,000 search-and-rescue missions each year, and have won worldwide recognition for their lifesaving skills.

Safety

The promotion of safety is a second major function of the Department of Transportation. Three agencies within the department oversee air, highway, and rail transportation. They are the Federal Aviation Administration, the National Highway Traffic Safety Administration, and the Federal Railroad Administration. A fourth agency that is independent of the department, the National Transportation Safety Board, provides a further check on safety.

Air Safety Every day some 160,000 aircraft take off and land at major airports in the United States. The Federal Aviation Administration (FAA) is the nation's air traffic cop. The FAA's air traffic controllers direct flights in and out of airports and also control traffic holding patterns over airports.

The FAA promotes air safety in other ways. It sets and enforces standards for the manufacture, operation, and maintenance of aircraft. It registers planes and approves the licensing of all civilian pilots and mechanics. It also conducts research in air safety technology and helps fund airport construction.

Road and Rail Safety One out of every two Americans owns a car today. Automobile usage consumes more petroleum than any other type of vehicle. The National Highway Traffic Safety Administration (NHTSA) promotes both traffic safety and fuel economy.

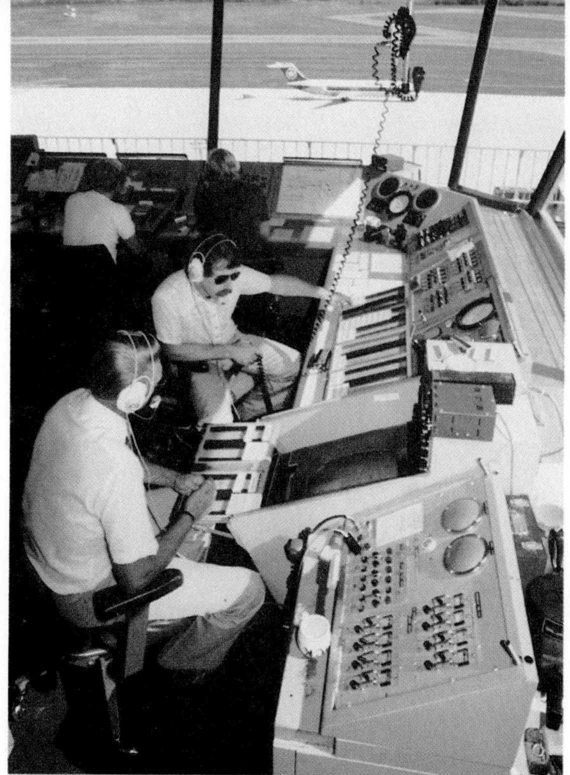

Air traffic controllers (above) use radar to guide incoming and outgoing flights at major airports. The Alaska Railroad (below), operated by the Federal Railroad Administration, provides transportation to encourage settlement and to stimulate industrial growth in Alaska.

Automobile accidents have killed more Americans than all the wars in United States history. To reduce the slaughter on the highways, the NHTSA sets safety standards for motor vehicles. It has the power to make manufacturers recall defective vehicles. It supports driver training programs, safety inspection programs, and programs to eliminate drunk driving.

The NHTSA also enforces fuel economy standards in the manufacture of automobiles. Its goal in this area is to reduce consumption of foreign oil. Today there are some American cars that get 40 miles (64.5 kilometers) or more to the gallon, due mostly to the efforts of the NHTSA.

In 1974 Congress set a national speed limit of 55 miles (88 kilometers) per hour. The NHTSA has mounted a public service campaign to support the 55-miles-per-hour (88-kilometers-per-hour) speed limit. This nationwide campaign has helped both to reduce traffic accidents and to conserve energy.

The Federal Railroad Administration (FRA) administers laws to promote safety on the railroads, in the same manner that the FAA promotes air safety and the NHTSA promotes motor vehicle safety.

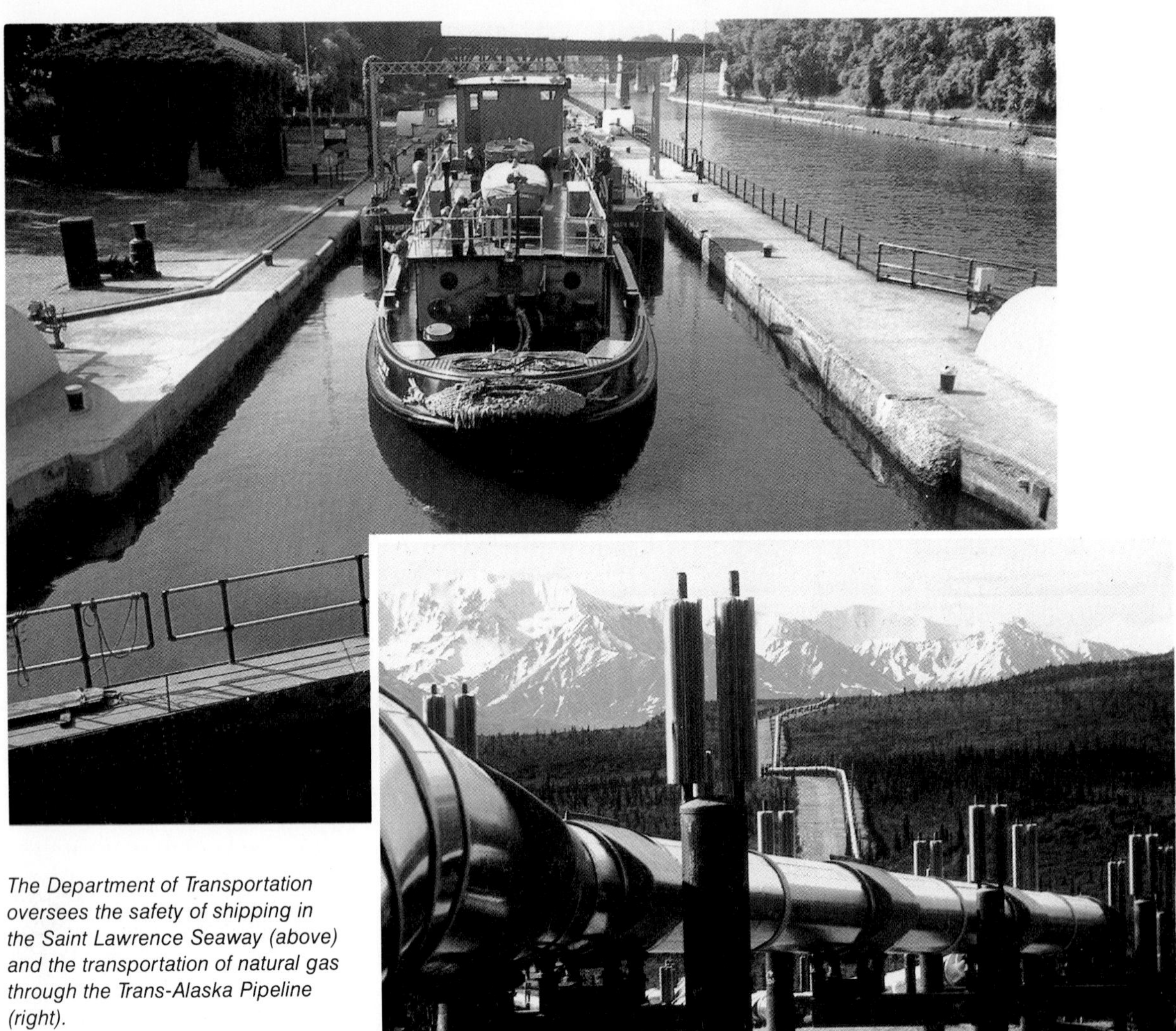

The Department of Transportation oversees the safety of shipping in the Saint Lawrence Seaway (above) and the transportation of natural gas through the Trans-Alaska Pipeline (right).

Watchdog Agencies Also promoting safe transport is the National Transportation Safety Board. Once a part of the Department of Transportation, it became an independent agency in 1975.

The safety board consists of five members appointed by the President and confirmed by the Senate. The board investigates the causes of all transport accidents of civil aircraft or passenger trains. It investigates all major accidents involving pipelines, freight trains, or ships. It also studies accidents between a motor vehicle and another form of transportation, such as a train and truck collision at a railroad crossing. The board makes all the results of these investigations public.

The board also evaluates the safety work done by other federal agencies and makes safety recommendations to them and to the transportation industry. The board hears appeals of decisions made by agencies within the Department of Transportation. If the FAA revokes a pilot's license, for example, the pilot may appeal the decision to the National Transportation Safety Board.

Construction and Maintenance

Several agencies within the Department of Transportation have as their primary responsibility the construction and maintenance of transportation systems. Among these agencies are the Federal Highway Administration, the Maritime Administration, the Urban Mass Transportation Administration, and the Saint Lawrence Seaway Development Corporation.

Road Building The most important of these agencies is the Federal Highway Administration, the nation's main road-building agency. Until the early

1900's the construction and maintenance of roads was financed almost entirely by state and local governments.

Then in 1916 the first federal highway program was established by the Federal Aid Road Act. The act provided road-building grants to the states, which had to match the money they received from the federal government. States no longer have to match grants on a dollar-for-dollar basis. But the system of grants-in-aid is still used in most federal highway programs.

Working with the states, the federal government has helped to construct 900,000 miles (1,440,000 kilometers) of highways, or about one fourth of the nation's network of roads. It is paying 90 percent of the cost of the Interstate Highway System, which will be completed in the 1990's.

The Federal Highway Administration also builds and maintains the roads in the national parks. It enforces safety regulations for the interstate trucking industry. Finally, it determines the tolls charged on bridges that cross navigable waters.

The Maritime Administration The Maritime Administration is in charge of programs to develop and maintain the United States merchant marine. The Maritime Administration guarantees loans to shipbuilders and subsidizes American shipping to meet foreign competition. It also researches ways to improve the overall quality of ships.

One of the federal government's main concerns in promoting the merchant fleet is to ensure that in time of war or national emergency ships will be available to support the armed forces and to meet vital transportation needs. The Maritime Administration maintains the nation's defense reserve fleet, numbering over 1,000 vessels. It also pays to have defense features built into the ships of the regular merchant fleet.

Urban Mass Transit One of the most important ways to conserve energy is to cut down on the use of private cars. Mass-transit systems save fuel and at the same time reduce pollution and traffic congestion. They also provide a means of travel for the

INSIGHT

The Interstate Highway System

Nothing has so changed the character of American life as the automobile. Each year the number of cars on United States highways increases. Americans travel more than 650 billion miles (1 trillion kilometers) annually on the nation's highways.

Unfortunately, the nation's highway system has not kept pace with increases in automobile traffic. Although the number of registered cars doubled in the 1950's, the number of miles of highway increased by only one third. Most roads were narrow and badly needed repair. As a result, traffic jams and rising accident rates plagued travel.

In 1956 President Eisenhower initiated the largest public works project in United States history—the construction of a national Interstate Highway System of high-speed, nonstop expressways.

Today a staggering 42,500 miles (68,000 kilometers) of interstate highways link the nation's major cities from coast to coast and carry the nation's travelers and commerce. Theoretically, a driver may use the interstate system to travel from New York City to San Francisco without ever having to stop at a traffic light.

The Interstate Highway System, originally estimated to cost $27 billion, has already run up a price tag of over $100 billion. The huge cost, however, has been offset by the system's benefits. It is estimated that the system has saved the public nearly $11 billion in lower vehicle costs, lower accident rates, and shorter traveling time. A study of the period between 1956 and 1980 estimates that the safer travel on interstate highways decreased highway fatalities by 75,000.

PROFILE

Models for Modern Mass Transit

Sleek, ultramodern subway cars rocket at speeds of up to 80 miles (129 kilometers) per hour along a network of 75 miles (121 kilometers) of track. The tracks run on elevated platforms in some places, plunge into underground tunnels below the city in others, and in one stretch run through a tube laid across the bottom of San Francisco Bay. A central computer dispatches and operates as many as 105 trains at a time. Electronic sensors guide the trains into the stations and open and close train doors. For passengers on the station platforms, electric signs indicate intervals between trains and flash the destination of each arriving train.

This is BART, the Bay Area Rapid Transit system. Opened in 1972 it is the first new subway system to be built in the United States in 60 years. It is also the first public transit system to use some of the same technology that put astronauts on the moon. BART's success in San Francisco has spawned a new generation of modern subway systems, including those in the cities of Atlanta, Baltimore, Buffalo, Miami, and Washington, D.C.

Modeled closely after BART, the "Metro" system in Washington, D.C., is by far the largest and most ambitious modern subway system in the country. The Metro's sleek aluminum cars, capable of traveling 75 miles (121 kilometers) per hour, float on air springs and run on tracks cushioned by fiberglass pads to reduce noise. The cars approach stations so quietly that flashing lights are used to signal passengers about a train's arrival. When the Metro is completed, it will cover 101 miles (163 kilometers) of track and will have cost a staggering $7 billion.

The cost of building a new subway system—approximately $100,000 a foot—has prompted city planners to look for ways to make existing transit systems more efficient. San Francisco, the city that built the first modern subway, has rehabilitated the 100-year-old cable car system. More than $10 million of the $58-million cost has been raised in private donations, not only from San Franciscans but also from people across the nation.

handicapped, the elderly, and others who cannot drive or afford automobiles.

Unfortunately, most of the United States mass-transit systems are old, inadequate, and inefficient. They were designed over 50 years ago. In most cities there was never any overall plan. Bus, subway, and streetcar systems grew up piecemeal over the years. The result is that many Americans now prefer driving cars rather than taking a bus or subway.

The Urban Mass Transportation Administration funds programs to build and improve mass-transit systems. Funding amounts to almost $4 billion a year. The money is spent to improve existing systems and to develop newer, cleaner, and more efficient ways of moving people in and out of cities to encourage them to leave their cars at home.

Section Check

1. Identify: Revenue Marine, Interstate Highway System, Bay Area Rapid Transit
2. Why was the Department of Transportation set up in 1966?
3. How does the Coast Guard promote law enforcement?
4. What three agencies promote transit safety in the United States?
5. What effect has the national speed limit had on reducing traffic deaths?
6. What are the advantages of mass-transit systems? Why do many people prefer driving a car to using mass transit?

2 THE DEPARTMENT OF COMMERCE

The Department of Commerce and Labor was established in 1903 to "foster, promote, and develop the foreign and domestic commerce, the manufacturing, the shipping and fishing industries ... of the United States." In 1913 Congress made the Department of Labor into a separate organization. From then on the redesignated Department of Commerce focused its attention on encouraging business and the free enterprise system.

As a member of the Cabinet the Secretary of Commerce advises the President on matters relating to business and industry. The President almost always appoints to this post someone who has been outstandingly successful in business. The Secretary of Commerce also directs the work of the various

Notable Secretaries of Commerce include Herbert Hoover (left), who served from 1921 until 1929, and Harry L. Hopkins (below), who served from 1938 until 1940. Lewis L. Strauss (bottom left), former head of the Atomic Energy Commission, served from 1958 until 1959, and Juanita M. Kreps (bottom right), the first woman appointed Secretary of Commerce, served from 1977 until 1979.

departmental agencies and ensures that the services of the department are made available to anyone who needs them.

The Department of Commerce is a complex of administrations, bureaus, offices, and services. Their functions, which range from taking the census to predicting the weather, vary greatly. But they have a common overall mission, to promote the nation's economic development.

The Department of Commerce has six main functions. It promotes foreign and domestic trade. It prepares statistical data on the nation's economy, does research in science and technology, and develops and maintains the United States merchant marine. It studies the weather. And it maintains several smaller agencies that promote and regulate various individual aspects of the nation's commerce.

International Trade

International trade plays a major role in the nation's economy. It accounts for almost 20 percent of the annual production of goods and services in the United States. It also provides jobs for millions of Americans. As a result, the Department of Commerce plays an important role in strengthening the position of the United States in world trade.

Study the graph of the major trading partners of the United States. What is the total value of the trade between the United States and Canada? What is the value of United States imports from West Germany?

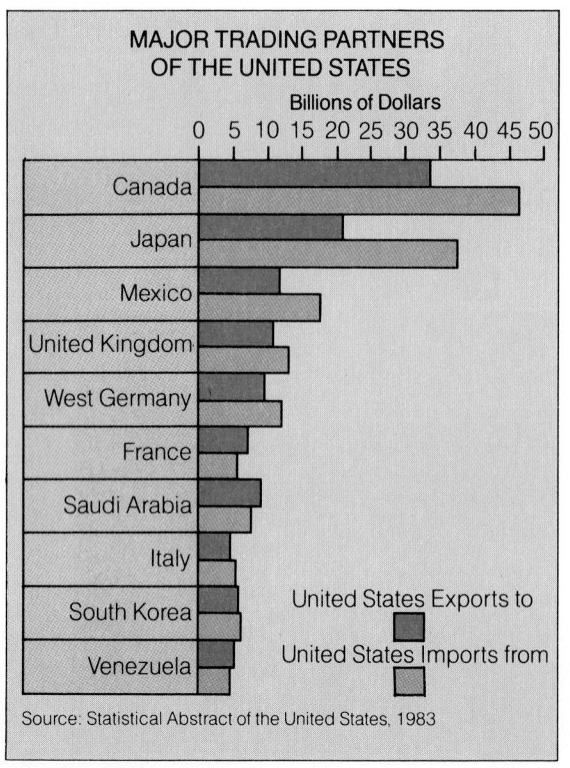

Fostering Foreign Trade Of the department's many divisions the one most directly concerned with world trade is the International Trade Administration (ITA). Over the past decade the price of foreign oil has increased 14 times over. Because the nation imports about 30 percent of the oil it uses each year, the United States has spent more than it has earned in international trade. In response, the ITA is trying to open new markets overseas for American products.

The International Trade Administration helps make United States international economic policy. The ITA focuses on such areas as export financing, tariffs and other trade barriers, exchange rates, investment regulations, and other policies that affect trade and investment. The ITA research staff keeps in close touch with changing economic conditions and the policies of countries around the world. It advises American business on trade and investment opportunities abroad. The ITA also takes part in negotiating trade agreements between the United States and other nations. The ITA's Foreign Commercial Service represents American trade and investment interests abroad through offices in 65 countries.

Regulating Foreign Trade In addition to promoting American exports the ITA also has regulatory responsibilities. It administers controls set on certain exports for reasons of national security, foreign policy, or short supply. Highly advanced electronic equipment and weapons, for example, are under strict control so that they are not sold to unfriendly nations. Regulating exports also serves as an instrument of foreign policy. For example, the President banned wheat sales to the Soviet Union after its invasion of Afghanistan in 1980. Another example is the general ban on trade with Iran after the seizure of the American embassy hostages. All United States exports are under license. Normally goods may be exported under "open license" without restriction. But by executive order, the President may place any commodity on a list of restricted exports.

The ITA is not concerned exclusively with international trade. Its Bureau of Domestic Business Development provides advice and assistance to the nation's business community. Its staff includes an

LEXICON

Balance of Trade

The ***balance of trade*** is the difference between what a nation earns from exports—the sale of its goods abroad—and its imports—what it spends to buy foreign products. When exports are greater than imports, a nation has a ***trade surplus,*** or a favorable balance of trade. When imports are greater than exports, a nation has a ***trade deficit,*** or an unfavorable balance of trade.

Over the decade of the 1970's, for example, the United States trade deficits totalled more than $105 billion. When the United States has a trade deficit, more dollars leave the country than are returned.

The value of the dollar is measured against the value of foreign currencies. The determination of the dollar's value is measured in the ***exchange rate,*** or the rate at which dollars can be traded for other currencies. When measured against a strong foreign currency, for example, the dollar is worth less—that is, more dollars are required to purchase foreign-made goods. The practical result is that Americans must pay more for foreign products. On the other hand, American products are cheaper for foreign buyers. When the value of the dollar declines, then, exports are likely to increase.

official who handles business people's complaints and tries to reduce their frustration with government red tape. The ITA staff also analyzes the effect of economic trends for different industries and makes recommendations on government policy and programs.

Economic Policies and Statistics

The Chief Economist of the Department of Commerce works both inside and outside the department. Outside the department the Chief Economist works with the President's Council of Economic Advisers, the Treasury, and the Federal Reserve Board in determining overall economic policy. Within the department the Chief Economist advises the Secretary of Commerce and other department officials on economic conditions and trends. The Chief Economist also supervises the department's statistical programs, especially those of the Bureau of the Census and the Bureau of Economic Analysis.

The Bureau of the Census collects a wide variety of statistical data about the American people and the nation's economy that is invaluable to people who want to know which way a particular industry, or the economy as a whole, is headed. The information

The Constitution provides for a census every 10 years. The information collected from single individuals and heads of households must be kept strictly confidential and be used only for statistical purposes.

Please fill out this official Census Form and mail it back on Census Day, Tuesday, April 1, 1980

1980 Census of the United States

LEXICON

The Gross National Product

The ***gross national product*** (GNP), published every three months by the Bureau of Economic Analysis, is a figure representing the total value of goods and services produced in the United States during the year. The GNP divided by the total population of a nation yields a nation's ***per capita income***—the income of the average person. The per capita income is useful in comparing the economies of different countries. It is also widely used to measure a nation's standard of living.

collected by the Census Bureau also helps businesses to locate markets for their products. For example, a company that manufactures toys needs to know which cities have the most children. A company that is trying to decide on which television stations to advertise its camping equipment needs to know not only which communities campers come from but also in which communities people watch the most television.

The Bureau of Economic Analysis prepares and interprets ***economic accounts*** of the United States. These are the yardsticks by which national income, productivity, and wealth are measured. The broadest measure of the nation's economic health is the gross national product (GNP). The bureau also publishes a journal called *Survey of Current Business.*

Science and Technology

The Department of Commerce seeks "to advance science and technology in order to foster, serve and promote the nation's economic development." It does so through the National Bureau of Standards (NBS) and the Patent and Trademark Office.

The gross national product (GNP) of the United States has risen rapidly in recent years. What does the GNP measure? If the population of the United States is approximately 235 million, what is the nation's per capita income for 1984?

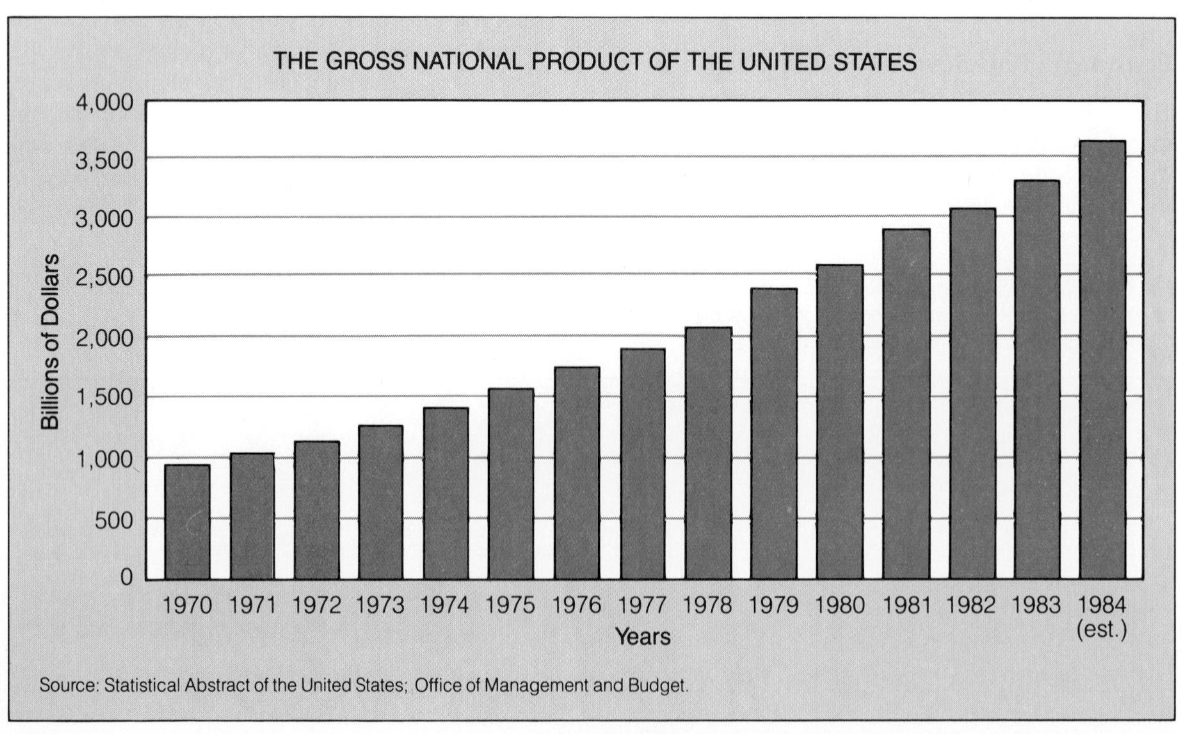

Standards of Measurement Modern industrial society depends upon accurate and uniform measurements. The National Bureau of Standards is the nation's official measurement laboratory. It sets the exact standards to be used in the measurement of just about everything—mass, length, time, temperature, and so on.

In addition to setting measurement standards the bureau conducts basic research into the properties of materials. It analyzes their chemical composition, physical structure, and behavior. These analyses have helped industry to develop many new and improved products.

The bureau's National Engineering Laboratory conducts research in such areas as building construction, fire safety, and consumer product safety. It provides its services to both private business and government agencies. For the Consumer Product Safety Commission, for example, the NBS has conducted research aimed at reducing injuries and deaths caused by flammable clothing and unsafe toys.

The National Bureau of Standards is not a regulatory agency and thus has no authority to impose its findings on either industry or the public. On the other hand, many of the bureau's findings have been enacted into law by Congress and serve as standards in government regulation.

Patents and Trademarks Although Congress first passed a patent law in 1790, it did not create the Patent Office until 1836. The Patent and Trademark Office protects the creative efforts of inventors and businesses. It does so by issuing patents and registering trademarks.

A ***patent*** is a license that grants an inventor exclusive rights to the manufacture, use, and sale of his or her discovery for a limited time. This protection is based on Article 1, Section 8, of the Constitution, which gives Congress the power "to promote the progress of science and useful arts."

There are three kinds of patents. A patent of invention applies to "any new and useful art, machine, manufacture, or composition of matter, or useful improvement thereof." A plant patent applies to new varieties of living plants. Both of these kinds of patents are good for 17 years. A patent of design applies to ornamental designed articles, such as a patterned fabric. It is good for 3½, 7, or 14 years and may be renewed. Other patents are rarely renewed, and then only by a special act of Congress.

Each year the Patent and Trademark Office issues more than 70,000 new patents. The office, however, only issues the patent. It does not prosecute those who infringe upon it or challenge it. The patent holder is responsible for taking any infringement to a federal District Court. In the past most patents were obtained by individual inventors. Today most patents are usually held by large corporations.

A ***trademark*** is a distinctive device that identifies the manufacturer or seller of a product sold in interstate or foreign commerce. A trademark may be a word or phrase, or it may be a symbol. A trademark is good for 20 years and may be renewed over and over. Each year the Patent and Trademark Office registers about 30,000 trademarks.

Commercial Navigation

A nation's ***merchant marine*** is its commercial fleet of ships. These ships may be privately or publicly owned. In the United States the merchant marine carries most foreign commerce and all domestic waterborne commerce. In time of war the merchant marine also serves as an auxiliary to the United States Navy.

The Federal Maritime Commission is an independent regulatory agency. The commission has five members, each of whom is appointed by the President and confirmed by the Senate for a five-year term. The commission regulates the rates, services, and employment practices of American ships engaged in foreign commerce and in domestic commerce offshore. Shipping on United States inland waters is regulated by the Interstate Commerce Commission.

The Federal Maritime Commission issues licenses to businesses that engage in oceangoing trade.

INSIGHT

How Federal Funds Are Distributed

The government distributes federal funds to business by providing direct subsidies in the form of cash grants. It also provides indirect subsidies in the form of cash grants to other sectors of the economy on which business depends, such as the transportation system. Tax laws that favor business are still another form of aid. Many federal agencies make or guarantee loans to business. Two such agencies are the Small Business Administration and the Export-Import Bank. The former promotes and encourages small business, while the latter helps to finance the export of American products. Finally, the federal government spends enormous sums of money outright—over $700 billion each year—to buy goods and services and to pay salaries and welfare benefits. Most of the goods and services are provided by American businesses. And the salaries and welfare benefits go to consumers who, in their turn, buy goods and services. Either way, business get its fair share.

Other Responsibilities

The Commerce Department exercises responsibility in a number of other areas. Through the United States Travel and Tourism Administration it establishes and maintains relations with government and industry officials to facilitate tourism policies and programs.

Through the National Oceanic and Atmospheric Administration (NOAA) it explores and charts oceanic resources. It also monitors and reports atmospheric conditions, including the daily weather and potentially destructive storms.

The Commerce Department, through the Economic Development Administration, conducts programs for long-range economic development in areas of the country with severe unemployment. The department funds public works projects and state and local economic development programs. It makes direct loans to help businesses expand job opportunities and construct plants and also guarantees private loans to businesses.

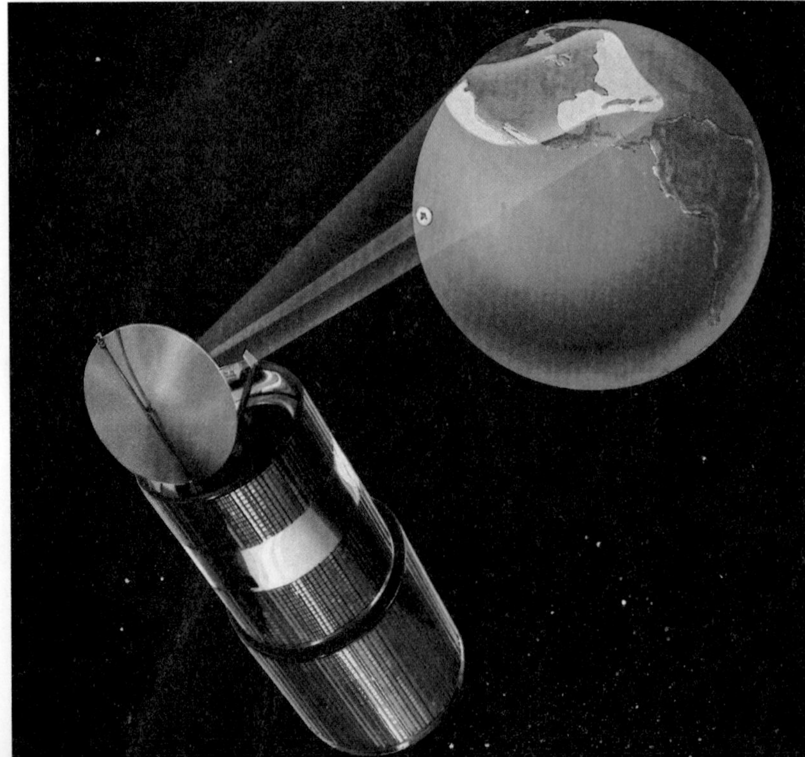

The Department of Commerce formulates policies that encourage the development of telecommunications satellites, such as Western Union's Westar *satellite.*

The Commerce Department, through the Minority Business Development Agency, coordinates federal efforts to establish and strengthen minority-owned businesses. It encourages state and local government and private organizations to support these businesses. It also acts as a clearinghouse for business information that is useful to minorities.

Through the National Telecommunications and Information Administration, the Commerce Department advises the President on policies relating to the promotion and regulation of the telecommunications industry—telephones, radio and television, microwave lines, and satellite systems.

Section Check

1. Define: balance of trade, trade surplus, trade deficit, exchange rate, economic accounts, gross national product, patent, trademark, merchant marine
2. Identify: International Trade Administration, Bureau of the Census, *Survey of Current Business*, Minority Business Development Agency, National Telecommunications and Information Administration
3. How does the Department of Commerce promote business? How does it regulate business?
4. How does information collected by the Census Bureau help business?
5. What are three main functions of the Bureau of Standards?

3 REGULATION OF COMMERCE

The power to regulate commerce is granted by Article 1, Section 8, Clause 3, of the Constitution. Some important terms will be defined before the ways in which commerce is regulated are discussed.

The Language of Commerce

The meaning of the term ***commerce*** is constantly expanding as Congress finds new ways of exercising the commerce power and as the Supreme Court rules on the constitutionality of those ways. Originally, commerce meant the goods that were bought and sold. It did not refer to the means by which they were bought and sold. Today commerce means both of these things. Thus it includes the advertising of goods, the transportation of goods, the working conditions under which goods are sold—all the means by which buying and selling takes place. It also includes the goods themselves. This interpretation was first handed down in 1824 by Chief Justice John Marshall in *Gibbons* v. *Ogden*.

Working conditions, salaries and wages, and business practices are among the aspects of interstate business monitored by the Commerce Department. What is the difference between interstate and intrastate commerce? What level of government regulates intrastate commerce?

Commerce . . . describes the commercial intercourse between nations, and parts of nations, in all its branches, and is regulated by prescribing rules for carrying on that intercourse.

Interstate vs. Intrastate Commerce ***Interstate commerce*** takes place between and among the states. ***Intrastate commerce*** is conducted within one state. The distinction is important, because only interstate commerce is subject to federal regulation. Intrastate commerce is regulated by the states. If state regulation of intrastate commerce conflicts with federal regulation of interstate commerce, the federal regulation takes precedence.

But it is not always easy to tell what is interstate commerce. Interstate commerce includes any transaction that crosses a state line. It also includes any transaction that is part of a transaction that crosses a state line. Therefore, the Supreme Court has ruled that goods are a part of interstate commerce when they start on a continuous journey that will take them across a state line. Goods generally cease being interstate commerce when the original package in which they were shipped is broken open, used, or sold by the party to whom they were shipped. This is called the ***original package doctrine.*** In some cases, however, goods cease being interstate commerce as soon as they reach the party to whom they were shipped.

Foreign Trade as Commerce Foreign commerce is any United States commerce that begins in, passes through, or ends in a foreign country. Like interstate commerce, foreign commerce becomes intrastate commerce under the original package doctrine. The effect of the original package doctrine is to prevent the states from interfering with foreign trade. Congress, however, has used its powers to regulate foreign commerce to prohibit the import of such goods as illegal drugs and diseased plants and animals. Congress has also restricted the export of certain goods, such as weapons.

Transportation as Commerce Commerce includes all forms of transportation that are used directly or indirectly to move goods intended for trade. These include railroads, ships, aircraft, motor vehicles, electrical power lines, and gas pipelines. Therefore, whenever any of these forms of transportation are used in interstate commerce, they are subject to federal regulation.

Communications as Commerce Radio and television, the telephone, and the telegraph are all used in the buying and selling of goods. Therefore, these forms of communication are included under the definition of commerce, and interstate communications are subject to federal regulation.

Restraints on Trade A ***trust*** is a group of companies within a single industry who agree to limit production, fix prices, or cooperate in other ways to reduce or eliminate competition. By the end of the 1800's trusts dominated most of the nation's major industries. To control the trusts Congress passed the Sherman Antitrust Act of 1890. The law prohibited every agreement "in restraint of trade or commerce among the several States, or with foreign nations." In 1911 the Supreme Court interpreted restraint to mean every agreement that was "unreasonably restrictive of competitive conditions."

In 1914 Congress passed the Clayton Antitrust Act. It imposed four specific controls on monopolies. It forbade any corporation to purchase the stock of a competitor. It forbade the same person to sit on the board of directors of two competing companies. It forbade exclusive agreements, whereby a dealer could handle only one company's products. And it forbade price cutting, price discrimination among different customers, and certain other practices designed to reduce or eliminate competition. Since then, certain groups—including telephone companies, farmers, and professional baseball players—have been exempted from some or all provisions of the Sherman and Clayton Acts.

The antitrust laws are enforced by the Federal Trade Commission (FTC). Companies that violate antitrust laws may be subject to criminal prosecution. They also may be prosecuted for damages in a civil suit brought by the federal government or by a private party. Suits filed by the federal government are prosecuted by the Antitrust Division of the Department of Justice. Companies that are found guilty of violating the antitrust laws may be fined as much as $1 million. Individuals who are found guilty of violations may be jailed for up to three years.

The Role of Regulatory Commissions

The regulation of business and industry has largely been given over to independent regulatory commissions rather than to bureaus within the Department of Commerce. The commissions that regulate commerce also regulate transportation because commerce includes transportation.

Each commission is organized as a bipartisan board of 5 to 11 members who serve staggered terms of 5 to 7 years. Members are appointed by the President with the consent of the Senate. They may be removed only for misconduct or neglect of duty. Each commission has broad regulatory power over one sector of the economy or one type of commercial activity.

Congress has given each commission the power to make, enforce, and interpret rules for the regulated industries. In much of their work the commissions use a quasi-judicial procedure. Following the format of a civil court they accept claims and complaints, hold hearings, and make rulings on a case-by-case basis. The independent regulatory commissions exercise enormous power, but this power does not go unchecked. Any abuse of authority is likely to bring loud protest from either the regulated industry or from public-interest advocates and consumer groups.

Congress can investigate a commission's policies and procedures. Congress can also narrow a commission's authority or abolish it altogether. In addition, Congress has control over the funding of commissions. In 1980 Congress, opposing Federal Trade Commission regulations, held up FTC appropriations. Only last-minute action by the FTC saved it from closing.

The President exerts influence as well, not over a commission's particular decisions, but over general regulatory policy. Through appointments, control over the budget, recommendations to Congress, and the President's position as the nation's leader, the chief executive plays a major role in shaping the environment within which the commissions operate.

Finally, the courts have the power to review a commission's decisions. This ensures that each commission conforms with the law and with the Constitution.

Thus, while the regulatory commissions are formally independent, they are subject to check by Congress, the President, and the courts. The commissions are ultimately answerable to the people, and they are judged by how well they serve the public interest.

Interstate Commerce Commission The first independent regulatory commission was the Interstate Commerce Commission (ICC). Its creation in 1887 was a response to the public outcry over scandal in the management of the railroad industry. Congress gave the ICC the responsibility for regulating the railroads in the public interest. In its first actions the ICC set "just and reasonable" rates and decided various matters related to railroad service. Over the years, the commission's authority has been broadened to include trucks, buses, express agencies, inland water and coastal shipping, oil pipelines, and other forms of interstate transport.

The commission approves company mergers and determines whether service is adequate. It grants the right to operate trucking companies, bus lines, and water carriers. It rules on applications to establish new routes or abandon old ones, and it must approve any discontinuation of passenger train service. The ICC settles controversies over the rates that carriers charge and approves any rate changes.

The 1935 Motor Carrier Act extended the jurisdiction of the Interstate Commerce Commission (ICC) to trucks, buses, and other vehicles engaged in interstate trade. What other forms of interstate transport are under ICC supervision?

ICC regulations have drawn attack on two main fronts. First, critics charge that the ICC has crippled the railroads by discouraging initiative, depressing rates, and draining off profits to subsidize money-losing lines. Second, they argue that the ICC has destroyed competition in the trucking industry. The commission controls who gets an operating certificate, what can be hauled, how it can be hauled, and where it can be hauled. The result, critics say, is costly inefficiency for which the public pays dearly.

Since 1976 Congress has begun to encourage ***deregulation*** in order to promote competition in the transportation industry. Congress has reduced the ICC's authority over the railroads and the truckers in particular. Today the ICC itself is engaged in a review of railroad and trucking regulations. In the words of a former chairman the goal is to "find the least amount of regulation necessary to maintain a sound, reliable, stable transportation system."

Federal Trade Commission Established in 1914 to enforce the Clayton Antitrust Act, the Federal Trade Commission (FTC) directs activities against "unfair methods of competition" and "unfair or deceptive acts or practices."

While the FTC seeks to prevent restraints on trade, most of its efforts today are directed toward preventing false or deceptive advertising. The commission regulates truth in packaging and labeling for textiles, furs, and a number of other consumer products. Labels must specify the contents of the package, the fiber content of the textile, or the common name of the fur, such as rabbit rather than lapin, coney, or French chinchilla. Accurate labeling enables consumers to make value comparisons for price. As required by the Truth in Lending Act the FTC seeks to protect consumers from businesses that offer misleading credit information. The commission also regulates credit agencies.

The FTC relies mainly on voluntary compliance with its regulations. It publishes trade regulation rules and offers legal advice to businesses. When voluntary compliance is not given, the FTC acts like a court. It hears complaints of unfair practices, investigates selected complaints, and issues a stipulation or a cease-and-desist order when it finds that a complaint is justified. A ***stipulation*** asks the guilty party to stop engaging in the unfair practice. A ***cease-and-desist order*** obliges the party to do so. A cease-and-desist order is issued only after a formal hearing and usually only if the offender has refused a stipulation. A cease-and-desist order can be enforced by the federal courts. Violation carries a heavy penalty. The FTC, however, is generally more interested in stopping unfair business practices than in punishing violators. As a result it usually leaves prosecution to the Antitrust Division.

For decades the FTC was criticized for not effectively protecting the public. In recent years, however, the FTC has become very aggressive and has come under heavy attack from business leaders and members of Congress who believe the commission has abused its authority, notably in its efforts to regulate advertising.

Under legislation passed in 1980 Congress has limited FTC powers to regulate advertising and has prevented the FTC from investigating the insurance industry without Congressional approval. The law

Federal Communications Commission (FCC) meetings are held concerning rate-increase requests and licensing considerations. List the types of communication regulated by the FCC.

ISSUES

The Equal-Time Rule

In the 1940 film *Knute Rockne—All American,* the crowds at Notre Dame cheered wildly as a young football star named George Gipp raced for a touchdown. Almost twenty-five years later *Knute Rockne—All American* caused a thorny problem for the Federal Communications Commission: Ronald Reagan, the actor who had played George Gipp, had become a candidate for governor of California. By airing any of the 50 films Reagan made in his career as an actor, a television station would be required to provide equal time to his political opponents.

If any television station permits a "legally qualified candidate for any public office to use a broadcasting station," the FCC's equal-time rule reads, "[it] shall afford equal opportunities to all other such candidates." According to the FCC, "use" is the same as "appearance" or "exposure" to the public "view or ear." If a candidate appears on the air, either on film or in a still photograph, the broadcasting station must make equal time available to other candidates. It doesn't matter whether or not the candidate speaks. Similarly, if a candidate's voice is heard and can be identified, the equal-time rule applies.

Not all broadcasts, however, trigger the equal-time rule. In 1959 Congress exempted certain television presentations, such as a newscast, a news interview, a news documentary, or on-the-spot coverage of a news event, from the equal-time rule. An appearance by a political candidate in a story on the evening news does not trigger the equal-time rule. Nor does an interview with a political candidate on a news program. In 1975 the FCC ruled that political debates are news events and are exempt from equal-time demands.

Curiously, although the equal-time rule was established to ensure fairness in political campaigns, it does not distinguish between political and nonpolitical appearances. Thus, if a business executive running for office were to do a television commercial advertising his or her business, all opponents could demand equal time. Any appearance by a political candidate, even as an actor, is subject to the provisions of the equal-time rule.

also requires the FTC to weigh the cost of any new rule against its benefits. Congress also voted itself the right to veto new rules issued by the FTC, but the Supreme Court declared this ***legislative veto*** unconstitutional in 1983.

Federal Communications Commission The Federal Communications Commission (FCC), established in 1934, regulates interstate and foreign communications by radio, television, telephone, wire, and cable. In most countries, radio, television, and telephone services are owned and operated by the government. In the United States they are privately owned but are subject to government regulation.

Because only a limited number of radio frequencies and television channels are available, the FCC controls them through licensing. A television license is usually worth millions of dollars in advertising revenues, and competition for a television license is intense and often highly political. Licenses for both radio and television are granted for a fixed period. Renewal, once virtually automatic, now requires hearings on the station's record of public service.

The Federal Communications Commission enforces regulations prohibiting obscene language over the airwaves. It also administers the ***fairness doctrine*** and the ***equal-time rule.*** The fairness

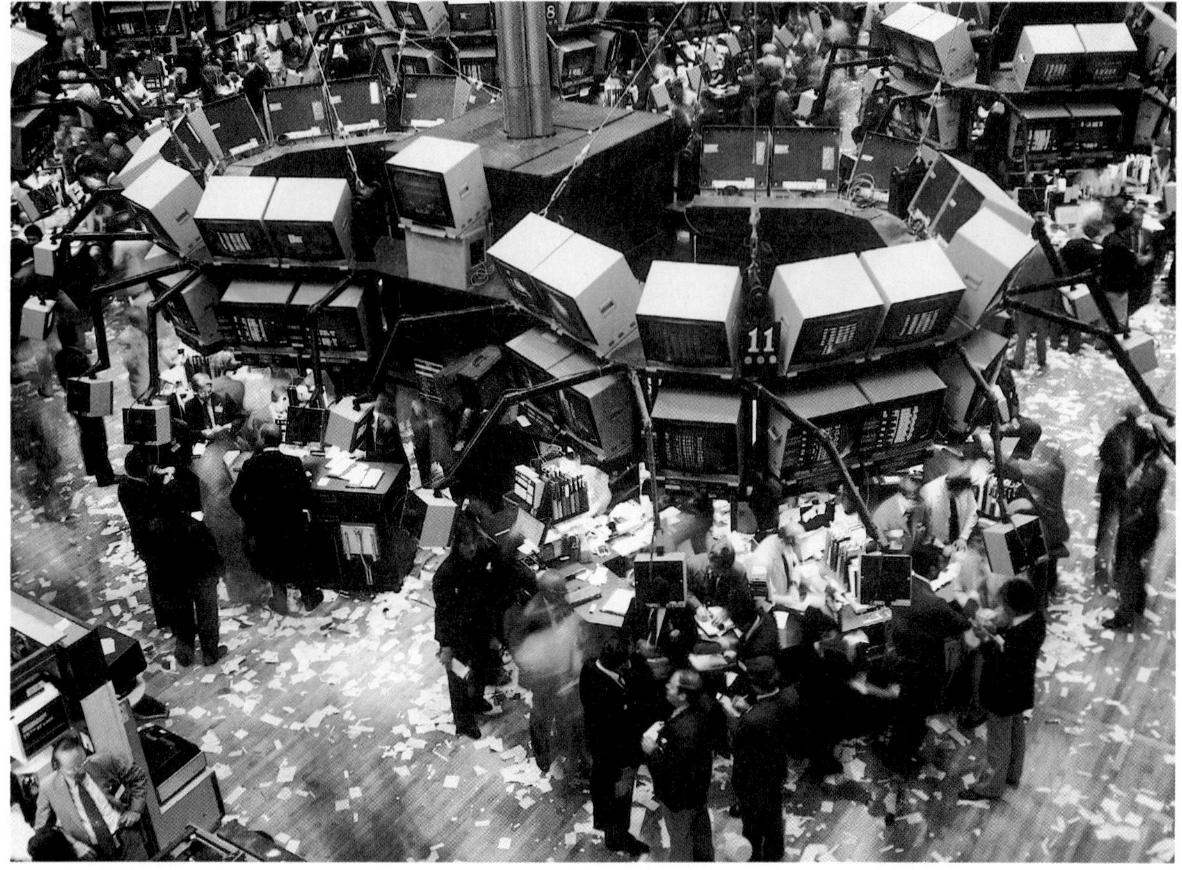

The New York Stock Exchange has been called "the nation's market place." The trading activities of the stock exchange are regulated by the Securities and Exchange Commission (SEC).

doctrine requires that stations present all sides of important public issues. The equal-time rule requires that all candidates for public office be given equal access to radio and television. If a television station provides paid or free time for one candidate, it must offer equal time to all opposing candidates.

The FCC also regulates the telephone, wire, and cable industries. It ensures that rates and services are fair and reasonable. In regulating the wire and telephone services the FCC shares responsibility with state utility commissions. The states control intrastate rates, while the FCC must approve rates charged for interstate telegrams and long-distance calls.

Securities and Exchange Commission Congress established the Securities and Exchange Commission (SEC) in 1934 as a result of Senate investigations into the causes of the stock market crash of 1929. The investigations revealed deception, fraud, and manipulation. Although there were state regulations governing the securities market, these regulations had proven ineffective, because the sale of securities is, in reality, an interstate business. National regulation was called for, and the SEC was established to provide it.

The SEC has five members, each of whom are appointed by the President and confirmed by the Senate for a five-year term. The SEC administers a number of laws against fraudulent and unfair practices. New stock issues must be registered with the SEC before they can be sold. The registration statement must give complete and honest information about the stock's value. For example, potential stockholders are entitled to know if there are any lawsuits pending against a company. The Securities Exchange Act of 1934 requires that all national securities exchanges, such as the New York Stock Exchange, register with the commission and adopt its rules. The Public Utility Holding Company Act of 1935 gives the commission regulatory powers over ***holding companies,*** or corporations that hold enough stock in other companies to be able to control their operations. The SEC also has broad regulatory authority over stockbrokers and investment companies.

Commodity Futures Trading Commission The Commodity Futures Trading Commission (CFTC) was established in 1975 to regulate the commodity futures markets, which handle lumber, metals, and most agricultural products. ***Futures*** are agreements to buy and sell a particular commodity at an agreed-upon price at a future date. A futures buyer, for example, purchases corn long before it is actually harvested. The buying of futures establishes a price for the commodity, which in turn tends to stabilize the market. The buying of futures also offers great rewards to the speculator. At the same time, however, futures buying carries great risk. Therefore, a speculator may be tempted to engage in dishonest trading practices. The CFTC seeks to prevent price manipulation, attempts at cornering or dominating the market in a particular commodity, and other forms of dishonesty. The CFTC approves all futures agreements, regulates the exchanges on which futures are traded, and licenses firms and brokers that deal in commodities.

Consumer Product Safety Commission Each year an estimated 36 million Americans are injured and 30,000 are killed in accidents related to consumer products. To reduce the number and severity of these accidents Congress established the Consumer Product Safety Commission (CPSC) in 1972.

The commission is responsible for setting mandatory product safety standards. Thousands of detailed regulations cover the design, construction, performance, and packaging of almost every conceivable consumer product. Standards are developed in cooperation with consumer organizations, with interested members of the general public, and with representatives from the different industries. Anyone may propose a standard. If the CPSC approves it, and if the standard is not challenged in the United States Court of Appeals of the District of Columbia, it becomes law.

The activities of the Chicago Board of Trade—the world's largest commodity exchange—and other commodities markets are regulated by the Commodity Futures Trading Commission (CFTC). How does the CFTC monitor commodities markets?

ISSUES

The Regulation Debate

Few subjects are as likely to start an argument as the issue of government regulation. Regulation has bitter critics and passionate defenders, and since the late 1970's the controversy has grown more intense. Today, there are 56 federal agencies with regulatory authority, ranging from the independent regulatory commissions to the Department of Labor's Occupational Safety and Health Administration (OSHA) and the Environmental Protection Agency (EPA). Together these 56 agencies influence virtually every aspect of American economy and society. Charles Schultze, former chairman of the President's Council of Economic Advisers, stated:

By now, regulation almost parallels the taxing and spending powers of government in terms of its influence and importance in the life of the nation. Finding ways to improve how it goes about regulating is the most important managerial task now facing the government.

Critics argue that overregulation has led to unwarranted government interference in private life. They say that regulation is strangling the economy because it has reduced competition, stifled innovation, destroyed jobs, and cut productivity. The cost of regulation, these critics contend, is a "hidden tax" that adds to inflation by raising the price of goods and services.

The increase in regulation can be measured in the number of pages in the *Code of Federal Regulations,* which has grown from 30,000 pages in the 1960's to more than 87,000 pages in the 1980's. Keeping up with all these detailed regulations can be both confusing and costly for businesses. Meeting the standards for a given product or a given service may require a dozen or more permits from as many agencies. Obtaining permits can take a company two or three years. And the cost of compliance runs into billions of dollars a year, although estimates range from a low of $2.6 billion to a high of $100 billion. One unintended result, according to critics, is that only large companies are able to cope with the cost and complexity of regulation. Small firms often do not have the resources to meet federal regulations and, as a result, may be forced out of business.

Those who defend regulation argue that to measure the costs of regulation without looking at its benefits is one-sided. Regulations, they point out, have promoted the interests of agriculture, labor, and business. Regulations have resulted in cleaner air and water, and safer work places. They have protected the general public by giving it safer products and more wholesome food. Most important, advocates argue, federal regulations have saved lives. Advocates cite as one example the regulations that control the use of cancer-causing chemicals. The value of life, advocates argue, cannot be measured in terms of monetary costs.

Fundamentally, however, the issue is not whether or not to regulate. The challenge is to improve regulation. Reform efforts seek to maintain the benefits that regulations are intended to achieve while, at the same time, reducing the number, complexity, and cost of regulations.

The commission also has the authority to ban the sale or shipment of hazardous consumer products. Its efforts to protect children have been especially vigorous. About 2,000 different children's toys have been banned as dangerous—often because they were flammable, had sharp edges or sharp points, or could have caused a small child to choke on them. Each year the CPSC bans additional toys as unsafe.

The Consumer Product Safety Commission has provoked as much controversy as other regulatory agencies. Its supporters claim that consumers need all the protection they can get from the enormous power of big business. The supporters recall the days when a consumer who was injured by a defective tool or an exploding jar had no recourse. To the victims of unsafe products the CPSC can hardly go too far.

Critics charge that the commission has unnecessarily intruded into business and has limited the consumer's choice. In a humorous jab at the commission's efforts one economist defined ***consumer*** as "a person who is capable of choosing a President but incapable of choosing a bicycle without help from a government agency."

In 1983 the Supreme Court declared that Congress could not veto the regulations of regulatory agencies. In response to the Court's decision the House of Representatives voted to strip the Consumer Product Safety Commission of its power to issue regulations. The Senate and the House, however, failed to reach an agreement on this issue.

Section Check

1. Define: original package doctrine, trust, deregulation, stipulation, cease-and-desist order, legislative veto, fairness doctrine, equal-time rule, holding company, futures
2. Identify: *Gibbons* v. *Ogden,* Sherman Antitrust Act, Truth in Lending Act, *Code of Federal Regulations*
3. What does the term *commerce* include?
4. What is the difference between interstate commerce and intrastate commerce?
5. What was the first independent regulatory commission?
6. Why do some business people object to federal regulation? Why has Congress encouraged deregulation since 1976?
7. Why was the SEC created?

SUMMARY

The Department of Transportation administers federal transportation programs and develops national transportation policies. It enforces the law on the high seas and promotes safety for transportation on land. It maintains and constructs highway and mass-transit systems, often in cooperation with state agencies. It also operates and maintains the United States portion of the Saint Lawrence Seaway. The Coast Guard is a part of the Department of Transportation during peacetime, but it is a part of the United States Navy during wartime.

The Department of Commerce promotes the interests of business through economic development and technological advancement in six ways. (1) It promotes foreign and domestic trade. (2) It collects and analyzes statistics on economic conditions and trends. (3) It sets and monitors measurement standards and protects the creative efforts of inventors and businesses through the issuing of patents and trademarks. (4) It enforces the law within the coastal waters of the United States and regulates shipping. (5) It monitors atmospheric and oceanic conditions and reports on weather conditions within the United States. (6) It promotes minority businesses, tourism, and the economic development of depressed areas.

According to the language of economics, the term *commerce* includes both goods that are bought and sold and the means by which they are bought and sold. Interstate commerce is subject to federal regulation. Interstate commerce is any transaction or part of a transaction that crosses a state line. Foreign commerce is United States commerce that begins in, passes through, or ends in a foreign country. Transportation of goods intended for trade is a form of commerce. Communication is also a form of commerce. The regulation of commerce also includes breaking up attempts to restrain trade through the formation of trusts and monopolies.

The regulation of business, for the most part, is done by independent regulatory commissions. The Interstate Commerce Commission regulates all forms of interstate surface transport. The Federal Trade Commission enforces antitrust laws and protects consumer interests by preventing false or deceptive advertising. The Federal Communications Commission regulates interstate and foreign communications within the United States. Two other major commissions include the Securities and Exchange Commission and the Commodity Futures Trading Commission.

Chapter 24 Review

Using Vocabulary

Answer the questions below by using the meaning of each underlined term.

1. Why does a favorable exchange rate usually mean an unfavorable balance of trade?
2. How can the gross national product and per capita income be used to measure a nation's standard of living?
3. How does the original package doctrine help to define interstate commerce?
4. How does a patent differ from a trademark?
5. What are futures?
6. How might a trade deficit affect a nation's commerce?

Understanding American Government

1. How have the functions of the United States Coast Guard changed over the years?
2. In what three areas does the federal government regulate traffic safety?
3. Compare the costs and the benefits of the Interstate Highway System.
4. How does the federal government protect the creative efforts of inventors and businesses?
5. How does federal promotion and regulation of commerce affect our national security?
6. What control does Congress have over independent regulatory commissions? What control does the President have? What control does the Supreme Court have?
7. How does the Federal Communications Commission regulate election campaigns?
8. What measures has the Securities and Exchange Commission taken to protect investments and potential investments in the stock market?
9. How has Congress's attitude toward the regulation of industry changed since 1790?

Extending Your Skills: Analyzing a Bar Graph

Study the graph on page 580. Then complete the items that follow.

1. The value of United States imports from Canada is about (a) \$10 billion; (b) \$25 billion; (c) \$45 billion.
2. The value of United States imports from Japan exceeds the value of United States exports to that nation by about (a) \$5 billion; (b) \$20 billion; (c) \$50 billion.
3. The combined value of United States exports to the United Kingdom, West Germany, and France is about (a) \$10 billion; (b) \$25 billion; (c) \$50 billion.
4. The value of United States imports from Japan is about twice as great as the value of United States imports from (a) Canada; (b) Saudi Arabia; (c) Mexico.

Government and You

1. What, if anything, do you think the government should do to reduce the number of automobile accidents?
2. Imagine that your community received funds from the federal government for improvements in transportation. Should the money be used to improve streets, roads, and highways or to develop mass-transit systems? Give reasons for your opinion.
3. Do you agree or disagree with the equal-time rule of the FCC? Explain.
4. Comment on the statement that a consumer is "a person who is capable of choosing a President but incapable of choosing a bicycle without help from a government agency."
5. Why do you think some people favor government regulation? Why do you think some people oppose government regulation?

Activities

1. Research the goods and services that are included when figuring the gross national product. Then make two lists, one showing the items that are included and one showing the items that are not included in determining the GNP.
2. Draw a poster that shows the major activities of one regulatory agency.
3. Construct a bar graph showing the number of antitrust suits filed by the federal government during each decade since the passage of the Sherman Antitrust Act.

Chapter 25

Natural Resources, Science, and Technology

Let us use wisely the resources we hold in trust for this and future generations.

CECIL D. ANDRUS

CHAPTER OVERVIEW

1 THE DEPARTMENT OF THE INTERIOR
Land and Water Resources / The National Park System / Fish and Wildlife Conservation / The Geological Survey / Mines and Mining

2 THE ENVIRONMENT AND OUTER SPACE
The Environmental Protection Agency / The National Oceanic and Atmospheric Administration / The National Aeronautics and Space Administration

3 THE DEPARTMENT OF ENERGY
The Energy Crisis / Energy Policies / Use of Fossil Fuels / Nuclear Energy / Renewable Energy / Regulation and Marketing / Defense Programs / The Nuclear Regulatory Commission / Continuing Support of Science

The Department of the Interior is responsible for maintaining the land and water resources of the United States. The Norris Dam, which controls flooding and creates electric power in the Clinch River region of eastern Tennessee, was built in the 1930's.

1 THE DEPARTMENT OF THE INTERIOR

The Department of the Interior was created in 1849. Originally it performed functions that were not assigned to other departments. Among other things, it took the census, managed public buildings, paid out federal pensions, and supervised United States marshals. The department also had jurisdiction over public lands, federal mining regulations, and Indian affairs. Today the Department of the Interior is the nation's principal conservation agency.

The department's activities in the area of conservation fall into three broad groups. First, the Interior Department manages more than 770 million acres (311 million hectares) of the nation's land and water resources. Second, it oversees the use of federal lands for recreation and protects the nation's wildlife. Finally, it engages in research on the nation's geology and its mineral resources.

The Department of the Interior is headed by the Secretary of the Interior, who, like the other Cabinet officers, is appointed by the President with Senate confirmation. Usually the President chooses someone from a state west of the Mississippi. A westerner is chosen because much of the department's work is done in the West, where most public lands and most Native Americans are located.

Land and Water Resources

Approximately one third of the land area of the United States is owned by the federal government. This land was acquired by treaty from foreign countries—Great Britain, France, Spain, Mexico, and Russia—and from states that ceded their western land claims to the federal government.

Although these public lands are extensive, they were originally much larger. Some 60 percent of what was once public land is now owned by private parties or by the states. It was sold or granted to homesteaders to encourage the settlement of the West; to railroads to encourage their expansion; and to the states to build roads, canals, and public colleges.

Land Management Various federal agencies have authority over portions of public land. But the major responsibility for public land lies with the Interior Department's Bureau of Land Management (BLM), which today administers more than 282 million acres (40 million hectares).

The BLM is responsible for the protection, orderly development, and use of public lands and resources. Resources include timber, minerals, oil and gas, geothermal energy, wildlife, rangeland vegetation, wild and scenic rivers, and designated conservation and wilderness areas. The BLM practices ***multiple-use management,*** trying to make sure that public lands and resources are used wisely in as many different ways as possible.

Public lands are an important source of revenue for the federal treasury. The sale of oil and gas leases, of grazing rights, of timber leases, and of leases for mining coal, oil shale, and other minerals brings in between $1 billion and $2 billion each year.

The use of public lands has often been a matter of controversy. The Bureau of Land Management consults special advisory councils and state and local governments before reaching any important decision on land use. It holds public hearings to give concerned citizens, oil companies, environmental groups, and other interested organizations an opportunity to make their opinions known.

In recent years a political battle has been raging over the future of virgin lands in Alaska and in portions of the western states. Commercial interests want to open these areas to timber harvesting, mineral exploitation, and recreational development. They argue that the country cannot afford to let these

Most federally owned lands have never been privately owned. The National Park System comprises about 20 percent of the federally owned lands. The remaining 80 percent provides forest and agricultural products, minerals, and energy resources.

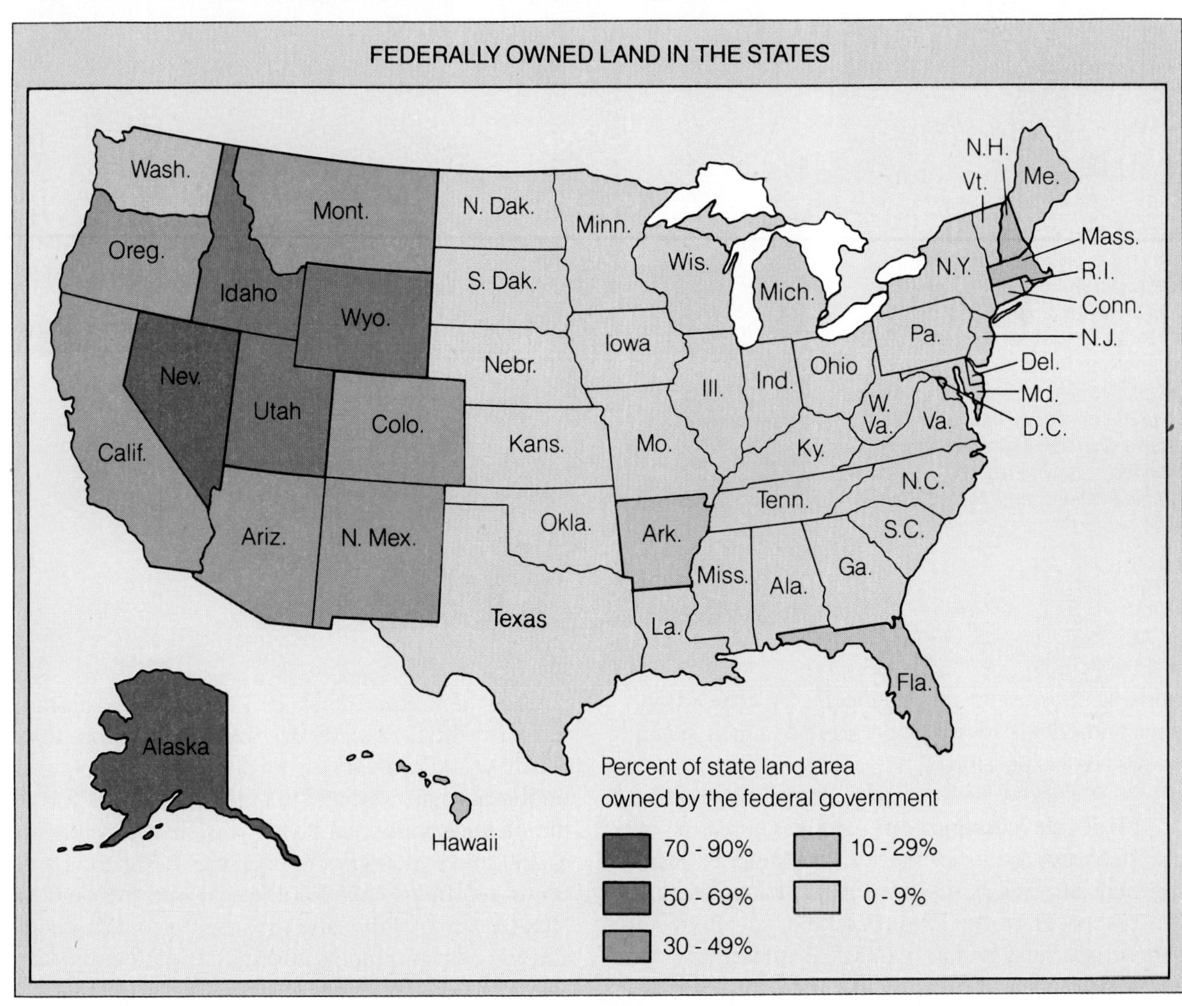

Among the persons who have served as Secretary of the Interior are (clockwise, from above) Albert Fall, who served from 1921 until 1923 and was later convicted and imprisoned for accepting bribes while in office; Harold Ickes, who held the post from 1933 until 1946; Stewart Udall, who served the Kennedy and Johnson administrations; and William Clark, who served from 1983 until 1985.

valuable resources go untapped. In opposition, environmentalists want to preserve as much virgin wilderness as possible.

Minerals Management A separate agency of the Department of the Interior, the Minerals Management Service, is responsible for administering the resources of the Outer Continental Shelf. All submerged land within 3 miles (5 kilometers) of shore belongs to the states, and Texas and Florida control submerged land 10.5 miles (16.8 kilometers) into the Gulf of Mexico. Land that is more than 3 miles (5 kilometers) from shore but submerged under less than 600 feet (183 meters) of water forms the Outer Continental Shelf. This shelf extends up to 250 miles (400 kilometers) into the Atlantic and up to 140 miles (225 kilometers) into the Gulf of Mexico. Some of the land in question contains valuable deposits of oil and natural gas. The Minerals Management Service leases deposit sites to private oil and gas companies. In recent years, annual revenue from offshore leases and ***royalties,*** or shares of the profit from sales has totaled more than $10 billion.

Reclamation Reclaiming arid and semiarid lands in the West by supplying water for irrigation and by building and operating dams and canals is the main function of the Bureau of Reclamation. The bureau's projects irrigate more than 17 million acres (6.8 million hectares) in 17 western states. The projects serve many purposes in addition to irrigation. They provide municipal and industrial water, hydroelectric power, flood control, and outdoor recreation. They regulate the flow of rivers, support fish and wildlife, and improve water quality. The projects are based upon the principle of repayment. Those who use the water and hydroelectric power return to the United States Treasury nearly 85 percent of the construction costs. Most projects are conducted by local authorities under the supervision of the bureau.

Water Research and Management Solving problems that involve water resources is the work of the Office of Water Research and Technology (OWRT). For example, the OWRT is trying to find a cheap and practical way of turning salt water into fresh water. Obviously, increasing the freshwater supply would help to alleviate water shortages in seaboard states such as California, where city dwellers, factories, and farmers all compete for a limited water supply. The OWRT works in cooperation with various other agencies, especially with the Water Resources Research Institutes at several state universities. In a world where the demand for water grows as the supply of water dwindles, the far-reaching research activities of the OWRT deserve to be better known.

An independent agency, the Tennessee Valley Authority (TVA) is mentioned here because, like the agencies of the Interior Department, it works to conserve and develop natural resources.

The dams operated by the Tennessee Valley Authority (TVA) supply electric power for homes, farms, factories, and mines in the Tennessee Valley region.

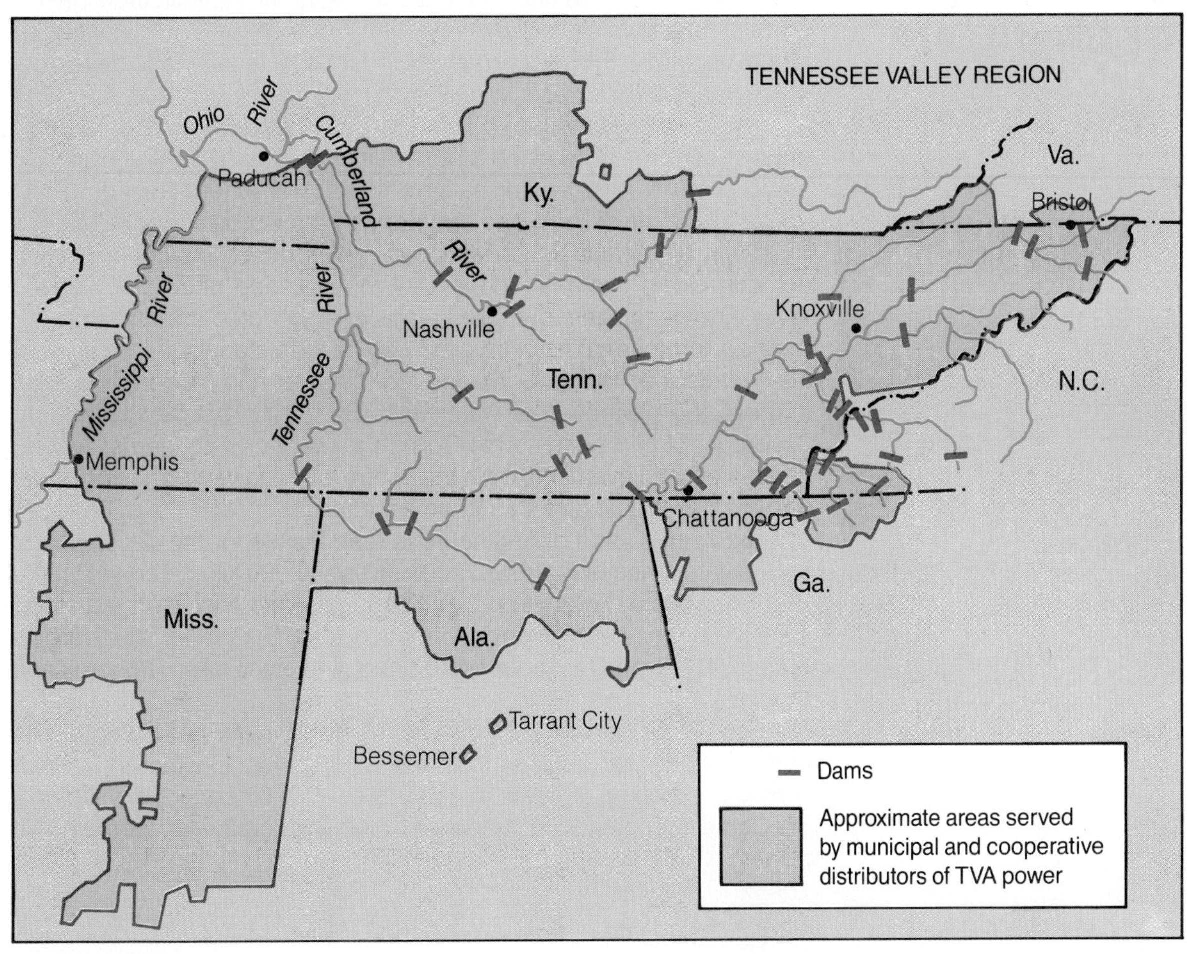

The TVA was created by Congress in 1933 to develop the resources of the Tennessee River valley. TVA dams provide electric power and control flooding in seven states: Alabama, Georgia, Kentucky, Mississippi, North Carolina, Tennessee, and Virginia. The Tennessee River is now a navigable waterway. The TVA promotes scientific farming and industrial growth. Since the mid-1970's, it has also placed emphasis on reforestation and soil conservation. All in all, the TVA has given the once-depressed Tennessee River valley a healthy present and a bright economic future.

The TVA is a ***government corporation,*** or a government agency established to conduct some form of business. It is funded partly by Congressional appropriations and partly by the sale of electric energy. Because this puts the agency in direct competition with private power companies, the TVA has been the object of considerable controversy. The Supreme Court upheld its right to sell electric power in *Ashwander* v. *TVA* (1936).

The TVA is governed by a board of directors, whose members are appointed by the President with Senate confirmation. The board appoints a general manager to supervise the agency's work. The TVA had 41,400 employees in 1983, making it the third-largest independent federal agency, after the U.S. Postal Service and the Veterans Administration.

PROFILE

United States Army Corps of Engineers

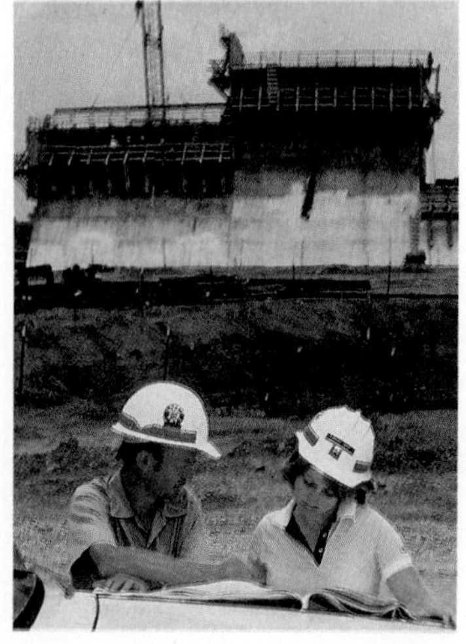

The United States Army Corps of Engineers is the world's largest engineering and construction organization. In time of war the engineers provide support on the battlefield for the movement and operation of the armed forces. In peacetime they design and build the facilities that keep the Army in combat readiness. These facilities include bases, ports, and missile sites all over the world. The Corps of Engineers also has a civil works mission, however, and today it is the major developer of the nation's water resources.

The Corps was founded in 1775. Then, because of the need for engineer officers, the United States Military Academy at West Point was established in 1802 as our nation's first school of engineering. From 1802 to 1864 West Point was operated by the Corps of Engineers.

During the early 1800's the Corps helped open the frontier to settlement. Given overall responsibility for exploring and surveying the West, Army engineers prepared maps and collected scientific data on the new territories. They surveyed early roads, canals, and railroads. They introduced iron bridges and took on river and harbor projects to improve the navigation of waterways. By the 1870's, navigation and flood control had become the Corps's primary civil concerns. Among its greatest achievements were the control of the lower Mississippi River and the construction of the Panama Canal.

Today the Corps of Engineers is responsible for the development and maintenance of roughly 25,000 miles (40,000 kilometers) of inland and intercoastal waterways. The Corps has improved and maintains some 500 commercial and recreational harbors. It is also largely responsible for the restoration and protection of the nation's shores and beaches.

The Corps operates 325 dams. Many of these are multipurpose dams that provide flood control as well as water for industrial and municipal use, irrigation, recreation, and power. With 66 generating stations, the Corps of Engineers is the nation's leading producer of hydroelectric power.

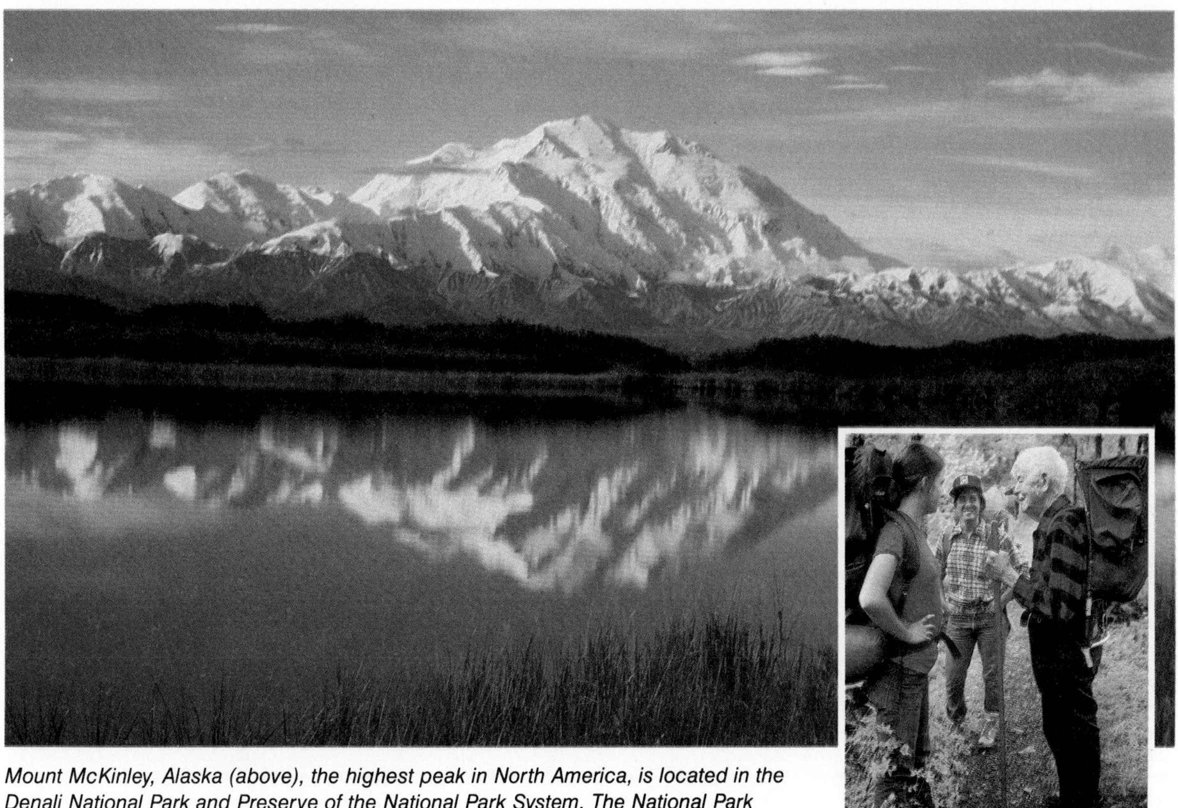

Mount McKinley, Alaska (above), the highest peak in North America, is located in the Denali National Park and Preserve of the National Park System. The National Park System, administered by the Department of the Interior, provides scenic trails for backpackers (right). What other services does the National Park System provide?

The National Park System

In 1872 Congress established Yellowstone National Park "for the benefit and enjoyment of the people." Today the National Park System includes some 333 sites covering 79 million acres (32 million hectares), of which 54 million acres (22 million hectares) are in Alaska. The system is administered by the National Park Service, established in 1916. Its mission is to conserve the natural beauty and historical heritage of the United States while providing areas for public recreation. The areas are to be administered in such a manner "as will leave them unimpaired for the enjoyment of future generations."

The divisions within the National Park System include parks and monuments, scenic parkways, riverways, seashores, and lakeshores. They include a variety of historic sites associated with important events and personalities in America's past—archeological sites of prehistoric Native American civilizations; important Revolutionary War and Civil War battlefields; homes of former Presidents; and such memorials as those dedicated to Washington, Jefferson, and Lincoln in Washington, D.C. The park system provides for recreation in the form of hiking, horseback riding, canoeing, swimming, and camping. But there are also restricted wilderness areas in many national parks. These wilderness areas, which are protected to preserve their original character, are open to hikers and campers. But they are without roads and are otherwise uninhabited.

Fish and Wildlife Conservation

The Department of the Interior has national responsibility for the conservation and management of fish and wildlife resources. The Fish and Wildlife Service was originally the Bureau of Fisheries, the nation's first federal conservation agency.

The Fish and Wildlife Service administers 410 National Wildlife Refuges. These refuges, which comprise more than 86 million acres (34 million hectares), provide a natural habitat for many endangered species as well as other wildlife. A number of refuges are located along the migratory routes of waterfowl and provide nesting and wintering areas for the birds. To keep federal inland waters stocked with fish, the service also operates 89 hatcheries.

An employee of the Fish and Wildlife Service attaches an identification band to a bird. The band, which will identify the bird if it is caught later, is an important tool used in migration research. What tasks are performed by the research centers of the Fish and Wildlife Service?

Finally, the service maintains 13 major research centers. These centers monitor fish and wildlife populations. They conduct research on animal nutrition and disease and on the ways in which changing environmental conditions affect wildlife.

The Fish and Wildlife Service works closely with other federal agencies, state conservation agencies, and private organizations. It also works in cooperation with other nations to protect endangered species.

The Geological Survey

The United States Geological Survey (USGS) is the scientific arm of the Department of the Interior. The USGS was established by Congress in 1879 to provide for "the classification of public lands and the examination of the geological structure, mineral resources, and products of the national domain." The USGS researches various aspects of geology and makes its findings available to the public. Its primary work is divided into five categories: topographic mapping, geology, water resources, conservation, and land information and analysis.

The United States Geological Survey prepares topographic maps that show the height and configuration of the land surfaces of the United States and its island territories. These maps are drawn in several scales and show both natural and artificial features. They include color photo-image maps as well as the conventional line maps. The USGS also prepares special topographic maps of Antarctica for use in the scientific exploration of the polar continent.

The USGS conducts research on the geology of the United States, the Outer Continental Shelf, and the Antarctic Region in order to learn more about the location, character, and potential use of mineral and energy resources. The USGS also conducts research on volcanoes and earthquakes.

For the National Aeronautics and Space Administration (NASA), the USGS mapped the surface of the moon to prepare for lunar exploration. USGS scientists studied the rock samples and other data gathered by Apollo astronauts.

The USGS collects and distributes data on the quantity and quality of the nation's surface water and

INSIGHT

Youth Conservation Corps

The Youth Conservation Corps (YCC) employs young men and women in summer projects to develop and maintain natural resources. Participants work in national parks, wildlife refuges, and fish hatcheries, and on other public lands. Corps activities include building trails and campgrounds, planting trees, tending hatcheries, gathering water samples, and studying animal habitats. Leaders skilled in the management of natural resources supervise all projects.

The YCC has three main objectives. First, it exists to accomplish needed conservation work on public lands. Second, it provides summer employment for youths 15 through 18 years of age from all social and economic backgrounds. Third, it aims to develop among participants an understanding of the nation's natural environment and heritage.

A United States Geological Survey (USGS) map shows Chesapeake Bay, an inlet of the Atlantic Ocean. The bay forms parts of the Virginia and Maryland coastlines. USGS maps are prepared from photographs taken from satellites in outer space. What other types of work does the USGS perform?

groundwater. It classifies federally owned lands according to the value of the oil, gas, uranium, and coal they contain. The USGS also identifies public lands that can be developed for waterpower and geothermal energy.

Mines and Mining

The Bureau of Mines, created in 1910, is primarily a research agency. Its goal is to help ensure that the nation has adequate mineral supplies. It collects and analyzes data on every aspect of the nation's mineral resources. The bureau's research includes studies on miners' health, mine safety, mining techniques, and environmental protection.

The Office of Surface Mining Reclamation and Enforcement seeks to protect the environment from the adverse effects of ***strip mining.*** In strip mining hilltops are removed to get at coal, and the wastes are dumped into streams, often clogging them and causing flooding. At the same time, the office seeks to ensure that the nation will have enough coal to meet its needs. It enforces minimum national standards for surface mining operations and promotes the reclamation of previously mined land. It also helps the states to develop and enforce their own regulatory programs. The Office of Surface Mining was created in 1977. This office has the power to enforce its own regulations by imposing penalties on violators.

Section Check

1. Define: multiple-use management, royalties, government corporation, strip mining
2. Identify: Bureau of Land Management, Outer Continental Shelf, Bureau of Reclamation, *Ashwander* v. *TVA,* United States Army Corps of Engineers, Yellowstone National Park
3. Why does the President usually choose someone from a state west of the Mississippi to head the Department of the Interior?
4. How do public lands provide revenue for the federal government?
5. Describe the work of the TVA.
6. What is the relationship between the United States Army Corps of Engineers and the nation's water resources?

Since the 1970's, manufacturing plants may no longer emit vast quantities of hazardous pollutants into the air. Plant emissions are now subject to regulation by the Environmental Protection Agency (EPA).

2 THE ENVIRONMENT AND OUTER SPACE

The Department of the Interior shares its concern for the environment with many other agencies at all levels of government. This section examines three of the most important ones. They are the Environmental Protection Agency, the National Oceanic and Atmospheric Administration, and the National Aeronautics and Space Administration.

The Environmental Protection Agency

A growing concern over the threat of pollution to human health and the natural environment led to the creation in 1970 of the Environmental Protection Agency (EPA). The EPA's mission is to clean and to prevent air, water, and noise pollution and to regulate the disposal of solid waste as well as toxic and radioactive substances. According to its own statement of purpose, the EPA "is designed to serve as the public's advocate for a livable environment."

Powers and Responsibilities The EPA is an independent executive agency whose administrator is appointed by the President with Senate confirmation. Before the EPA was created, some 40 federal agencies were responsible for administering federal laws on pollution control. With the creation of the EPA the work of pollution control came at last under one agency's control.

The EPA sets standards for environmental quality. Although it encourages voluntary compliance, it can enforce its own regulations if certain pollutants exceed specified levels. The EPA also monitors the levels of pollution to see whether environmental standards are as effective as they should be.

In addition to establishing and enforcing federal environmental standards, the EPA coordinates and supports antipollution activities by state and local governments and by private groups. It researches the effects of pollution and ways to improve the quality of the environment. The EPA coordinates this research with Canada, Mexico, and about 50 other nations.

Air Air pollution poses a serious threat to the nation's health. Until 1970 the control of air pollution was under the jurisdiction of the Department of Health, Education, and Welfare. By 1970, when the Environmental Protection Agency was created, over 200 million tons (181.5 million metric tons) of waste products were being released into the air each year. Over half of the nation's air pollution comes from cars and trucks, and its impact is visible in the smog that hangs over many United States cities. Air pollution is associated with a growing number of cases of emphysema and other respiratory diseases. In addition, pollution causes the loss of billions of dollars every year from the destruction of buildings, forests, and crops.

The first law to combat air pollution was the Federal Air Pollution Control Act of 1955. This act did little more than authorize the Public Health Service to research the subject. It was followed by the Clean Air Act of 1963 and the Air Quality Control Act of 1967—two laws that provided for control as well as research. The Air Quality Control Act obliged the states to adopt and implement ***air quality standards*** and authorized federal regulation of auto emissions.

The Clean Air Act Amendments of 1970 imposed tough auto emission standards nationwide. According to these standards, new cars sold in the United States after 1974 were supposed to emit 90 percent fewer pollutants than the 1970 models. In practice this requirement has not been met. Congress has postponed the deadline several times under pressure from the automobile manufacturers and the United Auto Workers, who claim that it takes time to meet such expensive and technologically demanding standards.

This law also required the EPA to set emission standards for industrial smokestacks and other stationary sources and air quality standards for all major pollutants. It directed the states to develop programs to meet these standards. And, like the previous laws, it provided for further research on the sources, nature, and effects of air pollution.

By 1979 the estimated value of the benefits of cleaner air had reached $21.4 billion a year. The Reagan administration, however, believed that the costs of reducing air pollution were too high for business to bear. It also was committed to easing government regulation in general. Accordingly, EPA funds for cleaner air were cut from $267 million in 1980 to $147 million in 1983, and the annual number of pollution cases referred by the EPA for prosecution dropped from more than 200 to about 50.

One result was a substantial increase in ***acid rain,*** or rain that contains a high proportion of acids—mostly sulfur dioxide, which is released when coal is burned. Acid rain is now causing annual damage of $2.5 billion a year to forests, crops, fisheries, buildings, and other property. Canada, whose travel and recreation industries are affected by acid rain from the United States, has called the situation "the single greatest irritant to the U.S.–Canadian relationship." Canada is currently insisting that the United States do something about lowering sulfur emissions.

In the early 1980's, the Environmental Protection Agency announced that it had been considering an experimental program aimed at cutting sulfur

Employees of the Environmental Protection Agency (EPA) work to control damage caused by an oil spill. A major goal of the EPA is to identify hazards and to prevent them from developing into critical situations.

emissions from power plants and factories in four to six states in the Midwest. The cost was estimated at $2.5 billion, but the program would reduce sulfur emissions by 3 million tons (2.7 million metric tons) a year. Many scientists, however, have declared that a reduction of at least 10 million tons (9 million metric tons) a year is needed.

Water Over the years, raw sewage and industrial chemicals have been dumped into many of the nation's rivers and lakes. These pollutants have found their way into the groundwater and contaminated drinking water in some communities. For example, in 1980 a mysterious illness affecting almost every resident in two Texas towns was traced to pollution of the public water supplies. Today even the oceans are becoming dangerously polluted by oil spills and by the wastes that reach them through the rivers and by direct dumping into the sea.

The issue of water pollution is not a new one. The Refuse Control Act of 1899 prohibited unlicensed pollution of interstate waters. Although this act was technically the first federal environmental protection law, it was not enforced until 1970.

Water pollution, like other forms of pollution, began to receive more attention in the 1950's and 1960's. The Water Pollution Act was passed in 1956 and the Clean Water Restoration Act in 1966. These acts provide federal funding to local governments for the construction of municipal sewage treatment facilities. They also provide grants to state governments for areawide waste-water management.

In 1970 Congress passed the Water Quality Improvement Act. This act regulates the dumping of oil into navigable waters. It was followed in 1972 by the Marine Protection, Research, and Sanctuaries Act. This act controls the dumping of wastes into the sea. Finally, the Safe Drinking Water Act of 1974 sets national quality standards for drinking water.

The EPA enforces standards for water quality by regulating industrial, agricultural, and other sources of pollution. In addition to these regulatory activities, the EPA administers the grants provided under the Water Pollution Control Act and the Clean Water Restoration Act.

Solid Waste The United States produces an enormous amount of garbage and solid waste. Each year, Americans throw away about 48 billion cans, 26 billion bottles and jars, 4 million tons (3.6 million metric tons) of plastic, 7 million television sets, 7 million cars and trucks, and 30 million tons (27 million metric tons) of paper. The EPA seeks to reduce the amount of solid waste produced. It encourages the use of returnable bottles instead of throw-aways. It seeks to recover materials from waste products, as in the recycling of aluminum cans and paper. In addition, under the Resource Conservation and Recovery Act of 1976, it is implementing a ban on open dumps.

Hazardous wastes present a special problem. The 1976 act defines ***hazardous wastes*** as discarded substances that may cause death or disease or that threaten public health or the environment. These wastes include chemical, radioactive, explosive, and flammable substances. The nation's oil, steel, chemical, and other industries produce 55 million tons (49.8 million metric tons) of hazardous wastes each year. Some are poured into steel drums and buried. Some are burned. And some are recycled. Under the 1976 law the EPA sets and enforces standards for handling hazardous wastes.

In 1980 the Carter administration established a $1.6 billion "superfund" designated to clean up some 15,000 hazardous waste dump sites around the country. The theory was that the EPA would clean up the sites itself rather than sue the businesses responsible for the dumping. After that, the EPA would get the chemical and oil businesses involved to reimburse the costs.

Scientists are only beginning to discover the dimensions of the problem of hazardous wastes. The health of some residents of Love Canal, near Niagara Falls, New York, was seriously damaged by toxic chemical wastes buried in the 1950's. The chemicals leaked through the soil into the yards and homes of the residents. More than 300 families had to be evacuated.

Toxic Substances and Pesticides Chemicals to control weeds, insects, and other pests have made an important contribution to agriculture. Improperly used pesticides, however, can cause illness or death. Furthermore, some pesticides leave residues that persist for many years. Their presence in food may cause a buildup of toxic substances in animal and human tissues. An example is the pesticide DDT, which is now banned.

The EPA has the power to limit or even ban the production and use of any chemical harmful to public health. The government requires that new chemical substances be tested before being marketed to determine their effects on human health and on plant and animal life. The EPA is particularly concerned about chemicals that may cause cancer, birth defects, or genetic damage.

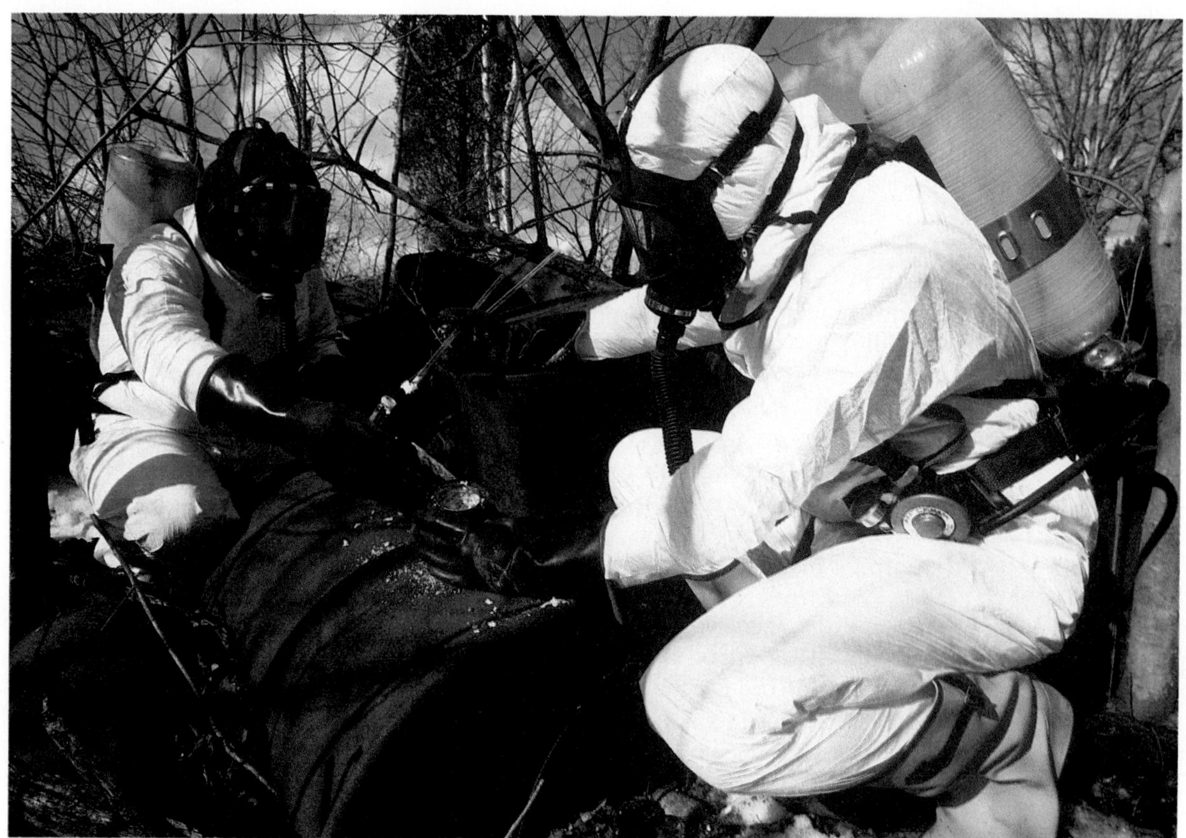

Workers at a hazardous waste site in New Jersey wear protective clothing and breathe with the aid of oxygen supplied from tanks to avoid contamination from toxic materials. What types of substances are defined as hazardous wastes?

Radiation Americans are exposed to radiation every day in the form of heat, light, and other electromagnetic waves from the sun and the solar system. Since the discovery of the X ray and the development of radio, television, microwave devices, lasers, and nuclear energy, levels of radiation have increased. Exposure to large doses of radiation poses a serious health hazard, for radiation can cause cancer and genetic defects. The EPA sets standards to protect the public from dangerous levels of radiation. Thus, for example, it regulates medical and dental X-ray procedures. It limits the planned release of radioactive material from nuclear power plants. It is also developing programs for the management and disposal of radioactive wastes.

The EPA maintains stations around the country that regularly check samples of air, water, milk, and human and animal tissues for unacceptable levels of radioactivity. If such samples reveal radioactivity levels that are too high, the EPA notifies the Nuclear Regulatory Commission or the appropriate federal or state agency.

Noise Certain occupations involve high levels of noise that can result in the loss of a worker's hearing. Environmental noise also takes its toll in hearing damage. Jet planes, trucks, motorcycles, and construction equipment are among the many sources of such noise. The EPA was responsible for identifying the sources of such noise, setting noise level standards, and suggesting techniques to control and reduce noise. Under the Reagan administration, however, the federal noise-control program has been dropped.

Environmental Impact The EPA administers the National Environmental Policy Act of 1969. The act requires any agency using federal funds to assess the ***environmental impact*** of certain new projects before undertaking them. Many state and local governments require similar environmental impact statements before projects, either public or private, may begin. If a project threatens to damage the environment, government officials or private citizens may take legal action to try to stop it.

Concern about a negative environmental impact has prevented the execution of or altered the design of major engineering projects, such as mining operations and the building of dams, highways, and nuclear power plants. Hearings and various legal actions sometimes postpone a project for several years. Concern for the environment provoked intense debate on the Alaska Pipeline project. Opponents of the pipeline feared that it would destroy the delicately balanced Alaskan environment and threaten the caribou and other wildlife. Advocates for the pipeline emphasized the nation's energy needs and the urgency of developing the oil fields of Alaska's North Slope. Eventually engineers designed and carried out the construction of the pipeline with sensitivity to environmental concerns. The environmental impact of the project is still unknown, however, and may not be known for many years.

Council on Environmental Quality The EPA works in cooperation with the Council on Environmental Quality, an agency within the Executive Office of the President. The Council conducts research and reviews federal environmental programs to determine their effectiveness. Its three members also assist the President in preparing an environmental quality report that is submitted to Congress each year together with the President's recommendations for legislative action.

The National Oceanic and Atmospheric Administration

The National Oceanic and Atmospheric Administration (NOAA) is a bureau of the Department of Commerce. It was created in 1970 by combining two older agencies, the Coast and Geodetic Survey and the Weather Bureau. It is the function of NOAA "to describe, understand, and predict" the state of the oceans and the atmosphere and the size and shape of the earth.

National Ocean Survey The scientists and engineers of the National Ocean Survey explore and map the oceans and chart their currents. They study the interaction of the sea with the land and atmosphere. They maintain navigational buoys, which—like traffic signals on the ocean—mark channels, currents, and reefs for ships. They also maintain data-collecting buoys all over the world. Satellites also provide important scientific information on the oceans and on the conditions of the land. The information collected by the National Ocean Survey is used not only by ships and aircraft but also by engineers, seismologists, and other scientists.

National Marine Fisheries Service The scientists of the National Marine Fisheries Service study the physical and biological resources of the

ISSUES

EPA Under Fire

Like the Office of Safety and Health Administration (OSHA) and the Federal Trade Commission, the Environmental Protection Agency (EPA) has come under heavy attack for overregulation. Critics cite the number and detail of EPA regulations. They also point to the costs of compliance—costs that industry passes on to the consumer in the form of higher prices. The EPA responds by saying that failure to control pollution leads to even greater costs—both in dollars and in human health.

Still another set of costs must be considered, those inherent in the trade-off between environmental protection and energy. For example, strict emission controls on automobiles result in greater fuel consumption. At the same time, concern for environmental impact may make it more difficult to produce fuel from alternative energy resources such as nuclear energy. Many environmentalists oppose offshore drilling, strip mining, and the production of synthetic fuels from low-grade coal and oil shale. Most Americans are aware that the search for energy cannot destroy the environment. They know that the challenge is to strike a balance between environmental concerns and the need for energy.

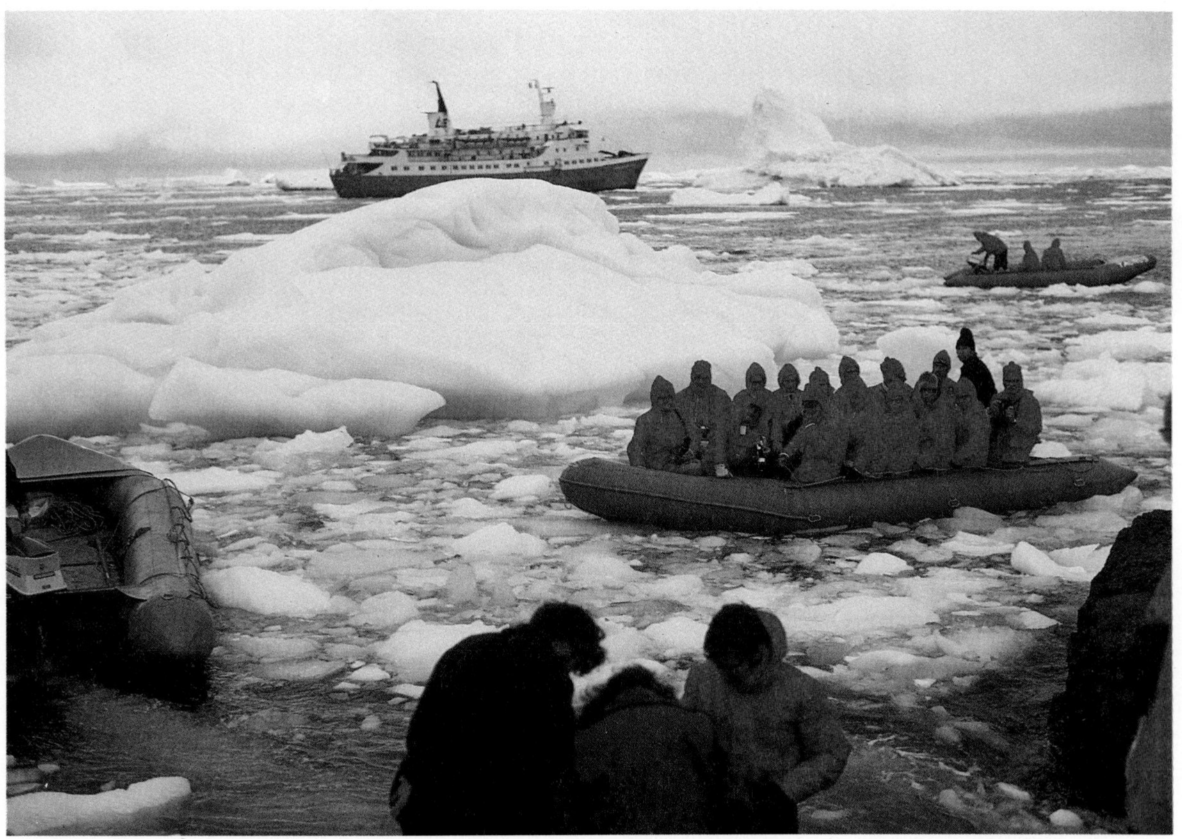

National Oceanic and Atmospheric Administration (NOAA) researchers endure harsh weather conditions to conduct experiments in Antarctica. The goal of NOAA research in Antarctica is to explain such phenomena as magnetism, gravity, and earthquakes.

ocean. The service has authority to manage and conserve commercial fishing grounds within 200 miles (321.8 kilometers) of the nation's shores. And it comes to the aid of fishers whose vessels have been seized in other nations' fishing grounds. The service also enforces the laws protecting marine animals such as whales, porpoises, seals, and sea lions.

National Weather Service One of the main divisions of NOAA is the National Weather Service (NWS). This agency provides weather forecasts to the general public and special reports for farmers, pilots, fishers, sailors, the space program, and the military. It issues warnings against hurricanes, tornadoes, floods, and the huge destructive waves called tsunamis, which are tidal waves caused by earthquakes. In addition to reporting the weather, the NWS studies ways to modify it, including cloud seeding and reducing the power of hurricanes.

The reports that are used to make weather forecasts come in from 400 weather stations situated across the 50 states, in foreign countries, and on ships at sea. NOAA satellites provide data on the weather and on atmospheric conditions.

The NWS also operates the National Hurricane Center in Miami, Florida. This center monitors hurricanes as they form and issues warnings to the islands of the Caribbean and the coastal regions of the United States, Mexico, and Central America.

The National Aeronautics and Space Administration

In the decade following World War II the United States led the world in missile research. In 1957, however, the Soviet Union launched *Sputnik I,* the world's first artificial satellite. The United States accelerated its own space program. The Department of Defense directed the military component of this program, but the National Aeronautics and Space Administration (NASA), a new independent executive agency, directed the civilian space effort. It was created in 1958, the year that the first American satellite, *Explorer I,* was launched.

Astronauts Sally K. Ride (above) and Guion S. Bluford, Jr. (right), worked as mission specialists on flights of the space shuttles, NASA's reusable spacecraft. Dr. Ride was the first American woman in space; Lt. Bluford was the first black American in space.

NASA was given broad authority to conduct civilian aeronautical and space research. Various government activities were transferred to the new agency which was to forge and expand a program for the exploration of space.

NASA has placed astronauts on the moon and returned them safely to earth. It has reached out in the exploration of the planets and opened the universe to greater human understanding. Its research centers and laboratories have tested research aircraft and missiles. They have studied the effects on the human system of living in space, and other aspects of space exploration.

Many benefits have come from this $100 billion investment in space research. Space technology is now used in business, industry, medicine, and education. New products range from quieter aircraft engines to the microcircuits and solid-state electronics that have revolutionized television sets, radios, cameras, and small calculators.

NASA satellites relay telephone calls and telecasts in a worldwide communications system. They enable us to watch live television coverage of events anywhere in the world. Satellites also make it possible to forecast the weather more accurately and to provide information on conditions at sea. Satellite data have deepened our knowledge of the earth's surface, oceans, and natural resources. NASA's research on the internal structure of the sun has helped to harness solar energy on earth. Its aeronautic research is developing safer, more efficient, and more environmentally acceptable air transport systems. And its work in protecting and monitoring the health of astronauts during space flights has resulted in the development of medical techniques and devices that can save lives and improve health care.

Section Check

1. Define: air quality standards, acid rain, hazardous wastes, environmental impact
2. Identify: Environmental Protection Agency, National Weather Service, *Sputnik I*, *Explorer I*
3. What are some of the effects of air pollution?
4. Why is Canada concerned about acid rain produced in the United States?
5. Name some benefits gained from space research.

3 THE DEPARTMENT OF ENERGY

The Department of Energy (DOE) was established in 1977 to provide a comprehensive and balanced national energy plan. The new department brought together major federal energy programs that had been scattered among various agencies.

The Department of Energy is responsible for research, development, and demonstration of energy technology. It promotes energy conservation and the search for new energy sources. It regulates the production, price, allocation, and use of energy. It markets federal power, such as that produced by federally operated hydroelectric plants. The DOE is also in charge of the nation's nuclear weapons program. The department maintains offices throughout the country to implement and to manage its programs. The Secretary of Energy supervises the department and is the President's major adviser on energy policy. Like other Cabinet secretaries, the Secretary of Energy is appointed by the President with Senate confirmation.

The Energy Crisis

The creation of the Department of Energy was a response to the world energy crisis. The crisis was spotlighted by the 1973–74 Arab oil embargo against the United States. The resulting long lines at the gas pumps brought home to every American the danger of the nation's dependency on imported oil. That continuing dependence was registered in the jolts given to the United States economy by periodic increases in the price of foreign oil. The energy crisis, however, was not simply the result of artificially created shortages or high prices. Its root cause was the enormous increase in energy consumed by industrialized nations since World War II. This rapid increase drastically reduced the world's limited petroleum resources.

Nearly one half of America's primary energy demand is met by oil. The United States produces fuel to meet approximately 79 percent of its energy needs, but 28 percent of the oil used in the United States is imported. In 1984 American dependency

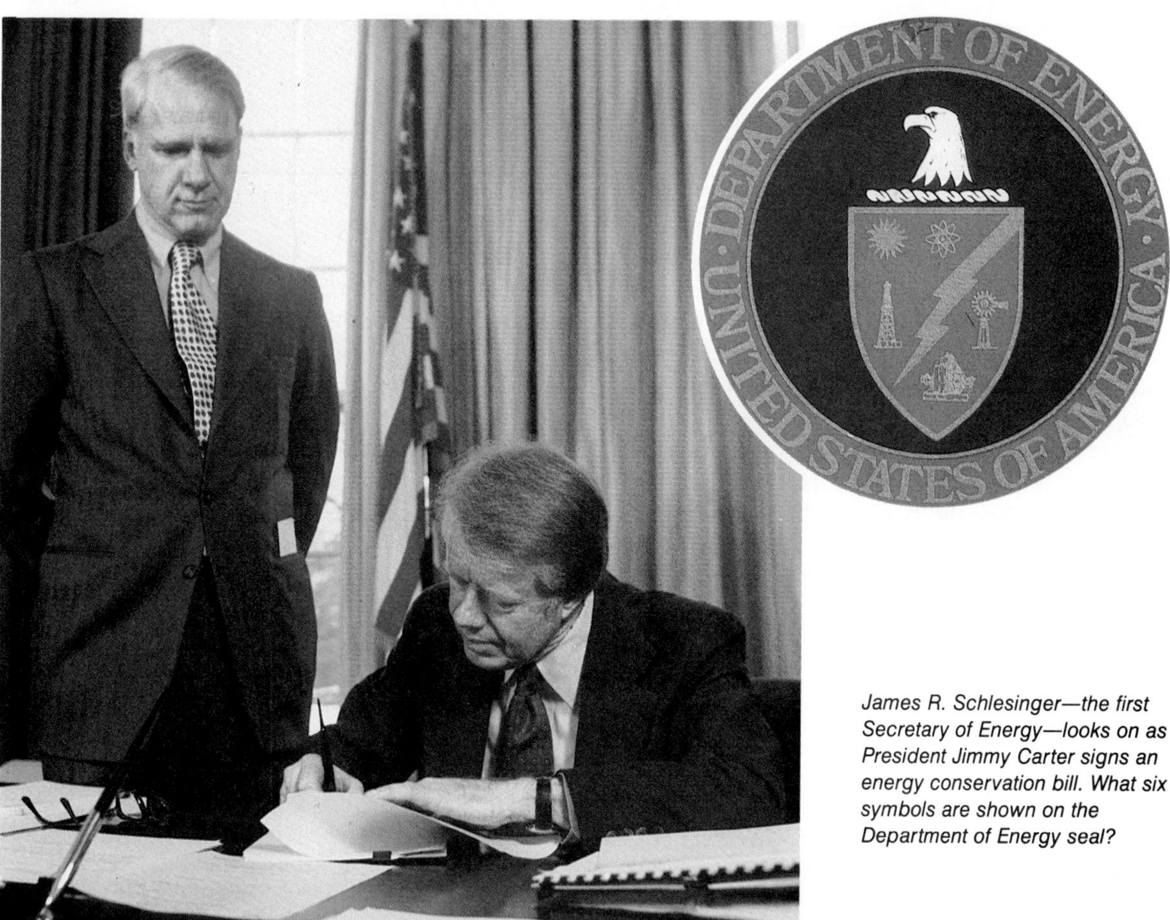

James R. Schlesinger—the first Secretary of Energy—looks on as President Jimmy Carter signs an energy conservation bill. What six symbols are shown on the Department of Energy seal?

The 13 member-nations of the Organization of Petroleum Exporting Countries (OPEC) meet annually to negotiate oil-pricing policies. Many nations that lack oil reserves have become dependent on oil imported from OPEC nations.

upon foreign oil amounted to 4.2 million barrels per day, two thirds of which came from the Organization of Petroleum Exporting Countries (OPEC). The major oil-producing nations have joined together in OPEC to maintain prices at agreed-upon levels by limiting the supply of oil to world markets. Its members include Iran, Nigeria, Gabon, Indonesia, Ecuador, Venezuela, and the seven Arab nations of Saudi Arabia, Libya, Iraq, Algeria, Kuwait, Qatar, and the United Arab Emirates.

Oil is a ***nonrenewable energy resource.*** Its supply is depleted with every barrel pumped from the ground. Over the past decade oil production has declined in the 48 coterminous states. This decline, however, has been offset by new production from Alaska and by advanced techniques for the recovery of oil. Still, domestic oil production does not meet the energy needs of the United States.

Energy Policies

The Department of Energy's goal is to aid the nation's orderly transition from an economy dependent upon oil to one reliant upon diversified energy sources. DOE policy calls for both reduction of demand and increase in the supply of energy.

Reduction of Demand The Department of Energy has undertaken three major efforts to reduce demand. They are conservation, decontrol, and emergency planning.

First, the DOE seeks to reduce energy consumption through more efficient use of energy. An important element of this program is making the public aware of the ways to conserve energy in homes and in personal transportation. Car pools, for example, conserve energy at the same time they ease traffic congestion and reduce air pollution. Reduced speed saves gas as well as lives.

A great deal of energy can also be saved through home insulation and weatherization. The federal government provides tax incentives to encourage people to make their homes more energy efficient. Weatherization assistance is available to low-income persons, the elderly, and the handicapped.

Second, in 1982 the federal government completed the phasing out of price controls on all domestically produced crude oil. It is expected that the resulting higher prices will reduce demand and also stimulate oil exploration and production. Coupled with this decontrol, a "windfall profits" tax was placed on income that oil producers receive as a result of the price increase.

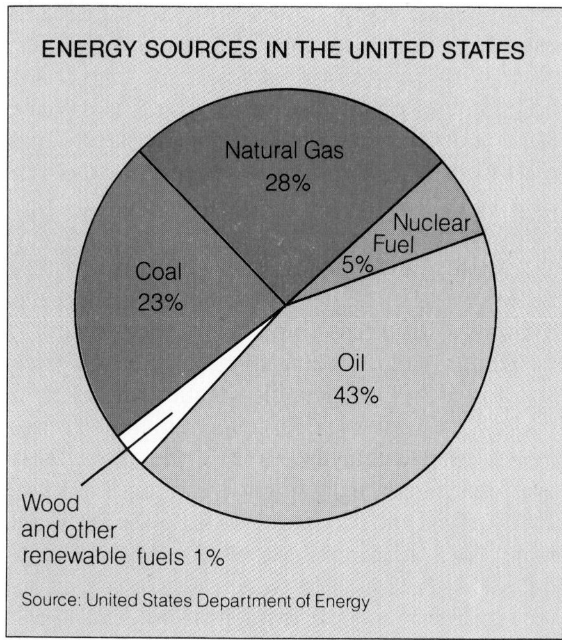

Various fuel sources are used to supply energy to consumers and businesses in the United States. What source supplies the most energy?

Third, a key element in the formulation of national energy policy is planning for possible shortages. The department is pursuing two approaches. One involves mandatory limits on the allocation of gasoline among the states in time of emergency. The other is a gasoline-rationing plan that would go into effect during a shortage. The DOE planning includes the storage of 750 million barrels of oil in underground salt caverns in Texas and Louisiana. The oil would be drawn out of this reserve only in a severe supply emergency.

Expansion of Supply The development of the Alaskan oil fields, offshore production, and the new technology of enhanced oil recovery from existing fields have expanded the domestic oil supply. However, the nation's energy future depends upon developing alternative sources that are environmentally acceptable substitutes for oil. That responsibility lies primarily within the private sector, but the federal government has assumed an important role in energy research and development.

Use of Fossil Fuels

Oil, gas, and coal are ***fossil fuels,*** formed millions of years ago from decomposed plant life. While oil and gas are in short supply, the United States has vast coal resources. It is estimated that nearly 4 trillion tons (3.6 trillion metric tons) of coal exist and that some 200 to 300 billion tons (181 to 272 billion metric tons) are economically recoverable with current technology. This is enough to supply the nation's energy needs for several hundred years, even with increased consumption. In addition to being used directly, coal can become a source of synthetic liquid and gas fuels. The Department of Energy seeks to encourage greater reliance on coal. As a result, it is engaged in research to find more efficient and environmentally acceptable uses of coal.

Much of the electricity generated in the United States is produced by coal-burning power plants. Sulfur emissions from coal-burning power plants, however, cause extensive environmental damage.

At the same time, the DOE seeks to expand domestic oil exploration and production through greater price incentives, the development of new technology, and the opening of new areas for exploration and development. The nation's ***oil reserves***—an estimated 334 billion barrels of oil—remain in the ground. Most of the supply in the oil reserves is too expensive to pump by conventional techniques at current prices. The strategy here is decontrol in order to make the recovery of oil reserves more economically attractive.

The DOE also seeks to provide incentives for commercial production of oil shale. The western shales are estimated to contain the equivalent of up to 1.8 trillion barrels of oil, about 40 percent of which may be recoverable.

Serious problems are involved in the use of fossil fuels. For example, the use of coal raises environmental concerns. Mining leads to the destruction of the land. The burning of coal emits sulfur and other noxious substances into the air and creates acid rain. The use of coal becomes more attractive, however, as research improves mining methods and emission controls to meet environmental standards.

There is also concern over the environmental impact of large-scale development of ***synthetic fuels***—fuels made from natural materials in a factory process. Environmentalists fear that extraction of coal and oil shale will scar the landscape and burning large amounts of fossil fuels or synthetic fuels will pollute the air. Others fear that synthetic fuel production will divert scarce water resources from agricultural and municipal consumption. Another major limitation is the expense of production. Improved technology, however, may reduce production costs and enhance environmental protection. In 1980 Congress created the Synthetic Fuel Corporation to make loans for promising synthetic fuel projects.

Nuclear Energy

Nuclear energy in recent years has generated about 13 percent of the electricity consumed in the United States. As of 1984 there were approximately 80 nuclear reactors in operation. The DOE's nuclear program involves research to improve the reliability and safety of nuclear power plants and the management and disposal of nuclear wastes. It is also engaged in research on the development of the breeder reactor, which produces more plutonium than it consumes.

American energy policy projects an increased use of nuclear power, but opposition to nuclear power has grown in recent years. The high cost of building and operating nuclear plants is a factor. Major opposition arises, however, from concern about reactor safety, a concern underscored by the accident in 1979 at the nuclear power plant on Three Mile Island.

Another area of concern is the management of nuclear wastes. The permanent and safe disposal of radioactive materials poses a serious problem to which the DOE is seeking solutions through extensive research. One possible solution would be to package the wastes and place them in mined repositories deep within the earth. Critics warn, however, that radioactivity might escape back into the environment and pose a danger to public health and safety. Not surprisingly, despite assurances of safety, the selection of nuclear waste sites has met strong resistance from people living near potential sites.

Renewable Energy

One of the goals of America's energy policy is greater reliance on ***renewable energy resources.*** Today renewable energy means primarily hydroelectric power. Other renewable energy resources include solar, geothermal, and wind power, as well as power from fuels made by mixing alcohol with gases formed from plant materials. Of these renewable energy resources, solar power offers the greatest potential as an inexhaustible source of future energy. If the price of oil continues to rise, solar power could become more economically competitive. At the same time, with the development of a market for solar energy systems, costs should be reduced significantly.

An area of long-term research is fusion, a process that would harness the energy of hydrogen in the oceans. Fusion may be an almost unlimited energy source and, in addition, may pose fewer environmental problems than coal and nuclear power. The technological problems of fusion are enormously complex, however, and the commercial development of energy from fusion is not expected until after the turn of the century.

Regulation and Marketing

The Department of Energy has regulatory authority over a wide range of energy-related activities. Federal law prohibits new power plants and major fuel-burning installations from using oil or gas unless the DOE grants an exemption. The department is

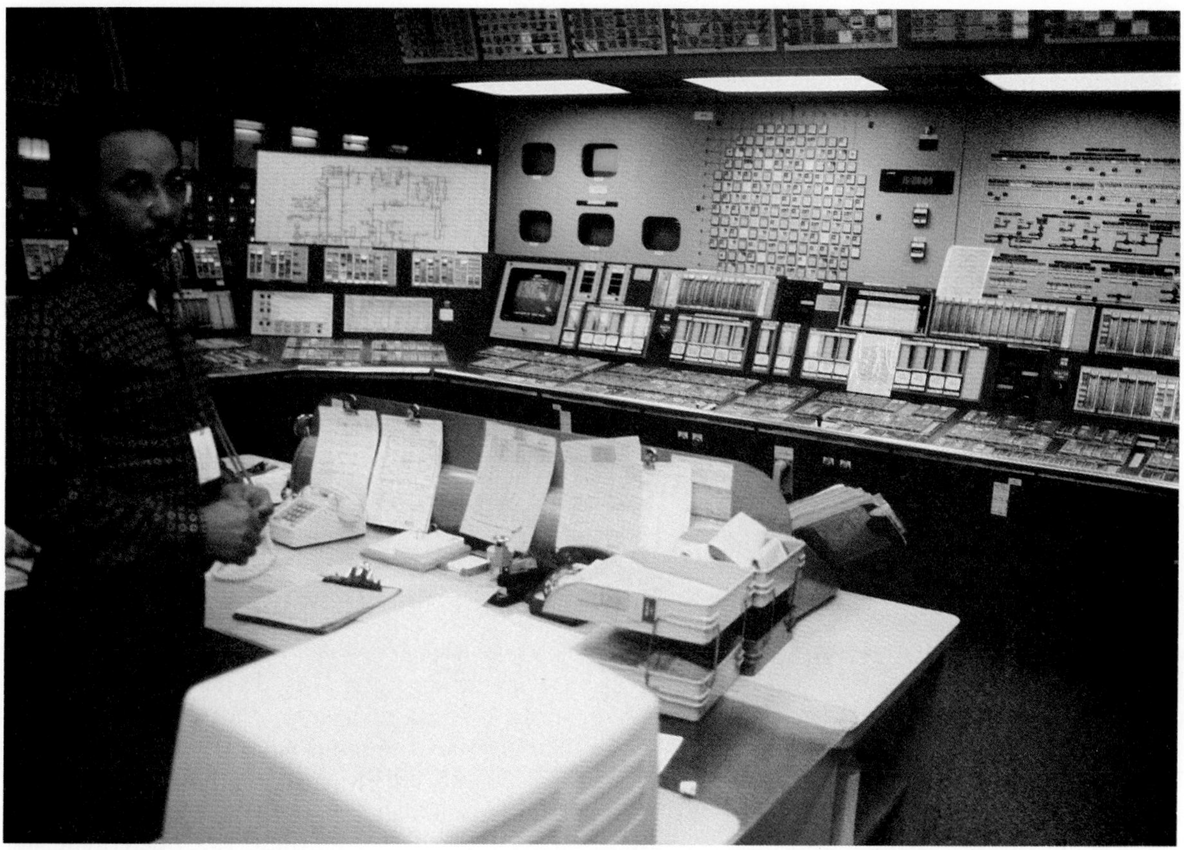

The operation of a nuclear power plant is directed from a computerized control room. The heat produced in the nuclear plant's reactor is used to generate electricity. What percentage of electricity consumed in the United States comes from nuclear energy?

responsible for encouraging the use of coal at existing power plants and major industrial installations.

The Federal Energy Regulatory Commission is an independent five-member commission within the Department of Energy whose members are appointed by the President with Senate approval. The commission sets rates for the interstate transportation and sale of natural gas and electricity. It has authority to establish rates for the transportation of oil by interstate pipeline. The commission also licenses hydroelectric power projects.

The Department of Energy markets federally generated hydroelectric power. The sale of electricity is handled by five regional Power Marketing Administrations. Sales account for about half of all hydroelectric power produced in the United States. The DOE also produces enriched uranium, the fuel used in nuclear power plants in the United States. The uranium production program serves domestic and foreign utilities, as well as the nation's defense requirements.

Defense Programs

The Department of Energy manages a variety of atomic energy defense programs in cooperation with the Department of Defense. These activities include:

- Design, testing, and production of nuclear weapons as authorized by the President. All tests are conducted at the Nevada test site.
- Production of nuclear material for weapons.
- Management of nuclear wastes.
- Protection of facilities, materials, and information relating to the United States nuclear defense program.
- Improvement of United States capability to detect, locate, and identify nuclear explosions anywhere in the world.
- Prevention of the proliferation of nuclear weapons beyond those nations which already have them.
- Control of exports of nuclear technology and materials contrary to United States national security.

A nuclear power plant in Plymouth, Massachusetts, is subject to periodic inspection by the Nuclear Regulatory Commission, as are all nuclear facilities in the United States. List the five basic functions of the Nuclear Regulatory Commission.

The Nuclear Regulatory Commission

The Nuclear Regulatory Commission (NRC), created in 1974 to replace the Atomic Energy Commission, is an independent regulatory commission. Its five members are appointed by the President with Senate approval and serve five-year terms.

In signing the act establishing the NRC, President Gerald Ford stated:

The highly technical nature of our nuclear facilities and the special potential hazards which are involved in the use of nuclear fuels fully warrant the creation of an independent and technically competent regulatory agency to assure adequate protection of public safety. NRC will be responsible for the licensing and regulation of the nuclear industry under the provisions of the Atomic Energy Act. This means that NRC will be fully empowered to see to it that reactors using nuclear materials will be properly and safely designed, constructed and operated to guarantee against hazards to the public from leakage or accident. NRC will also exercise strengthened authority to assure that the public is fully safeguarded from hazards arising from the storage, handling and transportation of nuclear materials being used in power reactors, hospitals, research laboratories or for any other purpose.

Basic Functions The Nuclear Regulatory Commission has five basic functions. First, it issues and reviews licenses for the construction and operation of nuclear power plants and for the use of nuclear materials in medicine, industry, and research. By the beginning of 1984, 80 nuclear reactors had been licensed to operate, and 50 others were at various stages of design and construction.

Second, the NRC establishes regulations, standards, and guidelines governing the licensed use of radioactive materials. These rules determine the location, design, construction, operation, and safeguarding of nuclear reactors and other facilities. They also govern the storage and handling of nuclear materials and the management of nuclear wastes.

Third, the NRC inspects nuclear plants periodically to make sure that they comply with regulations and standards. All licensees must meet NRC requirements for health and safety, security of nuclear materials and facilities, and environmental protection. Fourth, the NRC conducts research on safety in the use of nuclear energy. Finally, the NRC is responsible for licensing the export of nuclear reactors and the export and import of uranium and plutonium.

Three Mile Island The most serious accident ever to occur in the history of commercial nuclear power took place in March 1979 at the Three Mile Island Nuclear Station near Harrisburg, Pennsylvania. Escaping radioactive gases formed a huge bubble at the top of the reactor containment vessel. A major catastrophe was averted when the reactor cooled without releasing the gases. Nevertheless, the accident was a traumatic event for the American public and for the NRC.

The President's Commission appointed to investigate the accident found serious shortcomings.

In particular, the commission severely criticized the training of power plant personnel and the operating procedures they followed. The NRC responded by declaring a moratorium on the licensing of new nuclear power plants until it could review its entire regulatory program. The NRC moved to strengthen safety standards, inspection procedures, and emergency safeguards. It reaffirmed its primary goals in nuclear regulation—"protecting the public health and safety, safeguarding nuclear materials and facilities, and preserving environmental values."

Continuing Support of Science

From the founding of the Republic, the government has used and supported science and technology. Among the Founders, Benjamin Franklin and Thomas Jefferson were leaders in science as well as politics. The Constitution provided for the establishment of the census, standards in weights and measures, and patent laws. The government also sponsored expeditions, like that of Lewis and Clark (1804–1806), to explore the resources of the new nation.

Government support for science expanded with the outbreak of the Civil War. Research and development to meet military needs produced the ironclad *Monitor,* a major innovation in ship design. In 1862 the establishment of the land-grant colleges provided for agricultural research. A year later Congress created the National Academy of Sciences, an advisory organization of distinguished scientists.

National emergencies provide a strong push for public support of science. This was especially true during World War II. Research in behalf of the war effort led to breakthroughs in electronics, radar, nuclear energy, and medical science. This directed research laid the foundation for a permanent alliance between science and government.

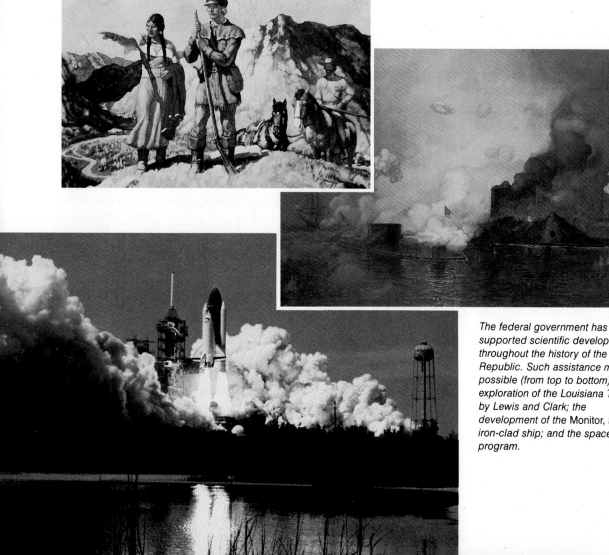

The federal government has supported scientific development throughout the history of the Republic. Such assistance made possible (from top to bottom) the exploration of the Louisiana Territory by Lewis and Clark; the development of the Monitor, *the first iron-clad ship; and the space-shuttle program.*

Many departments and agencies of the government support scientific research within their areas of particular concern. The Office of Science and Technology, within the Executive Office, helps the President to coordinate the research and development programs of the federal government. It is responsible for advising the President in a broad range of scientific and technical areas. The Office of Technology Assessment, within the legislative branch, helps Congress to evaluate the impact of science and technology on the lives of Americans and on the environment. It prepares reports for Congressional committees on the broad technological consequences of proposed legislation.

The National Science Foundation (NSF) also plays an important role in planning national science policy. Established in 1950 as an independent executive agency, the NSF "promotes the progress of science through the support of research and education in the sciences." It specializes in ***basic research,*** the study of the fundamental laws of nature. It also engages in ***applied research*** "directed toward the solution of more immediate problems of our society."

The NSF supports universities and other research institutions by awarding them grants and contracts. The foundation also sponsors major national and international science programs; an example is the United States Antarctic Program. The NSF has been especially active in the field of astronomy, and it supports a number of national research centers and observatories.

Section Check

1. Define: fossil fuels
2. Identify: OPEC, Federal Energy Regulatory Commission, Three Mile Island
3. What is the root cause of the energy crisis?
4. About what percentage of the energy needs of the United States are met by oil? About how much of the oil used by the United States is imported?
5. What are some ways in which individuals can conserve energy?
6. What is the strategic petroleum reserve, and what is its purpose?
7. What are two major problems with the use of fossil fuels?
8. Give three examples of renewable energy resources.
9. What are the main goals of the NRC?

SUMMARY

The Department of the Interior is the principal conservation agency of the United States. Headed by the Secretary of the Interior, the department manages the nation's land and water resources. The Department of the Interior is also concerned with recreation, parks, and wildlife. The National Park Service administers the national parks. The Fish and Wildlife Service protects the nation's wildlife.

Finally, the Department of the Interior does research on the geology and mineral resources of the United States. The Geological Survey studies various aspects of geology. The Bureau of Mines studies data related specifically to mining. The Office of Surface Mining Reclamation and Enforcement sets and enforces environmental protection standards for mining.

Three important federal agencies are concerned with the environment and outer space. The Environmental Protection Agency controls air and water pollution in general as well as pollution from such specific sources as solid waste, toxic substances, and radiation. The EPA also administers the federal law requiring an environmental impact statement for many public and private projects. Federal environmental policy and programs are reviewed by an executive agency, the Council on Environmental Quality.

The National Oceanic and Atmospheric Administration studies the oceans and the atmosphere. Its National Ocean Survey maps the oceans and charts their currents, while its National Marine Fisheries Service develops and conserves marine life. Its National Weather Service studies and forecasts the weather.

The National Aeronautics and Space Administration directs the civil space effort. It also conducts civilian aeronautical and space research, which has produced enormous benefits for business, industry, medicine, and education.

The Department of Energy was established to write the nation's energy policy and to administer a wide variety of federal energy programs. The DOE seeks to reduce the demand for energy. At the same time it seeks to increase the supply by developing a wide range of diversified energy sources.

The Nuclear Regulatory Commission is an independent agency whose job is to license and regulate the nuclear industry. The commission was created in 1974. Five years later, the accident at Three Mile Island brought home the critical importance of nuclear regulation.

Chapter 25 Review

Using Vocabulary

Answer the questions below by using the meaning of each underlined term.

1. What environmental impact might the strip mining of a fossil fuel have on a forested area?
2. What is the relationship between acid rain and the enforcement of air quality standards?
3. What government corporation is involved in the multiple-use management of the Tennessee River?
4. Would scientists use basic research or applied research in discovering solutions to the problem of hazardous wastes?
5. How does a nonrenewable energy resource differ from a renewable energy resource?

Understanding American Government

1. Why is conservation of resources important?
2. What is the nation's principal conservation agency?
3. How does the Bureau of Reclamation help people in 17 western states?
4. What is the relationship between the Geological Survey and the National Aeronautics and Space Administration?
5. Why has it been difficult to meet requirements for controlling auto emissions?
6. Why is it important to test chemicals before they are marketed?
7. Why do some people criticize the EPA? Why do some people support it?
8. What is the purpose of the Department of Energy?

Extending Your Skills: Drawing Conclusions from Maps

Study the map on page 597. Then complete the items that follow.

1. In Illinois, Texas, Pennsylvania, and Virginia, the percentage of federally owned land is between (a) 0 and 9 percent; (b) 10 and 29 percent; (c) 30 and 49 percent.
2. In Florida, Arkansas, and New Hampshire the percentage of federally owned land is between (a) 0 and 9 percent; (b) 10 and 29 percent; (c) 30 and 49 percent.
3. Among the states in which the federal government owns between 30 and 49 percent of the land are (a) North Dakota, South Dakota, and Indiana; (b) Idaho, Wyoming, and Utah; (c) Montana, California, and Arizona.
4. The states in which the federal government owns between 50 and 69 percent of the land are (a) Maine, Missouri, and Kansas; (b) Idaho, Wyoming, and Utah; (c) Kentucky, Washington, and Alaska.
5. The two states that have the highest percentage of federally owned land are (a) Alabama and New York; (b) Ohio and Colorado; (c) Nevada and Alaska.
6. Using data from the map, write a brief paragraph proving that the following statement is true: The highest percentage of state land area owned by the federal government is located in the western part of the United States.

Government and You

1. In the past the federal government has given or sold land to homesteaders, to railroads, and to states. Do you think the federal government should give or sell any of its land at the present time? If so, to whom and under what conditions?
2. Should the United States Army Corps of Engineers be involved in the development of the nation's water resources, or should the task be left to the private sector? Give reasons for your opinion.
3. What might you do to promote the conservation of natural resources?

Activities

1. Research and prepare a report on a conservation or antipollution program that is currently under way in your local community or in your state.
2. Choose one of the following and write a brief biography, emphasizing that person's contribution to conservation: (a) John Muir; (b) President Theodore Roosevelt; (c) Senator George W. Norris; (d) Rachel Carson.

Chapter 26

Human Resources

The time has come to break decisively with the past and to create the conditions of a new era. . . .

RICHARD M. NIXON

CHAPTER OVERVIEW

1 **THE DEPARTMENT OF HEALTH AND HUMAN SERVICES**
Public Health Maintenance / Health Insurance / Social Security / Human Development Services

2 **THE DEPARTMENT OF EDUCATION**
The Federal Role in Education / Aid to Elementary and Secondary Education / Aid to Higher Education

3 **THE DEPARTMENT OF HOUSING AND URBAN DEVELOPMENT**
Housing Support / Fair Housing / Urban Renewal

4 **OTHER HUMAN RESOURCE AGENCIES**
Volunteer Programs / Indian Affairs / Supporting the Arts and Humanities / Veterans Benefits

In 1955, President Dwight Eisenhower presents a citation from the Department of Health, Education, and Welfare to Dr. Jonas Salk (standing to the President's right), who developed the first polio vaccine. To Eisenhower's left is Oveta Culp Hobby, the first Secretary of the Department of Health, Education, and Welfare.

1 THE DEPARTMENT OF HEALTH AND HUMAN SERVICES

The Department of Health and Human Services (HHS) is the present name of the former Department of Health, Education, and Welfare (HEW). The change of title became necessary in 1979 with the creation of the Department of Education. But HHS continues its basic mission of providing services that protect and advance the quality of life for all Americans. Patricia Harris, former Secretary of HEW, stated:

The Department of Health and Human Services serves the most vulnerable people in our society, and its mission reflects the nation's commitment to a just and decent society for all persons.

The idea that the government has an obligation to help the unfortunate is relatively new. Historically the colonies, and later the states, established poor farms and similar institutions. In general the care of the elderly, the poor, and the sick was left to families and to private charity. ***Public welfare*** is an outgrowth of the Great Depression, which created the first real need for such widespread relief.

The origins of the public welfare system, however, go back almost 200 years to 1798, when Congress created the Marine Hospital Service to care for merchant seamen. The Marine Hospital Service was the first national public health agency. In 1912 its responsibilities were expanded, and it became the Public Health Service. That same year the Children's Bureau was created to combat the exploitation of children.

In 1935 the Social Security Act established the world's largest insurance program. These and other federal activities in the areas of health, education, social insurance, and human services were brought together in 1939 to form the Federal Security Agency (FSA). Following World War II, government programs in these fields expanded rapidly. In 1953 President Dwight D. Eisenhower recommended that the FSA be reorganized and raised to Cabinet status as the Department of Health, Education, and Welfare (HEW).

During the 1960's and 1970's, HEW programs grew and multiplied. By 1979 HEW had the largest annual budget of any agency in the federal government, a whopping $180 billion, or more than one third of all federal expenditures. Today HHS is responsible for more than 300 programs, and it still has the biggest budget of any federal agency. The bulk of its money goes to pay for Social Security, Medicare, and Medicaid benefits. Other funds, especially for the many public assistance programs, are administered chiefly through state and local agencies.

The Department of Health and Human Services is headed by a Secretary of Cabinet rank, under whose direction it performs four major functions. It protects the public health. It provides basic health care to poor, elderly, and disabled Americans. It administers social welfare programs. And it administers a broad range of human development services.

Public Health Maintenance

Protecting and advancing the health of all Americans are the basic tasks of the Public Health Service. Through its six major agencies the Public Health Service promotes medical research, develops medical facilities, trains health professionals, and works to control the spread of diseases.

Health Care and Disease Prevention The National Institutes of Health (NIH) conduct research into the causes, prevention, and treatment of disease. The NIH consists of 11 research institutes, each specializing in one field, such as cancer, heart disease, strokes, the aging process, cell biology, and environmental hazards. The NIH maintains hundreds of laboratories, as well as a 516-bed clinic where volunteer patients are studied and treated by specialists. The NIH also maintains the world's largest medical research library, the National Library of Medicine. From NIH research have come such advances as the first chemical cure for cancer and a vaccine against rubella, or German measles.

The Health Resources Administration (HRA) funds programs to develop health care services at the state and local levels. It also works with state and local planning agencies to make more and better health care services available. Through the National Center for Health Statistics, the HRA also collects data on national health trends, birth rates, death rates, and life expectancy.

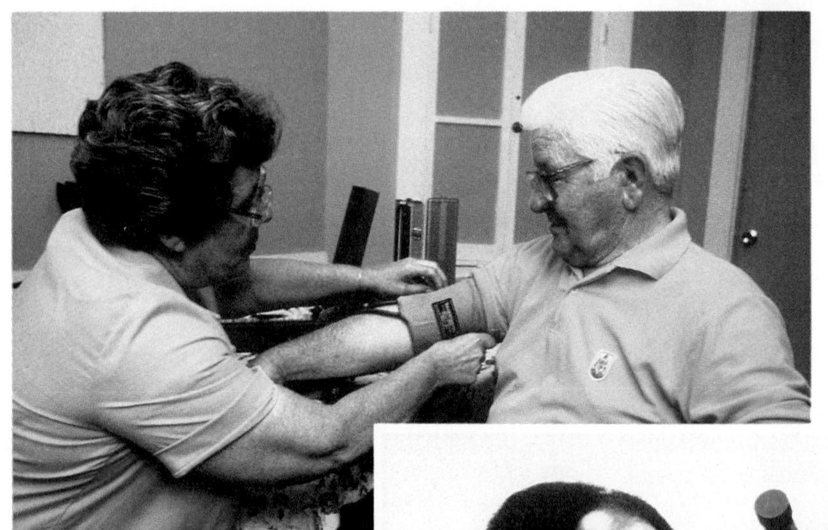

Health and Human Services (HHS) employees engage in a wide variety of public health-related activities. An HHS nurse administers a routine checkup (left) to a resident of a senior citizens' center. An HHS scientist (below) conducts biophysical research at the National Institute of Health.

The Health Services Administration (HSA) funds more than 600 community health centers, bringing health care to residents of the inner city and of isolated rural areas. Its migrant health program serves migrant workers and their families. Its National Health Service Corps recruits doctors, dentists, and nurses to work in areas where health care is unavailable or difficult to obtain.

The HSA also provides health care for merchant sailors and special medical services for the Coast Guard and for the Federal Bureau of Prisons. Its Indian Health Service provides direct care through hospitals, health centers, and field clinics to nearly a half million Native Americans and Eskimos.

Food and Drug Purity The federal government's role in guarding food and drug purity began with the passage of the Pure Food and Drug Act of 1906. Administration of the 1906 act, which imposed restrictions on the preparation and sale of food and drug products, was originally handled by a variety of federal agencies. In 1931 Congress established the Food and Drug Administration (FDA). In 1953 the FDA became part of the Department of Health, Education, and Welfare.

The FDA regulations seek to protect the public against adulterated food, useless or unsafe drugs, and dangerous cosmetics. In addition, they require manufacturers to list all ingredients accurately on product labels. Poisons must be identified as such, and the antidotes must appear on the labels. Narcotics must be labeled as habit-forming. The FDA is also responsible for making sure that radiation emission levels on such electronic products as television sets and microwave ovens are safe.

The FDA inspects factories, warehouses, and stores to ensure that its standards are being met. It approves the marketing of all new drugs. In order to be marketed, new drugs must first pass clinical tests to prove that they are effective and have no harmful side effects.

The FDA has limited power to enforce its regulations. If the FDA finds that new products are unsafe or contaminated, or that the claims made for them are false or misleading, it may sue to remove them from the market. Under the Reagan administration, however, the FDA has increasingly emphasized voluntary correction of problems by industry.

Alcoholism and Other Disorders The prevention and treatment of alcoholism, drug abuse, and mental illness are the concerns of the Alcohol, Drug Abuse, and Mental Health Administration. The agency conducts its own research into the causes of these disorders. It also funds research by state and local agencies. One of its most important organizations is the National Institute of Mental Health. Working with state and local authorities, this institute has established a network of community mental health centers.

Before the passage of the Pure Food and Drug Act of 1906, many manufacturers were able to make fraudulent claims—as in the advertisement above—concerning the merits of their products. What federal agency now protects the public from the inaccurate labeling of food and drugs?

Health Insurance

Health care is expensive. In the early 1980's the average American was paying more than $1,100 a year in medical bills. Obviously every American—except perhaps the very rich—needs some form of health insurance.

Most Americans are covered by private health insurance programs such as Blue Cross, Kaiser, Blue Shield, or Health Maintenance Organizations (HMO). Under these programs, the insured person pays a monthly fee that varies with age, occupation, and state of health. In return, the insurance company or HMO will pay all or part of that person's medical and hospital bills. The insured person's dependents may also be covered.

Not everyone, however, can afford private health insurance or health maintenance programs, because monthly fees may run as high as $250 for some families. National health insurance is one alternative to providing everyone with adequate medical care. Another alternative is providing national health insurance for only certain groups. Medicare and Medicaid provide such insurance for the poor, the elderly, and the disabled. These programs were created by Congress in 1965 and are managed by the Health Care Financing Administration, a division of the Department of Health and Human Services.

Medicare Health insurance for about 28 million elderly persons and 3 million disabled persons is provided by Medicare. Anyone age 65 or over who is entitled to Social Security or Railroad Retirement benefits is automatically protected by Medicare's hospital coverage. Disabled persons under age 65 who have been receiving Social Security disability benefits for two years are also protected. So are

PROFILE

The Disease Detectives

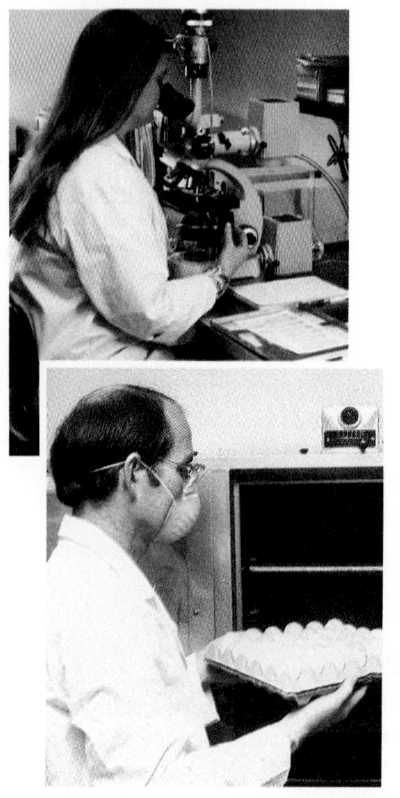

In the summer of 1976 a baffling disease began striking members of the American Legion at a convention in Philadelphia. Within several weeks 100 people were seriously ill and 29 were dead. Immediately federal investigators from the Centers for Disease Control (CDC), an arm of the Public Health Service, rushed to Pennsylvania to try to discover the cause of what was soon dubbed "Legionnaires' disease." Like detectives looking for clues, the investigators interviewed patients and their families, collected specimens, and examined the hotel where the convention took place. At the CDC laboratory the technicians studied blood and tissue specimens from the victims, searching for the virus or bacterium that had caused the disease. For months the scientists were baffled. Meanwhile another outbreak of the deadly disease occurred in Ohio. The CDC scientists intensified their efforts to solve the mystery. Finally, at the end of 1977, two of the CDC researchers announced that they had found the cause. The culprit was an organism that was in a class between viruses and bacteria. The investigation, the largest in CDC history, also turned up an antibiotic effective in treating Legionnaires' disease, technically known as Legionellosis.

Preventing and controlling infectious diseases and diseases spread by insects and other organisms is the work of the CDC. From their headquarters in Atlanta, the CDC scientists monitor and investigate the spread of diseases, conduct eradication and immunization programs, and enforce quarantines. The CDC licenses laboratories that engage in interstate commerce. The center also trains state and local health officials in the control of epidemics and helps them to develop disease-prevention programs. In addition it works closely with foreign governments and with the Immigration Service and the Customs Service to protect residents of the United States from diseases that originate abroad.

Each year the CDC investigates more than 1,500 outbreaks of disease throughout the world. With a staff of 3,500 physicians, lab technicians, researchers, and other experts, the CDC is the largest center in the world for the fight against disease.

★ ★

ISSUES

National Health Insurance

Over the past two decades the cost of health care has soared greatly. A day's stay in a hospital now averages more than $300, and that does not include doctors' fees or medication. Surgery can easily cost thousands of dollars. Nine out of ten Americans have some form of health insurance, but very often their coverage is inadequate to meet the full cost of a prolonged illness. The result, even for middle-class families, can be financial ruin.

For more than 30 years, one of the most intense battles in American politics has been over the issue of national health insurance. Various plans have been presented. In recent years Senator Edward Kennedy has put forward a comprehensive health insurance plan that would provide full coverage for all Americans. Other proposed plans back away from the cost of a full-coverage program and offer to pay family medical expenses above a certain level—say, $2,000 a year.

The proposed national health plans would use private insurance companies. Financing arrangements would vary, however. The Kennedy plan, for example, would be financed both from general tax revenue and from premiums paid by employees and their employers. The comprehensive plan stresses preventive medicine and includes measures to control costs.

People who favor national health insurance say that it would not only provide necessary protection but would also reduce medical costs while improving the quality of the care. Opponents, notably the members of the American Medical Association, disagree. They say that the comprehensive plan is likely to push medical costs still higher. Moreover, they say that the red tape, regulation, and bureaucratic structure of the program would ultimately reduce the quality of health care in the United States.

★ ★

insured workers and their dependents who require kidney dialysis or transplants. A second voluntary Medicare program helps pay for doctors, medical supplies, laboratory tests, and other health services. This additional protection is available to persons age 65 or older for a small monthly fee.

Medicare costs are high, and some experts predict that the program will run out of money by 1990. As a result, in November 1983 a federal advisory committee recommended certain changes in the Medicare law. These included raising the eligibility age to 67, increasing the voluntary premium for additional services, and decreasing the Medicare payment rate for hospitals.

Medicaid Doctor and hospital bills for low-income patients are paid through Medicaid. The program also provides insurance for people who are not poor enough to qualify for other welfare programs but whose income is insufficient to meet their medical expenses. Medicaid is jointly funded by federal and state governments and is administered by the states. It provides health care annually for at least 20 million people.

Social Security

The Social Security Act of 1935 was passed in response to the widespread poverty of the Great Depression. Never had so many Americans experienced poverty. Between 1929 and 1933 the number of unemployed workers in the United States rose from 2 million to nearly 14 million, or one out of every four workers. By 1935, 18 million Americans—one person out of every seven—were living on public relief.

The emergency relief programs started in 1933 with the implementation of President Franklin D.

Roosevelt's New Deal. Roosevelt soon urged the Congress to create permanent, long-range programs that would restore the nation's economic health. One of these programs was the Social Security Act of 1935. The act has been regularly amended over the years. Today its programs provide two broad categories of social welfare coverage: social insurance and public assistance. Both sets of programs are administered by the Social Security Administration of the Department of Health and Human Services, headquartered in Washington, D.C.

Social Insurance Old-Age, Survivors, and Disability Insurance (OASDI)—commonly known as Social Security—is the world's largest social insurance program. It is a compulsory savings plan designed to prevent destitution among the elderly, the families of deceased workers, and the disabled. During their working years, employees contribute a certain percentage of their income to Social Security. This contribution is matched by their employers. Self-employed persons also contribute to the system.

During the last 40 years, the Social Security system has paid billions of dollars in benefits to millions of persons. What groups of people contribute to the Social Security system? Who receives benefits from the system?

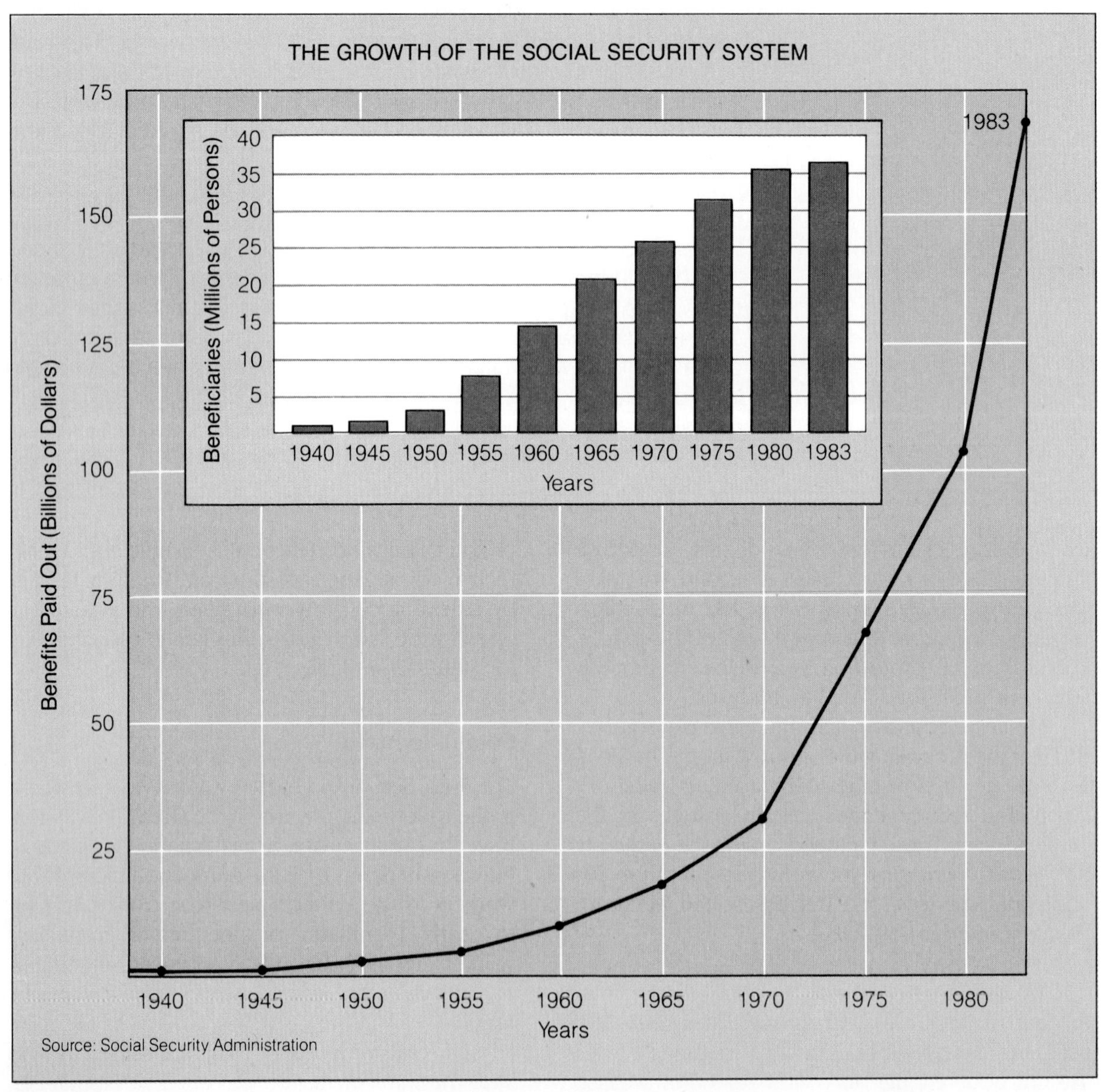

ISSUES

The Future of Social Security

As President Franklin D. Roosevelt signed into law the momentous Social Security Act he declared:

Today a hope of many years' standing is in large part fulfilled. We can never insure 100 percent of the population against 100 percent of the hazards and vicissitudes of life, but we have tried to frame a law which will give some measure of protection to the average citizen and to his family . . . against poverty-ridden old age.

Since its creation in 1935, Social Security has grown into the nation's largest and most successful social program. It currently protects more than 36 million Americans, or nearly one out of six. But the system is also in deep trouble, in part because it has grown so large. By the end of 1982, the Social Security Administration was paying out—every minute of every day—$20,000 more in benefits than it was collecting from payroll taxes. Experts agree that the Social Security fund will be bankrupt before long if the payout rate is not stabilized. Indeed, an official of the Social Security Administration recently estimated that under present law today's workers and retirees will be entitled to $5.6 trillion in benefits over their lifetimes.

Part of the Social Security system's problem has been its enormous success. In 1935, when Social Security began, it provided benefits only to working Americans. In 1939 Congress extended benefits to workers' dependents and survivors. During the 1950's Congress extended Social Security benefits to self-employed workers, to members of the armed forces, to disabled workers, and to others. The extension of benefits made the system more expensive. In 1975, for the first time, the payment of benefits exceeded the Social Security system's income from payroll taxes.

Demographic changes in the United States have added to the payout problem. Thanks to improved medical care and living conditions, the life expectancy of the average American has risen steadily in this century. Many American workers now live beyond retirement age, which increases the payout of benefits and drains the funding of the Social Security system. In addition, the birth rate has been declining. More retirees must now be supported by fewer working taxpayers. In 1945, for example, fewer than 42 workers were required to support one retiree. By 1950 there were only 17 workers to support each retiree. Today a single retiree is supported by 3.2 taxpayers. By the end of the century, it is expected that a single retiree will be supported by only 2 working taxpayers.

The future of Social Security will not be an easy one. Taxpayers may be called upon to assume an even greater burden in supporting the system. The elderly may have to receive fewer benefits if the system is to survive. Whatever the cost, most Americans are likely to agree that the Social Security system must be saved so that the United States can continue to shelter and protect its citizens from "the hazards and vicissitudes of life." Nevertheless, assuring the continued success of the Social Security system without adding to its problems will test the ingenuity and determination of each generation.

A portion of the Social Security tax is used to finance the Medicare program. The rest is pooled in special trust funds. When a worker's earnings stop or are reduced because of death, retirement, or disability, the worker or the worker's family is paid a monthly cash benefit. The amount of the benefit depends on the worker's age, the worker's earnings over the years, and the size of the worker's family.

Most beneficiaries are retired persons. At present the age for full retirement is 65, and the age for retirement with reduced benefits is 62. A 1983 amendment provides for full retirement at age 67 for all people born in 1960 and thereafter. The OASDI benefits are provided for certain dependents, such as a spouse who is 62 or older and unmarried children under the age of 18. Unmarried children, who are full-time students, may continue to receive benefits until the age of 22. When someone covered by the OASDI dies, surviving dependents are entitled to monthly benefits. If a person is disabled by illness or an accident, the OASDI pays benefits until that person can return to work. If the person cannot return to work, payments will continue until the age of full retirement. Almost all working Americans are now covered by the OASDI.

The money for the OASDI benefits comes from taxes paid by people who are currently working. It follows that the OASDI system must take in enough money each year to pay the benefits that are due each year. Since 1977, however, the system has been operating at a deficit.

Public Assistance Public assistance, commonly known as "welfare," provides cash and other benefits to people who are poor.* Unlike social insurance, which is essentially self-financed, public assistance comes from the general tax revenue fund. Two of the most important public assistance programs are administered by the Social Security Administration.

The Supplemental Security Income (SSI) program provides cash benefits to approximately 4 million poor people who are permanently disabled, aged, or blind. The SSI replaces a patchwork of state-administered programs with one direct and uniform federal program. For those who qualify under the SSI, the federal government provides a guaranteed minimum income, the size of which depends on a person's marital and family status. In effect the SSI provides assistance to old and to disabled people who do not qualify for the OASDI benefits.

Aid to Families with Dependent Children (AFDC) provides cash payments to 11 million persons, mostly to mothers and to children, who have little or no other income. AFDC is a joint federal-state program. Federal funding is handled by the Social Security Administration, which pays each child a monthly benefit. The state matches this payment with a payment of its own. However, AFDC is administered by the states. Eligibility requirements differ among the states, and each state sets its own level of payments. The result is that the average benefit paid to needy families varies enormously from state to state.

Most families who receive aid from the AFDC or the SSI programs are automatically eligible for food stamps. The ***food stamp program*** is administered by the Department of Agriculture through state and local welfare agencies.

From its beginning, the food stamp program has been marked by abuse and scandal. In 1965 less than a half million people received food stamps. By the early 1980's the number of food stamp recipients had grown to 23 million. Critics of the program have claimed that many recipients are not genuinely poor. Eligibility requirements now have been tightened to exclude those taking unfair advantage of the program. Nevertheless, many critics have urged that food stamps be replaced by cash payments to the poor and by basic welfare reform.

Welfare Reform The American welfare system has grown in an uncoordinated fashion in the 50-odd years since its creation. One program has been piled upon another, and responsibility has been divided among dozens of agencies with overlapping jurisdictions. More than 50 separate federal programs provide cash or services to various categories of the poor. The system is not only complicated, it is also wasteful and sometimes unjust. Conservatives and liberals alike agree that something must be done to reform the system.

Most people agree that a new welfare system should have the following goals:

- Provide adequate income for the elderly, the disabled, and other needy people who cannot work.

---

*The federal government defines a poor family as one whose income is below $7,190 if they live on a farm, or below $8,450 if they live elsewhere. Following this definition, data collected in the 1980 census reveal that one out of every eight Americans is poor. The 1980 Census data also reveal that the heads of two thirds of the poor families are employed, 40 percent full time. The heads of 35 percent of all poor families are women.

- Establish incentives to encourage those who can work to do so.
- Encourage families to stay together.
- Provide equal benefits to families or individuals in similar circumstances.
- Prevent fraud and abuse by welfare recipients and by those who provide services.
- Streamline administration so that it is simple, efficient, and as inexpensive as possible.

Human Development Services

The Office of Human Development Services administers a broad range of social and rehabilitation programs to serve the needs of the elderly, children of low-income families, persons with mental and physical handicaps, Native Americans, and other groups. Most of the programs are run by the states under grants from the federal government. They are administered by four different agencies.

Providing for the Aged More than 25 million Americans are age 65 or older. Many are isolated and forgotten. The Administration on Aging was established to identify the needs and concerns of older people and to coordinate federal policies and programs that affect them. Through grants to the states, the agency supports community-based nutrition and companionship programs. It also provides recreational activities, transportation, legal aid, and homemaker and home health services for older people. The primary goal of all these services is to keep the elderly out of institutions, to allow them to remain a part of the community, and to enable them to lead full and productive lives.

Protecting the Young The Administration for Children, Youth, and Families coordinates federal programs for children and their families. It funds programs for the protection of abused and neglected children, for help to runaway and homeless youths, and for high-quality day-care centers to meet the needs of working parents. Its Head Start program serves the needs of preschool children from low-income families. Head Start provides these children with medical and dental services, with improved nutrition, and with help in developing their language and learning abilities.

Many programs offered by the Office of Human Development Services enable elderly persons to take active roles in their communities. Retirees provide free counseling to teenagers (left) and teach a Head Start class (below).

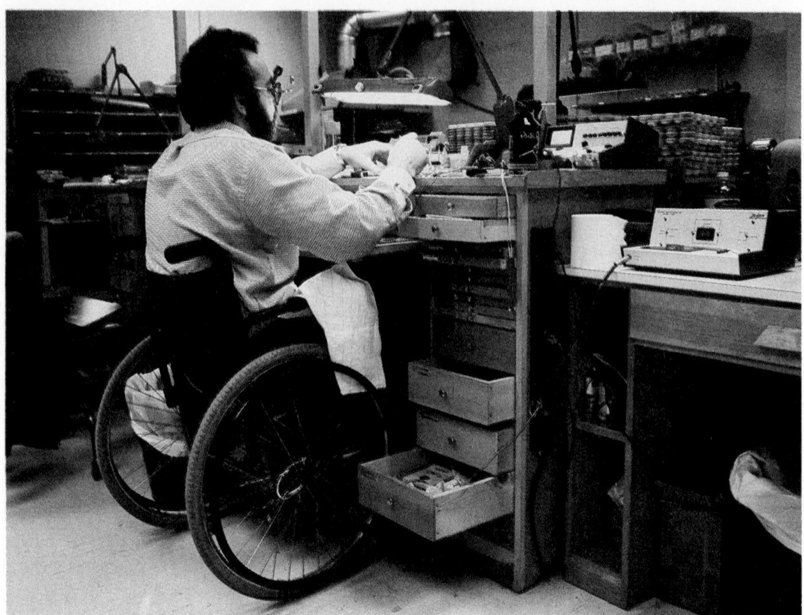

The Administration on Developmental Disabilities provides counseling and financial assistance to disabled persons. These services enable disabled persons to remain productive members of society.

Assisting the Disabled The Administration on Developmental Disabilities serves the needs of the physically and the mentally handicapped. It works through state agencies, providing vocational rehabilitation to train handicapped persons and place them in productive employment so they may help themselves. For example, federal standards now seek to eliminate architectural and transportation barriers that impede the mobility of people on crutches or in wheelchairs.

Aiding Native Americans One third of all Native Americans, Aleuts, and Eskimos live in poverty. The number of Native Americans who complete high school lags behind figures for the general population, while their unemployment is almost double. The average life expectancy among Native Americans is eight years below the national average.

The Administration for Native Americans works to help Native Americans, Eskimos, Aleuts, and Native Hawaiians achieve economic self-sufficiency. Grants are made directly to tribal groups and other Native American organizations. Financial support is flexible and provides for programs designed and operated by the Native Americans themselves. The administration works with the Bureau of Indian Affairs (BIA) and other federal agencies to coordinate programs and avoid overlap.

Work Incentive Program Most welfare recipients are not able to work. They are either too old, too young, or too severely handicapped. Those who are able to work, however, often lack skills and education. Unable to find steady employment, they come and go from the public assistance rolls. One of the major goals of the Department of Health and Human Services (HHS) is to help these people break out of the cycle of poverty and dependency so that they may become self-reliant and self-supporting members of society.

Administered jointly by the HHS and the Department of Labor, the Work Incentive Program (WIP) provides employment and social services to welfare recipients. Its purpose is to shift families off welfare dependency. The WIP gives able welfare recipients the skills and the opportunity to work.

Section Check

1. Identify: Marine Hospital Service, National Institutes of Health, Medicare, Medicaid, Social Security Act
2. What are the four major functions of the Department of Health and Human Services?
3. What are the six major agencies of the Public Health Service?
4. What are some arguments in favor of national health insurance? What are some arguments against it?
5. List three goals of welfare reform.
6. What programs are administered by the Office of Human Development Services?

2 THE DEPARTMENT OF EDUCATION

The Department of Education, created in 1979, is the nation's newest Cabinet-level agency. It pulls together a wide range of federal education programs. Its goal is "equal access to quality education."

The department was born in a storm of controversy. The National Education Association (NEA), the nation's largest teachers' organization, led the campaign for its creation. The aim was to give education a separate and presumably more effective voice and presence in federal government. The NEA campaign won President Carter's support, but local school officials were divided. Many of them feared that the new department would expand federal control over local school systems.

Congress, also concerned with the issue of federal interference in local matters, imposed explicit limits on the department's jurisdiction. Thus, interference with matters traditionally decided at state and local levels, such as curriculum, textbooks, testing, and the hiring of teachers requires specific Congressional authorization. Under the Reagan administration the department has shifted greater responsibility for educational policy and programs to the states and to local school districts.

In the United States, education is largely the responsibility of state and local governments. The Hope Eskimo School in Alaska is subject to that state's regulations.

A U.S. Postal Service stamp celebrates the importance of education in American life.

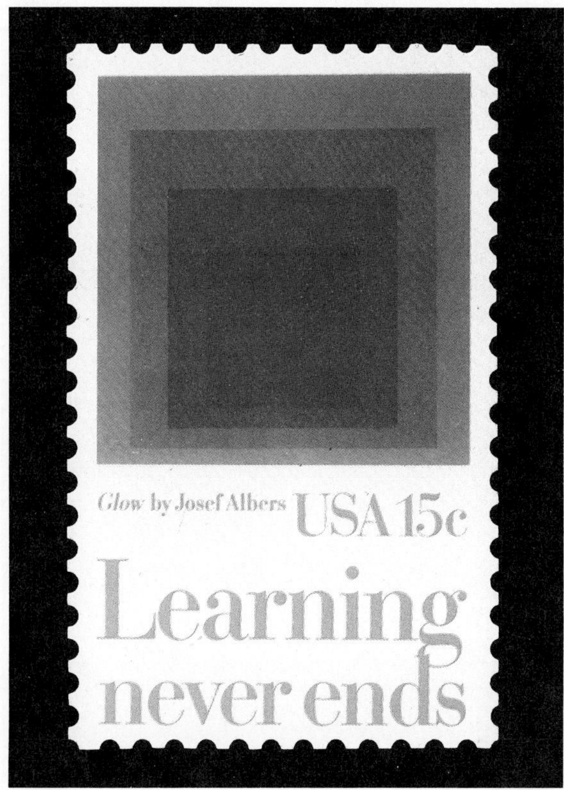

The Federal Role in Education

Responsibility for financing elementary and secondary education lies primarily with local government. The federal government supplies only 8 percent of the money for financing the public schools. As the chart on page 632 shows, federal concern for education goes back to the early days of the Republic, when the Northwest Ordinance of 1787 offered land grants for public schools. The act stated:

> .... *[K]nowledge being necessary for good government and the happiness of mankind, schools and the means for education shall ever be encouraged.*

The Morrill Act of 1862 provided grants of federal land to each state to establish colleges for agriculture and the mechanical arts. This act was a landmark piece of legislation because it represented the first attempt by any government in the world to offer higher education to all of its people. In 1867 Congress created the United States Office of Education, the forerunner of today's Department of Education.

The federal role in education expanded slowly. The Smith-Hughes Act of 1917 provided grants for public schools to promote vocational training in agriculture, home economics, trades, and industry.

MAJOR FEDERAL LEGISLATION TO AID EDUCATION

Date	Legislation	Purpose
1787	Northwest Ordinance	Offered land grants for public schools in the new territories
1802	Military Peace Establishment Act	Established the United States Military Academy at West Point, New York
1862	First Morrill Act	Provided land grants to each state for agricultural and mechanical colleges
1867	Department of Education Act	Created first United States Office of Education
1917	Smith-Hughes Act	Provided grants for vocational education in public high schools
1918	Vocational Rehabilitation Act (and later amendments)	Authorized funds for rehabilitation of World War I I veterans
1944	Servicemen's Readjustment Act (G.I. Bill)	Provided stipends and tuition assistance to veterans
1946	National School Lunch Act	Provided funds for low-cost lunch and milk programs in public schools
1950	Public Laws 81-874 and 81-815	Provided financial assistance and building-construction funds for public schools in federally impacted areas
1958	National Defense Education Act (and later amendments)	Provided funds for improved instruction of science, math, foreign languages; provided funds for guidance counseling, testing, and low-interest student loans
1965	Elementary and Secondary Education Act (and later amendments)	Guaranteed equal educational opportunity; supported educationally deprived children
1965	Higher Education Act (and later amendments)	Provided funds for library assistance, insured student loans, and aid to help low- and middle-income families meet the cost of higher education
1979	Department of Education Organization Act	Created the United States Department of Education
1981	Educational Consolidation and Improvement Act	Replaced many programs with block grants

Source: United States Department of Education

Federal aid to science education has included the funding of school science laboratories in the late 1950's (below) and of classroom computers in the 1980's (left). What event in 1957 caused Americans to be concerned about science education?

In 1946 the school lunch and milk programs were started. In 1950 Congress authorized aid to public schools in ***federally impacted areas*** of the nation. These are areas where federal activities substantially increase school enrollment—near a military base, for example—or where federally owned property reduces the tax base and with it the taxes that support the schools.

In 1957 the Soviet Union launched *Sputnik I,* the first satellite into space. The successful Soviet space shot aroused concern among Americans who feared that the United States was falling behind in education, especially in science and technology. In response to *Sputnik I,* Congress passed the National Defense Education Act (NDEA). The NDEA provided grants to states and to school districts to improve instruction in science, mathematics, and foreign languages. The NDEA was later amended to include civics, history, geography, and English. Underlying the NDEA was the recognition that the strength of the nation depends upon the education of its people.

While the number of federal programs continued to increase, the federal role in education remained small. In 1965, however, the federal role expanded dramatically with the passage of the Elementary and Secondary Education Act (ESEA). Today federal education programs range from preschool training to postdoctoral study. Some 150 education programs affect nearly all of the nation's 15,000 school districts, 2,500 colleges and universities, and a school population of nearly 60 million children and youths.

Aid to Elementary and Secondary Education

The Elementary and Secondary Education Act (ESEA), which established the first general federal aid-to-education program, has been amended and expanded

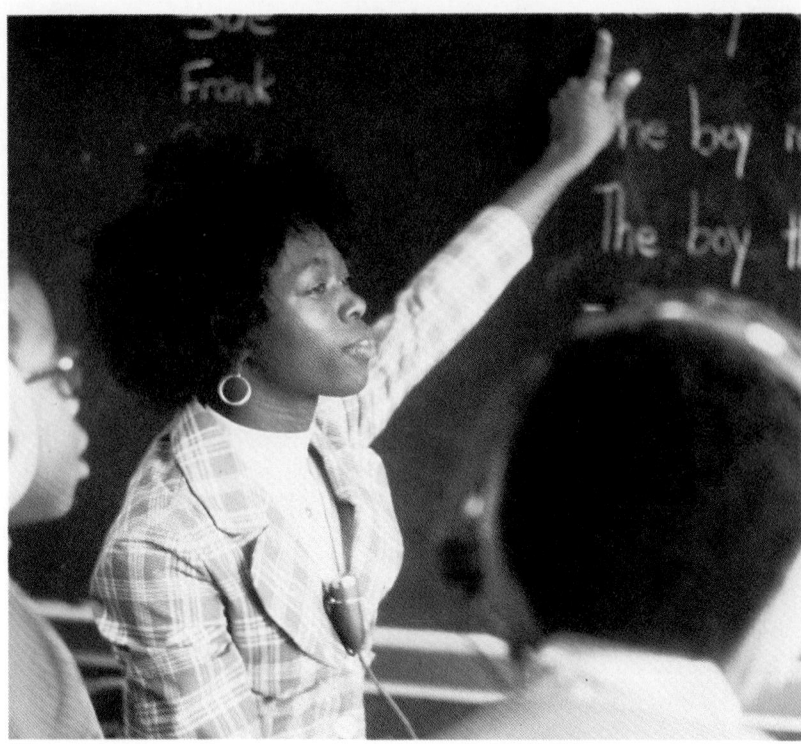

The Model Secondary School for the Deaf and the Kendall Demonstration Elementary School, both located on the Gallaudet College campus, are special schools funded by the federal government. List some other special education activities funded by federal programs.

several times. The ESEA provides grants to most of the nation's schools, both public and private. Its purpose is to ensure equal educational opportunity and to support "the special needs of educationally deprived children." The ESEA bases its grants on the number of children from low-income families in each district, and the moneys fund locally designed programs. The programs include education for minority children in urban ghetto areas, for children in rural Appalachia, for Hispanic and Native American children in the Southwest, and for the children of migrant workers.

The ESEA and other federal programs also fund a number of special activities. Bilingual education programs are designed to meet the needs of children who come from homes where English is not spoken. To help these children overcome the language barrier, bilingual education provides instruction in their own language while they learn English. The vast majority of the children enrolled in bilingual education programs speak Spanish, but bilingual programs are conducted in more than 60 languages and dialects, from Arabic to Vietnamese.

There are also special education programs for children with learning disabilities and for deaf, blind, and other handicapped children. Yet another program provides enriched education for children with special talents.

Aid to Higher Education

The Higher Education Act of 1965 and its amendments expanded federal aid to higher education. To help low- and middle-income families meet the rising costs of higher education, the act provided funds for scholarships, for work-study programs, and for low-interest loans to students. It also provided federal funds to improve libraries and to construct classrooms, laboratories, and other facilities. Most federal aid to higher education is now under the Higher Education Act.

Section Check

1. Define: federally impacted area
2. Identify: National Education Association, Northwest Ordinance, Morrill Act
3. About what percentage of the money for financing public schools comes from the federal government?
4. What is the basis for federal grants to education under the Elementary and Secondary Education Act?
5. What kinds of help does the federal government give to higher education?

---

3 THE DEPARTMENT OF HOUSING AND URBAN DEVELOPMENT

Congress created the Department of Housing and Urban Development (HUD) in 1965 as a response to rapid urbanization of areas surrounding central cities and the growing problems of the inner city. But it was during the Great Depression that the government created the Federal Home Loan Bank system to help Americans buy or rent decent housing. Today HUD administers some 70 federal programs in the two broad categories of housing support and urban renewal. In addition HUD administers the federal fair housing laws.

Housing Support

Federal support for housing consists of mortgage insurance, of tax incentives for the home buyer, and of public housing for low-income families.

Mortgage Insurance The Federal Housing Administration (FHA) was created in 1934 to provide mortgage insurance for people who wanted to buy homes. The FHA itself does not make loans. Instead it protects lending institutions, such as banks and savings and loan associations, against loss in case a home buyer fails to repay a loan. This protection encourages private lenders to make more loans at lower interest rates, for longer periods, and with lower down payments than they would otherwise. The insurance program is financed by a small charge added to each mortgage. But the record of mortgage repayment is so good that the FHA regularly returns money to the United States Treasury.

The FHA also insures loans to homeowners who want to make improvements to their property. Mortgage guarantees also are provided through the Veterans Administration and the Farmers Home Administration.

Tax Incentives In addition to mortgage and to home-improvement-loan insurance, the federal government promotes home ownership through tax incentives. Homeowners with outstanding home loans receive what amounts to a federal housing subsidy in the form of income tax deductions. In figuring their federal income tax, they can deduct the interest they pay on their mortgage loans from their taxable income, thus saving several hundred dollars a year in taxes.

Public Housing Today more than 65 percent of all American families own their homes. But millions of other Americans need help to buy homes or to rent decent houses or apartments. Since 1937 the federal government has provided grants and loans for low-rent public housing to the poor and to the aged. The program is administered by HUD's Housing Assistance Administration. The administration does not build, own, or operate housing projects. Instead, it makes long-term, low-interest loans to local housing authorities. These agencies, in turn, build and rent public housing. HUD subsidizes the agencies so that they can charge low rent.

As the percentage of elderly persons in the population increases, the need for low-cost housing for the aged becomes more critical. How does the Housing Assistance Administration help to meet this need?

From the beginning, public housing has been controversial. Some 2 million people live in public housing, but many do so only as a last resort. The huge housing projects are often impersonal and bureaucratic. Some have become high-rise slums where tenants live in constant fear of crime. Often residents will fight to keep a project from being built in their neighborhood. No community, however, is required to have public housing. As a result projects have frequently been rejected when put to a public referendum. One solution is ***scatter housing***, or replacing huge public housing projects with smaller projects throughout the city.

While HUD seeks to improve public housing, it has also been experimenting with ***rent subsidies*** for private housing. Under this program, local housing authorities help low-income families by paying a portion of the rent directly to the landlord. In place of both public housing and rent subsidies, many reform advocates favor a ***housing allowance*** for low-income families. This proposal calls for cash payments to the poor and to the aged to enable them to shop around for decent housing.

Urban renewal sometimes includes restoring homes to their original condition. This revitalized street is in Georgetown, the oldest section of Washington, D.C.

Fair Housing

An end to discrimination in the sale and in the rental of housing has been a major civil rights goal since the 1960's. For many years racial bias has kept minorities in segregated neighborhoods, denying them fair housing opportunities. The Civil Rights Act of 1968 has prohibited discrimination in housing on the basis of race, color, religion, sex, or national origin. Many states and cities have also passed fair housing or "open housing" laws. It is HUD that administers the federal law and investigates complaints of housing discrimination. Complaints are referred to state and local fair housing agencies when these agencies offer basically the same protection as that afforded under federal law.

Urban Renewal

The Department of Housing and Urban Development oversees a number of programs designed to stop the deterioration of American cities. The growth of the suburbs in the years following World War II weakened the financial resources of the central cities. Suburban shopping centers drew businesses and customers away from downtown sections. Public services in the cities were cut back, many buildings were left to decay, and old neighborhoods turned into slums.

To save the central cities, the federal government has funded a broad program of urban renewal. Through Community Planning and Development, HUD provides grants that municipal authorities can use to acquire run-down urban property. Once residents are relocated, the sites are prepared for new uses. Often the land is resold to private development companies who agree to clear it and rehabilitate it according to approved plans. Federal mortgage insurance is made available for the reconstruction projects.

Urban renewal has transformed once-blighted urban areas into attractive places to live and work. The projects attract middle-class residents as well as business and industry back to the inner city. The projects also create new jobs and stimulate additional development in the surrounding areas. Often renewal projects involve the construction of universities, hospitals, and civic centers. Over time, the city's investment is repaid by increased tax returns on the renewed property.

Urban renewal, however, has another side. All too often urban renewal means urban removal of the poor and elderly. Most of the people who are displaced by urban renewal programs cannot afford the higher rents that are usually charged in the buildings that replace their former homes. Many of these people must often move to another blighted, run-down area. In addition, urban renewal programs frequently destroy old ethnic neighborhoods, dispersing residents and lessening the cultural variety and flavor of the larger central cities.

In recent years a new emphasis has been placed on the rehabilitation of existing property and on the preservation and restoration of neighborhoods. Federal assistance is offered by HUD to neighborhood organizations for self-help development. The goals are to enable residents to improve their housing and to revitalize their communities.

Section Check

1. Define: scatter housing, rent subsidy, housing allowances
2. Identify: Federal Housing Administration, Civil Rights Act of 1968
3. How does mortgage insurance help home buyers?
4. What are some criticisms of public housing?
5. Describe three proposals for reforming public housing.
6. What are some positive results of urban renewal? What are some negative results?

4 OTHER HUMAN RESOURCE AGENCIES

Many other federal agencies are concerned with human resources. Some are agencies within Cabinet departments, such as the Bureau of Indian Affairs, which is part of the Department of the Interior. Others are independent executive agencies, such as ACTION and the Veterans Administration.

Volunteer Programs

ACTION was created in 1971 to bring together a number of federal volunteer programs. The best known are the Peace Corps and Volunteers in Service to America (VISTA). Other programs include Foster Grandparents, the Retired Senior Volunteer Program, and the Senior Companion Program, all of which offer older people the chance to serve their communities in various ways. ACTION volunteers have two goals. They help low-income people to help themselves. They also work to meet these people's basic needs.

The VISTA program is a national corps of volunteers who work to fight poverty in America. Since the program began in 1964, more than 70,000 people from all racial and economic backgrounds have

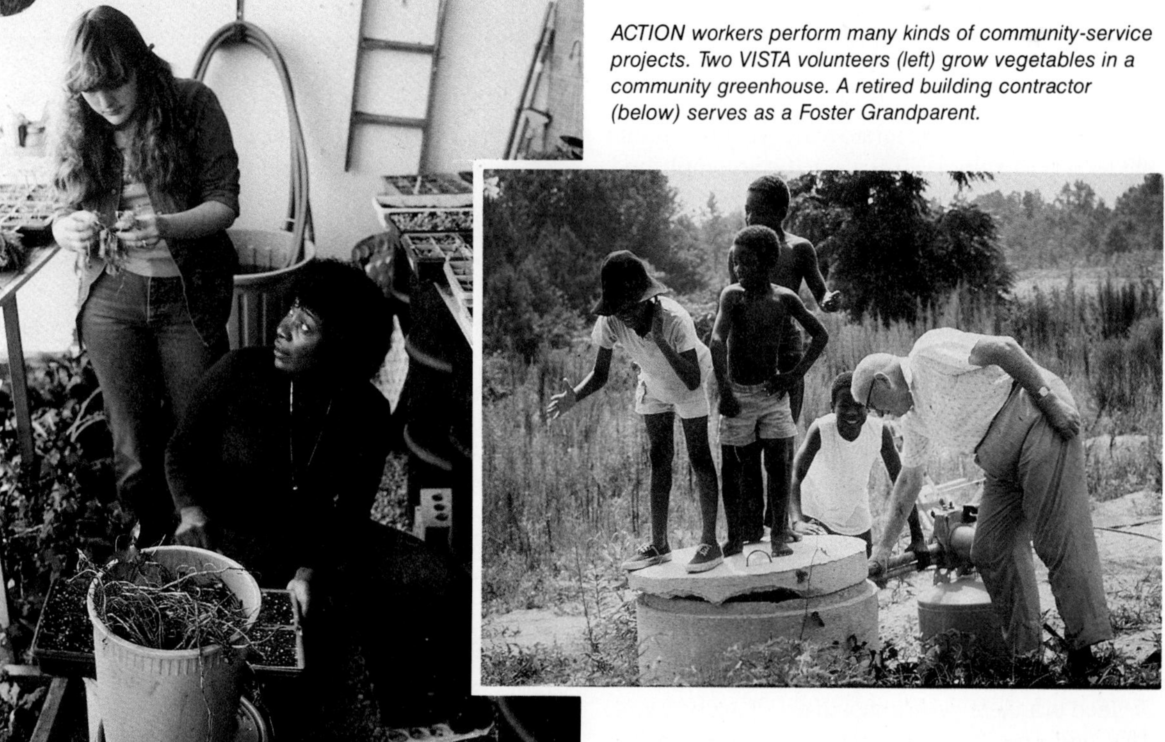

ACTION workers perform many kinds of community-service projects. Two VISTA volunteers (left) grow vegetables in a community greenhouse. A retired building contractor (below) serves as a Foster Grandparent.

served as VISTA volunteers. About two thirds of the volunteers are women, and almost half are between 18 and 27 years of age. Volunteers receive a small monthly allowance to cover the cost of food, housing, and incidentals. They serve for one or two years on a full-time basis in locally sponsored projects. They work among the poor, the needy, and the handicapped in urban and in rural areas, on Indian reservations, with migrant workers, and in institutions for the mentally ill. About half of the VISTA volunteers serve in their own communities.

Indian Affairs

The Bureau of Indian Affairs (BIA) was created in 1824 as a part of the War Department. In 1849 it was transferred to the Department of the Interior. It is the principal federal agency dealing with Native American groups, Aleuts, and Eskimos. The bureau is a service and support agency that helps these groups manage their own affairs under a special trust relationship with the federal government.

That relationship is the result of a long—and often shameful—history. In the early years of the Republic, the federal government treated each group of Native Americans as if it were a foreign country, dealing with each group by treaty. As the West was settled, these treaties were often broken. The lands of Native Americans were taken from them by force, and the tribes were moved onto reservations that were often on barren land far from their original homes.

In the 1870's the federal policy changed. The goal then became to integrate Native Americans into the society as a whole. This was to be accomplished, however, by destroying the Native American cultures. Accordingly, the tribes were officially abolished, and reservation lands were divided into small parcels and allotted to individuals. But this Americanization policy failed.

In 1933 federal policy changed again. The goal then became to preserve the Native American cultures, especially on the reservations. Native Americans were no longer to be integrated into society by destroying their own ways of life. Instead the allotment policy was abolished and tribal authority on the reservations was strengthened.

In 1953 Congress changed its Native American policy yet again. Until then, Native Americans had been considered ***wards*** of the government and, as such, under its care and protection. Then Congress decided that these people should no longer be wards. Civil and criminal authority over the reservations was taken away from tribal chiefs and given to the states, while tribal land was again distributed to individuals. The Bureau of Indian Affairs began a job-training and relocation program designed to turn Native Americans into urban workers.

Kenneth Smith—a member of the Wasco tribe in Oregon—serves as Assistant Secretary of the Interior for Indian Affairs. What is the federal government's current Native American policy?

This termination policy was as much a failure as previous policies. As a result, in 1963 the federal government again changed its policy. The relationship between the government and the tribes today stresses self-determination. In a special message to Congress in 1968, President Lyndon B. Johnson stated:

Our goal must be: A standard of living for Indians equal to that of the country as a whole; freedom of choice—an opportunity to remain in their homeland if they choose, without surrendering their dignity, and an opportunity to move to the towns and cities of America if they choose, equipped with skills to live in equality and dignity; full participation in the life of modern America, with a full share of economic opportunity and social justice.

There are nearly 1.5 million Native Americans, Aleuts, and Eskimos. Approximately half of them live on 266 reservations and other scattered piec land totaling more than 50 million acres.

The responsibility of the Bureau of Indian Affairs (BIA) does not extend to Native Americans who have chosen to leave the reservations. The BIA views its mission as threefold.

- Recognition and preservation of the inherent rights of tribal self-government, the strengthening of tribal capacity to govern, and the provision of resources for tribal government programs.
- Pursuit and protection of the sovereignty and the rights of Native American tribes, of Aleuts, and of Eskimos in dealing with other governmental entities and the private sector.
- Execution of the federal government's trust obligation to Native American tribes, Aleuts, and Eskimos.

The BIA seeks to promote full educational opportunity for Native Americans. Today most Native American students attend public schools. To serve areas that have no public schools, there are 213 federal schools. Since the founding of the Navajo Community College in 1969, several Native American groups have established junior-college programs. The bureau provides college scholarships for Native Americans, and so do some tribes.

The BIA also works with tribal groups to provide such services as child welfare, road maintenance, and housing. Special emphasis is placed on economic development and employment programs. The BIA also helps Native Americans make better use of reservation resources by encouraging the development of industry on or near reservations.

Supporting the Arts and Humanities

The National Foundation on the Arts and Humanities (NFAH) was created in 1965 to promote the

Elected officials representing the Apache tribes of Arizona meet at a regional council (left). A lumber yard provides employment for many Apaches on the White Mountain reservation in Arizona (below).

nation's progress in the arts and ***humanities***—the field of study that includes literature, languages, philosophy, and history. The National Endowment for the Arts, a division of the NFAH, seeks to make the arts widely available, to preserve the cultural heritage of the United States, to strengthen cultural organizations, and to help develop the nation's finest creative talent. The endowment makes grants to individual artists and to state and regional arts agencies. It supports projects in architecture, dance, film, music, painting, sculpture, and theater and makes grants to museums.

LEGACY

Wonders of the Smithsonian Institution

Enter the towering glass and steel structure of the Smithsonian Institution's National Air and Space Museum, and you have stepped into a living history of flight. The museum, which is visited by more people each year than any other museum in the world, contains everything from early flight balloons to a studio model of the U.S.S. *Enterprise* from the "Star Trek" television series. Here is the Wright brothers' original aircraft, *Kitty Hawk Flyer,* suspended above *Columbia,* the Apollo II command module that in 1969 made the first lunar landing. Here you can touch a moon rock collected by the Apollo crew, walk through America's first space station, and gaze at the *Spirit of St. Louis,* the plane Charles Lindbergh piloted on the first solo nonstop transatlantic flight in 1927.

Vast as it is, the National Air and Space Museum is just one of 13 museums that comprise the Smithsonian Institution, the largest complex of museums and art galleries in the world. The Smithsonian began in 1826, when English scientist James Smithson bequeathed his estate—100,000 gold sovereigns worth a half million dollars—to the United States "to found at Washington, under the name of the Smithsonian Institution, an establishment for the increase and diffusion of knowledge among men." Founded in 1846 by an Act of Congress, the Smithsonian Institution has grown from one small museum to a giant complex of research facilities, museums, galleries, and zoos unmatched anywhere in the world.

The Smithsonian's National Museum of Natural History, for example, displays a collection of more than 65 million specimens of animals, plants, fossils, rocks, and human artifacts—including the legendary Hope Diamond, the largest blue diamond in existence. At the National Museum of American History visitors thrill to the sight of the historic flag that inspired Francis Scott Key to write the poem that became the "Star Spangled Banner."

In 1889 Congress established the Smithsonian's National Zoological Park, which today exhibits approximately 2,500 animals. At the zoo's Conservation and Research Center in nearby Virginia, zoologists study animals on a 3,150-acre tract in order to improve their care in captivity and to encourage their breeding.

More than 23 million people visit the Smithsonian's museums, art galleries, and zoo every year. So vast is the collection of the Institute that only 1 percent of its holdings are on display at any one time, although the rest are available to scientists and scholars for study. Expeditions are constantly being made by the Smithsonian Institution to gather new facts and specimens from all parts of the world.

Veterans Benefits

Millions of Americans have served their nation in the armed forces. In this century they have faced major combat in two world wars, in Korea, and in Vietnam, as well as limited actions in Mexico, in Latin America, and in the Middle East. Since the Revolutionary War, Congress has awarded pensions to veterans disabled in the line of duty and to the spouses of those who died in battle. After World War I, benefits were expanded, and in 1930 the administration of these benefits was assigned to an independent agency, the Veterans Administration (VA).

The VA, with a work force of more than 236,000, is the third-largest agency in the federal government. The VA serves more than 30 million veterans and 60 million dependents and survivors. In recognition of the debt the American people owe to the men and women who served in the armed forces, Congress has provided a program of extensive benefits. These include compensatory payments to veterans or their survivors for disabilities or death related to military services. They also include pensions, based on financial need, for veterans disabled from causes unrelated to military service. Veterans receive assistance in finding employment, in obtaining low-cost life insurance, and in arranging for burial in federal cemeteries.

Since the passage of the G.I. Bill of Rights in 1944, over 16 million veterans have received education and training under VA programs. Sixty-five percent of all Vietnam veterans have benefited from these programs. The G.I. Bill has also provided VA-guaranteed home loans for nearly 9.5 million veterans. Finally, the Veterans Administration operates the largest hospital and health care system in the United States. Its 172 hospitals treat 1.3 million patients each year.

Section Check

---

1. Identify: VISTA, Bureau of Indian Affairs, National Foundation on the Arts and Humanities, James Smithson, Veterans Administration
2. Describe the typical VISTA volunteer and the places where volunteers work.
3. Describe the various policies of the federal government toward Native Americans.
4. What are some benefits Congress provides to veterans?

SUMMARY

The Department of Health and Human Services (HHS) is the federal government's health and welfare agency. It protects the public health through the six main agencies of the Public Health Service: the National Institutes of Health; the Food and Drug Administration; the Centers for Disease Control; the Health Resources Administration; the Health Services Administration; and the Alcohol, Drug Abuse, and Mental Health Administration.

The Department of Health and Human Services also administers Medicare and Medicaid. Medicare provides health insurance for elderly and disabled persons; Medicaid provides health insurance for the poor of all ages.

The Social Security Administration of the HHS administers social insurance and public assistance programs. Social insurance is provided through Old-Age, Survivors, and Disability Insurance, or Social Security, which is a workers' compulsory savings plan. Public assistance programs include Supplemental Security Income for the aged, blind, or disabled poor, and Aid to Families with Dependent Children for poor families with dependent children. The HHS also administers a variety of other social and rehabilitation programs through the Office of Human Development Services.

The Department of Education administers a wide range of federal education programs. These programs, which provide aid to elementary, secondary, and higher education, are designed to ensure that all Americans shall have "equal access to quality education."

The Department of Housing and Urban Development administers federal housing support programs. These various programs provide mortgage insurance for home buyers and public housing for low-income families. In addition HUD administers the federal fair housing laws and the urban renewal programs designed to restore America's deteriorating cities. There are many other human resource agencies. Important ones include ACTION, which administers VISTA and a number of other federal volunteer programs; the Bureau of Indian Affairs, which protects the interests of Native Americans; the National Foundation on the Arts and Humanities, which promotes and supports the humanities and the arts; and the Smithsonian Institution, which conducts research and maintains museums dedicated to art, history, and science. Finally, the Veterans Administration administers a wide range of programs that provide benefits to America's veterans.

Chapter 26 Review

Using Vocabulary

Answer the questions by using the meaning of each underlined term.

1. Would landlords prefer that people receive rent subsidies or housing allowances?
2. Is the theater part of the arts or the humanities?
3. What are two examples of a federally impacted area?

Understanding American Government

1. How does the federal government protect and advance the health of all Americans?
2. Which groups receive special health-care benefits from the federal government?
3. Compare the original beneficiaries of the Social Security Act with present-day beneficiaries. How might you explain any difference?
4. Give four reasons why the OASDI has been operating at a deficit for several years.
5. What limitation did Congress impose on the jurisdiction of the Department of Education? Why?
6. What three forms does federal support for housing take? Which form or forms benefit middle-class people? Which benefits poor people?
7. Describe the changes that have taken place in the attitude of the federal government toward Native Americans.
8. Describe the attitude of the federal government toward the arts and humanities.

Extending Your Skills: Comparing Graphs

Study the graphs on page 626. Then complete the items that follow.

1. The Social Security system in 1945 paid out benefits that totaled (a) $1 billion; (b) $10 billion; (c) $50 billion.
2. The number of beneficiaries of the Social Security system in 1975 was about (a) 10 million persons; (b) 21 million persons; (c) 32 million persons.
3. Between 1960 and 1983 the number of beneficiaries of the Social Security system (a) more than doubled; (b) more than tripled; (c) almost quadrupled.
4. Between 1960 and 1983 the amount of benefits paid out by the Social Security system increased about (a) 5 times; (b) 10 times; (c) 17 times.
5. Using data from the graphs, write a brief paragraph explaining the relationship that apparently exists between the number of beneficiaries of the Social Security system and the amount of benefits paid out by the Social Security system. Be prepared to read your paragraph to the class.

Government and You

1. Do you think the old, the poor, and the sick should be cared for through a national system of social welfare? Why or why not?
2. In what ways, if any, would you expand the Medicare program? Justify your answer.
3. Why is it difficult to reform the OASDI?
4. Do you think the federal government should support higher education? Why or why not?
5. Are there any changes you would recommend in current programs of urban renewal? Justify your answer.
6. Do you agree that all veterans, regardless of whether they saw active military service, are entitled to veterans' benefits? Why or why not?

Activities

1. Interview an official of your nearest Veterans Administration hospital or community mental health center, and report some of that institution's services and activities.
2. Prepare a series of bar graphs showing the changes in Social Security payments in 10-year intervals since the program began.
3. Write a brief biography of Upton Sinclair, Dr. Harvey Washington Wiley, or Dr. Frances O. Kelsey, stressing that person's contribution to the nation's health.
4. Draw a poster encouraging people to join the VISTA program.
5. Research an urban renewal project that has taken place during the past decade in one of the nation's 20 largest cities. Prepare a report noting the effects of the project.

UNIT 9

THE COURT SYSTEMS AND JUSTICE

Chapter 27

The Federal Judiciary, the Law, and the Courts

Scarcely any political question arises in the United States that is not resolved, sooner or later, into a judicial question.

ALEXIS DE TOCQUEVILLE

CHAPTER OVERVIEW

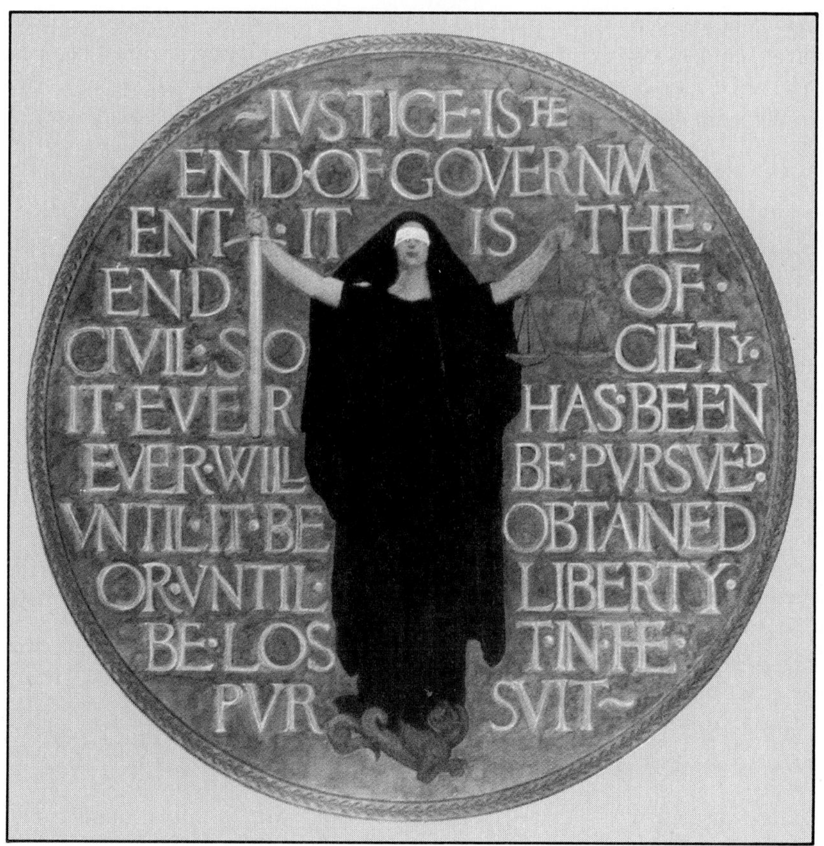

"Law"—a 1907 painting by Edwin Austin Abbey—quotes Alexander Hamilton: "Justice is the end [goal] of government. It is the end [goal] of civil society. It ever has been, ever will be pursued until it be obtained or until liberty be lost in the pursuit."

1 THE LAW

The government of the United States is a government of ***law***—the set of rules, rights, and obligations that are binding on a society. In contrast to custom or habit, law is a formal code of conduct that is enforced by the power of the nation. In the United States political ideals go beyond the desire for a merely orderly society. Americans strive for a free, just, and democratic society. To meet the goals of the nation, Americans require a body of laws that is clear, thorough, and flexible enough to adapt to changing times.

Law in a democratic society must reflect the will of the majority. Law must also guarantee the essential rights of the minority. Law must be predictable and just, applying equally to all people in all parts of the land. The nature of law in any society is a reflection of its values and ideals. In the United States those ideals are perhaps best represented by the words above the entrance to the Supreme Court: "Equal Justice Under Law."

Law in the United States can be classified by its source, by its subject matter, and by its level, or arena.

The Six Forms of Law

Law in the United States stems from six primary sources: the Constitution, statutes, rules and regulations, tradition, common sense, and international agreements. Thus, there are six forms of law.

Constitutional Law The basic structures of American government—the United States Constitution, state constitutions, and interpretations of the Supreme Court—establish the body of ***constitutional law.*** The Second Amendment of the Constitution is an example of constitutional law. It reads:

A well regulated Militia, being necessary to the security of a free State, the right of the people to keep and bear Arms, shall not be infringed.

The exact meaning of this sentence and how it applies, for example, to gun control legislation, would be an appropriate subject for constitutional law.

Statutory Law The thousands of laws, or statutes, that are passed each year by Congress, the state legislatures, city councils, and other lawmaking units make up the body of ***statutory law.*** Statutes can range from a Congressional decision to build a new aircraft carrier to a local leash law for the control of stray dogs. All statutes must conform to the basic requirement of constitutional law.

Administrative Law Rules and regulations issued by administrative agencies of the executive branch of government form ***administrative law.*** Congress delegates authority to the executive branch to make such rules as are necessary to carry out its administrative responsibility. For example, the regulations of the Federal Communications Commission must be followed by anyone operating a radio or television station.

Over the past 50 years administrative rules and regulations have increased in number and complexity. The volume of administrative law today is greater than that of statutory law. The federal courts may review any administrative law to ensure that it is in accord with constitutional and statutory law. The courts may also judge whether an action of an administrative agency is proper and within its authority.

Common Law Unwritten, judge-made law based upon custom, tradition, and precedent forms the body of ***common law,*** which originated in twelfth-century England when royal judges traveled around the country making decisions based on local custom. Under common law a judge decided each new case by citing a decision in a similar earlier case, an action called invoking the ***rule of* stare decisis,** a Latin term meaning "let the decision stand." Whenever a judge made a new decision, it established a rule that could then apply to similar cases. The decision, though not written as a statute, became a part of the body of common law.

Common law adapts to changing times and conditions. If there is a strong reason to do so, a judge may reverse an established decision in common law and create a new precedent. Today most of the principles of common law have been transformed by legislative bodies into statutory law. When constitutional, statutory, or administrative law cannot be applied to a case, American judges still rely on common law tradition.

Law of Equity What if the city, to make room for a new sidewalk, planned to chop down a beautiful shade tree in front of your home? What if someone decided to build a dam that would flood your property? Must you wait until after a wrong has been committed to seek legal assistance? The law of equity provides a common-sense remedy, a way of preventing an obvious wrong from occurring.

Like common law, ***equity*** is judge-made law. It derives from the idea of natural law, a law based on reason, and seeks to ensure justice where statutory or common law does not apply. The most common remedy under equity law is the ***injunction,*** a court order to prevent a specific person from performing a specific action.

International Law Treaties and agreements among nations, decisions of international courts, and international customs compose ***international law.*** International law is binding only if nations willingly submit themselves to it. There is no global police organization to enforce international law. A nation must be willing to accept the terms of a treaty or a decision of the International Court of Justice or a resolution of the United Nations.

Criminal and Civil Law

Law may also be classified according to its subject matter as either criminal or civil. Many states provide separate courts for criminal and civil proceedings.

Criminal law specifies offenses against the public. It defines illegal conduct and prescribes the appropriate punishment. A criminal case is brought by a government—federal, state, or local—against a person accused of violating a specific law.

Civil law governs the relations between individuals and defines their legal rights. It involves a wide range of matters, including property rights, business contracts, divorce, and injury due to negligence. In a civil case one party brings another party to court based on a ***suit,*** or legal claim. For example, someone may sue a manufacturer if the use of its product resulted in personal injury.

Most civil cases involve private persons or corporations, but the government can also be party to civil action. The federal government, for example, can bring an antitrust suit against a corporation engaged in restraint of trade.

To illustrate the difference between criminal and civil law, suppose a person has a car accident while driving under the influence of alcohol. In the accident another person is injured. The driver may be tried under criminal law for violating state laws about driving while intoxicated. The driver may also be sued in a civil action by the injured party to recover damages.

The function of the court is to settle disputes involving matters of law. All disputes, however, do not end up in court. Many are settled informally through negotiation or mediation with a third party because court action may take too much time and be too expensive. The number of cases, however, continues to grow each year.

Federal, State, and Municipal Law

Law may also be classified according to the level of government at which it is passed and enforced. There is federal law, state law, and municipal law. This division is reflected in the organization of the courts in the United States.

Section Check

1. Define: law, rule of *stare decisis,* equity, injunction, suit
2. What are the six forms of law?
3. How did common law originate?
4. What is the difference between criminal and civil law?

---

2 THE AMERICAN JUDICIAL SYSTEM

The courts in the United States resolve disputes between individuals and between the government and individuals. They operate with all six forms of the law. The courts interpret the federal and state constitutions; settle conflicts between statutory, constitutional, and administrative law; invoke and establish common law and equity; and may rule on treaties.

The Framers of the Constitution recognized the need for a court system in Article 3, Section 1, which establishes the right to create a complete judiciary.

The judicial Power of the United States, shall be vested in one Supreme Court, and in such inferior Courts as the Congress may from time to time ordain and establish.

The American judicial system, as it exists today, consists of thousands of courts.

The judiciary in the United States is basically a dual system that consists of a complete federal court system and 50 state court systems. There are more than 100 federal courts, including the Supreme Court, the Courts of Appeals, and the District Courts. Each of the states also maintains a separate court network that includes various levels of courts.

The Role of the Courts

The responsibility of the courts is to find the facts and determine the law with respect to a particular case. In the United States, before a case can be brought into court, there must be a real dispute between opposing parties. American courts rest upon an ***adversary system*** in which the two sides of a dispute argue before an unbiased jury and a neutral judge.

All disputes are not appropriate for court action. Some may be private. The referee cannot be sued because you think there was a wrong call on a football play. Increasingly, however, legal rights and obligations have expanded. This has been especially dramatic in the area of civil rights and in the efforts to end racial discrimination.

Other disputes may be inappropriate for the courts because they are political and involve questions that should be resolved by the elected representatives of the people, not by the courts. But the line between the political and the nonpolitical may be subject to disagreement. Where constitutional issues have been involved—especially those

The official record of the first Supreme Court session, which met in New York in 1790, is called the Fine Minute Book.

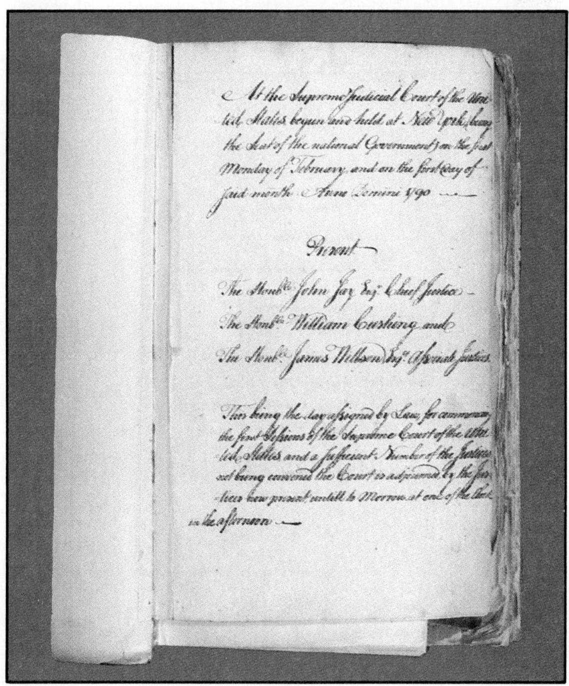

At the Supreme Judicial Court of the United States begun and held at New York, being the Seat of the national Government, on the first Monday of February, and on the first day of said month Anno Domini 1790 —

Present —

The Honble John Jay Esq. Chief Justice —
The Honble William Cushing and
The Honble James Wilson Esqrs. Associate Justices.

This being the day assigned by Law for commencing the first Session of the Supreme Court of the United States and a sufficient Number of the Justices not being convened the Court is adjourned by the Justices now present untill to Morrow at one of the Clock in the afternoon —

involving civil rights and civil liberties—some judges have been more willing than others to enter political areas.

Judges are to be impartial, but inevitably they are more than neutral umpires. The Constitution does not speak for itself. Its meaning must be interpreted. Laws are broadly written and sometimes vague. In applying law to concrete situations, judges give shape to law as it is enforced. In this sense judges make law.

The State Courts

Most legal business in the United States is handled at the state level. The state courts interpret the state constitution and the laws passed by state legislatures. They hear the great majority of all criminal and civil cases, about 10 million each year.

There are significant differences in structure among the 50 state court systems. Some states have a relatively simple, unified system. Other states have a complex system, with all sorts of special courts. In some states there are separate civil and criminal courts. To make all this more confusing, almost every state uses different names for its courts. The highest court, the court of last resort, usually is called the supreme court, but several states use other terms. Connecticut calls its court of last resort the Supreme Court of Errors.

A simplified model shows the typical structure of state court systems in the United States. About 90 percent of all court activity takes place at the state level.

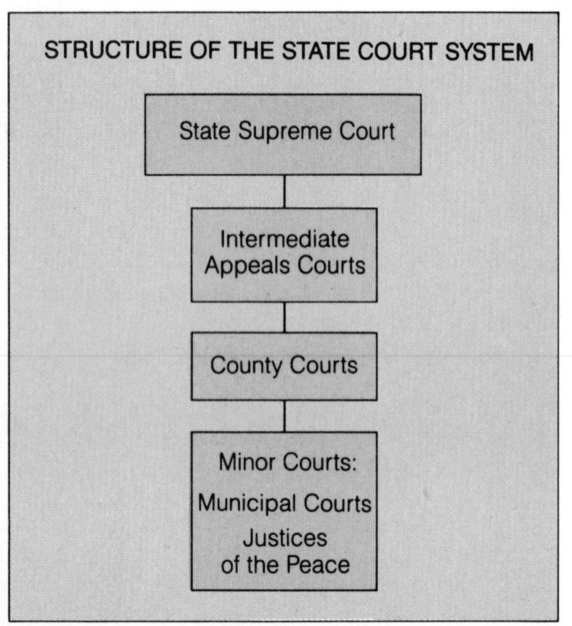

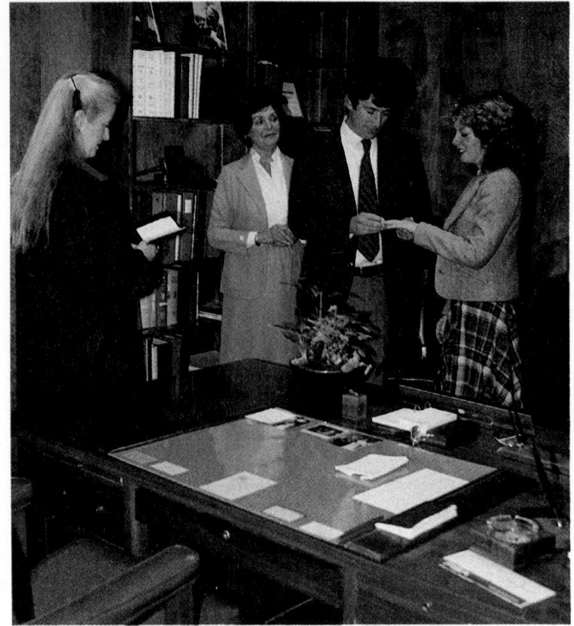

A judge performs a civil marriage ceremony. Although marriage laws vary from state to state, all state judges are empowered to conduct civil marriages. In some states, justices of the peace may also conduct civil marriage ceremonies.

Despite these variations, there is a basic pattern in the structure and organization of the state court systems. The systems can be viewed as pyramids with minor courts at the base and the state supreme court at the top.

Minor Courts Minor courts are basically of two types. The first minor court is handled by an official called the justice of the peace. The second type is the municipal court.

The office of ***justice of the peace*** originated in the Middle Ages and came to the American colonies from England. Today "JP" courts are found mainly in rural areas and small towns. A justice of the peace, or magistrate, handles petty criminal matters called ***misdemeanors*** and civil cases involving not more than $200. Much of a JP's case load may involve traffic violations. In addition a JP may issue hunting and fishing licenses and perform civil marriage ceremonies. A JP need not have a law degree, and JP court procedures are often informal.

A ***municipal court*** has jurisdiction within an urban area. A municipal judge generally has legal training, and the court procedures are formal. In most cities the municipal court is divided by function into separate courts for civil and criminal matters. Civil cases usually involve sums no greater than

$1,000. Criminal cases are limited to misdemeanors, such as littering or disturbing the peace. In addition, there may be a traffic court, a juvenile court, and a domestic relations court dealing with family legal matters.

The decisions of these minor courts may be appealed to the court at the next level, usually the county court. Ordinarily, judgments of the minor courts are not appealed because it is often too costly for the penalty involved. If there is an appeal, however, the case will be tried all over again. It is only in appeals from justices of the peace and municipal courts that a case is retried on appeal. In other cases review by the higher court is made by an examination of the record of the trial court.

County Courts Major civil cases and criminal cases involving more than petty misdemeanors are heard in the county courts. Sometimes called trial courts, superior courts, or district courts, the county courts are where most of the work of the state judicial system takes place. Trial by jury in state proceedings is most frequently conducted in county courts. The county courts, as the name implies, have jurisdiction within a county.

A number of special courts may be found at the county level, including courts for juveniles, orphans, domestic relations, and for the probate of wills, deeds, and estates. The judgment of a county court may be appealed, but only about 5 percent of county court cases are appealed.

INSIGHT

Small Claims Court

The case may involve a fence that is falling into a neighbor's yard or a mechanic who repaired someone's car and was never paid. The defendant, the one who is sued, and the plaintiff, the one who is suing, may be neighbors or friends. Though they may never have appeared in court before, they present their own cases. A judge listens to their stories, decides the case, and awards damages.

The court is a small claims court, one of thousands of local courts throughout the country established to hear minor disputes without the procedure of lengthy lawsuits and jury trials. As its name implies, a small claims court handles cases brought by individuals with small monetary claims against one another. Some states limit claims to $500; others allow claims up to $5,000. The average claim limit is between $750 and $1,000. Cases most commonly brought before a small claims court include breach of contract, failure to pay for goods or services, claims against landlords, claims for defective goods or improper service, and negligence.

The procedure for making a claim is simple. Usually the plaintiff files a claim with the clerk of the court. Filing fees range from $2 to $10. The clerk sets a date and notifies the defendant against whom the claim is made. Notification may be made by mail or in person by an officer of the court. In most states a small claim is heard within 30 days. That way the details of the case will be fresh in the minds of the plaintiff and the defendant. In rural or suburban areas the judge may be a justice of the peace or a town judge. In cities the small claims court may be part of the municipal court.

On the day of the hearing in court the plaintiff and the defendant usually speak for themselves, without the aid of a lawyer. This is in keeping with the court's role as a "people's court." The plaintiff and defendant testify under oath, present evidence, and answer questions. After the judge has heard all the evidence, a decision is made. Usually the decision involves an award of monetary damages. The decision of a judge in small claims court, as in any other court, is binding.

In California the highest court is called the supreme court. Its 7 members—a chief justice and 6 associate justices—are appointed by the governor of California for 12-year terms. The California state court system also includes 5 district courts of appeal.

Intermediate Appeals Courts In about half the states an appeal from a county court case is made directly to the state supreme court. Other states provide a system of intermediate appellate courts. These are usually dispersed around the state by region. Appellate judges review appeals from municipal and county courts within their jurisdictions. Review of appeals is based on an examination of the trial record of the lower court. Decisions of the appellate courts are usually final. Only a very few cases go on to the state supreme court.

State Supreme Court The highest court in the state system is known as the supreme court. The number of judges who sit on a state supreme court varies between three and nine. In most states the state supreme court is the court of last resort for both civil and criminal cases. Texas and a few other states, however, have separate civil and criminal appellate courts.

With respect to the meaning of the state constitution and state and local laws, the decision of the state supreme court is final. Unless a federal or constitutional question is involved, a case can go no further. Supreme court justices usually decide which cases they will hear. For the most part they accept only those cases that raise significant questions about the meaning or application of law.

Selection of State Judges The quality of justice may be only as good as the judges who serve on the courts. Because judges are expected to be impartial, they must be assured of reasonable independence and security. They must be free from pressure, both from inside and outside government. A politically influenced or otherwise biased judge may bring the courts and the law into disrespect.

In about two thirds of the states, judges are selected by popular election. Lower court judges usually serve short terms. Justices of the peace, for example, typically must face election every two years. County judges serve longer terms, from 5 to 10 years. Supreme court judges may be elected for a period of anywhere from 7 years to life.

Those who support election of judges argue that judges should be accountable to the people. Judges, according to this view, should reflect the values and attitudes of the community they serve. Critics of election argue that popular election draws the judiciary into the political arena. Justice may not be served by a judge concerned with reelection. Moreover, critics feel that elections give more importance to personality than to ability.

In a few states the legislature selects judges, but the most common alternative to election is appointment by the governor. This method is not free from political manipulation; nor is it guaranteed to bring more qualified judges to the bench. There long has been debate about the advantages of election versus appointment. The two systems, nevertheless, do not differ significantly in either the quality of the judges selected or in the nature of the decisions made.

There have been a number of efforts to reform the method by which judges are selected. Several states now use modified appointment plans, following the pattern first used by California and Missouri. These plans represent a compromise between election and appointment. When a vacancy occurs, a list of qualified candidates is prepared by a nonpartisan commission. The commission is composed of citizens, lawyers, and a judge. The governor makes an appointment from the list of nominees. After serving for a period of at least one year, a judge must then be approved in a popular election.

How can biased or corrupt judges be removed? In states providing for election, they can be defeated at the polls. In states providing for appointment, a judge may be impeached for gross misconduct or abuse of authority—for "high crimes and misdemeanors," in the words of the Constitution. Such charges are not brought lightly. In most states the lower house of the legislature impeaches the official. The trial is conducted in the upper house. If found guilty of the charges, the official is forced to step down from office. Several western states also permit a judge to be recalled from office by popular vote. Recall requires a special election on the basis of a citizens' petition. Some states have established commissions to investigate charges against judges. On the basis of such inquiries judges may be censured or removed from the bench.

The Jurisdiction of Federal Courts

As set forth in Article 3 of the Constitution, federal courts have authority according to subject matter or the parties involved. By subject matter federal courts have authority in cases (1) involving interpretation or application of the Constitution, federal law, or treaties; and (2) involving admiralty and maritime law, which is law relating to shipping on the high seas and on waterways within the United States. By the parties involved, federal courts have authority in cases (1) in which the United States is a party; (2) affecting foreign diplomats in the United States; (3) between two or more states; (4) involving a state and citizens of another state; (5) between citizens of different states; (6) between citizens of the same state claiming lands under grants of different states; and (7) between American citizens and foreign countries or the citizens of foreign countries.

Article 3, Section 1, of the Constitution organizes the judicial department of the United States. The Supreme Court is the only federal court specifically created by the Constitution. Other federal courts are established by Congress.

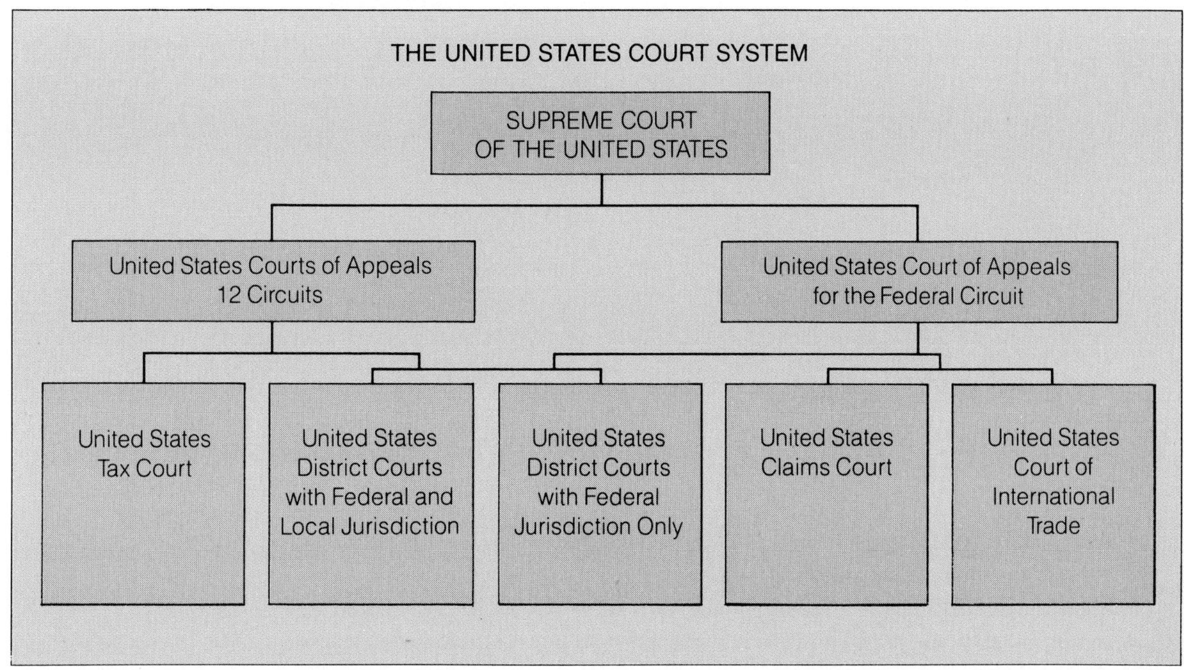

In some cases, between two states, for example, Congress has given the federal courts ***exclusive jurisdiction.*** This means that only federal courts may hear such cases. But in other cases, federal and state courts have equal authority, or ***concurrent jurisdiction.*** In a suit involving citizens of different states, for example, a state court may hear the case if both parties to the suit agree.

The Structure of the Federal System

Article 3 of the Constitution established the Supreme Court and granted Congress the power to create lesser courts. In the Judiciary Act of 1789 Congress established a system of federal courts that is organized on three levels—the District Courts, the Courts of Appeals, and the Supreme Court. The Federal court system also includes a number of special courts with jurisdiction over particular kinds of cases.

The United States District Courts The basic courts of the federal system are the United States District Courts. Federal civil and criminal cases begin in these courts. There are 94 District Courts with 515 judges. Each state has at least one District Court; most states have two; and the largest have four. There are District Courts for the District of Columbia and Puerto Rico, each with the same jurisdiction as the 89 District Courts in the 50 states. Each of the United States territories of the Virgin Islands, Guam, and the Northern Mariana Islands has a District Court. These courts also have jurisdiction over many local matters which, within the states, would be decided by state courts.

Federal civil and criminal cases originate at the district level—in the District Courts. Decisions in these cases may be appealed at the circuit level—in the Courts of Appeals. What law established the federal court system?

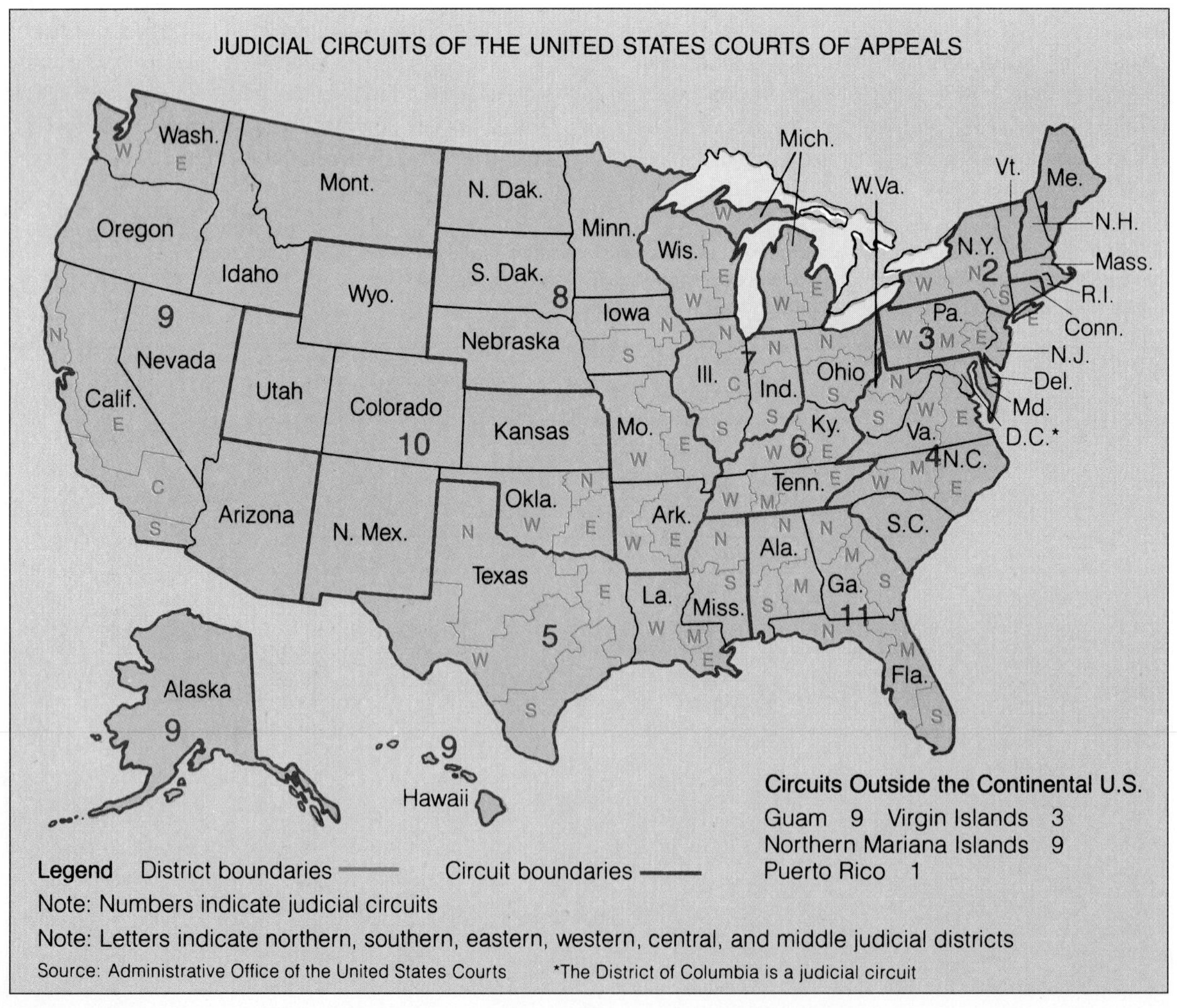

Military trials, or courts-martial, are governed by distinct military laws rather than by civilian laws. How did military personnel acquire the full constitutional protection of citizens?

The number of judges in each district varies from 1 to 27. Over the years the number of federal district judges has been increased, but the case load per judge still continues to grow. The large volume of cases often means long delays—sometimes as long as three years—before a case is actually brought to trial. The District Courts now hear about 200,000 cases each year. In most cases the verdict of the district judge is final. Less than 10 percent of these verdicts are appealed.

The United States Courts of Appeals Appeals from the District Courts and from various federal regulatory agencies are heard in the United States Courts of Appeals. Appeals usually number more than 25,000 cases each year. Except for a very few cases that are taken by the Supreme Court of the United States, the decisions of the Courts of Appeals are final.

The Courts of Appeals are organized into twelve circuits. Each circuit has 4 to 24 judges, headed by a Chief Judge. Normally, three judges sit together on a panel to review cases. No new factual evidence is introduced in an appellate review. It is based on an examination of the record of the District Court or administrative agency. Most cases are decided solely on the basis of the official documents submitted. In only the most important cases will the attorneys for each side make oral arguments before the court.

Special Courts The federal court system also includes five special courts with jurisdiction in specific kinds of cases: the Court of Claims, the United States Tax Court, the Court of International Trade, the Court of Customs and Patent Appeals, and the Court of Military Appeals.

The Court of Claims has authority to hear suits brought by citizens against the government of the United States. In theory the federal government cannot be sued except by its own consent. Otherwise the government could be disrupted by all sorts of unfounded claims. The government, however, does in fact allow itself to be sued, but the range of suits permitted is fairly narrow. Most arise out of disputes over public contracts or claims of personal injury caused by federal employees.

The United States Tax Court settles disputes between taxpayers and the Internal Revenue Service.

The Court of International Trade hears disputes arising out of duties imposed on goods imported into the United States and other disputes involving international trade.

The Court of Customs and Patent Appeals has appellate authority over the decisions of the Patent and Trademark Office and the Tariff Commission.

The Court of Military Appeals is a civilian court empowered to review decisions made by military courts. It has authority to apply and interpret military law. It is the court of last resort in military justice. Thus the Supreme Court does not have the power to review its decisions.

Military law is distinct from civilian law. It is governed by a concern for military efficiency and discipline. Until the 1960's military personnel had only limited constitutional rights. Today, as a result of a series of Supreme Court decisions and the passage of the Military Justice Act of 1968, men and women in the military have almost the same constitutional protections as do civilians. In addition, the Supreme Court held in 1969 that civilian courts had authority over "off-base, non-service connected" offenses committed by military personnel in the United States during peacetime.

Appointment of Federal Judges

The Constitution gives the President the power to appoint federal judges. Appointment requires confirmation by a simple majority of the Senate. A number of considerations may restrict the President's choice.

First, the President, following the custom of senatorial courtesy, is expected to consult informally with senators from the state where the judicial appointment is to be made. Thus a senator of the President's own party has approval power over an appointment if it involves his or her home state. In practice the senator often selects the federal judge.

Federal judgeships may be among the most important appointments a President can make because federal judges exercise great power. Political considerations bear heavily on a President's choice. Most judges are appointed from within the President's party. President Kennedy's appointments were 92 percent Democratic. President Nixon's appointments were 93 percent Republican. In many cases appointments to the bench may be a reward for political loyalty. In addition to party considerations, the President may be influenced by the policy positions of available candidates. Whether candidates are liberal or conservative and whether they share the President's views on matters likely to come before the court are important considerations.

The American Bar Association (ABA), the most distinguished organization of the legal profession, watches the appointment of federal judges very closely. Its Committee on the Federal Judiciary investigates the qualifications of each nominee for the federal courts. In a report to the Justice Department the nominees are rated on a scale from "Extremely Well Qualified" to "Not Qualified." The ABA evaluation on each candidate is an important factor in the selection process.

The Constitution prescribes no minimum qualifications for federal judges. In practice all are appointed from the legal profession. Some may be leading attorneys, others professors of law. Some come directly from politics—from Congress or state legislatures. While no previous experience is required for appointment to the federal bench, many come from state courts. By tradition, appointment to the Courts of Appeals is made from the ranks of federal district judges.

By and large the federal selection process works well. The quality of federal judges is relatively high. Some observers feel that the federal system should provide a model for the state selection process. "The genius of the federal system," writes one author, "may be its pluralism. The Justice Department, the senator, the ABA, special-interest groups, and the press are all permitted a voice." The lesson here, the author concludes, is "maximize, don't minimize, the participants in the process. Let everyone be heard and do it as openly as possible."*

Judges on the Court of Military Appeals, the Tax Court, and the District Territorial Courts serve fixed terms. All other federal judges are appointed for life. They serve on "good behavior" until their resignation, retirement, or death. There is no compulsory retirement age. The justification for ***life tenure*** rests on the importance of judicial independence. Life tenure acts to shield the judge from pressures that might influence judicial decisions.

All judges, unfortunately, are not above criticism. In any court system there may be biased, incompetent, or corrupt judges. The Constitution provides for the removal of these judges by impeachment and conviction. A judge guilty of gross misconduct or judicial tyranny may be impeached by a majority vote of the House of Representatives. The trial is then held in the Senate, with conviction by a two-thirds vote. The most common complaint about the federal impeachment system is that this process is too difficult. Short of impeachment, some judges guilty of misconduct have chosen to resign rather than face exposure and scandal. Of the 10 federal judges who have been impeached since the founding of the Republic, 4 were convicted and removed from the bench.

---

*Donald Dale Jackson, *Judges*. New York: Atheneum, 1974, p. 388.

Section Check

1. Define: justice of the peace, misdemeanor, exclusive jurisdiction, concurrent jurisdiction, life tenure
2. Identify: Small Claims Court, Judiciary Act of 1789, United States District Courts, Supreme Court, the American Bar Association
3. Explain the dual nature of the American judiciary system.
4. What basic pattern reveals itself in the structure and organization of the state court system?
5. What are the three basic levels of the federal courts?

3 THE SUPREME COURT

The United States Supreme Court is the highest court in the nation, the only court specifically mentioned in the Constitution. All other federal courts have been created by Acts of Congress. The Constitution does not name the number of judges to serve on the Supreme Court; that has been determined by Congress. In its first years the Court's membership varied between 5 and 10. In 1869 the number was set at 9, and there it has remained—a Chief Justice and 8 associate justices.

Jurisdiction

The Supreme Court has original and exclusive jurisdiction in cases involving foreign ambassadors, ministers, and consuls, and those in which a state is a party. It alone hears cases between two or more states. In other cases jurisdiction is shared with the District Courts. Since 1789 only 155 cases have originated in the high court. Today the majority of cases originating in the Supreme Court are between states, involving disputes over such subjects as water rights and boundaries.

The Supreme Court also hears appeals. Most cases that come to the Supreme Court are appeals of decisions handed down by federal courts or from the highest state courts. These appellate cases reach the Supreme Court normally by one of two routes: on appeal or by writ of certiorari.

Appeal In certain classes of disputes the losing party has a theoretical right to have the Supreme Court review the case. An ***appeal*** may apply where a state supreme court has declared a federal law unconstitutional, or where a state law is claimed to conflict with a federal law or the Constitution. One of the parties in such a case may ask the Supreme Court to review the ruling of a lower court. In theory the Court must hear the appeal in such cases. In reality, though, the Supreme Court chooses the cases it hears. It may reject an appeal on the grounds that it does not present a substantial federal question.

CHIEF JUSTICES OF THE UNITED STATES

Chief Justice	President by whom Appointed	Years of Service
John Jay	Washington	1789-1795
John Rutledge*†	Washington	1795
Oliver Ellsworth	Washington	1796-1800
John Marshall	John Adams	1801-1835
Roger B. Taney	Jackson	1836-1864
Salmon P. Chase	Lincoln	1864-1873
Morrison R. Waite	Grant	1874-1888
Melville W. Fuller	Cleveland	1888-1910
Edward D. White†	Taft	1910-1921
William Howard Taft	Harding	1921-1930
Charles Evans Hughes†	Hoover	1930-1941
Harlan F. Stone†	F.D. Roosevelt	1941-1946
Frederick M. Vinson	Truman	1946-1953
Earl Warren	Eisenhower	1953-1969
Warren E. Burger	Nixon	1969-

*While Congress was not in session Rutledge was appointed by President Washington on July 1, 1795. He presided over the August 1795 term of the Supreme Court. The Senate refused confirmation of his appointment on December 15, 1795.

†The following four men served as associate justices before being appointed Chief Justice: John Rutledge, 1789-1791; Edward White, 1894-1910, Charles E. Hughes, 1910-1916; and Harlan Stone, 1925-1941. Rutledge was appointed as associate justice in 1789 but resigned a year and a half later, having attended no sessions of the Court. Hughes resigned as associate justice in 1916 in order to seek the Presidency. White and Stone were associate justices when appointed Chief Justice.

The Chief Justice of the United States is the presiding officer of the Supreme Court. As leader of the third branch of government, the Chief Justice announces the decisions of the Court and assigns to the justices the responsibility of writing opinions for cases.

Certiorari When there is no theoretical right of appeal, a case may be brought before the Supreme Court on a ***writ of certiorari,*** a Latin word meaning "to be made certain." Certiorari applies when a party alleges that a lower court has made an error in its handling of a case. About 85 percent of the cases before the Court come by certiorari. The Court will accept only those petitions that raise significant federal questions. If at least four justices believe it to be sufficiently important, the Court will take the case. The Court has complete discretion in this circumstance. More than 90 percent of all certiorari petitions are denied.

By refusing to take a case, the Supreme Court allows the decision of the lower court to stand. The refusal does not necessarily imply the Court's approval of the decision. It may mean simply that the Court is not yet ready to make a ruling. Perhaps the justices do not believe that it is the best case for a ruling on the issue. Perhaps the case involves a political question that the Supreme Court does not want to address.

It is important to remember that whether a case is taken by appeal or certiorari, review is at the discretion of the Court. Former Chief Justice Frederick Vinson once said:

To remain effective, the Supreme Court must continue to decide only those cases which present questions whose resolution will have immediate importance far beyond the particular facts and parties involved.

The Court continues carefully to choose the cases it will hear.

In a given year more than 4,000 cases come before the Supreme Court. Most are readily dismissed. In only some 175 cases does the Court hand down full, written opinions. Even for those few cases taken, the road to the high court is long and often expensive. The average case may take from two to five years to reach the bench.

The Court at Work

The United States Supreme Court building stands across from the Capitol in Washington. The Court building is patterned after a Greek temple. Over the massive bronze doors at its entrance are carved the words "Equal Justice Under Law."

The formal sessions of the Supreme Court are held for 36 weeks each year, from October until June. Inside the Court the atmosphere is one of

In 1929 Chief Justice William Howard Taft (third from left) and six of his colleagues viewed an architect's model of the new Supreme Court building. Taft, the only person to have served as President and as Chief Justice of the United States, convinced Congress to appropriate funds for the new Supreme Court building.

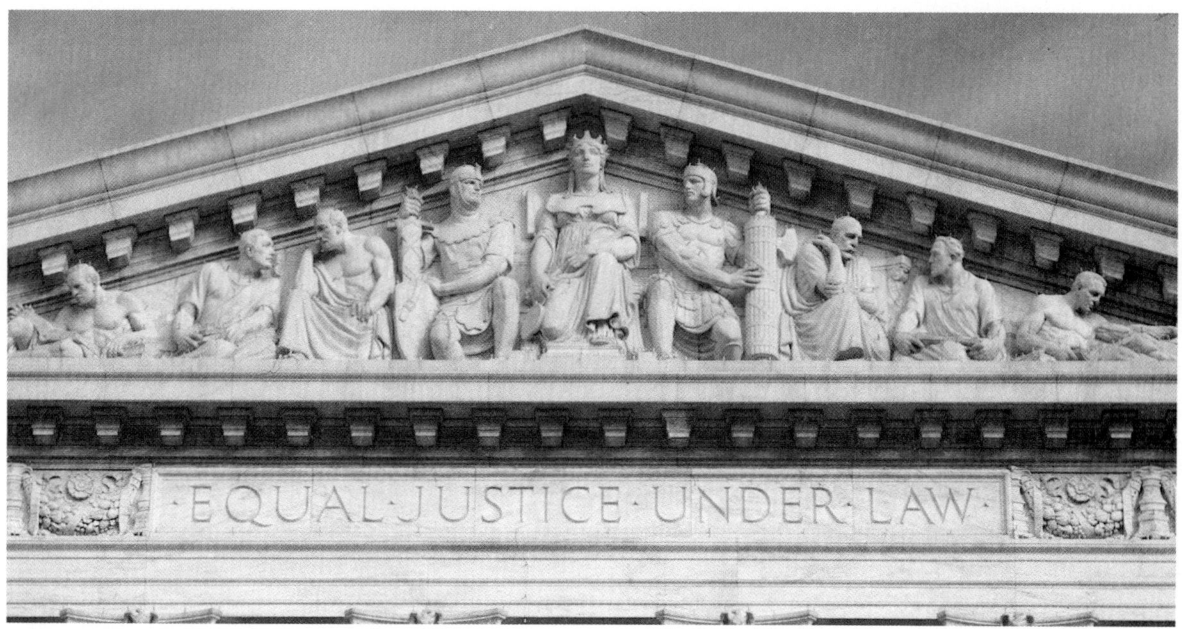

"Equal Justice Under Law"—the phrase over the entrance to the Supreme Court building—embodies the Court's spirit. This spirit has endured since the early days of the Republic.

silence and dignity. At the marshal's cry, "Oyez, oyez, oyez," those assembled in the courtroom rise. From the parted dark red drapes, the nine justices in black judicial robes appear. The Chief Justice sits at the center of the great bench. The associate justices are seated on each side in the order of seniority, or their appointment to the Supreme Court.

Oral Arguments For two weeks out of every month the Court hears oral arguments. Usually four cases are presented each day, three or four days a week. There are no witnesses or jurors. The justices have already read detailed ***briefs*** stating the arguments for each side. In oral arguments each attorney is normally allotted half an hour to present as convincing a case as possible. The justices often interrupt with questions. If the federal government is party to a case, the argument before the Court is presented by the United States solicitor general.

Conference The justices meet in conference on Wednesday afternoons and all day Friday. They consider new appeals and discuss the cases heard that week in oral argument. The conference is held in absolute secrecy. No one but the nine justices is present. No record is kept of the discussion or the votes taken. What is known of the conferences comes from the memoirs and private notes of the justices—usually available only many years later.

By tradition the justices all shake hands with each other as they enter the conference room. As the first order of business they consider as many as 100 new motions, petitions, and appeals. A case is placed on the conference list if at least one justice requests that it be considered. Otherwise it is placed on the "dead list." The Supreme Court receives more than 4,000 appeals each year. A few justices will read every request, but most rely on their law clerks to prepare summaries of each case. Only those cases presenting substantial federal questions are likely to be brought before the conference. In conference the justices discuss the merits of the case and vote whether to accept it for review. Under the informal "rule of four," the Court will accept a case only if four justices vote to grant review.

Also at the conference the justices consider each case presented that week in oral argument. Beginning with the Chief Justice, and then in the order of seniority, each justice expresses his or her views on the case. Discussion during these conferences may become quite heated. A tentative vote is usually taken, with the most junior justice voting first. After a decision is reached, the Court explains its reasoning in a formal written statement, called an opinion.

Opinions The opinions express the position of the Court. A ***unanimous opinion*** expresses the agreement of all justices voting on an issue. The

Court is unanimous about 30 percent of the time. The rest of the time, the Court reaches agreement by a majority vote and issues a ***majority opinion.*** When a decision is unanimous, or if the Chief Justice is in the majority, the Chief Justice writes the opinion or assigns it to another justice. If the Chief Justice is in the minority, the senior associate justice in the majority assigns the majority opinion. There is some effort to share the responsibility for writing majority opinions.

The justice to whom the majority opinion has been assigned may labor for months in preparing the draft. These drafts are circulated among all the justices. They comment, argue, and negotiate. Substantial changes may be required in order to retain the support of other justices. Perhaps additional changes may win over a dissenting justice to the majority. In the course of argument justices may shift positions. A divided vote in conference may change to unanimity. Shaped in this way, the opinion is often the work of many minds. A clear and meaningful decision should represent a solid majority. A number of separate concurring opinions will only be ambiguous and inconclusive in terms of policy. A narrow 5–4 vote will weaken the force of the decision. Such decisions may be reversed easily.

Thurgood Marshall's experience as an attorney for the National Association for the Advancement of Colored People (NAACP) and as a federal appellate judge made him exceptionally qualified to protect civil rights as a Supreme Court justice.

Each justice usually writes between 13 and 18 majority opinions each year, in addition to concurring and dissenting opinions. A ***concurring opinion*** is expressed when a justice agrees with the Court's decision, but not with the reasoning behind it. A ***dissenting opinion*** expresses opposition to the decision of the Court. Some of the important dissents of the past have become the majority opinions of the Court today.

Opinion Day Traditionally, Monday is Opinion Day at the Supreme Court. The justices deliver their opinions on each case, usually in summary form. The full opinions—often quite lengthy—are published later. The legal core of the Court's decision is binding on all lower courts, and the ruling becomes a part of constitutional law.

Appointment and the President

The selection of the justices of the Supreme Court is made by the President, with the "advice and consent" of the Senate. These appointments are likely to be among the most important decisions made by any President. The President's choice is limited by many of the same considerations that affect the selection of federal judges. The most important is senatorial confirmation. The Senate takes this power seriously and has refused to confirm 26 of the 136 nominations made for the Supreme Court. In recent years two nominations by President Nixon were rejected by the Senate. In one case the Senate raised serious questions as to the judicial ethics of the nominee. In the other the Senate found the nominee to be unqualified.

A number of other considerations influence the President's selection of Supreme Court Justices. Of fundamental importance is the candidate's judicial qualifications—integrity, experience, and legal scholarship. The President may make some effort to assure balanced representation on the Court. Thus the Court has come to reflect the geographic, religious, and ethnic diversity of the American people. In 1967 Thurgood Marshall became the first black ever to serve on the Supreme Court. In 1981 President Reagan appointed the first woman—Sandra Day O'Connor—to the Court.

SUPREME COURT APPOINTMENTS SINCE 1953

Administration	Chief Justice	Associate Justices							
	Frederick M. Vinson (1946-1953)	Hugo Black (1937-1971)	Felix Frankfurter (1939-1962)	Sherman Minton (1949-1956)	William O. Douglas (1939-1975)	Tom C. Clark (1949-1967)	Stanley Reed (1938-1957)	Robert H. Jackson (1941-1954)	Harold H. Burton (1945-1958)
Eisenhower	Earl Warren (1953-1969)			William Brennan (1956-)			Charles Whittaker (1957-1962)	John M. Harlan (1955-1971)	Potter Stewart (1958-1981)
Kennedy			Arthur Goldberg (1962-1965)				Byron White (1962-)		
Johnson			Abe Fortas (1965-1969)			Thurgood Marshall (1967-)			
Nixon	Warren Burger (1969-)	Lewis Powell (1972-)	Harry Blackmun (1970-)					William Rehnquist (1972-)	
Ford					John Paul Stevens (1975-)				
Carter									
Reagan									Sandra D. O'Connor (1981-)

Supreme Court in 1953 — Present-day Supreme Court

The President's power to appoint justices to the Supreme Court is granted in Article II, Section 2, of the Constitution. This power has enabled many Presidents to have a long-lasting influence on the Court's ideology. Which President may have had the greatest impact on the present-day Supreme Court?

Political considerations are also likely to sway the President's decision. The President tries to make a selection that is popular with important interest groups and with members of the party. The President will, of course, try to choose a candidate who shares a similar political philosophy.

Politics has influenced appointments to the Court from the beginning. President John Adams sought to perpetuate Federalist party power through the appointment of John Marshall as Chief Justice. Each succeeding President has sought to leave an imprint on the Court.

Judicial Independence

To some extent Presidents have tried to pack the Court, to appoint justices favorable to their own viewpoints. The most dramatic and controversial instance of this involved President Franklin D. Roosevelt. During his first term (1933–1936) much of his New Deal legislation was struck down by the Court as unconstitutional. To bypass the "nine old men," Roosevelt proposed to expand the Court's membership to fifteen. The "Court-packing Bill," as it was called, never got past the Senate. Ultimately,

A 1937 cartoon satirizes President Franklin Roosevelt's attempt to gain ideological control over the Supreme Court. What was Roosevelt's "court-packing" plan?

during his four terms in office, Roosevelt succeeded in replacing all nine Supreme Court justices with his own appointments.

No President can be assured that the justices appointed to the Court will perform as expected. This was as true for Roosevelt as other Presidents. Not only are the justices likely to exercise independent judgment, but their future judicial behavior may be very difficult to predict.

The 1974 case of *United States* v. *Nixon* provides a classic illustration of judicial independence. In his first three years in office Nixon attempted to transform the Court with the appointments of four conservative justices, including Chief Justice Warren Burger. In 1973 the Watergate scandal broke. Congress and the President locked in a tug-of-war over the infamous White House tapes—recordings of conversations held in the President's office. These tapes were believed to implicate the President in a cover-up of the scandal. Claiming executive privilege, Nixon refused to release the tapes as ordered by Federal District Judge John Sirica. In a deepening constitutional crisis, the Supreme Court agreed to hear the case. With Justice Rehnquist not participating, the Court ruled 8–0 against the President. Chief Justice Burger spoke for the unanimous Court: "No person, not even the President of the United States, is above the law." Fifteen days later, facing certain impeachment, President Nixon resigned.

Court Leadership

The Chief Justice may exercise great influence in shaping the character of the Supreme Court. The Court is known and characterized by the name of the Chief Justice. Thus we speak of the Warren Court and the Burger Court.

The Warren Court From 1953 until 1969, the Supreme Court reflected the commitment of Chief Justice Earl Warren to civil rights and civil liberties. Under Warren the Court became the custodian of the rights of the minority. The number of cases expanded as the poor and disadvantaged now sought access to the federal courts. The Supreme Court's decisions had far-reaching impact. Not surprisingly, they also provoked controversy and opposition. The unanimous 1954 *Brown* v. *Board of Education of Topeka* decision, which declared segregation in schools unconstitutional, is a landmark case in the struggle for racial equality in the United States. Opponents, however, denounced the ruling as a violation of states' rights and called for massive retaliation. In a series of cases, the Warren Court sought to protect the rights of criminal defendants. Critics accused the Court of "coddling criminals" and "handcuffing the police." In its decisions on the First Amendment freedoms of speech, press, assembly, and religion, the Warren Court was no less controversial.

Some of the Court's most vigorous critics were themselves justices. The Court was frequently divided, particularly in the area of criminal justice, where cases were often decided by a 5–4 vote. Many of its more thoughtful critics felt that the Court had too readily taken on political questions. Some felt the Warren Court was too liberal because it went beyond what the Constitution required—that it was reading its own values and preferences into the Constitution.

In response to criticism of the liberal Warren Court, Richard Nixon, in his 1968 Presidential campaign, promised to appoint conservative, "law-and-order" justices to the bench. Nixon wanted "strict constructionists who saw their duty as interpreting law and not making law." In 1969 Earl Warren retired as Chief Justice. To replace him, President Nixon appointed Warren Burger, a conservative judge on the Court of Appeals. He was soon joined by four new associate justices.

The Burger Court The appointment of Warren Burger brought a shift to the right in the Court's political center of gravity. Where the Warren Court had expanded access to the federal courts, the Burger

Earl Warren (above) served as Chief Justice of the United States for 16 years. In 1967 the Warren Court (from left to right, seated) included Justices Harlan, Black, Warren, Douglas, and Brennan, and (from left to right, standing) Justices Fortas, Stewart, White, and Marshall.

Court now sought to restrict it. The courts were overburdened, the Chief Justice argued, by problems that could be better handled by Congress and the state legislatures. Moreover, cases that did not clearly involve federal questions should be left to the state courts. Overall, the Burger Court sought to minimize federal intervention in state matters.

In its decisions the Burger Court reflected a generally conservative stance. In various rulings, for example, it "chipped away" at the protections given to criminal defendants. At the same time, however, other decisions gave conservatives little comfort. The Burger Court extended the right to counsel to poor defendants in misdemeanor trials. It strengthened the rights of prisoners. It took a strong stand against wiretapping without a warrant. In the area of civil rights the Court outlawed segregation in private schools, and it upheld court-ordered busing for racial integration of schools.

No Court's decisions can always be described as "liberal" or "conservative." Neither are the justices easily categorized. As the chart on this page shows, Justices Brennan and Marshall reflect the old Warren Court and are predictably liberal in their votes. Chief Justice Burger, Justice Rehnquist, and Justice O'Connor are conservative. The other justices, while generally conservative, are less predictable. They can swing either way. A justice might be counted as conservative in a criminal justice case, yet liberal on a First Amendment or civil rights question. And justices may change during their years on the bench.

(continued on page 664)

The ideological stance of the Burger Court is reflected in the voting patterns of its members.

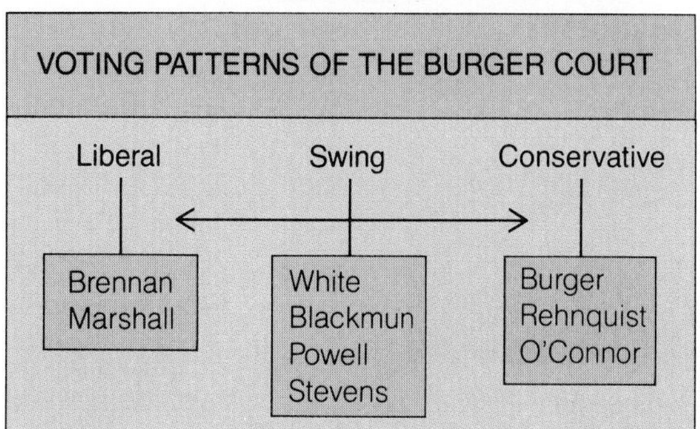

PROFILE

The Supreme Court Today

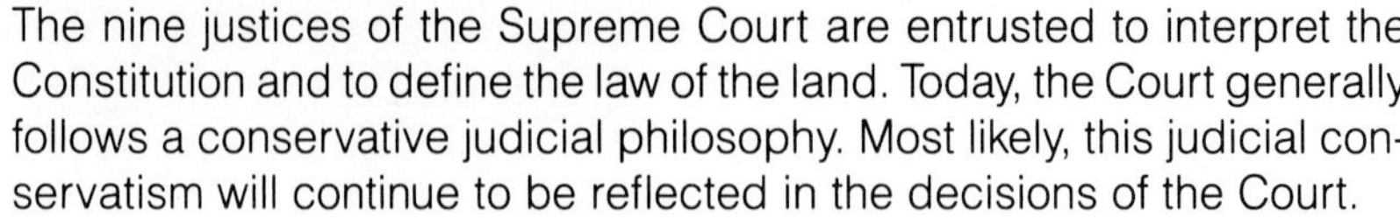

The nine justices of the Supreme Court are entrusted to interpret the Constitution and to define the law of the land. Today, the Court generally follows a conservative judicial philosophy. Most likely, this judicial conservatism will continue to be reflected in the decisions of the Court.

Warren Burger, Chief Justice

From a position of assistant attorney general in the Eisenhower administration, Warren Burger was appointed in 1955 to the Court of Appeals for the District of Columbia. President Nixon appointed him Chief Justice of the United States in 1969. Burger's position is generally conservative, especially with respect to criminal justice. He is a forceful advocate of a reduced role of the courts in American society.

William Brennan, Jr.

President Eisenhower appointed Brennan to the Supreme Court in 1957. He had served as a justice of the state supreme court of New Jersey. Brennan is highly regarded as a judicial scholar and wrote many of the key decisions of the Warren Court. Today, as a liberal on the more conservative Burger Court, he largely writes dissents.

Byron White

In college White was a scholar-athlete. He played professional football for Pittsburgh, then left for Oxford as a Rhodes Scholar. Active in Kennedy's 1960 Presidential campaign, he served as deputy attorney general in the Kennedy administration. He was appointed to the Court in 1962. White is usually to be found on the conservative side of the Court.

Thurgood Marshall

Long with the National Association for the Advancement of Colored People, Marshall led the NAACP's legal struggle against racial segregation. Before the Supreme Court in *Brown* v. *Board of Education* (1954), he successfully argued that segregation in public schools is unconstitutional. In 1961 he was appointed by President Kennedy to the Courts of Appeals. In 1965 he was named solicitor general by President Johnson. In 1967 Marshall became the first black to be appointed to the Supreme Court. There he has served as a forceful advocate for minorities and the nation's poor.

Harry Blackmun

Like many of his colleagues, Blackmun served on the Courts of Appeals before being appointed to the Supreme Court in 1970. He is a lifelong friend of fellow Minnesotan Chief Justice Warren Burger and shares Burger's conservativism. But Blackmun has demonstrated independence on the Court. Parting with the Chief Justice, he has joined the liberals in a number of decisions.

Lewis Powell, Jr.

A former president of the American Bar Association, Powell was appointed to the Court in 1971 from a distinguished legal practice. Described as a "moderate" and "careful conservative," he commands a position of influence on the Court. His sense of judicial self-restraint is balanced by a concern for individual rights.

William Rehnquist

Rehnquist is the most conservative member of the Court. He gained wide attention as an articulate speaker for the Nixon administration while serving as an assistant attorney general. He was appointed to the Court in 1971 by President Nixon.

John Paul Stevens

In 1975 President Ford appointed Stevens to the Supreme Court from the Courts of Appeals. A judicial and political moderate, Stevens is noted for his well-crafted opinions. He has been described as a "judge's judge."

Sandra Day O'Connor

Appointed in 1981, O'Connor is the first woman to serve as a member of the Supreme Court. Having served as majority leader of the Arizona state senate, she brings to the Court a background of practical political experience. As a judge on the Arizona appeals court, she was known for judicial restraint in leaving most questions to the legislative and executive branches.

Judicial Review

The most controversial power of the Supreme Court is ***judicial review,*** the power to declare a law or official action to be unconstitutional. This power is not granted expressly in the Constitution. It was asserted by the Court in *Marbury* v. *Madison* in 1803. In brief, the Court ruled that it had the authority to declare a section of the Judiciary Act of 1789 in conflict with the Constitution and therefore void.

Since 1803 the Court has invoked the power of judicial review over one thousand times. The most significant impact of judicial review comes from its ***deterrent effect*** on federal and state action. Because the Supreme Court has a veto over the other branches of government, the legislative and executive branches must be careful that all laws are drafted and enforced in accordance with the Constitution as interpreted by the Court.

The meaning of the Constitution is not always self-evident. People may in good faith disagree over its intent. The Supreme Court is empowered to resolve these differences. The Court interprets the Constitution and adapts its meaning to changing times. In *McCulloch* v. *Maryland* (1819), Chief Justice Marshall said that the Constitution was "intended to endure for ages to come and, consequently, to be adapted to the various crises of human affairs." One hundred years later, Justice Louis Brandeis wrote, "Our Constitution is not a strait jacket. It is a living organism. As such it is capable of growth—of expansion and adaptation to new conditions." Justice Charles Evans Hughes in 1907 stated it more bluntly: "We are under the Constitution, but the Constitution is what the judges say it is."

Activism and Self-Restraint

Judicial review, the Constitution, and the structure of the judicial system give the Supreme Court enormous power. How should this power be used? How active a role should the Supreme Court take in the making of public policy and law? Over its history the Supreme Court has swung between an active and a passive role. The more aggressive role has been labeled ***judicial activism.*** The more passive role has been described as a policy of ***judicial self-restraint.***

An activist justice feels that the Court is not simply a neutral reviewer of executive and legislative action. The Court, in this view, is a powerful instrument of social change, a creative governmental force. One of the most activist of justices was Hugo Black. About constitutional and legislative intent he wrote, "No higher duty, no more solemn responsibility, rests upon this Court, than that of translating into living law and maintaining this constitutional shield."

An activist Court may be either conservative or liberal. In the period from 1865 to 1937 a conservative Court actively sought to protect business interests from governmental regulation. The Court struck down numerous state and federal laws during this period. Between 1920 and 1937, 32 Acts of Congress were declared unconstitutional.

The Warren Court took judicial activism in another direction. From 1953 to 1969 it helped create political and social change in the United States. This Court outlawed racial segregation in public schools, strictly protected the rights of criminal defendants, and forced reapportionment of state legislatures.

In contrast to the position of judicial activism is that of judicial self-restraint. Those who favor self-restraint argue that the Court should avoid taking the initiative on social and political questions. Legislative acts should be upheld unless they are in clear violation of the Constitution. The Court should defer to the legislative and executive branches unless called upon to decide a particular issue.

Justice Felix Frankfurter was deeply committed to judicial self-restraint. He repeatedly argued that the Court should pass only on the constitutionality of laws—not on their wisdom. In a famous dissent Frankfurter stated that "as a member of this Court I am not justified in writing my private notions of policy into the Constitution, no matter how deeply I may cherish them or how mischievous I may deem their disregard." He was convinced that "the responsibility for legislation lies with legislatures, answerable as they are directly to the people."

The problem, as Justice Frankfurter found in the Court, is that justices differ in their interpretation of what Congress or the states can and cannot do. Ultimately the conflict between judicial activism and self-restraint involves debate over how far the Court can and should go. The line between interpreting and legislating may be very fine indeed.

Judicial Intervention

Among the most controversial forms of judicial activism are those involving lower federal courts. The issue focuses on recent intervention by the courts in areas of legislative and executive responsibility. In some districts, for example, federal courts have taken responsibility for running schools, hospitals, and prisons. Some people say that the political branches of government have been unwilling to make unpopular but necessary decisions. According to former Courts of Appeals Judge Shirley Hufstedler, "Resolving conflicts between people is not a popular task because there are always losers. Legislators understandably prefer to delegate these hard choices to someone else—namely judges." Such action further burdens the courts with decisions that are properly political.

Often, however, the courts have intervened to overturn or block decisions taken by the political branches of government. Chief Justice Burger has attacked what he sees as a takeover of legislative and executive authority by federal courts "under the guise of judicial review." In a 1978 Supreme Court decision Burger described the situation as "judicial review run riot." The case reversed a lower court decision which had delayed the development of three nuclear power plants. In a unanimous 7–0 opinion the Supreme Court condemned such judicial intervention: "Time may prove wrong the decision to develop nuclear energy. But it is Congress or the states within their appropriate agencies which must eventually make that judgment."

Judge Shirley Hufstedler (Ninth Circuit) was for many years the only woman serving in the federal appellate system.

Limitations on Judicial Authority

The Supreme Court is limited in many ways. One self-imposed limitation is the Court's respect for legislation. Of some 40,000 laws passed by Congress, the Court has held only 104 to be in violation of the Constitution. Of the many thousands of state laws enacted, only about 900 have been declared unconstitutional.

The Court achieves stability through the weight it gives to *stare decisis,* or judicial precedent. On occasion the Court reverses one of its earlier decisions. Generally, however, the Court is reluctant to overrule itself. The Court is more comfortable with gradual change than with dramatic reversals of policy.

The Constitution itself places significant checks upon the Court's authority. A ruling by the Court may be reversed by constitutional amendment. More frequently, when in conflict with the Court over the interpretation of a law, Congress may rewrite or repeal the legislation in question.

Another limitation involves enforcement of the Court's decisions. A ruling may be ignored or resisted. When President Jackson disagreed with Chief Justice John Marshall in an 1832 decision, he said: "John Marshall has made his decision. Now let him enforce it." The Supreme Court sets general policy. The lower federal and state courts apply that policy. Then the executive branches of the national and state governments enforce it. This is another example of the balance of powers in the United States government.

In general the Court is not likely to be out of step with the people over the long run. Only for short periods has it ever gone against the views of the electorate. The Court, of necessity, is a creature of its time. The justices generally share with their fellow citizens the prevailing social values and preferences. When the Court does fall out of step, it is only a matter of time before the old justices will be replaced by new Presidential appointments. Yet the Court will never be the mouthpiece of the executive branch, or even of the people. The Court will never yield its independence. The Supreme Court remains, as Woodrow Wilson once wrote, "the balance wheel of our whole constitutional system."

Section Check

1. Define: appeal, writ of certiorari, brief, judicial review, judicial activism, judicial self-restraint
2. Identify: Opinion Day, the Warren Court, the Burger Court, *United States* v. *Nixon* (1974), Sandra Day O'Connor
3. Distinguish between majority opinion, concurring opinion, and dissenting opinion in the decisions of the Supreme Court.
4. What considerations does the President make in selecting justices for the Supreme Court?
5. What is the central point in the conflict between judicial activism and judicial self-restraint?

4 THE DEPARTMENT OF JUSTICE

The Department of Justice and its various divisions are a part of the executive branch. As such, they are directly responsible to the President. This department also sees to the administration of justice and is closely connected with the judiciary.

The Department of Justice is a Cabinet-level department that is sometimes called the nation's largest law firm. It began in 1789 as the Office of the Attorney General, with a staff of two, and was reorganized in 1870 as the Department of Justice. Today, the department contains six divisions and a complex maze of bureaus, offices, and boards.

The Department of Justice performs six main functions. (1) It gives legal advice to the President. (2) It represents the United States government in court. (3) It enforces most federal criminal laws. (4) It supervises the work of United States attorneys and marshals. (5) It enforces the immigration, naturalization, and narcotics laws. And (6) it operates the federal prisons.

Attorney General

The Attorney General is the head of the Department of Justice, is a member of the Cabinet, and is appointed by the President and confirmed by the Senate. Today the Attorney General has three responsibilities. First, as chief law enforcement officer of the federal government, the Attorney General represents the United States in legal matters. Second, the Attorney General directs the activities of the Department of Justice. Finally, the Attorney General gives legal advice to the President and to the heads of the executive departments. The Attorney General's chief assistant and the second-ranking member of the department is the deputy attorney general.

Well-known United States Attorneys General are the first Attorney General, Edmund Randolph (below); Harlan Stone (bottom), who was appointed Attorney General by Calvin Coolidge and later became Chief Justice; and Robert Kennedy (right), who served his brother John F. Kennedy.

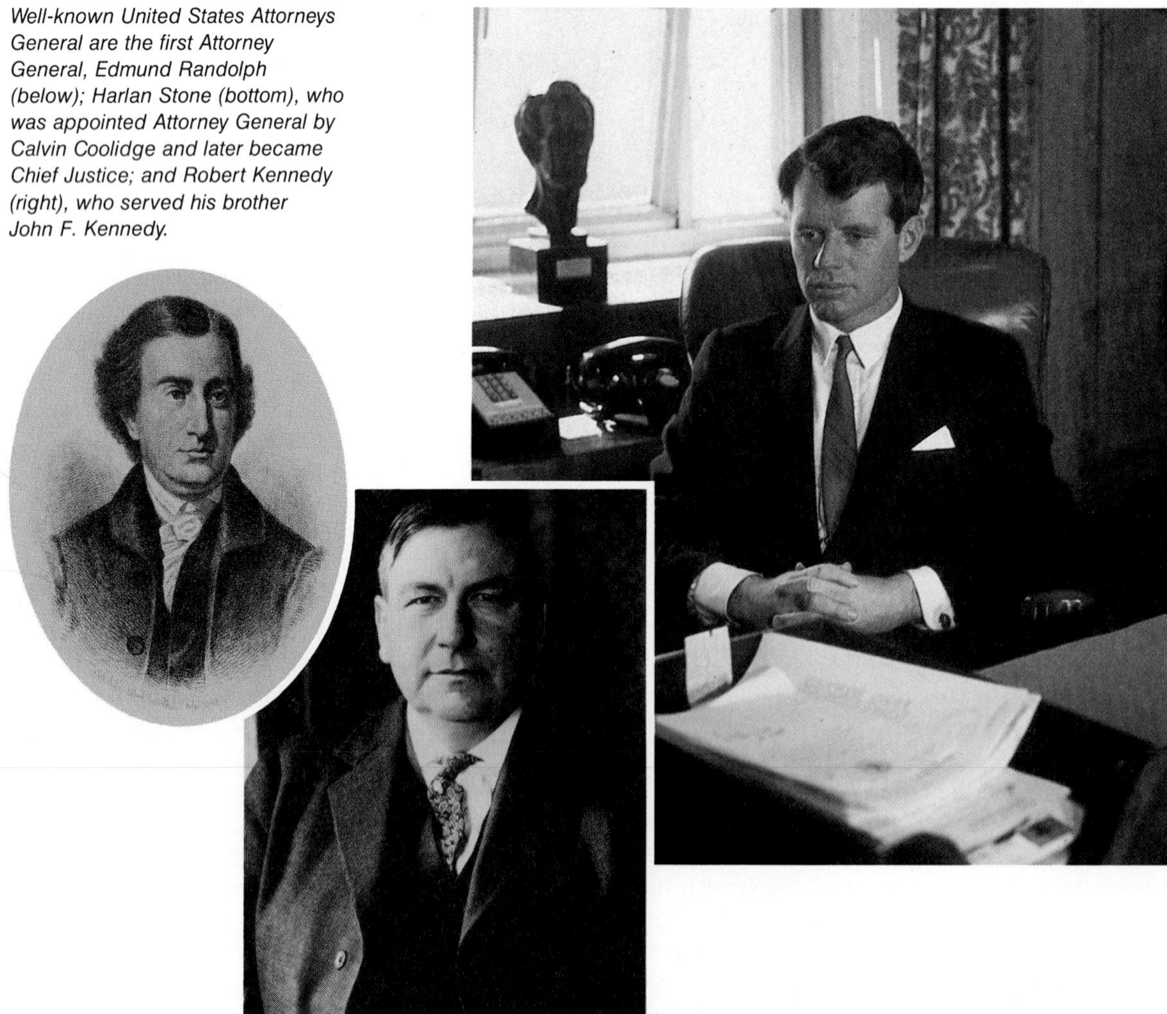

LEGACY

Justice

> Justice is founded in the rights bestowed by nature upon men. Liberty is maintained in the security of justice.
>
> *Inscription on the Department of Justice building, Washington, D.C.*

Solicitor General

The solicitor general is the Justice Department's third highest ranking officer and represents the federal government before the Supreme Court.* The government may appear in court as a plaintiff suing those who violate federal laws, or as a defendant being sued by individuals or states. In either event, the solicitor general decides what cases the government will ask the Supreme Court to review and what position the government should take in cases already before the Court. The solicitor general personally argues the more important cases before the Supreme Court. When the government loses a case in the federal district courts, the solicitor general must also decide whether or not to appeal the decision.

The Department's Divisions

There are six divisions within the Department of Justice. Each is concerned with a specific area of legal activity, and each is headed by an assistant attorney general.†

Antitrust Division The Antitrust Division enforces federal antitrust laws by investigating complaints that these laws have been violated and by prosecuting the violators. Its basic task is to maintain competition within the free enterprise system.

The division combats two main threats to economic competition. The first is ***conspiracy,*** a predetermined effort within an industry to fix prices or restrain trade. The second is ***monopoly,*** the control of a market by a single large enterprise.

Civil Division The Civil Division handles most of the noncriminal cases to which the government is a party. It represents the United States, its agencies, and its officials just as a private law firm represents a large corporation. It defends the federal government against suits brought by private persons, groups, or corporations. For example, somebody might sue the government for damages caused by the negligence of a government official or challenge the ruling of a federal agency. The Civil Division is also in charge of suits brought by the federal government, such as a suit against a corporation to recover money owed under contract.

Civil Rights Division The Civil Rights Division enforces federal civil rights laws. These laws prohibit various forms of discrimination in voting, education, employment, housing, the use of public accommodations, and the administration of federally funded programs.

Criminal Division The Criminal Division is the largest division of the Justice Department. It enforces all federal criminal laws except those specifically assigned to other units. Federal crimes under its jurisdiction include kidnapping, bank robbery, interstate auto theft, and aircraft hijacking. The Criminal Division has special sections to fight organized crime and narcotics. Its Internal Security section enforces laws involving sabotage, espionage, and treason.

Land and Natural Resources Division The Land and Natural Resources Division handles all civil suits involving federal lands and resources. It deals with boundary disputes, land titles, oil and mineral leases, water rights, and the private cutting of timber on government land. The division also represents the federal government in civil cases brought by Native Americans. It handles both civil and criminal cases involving air, water, and noise pollution and is generally responsible for the protection of the environment in the United States.

---

*In the lower courts, the government is usually represented by Department of Justice attorneys or United States attorneys or assistant attorneys. The solicitor general, however, *may* represent the government in any court.

†There are three other assistant attorneys general. One supervises the internal affairs of the Justice Department, one heads the Office of Legislative Affairs, and one heads the Office of Legal Counsel. All nine of the assistant attorneys general are appointed by the President and confirmed by the Senate.

Tax Division The Tax Division acts as lawyer for the Internal Revenue Service in disputes between the government and the taxpayer. Some of these disputes involve federal crimes such as tax evasion and fraud. Others involve honest differences over the interpretation of the tax laws. The Tax Division also helps the IRS to collect federal revenue.

United States Attorneys and Marshals

There are 94 federal District Courts in the United States and its possessions. For each of these courts, there is a United States attorney and a marshal.* Both officers are appointed to a four-year term by the President with Senate approval. Both are under the supervision of the Department of Justice and the Attorney General.

United States attorneys represent the government in the federal district court, handling both civil and criminal cases. Usually they act as chief prosecutor in cases that involve violations of federal law.

Marshals arrest people who violate federal laws. They also act as officers of the federal District Courts. In that capacity they are responsible for carrying out court orders, maintaining order in the courtroom, protecting witnesses and judges when necessary, and keeping custody of federal prisoners. Marshals are sometimes called upon to perform special law enforcement duties for the Attorney General, such as the control of civil disturbances and the enforcement of school desegregation.

The Federal Bureau of Investigation

The Federal Bureau of Investigation (FBI) is the best known of the federal law enforcement agencies. It was established in 1908 as the major fact-finding agency of the Department of Justice. It investigates all violations of federal law except those in areas specifically assigned to the United States Customs Service, the IRS, and the Secret Service. The jurisdiction of the FBI covers crimes related to domestic security, such as espionage, sabotage, and terrorism. It covers assault on a President or the assassination of a President or other federal official. It covers civil rights violations. It covers theft of government property and fraud against the government. And it covers such criminal activities as kidnapping, bank robbery, and the interstate transportation of stolen goods.

The director of the FBI is appointed by the President, with the consent of the Senate, for a 10-year term. The bureau's headquarters are in Washington, and it maintains 59 field offices in cities throughout the United States as well as several offices abroad. It has some 19,000 employees, of whom 7,870 are special agents. The rest are scientists, laboratory technicians, and office staff.

Most FBI agents have degrees in either law or accounting, the latter because investigation of such crimes as embezzlement requires expert knowledge of accounting practices. All agents undergo an intensive course at the FBI National Academy at Quantico, Virginia. Training ranges from physical conditioning and basic police skills to courses in advanced criminology and constitutional law. Courses at the academy are also open to select local and state law enforcement officials and to a few officials from foreign countries.

The FBI Laboratory has the most advanced instruments in the world for analyzing evidence, such as firearms, bloodstains, hair, and paint. Its facilities are available free of charge to all the law enforcement agencies in the United States.

The FBI's National Crime Information Center is a computer-based information network. Within seconds, it can relay data—on wanted persons or stolen property, for example—to law enforcement agencies throughout the country. The FBI also collects crime data from police departments across the nation and publishes regular statistical reports on crime.

State and local law-enforcement officers receive training at the FBI Academy Laboratory in Quantico, Virginia.

*At the present time, the United States attorney and marshal of Guam also serve the Northern Marianas. Thus, the actual numbers of attorneys and marshals total 93 each.

PROFILE

The FBI Lab

Each year the FBI Laboratory makes thousands of investigations using the most sophisticated scientific equipment available. Founded in 1932 by J. Edgar Hoover, the FBI Laboratory has grown from a single office equipped with a single microscope to a large research center where everything from scanning electron microscopes to powerful computers are used to examine evidence and track down clues in the fight against crime.

In the documents section of the lab, experts match handwriting or typewriter print samples to link a suspect to a crime. In one famous case, FBI technicians searched for the kidnapper of a one-month-old child by comparing the ransom note with writing specimens on file. After searching more than 2 million specimens, they matched the ransom note with the handwriting of an ex-convict on probation. The man was arrested and found guilty of kidnapping. Experts in the documents section also study shoe prints and tire treads found on the scene of a crime. So sophisticated are the techniques used today that technicians can examine a photograph of footprints in the snow and determine whether the person who made them was running or walking.

The FBI Laboratory's scientific analysis section uses advanced scientific equipment to study firearms, hairs and fibers, blood, paint chips, broken glass, and a wide variety of other physical clues that may connect a criminal with a crime. Lab technicians can examine a single human hair and determine the race, sex, and age of the person from whom it came. A speck of dirt no larger than a pinhead can be used to connect a person with a crime. In one well-known case, paint chips discovered on the clothing of a hit-and-run victim were found to be from a Buick, Pontiac, or Oldsmobile. When investigators turned up a suspect, the lab technicians compared the paint chips with the paint on the car, a 1965 Buick. The paint samples matched, and the driver of the car was arrested.

The FBI Laboratory's facilities are available without charge to all state, county, and municipal law enforcement agencies in the United States. Because the findings of the lab are often used in court, the FBI also furnishes experts to testify without cost in state and federal trials.

During the directorship of J. Edgar Hoover, who served as the head of the agency from 1924 to 1972, the capture of well-known criminals brought the FBI worldwide publicity. Today, the bureau concentrates its efforts on organized crime, the corruption of public officials, bank embezzlement and other forms of white-collar crime, and foreign espionage. The bureau has a long tradition of self-government, due largely to Hoover's refusal to be swayed by outside political pressure. Its public image, which was once highly favorable, suffered somewhat in the 1970's when the investigations that followed the Watergate scandal disclosed the use of such illegal practices as wiretaps, the harassment of radical groups, and the falsification of records. Today, the operations of the FBI are under close scrutiny by the Attorney General, various Congressional "watchdog" committees, and the press.

Other Bureaus

In addition to the FBI, the Justice Department contains a number of other bureaus, agencies, and offices. Some of the more important ones are the Immigration and Naturalization Service, the Drug Enforcement Administration, and the Bureau of Prisons.

The Immigration and Naturalization Service administers the immigration and nationality laws, which have been discussed at length in Chapter 7.

The Drug Enforcement Administration (DEA) is the leading federal agency in the grim battle against the illegal use of narcotics. A large percentage of all crimes are committed by people under the influence of drugs they have obtained illegally or by addicts seeking money to buy illegal drugs. In addition, organized crime is heavily involved in the sale and traffic of illegal drugs. Many suicides, accidental deaths, and injuries are caused by drug abuse. The DEA enforces the federal drug laws and works closely with state and local authorities to prevent drug abuse. It also works with other nations to suppress the international traffic in illegal drugs.

The Bureau of Prisons is responsible for the custody of persons convicted of federal crimes and sentenced to serve time in prison.

Section Check

---

1. Define: conspiracy, monopoly
2. Identify: Federal Bureau of Investigation, Immigration and Naturalization Service, Drug Enforcement Administration, Bureau of Prisons
3. How do the functions of the Attorney General differ from those of the solicitor general?
4. What two federal officers are found in a federal District Court?
5. Why do many FBI agents have degrees in accounting?
6. In what three ways does the FBI help other law enforcement agencies in the United States?

SUMMARY

The government of the United States is a government of laws. Law may assume six different forms: constitutional, statutory, administrative, common, equity, and international. Law may be classified by its subject matter as either civil or criminal.

The United States has a dual court system with separate federal and state networks. Most legal business is conducted at the state level. Each state has a pyramid-shaped structure with minor courts at the base and a state supreme court at the top. State judges are selected through such methods as election, legislative appointment, and gubernatorial appointment.

The federal system is organized on three levels. They are the District Courts, the Courts of Appeals, and the Supreme Court. Federal judges are selected by the President. But senators, the American Bar Association, and other sources lend their judgment to the decision-making process.

The Supreme Court is the highest court in the land. Most of its cases involve review of a lower court decision under a writ of certiorari. The Court expresses itself through unanimous, majority, concurring, or dissenting opinions. Supreme Court justices are appointed by the President. These appointments may be among the most important choices a President will make.

Judicial review is one of the Supreme Court's most important powers. By this power the Court may declare any law to be in violation of the Constitution and therefore void. Different Supreme Courts have varied over the years in using their power of judicial review. Aggressive use of this power is called judicial activism. A more passive approach to the Court's role is known as judicial self-restraint. The Court's independence is a basic protection of the constitutional system of checks and balances.

The Department of Justice is the nation's highest law enforcement agency. It is headed by the Attorney General, assisted by the deputy attorney general. The solicitor general represents the federal government before the Supreme Court.

There are six divisions within the Department of Justice. The Antitrust Division enforces federal antitrust laws. The Civil Division represents the United States in civil lawsuits. The Civil Rights Division enforces federal civil rights laws. The Criminal Division enforces federal criminal laws. The Land and Natural Resources Division handles civil suits that involve federal land and resources. And the Tax Division represents the IRS in court.

United States attorneys and marshals work under the supervision of the Department of Justice. United States attorneys represent the government in the federal district courts. United States marshals arrest people who violate federal laws and act as officers of the federal district courts.

The Justice Department contains various bureaus and agencies. The Federal Bureau of Investigation (FBI) investigates all violations of federal law, except those in areas specifically assigned to other agencies. The Immigration and Naturalization Service administers the immigration and nationality laws. The Drug Enforcement Administration enforces the federal drug laws. The Bureau of Prisons supervises the federal prisons.

Chapter 27 Review

Using Vocabulary

Answer the questions by using the meaning of each underlined term.

1. How does constitutional law differ from statutory law?
2. What is the relationship of *stare decisis* to common law?
3. Why is a misdemeanor more likely to be a part of criminal law rather than civil law?
4. When might a justice of the Supreme Court be expected to deliver a concurring opinion? A dissenting opinion?
5. What does appeal and writ of certiorari have to do with judicial review?
6. How does judicial activism differ from judicial self-restraint?

Understanding American Government

1. What are some matters governed by international law?
2. Why do we call the American court system a dual system?
3. Describe the structure of the federal court system.
4. What are some special courts in the federal system?
5. What considerations does the President make in the selection of federal judges?
6. Why is it important that a clear and meaningful decision of the Supreme Court represent a solid majority?
7. Why have some Presidents tried to pack the Supreme Court?
8. Why is judicial review important?

Extending Your Skills: Making Comparisons from a Chart

Study the chart on page 659. Then complete the items that follow.

1. Which President appointed the first woman to the Supreme Court?
2. In the time span shown on the chart, which President appointed the most justices?
3. Which President had no opportunity to appoint any Supreme Court justices?
4. Which justice on the present Court has served the longest?
5. Which President made the most appointments to today's Supreme Court?
6. Using data from the chart, prove each of the following statements: (a) Supreme Court appointments extend a President's influence beyond the Presidential term of office. (b) There is less change in the Supreme Court than in the Presidency.

Government and You

1. Which of the six forms of law are likely to be the fairest? Which are likely to be the most arbitrary? Which forms do you think will best protect your basic rights as a citizen? Why?
2. State judges are selected by several different methods: election, appointment by the governor, appointment by the legislature, and modified appointment plans. Which of these methods is best in your opinion? Why?
3. What purpose is served by the Supreme Court presenting majority, concurring, and dissenting opinions? Why are dissenting opinions important in our judicial history?
4. The Supreme Court is fiercely independent. Sometimes the Court will go against the wishes of Congress, the President, and perhaps even the American people. Should this independence be supported? Or should the Court be more responsive to popular opinion?
5. Justice Charles Evans Hughes said: "We are under the Constitution, but the Constitution is what the judges say it is." What did he mean by this statement? Do you agree or disagree with it?

Activities

1. Make a wall chart of our federal court system. For each branch include the following information: jurisdiction, original and appellate; number of judges; how judges are elected; the judges' term of office.
2. Prepare a biographical report on a Supreme Court justice of the past.

Chapter 28

Criminal Justice and the Rights of the Accused

A free man shall be punished for a small fault only according to the measure thereof, and for a great crime according to its magnitude. . . . None of these punishments shall be imposed except by the oath of honest men of the neighborhood. No free man shall be taken, imprisoned, dispossessed, outlawed, banished, or in any way destroyed, nor will We proceed against or prosecute him, except by the lawful judgment of his peers and by the law of the land. To no one will We seel, to none will We deny or delay right or justice.

THE MAGNA CARTA

CHAPTER OVERVIEW

Aaron Burr (far left)—Vice President from 1801 to 1805—was the first person tried for treason against the United States. According to the Constitution, "No person shall be convicted of treason unless on the testimony of two witnesses . . ." Burr was acquitted in 1807 because only one witness testified against him.

1 THE RIGHTS OF THE ACCUSED

The Framers of the Constitution gave special prominence to criminal procedure and the rights of those accused of crimes. The procedures of criminal justice guaranteed by the Constitution are essential to the personal freedom of all citizens. They are so important that Justice Felix Frankfurter once said, "The history of liberty has largely been the history of observance of procedural safeguards." These safeguards, he said, have frequently "been forged in controversies involving not very nice people." Their purpose, however, is not "to convenience the guilty, but to protect the innocent." The procedure that protects one protects all in a free society.

Because crimes are often committed by "not very nice people," the procedural guarantees of the Constitution are sometimes seen as favoring the criminal. "Why should criminals have all these rights?" some may ask. Citizens are shocked when they see a person who appears "obviously guilty" set free on a technicality of criminal law. Magazine articles regularly appear with titles such as "Let's Stop Protecting the Guilty!" or "Take the Handcuffs Off the Police!" Before police can complete their paperwork, people they have arrested may be released. Community outrage builds when "the criminals are out of jail before their victims are out of the hospital."

These are legitimate concerns. The rights of the victim and of society are of the greatest importance. Yet people accused of crimes are not necessarily guilty, and, even if guilty, they deserve constitutional protections. And what if a person is wrongly accused? The Constitution requires a fair hearing for all those accused of crime.

The American judicial system is based on a ***presumption of innocence.*** Under this presumption a person is innocent until proven guilty in a fair trial. The burden of society is to prove that guilt beyond a reasonable doubt. The denial of constitutional rights to any accused citizen is a threat to the freedom of all citizens.

Due Process and Criminal Justice

The Fifth Amendment guarantees that "no person shall be ... deprived of life, liberty, or property without due process of law." ***Due process*** means, at a minimum, fair and regular procedures. Due process occupies a special role in criminal justice. The procedural guarantees of due process embodied in the Bill of Rights are essential to the discovery of truth. They are vital to the exposure of mistake, bias, and falsehood.

The procedural requirements of the Bill of Rights guarantee the accused the right to a fair trial. This does not refer simply to what goes on in the courtroom. It includes the whole of the criminal justice process, from the moment the investigation of a crime begins until a verdict is determined and a sentence imposed.

At each stage of criminal law there are specific procedural requirements. Some of these are imposed on both federal and state authorities by the Constitution. These are minimum standards with which all governments must comply. In addition, the federal government and the 50 states each have their own procedural requirements. Inevitably, this has resulted in considerable variation between federal and state practices. In recent years, however, differences have been reduced as more uniform standards and procedural requirements have been adopted by the state governments.

ISSUES

Victims' Rights

Of the first ten amendments to the Constitution five directly address the rights of persons accused of committing crimes. Subsequent court rulings have strengthened and expanded the procedures for protecting the rights of the accused. These rights are the foundation of our judicial system. But what about the victims of crime? Do they have rights that need to be defended?

In 1982 California voters enacted what has been called a "bill of rights" for crime victims. The proposition requires some people convicted of crimes to make restitution to their victims. It also places a limit on the use of the insanity defense and provides victims with a say in their assailants' sentencing and parole.

Although California's bill on victims' rights is controversial, it does represent a national trend toward protecting the victims of crime. Thirty-three states and the District of Columbia have set up funds to compensate crime victims for their injuries—some by fines imposed on convicts, some with tax money, and some from a combination of both. Officials in more than 200 communities have established special units to keep victims posted on the progress of cases against their attackers. Such units also encourage victims and witnesses to appear in court by providing transportation, child care, and paid time off from work. Several communities have adopted measures that allow a victim to influence the sentencing of a criminal—either by addressing a judge before a convict is sentenced or by submitting a written statement.

The courts have also been increasingly sympathetic to lawsuits brought by victims against their attackers and others blamed for negligence in allowing crimes to occur. In one such case members of a parole board were found guilty of negligence in releasing a prisoner who went on to commit murder. In another a woman attacked in a hotel room successfully sued the hotel for not providing sufficient security.

But the issue of victims' rights remains controversial. Some opponents charge that certain aspects of bills on victims' rights are unconstitutional—because they conflict with the rights of the accused.

Later in this chapter the various stages of criminal justice, from arrest to trial, conviction, and punishment will be studied. But the first step is an examination of the basic rights of the accused, as listed in the Constitution and as determined by Supreme Court decisions. There are nine basic protections in criminal justice: (1) the writ of habeas corpus; (2) freedom from ex post facto laws and bills of attainder; (3) freedom from unreasonable search and seizure; (4) the right to legal counsel; (5) protection against self-incrimination; (6) freedom from unnecessary imprisonment; (7) the requirement of formal charges; (8) the right to trial by jury; and (9) freedom from cruel and unusual punishment.

The Writ of Habeas Corpus

Habeas corpus is a Latin expression meaning "you should have the body." The ***writ of habeas corpus*** is a written order delivered by a judge. It forces a law enforcement officer to bring a prisoner to court and to show proof why the prisoner should remain in jail. If proof cannot be demonstrated, the judge may free the prisoner. The writ of habeas corpus is designed to prevent arbitrary arrest and imprisonment.

Arbitrary arrest today is not as common an occurrence as in the past. Today the writ of habeas corpus is used primarily to secure release from prison after people have been convicted. But it may be used in this way only after regular appeal has failed. The writ will be granted only if defendants were convicted in violation of their constitutional rights. Very few petitions for such release on a writ of habeas corpus are accepted, and in recent years, the Supreme Court has restricted its use.

Article 1, Section 9, of the Constitution provides that the "privilege of the writ of habeas corpus shall not be suspended, unless when in cases of rebellion or invasion, the public safety may require it." There have been very few suspensions. After the Civil War, in 1866, the Supreme Court held that the writ could be suspended only in those areas of the country where there were actual military operations. In recent times the privilege of habeas corpus has been suspended only once—in Hawaii during World War II. The Supreme Court later ruled that the suspension had been improper.

Prohibition of Ex Post Facto Laws and Bills of Attainder

In Article 1, Sections 9 and 10, the Constitution forbids both federal and state governments from passing ex post facto criminal laws and bills of attainder.

An ***ex post facto law*** prohibits an action ***after*** it has already taken place. The Constitution guarantees that no person shall be convicted and punished for an act that was not a crime at the time it was committed. The prohibition concerns criminal

President Abraham Lincoln used his power as commander in chief to suspend the writ of habeas corpus during the Civil War. Lincoln believed that the action was necessary to preserve the Union.

laws only because civil laws may be retroactive. A tax, for example, may be imposed on income already earned.

A ***bill of attainder*** is a legislative act that imposes punishment without trial upon a specified individual or group. The English Parliament passed many such bills during the colonial era, but few have been introduced in modern times. In 1943, though, an appropriations act included a section that forbade the payment of salary to three specific government employees. Congress objected to the political views of these people and sought to deny them their jobs. They had been labeled by the House Internal Security Committee as "crackpot, radical bureaucrats," and members of Communist groups. The Supreme Court ruled, in *United States* v. *Lovett* (1946), that this was a bill of attainder and thus in violation of the Constitution.

SUPREME COURT OF THE STATE OF NEW YORK
COUNTY OF NEW YORK

IN THE NAME OF THE PEOPLE OF THE STATE OF NEW YORK
TO ANY POLICE OFFICER IN THE CITY OF NEW YORK

Proof by affidavit having been made this day before me by
________ that there is probable cause for believing that
certain property, to wit, ________
evidence of the possession of narcotics and the means of committing a narcotics
crime is in the possession of ________
or may be found in ________

YOU ARE THEREFORE COMMANDED, ________
without prior notice, pursuant to Section 690.35 (3b) Criminal Procedure Law,
to make a search of ________
in premises ________
utilized by ________ and of the person of ________
for ________ evidence of the possession of narcotics and the means
of committing a narcotics crime, and if you find any such property or evidence
or any part thereof to bring it before the court without unnecessary delay.

WARRANT MUST BE EXECUTED WITHIN TEN (10) DAYS OF DATE OF ISSUANCE

DATED IN THE CITY OF NEW YORK, this ____ day of ________

Time: ---------

____
Justice of the Supreme Court

SNC20(9-[illegible])

Search warrants permit law-enforcement officers engaged in the investigation of crimes to conduct lawful searches and seizures.

Freedom from Unreasonable Search and Seizure

The Constitution guarantees freedom from unreasonable searches and seizures. The Fourth Amendment reads:

The right of the people to be secure in their persons, houses, papers, and effects, against unreasonable searches and seizures, shall not be violated, and no Warrants shall issue, but upon probable cause, supported by Oath or affirmation, and particularly describing the place to be searched and the persons or things to be seized.

The Court has specified that a valid ***search warrant*** must rest on the showing of ***probable cause,*** reasonable grounds for believing that an offense has been committed as charged. The warrant must specify the place to be searched and the particular items to be seized.

The search warrant is valid only for the place and goods described. A police officer in the course of a search with a warrant, however, may stumble unexpectedly on stolen or illegal property. The Court has held that although not specified in the warrant, such property may be seized legally if it is in "plain view."

Because of the urgent nature of many law enforcement situations, the Supreme Court has recognized a number of exceptions to the general requirement that a search may be conducted only under a warrant. In fact, most searches are made without warrant. Among the various exceptions are (1) search incident to arrest; (2) exigent circumstances; (3) stop-and-frisk actions; and (4) consent searches.

The most significant exception to the requirement for a search warrant is ***search incident to arrest.*** When an individual is arrested with probable cause, an officer may engage in a warrantless search. This exception arises from the need of officers to protect themselves by disarming the accused. It also serves to preserve evidence of the crime. A reasonable search can extend into the area within the "immediate control" of the person arrested to prevent the person from grabbing a weapon or destroying evidence. A more extensive search of the premises requires either consent or a search warrant—unless there are "exigent circumstances."

Situations where an immediate search may be necessary in order to prevent destruction or removal of evidence is an ***exigent circumstance.*** The time taken to get the warrant may result in the loss of the evidence. A police officer, for example, may be in hot pursuit of a robber. The robber runs into a building. If the officer first had to obtain a warrant to enter the building, the culprit would surely escape. An exigent circumstance permits the officer to enter the building without a warrant to search for the person and the evidence.

Another exception to the warrant requirement is the ***stop-and-frisk action.*** A police officer may stop and question someone who is acting suspiciously or who may be carrying a weapon. For the officer's protection a "pat down" for concealed weapons is permitted, but the search may go no further unless an arrest is made. In *Adams* v. *Williams* (1972) the Court ruled that a "tip" from a reliable informant was probable cause for a stop-and-frisk.

A search, of course, may be conducted without a warrant on the basis of ***voluntary consent,*** which is consent without force or coercion.

Wiretapping One special aspect of search and seizure law involves ***electronic surveillance***—"bugging" and "wiretapping." Does the Fourth Amendment's guarantee of freedom from unreasonable search and seizure extend to private conversation? In *Olmstead* v. *United States* (1928) the Supreme Court said that only material things—the person, home, and belongings—are protected. If the police do not actually enter the premises, the Court contended, tapping a telephone from outside does not constitute "search and seizure." Justices Holmes and Brandeis dissented. They argued that the wiretapping was unconstitutional.

In *Katz* v. *United States* (1967) the Supreme Court overturned the *Olmstead* ruling. Katz had been convicted of illegal gambling. The evidence came from a recording device the Federal Bureau of Investigation had placed in Katz's favorite public telephone booth where he sent and received gambling information. The Court ruled that the wiretap was a warrantless, illegal search. "The Fourth Amendment," the Court held, "protects people—not simply 'areas'—against unreasonable searches and seizures."

For a wiretap to be legal, it must be authorized by a magistrate in a warrant. The Crime Control Act of 1968 imposes a number of restrictions on issuing warrants for electronic surveillance. Probable cause must be established, and the court order must specify the place, person, and particular conversation sought.

Despite both federal and state laws restricting electronic surveillance, wiretapping without warrant is widespread. It is used both by government authorities and private individuals. Evidence secured either directly or indirectly from such illegal surveillance, however, is not admissible in court.

Exclusionary Rule Illegally obtained evidence is not admissible in the courts. Under the ***exclusionary rule*** evidence may be admitted only if it is secured by a warrant or under one of the recognized exceptions to the warrant requirement. The exclusionary rule was established for federal courts in *Weeks* v. *United States* (1914). Then, in *Mapp* v. *Ohio* (1961), the Court held that the exclusionary rule was binding on the states.

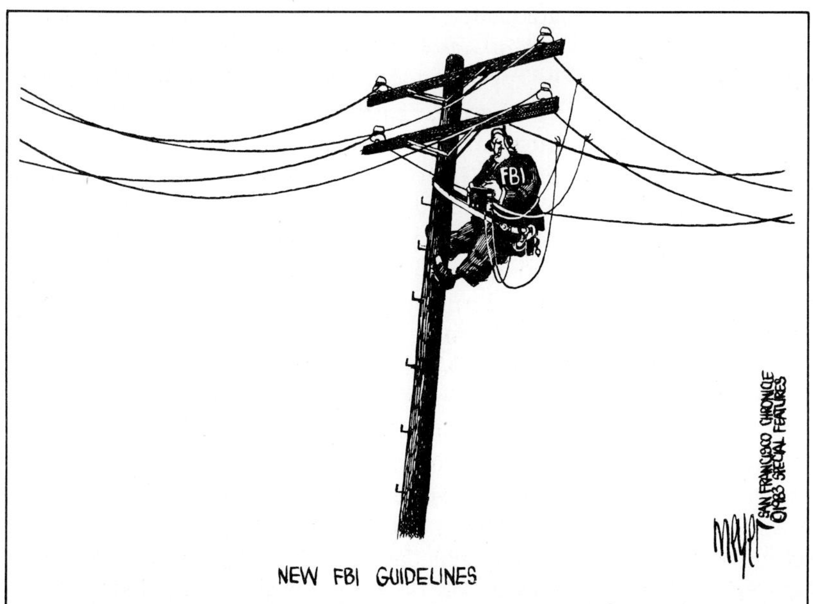

Wiretapping by the Federal Bureau of Investigation (FBI) to collect evidence against criminal suspects is criticized in a recent cartoon. Under what circumstance is a wiretap considered legal?

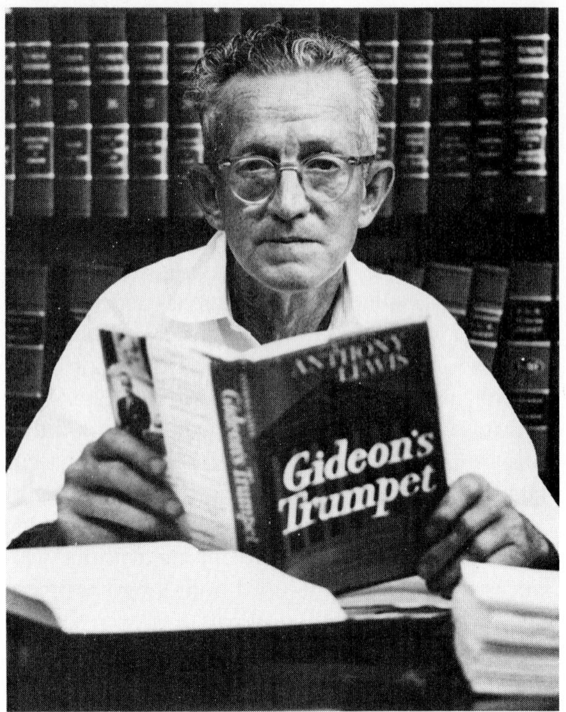

DIVISION OF CORRECTIONS

CORRESPONDENCE REGULATIONS

MAIL WILL NOT BE DELIVERED WHICH DOES NOT CONFORM WITH THESE RULES

No. 1 -- Only 2 letters each week, not to exceed 2 sheets letter-size 8 1/2 x 11" and written *on one side only*, and if ruled paper, do not write between lines. *Your complete name* must be signed at the close of your letter. *Clippings, stamps, letters* from other people, *stationery* or *cash must not be enclosed* in your letters.

No. 2 -- All *letters* must be addressed in the *complete prison name* of the inmate. *Cell number*, where applicable, and *prison number* must be placed in lower left corner of envelope, with your complete name and address in the upper left corner.

No. 3 -- *Do not send any packages without a Package Permit.* Unauthorized *packages* will be destroyed.

No. 4 -- *Letters* must be written in English only.

No. 5 -- *Books, magazines, pamphlets,* and *newspapers* of reputable character will be delivered *only if* mailed direct from the publisher.

No. 6 -- *Money* must be sent in the form of *Postal Money Orders* only, in the inmate's complete prison name and prison number.

INSTITUTION ______ CELL NUMBER ______

NAME ______ NUMBER ______

In The Supreme Court of The United States
Washington D.C.
clarence Earl Gideon
Petitioner | Petition for awrit
VS. | of Certiorari Directed
H.G. Cochran, Jr, as | to The Supreme Court
Director, Divisions | State of Florida.
of corrections State |
of Florida | No. 890 Misc.
OCT. TERM 1961
U. S. Supreme Court

To: The Honorable Earl Warren, Chief Justice of the United States

Comes now The petitioner, Clarence Earl Gideon, a citizen of The United States of America, in proper person, and appearing as his own counsel. Who petitions This Honorable Court for a Writ of Certiorari directed to The Supreme Court of The State of Florida, To review The order and Judgement of the court below denying The

While in prison, Clarence Earl Gideon wrote to the Supreme Court, explaining that he had been denied a fair trial because he was too poor to pay a lawyer. Eventually, the Supreme Court ruled that Gideon had been denied due process.

The exclusionary rule is justified in two ways. If police know that illegally obtained evidence may not be used, they will be more likely to follow constitutional warrant requirements. A second justification is that the government is not above the law. Justice Tom Clark said in the *Mapp* decision: "Nothing can destroy a government more quickly than its failure to observe its own laws, or worse, its disregard of the charter of its own existence."

Critics question whether the rule does prevent police misconduct. The police have to deal with immediate situations. They must make split-second decisions. They may not have the time to consider the judicial implications of their actions. Also, critics argue that respect for the law is undermined when people who seem clearly guilty are set free because the evidence against them cannot be used in court. As Justice Benjamin Cardoza once asked, "Is the criminal to go free because the constable blundered?"

Chief Justice Warren Burger has been a strong critic of the exclusionary rule. But he is not ready to abandon it until a meaningful substitute is developed. The problem is that alternatives have been difficult to develop. One, now used in several states, is to admit illegally obtained evidence into court if the police officer acted "in good faith."

The Right to Counsel

Among the most important rights a defendant has is the ***right to counsel,*** which is guaranteed by the Sixth Amendment. One problem with this guarantee arises when a person cannot afford the cost of legal counsel. Over the years the Supreme Court has gradually extended the right to counsel. In *Gideon* v. *Wainwright* (1963) it required that an attorney be appointed for those too poor to hire their own.

Clarence Earl Gideon had been convicted of theft in a Florida poolroom. Although only a poor drifter, Gideon knew that the Constitution guaranteed him a fair trial. Yet because he was so poor, he had undergone his trial without a lawyer. How could he have a fair trial without an attorney? The Court agreed, ruling that any person too poor to hire an attorney must be provided one by the state. Gideon won a new trial and was eventually acquitted.

The Court's decision in *Gideon* applied only to serious crimes called felonies. In 1972 the Court extended the right of appointed counsel to misdemeanor cases involving possible imprisonment.

What is the scope of the right to legal counsel? Is the defendant guaranteed representation by a lawyer only during the trial itself? In 1960 Chicago police questioned Danny Escobedo about the murder of his brother-in-law. Escobedo asked to see a lawyer, but his request was refused. During a lengthy interrogation, he eventually confessed to the murder. Escobedo's conviction was overturned on appeal. The Supreme Court ruled in *Escobedo* v. *Illinois* (1964) that the right to legal counsel applies as soon as the suspect is accused of a crime by police, even during preliminary questioning.

Protection Against Self-Incrimination

The right to remain silent relies on the Fifth Amendment guarantee against ***self-incrimination*** that says no person "shall be compelled in any criminal case to be a witness against himself." This means that defendants need not testify in their own trials, unless they wish to do so. Also, if their testimony would tend to be self-incriminating, people may refuse to answer questions as witnesses in the trial of another person or in a hearing. Refusal to answer under these circumstances is known as "taking the Fifth."

Protection against self-incrimination also implies that forced or coerced confessions whether true or false are not admissible evidence. A confession must be voluntary to be allowed as evidence. Coercion, or involuntary testimony, need not be in the form of rapid, hostile questioning—the so-called third degree. Subtle psychological pressure and trickery also constitute coercion. In many circumstances it may be difficult to determine whether a confession is, in fact, voluntary.

In several crucial decisions in recent years the Supreme Court has ruled that protection against self-incrimination also requires that accused persons be fully advised of their rights. *Miranda* v. *Arizona* (1966) greatly extended the protections against self-incrimination. Ernesto Miranda had been arrested in 1963 for the rape and kidnapping of a woman near Phoenix, Arizona. The victim had picked Miranda out of a police lineup. Questioned by the police, without being advised of his rights, Miranda confessed. In a hotly debated 5–4 vote the Court overturned the conviction.* The Court ruled that the protection against self-incrimination requires that all accused persons be given the following information before questioning: (1) they have a right to remain silent; (2) anything they say may be held against them; (3) they have a right to an attorney; (4) an attorney will be provided for those too poor to afford one.

The *Miranda* decision has created a storm of protest. Law enforcement officials have complained that the ruling would handicap questioning and greatly reduce the number of confessions. The application of the exclusionary rule has meant that no statement from an improperly informed defendant would be admissible in court. Those who have supported the decision have argued that if constitutional rights are to be meaningful, they must be known.

As it has turned out, the police have learned to live with the *Miranda* decision. Some police even carry cards with the *Miranda* rights of the accused listed. Fears that the *Miranda* decision would seriously weaken law enforcement efforts have not proven to be true.

Today law-enforcement officers throughout the United States must read the Miranda *rights to the suspects they have apprehended.*

MIRANDA WARNING

1. You have the right to remain silent.
2. Anything you say can and will be used against you in a court of law.
3. You have the right to talk to a lawyer and have him present with you while you are being questioned.
4. If you cannot afford to hire a lawyer, one will be appointed to represent you before any questioning, if you wish one.

WAIVER

AFTER THE WARNING AND IN ORDER TO SECURE A WAIVER, THE FOLLOWING QUESTIONS SHOULD BE ASKED AND AN AFFIRMATIVE REPLY SECURED TO EACH QUESTION.

1. Do you understand each of these rights I have explained to you?
2. Having these rights in mind, do you wish to talk to us now?

SAN FRANCISCO POLICE DEPARTMENT

*When a conviction is overturned, it may be returned to the lower court for a new trial. Miranda was tried again without his "tainted" confession and was convicted.

Freedom from Unnecessary Imprisonment

In American justice an accused person is presumed innocent until proven guilty. This presumption leads to an attempt to prevent unnecessary time in jail by the defendant until a verdict is rendered. Two separate rights apply here. The first is the provision for ***bail***—money put up by a defendant as a pledge to return to court for trial. The defendant is released from jail; if the defendant does not return for trial, the bail is forfeited. In capital cases, where the death penalty is involved, the defendant may be held without bail. The reasoning here is that no amount of money could guarantee a person's return to face the death penalty.

The Eighth Amendment requires that bail not be "excessive," but some people are too poor to afford even a small amount. For this reason the courts now allow release of defendants on their own recognizance, a release without bail if the defendant can demonstrate trustworthiness. To give a defendant release on recognizance, a judge must examine such factors as length of residence in the community, family ties in the community, employment record, and any prior criminal record.

Those persons unable to make bail or to secure release on their own recognizance must remain in jail while they await trial.

The Sixth Amendment guarantees that "the accused shall enjoy the right to a speedy and public trial." Charges have actually been dismissed in several cases because the state took too long to try the defendant. Justice delayed is justice denied. With crowded courtrooms a problem, Congress has sought to firm up the guarantee of a speedy trial. The Speedy Trial Act of 1974 has established a maximum of 100 days between arrest and trial in federal courts. A number of states have passed similar laws that, with some variation, now follow the federal requirements.

Requirement of Formal Charges

The Sixth Amendment provides that the accused has a right "to be informed of the nature and cause of the accusation." Formal charges are made only after it has been determined by the District Attorney or prosecutor that there is enough evidence to bring the defendant to trial. Formal charges may be brought in two ways: by grand jury indictment or by information.

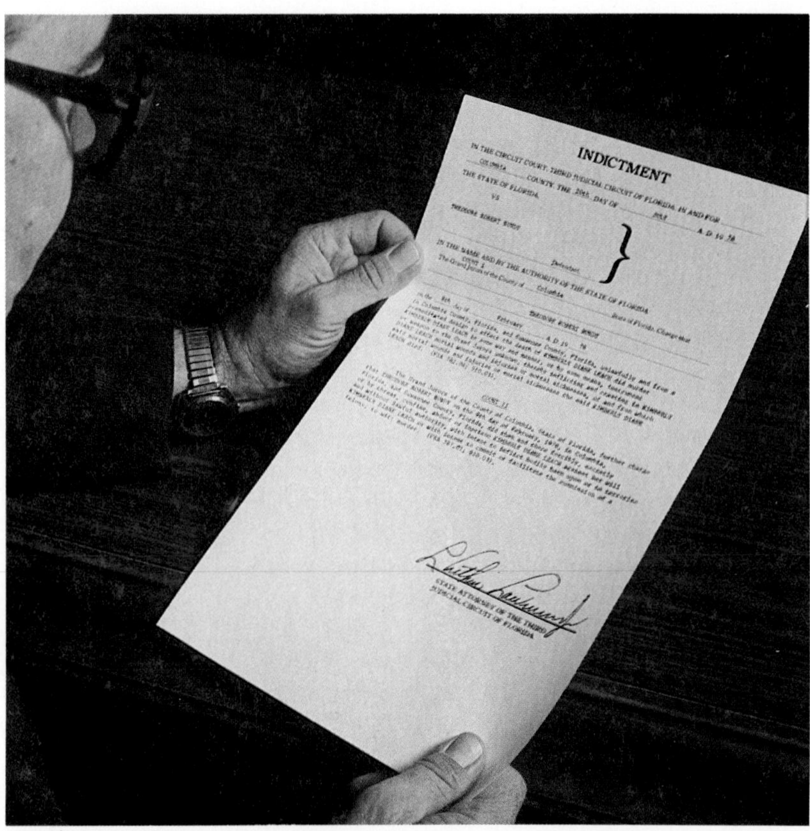

A Florida judge studies a bill of indictment, or true bill, accusing a person of murder. The form and language of an indictment are determined by state law. Through what means other than indictment may formal criminal charges be brought against a person?

INSIGHT

The Requirement of Unanimity

The requirement of unanimity means that all jurors must reach agreement on either a guilty or not guilty verdict. In about 6 percent of all trials, a single juror may hold out against all the rest. Then a unanimous verdict cannot be reached and the jury is said to be deadlocked, or "hung." Then the judge will dismiss the jury. A new trial before another jury may then be ordered.

The Fifth Amendment protects people against ***double jeopardy,*** which guarantees that no person shall "be subjected, for the same offense, to be twice in jeopardy of life and limb." Very simply this means that defendants found not guilty may not be tried again for the same crime. But when a defendant is not acquitted of the charges—for example, in the case of a hung jury—or when a conviction is overturned by a higher court, a new trial does not violate the right against double jeopardy.

An ***indictment*** is the formal written charge of a crime. The Fifth Amendment requires that indictments in federal criminal proceedings be made by grand jury. This requirement is not binding on the states. Nevertheless, many state constitutions require the use of grand jury indictments to initiate criminal proceedings.

A ***grand jury*** may consist of 6 to 23 members. Its responsibility is not to determine innocence or guilt. It must decide only whether the evidence presented by a government's attorney is sufficient to justify prosecution. Grand jury proceedings are secret, and decisions are reached by majority vote. If a grand jury decides that there is probable cause to believe the accused guilty of an alleged offense, it will bring "a true bill" of indictment. This formally specifies the crime for which the defendant will be brought to trial.

Most states do not require grand juries. Rather than indictment, formal charge is by ***information.*** In this procedure a complaint is filed before a magistrate, specifying charges. The defendant is asked to plead guilty or not guilty. If the plea is guilty, a sentence is determined. If the plea is not guilty, the magistrate holds a ***preliminary hearing,*** a kind of mini-trial without jury. In it evidence is introduced and witnesses may be called by both prosecution and defense attorneys. If the charges are not adequately supported, they will be dropped and the case dismissed. If the magistrate is satisfied that there is probable cause to believe the defendant guilty, the prosecutor then files an information. This is the formal charge which serves as the basis for trial.

The Right to Trial by Jury

The Sixth Amendment guarantees the accused the right to trial by jury. The jury system involves the citizen in the administration of justice. It provides for community participation and shared responsibility. Although serving on a jury may be an inconvenience for some people, it is an important duty of citizenship. The rights of citizenship do not come without responsibilities.

Traditionally a jury is composed of 12 persons, though nowhere in the Constitution is a specific number mentioned. In 1970 the Supreme Court upheld the constitutionality of state laws that provided for juries of fewer than 12 persons. What is important, the Court said, is that the number be large enough to promote group deliberation and to be a fair, representative cross section of the community.

In all federal trials the verdict of the jury must be unanimous. The Supreme Court held in 1972, however, that due process did not impose the rule of unanimity on the states. If a state wished to permit the jury verdict to be based on a substantial majority, rather than unanimous agreement, the state could do so.

Juries are to be representative of a fair cross section of the community. Their members are to be selected at random, so that each citizen has an equal chance of being called to serve. It is not required that each jury be proportionately representative, with a certain percentage of women, blacks, Catholics, and any other minority group present in the community. No section of the population, however, may

LEXICON

Classes of Crimes

Crimes are divided into two categories—felonies and misdemeanors. ***Felonies*** are major crimes that carry punishments ranging from lengthy prison sentences to death. Among these are murder, rape, kidnapping, arson, and robbery. ***Misdemeanors*** are less serious crimes. In general they carry fines and not more than one-year imprisonment. They include the violation of city ordinances, disturbing the peace, gambling, drunkenness, and cruelty to animals.

be systematically excluded from jury service. The law demands that no citizen be excluded because of "race, color, religion, sex, national origin, or economic status."

The Sixth Amendment guarantees the right to an "impartial jury." To secure such a jury, the lawyers on both sides question each person selected for service. Prospective jurors who are unable to reach a decision impartially, based only upon the evidence presented in court, are excluded from service.

Freedom from Cruel and Unusual Punishment

The Eighth Amendment prohibits "cruel and unusual punishments." The prohibition involves the form and the severity of punishment. Such punishments are clearly excessive, inherently unfair, or unnecessarily degrading. But where is the line between just punishment and cruel or unusual punishment? Clearly a jail sentence is permitted by the Eighth Amendment, while torture is obviously prohibited.

The Eighth Amendment has been used to restrict the use of such severe measures as solitary confinement. It has also been used to improve prison conditions in the United States. In *Hold* v. *Sarver* (1970) a District Court applied the "cruel and unusual punishments" clause to require improvements in Arkansas state prisons, ruling that the "System as it exists today . . . is unconstitutional."

Is the death penalty, or ***capital punishment,*** a "cruel and unusual punishment" and thus unconstitutional? The Supreme Court considered this question in *Furman* v. *Georgia* (1972). The 5–4 decision was inconclusive. There was no single majority opinion. Two justices believed that the death penalty was unconstitutional. They argued that it was simply unacceptable in contemporary society. Three justices, in separate opinions, refused to hold that

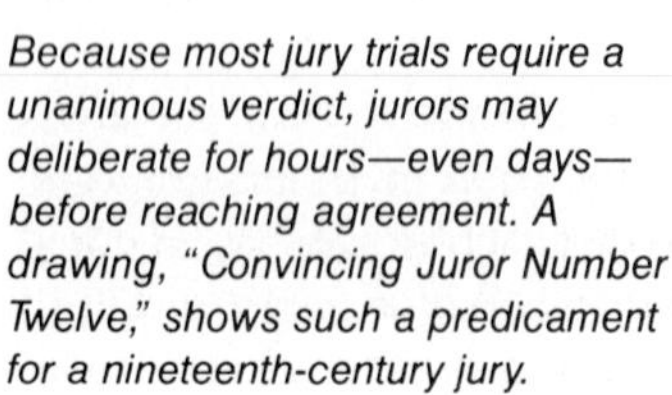

Because most jury trials require a unanimous verdict, jurors may deliberate for hours—even days—before reaching agreement. A drawing, "Convincing Juror Number Twelve," shows such a predicament for a nineteenth-century jury.

The pillory was used to enforce Puritan standards of morality in New England during the 1600's. Many colonists felt that the use of the pillory and other public punishments was cruel and unusual.

the death penalty in itself was unconstitutional. Rather, they held that capital punishment was invalid because of the arbitrary, unequal, manner in which it was imposed by judges. For example, convicted blacks were executed more often than whites convicted for the same type of crime.

The Court thus held that although existing laws were invalid, the death penalty was permitted by the Constitution. If capital punishment was to be abolished, it was a matter for Congress and the state legislatures, not the courts, to decide. After the *Furman* decision 36 states enacted new laws providing for capital punishment. These state laws were carefully drafted in order to meet the Supreme Court's requirements that the death penalty not be imposed arbitrarily.

In *Gregg* v. *Georgia* (1976) the Court reviewed the various laws passed. Several failed to meet the Court's standards, but others met the requirements of due process. The laws were held constitutional. In general, the Court has approved those statutes that require a two-stage trial in capital cases. First, guilt or innocence is determined. If guilt is determined, then the guilty person faces a separate hearing to decide if the death penalty should be applied. In 1977 the first execution in 10 years in the United States took place in Utah.

Section Check

1. Define: presumption of innocence, writ of habeas corpus, ex post facto law, bill of attainder, exclusionary rule, felony, indictment, grand jury, double jeopardy, capital punishment
2. Identify: bill of victims' rights, Clarence Earl Gideon, Danny Escobedo, Ernesto Miranda
3. What are the nine basic rights of the accused?
4. What are the situations in which a search may be conducted without a warrant?
5. What does it mean when a witness "takes the Fifth"?

2 JUSTICE AT WORK

Section 1 examined the constitutional rights of the accused. In order to see how these rights work, Section 2 will examine each stage of the criminal justice system. First, a case that does not go to trial will be examined. Then trial procedure will be examined in detail.

Case Study: *The State* v. *John Harris*

Officer Tom Green was on routine patrol late one night in a neighborhood where there had been several recent burglaries. He was on the lookout for an automobile that had been reported as "suspicious." A car matching the report's description was parked in front of a vacant lot, its engine still warm. Officer Green called in for assistance. He then watched attentively and waited.

Arrest Within a few minutes two young men approached the car. They carried a tape recorder and a portable television set. Green arrested the young men, who offered no resistance. To protect himself and to prevent the destruction of any additional evidence, Green conducted a search at the time of arrest. He found no weapons. He then advised the young men of their *Miranda* rights to remain silent and to have an attorney present.

During an arrest, suspects are read their Miranda *rights. What constitutional protections do the* Miranda *rights guarantee?*

A suspect is fingerprinted when booked for a crime. What else takes place at the time of booking?

Booking The young men were John Harris, 19 years of age, and his friend Bill Parker, 16. They were taken to the police station. There the sergeant on duty reviewed the circumstances of the arrest. In his judgment there was probable cause to hold the young men in custody. Because Bill was 16, he was turned over to the juvenile authorities. (His case will be discussed later.) John, because he was 19, was booked as an adult accused of a crime. His arrest was recorded. He was photographed and fingerprinted. John was permitted to make one telephone call. He nervously called his parents to explain his situation and asked that they contact their lawyer.

Initial Appearance The law requires that the defendant be brought before a magistrate or justice of the peace "without unreasonable delay." This usually means no more than 24 hours from the time of arrest. After his night in jail, John was taken into the municipal court for his initial appearance. His parents were already there, together with their attorney, Ann Miles. If his family had been unable to afford a lawyer, the court would have appointed counsel to represent John.

John and his lawyer approached the bench. John was again advised of his constitutional rights. The judge read the charge against him: burglary, a felony crime. Bail was set at $1,000. Upon payment of his bail, John was released to await trial.

Indictment John's case then went to the District Attorney. On the facts of the case, the D. A. decided to ask the grand jury to bring formal charges. The grand jury, in secret session, must determine whether there is probable cause to believe the defendant guilty. After studying the evidence, the grand jury voted to indict John for burglary.

Arraignment The defendant's first appearance in the court in which he will be tried is at the ***arraignment***, a formal hearing at which the charges are read. The defendant enters his plea of guilty or not guilty. John's lawyer explained the implications of each plea. If he were to plead not guilty, his case would be tried in court before a jury. If John were to plead guilty, the sentence would be imposed by the judge without trial.

Plea Bargaining John had been arrested once before—for auto theft. He had been found guilty and was sentenced to one year probation. If John were to be found guilty of burglary, this previous conviction would weigh heavily against him in the determination of sentence. Ms. Miles thought that the prosecutor might be willing to recommend the minimum sentence in exchange for a plea of guilty.

John entered a plea of guilty on the basis of a bargain with the District Attorney. The judge sentenced him to two years imprisonment. He would be eligible for release on parole after eight months.

John's case was settled by negotiation between the prosecutor and the defendant in what is called a ***plea bargain.*** In the bargain the defendant pleads guilty in exchange for a promise of leniency—usually a reduction of charges or a reduced sentence. In the American system 90 percent of all convictions result from a guilty plea, never involving a trial. Most of these are a result of plea bargains. The Supreme Court has recognized plea bargaining as "an essential component of the administration of justice." Chief Justice Burger has said:

Plea bargaining leads to prompt and largely final disposition of most criminal cases; it avoids much of the corrosive impact of enforced idleness during pretrial confinement for those who are denied release pending trial; it protects the public from those accused persons who are prone to continue criminal conduct even while on pretrial release; and, by shortening the time between charge and disposition, it enhances whatever may be the rehabilitative prospects of the guilty when they are ultimately imprisoned.

During the arraignment (above) the suspect—upon the advice of counsel—enters a plea of guilty or not guilty. If the suspect pleads guilty, a trial is unnecessary. The judge determines the sentence (below) for the guilty person. Why does the court allow plea bargaining?

Before a trial begins, a defense attorney questions prospective jurors to eliminate those who appear to favor the prosecution. Through what other means may attorneys exclude prospective jurors?

Nevertheless, plea bargaining has come under a strong attack. Some critics argue that the threat of a severe sentence might lead an innocent person to plead guilty to lesser charges. Perhaps a poor person, unable to post bail, might plead guilty—even though innocent—to secure immediate release on probation or a brief sentence. Such abuse is minimized by requiring that the bargain be closely reviewed by the judge. Some critics feel that excessive use of plea bargaining limits the deterrent effect of severe sentences. Criminals, by this reasoning, would be secure in the knowledge that a plea bargain will produce a lighter sentence. Still, most authorities feel that, despite its faults, plea bargaining has a secure place in our criminal justice system.

Trial Procedures

In some 10 percent of cases reaching arraignment, however, a trial is required. If John Harris had entered a plea of not guilty, he would have gone to trial.

Criminal justice in the United States employs an adversary system to determine innocence or guilt. The adversary system rests on the assumption that the truth is most likely to emerge when the opposing sides in the trial confront each other in the open courtroom. In a criminal trial the defendant, represented by counsel, faces the prosecuting attorney for the state. Each side offers evidence, calls and questions witnesses, and advances legal claims on its own behalf.

The judge, a guardian of due process, acts as a neutral umpire between the two adversaries and decides questions of law. Without partiality the judge determines what evidence may be admitted legally, ensures that the evidence introduced is reliable and relevant, and decides how the law applies to the case and instructs the jury to its responsibility.

The members of the jury decide questions of fact. They must determine what actually happened. They must evaluate the witnesses and weigh the evidence. Each juror is to be impartial and listen to both sides with an open mind. Ultimately it is the responsibility of the jury to give a verdict of guilty or not guilty.

Pretrial Motions Before the trial actually begins, a number of motions may be filed with the court. The defense, for example, may seek to have certain evidence excluded from the trial. It may claim that the evidence had been seized illegally in violation of the defendant's Fourth Amendment rights. Another motion may seek a ***change of venue,*** a shift in the location of the trial. A change of venue is sometimes necessary because local feelings and publicity may be harmful to the defendant's right to a fair trial. After all the pretrial motions have been ruled upon by the judge, the case goes to trial.

Jury Selection Prospective jurors are examined by both defense and prosecuting attorneys. Those who are prejudiced, or show bias, toward either side are excluded. Each side is also permitted to exercise ***peremptory challenges***—actions that exclude a specified number of potential jurors without cause. When the required number of jurors (usually 12) has been selected, the trial is ready to begin.

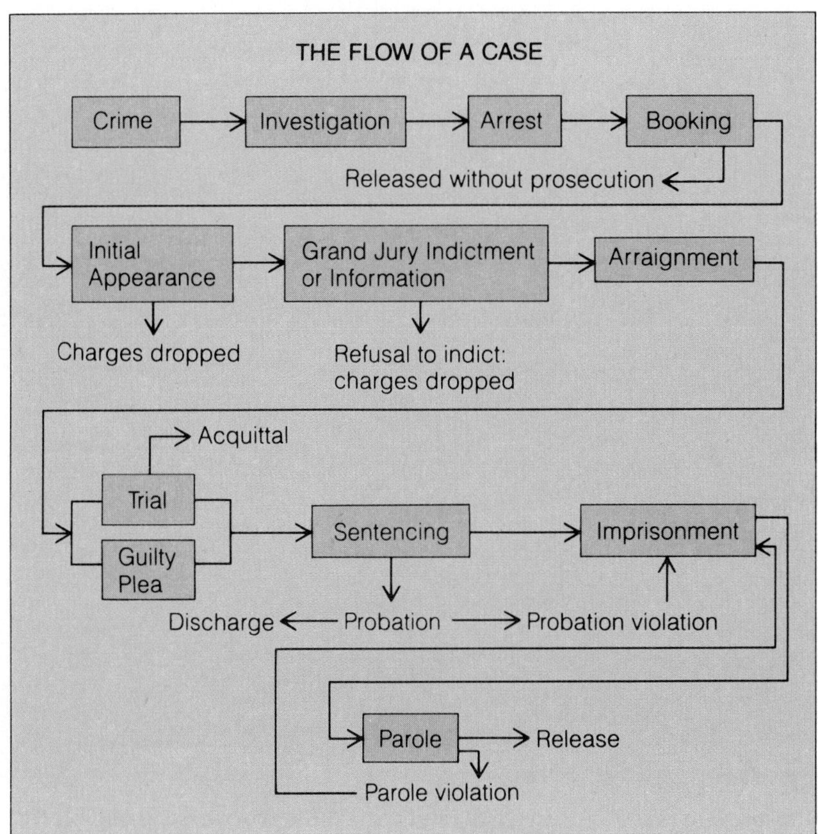

A flow chart shows the typical steps in a criminal case—from the commission of the crime to release of the defendant from prison. What steps may follow the arraignment?

Opening Statements The prosecuting attorney states the charges against the defendant and the reasoning on which the state will base its case. The defense attorney then follows with the counterargument by which the accused will be defended.

Presentation of Evidence Each side presents evidence in its own behalf, normally in the form of witnesses. In giving testimony, witnesses are sworn to tell the truth. False testimony is ***perjury,*** for which the witness may be imprisoned. The Sixth Amendment guarantees the right of the defendant to confront and cross-examine witnesses. Cross-examination may show a witness to be untrustworthy, biased, or unreliable. The Fifth Amendment guarantees that accused persons need not be witnesses against themselves or take the stand in their own defense.

A Trial's Conclusion The prosecution and the defense conclude their cases by presenting a summary of the evidence to the jury. The judge instructs the jury on how the law applies to their determination of the facts. The judge emphasizes that the defendant is presumed innocent until proven guilty beyond a reasonable doubt. The burden of proof is on the prosecution. In secrecy the jurors consider the innocence or guilt of the defendant. If opinion is divided, the jurors must then argue among themselves in an attempt to reach a decision. In federal courts and in most states the verdict must be unanimous. The jury returns to the courtroom, and the verdict is given to the judge. If found not guilty, the defendant receives an ***acquittal*** of all charges. If the defendant is found guilty, the judge will then determine the appropriate sentence. This is sometimes done with a recommendation from the jury. In some states the jury determines the sentence as well as the verdict.

Appeal If found guilty, the defendant has the right of appeal. Most defendants accept the verdict of the trial court as final. Appeal may involve considerable expense. Moreover, unless there is substantial basis for appeal, the likelihood of winning is very small.

An appeal is a request for a higher ***appellate*** (or appeals) court to review the decision. Appeal most frequently rests on the claim that the defendant did not receive a fair trial because of a legal

The foreman—the presiding officer of the jury—reads the verdict to the court. In some states the jury may also recommend an appropriate sentence to the judge.

error. This might involve error by the judge in procedure or in the interpretation of law. The error must be sufficient to prejudice the outcome of the trial. If the appellate court finds a serious error, the decision of the trial court is reversed. In most instances, the case is returned to the lower court for a new trial.

Appeal from the trial court may be made only by the defendant. The prosecutor may not appeal if the defendant is acquitted because a defendant that has been acquitted may not be tried again for the same crime. There is one exception to this rule. A single criminal act may violate both state and federal laws. Although acquitted by a state court, a person may be tried again in a federal court.

Sentencing In determining the appropriate sentence, the judge takes into consideration the circumstances of the offense as well as the defendant's background and previous record. Special leniency, for example, may be given to a person with no previous criminal record.

Flexibility in sentencing is subject to abuse. For the same crime, sentences often vary greatly. Uncertainty, both for the offender and society, may reduce respect for the law. In addition, the time actually served in prison is uncertain. With "good behavior" a prisoner usually is released on ***parole*** before serving the full term. Most prisoners are eligible for parole after serving one third of their sentences.

There is growing criticism today of sentencing procedures and the parole system. Prison sentences are supposed to rehabilitate convicted criminals so they can return as productive members of society; the system is also designed to deter criminal acts, to convince persons that crime does not pay. But deterrence seems ineffective, partly because sentences are uncertain, and very few people are rehabilitated by prison. Crime rates continue to rise, and 50 to 70 percent of those released from prison are convicted again. Recognizing the problem, Congress and many states are seeking fundamental reforms in sentencing procedures and the parole system.

Section Check

1. Define: arraignment, plea bargain, change of venue, peremptory challenge, perjury, acquittal
2. How does plea bargaining relieve the load on the court system?
3. Explain the roles of a judge, jury, prosecutor and defense attorney in a trial.

3 THE JUVENILE JUSTICE SYSTEM

The juvenile justice system is separate and distinct from the criminal justice system. It falls within the area of civil, not criminal, law. The system, as it existed until recently, evolved over one hundred years to provide special attention to young offenders and to separate them from hardened criminals. It tended to emphasize compassion, individual treatment, and rehabilitation. The proceedings, held in private and without a jury, were informal. They did not have the adversary character of a criminal trial. The rules of criminal procedure, with all their technicalities, did not apply. In denying these rules, the state was acting ***in loco parentis*** ("in place of parents").

Due Process in Juvenile Court

In 1967 the Supreme Court heard a case challenging the authority of the juvenile court. The case, known as *In re Gault,* involved Gerald Gault, a 15-year-old Arizona youth. He had been accused by a neighbor of making an anonymous telephone call in which he had used lewd and offensive language. On the basis of the complaint Gerald was picked up by the sheriff and taken to the Children's Detention Home.

The juvenile court judge found Gerald to be a "delinquent child" and committed him to the State Industrial School in Arizona, a juvenile reformatory, for a maximum of six years. Had Gerald been tried in a state criminal court as an adult, the penalty for his misdemeanor would have been a maximum fine of $50 or no more than two months in prison.

Juvenile proceedings in Arizona offered no right of appeal. Gerald's parents filed a writ of habeas corpus to secure his release. They argued that the proceedings of the juvenile court were in violation of the due process clause of the Fourteenth Amendment. Gerald, they claimed, had been denied his constitutional rights.

Gerald's parents had received no formal notice of the charge against their son. They had had no opportunity to decide on a course of action or prepare his defense. Neither Gerald nor his parents had been advised of their right to counsel. The proceedings were conducted without the assistance of an attorney. The woman who had filed the complaint against Gerald did not appear in court. Thus Gerald had been denied the right to confront and cross-examine the witness against him. There was some doubt as to whether Gerald had actually admitted making the phone call. In any case, he had not been advised of his right to remain silent. The trustworthiness of a confession is always suspect in the criminal trial of an adult. Surely, in the case of a young person, the greatest care must be taken to ensure that a confession is voluntary. A confession may be coerced or suggested, or it may be the product of fantasy, fright, or despair.

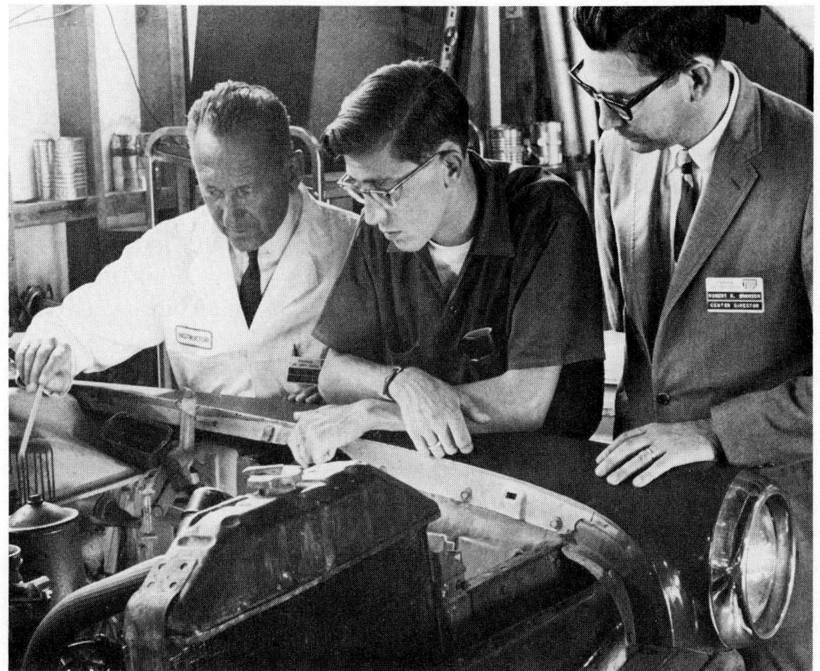

Constitutional protections for juveniles were guaranteed by the Supreme Court's ruling in In re Gault. *Gerald Gault (center)—shown here at a vocational school—had been denied due process by the Arizona juvenile courts.*

PROFILE

A Jury of Their Peers

In Denver, Colorado, a 15-year-old boy named Tom has been caught breaking into a vending machine. The police release him to the custody of his parents, and several days later he stands before a jury. "Why did you do it?" one jury member asks. Another wants to know how Tom gets along with his parents and what he does with his free time. Tom answers all the questions, embarrassed and apprehensive. After deliberating in private, the jury returns to hand down an unusual verdict. Tom will have to get a part-time job to pay back the money, and for the next 18 months he will have to call his counselor once a week and write a monthly report on his conduct.

The jury and its unusual verdict are part of an innovative program in Denver designed to confront the thorny problem of juvenile crime. Teenage offenders face a jury of their peers, other teenagers, some of whom have been in trouble with the law themselves. Only first-time offenders who have already admitted their guilt are allowed to appear before the student jury. They must agree, in writing, to abide by the sentence the jury imposes. The jury considers all but the most serious crimes—theft, assault, possession of dangerous weapons—and its sentence has the force of law. Jury members, who volunteer for duty, are selected by the Denver district attorney's office, which supervises the program.

From its beginning the program has been a success. A total of 126 teenagers have gone before the student jury. Only 18 of those offenders have failed to meet the requirements of their sentences—which include staying out of further trouble with the law. Zoralee Steinberg, one of the founders of the student jury program, credits the teenagers themselves with its success. "The students on the jury know the problems and pressures of being a teenager," she says. "They understand better than anyone what led these youngsters into committing a crime, and what will keep them from doing it again."

In its decision the Supreme Court held that the action of the juvenile court was a denial of due process. "The essential difference between Gerald's case and a normal criminal case," the Court ruled, "is that safeguards available to adults were discarded in Gerald's case." Speaking for the Court, Justice Abe Fortas declared, "Under our Constitution, the condition of being a boy does not justify a kangaroo court." When speaking of a ***kangaroo court,*** Justice Fortas referred to a court in which a fair trial is impossible.

In *In re Gault* the Supreme Court held that where possible commitment to an institution such as a reform school was involved, four constitutional rights must be guaranteed: (1) the right to formal notice of the charges; (2) the right to be represented by counsel; (3) the right to confront one's accusers and to cross-examine witnesses; and (4) protection against self-incrimination. In addition, the court ruled that in juvenile proceedings—as in adult trials—the standard of proof should be "guilt beyond a reasonable doubt."

In extending these fundamental constitutional protections to juvenile proceedings, the Court was not requiring that the juvenile court conform to all the requirements of a criminal trial. What was required, however, was that "the hearing must measure up to the essentials of due process and fair treatment." The trend in most states, though, is toward extending to juveniles most of the rights that adults have in criminal cases. It is likely that the trend of extending adult rules to juveniles will continue.

In re Gault is the landmark case in the rights of juvenile defendants. In that case, speaking for the Court, Justice Fortas affirmed the fundamental principle of American justice.

Due process of law is the primary and indispensable foundation of individual freedom. It is the basic and essential term in the social compact which defines the rights of the individual and delimits the powers which the state may exercise.

Case Study: Juvenile Justice Procedures

All states must meet the standards required by due process of law. The federal character of American government, however, permits considerable variation among the state systems of juvenile justice. The maximum age subject to jurisdiction of the juvenile court varies, for example, from 16 to 20. In most states older youths who have committed serious crimes may be turned over to a regular criminal court to be tried as adults. In some states juvenile court is still fairly informal; in others the proceedings have a formal adversary character—complete with prosecutor and jury. Many states now also provide appeal procedures through the civil courts.

In order to see how juvenile proceedings work, the case of Bill Parker will be examined. Bill, as you read earlier in this chapter, was arrested for burglary along with John Harris. Because he was only 16 years old, Bill was placed in the custody of the juvenile authorities. At the juvenile detention center the "intake officer" called Bill's parents. They were told that a delinquency petition would be filed with the juvenile court. He was to make his initial appearance the next day.

Initial Appearance Bill's parents met him at the court. The judge, Elizabeth Mayhew, formally gave notice of the charge. She advised Bill of his right to remain silent and to have counsel. As Bill's parents were unable to afford a lawyer, the judge appointed one to represent him.

There is no right to bail in juvenile proceedings. Following general practice, however, Bill was released in the custody of his parents. If Judge Mayhew had believed that Bill would not show up at the scheduled hearing, she could have had Bill held in custody.

PROFILE

The Judge and the Comics

Who is that mysterious masked man who races across the city as quick as lightning, stopping criminals with superhuman strength?

His name is *Relampago*—"lightning" in Spanish—and he is the comic book creation of Judge Marbarito C. Garza, a judge in the county court system of Corpus Christi, Texas. Like most superheroes, *Relampago* possesses extraordinary strength and breathtaking speed, which he uses to battle successfully against crime. What makes him special is his Spanish heritage. Once a petty criminal named Marcos Zapata, he was transformed into a superhero by a witch after being shot in an attempted burglary. *Relampago*'s costume is adorned with Mexico's symbol of the eagle and the snake. In two issues of the comic book *Relampago* breaks up a drug ring, captures robbers and thieves, and battles a law-breaking motorcycle gang.

Judge Garza is considered one of the strictest judges in the county court, especially when he lectures young people who have broken the law. He created *Relampago* to promote a positive symbol of law enforcement for Mexican-American children in the Southwest. Judge Garza wrote and designed each issue, enlisting the help of Sam Gonzalez, a local artist, to do the drawings. A second generation Mexican-American himself, Judge Garza learned English by reading comic books, and he has held a lifelong interest in them.

In some states, juvenile defendants and their parents (left) are required to make an initial appearance before a judge. Juvenile defendants have the right to testify at their adjudication hearings (right) but as guaranteed by the Fifth Amendment, cannot be compelled to testify against themselves. What two options may the judge exercise during the disposition hearing?

The Adjudication Hearing The juvenile court hearing is the equivalent of a trial in a criminal case. The purpose of the adjudication hearing is to determine guilt or innocence. The police officer who had taken Bill into custody was called as a witness. The officer was questioned by a prosecutor and cross-examined by the defense attorney. On the advice of his lawyer Bill decided to testify in his own defense. Had he not chosen to do so, he could have remained silent, protected by the Fifth Amendment privilege against self-incrimination. After hearing the evidence, Judge Mayhew found Bill to be delinquent.

The Disposition Hearing In juvenile cases the judge has two principal options in the disposition hearing. First the youth may be placed on ***probation,*** in the custody of parents, a guardian, or in a foster home. Probation is subject to certain conditions and is usually for a period of one year. Second the youth may be committed to a state training or reform school.

Bill had been found guilty of a serious offense, but he had never been in trouble before. With concern for his rehabilitation Judge Mayhew decided that Bill's best interest would be served by probation. For a period of one year Bill would be placed under the supervision of a probation officer. If Bill violated the rules of probation, he would be returned to the juvenile court for further action that might include being committed to a reform school.

The files relating to a juvenile case are kept separately from criminal records of adults. Their contents are not open to public inspection. After a youth is discharged, the files and records of the case may be sealed.

Though the juvenile system is separate and distinct, it reflects the same values and priorities as the criminal justice system. In the United States the power of law enforcement officials and courts is limited by design to ensure, as much as is possible, that innocent people are not wrongly punished. The rights of the accused are cherished and defended, not to coddle criminals, but to protect the innocent. These

INSIGHT

The Rules of Juvenile Probation

Probation rules may vary. Those below, to which the youth must agree, are typical.

1. I will obey all laws.
2. I will obey my parents.
3. I will attend school regularly and obey all school rules.
4. I will remain in my home at night except when my parents give me permission to be at a specific place.
5. I will notify the county juvenile court before making any change of address, school, or employment.
6. I will remain within the limits of the county, except for routine trips with my parents. I will leave the county only after receiving permission from a probation officer of the juvenile court.
7. I will report to my probation officer as directed and I will cooperate in every way to ensure the success of the terms of probation.

rights are, of course, balanced against the need to maintain effective law enforcement. The federal government attempts to give a certain latitude to the states, while establishing the uniformly fair procedures required by the Constitution. Above all, a person is considered innocent until proven guilty; and the burden of proof of guilt beyond a reasonable doubt falls upon the state. These elements, whether in juvenile or adult criminal law, lie at the heart of justice in the United States.

Section Check

1. Define: *in loco parentis,* probation, kangaroo court
2. Identify: *In re Gault,* jury of one's peers, probation rules
3. Distinguish between an adjudication hearing and a disposition hearing.

SUMMARY

Civil liberties safeguard individual freedom. To protect our freedom from unlimited and arbitrary government, the Constitution and the Bill of Rights give special emphasis to the rights of the accused. These rights are embodied in the concept of due process of law. Due process means, at a minimum, procedural regularity and fundamental fairness.

The Constitution provides nine basic protections for the accused: the writ of habeas corpus; prohibition of ex post facto laws and bills of attainder; the freedom from unreasonable search and seizure; the right to counsel; protection against self-incrimination; protection against unnecessary imprisonment; requirement of formal charges; the right to trial by jury; and the freedom from cruel and unusual punishment.

Ninety percent of all criminal convictions are the result of a guilty plea by the defendant. A trial is involved only 10 percent of the time. Most guilty pleas are the result of plea bargains, agreements between the prosecutor and the defendant in which a guilty plea is exchanged for a lesser sentence. When a trial does result, the following stages are involved: pretrial motions, jury selection, opening statements, presentation of evidence, closing arguments, judge's instructions to the jury, jury's deliberation, verdict, and sentencing.

The juvenile justice system is distinct from the adult criminal justice system. Juvenile court is classified as a civil, not a criminal, court. The Supreme Court ruling in *In re Gault* extended many of the basic rights of accused adults to juvenile defendants. The stages of a juvenile court case are initial appearance, adjudication hearing, and disposition hearing.

In both juvenile and adult criminal court the law attempts to protect the innocent. American justice depends on fair, equal, and uniform treatment of all persons.

Chapter 28 Review

Using Vocabulary

Answer the questions by using the meaning of each underlined term.

1. Why are the writ of habeas corpus, the right to counsel, and presumption of innocence an important part of due process?
2. When might a court act in loco parentis?
3. Does an arraignment or an indictment come first in criminal court procedures?
4. How does parole differ from probation?
5. How might double jeopardy protect a person from capital punishment?
6. When does a peremptory challenge take place?
7. What is a kangaroo court?
8. How might a change of venue protect the rights of an accused person?

Understanding American Government

1. Why did the Framers of the Constitution give special prominence to criminal justice procedures and the rights of the accused?
2. What is the basic philosophy of the American judicial system?
3. For what reasons are law enforcement officers allowed to make a search incident to arrest?
4. What are two justifications for the exclusionary rule?
5. Explain how *Gideon* v. *Wainwright* extended the right to counsel.
6. Explain how *Miranda* v. *Arizona* extended the protections against self-incrimination.
7. Explain how formal charges are brought by grand jury indictment or by information.
8. Explain the flow of an adult criminal law case from arrest to trial and acquittal or sentencing.
9. Explain how the juvenile justice system differs from criminal justice procedures for adults.

Extending Your Skills: Reading a Flow Chart

Study the chart on page 687. Then complete the items that follow.

1. Arrange the following steps in the correct order of their occurrence: booking, arrest, indictment, trial, arraignment.
2. What is a likely occurrence if probation is violated? If parole is violated?
3. At what different times may charges be dropped?
4. Using the steps listed in the flow chart, write a brief paragraph explaining how an individual's rights are protected through the flow of a case.

Government and You

1. Explain how the Magna Carta forms a basis for the United States justice system.
2. Under the exclusionary rule, illegally obtained evidence is not admissible in court. Some jurists are critical of this rule, including Justice Benjamin Cardoza, who asked, "Is the criminal to go free because the constable blundered?" Do you agree or disagree with Justice Cardoza? Why?
3. In a case study in this chapter John Harris received a light sentence because he made a plea bargain. Do you approve or disapprove of plea bargaining, based on your understanding of the justice system in the United States? What might happen if plea bargaining were abolished?
4. Until recently juvenile courts were quite different from adult criminal courts. There are still major differences. Do you think juvenile courts should more closely follow adult criminal procedures? Why or why not?

Activities

1. Prepare a report on one of the reforms in criminal justice procedures under the Warren Court—*Gideon* v. *Wainwright, Escobedo* v. *Illinois,* or *Miranda* v. *Arizona.* Include in your report the public's reactions to the Supreme Court's decisions.
2. Prepare a bulletin-board display that shows the steps as a case moves through criminal court.
3. Make a scrapbook of newspaper and magazine clippings about the criminal justice system at work in one week.

UNIT 10

STATE AND LOCAL GOVERNMENT

Chapter 29

State Government

Despite the glamor of national politics, states and communities carry on the greatest volume of public business, make the majority of policy decisions, and direct the bulk of public programs. They have the major responsibility for maintaining domestic law and order, for educating the children, for moving Americans from place to place, and for caring for the poor and the ill. They regulate the provision of water, gas, electric, and other public utilities; share in the regulation of insurance and banking enterprise; regulate the use of land; and supervise the sale and ownership of property. Their courts settle by far the greatest number of civil and criminal cases.

THOMAS R. DYE

CHAPTER OVERVIEW

The Texas state capitol in Austin is the center of governmental activity in the state. Austin has served as the capital of Texas since 1845; the state capitol was completed in 1888.

1 THE STATE CONSTITUTIONS

In the American federal system the national and state governments are constitutionally separate, but they share powers. The United States Constitution does not list the powers of the state governments. The states existed before the Constitution was adopted, and they retained all the powers that the Constitution did not expressly grant to the national government and did not expressly deny to the states. These ***reserved powers*** are specifically recognized in Amendment 10.

The powers not delegated to the United States by the Constitution, nor prohibited by it to the States, are reserved to the States respectively, or to the people.

Basis for Government

Within the limits of its own constitution, each state has the power to:

1. tax and spend for the general welfare of its citizens;
2. regulate the ownership and use of property;
3. define and punish illegal conduct;
4. regulate and administer records of birth, death, marriage, and divorce;
5. provide for public education, health, and welfare;
6. provide for roads, canals, and public transportation;
7. exercise authority over the creation, organization, and conduct of local government.

Each state (see chart on page 698) is free to exercise these powers as it sees fit. Like the national government, each state government has a legislative, executive, and judicial branch. These three branches exercise the powers reserved to the state.

Each state has its own written constitution, which defines the powers of state government and specifies which branch of government exercises which powers. It also restricts the government's exercise of power. In all these ways it guarantees the fundamental rights of citizens.

The United States Constitution is the supreme law of the land. No state constitution may conflict with it. By the same token, each state's constitution is the supreme law of that state. No other state or local law may conflict with the provisions of the state constitution.

PROFILES OF THE STATES

State	Year of Statehood	1980 Population	Reps. in Congress	Area sq. mi.	Area sq. km.	Capital	Largest City
Alabama	1819	3,890,061	7	51,609	133,667	Montgomery	Birmingham
Alaska	1959	400,481	1	586,412	1,718,807	Juneau	Anchorage
Arizona	1912	2,717,866	5	113,909	295,024	Phoenix	Phoenix
Arkansas	1836	2,285,513	4	53,104	136,539	Little Rock	Little Rock
California	1850	23,668,562	45	158,693	411,015	Sacramento	Los Angeles
Colorado	1876	2,888,834	6	104,247	270,000	Denver	Denver
Connecticut	1788	3,107,576	6	5,009	12,973	Hartford	Bridgeport
Delaware	1787	595,225	1	2,057	5,328	Dover	Wilmington
Florida	1845	9,739,992	19	58,560	151,671	Tallahassee	Jacksonville
Georgia	1788	5,464,265	10	58,876	152,489	Atlanta	Atlanta
Hawaii	1959	965,000	2	6,450	16,706	Honolulu	Honolulu
Idaho	1890	943,935	2	83,557	216,413	Boise	Boise
Illinois	1818	11,418,461	22	56,400	146,076	Springfield	Chicago
Indiana	1816	5,490,179	10	36,291	93,995	Indianapolis	Indianapolis
Iowa	1846	2,913,387	6	56,290	145,791	Des Moines	Des Moines
Kansas	1861	2,363,208	5	82,264	213,064	Topeka	Wichita
Kentucky	1792	3,661,433	7	40,395	104,623	Frankfort	Louisville
Louisiana	1812	4,203,972	8	48,523	125,875	Baton Rouge	New Orleans
Maine	1820	1,124,660	2	33,215	86,017	Augusta	Portland
Maryland	1788	4,216,446	8	10,577	27,394	Annapolis	Baltimore
Massachusetts	1788	5,737,037	11	8,257	21,386	Boston	Boston
Michigan	1837	9,258,344	18	58,216	150,779	Lansing	Detroit
Minnesota	1858	4,077,148	8	84,068	229,736	St. Paul	Minneapolis
Mississippi	1817	2,520,638	5	47,716	123,584	Jackson	Jackson
Missouri	1821	4,917,444	9	69,686	180,487	Jefferson City	St. Louis
Montana	1889	786,690	2	147,138	381,087	Helena	Billings
Nebraska	1867	1,570,006	3	77,227	200,018	Lincoln	Omaha
Nevada	1864	799,184	2	110,540	286,299	Carson City	Las Vegas
New Hampshire	1788	920,610	2	9,304	24,097	Concord	Manchester
New Jersey	1787	7,364,158	14	7,836	20,295	Trenton	Newark
New Mexico	1912	1,299,968	3	121,666	315,115	Santa Fe	Albuquerque
New York	1788	17,557,288	34	49,576	128,405	Albany	New York City
North Carolina	1789	5,874,429	11	52,586	136,198	Raleigh	Charlotte
North Dakota	1889	652,695	1	70,665	183,022	Bismarck	Fargo
Ohio	1803	10,797,419	21	41,222	106,765	Columbus	Cleveland
Oklahoma	1907	3,025,266	6	69,919	181,090	Oklahoma City	Oklahoma City
Oregon	1859	2,632,663	5	96,981	251,181	Salem	Portland
Pennsylvania	1787	11,866,728	23	45,333	117,412	Harrisburg	Philadelphia
Rhode Island	1790	947,154	2	1,214	3,144	Providence	Providence
South Carolina	1788	3,119,208	6	31,055	80,432	Columbia	Columbia
South Dakota	1889	690,178	1	77,047	199,552	Pierre	Sioux Falls
Tennessee	1796	4,590,750	9	42,244	109,412	Nashville	Memphis
Texas	1845	14,228,383	27	267,339	692,408	Austin	Houston
Utah	1896	1,461,037	3	84,916	219,932	Salt Lake City	Salt Lake City
Vermont	1791	511,456	1	9,609	24,887	Montpelier	Burlington
Virginia	1788	5,346,279	10	40,817	105,716	Richmond	Norfolk
Washington	1889	4,130,163	8	68,192	176,617	Olympia	Seattle
West Virginia	1863	1,949,644	4	24,181	62,629	Charleston	Charleston
Wisconsin	1848	4,705,335	9	56,154	145,439	Madison	Milwaukee
Wyoming	1890	470,816	1	97,914	253,687	Cheyenne	Casper
District of Columbia		637,651	—	69	174		Washington

The First Constitutions The first state constitutions were modeled after the old colonial charters. Between 1776 and 1780 all 13 of the original states adopted constitutions based more or less closely on these charters. In 12 of these states the legislatures approved the new constitutions without submitting them to popular votes. Only in Massachusetts was the constitution drawn up by a popularly elected convention and then approved by the people themselves. The Massachusetts Constitution, which was adopted in 1780, introduced the method by which most subsequent constitutions have been drafted. All of the present state constitutions were drawn up by popular assemblies, and only four* were adopted without first being submitted to a popular vote.

The first state constitutions were brief, general, and flexible in character. They granted broad authority to the legislatures and imposed few restrictions on how legislative power was to be used. They recognized that the power of the government originated with the people, and they were careful to preserve the people's sovereign rights. All 13 of the original state constitutions maintained the separation of powers and to some extent a system of checks and balances. In practice the early legislatures enjoyed more power than either of the other two branches. In all but Massachusetts and New York the governor was chosen by the legislature, and in most states the governor could serve only one term. Only Massachusetts and South Carolina gave the governor the power of veto. Remembering the excesses of the royal governors, the framers of the state constitutions were determined to keep power firmly in the hands of the people.

State Constitutions Today In their basic form state constitutions today are very much alike—and in many ways very like the first constitutions. Every state constitution provides for a separation of powers and a system of checks and balances among the legislative, executive, and judicial branches. All but the Nebraska Constitution provide for a bicameral legislature. Each limits the powers that are vested in the government. Each is based on the concept of popular sovereignty—that is, on the belief that the power of the government originates with the people. And each gives the state courts the power of judicial review—the power to declare an act of the government unconstitutional. Finally, every state constitution includes a bill of rights that includes most or all of the protections that are listed in the United States Bill of Rights. Usually a state bill of rights includes other protections—the right to leave the state, for example, or the right to engage in collective bargaining.

*Those of Vermont (1793), Mississippi (1890), South Carolina (1895), and Delaware (1897).

Samuel Adams, governor of Massachusetts from 1794 until 1797, was influential in the drafting of that state's 1780 constitution. Much of Adams's power as governor derived from his constitutional authority to veto acts of the state legislature.

Contents of State Constitutions

Each state constitution describes in detail the powers, structures, and procedures of state government. It specifies what each branch of the government can and cannot do. It spells out the laws that govern the relationships between state and local government. It specifies how the state can spend and borrow money. It spells out the tax laws. It includes provisions for public education. It tells how elections are to be held, how laws are to be drafted and adopted, and how public officials can be recalled.

THE STATE CONSTITUTIONS*

State	Date of Present Constitution	Number of Words	Number of Amendments	Number of Previous Constitutions
Alabama	1901	129,000	383	5
Alaska	1959	12,880	16	—
Arizona	1912	28,779	102	—
Arkansas	1874	40,469	67	4
California	1879	33,000	438	1
Colorado	1876	39,800	101	—
Connecticut	1965	7,900	16	3
Delaware	1897	18,700	107	3
Florida	1969	25,000	32	5
Georgia	1977	48,000	193	8
Hawaii	1959	17,450	74	—
Idaho	1890	21,323	94	—
Illinois	1971	13,200	2	3
Indiana	1851	10,225	34	1
Iowa	1857	12,500	43	1
Kansas	1861	11,865	80	—
Kentucky	1891	23,500	25	3
Louisiana	1975	35,387	8	10
Maine	1820	13,500	146	—
Maryland	1867	40,775	189	3
Massachusetts	1780	36,612	115	—
Michigan	1964	20,000	13	3
Minnesota	1858	9,491	103	—
Mississippi	1890	23,500	48	3
Missouri	1945	40,134	52	3
Montana	1973	11,812	7	1
Nebraska	1875	18,802	176	1
Nevada	1864	19,735	94	—
New Hampshire	1784	9,175	75	1
New Jersey	1948	17,086	28	2
New Mexico	1912	27,066	99	—
New York	1885	47,000	191	3
North Carolina	1971	10,500	19	2
North Dakota	1889	30,000	110	—
Ohio	1851	36,300	140	1
Oklahoma	1907	68,500	107	—
Oregon	1859	25,000	169	—
Pennsylvania	1968	21,675	15	4
Rhode Island	1843	19,026	43	1
South Carolina	1896	22,500	443	6
South Dakota	1889	23,250	89	—
Tennessee	1870	15,300	31	2
Texas	1876	61,000	247	4
Utah	1896	17,300	64	—
Vermont	1793	6,600	48	2
Virginia	1971	18,500	13	5
Washington	1889	29,350	73	—
West Virginia	1872	25,500	53	1
Wisconsin	1848	13,435	116	—
Wyoming	1890	27,600	47	—

*As of December 31, 1981. The figures are subject to various qualifications, and length of the constitutions for some states is in estimated number of words.

Source: *The Book of the States*

Most state constitutions begin with a statement of purpose called a ***preamble.*** Most also include a ***schedule***—a set of rules for putting new laws or provisions into effect. Sometimes provisions in a state constitution become outdated when times change or when new laws are passed. These provisions, which no longer have any legal force, remain a part of the constitution unless they are removed. They are known as ***dead letter provisions.***

In order to remove these dead letter provisions—and for other reasons as well—every state constitution includes procedures for change.

Changing State Constitutions

The earliest changes in state constitutions were made in response to abuses of legislative authority. In exacting detail, state constitutions listed what the government could not do. They specified how much public money the government could spend and what it could be spent for. From the 1820's to the 1850's changes were made in many government procedures. New offices were added to state governments. Executive and judicial offices, once filled by appointment, were made elective to make state government more directly accountable to the people.

During the latter half of the nineteenth century, state constitutions grew in detail. Various interest groups—agriculture, business, and labor—staked out claims for special protection and advantage. By the end of the century new state constitutions were becoming thoroughly unwieldy. As constitutions grew longer, they became essentially ***statutory codes***—that is, collections of specific laws on just about everything. The California Constitution, for example, specified that "fruit and nut-bearing trees under the age of four years" were exempt from taxation. The Illinois Constitution devoted a whole article to public warehouses. Detail gives rigidity to state constitutions and requires that they be added to or updated frequently to reflect changing times (see chart on page 700).

INSIGHT

Dead Letter Laws

In the city of China Grove, North Carolina, it is against the law to sneeze or whistle in public. A statute on the books in the state of California makes it illegal to require anyone to purchase a horror comic book. In the state of Arkansas a current statute forbids students from insulting one another.

These are only a few of thousands of dead letter laws that remain on the books in many cities and states—even though the laws are rarely, if ever, enforced today. Some dead letter laws give an interesting glimpse into how times have changed. A California statute, for example, enacted in 1872 but still on the books today, makes it illegal to reproach someone for not accepting a challenge to fight a duel. An ordinance in Evanston, Illinois, forbids anyone from making ice cream sodas on the Sabbath—the same ordinance that inspired a druggist to invent the "Sunday," now called the "sundae." In New York City a man unlucky enough to be arrested twice for turning around on a city street to stare at a woman is liable for an unusual punishment: according to a city ordinance, he can be sentenced to wear a pair of horse's blinders. In one of the strangest examples of a dead letter law, an ordinance in a small Chicago suburb makes it illegal for anyone to give lighted cigars to domesticated animals kept as pets.

Why do such laws remain on the books? In most cities and states it is easier to pass a law than to revoke one. Legislation must be repealed or declared unconstitutional, a procedure which in some cases can require a court hearing and a vote in the legislature. For that reason, most dead letter laws remain on the books—a reminder that laws change as times and customs change.

A constitution may be changed by amendment or by revision. An amendment alters only one, or at most a few, provisions of the constitution. A revision alters all or most of the original document. Most changes in state constitutions are made by amendment. State constitutions have been amended more than 3,000 times. The California Constitution has 438 amendments; the Texas Constitution, 247. Georgia's 1945 constitution was amended 830 separate times before the state adopted a revised constitution in 1977.

A constitutional change may be formal or informal. As explained in Chapter 3, the United States Constitution has often been changed both ways. State constitutions can also be changed formally and informally. But in practice informal change rarely takes place at the state level because state constitutions are rigid and specific. Unlike the federal Constitution, they spell out the powers, structures, and procedures of the government in detail. Then too, state courts, unlike the federal courts, have tended to interpret state constitutions strictly, a practice that has further discouraged the use of informal methods of change.

So when changes are made in a state constitution, it is most often done formally by means of an amendment.

Formal Amendments Formal amendments are made in one of three ways. They may be proposed by a constitutional convention. They may be proposed by the state legislature. Or they may be proposed by popular initiative. Regardless of how they are proposed, in 49 of the 50 states they must be approved by the voters.

Most amendments to state constitutions are made by legislative proposal. Provisions vary among the states, but the typical pattern requires a two-thirds vote of each chamber of the legislature to propose an amendment. In every state except Delaware the proposed amendment must then be submitted to the voters for ratification. In Delaware the legislature ratifies amendments.

Seventeen states, mostly in the West, permit proposal of amendments by ***popular initiative,*** a procedure enabling interested citizens to place a constitutional amendment on the ballot. Citizens do this by circulating a petition supporting the proposal. If the petition is signed by the required number of registered voters—from 3 percent in Massachusetts to 15 percent in Arizona and Oklahoma—the proposal is placed on the ballot, where the whole electorate approves or rejects it.

Popular initiative, like the process of legislative proposal, varies from state to state. One well-known example of an initiative proposal was California's Proposition 13, which in 1978 amended the state constitution to limit property taxes. The success of Proposition 13 was at least partly responsible for similar initiatives in several other states.

Constitutional Conventions To date, at least 230 conventions have been held to rewrite state constitutions. ***Constitutional conventions*** are called for the purpose of revising the constitution. In some states, however, they can be used to propose amendments. The legislature of every state has the power to call a convention, but in all but seven states* the voters must approve the decision to do so. Fourteen states† require the legislature to submit the question of a constitutional convention to the voters at intervals of 9 to 20 years. This requirement is based on the assumption that every generation should have a chance to revise its basic law.

---

*Alaska, Georgia, Louisiana, Maine, South Carolina, South Dakota, Virginia

†Alaska, Connecticut, Hawaii, Illinois, Iowa, Maryland, Michigan, Missouri, Montana, New Hampshire, New York, Ohio, Oklahoma, Rhode Island

Citizens of Cambridge, Massachusetts, sign a petition to place an amendment to the state constitution on the ballot.

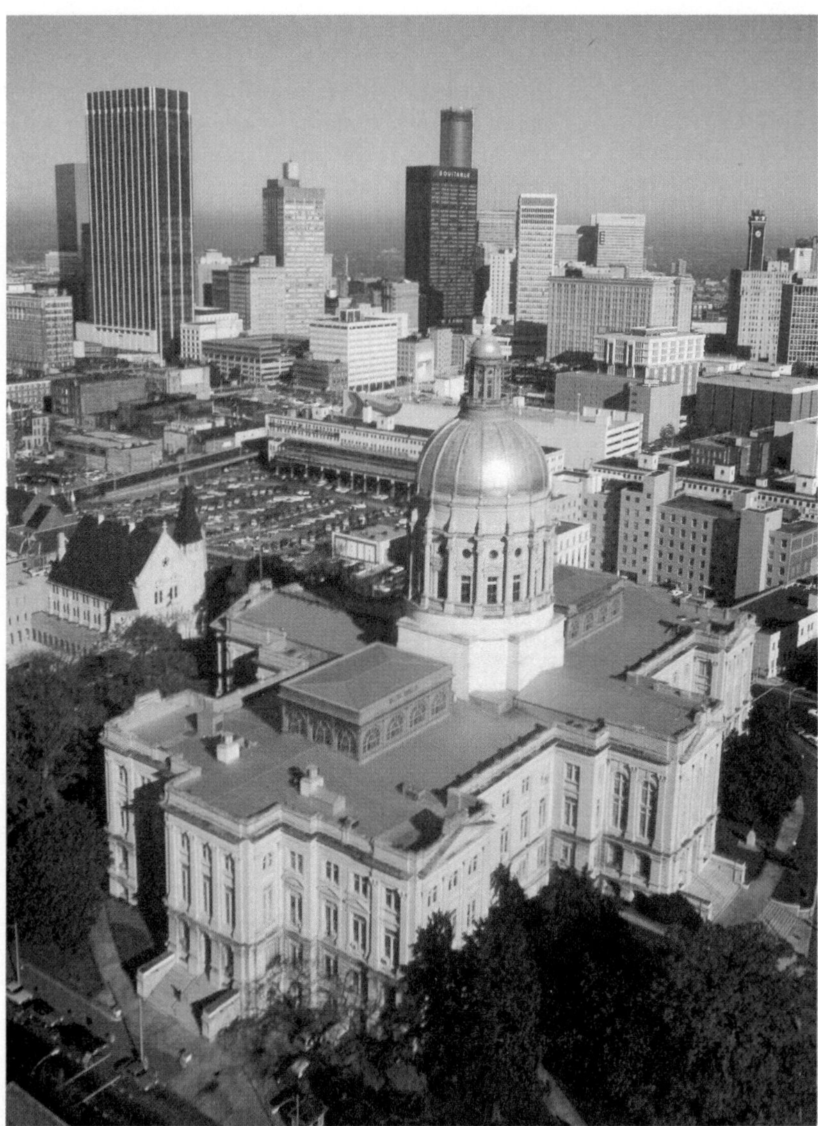

The Georgia state capitol in Atlanta is modeled after the United States Capitol in Washington, D.C. Atlanta has been the capital of Georgia since 1868.

If the voters approve the convention, they must then elect delegates. When the delegates have done their work, the new constitution is submitted to the voters for ratification. The voters may be asked to accept or reject it as a whole. Or they may be permitted to vote on it section by section. Thus a constitutional convention generally involves three separate popular elections.

A number of states have used ***constitutional commissions*** in rewriting their constitutions. These commissions are usually made up of selected state officials, together with leading citizens who are experts in fields that are relevant to the task of constitutional revision. Such commissions may be established for study purposes before the constitutional convention is called.

During the 1960's and 1970's most states considered major constitutional revisions. Citizens in 10 states actually approved new constitutions. The reforms tended to strengthen the powers of the governor, to make the bureaucracy more professional, and to reorganize the court system.

Need for Reform Most state constitutions are in need of reform. Practically all are out of date, too long, or both. Many—even the newest ones—do not address important current problems. Changes that have radically altered people's lives are often not reflected in the law that governs them.

Most state constitutions are simply too long. The first state constitutions kept to the basics; the longest one—that of Massachusetts—contained only about

12,000 words. Today only 9 approach that limit; the average length is around 37,000 words. By contrast, the Constitution has only 6,700 words.

And yet, in the face of the need for reform, proposals for revision draw strong opposition because any change in a state constitution is likely to benefit one group or interest at the expense of another. If enough groups object to one section or another, the proposed revision will be defeated.

Sometimes the defeat is stinging indeed. In Texas, for example, work on revising the 1876 constitution took five years and cost $7 million. When the proposed revision was placed before the voters, it was turned down by 73 percent of the voters.

Different States, Different Constitutions

In their basic form the state constitutions are very much alike. It is in their details that they differ. Different constitutions give different formal powers to the three branches of government. But even when the structures of government appear to be very similar, their style of operation may vary widely from one state to the next. One must always look beyond the formal, written constitution to see how the institutions of government actually work. A constitution establishes a framework and lays down basic rules. Within that framework the structures and process of government are shaped by changing times and by conditions peculiar to each state.

No two states are alike. They vary with respect to urbanization and industrialization. They vary in their racial, ethnic, and religious makeup. These and other factors give each state its own unique political character. It is important to remember these differences as basic patterns of state government are studied.

Section Check

1. Define: preamble, schedule, statutory code, popular initiative, constitutional commission
2. Identify: Amendment 10, dead letter provision, California's Proposition 13
3. What are the two methods for changing a state constitution?
4. How many popular elections are usually required during the entire process of a constitutional convention? What is the purpose of each?
5. Why do most state constitutions need reform?

2 THE STATE LEGISLATURES

The legislature is the branch of government that makes the laws. Under the earliest constitutions the legislatures were the central institutions of state government. During the nineteenth century legislative powers were cut back, and legislative prestige declined. Today legislatures vary widely in their power, prestige, and performance.

Bicameral Legislatures

The state legislatures have a variety of names. Most often a lawmaking body is simply called the legislature. Sometimes it is called the general assembly, the legislative assembly, or the general court. With the exception of Nebraska, which has a single-house

The unicameral legislature of Nebraska meets in the state capitol in Lincoln. The capitol, with its 400-feet high (120-meters high) tower, was completed in 1932. Omaha was the capital of Nebraska from 1855 until 1867. Lincoln has served as the capital since that time.

STATE LEGISLATURES

State	Senate Seats	Senate Term (years)	House Seats	House Term (years)
Alabama	35	4	105	4
Alaska	20	4	40	2
Arizona	30	2	60	2
Arkansas	35	4	100	2
California	40	4	80	2
Colorado	35	4	65	2
Connecticut	36	2	151	2
Delaware	21	4	41	2
Florida	40	4	120	2
Georgia	56	2	180	2
Hawaii	25	4	51	2
Idaho	35	2	70	2
Illinois	59	2 or 4	177	2
Indiana	50	4	100	2
Iowa	50	4	100	2
Kansas	40	4	125	2
Kentucky	38	4	100	2
Louisiana	39	4	105	4
Maine	33	2	151	2
Maryland	47	4	141	4
Massachusetts	40	2	160	2
Michigan	38	4	110	2
Minnesota	67	4	134	2
Mississippi	52	4	122	4
Missouri	34	4	163	2
Montana	50	4	100	2
Nebraska	49	4	unicameral	
Nevada	20	4	40	2
New Hampshire	24	2	400	2
New Jersey	40	4	80	2
New Mexico	42	4	70	2
New York	60	2	150	2
North Carolina	50	2	120	2
North Dakota	50	4	100	2
Ohio	33	4	99	2
Oklahoma	48	4	101	2
Oregon	30	4	60	2
Pennsylvania	50	4	203	2
Rhode Island	50	2	100	2
South Carolina	46	4	124	2
South Dakota	35	2	70	2
Tennessee	33	4	99	2
Texas	31	4	150	2
Utah	29	4	75	2
Vermont	30	2	150	2
Virginia	40	4	100	2
Washington	49	4	98	2
West Virginia	34	4	100	2
Wisconsin	33	4	99	2
Wyoming	30	4	62	2

Source: *The Book of the States*

A diversity exists among state legislatures because the federal system in the United States permits each state to structure its own government. Thus, the constitution of each state specifies the membership and structure of the state's legislature.

legislature, every state has a ***bicameral,*** or two-house, legislature. Following the terminology of Congress, the upper house is called the senate. The lower house in most states is known as the house of representatives. In a few states it is called the house of delegates, the assembly, or the general assembly.

The size of a state legislature is important. It must be large enough to represent the many interests of the people. At the same time, it must be small enough to work effectively. State legislatures come in all sizes, and not all are directly proportionate to the population of the state. The largest is that of New Hampshire, which has 424 members representing a state population of about 900,000. The smallest is that of Nevada, with 60 members for a population of 800,000. New York and California, the two most populous states, have legislatures of 210 and 120 members respectively.

In bicameral legislatures the upper house is usually smaller than the lower house, ranging in size from 20 to 67, with an average of about 40 members. The size of the lower house varies much more—from 40 to 400, with an average of 100 members.

State legislatures are bicameral for largely historical reasons. The legislatures of the original states were organized in the same way as the early colonial legislatures. These colonial legislatures were divided into an upper house, consisting of the governor's council, and a lower house, consisting of the people's elected representatives. When the colonies became independent, the national government followed the established colonial pattern.

Today some people believe that state legislatures should be ***unicameral***—that is, should consist of just one house. These people argue that in a bicameral system one house does not always act as a check on the other—which is one of the main reasons for having two houses in the first place. They believe that public opinion, the media, and the governor's veto act as better checks against poor legislation.

Supporters of bicameralism argue that the system works well in Congress, but opponents reply that Congress represents a federation of states. They argue that the bicameral system is not necessarily appropriate for state legislatures, each of which represents a single state.

Nebraska's unicameral legislature is composed of 49 members called senators, who are elected in a nonpartisan election to 4-year terms. Nebraska is the only state in which legislators are chosen in nonpartisan elections.

The Illinois constitution states that the regular session of the senate begins on the second Wednesday in January. It does not, however, specify the length of regular senate sessions.

Legislative Sessions

Forty-three states hold annual legislative sessions. Most of the others meet in regular session every other year. California holds a continuous two-year session. In some states the constitution limits the length of the legislative session—from 20 days in Utah and Wyoming to six months in Delaware and Missouri. In recent years the trend has been toward annual sessions and longer periods.

In every state the governor may also call the legislature into ***special session.*** In about half the states the legislature itself may call a special session. Special sessions are called fairly often, especially in states where regular sessions are limited or are held only every other year. The purpose of a special session is to enable the legislature to consider urgent business without having to wait for the next regular session. A few states also hold a ***veto session*** after each regular session. Its purpose is to consider any bills that the governor vetoed after the regular session had adjourned.

The Legislators

The qualifications for legislators are set forth in the constitution of each state. In most states members of the lower house must be at least 21 years old; in a few they need be only 18. Members of the upper house must usually be a little older—25 in most states and 30 in a few. Legislators must almost always be citizens of the United States and legal residents of the state in which they serve. Legislators are elected by the people, usually in November.

Members of the upper house serve four-year terms in most states; members of the lower house, two-year terms. For this reason, and also because the lower house is larger, there are usually more new members in the lower house than in the upper house in any given term.

But turnover is high in both houses; each year more than one fourth of all state legislators come in as new members serving their first term. This high turnover is largely a matter of money. Since legislative sessions rarely last more than a few months each year, most state legislators have only a part-time job, and they are usually paid a part-time salary. In a few states legislators' salaries are specified in the constitution but in most states the legislature sets its own salary. New York and California pay the highest legislative salaries, but few states pay enough for anyone to live on. Several states simply give an allowance for each day the legislature is in session. Under these circumstances a legislator must either be independently wealthy or hold another job, one that he or she can leave to attend the sessions of the legislature. Not surprisingly, lawyers make up the largest single occupational group among state legislators.

Even for those who can interrupt their work to attend sessions, the spirit of public service is not always enough to offset the financial hardship. Many legislators serve only a term or two and return voluntarily to their regular occupations. For others the legislature is a stepping-stone to higher political office. Under these conditions it is difficult for state legislatures to develop a stable and experienced membership.

Legislative Apportionment

The legislature is the representative assembly of the people. It acts in the name of the people and, ideally, in their behalf. But until the 1960's most state legislatures were not genuinely representative.

The seats in the state legislature are distributed among districts within the state in a process known as ***apportionment.*** The state constitution specifies how seats should be apportioned. With the passage of time apportionment has failed to reflect shifts in population.

Representative Imbalance In 1900 the United States was still a predominantly rural, agricultural society. But starting at the turn of the century, industrialization and urbanization transformed American society. By 1960, 70 percent of the people lived in urban areas. In most cases legislative districts had not been altered in over 50 years. As a result rural interests were overrepresented in state legislatures and urban interests were underrepresented. In Florida, for example, 20 percent of the state's population in 1960 lived in and around Miami. Yet Dade County, the legislative district in which Miami is located, elected only 3 of the 95 members of the house of representatives and only 1 of the state's 38 senators. In state after state there was a similar imbalance between rural and urban interests.

There were two reasons for rural-urban imbalance. First, many state constitutions apportioned seats on the basis of a political unit. No account was taken of population. Each county, for example, regardless of size, might be given the same number of seats. Second, many states ignored the constitutional requirement to reapportion legislative seats according to population shifts, following the federal census every 10 years. Perhaps legislators from small towns

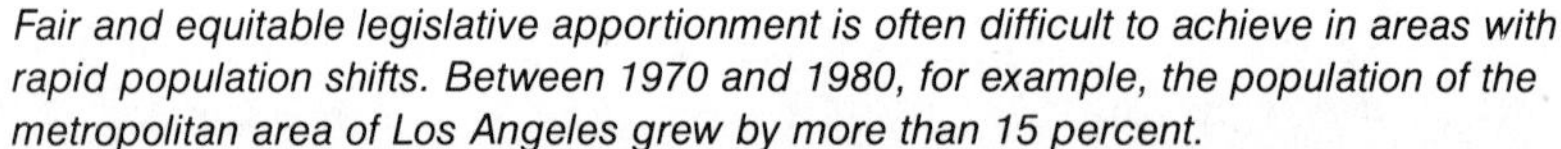

Fair and equitable legislative apportionment is often difficult to achieve in areas with rapid population shifts. Between 1970 and 1980, for example, the population of the metropolitan area of Los Angeles grew by more than 15 percent.

were not anxious to reapportion themselves out of a job. Perhaps, too, their constituents did not wish to lose the influence they enjoyed within the state legislature.

Obviously, urban leaders wanted a fair representation. They charged that the rural-dominated legislatures were unresponsive to the needs of the cities. They argued that the people who lived in the cities had been reduced to the status of second-class citizens. All across the country the call went out for reapportionment. The time had come to reapportion legislative seats to give fair representation to urban areas.

Court-Enforced Actions In Tennessee, where the legislature had not been reapportioned since 1901, the efforts of a group of urban voters brought the matter ultimately to the United States Supreme Court. The case was *Baker* v. *Carr* (1962). In one of the most significant decisions of the twentieth century, the Court held that citizens have the right to challenge unequal representation through the federal courts. *Baker* v. *Carr* marked the beginning of the reapportionment revolution. But *Baker* v. *Carr* was only the first step. The Supreme Court had decided that the federal courts had jurisdiction over cases in which unequal representation was alleged. But it had not decided the important question of whether representation should be based on area or on population.

This question was answered in the landmark case of *Reynolds* v. *Sims* (1964). In this case the Supreme Court stated:

The fundamental principle of representative government in this country is one of equal representation for equal numbers of people, without regard to race, sex, economic status, or place of residence within a state.

In other words, voting equality means one person, one vote. This principle was to be applied to both houses of a state legislature. Thus, the Court rejected the federal analogy—the argument that representation in the upper house might be based on geographic units, as it is in the United States Senate, while representation in the lower house was based on population. Speaking for the Court, Chief Justice Earl Warren declared:

Legislators represent people, not trees or acres. Legislators are elected by voters, not farms or cities or economic interests.

From now on, apportionment was to be based on population—and population alone.

As a result of these Supreme Court decisions, the states reapportioned their legislatures. Districts were redrawn so that each district had approximately the same number of people. "The weight of a citizen's vote," the Chief Justice stated in *Reynolds*, "cannot be made to depend on where he lives."

The impact of reapportionment was felt across the nation, but it was felt in different ways. Except in the few predominantly agricultural states, rural interests lost control of the state legislatures. In the heavily populated northern states reapportionment favored the growing suburbs rather than the central cities. In the South it gave new power to the cities and changed the basic character of state politics. In Georgia, for example, the most populous county, containing Atlanta, increased its representation in the state senate from one member to seven. One of the new senators elected was the first black to serve in the Georgia legislature since Reconstruction.

Political Parties and Interest Groups

Politics in the United States is organized primarily through political parties, but the role of parties in state government varies from state to state. Political parties are likely to play an important role in states where there is close two-party competition. In other states political parties often play little or no role in legislative decision making because legislators may be divided along other lines—urban versus rural, business versus labor, or liberal versus conservative. In all but one state, however, a candidate for the state legislature seeks election as the nominee of a political party. The one exception is Nebraska, where legislators are not identified on the ballot by party label.

Interest groups play an important role in state government—far too important, say their critics. Interest groups organize around virtually every issue. Permanent interest groups have been established in such fields as business, labor, agriculture, oil and gas, highways, health, and education. Other interest groups come together on a one-time basis to support or oppose a particular bill. Permanent interest groups usually have an office in the state capital and a full-time group representative or ***lobbyist***, who keeps in continuous touch with members of the legislature.

Interest groups often find it easier to exert their influence at the state level than at the national level. The national government is a wide arena in which many diverse interests must compete for attention. A state is more easily dominated by the activity of a given interest group. Patterns of domination vary with the character of the state, its society, and its economy. Most states follow one of four patterns.

1. An alliance of two or three major interest groups dominates state politics.
2. A single interest predominates.
3. Two dominant groups, such as business and labor, conflict.
4. Many diverse interests compete with each other for influence.

The legislator's job is to manage interest groups, not to be managed by them. The legislator is the broker in the process of bargaining and compromise that is the essence of political life.

Powers of State Legislatures

The legislature has all the powers that the state constitution does not grant exclusively to some other branch of government and that are not prohibited to it by the state constitution or by the United States Constitution. These powers may be legislative or nonlegislative.

Legislative Powers All of the powers a state legislature exercises when it makes law are legislative powers. Wide ranging and extremely varied, they include the power to maintain the public schools, to regulate business, to borrow money, to define and punish crimes, and to collect taxes. A state legislature may enact any law that does not conflict with the Constitution, with federal law, or with its state constitution—essentially, its reserved powers.

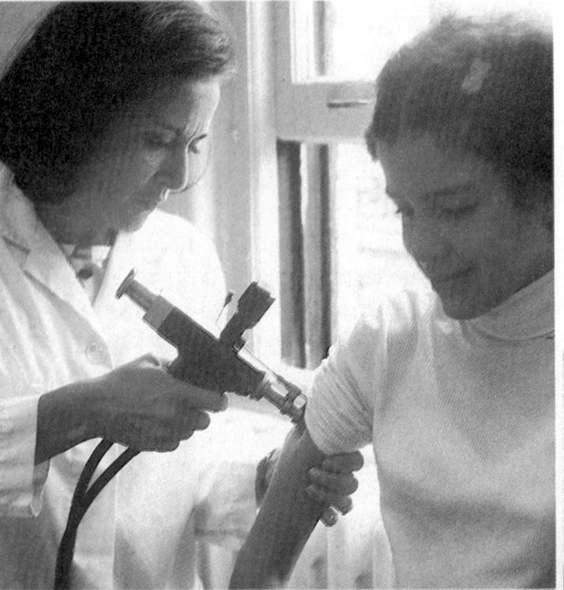

Among the legislative powers of state legislatures are the authority to require periodic safety inspections for automobiles registered in the state (below) and the authority to immunize children against communicable diseases (left). List other legislative powers of the state legislatures.

What goes on in the state legislature only occasionally makes headlines. Few of the issues it considers are earthshaking. Yet state law touches almost every aspect of our lives—whether we know it or not. Many years ago, a member of the Oregon legislature described his experience after he was first elected.

*I arrived at our new marble Capitol expecting to spend most of my time considering momentous issues—social security, taxes, conservation, civil liberties. Instead we devoted long hours to the discussion of regulations for the labeling of eggs. We have argued about the alignment of irrigation ditches, the speed of motorboats on mountain lakes, the salaries of justices of the peace, and whether or not barbers and beauty parlor attendants should be high school graduates. For two days we wrangled about a bill specifying the proper scales for weighing logs and lumber.**

None of these questions concerns large numbers of people. Yet each question concerns a few people vitally.

One of the most important legislative powers is the ***police power***—the authority to promote and protect the health, safety, morals, and welfare of the people. This power is nowhere precisely defined, but it is the foundation for the broad scope of state regulatory activity. It includes far more than law enforcement. It is the basis for laws that require automobile safety inspections, building codes, sanitation laws, the licensing of doctors and nurses, compulsory vaccination, and compulsory school attendance. The list could go on and on.

A state legislature also holds the purse strings. The ***power of the purse*** gives the legislature control over the tax and appropriation measures of the state budget. The legislature alone has the power to authorize state spending for whatever purpose. Roads, the construction of schools and hospitals, welfare programs, teachers' salaries—appropriations for all of these things are determined by the state legislature.

Nonlegislative Powers A legislature exercises certain other powers called nonlegislative powers. These fall into three categories. ***Executive powers***—the power to appoint certain state officials or to approve the governor's appointments—are vested in the legislature in some of the states. ***Judicial powers*** include the power to impeach executive and judicial officers. This power is vested in the legislature in all states except Oregon. In every state the legislature also has the power to judge disputes involving its own members. Finally, the ***constituent power***—the power to amend or revise the state constitution—is considered a nonlegislative power.

*Richard L. Neuberger, "I Go to the Legislature," *Survey Graphic,* July 1941, p. 374.

Legislative Organization and Procedure

All of the state legislatures are organized in much the same way, and all of them use similar procedures. Although their specific powers vary from state to state, the presiding officers of the house and senate are typically the key figures in the legislative process.

Presiding Officers The presiding officer of the house is the speaker. The speaker is elected formally by the entire membership of the house. In practice the choice is made by the members of the

Willie L. Brown, Jr., is the speaker of the California assembly, the lower house of that state's legislature. In California the speaker is chosen by the entire membership of the assembly. Assembly members serve two-year terms.

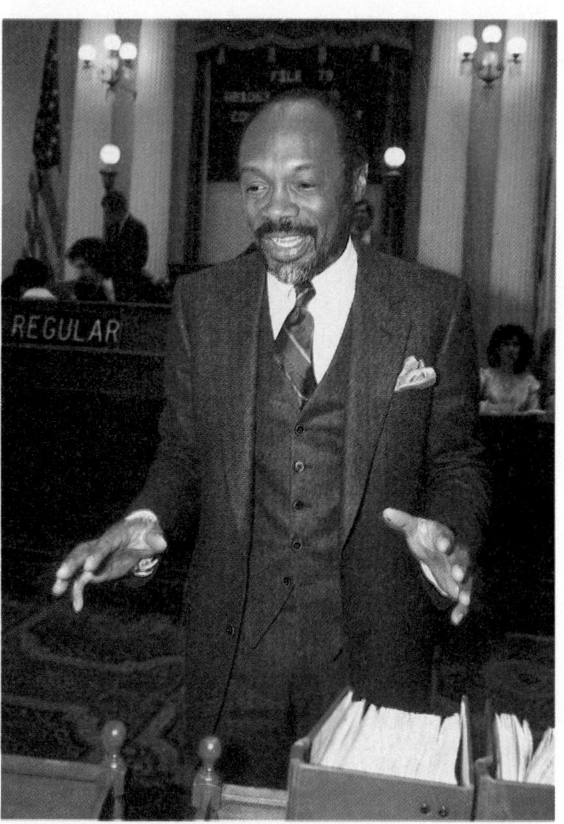

majority party. In 30 states the lieutenant governor presides over the senate; in the others the presiding officer is selected by the majority party.

The presiding officers are very powerful figures indeed. They recognize members who seek the floor—thus controlling who gets to speak and when. They interpret and apply the rules. They refer bills to committee. But above all, the presiding officers control committee appointments.

Committees Much legislative work is done by committees. There are usually 20 or so permanent, or standing, committees in each house. Most standing committees have jurisdiction over a particular subject—highways or education, for example. Each legislator typically serves on two or three committees, and each committee may have from 10 to 40 members. Joint committees—standing committees made up of members of both houses—in about half the state legislatures are used to save time and money. ***Interim committees*** work between legislative sessions. They study a specific problem in detail and present their findings to the next session.

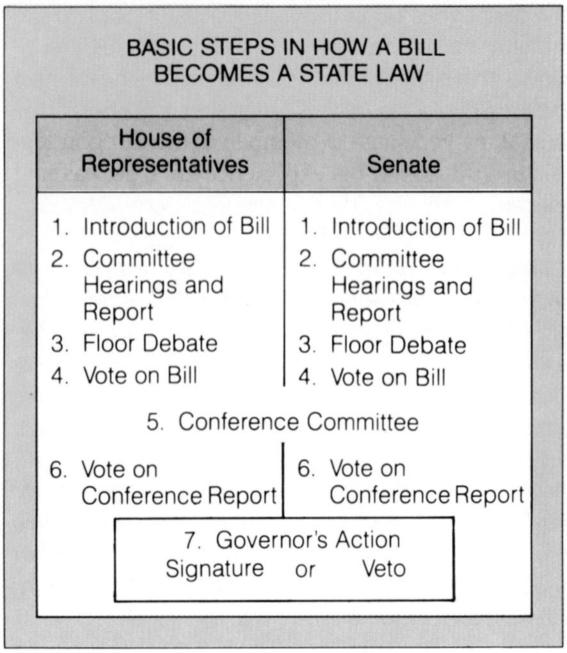

BASIC STEPS IN HOW A BILL BECOMES A STATE LAW

House of Representatives	Senate
1. Introduction of Bill 2. Committee Hearings and Report 3. Floor Debate 4. Vote on Bill	1. Introduction of Bill 2. Committee Hearings and Report 3. Floor Debate 4. Vote on Bill
5. Conference Committee	
6. Vote on Conference Report	6. Vote on Conference Report
7. Governor's Action Signature or Veto	

A simplified chart describes the typical legislative procedure by which a bill becomes a state law. What step follows the conference committee's passage of the bill?

Procedure The procedure for passing bills in state legislatures is roughly similar to the procedure used in Congress.* The specifics differ among the states, but they are almost always complicated. Mastery of procedure is the mark of a skilled legislator. The typical process by which a bill becomes a law is presented in the chart on this page.

The idea for a bill may originate with a legislator. More often bills originate with the governor, a state administrative agency, or an interest group. Occasionally an individual provides the idea for a bill. But only a member of the legislature may introduce a bill. Except for revenue legislation, which must be introduced in the lower house, bills may be introduced in either house. Important bills are often introduced in both houses at the same time.

After a bill is introduced, the presiding officer refers it to the appropriate standing committee. The committee conducts hearings on the merits of the bill, and witnesses, pro and con, are invited to testify. The committee closely examines each provision of the bill, makes amendments, and may even rewrite it. In many states, a committee may simply ignore a bill—in effect killing it.

If the bill is reported favorably back to the originating house, it is placed on the calendar and is brought to the chamber floor for debate. Amendments are considered and put to a vote. If the final bill is passed, it then goes to the other house, where the whole procedure is repeated.

There are several ways of taking a vote. The common method is the voice vote. The presiding officer puts the question to the house and then judges from the volume of the response whether there are more "yeas" or "nays." If the presiding officer's judgment is challenged, the question is often settled by a standing vote. Here the members for and then those against a motion rise, and the presiding officer counts them. In a teller vote the members file past and are counted by two tellers, one for the motion and one against it. And in a record vote or roll-call vote, each member who is present gives one of three responses—"yea," "nay," or "present" (not voting) and the response is recorded next to the member's name. Members who are not present are recorded "absent." A role-call vote is time-consuming, but it provides a permanent record that shows how each legislator voted on the issue in question.

A bill must pass both houses in order to become a law. Sometimes it passes both houses, but in two

*See Chapter 16, "Congress in Action." For details of the legislative procedure in their own state, students may refer to the legislative manual, available in many libraries. A more general description of the process may be found in the legislative guide published in most states by the League of Women Voters.

different forms. When this happens, a conference committee may be appointed to iron out the differences in each house's bill. The committee is made up of members from each house, and it reaches agreement on the wording for a bill. Once the conference report has cleared both houses, the bill is submitted to the governor for action.

When the governor signs it, the bill becomes state law. In every state except North Carolina, however, the governor can refuse to approve a bill. This veto power gives the governor a strong voice in the legislative process. The legislature can override the governor's veto, but a two-thirds vote is usually required, and this is difficult to achieve. For this reason the governor can often sway the legislature simply by threatening to veto a bill. In most states the governor also has an ***item veto,*** that is, the power to veto specific sections or items—usually of an appropriations bill—while signing the rest of the bill into law.

Citizens and Legislation

In some states the voters play an active role in the legislative process. They do this by means of two devices: the referendum and the initiative.

There are three forms of referendum. In all three a legislative bill is referred directly to the voters for approval. In the ***popular referendum*** the people may petition to vote on a bill already passed by the legislature. In other words, the people have the veto power. Unlike the governor's veto, the people's veto may not be overridden by the legislature. Twenty-four states have some form of popular referendum.

In the ***mandatory referendum*** a bill must be referred to the voters. Except in Delaware, any proposed amendment to the state constitution must be approved by the voters. In some states certain other kinds of legislative measures also call for a mandatory referendum.

The ***optional referendum*** is seldom used; here the legislature chooses to refer a measure to the voters. Usually it does so in order to avoid having to take a stand on a difficult or politically ticklish question.

The popular initiative may be used not only to propose a constitutional amendment, but also, in 21 states, to propose an ordinary statute. A required number of voters must sign a petition that describes the proposal for an amendment or law. In the case of a ***direct initiative*** the proposal is placed on the ballot. If the voters approve the initiative, it becomes law directly. This is the method that is used for constitutional amendments. In the case of an ***indirect initiative*** the proposal goes first to the legislature. If the legislature fails to enact the proposal, it, too, goes on the ballot.

These methods of direct legislation may be seen as a way of safeguarding the popular sovereignty. They ensure that, while the legislature makes the laws, its power to do so is subject to the wishes of the people.

Section Check

1. Define: police power, power of the purse, item veto, interim committee, referendum, initiative
2. Identify: *Baker* v. *Carr* (1962), *Reynolds* v. *Sims* (1964)
3. How are most state legislatures organized?
4. What is meant by the executive, judicial, and constituent powers of state legislatures?
5. What are the different ways of holding a vote in state legislatures?
6. What are the three forms of referendum?

3 THE STATE EXECUTIVE OFFICES

The ***governor,*** as the chief executive of each state, enjoys the prestige of the state's highest office. It is to the governor that the state's people look for leadership. But the power a governor actually commands has varied widely over time and still varies from state to state.

Development of the Governor's Office

In colonial America the governor was the representative of the British Crown. By the time the Revolution took place, the conflict between the royal governor and the elected legislature had bred distrust of executive authority. The first state constitutions, written between 1776 and 1780, reflected this distrust. In all but two states the governor was chosen by the state legislature. In most states the governor served only a one-year term. A governor's powers were limited. Generally a governor was little more than a figurehead.

The Constitution established a balanced relationship between the executive and legislative branches of the national government. In so doing, it set an example for the states. Over the next 50 years the governors gradually came to be elected by the people. They gained the veto power, and their administrative powers increased.

The expansion of their office gave the governors independent authority, yet their powers remained relatively weak. Governors were no longer dominated by the legislatures because the rise of Jacksonian democracy in the 1820's weakened the governors' control over the executive branch. Numerous executive and judicial officials, formerly appointed by the governors, were now elected by popular vote. Elected officials typically included lieutenant governors, attorneys general, secretaries of state, and the superintendents of education. These elected officials had their own constituencies and were often political rivals. The intent was to make state government more responsive to the people. The result in practice was to divide executive responsibilities and to make it more difficult for the people to hold any one official accountable for state policy and action.

Toward the end of the nineteenth century state activities expanded to meet the challenge of urbanization and industrialization. New agencies, boards, and commissions were created. Most of these were beyond control of the chief executives. Many of the officials were elected, but even when they were appointed, they usually served long terms and were hard to remove.

By the end of the 1800's the governors had gained important political powers. As state party leaders, the governors became increasingly influential in the legislature. In most states governors obtained the power to call special sessions, to prepare and submit the state budgets, and to exercise item vetos over appropriations bills. However, they still had no effective control over the administration of their executive offices.

The movement for administrative reorganization of the executive branch of state government began in about 1910. Its goal was to promote efficiency and economy in state government by concentrating executive power in the hands of the governor. Illinois took the lead in 1917, when it completely reorganized its executive branch. In place of a hundred or so agencies, nine new departments were created. Each was headed by a single director, appointed by and directly responsible to the state's governor. Other states soon followed suit. They reduced the number of their elected officials and consolidated their executive offices under the control of the governors. In many states the governors were also given longer terms of office and greater budgetary powers.

The reorganization efforts enhanced the governorship while making state governments more responsible and more effective. But the formal powers of the governorship still vary widely from state to state.

The Governor's Office Today

As the central position in state government, the governor's office is an attractive political prize. Election as governor may be the peak of a career in state public life or a stepping-stone to the Senate, the Vice Presidency, or the Presidency itself. In 1980 both major-party candidates for the Presidency had once served as state governors—Jimmy Carter in Georgia and Ronald Reagan in California.

Qualifications In most states the constitution prescribes the formal qualifications for governor. The minimum age requirement is usually set at 30 years. The governor must be a United States citizen and must usually have resided in the state for a certain period. Only two states—Kansas and Ohio—set no formal qualifications for the office of governor.

The formal qualifications establish legal eligibility for the office. But to be elected, candidates must also demonstrate integrity, experience, and leadership. Most candidates have long records of public service, and many have served in the legislature or in an executive office—often as lieutenant governors or attorneys general. To be elected, candidates must be acceptable to the major political, ethnic, and business interests within each state. Last but not least, they must have the personal and political appeal to win votes.

Selection The governor is elected by the people. In most states candidates from the major parties are nominated in primary elections. In a few states they are chosen by conventions. In almost half the states the governor and lieutenant governor run as a team and are elected together, like the President and Vice President of the United States. In all but four states a plurality is required to win a gubernatorial election.*

---

*The four are Georgia, Louisiana, Mississippi, and Vermont. If no candidate wins a clear majority in the first two states, a run-off election is held. In the last two states the legislature chooses the winner.

The governor's official residence in Olympia, Washington, stands on a hill overlooking the state capitol. The governor of Washington serves a four-year term, and may be reelected an unlimited number of times.

Term and Salary In most states the governor serves a four-year term. In Arkansas, New Hampshire, New Mexico, and Virginia the term is two years. In about half the states there is no limit on the number of terms a governor may serve. Twenty-four states restrict the governor to two consecutive terms. In Kentucky, Mississippi, New Mexico, and Virginia the governor cannot run for reelection.

Governors' salaries vary from state to state, but compared to state legislators, governors are generally well paid. The average annual salary is around $56,000. Most states also give their governors an expense account and an official residence.

Removal and Succession In every state except Oregon, a governor may be impeached. In impeachment the lower house of the state legislature brings a formal charge of misconduct against the governor or another high state official. The upper house holds the trial. If convicted, the governor is removed from office. Since 1900 four governors have been removed from office by impeachment.* In most states the official who has been impeached is barred thereafter from holding public office in that state.

In 15 states the governor may also be removed by popular ***recall.*** In this procedure those who wish to remove the governor circulate a petition. If they gather the required number of signatures, a special election is held to decide whether the governor shall be dismissed. Only one governor, Lynn J. Frazier of North Dakota in 1921, has ever been removed from office by recall.

When a governor is removed, resigns, or dies, the line of succession is specified in the constitution of each state. In 43 states the lieutenant governor assumes the office of chief executive. In four states it goes to the president of the senate, and in the remaining three states it goes to the secretary of state.

*William Selzer of New York, 1913; James E. Ferguson of Texas, 1917; J. C. Walton of Oklahoma, 1923; and Henry S. Johnston of Oklahoma, 1929.

Current governors include Mario Cuomo (left) of New York, George Nigh (above left) of Oklahoma, and William F. Winter (above right) of Mississippi. As head of the executive branch of state government, a governor's primary responsibility is to enforce the laws passed by the state's legislative branch.

Powers of the Governorship

The governors are the central figures of state governments and hold certain specific powers. One of the most important is the executive power to appoint and remove lower officials.

Executive Powers Governors work best with assistants whom they choose themselves. Choice does not guarantee effective administration, but governors who can appoint department heads are likely to be stronger than those who lack this power.

In most states the governor shares executive authority with other elected officers. Typically these officers include the lieutenant governor, the attorney general, and the secretary of state. Other officers, although they are appointed by the governor, must be confirmed by the state's upper house. And the legislature often sets its own requirements for appointees to the boards and commissions it creates, giving the governor little control over the appointments. Finally, state law requires that members of the civil service be hired on the basis of merit and fired only for cause. All these limitations affect the governor's power of appointment and removal. Administrative reorganization has strengthened the governorship in most states, but a governor's opportunity for control over administration varies widely.

The power of supervision is closely related to the power of appointment and removal. It is part of a governor's job to supervise the administration of state government, the actual details of which are handled by hundreds of boards, commissions, and agencies and by the thousands of individuals within them. A governor's ability to control all these agencies is determined partly by the formal powers vested in the office by the state constitution. It is also determined partly by such informal powers as the governor's control over the party and ability to influence public opinion. A governor who knows how to make good use of these informal powers is likely to be a strong administrator.

A major source of executive power is the governor's formulation of the ***state budget.*** The budget is an estimate of the revenues and expenditures

Martha Layne Collins, who had been the lieutenant governor of Kentucky, celebrates her election to the governorship. Collins won almost 55 percent of the vote in a three-way contest.

needed to carry out state operations for a specific period, usually a year. The budget sets priorities of program and policy objectives.

In all but a few states, the governor prepares the budget and submits it to the legislature. The legislature must pass the budget, and no state monies may be spent without legislative appropriation. The legislature can and does make changes, but the final budget is basically the same as the one submitted by the governor. By giving money to or withholding money from an agency, the governor can exercise considerable control.

The governor also has certain military powers as the commander in chief of the state's National Guard. The governor also has responsibility for organizing ***civil defense***—the protection of the civilian population—in the event of an enemy attack against the United States.

Legislative Powers Like the three branches of the national government, the three branches of state government share powers in a system of checks and balances. The state's chief executive is also the state's chief legislator. A governor's ability to play this role depends partly on popular support and on the support of the governor's own party. But most state constitutions give the governor three important legislative powers.

LEGACY

The National Guard

The National Guards are the volunteer armed forces of the states. Originally called the "militia," the first unit was organized in the Massachusetts Bay Colony in 1636. As bands of Minutemen, they fought at the battles of Lexington and Concord in the American Revolution.

The men and women of today's National Guard have regular civilian occupations in normal times. But they are organized, equipped, and trained to meet the call for emergency action. In time of peace a state's National Guard units are under the control of the state governor. They stand in readiness to provide aid in time of natural disaster or to preserve the peace and public safety in the event of civil disorder. The federal government calls up National Guard units in time of war or national emergency. National Guard units have served on active duty in World Wars I and II, in Korea, and in Vietnam.

The first is the power to recommend legislation. It is exercised through messages and through the state budget. Governors typically present their programs in an annual State of the State Address at the beginning of a legislative session. From time to time they may also send messages to the legislature calling for the enactment of a particular bill. Finally, governors may send informal messages—in private talks with legislative leaders, in public appeals to the voters—to help promote a particular piece of legislation.

Governors also wield considerable legislative clout through their control of the state budget. Governors have the power, in effect, to fund the programs they wish to promote and to cut off funds from others.

Second, governors of all 50 states have the power to call the legislature into special session. In some states they may specify what the legislature can consider in special session. In theory, special sessions are called in order to consider urgent business. In practice, the governor may threaten to call a special session if the legislature fails to pass a bill during the regular session. Thus the legislative power of the governor is greater than appears at first glance.

Third, in every state but North Carolina, the governor has the veto power. This is a formidable weapon for influencing legislative outcome. A veto is not easy to override, and by threatening to veto a bill, the governor can often influence the legislature.

Judicial Powers The governor also has certain judicial powers. These are the so-called powers of ***executive clemency***—powers to lighten or overturn the sentences of people who have been convicted of state crimes. A governor may issue a ***pardon,*** which is the power to release a person from punishment. Pardons are usually granted to correct mistakes in conviction or to release offenders who have been rehabilitated. In about half the states the pardoning power is the governor's alone. In others an advisory pardon board makes recommendations to the governor.

The governor may also commute a sentence—reduce its severity—or grant a reprieve. A reprieve is a delay in punishment granted so that the court may consider new evidence or to allow time for further appeal. The governor may also reduce or cancel a fine. Finally, the governor may have the power to parole. Usually this power is exercised by the state parole board. The exact nature of all of these powers varies from state to state, but in each state the governor has some or all of them.

Other Roles Governors greet visiting dignitaries, dedicate new buildings, and make public appearances at a host of gatherings. They open state fairs; they speak on any number of occasions; they crown the winners of beauty contests, pie-eating contests, and calf-roping contests. At public events of every kind governors represent their states.

Governors also represent their states in negotiations with other levels of government and with other states. They negotiate with local governments to determine state and local responsibilities—to decide who, for example, pays what towards the cost of public education. They negotiate with other state governments on problems of mutual concern—air and water pollution, for example. Finally, they negotiate with the federal government—for highway funds, welfare assistance, aid to education, for moneys from a vast number of federal programs. In national conferences, before congressional committees, and in the offices of various federal agencies, governors represent the views and interests of their states.

Governor George Deukmejian of California hosts Queen Elizabeth II of Great Britain during her visit in 1983. Describe other situations in which governors represent their states.

PROFILE

The Governorship in America

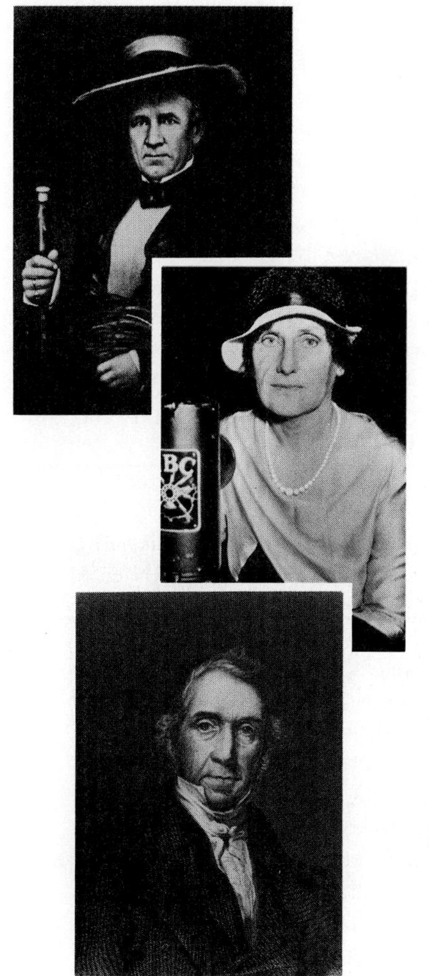

The first American governors represented the British king in the 13 colonies. As the struggle for independence grew, the men chosen to preside over the colonies were often revolutionary leaders. A year after Patrick Henry delivered his famous words, "Give me Liberty, or give me Death," he was elected governor of Virginia (1776–1779). He was followed in that office by Thomas Jefferson (1779–1781).

Several of the men who staked out the American continent went on to serve the nation as territorial governors. Meriwether Lewis and William Clark, whose expedition was the first to cross the continent by way of its two great rivers, were later appointed governors. Lewis presided over the Louisiana territory, Clark over the territory of Missouri. John C. Frémont, called "the Pathfinder," who led an early expedition into California, later served as governor of the Arizona territory.

Military leaders also sat in the governor's office. Henry "Light-Horse Harry" Lee, a daring Revolutionary Army cavalry officer, went on to hold Virginia's highest office. Sam Houston (top), commander in chief of the Texas Army in the war for independence from Mexico, has the singular distinction of serving as governor in two different states—Tennessee (1827–1829) and Texas (1859–1861).

Throughout its history the governorship has been a stepping stone to higher office. Twenty-one Presidents and Vice Presidents held office as governors before they entered national politics. Four governors—John Jay, Salmon P. Chase, Charles Evans Hughes, and Earl Warren—went on to the Supreme Court. In one reversal, Alexander Stephens was elected governor of Georgia after serving as Vice President of the Confederacy.

Women entered the American governorship late. Nellie Tayloe Ross (center) was elected governor of Wyoming in 1925—the first woman to serve as governor. (She later served as director of the United States Mint, another first for a woman.) Only 15 days after Nellie Tayloe Ross became governor, Miriam A. Ferguson began the first of her two terms as governor of Texas. Lurleen Wallace of Alabama, Ella Grasso of Connecticut, and Dixy Lee Ray of Washington also served as governors. In 1984 Martha Layne Collins was elected governor of Kentucky and Madeleine Kunin was elected governor of Vermont.

Perhaps the most successful candidate for governor was Thomas Chittenden of Vermont, who ran for 20 successive terms and was elected for 19. The most persistent candidate was Marcus Morton (bottom), who ran for the Massachusetts governorship 17 times. He was elected only twice, and won one of these elections—in 1839—by a single vote.

Governors are political leaders, too. As the states' most prominent officials, governors are the center of public attention. Television, radio, and newspapers cover the governors' news conferences, meetings, and public appearances. This media attention enables governors to focus public opinion on the issues they believe to be important.

Governors are usually party leaders, though their roles as heads of their political parties are often challenged by a big-city mayor, a United States senator, or the leader of an opposition group. Yet governors have little formal authority over party members. They are leaders by virtue of political skill; their power depends on their ability to persuade.

Other Executive Officers

Governors usually share executive authority with other elected officers.* These state officers typically include the lieutenant governor, the attorney general, the state treasurer, the auditor or comptroller, and the secretary of state. In some states they also include the superintendent of public instruction.

The Lieutenant Governor Forty-three states have a lieutenant governor. In all but Tennessee and Utah the post is elective. The lieutenant governor is elected at the same time as the governor and serves the same term of office. The role is rather like that of the Vice President. The lieutenant governor takes over the job of governor if the office becomes vacant and typically presides over the state senate, casting the deciding vote in case of a tie. Beyond that, most lieutenant governors have little to do. A notable exception is the lieutenant governor of Texas. His or her power over committee appointments and over the agenda of the upper house has made him or her the state senate's most powerful leader.

The Attorney General The attorney general is the chief legal officer of the state. In 42 states the attorney general is elected; in the others he or she is appointed by the governor, by the legislature, or in one state (Tennessee), by the supreme court.

The attorney general serves as legal adviser to the governor, to the legislature, and to state agencies. This officer represents the state in legal actions and has important law-enforcement powers. In some states—California, for example—the attorney general also has general supervisory powers over district attorneys and sheriffs. The ***legal opinions*** of the attorney general—that is, formal interpretations of state law—have the force of law in state affairs, unless they are overruled by a court.

In most states the attorney general is second only to the governor in power. This office, like the office of lieutenant governor, is often seen as a stepping-stone to the governorship.

The State Treasurer The state treasurer, elected in 39 states, is in charge of state funds. He or she oversees the investment of state money, acts as the state's paymaster, and, in some states, collects taxes. The treasurer's most important duty is to make payments for the state payroll and for goods and services purchased by the state.

The Auditor Closely related to the office of treasurer is that of the auditor, or comptroller. The auditor is the state's financial watchdog and determines in advance whether or not the spending of state agencies is authorized by law.

The legality of state spending must also be verified—that is, the auditor must examine the accounts of any agency that spends state money in order to make sure that the money was, in fact, spent legally. Although one elected official performs both of these functions in most states, there are strong arguments for having them performed by two separate officials, the first appointed by the governor, the second appointed by the legislature. Such an arrangement—which now exists in only 12 states—provides a better check against waste and fraud.

The Secretary of State The United States Secretary of State is in charge of America's relations with foreign countries. At the state level this officer has a totally different responsibility as the keeper of official records and documents. The secretary of state issues business licenses and charters corporations. As the state's chief election officer, the secretary of state also administers the election laws, prepares and distributes ballots, and receives the election results. As a rule, the office is elective. The office exists in every state except Alaska and Hawaii.

*In Maine, New Jersey, and Tennessee the governor is the only executive officer elected by the people.

Nancy Dick is the lieutenant governor of Colorado. What is the lieutenant governor's role in state government? How is a lieutenant governor usually chosen?

March Fong Eu, the secretary of state of California, affixes the state seal to a legal document. List five other responsibilities of a secretary of state.

The Superintendent of Public Instruction The public school system is administered by the superintendent of public instruction, sometimes called the commissioner of education. This officer is elected in 18 states. In the other states the superintendent is appointed either by the governor or by the state board of education. This board sets general education policy. Its members are usually appointed by the governor, although in a few states they are elected. In most states the superintendent serves on the board and acts as its chief administrative officer. He or she usually establishes and enforces statewide standards in school curriculum, certifies teachers, and controls state funding to local school districts.

State Boards In addition to the executive offices there are many minor offices, some appointive and others elective. In addition there are dozens of state boards, each of which administers certain institutions or certain laws within the state. Schools are administered by the state board of education. The parole of state prisoners is usually handled by the parole board. Laws relating to public health may be administered by the state board of health, laws relating to banking by the banking commission. Many state boards also issue commercial and professional licenses; for example, to practice medicine within a state, a physician must be licensed by the state board of medical examiners. State boards, commissions, and other agencies, and the titles of the officers who head them, vary widely from state to state. A complete list of these organizations may be found in the blue book, or directory, of each state.

Reorganizing the Bureaucracy

Because the executive branch contains so many boards, commissions, and agencies—most of which were established piecemeal as the need for them arose—the administration of many state governments has become a bureaucratic nightmare. Even in the best of circumstances the overlapping of duties among agencies leads to inefficiency and waste.

Most states have made some effort to bring order out of chaos by reorganizing their bureaucracies. Some have been more successful than others. Alaska, California, Hawaii, Michigan, Missouri, New Jersey, New York, and North Carolina have been cited as the best examples of efficiently organized state government.

More and more states are beginning to reorganize bureaucracy along the five guidelines proposed by the Council of State Governments.

1. Consolidate all agencies into a few departments, each of which performs a given function.
2. Establish clear lines of authority from the governor down.
3. Establish staff agencies that are directly responsible to the governor.
4. Eliminate boards, commissions, and agencies that have more than one head.
5. Establish an independent auditor to verify that state money has been spent legally.

Section Check

1. Define: governor, impeachment, recall, special session, executive clemency, legal opinion
2. Identify: National Guard, State of the State Address, parole board, Nellie Tayloe Ross
3. Name one legislative and one judicial power given to governors by state constitutions.
4. Who are the other usual elected officials of most states besides governors?
5. Why is it often difficult for the people in a state to hold any one official accountable for state policy?

The University of Georgia at Athens, chartered in 1785, was the first state-funded institution of higher education in the United States. What role do state governments play in higher education today?

4 STATE GOVERNMENTS IN ACTION

In this chapter much has been said about legislative programs and state spending. Now it is time to look a little more closely at state programs and state spending, and those who benefit from them.

Education

Education is the largest single item in state budgets. One third of all the money spent by the states is allocated for education. Most of this money supports state colleges and universities. Elementary and secondary schools are supported mainly by local taxes, so they receive only a small amount of state funding. The rules that govern school taxes are set by the laws and constitutions of the states.

Responsibility for operating the public schools rests with the local community. However, state government plays an important supervisory role. The state sets minimum standards for elementary and secondary schools. It may require all schools to offer certain courses. It may set certain qualifications for teachers. It may require schools to hold classes for a minimum number of days each year. Although the state governments set the standards for schools, they generally leave the implementation of these standards to the local school boards.

At the level of higher education, most states have a separate system of colleges and universities, funded primarily by the state. Students at state colleges pay tuition, but the tuition is considerably lower than that charged by private institutions. State colleges generally charge a higher tuition fee to students who enroll from out of state.

The first state university was the University of Georgia, chartered by the state legislature in 1785. Today there are over 700 state colleges and state universities. The New York State University system alone includes some 32 colleges. Three quarters of America's 9 million college students today attend public, tax-supported institutions.

Highways

The construction and maintenance of roads and highways is one of the states' biggest responsibilities. Of the nation's 3 million miles (4.8 million kilometers) of paved roads, the states administer some 800,000 miles (1,280,000 kilometers). This vast system is funded in a cooperative effort by the federal and state governments. One tenth of all the money spent by the states is spent on building and maintaining roads and highways.

But the administration of state highways involves more than construction and maintenance. The states also write their own driving laws, set the speed limits, and set safety standards.

The states also register vehicles and license drivers. They decide what qualifications a driver must have to obtain a license, and they administer the driving test. These qualifications vary from one state to the next. In Colorado, for example, one must be 21 years old to get a regular driver's license, but in Mississippi one can get a regular license at 15.

Highways may be financed by ***user taxes***—that is, by taxes on gasoline, oil, and vehicle registrations. They may also be financed by general bond issues. In New Jersey and a few other states, highways are financed from general fund appropriations.

Public Welfare and Insurance Benefits

Almost one third of the money spent by the states goes to pay for public welfare and insurance benefits. Every state provides welfare assistance to people in need, but each state sets its own rules for eligibility and amount of payments as well as other conditions. Many programs are jointly administered with other levels of government. The states also administer Medicaid, the federally assisted medical program for the poor.

Welfare assistance costs are shared by the state and the federal government. Such assistance provides medical care and cash payments to the aged, the disabled, and dependent children. More than 15 million Americans benefit from welfare.

Each state also has various insurance programs. Unemployment insurance provides income for a limited time to people who are laid off or who lose their jobs. Pensions provide retirement income to men and women who have worked a certain length of time for the state. In addition, each state administers worker's compensation programs that provide income to employees who are unable to work as a result of job-related injury.

Insurance benefits are paid out of insurance reserves. The reserves come from payroll taxes and from the interest on these payments. Insurance benefits represent a big slice of the budget in most states.

Public Health

Most states spend a great deal of money on public health programs run by various state agencies. State health agencies have a broad range of concerns. In general, they seek to promote personal and environmental health.

Today state governments play active roles in providing health, safety, and welfare services for their citizens. Each state administers programs that help unemployed persons (left) and persons with physical disabilities (below).

The states operate some 575 hospitals. (Cities and counties operate another 1,700 hospitals.) Many state hospitals are run in cooperation with a state university medical school. Such cooperation provides practical experience for medical students and enables hospitals to conduct basic medical research. The states also have special hospitals for the mentally ill.

Personal health programs also include immunization, control of communicable disease, maternal and child health care, help for the disabled, and a wide variety of mental health supports. State agencies provide direct personal health services to 58 million persons each year.

The states also regulate the practice of medicine. Physicians, dentists, nurses, and other health care providers must be licensed by the state in which they wish to practice. Hospitals, nursing homes, and similar institutions must also be licensed by the state. The state also regulates the sale of drugs.

Environmental health programs are designed to promote public health by cleaning up the surroundings where people live, work, and recreate. Such programs include providing public sanitation, promoting occupational safety and health, and regulating air and water quality. In recent years states have begun to institute programs to control radiation and chemical wastes.

Concern for environmental health is relatively new. As recently as the 1930's there were very few states with laws governing air and water quality, for example. The pioneer state in this respect has been Oregon, which has often been the first to pass tough antipollution laws that were later adopted by other states. The most famous of these, passed in 1971, outlaws pull-tab beverage cans and nonreturnable bottles. This antilitter law, which was strongly opposed by the beverage and container interests, has reduced litter along Oregon's roads and highways. A number of other states, New York among them, have since passed similar laws.

Conservation

Conservation programs are closely related to environmental health programs. Both deal with the environment and may be handled by the same state agencies. But health programs seek to clean up the environment. Conservation programs seek to preserve it—that is, to conserve land, water, forests, wildlife, and other national resources.

States have been active in conservation since the early part of the century, although their efforts have often come into conflict with commercial interests. Over the years state park systems have preserved millions of acres of unspoiled land for the people to enjoy. In Florida, for example, which first appropriated funds for parks in 1935, the state park system now covers some 177,000 acres (71 600 hectares). Fish and game laws in every state are designed to control the killing of wildlife. Other laws are designed to prevent soil erosion, the clear-cutting

About one fourth of Alaska's lands are set aside as wildlife refuges, national parks, and other conservation areas. The state government of Alaska takes an active role in maintaining and protecting natural resources.

Company B of the Texas Rangers posed for this 1909 photograph in Amarillo, Texas. Today the Texas Rangers are still active law-enforcement officers. The group is now a division of the Texas Department of Public Safety.

of timber, the use of motor vehicles in fragile ecologies, and the destruction of the environment in other ways. Oregon, again, has long been a leader in conservation. For example, all of the Oregon beaches are state property up to the vegetation line. This fact has limited commercial exploitation to the area above that line.

Reclamation programs in some states require certain industries to repair the damage that they have done to the natural environment. In Pennsylvania, for example, strip-mining firms must grade and reseed the areas that they have mined. These firms are required to post a very high bond, which is released only when the plants have begun to grow. Such reclamation programs cannot restore the environment to its premining condition, but they can, and do, cover up the worst of the scars.

Law Enforcement and Corrections

Each state has a police system to preserve law and order. The first state police force was the Texas Rangers. They were organized in 1835, when Texas was still a republic. The first regular state police department was established by Pennsylvania in 1905. The biggest push in the development of state police systems came with the automobile. As cars became common on state roads and highways, speed laws and other traffic laws had to be established, and state police departments were needed to enforce them. What we know today as the highway patrol was born in the first 20 years of this century.

The authority of the state police differs from state to state. In most states they are responsible for enforcing state laws outside of cities. They also provide emergency services for civil defense and in time of natural disaster. State police departments keep a central file of fingerprints and criminal histories. Usually they also maintain a criminal investigation laboratory and provide services to local police.

Each of the 50 states has its own prison and correctional system. Almost all the convicted criminals serving time in penitentiaries are in state-run institutions. The states also operate reformatories for juvenile offenders.

Regulation and Licensing

The states promote public health and safety and ensure fair business practices by regulation and licensing. States regulate public utilities by setting the rates that telephone, water, gas, and electric companies charge. These companies may be either privately or publicly owned, but they operate under government franchise and have no competition. For this reason they are required by law to give adequate service at reasonable rates. The details of state regulatory activities vary, but most states regulate:

1. the chartering of banks and the activities of insurance companies;
2. the licensing of certain types of businesses;
3. the activities of labor unions, and collective bargaining between unions and management;
4. safety and health standards for the workplace: proper heating, light, ventilation, adequate fire escapes, and fire prevention measures;
5. intrastate transportation facilities such as bus lines, truck lines, and railroads;
6. the sale of alcoholic beverages.

Most states also have regulations that:

1. restrict child labor;
2. ensure equal employment opportunity, forbidding discrimination in employment on the basis of race, religion, national origin, or sex;
3. protect consumers against fraud and false advertising.

Finally, to safeguard the public, the states license members of certain trades and professions. These include lawyers, doctors, dentists, veterinarians, plumbers, electricians, and many more.

Section Check

1. Define: reclamation program, user tax
2. Identify: school board, Medicaid
3. What is the area of greatest expense on state budgets?
4. What are the different methods for financing state highways?
5. What is the difference between conservation programs and environmental health programs?
6. Why do the states practice regulation and licensing?

---

5 BESIDES THE STATES . . .

In addition to the 50 states the United States has sovereignty, or authority, over a number of islands and the District of Columbia.

Territories

A ***territory*** is an area belonging to the United States that is not a part of any state. The Constitution does not give the United States the expressed power to acquire territory. But the Supreme Court has held that the United States has the inherent power to do so. This inherent power is based in international law, which holds that a country may acquire territory by discovery and occupation, by cession, or by conquest. The power to acquire territories is also implied by the power to make treaties (and so to gain territory by treaty); the power to make war (and so to gain territory by conquest); and the power to admit new states (and so to gain the territory from which to make them). All of these powers are expressly granted by the Constitution, and the United States has gained territory by all three means.

The earliest territories were part of the North American continent. As the United States expanded westward across the continent, it acquired new territories that eventually became states. The last were Alaska and Hawaii, admitted to the Union in 1959.

Today the United States has no territories on the North American continent. Its territories are all islands—several thousand of them—in the Pacific Ocean and in the Caribbean. Many are uninhabited, some so tiny that they cover only a few acres.

The legal status of the territories differs, but all are subject to the jurisdiction of Congress. Article 4, Section 3, of the Constitution gives Congress the power to "make all needful rules and regulations respecting the territory . . . belonging to the United States."

The legal status of the major territories takes three basic forms. An ***organized territory*** is governed under an ***organic act,*** a document that resembles a state constitution, except that it is enacted by Congress and can be changed or revoked by Congress. Guam and the U.S. Virgin Islands are organized territories.

An ***unorganized territory*** does not have an organic act. Today the only unorganized territory is American Samoa.

A ***commonwealth*** is a territory that enjoys a high degree of self-rule. It has a constitution, drafted and adopted by its own residents. Until 1981, when the Northern Mariana Islands became a commonwealth, Puerto Rico was the only commonwealth territory.

The Trust Territory of the Pacific Islands is a special case. It is now largely independent, but it keeps some ties with the United States, as will be explained presently.

Residents of Guam, the U.S. Virgin Islands, and Puerto Rico are American citizens, holding many of the same rights and privileges as the residents of the states. They do not, however, have voting representatives in Congress, and they cannot vote in Presidential elections. Residents of Samoa are American nationals; that is, they are protected by the United States, but they are not citizens.

The Department of the Interior administers American Samoa, Guam, and the U.S. Virgin Islands. Other smaller islands that belong to the United States are administered either by the Department of the Interior or by other federal agencies, such as the Navy and the Air Force.

Guam The Pacific island of Guam lies 3,700 miles (5,950 kilometers) west of Hawaii. It has a population of about 106,000, of which 20 percent are United States military personnel. The island, which originally belonged to Spain, was acquired by conquest and treaty in 1898 following the Spanish-American War. Until 1950 Guam was administered by the Navy; it is still the site of important naval and air force bases.

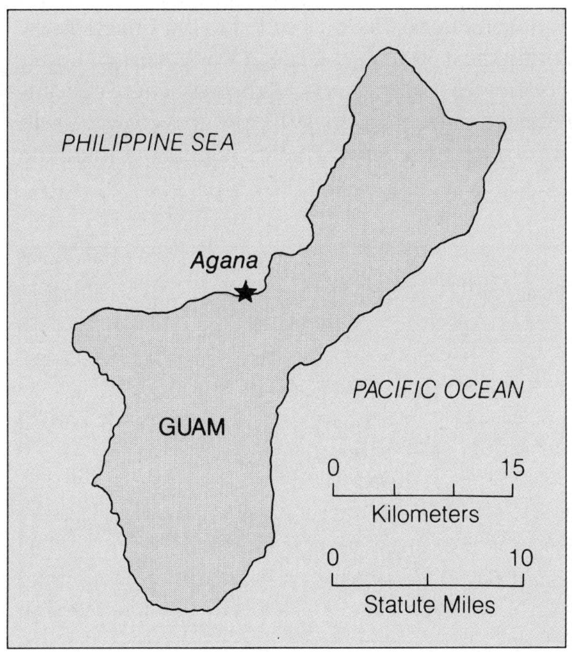

Guam's present government was organized by an organic act that was passed by Congress in 1950. At that time the island was brought under the administration of the Department of the Interior, and the Guamanians (previously American nationals) were made citizens of the United States. Until 1970 the President appointed the territorial governor. Now the residents of Guam elect their governor themselves. Guam has a unicameral legislature and sends a nonvoting delegate to Congress.

U.S. Virgin Islands The U.S. Virgin Islands are located in the Caribbean Sea approximately 1,000 miles (1,600 kilometers) southeast of Miami. The population of the islands is some 96,000, most of whom live on the islands of St. Thomas, St. Croix, and St. John. The 50 islands comprising the group were purchased from Denmark in 1917 for $25 million. Like Guam, the U.S. Virgin Islands are administered by the Department of the Interior. The islanders became citizens in 1927. They elect their own governor and their own unicameral legislature. They, too, send a nonvoting delegate to Congress.

American Samoa American Samoa, the most southerly of all United States territories, is a group of Pacific islands lying 2,300 miles (3,700 kilometers) southwest of Hawaii. The seven islands of American Samoa have a total population of 32,000. Samoa was acquired in 1900 through a treaty with Great Britain and Germany and a series of agreements with the island chiefs.

American Samoa was administered by the Navy until 1951, when responsibility was transferred to the Department of the Interior. In 1960 the first constitution for the territory was approved by Samoan voters and ratified by the Secretary of the Interior, who appointed the governor until 1977. The Samoans have since elected their own governor. The American Samoan legislature is composed of an elected house of representatives and a senate composed of local chiefs selected according to Samoan custom.

Northern Mariana Islands The Northern Mariana Islands, home for about 17,000 people, lie near Guam in the western Pacific along a 500-mile (800-kilometer) arc south of Japan. From 1947 until 1981 the United States administered the Marianas. Although they were supervised by the Department of the Interior, the islands were not American possessions. The Marianas were taken from the Japanese in World War II and were administered under United Nations trusteeship.

LEGACY

The Panama Canal

By treaty with the Republic of Panama in 1903, the United States was given jurisdiction over the Canal Zone. The Zone extended 5 miles (8 kilometers) on each side of the Panama Canal. The Zone was administered by a governor appointed by the President. The governor also served as the head of the Panama Canal Company, responsible for the operation of the Canal. In 1979 the new Panama Canal Treaties abolished the Canal Zone and placed the territory under Panamanian jurisdiction. A new Panama Canal Commission, an agency of the United States Government, will continue to operate the Canal until the year 2000.

In 1975 the people of the Northern Marianas voted to establish a commonwealth in political union with the United States. During the transition period the Northern Marianas adopted a constitution and elected their own governor. In 1976 the Northern Marianas gained provisional commonwealth status—the newest territory to be brought under American sovereignty. Full commonwealth status and citizenship for the Northern Marianas will come with the termination of trusteeship sometime in the 1980's.

Trust Territory of the Pacific Islands These islands cover a water area of 3 million square miles (7.7 million square kilometers)—about the size of the continental United States. They lie in the western Pacific between Hawaii and the Philippines. The total land area is 516 square miles (1,300 square kilometers)—half the size of Rhode Island. Of the 2,100 islands only 100 are inhabited, with a total population of about 117,000. They include two major groups of islands, the Caroline Islands and the Marshall Islands.

During World War II these islands were controlled by Japan. They were occupied by United States forces in 1944, and after the war the United States assumed responsibility for them. They were administered through the Department of the Interior under a trusteeship agreement with the United Nations. The chief executive of the Trust Territory of the Pacific Islands was a high commissioner appointed by the President.

During the 1970's the United States began negotiations on the future political status of the Trust Territory. The Trust Territory at this time consists of three divisions: the Republic of Palau, the Republic of the Marshall Islands, and the Federated States of Micronesia. By agreement the islands are moving toward self-rule under a unique political arrangement. If approved by the people, by Congress, and by the United Nations, the Compact of Free Association will give to the governments of all three Pacific islands authority for their domestic and foreign affairs. The United States, however, will retain responsibility for defense and also provide economic assistance and certain domestic services such as weather service, postal service, aviation, and emergency assistance.

Puerto Rico Puerto Rico lies in the West Indies, some 900 miles (1,450 kilometers) from Florida. The island was discovered by Christopher Columbus and for more than 400 years remained under Spanish rule. In 1898, after the Spanish-American War, Puerto Rico was ceded to the United States. For the next 50 years the island was governed under a series of organic acts. Although Puerto Ricans received citizenship in 1917, progress toward self-government was slow. The President appointed the

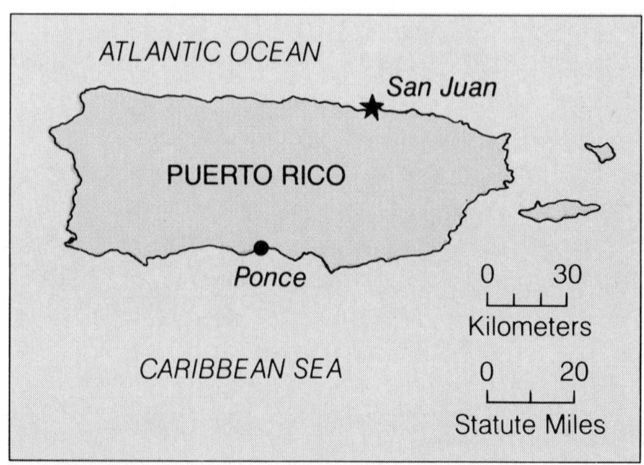

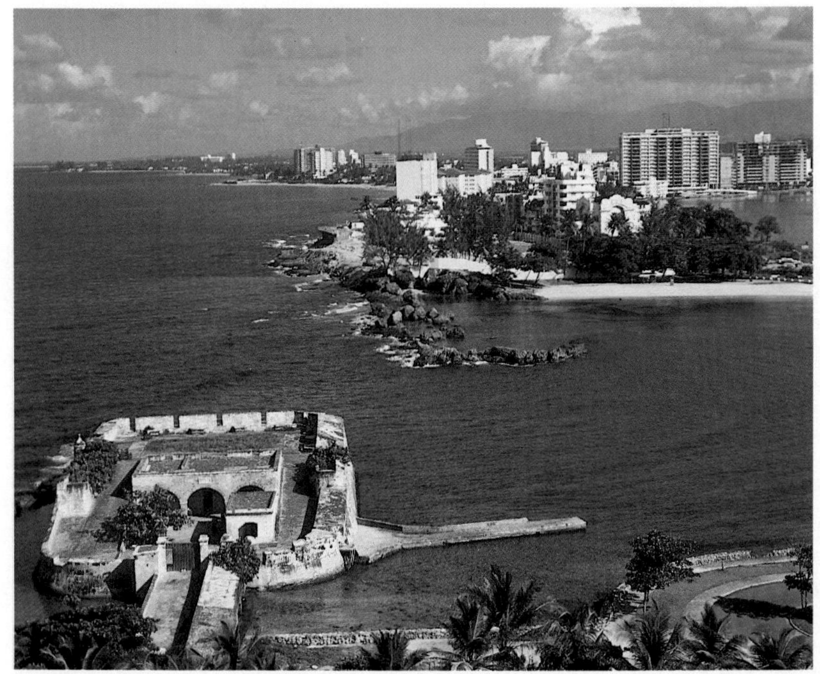

The port city of San Juan, the capital of Puerto Rico, was founded by Spanish colonists in the sixteenth century. Puerto Rico, ceded to the United States in 1898, became a commonwealth in 1952. In what ways does a commonwealth resemble a state?

governor and all the major officials until 1947, when Puerto Rico was given the right to elect its own governor.

Pressure built in Puerto Rico for a change in political status and Congress gave permission for the island to draft a constitution, which was ratified by popular vote in 1952. Since then the island has been officially known as the Commonwealth of Puerto Rico. Its elected government has authority over internal affairs, but Puerto Rico remains ultimately subject to the will of Congress.

In many ways Puerto Rico resembles a state. Its governor is elected for a four-year term and has powers similar to those of the state governors. Its legislature consists of a house of representatives and a senate. Its judicial branch is headed by the Puerto Rico Supreme Court. Puerto Rico is subject to most federal laws and receives most of the same federal services as the states. Like other Americans, residents of Puerto Rico are subject to military service.

Despite these similarities Puerto Rico is not a state. Its 3.2 million residents cannot vote in Presidential elections.* Puerto Rico has no voting representative in Congress, but elects one resident commissioner to the House of Representatives. The commissioner represents the island's interests, votes in committees, and takes part in debate, but is not entitled to vote on final legislation. Finally, residents pay no federal income taxes on the money they earn in Puerto Rico.

Since the early 1970's there has been a movement to make Puerto Rico the 51st state. The issue is a matter of great debate in Puerto Rico. Public opinion polls indicate that a majority of the people want statehood. A large minority want to remain a commonwealth, however, and a few want independence for Puerto Rico.

The District of Columbia

The District of Columbia—Washington, D.C.—is the nation's capital. It occupies a unique position within the federal system—not a state, not a territory.

The Framers of the Constitution decided that the capital for the new government should be located outside the control of any state. In 1790 Congress approved a site selected by George Washington along the Potomac River. This site was named the District of Columbia after Christopher Columbus. It consisted of a 67-square-mile (174-square-kilometer) area carved from the state of Maryland and separated from Virginia by the Potomac River.

The area within the District where the federal buildings would be located was named the City of Washington. The plan of the city was designed in

*But since they are citizens, Puerto Ricans who move to any of the 50 states automatically acquire the same rights and responsibilities as the other residents of that state, including the right to vote in local and national elections.

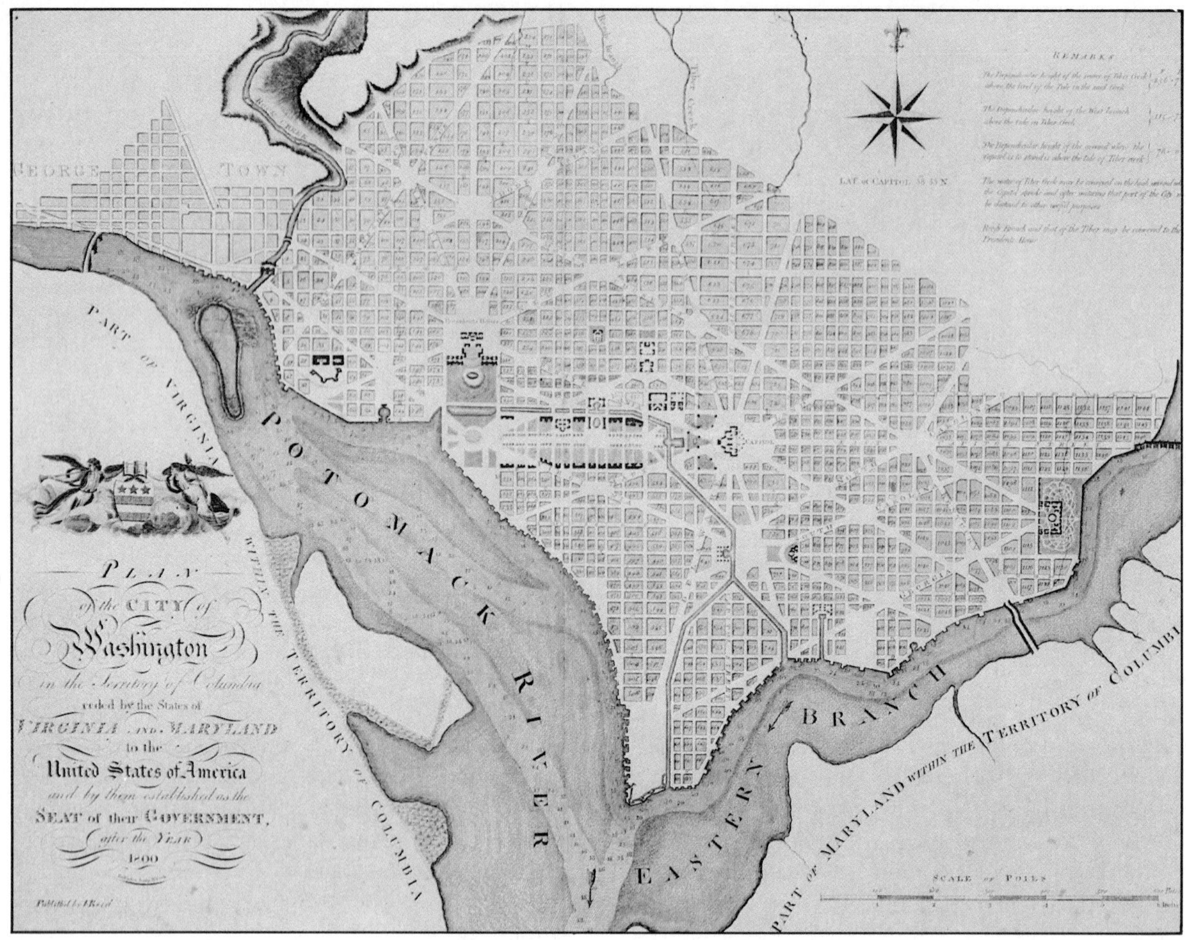

An 1800 map of the District of Columbia charts the location of the White House, the Capitol, and the major avenues named after states of the Union. What institution has constitutional authority over the District of Columbia?

1791 by Pierre-Charles l'Enfant, an army engineer who had come from France with General Lafayette to fight in the American Revolution. With its wide avenues and vistas Washington was to become one of the world's most beautiful cities—a city of great public buildings, monuments, museums. On December 1, 1800, Washington was named the nation's capital.

Over the next 200 years the city grew and spread. Today Washington, D.C., and the District of Columbia are one and the same. The site that was chosen almost 200 years ago to be the nation's capital is now the home of 638,000 people.

Under the Constitution, Congress has final legislative authority over the District of Columbia. In its early history, the District enjoyed limited self-government and elected a mayor and council. This agreement ended in 1874. For the next hundred years the District was governed by a board of three commissioners appointed by the President. There was no city council. Congress handled all the problems a city council usually handles, even passing laws for the licensing of dogs.

All this time the citizens of the District continued to push for home rule. The movement gained strength with the support of five successive Presidents—Truman, Eisenhower, Kennedy, Johnson, and Nixon. Congress passed a widely supported Home Rule Act in 1973. The act was approved by District residents, and in 1975 an elected mayor and council took office.

Under home rule the District functions like a city and also like a state. The mayor is the chief executive of the District government, holding the powers of a city mayor and also most of the powers of a state governor. The council is the city's legislative body; its powers are similar to those of a state legislature.

There are safeguards to protect the federal interest in the nation's capital. Legislation enacted by the District council is sent to Congress for review. The law takes effect after 30 working days unless it is vetoed by both houses of Congress. In addition, under its constitutional authority, Congress can enact laws on any subject dealing with the District of Columbia.

The Home Rule Act provides many new opportunities for citizens to participate in local government. Advisory Neighborhood Commissions are elected for each of 36 areas of the city. The commissions advise the council, the mayor, and various agencies of the District government on matters that affect their neighborhoods. They help to make decisions concerning streets, parks and recreation, education, public health, public safety, and a variety of social services.

The campaign for home rule was accompanied by a movement to give residents of the District the right to vote. The Twenty-third Amendment, adopted in 1961, gave the District three electoral votes in Presidential elections. However, its residents still had no representative in Congress. In 1970 Congress granted the District authority to elect a nonvoting delegate to the House of Representatives. In 1978 Congress proposed an amendment to the Constitution that would give the District voting representation in both the House and the Senate "as though it were a state." The proposal provides for the election of two senators and the number of representatives that the District's population would warrant if it were a state. This amendment is now before the states. To be adopted, it must be ratified by the legislatures of three fourths of the states within seven years—that is, by August 1985.

Section Check

---

1. Define: organic act, organized territory, commonwealth
2. Identify: American national, Panama Canal Commission, District of Columbia, Puerto Rico, Pierre-Charles l'Enfant, Home Rule Act
3. What are the two organized territories?
4. What are the two commonwealths?
5. What are the two major island groups of the Trust Territory of the Pacific Islands?
6. By what means did the District of Columbia gain three electoral votes in Presidential elections?

SUMMARY

Every state has its own constitution, which spells out the basic powers, structures, and procedures of state government. The first constitutions were brief and flexible, but today most state constitutions are highly detailed. State constitutions change with the times, usually by means of formal amendments. Most state constitutions need to be reformed; they are out-of-date or too long or both. In their basic form all state constitutions are very much alike, but they differ in their details as the states themselves differ.

The state legislature is the branch of government that makes the laws. Every state holds regular legislative sessions. The legislators in each state are elected by the people; their terms and qualifications vary. Legislators' salaries are usually low, and this makes for a high turnover in both houses. Since the move for reapportionment that took place in the 1960's, seats in the state legislature have been apportioned on the basis of population alone.

The state legislature has all the powers that the state constitution does not grant exclusively to some other branch of government, and that are not prohibited to it by the state constitution or by the Constitution. In some states voters engage in direct legislation by means of the referendum and the initiative.

The state executive branch consists of the governor, various other executive officers, and many boards, agencies, and commissions. Other executive officers include the lieutenant governor, the attorney general, the state treasurer, the auditor, the secretary of state, and the superintendent of public instruction. Dozens of state boards administer certain laws or institutions. The result has often been a tangled bureaucracy in need of reform.

The state government plays an important role in public education, builds and maintains state highways, provides public welfare and insurance benefits, promotes public health, conserves natural resources, preserves law and order, and regulates business and labor.

Besides the states the United States has sovereignty over six territories: Guam, the U.S. Virgin Islands, American Samoa, the Northern Mariana Islands, the Trust Territory of the Pacific Islands, and Puerto Rico. Some enjoy limited self-rule, but all are subject to the jurisdiction of Congress. The District of Columbia—Washington, D.C.—is subject to the final jurisdiction of Congress, but since the Home Rule Act took effect, the District has functioned for the most part like a combination city-state.

Chapter 29 Review

Using Vocabulary

Answer the questions by using the meaning of each underlined term.

1. What needs to be done to remove a dead letter provision from a statutory code?
2. What is the purpose of a constitutional commission?
3. When might voters exercise recall, direct initiative, and popular referendum?
4. Why is the item veto an important power of a governor?
5. When might executive clemency be granted and by whom?
6. What is a constituent power and who may exercise it?
7. What is the main task of an interim committee?
8. What is the importance of an organic act to a territory?

Understanding American Government

1. How are state constitutions similar to the Constitution?
2. The Constitution can be changed by formal and informal amendment. State constitutions can also be changed by either method, but in practice informal amendments are rarely used at the state level. Why is this so?
3. Trace the historical growth of power for state governors.
4. How is the role of lieutenant governor similar to that of Vice President?
5. What role do the states play in supervising education?
6. Why do the states regulate public utilities?
7. How is Puerto Rico different from the 50 states?
8. Under the Home Rule Act how does the District of Columbia function like a city and also like a state?

Extending Your Skills: Using Information from a Chart

Study the chart on page 698. Then complete the items that follow.

1. What five states have the largest populations? How many representatives does each of these states have?
2. What relationship exists between a state's population and its number of representatives in Congress?
3. What three states were the first to enter the Union? When did the state in which you live enter the Union?
4. Prove or disprove the following statements using data from the chart: (a) The largest states in area always have the largest populations. (b) The largest city in a state is usually the capital city of the state.

Government and You

1. Does your state have a bicameral legislature? Are any groups proposing switching to a unicameral body? Do you think a unicameral legislature would be an improvement? Why or why not?
2. The reapportionment based on "one person, one vote" in the 1960's affected each state in a different way. How was your state affected by reapportionment?
3. Has your state ever had a woman as governor? How many women are now serving as governors in the United States? Why have so few women been elected to this position?
4. The low pay of state legislators is partly responsible for a high turnover rate from session to session. What are some other reasons? Should the pay of state legislators be raised? Why is this pay fairly high in a few states?
5. At present the District of Columbia has no voting representatives in Congress. Do you think the residents of this area should have such representation? What are the reasons for your answer?

Activities

1. Prepare a biographical report on the governor of your state.
2. Study the process of how a piece of legislation passes through the state legislature. Make a chart showing the steps in this process.
3. Make a scrapbook about your state constitution. How long is it? When was it first written? How many amendments does it have?

Chapter 30

Local Government

In no country in the world does the law hold so absolute a language as in America; and in no country is the right of applying it vested in so many hands.

ALEXIS DE TOCQUEVILLE

CHAPTER OVERVIEW

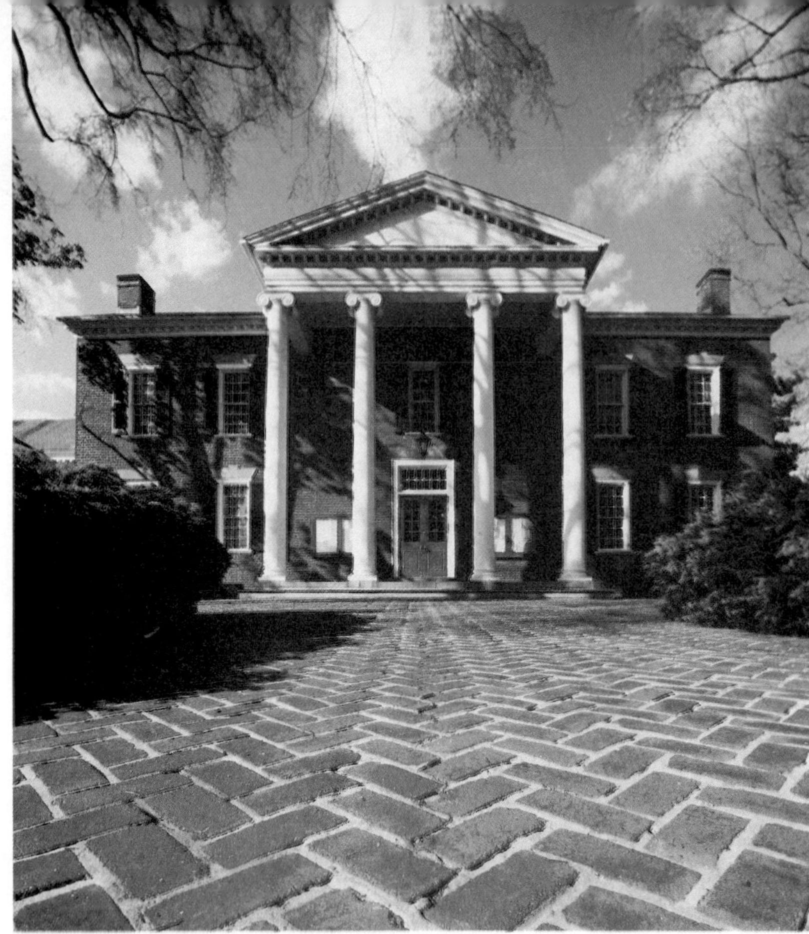

The courthouse of Albermarle County, Virginia, is located in the city of Charlottesville. Charlottesville serves as the county seat—the county's administrative center. Albermarle County has a population of about 40,000.

1 COUNTIES

There are in the United States some 80,000 units of government. Almost all are local governments. These include cities, counties, townships, and a variety of special districts.

Local governments are created by the states. They are agents of the state and exercise only those powers given them by the state. The states have the power to create, alter, or abolish any unit of local government.

Local governments are not created according to some overall plan. They are created, layer on layer, to solve new problems or to meet new needs. The result is a crazy quilt of overlapping jurisdictions.

During much of the nineteenth century, state legislatures supervised local governments. They even passed ordinances for particular towns and cities. As local governments took on more responsibility for roads, education, health, welfare, and public safety, direct supervision of local governments shifted to the state executive branch. At the same time, constitutional amendments frequently granted local governments some measure of control in managing their affairs. Today state control over local governments varies from state to state and for different kinds of local government within each state.

The states are divided geographically into more than 3,000 ***counties.*** In Louisiana, counties are called *parishes,* and in Alaska they are called *boroughs.* Only

All but a few of the units of government in the United States are at the local level. What institution has direct supervision over local units of government today?

LAYERS OF GOVERNMENT

Type of Government	Number of Units
National government	1
State governments	50
Counties	3,041
Municipalities	19,083
Townships	16,748
School districts	15,032
Other special districts	28,733
Total	82,688

Source: Bureau of the Census, Department of Commerce

two states have no counties—Connecticut and Rhode Island.* The number of counties in each state ranges from 3 in Delaware and Hawaii to 254 in Texas. The largest is California's San Bernardino County, which covers 20,117 square miles (52,304 square kilometers). The smallest is Arlington County in Virginia with 26 square miles (67.6 square kilometers). Population also varies—from 7.4 million in Los Angeles County to 91 in Loving County, Texas—but the population of most counties is under 50,000.

As the great variety in county population patterns suggests, counties differ in power and function from state to state. In New England, for example, they are relatively unimportant, while in the South and West they are very strong. In the Midwest they share their power with townships. Counties are generally less powerful in urban areas, where the functions of county and city are intertwined. Counties tend to be overshadowed by municipal governments. In rural areas, however, counties hold their own as the basic unit of local government.

*In various parts of other states there is no separately organized county government. In most of these areas a county government forms part of a city government. A few cities, such as San Francisco and Honolulu, are also counties.

The Functions of Counties

Counties exist as administrative units of state government, although in a few states counties are permitted to operate more independently under home rule. As units of state government, they administer state laws and whatever county ordinances, or laws, the state permits them to enact.

Traditionally, in rural areas county officials enforce the law and maintain jails. They are responsible for building and repairing roads. They assess property and collect taxes. They administer elections and welfare and public health programs. They record property deeds, birth certificates, marriage licenses, and other documents. In some counties officials also have responsibility for public schools. Officials in urban counties share responsibility with city officials for these same functions. In addition, urban counties often provide city services, for example, bus lines, water and sewer service, or ambulance service, to ***unincorporated areas*** of the county—areas outside the city limits. The terms *incorporated* and *unincorporated* refer to the legal status of a local unit of government. A city is a municipal corporation and operates under a state charter. The area within the boundaries of the city is thus incorporated. The area of the county that is not

A major responsibility of county governments is the construction and maintenance of roads, bridges, and other public works. List other responsibilities of county governments.

included within the city remains unincorporated. One town in each rural county is designated as the ***county seat.*** The courthouse—the center of county government—is located here. The county seat is typically the business, agricultural, and social center of the county.

The Structure of County Government

County government typically consists of a county board, a set of elected officials, a number of special boards or commissions, and an appointed bureaucracy.

County Board A county is governed by an elected board, which is known variously as the board of commissioners, board of supervisors, fiscal court, police jury, or county board. Elected boards may have as few as 3 members or as many as 80. Members of the more numerous, smaller-size boards are known as ***county commissioners.*** They are elected specifically to the board, usually for a four-year term, and hold no other office. Members of the larger-size boards are known as ***county supervisors.*** They are elected from subdivisions within the county called ***townships,*** and each supervisor is usually an officer of the township as well.

The powers of the county board are assigned by the state. These powers are both legislative and executive. As legislators the members of the board levy taxes and appropriate funds for the county. They may also pass ordinances. As executives they manage county property and appoint county employees. They also administer various programs for public health, welfare, and the construction and maintenance of roads.

In many counties, the chief administrative officer is the sheriff. The sheriff prevents breaches of the peace and supervises prisoners. What other functions does a sheriff typically perform?

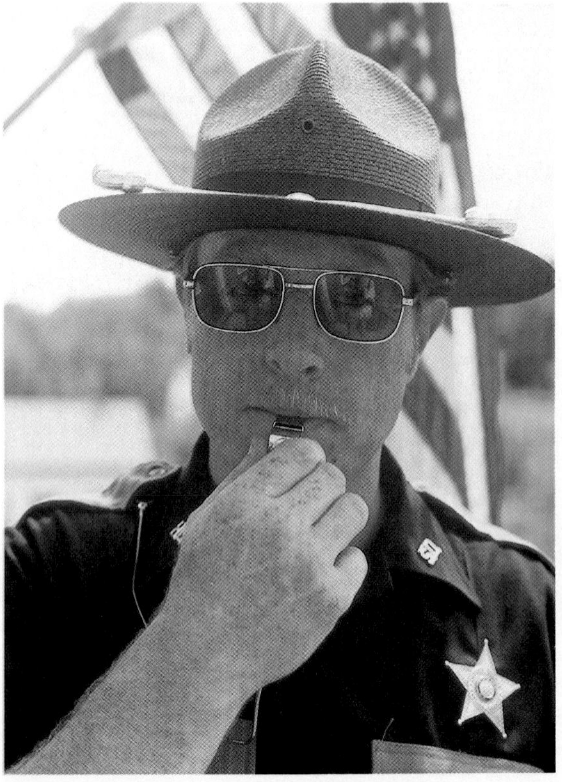

Elected Officials The county board shares its authority with a number of elected officials. Typically these include the following.

The ***sheriff*** provides police protection in unincorporated areas of the county, maintains the jail, and acts as an officer of the county court by summoning jurors and enforcing court orders. In some states the sheriff also serves as the county tax collector.

The ***county attorney*** is variously called district attorney, county attorney, or prosecutor. This important official represents the state and county in civil suits, conducts criminal investigations, and prosecutes those who violate the law.

The ***county clerk*** registers deeds and mortgages, births, marriages, divorces, and deaths; issues licenses; and supervises elections. The county clerk may also act as secretary to the county board.

The ***assessor*** determines the value of property for tax purposes. The ***treasurer*** collects, maintains, and pays out county funds. The ***auditor*** keeps county financial records and tax rolls and authorizes payments to meet approved obligations. The ***coroner,*** or ***medical examiner,*** conducts medical investigations into deaths by violence and deaths unattended by a physician. The ***county superintendent of schools*** supervises the county's public elementary and secondary schools.

Other County Officials Many counties have special boards or commissions, elected or appointed, that supervise county functions. These typically include a board of road reviewers, a library board, a hospital board, and a board of public health. Some counties have a special board in charge of proposals for reform. The work of the county, like the work of the state, is done by a vast network of employees, most of whom are appointed by the county board. County employees number some 2 million nationwide.

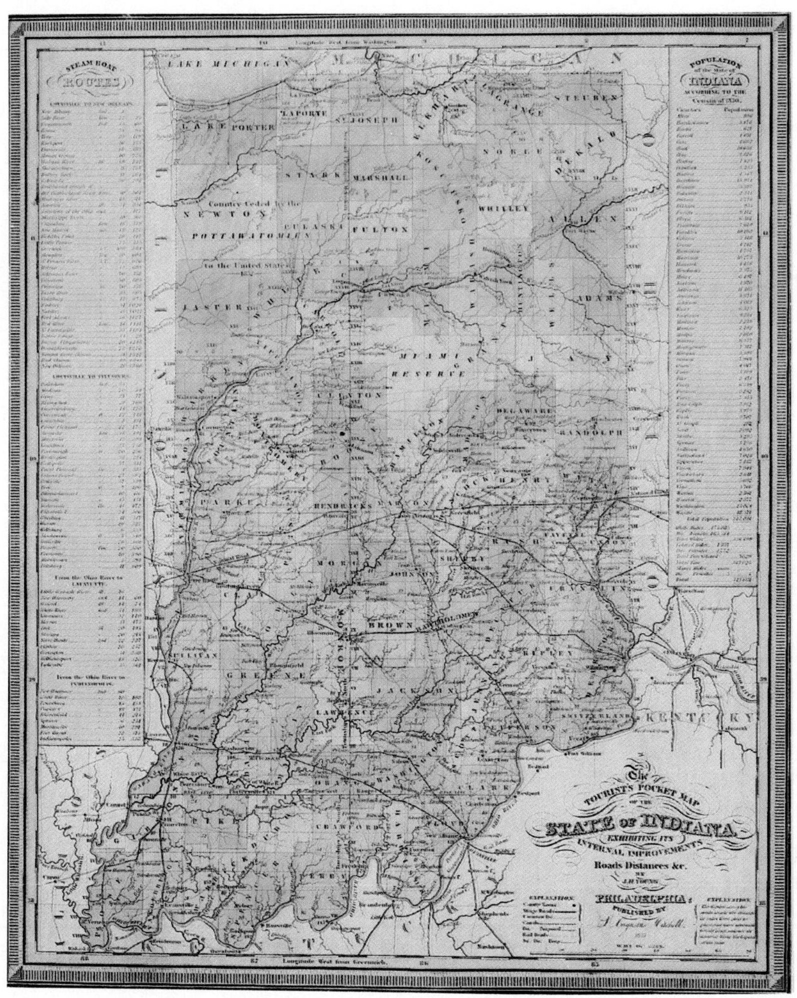

An 1837 map of Indiana shows that state's division into 63 counties. Today Indiana has a total of 92 counties. Other units of local government in Indiana include cities, towns, and townships.

Problems in County Government

There are four major problems in county government. The first is public indifference. Most people know less about their county government than they know about their state or city government—and most people seem unaware that it makes any real difference how their county is governed. The second problem is that county government is fragmented. Typically authority is parceled out among various elected officials and boards. As a result, it is difficult to hold the government accountable to the people. Third, the list of county officials to be elected is often so long that people cannot vote intelligently or judge the professional qualifications of the candidates. And fourth is the number and size of the counties themselves. Most were laid out long before the days of rapid transportation; as a result most states have many small counties when it would be far more efficient to have a few large ones.

Proposals for Reform

Reformers who feel that county government should be strengthened have put forth numerous proposals. Among the most significant proposals are new patterns of reorganization that would strengthen the executive branch of county government. Many counties throughout the country have adopted reorganization proposals in an attempt to strengthen county government.

New Patterns of Organization The first—and, many people feel, the best—of the new organizational patterns is the ***county manager plan.*** Under this plan the county board keeps its legislative powers, while its executive powers are given over to a county manager—a professional administrator, hired by the board and answerable to the board. The county manager appoints all the other administrative officers and oversees their work. Thus the county board makes policy, while the county manager administers policy. The county manager plan makes for clearer lines of responsibility, more professionalism, and a shorter ballot. It has been adopted by some 50 counties.

The ***elected chief executive plan*** resembles the county manager plan and has most of the same advantages. But electing the chief executive can be a disadvantage because a popular political figure—one who wins votes—is not necessarily a good administrator. The elected chief executive plan has been adopted by some 50 counties.

The ***chief administrative officer (CAO) plan*** is a variation of the county manager plan, but the CAO, unlike the county manager, has only very limited authority. The county board makes the policy; the CAO simply carries out its directives. This plan is the most popular of the three, having been adopted by some 600 counties.

Home Rule What the county can do is determined by the state constitution and state law. Twenty-eight states, however, now provide for some form of ***home rule,*** or self-government. The counties' decisions must be ratified by the local voters in every home rule state except Wisconsin.

Because it gives the counties power to change their own governmental structure, home rule would seem to be an important avenue of reform. But it has been little used. Almost 1,500 counties are now entitled to exercise home rule, but only about 100 have done so.

Consolidation Another reform, recommended for economy and improved delivery of services, is ***consolidation.*** One form involves the combination of two or more adjacent counties into a larger unit of government. Although many counties are small and inefficient, few such consolidations have been made—and none recently. The last took place in 1923 when Campbell and Milton counties became part of Fulton County, Georgia.

Three factors account for the lack of consolidation. Rural residents take pride in their counties and do not want to see them disappear. County officials and employees want to keep their jobs. And business interests in the county seats do not want to lose the patronage of local government.

Another form of consolidation involves the combination of a city and its surrounding county into a single unit of government. Denver and San Francisco are notable examples. This form of consolidation has taken place only a half dozen times.

Section Check

1. Define: county, unincorporated area, county seat, commissioner, sheriff, county attorney, assessor, coroner
2. Identify: county manager plan, chief administrative officer plan, elected chief executive plan, home rule
3. What powers do the states have over local governments?
4. Why do county governments tend to be more powerful in rural areas?
5. What are the main problems with county governments?

2 TOWNS, TOWNSHIPS, AND SPECIAL DISTRICTS

Towns and townships are the least common unit of local government. They are found in only twenty states, almost all in New England and in the Midwest. By contrast, cities are found in every state, counties in all but two states, and special districts in every state but one.

Towns and Townships

In New England the major unit of local government is the town. Except for the areas around a few incorporated cities, each state is divided into towns. Each town includes one or more villages and their surrounding countryside. The town provides most of the government services that are provided by cities and counties in other states.

The ***town meeting*** is the governing authority of the New England town. Meetings are usually held once a year and are open to all qualified voters, who approve the budget, levy taxes, and pass new laws. They elect a town clerk, a tax collector, a constable, a road commission, and a school board. They also elect a board of three to five ***selectmen*** to manage the town's affairs between annual meetings.

In the small New England towns the town meeting still maintains the tradition of direct democracy dating back to colonial times. In the larger towns this is no longer so. There, as the population has grown—and the town's problems have grown more complex—the practice of direct democracy has given way to a representative system. Delegates elected by the voters attend the town meeting. The selectmen then make many of the decisions that the voters themselves used to make at the annual town meetings. And many towns have hired town managers to supervise the administration of services.

In 16 northern states from New York through the Midwest some—though not all—counties are divided into ***townships.*** In a few states townships were created piecemeal as areas were settled and the need for local government arose. In most, the townships are the units that were used originally for surveying land. Typically these units were six miles square.

Some townships hold annual meetings. All have elected township boards. Board members may be elected specially to that office. Or they may be elected to some other township office that entitles them to serve on the board. Township officers include a supervisor, a clerk, an assessor, a treasurer, a constable, a road commission, and a justice of the peace.

Unlike a town, a township does not include villages. Any village within a township usually has its own separate government. A township's functions are essentially those of a county: road maintenance, weed control, and so forth. In many places townships have disappeared and their functions have been transferred to county governments. In a few states, however, urban townships have grown stronger. In these states they are taking on the powers of the city and are providing many of the same services that cities normally provide.

Special Districts

A ***special district*** is a unit of local government created to provide a single service or a few related services. It is usually established to deal with problems that cut across the boundaries of other local government units. Thus a special district may be created to provide fire protection, sewer service, or public transportation in an area that is not served by any local governments or that is served by several local governments. Special districts are also created to maintain airports and parks, to provide water service or police protection, and to construct public housing. And special districts may be created for soil conservation, irrigation, or mosquito control. Special districts may also be created for financial reasons—to secure a broader tax base, to finance a service out of users' fees, or to take advantage of a federal grant.

Special districts are created under state law and governed by small elected boards. They have the power to levy taxes or impose fees to pay for the services that they provide.

Citizens of Antrim, New Hampshire, gather for their annual town meeting, a tradition practiced in that community since the 1700's. The town meeting is a form of direct democracy.

There are more than 41,000 special districts in the United States. About 40 percent of them are school districts. As separate units of government all these special districts are piled one on top of the other in overlapping layers. Local government is thus further fragmented, and the coordination of services is often difficult to achieve.

School Districts

Public education is the largest and most costly activity of state and local government. As early as 1647 Colonial Massachusetts required towns to provide education to children from public funds. Compulsory schooling began in 1852, and today the standard in all states is that public education shall be free, compulsory, and universal. Public education is organized by ***school districts,*** the most common type of special district. They are also the oldest: the first school districts were established in New York in 1812. Today public schools are run by local school districts in about half the states. In the other states, the city, county, or town runs the schools. School districts come in all shapes and sizes, and their boundaries do not necessarily follow those of the city or county. At one time there were more than

The primary responsiblity for administering public education (above) belongs to local governments. Horace Mann, the noted Massachusetts educator (right), was a leader in the establishment of public schools in the United States. Mann was often called the "father of the common schools."

100,000 school districts, but over the past 40 years, through consolidation, their number has been reduced to about 15,000.

Most school districts are governed by an elected ***school board*** that makes basic policy and that appoints a superintendent to administer the system. School districts, operating under state law, have the power to tax, to borrow money, to build schools, and to hire teachers. But in all of this the state—and increasingly the national government—plays an important role. Indeed, perhaps nowhere is the "marble cake" of governmental relations so clearly evident as in public education.

State law specifies what kind of taxes school districts may levy (usually property taxes). And state law sets the tax rates. State law determines the number of school days in each year. It determines the number of years of compulsory education. State law sets the minimum teachers' salaries and the requirements for teacher certification. It specifies the general content of what is to be taught. Many states select the textbooks used in the public schools, and some give statewide examinations.

The state education agency oversees local school districts to make sure they follow state policies. The agency also handles state grants to school districts. Through these grants state governments finance more than 40 percent of the total cost of public schools. The details of these grants vary from state to state, but the basic goal is always the same: to provide an equal education for all. By helping poorer districts, the state can make sure that basic standards are met in all schools.

Section Check

1. Define: town, town meeting, selectman, township, special district, school board
2. What kinds of decisions are reached at New England town meetings?
3. How do towns and townships differ?
4. What are some services provided by special districts?
5. Why are there so many special districts?

3 CITIES

The most important unit of local government today is the ***municipality,*** for the United States has grown from a small, largely rural nation to an enormous, largely urban one. In 1790, when the first census was taken, the nation's total population was just under 4 million. Just over 5 percent of the population lived in the cities. To put it another way, the entire urban population of the United States at that time was about the same as the population of Mobile, Alabama, today.

Today 75 percent of all Americans are concentrated in the cities and suburbs of more than 300 ***metropolitan areas.*** Each metropolitan area is an urban complex containing a ***central city*** with a population of at least 50,000 and its surrounding suburbs, with a total population of at least 100,000 (75,000 in New England). ***Suburbs*** are the smaller towns and unincorporated residential areas on the outskirts of a city. The name of the central city usually is attached to the area (Greater Houston, for example), and the telephone company typically issues a single directory. These metropolitan areas, however, occupy only about 10 percent of the land.

The shift to an urban population has had enormous consequences for local government. When most people lived in rural areas, the counties, towns, and townships were the basic units of government. Now their responsibilities have been largely taken over by the cities. But the issue is more complex than that, for people who live in densely settled areas often have different needs and more complicated problems than people who live in rural areas. To meet these needs, to solve these problems—that is the job of city government today.

The City and the State

The term ***city*** means different things in different states. In some states a city is any municipality, no matter how small. In most states only the larger municipalities are called cities, while the smaller ones may be called villages, boroughs, or towns. State law, the constitution, and sometimes local custom define the term in each state.

Like every other unit of local government, the city is subject to the state. Originally it received its powers directly from the state legislature. But as cities grew, conflicts came with the rural-dominated state legislatures. Gradually control of the cities shifted from the legislatures to the cities themselves. State constitutions specify the powers of city government and spell out many of its functions in detail. They also deal with ***incorporation***—the process by which a city becomes a legal body.

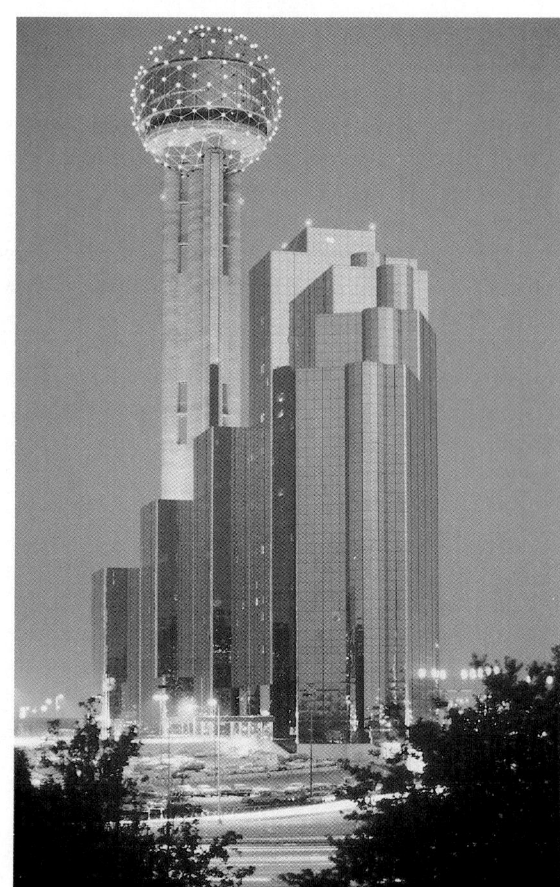

Reunion Tower is a landmark of the Dallas, Texas, skyline. The population of Dallas, the seventh largest city in the United States, is nearly 1 million.

A city—unlike a county—is created at the request of its residents. A city is incorporated by the state after its residents request incorporation, and it meets certain requirements spelled out in the state constitution or in state laws. Usually it must have a minimum number of residents, perhaps two or three hundred. Other requirements vary from state to state. If the community meets all the legal requirements, the state will declare it incorporated. The incorporation may then be subject to approval by the voters. In a few states a city can become incorporated only by a special legislative act called a ***charter.***

City Charters

In the United States, cities are incorporated under a charter from the state. The city—as a ***municipal corporation***—is a legal body holding the right to make contracts, the right to sue in the courts, and the right to buy and sell property. In effect the act of incorporation bestows on the city some of the same legal rights that a person has.

The charter is the city's constitution. It names the city and defines its boundaries. It outlines the structure of the city's government and lists that government's powers and functions. It makes provisions for the election or appointment of public officials and prescribes their duties. And it sets forth the laws that govern the city's finances.

Four different kinds of charters govern city operations. They are the special charter, the general charter, the optional charter, and the home rule charter. Each type of charter, however, varies from state to state.

The Special Charter The earliest city charters were granted by the state legislatures, which wrote a separate special charter for each city. A few states still issue special charters, but most states have abandoned the practice as too time-consuming because a city government incorporated under a special charter cannot be changed except by the direct action of the legislature.

The General Charter Several states now classify cities—usually according to size—and provide a general charter for the cities within each classification. This practice makes for equal treatment of similar cities, while at the same time it allows for flexibility. It is also far more efficient than the special charter process. Its disadvantage is that two cities of the same size may, in fact, have very little else in common.

The Optional Charter To get around this disadvantage, several states now prefer the optional charter plan. They permit all cities (or all cities of a certain size) to choose among several charters provided by state law. Usually the city's voters must approve the choice. The optional charter practice offers a more individualized approach than that provided by the general charter. But its use is still less satisfactory than the fourth and final alternative of home rule.

The Home Rule Charter Forty states give cities the power to draw up and amend their own charters in a practice known as home rule.

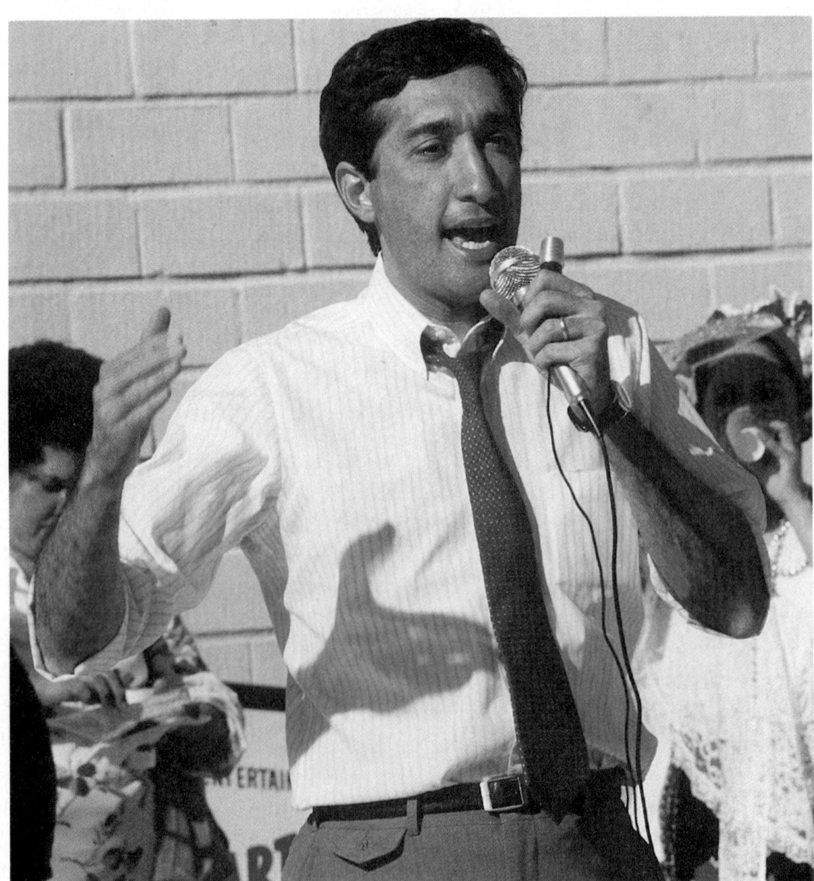

Henry Cisneros was the first Hispanic elected mayor of a major American city—San Antonio, the nation's tenth largest. Cisneros was reelected in 1983 with more than 94 percent of the vote.

A cartoon, "Mayor Jimmy Walker and Himself," portrays the popular mayor of New York, who served from 1925 until 1932. Walker was one of many big-city mayors who wielded great power over their cities during the first part of the century.

In some states incorporation by home rule is required by the state constitution. In other states it is permitted by state constitutions. Home rule can also be granted by the state legislature. If the legislature can grant home rule, it can also take it away—so legislative home rule is a less secure grant of power than constitutional home rule.

Some states grant home rule to any municipality. Others grant it only to cities of a certain size. The requirements vary from state to state, but most of the nation's larger cities have some measure of home rule.

Under home rule local voters elect a group of citizens to draft a city charter. Or the charter may be drafted by the city council. The charter is then placed before the voters for their approval or rejection. In some states the legislature must approve the charter. Amendments to a city charter may be proposed by the city council or by initiative petition, but an amendment must be ratified by the voters.

Home rule gives a city the power to manage its own affairs. But a home rule charter and all municipal laws must conform to the state constitution and state law. When they conflict, state law is supreme.

Home rule introduces an element of federalism into state-local relations. It limits state interference in local affairs. But home rule inevitably gives rise to disputes over jurisdiction because few problems are confined by municipal boundaries. Some problems, like pollution or crime, may extend over a wide area, and solutions may require the cooperation of many different units of government. Others, like education or welfare, may cost too much for the municipal government to handle alone. Its powers and functions are intertwined with those of the state.

According to its advocates home rule strengthens democracy. It encourages citizens to participate in local government. These advantages, and the fact that it offers a highly individualized approach to city government, make the home rule charter the most popular means of incorporation among the states today.

The Structure of City Government

Three basic forms of ***municipal government*** are the mayor-council plan, the commission plan, and the council-manager plan.

The Mayor-Council Plan During the nineteenth century nearly all cities had the mayor-council form of government. Today about half of the nation's 19,000 cities operate under this plan. The basic feature of the mayor-council form is a separation of powers between an elected mayor serving as the city's chief executive and an elected council serving as its legislative body.

The elected council is typically a unicameral body with five or seven members, though it may have as many as fifty. Its powers vary according to the role of the mayor. But in all cases, the council passes local laws, usually called city ordinances, and controls the purse strings.

Members of the typical council serve a four-year term. In cities that are exceptions, members may serve anywhere from one to six years. Council members are elected in either partisan or nonpartisan elections—that is, with or without political party labels. They are elected from wards or districts, from the city at large, or by a combination of both systems.

How the council is elected has a major impact on representation and the distribution of power within the city. In the ***ward system of election***

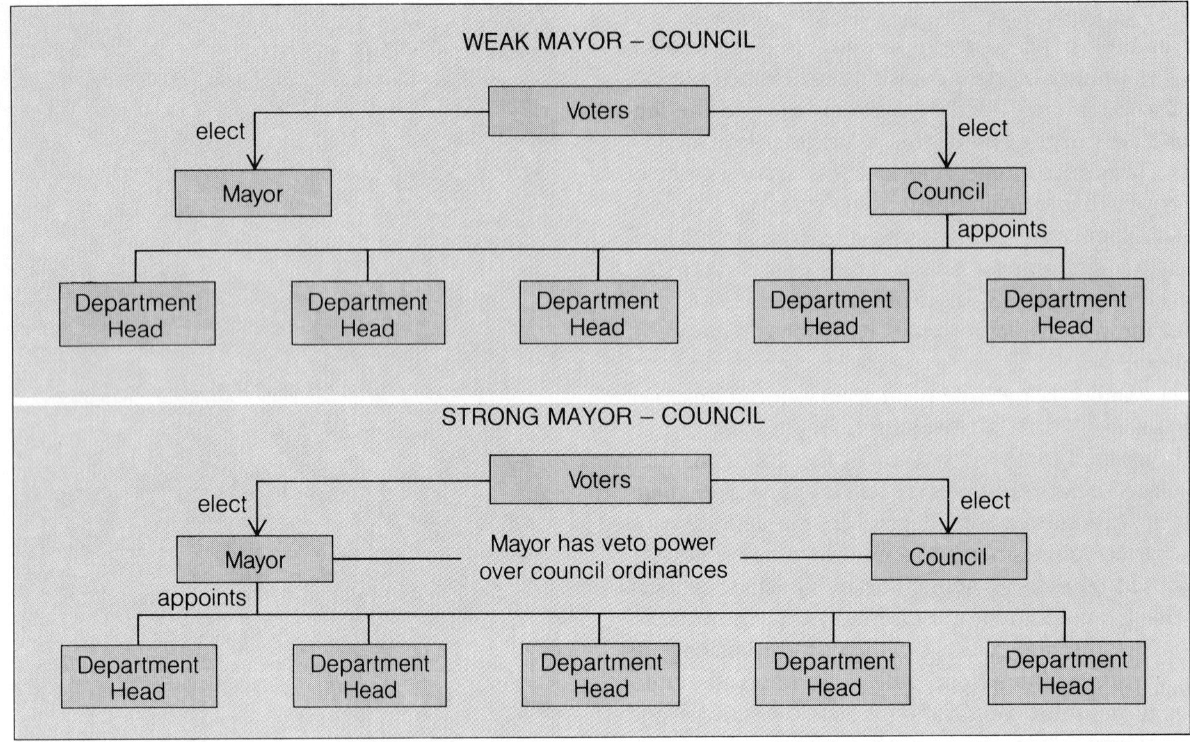

Study the differences between the weak mayor-council and the strong mayor-council forms of government. Who appoints city department heads under each form of government?

the city is divided into districts for the purpose of electing council members—or aldermen, as they are sometimes called. People who favor the ward system argue that it provides a council more representative of neighborhood and minority interests. Council members elected by wards are more likely to know the people they represent and to be responsive to their needs. Large and ethnically diverse cities tend to prefer the ward system.

Critics of the ward system argue that it emphasizes special neighborhood interests and ignores the needs and interests of the city as a whole. For this reason many cities have adopted a city-wide ***at-large system of election.*** Proponents of the at-large system feel that it best serves the needs of the majority. Small and ethnically homogeneous cities tend to prefer the at-large system of election. Some cities have compromised by adopting a combination of both the ward and the at-large systems.

The most important difference among cities with the mayor-council plan lies in the power of the mayor. Most cities have what is called the ***weak-mayor form*** of government. Under this form the mayor shares executive authority with the city council and often with other elected officials as well. The mayor presides over the council, but the role is largely ceremonial. Typically, the mayor lacks the veto power. And the council—not the mayor—appoints department heads and prepares the budget.

Over the years, as cities have grown in size and complexity, the office of the mayor has been strengthened in order to make city management more effective, to provide strong political leadership, and to lay down clear lines of responsibility. Today the ***strong-mayor form*** of government is used in most large cities. Under this form executive authority is concentrated in the hands of the mayor. The mayor has the power to appoint and remove department heads, to prepare the budget, and to veto city council ordinances. In a few cities the mayor is assisted by a chief administrative officer. This officer, who is appointed by the mayor, is an expert in city management who supervises the budget and coordinates the operations of city government, leaving the mayor free to concentrate on issues of policy.

Weaknesses of the strong-mayor form are three. First it is complex. Second it can give rise to conflict between the mayor and the council. Third it depends for its success on the abilities of one person—the mayor.

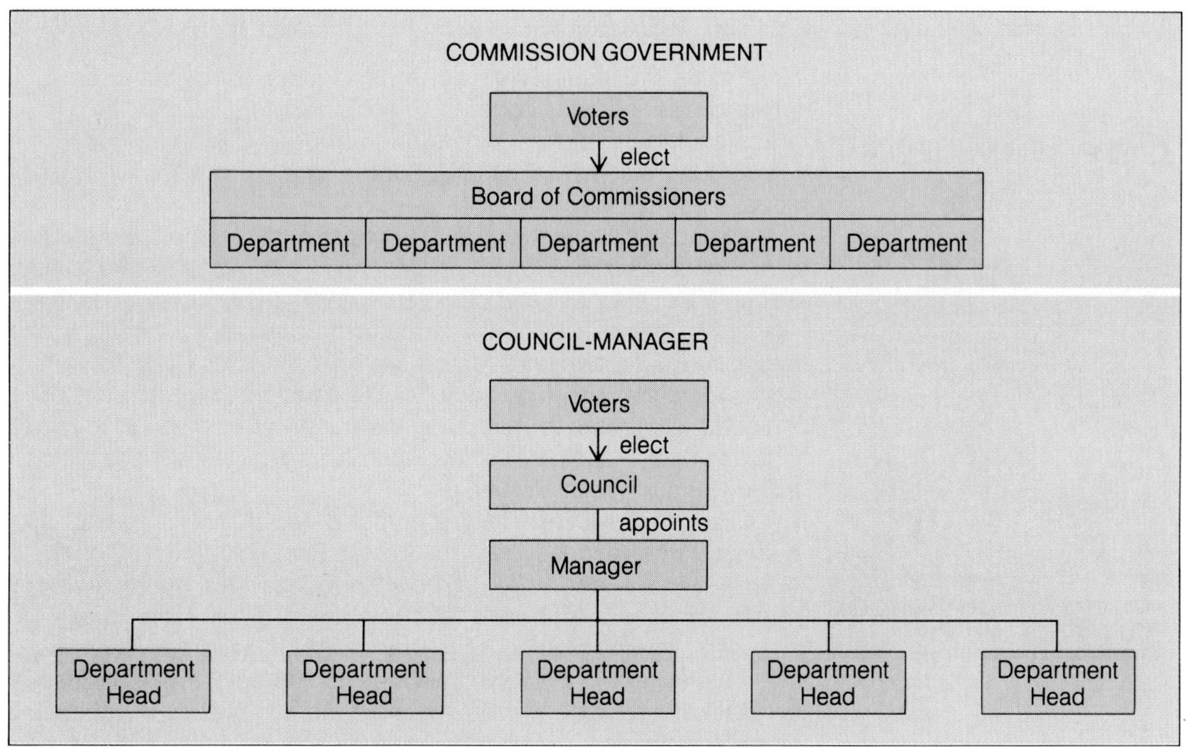

The commission form of government is rarely used today, while the council-manager form is very popular. What is the major disadvantage of commission government? Who administers the city under council-manager government?

The Commission Plan New forms of government have often emerged in response to changing conditions. Sometimes reforms have been the product of crisis. In 1900 a hurricane and high waves destroyed much of Galveston, Texas. The city government was unable to cope with the emergency. On the recommendation of local businessmen the state legislature placed control of the city in the hands of five commissioners. The measure appealed to reformers, who wanted more efficient city government, free from party politics. By 1917 more than 500 cities had adopted the commission plan.

Under the commission plan legislative and executive functions are combined in a single board, or commission. Typically this commission is composed of five elected members who act as a city council to pass ordinances and control the purse strings. Individually, each commissioner is in charge of a city department. One commissioner is chosen as mayor, but the mayor's role is largely ceremonial.

Commissioners typically serve a two- or four-year term. They are usually elected in nonpartisan elections from the city at large. They serve full time, unlike the members of the city council, who generally have outside jobs.

The commission plan of city government is simple, and it makes for a short ballot. These advantages made the plan popular in the early part of the twentieth century. But its divided leadership soon showed itself as a disadvantage. Without a chief executive it was difficult to fix responsibility. Departments tended to go off in separate directions. Sometimes commissioners competed for power. Often they lacked real expertise in administration. After 1920, cities began to abandon the commission plan, and even Galveston turned to the mayor-council form in 1960. A little more than 100 cities now operate under a commission form of government. These cities have adopted reforms to coordinate the functions of city government, and most of them hire a professional administrator to manage each department.

The Council-Manager Plan During the twentieth century the mayor-council plan was modified to create the council-manager plan. Under this plan an elected council appoints a professional administrator, the ***city manager,*** to run the city government. The post is nonpolitical. A weak mayor is elected separately or chosen from within the

INSIGHT

City-Business Courtship

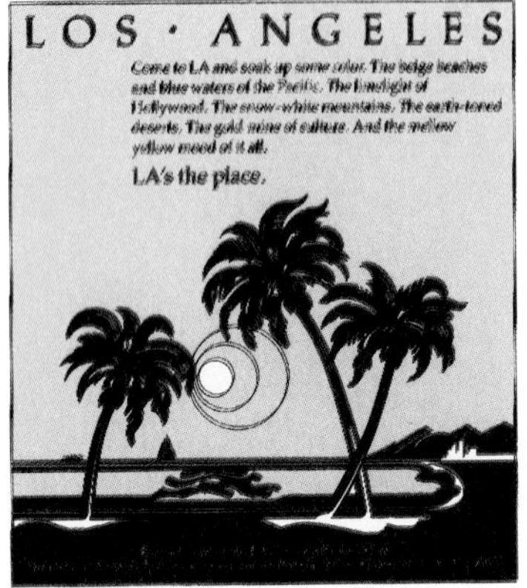

"Take stock in Greater Syracuse," reads one full-color advertisement in a recent business magazine. "Philadelphia Style . . . Come and Get It," reads another. "Peaches, pineapples, oranges & grapefruit are great . . . but there's nothing like the Big Apple," proclaims a flashy two-page ad for New York City.

American cities actively court big business, seeking headquarters, plants, or new offices to boost local economies. Most cities were founded as centers of business and commerce. Today the economic health and vitality of American cities still depend on business. Cities may offer business ***tax incentives***—tax breaks to make it less expensive for a company to set up and operate. City government may also ease building code restrictions to encourage the construction of new office buildings and plants. Some cities have even issued municipal bonds to raise money for ailing local industries.

Cities have successfully encouraged new business by improving public services and facilities. The Boston Redevelopment Authority, for example, has successfully attracted new business by improving its public transportation system and rebuilding deteriorating areas into shops, malls, and new housing. The construction of new office buildings has revitalized the downtown area, encouraging more businesses to locate there. Boston's redevelopers have also placed a high priority on making their city safe from crime—an important attraction for many businesses.

Every city offers unique attractions. Boston considers the excellence of its universities an important selling point for new businesses. New York counts on its reputation as a banking and financial center as well as its cultural offerings. Detroit and other Michigan cities attract new business on the strength of their public and private school systems—an important asset for any city. Almost as important is each city's image. Magazine advertisements, television commercials, and even bumper stickers have been used to promote cities. Chicago's former Mayor Jane Byrne even offered a prize for a new song for Chicago. She hoped that a song celebrating Chicago would evoke in its listeners as much enthusiasm for the "Windy City" as the song *New York! New York!* does for the "Big Apple."

council. The council is usually small with five to nine members. These members, elected at large on a nonpartisan ballot, have the power to make city policy, and they hire and fire the city manager.

The city manager is responsible for running the city government, preparing the budget, spending the funds appropriated by the council, and hiring and firing all city employees. The city manager executes the policies set by the council and is often an important source of policy suggestions. The council, for its part, must not interfere in the city manager's day-to-day administration of the government.

The council-manager plan is especially popular among small and medium-sized cities. About 3,000 cities have adopted it. It has many advantages. It is simple, it clarifies who is responsible for both policy and administration, it is efficient, and it is economical. It emphasizes professionalism, expertise, and businesslike administration. The council-manager plan, however, has had little appeal for the largest cities because it does not provide for strong political leadership. It gives less representation to special interests and minorities. And it offers no satisfactory mechanism for bargaining.

The Functions of Cities

A city's major function is to provide its residents with services. Sometimes these services are provided by the city alone. More often they are provided by the city in cooperation with other levels of government. City governments frequently administer state and federal programs. Many urban services are financed, wholly or in part, by the state or by the federal government. All city services must conform to state law, and they may be subject to the supervision of state agencies.

The services that cities provide vary with their size and wealth. One of the most important is public education. Schools are typically administered through special districts, but many cities have their own school boards. A number of cities and counties operate community colleges. New York City, for example, has its own university system.

Services that cities provide include the following:

1. police and fire protection;
2. construction and maintenance of streets, sidewalks, street lights, and traffic signs;
3. garbage collection, waste treatment, and sanitary services;
4. water, gas, and electric service;
5. parks and recreational facilities;
6. public transportation systems;
7. public health services;
8. welfare for the needy;
9. slum clearance and public housing;
10. hospitals, clinics, and nursing homes;
11. libraries and museums;
12. animal shelters;
13. airports;
14. auditoriums, convention centers, and sports arenas.

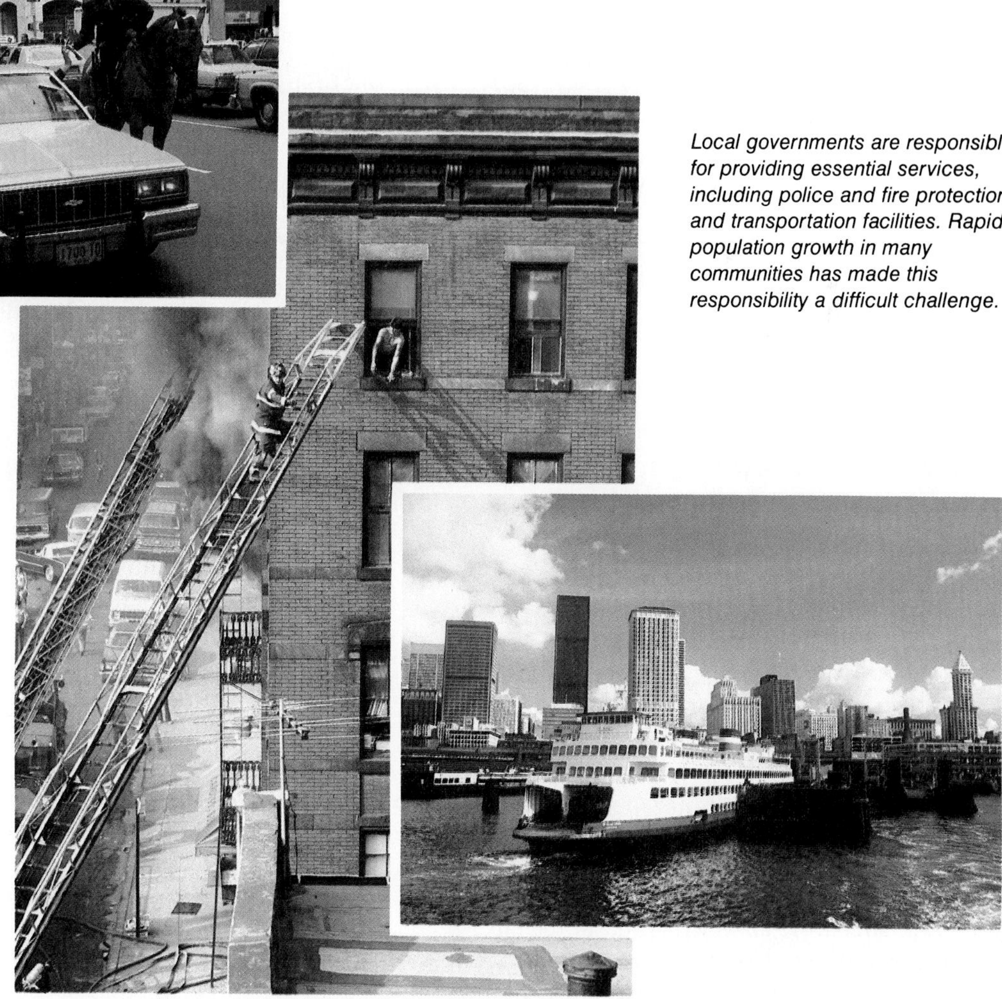

Local governments are responsible for providing essential services, including police and fire protection and transportation facilities. Rapid population growth in many communities has made this responsibility a difficult challenge.

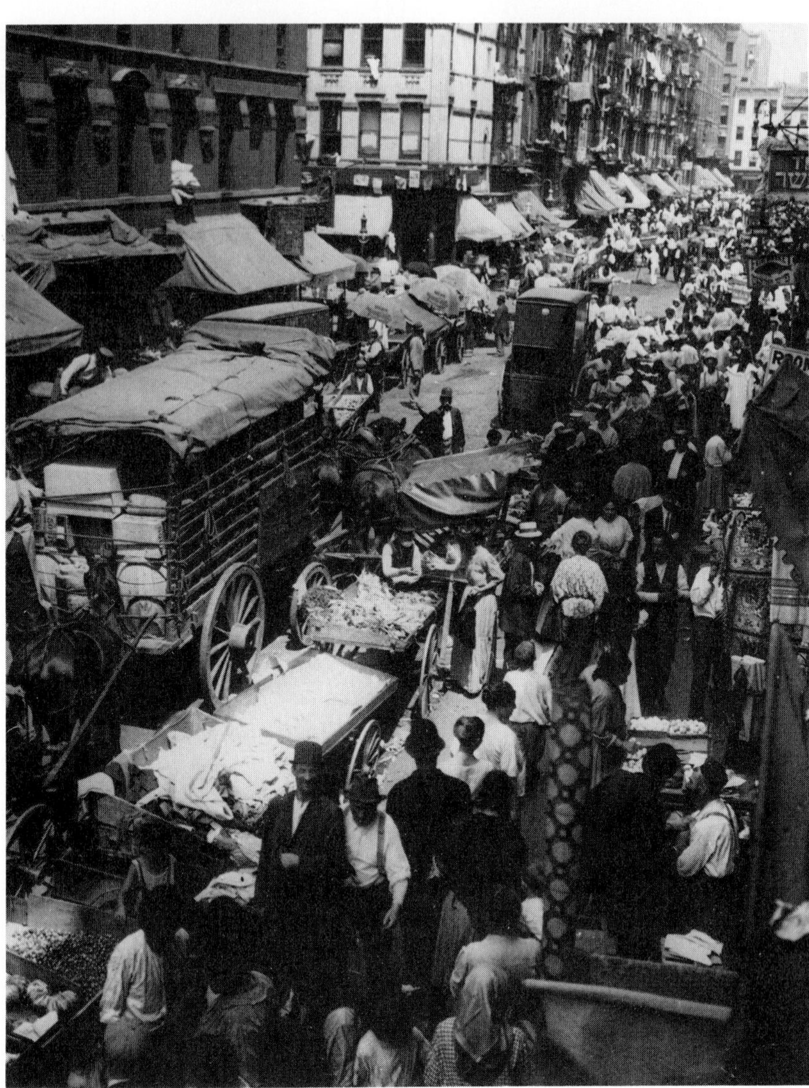

At the turn of the century, overcrowding, inadequate health facilities, and crime were among the common urban problems of major cities in the United States. List some common problems of major cities today.

The Problems of Cities

Since the earliest civilizations, the city has been the center of culture, commerce, and political life. But the city has always had special problems. Congestion, slums, crime, and rootlessness are ageless, as every reader of Charles Dickens knows. By the mid-twentieth century, however, many observers had begun to speak of an "urban crisis" in the United States. The portrait these observers painted was bleak. According to them, basic services had not kept pace with the cities' growth. Cities were choked by polluted air and traffic congestion. Public transportation was inadequate, housing was deteriorating, and the schools were turning out graduates who could not read. There was so much crime in the streets that law and order seemed to have broken down. The white middle class was moving to the suburbs of metropolitan areas, and racial tensions began flaring in the inner cities. City life, it seemed, was becoming one long round of danger, harassment, and frustration.

Not everyone is prepared to accept this portrait of urban crisis. Those who defend the city emphasize the diversity and vitality of urban life. Cities are centers of creativity, innovation, and opportunity. But cities do have problems, and the tasks of urban government are growing more difficult every day.

City Planning Most cities in the United States were not planned. They simply grew—a factory here, an office building there, one main thoroughfare following another. Schools and gas stations and homes sprang up wherever there was room, wherever land was cheap, or wherever people wanted to build them.

LEGACY

Art in the Center

Walkers in Chicago's famous Loop—the business district that received its name from the elevated tracks that circled the area—come face to face with sculptures by the world's most famous modern artists. Since the placement of the sphinx-like woman by Pablo Picasso in Daley Plaza, Chicago city planners have encouraged public art.

In 1978 Chicago passed an ordinance that requires that 1 percent of the total construction cost of every public building be set aside for art. Another program, Art in the Center, accepts donations of sculpture such as Joan Miro's "Chicago" or Marc Chagall's mural "The Four Seasons." Under this program the work of art and the land beneath it become city property.

Federal buildings under the General Services Administration's Art-in-Architecture Program set aside five eighths of 1 percent of construction costs for public art. Thus Chicagoans can enjoy Alexander Calder's "Flamingo" and Claes Oldenburg's "Batcolumn," each on the site of a federal building.

Today cities must plan for the future. They must anticipate problems and needs before they arise—and before it is too late. Are new schools needed? Where should they be located? Will public transportation be adequate for the coming decade? Are there enough parks and recreational facilities? Should streets and public utilities be extended to outlying areas? The goals of city planning are orderly growth and improvement in the quality of urban life.

Planning also seeks to correct past mistakes. It seeks especially to revitalize the ***inner city***—the oldest, central neighborhoods where unplanned growth has had time to do the most damage. Pittsburgh, for example, has cleaned its inner-city air of industrial pollution and rebuilt the heart of its business district. Detroit's Renaissance Center symbolizes the rebirth of a once blighted area. But there is more to revitalizing the city than tearing down slums to build skyscrapers. City revitalization also means restoring existing buildings. It means providing adequate housing for people at all income levels. City revitalization—indeed, all of city planning—is a matter of public spirit and of civic pride for urban dwellers.

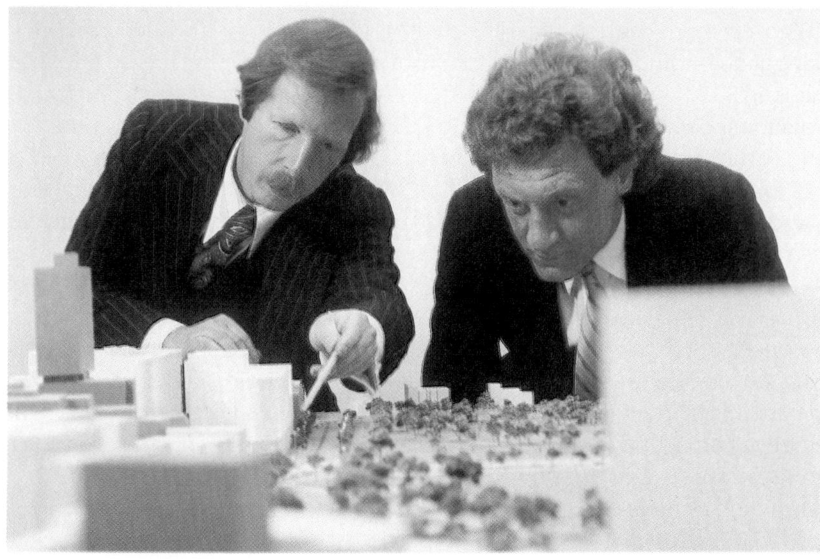

A city planner—working from a master plan—presents a model of a proposed urban renovation to a city official. What are some of the questions city planners try to answer as they develop plans for a city's future?

Houston is the leading industrial center and the largest city in Texas. Uncontrolled planning and a lack of zoning ordinances, however, have created urban problems in Houston—crowded highways, pollution, and inadequate public services.

Civic pride, then, is one of the factors that encourage city planning. Enlightened self-interest is another. A well-planned city is a more pleasant city to live in. It attracts more business, and its property values stay high. Finally, the federal government has encouraged city planning by making it a condition for most federal assistance programs.

Nowadays most cities have a planning commission or some similar agency with a professionally trained staff. It is the commission's job to draw up a master plan if the city does not already have one. And it is its job to see that the master plan is actually used to guide the city's growth.

Zoning One of the main concerns of city planning is how land is used. During the nineteenth century, cities grew without any particular order. Factories, businesses, and homes might be found anywhere within the city. Chicago's stockyards, for example, were located right in the middle of a residential neighborhood.

Uncontrolled land use began to change in 1916, when New York City adopted the first comprehensive ordinance controlling the use of land. Other cities soon followed suit. Today nearly every city of any size controls the use of land through ***zoning***—the division of a city into districts, each of which may be used only for certain purposes. Most cities have three kinds of zones: residential, commercial, and industrial. Each of these zones may be divided into subzones. For example, one residential area may be reserved for single-family homes and another for duplexes and apartments. Heavy industry may be concentrated in one place, and light industry in another. In addition, zoning laws usually impose other restrictions on land use. They may regulate the height and size of buildings. They may specify how close together two houses may be built. They may even say where a building must be placed on the lot.

Zoning has many obvious advantages. It helps the city to plan for future growth. It helps the city to provide for efficient services by separating residential, commercial, and industrial areas. It protects property values in residential areas by keeping out businesses and factories. It can even be used to make a community more beautiful.

Some people opposed to zoning consider it government interference in their property rights. They argue that people should be able to do anything they want with their own property. The Supreme Court confronted this question in 1926. In a case that involved the zoning laws of Euclid, Ohio, the Court upheld zoning laws as a proper exercise of police power, saying that the power to zone property was part of the community's power to protect the health, safety, and welfare of the people.

Zoning must not be used in a discriminatory manner. That is, it must not deprive people of the liberty to use their property as they like—or of the property itself—without due process of law. The right to due process is guaranteed by the Fourteenth Amendment and is reaffirmed in most state constitutions. In addition, zoning must be reasonable.

PROFILE

Urban Renaissance

In the mid 1960's the Inner Harbor area of Baltimore, Maryland, was an urban wasteland of rotting wharves, empty warehouses, and deserted railroad yards. Residents and businesses had abandoned the area, where only crime seemed to flourish. Many Baltimore residents considered the downtown district lost—a victim of the urban blight that threatens many other American cities.

Today Baltimore's Inner Harbor is an urban showcase of shops and cafes, restaurants and galleries that draws close to 20 million visitors a year. Jugglers perform, musicians play, visitors stroll past the wharves that were once in danger of falling into ruin. Where vacant warehouses stood before, new businesses have created more than 2,000 jobs and earned more than $40 million dollars in one of the most successful examples of recent urban redevelopment.

The program to revitalize Baltimore spanned 25 years and cost $1.5 billion. Business leaders, government leaders, preservationists, and city residents joined together in their effort to save the city. The program began with the construction of a new downtown high-rise office complex and a large convention center. New hotels went up, as well as a concert pavilion for cultural attractions. But Baltimore's renaissance also included saving old buildings in residential neighborhoods. A homesteading program preserved many of the city's nineteenth-century red brick row houses. A similar program, called "shopsteading," encouraged businesses to save old storefronts. Local businesses have also supported the city's restoration program by pitching in up to 5 percent of their annual income to support civic causes. As one city planner noted, "Nothing happens here by itself. People have to make it happen."

Baltimore is only one of many American cities rebuilding itself after decades of decline. St. Louis is turning an abandoned railroad terminal into a hotel and office complex. Milwaukee has restored a 1915 city landmark and constructed around it a three-level shopping mall in the heart of its downtown area. In Boston the construction of a new shopping and office complex called Faneuil Hall Marketplace has brought about what a former mayor of Boston called "the greatest development boom" in the city's 350-year history. Such programs prove the continuing strength and vitality of the American city.

Zoning laws apply only to new uses of land or to land that is about to be developed. They cannot be used to prevent people from using the land as they have done in the past. Most cities also grant ***variances,*** or exceptions, in cases where zoning laws would impose undue hardship. Variances are considered by a special zoning board of appeals.

Zoning decisions often set off major political battles within the community. A land developer, for example, may seek zoning for high-density multiple-family housing in a newly developed area. A citizens' environmental group may be committed to low-density single-family housing or perhaps to the preservation of a "green belt." Zoning battles may occur over the construction of freeways. In recent years many cities have faced zoning conflict over urban growth. Business and real estate interests typically favor growth. They want to attract new business and industry to stimulate the economy and create new jobs. On the other side, there are those who favor strict controls on growth or, in some cases, "no growth." They fear urban sprawl, congestion, pollution, and a decline in the quality of life.

City planning, then, can be a thorny issue. It is not that most people oppose city planning as such. But what, exactly, is a well-planned city? Often this term means different things to different people.

The Rise of the Suburbs As the chart on page 753 shows, the United States is an urban nation. Some of the most serious problems urban areas face today are caused by the rise of the suburbs. Suburban growth has been amazing. Between 1950 and 1980 the population of the suburbs grew by 100 percent. During this time the population of the central cities grew slowly or declined. Today more people live in the suburbs than in the central cities.

People move to the suburbs of central cities for many reasons. They are drawn by cheaper houses and lower taxes; by less crime and newer schools; and by open space, privacy, and clean air. But besides people the suburbs have attracted shopping centers, office buildings, restaurants, gas stations, and motels. Industries too have moved to the suburbs, drawn, like the people themselves, by cheap land and lower taxes—and sometimes by the absence of zoning

LEXICON

Daylighting, Piggybacking, and Shoehorning

In New York City a condominium stands atop the Museum of Modern Art. The sleek CitiCorp Building perches on stainless steel stilts above a church. In Houston a shimmering skyscraper rises to rival the Emerald City where the Wizard of Oz once held court. In scores of American cities exciting new architecture reflects the hopes of city planners and the limits of local zoning ordinances.

Zoning ordinances in cities like New York control not only a building's ground-floor plan, called its ***footprint,*** but also the measure of how much sky remains visible around a building, called ***daylighting.*** In New York, city planners also consider ***piggybacking,*** building a new structure on top of an old building, and ***shoehorning,*** slipping a new building between two existing structures.

But not all cities enact zoning ordinances. In Houston there are no zoning restrictions. This unrestricted development reflects the freewheeling spirit of a young and rapidly growing city. But Houston city planners see serious problems ahead. Public transportation is already straining to meet the needs of the sprawling city. In the last few years traffic congestion has doubled the time it takes to cross Houston by car. A serious housing shortage looms on the horizon as Houston grows. In the future, say Houston city planners, they may turn to zoning as a way to control the city's growth without sacrificing its unique vitality. For the present, Houston's downtown office buildings are architectural wonders, and the city's skyline is one of the most exciting in America.

codes and other strict controls on growth. Ironically, many of the problems suburbanites had hoped to escape—congestion, pollution, and crime—have followed them to the suburbs.

The rise of the suburbs has had a deep impact on the central cities, changing their social and political character. The people who have moved to the suburbs have been predominantly white, middle class, and relatively young. As a result, the central cities have an older population and a higher proportion of blacks and other minorities, including the poor. To a limited degree the makeup of central cities and suburbs has begun to change in recent years. More middle-class blacks and Hispanics are moving to the suburbs, and some wealthier whites are returning to the high-rise apartments and condominiums of the revitalized central cities.

The rise of the suburbs has affected the financial position of the central cities. Most people who live in the suburbs work in the central city, but they pay no taxes to support the services provided by the city in which they are employed. With the middle-class exodus to the suburbs the central cities have lost an important source of revenue. The loss of businesses and industries has cut further into the city tax base. The central cities have less money with which to finance services, while at the same time the people who still live there are the very ones who need these services the most. The result is that central cities are less and less able to cope with the pressing problems of urban life.

The Metropolitan Area The difficulty central cities face in dealing with urban problems is increased by the fragmentation of local government. A metropolitan area frequently spreads over several counties. In addition to the central city, it may include dozens of suburban towns and a maze of special districts. Each of these units of government may provide some, all, or none of the same services as another unit—and residents of a given area may be getting their services from three or four different units of government at once. No wonder that good service is often hard to come by, or that it is sometimes a puzzle to tell who is responsible for what!

Various efforts have been made to solve the problems of these metropolitan areas. Special districts have been formed to handle one specific areawide service, such as public transportation. A few cities and counties have consolidated to form a single metropolitan government. Others have assigned specific functions to specific levels of government. The county or a special "metro" government may

URBAN AMERICA TODAY

State	Percent Urban	Percent Rural
Alabama	60.0	40.0
Alaska	64.3	35.7
Arizona	83.8	16.2
Arkansas	51.6	48.4
California	91.3	8.7
Colorado	80.6	19.4
Connecticut	78.8	21.2
Delaware	70.6	29.4
Florida	84.3	15.7
Georgia	62.4	37.6
Hawaii	86.5	13.5
Idaho	54.0	46.0
Illinois	83.3	16.7
Indiana	64.2	35.8
Iowa	58.6	41.4
Kansas	66.7	33.3
Kentucky	50.9	49.1
Louisiana	68.6	31.4
Maine	47.5	52.5
Maryland	80.3	19.7
Massachusetts	83.8	16.2
Michigan	70.7	29.3
Minnesota	66.9	33.1
Mississippi	47.3	52.7
Missouri	68.1	31.9
Montana	52.9	47.1
Nebraska	62.9	37.1
Nevada	85.3	14.7
New Hampshire	52.2	47.8
New Jersey	89.0	11.0
New Mexico	72.1	27.9
New York	84.6	15.4
North Carolina	48.0	52.0
North Dakota	48.8	51.2
Ohio	73.3	26.7
Oklahoma	67.3	32.7
Oregon	67.9	32.1
Pennsylvania	69.3	30.7
Rhode Island	87.0	13.0
South Carolina	54.1	45.9
South Dakota	46.4	53.6
Tennessee	60.4	39.6
Texas	79.6	20.4
Utah	84.4	15.6
Vermont	33.8	66.2
Virginia	66.0	34.0
Washington	73.5	26.5
West Virginia	36.2	63.8
Wisconsin	64.2	35.8
Wyoming	62.7	37.3

Source: U.S. Census, 1980. The urban population consists basically of all persons living in places of 2,500 inhabitants or more.

Mayors of cities with populations of more than 30,000 persons are eligible for membership in the United States Conference of Mayors. The conference, which meets twice each year, is a forum through which mayors exchange information and debate issues affecting city government.

be responsible for areawide services—fire protection or sewer service, for example—while the city and suburbs retain control over strictly local matters. Still others have resorted to ***annexation,*** the extension of municipal boundaries to bring new land into the city limits. Annexation usually occurs as population density increases on the outskirts of a city. The procedures for annexation are set by state law and vary among the states. Generally the voters of both the central city and the area concerned must vote in favor of annexation.

Intergovernmental Relations

In the American federal system the national, state, and local governments share many responsibilities. In Chapter 4 the relationship between the national and state levels of government involving both conflict and cooperation was discussed. Similarly, in the relations among the states and between the state and local governments, there is both conflict and cooperation.

The states are often competing with each other—to attract business and industry, to secure a larger share of federal aid, and to advance their own interests in general. Cities and various other units of local government also compete, and among the different governments of the same metropolitan area, conflict can be intense. But at each level, governments face common problems and have mutual interests best served by cooperation.

We have seen how governments work together to solve some of the problems of the metropolitan area. ***Interstate compacts*** are designed to solve the problems faced by two or more states. These compacts are an instrument of regional cooperation; more than 160 of them are in force today. One well-known compact established the Port of New York Authority. Under this agreement New York and New Jersey together regulate New York Harbor and share in the construction and management of interstate bridges, tunnels, bus terminals, and airports.

The Council of State Governments coordinates interstate relations in areas of common concern. This agency is maintained by the states. It serves as the central office for the National Governors' Association, the National Conference of State Legislatures, and similar organizations for state chief justices, attorneys general, budget officers, and other state officials.

A number of organizations serve the same function for local government officials. Among the most important are the United States Conference of Mayors, the National League of Cities, and the National Association of Counties.

The United States Advisory Commission on Intergovernmental Relations includes representatives from all levels of government. It studies the proper role of the federal government in relation to state and local governments. The future of American federalism depends upon balance and cooperation in intergovernmental relations. For "a more perfect union," governments at each level must work together in partnership.

Section Check

1. Define: municipality, metropolitan area, incorporation, charter, city manager, tax incentive, inner city, zoning, variance, piggybacking, central city
2. Identify: mayor-council plan, ward system of election, weak-mayor form of government, commission plan, council-manager plan, Art in the Center Program, Detroit's Renaissance Center
3. What are the four types of city charters?
4. Explain the advantages and disadvantages of the strong-mayor system.
5. Why do most cities pass zoning ordinances?

---

4 FINANCING STATE AND LOCAL GOVERNMENT

In recent years the cost of state and local government has skyrocketed. At the turn of the century state and local governments spent a total of less than $1 billion a year. By 1960 this figure had increased to slightly over $60 billion. In 1970 it was $148 billion. By 1980, the total expenditure of state and local government had reached a whopping $434 billion a year. To put it another way, in 1900, state and local government cost about $13 for each person. In 1980 the per-person cost had increased to roughly $2,000 per person.

Part of the answer for this amazing surge in the cost of government lies in inflation. But the cost of government has also been affected by the huge growth in government itself. And if government has grown so huge, it is because over the years the people have expected the government to provide more and more services.

Since 1950 the number of state and local employees has grown by more than 300 percent—from 4 million in 1950 to more than 13 million today. Today state and local governments employ more than four times as many people as the national government.

This increase reflects an enormous expansion of services and activities. State and local governments today provide a range of services—many of

Citizens have grown to expect an increasing number of services from government. Thus, the power to raise and spend money has become vital to the functioning of state and local government.

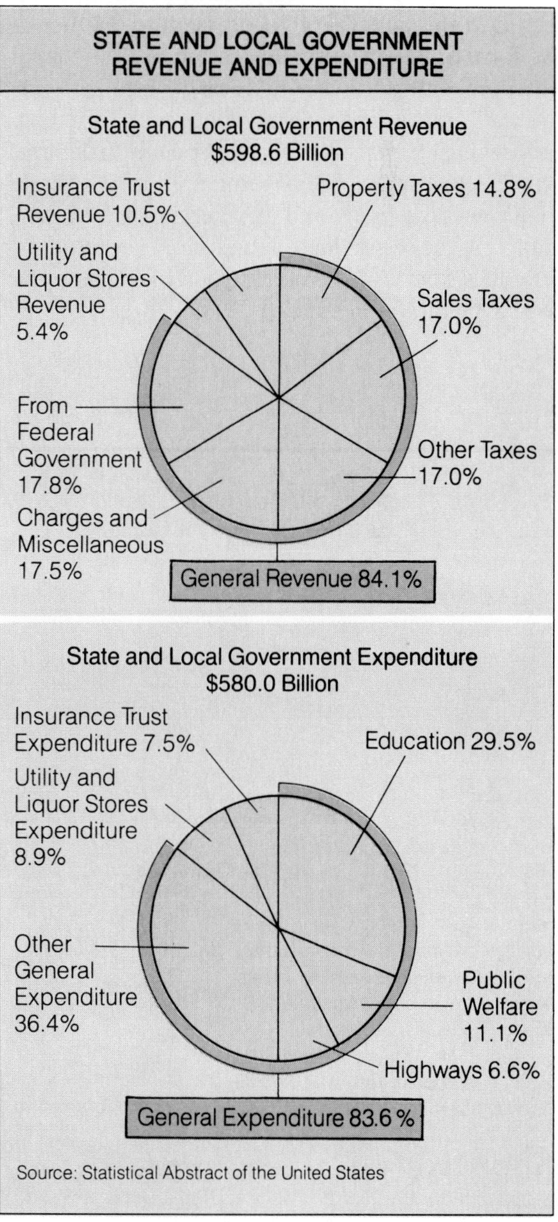

them unheard of 80, or even 30, years ago. Education, highways, public welfare, and public health account for almost three fourths of the states' annual expenditures. Local governments must also carry expenses for police and fire protection, sewerage and sanitation, public housing and urban renewal, and parks and recreation.

Taxes

State and local governments derive most of their ***revenue,*** or income, from taxes. Tax revenues in the early 1980's amounted to more than $250 billion. Intergovernmental grants provide another source of revenue. In these grants money is transferred from one level of government to another in the form of federal revenue sharing or in the form of federal grants to state and local governments. Or the states may share their revenues with local governments or give them grants for specific programs. Finally, state and local governments may operate their own businesses. And they may borrow money, subject to the restrictions of their state constitutions. Revenues from all these nontax sources totaled more than $200 billion in the early 1980's.

Powers of Taxation A ***tax*** is a compulsory charge made by the government to raise money for public purposes. The states derive their power to tax from the Constitution, and local governments derive their power to tax from the states. But the power to tax is limited by the federal and state constitutions, and in the case of local governments, by state laws as well.

The states' power to tax is limited in several ways. The Constitution—Article 1, Section 10—forbids the states to impose taxes on imports or exports. Neither may the states interfere with interstate commerce by means of taxation. As established in *McCulloch* v. *Maryland* (1819), states may not tax the activities of the federal government, because "the power to tax involves the power to destroy." Under the Fourteenth Amendment, states may not use their taxing power to deny persons equal protection of the law. Nor may they use taxes to deprive persons of their property without due process.

"Equal protection" requires that classifications of persons for tax purposes be *reasonable.* A tax based on race, religion, national origin, or political belief, for example, would be forbidden. "Due process" requires that taxes be drawn up and

Local parks and recreational facilities are funded through taxes and federal revenue sharing. A park ranger (above) conducts a tour of an early Spanish settlement in St. Augustine, Florida. Freeway Park (right) is a popular retreat in Seattle, Washington.

Taxes provide the funds to operate a sewage-treatment plant (left) as well as the funds to equip and operate schools (below). From what sources do state and local governments derive the power to tax?

administered fairly. They must be imposed only for public purposes, and they must not be so heavy as to confiscate property.

The states' power to tax is also limited by the state constitutions. Often the constitutions specify the types of taxes that the states may impose. Sometimes they even specify the amounts. The state constitutions generally exempt certain types of property from taxation. For example, taxes are not usually imposed on property used for religious, charitable, or educational purposes.

Within these restrictions and their specific applications, state legislatures may enact whatever taxes they choose. Local governments operate under far greater limitations. They may impose only those taxes which the state constitutions or the state legislatures permit. In practice most local governments have extremely restricted powers of taxation.

Principles of Taxation There is no such thing as a popular tax—but taxes should be fair. They should be fixed and certain. They should be levied in such a way as to make it as convenient as possible for people to pay them. Taxes should not be higher than necessary.

Most tax systems fall into one of three categories. In ***proportional taxation*** each person pays a tax that equals exactly the same percentage of income. In ***progressive taxation*** each person pays a graduated tax based upon income. People with high incomes, for example, pay proportionately higher taxes than people with lower incomes. In ***regressive taxation*** everyone, regardless of income, pays the same amount. Regressive taxation results in people with low incomes paying a greater percentage in taxes than people with high incomes. Of the 50 states 30 have regressive tax systems, 15 have proportional tax systems, and only 5 have progressive tax systems.

Sales Taxes A sales tax is a tax placed on the sale of goods. It is paid by the purchaser at the time a sale is made. A ***general sales tax*** is a tax placed on the sale of almost all goods. A ***selective sales tax*** is placed on certain items. An example of a selective tax is an ***excise tax,*** a tax levied on luxury items. The sales tax is the largest single source of revenue for state governments, producing about half of all state revenue. Many cities and some counties also levy a sales tax.

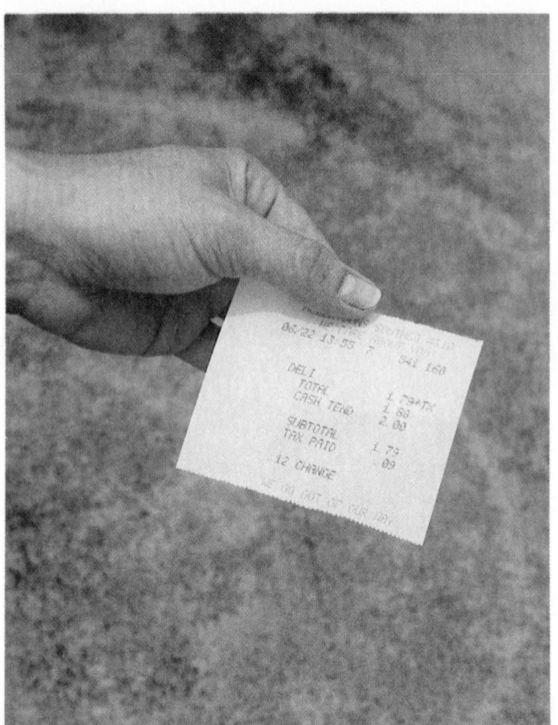

The sales tax is calculated as a percentage of the purchase price of a product. The seller of the product collects the tax and sends it to the state or local taxing authority. Why is the sales tax often favored over other types of taxation?

All states with the exception of Alaska, Delaware, Montana, New Hampshire, and Oregon impose a general sales tax, and its use is increasing among cities. Everyone, regardless of income, pays at the same rate, typically 4 percent. All states have a selective sales tax on liquor, cigarettes, and gasoline, and most levy a selective sales tax on amusements, hotel accommodations, and automobiles, among other things. The selective sales tax produces almost a quarter of all state revenue.

The sales tax is generally favored for several reasons. State legislatures like it because it is easy to administer and produces a great deal of money for the state. And citizens tend to favor it because it is relatively painless. Because they usually pay it a few cents at a time, they do not feel the bite as much as they do in the case of a larger annual tax payment. Many people favor the sales tax because it requires all citizens to contribute to the support of their government.

Its disadvantage is that it is a regressive tax. Everyone, regardless of income, pays at the same rate. For this reason the sales tax falls most heavily on people with low incomes for whom the sales tax represents a greater proportion of their earnings. Some states have sought to reduce the sales tax burden on people with lower incomes by exempting basic necessities such as food, clothing, and medicine from the sales tax.

Income Taxes An ***income tax,*** which is a tax placed on personal or corporate income, produces over one third of all state revenue. Forty-six states have corporate income tax, while 43 have personal income tax. A few cities also levy a municipal income tax.

Individual income taxes are usually progressive—that is, the rate at which a person is taxed goes up as income increases. Corporations are usually taxed at a fixed percentage rate. On the whole, state and local income taxes are relatively low. States tend to be cautious about raising taxes because the federal income tax is already so high. They are also cautious because higher taxes might drive business and industry out of the state and into another where taxes are lower.

Property Taxes The ***property tax*** is the major source of revenue for local governments, accounting for some 85 percent of the tax moneys collected by cities, counties, townships, school districts, and other special districts. At one time the property tax was also an important source of state revenue, but today the states make relatively little use of this tax.

Property taxes may be levied on either ***real property***—land and the buildings on that land—or ***personal property***—movable objects that may be ***tangible,*** such as furniture, jewelry, and livestock, or ***intangible,*** such as bank accounts, stocks, and bonds. In actual practice personal property is taxed much less often than real property.

Before a tax can be levied on property, the property's value must be determined in a process known as ***assessment*** by an elected or appointed assessor. The assessment is usually made once a year in the case of personal property and once every two or four years in the case of real property.

The property tax is perhaps the most controversial of all taxes. There are three arguments in its favor. It is a dependable source of revenue. The tax rate is easily adjusted to meet changing needs. And because their property is protected by the government, it is fair that property owners should pay taxes to support that government.

But there are also several arguments against the property tax. First, personal property is easy to hide. Second, it is very hard to ensure that property will be assessed fairly. Assessors are seldom trained specialists, and the way in which property is assessed varies widely. So, too, do the rates at which property is taxed. This means that property taxes may be high in one city and low in another, but they may also vary within the same city.

But the strongest argument, and the one most often cited, is that the property tax is not related to the ability to pay. A house is taxed according to what it would sell for today—not according to what the owner originally paid for it. As housing costs go up, so do property taxes. As a result many people have been squeezed by property taxes that have risen faster than their incomes. The burden of taxation is placed on the people who own real estate, but these people are not necessarily wealthy.

ISSUES

The Tax Revolt

In 1978 the voters of California passed a revolutionary proposal to cut their own taxes—a move which many observers saw as the beginning of a nationwide tax revolt. The California ballot initiative, called Proposition 13 or the Jarvis-Gann Amendment, cut property taxes by 30 percent. It further required a two-thirds majority of the state legislature to pass new taxes. Proposition 13 cut $7 billion in annual taxes from a total budget of $24 billion. State and local governments depended on those tax revenues to fund a wide variety of programs and services. But supporters of the initiative saw it as a victory against uncontrolled government spending. Opponents feared that it would create havoc in city and state budgets and seriously undermine many of the services paid for by tax revenues, including police and fire protection, health care, and education programs. As the controversy raged, even economists failed to agree on what effect Proposition 13 would have.

Still, a majority of Americans welcomed a tax cut. When Proposition 13 passed in California, a Gallup poll showed that 57 percent of the public favored a cut in their own state. Tax cut initiatives were already under way in a number of states. Predictions of a nationwide tax revolt seemed justified. By 1980 limits on taxes or spending had been passed in 19 states.

In that year, however, the tax revolt suffered a startling setback. The same voters in California who had passed Proposition 13 by a 65 percent majority rejected a second initiative to cut state income taxes. Many thousands of state and city employees had been laid off their jobs as a result of Proposition 13. Municipal governments had been forced to cut back police and fire departments. Voters now seemed to fear that this new tax cut would further cut back or eliminate essential services.

The effects of California's Proposition 13 are still being measured. In 1978, at the time of the passage of Proposition 13, California enjoyed a $6.1 billion state budget surplus. Instead of cutting many government services, the state elected to dip into its surplus. By the 1980's, however, with tax revenues cut and the cost of government services still running high, the state had depleted its surplus and was forced to borrow more than a billion dollars to meet its payroll. Many city and state programs were again in danger of being drastically reduced or eliminated entirely. In California and across the nation, the basic question of the tax revolt was still to be answered: how can taxes be cut without cutting the basic services that citizens have come to expect?

For example, an elderly couple living on Social Security purchased their home 40 years ago for $10,000. Now they are living on $400 a month. But because property values have gone up, their house is worth $200,000—and their property tax is $2,000 a year.

Some local and state governments have tried to remedy inequities in assessed valuations and property taxes. A number of states have provisions called "circuit breakers" that take into account the ability to pay. Several states also exempt people over the age of 65 from property taxes. But the matter of exemptions is itself a source of controversy. About 80 percent of real estate is subject to taxation. Government property is tax-exempt, as is property owned by private schools, and churches. Whenever property is removed from the tax rolls, other taxpayers have to make up the difference.

One of the most intense controversies over the property tax concerns the public schools. Except in Hawaii, school districts are financed primarily by local property taxes. The amount of money available to finance public education thus depends on the wealth of the school district, and this varies widely within each state. The states provide funding to bring each district up to a minimum standard. But poor districts, often with high taxes, still cannot spend as much on their schools as wealthier districts in the same state.

In 1971 the parents of Tony Serrano took the issue of unequal financing among school districts to court. Tony attended school in a poor California district. His parents argued that the unequal financing resulting from the use of the property tax violated the California Constitution. The California Supreme Court agreed. In *Serrano* v. *Priest* the court ruled that the quality of a child's education must not depend on the wealth of his or her parents or community.

The issue was addressed again in 1973, this time by the United States Supreme Court. The case was *San Antonio Independent School District* v. *Rodriguez.* The question before the Court was whether using the local property tax to finance schools violated the equal protection clause of the Fourteenth Amendment. In a 5–4 decision the Court held that it did not. The Court recognized the problem, but it stated that "the ultimate solution must come from lawmakers and from the democratic pressures of those who elect them." Today the states are exploring new ways to finance public education. Meanwhile the property tax is still the most important source of local revenue for the support of schools.

Other Taxes Business taxes of some kind are imposed in every state. All states impose business license taxes, fees that permit individuals or corporations to do business in the state. Business license taxes are also imposed by many local governments. Other business taxes imposed in some states include severance taxes, documentary and stock transfer taxes, and capital stock taxes. ***Severance taxes*** are taxes levied on the removal of natural resources such as minerals, timber, or oil. ***Documentary*** and ***stock transfer taxes*** are taxes levied on the recording, registering, and transferring of documents. ***Capital stock taxes*** are taxes levied on the stock issued by a business. They are less common than the other kinds of business taxes.

Most states also impose various kinds of property transfer taxes. ***Estate taxes*** are levied on the estate of someone who has died. ***Inheritance taxes*** are levied on a beneficiary's share of the estate of the deceased person. Every state except Nevada levies one or the other of these so-called death taxes. Some states also impose a ***gift tax***—that is, a tax levied on a large cash gift to another person. Sometimes such gifts are made in order to avoid paying a death tax; the purpose of the gift tax is to close this tax loophole.

Nontax Sources of Revenue

Whether for schools or for the support of other services, local governments depend increasingly on ***intergovernmental grants.*** These grants may come from the state or from the federal government.

State aid to local governments takes two forms. Many states provide support through tax sharing. According to a formula established by law, the state turns over a certain amount of its tax revenue to local governments. Sometimes the money may be used as the receiving government sees fit. Sometimes the state government has a say in how the money will be used.

Most state assistance to local governments comes in the form of grants for specific programs. Almost all of this money goes to four areas: education, public welfare, public health and hospitals, and highways. Of these, education gets the lion's share. Grants, like tax-sharing funds, are generally distributed according to a specific formula.

The state also serves as a channel for distributing federal aid to local governments. In addition the states themselves receive federal aid. Federal aid is an important source of funding for state and local governments.

An important source of revenue for Oregon is the severance tax paid by lumbering industries in the state. More than half the states levy severance taxes. List other types of business taxes imposed by some states.

Government-Operated Businesses Every state owns and operates various businesses. So do many cities. The revenue from these businesses goes to support the government that runs them.

Many state governments are in the transportation business. These governments own and operate ferries, toll bridges, and toll roads. Cities may own and operate their own bus lines.

Many cities are landlords. They rent out space in housing projects, office buildings, and other city-owned property. Many other cities own their own utility systems.

Some state governments are in banking; others are in the manufacturing business. Eighteen states sell liquor through state-operated stores. Sixteen states run public lotteries, the proceeds from which go to support state government.

Borrowing When a state or city takes on a major public works project, it often borrows the money. Most state and local governments borrow by issuing bonds. The bond buyer, in effect, loans the issuer money for a fixed term after which the loan must be repaid with interest.

State constitutions normally restrict the state and local governments' power to borrow. This is because in the past many state and local governments have often borrowed more than they could repay. Typically the state constitution requires the voters to approve the issuing of the bonds. This may be done in a special bond election, or the bond issue may appear on the regular ballot. Often the voters will approve, but it is not unusual for bond issues to be voted down. Bonds are sold with the obligation to repay the lender with interest. Public bonds are an attractive investment because the interest earned is not taxed by the federal government.

In spite of the limits placed on borrowing by state constitutions, state and local indebtedness has risen steadily over the years. By the early 1980's, state debts totaled more than $125 billion and local government debts totaled almost $250 billion.

Many states raise revenue by imposing tolls on the use of certain highways and bridges. Much of the revenue collected from toll fees is used to maintain state roads and bridges.

The State Budget

The enormous sums of money taken in—and spent—by the state government must all be accounted for in detail. As is explained in Chapter 29, this is primarily the governor's job. In all states except Mississippi, South Carolina, and Texas, the governor alone has the power to prepare the state budget and—once the legislature has appropriated the funds—to execute it. In most states the governor is assisted in this task by a budget director and a professional staff. In cities with a strong mayor-council or a council-manager government, the mayor or city manager has these powers.

A state budget is both an estimate and a plan. It is an estimate of revenue and expenses and a plan for balancing the two. It is a plan for determining how much money is coming in, how much money is needed for what, and where the available money will go. Simply put, the budget is a plan for keeping track of the state's money.

Until the 1920's the state budget was scarcely planned at all. It was appropriated piecemeal by the legislature and allocated to the various state agencies. Each agency had to fight for its slice of the pie. The agency with the most political clout got the biggest slice. The legislature often had no idea how much money had been spent—or what it had been spent for.

The budget process nowadays is far more efficient, economical, and fair. This budgetary process is essentially the same for all state and local governments. It consists of six steps.

First, each agency prepares an estimate of its expenses for the next fiscal year. Second, the budget agency, appointed by and answerable to the governor, reviews the estimates. When necessary, the estimates are then revised. Third, the revised estimates and all the data to support them are consolidated into a statewide financial program. Then the governor presents this program to the legislature. Fourth, the legislature considers each part of the budget. It accepts or rejects each expenditure and appropriates the necessary funds. If new sources of revenue are needed, the legislature enacts the necessary measures. Fifth, the approved budget goes back to the governor, who executes it. Sixth, the state auditor performs an independent check to make sure that the state money was actually spent as budgeted.

State and local governments today take in—and spend—more and more money every year. Under these circumstances it becomes increasingly important that the legislature—and the people—know exactly where the money goes.

Section Check

1. Define: proportional taxation, progressive taxation, regressive taxation, excise tax, assessment, severance tax, estate tax
2. Identify: circuit breaker, Proposition 13
3. How has the Fourteenth Amendment provided guidelines for governments to draw up fair taxing systems?
4. Why is a sales tax generally favored over other forms of taxation?
5. What arguments are made for and against the property tax?

SUMMARY

There are about 80,000 units of local government in the United States. All local governments are agents of the state, and the powers they exercise are delegated to them by the state.

In rural areas the county is usually the basic unit of local government. The major problems in county government are public indifference, a fragmented structure with no chief executive, a long ballot of elected officials, and the inefficiently small size of most counties. Many proposals have been made for reforming county government.

Towns and townships are found in only 20 states. In New England the major unit of local government is the town, and the town meeting is its governing authority. In the Midwest the states are divided into townships that have functions similar to those of a county. A special district is a unit of local government created to provide a single service or a few related services. School districts are the most common type of special district.

The city is the most important unit of local government. Three basic forms of city government are the mayor-council plan, the commission plan, and the council-manager plan.

Rapid urban growth has created many problems for the cities, whose major functions are to provide their residents with services. The cities' failure to plan in the past has resulted in a hodgepodge of disorderly growth. But cities nowadays have planning commissions to correct past mistakes and to provide for orderly future development. Zoning is an important element in city planning. The rise of the suburbs has altered the character and reduced the tax base of the central cities. And the metropolitan areas are faced with problems involving urban sprawl and fragmentation. These problems can be solved only by cooperation among the various units of local government.

In recent years the costs of state and local governments have risen as government units have been called upon to provide more and more services. Governments get the revenue to meet their costs from taxes and nontax sources.

The states' power to tax is derived from the United States Constitution, and the local governments' power to tax is derived from the states. Tax systems fall into three categories: proportional taxation, progressive taxation, and regressive taxation.

A sales tax is a tax placed on the sale of goods. An income tax is a tax placed on personal and corporate income. A property tax is a tax placed on real or personal property. Revenue from the property tax is used to finance the public schools. Other kinds of state and local taxes include business taxes, property transfer taxes, and severance taxes.

State and local governments also have various nontax sources of revenue. Intergovernmental grants are funds transferred from one level of government to another. State grants may take the form of tax sharing or of specific grants to local governments. Federal aid to state and local governments is another form of intergovernmental grant. Many state and local governments own and operate businesses. Borrowing, usually by means of a voter-approved bond issue, is another source of revenue for state and local governments.

The state budget is a plan for keeping track of a state's money. In almost all states the governor prepares the state budget, the legislature approves it and appropriates the necessary funds, and the governor then executes it. The budget process provides an efficient, economical, and fair way of determining how the money is spent.

Chapter 30 Review

Using Vocabulary

Answer the questions by using the meaning of each underlined term.

1. What is the relationship of a township to a county?
2. When a person wants an exception to zoning, why does that person seek a variance rather than a charter?
3. How can a suburb, a central city, and an inner city each be part of a metropolitan area?
4. When is personal property tangible property?
5. How does an excise tax differ from an estate tax?
6. What is an argument against regressive taxation?
7. If an area is unincorporated, is it under the jurisdiction of the county or the jurisdiction of the nearest municipal government?

Understanding American Government

1. Give the main advantages of each of these three plans for reorganizing county government: county manager, chief administrative officer, elected chief executive.
2. How does the power of county governments vary in different areas? Where are county governments strongest?
3. How have town meetings changed as population has grown in the larger New England towns?
4. What are the strengths and weaknesses of the strong-mayor system?
5. What factors have encouraged cities to plan more effectively?
6. How has the rise of the suburbs affected the central cities?

Extending Your Skills: Comparing Plans of Government

Study the charts on pages 744 and 745 and reread pages 743–746. Then complete the items that follow.

1. What is the major difference between the weak mayor-council form of government and the strong mayor-council form of government?
2. How are the commission plan of government and the council manager plan of government similar? How are they different?
3. To whom are the department heads responsible under the weak mayor-council form of government? Under the strong mayor-council form? Under the council-manager plan?
4. Under all four forms of government, who holds the ultimate control of the government?
5. Based on your study of the charts and your readings, choose one of these forms of government, and in a brief paragraph explain why you think it would be the best suited to your city, town, or community.

Government and You

1. What is the name of your county, parish, or borough? Do you think counties are important structures in our political system? What functions does your county government fulfill?
2. Do you live in a city or near one? Which form of government does it use? What kind of charter does it have? In how many special districts do you reside?
3. Does your state have a sales tax? Some say the sales tax is unfair because it is regressive—that is, everyone pays the same rate regardless of income. Where do you stand on the issue of a sales tax? Explain.
4. Some observers think that our cities are dying. Do you agree or disagree? Why?
5. With many middle-income families moving to the suburbs, central cities have lost an important source of tax revenue. What effects has the loss of revenue had on many central cities? What might central cities do to reverse the flight of people to the suburbs?

Activities

1. Prepare a written report on the founding of your town or city, or the city nearest to you. Present your report to the class.
2. Secure information on zoning in your community or a community nearby. Then prepare a map of its zoning plan.

THE REFERENCE SHELF

UNITED STATES POLITICAL MAP
WORLD POLITICAL MAP
GOVERNMENTS OF THE WORLD
CHRONOLOGY
ALMANAC
GLOSSARY
INDEX

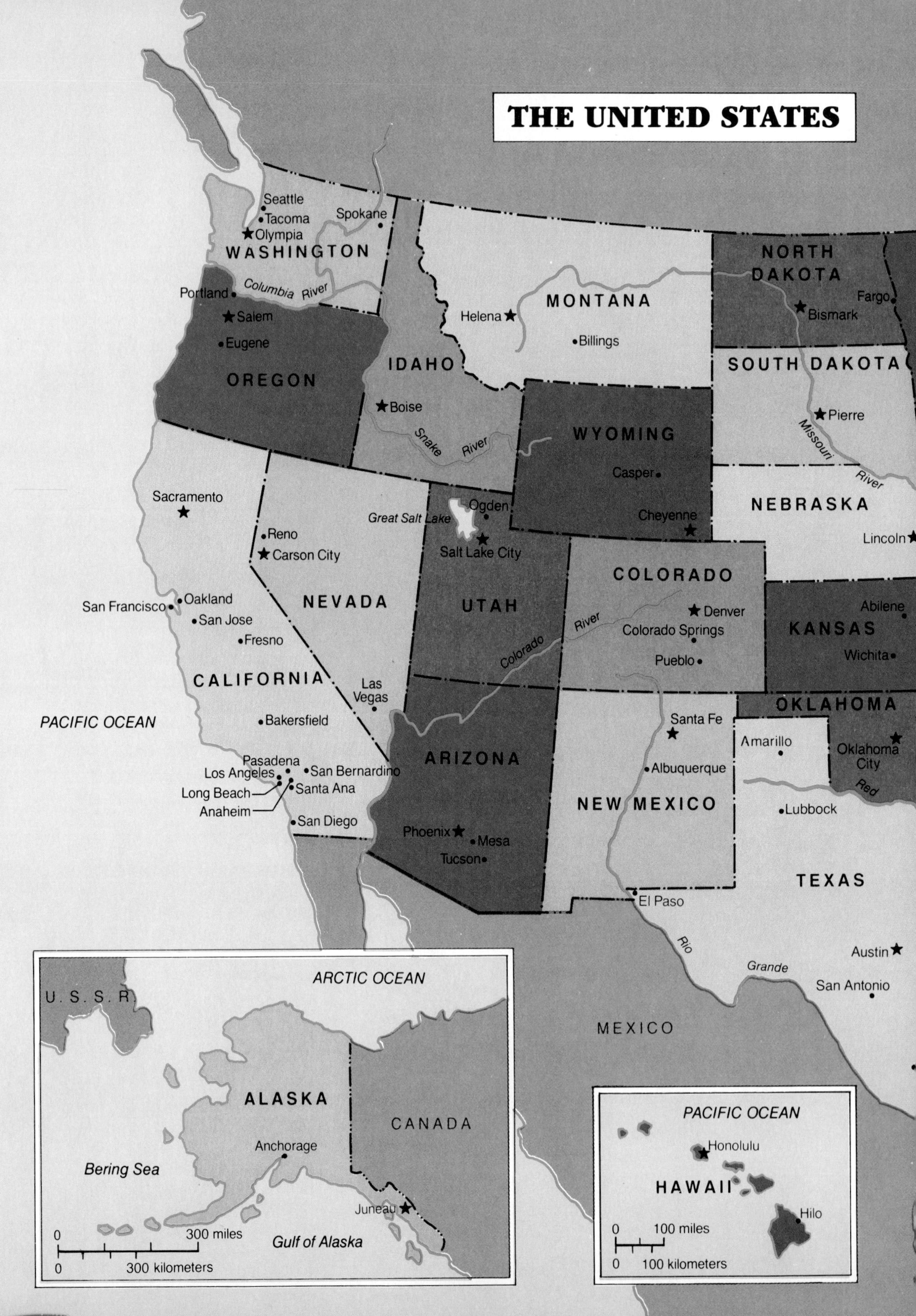
THE UNITED STATES
Seattle
Tacoma
Olympia
Spokane
WASHINGTON
Columbia River
Portland
Salem
Eugene
OREGON
IDAHO
Boise
Snake River
MONTANA
Helena
Billings
NORTH DAKOTA
Fargo
Bismark
SOUTH DAKOTA
Pierre
Missouri River
WYOMING
Casper
Cheyenne
NEBRASKA
Lincoln
Sacramento
Reno
Carson City
NEVADA
Great Salt Lake
Ogden
Salt Lake City
UTAH
COLORADO
Denver
Colorado Springs
Pueblo
Colorado River
KANSAS
Abilene
Wichita
San Francisco
Oakland
San Jose
Fresno
CALIFORNIA
Las Vegas
PACIFIC OCEAN
Bakersfield
Pasadena
Los Angeles
San Bernardino
Long Beach
Santa Ana
Anaheim
San Diego
ARIZONA
Phoenix
Mesa
Tucson
NEW MEXICO
Santa Fe
Albuquerque
OKLAHOMA
Oklahoma City
Amarillo
Red
Lubbock
TEXAS
El Paso
Rio Grande
Austin
San Antonio
MEXICO
ARCTIC OCEAN
U. S. S. R.
ALASKA
CANADA
Anchorage
Bering Sea
Juneau
Gulf of Alaska
0
300 miles
0
300 kilometers
PACIFIC OCEAN
Honolulu
HAWAII
Hilo
0
100 miles
0
100 kilometers

CANADA
MINNESOTA
Duluth
St. Paul
Minneapolis
WISCONSIN
Green Bay
Milwaukee
Madison
Lake Superior
MICHIGAN
Lake Michigan
Lake Huron
Flint
Lansing
Detroit
Lake Erie
Lake Ontario
St. Lawrence River
N.H.
MAINE
VT.
Augusta
Montpelier
Portland
Concord
NEW YORK
Hudson River
Syracuse
Albany
Rochester
Buffalo
Erie
Boston
MASS.
Providence
R.I.
CONN.
Hartford
New York City
Newark
PA.
Harrisburg
Trenton
N.J.
Philadelphia
Pittsburgh
Cleveland
Toledo
OHIO
Columbus
Dayton
Cincinnati
Baltimore
Dover
DEL.
Annapolis
MD.
Washington, D.C.
W. VA.
Charleston
Richmond
VIRGINIA
Norfolk
Roanoke
IOWA
Cedar Rapids
Des Moines
Davenport
Omaha
Chicago
Gary
Peoria
ILLINOIS
Springfield
Indianapolis
IND.
Ohio River
MISSOURI
Mississippi River
Topeka
Jefferson City
St. Louis
Springfield
Frankfort
Louisville
Lexington
KENTUCKY
Winston-Salem
Raleigh
Knoxville
NORTH CAROLINA
Nashville
TENN.
Memphis
Tulsa
ARKANSAS
Little Rock
River
Columbia
SOUTH CAROLINA
Charleston
Huntsville
Atlanta
Birmingham
Macon
Montgomery
Columbus
MISS.
GEORGIA
ALABAMA
Jackson
Dallas
Fort Worth
Shreveport
LA.
Waco
Mobile
Jacksonville
Biloxi
Tallahassee
Baton Rouge
New Orleans
Beaumont
Houston
Galveston
FLORIDA
Orlando
Tampa
St. Petersburg
Lake Okeechobee
Fort Lauderdale
Miami
ATLANTIC OCEAN
THE BAHAMAS
Gulf of Mexico
Corpus Christi
Key West
Straits of Florida
CUBA
National capital
State capitals
Other cities
0
500 miles
0
500 kilometers

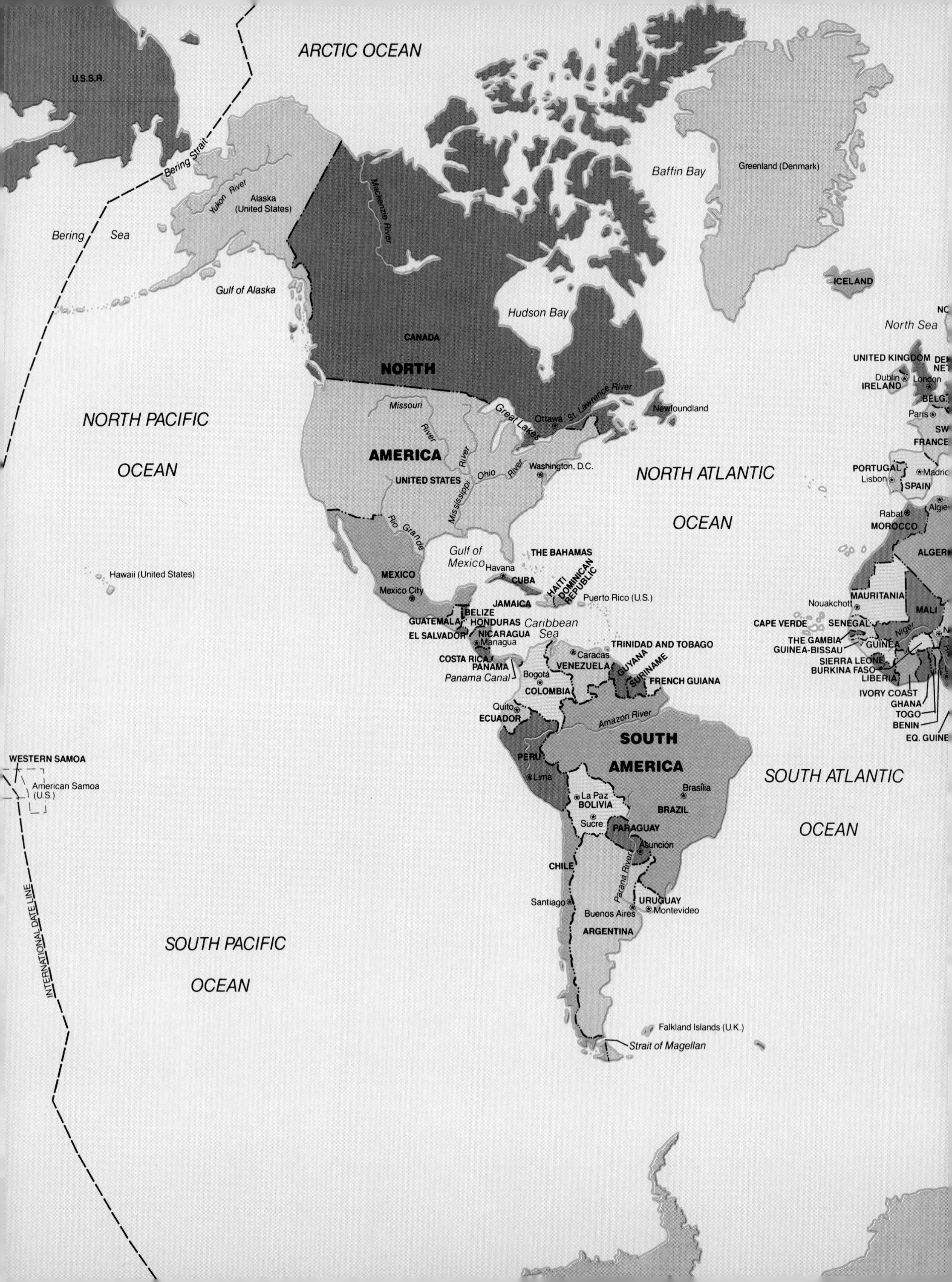

ARCTIC OCEAN
U.S.S.R.
Bering Strait
Yukon River
Alaska (United States)
Bering Sea
Gulf of Alaska
Mackenzie River
Baffin Bay
Greenland (Denmark)
ICELAND
Hudson Bay
CANADA
NORTH
AMERICA
North Sea
UNITED KINGDOM
Dublin
London
IRELAND
BELG.
Paris
FRANCE
Newfoundland
Ottawa
St. Lawrence River
Great Lakes
Missouri River
Ohio River
Mississippi River
Washington, D.C.
UNITED STATES
NORTH PACIFIC OCEAN
NORTH ATLANTIC OCEAN
PORTUGAL
Lisbon
SPAIN
Rabat
MOROCCO
Rio Grande
Gulf of Mexico
THE BAHAMAS
Havana
CUBA
HAITI
DOMINICAN REPUBLIC
Puerto Rico (U.S.)
Hawaii (United States)
MEXICO
Mexico City
JAMAICA
BELIZE
GUATEMALA
HONDURAS
EL SALVADOR
NICARAGUA
Managua
Caribbean Sea
COSTA RICA
PANAMA
Panama Canal
TRINIDAD AND TOBAGO
Caracas
VENEZUELA
GUYANA
SURINAME
FRENCH GUIANA
Bogotá
COLOMBIA
Quito
ECUADOR
Amazon River
MAURITANIA
Nouakchott
MALI
CAPE VERDE
SENEGAL
THE GAMBIA
GUINEA-BISSAU
GUINEA
Niger
SIERRA LEONE
BURKINA FASO
LIBERIA
IVORY COAST
GHANA
TOGO
BENIN
WESTERN SAMOA
American Samoa (U.S.)
SOUTH AMERICA
PERU
Lima
La Paz
BOLIVIA
Sucre
Brasília
BRAZIL
PARAGUAY
Asunción
SOUTH ATLANTIC OCEAN
CHILE
Paraná River
Santiago
URUGUAY
Buenos Aires
Montevideo
ARGENTINA
INTERNATIONAL DATE LINE
SOUTH PACIFIC OCEAN
Falkland Islands (U.K.)
Strait of Magellan

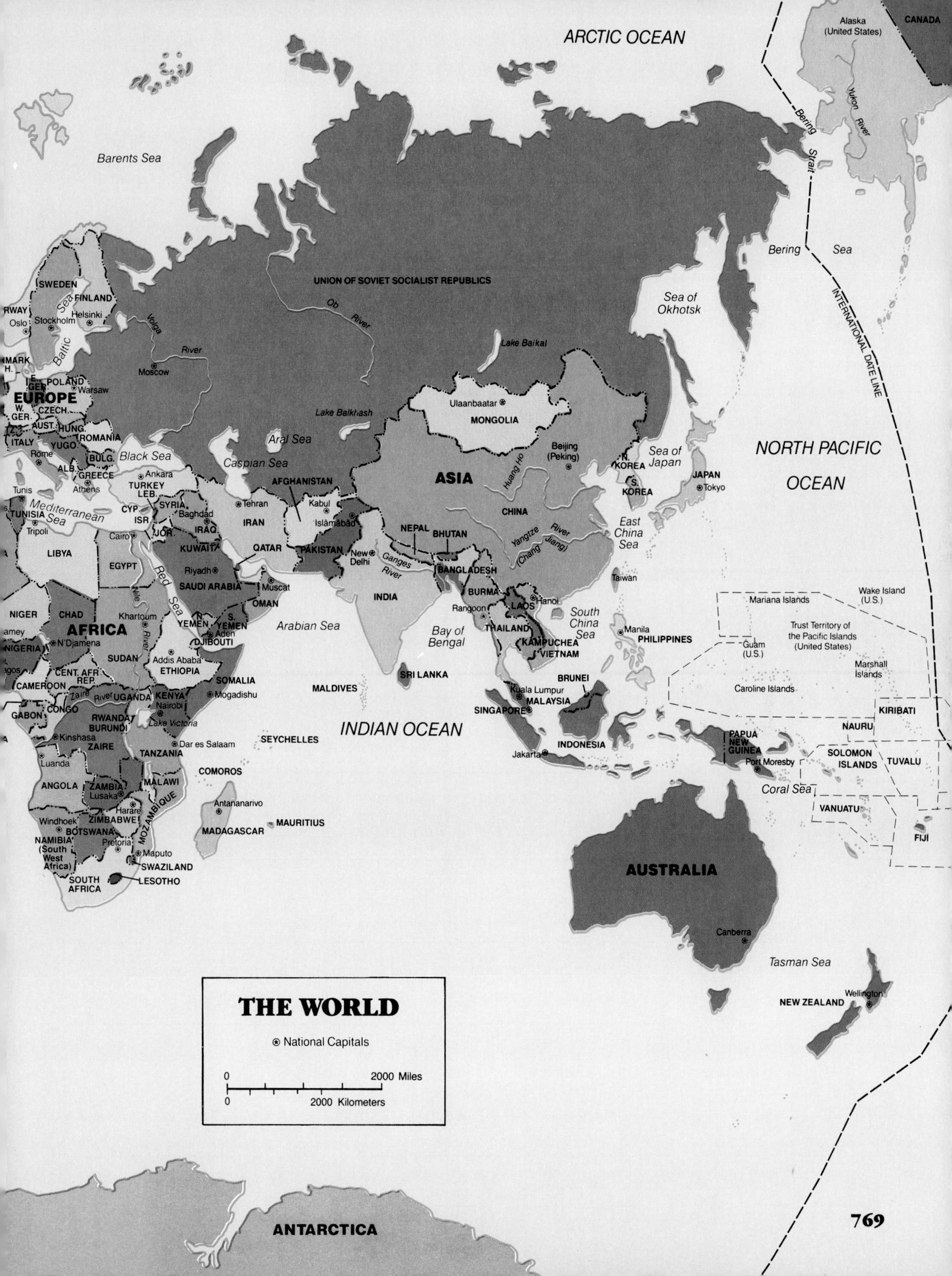

ARCTIC OCEAN
CANADA
Alaska (United States)
Yukon River
Bering Strait
Barents Sea
Bering Sea
INTERNATIONAL DATE LINE
SWEDEN
FINLAND
Baltic Sea
Oslo
Stockholm
Helsinki
UNION OF SOVIET SOCIALIST REPUBLICS
Ob River
Volga River
Moscow
Lake Baikal
Sea of Okhotsk
POLAND
Warsaw
EUROPE
E. GER.
W. GER.
CZECH.
AUST.
HUNG.
ROMANIA
ITALY
YUGO.
BULG.
ALB.
GREECE
Rome
Athens
Black Sea
Ankara
TURKEY
LEB.
SYRIA
CYP.
ISR.
JOR.
Tunis
TUNISIA
Tripoli
Mediterranean Sea
Lake Balkhash
Aral Sea
Caspian Sea
Ulaanbaatar
MONGOLIA
Beijing (Peking)
Huang Ho
ASIA
CHINA
N. KOREA
S. KOREA
Sea of Japan
JAPAN
Tokyo
NORTH PACIFIC OCEAN
AFGHANISTAN
Kabul
Islāmābād
Tehran
IRAN
Baghdad
IRAQ
KUWAIT
QATAR
PAKISTAN
NEPAL
BHUTAN
New Delhi
Ganges River
Yangtze River (Chang Jiang)
East China Sea
LIBYA
EGYPT
Cairo
Riyadh
SAUDI ARABIA
Muscat
OMAN
BANGLADESH
INDIA
Taiwan
Red Sea
Nile River
CHAD
NIGER
AFRICA
Khartoum
N. YEMEN
S. YEMEN
Aden
DJIBOUTI
Arabian Sea
Bay of Bengal
BURMA
Rangoon
LAOS
Hanoi
THAILAND
KAMPUCHEA
VIETNAM
South China Sea
Manila
PHILIPPINES
Mariana Islands
Wake Island (U.S.)
Trust Territory of the Pacific Islands (United States)
Guam (U.S.)
Marshall Islands
Caroline Islands
N'Djamena
NIGERIA
SUDAN
Addis Ababa
ETHIOPIA
SOMALIA
Mogadishu
SRI LANKA
MALDIVES
BRUNEI
Kuala Lumpur
MALAYSIA
SINGAPORE
CENT. AFR. REP.
CAMEROON
GABON
CONGO
Zaire River
UGANDA
KENYA
Nairobi
RWANDA
BURUNDI
Lake Victoria
Kinshasa
ZAIRE
Dar es Salaam
TANZANIA
SEYCHELLES
INDIAN OCEAN
INDONESIA
Jakarta
PAPUA NEW GUINEA
Port Moresby
KIRIBATI
NAURU
SOLOMON ISLANDS
TUVALU
Luanda
ANGOLA
ZAMBIA
Lusaka
MALAWI
COMOROS
MOZAMBIQUE
Harare
ZIMBABWE
Antananarivo
MADAGASCAR
MAURITIUS
Coral Sea
VANUATU
FIJI
Windhoek
BOTSWANA
NAMIBIA (South West Africa)
Pretoria
Maputo
SWAZILAND
LESOTHO
SOUTH AFRICA
AUSTRALIA
Canberra
Tasman Sea
NEW ZEALAND
Wellington
THE WORLD
National Capitals
0
2000 Miles
0
2000 Kilometers
ANTARCTICA

GOVERNMENTS OF THE WORLD

Nation Population Capital	Official Name of Nation	Chief of State/ Chief Executive	Legislature	Party System	Suffrage/Age
Afghanistan 14,177,000 Kabul	Democratic Republic of Afghanistan	President (head of Communist party)/ Prime Minister	Revolutionary Council (unicameral)	Single party	Universal/18
Albania 2,846,000 Tiranë	People's Socialist Republic of Albania	Chairman, Presidium of People's Assembly/ Premier	People's Assembly (unicameral)	Single party	Universal, compulsory/18
Algeria 20,695,000 Algiers	Democratic and Popular Republic of Algeria	President (military leader)/ President (military leader)	National Popular Assembly (unicameral)	Single party	Universal/19
Andorra 38,000 Andorra	Principality of Andorra	Co-princes: President of France and Spanish Bishop of Urgel	General Council (unicameral)	None	Universal/21 and 3rd generation Andorrans
Angola 7,567,000 Luanda	People's Republic of Angola	President/President	People's Assembly (unicameral)	Single party	Universal, compulsory/18
Antigua and Barbuda 78,000 St. Johns	Antigua and Barbuda	British Monarch[1] (ceremonial)/ Prime Minister	Parliament (bicameral)	Multiparty	Universal/18
Argentina 29,627,000 Buenos Aires	Argentine Republic	President/President	National Congress (bicameral)	Multiparty	Universal, compulsory/18
Australia 15,265,000 Canberra	Commonwealth of Australia	British Monarch[1] (ceremonial)/ Prime Minister	Federal Parliament (bicameral)	Multiparty	Universal/18
Austria 7,574,000 Vienna	Republic of Austria	President/Chancellor	Federal Assembly (bicameral)	Multiparty	Universal/19
The Bahamas 223,000 Nassau	The Commonwealth of the Bahamas	British Monarch[1] (ceremonial)/ Prime Minister	Parliament (bicameral)	Two party	Universal/18

See footnotes at the end of the chart.

GOVERNMENTS OF THE WORLD

Nation Population Capital	Official Name of Nation	Chief of State/ Chief Executive	Legislature	Party System	Suffrage/Age
Bahrain 393,000 Manama	State of Bahrain	Emir/Emir with Prime Minister	None	None	None
Bangladesh 96,539,000 Dhaka	People's Republic of Bangladesh	President/Chief Martial Law Administrator	Parliament (unicameral)	Multiparty (banned)	Universal/18
Barbados 251,000 Bridgetown	Barbados	British Monarch[1] (ceremonial)/ Prime Minister	Parliament (bicameral)	Two party	Universal/18
Belgium 9,865,000 Brussels	Kingdom of Belgium	King/Prime Minister	Parliament (bicameral)	Multiparty	Universal/18
Belize 154,000 Belmopan	Belize	Governor General/ Prime Minister	National Assembly (bicameral)	Two party	Universal/21
Benin 3,754,000 Porto-Novo (official); Cotonou (de facto)	People's Republic of Benin	President/President	National Revolutionary Assembly (unicameral)	Single party	Universal/adult[2]
Bhutan 1,386,000 Thimphu	Kingdom of Bhutan	King/King	National Assembly (unicameral)	(illegal)	Each family has one vote
Bolivia 5,883,000 La Paz, Sucre	Republic of Bolivia	President/President	National Congress (bicameral)	Multiparty	Universal, compulsory/18, if married; 21, if single
Botswana 1,003,000 Gaborone	Republic of Botswana	President/President	Legislative Assembly (bicameral)	Multiparty	Universal/21
Burkina Faso (Upper Volta) 6,569,000 Ouagadougou	Burkina Faso	President (military leader)/ Prime Minister (military leader)	General Assembly of the People's Salvation Council (unicameral)	(suspended)	Universal/adult[2]

See footnotes at the end of the chart.

GOVERNMENTS OF THE WORLD

Nation Population Capital	Official Name of Nation	Chief of State/ Chief Executive	Legislature	Party System	Suffrage/Age
Brazil 131,305,000 Brasilia	Federative Republic of Brazil	President /President	National Congress (bicameral)	Multiparty	Compulsory/18 (except illiter-ates)
Brunei 209,000 Bandar Seri Begawan	State of Brunei	Sultan/Sultan	Legislative Council (unicameral)	Single party	Universal/21
Bulgaria 8,944,000 Sofia	People's Republic of Bulgaria	President/Premier	National Assembly (unicameral)	Two party[3]	Universal, compulsory/18
Burma 37,061,000 Rangoon	Socialist Republic of the Union of Burma	President[4]/ Chairman of Council of State[4]	National Assembly (unicameral)	Single party	Universal/18
Burundi 4,561,000 Bujumbura	Republic of Burundi	President (military)/President (military)	National Assembly (unicameral)	Single party	Universal
Cameroon 9,251,000 Yaoundé	United Republic of Cameroon	President/President	National Assembly (unicameral)	Single party	Universal/21
Canada 24,882,000 Ottawa	Canada	British Monarch[1] (ceremonial)/ Prime Minister	Parliament (bicameral)	Multiparty	Universal/18
Cape Verde 297,000 Praia	Republic of Cape Verde	President/ Prime Minister	National People's Assembly (unicameral)	Single party	Universal/15
Central African Republic 2,512,000 Bangui	Central African Republic	President (military leader)/ President (military leader)	None	None	Universal/21
Chad 4,990,000 N'Djamena	Republic of Chad	President/President	None	(illegal)	Universal

See footnotes at the end of the chart.

GOVERNMENTS OF THE WORLD

Nation Population Capital	Official Name of Nation	Chief of State/ Chief Executive	Legislature	Party System	Suffrage/Age
Chile 11,486,000 Santiago	Republic of Chile	President of Military Junta/ President of Military Junta	None	Multiparty	None (elections prohibited)
China 1,059,802,000 Beijing (Peking)	People's Republic of China	Chairman of National People's Congress[5]/ Premier[5]	National People's Congress (unicameral)	Single party	Universal/18
Colombia 27,663,000 Bogotá	Republic of Colombia	President/President	Parliament (bicameral)	Two party	Universal/18
Comoros 442,000 Moroni	Federal Islamic Republic of the Comoros	President/President	Federal Assembly (unicameral)	Single party	Universal/adult[2]
Congo 1,694,000 Brazzaville	People's Republic of the Congo	President (military leader)/ Prime Minister (military leader)	National Assembly (unicameral)	Single party	Universal/18
Costa Rica 2,599,000 San José	Republic of Costa Rica	President/President	Legislative Assembly (unicameral)	Multiparty	Universal/16
Cuba 9,852,000 Havana	Republic of Cuba	President (military leader)/ President (military leader)	National Assembly of the People's Government (unicameral)	Single party	Universal/16
Cyprus 653,000 Nicosia	Republic of Cyprus	President/President	House of Representatives (unicameral)	Multiparty	Universal/21
Czechoslovakia 15,420,000 Prague	Czechoslovak Socialist Republic	President/Premier	Federal Assembly (bicameral)	Single party	Universal/18
Denmark 5,115,000 Copenhagen	Kingdom of Denmark	Monarch/ Prime Minister	Parliament (unicameral)	Multiparty	Universal/21

See footnotes at the end of the chart.

GOVERNMENTS OF THE WORLD

Nation Population Capital	Official Name of Nation	Chief of State/ Chief Executive	Legislature	Party System	Suffrage/Age
Djibouti 316,000 Djibouti	Republic of Djibouti	President/President	National Assembly (unicameral)	Single party	Universal
Dominica 74,000 Roseau	Commonwealth of Dominica	British Monarch[1] (ceremonial)/ Prime Minister	House of Assembly (unicameral)	Multiparty	Universal/18
Dominican Republic 6,248,000 Santo Domingo	Dominican Republic	President/President	National Congress (bicameral)	Multiparty	Universal, compulsory/18 or married
Ecuador 8,811,000 Quito	Republic of Ecuador	President/President	Chamber of Representatives (unicameral)	Multiparty	Universal/18
Egypt 45,851,000 Cairo	Arab Republic of Egypt	President/President	People's Assembly (unicameral)	Multiparty	Universal/18
El Salvador 4,685,000 San Salvador	Republic of El Salvador	President/President	Constituent Assembly (unicameral)	Multiparty	Universal/18
Equatorial Guinea 268,000 Malabo	Republic of Equatorial Guinea	President of Supreme Military Council/ President of Supreme Military Council	National Assembly (unicameral)	Single party (suspended)	Universal/adult[2]
Ethiopia 31,265,000 Addis Ababa	Socialist Ethiopia	Chairman, Provisional Military Administrative Council/Chairman, Provisional Military Administrative Council	None	None	Universal/21
Fiji 676,000 Suva	Fiji	British Monarch[1] (ceremonial)/ Prime Minister	Parliament (bicameral)	Multiparty	Universal/adult[2]
Finland 4,850,000 Helsinki	Republic of Finland	President/ Prime Minister	Parliament (unicameral)	Multiparty	Universal/18

See footnotes at the end of the chart.

GOVERNMENTS OF THE WORLD

Nation Population Capital	Official Name of Nation	Chief of State/ Chief Executive	Legislature	Party System	Suffrage/Age
France 54,604,000 Paris	French Republic	President/Premier	National Assembly (bicameral)	Multiparty	Universal/18
Gabon 921,000 Libreville	Gabonese Republic	President/President	National Assembly (unicameral)	Single party	Universal/18
The Gambia 638,000 Banjul	Republic of The Gambia	President/President	House of Representatives (unicameral)	Multiparty	Universal/adult[2]
German Democratic Republic 16,724,000 East Berlin	German Democratic Republic	Chairman, Council of State/Chairman, Council of Ministers (Premier)	People's Chamber (unicameral)	Multiparty	Universal/18
Germany, Federal Republic of 61,543,000 Bonn	Federal Republic of Germany	President/Chancellor	Parliament (bicameral)	Multiparty	Universal/18
Ghana 13,367,000 Accra	Republic of Ghana	Chairman of Military Council/Chairman of Military Council	None	(illegal)	Universal/21
Greece 9,898,000 Athens	Hellenic Republic	President/ Prime Minister	Parliament (unicameral)	Multiparty	Universal/18
Grenada 111,000 St. Georges	Grenada	British Monarch[1] (ceremonial)/ Prime Minister	Parliament (unicameral)	Multiparty	Universal/adult[2]
Guatemala 7,714,000 Guatemala	Republic of Guatemala	President/President	Constituent Assembly (unicameral)	Multiparty	Universal/18
Guinea 5,430,000 Conakry	People's Revolutionary Republic of Guinea	President/President	People's National Assembly (unicameral)	Single party	Universal/18

See footnotes at the end of the chart.

GOVERNMENTS OF THE WORLD

Nation Population Capital	Official Name of Nation	Chief of State/ Chief Executive	Legislature	Party System	Suffrage/Age
Guinea-Bissau 827,000 Bissau	Republic of Guinea-Bissau	President (military leader)/ Prime Minister	None	Single party	Universal/15
Guyana 834,000 Georgetown	Cooperative Republic of Guyana	Executive President/ Executive President	National Assembly (unicameral)	Multiparty	Universal/18
Haiti 5,666,000 Port-au-Prince	Republic of Haiti	President-for-Life/ President-for-Life	National Assembly (unicameral)	Multiparty (inactive)	Universal/18
Honduras 4,276,000 Tegucigalpa	Republic of Honduras	President/President	National Congress (unicameral)	Multiparty	Universal, compulsory/21
Hungary 10,691,000 Budapest	Hungarian People's Republic	President/Chairman, Council of Ministers	National Assembly (unicameral)	Single party	Universal/18
Iceland 236,000 Reykjavík	Republic of Iceland	President/ Prime Minister	Parliament (bicameral)	Multiparty	Universal/20
India 740,009,000 New Delhi	Republic of India	President (ceremonial)/ Prime Minister	Parliament (bicameral)	Multiparty	Universal/21
Indonesia 160,932,000 Jakarta	Republic of Indonesia	President/President	People's Consultative Assembly (unicameral)	Multiparty	Universal/17 or married
Iran 42,490,000 Tehran	Islamic Republic of Iran	Ayatollah (religious leader)/ Prime Minister	Islamic Consultative Assembly (unicameral)	Two party	Universal/15
Iraq 14,509,000 Baghdad	Republic of Iraq	President/President	National Assembly (unicameral)	Single party	Universal/adult[2]
Ireland 3,534,000 Dublin	Ireland, Eire (Gaelic)	President/ Prime Minister	Parliament (bicameral)	Multiparty	Universal/18

See footnotes at the end of the chart.

GOVERNMENTS OF THE WORLD

Nation Population Capital	Official Name of Nation	Chief of State/ Chief Executive	Legislature	Party System	Suffrage/Age
Israel 3,957,000 Jerusalem[6]	State of Israel	President (ceremonial)/ Prime Minister	Knesset (unicameral)	Multiparty	Universal/18
Italy 56,345,000 Rome	Italian Republic	President/Premier	Parliament (bicameral)	Multiparty	Universal/18, except 25 in senatorial elections
Ivory Coast 8,890,000 Abidjan	Republic of the Ivory Coast	President/President	National Assembly (unicameral)	Single party	Universal/21
Jamaica 2,335,000 Kingston	Jamaica	British Monarch[1] (ceremonial)/ Prime Minister	Parliament (unicameral)	Two party	Universal/18
Japan 119,205,000 Tokyo	Japan	Emperor (ceremonial)/ Prime Minister	Diet (bicameral)	Multiparty	Universal/20
Jordan 3,436,000 Amman	Hashemite Kingdom of Jordan	King/King	National Assembly (bicameral)	None	Universal/20
Kampuchea (Cambodia) 5,996,000 Phnom Penh	A civil war exists between two rival governments — Democratic Kampuchea and the People's Republic of Kampuchea.				Universal/18
Kenya 18,580,000 Nairobi	Republic of Kenya	President/President	National Assembly (unicameral)	Single party	Universal/21
Kiribati 60,000 Tarawa	Republic of Kiribati	President/President	Parliament (unicameral)	Two party	Universal/adult[2]
Korea, North 18,802,000 Pyongyang	Democratic People's Republic of Korea	President (General Secretary of Communist Party)/Premier	Supreme People's Assembly (unicameral)	Single party	Universal/17
Korea, South 41,287,000 Seoul	Republic of Korea	President/ Prime Minister	National Assembly (unicameral)	Multiparty	Universal/20

See footnotes at the end of the chart.

GOVERNMENTS OF THE WORLD

Nation Population Capital	Official Name of Nation	Chief of State/ Chief Executive	Legislature	Party System	Suffrage/Age
Kuwait 1,652,000 Kuwait	State of Kuwait	Emir/Emir	National Assembly (unicameral)	None	Males/21
Laos 3,647,000 Vientiane	Lao People's Democratic Republic	President/ Prime Minister	National Congress of People's Representatives (unicameral)	Single party	Universal/18
Lebanon 2,598,000 Beirut	Republic of Lebanon	President (Maronite Christian)/ Prime Minister (Sunni Muslim)	National Assembly (unicameral)	Multiparty	Compulsory: males/21; women with elementary education/21
Lesotho 1,438,000 Maseru	Kingdom of Lesotho	King/Prime Minister	Interim National Assembly (unicameral)	Two party	Universal/adult[2]
Liberia 2,091,000 Monrovia	Republic of Liberia	Commander in chief of the Armed Forces/ Commander in chief of the Armed Forces	None	None	Universal/18 and property owners
Libya 3,498,000 Tripoli	Socialist People's Libyan Arab Jamahiriya	Military Dictator/ Military Dictator	General People's Congress (unicameral)	None	Universal/adult[2]
Liechtenstein 26,000 Vaduz	Principality of Liechtenstein	Grand Duke/ Prime Minister	Parliament (unicameral)	Multiparty	Males/20
Luxembourg 336,000 Luxembourg	Grand Duchy of Luxembourg	Grand Duke/ Prime Minister	Chamber of Deputies (unicameral)	Multiparty	Universal, compulsory/18
Madagascar 9,389,000 Antananarivo	Democratic Republic of Madagascar	President (military leader)/ President (military leader)	National Popular Assembly (unicameral)	Multiparty (limited)	Universal/18
Malawi 6,612,000 Lilongwe	Republic of Malawi	President/President	National Assembly (unicameral)	Single party	Universal/21

See footnotes at the end of the chart.

GOVERNMENTS OF THE WORLD

Nation Population Capital	Official Name of Nation	Chief of State/ Chief Executive	Legislature	Party System	Suffrage/Age
Malaysia 14,995,000 Kuala Lumpur	Malaysia	Paramount Ruler (monarch)/ Prime Minister	Parliament (bicameral)	Multiparty	Universal/20
Maldives 168,000 Male	Republic of Maldives	President/President	People's Council (unicameral)	None	Universal/21
Mali 7,393,000 Bamako	Republic of Mali	President (military leader)/ President (military leader)	National Council (unicameral)	Single party	Universal/21
Malta 363,000 Valletta	Republic of Malta	President/ Prime Minister	House of Representatives (unicameral)	Two party	Universal/18
Mauritania 1,591,000 Nouakchott	Islamic Republic of Mauritania	Military leader/ Military leader	None (suspended)	None (suspended)	Universal/adult[2]
Mauritius 1,002,000 Port Louis	Mauritius	British Monarch[1] (ceremonial)/ Prime Minister	Legislative Assembly (unicameral)	Multiparty	Universal/18
Mexico 75,702,000 Mexico City	United Mexican States	President/President	National Congress (bicameral)	Multiparty	Universal, compulsory/18
Monaco 28,000 Monaco	Principality of Monaco	Prince/Minister of State (French civil servant)	National Council (unicameral)	Multiparty	Universal/adult[2]
Mongolia 1,809,000 Ulaanbaatar	Mongolian People's Republic	General Secretary of Communist Party and Chairman of National Assembly/Chairman of Council of Ministers	People's Great Hural (unicameral)	Single party	Universal/18
Morocco 22,889,000 Rabat	Kingdom of Morocco	King/Prime Minister	Chamber of Representatives (unicameral)	Multiparty	Universal/20
Mozambique 13,047,000 Maputo	People's Republic of Mozambique	President/President	People's Assembly (unicameral)	Single party	Universal, compulsory/ adult[2]

See footnotes at the end of the chart.

GOVERNMENTS OF THE WORLD

Nation Population Capital	Official Name of Nation	Chief of State/ Chief Executive	Legislature	Party System	Suffrage/Age
Nauru 8,000 Yaren district	Republic of Nauru	President/President	Parliament (unicameral)	Two party	Universal/adult[2]
Nepal 16,179,000 Kathmandu	Kingdom of Nepal	King/Prime Minister	National Assembly (unicameral)	(illegal)	Universal/21
Netherlands 14,374,000 Amsterdam; The Hague	Kingdom of the Netherlands	Monarch/ Prime Minister	States General (bicameral)	Multiparty	Universal/18
New Zealand 3,142,000 Wellington	New Zealand	British Monarch[1] (ceremonial)/ Prime Minister	House of Representatives (unicameral)	Multiparty	Universal/18
Nicaragua 2,812,000 Managua	Republic of Nicaragua	President/President	Council of State (unicameral)	Multiparty (restricted)	Universal/16
Niger 6,083,000 Niamey	Republic of Niger	President, Supreme Military Council/ President, Supreme Military Council	None	(illegal)	None (elections suspended)
Nigeria 85,219,000 Lagos	Federal Republic of Nigeria	Head of Federal Military Government[3]/ Chairman of Supreme Military Council[3]	None	(illegal)	None (elections suspended)
Norway 4,131,000 Oslo	Kingdom of Norway	King/Prime Minister	Parliament (bicameral)	Multiparty	Universal/20
Oman 978,000 Muscat	Sultanate of Oman	Sultan/Sultan	None	None	None
Pakistan 96,874,000 Islamabad	Islamic Republic of Pakistan	President (Chief Martial Law Administrator)/ President (Chief Martial Law Administrator)	None	Multiparty	Universal/18

See footnotes at the end of the chart.

GOVERNMENTS OF THE WORLD

Nation Population Capital	Official Name of Nation	Chief of State/ Chief Executive	Legislature	Party System	Suffrage/Age
Panama 2,059,000 Panama	Republic of Panama	President/President	National Assembly of Community Representatives (unicameral)	Multiparty	Universal, compulsory/18
Papua New Guinea 3,259,000 Port Moresby	Papua New Guinea	British Monarch[1] (ceremonial)/ Prime Minister	House of Assembly (unicameral)	Multiparty	Universal/adult[2]
Paraguay 3,526,000 Asunción	Republic of Paraguay	President (military leader)/ President (military leader)	Legislature (bicameral)	Multiparty	Universal, compulsory/ 18–60
Peru 19,161,000 Lima	Republic of Peru	President/President	National Congress (bicameral)	Multiparty	Universal/18
Philippines 53,162,000 Manila	Republic of the Philippines	President/President with Prime Minister	National Assembly (unicameral)	Multiparty	Universal/18
Poland 36,556,000 Warsaw	Polish People's Republic	President/Premier	Legislature (unicameral)	Single party	Universal, compulsory/18
Portugal 10,008,000 Lisbon	Portuguese Republic	President (military leader)/ Prime Minister	Assembly of the Republic (unicameral)	Multiparty	Universal/18
Qatar 267,000 Doha	State of Qatar	Emir/Emir	State Advisory Council (unicameral)	None	None
Romania 22,649,000 Bucharest	Socialist Republic of Romania	President/ Prime Minister	Grand National Assembly (unicameral)	Single party	Universal, compulsory/18
Rwanda 5,644,000 Kigali	Republic of Rwanda	President (military leader)/ President (military leader)	National Development Council (unicameral)	Single party	Universal/adult[2]

See footnotes at the end of the chart.

GOVERNMENTS OF THE WORLD

Nation Population Capital	Official Name of Nation	Chief of State/ Chief Executive	Legislature	Party System	Suffrage/Age
St. Christopher-Nevis 45,000 Basseterre	State of St. Christopher-Nevis	British Monarch[1] (ceremonial)/ Prime Minister	House of Assembly (unicameral)	Multiparty	Universal/adult[2]
St. Lucia 119,000 Castries	St. Lucia	British Monarch[1] (ceremonial)/ Prime Minister	Parliament (bicameral)	Multiparty	Universal/adult[2]
St. Vincent and the Grenadines 128,000 Kingstown	St. Vincent and the Grenadines	British Monarch[1] (ceremonial)/ Prime Minister	House of Assembly (unicameral)	Multiparty	Universal/adult[2]
San Marino 22,000 San Marino	Republic of San Marino	Two Secretaries of State/Two Secretaries of State	Grand and General Council (unicameral)	Multiparty	Universal/adult[2]
São Tomé and Principe 88,000 São Tomé	Democratic Republic of São Tomé and Principe	President/President	National Popular Assembly (unicameral)	Single party	Universal/18
Saudi Arabia 10,443,000 Riyadh	Kingdom of Saudi Arabia	King[4]/ Prime Minister[4]	None	None	None
Senegal 6,335,000 Dakar	Republic of Senegal	President/ Prime Minister	National Assembly (unicameral)	Multiparty	Universal/adult[2]
Seychelles 65,000 Victoria, Mahé Island	Republic of Seychelles	President/President	People's Assembly (unicameral)	Single party	Universal/adult[2]
Sierra Leone 3,705,000 Freetown	Republic of Sierra Leone	President/President	House of Representatives (unicameral)	Single party	Universal/21
Singapore 2,503,000 Singapore	Republic of Singapore	President/ Prime Minister	Parliament (unicameral)	Multiparty	Universal, compulsory/20

See footnotes at the end of the chart.

GOVERNMENTS OF THE WORLD

Nation Population Capital	Official Name of Nation	Chief of State/ Chief Executive	Legislature	Party System	Suffrage/Age
Solomon Islands 256,000 Honiara	Solomon Islands	British Monarch[1] (ceremonial)/ Prime Minister	National Parliament (unicameral)	Multiparty	Universal/21
Somalia 6,248,000 Mogadishu	Somali Democratic Republic	President (military leader)/ President (military leader)	National People's Assembly (unicameral)	Single party	None
South Africa 30,938,000 Pretoria	Republic of South Africa	State President[4]/ Prime Minister[4]	House of Assembly (tricameral)[7]	Multiparty (restricted to whites, coloureds, Indians)[7]	Whites, coloureds, and Indians/18[7]
Soviet Union 272,308,000 Moscow	Union of Soviet Socialist Republics	Chairman of the Presidium of the Supreme Soviet/ Premier (Chairman of Council of Ministers)	Supreme Soviet (bicameral)	Single party	Universal/18
Spain 38,234,000 Madrid	Spanish State	Monarch/ Prime Minister	Cortes Generales (bicameral)	Multiparty	Universal/18
Sri Lanka 15,647,000 Colombo	Democratic Socialist Republic of Sri Lanka	President/President	Parliament (unicameral)	Multiparty	Universal/18
Sudan 20,585,000 Khartoum	Democratic Republic of the Sudan	President/President	National People's Assembly (unicameral)	None	Universal/adult[2]
Suriname 353,000 Paramaribo	Republic of Suriname	President (ceremonial)/ Military Commander	None	(illegal)	(elections suspended)
Swaziland 632,000 Mbabane	Kingdom of Swaziland	Queen Regent/ Prime Minister	Parliament (bicameral)	None	Universal/adult[2]
Sweden 8,331,000 Stockholm	Kingdom of Sweden	Monarch/ Prime Minister	Parliament (unicameral)	Multiparty	Universal/18

See footnotes at the end of the chart.

GOVERNMENTS OF THE WORLD

Nation Population Capital	Official Name of Nation	Chief of State/ Chief Executive	Legislature	Party System	Suffrage/Age
Switzerland 6,463,000 Bern	Swiss Confederation	President/President	Parliament (bicameral)	Multiparty	Universal/20
Syria 9,739,000 Damascus	Syrian Arab Republic	President/President	People's Council (unicameral)	Multiparty (one dominant party)	Universal/18
Taiwan 18,810,000 Taipei	Taiwan	President/Premier	National Assembly (unicameral)	Single party	Universal/20
Tanzania 20,524,000 Dar es Salaam	United Republic of Tanzania	President/ Prime Minister	National Assembly (unicameral)	Single party	Universal/18
Thailand 50,731,000 Bangkok	Kingdom of Thailand	King/Prime Minister	National Assembly (bicameral)	Multiparty	Universal/20
Togo 2,823,000 Lomé	Republic of Togo	President/President	National Assembly (unicameral)	Single party	Universal/adult[2]
Tonga 104,000 Nuku'alofa	Kingdom of Tonga	King/Premier	Legislative Assembly (unicameral)	None	Literate taxpayers/21
Trinidad and Tobago 1,211,000 Port-of-Spain	Republic of Trinidad and Tobago	President/ Prime Minister	Parliament (bicameral)	Multiparty	Universal/18
Tunisia 7,020,000 Tunis	Republic of Tunisia	President/ Prime Minister	National Assembly (unicameral)	Single party	Universal/21
Turkey 49,155,000 Ankara	Republic of Turkey	President (military leader)/ Prime Minister (military leader)	Grand National Assembly (unicameral)	(suspended)	Universal/21
Tuvalu 8,000 Funafuti	Tuvalu	British Monarch[1] (ceremonial)/ Prime Minister	Parliament (unicameral)	None	Citizens/18

See footnotes at the end of the chart.

GOVERNMENTS OF THE WORLD

Nation Population Capital	Official Name of Nation	Chief of State/ Chief Executive	Legislature	Party System	Suffrage/Age
Uganda 13,819,000 Kampala	Republic of Uganda	President/President	National Assembly (unicameral)	Multiparty	Universal/adult[2]
United Arab Emirates 1,374,000 Abu Dhabi	United Arab Emirates	President/ Vice President is Prime Minister	Federal National Council (unicameral)	None	None
United Kingdom 56,078,000 London	United Kingdom of Great Britain and Northern Ireland	British Monarch/ Prime Minister	Parliament (bicameral)	Multiparty	Universal/18
United States 234,193,000 Washington, D.C.	United States of America	President/President	Congress (bicameral)	Two party	Universal/18
Uruguay 2,916,000 Montevideo	Oriental Republic of Uruguay	President/President	National Assembly (bicameral)	Multiparty	Universal/18
Vanuatu 127,000 Port-Vila	Republic of Vanuatu	President/ Prime Minister	Parliament (unicameral)	Single party	Universal/adult[2]
Vatican City 1,000 Vatican City	State of the Vatican City	Supreme Pontiff of the Roman Catholic Church/ Supreme Pontiff of the Roman Catholic Church	None	None	Cardinals/less than 80
Venezuela 17,993,000 Caracas	Republic of Venezuela	President/President	National Congress (bicameral)	Multiparty	Universal, compulsory/18
Vietnam 57,036,000 Hanoi	Socialist Republic of Vietnam	General Secretary of Communist Party/ Chairman, Council of State	National Assembly (bicameral)	Single party	Universal/18
Western Samoa 160,000 Apia	Independent State of Western Samoa	Head of State (native chief)/ Prime Minister	Legislative Assembly (unicameral)	None	(see footnote 8)

See footnotes at the end of the chart.

GOVERNMENTS OF THE WORLD

Nation Population Capital	Official Name of Nation	Chief of State/ Chief Executive	Legislature	Party System	Suffrage/Age
Yemen, North 5,744,000 Sanaa	Yemen Arab Republic	President (military leader)/ Prime Minister	People's Constituent Assembly and General People's Congress (bicameral)	Multiparty	Universal/21
Yemen, South 2,086,000 Aden	People's Democratic Republic of Yemen	Chairman of the Presidium of the Supreme Peoples' Council[4]/ Prime Minister[4]	Supreme People's Council (unicameral)	Single party	Universal/18
Yugoslavia 22,826,000 Belgrade	Socialist Federal Republic of Yugoslavia	President[9]/ President[9]	Federal Assembly (bicameral)	Single party	Universal/18
Zaire 31,250,000 Kinshasa	Republic of Zaire	President/ Prime Minister	National Legislative Council (unicameral)	Single party	Universal, compulsory/18
Zambia 6,346,000 Lusaka	Republic of Zambia	President/ Prime Minister	National Assembly (unicameral)	Single party	Universal/adult[2]
Zimbabwe 8,376,000 Harare	Republic of Zimbabwe	President/ Prime Minister	Parliament (bicameral)	Multiparty (one dominant party)	Universal/18

Footnotes

1. The British monarch is represented by a governor-general.
2. The meaning of the term *adult* varies with the customs of the country.
3. Only Communist party holds power; other party is a puppet.
4. Both positions are held by the same person.
5. Real power is held by the General Secretary of the Communist Party.
6. Many nations recognize Tel Aviv as the capital of Israel.
7. In South Africa, *coloureds* are people of mixed race. Blacks are denied suffrage. Membership in each house of the legislature is segregated.
8. Forty-five members of the legislature are elected by heads of families; two other members of the legislature are elected by universal adult suffrage.
9. The State Presidency is a collective, rotating policymaking body composed of representatives from each republic and province; one representative presides as president for one year.

Source: *The World Factbook*; various other references.

Significant Events in American Government

History, by apprising [people] of the past, will enable them to judge of the future; it will avail them of the experience of other times and other nations.

THOMAS JEFFERSON

1215

★ The Magna Carta establishes the principle of limited government by placing restraints on the power of the English monarch.

The Magna Carta

1265

★ A representative Parliament is established in England.

1619

★ Landowners in the colony of Virginia elect the House of Burgesses, the first representative lawmaking body in the New World.

1620

★ Forty-one adult male Pilgrims sign the Mayflower Compact in which they agree to obey the laws they will pass and the officers they will elect.

1636

★ The first militia—now known as the National Guard—is organized in Massachusetts.

1641

★ Massachusetts adopts a Body of Liberties guaranteeing free elections, no taxation without representation, trial by jury, and due process of law.

1644

★ The charter of the new colony of Rhode Island grants individual religious freedom, thus separating church from state.

1689

★ The English Bill of Rights secures the supremacy of Parliament over the English crown and lists specific individual rights.

1690

★ John Locke publishes his *Second Treatise on Civil Government.*

1765

★ The Stamp Act Congress drafts a Declaration of Rights and Grievances protesting Britain's levying of taxes without the consent of the colonial legislatures.

1774

★ The First Continental Congress sends a Declaration of Rights to the king of Great Britain asserting that Parliament does not have the right to pass laws for the colonies.

1775–1781

★ The Second Continental Congress guides the 13 colonies through the Revolutionary War.

Signing the Declaration of Independence

1776

★ The Declaration of Independence is signed.

★ Adam Smith examines the nature of capitalism in *An Inquiry into the Nature and Causes of the Wealth of Nations*.

1780

★ Massachusetts drafts its state constitution by popular convention, thus introducing the method by which most subsequent state constitutions have been drafted.

1781

★ The Articles of Confederation go into effect.

1783

★ The Treaty of Paris recognizes the independence of the United States.

1785

★ The University of Georgia is founded, becoming the first state university in the nation.

1786–1787

★ Shays's Rebellion helps swing public opinion in favor of revising the Articles of Confederation.

1787

★ The Northwest Ordinance provides for the governing of the Northwest Territory, establishes the basis on which new states enter the Union, and offers land grants for public schools in the territories.

★ The Constitutional Convention drafts the Constitution.

★ Delaware, Pennsylvania, and New Jersey ratify the Constitution.

1787–1788

★ Alexander Hamilton, John Jay, and James Madison argue in favor of ratifying the Constitution in a series of articles later published as *The Federalist.*

1788

★ Georgia, Connecticut, Massachusetts, Maryland, and South Carolina ratify the Constitution; New Hampshire becomes the ninth state to ratify the Constitution; and the Constitution becomes the supreme law of the land.

★ Virginia and New York ratify the Constitution, thus assuring the new government's success.

1789

★ New York City is chosen as the nation's temporary capital.

★ George Washington takes office as first President of the United States.

★ Congress creates the Departments of State, Treasury, and War and the Offices of Attorney General and Postmaster General.

★ Congress establishes a system of federal courts headed by the Supreme Court.

★ North Carolina becomes the twelfth state to ratify the Constitution.

1 George Washington

1789–1793

★ The Cabinet system develops.

1790

★ The first national census is taken.

★ Congress approves a site selected by George Washington along the Potomac River for the permanent capital of the nation.

★ Rhode Island, the last of the original 13 states to ratify the Constitution, becomes part of the Union.

1791

★ The first 10 amendments to the Constitution, known as the Bill of Rights, are ratified. The Bill of Rights guarantees basic civil rights to Americans.

★ Vermont enters the Union as the fourteenth state.

1792

★ Congress establishes a national currency system based on gold and silver.

★ Congress holds its first investigation.

★ Kentucky enters the union as the fifteenth state.

1792–1794

★ Political parties develop.

1793

★ George Washington is inaugurated for a second term.

1796

★ Tennessee enters the Union as the sixteenth state.

2 John Adams

1797
★ John Adams is inaugurated as the second President.

1798
★ The Eleventh Amendment, which provides that a state can be sued only in its own courts, is ratified.
★ The Sedition Act of 1798 provides for fines and imprisonment for writing, saying, or printing anything "false, scandalous, and malicious" against the government.
★ The first national public health agency, the Marine Hospital Service, is established.

1800
★ Washington, D.C., becomes the nation's permanent capital.
★ The Library of Congress is founded.

3 Thomas Jefferson

1801
★ John Marshall is appointed Chief Justice of the United States.
★ Thomas Jefferson is inaugurated as the third President.

1802
★ The United States Military Academy at West Point, New York, is established.

1803
★ *Marbury* v. *Madison* reinforces the legal principle of judicial review.
★ Ohio enters the Union as the seventeenth state.

1803–1806
★ Meriwether Lewis and William Clark explore the Louisiana Purchase.

1804
★ The Twelfth Amendment, instructing electors to cast separate ballots for President and Vice President, is ratified.

1805
★ President Jefferson begins a second term in office.

4 James Madison

1809
★ James Madison begins his first term as President.

1812
★ Congress makes its first foreign-aid appropriation.
★ The first school district is established in New York.
★ Louisiana enters the Union as the eighteenth state.

1813
★ President Madison is inaugurated for a second term.

1816
★ Indiana enters the Union as the nineteenth state.

1817

★ James Monroe is inaugurated as the fifth President.

★ Mississippi enters the Union as the twentieth state.

5 *James Monroe*

1818

★ Illinois enters the Union as the twenty-first state.

1819

★ *McCulloch* v. *Maryland* interprets the elastic clause to uphold all legislation whose purpose is consistent with Congressional powers, establishes the principle of national supremacy, and holds that states may not tax the activities of the federal government.

★ Alabama enters the Union as the twenty-second state.

1820

★ Maine enters the Union as the twenty-third state.

1821

★ Monroe begins a second term in office.

★ Missouri enters the Union as the twenty-fourth state.

1824

★ *Gibbons* v. *Ogden* establishes the authority of the federal government over interstate commerce and expands the definition of interstate commerce to include not only goods but also the means by which they are bought and sold, as well as any trade that affects more than one state.

6

7

1825

★ The House of Representatives selects John Quincy Adams as the sixth President after none of the Presidential candidates win a majority of the electoral votes.

1829

★ Andrew Jackson begins his first term as President.

1829–1837

★ Andrew Jackson gives form to the modern Cabinet, makes extensive use of the veto, and brings his own people into office at every level of the federal government.

1831

★ The Anti-Mason party holds the first national nominating convention for President and Vice President, and the convention system soon replaces the caucus system.

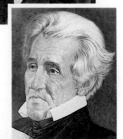

8

6 *John Quincy Adams*
7 *Andrew Jackson*
8 *Martin Van Buren*

1832

★ President Jackson is inaugurated for a second term.

1833

★ *Barron* v. *Baltimore* holds that the Bill of Rights applies only to the federal government.

9 William H. Harrison
10 John Tyler
11 James K. Polk
12 Zachary Taylor
13 Millard Fillmore
14 Franklin Pierce

1835

★ The first state police force, the Texas Rangers, is organized.

1836

★ Arkansas enters the Union as the twenty-fifth state.

1837

★ Martin Van Buren is inaugurated as President.

★ Michigan enters the Union as the twenty-sixth state.

1841

★ William Henry Harrison is inaugurated as the ninth President. Upon his death one month later, John Tyler becomes the first Vice President to succeed to the Presidency.

1845

★ James K. Polk is inaugurated as the eleventh President.

★ Florida is the twenty-seventh state to join the Union; Texas becomes the twenty-eighth state to enter the Union.

1846

★ The Smithsonian Institution is founded in Washington, D.C.

★ Iowa enters the Union as the twenty-ninth state.

1848

★ The first Women's Rights Convention is held in Seneca Falls, New York.

★ Henry David Thoreau writes "Civil Disobedience," advocating nonviolent resistance in matters of conscience, such as the abolition of slavery.

★ Wisconsin enters the Union as the thirtieth state.

1849

★ Zachary Taylor is inaugurated as the twelfth President.

★ The Department of the Interior is established.

1850

★ President Taylor's death brings Vice President Millard Fillmore into office.

★ California is the thirty-first state to enter the Union.

1852

★ Compulsory public schooling begins.

1853

★ Franklin Pierce is inaugurated as President.

1857

★ James Buchanan is inaugurated as the fifteenth President.

★ The *Dred Scott* decision holds that blacks are not citizens and that it is illegal to forbid slavery in the western territories because it would deprive slaveholders of property without due process.

1858
★ Minnesota is the thirty-second state to enter the Union.

1859
★ Oregon enters the Union as the thirty-third state.

1861
★ Abraham Lincoln is inaugurated as the sixteenth President.
★ *Kentucky* v. *Dennison* holds that a state governor may refuse to give up a fugitive to another state.
★ Kansas is the thirty-fourth state to join the Union.

15

16

15 *James Buchanan*
16 *Abraham Lincoln*

1861–1865
★ The North's victory in the Civil War preserves the Union. Abraham Lincoln establishes the precedent that in times of crisis the President commands extraordinary power.

1862
★ The Department of Agriculture is established.
★ The Homestead Act passes, giving 160 acres of public land in the Midwest and West to anyone farming them for five years.
★ The first Morrill Act passes, giving 11 million acres of public land to the states for agriculture and mechanical-arts colleges.

1863
★ The national government employs military conscription for the first time.
★ West Virginia is the thirty-fifth state to enter the Union.

1864
★ Nevada enters the Union as the thirty-sixth state.

1865
★ President Lincoln is inaugurated for a second term. On April 14, Lincoln is assassinated by John Wilkes Booth. Vice President Andrew Johnson succeeds Lincoln as President.
★ The Thirteenth Amendment, abolishing slavery, is ratified.

17 *Andrew Johnson*

1867
★ Nebraska becomes the thirty-seventh state to join the Union.

1867–1877
★ The period of Radical Reconstruction in the South sets up black suffrage, eliminates property requirements for voting and holding office, and establishes a system of public schools.

1868
★ The Fourteenth Amendment, granting former slaves the rights of citizenship, nullifying the Three-Fifths Compromise, and canceling all debts owed by the Confederate government, is ratified.
★ Andrew Johnson is impeached.

18 *Ulysses S. Grant*

1869

★ Congress sets the number of Supreme Court justices at nine.
★ Ulysses S. Grant is inaugurated as the eighteenth President.

1870

★ The Fifteenth Amendment, extending the voting franchise to black males, is ratified.

1872

★ Susan B. Anthony, a leader of the women's movement, is arrested and convicted for voting illegally.
★ Congress establishes Yellowstone as the first national park.

1873

★ President Grant begins his second term.
★ Congress limits the coinage of silver, beginning a 23-year battle over the issue of free silver.
★ The *Slaughterhouse Cases* hold that the Bill of Rights is not incorporated within the Fourteenth Amendment and thus applies only to the federal government.

1876

★ Colorado enters the Union as the thirty-eighth state.

1877

★ Rutherford B. Hayes takes the Presidential office after a special electoral commission gives him 20 disputed electoral votes.

1879

★ *Reynolds* v. *United States* upholds the prohibition of the Mormon practice of polygamy on the grounds that religious actions may be subject to government regulation for the health, safety, and convenience of the community.

1881

★ The American Federation of Labor (AFL), the nation's first federation of craft unions, is organized.
★ James A. Garfield is inaugurated as President. After he dies from an assassin's bullet, Vice President Chester A. Arthur becomes the twenty-first President.

1881–1891

★ Jim Crow legislation is passed in the South.

1882

★ Congress passes the Chinese Exclusion Act.

1883

★ The *Civil Rights Cases* hold that the Fourteenth Amendment applies only to state action and that Congress cannot prohibit discrimination by private individuals.
★ The Pendleton Act establishes the framework for a system of government employment based on merit.

19

20

21

19 *Rutherford B. Hayes*
20 *James A. Garfield*
21 *Chester A. Arthur*

1885

★ Grover Cleveland is inaugurated as the twenty-second President.

1887

★ Congress establishes the first federal regulatory agency, the Interstate Commerce Commission.

1888

★ The secret ballot is introduced from Australia.

1889

★ Benjamin Harrison is inaugurated as President.
★ North Dakota enters the Union as the thirty-ninth state.
★ On the same date, South Dakota follows as the fortieth state.
★ Montana enters the Union as the forty-first state.
★ Washington is the forty-second state to enter the Union.

1890

★ Idaho is the forty-third state to enter the Union.
★ Wyoming enters the Union as the forty-fourth state. It becomes the first state with women's suffrage.
★ The Sherman Antitrust Act aims at controlling monopolies.

1892

★ Mechanical voting machines are introduced.

1893

★ After four years out of office, Grover Cleveland is again inaugurated as President.

1896

★ *Plessy* v. *Ferguson* holds that racial segregation can be required by law so long as the separate facilities are equal.
★ Utah is the forty-fifth state to enter the Union.
★ *In re Debs* holds that President Grover Cleveland was justified in sending federal troops to Chicago to break the Pullman railroad strike because the President must protect national property, enforce national law, and maintain national functions, such as mail delivery.

1897

★ William McKinley is inaugurated as President.

1898

★ The Supreme Court upholds literacy tests, the poll tax, and residency and property requirements for voting.

1899

★ The first national environmental protection law is passed, but it is not enforced until 1970.

1900

★ Congress establishes the gold standard for the national currency.

22
24

23

22 and 24 Grover Cleveland
23 Benjamin Harrison

25 William McKinley

CHRONOLOGY

26 *Theodore Roosevelt*

1901

★ President McKinley begins his second term in office. In the same year, McKinley is shot, and Vice President Theodore Roosevelt takes office as the twenty-sixth President.

1903

★ Wisconsin becomes the first state to use the direct primary for choosing candidates for Congress and state offices.
★ Congress establishes the Department of Commerce.
★ The United States receives jurisdiction over the Panama Canal Zone.

1905

★ Pennsylvania establishes the first regular state police department.
★ Theodore Roosevelt is inaugurated as President in his own right.

1906

★ The Pure Food and Drug Act imposes restrictions on the preparation and sale of food and drugs.

1907

★ Oklahoma is the forty-sixth state to enter the Union.

1908

★ The Federal Bureau of Investigation (FBI) is established as the major fact-finding agency of the Department of Justice.

27 *William H. Taft*

1909

★ William H. Taft is inaugurated as President.

1910

★ A House revolt against Speaker Joe Cannon eliminates the speaker's power to appoint members to House committees and decentralizes power among committee chairpersons.

1911

★ Membership in the House of Representatives is fixed by Congress at 435.

28 *Woodrow Wilson*

1912

★ New Mexico is the forty-seventh state to enter the Union.
★ Arizona enters the Union as the forty-eighth state.

1913

★ After defeating Taft and Roosevelt, Woodrow Wilson is inaugurated as President.
★ The Sixteenth Amendment, giving Congress the power to levy a direct tax on incomes, is ratified.
★ The Seventeenth Amendment, providing for the direct election of United States senators, is ratified.
★ The Federal Reserve System is established.
★ Congress establishes the Department of Labor.

1914

- ★ The Clayton Antitrust Act forbids certain practices in restraint of trade.
- ★ The Federal Trade Commission is established.
- ★ *Weeks* v. *United States* establishes the exclusionary rule for federal courts.

1915

- ★ The Supreme Court declares the "grandfather clause" unconstitutional.

1916

- ★ Jeannette Rankin of Montana is the first woman elected to the United States Congress.
- ★ The first federal highway program is begun.

1917

- ★ President Wilson is inaugurated for a second term.
- ★ The Senate adopts a strict Cloture Rule.
- ★ Illinois becomes the first state to reorganize its executive branch.

1917–1918

- ★ Woodrow Wilson utilizes the war power to assume wide control over the nation's economy.

1918

- ★ Congress passes the Sedition Act of 1918.

1919

- ★ The Eighteenth Amendment, prohibiting the manufacture, sale, or shipment of alcoholic beverages, is ratified.
- ★ *Schenck* v. *United States* holds that freedom of speech may be restricted if a "clear and present danger" exists.

1919–1920

- ★ The Senate rejects the Treaty of Versailles that ends World War I.

1920

- ★ The United States becomes an urban nation. The Census Bureau determines that 51 percent of the United States population lives in urban areas.
- ★ The Nineteenth Amendment, extending the franchise to women, is ratified.

1921

- ★ Warren G. Harding is inaugurated as President.
- ★ New York and New Jersey enter into an interstate compact to create the Port of New York Authority to manage and develop transportation factilities in the New York City area.
- ★ Lynn J. Frazier, governor of North Dakota, is removed from office by recall.
- ★ Former President William H. Taft is appointed Chief Justice of the United States.

29 Warren G. Harding

30 *Calvin Coolidge*

1923

★ Upon Harding's death, Calvin Coolidge takes office as the thirtieth President.

1924

★ The Child Labor Amendment is defeated.
★ Native Americans receive citizenship.
★ The National Origins Act establishes immigration by quota.

1925

★ *Gitlow* v. *New York* extends the protection of freedom of speech and press to actions by the states.
★ Nellie Taylor Ross of Wyoming becomes the first woman governor of a state.
★ Coolidge is inaugurated as President in his own right.

1928

★ *Olmstead* v. *United States* holds that wiretapping does not constitute unreasonable search and seizure.

31 *Herbert Hoover*

1929

★ Herbert Hoover is inaugurated as President.
★ The stock market crashes, and the Great Depression begins.

1930

★ The Veterans Administration is established.

1932

★ The Norris-LaGuardia Act outlaws yellow-dog contracts and restricts the use of injunctions.

1933

★ Franklin D. Roosevelt is inaugurated as the nation's thirty-second President after winning a landslide victory over incumbent President Hoover.
★ The Twentieth Amendment, shortening the time between the President's election and inauguration and between Congressional elections and the next Congressional session, is ratified.
★ The Twenty-first Amendment, repealing the Eighteenth Amendment and ending national prohibition, is ratified.
★ The gold reserve system replaces the gold standard.
★ The Tennessee Valley Authority (TVA) is created by Congress to develop the electric power and other resources of the Tennessee River valley.

1933–1938

★ Under the New Deal, the federal government takes an active role in trying to solve the nation's economic and social problems.

1934

★ The Federal Communications Commission is established.
★ The Securities and Exchange Commission is established to regulate the stock market.

1935

- ★ The Social Security Act establishes the world's largest insurance program.
- ★ The Wagner Act gives workers in interstate commerce the right to organize and bargain collectively and outlaws certain unfair labor practices, such as company unions.
- ★ The Congress of Industrial Organizations (CIO), the nation's first federation of industrial unions, is organized.
- ★ George Gallup conducts the first nationwide scientifically constructed political opinion poll.

1936

- ★ *United States* v. *Curtiss-Wright* holds that the conduct of foreign affairs is an exclusive power of the President.
- ★ *Ashwander* v. *TVA* upholds the right of the TVA to sell electric power in competition with private power companies.

1937

- ★ President Roosevelt is inaugurated for a second term.
- ★ *National Labor Relations Board* v. *Jones & Laughlin Steel Corp.* expands the commerce clause to allow federal regulation of intrastate activities in such areas as minimum wages, child labor, and agricultural production.
- ★ The Supreme Court includes freedom of assembly within the meaning of due process, thus extending part of the Bill of Rights to the states.

32 Franklin D. Roosevelt

1938

- ★ The Fair Labor Standards Act sets a maximum work week and a minimum wage and restricts the use of child labor.

1939

- ★ The Executive Office of the President is established.

1940

- ★ The Supreme Court includes the free exercise of religion within the meaning of due process, thus extending part of the Bill of Rights to the states.
- ★ The Alien Registration Act requires aliens to register.

1941

- ★ Franklin D. Roosevelt becomes the first President to serve a third term.

1942

- ★ *Wickard* v. *Filburn* expands the power of Congress over interstate commerce.

1943

- ★ Income-tax withholding is instituted.
- ★ *West Virginia State Board of Education* v. *Barnette* holds that public school children who refuse to salute the flag for religious reasons cannot be expelled from school.

1944

- ★ *Smith* v. Allwright holds that the white primary is unconstitutional.
- ★ The Servicemen's Readjustment Act, popularly called the G.I. Bill, provides federal funds to veterans who wish to go to school.

33 *Harry S Truman*

1945

- ★ The United States participates in the founding of the United Nations.
- ★ President Roosevelt begins a fourth term in office. After Roosevelt's death, Vice President Harry S Truman assumes the Presidency.

1946

- ★ *United States* v. *Lovett* holds that denying salary payments to three specific government employees because of their political views is unconstitutional.

1947

- ★ The National Security Council (NSC) and the Central Intelligence Agency (CIA) are established.
- ★ *Everson* v. *Board of Education* includes the prohibition on the establishment of religion within the meaning of due process, thus extending part of the Bill of Rights to the states.
- ★ The Taft-Hartley Act prohibits certain labor union practices; bans strikes against the federal government; outlaws the closed shop; and gives states the power to pass right-to-work laws.

1948

- ★ Truman issues executive orders ending discrimination in federal employment and desegregating the armed forces.
- ★ *McCollum* v. *Board of Education* rules that religious instruction may not be carried out during school hours within public school buildings.

1948–1952

- ★ The Marshall Plan helps Western Europe regain economic and political stability.

1949

- ★ Truman is inaugurated as President in his own right.
- ★ The United States signs a collective security agreement with non-Communist nations and forms the North Atlantic Treaty Organization (NATO).
- ★ The Departments of the Army, the Navy, and the Air Force are combined to form the Department of Defense.

1951

- ★ The Twenty-second Amendment, limiting a President to two terms, is ratified.
- ★ President Truman maintains civilian control over the military by firing General Douglas MacArthur.
- ★ *Dennis* v. *United States* holds that the government may restrict the speech of those who advocate its overthrow.

1952

★ Puerto Rico becomes the nation's first commonwealth.
★ The Immigration and Nationality Act, known as the McCarran-Walter Act, lifts the racial barrier against Asian immigrants but continues the national-origins quota system for all immigrants except those from the Western Hemisphere.

1953

★ Dwight D. Eisenhower is inaugurated as the thirty-fourth President.
★ Earl Warren is appointed Chief Justice of the United States.

34 *Dwight D. Eisenhower*

1953–1954

★ The McCarthy Investigations inquire into Communist influence and subversive activities in the United States.

1954

★ *Brown* v. *Board of Education of Topeka* holds that racial segregation in public school is unconstitutional, thus overthrowing the "separate but equal" doctrine of *Plessy* v. *Ferguson.*

1955

★ Dr. Martin Luther King, Jr., organizes a nonviolent bus boycott in Montgomery, Alabama, to eliminate discrimination in public transportation.
★ The AFL and the CIO merge.

1956

★ Work begins on the national Interstate Highway System.

1957

★ The Civil Rights Act gives the Justice Department the power to file suits on behalf of blacks who are denied the right to vote.
★ President Dwight D. Eisenhower sends federal troops into Little Rock, Arkansas, to enforce school desegregation.
★ *Roth* v. *United States* establishes a threefold test for determining whether material is obscene and thus without First Amendment protection.
★ *Yates* v. *United States* holds that advocating the overthrow of the government can be curtailed only if it incites immediate or probable action.

1958

★ *NAACP* v. *Alabama* holds that freedom of assembly is part of free speech and that a state may not interfere with it.

1959

★ The Landrum-Griffin Act requires unions to file financial reports on pension funds and to hold elections by secret ballot.
★ Alaska enters the Union as the forty-ninth state.
★ Hawaii is the fiftieth state to enter the Union.

35 *John F. Kennedy*

36 *Lyndon B. Johnson*

1960

★ *The New York Times Company* v. *Sullivan* holds that libel law applies one way to private citizens and another way to public figures, because criticism of public officials is a necessary part of a democracy.

★ The first televised debates between Presidential candidates are held.

1961

★ John F. Kennedy, the first Roman Catholic President, is inaugurated.

★ The Twenty-third Amendment, allowing residents of the District of Columbia to vote in Presidential elections, is ratified.

★ *Mapp* v. *Ohio* applies the exclusionary rule to the states.

1962

★ *Engle* v. *Vitale* holds that official prayers in the public schools violate the principle of separation of church and state.

★ *Gideon* v. *Wainwright* holds that the state must provide legal counsel for persons too poor to hire their own counsel.

★ *Baker* v. *Carr* holds that citizens may challenge unequal representation in state legislatures through the federal court system.

1963

★ The Equal Pay Act requires employers to pay the same wages to men and women for equal work.

★ *Edwards* v. *South Carolina* holds that people may assemble peaceably without state interference.

★ Upon the assassination of President Kennedy, Vice President Lyndon B. Johnson succeeds to the Presidency.

1964

★ The Twenty-fourth Amendment, abolishing the poll tax in national elections, is ratified.

★ The Civil Rights Act, which outlaws racial discrimination in public accommodations affecting interstate commerce, is passed.

★ *Heart of Atlanta Motel* v. *United States* holds that discrimination restricts the flow of interstate commerce and can be regulated through legislation.

★ *Wesberry* v. *Sanders* holds that the boundaries of Congressional districts must be drawn so that each contains approximately the same number of people.

★ *Reynolds* v. *Sims* holds that representation in state legislatures must be based on population because voting equality means one person, one vote.

★ *Escobedo* v. *Illinois* holds that the right to legal counsel applies as soon as the suspect is accused of a crime by police.

★ Punch-card ballots tallied by computers are introduced.

1964–1969

★ Under the Great Society, federal funding increases in such areas as education, housing, and national health insurance.

1965

- ★ Johnson is inaugurated as President in his own right.
- ★ The Supreme Court holds that the Ninth Amendment guarantees the right to privacy.
- ★ The Department of Housing and Urban Development is established.
- ★ The Voting Rights Act provides for direct federal action to guarantee voting rights and limits the use of literacy tests.
- ★ Medicare and Medicaid provide national health insurance for the poor, the elderly, and the disabled.
- ★ The national origins quota system for immigrants is abolished and replaced by a preference system.

1966

- ★ The Supreme Court declares the poll tax unconstitutional in all elections.
- ★ The Department of Transportation is established.
- ★ *Miranda* v. *Arizona* holds that accused persons must be fully advised of their legal rights.
- ★ *Sheppard* v. *Maxwell* holds that a judge must protect a person's right to a fair trial if that trial is being damaged by prejudicial media coverage.

1967

- ★ The Twenty-fifth Amendment, providing for Presidential succession in the event of removal, death, or resignation of the incumbent, is ratified.
- ★ Thurgood Marshall becomes the first black appointed to the Supreme Court.
- ★ *Katz* v. *United States* holds that wiretapping without a warrant is an illegal search.
- ★ *In re Gault* extends due process to juvenile proceedings.

1968

- ★ The Civil Rights Act prohibits discrimination in the sale or rental of most private housing.
- ★ *Jones* v. *Mayer* holds that racial discrimination in the sale or rental of property violates due process.

1969

- ★ Richard M. Nixon is inaugurated as President.
- ★ Warren Burger is appointed Chief Justice of the United States.
- ★ *Tinker* v. *Des Moines School District* holds that students are entitled to First-Amendment rights.

37 Richard M. Nixon

1970

- ★ The Office of Management and Budget is established.
- ★ *Welsh* v. *United States* holds that status as a conscientious objector may be granted for deeply held moral and ethical beliefs as well as for beliefs in an organized religion.
- ★ The Envinronmental Protection Agency is established.
- ★ Amendments to the Clean Air Act impose nationwide auto-emission standards.

1971

- ★ The Twenty-sixth Amendment, lowering the voting age to 18, is ratified.
- ★ President Nixon announces that the United States will no longer use the gold standard to determine the value of the dollar in international trade.
- ★ *Swann* v. *Charlotte-Mecklenburg Board of Education* holds that busing can be used to integrate urban schools.
- ★ *Serrano* v. *Priest* holds that the quality of a child's education must not depend on the wealth of his or her parents or community.
- ★ The *Pentagon Papers Case* holds that pre-publication censoring of historical information violates freedom of speech.
- ★ Oregon passes an antilitter law that prohibits throwaway bottles and cans.

1971–1976

- ★ Congress passes a series of laws regulating campaign funding practices, including optional public financing for Presidential candidates.

1972

- ★ Revenue sharing between the federal government and state and local governments is adopted.
- ★ *Wisconsin* v. *Yoder* holds that if compulsory school attendance threatens the survival of a religious community, such as the Amish, the free expression of religion is more important than the state's interest in education.
- ★ *Adams* v. *Williams* holds that a "tip" from a reliable informant is probable cause for a stop-and-frisk action without a search warrant.
- ★ *Furman* v. *Georgia* holds that capital punishment, although not cruel and unusual, cannot be applied in an arbitrary, unequal manner.

1973

- ★ President Nixon is inaugurated for a second term.
- ★ *Miller* v. *California* emphasizes the use of "community standards" for determining when material is obscene and thus without First-Amendment protection.
- ★ *San Antonio Independent School District* v. *Rodriguez* holds that use of the local property tax to finance schools does not violate the equal protection clause.
- ★ Congress passes the War Powers Resolution requiring the President to report to Congress within 48 hours after committing American forces to combat abroad.
- ★ The Watergate Hearings investigate illegal campaign practices and abuses of Presidential power.
- ★ Vice President Spiro Agnew resigns from office. Under the provisions of the Twenty-fifth Amendment to the Constitution, President Nixon chooses Gerald R. Ford to fill the Vice-Presidential vacancy.
- ★ Washington, D.C., receives home rule.

1974

38 *Gerald R. Ford*

- ★ *United States* v. *Nixon* recognizes executive privilege but holds that it must yield to the rule of law and the need for evidence in a criminal trial.
- ★ Richard M. Nixon becomes the first President to resign from office; Vice President Gerald R. Ford succeeds him as President.
- ★ President Ford chooses Nelson Rockefeller to fill the Vice-Presidential vacancy.
- ★ The Privacy Act places limits on the kinds of records that may be kept, limits public disclosures of personal information, and permits individuals to find out what information the government may have about them.
- ★ The Budget and Impoundment Control Act aims at more effective Congressional control over spending.
- ★ A national speed limit of 55 miles-per-hour is set.

1975

- ★ *Sosna* v. *Iowa* holds that a state may not make new residents wait an unreasonable length of time before they are eligible to receive welfare, to vote, to seek a divorce, or to attend a state university.
- ★ The CIA Investigations produce evidence of illegal and improper spying on American citizens by the CIA.
- ★ Congress outlaws all literacy tests for voting and extends the protection of the Voting Rights Act to members of language minorities.

1976

- ★ *Gregg* v. *Georgia* holds that statutes requiring a two-stage trial in capital cases meet the requirements of due process.

1977

39 *Jimmy Carter*

- ★ Jimmy Carter is inaugurated as the thirty-ninth President.
- ★ Congress establishes the Department of Energy.

1978

- ★ A proposed amendment giving the District of Columbia representation in Congress and the power of a state in amending the Constitution is submitted to the states for ratification.
- ★ *Bakke* v. *The Regents of the University of California* holds that the use of racial quotas in admissions violates due process but that race may be considered as one factor in developing an admissions policy.
- ★ Proposition 13, a popular initiative proposal in California, amends the state constitution to limit property taxes and sets off similar initiatives in other states.
- ★ The Civil Service Reform Act gives more flexibility and responsibility to individual federal agencies.

1979

- ★ Congress establishes the Department of Health and Human Services.
- ★ Congress establishes the Department of Education.

40 Ronald Reagan

1981

Ronald Reagan is inaugurated as the fortieth President.

★ President Reagan pledges to reduce the size of the federal government by returning certain responsibilities to state and local governments.

★ Sandra Day O'Connor is the first woman appointed to the Supreme Court.

1982

★ The Equal Rights Amendment is defeated.

1983

★ Sally K. Ride is the first American woman to travel in space.

★ Guion S. Bluford, Jr., is the first black American astronaut to travel in space.

★ The United States invasion of Grenada and the presence of United States Marines in Lebanon raise questions about the Presidential power to commit combat troops overseas.

★ *Immigration and Naturalization Service* v. *Chadha* declares one legislative veto unconstitutional and raises questions about the constitutionality of other legislative vetoes.

1984

★ Democrat Geraldine Ferraro is the first woman nominated for the Vice Presidency by a major political party.

1985

★ Ronald Reagan is inaugurated for a second term.

Almanac of Federal Agencies

Congress shall have power to make all laws which shall be necessary and proper for carrying into execution . . . all . . . powers vested . . . in the government of the United States, or in any department thereof.

THE CONSTITUTION

ACTION (Independent Executive Agency) Includes the Peace Corps, VISTA, and other volunteer service programs. The Peace Corps sends volunteers to conduct programs in economic and social development in foreign countries. VISTA (Volunteers in Service to America) works to fight poverty in urban and rural areas, on Indian reservations, on farms with migrant workers, and in institutions for the mentally ill.

Administration on Aging (Office of Human Development Services) Provides recreational activities, transportation, legal aid, and housekeeping and home health services for older Americans.

Administration for Children, Youth, and Families (Office of Human Development Services) Administers funding for the Head Start program, day-care centers, and programs for abused and neglected children.

Administration on Developmental Disabilities (Office of Human Development Services) Provides vocational rehabilitation for physically and mentally handicapped persons and encourages the elimination of architectural and transportation barriers for users of wheelchairs and crutches.

Administration for Native Americans (Office of Human Development Services) Funds industrial, educational, and other self-help programs developed on reservations by Native Americans.

Agency for International Development (International Development Cooperation Agency) Administers most of the nation's economic and technical foreign-aid programs.

Alcohol, Drug Abuse, and Mental Health Administration (Public Health Service) Conducts research on alcoholism, drug abuse, and mental disorders, and administers programs for their prevention. The National Institute of Mental Health—a part of the Alcohol, Drug Abuse, and Mental Health Administration—maintains a network of community mental health centers.

Amtrak See *National Railroad Passenger Corporation.*

Arms Control and Disarmament Agency (Independent Executive Agency) Negotiates and implements international agreements on arms control, keeps track of the movement of arms throughout the world, and advises the President and other government officials on arms control.

Army Corps of Engineers (Division of the United States Army) Builds bridges and military installations during wartime and constructs flood control and other navigation projects in peacetime.

Bureau of Alcohol, Tobacco, and Firearms (Department of the Treasury) Collects taxes on liquor and tobacco products and works to keep guns out of the hands of criminals.

Bureau of the Census (Department of Commerce) Collects data on the nation's population and on other matters such as manufacturing, commerce, agriculture, housing, and transportation.

Bureau of Economic Analysis (Department of Commerce) Prepares economic accounts of the nation and publishes the *Survey of Current Business.*

Bureau of Engraving and Printing (Department of the Treasury) Designs, engraves, and prints all the nation's paper money.

Bureau of Government Financial Operations (Department of the Treasury) Serves as the government's bookkeeper. It maintains a central accounting system, pays out federal funds, and publishes reports on the government's financial operations.

Bureau of Indian Affairs (Department of the Interior) Assists Native Americans on reservations by providing child welfare services, maintaining schools and roads, and encouraging industrial development.

Bureau of International Labor Affairs (Department of Labor) Represents the nation's labor interests in world affairs through such means as sponsoring exchange programs with union officials of other countries and participating in the International Labor Organization.

Bureau of Labor Statistics (Department of Labor) Conducts research and publishes data on labor-related matters.

Bureau of Land Management (Department of the Interior) Administers public lands and their resources, including timber, minerals, oil and gas, wildlife, and wilderness areas.

Bureau of Mines (Department of the Interior) Conducts research on the nation's mineral resources and on the health and safety of miners.

Bureau of the Mint (Department of the Treasury) Manufactures and distributes the nation's coins.

Bureau of Prisons (Department of Justice) Supervises federal prisons.

Bureau of Public Debt (Department of the Treasury) Manages the national debt by supervising the loans that the government takes out to pay its expenses.

Bureau of Reclamation (Department of the Interior) Supplies water for irrigation to arid and semiarid lands in the West.

Centers for Disease Control (Public Health Service) Works to protect the public health by controlling diseases and setting occupational health and safety standards.

Central Intelligence Agency (Independent Executive Agency) Gathers political, economic, and military information about other nations and carries out covert actions that support American foreign policy objectives.

Commodity Futures Trading Commission (Independent Regulatory Commission) Regulates trading practices on the commodity futures markets.

Congressional Budget Office (United States Congress) Provides the House and Senate budget committees with economic data and analyzes alternative policy choices.

Consular Affairs (Department of State) Maintains consular offices in major cities around the world to look after Americans and United States commercial interests abroad.

Consumer Product Safety Commission (Independent Regulatory Commission) Works to protect consumers from unsafe products.

Council of Economic Advisers (Executive Office of the President) Assists the President in making economic policy.

Council on Environmental Quality (Executive Office of the President) Reviews federal environmental programs and helps the President prepare an annual environmental quality report.

Defense Intelligence Agency (Department of Defense) Gathers information about the military capabilities and intentions of foreign nations.

Defense Nuclear Agency (Department of Defense) Manages the nation's stockpile of nuclear weapons and coordinates weapons development and testing with the Department of Energy.

Department of Agriculture (President's Cabinet) Works to help farmers receive adequate prices. It also administers the Food Stamp Program, promotes agricultural research and education, and works to maintain adequate reserves of farm products.

Department of Commerce (President's Cabinet) Promotes domestic and foreign business by preparing data on the nation's economy, doing research in science and technology, and maintaining the nation's merchant marine.

Department of Defense (President's Cabinet) Maintains and directs the nation's armed forces and advises the President and Congress on defense policy.

Department of Education (President's Cabinet) Administers promotional and improvement programs in education. These include bilingual and compensatory education, and programs for the deaf, the blind, and children with special talents.

Department of Energy (President's Cabinet) Works to meet the nation's energy needs by promoting conservation, looking for new energy sources, and regulating the production and price of energy.

Department of Health and Human Services (President's Cabinet) Protects public health, provides basic health care to certain groups, and administers social welfare and human development programs.

Department of Housing and Urban Development (President's Cabinet) Administers mortgage insurance and other programs to help Americans buy or rent decent housing. The Department also administers federal fair-housing laws and provides grants and insurance for urban-renewal programs.

Department of the Interior (President's Cabinet) Works to conserve and develop the nation's natural resources and maintains the National Park System.

Department of Justice (President's Cabinet) Enforces federal laws (anti-trust, civil rights, and criminal) and gives legal advice to the President and the Cabinet.

Department of Labor (President's Cabinet) Serves the needs of workers by administering unemployment compensation, setting fair employment and occupational safety standards, collecting labor statistics, operating a national network of employment agencies, and promoting sound labor-management relations.

Department of State (President's Cabinet) Advises the President in the formulation and execution of foreign policy. The department's primary objective in foreign relations is to promote the long-range security and well-being of the United States.

Department of Transportation (President's Cabinet) Helps construct and maintain federal highways and urban mass-transit systems; enforces federal law on the high seas; promotes air, highway, and railroad safety; and maintains and operates part of the Saint Lawrence Seaway.

Department of the Treasury (President's Cabinet) Formulates and recommends economic, financial, and tax policies; serves as the financial agent for the federal government; enforces the law; and manufactures coins and currency.

Domestic Policy Staff (Executive Office of the President) Reviews ongoing domestic progams and recommends policy choices in the domestic area.

Drug Enforcement Administration (Department of Justice) Enforces federal drug laws.

Economic and Business Affairs (Department of State) Carries out established trade policies and oversees international finance and development.

Economic Development Administration (Department of Commerce) Funds public works projects in areas of the country with high unemployment rates and lends money to businesses to expand job opportunities.

Environmental Protection Agency (Independent Executive Agency) Sets standards for environmental quality, regulates the disposal of solid waste and toxic and radioactive substances, and administers federal law regarding environmental impact statements for many public and private projects.

Executive Office of the President (Executive Branch) Serves the President in the performance of the many detailed activities of the office.

Export-Import Bank (Independent Executive Agency) Helps finance the export of American goods and services.

Farm Credit Administration (Independent Executive Agency) Providing loans to farmers to buy or improve land, buildings, and farm equipment.

Federal Aviation Administration (Department of Transportation) Promotes air safety by controlling flights in and out of airports, registering planes, licensing pilots and mechanics, operating navigational aids, and requiring antihijacking security.

Federal Bureau of Investigation (Department of Justice) Investigates most kinds of federal crimes; collects evidence on law suits involving the federal government; and gathers information on individuals and groups considered dangerous to national security.

Federal Communications Commission (Independent Regulatory Commission) Regulates interstate and foreign communications by radio, television, telephone, wire, and cable.

Federal Deposit Insurance Corporation (Government Corporation) Protects people's savings in member institutions by insuring individual accounts up to $100,000.

Federal Energy Regulatory Commission (Independent Regulatory Commission) Sets rates for the interstate transport and sale of natural gas, electricity, and oil, and licenses hydroelectric power projects.

Federal Highway Administration (Department of Transportation) Supervises federal aid for highway construction and improvement, builds and maintains roads in national parks and other federal lands, and enforces safety regulations for interstate truckers.

Federal Home Loan Bank Board (Independent Executive Agency) Supervises most of the nation's savings and loan associations.

Federal Housing Administration (Department of Housing and Urban Development) Provides mortgage insurance for home buyers and insures home improvement loans.

Federal Labor Relations Authority (Independent Executive Agency) Helps to prevent or to settle labor-management disputes within government, oversees federal employee unions, and investigates complaints of unfair labor practices.

Federal Maritime Commission (Independent Regulatory Commission) Regulates the rates, services, and employment practices of United States ships engaged in foreign commerce and in domestic commerce in offshore waters.

Federal Mediation and Conciliation Service (Independent Executive Agency) Helps prevent or settle labor-management disputes that affect interstate commerce.

Federal Railroad Administration (Department of Transportation) Administers laws to promote safety on railroads.

Federal Reserve Board (Independent Regulatory Commission) Oversees the nation's banking system and administers monetary policy by expanding or contracting the money supply.

Federal Trade Commission (Independent Regulatory Commission) Works to maintain competition and to protect consumers from false or deceptive advertising and other unfair practices.

Fish and Wildlife Service (Department of the Interior) Protects the nation's wildlife by administering National Wildlife Refuges, operating fish hatcheries, and doing research on animal nutrition and disease.

Food and Drug Administration (Public Health Service) Protects the public against adulterated food, useless or unsafe drugs, and dangerous cosmetics.

General Accounting Office (Independent Agency of the United States Congress) Checks to make sure that federal money is being spent legally and supervises the recovery of debts owed to the federal government.

General Services Administration (Independent Executive Agency) Manages the federal government's property and records.

Government Printing Office (Independent Organization) Publishes thousands of pamphlets and books each year, including *The Congressional Record* and the *Statistical Abstract of the United States.*

Health Care Financing Administration (Department of Health and Human Services) Administers Medicare and Medicaid.

Health Resources Administration (Public Health Service) Funds programs to develop health-care services at the state and local levels and collects data on such matters as birth and death rates, life expectancy, and national health trends.

Health Services Administration (Public Health Service) Funds community health centers, serves migrant workers and their families, and provides health care for merchant sailors, members of the Coast Guard, Native Americans, and Eskimos.

Heritage Conservation and Recreation Service (Department of the Interior) Oversees the use of federal lands for recreation.

Housing Assistance Administration (Department of Housing and Urban Development) Lends money to local housing authorities for the construction of public housing projects for the poor and the aged, and also gives rent subsidies to low-income families.

Immigration and Naturalization Service (Department of Justice) Administers the nation's immigration laws, advises people who wish to become naturalized, and patrols the nation's borders to prevent the unlawful entry of aliens.

Intelligence and Research (Department of State) Analyzes the flow of information coming into the department and other agencies from around the world and prepares reports on problems and trends in international affairs.

Internal Revenue Service (Department of the Treasury) Collects individual and corporate income taxes, checks tax returns, and issues refunds.

International Organization Affairs (Department of State) Coordinates American participation in the United Nations and other international organizations.

International Trade Administration (Department of Commerce) Secures new markets for United States goods overseas and regulates the export of such items as electronic equipment and weapons.

Interstate Commerce Commission (Independent Regulatory Commission) Regulates the interstate movement of people and goods by land and water, including rates, service, and routes.

Joint Chiefs of Staff (Department of Defense) Provides military advice to the President, the National Security Council, and the Secretary of Defense. The Joint Chiefs also prepares strategic plans for the armed forces in the event of war and directs combat operations. Individual members administer the military services.

Library of Congress (Independent Organization) Does research for Congress and serves as the national library, holding all copyright material, providing cataloging information to other libraries, and furnishing special materials for the blind.

Maritime Administration (Department of Transportation) Promotes the merchant marine by subsidizing American shipbuilders to meet foreign competition and by conducting research on how to improve ship quality.

Merit Systems Protection Board (Independent Executive Agency) Protects the rights of individual employees and oversees the federal merit system.

Mine Safety and Health Administration (Department of Labor) Enforces mine safety standards and protects the health of miners.

Minerals Management Service (Department of the Interior) Administers the resources of the Outer Continental Shelf by leasing sites to private oil and gas companies.

Minority Business Development Agency (Department of Commerce) Helps minority-owned businesses with information and other aid.

National Aeronautics and Space Administration (Independent Executive Agency) Directs the nation's civilian space effort. Among other accomplishments, it has placed astronauts on the moon, and it relays telephone calls and telecasts in a worldwide satellite communications system.

National Bureau of Standards (Department of Commerce) Sets measurement standards of mass, length, time, and temperature for science, industry, and commerce; conducts research into the properties of materials.

National Foundation on the Arts and Humanities (Independent Executive Agency) Supports programs in the arts and humanities. The National Endowment for the Arts, a division of the National Foundation on the Arts and Humanities, helps develop the arts by making grants to artists and nonprofit organizations.

National Highway Traffic Safety Administration (Department of Transportation) Promotes traffic safety and fuel economy.

National Institutes of Health (Public Health Service) Does research into the causes and prevention of disease.

National Institute of Mental Health See *Alcohol, Drug Abuse, and Mental Health Administration.*

National Labor Relations Board (Independent Executive Agency) Administers the federal laws on labor-management relations, works to prevent unfair labor practices by employers and unions, and supervises labor union elections.

National Oceanic and Atmospheric Administration (Department of Commerce) Explores and charts oceanic resources and monitors and reports atmospheric conditions. The National Ocean Survey—an agency of the National Oceanic and Atmospheric Administration—maps oceans, maintains navigational and data-collecting buoys and data-collecting satellites, and studies the interaction of the sea with the land and the atmosphere. The National Marine Fisheries Service studies the physical and biological resources of the ocean, manages commercial fishing grounds within 200 miles (321 kilometers) of the United States coasts, and enforces laws protecting marine animals such as whales and seals. The National Weather Service issues forecasts, reports the weather, and studies ways to modify it.

National Park Service (Department of the Interior) Administers national parks, monuments, historic sites, and other areas in the National Park System.

National Railroad Passenger Corporation (Government Corporation) Operates almost all intercity passenger trains in the nation.

National Science Foundation (Independent Executive Agency) Engages in basic and applied research in engineering, physical sciences, and social sciences and supports programs to improve science education.

National Security Agency (Department of Defense) Is responsible for making and breaking security codes and for electronic surveillance.

National Security Council (Executive Office of the President) Advises the President on foreign policy and the integration of that policy with domestic concerns and military policy.

National Telecommunications and Information Administration (Department of Commerce) Advises the President on policies about promoting and regulating telecommunications.

National Transportation Safety Board (Independent Executive Agency) Helps maintain public safety by investigating major transportation accidents, evaluating the safety work done by other federal agencies, and hearing appeals of decisions made by bureaus in the Department of Transportation.

National Weather Service See *National Oceanic and Atmospheric Administration.*

Nuclear Regulatory Commission (Independent Regulatory Commission) Assures public safety in the production of nuclear power by licensing and regulating nuclear power plants, materials, and the disposal of radioactive wastes.

Occupational Safety and Health Administration (Department of Labor) Promotes safe and healthful working conditions.

Office of the Comptroller of the Currency (Department of the Treasury) Supervises national banks to make sure they are complying with federal laws and are in sound financial condition.

Office of Human Development Services (Department of Health and Human Services) Administers social and rehabilitation programs to serve elderly people, children from low-income families, people with mental and physical handicaps, Native Americans, and other groups.

Office of Labor-Management Relations (Department of Labor) Conducts and publishes research on collective bargaining and helps state and local governments resolve labor disputes.

Office of Management and Budget (Executive Office of the President) Assists the President in preparing the annual budget, oversees budgetary expenditures, and coordinates proposed legislation coming from executive departments and agencies.

Office of Personnel Management (Independent Executive Agency) Coordinates the recruitment, training, and promotion of federal employees.

Office of Science and Technology (Executive Office of the President) Advises the President on science and technology.

Office of Surface Mining (Department of the Interior) Enforces environmental protection standards for surface mining operations and promotes the reclamation of land that has been strip-mined.

Office of Technology Assessment (United States Congress) Helps Congress evaluate the impact of science and technology on people and on the environment.

Office of Water Research and Technology (Department of the Interior) Works to solve problems of water resources.

Office of Workers' Compensation (Department of Labor) Administers the compensation program for federal employees and tries to protect federal workers against job-related injuries.

Patent and Trademark Office (Department of Commerce) Protects the creative efforts of inventors and businesses by issuing patents and registering trademarks.

Peace Corps See *ACTION.*

Public Health Service (Department of Health and Human Services) Protects the public's health by promoting medical research, developing medical facilities, training health professionals, and improving the treatment of diseases.

ALMANAC

Rural Electrification Administration (Department of Agriculture) Provides loans to bring electric power and telephone service to rural areas.

Secret Service (Department of the Treasury) Stops counterfeiting and protects the President and the First Family, the Vice President and his or her family, major political candidates, and visiting heads of state.

Securities and Exchange Commission (Independent Regulatory Commission) Protects investors in the stock market against fraudulant and unfair practices.

Selective Service System (Independent Executive Agency) Administers the nation's military draft.

Small Business Administration (Independent Executive Agency) Helps small businesses by making or guaranteeing loans and by providing management counseling and training.

Smithsonian Institution (Independent Organization) Contains art galleries, museums, a zoo, a cultural center, and research facilities in science.

Social Security Administration (Department of Health and Human Services) Administers federal social insurance and public assistance programs.

Synthetic Fuels Corporation (Department of Energy) Makes loans for synthetic fuel projects.

Tennessee Valley Authority (Government Corporation) Develops the resources of the Tennessee River valley, including building dams for electric power and flood control, improving waterways, and encouraging reforestation and soil conservation.

United States Air Force (Department of Defense) Maintains a constant alert to defend United States territory, provides military air transportation, and in wartime gives air support to land and naval combat forces.

United States Army (Department of Defense) Is responsible for military operations on land; it includes infantry, armor, and artillery.

United States Coast Guard (Bureau of the Department of Transportation in peacetime and a division of the United States Navy in wartime) Protects life and property at sea and enforces United States maritime laws. It patrols for smuggling, fights oil spills, keeps watch on icebergs in shipping lanes, and goes out on search-and-rescue missions to aid sailors and fishers.

United States Customs Service (Department of the Treasury) Levies and collects taxes on imports; processes people, carriers, cargo, and mail in and out of the country; and tries to prevent smuggling.

United States Geological Survey (Department of the Interior) Studies various aspects of geology, including volcanic activity and mineral and energy resources, and prepares topographical maps.

United States Information Agency (Independent Executive Agency) Maintains officers at American embassies to arrange educational and cultural exchanges and to provide information about life in the United States and about its foreign policy.

United States Marine Corps (Division of the United States Navy) Provides combat troops to secure and fortify land bases in naval campaigns and provides close air support for ground forces landing on foreign shores.

United States Navy (Department of Defense) Is responsible for military operations at sea.

United States Parole Commission (Department of Justice) An independent unit that administers the parole system for federal prisoners.

United States Postal Service (Independent Executive Agency) Delivers the mail.

United States Travel and Tourism Administration (Department of Commerce) Promotes tourism in the United States.

Urban Mass Transportation Administration (Department of Transportation) Directs programs to build and improve mass-transit systems.

Veterans Administration (Independent Executive Agency) Administers disability payments, pensions, hospitals, educational training, and other programs to help veterans and their families.

VISTA See *ACTION*.

White House Office (Executive Office of the President) Determines who and what should receive the President's personal attention, writes Presidential speeches, and maintains liaison with executive departments, Congress, the mass media, interest groups, and the general public.

Women's Bureau (Department of Labor) Investigates women's employment opportunities and working conditions and advises federal and state governments about them.

Youth Conservation Corps (Department of the Interior) Operates summer projects to develop and maintain natural resources. Examples include building trails and campgrounds, planting trees, and tending hatcheries.

Glossary of Terms

. . . [K]nowledge being necessary to good government and the happiness of [humankind], schools and the means of education shall be forever encouraged.

THE NORTHWEST ORDINANCE

This glossary contains many of the terms you need to understand American government. The page number in parentheses after each definition refers to the page on which the term is introduced in the text. You may find it useful to turn to the page listed to read more about the term. The terms appear in boldface type when they are introduced and discussed in the textbook.

A

absentee ballot An official list of candidates for elective offices and the vote cast before an election, usually by mail, by a registered voter who is unable to vote on election day. (332)

acid rain A form of precipitation with a high proportion of sulfuric and other acids that is environmentally damaging. (605)

acquittal A formal declaration by a court that a person accused of a crime is innocent. (687)

acreage allotment A governmental means of controlling crop production by assigning a certain number of acres to each farmer for planting. (553)

act of admission A law passed by Congress admitting a territory into the Union as a state on an equal footing with the other states. (120)

administrative law The rules and regulations issued by administrative agencies of the executive branch of government. (646)

advance personnel Staff members who precede a political candidate on the campaign trail and arrange the details for personal appearances. (306)

adversary system The basis of United States courts, in which the two sides of a dispute argue before an unbiased jury and a neutral judge. (647)

advice and consent The constitutional requirement of senatorial approval of certain Presidential appointments. (440)

adviser A White House staff member who helps the President make and implement policy. (450)

advocate A person who defends or pleads a cause; a supporter. (510)

affirmative action A policy of preferential treatment of minorities and women to ensure nondiscrimination in hiring, promotion, school admissions, and participation in political conventions. (173, 300, 561)

affirmative action hiring program A program that seeks to eliminate from all aspects of federal employment such nonmerit considerations as race, religion, sex, age, and political party affiliation. (520)

air quality standard A rule that sets limits on the amount of waste products allowed in the air before businesses are required to develop cleanup programs. (605)

amnesty A general pardon, before arrest or conviction, to all members of a group who have violated the law. (440)

anarchy The absence of rules or government. (17)

annexation The extension of municipal boundaries to bring new land into the city limits; the addition of a region or country to a sovereign state. (754)

appeal A request by a party to a case that a higher court review the decision of a lower court. (655)

appellate A term that refers to a court with the power to reexamine and reverse or reaffirm the decisions of a lower court. (687)

applied research The use of the fundamental laws of nature to solve an immediate problem; see *basic research*. (618)

apportionment The distribution of seats in the House of Representatives among states according to their population, as required by the Constitution; the distribution of seats in a state legislature among districts within the state. (207, 708)

appropriation A legislative grant of money for a specific purpose. (398)

arbitration The submission of a dispute to a binding settlement by an impartial third party. (569)

arraignment A formal court hearing at which the charges against a defendant are read. (685)
assessment The process by which the value of property is determined for tax purposes. (758)
assessor The county official who determines the value of property for tax purposes. (736)
at-large system of election The election of city council members by city voters as a whole; see *ward system of election*. (744)
auditor The county official who keeps financial records and tax rolls and who authorizes payments to meet approved obligations. (744)
authoritarian A term that refers to a type of dictatorship that limits power to political control; see *totalitarian*. (27)
authorization act An act by which Congress establishes a program, specifies its general purpose, and estimates how much money will be needed to finance it without actually providing the money; see *appropriation*. (398)
authorized Permitted by law. (398)

B

bail The money put up by a defendant as a pledge to return to court for a trial. (680)
balanced ticket A slate of candidates representative of varying geographic regions, ideologies, ethnic backgrounds, or religions selected in order to broaden a party's appeal and strengthen its chances of winning the election. (305)
balance of trade The difference between what a nation earns from exports and what it spends on imports. (581)
balancing doctrine The theory that the freedoms guaranteed by the First Amendment are as important as other freedoms and must be balanced against competing rights. (135)
bandwagon A propaganda technique that encourages people to support an idea or candidate because it is the popular thing to do. (278)
bandwagon effect The tendency for people to rally in support of a seeming winner in a campaign. (301)
basic research The study of the fundamental laws of nature; see *applied research*. (618)
bellwether A characteristic, usually of a voting district, representative of a voting pattern in an election. (278)
bicameral See *bicameral legislature*. (37, 706)
bicameralism The legislative system under which Congress is composed of a Senate representing the states and a House of Representatives representing the people. (65)
bicameral legislature A legislature composed of two houses. (341)
bilingual education The practice of using two languages in teaching children—in the United States, English and a child's in-home language. (213)
bill A proposed law. (389)
bill of attainder A legislative act prohibited by the Constitution that imposes punishment without trial upon a specified individual or group. (676)
bill of rights A constitutional list of civil and personal guarantees. (43)
bimetallic system A practice in the United States between 1792 and 1873 of minting both gold and silver coins; see *gold standard*. (533)
binding decisions Governmental acts that have the force of law. (20)
bipartisan See *bipartisan group*. (512)
bipartisan group A commission or meeting composed of members of the two major political parties. (366)
blanket primary An election for the nomination of candidates in which candidates for the same office are grouped together on the ballot without regard to party; also called a wide-open primary. (296)
block grant An award of federal funds given to a state or local government that has few or no restrictions upon its use; see *grant-in-aid*. (123)
brief A written presentation that details the legal arguments of a case. (657)
broad construction An interpretation of the Constitution which holds that Congress has the authority to use any proper means to carry out the expressed powers of the Constitution; see *implied powers*. (113)
broad constructionist A person who supports a broad interpretation of the Constitution. (383)
bureau The largest unit within a department of the federal bureaucracy; sometimes called an office, administration, or service. (510)
bureaucracy Any large organization characterized by specialization of function, hierarchical form, and standardized procedures. (503)
bureaucrat A person who works in a bureaucracy. (503)
bylaws Rules that govern a group. (250)

C

Cabinet The group of Presidential advisers formed of the secretaries of the major executive departments and other officials appointed by the President. (454)
campaign The various activities in which a candidate engages that are designed to bring about an election victory. (278)
candidate appeal The attractiveness of a person running for office, often based on the public's perception of past achievements or personality rather than on stated policy positions. (334)
candidate image The way a candidate is viewed by the public. (335)
capitalism An ideology as well as an economic system based on private ownership of property and the means of production and on competition for profit in a market economy. (487)

capital punishment The death penalty. (682)
capital stock tax A tariff levied on the stock issued by a business. (760)
case work Actions by public officials that help constituents with their problems. (353)
categorical grants An award of federal funds given to a state or local government under certain stated conditions. (122)
categorical group A body of people organized on the basis of a specific common characteristic. (249)
cease-and-desist order A command issued by a court or an independent regulatory commission that requires a guilty party to stop engaging in an unfair practice. (588)
censure A formal reprimand or condemnation. (356)
census A count of the population taken by government at stated intervals of time. (204)
central city A territorial and governmental unit with a population of at least 50,000 that forms the core of a metropolitan area. (741)
change of venue The shifting of the locale of a trial to ensure a fair trial. (142, 686)
charter A written governmental grant giving a colony, a group of citizens, or a commercial company the right to organize. (37) A special act by a state legislature allowing a city to become a legal body. (741)
charter colony An English colony in North America in which the people had been granted the right of self-government. (39)
checks and balances A feature of a governmental system whereby the major branches of government share certain powers to permit each branch to check or restrain the other branches. (65)
chief administrative officer plan A proposal for reforming county government that divides responsibility by having the county board make policy and an appointed chief administrative officer or county officer carry it out. (738)
citizenship The condition of being a member of a nation or state. A citizen is granted rights by the nation or states and in return is required to fulfill certain obligations, such as obedience to the laws. (196)
city A unit of local government subject to the state. (741)
city manager A professional administrator appointed by an elected city council to run the city government. (745)
civic duty A citizen's obligation to vote, to serve on a jury, or to perform some other function for the public good. (332)
civil defense A department of state and local government charged with the protection of the civilian population in times of emergencies, such as a foreign military attack. (717)
civil disobedience The deliberate and public violation of the law by a citizen desiring to focus attention on an issue; see *passive resistance.* (144)
civilian supremacy The constitutional principle that the President is the supreme commander of the armed forces in both peace and war. (443)
civil law The rules enacted by legislative groups that govern the relationships between individuals and define their legal rights; see *criminal law.* (646)
civil liberties The personal rights of all citizens, including the freedoms of speech, assembly, religion, and the press; the right of privacy; the right to travel; and the right to a fair trial. (133, 486)
civil service A program of public employment through merit; see *spoils system.* (357, 519)
classical liberalism A political philosophy of Europe's middle class in the 1700's that stressed the ideas of equality, the right to property, and limited government. (232)
class struggle The phrase used by Karl Marx to describe the conflict between those with economic power and those without it, a conflict that Marx believed would ultimately end in a workers' revolution; see *Communism.* (489)
client A person or group served by the agencies and bureaus of the federal government. (516)
closed primary An election for the nomination of candidates in which only party members may vote. (296)
closed shop A workplace where only union members are hired. (569)
cloture rule A special motion in a legislative body to stop debate on a bill. (394)
coalition An alliance of parties or states—usually temporary—to secure a common goal. (25, 287)
coattail effect The influence of one candidate's popularity on winning support for less popular candidates. (347)
coattails See *coattail effect.* (278)
code of ethics A set of rules that governs the activities of an organization's members. (355)
cold war A period of political and ideological competition that has ensued since World War II between the United States and the Soviet Union. (460)
collateral Security for a loan. (552)
collective bargaining The process in which a union representing employees negotiates with an employer on the terms of a contract. (564)
collective naturalization The process by which Congress grants citizenship to a large group of people at the same time. (197)
collective security agreement An international agreement in which each signatory agrees to defend the others against armed attack. (461)
commerce The production, buying, selling, and transporting of goods. (127) The goods themselves. (585)
committee report A document issued by a Congressional committee describing the reasons for its actions with regard to a bill and explaining the bill's scope and purpose. (391)

common law A body of law based on customs, traditions, and prior judicial decisions rather than on written statutes. (37, 646)

commonwealth A territory of the United States with a constitution and a high degree of self-rule, subject to the jurisdiction of Congress. (726)

Communism An economic, political, and social ideology based on the theories of Karl Marx in which all property and means of production are owned by the people. In practice, Communism has become a totalitarian political system in which the Communist party has exercised complete control over the people. (489)

company union A group of workers that is organized by an employer with the purpose of preventing outside unionization; now illegal. (565)

compromise The settlement or resolution of conflict with each side making concessions in order to achieve a common goal. (22)

concurrent jurisdiction The equal authority of federal and state courts to hear a case. (652)

concurrent power In a federal system, those powers which the states share with the national government. (112)

concurrent resolution A measure passed by both houses of Congress that neither requires a signature from the President nor has the force of law; often used for internal Congressional matters or as an expression of opinion. (389)

concurring opinion A statement issued when a justice agrees with a court's decision but not with the reasoning behind it. (658)

confederation A form of government or a league in which states join together for some common purpose while keeping their independence for all other purposes. (24)

conference committee A temporary group of legislators from both houses created to resolve differences in each house's version of the same bill. (371, 394)

conference report The compromise bill worked out by a conference committee; see *conference committee.* (394)

confirmation power The authority to grant formal approval of an appointment; usually refers to Senate approval of a President's appointees. (386)

conflict Disagreement. (21)

conflict of interest The situation that arises when a public official acts in an official capacity to benefit personally from the action. (356)

consensus Agreement. (23)

conservation payment A grant to farmers for not growing crops or grazing animals on their land. (554)

conservative A person who seeks to preserve existing political, social, or economic institutions; a program that favors existing political, social, or economic institutions; of or relating to a philosophy of conservatism. (230)

consolidation The combination of two or more adjacent units of government into a larger unit. (738)

conspiracy In commerce, a predetermined effort within an industry to fix prices or to restrain trade. (667)

constituency The body of voters to whom an elected official is politically responsible. (63)

constituent power The power sometimes vested in a state legislature to amend or to revise the state constitution. (711)

constitution The fundamental laws, ideals, and principles by which a nation or a state is governed; may be unwritten (as in Great Britain) or written (as in the United States). (61)

constitutional commission A group set up to revise a state constitution. (703)

constitutional convention A meeting called for the purpose of revising a constitution. (702)

constitutional monarchy A form of government headed by a king or queen whose powers are primarily ceremonial; real power lies with an elected parliament. (23)

consulate The office of a foreign service official appointed to oversee the various commercial business interests of a nation. (200)

consumer A user of goods and services. (593)

copyright The exclusive legal right to reproduce, publish, and sell a literary, musical, or artistic work. (378)

containment A post–World War II policy of the United States aimed at keeping Communism from spreading outside its existing boundaries; see *cold war.* (461)

coroner The county official who conducts medical investigations into deaths by violence and deaths unattended by a physician; also called a medical examiner. (736)

corporate income tax A fee levied on corporations by a unit of government. (541)

county A political subdivision found in most states. (734)

county attorney The official who represents the state and county in civil suits, conducts criminal investigations, and prosecutes those who violate the law; also called the district attorney or the prosecutor. (736)

county clerk The official who registers deeds, mortgages, births, marriages, divorces, and deaths; issues licenses; and supervises elections in a county. (736)

county commissioner An official elected to the board governing a county; see *county supervisor.* (736)

county court A type of court that originated in the Southern colonies in which a justice of the peace levied taxes, tried certain cases, and carried on other kinds of public business. (39)

county extension agent An employee of the Department of Agriculture who communicates new techniques and information to farmers by coming directly into farm communities. (555)

county manager plan See *chief administrative officer plan.* (737)

GLOSSARY

county seat The town that serves as the center of county government. (736)

county superintendent of schools An official who supervises a county's public elementary and secondary schools. (736)

county supervisor An official, elected to the board governing a county, who is an officer of the township as well as of the board. (736)

covert action A special activity conducted abroad by the Central Intelligence Agency to influence opinions and events in support of the foreign-policy objectives of the United States. (470)

craft union A labor organization composed of skilled workers whose members practice the same trade; see *industrial union.* (563)

credentials committee The group at a political convention that decides which delegates may participate. (303)

criminal law The body of statutes that specifies offenses against the public and prescribes the appropriate punishment. Criminal cases are brought by a unit of government against a person; see *civil law.* (646)

cross-cutting interests Divided loyalties. (282)

crossover vote A situation in which voters registered as members of one political party vote for another party's candidates in an open primary. (296)

currency Paper money. (533)

customs The cultural patterns that distinguish a society or group from other societies or groups. (17)

customs duty See *tariff.* (542)

D

dark horse A little-known candidate who wins a surprise election victory. (278, 304)

daylighting A characteristic of a zoning ordinance that provides for a specific amount of space between buildings. (752)

dead letter provision An ordinance or other law that remains on the books but no longer has any legal force. (701)

deadlock A complete standstill resulting from the opposition of two equally powerful, uncompromising persons or factions. (304)

de facto In practice. (157)

***de facto* segregation** The separation of groups—based on race, religion, or other characteristics—in practice rather than by law. (159)

defector A person who flees his or her homeland for political reasons; commonly applies to people escaping Communist oppression. (193)

deficit spending A governmental policy of spending more money than it receives. (21, 546)

de jure By law. (157)

delegated powers The powers granted to the national government by the Constitution; see *expressed powers, implied powers, inherent powers.* (109)

democracy A government that is run by the people who live under it. (29, 42)

democratic socialism A form of political expression in which the government's role in the economy is determined by free elections. (489)

demographic data Statistical information about population. (204)

demography The study of population and population statistics. (204)

deportation The forcible removal of a person from a country. (195)

depression A severe and prolonged economic slump in which prices drop, business productivity slows down, and unemployment increases; see *inflation.* (545)

deregulation The policy of reducing government control over particular economic activities or industries in order to promote competition. (588)

deterrence Since World War II, a policy of the United States that discourages aggression by the threat of retaliation. (461)

deterrent effect The influence of a policy of restraint; refers to the impact judicial review has on the drafting and enforcement of laws by the legislative and executive branches; see *judicial review.* (664)

détente A period characterized by the relaxation of tensions between the United States and the Soviet Union; see *cold war.* (464)

dictatorship A form of government in which power is concentrated in the hands of one person or a select few, with the rulers accountable only to themselves and holding power by force. (26)

dictatorship of the proletariat The Communist government that was established as a result of the workers' revolution; see *class struggle.* (489)

diplomacy International negotiations. (458)

diplomatic recognition The exchange of diplomatic representatives with a foreign nation. (443)

direct democracy A form of government in which the citizens participate directly in making decisions. (29)

direct initiative An electoral process whereby citizens may vote directly on a law. (713)

direct popular election A system under which elected officials are chosen directly by the voters. (318)

direct primary An election within a political party in which voters select the party's candidates for the general election. (295)

direct tax A fee levied by a unit of government and paid directly to the government by the individual business or corporation on which it is levied; for example, an income tax or a property tax. (539)

discharge petition A request by a majority of the House of Representatives that a bill blocked by a committee be brought to the House floor for consideration. (391)

discount rate The interest that member banks pay when they borrow money from their Federal Reserve Bank to make loans to their own borrowers. (537)

disfranchisement The denial of the right to vote by such means as literacy tests, residence and property requirements, and the poll tax. (168)

dissenting opinion A statement issued when a Supreme Court justice opposes the majority decision. (658)

divine right A belief that a monarch's authority to rule came from God. (22)

division of powers A constitutional principle under which authority is divided between the national government and the states. (109)

documentary tax A fee levied, usually by state or local government, on the recording and registering of a document. (760)

double jeopardy The condition of being tried a second time for the same criminal offense within the same court system. (681)

dove In popular language, a person who is antiwar. (278)

due process The constitutional guarantee of applying fair and regular legal procedures in courts of law. (134, 674)

duty See *tariff.* (528)

dyed-in-the-wool A term that is descriptive of an individual who is steadfast in loyalty. (278)

E

economic account Data prepared and interpreted by the Bureau of Economic Analysis, used to measure national income, productivity, and wealth of the United States. (582)

economic sanction A collective boycott and trade restriction imposed on a nation to persuade it to change one or more actions. (495)

elastic clause The name given to Article 1, Section 8, Clause 18, of the Constitution because its use has enabled Congress to stretch the expressed powers; see *implied powers.* (100, 110, 383)

elected chief executive plan A proposal for reforming county government by having the board make policy and an elected chief executive administer it. (738)

electoral college A group of people chosen by the voters to formally elect the President and Vice President of the United States. (312)

electoral process The sequence of nomination, campaigning, and election by which voters in a democracy choose public officials. (294)

electorate Those eligible to vote. (321)

electronic surveillance The use of wiretaps and similar devices to obtain information. (677)

eligibility requirement A rule specifying who is entitled to receive the benefits of a program. (550)

emergency powers Actions the President can take in time of war. (413)

enabling act A Congressional act directing a territory to draft a state constitution and thus become eligible for admission into the Union. (120)

environmental impact The effect of an action on the environment. (607)

equality A fundamental principle of American government, set out in the Declaration of Independence, which holds that all people have the same rights before the law. (41)

equal-time rule A Federal Communications Commission requirement which specifies that all candidates for public office be given equal access to radio and television. (589)

equity A body of law based on natural law and applied in the absence of statutory or common law. (646)

establishment clause The constitutional prohibition against national or state actions that promote or establish religion. (146)

estate tax A fee levied on property left by someone who has died. (542, 760)

exchange rate The amount for which a nation's currency can be redeemed in another currency. (581)

excise tax A fee levied by government on the manufacture, sale, use, or transfer of such goods and services as liquor, tobacco, firearms, gasoline, air travel, and telephone service. (541, 757)

exclusionary rule A judicial decision which states that evidence obtained without either a warrant or one of the recognized exceptions to a warrant is inadmissible in court. (677)

exclusive jurisdiction The sole right of a court to hear a case. (652)

exclusive powers Actions that the Constitution grants only to the national government. (110)

executive A person or group of persons having the duty and power to put laws into effect. (37)

executive agreement A written Presidential pact with a foreign head of state that does not require the consent of the Senate. (442)

executive calendar The Senate's official list of nonlegislative business, such as treaties and confirmation of appointments. (391)

executive clemency The power of an executive to lighten or overturn the punishment of people who have been convicted of a crime. (718)

executive power A nonlegislative power sometimes vested in a legislature to appoint certain officials or to approve the executive's appointments. (711)

executive privilege The right of a President to withhold information from Congress and the courts, originally limited to the protection of military secrets or confidential treaty negotiations, but now used to protect decision-making processes within the executive branch. (444)

exigent circumstance A situation that calls for an immediate search to prevent the destruction or removal of evidence. (676)

export duty A tax on goods that are for sale outside a nation. (53)

***ex post facto* law** An act of the legislature, prohibited by the Constitution, that declares an action illegal after the action has taken place. (675)

expressed Stated orally or in writing; see *expressed powers.* (382)

expressed powers Those powers of the national government that are described or enumerated in the Constitution; see *implied powers.* (110, 382)

expulsion The removal of a member from an organization for wrongdoing. (356)

extradition A request made by one state to another state or by one nation to another nation to send back a suspected criminal for trial or punishment. (118)

F

faction A group pursuing particular goals within a larger organization. (250)

fairness doctrine A Federal Communications Commission requirement stating that radio and television stations must present all sides of important public issues. (589)

false association A propaganda technique that falsely identifies opponents with unpopular causes. (245)

fascism A nationalist dictatorial movement, emphasizing the state over the individual and opposed to both Communism and democracy, that arose in Italy in the 1920's under Benito Mussolini. (27)

fat cat A wealthy political contributor. (278)

federal budget An estimate of the amount of money the government expects to collect and spend during a 12-month period. (543)

federal bureaucracy The departments and agencies of the executive branch of the federal government. (449)

federalism See *federal system.* (62)

federally impacted area An area where federal activities substantially increase school enrollment, such as around an army base or where federally owned property reduces the tax base supporting the schools. (633)

federal system A form of government in which power is divided between a central government and regional governments. (24, 109)

felony A major crime—such as murder, rape, and robbery—that carries a punishment ranging from a lengthy prison sentence to death. (682)

field manager A person in a candidate's organization who coordinates campaign efforts within a particular area. (306)

filibuster A legislative tactic for delaying a bill in which one or more lawmakers continue talking as long as possible. (393)

fiscal policy A governmental plan to use its taxing and spending powers to influence the nation's economy. (546)

fiscal year A 12-month accounting period used by government and many businesses. (543)

floor manager A legislator who guides a bill through debate, usually the chairperson of the committee or subcommittee that previously reported out the bill. (392)

follow the crowd A propaganda technique that urges people to do something so they will not be left behind everyone else. (245)

food stamp program A program administered by the Department of Agriculture to improve family nutrition by providing free or low-cost coupons used to pay for food. (628)

footprint The ground floor plan of a building. (752)

forecast The outlook for the future. (220)

foreign-intelligence activities The acquisition and evaluation of information about the capabilities and intentions of foreign governments. (469)

fossil fuel An energy resource such as oil, gas, or coal that was formed millions of years ago from decomposed plant life. (613)

franking privilege Free postage for official mail sent out by members of Congress to their constituents. (356)

freedom of assembly The constitutional right of the people to form groups peaceably to gain political recognition and power. (143)

freedom of speech The constitutional right to discuss an unpopular or unusual opinion as long as it does not incite an immediate breach of the peace. (136)

freedom of the press The constitutional guarantee that people will have access to all opinions. (136)

free exercise clause The constitutional protection afforded to individuals to express or not to express religious beliefs without government interference. (146)

free rider A worker who benefits from collective bargaining without paying union dues or supporting the union in other ways. (569)

free silver See *free silver policy.* (533)

free silver policy A policy, popular in the late 1800's, that advocated the unlimited coinage of all silver mined. (276)

front runner The candidate in a group of candidates who seems most likely to win the election. (278)

futures Agreements to buy and sell a particular commodity at an agreed-upon price at a future date. (591)

G

gag order A court order forbidding the news media from publishing or broadcasting certain information about a case; usually considered unconstitutional except in compelling circumstances during wartime. (142)

gatekeeper A personal assistant to the President who screens visitors and written material. (450)

general sales tax A tax placed on the sale of almost all goods. (757)

gerrymandering The drawing of a district's boundaries by a majority party in a legislature to secure as many legislative seats as possible. (343)

gift tax A fee levied on the transfer of property. (542, 760)

glittering generality A propaganda technique that uses a high-sounding phrase with little substance to sway opinions. (244)

gold reserve A monetary system, used between 1933 and 1971, under which a supply of gold equal to at least 25 percent of all the paper money in circulation in the United States was held by the federal government to back United States currency. (534)

gold standard A monetary system in which the value of paper money and coins is measured in terms of gold. (276, 533)

government The institutions through which laws are made and enforced. (17)

government corporation A government agency that operates a commercial enterprise and is run like a private business. (514, 600)

government securities Interest-bearing bonds and notes issued by a government. (537)

governor The chief executive of a state. (713)

graduated tax See *progressive tax.* (540)

grandfather clause The provision in the laws of Southern states permitting a person to vote without taking the literacy test or paying the poll tax if he or one of his ancestors had been entitled to vote in 1866. Directed against blacks, it was declared unconstitutional in 1915. (168)

grand jury A group of 6 to 23 persons who decide whether the evidence presented by a government attorney is sufficient to justify prosecution of the accused person. (681)

grant-in-aid Federal funds given to state and local governments for a specified purpose; see *block grant.* (122)

grass roots At the local level. (263)

gross national product A figure representing the total value of goods and services produced in a nation during a year. (582)

guns and butter A public policy of funding new domestic programs and producing war supplies at the same time. (508)

H

hawk In popular language, a person who believes war is the best solution to a specific problem or situation. (278)

hazardous wastes Discarded substances that may cause death or disease and that threaten public health or the environment. (606)

hierarchy A ranking of bureaucrats with authority flowing downward from the top. (503)

holding company A corporation that holds enough stock in another company to control its operations. (590)

home rule Self-government by a township, a city, a county, or another dependent political unit. (738)

housing allowance A cash payment made directly to the poor or the aged to enable them to afford decent housing; see *rent subsidy.* (636)

humanities The field of study that includes literature, languages, philosophy, and history. (640)

human rights The modern term for natural rights. (42)

I

ideology A set of doctrines or closely related beliefs that seeks to explain some aspect of the world. (27) A program of revolutionary action that seeks to change the world. (229)

illegal alien A person who enters a country without permission or proper documents. (194)

implied powers Those powers of the national government that are not described in the Constitution but are suggested by those powers that are described; see *expressed powers.* (110, 382)

impoundment Presidential refusal to allow executive agencies to spend money appropriated by Congress. (399, 417)

inaugural address The speech delivered by the President after taking the oath of office, which sets the tone and spirit of the new administration. (434)

income tax A fee placed on personal or corporate income. (758)

incorporation The process by which a city becomes a legal body with governmental power. (741)

incumbent The holder of an office. (335)

independence of judgment A philosophy of representative government which holds that officials should exercise their own wisdom and conscience for the public good rather than serve as agents for local interests. (349)

independent executive agency A government bureau that is not part of any Cabinet department. (510)

independent regulatory commission An agency in the executive branch that combines quasi-legislative and quasi-judicial functions. (512)

independent union A union not affiliated with the AFL–CIO, such as the International Brotherhood of Teamsters or the United Mine Workers of America. (564)

indictment The formal written charge of a crime, often made by a grand jury. (681)

indirect initiative A procedure whereby a proposal is placed on the ballot to be voted on directly by the citizens. (713)

indirect tax A fee such as a sales or excise tax, levied on an article for sale and usually collected by a business that passes it on to the government. (539)

individualism A political and economic theory that stresses individual initiative and action. (232)

industrial union An organized group of skilled and unskilled workers in the same industry; see *craft union.* (563)

inflation An economic situation characterized by increased prices for goods and services and a decline in the purchasing power of money; see *depression.* (537)

information A formal charge of a crime, consisting of a complaint filed before a magistrate. (681)

inherent powers Those powers belonging to the national government because it exists as a government in the world community, such as the power to define the nation. (110)

inheritance tax A fee levied on a beneficiary's share of an estate. (760)

injunction A court order requiring an individual or a company to refrain from performing a specific action. (565, 646)

in loco parentis A Latin phrase meaning "in place of a parent" that refers to the role of the state in the operation of the juvenile justice system. (689)

inner city The oldest, central neighborhoods of a city or urban area. (749)

intangible Descriptive of personal property that is not physical in nature, such as the value of a stock certificate; see *tangible.* (758)

interest group An organized group whose members share a common goal and work to influence governmental policy. (248)

intergovernmental grant A grant of money from the state or the federal government to a local government for schools or for the support of other services provided by the local government. (760)

interim committee A committee, generally of a state legislature, that works on a specific problem between legislative sessions. (712)

internationalism A policy of active involvement in foreign affairs pursued by the United States since the end of World War II. (460)

international law The body of rules found in treaties and agreements among nations, decisions of international courts, and certain international customs that determine the conduct of nations. (646)

interstate commerce Buying and selling that takes place between and among the states. (585)

interstate compact An agreement between two or more states that deals with a common problem. (119, 754)

intrastate commerce Buying and selling that is conducted within the borders of one state. (585)

isolationism A policy of minimal involvement in foreign affairs pursued by the United States for much of the nineteenth century and part of the twentieth century. (458)

issue A matter over which there is public disagreement and debate. (23)

item veto The power exercised by a state governor to reject a particular portion, or item, within a bill. (448, 713)

J

joint committee A legislative committee composed of an equal number of members from both houses. (371)

joint resolution A legislative matter, usually about a limited or temporary concern, that must be passed by both houses of Congress and signed by the President to have the force of law. (389)

judicial Having the duty and power to administer justice. (37)

judicial activism A term that describes a more aggressive role taken by the courts in interpreting the Constitution. (264, 664)

judicial power The power vested in almost all state legislatures to impeach executive and judicial officers and to judge disputes involving their own members. (711)

judicial review The power of the courts to declare acts of the legislative and executive branches unconstitutional. (67, 664)

judicial self-restraint A term that describes a passive role taken by the courts in interpreting the Constitution. (664)

junket A trip taken abroad at government expense usually by a member of Congress. (357)

jus sanguinis The principle of citizenship on the basis of the citizenship of one's parents. (196)

jus soli The principle of citizenship on the basis of one's place of birth. (196)

justice of the peace A legal office that originated in the Middle Ages and exists today mainly in rural areas and small towns. (648)

K

kangaroo court A court in which a fair trial is impossible. (690)

keynote speaker A person who speaks in the evening of the first day of a convention and who praises the party and sets forth its goals in grand oratorical tradition. (303)

L

labor force That part of a nation's population who are employed or actively looking for work. (214)

laissez-faire A governmental policy of noninterference with business and industry beyond the enforcement of contracts and the protection of private property. (274, 488)

lame duck An officeholder whose term has not yet expired but who has not been reelected or reappointed to the office and thus has little governing power. (278, 436)

language minority In the United States, a person who speaks little or no English. (169)

law A set of rules, made and enforced by government, that is binding on society as a whole. (18, 645)

legal opinion Formal interpretation of a law by a chief officer, such as a state's attorney general, that has the force of law unless overturned by a court. (720)

legislative Having the duty and the power to make laws. (37)

legislative calendar The official list of bills to be considered by each chamber of Congress. (391)

legislative oversight The Congressional power to supervise executive activities. (395)

legislative powers Those powers of Congress that derive from Article 1 of the Constitution and involve the areas about which Congress may make laws. (382)

legislative veto The power of Congress to annul certain actions of regulatory commissions and government agencies; the Supreme Court has ruled that in some instances the legislative veto is unconstitutional. (589)

legitimacy Rightful authority. (18)

liaison Contact person. (261) A person who tries to secure cooperation between two units of government. (451)

libel The injuring of someone's reputation falsely through the printed word; see *slander*. (141)

liberal A person seeking significant change in a society's political, social, or economic institutions; a program that favors change and reforms; of or relating to a philosophy of liberalism. (230)

liberty A fundamental principle of American government, set out in the Declaration of Independence, which holds that people should be free from unwarranted political, economic, and social restraints. (42)

life tenure The right of a judge to serve on "good behavior" until resignation, retirement, or death, rather than for a fixed term. (654)

limited government A government whose power is restricted to protect fundamental human rights; a basic principle of the United States system of government which states that government may do only those things the people have empowered it to do. (62)

literacy test A requirement, usually part of a state constitution, that a prospective voter be able to read and understand certain written material. (168)

lobby See *pressure group*. (251)

lobbying Any organized effort by individuals or groups to influence public policy, especially efforts to influence legislative action. (262)

lobbyist A person who works to influence governmental decision makers. (709)

lockout An action closing a factory or other place of employment in order to force a union to accept management's terms in a dispute. (569)

long ballot A ballot that contains candidates for almost all public offices; see *short ballot*. (325)

loophole An inconsistency in the law, especially a tax law, that makes it possible for some people to avoid obeying the law. (540)

lynching The illegal execution of a person, usually by hanging. (157)

M

mace An ornamental staff used as a symbol of authority in the United States House of Representatives. (368)

majority opinion A ruling issued by a majority of the justices voting on a case. (658)

majority rule Decision making by more than half of a group's membership. (31)

malapportionment The unequal division of seats in the House of Representatives resulting from inequalities in the size or population of Congressional districts. (342)

mandate The will of the voters as expressed to their representative. (337)

mandated delegate A representative elected to express the will of his or her constituents. (349)

mandatory referendum A requirement of voter approval attached to certain legislative measures such as proposed amendments to a state constitution. (713)

market quota A limitation on the amount of a crop each farmer may sell. (554)

mass media The agencies of television, radio, newspapers, and magazines that help to shape public opinion. (241)

matching funds The amount of money a state or local government is required to put up in order to receive money from the federal government. (122)

means of production Resources such as land, factories, machines, and labor. (489)

media coverage The reporting of a campaign or a candidate by television, radio, newspapers, and magazines. (301)

medical examiner See *coroner*. (736)

merchant marine A nation's privately and publicly owned commercial ships and their personnel. (583)

merit system The practice of awarding government jobs on the basis of competitive examination; see *spoils system*. (520)

merit system principles The nine legally established principles of the federal civil service. (521)

message power The constitutional requirement that the President provide Congress with program and budget information and propose legislation on a regular basis. (445)

metropolitan area An urban complex containing a central city and its surrounding suburbs, with a total population of at least 100,000 (75,000 in New England). (741)

military-industrial complex The close connection between the United States military establishment and the huge arms industry. (475)

militia Citizen soldiers. (39)

minimum wage The lowest wage that an employer can legally pay an employee. (560)

minority rights Political rights that cannot be abolished in a democracy even though they are held by, or apply to, less than half the population. (31)

misdemeanor A minor criminal matter, such as the violation of a traffic law, that carries a fine and less than one year's imprisonment. (648, 682)

mixed economy An economic system in which private ownership and market competition are regulated extensively by government. (488)

monarchy A government that is headed by a king or queen. (23)

monetary policy Government actions that expand or contract the supply of money and credit. (537)

monopoly The control of a market by a single enterprise. (667)

moral principles Religious or ethical beliefs. (17)

multi-party system The existence of three or more parties seriously competing for the control of government. (280)

multiple-use management The policy of utilizing public lands and resources in a variety of ways. (597)

municipal corporation A city as a legal body with the right to make contracts, sue in the courts, and buy and sell property. (741)

municipal court A court having jurisdiction within an urban area. (648)

municipal government The government of a municipality. (743)

municipality A city or town with local self-government. (741)

N

name-calling A propaganda technique that describes policies or individuals with loaded words instead of presenting the policies or individuals on their merits. (244)

national committee The agency of a political party that provides ongoing national party leadership. (287)

national convention A political party's meeting held once every four years to nominate candidates for President and Vice President, ratify the platform, adopt party rules, and elect officers. (287)

national debt The total amount of money owed by the federal government. (544)

nationalism The common spirit that unites people—usually those with a similar culture, language, or territory—in the desire to be self-governing. (460, 483)

nationalization The taking over by a government of the ownership and management of private companies. (489)

national origins quota system The system that formed the basis of United States immigration policy between 1924 and 1952; admitted immigrants from any particular European country in numbers proportionate to the percentage of people in that national origin in the United States in 1890. (186)

naturalization The process by which a person gains citizenship at some time after birth. (186)

natural rights Those rights which are inherent with humanity and which cannot be taken away by government. (42)

nominating process The established procedures by which a political party chooses its candidates for public office. (294)

nomination by petition A process of collecting the signatures of a certain number of registered voters to place a candidate's name on a ballot; generally used in nonpartisan elections. (297)

nomination by self-announcement A procedure by which a candidate announces that he or she wishes to run for an office in the party primary. (297)

nonaligned nation A nation that is not allied with either the United States or the Soviet Union. (483)

nonlegislative powers Those powers of Congress which derive from parts of the Constitution other than Article 1 and which give Congress certain authority with regard to the executive branch. (382)

nonpartisan election An election in which party labels do not appear on the ballot. (327)

nonrenewable energy resource A resource, such as oil, whose supply is depleted with use. (612)

North-South dialogue The discussions in the United Nations between the non-Communist industrialized nations and the developing nations of the Third World concerning economic and political problems. (493)

O

obscenity Material that is considered offensive, that lacks any serious literary, artistic, political, or scientific value, and that thus loses its First Amendment protection. (140)

office-group ballot A type of ballot on which candidates of all parties are grouped together according to the office for which they are running. (325)

off-year election An election held in a year when the Presidency is not contested. (289)

oil reserves Untapped petroleum supplies. (614)

open-market operation The buying and selling of government securities by the Federal Reserve Board so as to regulate the supply of money and credit throughout the nation. (537)

open primary An election for nomination purposes in which the voters make no public declaration of party affiliation. (296)

open shop A workplace where workers have the option of joining a union; see *union shop*. (569)

opinion leader A person whose views are likely to have considerable influence on other members of a group. (240)

optional referendum A measure that a legislature chooses to refer to the voters, often so that it can avoid taking a stand on an issue. (713)

organic act A document, resembling a state constitution, that is enacted by Congress to govern an organized territory. (726)

organized territory A territory governed under an organic act. (726)

original jurisdiction The authority of a court to hear a case first. (106)

original package doctrine The criterion which holds that goods cease being interstate commerce when the original package in which they were shipped is opened, used, or sold by the party to whom they were shipped. (586)

P

page A youth between 16 and 18 years of age appointed under patronage to run errands, carry messages, distribute documents, and answer the telephone for members of Congress. (376)

pardon The legal release of a person from imposed punishment. (440, 718)

parity In agriculture, the balance between the minimum price for certain crops and a farmer's expenditures that gives the farmer the same purchasing power as a city dweller. (552)

parliamentarian A specialist in the rules of procedure and in the technicalities of the legislative process. (364)

parliamentary system A form of government in which the chief executive must belong to the legislature and is responsible to it. (25)

parole The conditional release of a prisoner from jail before the full term of punishment is served. (688)

partisanship Party loyalty. (333)

party caucus A closed meeting of party leaders to decide upon nominations, legislative proposals, or other business on which party unity is desired. (291)

party-column ballot A type of ballot on which candidates are listed by party in columns. (325)

party purist A person loyal to a candidate or committed to a particular issue rather than to a political party. (290)

party regular A supporter of a political party whose first interest is seeing that the party wins the election. (278, 290)

party responsibility A philosophy of representative government which holds that elected officials should support a national party program rather than serve as agents for local interests. (352)

passive resistance The nonviolent refusal to obey a law. (144)

passport A formal document issued by a nation to its citizens for travel abroad. (196)

patent A license, usually issued by a government, that grants to an inventor exclusive rights for a limited time to the manufacture, use, and sale of his or her discovery. (583)

patronage Political assistance in the form of jobs, contracts, and favors offered by a political machine to individuals and organizations in exchange for votes and money. (276, 289)

payroll tax A fee levied on employers and their employees and currently used to support the Social Security system and unemployment compensation programs. (541)

per capita income The income of the average person, obtained by dividing the gross national product by the total population of a nation. (582)

peremptory challenge The exclusion, without cause, of a prospective juror by an attorney. (686)

perjury False testimony under oath. (687)

personal organization The campaign staff of a nominee as distinguished from a party national committee. (306)

personal property Movable objects such as furniture, jewelry, livestock, bank accounts, stocks, and bonds; see *real property*. (758)

petition The application by a state for admission to the Union; also, a formal written request, usually with a specific number of signatures attached, made to a government, an election commission, or other governmental agency. (120)

pigeonhole To lay aside a bill or other legislation; to hold back action, usually in committee. (374)

piggybacking The building of a new structure on top of an old building. (752)

plain-folk approach A propaganda technique that attempts to identify a candidate as an average person. (245)

plank A position in a party platform. (304)

platform A political party's statement of policy on the issues, usually designed to win the support of various groups and to unite the party. (272)

plea bargain The settlement of a case by negotiation between the prosecution and the defense in which the defendant usually pleads guilty in exchange for a reduction of charges or a reduced sentence. (685)

plurality The greatest number of votes cast for a candidate in an election consisting of more than two candidates. (280, 296)

pocket veto The executive's rejection of a bill by failing to sign it before the legislature adjourns. (394, 447)

police power A government's authority to promote and protect the health, safety, morals, and welfare of its people. (711)

political machine The tightly controlled organization of a political party within a particular city, county, or state. (275, 289)

political party An organization of persons who join together to win elections, control government, and determine public policy. (271)

political rights Those rights that allow people to participate freely and effectively in government. (486)

GLOSSARY

political system The process by which a society governs itself. (22)

politics The process by which government decisions are made. (22)

poll watcher A person who oversees a polling place to make sure that an election is conducted fairly. (324)

popular initiative A procedure whereby interested citizens place an amendment to the state constitution on the ballot by obtaining a required number of signatures on a petition. (702)

popular referendum A petition by citizens calling for a vote on a bill passed by the legislature. (713)

popular sovereignty The principle that the people exercise supreme governmental authority. (30, 42, 62)

pork barrel See *pork-barrel project.* (278)

pork-barrel project A project that benefits the constituents of a member of Congress and thus enhances the member's chances for reelection. (372)

port of entry One of 300 official border crossing points, seaports, and international airports through which people and goods enter the United States. (528)

poverty line The federally determined income figure below which an individual or a family is considered too poor to buy adequate food, shelter, and health services. (216)

power of the purse Legislative control over taxes and appropriations. (395, 711)

pragmatism A philosophy that adopts a practical rather than an ideological approach to politics. (230)

preamble A constitution's statement of purpose. (701)

precedent A decision that serves as an example for a later decision; see *rule of* stare decisis. (37)

precinct A voting district. (324)

preference system A ranking of most-favored immigrants; since 1965, the basis of American immigration policy. (189)

preliminary hearing A judicial hearing similar to a nonjury trial during which witnesses are called and evidence is submitted so that a magistrate may determine if there is probable cause to continue proceedings in the case. If no probable cause is found, charges are dismissed. (681)

President-elect A person elected to the office of President but who has not yet been inaugurated. (437)

Presidential debates A series of televised debates, first held in 1960 and generally held every four years, between major Presidential candidates. (308)

Presidential disability A situation in which the President is unable to perform the duties of the office; in this situation the Vice President becomes Acting President until the President is able to perform the duties of the office. (437)

presidential system A form of government in which the legislative and executive branches are separate and independent of each other, with each checking and balancing the actions of the other. (25)

press staff The people responsible for a politician's relations with the news media. (21, 453)

pressure group A specialized association that exists primarily to protect and to promote the specific interests of its members by favorably influencing government policy. (251)

presumption of innocence The judicial principle held in the United States that a person is innocent until proven guilty in a fair trial. (673)

primary system A system of elections within a party to choose the party's nominee for each office. (291)

private bill A bill introduced on behalf of a specific person or with regard to a particular place. (389)

probable cause A term that describes the grounds for a legal search warrant as reasonable and justified. (676)

probation The conditional suspension of a court sentence upon the guarantee of good behavior by the person convicted of a crime. (692)

progressive tax A fee imposed by governmental authority, such as the federal income tax, the rate of which increases as income increases. (542)

progressive taxation See *progressive tax.* (757)

proletariat According to Marxist philosophy, the working class. (489)

promotion The effort by the federal government to improve the condition of particular parts of the economy or of the economy as a whole. (550)

propaganda The manipulation of information in order to influence attitudes. (27, 244)

property tax An assessment placed on land, buildings, and other real property. (758)

proportional representation A system that allocates membership in a legislative body according to the percentages of votes cast for each political party; a system in a legislative body that is based on the concept that each legislator is representing approximately the same number of constituents. (280)

proportional tax A duty that applies the same rate to each person's income regardless of its size; also called a flat-rate tax. (542)

proportional taxation See *proportional tax.* (757)

proprietor An individual to whom the English monarch granted land and political authority in a North American colony. (39)

proprietary colony An English colony in North America in which the governor was appointed by the proprietor. (39)

protective tariff A duty levied on imports set high enough to keep a particular foreign product out of the country. (127, 542)

public bill A bill that deals with matters of general concern and applies to the nation as a whole. (389)

public disclosure The requirement that interest groups reveal income and expenditures, who is working for them, and what contacts they have with government officials. (266)

public opinion The preference expressed by a significant number of people about a political issue. (225)
public sector The government. (261)
public welfare The care by government of the elderly, the poor, and the sick. (621)

Q

quarantine A period of isolation placed on plants and animals being brought into the country in order to prevent the entrance of diseases. (528)
quorum The minimum number of persons who must be present for a legislative body to conduct business. (392)

R

radical An individual or a government promoting swift, extreme, and far-reaching change; of or relating to a philosophy of radicalism. (27)
rally To gather party supporters together for an election or other political action. (278)
random sample A sample drawn in such a way that everyone in the total population being surveyed has an equal chance of being selected. (233)
rank-and-file The members of political or labor organizations. (278)
ratification Formal approval. (44)
reactionary An individual or a government seeking to prevent change. (27)
real property Land and the buildings on that land; see *personal property*. (758)
reapportionment A new distribution of the 435 seats in the House of Representatives among the 50 states, undertaken every 10 years to reflect changes in population. (342)
recall A procedure in which a special election, called after a required number of signatures has been collected, is held to decide whether a public official shall be dismissed from office. (715)
red tape In popular language, the routine attention to forms and details that often results in delay. (504)
regressive tax A tax, such as a general sales tax, in which each person pays the same amount regardless of income and which thus places more of a burden on lower-income households than on higher-income households. (542, 757)
regressive taxation See *regressive tax*. (757)
regular See *party regular*. (278)
regulation Government control over particular economic activities through such means as licensing and setting standards in a particular area. (550)
regulatory taxation The governmental use of taxes to promote desirable activities or to suppress dangerous or undesirable activities. (542)
renewable energy resource A resource, such as hydroelectric power, the supply of which is not depleted with use. (614)
rent subsidy A partial payment of rent to a landlord by a governmental unit, usually to assist low-income families; see *housing allowance*. (636)
representative government A form of government in which the people elect representatives to run the government for them. (62)
reprieve A postponement of punishment that has been legally imposed. (440)
republic A form of government that does not have a monarch at its head. (23) A form of government in which voters elect representatives who make public policy. (61)
reserved powers Those powers which the Constitution grants neither to the national government nor to the states. (111, 697)
reserve requirement The percentage of funds that each member bank must deposit with its Federal Reserve Bank. (537)
resolution A formal expression of opinion by either the House of Representatives or by the Senate that requires approval by neither the other house nor the President. (389)
restrictive covenant An agreement, now illegal, which required that certain properties be sold only to whites or Christians. (159)
revenue Income. (529, 756)
revenue sharing An arrangement under which the national government gives an annual share of federal tax money to state and local governments without specifying how the funds must be used. (124)
reverse discrimination The situation in which affirmative action programs conflict with the constitutional right of equal protection. (174)
rider A provision unrelated to the subject of a bill but attached to the bill in order to attain the provision's passage. (448)
right of privacy The right of individuals to have their thoughts, beliefs, and personal lives free from government surveillance, interference, or control. (151)
right to counsel The constitutional right of a defendant to the assistance of an attorney. (678)
right-to-work law A state law that establishes the open shop. (569)
roll-call vote A type of vote in which each legislator records his or her position; also called a record vote. (393)
royal colony An English colony in North America in which the governor and council were appointed by the English monarch and an assembly was elected by voters. (39)
royalties Shares of the profit from sales. (599)
rule of *stare decisis* A decision by a judge made by citing a decision in a similar earlier case; see *precedent*. (646)
running mate A candidate chosen to run with another candidate on a political ticket. (278)

GLOSSARY

runoff election An election held subsequent to a primary election to determine the majority nominee from among the candidates receiving the highest pluralities. (296)

rural electrification A federal program of loans to farm cooperatives and local governments to provide electric service and telephone service to rural areas. (556)

S

safe seat A legislative district in which one party usually wins elections by a large majority. (345)

sample A representative part selected from a larger whole. (206)

sampling error A mathematically determined range of error in any measurement of public opinion. (234)

scatter housing A form of public housing in which small projects are scattered throughout the city instead of being concentrated in a huge development. (636)

schedule A set of rules for putting new laws or constitutional provisions into effect. (701)

school board The governing body, which may be elected or appointed, of a school district. (740)

school district A type of special district created by state or local government to run the public schools within a specific area. (739)

search incident to arrest The right of a police officer to search an individual arrested with probable cause despite the absence of a search warrant. (676)

secret ballot A system of voting that originated in Australia in which votes are cast privately and anonymously. (325)

segregation The legal separation of people in public facilities, usually on a racial basis. (157)

select committee A legislative committee set up to deal with a particular problem or to conduct a study or an investigation. (370)

selective sales tax A tax placed on the sale of specific items. (757)

selectman The official who manages the affairs of a New England town between annual town meetings. (738)

self-incrimination The giving of evidence or the answering of questions that would tend to subject one to criminal prosecution. (679)

senatorial courtesy An unwritten rule of the Senate which requires that executive appointments of individuals from or in a particular state must first be approved by the senator of the same party from that state. (386)

seniority Length of service; often used in a legislature to determine committee assignments. (368)

separate but equal The doctrine, established in 1896 and declared unconstitutional in 1954, that racial segregation was legal so long as the facilities available to both whites and blacks were equal. (159)

separation of church and state The constitutional prohibition against making any religion an official arm of government. (146)

separation of powers A constitutional principle that prevents any one branch of government from dominating the other two branches. (63)

sequestering The isolation of jury members to prevent their being reached by any publicity during the course of a trial. (142)

severance tax A duty levied on the removal of certain natural resources such as minerals, timber, or oil. (760)

sheriff The county official who provides police protection in unincorporated areas, maintains the jail, and acts as a court officer. (736)

shoehorning Slipping a new building between existing structures. (752)

shoo-in A candidate who is a certain and easy winner in an election. (278)

short ballot An electoral form that usually contains the names of candidates for only policy-making offices; see *long ballot.* (327)

single-issue voting Making a choice in an election on the basis of only one issue rather than on an overall ideology or political position. (337)

single-member district A district that elects only one legislator. (280)

sit-down strike A work-stoppage technique in which workers remain inside a plant but do not work. (564)

slander The injuring of someone's reputation falsely through the spoken word; see *libel.* (141)

social contract A political theory which states that people permanently agree to surrender their individual sovereignty to the state in order to live in a civilized society. (22, 38)

socialism A political ideology that seeks to replace private ownership of property with public ownership. (488)

socialization The learning process by which people in a society come to share common values, beliefs, and attitudes. (238)

society An organized group. (17)

sovereignty The absolute power or authority to make final decisions. (22)

special district A unit of local government created to provide a single service or a few related services, such as fire protection. (739)

specialization of function A characteristic of bureaucracy that involves the performance of tasks through separate, specialized units. (503)

special session A legislative meeting called by the executive or by the legislative leadership to consider urgent business before the next regular session of the legislature. (707)

splinter group An organization formed by disaffected members of one of the two major political parties. (286)

spoils system The practice of awarding government jobs on a partisan basis; see *merit system.* (520)
stacking the deck A propaganda technique that favors only one side of an argument by means of exaggeration, truth-bending, half-truths, or lies. (245)
stagflation A combination of economic stagnation and inflation that plagued the United States economy in the 1970's. (546)
standard-bearer The leader of an organization, a movement, or a political party. (278)
standardized procedures Regulations that specify what is required in each situation and thus ensure that clients of a bureaucracy are treated equally. (503)
standing committee A permanent committee of a legislative body. (369)
standing vote A vote in which legislators who favor a bill stand up and are counted, followed by those opposed. There is no permanent record of how a legislator votes. (393)
state A political unit, structured by government and composed of citizens, that has sovereignty within a clearly defined territory. (22)
state budget An estimate of the revenues and expenditures needed to carry out state operations for a specific period, usually a year. (716)
state committee The agency of a political party that provides ongoing state party leadership. (289)
states' rights The theory that each state should have the power to interpret federal laws. (55)
statistics Numerical facts that are collected and classified systematically. (204)
status quo The existing state of affairs. (249)
statutory code A listing of specific laws. (701)
statutory law The laws passed by Congress, state legislatures, city councils, and other lawmaking units of government. (646)
stipulation A request issued by a court or an independent regulatory commission asking the guilty party to stop engaging in an unfair practice. (588)
stock transfer tax A tax that is levied on the transfer of stock. (760)
stop-and-frisk action A warrantless search for concealed weapons conducted by a police officer on someone who is acting suspiciously or who is suspected of carrying a weapon. (677)
straight ticket A ballot on which a person votes for all the candidates nominated by one political party. See *ticket splitting.* (325)
straw poll An informal survey of public opinion. (233, 278)
straw vote See *straw poll.* (278)
strict construction An interpretation of the Constitution which holds that the Constitution is a treaty entered into by sovereign states and that the authority of the national government is limited to the expressly delegated powers. (113)
strict constructionist A person who supports a strict construction of Article 1, Section 8, Clause 18, of the Constitution dealing with the powers of Congress; see *expressed powers.* (383)
strings Guidelines or legal requirements. (122)
strip mining A method of mining in which surface materials—soil and rock—are removed to reach underlying ore. (603)
strong-mayor form A form of municipal government in which executive authority is concentrated in the hands of the mayor. (744)
subcommittee A smaller body of a legislative committee, with a specialized area of concern. (370)
subsidy A grant of financial aid by the government to an individual, a company, or an industry. (550)
suburb A small town or unincorporated residential area on the outskirts of a city. (741)
subversive A person who is potentially dangerous to national security. (188)
suffrage The right to vote. (37, 321)
suit A legal claim in civil law. (646)
summit conference A face-to-face meeting of two or more heads of state. (463)
sunset legislation Laws that end the operation of an agency or program after a specified time. (398)
supremacy clause Article 6, Section 2, of the Constitution, which states that the Constitution is the supreme law of the land. (113)
surplus crop A crop that the government buys and stores to maintain target prices. (553)
synthetic fuel A fuel made from natural materials in a factory process rather than by nature. (614)

T

tangible Descriptive of personal property that is physical in nature, such as furniture, jewelry, and livestock; see *intangible.* (758)
tariff A tax on goods imported into the United States from other countries. (528)
tax A compulsory charge made by the government to raise money for public purposes. (756)
taxable income A person's total income minus exemptions and deductions. (540)
tax incentive A tax reduction, usually offered to encourage business development. (746)
territorial integrity The constitutional guarantee of the physical boundaries and legal existence of each state. (116)
territory An area belonging to the United States that is not a part of any state. (726)
test case A legal action to establish some claimed right or to challenge the constitutionality of a law. (264)
testimonial A propaganda technique that tries to ensure the acceptance of a candidate or idea through the endorsement of a movie star, sports personality, or other celebrity. (245)

GLOSSARY

third party A political party other than the two major parties. (284)

ticket splitting The act of voting for candidates of different parties for different offices; see *straight ticket.* (325)

totalitarian A term that refers to a type of dictatorship that seeks to control not only politics but also economic, social, religious, cultural, and personal matters; see *authoritarian.* (27)

town meeting A form of local government in New England in which all the citizens meet together to levy taxes, elect officers, and pass laws. (39, 738)

township A political unit, often a subdivision of a county, found in many northern states. (736, 739)

trade association An interest group that advances the interests of American business. (252)

trade deficit An excess in the value of a nation's imports over its exports; also called an unfavorable balance of trade. (581)

trademark A distinctive device that identifies the manufacturer or seller of a product. (583)

trade surplus An excess in the value of a nation's exports over its imports; also called a favorable balance of trade. (581)

treasurer The official who collects, maintains, and pays out funds for a governmental unit, such as the county. (736)

trend General direction. (207)

trial balloon A project or idea that is released to the media by the government or by a candidate in order to test public opinion. (300)

trust A group of companies within a single industry who agree to limit production, fix prices, or cooperate in other ways to reduce or eliminate competition within the industry. (586)

two-party system The existence of two major groups with differing political philosophies that compete for the control of government. (280)

tyranny The unjust use of power. (63)

U

umbrella association An organization that links many groups together. (252)

unanimous opinion A statement issued when all the justices voting on a case concur. (657)

unconstitutional Contrary to the Constitution; see *judicial review.* (67)

underdog The candidate least favored to win. (278)

unemployment insurance Government payments for a limited time to workers who have lost their jobs. (559)

unicameral A term referring to a legislature that consists of one house. (706)

unincorporated area A part of a county that is not part of a city, town, village, or other incorporated area. (735)

union shop A workplace where workers need not be union members in order to be hired but must join the union within a period of time; see *open shop.* (568)

unitary system A form of government in which all legal power is held by the central government. (24)

unit rule A winner-take-all system, used by the Democratic party until 1972, in which all delegates from a state to the national convention were bound to support the candidate favored by the majority of the delegates from that state. (299) A feature of the electoral college system in which the candidate who receives the largest number of popular votes in a state receives all the state's electoral votes. (316)

unorganized territory An area that does not have an organic act; see *organic act.* (726)

user tax A duty on gasoline, oil, and vehicle registration, generally used to finance highways. (723)

V

variance An exception to a zoning law. (751)

verdict Judgment or decision. (337)

veterans' preference The addition of extra points to the civil service examination scores of honorably discharged veterans and of disabled veterans and certain members of their families. (523)

veto The right of a chief executive to reject a bill and prevent it from becoming law. (37, 394)

veto override The repassing by the legislature of a bill vetoed by the chief executive. (448)

veto power See *veto.* (447)

veto session A special meeting called by a state legislature's leadership after the regular session has adjourned to consider bills vetoed by the governor. (707)

visa A travel permit for a limited stay in a particular country. (192)

voice vote A procedure by which legislators in chorus call out "aye" or "no" on a bill. There is no permanent record of how a legislator votes. (393)

voluntary consent Consent given without force or coercion to a warrantless search. (677)

vote projection and prediction system A system based on a computer analysis of a few selected precincts that enables the three major television networks to predict the winner of an election on the basis of only a small number of votes. (312)

W

wage and price controls Limits on how much workers can earn and businesses can charge, usually imposed only during wartime. (546)

wage and price guidelines Recommendations by the President's economic advisers that establish official permissible rates of increase in wages and prices. (546)

ward A person under the care and protection of a guardian or a court. (638)

ward system of election The election of city council members of districts within a city; see *at-large system of election.* (743)

warrant A written order by a judge giving authority for something, such as searching a particular person or place for a particular item. (676)

watchdog committee A group that oversees what politicians and public officials do. (278)

weak-mayor form A form of municipal government in which the mayor shares executive authority with the city council. (744)

whistle-blower A government employee who draws public attention to mismanagement, waste, corruption, or other wrongdoing within a government agency. (521)

wide-open primary See *blanket primary.* (296)

wire service An organization, such as United Press International or the Associated Press, that maintains reporters all over the world and provides information to subscribers on major world news events. (243)

withholding An automatic deduction taken from wages or salaries. (540)

write-in campaign An organized effort to convince voters to write in the name of a candidate not listed on the ballot. (325)

writ of certiorari A request that the Supreme Court review the decision of a lower court that has allegedly made an error in its handling of a case. (656)

writ of habeas corpus A written order by a judge requiring a police officer to bring a prisoner to court and to show proof why the prisoner should remain in jail. (675)

writ of mandamus A court order compelling an official to perform a specified act. (106)

Y

yellow-dog contract An agreement, now illegal, in which a worker promised an employer not to join a union. (565)

Z

zoning The control of land use within a city or a county by dividing it into districts, each of which may be used only in a specified manner. (750)

GLOSSARY

INDEX

Page numbers in *italics* that have *c, m, p,* or *fn* written before them refer to charts, diagrams, or graphs and their captions (*c*); maps and their captions (*m*); photographs and their captions (*p*); or footnotes (*fn*).

A

INDEX

INDEX

C

INDEX

INDEX

INDEX

D

E

INDEX

INDEX

F

INDEX

INDEX

INDEX

H

INDEX

J

INDEX

K

INDEX

M

INDEX

INDEX

O

S

INDEX

INDEX

T

INDEX

INDEX

INDEX

INDEX

ACKNOWLEDGMENTS

ACKNOWLEDGMENTS: Positions are shown in abbreviated form as follows: t–top, c–center, b–bottom, l–left, r–right.

COVER: ©J. Alex Langley/DPI

MAPS and CHARTS: Harcourt Brace Jovanovich

CITIZEN'S HANDBOOK OF SKILLS: p. 11(l), by Permission of Bill Mauldin and Wil-Jo Associates; 11(r), ©1958 Tom Little, by The New York Times Company.

UNIT ONE: p. 15, ©Robert Llewellyn; 17, Bettmann Archive; 18, "Amenhotep III and His Mother," The Metropolitan Museum of Art; 20(t), A. J. Miller: "Fort Laramie," Beinecke Rare Book Library, Yale University; 20(b), William Gropper: "Construction of the Dam," Courtesy, Public Building Service, General Services Administration; 21, "Washington Reviewing the Western Army," The Metropolitan Museum of Art, gift of Edgar William and Bernice Chrysler Garbisch; 23, Granger Collection; 24, "House Of Commons," 1793, National Portrait Gallery, London; 26, UPI/Bettmann Newsphoto; 28(t), Culver Pictures; 28(b), UPI/Bettmann Newsphoto; 29(t), Granger Collection; 29(b), Scala/Art Resource; 30, Granger Collection; 31, Granger Collection; 33, *Orlando Sentinel*; 36, Bettmann Archive; 37(l), National Portrait Gallery, London; 37(r), National Portrait Gallery, London; 38, Percy Moran: "Signing the Mayflower Compact," Museum of the Pilgrim Society; 40(t), Granger Collection; 40(b), Granger Collection; 41, Granger Collection; 42, National Portrait Gallery, London; 43, Library of Congress; 45, National Archives; 49, John Trumbull: "Declaration Of Independence," 1786, ©Yale University Art Gallery; 51(l), The Thomas Gilcrease Institute of American History and Art, Tulsa, Oklahoma; 51(r), Gilbert Stuart: "The Lansdowne Portrait of George Washington," 1798, The Pennsylvania Academy of Fine Arts, Bequest of William Bingham; 53, "Convention at Independence Hall," Pennsylvania Historical and Museum Commission; 55, Rembrandt Peale: "Thomas Jefferson," The New York Historical Society; 58(t), Thomas Sully: "Patrick Henry" ca. 1815, Colonial Williamsburg Foundation; 58(b), John Trumbull: "Alexander Hamilton," National Gallery of Art, Smithsonian Institution, Washington, gift of the Avalon Foundation; 61, Granger Collection; 62, Historical Pictures Service, Chicago; 66, Jehangir Gazdar/Woodfin Camp and Associates; 67, Bill Fitz-Patrick/The White House; 68, National Archives; 99(inset), René Burri/Magnum Photos; 99(b), Joseph H. Hidley: "View of Poestenkill, New York," ca. 1855, The Metropolitan Museum of Art, gift of Edgar William and Bernice Chrysler Garbisch; 100, Bettmann Archive; 101, Bettmann Archive; 102(t), Wide World Photos; 102(b) Bettmann Archive; 104, National Archives; 105, Granger Collection; 109, Globe Photos; 110(t), Library of Congress; 110(b), Library of Congress; 111, Fred Ward/Black Star; 112, Cary Wolinsky/Stock Boston; 114(l), National Portrait Gallery, Smithsonian Institution, Washington; 114(c), Granger Collection; 114(r), United States Supreme Court; 115, Historical Pictures Service, Chicago; 115(inset), Bettmann Archive; 117, Granger Collection; 118, HBJ Photo/Elliott Varner Smith; 120, Hawaii Newspaper Agency Library; 121, Wally McNamee/Woodfin Camp and Associates; 122, James R. Holland/Stock Boston; 123(l), John Troha/Black Star; 123(r), Tim Kelly/Black Star; 124, The United States Equal Employment Opportunity Commission; 125, David Aronson/Stock Boston; 126, UPI/Bettmann Newsphoto; 128, UPI/Bettmann Newsphoto.

UNIT TWO: p. 131, Karl Kummels, Shostal; 133, Martin A. Levick/Black Star; 134, Dennis Brack/Black Star; 135(l), Yousef Karsh/Woodfin Camp and Associates; 135(r), United States Supreme Court; 136, Granger Collection; 137(t), United States Supreme Court; 137(b), United States Supreme Court; 138, UPI/Bettmann Newsphoto; 139, Wide World Photos; 141, Martin A. Levick/Black Star; 142, UPI/Bettmann Newsphoto; 143, Owen Franken/Stock Boston; 144(t), Thoreau Lyceum; 144(c), Granger Collection; 144(b), C. Roy Moore/Black Star; 145(l), UPI/Bettmann Newsphoto; 145(r), UPI/Bettmann Newsphoto; 147(l), The Rhode Island Historical Society; 147(tr), Granger Collection; 147(br), ©Paul Conklin; 149, Library of Congress; 150, Larry Lambert/Picture Group; 151, Erich Hartmann/Magnum Photos; 152(both), ©Paul Conklin; 156, Granger Collection; 157, Missouri Historical Society; 158, Library of Congress; 159, Library of Congress; 160, Brown Brothers; 161, UPI/Bettmann Newsphoto; 162, Burt Glinn/Magnum Photos; 163, Jerry Berndt/Picture Group; 164, Wide World Photos; 165, Robert Kelley, Life Magazine, ©1963, Time, Incorporated; 166, Wide World Photos; 167, Historical Pictures Service, Chicago; 169, Daniel Brody/Stock Boston; 170(l), Brown Brothers; 170(c), Historical Pictures Service, Chicago; 170(r) Bettmann Archive; 171, The National Portrait Gallery, Smithsonian Institution, Washington, gift of the National Woman's Suffrage Association through Mrs. Carrie Chapman Catt; 172, Wide World Photos; 173, Wide World Photos; 175, Rick Browne/Picture Group.

UNIT THREE: p. 177, J. L. Atlan/Sygma; 179, from the collection of Mr. August A. Busch, Jr., Anheuser-Busch, Incorporated; 180, Granger Collection; 181, Granger Collection; 182, UPI/Bettmann Newsphotos; 183, Edward Laning: "Ellis Island Arrivals," 1937, one of the WPA mural series for the Aliens' Dining Room, Ellis Island, Courtesy, Public Buildings Service, General Services Administration; 184, Granger Collection; 185, Eric Carle, Shostal; 186, Wide World Photos; 187, UPI/Bettmann Newsphoto; 189, Wide World Photos; 193(t), Gilles Peress/Magnum Photos; 193(c), UPI/Bettmann Newsphoto; 193(b) Roger Sandler/Picture Group; 194, Alex Webb/Magnum Photos; 194(inset), Scott Newton/Picture Group; 196, Wide World Photos; 198, Library of Congress; 199, Bettmann Archive; 201, Wide World Photos; 204, Barbara Alper/Picture Group; 205, Ellis Herwig/Stock Boston; 205(inset), Seal, United States Department of Commerce, Bureau of the Census; 206, Smithsonian Institution, Washington; 207, Robert McElroy, Woodfin Camp and Associates; 212, Yoram Kaharal/Peter Arnold; 213, HBJ Photo; 214, Philip Jon Bailey/Taurus Photos; 217, Owen Franken/Stock Boston, 218, John Running/Stock Boston; 220, Eli Heller/Picture Group.

UNIT FOUR: p. 223, Ad Art Associates; 225, Susan Meiselas/Magnum Photos; 233, Wide World Photos; 235, *Philadelphia Inquirer Daily News*; 237, UPI/Bettmann Newsphoto; 239, Jeff Albertson/Stock Boston; 241, Reni Newsphotos Incorporated, Courtesy, NBC News "Meet The Press"; 242(tl), John Ficara/Woodfin Camp and Associates; 242(tr), CBS–TV News; 242(bl), Courtesy of Producers, Incorporated; 242(br), Robert McElroy/Woodfin Camp and Associates; 244, Bob Sacha/ABC News; 248, Mark Godfrey/Archive Pictures, Incorporated; 250, John Ficara/Woodfin Camp and Associates; 251, Chuck Fishman/Contact/Woodfin Camp Associates; 253(t), George Meany Memorial Archives; 253(c), Bettmann Archive; 253(b), AFL–CIO Archives; 254, Granger Collection; 254(inset),

George Mars Cassidy/Globe Photos; 255, Dale Ahearn/Sullivan and Associates; 257(t), ©Paul Conklin; 257(b), René Burri/Magnum Photos; 259, ©Bettye Lane; 260(t), Greenpeace; 260 (inset), HBJ Photo; 260(b), Peter Marlow/Sygma Photos; 263, Owen Franken/Stock Boston; 267, ©1978 Herblock, from *Herblock on All Fronts* (New American Library, 1980).

UNIT FIVE: p. 269, Smithsonian Institution, Washington; 271, Granger Collection; 273, Granger Collection; 274, The National Portrait Gallery, Smithsonian Institution, Washington; 275(tl), Historical Pictures Service, Chicago; 275(tr), Historical Pictures Service, Chicago; 275(b), Nebraska State Historical Society; 277, Bettmann Archive; 278, HBJ Cartoon; 279, Wide World Photos; 280, Clyde Peterson in *Houston Chronicle;* 283(l), Cornell Capa/Magnum Photos; 283(r), Lee Goff/Magnum Photos; 286, Burt Glinn/Magnum Photos; 288(l), ©Paul Conklin; 288(r), Peter Southwick/Stock Boston; 290, ©Michael D. Sullivan/Sullivan and Associates; 294, Randy Taylor/Sygma Photos; 295, Library of Congress; 297(l), Brad Bower/Picture Group; 297(r), Dennis Brack/Black Star; 298, John F. Kennedy Library, Courtesy, The Charleston, West Virginia *Gazette;* 299, Don Heing/Picture Group; 302, Granger Collection; 303, Owen Franken/Stock Boston; 304, Bettmann Archive; 305, UPI/Bettmann Newsphoto; 307, Granger Collection, 308, UPI/Bettmann Newsphoto; 310, Library of Congress; 314, HBJ Photo; 315(t), Allen Tannenbaum/Sygma Photos; 315(l), Liss/Gamma Liason; 315(r), Randy Taylor/Sygma Photos; 315(b), Bruce Hoertell/Gamma Liason; 317 (both), Granger Collection; 321, Granger Collection; 322, Brown Brothers; 323, Bettmann Archive; 324, Susan Ylvisaker/Jeroboam, Incorporated; 325, Brown Brothers; 326(tl), Courtesy, Secretary of State of Indiana; 326(tr), Courtesy, City and County of San Francisco, California; 326(b), René Burri/Magnum Photos; 331, By John Fischetti, ©1972, *Chicago Daily News,* Courtesy, News America Syndicate; 335, UPI/Bettmann Newsphoto; 335(inset), HBJ Photo; 336, Sygma; 336(inset), Owen Franken/Stock Boston.

UNIT SIX: p. 339, Globe Photos; 341, B. S. Cavanaugh/Globe Photos; 343, Library of Congress; 345, Shepard Sherbell/Picture Group; 346(tl), Shepard Sherbell/Picture Group; 346(tc), Wide World Photos; 346(tr), Wide World Photos; 346(bl), UPI/Bettmann Newsphoto; 346(bc), UPI/Bettmann Newsphoto; 346(br), UPI/Bettmann Newsphoto; 347, Bob East, III/Picture Group; 349, The Corcoran Gallery of Art, Museum Purchase, 1911; 350(tl), Shepard Sherbell/Picture Group; 350(cl), Shepard Sherbell/Picture Group; 350(bl), Shepard Sherbell/Picture Group; 350(br), Penelope Bretse/Gamma Liason; 353, ©Paul Conklin; 354(tl), Diane Walker, Time, Incorporated; 354(bl), Shepard Sherbell/Picture Group; 354(br), Stephen R. Brown/Picture Group; 355, UPI/Bettmann Newsphoto; 356, Al Stephenson/Picture Group; 357, ©Paul Conklin; 358, UPI/Bettmann Newsphoto; 361, Granger Collection; 362, Dennis Brack/Black Star; 363(l), UPI/Bettmann Newsphoto; 363(r), Susan McElinney/Archive Pictures, Incorporated; 365(l), UPI/Bettmann Newsphoto; 365(r), Steven Falk/Picture Group; 367(t), Dennis Brack/Black Star; 367(b), Shepard Sherbell/Picture Group; 368, Wide World Photos; 371(t), Charles Harbutt/Archive Pictures, Incorporated; 371(c), Ellis Herwig/Stock Boston; 371(b), John Ficara/Woodfin Camp and Associates; 373(l), Wide World Photos; 373(c), UPI/Bettmann Newsphoto; 373(r), UPI/Bettmann Newsphoto; 374, ©1970 Herblock, "The Godfather," from *State of the Union* (Simon and Schuster, 1972); 375, ©Paul Conklin; 376, Bettmann Archive; 377, ©Robert Llewellyn; 379, HBJ Photo; 382, Architect of the United States Capitol; 384, UPI/Bettmann Newsphoto; 385(l), Historical Pictures Service, Chicago; 385(r), Dennis Brack/Black Star; 386, ©Paul Conklin; 387, UPI/Bettmann Newsphoto; 388, *Congressional Quarterly;* 389, *Congressional Quarterly;* 390, Shostal; 390 (inset), Shepard Sherbell/Picture Group; 392, Art Stein/Photo Researchers; 393, Shepard Sherbell/Picture Group; 394, Wide World Photos; 395 (inset), UPI/Bettmann Newsphoto; 395, Wide World Photos; 397, Wide World Photos, 397(inset), Mark Godfrey/Archive Pictures, Incorporated; 399, ©Paul Conklin.

UNIT SEVEN: p. 403, George Galicz, Photo Researchers; 405, A. Sloan/Gamma Liason; 406, The Free Library of Philadelphia; 407, Courtesy, The Henry Francis du Pont Winterthur Museum; 408(t), Independence National Historical Park Collection; 408(b), National Portrait Gallery, Smithsonian Institution, Washington; 409(t), Granger Collection; 409(b), Library of Congress; 411(all), White House Historical Association, photograph by the National Geographic Society; 413, UPI/Bettmann Newsphoto; 414, White House Historical Association, photograph by the National Geographic Society; 415, White House Historical Association, photograph by the National Geographic Society; 416, White House Historical Association, photograph by the National Geographic Society; 417(both), White House Historical Association, photograph by the National Geographic Society; 418, Lyndon Baines Johnson Library; 419(both), Lyndon Baines Johnson Library; 420(both), White House Historical Association, photograph by the National Geographic Society; 421, White House Historical Association, photograph by the National Geographic Society; 422(inset), Mario Ruiz/Picture Group; 422, Johnson/Gamma Liason; 423(both), Sloan/Gamma Liason; 424, Bill Fitz-Patrick/The White House; 426(all), White House Historical Association, photograph by the National Geographic Society; 427(all), White House Historical Association, photograph by the National Geographic Society; 430(l), Dennis Brack/Black Star; 430(r), UPI/Bettmann Newsphoto; 434, Currier and Ives, Courtesy, The Museum of the City of New York; 435, P. C. Steffen, Photo Researchers; 436(t), UPI/Bettmann Newsphoto; 436(b), Wide World Photos; 438, Dirck Halstead/Gamma Liason; 439, Michael Norcia/Globe Photos; 440, Courtesy John Blecha, March of Dimes Birth Defects Foundation; 441, Bettmann Archive; 442, Wide World Photos; 443, Magnum Photos; 445, Wide World Photos; 447, Robert Knudsen, Courtesy, the John F. Kennedy Library; 448, Michael Evans/The White House; 451(t), White House Photos/Black Star; 451(b), UPI/Bettmann Newsphoto; 452(tl), Dirck Halstead/Gamma Liason; 452(bl), Bill Fitz-Patrick/The White House; 452(br), Karl Schumacher/The White House; 458, Pete Souza/The White House; 459, National Archives; 460, Bettmann Archive; 463(t), Constantine Manos/Magnum Photos; 463(b), Wide World Photos; 464, Globe Photos; 465, Globe Photos; 467, Stephanie Maze/Woodfin Camp and Associates; 468, Wide World Photos, 469, UPI/Bettmann Newsphoto; 470, UPI/Bettmann Newsphoto; 471(t), ©Paul Conklin; 471(b), Susan Meiselas/Magnum Photos; 473(inset), Philip Jon Bailey/Stock Boston; 473, Kryn Taconis/Magnum Photos; 474, Globe Photos; 475, Owen Franken/Stock Boston; 477, Gilles Peress/Magnum Photos; 478(tl), Alon Reininger/Contact Stock Images; 478(tr), Owen Franken/Stock Boston; 478(bl), ©Paul Conklin; 478(br), Geoff Payne/Picture Group; 482, UPI/Bettmann Newsphoto; 482(inset), UPI/Bettmann Newsphoto; 486, D. K. P./Magnum Distribution; 488, Granger Collection; 489(t), Bettmann Archive; 489(b), Wide World Photos; 490, Tass from Sovfoto; 491, Maggie Steber/Stock Boston; 493, David Forbert, Shostal; 495, Chuck Fishman/Contact/Woodfin Camp and Associates; 497(t), United Nations; 497(tc), United Nations; 497(bc), UPI/Bettmann Newsphoto; 497(bl), UPI/Bettmann Newsphoto; 497(br), Wide World Photos; 498, ©Paul Conklin.

UNIT EIGHT: p. 501, UPI/Bettmann Newsphoto; 503, Dennis Brack/Black Star; 504, John Marmaras/Woodfin Camp and Associates; 505, Historical Pictures Service, Chicago; 506, Brown Brothers; 506(inset), Bettmann Archive; 507(t), Wide World Photos; 507(b), UPI/Bettmann Newsphoto; 508, James Stoots, Jr., Lawrence Livermore National Laboratory; 512, NASA; 514(l), Larry Smith/Black Star; 514(r), ©Michael D. Sullivan/Sullivan and Associates; 515, United States Arms Control and Disarmament Agency; 516(t), United States Small Business Administration; 516(b), United States Department of Education; 517, United States Office of Management and Budget; 518(t), Historical Pictures Service, Chicago; 518(b), by John Fischetti, ©1978 *Chicago Sun-Times,* Courtesy of News America Syndicate; 519, Courtesy, United States Office of Personnel Management; 520, Granger Collection; 522, Dennis Stock/Magnum Photos; 523, Dennis Brack/Black Star; 527, United States Department of the Treasury; 528(tl), Granger Collection; 528(tr), Bettmann Archive; 528(bl), Granger Collection; 528(bc), Brown Brothers; 528(br), United States Department of the Treasury; 529(t), Billy Grimes/Black Star; 529(b), Internal Revenue Service; 530(t), Mark Godfrey/Archive Pictures, Incorporated; 530(b), Larry Downing/Woodfin Camp and Associates; 531(t), United States Department of the Treasury, Savings Bond Division; 531(b), Johnson/Gamma Liason; 532, Fred

Ward/Black Star; 533, Smithsonian Institution, Washington; 534, Fred Ward/Black Star; 535, Ad Art Associates; 536(both), Bettmann Archive; 539, Stacey Pick/Stock Boston; 550, George Hall/Woodfin Camp and Associates; 551(l), Granger Collection; 551(c), UPI/Bettmann Newsphoto; 551(r), Wide World Photos; 552, Stacey Pick/Stock Boston; 553, Brad Bower/Picture Group Incorporated; 554, Chuck Fishman/Contact/Woodfin Camp and Associates; 555, Bill Gillette/Stock Boston; 556, Bryce Flynn/Picture Group Incorporated; 556(inset), HBJ Photo; 557, Adam Woofitt/Woodfin Camp and Associates; 558(tl), Brown Brothers; 558(tc), United States Department of Labor; 558(tr), UPI/Bettmann Newsphoto; 558(bl), United States Department of Labor; 558(br), United States Department of Labor; 560, UPI/Bettmann Newsphoto; 561, Brown Brothers; 562, Ian Berry/Magnum Photos; 563, Granger Collection; 564, UPI/Bettmann Newsphoto; 565, The Archives of Labor and Urban Affairs, Wayne State University; 567(t), Brown Brothers; 567(c), Historical Pictures Service, Chicago; 567(bl), Wally McNamee/Woodfin Camp and Associates; 567(br), UPI/Bettmann Newsphoto; 569, Photoworld/FPG; 573, Ian Berry/Magnum Photos; 574(t), United States Department of Transportation; 574(b), Charles Harbutt/Archive Pictures, Incorporated; 575(t), Jim Merrithew/Picture Group; 575(b), Norris J. Klesman/Picture Group; 576, Erich Hartmann/Magnum Photos; 576(inset), Dennis Stock/Magnum Photos; 577, Kevin Horan/Picture Group; 578, Donald Dietz/Stock Boston; 579(tl), Brown Brothers; 579(tc), United States Department of Commerce; 579(tr), Brown Brothers; 579(bl), UPI/Bettmann Newsphoto; 579(br), UPI/Bettmann Newsphoto; 581, United States Department of Commerce; 583, Federal Maritime Commission; 584, Courtesy, Hughes Aircraft Company; 585, Franklin Wing/Stock Boston; 587, Craig Aurness/Woodfin Camp and Associates; 588, Mark Godfrey/Archive Pictures, Incorporated; 589, Bettmann Archive; 590, Andy Levin/Black Star; 592, Kevin Horan/Picture Group; 596, Courtesy, Tennessee Valley Authority; 598(tl), Brown Brothers; 598(t), Granger Collection; 598(c), United States Department of the Interior; 598(tr), UPI/Bettmann Newsphoto; 598(b), Wide World Photos; 599, Courtesy, Tennessee Valley Authority; 600, Courtesy, Corps of Engineers; 601(l), ©Carol J. Arnold; 601(r), Ethan Hoffmann/Archive Pictures, Incorporated; 602, Storey Litchfield/Stock Boston; 603, United States Geological Survey; 604, Robert Eckert/Stock Boston; 605, Doug Bruce/Picture Group; 607, Mike Yamashita/Woodfin Camp and Associates; 609, Ira Kirschenbaum/Stock Boston; 610(both), NASA; 611, Dennis Brack/Black Star; 611(inset), United States Department of Energy; 612, Wide World Photos; 613, George Hall/Woodfin Camp and Associates; 615, Paul Suszyniski/Picture Group; 616, Stuart Cohen/Stock Boston; 617(t), Bettmann Archive; 617(c), Bettmann Archive; 617(b), Wide World Photos; 621, UPI/Bettmann Newsphoto; 622(t), Ellis Herwig/Stock Boston; 622(b), United States Department of Health and Human Services; 623, Granger Collection; 624(both), Centers for Disease Control, Atlanta, Georgia; 627, UPI/Bettmann Newsphoto; 629(t), ©Paul Conklin; 629(b), Mark Brown/VISTA; 630, Kevin Horan/Picture Group; 631(t), ©Steve McCutcheon; 631(b), United States Postal Service; 633(t), Rick Browne/Picture Group; 633(b), Sybil Shelton/Monkmeyer Press Photo; 634, Charles Shoup/Learning Center, Gallaudet College; 635, Ann McQueen/Stock Boston; 636, Bannett, DPI; 637(l), Rick Reinhard/VISTA; 637(r), VISTA; 638, United States Department of the Interior; 639(t), John Running/Stock Boston; 639(b), ©John Running; 640, Mark Phillips/Picture Group.

UNIT NINE: p. 643, ©Paul Conklin; 645, Historical Pictures Service, Chicago; 647, J. M. Buchanan/National Archives; 648, HBJ Photo/Karen Rantzman; 650, Supreme Court of California; 653, Wide World Photos; 656, Bettmann Archive; 657, Chuck Fishman/Contact/Woodfin Camp and Associates; 658, Yoichi R. Okamoto/Photo Researchers; 660, Brown Brothers; 661(l), United States Supreme Court; 661(r), UPI/Bettmann Newsphoto; 662(all), UPI/Bettmann Newsphoto; 663(t), UPI/Bettmann Newsphoto; 663(b), The Supreme Court Historical Society; 665, UPI/Bettmann Newsphoto; 666(l), Granger Collection; 666(c), Bettmann Archive; 666(r), Erich Hartmann/Magnum Photos; 668, United States Department of Justice, Federal Bureau of Investigation; 669, United States Department of Justice, Federal Bureau of Investigation; 673, Brown Brothers; 675, Library of Congress; 677, Tom Meyer from *San Francisco Chronicle,* ©1983 Special Features; 678(l), Flip Schulke/Black Star; 678(r), National Archive; 680, 682, Bettmann Archive; 683, Granger Collection; 686, HBJ Photo; 688, HBJ Photo; 695, ©Christopher Springmann; 689, Wide World Photos; 691, ©by Judge Margarito C. Garza, 1977.

UNIT TEN: p. 695, ©Christopher Springmann; 697, Holleman Color Labs, Incorporated; 699, John Singleton Copley: "Samuel Adams," 1770–1772, Museum of Fine Arts, Boston; 702, Owen Franken/Stock Boston; 703, Al Stephenson/Woodfin Camp and Associates; 704, UPI/Bettmann Newsphoto; 706, Nebraska Unicameral Information Office; 707, George Mars Cassidy/Globe Photos; 708, Cary Wolinsky/Stock Boston; 710(t), Alex Webb/Magnum Photos; 710(b), Hamilton Test Systems; 711, ©Ed Kashi; 715, Tricia Hines/West Stock; 716(l), Charles Steiner/Picture Group; 716(r), Shepard Sherbell/Picture Group; 717, Patrick Pfister/Picture Group; 718, ©Ben Martin; 719(t), Library of Congress; 719(c), Bettmann Archive; 719(b), Massachusetts Historical Society; 720, Office of the Lt. Governor of Colorado; 721, Office of the Secretary of State of California; 722, Special Collections Division, University of Georgia Libraries; 723(t), Andrew Sacks/Black Star; 723(b), Jeff Lowenthal/Woodfin Camp and Associates; 724, Dennis Stock/Magnum Photos; 725, ©N. H. Rose Collection, Texas Memorial Museum, Austin; 729, Carl Mydans/Black Star; 730, White House Historical Association; 734, ©Robert Llewellyn; 735, Bruce Kliewe/Jeroboam, Incorporated; 736, Eve Arnold/Magnum Photos; 737, Indiana Historical Society Library; 739, Rick Friedman/Black Star; 740(l), Historical Pictures Service, Chicago; 740(r), The National Portrait Gallery, Smithsonian Institution, Washington; 741, Shelly Katz/Black Star; 742, Herman J. Kokojan/Black Star; 743, Humanities Research Center, The University of Texas at Austin; 746, Greater Los Angeles Visitors and Convention Bureau; 747(l), Newton Nelson/Globe Photos; 747(c), George Lorincy/Globe Photos; 747(r), Jay Lurie/West Stock; 748, National Archives; 749(t), HBJ Photo/Eric Arnesen; 749(b), Sepp Seitz/Woodfin Camp and Associates; 750, Roger Tully/Black Star; 751, Jim Sugar/Black Star; 754, Wide World Photos; 756(t), Paul Fusco/Magnum Photos; 756(b), Spencer Church/West Stock; 757(l), Tom Tracy/Black Star; 757(r), Bohdan Hrynewych/Picture Group; 758, Ad Art Associates; 759, Lester Sloan/Woodfin Camp and Associates; 761, Michael Collier/Stock Boston; 762, HBJ Photo.

CHRONOLOGY: p. 787, Bettmann Archive; 788, Yale University Art Gallery; 790(t), Granger Collection; 790(c), Bettmann Archive; 790(b), Granger Collection; 791(top three), Granger Collection; 791(b), White House Historical Association, photographs by the National Geographic Society; 792(t), Granger Collection; 792(tc), Bettmann Archive; 792(cl), White House Historical Association, photograph by the National Geographic Society; 792(cr), Granger Collection; 792(bc), Granger Collection; 792(b), Bettmann Archive; 793(all), Granger Collection; 794(t), Granger Collection; 794(c), White House Historical Association, photograph by the National Geographic Society; 794(bottom two), Granger Collection; 795(t), Granger Collection; 795(c), White House Historical Association, photograph by the National Geographic Society; 795(b), Granger Collection; 796(t), Granger Collection; 796(c), Bettmann Archive; 796(b), Granger Collection; 797, White House Historical Association, photograph by the National Geographic Society; 798(t), Granger Collection; 798(b), Granger Collection; 799, Granger Collection; 800, Granger Collection; 801, The Dwight D. Eisenhower Library; 802(t), Granger Collection; 802(b), Wide World Photos; 803, Granger Collection; 805(t), Wide World Photos; 805(b), Wide World Photos; 806, Wide World Photos.

A 5
B 6
C 7
D 8
E 9
F 0
G 1
H 2
I 3
J 4